Psychology's Roots

The first laboratory dedicated to the new science of psychology was founded by Wilhelm Wundt at the University of Leipzig in Germany in 1879. But psychology's roots go back further than that. Philosophers and scientists have long been interested in understanding how the mind works. Early schools of thought like structuralism and functionalism developed into contemporary perspectives, each defined by different sets of interests, prompting different kinds of questions.

BIOPSYCHOSOCIAL PERSPECTIVE

Examine the biological, psychological, and sociocultural factors influencing behavior.

What biological, psychological, and social factors influence the way I manage my allergy to tree pollen?

HUMANISTIC PERSPECTIVE

Carl Rogers 1902–1987

Abraham Maslow 1908–1970

Maintain an optimistic focus on human behavior; believe that each person is a master of his own fate.

Will tending to and nurturing this tree help me reach my fullest potential?

SOCIOCULTURAL PERSPECTIVE

Mamie Phipps Clark 1917–1983

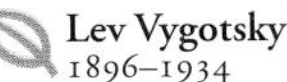

Lev Vygotsky 1896–1934

Understand behavior by examining influences of other people and the larger culture.

How do cultures differ in their attitudes toward nature?

PSYCHOANALYTIC PERSPECTIVE

Sigmund Freud 1856–1939

Interested in abnormal functioning and unconscious thought; personality is shaped by unconscious conflict.

How do your feelings about the size of this tree relate to your unconscious aggression toward your father?

EVOLUTIONARY PERSPECTIVE

Charles Darwin 1809–1882

Use knowledge about evolutionary forces to understand behavior.

Is my fear of heights inherited? Could it have contributed to my survival?

BEHAVIORAL PERSPECTIVE

B. F. Skinner 1904–1990

Ivan Pavlov 1849–1936

John Watson 1878–1958

Interested in studying only behavior that can be observed and measured.

Is spending time relaxing under this tree reinforced? If yes, I will come back again.

COGNITIVE PERSPECTIVE

George Miller 1920–2012

Renewed focus on mental processes, including physiological explanations.

How am I able to remember where this tree is in the forest?

STRUCTURALISM

Edward Titchener 1867–1927

Margaret Floy Washburn 1871–1939

Wilhelm Wundt 1832–1920

Used reports of subjective experience (introspection) to describe the structure of the mind.

Wilhelm Wundt, "Father of Psychology," founded the first laboratory dedicated to psychology.

Describe in detail each element of this tree, including color, shape, size, etc.

BIOLOGICAL PERSPECTIVE

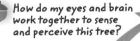

Use knowledge about underlying physiology to explain behavior and mental processes.

How do my eyes and brain work together to sense and perceive this tree?

FUNCTIONALISM

Mary Whiton Calkins 1863–1930

William James 1842–1910

Interested in how the mind functions to help us adapt and survive.

How does resting under this tree promote my long-term survival?

PHILOSOPHICAL AND SCIENTIFIC ROOTS

Plato 427–347 BCE

Aristotle 384–322 BCE

Descartes 1596–1650

Gustav Fechner 1801–1887

Ancient and modern philosophers and scientists explored the connection between mind and body.

Does this tree exist in the physical world or only in my mind?

Presenting Psychology

SECOND EDITION

Deborah M. Licht
Pikes Peak Community College
Colorado

Misty G. Hull
Pikes Peak Community College
Colorado

Coco Ballantyne

New York

Senior Vice President, Content Strategy: Charles Linsmeier
Program Director, Social Sciences: Shani Fisher
Executive Program Manager: Matt Wright
Assistant Editor: Un Hye Kim
Developmental Editors: Burrston House
Senior Marketing Manager: Clay Bolton
Marketing Assistant: Chelsea Simens
Director of Media Editorial and Assessment, Social Sciences: Noel Hohnstine
Associate Media Editor: Nik Toner
Media Project Manager: Jason Perkins
Director, Content Management Enhancement: Tracey Kuehn
Senior Managing Editor: Lisa Kinne
Senior Workflow Project Supervisor: Susan Wein
Senior Content Project Managers: Elizabeth Geller, Edward Dionne, Martha Emry
Director of Design, Content Management: Diana Blume
Design Services Manager: Natasha Wolfe
Art Manager: Matthew McAdams
Senior Photo Editor: Cecilia Varas
Photo Researcher: Donna Ranieri, Lumina Datamatics, Inc.
Designer: Lumina Datamatics, Inc.
Infographic Designer: DeMarinis Design LLC
Infographic Illustrator: Anne DeMarinis
Illustrations: Todd Buck, Evelyn Pence, Eli Ensor
Cover Designer: Michael Di Biase
Printing and Binding: LSC Communications
Cover Photos: Vintage Brain image: Original lithograph by E.J. Stanley 1901; Daisy: Le Do/Shutterstock; Hot Air Balloon: Brandon Bourdages/Shutterstock; Lock: revers/Shutterstock; Female Portrait: WAYHOME studio/Shutterstock; Male Portrait: Filipe Frazao/Shutterstock; Rubber Duck: F. JIMENEZ MECA/Shutterstock; Umbrella: drohn/Shutterstock.
Cover Illustrations on Book Pages: Evelyn Pence

Put Your Heads Together icon: GN ILLUSTRATOR/Shutterstock; Design icons: Marie Nimrichterova/Shutterstock; Idalba Granada / Alamy.

Library of Congress Control Number: 2018957944

Paperback:
ISBN-13: 978-1-319-09416-4
ISBN-10: 1-319-09416-3
Loose-leaf:
ISBN-13: 978-1-319-17104-9
ISBN-10: 1-319-17104-4

Printed in the United States of America
1 2 3 4 5 6 22 21 20 19 18

Worth Publishers
One New York Plaza
Suite 4500
New York, NY 10004-1562
www.macmillanlearning.com

For Eve.

About the Authors

Edee Chesire.

DEBORAH LICHT is a professor of psychology at Pikes Peak Community College in Colorado Springs, Colorado. She received a BS in psychology from Wright State University, Dayton, Ohio; an MA in clinical psychology from the University of Dayton; and a PhD in psychology (experimental psychopathology) from Harvard University. She has over two decades of teaching and research experience in a variety of settings, ranging from a small private university in the Midwest to a large public university in Copenhagen, Denmark. Deborah has taught introductory psychology, psychology of the workplace, abnormal psychology, the history of psychology, child development, and elementary statistics, in traditional, online, and hybrid courses. Working with community college students for over a decade has been very inspiring to Deborah; the great majority of students who attend community colleges often must overcome many challenges in pursuit of their dreams. Deborah continues to be interested in research on causal beliefs, particularly in relation to how college students think about their successes and failures as they pursue their degrees.

Steve Hull.

MISTY HULL is a professor of psychology at Pikes Peak Community College in Colorado Springs, Colorado. She has taught a range of psychology courses at Pikes Peak Community College, including introductory psychology, human sexuality, and social psychology in a variety of delivery formats (traditional, online, and hybrid). Her love of teaching comes through in her dedication to mentoring new and part-time faculty in the teaching of psychology. She received her BS in human development and family studies from Texas Tech University in Lubbock, Texas, and an MA in professional counseling at Colorado Christian University in Lakewood, Colorado. Misty has held a variety of administrative roles at Pikes Peak Community College, including as interim associate dean and coordinator of the Student Crisis Counseling Office. In addition, she served as the state psychology discipline chair of the Colorado Community College System from 2002 to 2010. One of her many professional interests is research on the impact of student persistence in higher education.

Kevin Luker.

COCO BALLANTYNE is a New York–based journalist and science writer with a special interest in psychology. Before collaborating with Misty Hull and Deborah Licht on *Scientific American: Psychology* and *Scientific American: Presenting Psychology,* Coco worked as a reporter for *Scientific American* online, covering the health, medicine, and neuroscience beats. She has also written for *Discover* magazine and *Nature Medicine.* Coco earned an MS from the Columbia University School of Journalism, where she received a Horgan Prize for Excellence in Critical Science Writing. Prior to her journalistic career, Coco worked as a teacher and tutor, helping high school and college students prepare for standardized tests such as the SAT, GRE, and MCAT. She also worked as a physics and math teacher at Eastside College Preparatory School in East Palo Alto, California, and as a human biology course associate at Stanford University, where she earned a BA in human biology.

Brief Contents

Contents

Mark Hess/Illustration Source.

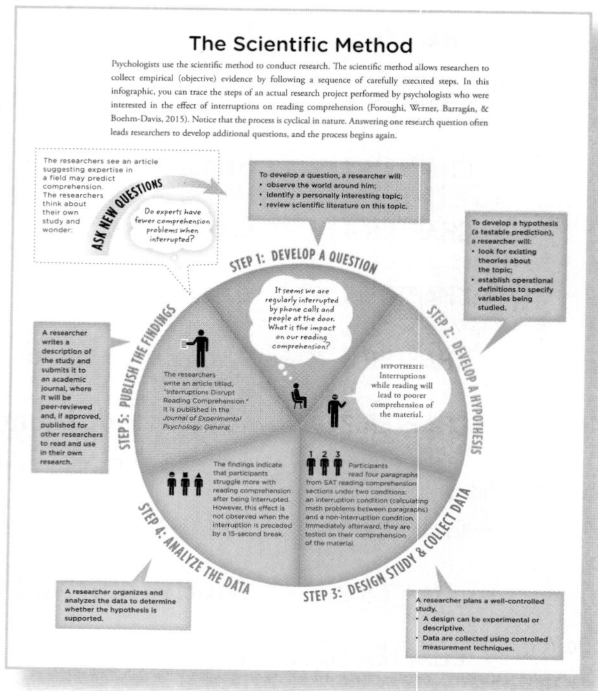

The Scientific Method
Psychologists use the scientific method to conduct research. The scientific method allows researchers to collect empirical (objective) evidence by following a sequence of carefully executed steps. In this infographic, you can trace the steps of an actual research project performed by psychologists who were interested in the effect of interruptions on reading comprehension (Foroughi, Werner, Barragán, & Boehm-Davis, 2015). Notice that the process is cyclical in nature. Answering one research question often leads researchers to develop additional questions, and the process begins again.
The researchers see an article suggesting expertise in a field may predict comprehension. The researchers think about their own study and wonder:
ASK NEW QUESTIONS
Do experts have fewer comprehension problems when interrupted?
To develop a question, a researcher will:
• observe the world around him;
• identify a personally interesting topic;
• review scientific literature on this topic.
To develop a hypothesis (a testable prediction), a researcher will:
• look for existing theories about the topic;
• establish operational definitions to specify variables being studied.
STEP 1: DEVELOP A QUESTION
It seems we are regularly interrupted by phone calls and people at the door. What is the impact on our reading comprehension?
STEP 2: DEVELOP A HYPOTHESIS
HYPOTHESIS: Interruptions while reading will lead to poorer comprehension of the material.
STEP 3: DESIGN STUDY & COLLECT DATA
Participants read four paragraphs from SAT reading comprehension sections under two conditions: an interruption condition (calculating math problems between paragraphs) and a non-interruption condition. Immediately afterward, they are tested on their comprehension of the material.
A researcher plans a well-controlled study.
• A design can be experimental or descriptive.
• Data are collected using controlled measurement techniques.
STEP 4: ANALYZE THE DATA
The findings indicate that participants struggle more with reading comprehension after being interrupted. However, this effect is not observed when the interruption is preceded by a 15-second break.
A researcher organizes and analyzes the data to determine whether the hypothesis is supported.
STEP 5: PUBLISH THE FINDINGS
The researchers write an article titled, "Interruptions Disrupt Reading Comprehension." It is published in the Journal of Experimental Psychology: General.
A researcher writes a description of the study and submits it to an academic journal, where it will be peer-reviewed and, if approved, published for other researchers to read and use in their own research.

CHAPTER 2 Biology and Behavior 40

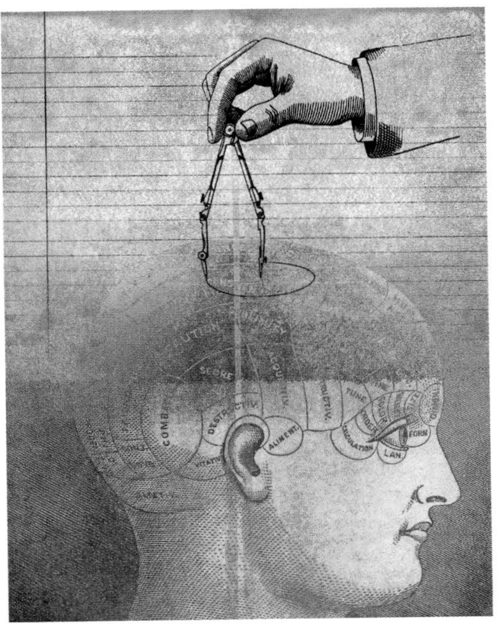

Roy Scott/Getty Images.

CHAPTER 3 Sensation and Perception 80

Mark Richards / Photo Edit.

CHAPTER 4 Consciousness 120

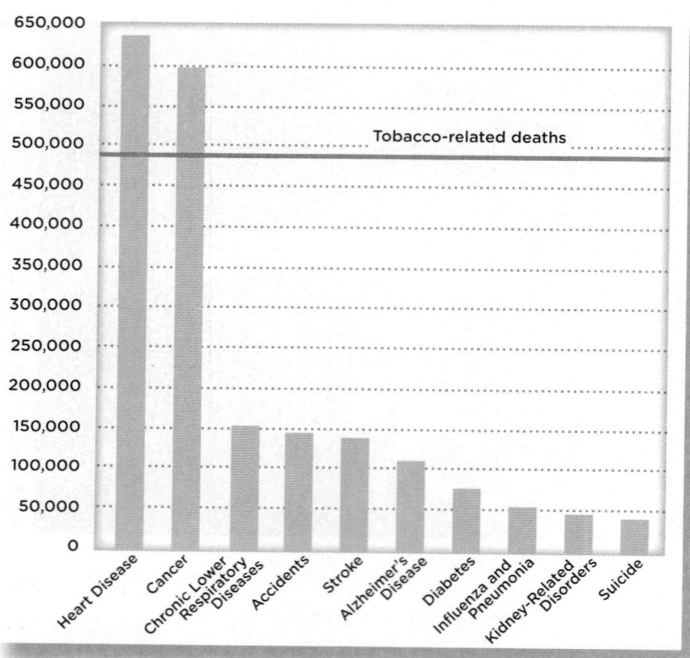

CHAPTER 5 Learning 162

Galina Ermolaeva/ Dreamstime.com.

CHAPTER 6 Memory 200

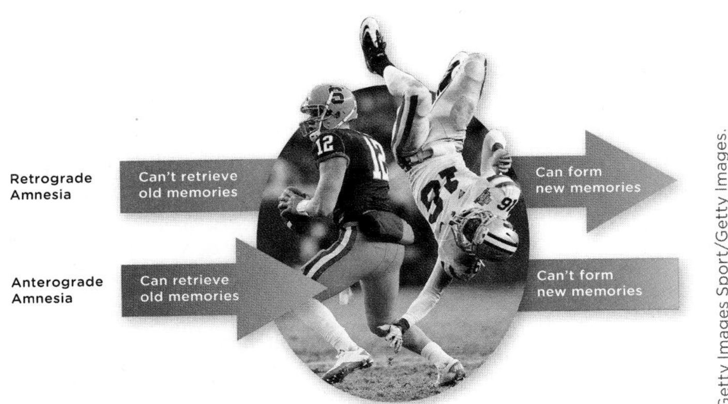

Getty Images Sport/Getty Images.

CHAPTER 7 Cognition, Language, and Intelligence 240

Mark Olencki - Wofford College.

CHAPTER 8 Human Development 278

Yvan Travert/Corbis.

CHAPTER 9 Motivation and Emotion 326

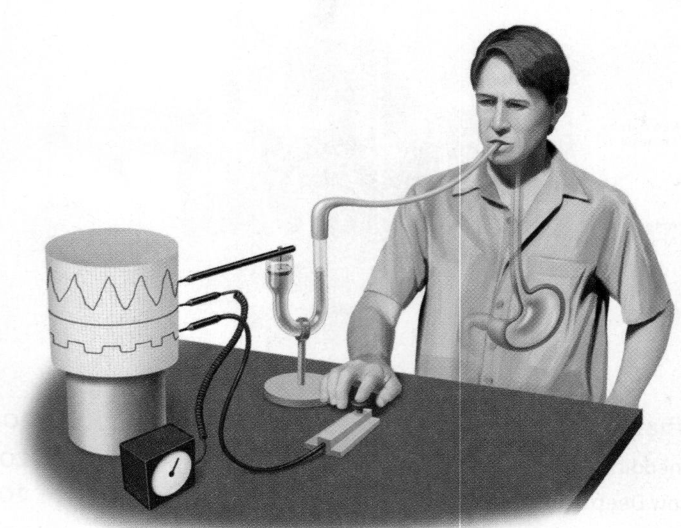

CHAPTER 10 Personality 366

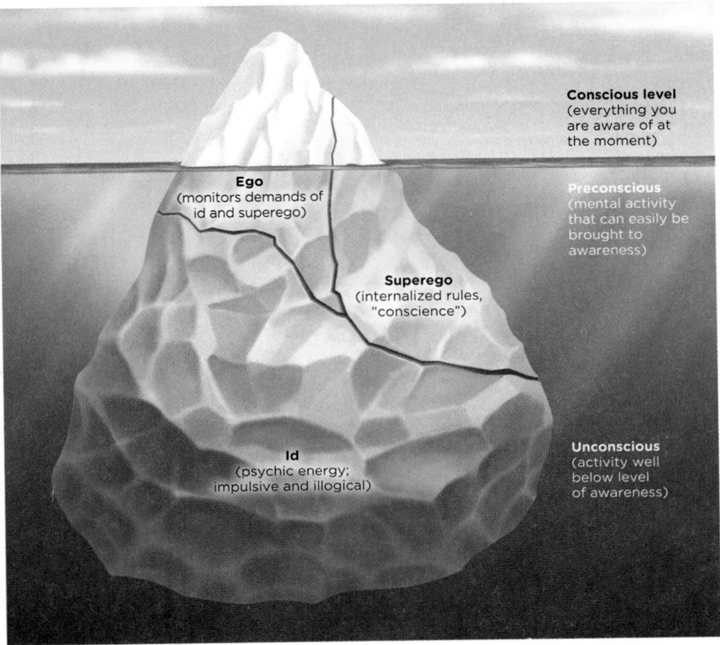

CHAPTER 11 Social Psychology 402

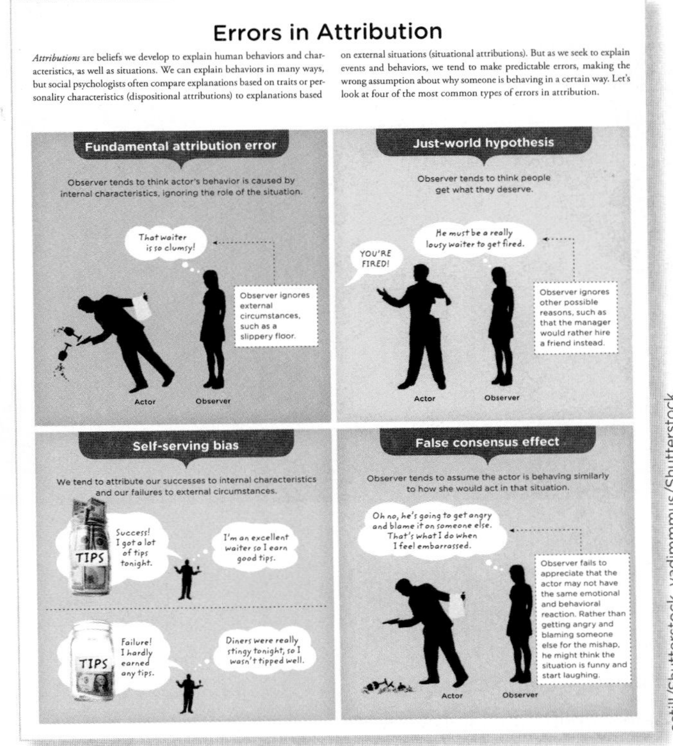

ostill/Shutterstock, vadimmmus/Shutterstock.

CHAPTER 12 Stress and Health 440

Richard Graulich/ZUMA Press/Newscom.

CHAPTER 13 Psychological Disorders 472

Tokyo Space Club/Corbis/VCG/Getty Images.

CHAPTER 14 Treatment of Psychological Disorders 512

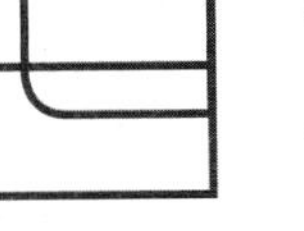

National Portrait Gallery, Smithsonian Institution / Art Resource, NY.

Preface

This is *your* book

The second edition of *Scientific American: Presenting Psychology* stems from a multi-year collaboration between the authors and instructors and students across the nation. Before we even embarked on this edition, the Scientific American: Psychology series had already been formally reviewed by over 1,300 instructors and students. This edition benefited from an additional 100+ instructor reviews and almost 900 student reviews—all of this in addition to the semester-by-semester feedback we have been gathering from our own students. We have also met with our colleagues in more than 20 focus groups, listening to their feedback and brainstorming ways to address unmet needs in the classroom. One of the main themes that has emerged through these discussions is the need for more active learning. Instructors around the country are calling for more features that compel students to interact with each other, and to become active agents in their own learning process. As you will see in the upcoming pages, we have addressed this need from many angles, adding new features to the book and its supplements.

It's all about solving problems: 10 challenges we address

For years, our publisher has been conducting extensive research on barriers to student learning. Using the data gathered from this research, along with evidence collected through reviews, focus groups, and our own interactions with students, we have identified what we believe to be the 10 greatest challenges that emerge in the introductory course. This book was created to address these 10 challenges in a way that no other textbook does—consciously, systematically, and comprehensively. Let's take a look at how we tackle them.

"A must have for teaching psychology because there is not another textbook like it."

—JoAnne Shayne, *Southern New Hampshire University*

1. Creating relevance and student engagement

NEW

A DAY NOT TO REMEMBER Thursday, October 9, 2014: Christy Sheppard can only recall bits and pieces of that rainy day in Colorado Springs. She remembers leaving her house just before 9:00 A.M., and glancing in the rearview mirror to see if the garage door was closed. Yet, she has no recollection of driving to a local school, getting out of her car, and finding her way to the room where she took a fitness exam administered by the Colorado Springs Police Department. Christy doesn't recall interacting with her fellow officers, or anything about the test itself—not one push-up, sit-up, agility exercise, or shuttle run.

Feeling the Pressure
A 27-year veteran of the Colorado Springs Police Department, Christy Sheppard has taken—and passed—many police fitness exams. Yet, the stakes seemed higher on that testing day in the fall of 2014. "I was worried, being a minority, a female, and a brand new lieutenant," Christy explains. "In my mind I was thinking, *I don't want to be the guy that fails.*" Courtesy of Veronica Garfield Newhoff.

Our market research strongly suggests that the greatest challenge of teaching introductory psychology is generating student interest and engagement in the subject matter. We also know from our own teaching experience that students learn and remember material better when they see how it applies to the lives of real people. We capture the student's interest from the get-go, launching each chapter with a story about a person (or people) whose experiences help us understand and apply psychological concepts. Unlike the isolated case studies and opening vignettes commonly seen in other textbooks, our *Integrated Stories* are written in a journalistic style and *woven throughout* the chapters, offering memorable examples that reinforce important concepts at key intervals.

Associated with these stories are *Online Video Profiles,* which are free to all students. These custom videos bring our story subjects to life and provide valuable insights into each one's character. Assessable versions of the videos, found in LaunchPad, provide thoughtful questions that tighten the link between the story and chapter content, creating a more relevant and memorable learning experience. Many instructors have found these unique videos to be an excellent prelecture activity or assignment resource.

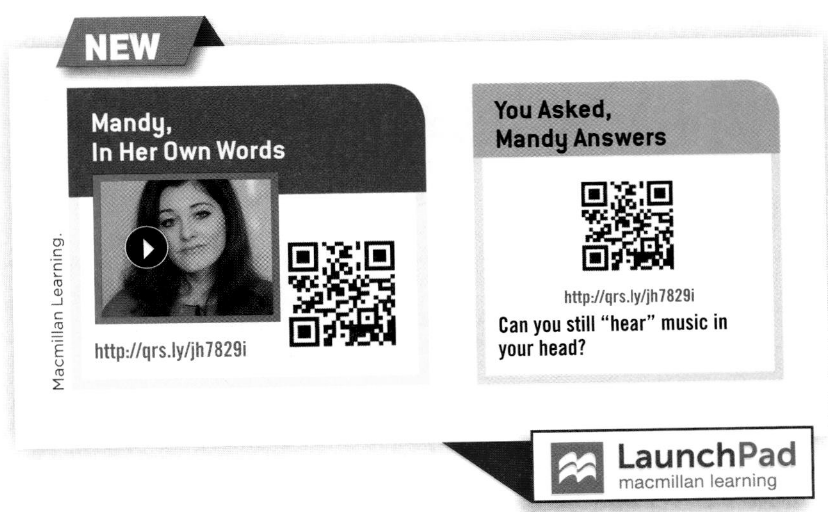

NEW
Mandy, In Her Own Words
http://qrs.ly/jh7829i
Macmillan Learning.
You Asked, Mandy Answers
http://qrs.ly/jh7829i
Can you still "hear" music in your head?
LaunchPad
macmillan learning

"The storytelling aspect differentiates this text from any other I've reviewed. Incredibly engaging, easy to read, yet grounded in theory. This is jam-packed with pedagogically sound techniques to engage readers of all abilities."

—Cari Stevenson, *Kankakee Community College*

1. Creating relevance and student engagement

Students want to know why studying psychology is important. How does it relate to their lives and when will they ever use it? We explore topical, high-interest subjects with real-world relevance in our *Integrated Thematic Features*. Organized around key themes in psychology, these features are seamlessly woven into the running text (not relegated to "boxes" that students will skip over). Look for these titles: Across the World, Believe It . . . Or Not, Didn't See That Coming, Think Critically, Social Media and Psychology, Think Positive, Career Connections, Apply This, and From the Pages of *Scientific American*.

SOCIAL MEDIA AND PSYCHOLOGY

CAN'T GET ENOUGH Is it difficult for you to sit through a movie without posting a new selfie on Instagram? Are you constantly looking at your Facebook News Feed in between work e-mails? Do you sleep with your iPhone? If you answered "yes" to any of the above, you are not alone. People around the world, from India to the United States, are getting hooked on social media—so hooked in some cases that they are getting treatment for social media or Internet "addiction"

THE URGE TO USE MEDIA WAS HARDER TO RESIST THAN SEX, SPENDING MONEY, ALCOHOL. . . .

NEW

DIDN'T SEE THAT COMING

SEXY SMELLS? Animals of all different kinds use pheromones to communicate with members of the same species. Rats, for example, release pheromones to mark territory and warn other rats of danger, and female elephants invite males to mate by secreting a pheromone in their urine (Tirindelli, Dibattista, Pifferi, & Menini, 2009).

THEIR ARMPITS SMELLED ENTICING.

NEW

CAREER CONNECTIONS

REINFORCEMENT IS GOLDEN Reinforcement is one of the most effective ways to change behaviors, but many people fail to take full advantage of its power. Would you believe that 37% of business managers report that they *never* offer positive reinforcement? Yet this type of input is key to maintaining good work relationships. Managers who offer positive reinforcement are actually perceived as more effective than those who offer mere criticism (Zenger & Folkman, 2017, May 2). What's more, workers tend to be more engaged when supervisors emphasize their strengths rather than homing in on their weaknesses (Fessler, 2017, June 22; Harter, & Adkinds, 2015,

EFFECTIVE MANAGERS USE POSITIVE REINFORCEMENT

NEW

THINK POSITIVE

GOING WITH THE FLOW People often make the mistake of viewing happiness as a goal they will attain at some point in the future, when all of life's pieces fall into place: "Once I start making a lot of money and buy a house, I will be happy," or, "If I just lose 10 pounds, I will finally be content." What they don't realize is that happiness may be within grasp, right here and right now. Sometimes it's just a matter of getting into the "flow."

Have you ever felt completely absorbed in a challenging task, guided by a focus so intense that everything else, including the past and future, faded from your awareness? Some people

IS IT THE SECRET TO ACHIEVING HAPPINESS?

1. Creating relevance and student engagement

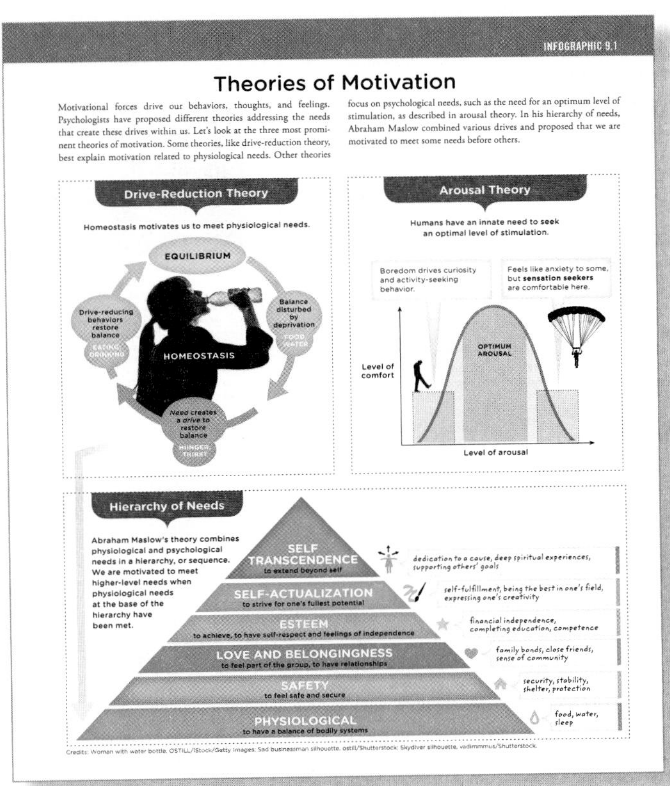

Sometimes "showing" is just as powerful as "telling." This is why we have included hundreds of thought-provoking photos and figures, as well as 52 full-page *Infographics* that primarily focus on presenting the hardest-to-teach topics.

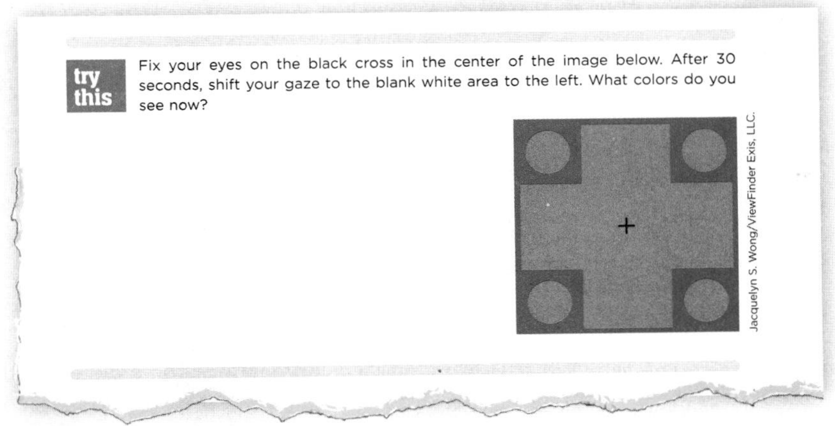

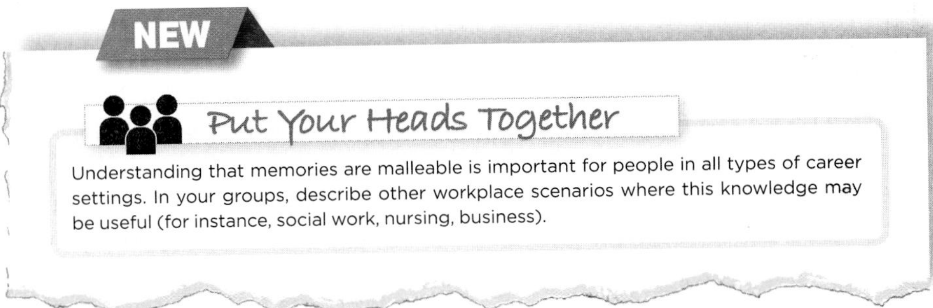

Another source of engagement is our new *Put Your Heads Together* feature, which prompts students to apply material and generate ideas in small groups. These 57 activities are interspersed throughout, available to any student with a book in hand. *Put Your Heads Together* was created in response to instructors' requests for more active learning exercises and recent research confirming the impact of such activities on concept understanding and retention. In our own classrooms, we have noted that these "learning by doing" tools are very effective and growing in popularity.

"I feel like my mind has been read with this text. All of my top complaints have been heard and addressed. I know I am not unique, but it feels like this text was written for me... Thank you!!"

—Christine Greco-Covington, *Brookdale Community College*

2. Demonstrating psychology is a science

In Chapters 0 and 1, we establish that psychology is a rigorous science, detailing the steps of the scientific method and emphasizing the importance of critical thinking. Using a variety of tools and features (some shown here), we continue to drive home this essential message in every subsequent chapter, encouraging students to evaluate research claims and consider the strengths and limitations of different methodologies.

Apply This ↓

DON'T BELIEVE EVERYTHING YOU READ

As you venture deeper into the study of psychology, you may find yourself becoming increasingly skeptical of media reports on psychological research. We encourage a healthy dose of skepticism. Although many news stories on scientific findings are accurate and balanced, others are flawed and overhyped. Look at these headlines about a 2017 study investigating the relationship between screen time and language development in toddlers:

"Tablets and smartphones damage toddlers' speech development."
(Snapton, 2017, May 4)

"The scary reason you need to limit your child's screen time ASAP."
(Jung, n.d.)

"Your iPhone could really mess up your baby."
(Brown, 2017, May 4)

It sounds as if screen time is *causing* speech problems in children. We must have a cause-and-effect relationship, right? Wrong. The following is a rough description of the research, which was presented at the 2017 Pediatric Academic Societies Meeting in San Francisco. The study focused on approximately 1,000 children ages 6–24 months. The parents reported the amount of time their kids spent playing on iPhones, tablets, and other handheld devices, and filled out a questionnaire aimed at assessing their children's language development. Upon reviewing the data, the

Overhyped Associations
In 2017 researchers presented a study revealing a correlation between toddler speech delays and the use of handheld devices like iPhones and iPads (Ma et al., 2017). The findings could easily be interpreted as "screen time leads to speech delays," but this is a reckless conclusion. Think of all the other variables that might impact language development: parenting

THINK CRITICALLY

CAN YOU PREDICT THE FUTURE? ESP, psychic powers—call it what you will, there is no scientific evidence to support its existence (Farha, 2007; Wiseman & Watt, 2006). Nevertheless, a handful of respected researchers have published research suggesting it exists. In 2011 Cornell University's Daryl Bem set off a firestorm of controversy with a journal article offering evidence for ESP. The article, which reported nine ex[…] 1,000 participants, suggested that human beings have […] future (Bem, 2011). When examining this work, othe[…] flaws in Bem's statistical analysis and tried without succ[…] (Ritchie, Wiseman, & French, 2012; Wagenmakers, W[…] der Maas, 2011).

THERE IS NO SCIENTIFIC EVIDENCE TO SUPPORT ITS EXISTENCE

Despite ESP's lack of scientific credibility, many pe[…] Most often, their "evidence" comes in the form of pers[…]

Overdose Death Toll
A woman marches during Overdose Awareness Day in the summer of 2017. The number one cause of death

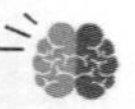

THINK CRITICALLY

AMERICA'S OPIOID EPIDEMIC Fifteen years ago, heroin use in the United States was relatively rare. Since then, the number of adults who have used this dangerous drug has jumped "almost 5-fold," from 0.33% to 1.6% (Martins et al., 2017, p. E5). What is behind this massive increase? One important factor is overuse of opioid painkillers such as Vicodin (hydrocodone) and OxyContin (oxycodone) (Barnett, Olenski, & Jena, 2017). Doctors prescribe these drugs for pain, but some patients get hooked and then turn to heroin as an alternative. Imagine a patient arriving at the emergency room and complaining of severe pain; the doctor writes a prescription for an opioid painkiller, and the patient (or perhaps a friend or family member of the patient) becomes dependent on it.

"THE WORST DRUG OVERDOSE EPIDEMIC IN AMERICAN HISTORY"

From the pages of SCIENTIFIC AMERICAN

"SUPER AGERS" HAVE BRAINS THAT LOOK YOUNG

Older adults who perform like young people on tests of memory have a shrink-resistant cortex.

As we get older, we start to think a little bit more slowly, we are less able to multitask, and our ability to remember things gets a little wobblier. This cognitive transformation is linked to a steady, widespread thinning of the cortex, the brain's outermost layer. Yet the change is not inevitable. So-called super agers retain their good memory and thicker cortex as they age, a recent study suggests.

Our partnership with the highly respected publication *Scientific American* tacitly reinforces the notion that psychology is a science. Equally important, it provides us with the opportunity to feature the work of leading science journalists. Every chapter includes a *From the Pages of Scientific American* feature that describes impactful research in the field.

"This book is in a league of its own. I am not aware of anything that compares with it. It is unique and visionary; every 'i' is dotted and every 't' crossed as far as I am concerned in terms of what an ideal text would be."

—Jan Mendoza, *Golden West College*

2. Demonstrating psychology is a science

In addition to reinforcing scientific concepts such as replicability and experimental control, Infographics teach students how to be consumers of scientific information from all sources, be it a journal article or media report:

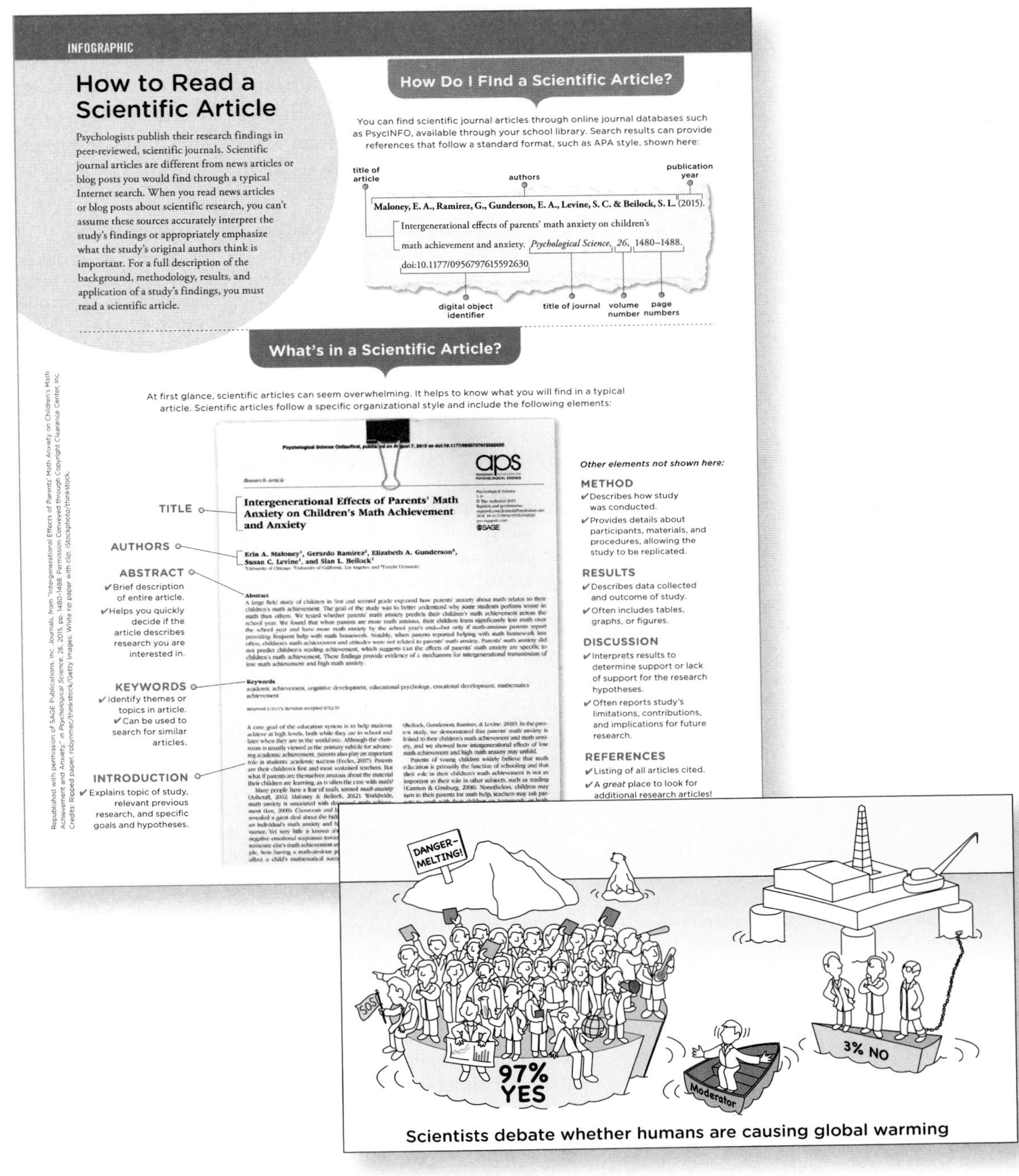

"This seems like the best text I've come across. By far."

—Justin Huft, *Saddleback College*

3. Helping students see the "big picture"

To help students see conceptual links across chapters, we have strategically placed *Connections* features in the margins. More detailed than typical cross-references, these brief summaries complement what many instructors do in the classroom—point out the relationships between topics currently being presented and material previously covered. Many students won't automatically make a connection between perception and memory, or see how transference might relate to obedience, but the Connections spell it out without requiring readers to flip back pages and locate the linked topic. Because making connections is so crucial (not only to us, but to the hundreds of instructors who have used and reviewed this text), we have included assessment questions directly related to these links in our *Test Bank*.

Surprisingly, compliance often occurs **outside of our awareness**. Suppose you are waiting in line at a copy machine, and a man asks if he can cut in front of you. Do you allow it? Your response may depend on the wording of the request. Researchers studying this very scenario—a person asking for permission to cut in line—have found that compliance is much more likely when the request is accompanied by a reason. Saying, "Excuse me, I have five pages. May I use the [copy] machine?" will not work as well as "Excuse me, I have five pages. May I use the [copy] machine, *because I am in a rush?*" People are more likely to comply with a request that includes

CONNECTIONS

In **Chapter 4,** we discussed automatic processing, cognitive activity that occurs with little or no conscious effort. Automatic processing can guide behaviors, including those associated with compliance.

learn behaviors through classical conditioning, operant conditioning, and observational learning (Chapter 5). Let's take a look at how operant conditioning can help us understand the relationship between learning and motivation. When a behavior is reinforced (with **positive or negative *reinforcers***), an association is established. This association between a behavior and its consequence becomes the **incentive,** or reason, you are motivated to repeat the behavior. Imagine you have been avoiding a particular term paper assignment. You decide to treat yourself to an hour of watching Netflix for every three pages you write. Adding a reinforcer (Netflix) increases your writing

CONNECTIONS

In **Chapter 5,** we introduced positive and negative reinforcers, which are stimuli that increase future occurrences of target behaviors. In both cases, the behavior becomes associated with the reinforcer. Here, we see how these associations become incentives.

CONNECTIONS

In **Chapter 2,** we discussed the properties that allow neurons to communicate. When enough sending neurons signal a receiving neuron to pass along its message, their combined signal becomes excitatory and the neuron fires. Similarly, if enough odor molecules bind to an olfactory receptor neuron, an action potential occurs.

as a lock acts as a docking site for a key; **Figure 3.4**). When enough odor molecules attach to an **olfactory receptor neuron, it fires.** This is how *transduction* occurs in the chemical sense of olfaction.

WHAT'S UP WITH THAT SMELL? Olfactory receptor neurons project into a part of the brain called the *olfactory bulb,* where they converge in clusters called *glomeruli* (Figure 3.4). From there, signals are passed along to higher brain centers, including the hippocampus, amygdala, and olfactory cortex (Firestein, 2001; Seubert, Freiherr, Djordjevic, & Lundström, 2013). The other sensory systems relay information through the thalamus before it goes to higher brain centers, but not the olfactory system; its wiring is on a fast track to the olfactory cortex. There is another reason smell is special. Olfactory receptor neurons are one of the few types of neurons that

"Great chapter connections, captivating personal stories of real people that make students want to read more, cool themes that capture student interest, and a book design that captures in-book activities that you can use for discussion. *All in one book.*"

—Nickolas Shizas, *Moraine Valley Community College*

4. Teaching and mastering the toughest concepts

We understand that difficult concepts require multiple examples underscoring connections with everyday life; we also know that students benefit from expanded assessment opportunities. But sometimes more narrative examples and intensive assessment are not enough; in order for things to really "click," a student must see the information presented in a new light. This is why we use Infographics, tables, figures, and photos to tackle challenging topics throughout the text.

There are 52 Infographics appearing throughout the chapters. Patterned after the visual features in *Scientific American,* these full-page visual presentations combine concepts and/or data into a single storyboard format. Most illuminate concepts identified through research as the most challenging for instructors to teach and students to master. The Infographics have received some of the most enthusiastic feedback from our student reviewers. Assessable versions are available through LaunchPad.

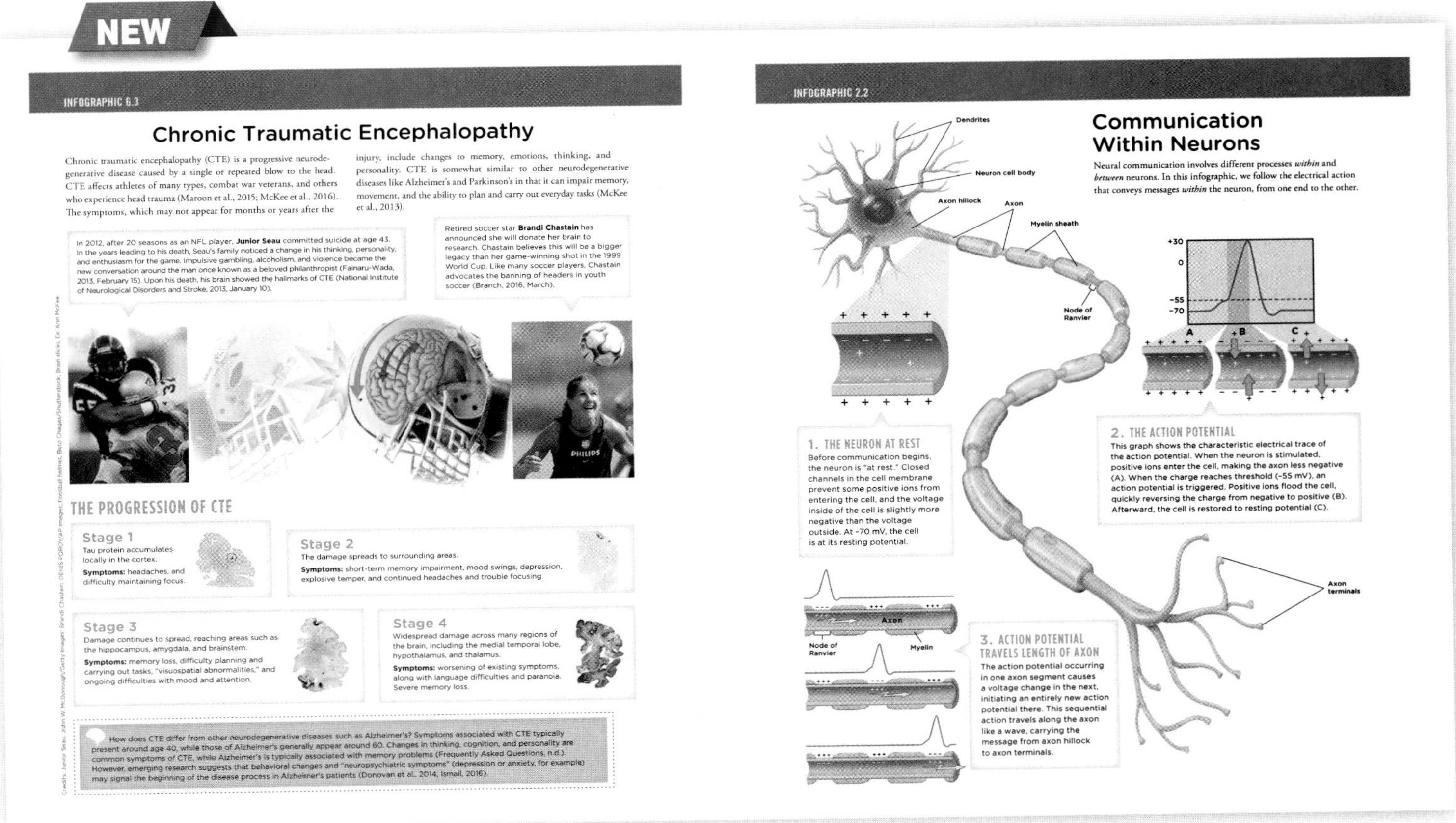

> "This is the best introductory text I've come across."
>
> —Rachel Laimon, *Mott Community College*

4. Teaching and mastering the toughest concepts

Tables and figures show how concepts can be organized.

NEW

TABLE 5.1 CLASSICAL CONDITIONING: STIMULUS AND RESPONSE

Stimulus	Response	Dog and Buzzer
Neutral stimulus (NS) does not cause an automatic response.	No relevant response to NS.	Buzzer (NS) initially does not cause dog to salivate.
Unconditioned stimulus (US) causes *unlearned* response.	**Unconditioned response (UR)** is automatic and is triggered by US.	Meat is always a US (the dog never has to learn how to respond to it). Dog's salivation is initially a UR to meat.
Conditioned stimulus (CS) causes *learned* response. Always different from US.	**Conditioned response (CR)** is learned from pairing with US.	Buzzer (CS) causes dog to salivate (CR).

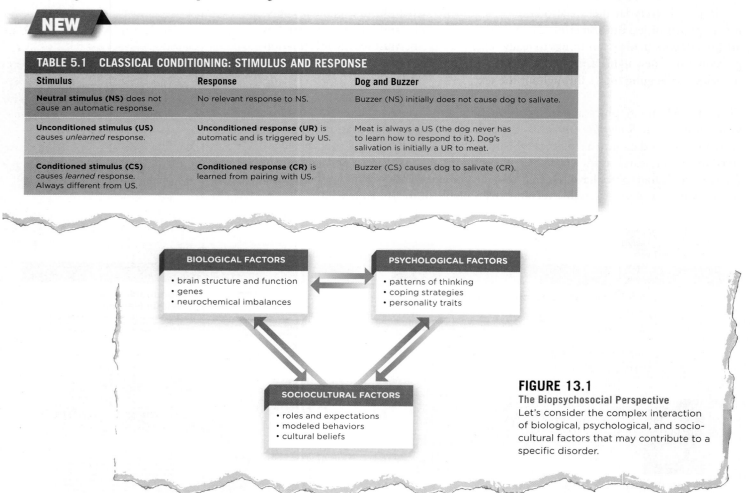

FIGURE 13.1
The Biopsychosocial Perspective
Let's consider the complex interaction of biological, psychological, and sociocultural factors that may contribute to a specific disorder.

And when it comes to explaining certain abstractions, a photo can be worth a thousand words.

Motion Parallax
As you walk along a busy street, nearby objects appear to move by faster than objects faraway. This monocular cue, known as motion parallax, also helps with depth perception when you are sitting still and objects in the environment are moving around you (for example, cars driving past at different distances).
Martin Botvidsson/Getty Images.

"This textbook is in a different league, essentially."

—Jonathan Sparks, *Vance-Granville Community College*

5. Illustrating real-world applications

NEW

Put Your Heads Together

In your groups, discuss the following: **A)** How is a split-brain operation different from a hemispherectomy? **B)** If you were faced with a hypothetical decision to undergo a hemispherectomy, which half of your brain would you choose to have removed and why? **C)** What functions might you lose as a result?

Put Your Heads Together

In your group, **A)** pick a character from a fairy tale, TV show, or movie, and describe some aspects of his or her personality. **B)** Now consider the six theoretical perspectives presented in Table 10.1, and pick at least three of them to explain how these characteristics might have developed.

Any time we see an opportunity to apply psychological findings to students' lives, we seize upon it. In addition to pointing out psychology-in-action via traditional avenues (research studies, photo captions, tables, figures, and so on), we have created several special features that compel students to *apply* key concepts and thereby make connections to their own lives.

This edition features 57 new Put Your Heads Together features that offer quick, engaging activities to generate class participation and stimulate discussions.

Also appearing throughout the chapters are *Try This* exercises, which prompt students to apply key concepts by performing simple activities. Typically fast and easy to do, these activities are designed to reinforce chapter content and engage students.

try this Next time you are outside in a crowded area, look up and keep your eyes toward the sky. Do some people change their gazes to match yours, even though there is no other indication that something is happening above?

Heather Shimmin/Shutterstock.com.

try this Stare at the photo of the monkey and then shut your eyes for several seconds. Did you see the image in your mind's eye and, if so, how long did this iconic memory last?

Georgegid/Shutterstock.com.

"I have reviewed several textbooks over the past couple of years, and this is superior to all of those."

—Stacey Frank, *Tri-County Technical College*

5. Illustrating real-world applications

Instructors want to make sure that students develop psychological literacy and acquire the critical thinking skills needed for success in real-life situations. *Your Scientific World* was created with such goals in mind. These new online immersive learning activities place students in role-playing scenarios requiring them to think critically and apply their knowledge of psychological science to solve real-world problems. Your Scientific World activities appear at the end of each chapter and can be assigned and assessed through LaunchPad. Students can also perform these activities on their own and see their results.

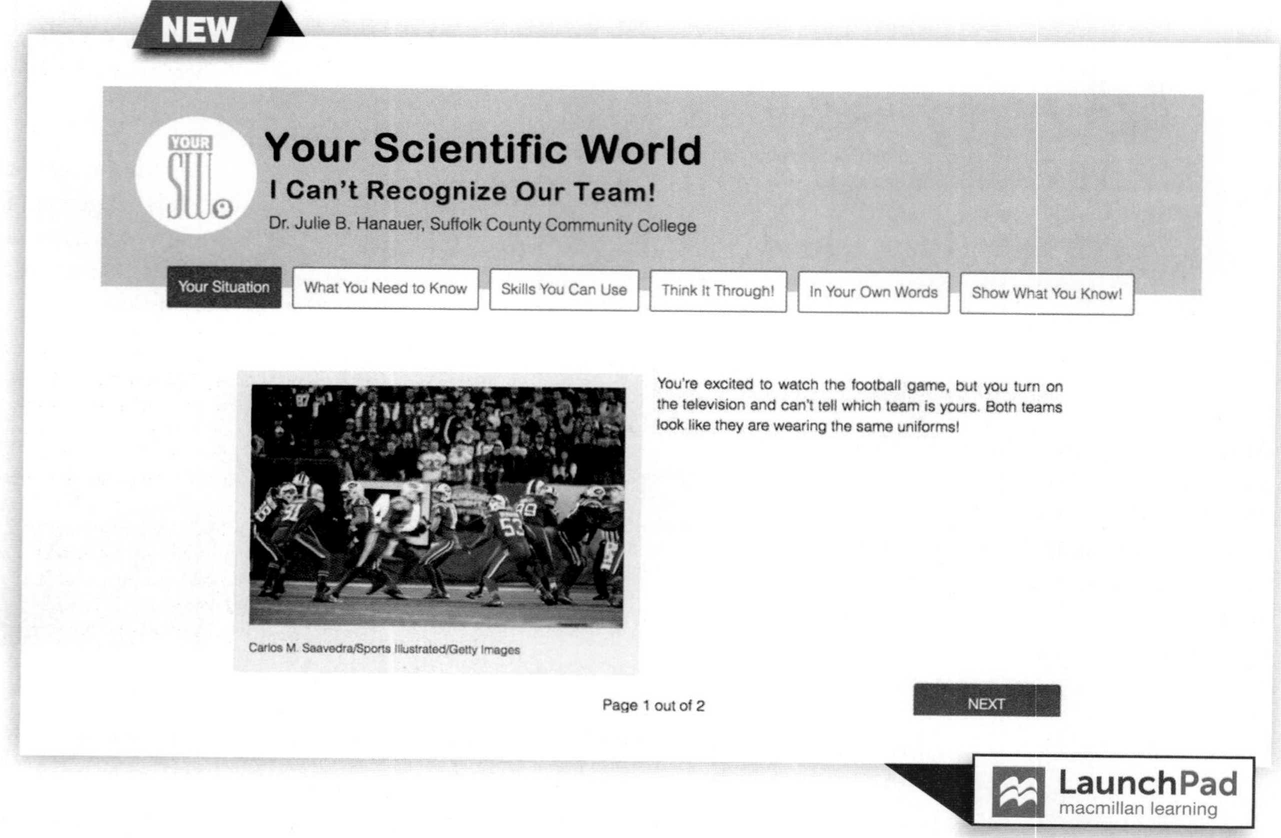

"This is a very captivating book to read, with high level examples from the real world and popular culture. I love how accessible the examples are for the students. Everyday language, explanations that are clear and relevant, like the ones on conditioning and dogs. I also think the infographics are special and unique."

—Deanna DeGidio, *Northern Virginia Community College*

"The partnership with *Scientific American* is invaluable."

—Justine Egan-Kunicki, *Community College of Rhode Island*

6. Keeping it positive

Many students enter the course thinking that psychology is all about abnormal and maladaptive patterns of human behavior. Our new *Think Positive* feature underscores the many ways psychological findings can guide us in a positive direction, helping us become the best possible versions of ourselves.

NEW

THINK POSITIVE

THE VERSATILE BRAIN Brandon and Christina provide breathtaking illustrations of neuroplasticity—the brain's ability to heal, grow new connections, and make do with what is available. These amazing changes can occur under a variety of circumstances—after a stroke, in the face of blindness, and even adapting to motherhood (Convento, Russo, Zigiotto, & Bolognini, 2016; Hasson, Andric, Atilgan, & Collignon, 2016; Kim, Strathearn, & Swain, 2016). Your brain can change, too. Every time you acquire knowledge or learn a new skill, whether it's cooking Pad Thai or plucking out melodies on a guitar, new networks of communication are sprouting between your neurons (Barss, Pearcey, & Zehr, 2016; Vaquero et al., 2016). Expose yourself to new information and activities, and your brain will continue to develop and adapt. There is no limit to the amount you can learn!

YOUR BRAIN CAN CHANGE, TOO

NEW

THINK POSITIVE

RIGHT HERE, RIGHT NOW In the very first chapter of this book, we introduced *positive psychology*, "the study of positive emotions, positive character traits, and enabling institutions" (Seligman & Steen, 2005, p. 410). Rather than focusing on mental illness and abnormal behavior, positive psychology emphasizes human strengths and virtues. The goal is well-being and fulfillment, and that means "satisfaction" with the past, "hope and optimism" for the future, and "flow and happiness" at the current time (Seligman & Csikszentmihalyi, 2000, p. 5).

FOCUS ON YOUR BREATHING. . . .

As we wrap up this chapter on stress and health, we encourage you to focus on that third category: flow and happiness in the present. No matter what stressors come your way, try to stay grounded in the here and now. The past is the past, the future is uncertain, but this moment is yours. Finding a way to enjoy the present is one of the best ways to reduce stress. Easier said than done, you may be thinking.

DEFYING STIGMA: ROSS AND MELISSA LEARN TO THRIVE It took years of hard work for Ross to get on top of his disorder. He quit using alcohol, caffeine, nicotine, and marijuana, and imposed a new structure on his life—waking up and going to sleep at the same time each day, eating regular meals, and exercising. He also started being open and honest in his relationships with friends, family, and his therapist. Most important, he confronted his self-hatred, working hard to identify and appreciate things he liked about himself. "What was missing was me being an active member in my treatment," Ross says, "and doing things outside of treatment [to get better]." After graduating cum laude from American University, Ross became a mental health advocate, giving presentations at high schools and colleges across America. Today, he is busy running his own consulting group, Human Power Project, which designs cutting-edge mental health curricula for middle and high schools. His battle with bipolar disorder is ongoing ("I'm not cured," says Ross), but he continues

Our Integrated Stories center on people who remain optimistic, hardworking, and kind to others—no matter how hard life gets.

"These features are really innovative and I really like that they are integrated into the text."

—Michaela Porubanova, *Farmingdale State University*

6. Keeping it positive

To illustrate the application value of research findings related to positive psychology, we have added a new Infographic on pathways to happiness.

NEW

INFOGRAPHIC 9.4

Pathways to Happiness

When it comes to being happy, there is no "magic bullet," but the latest research suggests we may be able to cultivate positive emotions and well-being through a variety of activities, many of which do not involve spending money. That being said, money does play a role—and it's not so much about how much you have, but how you choose to use it.

YES! Going to college
Higher levels of education have been linked to greater happiness (Trostel, 2015, October 14).

YES! Achieving "flow"
While studying, working, or pursuing an interest, allow yourself to become completely absorbed in challenging and rewarding tasks (Csikszentmihalyi, 1999; Culbertson, Fullagar, Simmons, & Zhu, 2015).

NO! Buying new stuff
Buying new things may provide temporary pleasure, but it is unlikely to increase long-term happiness (Donnelly, Ksendzova, Howell, Vohs, & Baumeister, 2016; Lyubomirsky et al., 2005).

YES! Prioritizing relationships
Cultivating deep and meaningful relationships with family and friends seems to bolster happiness (Helliwell, Layard, & Sachs, 2018).

YES! "Buying time"
Paying for timesaving services, such as grocery delivery, is associated with "greater life satisfaction" (Whillans, Dunn, Smeets, Bekkers, & Norton, 2017, p. 1).

NO! Becoming a millionaire
Salary increases may boost happiness, but "most data suggest that after basic needs have been met, additional income is not associated with increases in well-being" (Mogilner & Norton, 2016, p. 12).

MAYBE Moving your body
Physically active people are generally happier than their sedentary peers (Lathia, Sandstrom, Mascolo, & Rentfrow, 2017).

YES! Counting your blessings
Being grateful for what you have may lead to less stress and greater well-being (Emmons & McCullough, 2003; Krejtz, Nezlek, Michnicka, Holas, & Rusanowska, 2016).

MAYBE Buying experiences
Investing in vacations, restaurant meals, and other activities is more likely to promote "enduring happiness" than purchasing material items (Gilovich & Kumar, 2015).

YES! Being kind and generous
Whether you are buying a gift or donating to charity, spending money on others is likely to increase your happiness (Dunn, Aknin, & Nortin, 2014; Park et al., 2017).

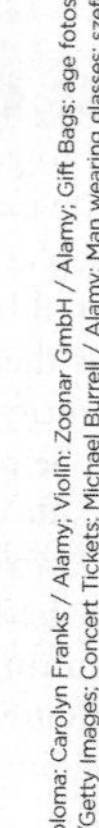

Top: Cap/diploma: Carolyn Franks / Alamy; Violin: Zoonar GmbH / Alamy; Gift Bags: age fotostock / Alamy; Delivery Van: Jakub Krechowicz / Alamy; Fruit: jean-paul chassenet / Alamy; Exercise Mat/Kettle Bells: Milic Djurovic / Alamy; Gift with bow: Milkos/Getty Images; Concert Tickets: Michael Burrell / Alamy; Man wearing glasses: szefei/AGE Fotostock; Heart Thank you note: stockcam/Getty Images; US Money: LAMB / Alamy; Figures holding hands: Strejman/Shutterstock

7. Embracing diversity

Our Integrated Stories, photos, in-text examples, and numerous application exercises provide exposure to a broad array of backgrounds. The recurring *Across the World* thematic feature is dedicated to exploring the impact of culture on human thoughts, emotions, and behavior.

ACROSS THE WORLD

WHEN TO REVEAL, WHEN TO CONCEAL Although the expression of some basic emotions appears to be universal, culture acts like a filter, determining the appropriate contexts in which to exhibit them. A culture's **display rules** provide the guidelines for when, how, and where an emotion is expressed. In North America, where individualism prevails, people tend to be fairly expressive. Showing emotion, particularly positive emotions, is socially acceptable. This is less the case in the collectivist (community-oriented) societies of East Asia, where concealing emotions is more the norm. Display rules are taught early in life, as parents

CAN YOU FEEL THE CULTURE?

ACROSS THE WORLD

CULTURE OF PERSONALITY Have you heard the old joke about European stereotypes? It goes like this: In heaven, the chefs are French, the mechanics German, the lovers Italian, the police officers British, and the bankers Swiss. In hell, the cooks are British, the police officers German, the mechanics French, the lovers Swiss, and the bankers Italian (Mulvey, 2006, May 15). This joke plays upon what psychologists might call "national stereotypes," or preconceived notions about the personalities of people belonging to certain cultures. Are such stereotypes accurate?

PLEASE LEAVE YOUR STEREOTYPES AT THE BORDER!

The Integrated Stories have been carefully researched and selected to represent people from all walks of life, providing a diverse mosaic of gender, culture, race, age, nationality, and occupation. Approximately 65% of the stories focus on the lives of people who are ethnic/racial minorities, and 23% relate the experiences of individuals with disabilities.

NEW

Humanistic, Learning, and Trait Theories

ON A POSITIVE PATH After Saifa's testes were removed and he began taking female hormones, doctors expected (or hoped) he would blossom into a lovely young woman. But as Saifa recalls, "I did not succumb to the pressure to be more feminine, but actually gravitated toward masculinity" (Wall, 2015, p. 118). He excelled in school and eventually became a leader at Williams College, spearheading campus demonstrations against police brutality and anti-gay hate crimes. A few years after graduating, Saifa decided to make the biological and social transition to manhood; he changed his name to Sean Saifa Wall, began taking testosterone, and underwent a double mastectomy.

Saifa had assumed control of his body and his life like never before, yet he could not shake the feelings of loneliness and self-hatred. To do this, he would need to confront a lifetime of trauma, which included the loss of his father—first to prison and then to AIDS—and life-changing medical interventions that occurred before he was old enough to give informed consent. Saifa courageously faced these traumas by

Courtesy Sean Saifa Wall.

Every Body Is Beautiful
Saifa advocates for the legal rights of children with intersex traits.

7. Embracing diversity

NEW

BEFORE HE WAS THE DOG WHISPERER December 23, 1990: Cesar Millan had made up his mind; it was time to leave Mexico and start a new life in America. He was 21 years old, spoke no English, and had exactly $100 in his pocket. Since the age of 13, Cesar had dreamed of becoming the greatest dog trainer in the world. Now he was ready to pursue that goal, even if it meant saying goodbye to everything he knew and cherished—his family, his homeland, and his culture (Millan & Peltier, 2006).

From his home in Mazatlán, Cesar traveled to the dangerous border city of Tijuana, where he met a human smuggler who said he would get him into the United States for a fee of—you guessed it—$100. Trudging over muddy terrain, darting across a busy freeway, and hiding in a frigid trench of water, Cesar stuck with the smuggler. When he finally reached San Diego, he was "dripping wet, filthy, thirsty, [and] hungry." But, as Cesar recalls in his book *Cesar's Way,* "I was the happiest man in the world" (Millan & Peltier, 2006, p. 39).

For more than a month, Cesar slept under a freeway and lived on hotdogs from 7-Eleven (Partisan Pictures, 2012). Technically, he was "homeless," but he didn't feel like a drifter. "I never felt lost," Cesar recalls, "I always knew what I wanted." Cesar got a job at

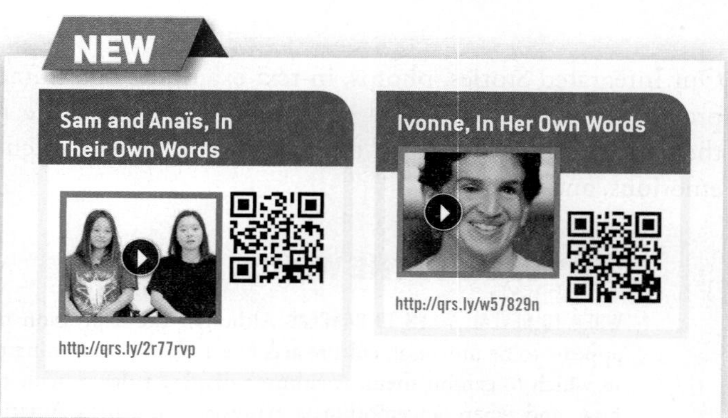

Photos throughout celebrate the strength and resilience of all human beings, especially those who have overcome significant challenges.

Faster Together? Athletes compete in the 5,000-meter T54 event of the 2016 Paralympics in Rio. Through social facilitation, competitive athletes may help each other perform better. Kyodo via AP Images.

Higher Education for All A student (left) works with his teacher at Syracuse University (SU), which has an "InclusiveU" program that serves students with intellectual disabilities. Students in InclusiveU take regular college classes, pursue internships, and participate in athletics. "At SU, we celebrate disability because it makes our campus stronger, more diverse, and much more interesting" (Syracuse University, n.d., para. 3). HEATHER AINSWORTH/The New York Times.

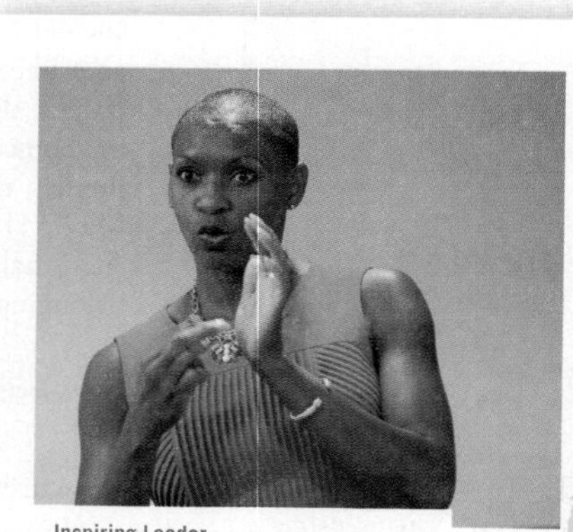

Inspiring Leader When Claudia Gordon lost the ability to hear at 8 years old, she thought she was "the only deaf person in the world" (Baggetto, 2010, para. 5). Gordon eventually became a leader in the deaf community and in society at large, serving in the Obama administration as public engagement advisor for the disability community. SourceAmerica.

"While I was reviewing the text and referring back to other intro psych texts, I could not think of other texts that had such well-designed features."

—Leslie Bartley, *Florida Southwest State College*

"I like the real life, current examples, the conversational style, and the multitude of ways in which the authors have made psychology user friendly to newcomers."

—Anthony Scioli, *Keene State College*

8. Dispelling myths

Many students have trouble distinguishing between pseudoscience and actual science. We begin to chip away at this challenge right away in Chapter 0 (Table 0.1, Dispelled: Five "Commonsense" Myths) and then continue to refute these and many other misconceptions in future chapters, always emphasizing the role of critical thinking.

TABLE 0.1 DISPELLED: FIVE "COMMONSENSE" MYTHS

Myth	Reality
"Blowing off steam" or expressing anger is good for you.	Unleashing anger actually may make you more aggressive (Lilienfeld et al., 2010).
Most older people live sad and solitary lives.	People actually become happier with age (Lilienfeld et al., 2010).
Punishment is a great way to change behavior in the long term.	Punishment can lead to unwanted results (see Chapter 5). Myths like this can have a lasting impact on perceptions of discipline (Furnham & Hughes, 2014).
Eating "comfort foods" makes you feel happier.	So-called comfort foods are not unique in their mood-enhancing effects; it appears that a wide variety of foods can improve our moods (Wagner, Ahlstrom, Redden, Vickers, & Mann, 2014).
Listening to Mozart and other classical music will make an infant smarter.	There is no solid evidence that infants who listen to Mozart are smarter than those who do not (Hirsh-Pasek, Golinkoff, & Eyer, 2003).

Here are a few examples of commonsense "wisdom" that have been debunked by psychological research.

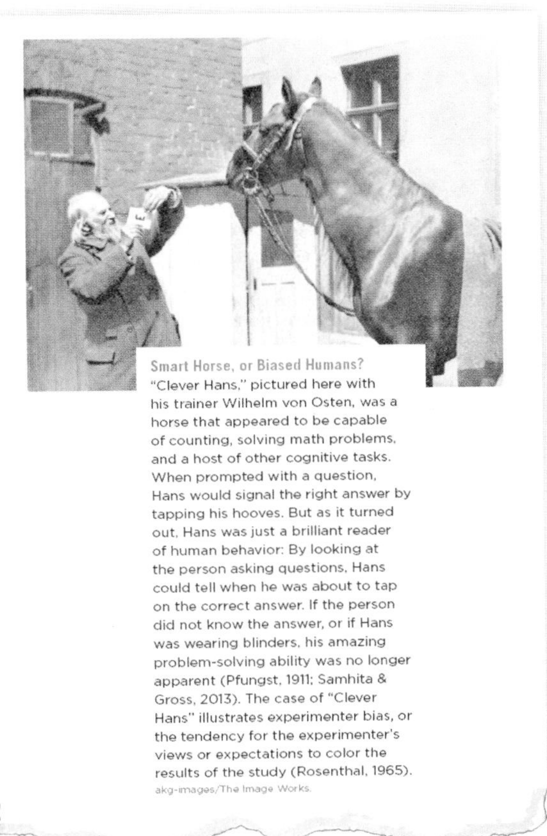

Smart Horse, or Biased Humans?
"Clever Hans," pictured here with his trainer Wilhelm von Osten, was a horse that appeared to be capable of counting, solving math problems, and a host of other cognitive tasks. When prompted with a question, Hans would signal the right answer by tapping his hooves. But as it turned out, Hans was just a brilliant reader of human behavior: By looking at the person asking questions, Hans could tell when he was about to tap on the correct answer. If the person did not know the answer, or if Hans was wearing blinders, his amazing problem-solving ability was no longer apparent (Pfungst, 1911; Samhita & Gross, 2013). The case of "Clever Hans" illustrates experimenter bias, or the tendency for the experimenter's views or expectations to color the results of the study (Rosenthal, 1965).
akg-images/The Image Works.

Bogus Fortune?
What do you think about the message delivered in this fortune cookie? Because the statement is sufficiently vague and complimentary, it could apply to just about any person on the planet—and therefore, many people fall for it. We call this phenomenon the Barnum effect.
Image Source/Getty Images.

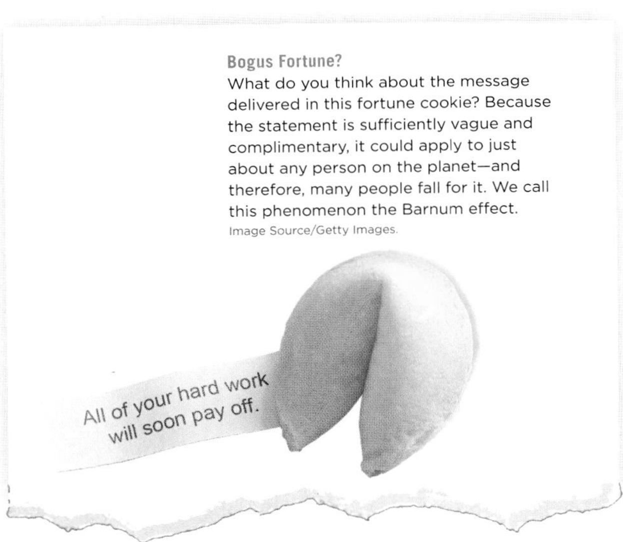

All of your hard work
will soon pay off.

"It is an exciting and innovative new textbook that will draw in your students and make them want to learn more about psychology."

—Sabra Jacobs, *Big Sandy Community and Technical College*

8. Dispelling myths

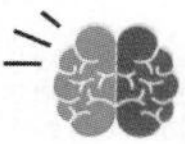

THINK CRITICALLY

THE INSANITY PLEA Perhaps you have heard the term "insanity" used in a legal setting. "The defendant got off on an insanity plea," or "The defense failed to demonstrate insanity." What do these statements mean? **Insanity** is a legal determination of the degree to which a person is responsible for his criminal behaviors. Those deemed legally insane are thought to have little or no control over or understanding of their behaviors at the time they committed their crimes. Therefore, they are given psychological treatment in a locked psychiatric facility rather than criminal punishment such as imprisonment or the death penalty. In America, 46 states offer a form of the insanity defense; only Idaho, Kansas, Montana, and Utah do not (Cevallos, 2015, July 17; "The Insanity Defense Among the States," n.d.). **Many people believe** that the insanity defense is frequently used, but it's invoked in only about 1% of cases. Of those cases, just 10–25% of insanity defenses are successful (Torry & Billick, 2010). Among those who avoided prison after entering an insanity plea was John Hinckley Jr., the man who attempted to assassinate President Ronald Reagan in 1981 (PBS, 2014).

IT'S INVOKED IN ONLY ABOUT 1% OF CASES

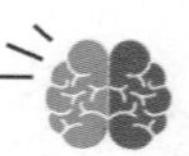

THINK CRITICALLY

6 SLEEP MYTHS

- **Drinking alcohol helps you sleep better:** Alcohol helps people fall asleep, but it undermines sleep quality and may cause night awakenings (Ebrahim, Shapiro, Williams, & Fenwick, 2013).
- **Yawning means you are exhausted:** Unlikely. Yawning appears to be related to temperature, and functions to help keep the brain cool (Massen, Dusch, Eldakar, & Gallup, 2014).
- **Everyone needs 8 hours of sleep each night:** Experts recommend we get more than 7 hours of sleep each night (Watson et al., 2015), but sleep needs can range greatly from person to person. Some people do fine with 6 hours; others genuinely need 9 or 10 (Schoenborn et al., 2013).

HAVE YOU FALLEN FOR ANY OF THEM?

"This text stands out from other texts with its various features and emphasis on making the information relevant and applicable, while still making it clear that psychology is a science and featuring relevant research studies."

—Brooke Hindman, *Greenville Technical College*

9. Testing works: More opportunities for assessment

We've read the research and seen it play out in the classroom: Students learn better when they are given ample opportunities to be tested on the material. But testing needn't be restricted to high-stakes exams and stressful pop quizzes. We have built assessment into our learning rubric, by using end-of-section *Show What You Know* and end-of-chapter *Test Prep* questions that reward students for reading carefully, thinking critically, and applying concepts. Each question is connected to a learning objective and answers are provided at the back of the book, in Appendix C.

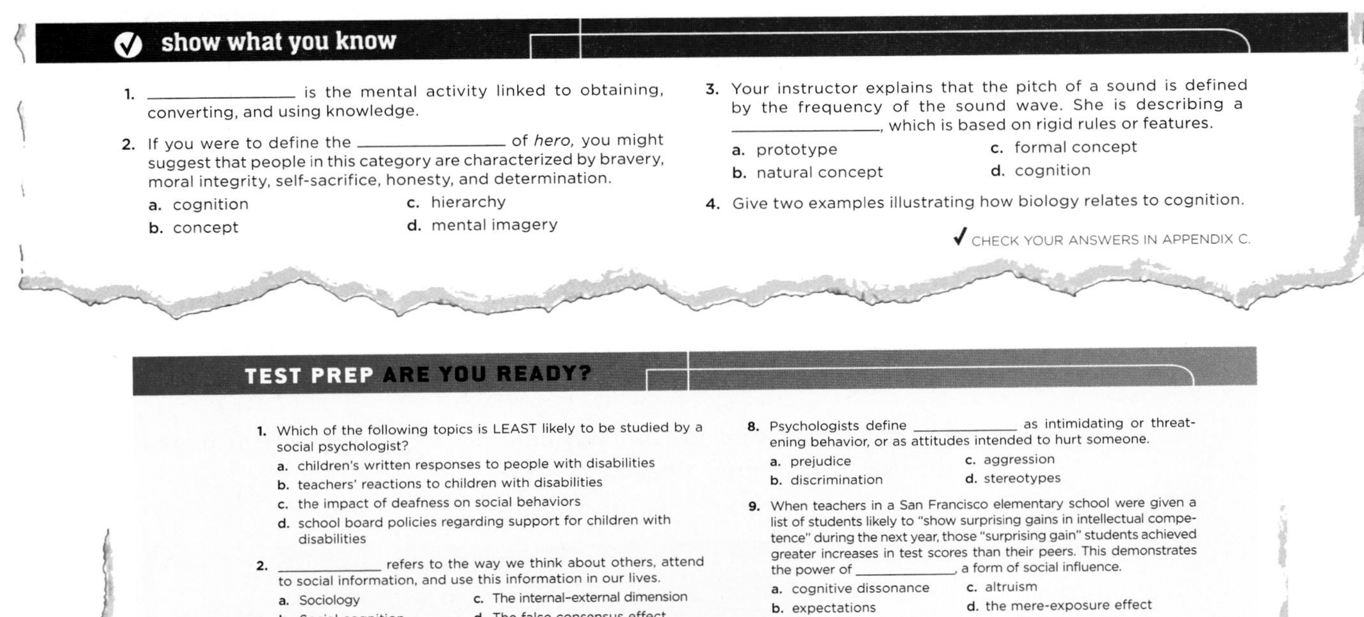

show what you know

1. ______________ is the mental activity linked to obtaining, converting, and using knowledge.
2. If you were to define the ______________ of *hero*, you might suggest that people in this category are characterized by bravery, moral integrity, self-sacrifice, honesty, and determination.
   a. cognition c. hierarchy
   b. concept d. mental imagery
3. Your instructor explains that the pitch of a sound is defined by the frequency of the sound wave. She is describing a ______________, which is based on rigid rules or features.
   a. prototype c. formal concept
   b. natural concept d. cognition
4. Give two examples illustrating how biology relates to cognition.

✓ CHECK YOUR ANSWERS IN APPENDIX C.

TEST PREP ARE YOU READY?

1. Which of the following topics is LEAST likely to be studied by a social psychologist?
   a. children's written responses to people with disabilities
   b. teachers' reactions to children with disabilities
   c. the impact of deafness on social behaviors
   d. school board policies regarding support for children with disabilities
2. ______________ refers to the way we think about others, attend to social information, and use this information in our lives.
   a. Sociology c. The internal–external dimension
   b. Social cognition d. The false consensus effect
3. Sometimes we attribute people's behaviors to their traits or personality characteristics, and underestimate the powerful influence of the environment. This is known as:
   a. the just-world hypothesis. c. a dispositional attribution.
   b. the false consensus effect. d. the fundamental attribution error.
4. The desire to help others with no expectation of payback is called:
   a. groupthink. c. altruism.
   b. deindividuation. d. conformity.
5. When it comes to decorating his house, your neighbor seems to follow the lead. If he sees others hanging lights, he immediately
8. Psychologists define ______________ as intimidating or threatening behavior, or as attitudes intended to hurt someone.
   a. prejudice c. aggression
   b. discrimination d. stereotypes
9. When teachers in a San Francisco elementary school were given a list of students likely to "show surprising gains in intellectual competence" during the next year, those "surprising gain" students achieved greater increases in test scores than their peers. This demonstrates the power of ______________, a form of social influence.
   a. cognitive dissonance c. altruism
   b. expectations d. the mere-exposure effect
10. According to Sternberg, love is made up of three elements:
   a. passion, mere exposure, and proximity.
   b. proximity, similarity, and passion.
   c. romantic love, mere exposure, and similarity.
   d. passion, intimacy, and commitment.
11. Social psychology explores the way individuals behave in relation to others and groups, while sociology examines the groups themselves. Give several examples of how these two fields might approach the same overall topic (for example, prosocial behavior of college students versus the impact of social support structures in higher education).

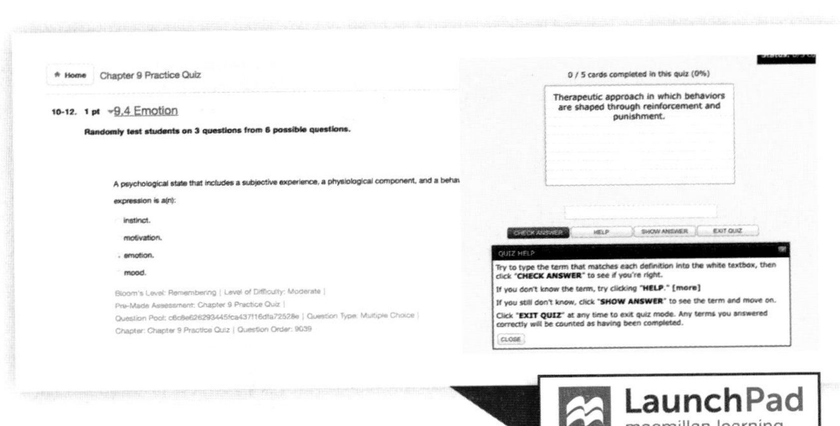

In addition to the Show What You Know and Test Prep, there are ample assessment opportunities beyond the book, including chapter-based practice quizzes and flashcards.

9. Testing works: More opportunities for assessment

Assessable versions of the Infographics and Online Video Profiles are available in LaunchPad, offering students an interactive way to gauge their understanding of the material. Questions for these activities are written by the authors.

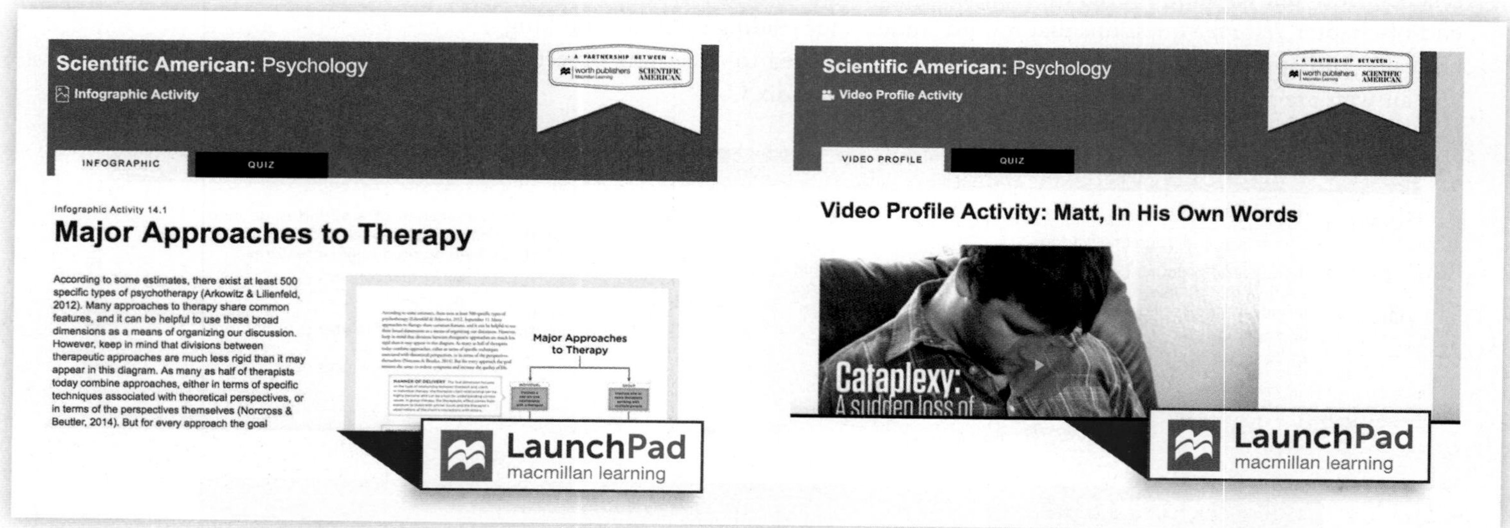

In LaunchPad, students can also find quizzes on the content presented in From the Pages of *Scientific American* features.

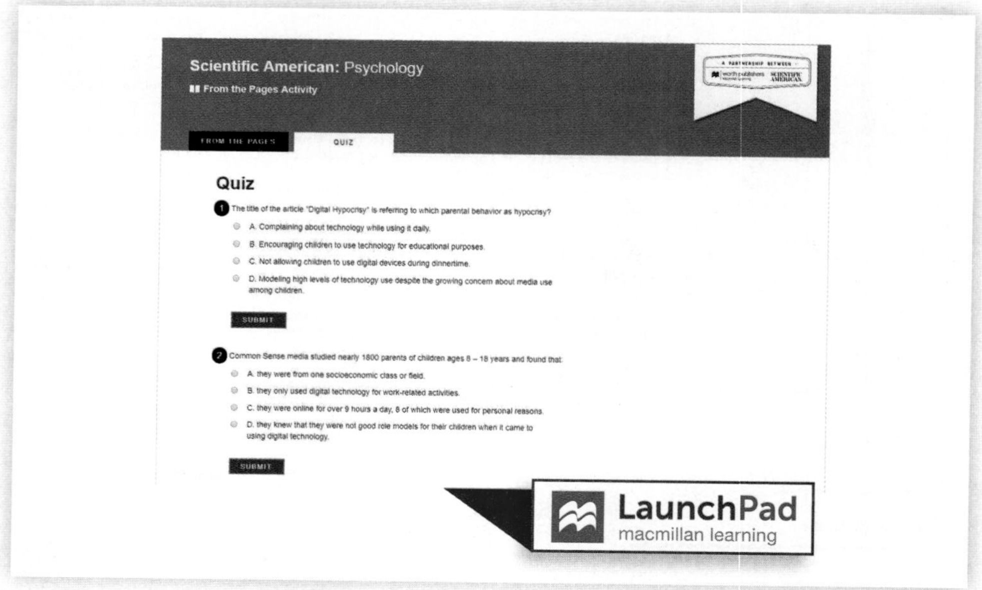

"LearningCurve, I believe, is a huge comparative advantage."

—Clifton Long, *Saddleback College*

"A brief textbook with lots of great illustrations/graphics where there are ideas for in-class activities and other assignments/activities asking students to apply the information. It is well written, engaging, and relevant to students' lives."

—Emily Keener, *Slippery Rock University*

9. Testing works: More opportunities for assessment

LearningCurve quizzing combines adaptive question selection, personalized study plans, and state-of-the-art question analysis reports. With thousands of questions written by authors Deborah Licht and Misty Hull, LearningCurve provides a unique learning experience—as opposed to a generic set of questions intended for use with any introductory psychology textbook—engaging students while helping them master concepts.

LearningCurve features an updated interface that makes it easy to utilize features such as the integrated e-book, Study Plan, and Hints.

After assigning a LearningCurve activity, instructors can track the progress and success of students—both individually and as a group—and use the data to guide their lectures.

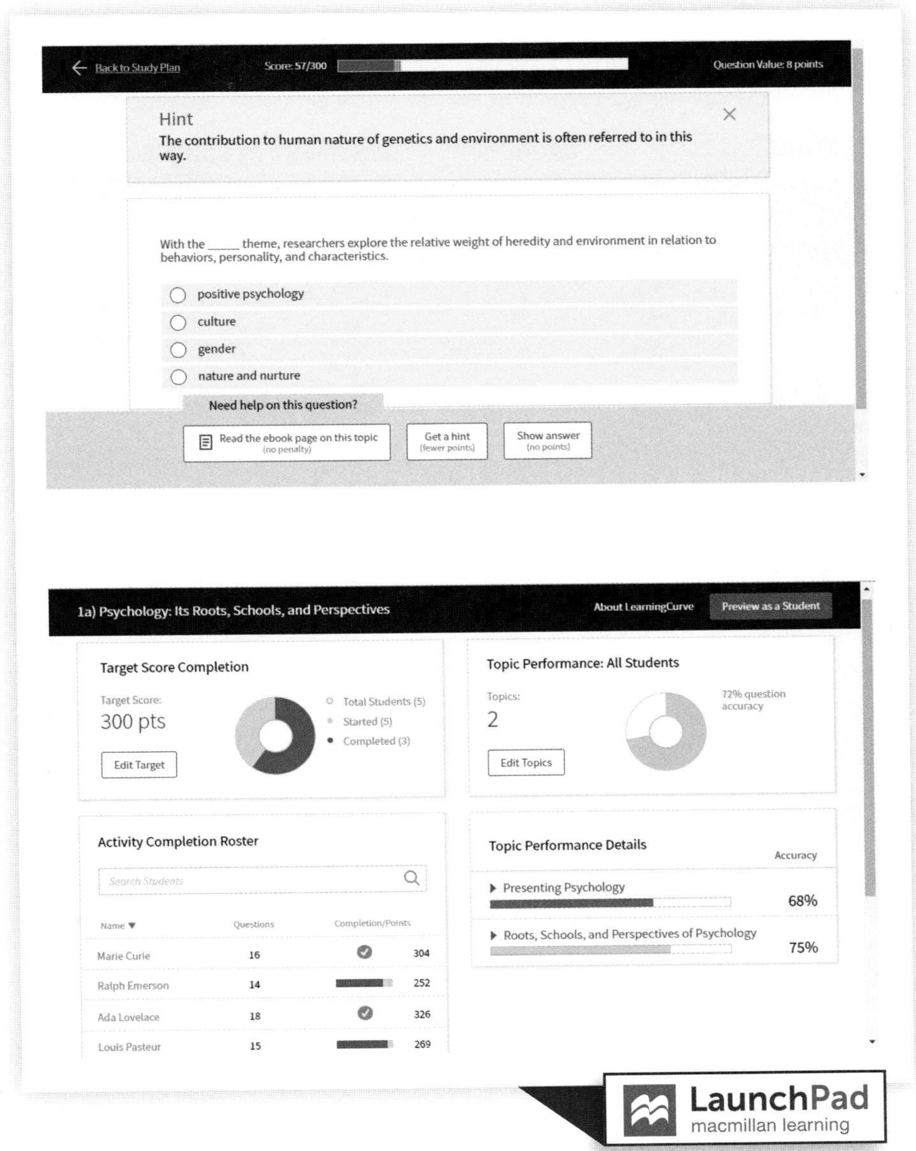

"I like the exercises in LearningCurve. It seems like it really functions like the 'mentor' the students need when they are not in the classroom."

—Julia Hoigaard, *Fullerton College*

"The supplements for the book being reviewed are of a much higher quality. I especially like that the [assessment] quiz bank is generated by the [text] authors."

—Laura Lozen-Collins, *Moraine Valley Community College*

9. Testing works: More opportunities for assessment

Instructors can easily adapt LearningCurve quizzes to address the exact content they cover in their course, having their students only focus on the concepts they need to learn.

FEATURE	LAUNCHPAD ASSESSMENT RESOURCE
LearningCurve	LearningCurve study plans and instructor reports are organized around sections in the book. There are multiple LearningCurve activities in each chapter to help students pinpoint areas where they need further review.
Test Bank	An extensive Test Bank is provided for each chapter, including multiple choice, true/false, and essay questions. Access to the Test Bank is available through LaunchPad and in the Diploma test-creation program (software included). Each question is tagged to the related learning objective and section from the book as well as an APA outcome.
Practice Quizzes	Each chapter-based Practice Quiz uses pools of questions so students get a different mix of questions each time they take the quiz in LaunchPad.
Show What You Know/ Test Prep	In the e-book in LaunchPad, students can immediately test themselves using the "Show Answer" button with each question.
Your Scientific World	Each of these immersive simulations ends with a "Show What You Know" quiz to help cement students' understanding of what they learned in the activity.
Video Profile Activities	Author-written questions for each Video Profile provide a capstone exercise for students tying together major concepts from the entire chapter.
Infographic Activities	Each Infographic Quiz is written by the authors to deepen students' understanding of the content and their visual literacy in reading the Infographics.
From the Pages of *Scientific American* Activities	In LaunchPad, each *Scientific American* article featured in the book becomes an assessable quiz featuring questions connecting the article to what students are learning.
Concept Practice	Concept Practice helps students understand psychology's foundational ideas. Each brief activity (only five minutes to complete) addresses one or two concepts, in a consistent format—review, practice, quiz, and conclusion—in which each section must be completed before students can move forward.
Topic Tutorials & Quizzes (PsychSim6)	*PsychSim's* interactive psychology simulations immerse students in the world of psychological research by placing them in the role of scientist or subject in activities that highlight important concepts, processes, and experimental approaches. Each simulation is accompanied by a quiz to assess students' understanding of the activity.
Video Activities	Over 100 videos from Worth's acclaimed video collection are made assessable through Video Activities to further illustrate concepts from the text.

NEW! Achieve: Read & Practice

Achieve: Read & Practice is the marriage of Worth's LearningCurve adaptive quizzing and our mobile, accessible e-book in one easy-to-use and affordable product. With Achieve: Read & Practice, instructors can arrange and assign chapters and sections from the e-book in any sequence they prefer, assign the readings to their class, and track student performance.

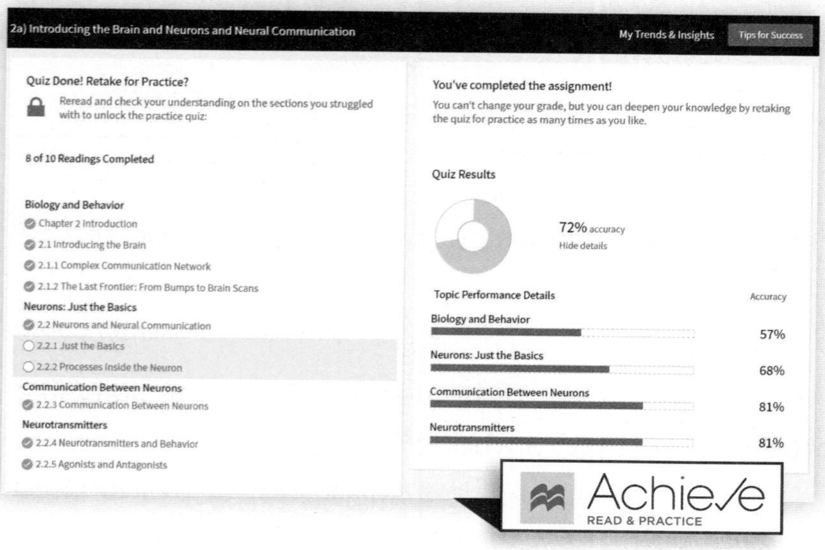

Assignments come with LearningCurve quizzes, offering individualized and adaptive question sets, immediate feedback, and e-book references for correct and incorrect answers. If students struggle with a particular topic, they are encouraged to reread the material and check their understanding by answering additional questions before being given the option to quiz themselves again.

The Read & Practice Trends & Insights dashboard provides analytics for student performance individually and for the whole class, by chapter, section, and topic, helping instructors prepare for class and one-on-one discussions.

10. Creating interactive, technology-based learning in partnership with the authors

A student's learning experience does not end with the printed text; nor does our authorship. From the inception of this project, we have been involved in the development of Worth's acclaimed online learning experience, LaunchPad, which includes a full e-book, LearningCurve quizzing, student self-assessment, simulations, videos, instructor resources, and an easy-to-use gradebook. Not only have we curated LaunchPad's content for easier assignability; we have been intimately involved in its development, writing questions for LearningCurve, Infographic Activities, and Video Profile Activities. Each online activity is carefully aligned with the content of this new edition's goals and the outcomes of the American Psychological Association (APA). We have also generated new features that reinforce the book's increased emphasis on active learning.

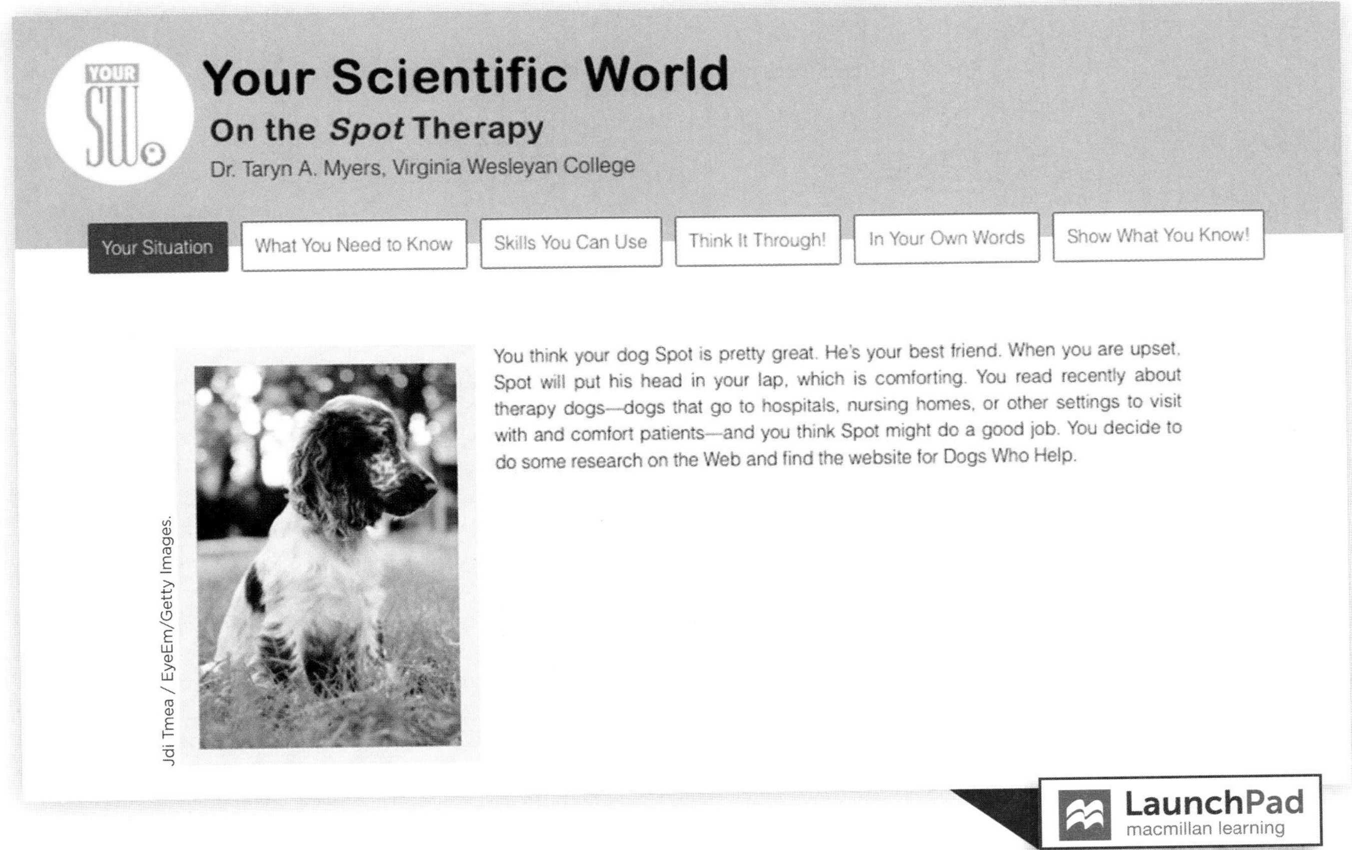

"This is a captivating and well-written textbook that is fully integrated with its online resources."

—Gene Ano, *Mt. San Antonio College*

"It is a great, clear, well-organized resource that is worth looking into. New features are amazing. As is the fact that everything was developed by the authors themselves. It fits my teaching style and addresses things I could not find in other textbooks."

—Kseniva Orlovska, *Fullerton College*

10. Creating interactive, technology-based learning in partnership with the authors

The Test Bank, created exclusively for this book, has recently undergone a complete review and revision process by an exceptional team of psychology professors, including Scott Cohn, Western State Colorado University; Vicki Ritts, St. Louis Community College-Meramec; and Laura Lauzen-Collins, Moraine Valley Community College. It includes more than 4,000 questions, each keyed to a specific learning objective, page and section reference, and APA learning goal. Instructors can access and assign assessments, edit questions, add new questions, format assessments, and more. They can also download the Test Bank in Diploma format for use off-line.

In LaunchPad, instructors can tailor their assessments using the searchable question bank, which includes the Test Bank, Web Quizzes, and Practice Quizzes. With the new filtering feature, it is possible to search for questions according to topic, APA outcome, level of difficulty, Bloom's level, question type, and source.

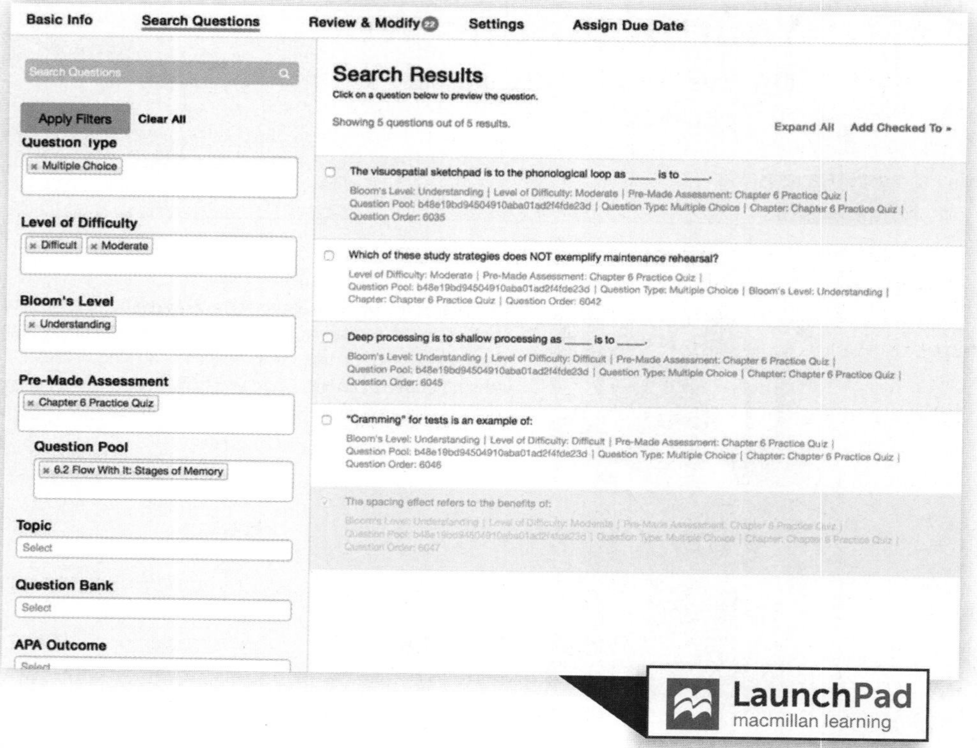

Instructor's Resource Manual

Within LaunchPad, you will find the perfect tool for busy instructors who want to make the introductory psychology course more engaging for their students—the *Instructor's Resource Manual (IRM)*. It is a resource specifically for this text and revised for the second edition by Charity Peak of Regis University and the Association of College and University Educators. The IRM contains chapter objectives; chapter summaries; lecture, discussion, and active-learning activity suggestions organized by section; multimedia suggestions from Worth's rich video and student media offerings; plus tips for embracing new classroom technology and teaching online.

We offer integration with LMS providers such as Canvas, BlackBoard, Moodle, and Brightspace. Learn more and request access at launchpadworks.com.

In a Nutshell

The second edition of *Scientific American: Presenting Psychology* represents our most complete and sincere effort to tear down barriers for instructors teaching psychology and students learning psychology. Removing those barriers involves listening to you and your students, devising creative solutions, generating evidence-based pedagogical tools, and creating state-of-the-art learning resources. We are confident that the integrated approach to addressing the 10 challenges described above represents a unique, enhanced tool that will stimulate student interest and elevate learning. We could never accomplish this without the valuable feedback of people like you. This text is the product of collaborations and conversations with students and faculty across the country, and it always will be.

What's New, Chapter by Chapter

It's a given that every chapter contains research updates, fresh examples, and new photos, but there are also several chapter-specific changes, outlined below:

Chapter 0: Are You Ready for This?

- Brand new and optional chapter introducing students to psychology; establishes that psychology is a scientific discipline driven by critical thinking; shows how the knowledge and skills acquired in this course promote success in school, career, and life in general
- Updated figure illustrating areas of specialization and places of work for psychologists in the United States
- Coverage of confirmation bias and how it relates to "fake news"
- New Didn't See That Coming feature giving students an opportunity to test their precourse knowledge of psychology
- New table outlining the characteristics of critical thinkers
- New table explaining how to cultivate 21st-century skills
- New Infographic prompting students to reflect on their use of learning resources
- New Put Your Heads Together feature

Chapter 1: Introduction to the Science of Psychology

- New Integrated Story of Anaïs Bordier and Samantha Futerman, identical twins separated at birth and reunited at age 25 with the help of social media
- New Online Video Profile to accompany the story of Anaïs and Samantha
- Expanded treatment of twin research and the nature and nurture theme
- New Infographic on critical thinking, using the example of global warming
- New figure illustrating how the wording of survey questions can sway responses
- New From the Pages of *Scientific American* feature exploring how parents often fail to set a good example for their children when it comes to limiting screen time
- Expanded coverage of third variables and experimenter bias
- New Across the World feature examining happiness in different countries
- Updated Apply This feature on psychology in the media; explores how correlations can be misrepresented as cause-and-effect relationships
- New Think Positive feature introducing positive psychology
- Four new Put Your Heads Together features

Chapter 2: Biology and Behavior

- Refined coverage of neural communication
- New table detailing the surprising effects of key neurotransmitters
- New table describing the functions of various regions in the brain's cortex
- New photo, caption, and video about the "brain–computer interface," an emerging technology that has enabled voluntary movement in a man with quadriplegia
- New table describing the functions of various brain regions below the cortex
- New From the Pages of *Scientific American* feature about the unique brain characteristics of "super agers"
- New Think Positive feature on neuroplasticity
- New Career Connections feature on active learning and the brain
- Three new Put Your Heads Together features

Chapter 3: Sensation and Perception

- New Integrated Story of Mandy Harvey, a singer/musician who is completely deaf
- New Online Video Profile to accompany the story of Mandy
- New table presenting mnemonic devices to remember the characteristics of sound and light waves
- New Didn't See That Coming feature on the debatable existence of "human pheromones"
- New From the Pages of *Scientific American* feature explaining the perceptual changes that may occur when we watch events replayed in slow motion
- New Infographic on perceptual illusions
- Three new Put Your Heads Together features

Chapter 4: Consciousness

- New Integrated Story of Dr. Divya Chander, a neuroscientist and anesthesiologist who has studied consciousness using technologies such as optogenetics
- New table outlining strategies for effective multitasking
- New Didn't See That Coming feature examining how screen time in the evening affects sleep
- Realigned coverage of the sleep stages
- New From the Pages of *Scientific American* feature reporting the average sleep duration of people living in countries around the world
- New Think Critically feature about America's opioid epidemic
- New Infographic on the effects of psychoactive drugs
- Four new Put Your Heads Together features

Chapter 5: Learning

- New Integrated Story of the "dog whisperer" Cesar Millan; examines how learning processes have played a role in his life and work
- New Online Video Profile to accompany the story of Cesar
- New table presenting terms to describe the stimulus and response in classical conditioning
- Updated Didn't See That Coming feature on saving wildlife with conditioned taste aversion
- New Infographic explaining four partial reinforcement schedules

- New From the Pages of *Scientific American* feature describing recent research on the psychological effects of spanking
- New Career Connections feature about the value of positive reinforcement in the workplace
- New table comparing classical and operant conditioning
- New Think Positive feature about finding a purpose and learning throughout life
- Five new Put Your Heads Together features

Chapter 6: Memory

- Updated coverage of multitasking and memory
- New From the Pages of *Scientific American* feature explaining which types of reminders are most effective
- New Try This exercise illustrating encoding failure—uses altered versions of the Apple logo as opposed to the traditionally utilized coins
- New Didn't See That Coming feature and video about highly superior autobiographical memory (HSAM)
- New Career Connections on memory accuracy and legal cases
- Introduction of chronic traumatic encephalopathy (CTE), a neurodegenerative disease caused by repetitive head trauma
- New Infographic exploring the causes and symptoms of CTE
- Five new Put Your Heads Together features

Chapter 7: Cognition, Language, and Intelligence

- New Integrated Story of former NFL linebacker Harry Carson, who suffers from language difficulties that appear to be linked to repeated head injuries sustained on the football field
- Discussion of CTE research, both its history and recent developments
- New Career Connections feature on dyslexia in the workplace
- New From the Pages of *Scientific American* feature on the potential drawbacks of high emotional intelligence
- Four new Put Your Heads Together features

Chapter 8: Human Development

- New Integrated Story about the multigenerational family of Ericka Harley, who works for a nonprofit organization that supports teen parents striving to attain college degrees
- New Online Video Profile to accompany the story of Ericka and her family
- New table illustrating newborn reflexes (photos included)
- New figure on language disparities among toddlers of different socioeconomic status
- New Infographic on Erikson's psychosocial stages
- New Social Media and Psychology feature about how frequent media use impacts the mental health of teenagers
- New From the Pages of *Scientific American* feature on the relationship between teenage well-being and screen time
- New table summarizing Kohlberg's stages of moral development
- New Career Connections feature identifying professions that require knowledge of human development
- New Think Positive feature about resilience in the face of hardship
- Four new Put Your Heads Together features

Chapter 9: Motivation and Emotion

- New Integrated Story of Marine Corps combat veteran Ibrahim Hashi
- Updated Integrated Story and Online Video Profile of Paralympian runner and triathlete, Ivonne Mosquera-Schmidt (previously appeared in Chapter 5)
- Updated coverage of social media and its role in satisfying needs
- Updated treatment of same-sex attraction and the sexual orientation continuum
- New Think Positive feature about maximizing happiness by taking advantage of what Mihaly Csikszentmihalyi calls "flow"
- New Career Connections feature on showing emotions at work
- New Infographic on pathways to happiness
- New From the Pages of *Scientific American* feature on the psychological effects of family rituals
- Four new Put Your Heads Together features

Chapter 10: Personality

- New Integrated Story about the personality development of intersex activist Sean Saifa Wall
- New Online Video Profile to accompany the story of Saifa
- Augmented coverage of temperament and personality
- New table on the "neo-Freudians" (photos included)
- New From the Pages of *Scientific American* feature on personality changes over the life span
- New Career Connections feature on personality testing in the workplace
- Four new Put Your Heads Together features

Chapter 11: Social Psychology

- New Integrated Story about Alexa and Dennis Conforti, a married couple that met on the dating app Tinder
- New Social Media and Psychology feature on the attributions people make about self-portraits, or "selfies"
- New Career Connections feature exploring how the risky shift might influence professional decisions
- New From the Pages of *Scientific American* feature about the romantic benefits of eating garlic
- Four new Put Your Heads Together features

Chapter 12: Stress and Health

- New Integrated Story of veteran police officer Christy Sheppard, who has experienced significant stressors on the job
- New Online Video Profile to accompany the story of Christy
- New Think Critically feature exploring how poverty impacts the developing brain
- New From the Pages of *Scientific American* feature about how financial stress influences pain perception
- New Infographic on health psychology and the biopsychosocial perspective
- New Across the World feature on "blue zones," regions of the world where people enjoy exceptional health and longevity
- New table describing the characteristics of people living in the so-called blue zones
- Expanded coverage of healthy living strategies, including a discussion of nutrition
- New Think Positive feature about using mindfulness meditation to reduce stress

- New figure instructing students how to engage in mindfulness meditation
- Three new Put Your Heads Together features

Chapter 13: Psychological Disorders

- New Across the World feature augmenting the discussion of cultural variation and psychological disorders
- New Infographic on fighting stigma
- New Career Connections feature on developing mental health literacy
- New From the Pages of *Scientific American* feature exploring the relationship between football-related head injuries and problems with mood and cognition
- Discussion of autism spectrum disorder—its symptoms and hypothesized causes
- Updated coverage of eating disorders (content previously discussed in Chapter 9)
- New table on treatments for eating disorders
- Five new Put Your Heads Together features

Chapter 14: Treatment of Psychological Disorders

- New Integrated Story of Dr. Nneka Jones Tapia, a clinical psychologist and warden of Chicago's massive Cook County Jail
- Expanded discussion of psychological disorders among jail and prison inmates
- New table describing the variables that may affect psychotherapy outcomes
- New From the Pages of *Scientific American* feature exploring the role of memory in exposure therapy
- Updated discussion on the efficacy of self-help groups
- New table providing the names and treatment targets of medications for psychological disorders
- New discussion about the possibility of using smartphones to help diagnose psychological disorders and facilitate treatment
- Four new Put Your Heads Together features

Alignment with APA Learning Guidelines 2.0

ALIGNMENT WITH APA LEARNING GUIDELINES 2.0

GOAL 1: KNOWLEDGE BASE IN PSYCHOLOGY

AMERICAN PSYCHOLOGICAL ASSOCIATION LEARNING OUTCOMES

1.1 Describe key concepts, principles, and overarching themes in psychology

1.2 Develop a working knowledge of psychology's content domains

1.3 Describe applications of psychology

***Scientific American: Presenting Psychology,* 2e, Learning Objectives/Content**

CHAPTER 0: LO 1–LO 5

CHAPTER 1: LO 1–LO 10

CHAPTER 2: LO 1–LO 16

CHAPTER 3: LO 1–LO 14

CHAPTER 4: LO 1–LO 12

CHAPTER 5: LO 1–LO 15

CHAPTER 6: LO 1–LO 15

CHAPTER 7: LO 1–LO 12

CHAPTER 8: LO 1–LO 18

CHAPTER 9: LO 1–LO 13

CHAPTER 10: LO 1–LO 14

CHAPTER 11: LO 1–LO 12

CHAPTER 12: LO 1–LO 11

CHAPTER 13: LO 1–LO 11

CHAPTER 14: LO 1–LO 12

APPENDIX A: Introduction to Statistics

APPENDIX B: Careers in Psychology

INTEGRATED THEMATIC FEATURES in each chapter

ALIGNMENT WITH APA LEARNING GUIDELINES 2.0 (CONTINUED)

CONNECTIONS in Chapters 1–14 and Appendix A

INFOGRAPHICS in each chapter

TRY THIS application activities in Chapters 3, 5–6, 9, 11–12, 14 and Appendix A: Introduction to Statistics

APPLY THIS application features in Chapters 1–3, 8–9, and 11–12

PUT YOUR HEADS TOGETHER group activities in each chapter

YOUR SCIENTIFIC WORLD interactive, problem-based learning activities for each chapter

LAUNCHPAD RESOURCES

LEARNINGCURVE

INSTRUCTOR'S RESOURCE MANUAL

GOAL 2: SCIENTIFIC INQUIRY AND CRITICAL THINKING

AMERICAN PSYCHOLOGICAL ASSOCIATION LEARNING OUTCOMES

2.1 Use scientific reasoning to interpret psychological phenomena

2.2 Demonstrate psychology information literacy

2.3 Engage in innovative and integrative thinking and problem solving

2.4 Interpret, design, and conduct basic psychological research

2.5 Incorporate sociocultural factors in scientific inquiry

Scientific American: Presenting Psychology, 2e, Learning Objectives/Substantive Content

Inside front cover: Infographic: How to Read a Scientific Article

CHAPTER 0: LO 2–LO 3; *Didn't See That Coming*: What Do You Know?; Table 0.1: Dispelled: Five "Commonsense" Myths; Table 0.2: What Critical Thinkers Do; Table 0.5: Look for These

CHAPTER 1: LO 5–LO 9; *From the Pages of Scientific American:* Digital Hypocrisy; *Across the World:* The Happiest Places on the Planet; *Didn't See That Coming:* SpongeBob on the Brain; *Think Positive:* Introducing Positive Psychology; Infographic 1.1: The Scientific Method; Infographic 1.2: Critical Thinking; Infographic 1.3: The Correlation Coefficient: What's in a Number?; Infographic 1.4: The Experimental Method; Figure 1.1: Raw Data; Figure 1.2: It Depends How You Ask; Figure 1.3: Happiness Hotspots; Table 1.1: Current Perspective in Psychology; Table 1.2: Research Methods: Advantages and Drawbacks

CHAPTER 2: LO 2 and 10; *Social Media and Psychology:* Facebook in the Brain; *From the Pages of Scientific American:* "Super Agers" Have Brains That Look Young; Infographic 2.1: Ways to Study the Living Brain; Figure 2.5: The Split-Brain Experiment

CHAPTER 3: LO 11; *Didn't See That Coming:* Sexy Smells?; *From the Pages of Scientific American:* Slo-Mo Made Him Do It; Infographic 3.3: Perceptual Illusions; Infographic 3.4: Gestalt Organizing Principles: The Whole Is Greater; *Think Critically:* Can You Predict the Future?

CHAPTER 4: *Didn't See That Coming:* Are Screens Ruining Your Rhythm?; *From the Pages of Scientific American:* Who Gets the Most Sleep?; *Think Critically:* 6 Sleep Myths; *Think Critically:* America's Opioid Epidemic; *Social Media and Psychology:* Can't Get Enough; *...Believe It...Or Not:* False Claims About Hypnosis; Infographic 4.3: Psychoactive Drugs

CHAPTER 5: *Didn't See That Coming:* Rescuing Animals with Classical Conditioning; *Think Critically:* Chickens Can't Play Baseball; *From the Pages of Scientific American:* What Science Really Says About Spanking; *Across the World:* Mind Your Manners; Infographic 5.1: Learning Through Classical Conditioning; Infographic 5.2: Learning Through Operant Conditioning; Infographic 5.3: Schedules of Reinforcement; Infographic 5.4: Learning: Punishment and Reinforcement; Figure 5.1: Higher Order Conditioning; Table 5.2: Real-Life Examples of Classical Conditioning

CHAPTER 6: *Social Media and Psychology:* Multitasking: Your Memory's Worst Enemy?; *From the Pages of Scientific American:* Stop Sending Yourself Reminder E-mails; *Didn't See That Coming:* Highly Superior Autobiographical Memory; *Career Connections:* Memory and the Law; Infographic 6.1: Study Smarter: Methods of Improving Your Memory; Infographic 6.3: Chronic Traumatic Encephalopathy; Figure 6.3: How Fast It Fades; Figure 6.5: Digit Span Test

CHAPTER 7: LO 7 and 11; *Think Critically:* Does Gender Matter?; *Didn't See That Coming:* The Perks of Being Bilingual; *...Believe It...Or Not:* Do Animals Use Language, Too?; *From the Pages of Scientific American:* The Dark Side of Emotional Intelligence; Infographic 7.1: Concepts and Prototypes; Infographic 7.2: Problem Solving; Infographic 7.4: How Smart Are Intelligence Tests?; Figure 7.1: Manipulating Mental Images; Figure 7.2: Scanning Mental Images; Table 7.2 Theories of Intelligence

CHAPTER 8: LO 3 and 18; *...Believe It...Or Not:* Genie the "Feral Child"; *From the Pages of Scientific American:* The "Goldilocks" Level of Teen Screen Use; *Social Media and Psychology:* Have Teens Gone Overboard?; *Think Critically:* The Case of Bruce Reimer; *Across the World:* Death in Different Cultures; Infographic 8.1: Research Methods in Developmental Psychology; Infographic 8.3: Piaget's Theory of Cognitive Development; Infographic 8.4 Erikson's Eight Stages; Figure 8.3: Language Disparities

CHAPTER 9: *Social Media and Psychology:* Network Needs; *Think Critically:* Sext You Later; *...Believe It...Or Not:* Just How Accurate Are Polygraph Tests?; *Across the World:* When to Reveal, When to Conceal; *From the Pages of Scientific American:* The More Rituals the Merrier; *Think Positive:* Going with the Flow; Infographic 9.3: The Anatomy of Fear; Infographic 9.4: Pathways to Happiness; Figure 9.3: Cannon and Washburn's Classic Hunger Study

CHAPTER 10: LO 12–LO 14; *Think Critically:* The Funny Thing About Personality; *...Believe It...Or Not:* How Birth Order May Affect Your Personality; *From the Pages of Scientific American:* Once Dependable, Always Dependable?; *Across the World:* Culture of Personality; *Social Media and Psychology:* It's Written All Over Your Facebook; Infographic 10.1: Ego Defense Mechanisms; Infographic 10.2: The Social-Cognitive Perspective on Personality; Infographic 10.3: Examining the Unconscious: Projective Personality Tests

CHAPTER 11: LO 10; *Social Media and Psychology:* What's in a Selfie?; *Think Critically:* Something Doesn't Feel Right; *Across the World:* Slackers of the West; *...Believe It...Or Not:* The Stanford "Prison"; *From the Pages of Scientific American:* In Human Attraction, You Are What You Eat; Infographic 11.2: Milgram's Shocking Obedience Study; Infographic 11.3: Thinking About Other People: Stereotypes, Discrimination, and Prejudice; Figure 11.2: Asch's Conformity Experiment

ALIGNMENT WITH APA LEARNING GUIDELINES 2.0 (CONTINUED)

CHAPTER 12: LO 2 and 3; *Think Critically:* Does Poverty Change the Brain?; *Across the World:* "Blue Zones"; *From the Pages of Scientific American:* Financial Stress Hurts, Literally; *Across the World:* The Stress of Starting Anew; Infographic 12.1: Stressed Out; Infographic 12.2: Physiological Responses to Stress; Infographic 12.3: Health Psychology; Infographic 12.4: The Process of Coping; Figure 12.1: The Hassles and Uplifts Scale

CHAPTER 13: LO 8; *Across the World:* Consider the Culture; *Think Critically:* The Insanity Plea; *...Believe It...Or Not:* A Label Can Change Everything; *From the Pages of Scientific American:* Striking Evidence Linking Football to Brain Disease Sparks Calls for More Research; *...Believe It...Or Not:* Four Sisters with Schizophrenia; *Across the World:* A Cross-Cultural Look at Eating Disorders; Infographic 13.1: Fighting Stigma; Figure 13.2: Seligman's Research on Learned Helplessness; Table 13.3: Anxiety Disorders

CHAPTER 14: LO 9; *Didn't See That Coming:* Virtual Reality Exposure Therapy; *From the Pages of Scientific American:* For Arachnophobia, a New Twist on Exposure Therapy; *Across the World:* Know Thy Client; *Social Media and Psychology:* Therapist or Friend?; Infographic 14.3: Biomedical Therapies;

APPENDIX A: Introduction to Statistics

DIVERSE CHARACTER profiles integrated throughout each chapter

INTEGRATIVE CONNECTIONS found in Chapters 2–15 and Appendix A

TRY THIS application activities in Chapters 1–3, 5–7, 9–10, 12, 14–15, and Appendix A: Introduction to Statistics

APPLY THIS application features in Chapters 1–3, 8–9, and 11–12

PUT YOUR HEADS TOGETHER group activities in each chapter

YOUR SCIENTIFIC WORLD interactive, problem-based learning activities for each chapter

LAUNCHPAD RESOURCES

LEARNINGCURVE

INSTRUCTOR'S RESOURCE MANUAL

GOAL 3: ETHICAL AND SOCIAL RESPONSIBILITY IN A DIVERSE WORLD

AMERICAN PSYCHOLOGICAL ASSOCIATION LEARNING OUTCOMES

3.1 Apply ethical standards to evaluate psychological science and practice

3.2 Build and enhance interpersonal relationships

3.3 Adopt values that build community at local, national, and global levels

***Scientific American: Presenting Psychology*, 2e, Learning Objectives/Substantive Content**

CHAPTER 1: LO 10; *From the Pages of Scientific American:* Digital Hypocrisy; *Across the World:* The Happiest Places on the Planet; *Think Positive:* Introducing Positive Psychology; Infographic 1.1: Critical Thinking

CHAPTER 2: *Social Media and Psychology:* Facebook in the Brain; *Think Positive:* The Versatile Brain

CHAPTER 4: *Think Critically:* America's Opioid Epidemic; *Social Media and Psychology:* Can't Get Enough

CHAPTER 5: LO 6; *From the Pages of Scientific American:* What Science Really Says About Spanking; *Across the World:* Mind Your Manners; *Think Positive:* You Are a Valuable Member of the Pack

CHAPTER 6: *Career Connections:* Memory and the Law

CHAPTER 7: LO 11

CHAPTER 8: *Social Media and Psychology:* Have Teens Gone Overboard?; *From the Pages of Scientific American:* The "Goldilocks" Level of Teen Screen Use; *Across the World:* Death in Different Cultures; *Think Positive:* Resilient in the Face of Hardship

CHAPTER 9: *Social Media and Psychology:* Network Needs; *Across the World:* When to Reveal, When to Conceal; *Career Connections:* Showing Emotions at Work; *From the Pages of Scientific American:* The More Rituals the Merrier

CHAPTER 10: *Across the World:* Culture of Personality; *Social Media and Psychology:* It's Written All Over Your Facebook

CHAPTER 11: LO 5–8, 11 and 12; *Social Media and Psychology:* What's in a Selfie?; *Apply This:* Cut the Loafing; *Across the World:* Slackers of the West; *From the Pages of Scientific American:* In Human Attraction, You Are What You Eat; *Career Connections:* Beware of the Risky Shift; Infographic 11.3: Thinking About Other People: Discrimination, Stereotype, and Prejudice; Figure 11.3: When Do We Conform?

CHAPTER 12: *Across the World:* The Stress of Starting Anew; *Across the World:* "Blue Zones"

CHAPTER 13: *Across the World:* Consider the Culture; *Across the World:* A Cross-Cultural Look at Eating Disorders

CHAPTER 14: LO 9; *Across the World:* Know Thy Client; *Social Media and Psychology:* Therapist or Friend?

DIVERSE CHARACTER profiles integrated throughout each chapter

PUT YOUR HEADS TOGETHER group activities in each chapter

GOAL 4: COMMUNICATION

AMERICAN PSYCHOLOGICAL ASSOCIATION LEARNING OUTCOMES

4.1 Demonstrate effective writing for different purposes

4.2 Exhibit effective presentation skills for different purposes

4.3 Interact effectively with others

***Scientific American: Presenting Psychology*, 2e, Learning Objectives/Substantive Content**

Inside front cover: Infographic: How to Read a Scientific Article

CHAPTER 7: LO 8 and 9; *Didn't See That Coming:* The Perks of Being Bilingual; Infographic 7.3: The Building Blocks of Language

CHAPTER 8: LO 8

ALIGNMENT WITH APA LEARNING GUIDELINES 2.0 (CONTINUED)

CHAPTER 9: *Social Media and Psychology:* Network Needs; *Across the World:* When to Reveal, When to Conceal; *Career Connections:* Showing Emotions at Work

CHAPTER 10: *Think Critically:* The Funny Thing About Personality; *Social Media and Psychology:* It's Written All Over Your Facebook

CHAPTER 11: LO 3–6 and 12; *Social Media and Psychology:* What's in a Selfie?; *Apply This:* Cut the Loafing; Infographic 11.1: Errors in Attribution

CHAPTER 14: LO 9 and 10; *Across the World:* Know Thy Client; *Social Media and Psychology:* Therapist or Friend?

SHOW WHAT YOU KNOW and **TEST PREP: ARE YOU READY?** assessment questions in each chapter

PUT YOUR HEADS TOGETHER group activities in each chapter

YOUR SCIENTIFIC WORLD interactive, problem-based learning activities for each chapter

TEST BANK essay questions

LAUNCHPAD RESOURCES

LEARNINGCURVE

INSTRUCTOR'S RESOURCE MANUAL

GOAL 5: PROFESSIONAL DEVELOPMENT

AMERICAN PSYCHOLOGICAL ASSOCIATION LEARNING OUTCOMES

5.1 Apply psychological content and skills to career goals

5.2 Exhibit self-efficacy and self-regulation

5.3 Refine project-management skills

5.4 Enhance teamwork capacity

5.5 Develop meaningful professional direction for life after graduation

***Scientific American: Presenting Psychology*, 2e, Learning Objectives/Substantive Content**

CHAPTER 0: LO 1 and 5; Figure 0.2: Fields of Psychology

CHAPTER 1: LO 1; Infographic 1.2: Critical Thinking; *From the Pages of Scientific American:* Digital Hypocrisy; *Apply This:* Don't Believe Everything You Read

CHAPTER 2: *Apply This:* Where's My Morning Antagonist?

CHAPTER 4: *Think Critically:* 6 Sleep Myths; Table 4.4: How to Get a Good Night's Sleep; *Social Media and Psychology:* Can't Get Enough

CHAPTER 5: *Think Positive:* You Are a Valuable Member of the Pack

CHAPTER 6: LO 6; *Social Media and Psychology:* Multitasking: Your Memory's Worst Enemy?; *From the Pages of Scientific American:* Stop Sending Yourself Reminder E-mails; Infographic 6.1: Study Smarter: Methods of Improving Your Memory

CHAPTER 7: LO 5–LO 7; *Didn't See That Coming:* The Perks of Being Bilingual; *From the Pages of Scientific American:* The Dark Side of Emotional Intelligence; Infographic 7.2: Problem Solving

CHAPTER 8: *Social Media and Psychology:* Have Teens Gone Overboard?; *From the Pages of Scientific American:* The "Goldilocks" Level of Teen Screen Use; *Apply This:* Move It or Lose It

CHAPTER 9: LO 1–LO 5 and 9; *Social Media and Psychology:* Network Needs; *Think Positive:* Going with the Flow; Table 9.3: Weight Loss: Making It Fit

CHAPTER 10: LO 6 and 7; *Social Media and Psychology:* It's Written All Over Your Facebook; Infographic 10.1 Ego Defense Mechanisms; Infographic 10.2: The Social-Cognitive Perspective on Personality

CHAPTER 11: LO 2–LO 6, 8, 10–12; *Social Media and Psychology:* What's in a Selfie?; *Think Critically:* Something Doesn't Feel Right; *Apply This:* Cut the Loafing; Infographic 11.1: Errors in Attribution; Figure 11.3: When Do We Conform?

CHAPTER 12: LO 7, 9, and 11; *Across the World:* The Stress of Starting Anew; *Apply This:* Everyday Stress Relievers; *Think Positive:* Right Here, Right Now; Infographic 12.1: Stressed Out; Infographic 12.3: Health Psychology; Infographic 12.4: The Process of Coping; Figure 12.3: Breathe In, Breathe Out; Table 12.1 Living Longer

CHAPTER 13: Infographic 13.1: Fighting Stigma; Infographic 13.2: Suicide in the United States

CHAPTER 14: LO 11 and 12; *Didn't See That Coming:* Virtual Reality Exposure Therapy; *From the Pages of Scientific American:* For Arachnophobia, a New Twist on Exposure Therapy; *Across the World:* Know Thy Client; *Social Media and Psychology:* Therapist or Friend?

APPENDIX B: Careers in Psychology

CAREER CONNECTIONS features in Chapters 2, 5–9, 11 and 13

PUT YOUR HEADS TOGETHER group activities in each chapter

LAUNCHPAD RESOURCES

LEARNINGCURVE

INSTRUCTOR'S RESOURCE MANUAL

Psychology Content on the MCAT

The Medical College Admission Test (MCAT) began to include psychology on its exam in 2015. The requirements stipulate that 25% of the test will include questions pertaining to the "Psychological, Social, and Biological Foundations of Behavior." Many of these topics are covered during the introductory psychology course, so we've made a useful chart that aligns the psychology topics to be covered on the MCAT with the location of that material in the book. This chart is available for download from the "Instructor Resources" section of the *Scientific American: Presenting Psychology* page at macmillanlearning.com.

Acknowledgments

Nearly a decade ago, the three authors came together to discuss the possibility of creating a bold new psychology textbook. We dreamed of creating an introductory text that would bring relevance and student engagement to a whole new level. We believe that dream has now materialized, but it would not have been possible without the hard work and talent of reviewers, focus group attendees, students, interview subjects, contributors, and editors.

Catherine Woods, you have been with us from the beginning, and we are thankful for your ongoing support and oversight. Executive Program Manager, Matt Wright, you have been a wonderful addition to this team. Thank you for being so responsive to us as an author team; you address problems directly and effectively, and that is the mark of good leader. It's clear you are invested in this project and want to take things to the next level. Assistant Editor Un Hye Kim, thank you for managing so many aspects of the project—we don't know how you kept track of it all! You were always on top of things and ready to jump in to help, and we are grateful for your excellent work. Nick Rizzuti, you came aboard toward the end, but thank you for jumping right in!

Brad Rivenburgh and Glenn and Meg Turner of Burrston House, you came to this project just when we were in great need of your extensive publishing experience and vast fund of research knowledge. Thank you for your indefatigable efforts assembling panels of reviewers, and distilling their feedback into practical suggestions for us to consider. The student and instructor focus groups you have organized are essential to the ongoing success of the project. Meg, your work reaching out to schools and connecting with instructors is critical; we understand how much energy and persistence it requires, and we cannot thank you enough. Glenn, what would we do without your wisdom and guidance? The edits provided by you and Brad have been invaluable!! (double exclamation mark intended). Brad, your attention to detail and your ability to manage so many tasks simultaneously is remarkable. We have said it a million times, and we will say it again: We never could have made this book without Burrston House. You are our greatest champions, our trusted advisors, and our dear friends.

Anne DeMarinis, Dawn Albertson, and Matt McAdams, thank you for making the infographics come to life so elegantly. Senior Photo Editor Cecilia Varas and photo researcher Donna Ranieri of Lumina Datamatics, the photos keep getting better with every edition, thanks to your tireless efforts to track down images and secure permissions. We know that some of our requests require you to jump through hoops, but you are always willing to take on the challenge, and the results are outstanding. We are so lucky to have you on our team!

Producing a high-quality college textbook is a formidable task, but we had the experts in our corner. Senior Content Project Manager Liz Geller, thank you for being an excellent project manager. You run a tight ship, and your dedication to producing a top-quality product is obvious. Martha Emry, thank you for taking the helm in the middle of production, and Edward Dionne, you have done a great job managing the transition. Director, Content Management Enhancement, Tracey Kuehn, you made the transition from development to production more manageable—and perhaps more importantly, you kept us sane during that first production experience. Copy editor Patti Brecht, we are grateful to you for answering our innumerable questions about hyphens, semicolons, uppercase letters, and other copy issues, and Cheryl Adam, we appreciate all your help in keeping track of all those citations. Chris Hunt and Ellen Brennan, we are so impressed with your work on the name and subject indexes, respectively. We are lucky to have you both on our team. Director of Design Diana Blume, Design Services Manager Natasha Wolfe, and Blake Logan for Lumina Datamatics, you have done a remarkable job presenting densely packed information in a clear and stimulating visual format. Thank you for taking the time to discuss the design and listen to our thoughts; this collaboration between the designers and the authors has made a huge difference, and we look forward to working together in the future.

To all the managers, designers, illustrators, editors, and other team members with whom we did not have direct contact, please know that we are thoroughly impressed with your work. A huge thanks to Senior Workflow Project Supervisor Susan Wein, Senior Managing Editor Lisa Kinne, Art Manager Matt McAdams, and illustrators Todd Buck, Evelyn Pence, and Eli Ensor.

Peter Levin, John Philp, and Barbara Parks of Splash Studios, your videos give us goose bumps, and some of them move us to tears. Thank you for conveying the chapter stories in a way that is real, yet respectful of the interview subjects. No one could have done it better.

Noel Hohnstine and Nik Toner, you have provided essential support in the development and refinement of our supplements and online learning activities. Noel, it has been wonderful having you on our weekly calls and hearing about the work you are doing to create a better online learning experience for students. We have been so impressed with your efficiency and dedication to our project. Scott Cohn, Program Assessment Lead, we have been looking for you for years, and finally you have joined our team! The outstanding work that you, Vicki Ritts, and Laura Lauzen-Collins have done on the Test Bank speaks for itself. The three of you understand and appreciate our vision, and that is priceless. Charity Peak, your work on the Instructor's Resource Manual is critical; thank you for sharing your expertise.

Marketing Manager Clay Bolton, we love the fresh perspective and openness you bring to the sales effort. We think you have the ability to make a big impact, and we look forward to cultivating a strong and interactive relationship with you and the sales team.

We have benefited in countless ways from an exceptional group of academic reviewers. Some have been our greatest champions, and others our sharpest critics. We needed both. Thank you for the hundreds of hours you spent examining this text, writing thoughtful critiques, and offering bright ideas—many of which we have incorporated into our text. This is your book, too.

Karen Amesbury, *Luzerne County Community College*
Gene Ano, *Mt. San Antonio College*
Lauren Appelbaum, *Pasadena City College*
Robyn Arnett, *Wake Technical Community College*
Sherry Ash, *San Jacinto College*
Sheryl Attig, *Tri-County Technical College*
Kevin Autry, *Cal Poly Pomona*
Mitch Baker, *Moraine Valley Community College*
Cynthia Barkley, *California State University–East Bay*
Joanna Barr, *North Shore Community College*
Leslie Bartley, *Florida South Western State College*
Dave Baskind, *Delta College*
Stacey Baugh, *Trinity Washington University*
Jesse Bengson, *Sonoma State University*
Lisa Bergeron Wood, *College of the Ouachitas*
Tawanda Bickford, *Hennepin Technical College*
Shiloh Blacksher, *Mt. San Antonio College*
Gerald Braasch, *McHenry County College*
Nicole Brandt, *Columbus State Community College*
Frank Calabrese, *Community College of Philadelphia*
Jarrod Calloway, *Northwest Mississippi Community College*
Carrie Canales, *West Los Angeles College*
Richardo Castillo, *Santa Ana College*
Christie Cathey, *Missouri State University*
Kenyatta Collins, *Atlantic Cape Community College*
Judy Colson, *Quinsigamond Community College*
Deborah Conway, *Community College of Allegheny County*
Cynthia Cornejo, *Prairie State College*
Cheryl Cotton, *Wor-Wic Community College*
Deanna DeGidio, *Northern Virginia Community College*
Bonnie Dennis, *Virginia Western Community College*
Mark Dennis, *Sacramento City College*
Kimberly Duff, *Cerritos College*
Justine Egan-Kunicki, *Community College of Rhode Island*
Nicholas Fernandez, *El Paso Community College*
Lisa Fozio-Thielk, *Waubonsee Community College*
Nathalie Franco, *Broward College Central*
Stacey Frank, *Tri-County Technical College*
Desiree Franks, *Northeast Wisconsin Technical College*
Tina Garrett, *Holmes Community College*
Lynn Garrioch, *Colby-Sawyer College*
Karen Gee, *Mission College*
Stan Gilbert, *Community College of Philadelphia*
Christine Greco-Covington, *Brookdale Community College*
Erinn Green, *University of Cincinnati*
Christine Grela, *McHenry County College*
Jillene Grover Seiver, *Bellevue College*
Brett Heintz, *Delgado Community College*
Ann Hennessey, *Los Angeles Pierce College*
Brooke Hindman, *Greenville Technical College*
Julia Hoigaard, *Fullerton College*

Rebecca Howell, *Forsyth Technical Community College*
Vivian Hsu, *Penn State University–Abington*
Ray Huebschmann, *Georgia State University–Perimeter College*
Justin Huft, *Saddleback College*
Alishia Huntoon, *Oregon Institute of Technology*
Sabra Jacobs, *Big Sandy Community and Technical College*
Heather Jennings, *Mercer County Community College*
Samuel Jones, *Jefferson State Community College*
Emily Keener, *Slippery Rock University of Pennsylvania*
Jacqueline Kikuchi, *University of Rhode Island*
Andrew Kim, *Citrus College*
Heather LaCost, *Waubonsee Community College*
Cindy Lahar, *University of South Carolina*
Rachel Laimon, *Mott Community College*
Laura Lauzen-Collins, *Moraine Valley Community College*
Brian Littleton, *Mott Community College*
Clifton Long, *Saddleback College*
Jeff Love, *Penn State University*
Tammy Mahan, *College of the Canyons*
Michael Mangan, *University of New Hampshire*
George Martinez, *Somerset Community College*
Randy Martinez, *Cypress College*
Catherine Matson, *Triton College*
Donna McElroy, *Atlantic Cape Community College*
Valerie Melburg, *Onondaga Community College*
Jan Mendoza, *Golden West College*
Stefanie Mitchell, *San Jacinto College*
Kristie Moore, *Angelo State University*
Jill Morgan, *Hinds Community College*
Katherine Neidhardt, *Cuesta College*
Hayley Nelson, *Delaware County Community College*
Laura Ochoa, *Bergen Community College*
Kseniva Orlovska, *Fullerton College*
Jennifer Ounjian, *Contra Costa College*
Rena Papafratzeskakou, *Mercer County Community College*
Andrea Phronebarger, *York Technical College*
Michaela Porubanova, *Farmingdale State University*
Sadhana Ray, *Delgado Community College*
Vicki Ritts, *St. Louis Community College*
MaryLou Robins, *San Jacinto College*
Erin Rogers, *Florida State College at Jacksonville*
Rodger Rossman, *College of the Albemarle*
Mariena Salters, *Georgia State University-Perimeter College*
Veronica Sanchez, *Cerritos College*
LaTasha Sarpy, *Bunker Hill Community College*
Alex Schwartz, *Santa Monica College*
Anthony Scioli, *Keene State College*
JoAnne Shayne, *Southern New Hampshire University*
Nick Shizas, *Moraine Valley Community College*
Staci Simmelink-Johnson, *Walla Walla Community College*
Michelle Slattery, *North Central State College*
Cindy Sledge, *Lone Star College*
Jonathan Sparks, *Vance-Granville Community College*
Cari Stevenson, *Kankakee Community College*
Anita Tam, *Greenville Technical College*
Felicia Thomas, *Cal Poly Pomona*
Inger Thompson, *Glendale Community College*
Regina Traficante, *Community College of Rhode Island*
Margot Underwood, *Joliet Junior College*
Lora Vasiliauskas, *Virginia Western Community College*
Dessiree Weeks, *Central Carolina Technical College*
Linda Weldon, *Community College Baltimore County*
Brian Wiley, *Florida State College at Jacksonville*
Keith Williams, *Stockton University*
Janis Wilson Seeley, *Luzerne County Community College*
Samantha Wolfe, *Grand Rapids Community College*
Marc Wolpoff, *Riverside Community College*
James Wright, *Forsyth Technical Community College*
Brandy Young, *Cypress College*
Valerie Young, *Northeast Lakeview College*
Clare Zaborowski, *San Jacinto College*

There is one "unofficial" reviewer whose contributions cannot be quantified. Working behind the scenes from start to finish, reading every line of this text alongside us was Dr. Eve Van Rennes. Dr. Van Rennes, thank you for your intelligent critiques and unwavering support.

It goes without saying that this project would not have been the same without the hard work and dedication of our author team. Every sentence in this textbook has been a group effort: We have written and reviewed everything together. Our minds work differently and we have distinct skill sets, but we recognize and appreciate those in each other. Writing this book was a grueling task (who knew three women could live on just a few hours of sleep every night?), but we have encouraged and supported each other along the way. We are more than a work team—we are lifelong friends. We should acknowledge that none of us would have written these words if it hadn't been for our parents and grandparents, who made our education their top priority.

Last, but certainly not least, we would like to thank the extraordinary people whose life stories are woven throughout these chapters. We selected you because your stories touched and inspired us. Learning about your lives has helped us become more thoughtful and compassionate people. We believe you will have the same effect on college students across the country.

Deborah M. Licht
Misty G. Hull
Coco Ballantyne

CHAPTER 0

Mark Hess/Illustration Source.

Are You Ready for This?

Welcome to Psychology

TRAPPED IN A MINE, 33 MEN FACED DEATH...and how their remarkable story relates directly to this course

Thursday, August 5, 2010: It was a crisp morning in Chile's sand-swept Atacama Desert. The mouth of the San José copper mine was quiet and still, just a black hole in the side of a mountain. You would never know an avalanche was brewing inside. That morning, 33 men entered that dark hole thinking they would go home to their families at the end of their 12-hour shift. Unfortunately, this is not how the story unfolded (Franklin, 2011).

At about 11:30 A.M., a loud splintering sound reverberated through the mine's dim caverns. Approximately 2 hours later, a section of tunnel collapsed some 1,300 feet underground (a depth of 4 football fields), sending a whoosh of stones and dirt howling through the shaft (Associated Press, 2010, August 25; Franklin, 2011). As miners scrambled through dark passageways slipping on loose rocks and gravel, the mountain shook again, delivering a fresh downpour of debris. The final cave-in, occurring hours later,

Los 33
These are the 33 survivors of Chile's 2010 mining disaster. How do you think being trapped underground affected these men's thoughts, emotions, and behaviors—that is, how might it have impacted their psychological processes? CLAUDIO ONORATI/AP Images.

ended with an enormous thunk—the sound of a massive 700,000-ton boulder plugging their only viable escape (Franklin, 2011).

The miners trapped inside began making their way to *el refugio**, a safety shelter half a mile underground at the base of the mine. About the size of a studio apartment, the shelter contained two oxygen tanks, a few medical supplies, and enough food to sustain 10 miners for 2 days. Once all 33 men had arrived, they closed the doors, turned off their lamps to save energy, and began to ponder what had just occurred. As journalists throughout the world would soon report, they had been buried alive (Franklin, 2011).

Take a minute and put yourself in the place of the Chilean miners. There you are crowded among 32 sweaty men in a small, dark hole half a mile beneath the earth's surface, where the temperature is approximately 90°F and the humidity 90% (Cohen, 2011). The main supply of drinking water is tainted with oil and dirt, and your daily food ration amounts to one spoonful of canned tuna fish and a few sips of milk (Franklin, 2011). Crouched on the wet rock floor, you wonder what your family is doing. Surely, they will worry when you don't show up for dinner tonight. Maybe a rescue team is on its way. But maybe not.

How Is It Relevant?

At this point, you may be wondering how this story relates to the study of psychology. Like any human story, the Chilean miner saga has *everything* to do with psychology. In fact, many of its themes relate directly to content in the coming chapters. You could study the men's experience from a *stress and health* perspective (Chapter 12), exploring how being trapped in the mine impacted their health and well-being, or how their behaviors were *motivated* by a variety of needs (Chapter 9). You might examine how the miners' *personalities* impacted their behaviors (Chapter 10), or take the *social psychology* perspective by investigating relationships and group dynamics (Chapter 11). *Memory* is another angle, as traumatic memories may increase the risk of developing a *psychological disorder,* which could lead to the need for *treatment* (Chapters 6, 13, and 14). Venture into these pages, and you will see how psychology is germane to all human stories, including your own.

Now that we have established that psychology is relevant, let's familiarize ourselves with the field.

*To get an idea what it was like inside the mine, go to YouTube and search the phrase "Chilean miners refuge." The story of the Chilean miners is largely based on Jonathan Franklin's *33 Men: Inside the Miraculous Survival and Dramatic Rescue of the Chilean Miners*. Publisher: G.P. Putnam's Sons.

FIGURE 0.1
What Is an LO?
Throughout this book, you will find callouts like this one. LO stands for Learning Objective, which is a statement pointing to essential content you should understand and be able to apply.

This Is the Field, and These Are the Players

LO 1 Define psychology.

Psychology is the scientific study of behavior and mental processes. Running, praying, and shouting were observable behaviors the miners displayed when the mountain collapsed, all potentially a focus of study in psychology. And although their thoughts and emotions were not observable, they too are valid topics of psychological research. *Psychologists* are scientists who work in a variety of fields, each of which centers on the study of behavior and underlying mental processes. People often associate psychology with therapy, and many psychologists do provide therapy. These *counseling psychologists* and *clinical psychologists* might also research the causes and treatments of psychological disorders (Chapters 13 and 14; Appendix B: Careers in Psychology). But clinical practice is just one slice of the gigantic psychology pie. There are psychologists who spend their days in the lab studying interactions between people, and those who assess the capabilities of children in schools. Psychologists may be found poring over brain scans in major medical centers, studying crimes and their perpetrators, analyzing how humans interact with products and technology, and working with athletes to enhance their performance. Did you know, for example, that the U.S. Olympic Committee employs sport psychologists to help athletes meet their full potential (Psychology, n.d.)?

Psychology is a broad scientific field that includes various perspectives and subfields, many of which correspond to chapters in this book (**Figure 0.2**). Chapter 1, for example, dives into the subfield of experimental psychology, exploring how psychologists design and carry out studies. Some of the content may surprise you: For instance, you probably know that if people are given a sugar pill but *believe* they are being treated with a medicine, they often experience benefits similar to those conferred by the drug—but did you know they can also experience similar side effects (Colloca, 2017)? Understanding such concepts is

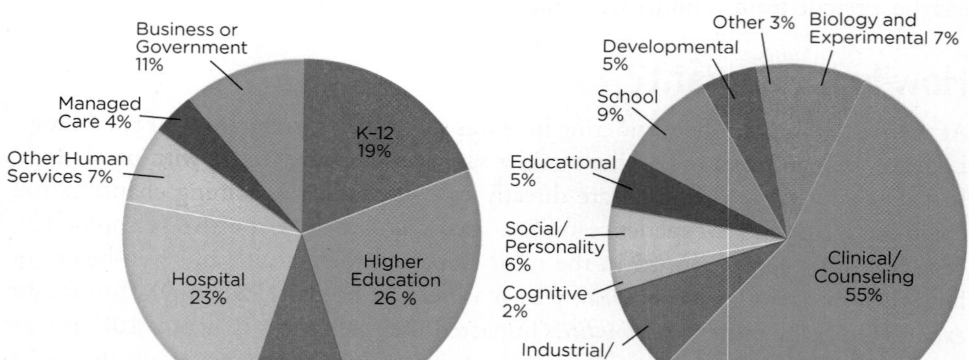

FIGURE 0.2
Fields of Psychology
These pie charts show the primary place of work for full-time doctorate-level psychologists working in 2014, along with their areas of specialty. As you can see, psychologists work in diverse contexts and specialize in many subfields. In the photo on the left, sport psychologist Dr. Michael Gervais stands on the sidelines of the football field, offering support to the Seattle Seahawks. Information from APA Center for Workforce Studies (2015) and U.S. Bureau of Labor Statistics (2014). Photo: Tom Hauck/AP Images.

important for psychologists conducting experiments, medical professionals caring for patients, and business people working in the pharmaceutical industry. Another chapter in this book, Chapter 8, is devoted to the subfield of developmental psychology, which centers on growth and change throughout the human life span. Researchers in this subfield study a range of characteristics across people of different ages; for example, they may compare how young adults and older adults express positive emotions (Rohr, Wieck, & Kunzmann, 2017), or how health behaviors change starting in high school and through the twenties (Ames, Leadbeater, & MacDonald, 2018). Knowledge of human development is crucial for psychologists working with children, nurses caring for the elderly, social workers dealing with families, and virtually any professional who interacts with people.

FIGURE 0.3
What Is This?
Throughout this book, you will find parenthetical notes like this one. These citations tell you the source of research or findings being discussed, in this case an article published by Ames, Leadbeater, & MacDonald in 2018. If you want to know more about a topic, you can look up the source and read the original article or book. Information provided in this brief citation allows you to locate the full reference in the alphabetized reference list at the back of the textbook: Look for Ames, M. E., Leadbeater, B. J., & MacDonald, S. W. S. (2018) on page R-3. Failing to cite the proper source of information is considered plagiarism—a serious academic offense. There are many systems and formats for citing sources, but this textbook uses the APA style established by the American Psychological Association (APA, 2010b). See the Infographic "How to Read a Scientific Article" on the inside front cover; learning how to read academic articles will help you in many classes, including psychology.

Isn't Psychology Just Common Sense?

Describe the hindsight bias and how it leads to misconceptions about psychology.

In our own classes, we find that many students begin the course with misconceptions about psychology. Research suggests this problem is relatively common, and not limited to college students (Ferguson, 2015; Hughes, Lyddy, & Lambe, 2013). Before taking psychology, students fall for about 50% of the psychological myths they have heard; for example, "alcohol kills brain cells" (it doesn't kill them, but it can damage structures important for communication between them); "humans have five senses" (we have more than five senses); and "suicides are especially likely during the Christmas holidays" (the rate of suicide is at its lowest in the month of December; CDC, 2013b; Furnham & Hughes, 2014, pp. 258–259). Through careful research, psychologists have determined that many common assumptions about behaviors are simply not true. Popular culture abounds with psychological myths conveying "misinformation about human nature" (Lilienfeld, Lynn, Ruscio, & Beyerstein, 2010, p. 43). Discover some of these popular misconceptions in **Table 0.1.** Have you fallen for any of them?

In addition to clinging to misconceptions, many students assume that psychology is simply "common sense," or a collection of knowledge that any reasonably smart person can pick up through everyday experiences. The problem is that common sense and "popular wisdom" are not always correct (Lilienfeld, 2012). For

TABLE 0.1 DISPELLED: FIVE "COMMONSENSE" MYTHS

Myth	Reality
"Blowing off steam" or expressing anger is good for you.	Unleashing anger actually may make you more aggressive (Lilienfeld et al., 2010).
Most older people live sad and solitary lives.	People actually become happier with age (Lilienfeld et al., 2010).
Punishment is a great way to change behavior in the long term.	Punishment can lead to unwanted results (see Chapter 5). Myths like this can have a lasting impact on perceptions of discipline (Furnham & Hughes, 2014).
Eating "comfort foods" makes you feel happier.	So-called comfort foods are not unique in their mood-enhancing effects; it appears that a wide variety of foods can improve our moods (Wagner, Ahlstrom, Redden, Vickers, & Mann, 2014).
Listening to Mozart and other classical music will make an infant smarter.	There is no solid evidence that infants who listen to Mozart are smarter than those who do not (Hirsh-Pasek, Golinkoff, & Eyer, 2003).

Here are a few examples of commonsense "wisdom" that have been debunked by psychological research.

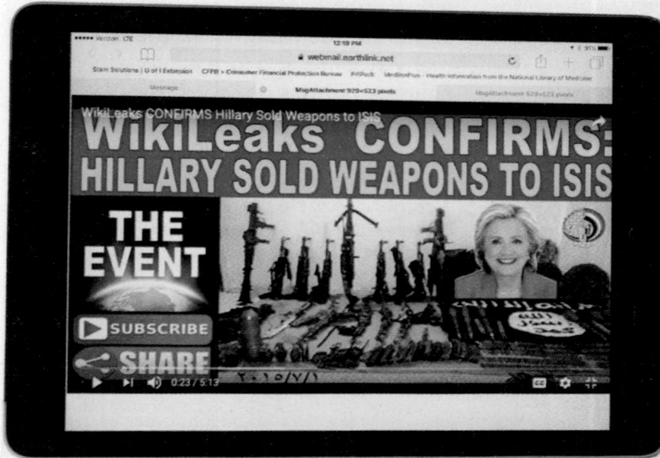

Deconstructing "Fake News"
Fake news has become such a pressing issue that high school students, like these juniors from Annandale High School in Washington, D.C. (top), are taking classes on "fighting fake news" (Contrera, 2017, September 4). Why are people susceptible to phony and misleading news stories like this one pictured in the bottom photo? If the scoop reaffirms something we already think is true, we may fall prey to a cognitive error known as the *confirmation bias,* which is the tendency to look for evidence that upholds our beliefs, and overlook information that contradicts them. Top: Bill O'Leary/The Washington Post via Getty Images. Bottom: The Photo Works/Alamy.

example, common sense might suggest that bystanders are more inclined to help a person in distress when others are nearby; the more people present, the more likely someone will offer aid. But research has repeatedly shown that the opposite occurs—bystanders are less likely to offer aid when many people are around. This "bystander effect" is not observed in all situations; for example, helping behaviors may depend on the thought processes of the people involved and the number of helpers needed (Greitemeyer & Mügge, 2015; Thomas, De Freitas, DeScioli, & Pinker, 2016). Nevertheless, this is a case in which common sense does not match the findings of psychological research.

The impression that psychological findings are obvious might be related to the *hindsight bias,* or the "I knew it all along" feeling (Chapter 7). When a student learns about the results of a psychology study, she may believe she knew it all along because it seems logical in retrospect. But could she have predicted the outcome beforehand? Not necessarily. We fall prey to the hindsight bias in part because we are constantly seeking to explain events. Once something occurs (for example, we hear about the findings of a study), we come up with a way to explain it, and then everything seems to make sense (Lilienfeld, 2012). If you like sports, you may fall prey to the hindsight bias when you "Monday morning quarterback," that is, point out how players and coaches could have avoided mistakes in a game you watched. Sure, you may come up with solutions that never occurred to the coaches and players, but unlike you, they did not have the luxury of thinking about it for several hours! In other words, they did not have hindsight.

Students sometimes insist that life has already taught them all they need to know about psychology. Learning from experience is a critical ability that helps us survive and adapt, but it cannot take the place of scientific findings. Suppose a man believes he knows everything about child development because he has raised three children. This type of *anecdotal evidence,* or personal observation, is valuable, but it is not the same as studying family members like an objective scientist. As you learn more about the human mind, you will see that it is quite prone to errors (Chapters 6 and 7).

It's a Science

Unlike common sense, which is based on casual observations, psychology is a science in the true sense of the word. *Science* is a systematic approach to gathering knowledge through careful observation and experimentation. It requires analyzing data and sharing results in a manner that permits others to duplicate and therefore verify work. Just like chemistry, biology, and all scientific disciplines, psychology is grounded in research using the scientific method. Did you know that many colleges categorize psychology as a part of their STEM (science, technology, engineering, and math) programs? As you read through this textbook, you will encounter examples of how psychology employs many of the essential components of science, including the peer-review process, evidence with citations, replication of research, and the use of theories, hypotheses, and statistical analyses.

Now that we have established what psychology is and isn't, why not get a sense of your knowledge coming into the course? How much do you really know about the science of psychology?

DIDN'T SEE THAT COMING

WHAT DO YOU KNOW? Many students are surprised to discover how often their commonsense knowledge is at odds with scientific findings. See how much you know by taking the quiz below, and then checking your answers on page 0-6.

Chapter 1: *Introduction to the Science of Psychology*

1. Who is considered the "father" of psychology?
   a. Sigmund Freud
   b. William James
   c. Wilhelm Wundt
   d. Edward Titchener

Chapter 2: *Biology and Behavior*

2. Which of the following statements about the brain is FALSE?
   a. People are born with all the brain cells they will ever have.
   b. "Seeing stars" after a blow to the head is likely caused by disruption of activity in the occipital lobes.
   c. Albert Einstein's brain weighed the same as that of the average person.
   d. People can function normally in their day-to-day lives even with an entire hemisphere of their brain missing.

Chapter 3: *Sensation and Perception*

3. Which of the following statements about sensation is FALSE?
   a. Our ability to detect faint stimuli (the sound of a mosquito buzzing, for example) is partly dependent on our psychological state.
   b. The human eye has a blind spot.
   c. Advertisers can get people to buy products by using subliminal messages.
   d. Male testosterone levels are affected by the smell of female armpit secretions.

Chapter 4: *Consciousness*

4. Which of the following statements about sleep is TRUE?
   a. Drinking alcohol helps you get better sleep.
   b. The blue light emitted by smartphones and tablets interferes with the activity of the sleep hormone melatonin.
   c. Yawning indicates that someone is exhausted.
   d. You can catch up on days or weeks of sleep loss with one night of "super-sleep."

Chapter 5: *Learning*

5. Research suggests that childhood exposure to media violence is associated with later aggressive behaviors. This is an example of a:
   a. cause-and-effect relationship.
   b. prosocial relationship.
   c. correlation.
   d. conditioned emotional response.

Chapter 6: *Memory*

6. Which of the following statements about memory is FALSE?
   a. Adults can "remember" events that never happened after viewing doctored photos that portray the fake events.
   b. Memories are located in specific regions of the brain.
   c. Researchers study sea slugs to learn about the neural changes underlying memory formation.
   d. A string around your finger is *not* a good reminder to do something.

Chapter 7: *Cognition, Language, and Intelligence*

7. When comparing the cognitive abilities of males and females, researchers have found that:
   a. girls tend be better than boys at mental rotation tasks.
   b. boys tend to perform better than girls on tests of verbal ability.
   c. men and women differ significantly in their cognitive abilities.
   d. men and women are far more alike than different in cognitive abilities.

Chapter 8: *Human Development*

8. Which of the following statements about human development is FALSE?
   a. There are times in fetal development when the brain is producing approximately 250,000 new neurons per minute.
   b. Happiness generally decreases with age, and negative emotions are more frequent in the elderly.
   c. By the age of 6, most children have a vocabulary that represents learning about one new word every 2 hours awake.
   d. Poor attachment during infancy can have long-term health consequences, influencing the development of illnesses like asthma and diabetes.

Chapter 9: *Motivation and Emotion*

9. Which of the following statements about happiness is NOT true?
   a. Family traditions make the holidays less pleasurable and reduce happiness.
   b. The simple act of smiling can make a person feel happier.
   c. Being completely absorbed in challenging tasks can promote happiness.
   d. Recording positive thoughts and feelings of gratefulness can increase happiness.

Chapter 10: *Personality*

10. Which of the following statements about birth order is TRUE?
   a. Firstborn children are conscientious and high achieving, and become leaders in the workforce.
   b. Youngest children are coddled by their parents, but tend to be rebellious as they grow up.
   c. Middle children get lost in the family shuffle, so they learn to be self-sufficient.
   d. Researchers have been unable to find any consistent connections between birth order and specific personality characteristics.

Chapter 11: *Social Psychology*

11. Social psychology research suggests all the following EXCEPT:
   a. People working in groups are more likely to slack off when individual contributions are hard to ascertain.
   b. The male hormone testosterone plays a role in aggressive behavior.
   c. Attractive people are generally perceived as being more intelligent.
   d. Women and men show similar degrees of physical aggression.

Chapter 12: *Stress and Health*

12. Which of the following is NOT a characteristic associated with living a long, healthy life?
   a. strong social support
   b. alcohol abstinence
   c. incorporating natural movement into daily life
   d. eating until one feels 80% full

Chapter 13: *Psychological Disorders*

13. Insanity is a legal determination of the degree to which people are responsible for their criminal behaviors. Those deemed legally insane are thought to have had little or no control over their behaviors at the time they committed their crimes. In what percentage of U.S. criminal cases is the insanity defense used?
   a. 1% **b.** 5% **c.** 10% **d.** 15%

Chapter 14: *Treatment of Psychological Disorders*

14. Which of the following statements about psychological treatment is TRUE?
   a. Only medical doctors can prescribe medications for people with psychological disorders.
   b. Neurosurgery is no longer used as a treatment for psychological disorders.
   c. Some antidepressants increase the risk of suicidal thoughts and behaviors among a small number of teenagers.
   d. Self-help groups such as Alcoholics Anonymous are typically run by licensed psychologists. !

ANSWERS: 1. c.; 2. a.; 3. c.; 4. b.; 5. c.; 6. b.; 7. d.; 8. b.; 9. a.; 10. d.; 11. d.; 12. b.; 13. a; 14. c

This Is Critical

How did you do? If you are like most students entering the class, you did not pass with flying colors, and that is 100% okay! The point of introductory psychology is for students to learn core concepts and develop psychological literacy, or "the ethical application of psychological skills and knowledge" (Murdoch, 2016, p. 189)—an important goal, according to the American Psychological Association (APA, 2013a). A student who has achieved psychological literacy can responsibly apply the lessons learned in psychology to everyday life. Suppose someone tells you the following: "People with mental illness are dangerous and prone to committing violent crimes." If you have a high degree of psychological literacy, you will not automatically accept this as truth, but draw on your psychology knowledge and thoughtfully assess the claim: *Actually, the research suggests that only a small percentage of crimes are clearly attributable to symptoms of psychological disorders; in fact, people who struggle with mental illness are more likely to be victims of violence than perpetrators of violence* (Desmarais et al., 2014; Peterson, Skeem, Kennealy, Bray, & Zvonkovic, 2014; Skeem, Kennealy, Monahan, Peterson, & Applebaum, 2016). Psychological literacy is not just about tapping into acquired knowledge; it also hinges on *critical thinking*.

Are You a Critical Thinker?

Critical thinking involves weighing pieces of evidence, and considering the source and quality of information before accepting it as valid. But it goes far beyond verifying the facts (Davies, 2015; Yanchar, Slife, & Warne, 2008). The process also entails synthesizing evidence (bringing it together), thinking beyond definitions, focusing on underlying concepts and applications, and being open-minded and skeptical at the same time. Like any scientific discipline, psychology is driven by critical thinking—disciplined thinking that is clear, rational, and always open to the consideration of new ideas. **INFOGRAPHIC 1.2** on page 16 shows how critical thinking is useful for tackling problems, even ones that may at first seem unrelated to psychology.

Critical thinking is an invaluable skill, whether you are a psychologist planning an experiment, a citizen preparing to vote in an election, or a student trying to earn a good grade in psychology class. Has anyone ever told you that choosing "C" on a multiple-choice question is your best bet when you don't know the answer? Research suggests this is not a winning strategy (Skinner, 2009). Accepting this type of advice without thinking critically can be a barrier to developing better strategies. Next time you're offered a tempting morsel of folk wisdom, think before you bite: Is there solid scientific evidence to support this claim? **Table 0.2** explains how a critical thinker would evaluate a commonsense claim.

The American Psychological Association (APA) views critical thinking as an essential skill for all undergraduate psychology majors. To achieve the APA's goal of Scientific Inquiry and Critical Thinking, students must be able to think critically about psychological claims, determine whether a source is objective (free of bias) and credible, and distinguish between real science and *pseudoscience* (APA, 2013a). To understand the meaning of pseudoscience, let's take a quick trip back into the Chilean miner story.

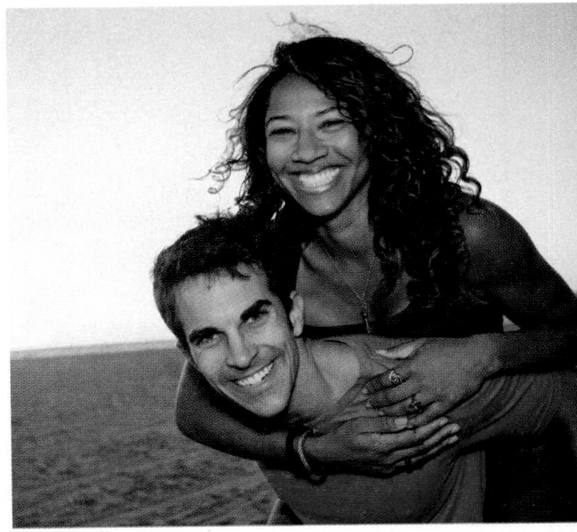

"Birds of a Feather?"
Do opposites really attract, as the saying goes? Put on your critical thinking cap, and you may begin to question this piece of commonsense "wisdom." Psychological research suggests that similarity is a better predictor of romantic attraction, as we are drawn to those who share our interests, viewpoints, and values. Age, education, occupation, and even personality tend to be similar among those who are close (Brooks & Neville, 2016; Lott & Lott, 1965; YouYou, Stillwell, Schwartz, & Kosinski, 2017). Peathegee Inc/Getty Images.

TABLE 0.2 WHAT CRITICAL THINKERS DO

Is it true that "opposites attract"? In other words, are people really drawn to romantic partners different from themselves? To evaluate this claim with critical thinking, you must do the following:

Be skeptical	Why should I believe this? Is there any supporting evidence?
Think deeply	What is meant by "opposites"? Are we referring to people with dissimilar personalities, interests, ethnic backgrounds, educational levels, socioeconomic statuses?
Draw on existing knowledge	My psychology professor recently lectured on interpersonal attraction. What did I learn from that presentation?
Ask questions	What factors are most important in determining whom we find attractive? Can these factors change as we age?
Consider alternative explanations	Maybe the opposite is true: People are attracted to those who are similar. Do "birds of a feather flock together"?
Reflect on your own emotional reactions	I am attracted to people who are different from me. But my personal experience does not constitute scientific evidence.
Tolerate uncertainty	The rules of attraction may not be universal, and they could fluctuate over a person's lifetime.
Keep an open mind	The idea that "opposites attract" is generally not supported by scientific research; however, it may be true for certain traits or certain people.

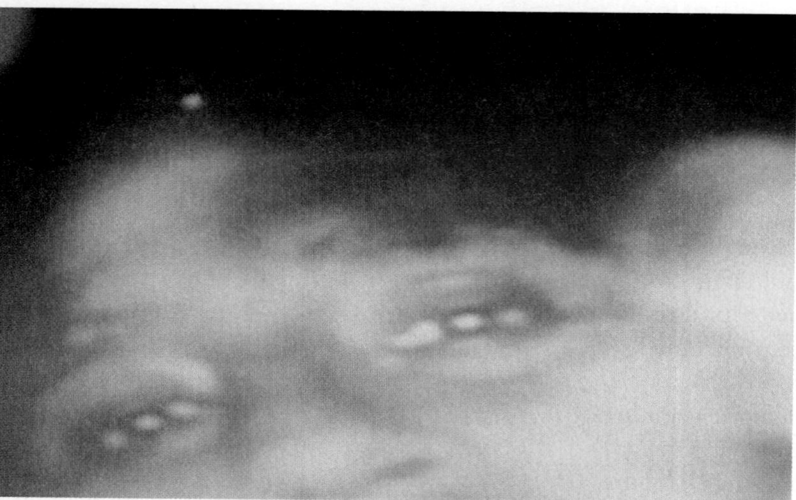

Hello from Below
What do you see in the eyes of miner Florencio Ávalos? At the time this photo was captured, the men had been trapped underground for over two weeks. How do you think this prolonged period with no sunlight affected the men's sleep–wake cycles? After reading Chapter 4, you will be able to answer this question. © Ho New/Reuters/Landov.

THE FIRST 17 DAYS Immediately following the mine collapse, the 33 trapped miners switched into survival mode. When faced with a life-or-death situation, the brain responds by unloading stress hormones. This "fight-or-flight" response, discussed further in Chapters 2 and 12, leads to a boost of physical energy, alertness, and an overwhelming sense of urgency to deal with a threat. The miners found it difficult to stay calm and think rationally. Some put themselves at great risk to search for escape routes; others impulsively stole cookies and milk from the food cabinet—provisions they knew were supposed to be shared by all (Tobar, 2014).

Several days passed without a sign from the world above, and the miners grew weak and weary. To stretch their food supply, they limited their daily intake to one spoonful of tuna fish, half a glass of milk, and one cracker—about 100 calories (Franklin, 2011). By Day 16, each of the miners had lost about 20 pounds (Healy, 2010, August 23). They had been hearing the hum of drills for days, a sure sign that a recovery effort was under way, but no rescue team had reached the part of the mine where they were trapped. Finally on the 17th day, a miracle came crashing through the roof of their dank dungeon: the tip of a drill bit. The rescue team had found them (Franklin, 2011).

Above ground, rescuers waited anxiously as the drill slowly emerged from the mine. The tip of the bit surfaced with bags of letters attached—clues that at least one man had survived. But the real celebrations began with the discovery of a note scrawled in red marker: "Estamos bien en el refugio los 33" or "We are okay in the shelter, the 33 of us." It was a miracle: All 33 men were alive (Franklin, 2011, p. 124).

News of the trapped miners was headlined, broadcast, and tweeted across the globe. People were amazed that all the miners had survived, and some tried to understand the events from a mystical perspective. Various believers in numerology, for example, suggested that the number 33 played a special role in the miners' story.

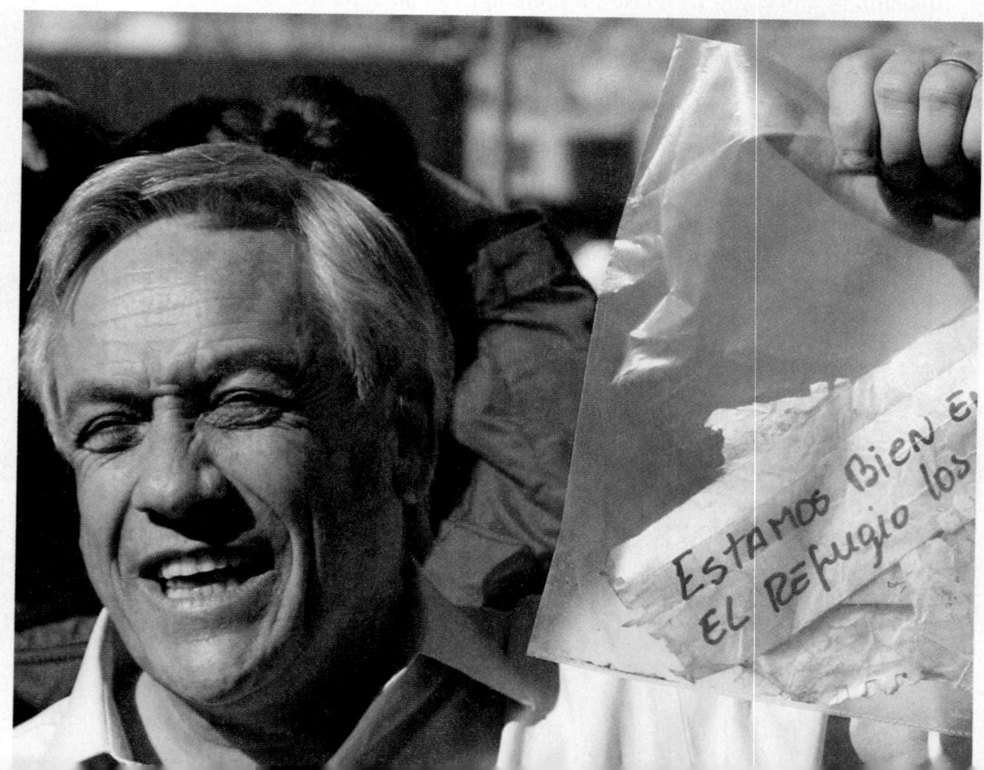

Estamos Bien
Chilean President Sebastián Piñera holds a bag of notes from the miners, one of which reads, "Estamos bien en el refugio los 33" or "We are okay in the shelter, the 33 of us." The rescuers—and eventually people all around the world—went wild in celebration. Now the challenge was drilling a hole wide enough to hoist the men to safety. © DPA/ZUMApress.com.

They noted, for example, that it took 33 days to drill the rescue tunnel for the 33 men, and that the eventual rescue began on 10/13/10, which adds up to 33 (Agence France Presse, 2010, October 14). These pieces of "evidence" may be intriguing, but they are nothing more than coincidence; and if you looked hard enough, you could probably find a different number pattern related to the Chilean miner story.

Bogus Fortune?
What do you think about the message delivered in this fortune cookie? Because the statement is sufficiently vague and complimentary, it could apply to just about any person on the planet—and therefore, many people fall for it. We call this phenomenon the Barnum effect. Image Source/Getty Images.

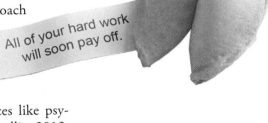

All of your hard work
will soon pay off.

LO 3 Evaluate pseudopsychology and its relationship to critical thinking.

PSEUDOPSYCHOLOGY In your everyday life, you will encounter many "disciplines," such as numerology, which present themselves as psychological science but lack scientific backing. They fall into the category of *pseudopsychology,* an approach to explaining and predicting behavior and events that appears to be psychology but is not supported by objective evidence. Another familiar example is astrology, which uses a chart of the heavens called a horoscope to "predict" everything from the weather to romantic relationships. Surprisingly, many people have difficulty distinguishing between pseudosciences like astrology, and true sciences like psychology, even after earning a college degree (Impey, Buxner, & Antonellis, 2012; Schmaltz & Lilienfeld, 2014).

How then does astrology often seem to be accurate in its descriptions and predictions? Consider this excerpt from a monthly Taurus horoscope: "You can run but you can't hide from love. . . . Money may flow freely in and out, but you won't do anything rash or irresponsible with your resources" (Horoscope.com, 2017). If you really think about it, this statement could apply to just about any human being in the world. We can all "run from love." And, doesn't money always come and go, requiring us to think carefully about our spending? How could you possibly prove such a statement wrong? You couldn't. This is one of the many reasons astrology is not science. A telltale feature of a pseudopsychology, like any pseudoscience, is its tendency to make assertions so broad and vague that they cannot be refuted (Stanovich, 2013). Astrology, numerology, tarot readings, and other forms of pseudopsychology do not rest on a solid foundation of critical thinking.

You have now learned that psychology is neither common sense nor pseudoscience, but a true science driven by critical thinking. We will soon explore how psychology can help you achieve your education and career goals. But first, let's discover the fate of the miners. What happened with the rescuers' effort, and how did the ordeal impact the men's psychological health?

The Rescue Capsule
A rescuer climbs into the Phoenix capsule, ready to venture underground and meet the miners. AFP/Getty Images.

Why Psychology Is Important

THE RESCUE Tuesday, October 12, 2010: The miners had been dreaming of this day for the past 10 weeks. An elevator-like contraption known as the "Phoenix" would soon be lowered down a rescue tunnel to retrieve them. One by one, each miner would return to the surface of the earth and into the arms of family and friends. There would be a few onlookers, including Chilean President Sebastián Piñera, a thousand journalists, and 1 billion people watching on live television (Craze & Crooks, 2010, October 13).

The rescue effort spanned two days and brought all 33 men to safety. Now everyone wondered how the miners would cope with their new

Tears of Joy
Darío Segovia's family members erupted in celebration as they witnessed him emerge from the mine on October 13, 2010. They had waited 10 weeks for him to come home. Natacha Pisarenko/AP Images.

celebrity status. Reporters, publishing companies, and Hollywood all wanted a piece of Los 33.

As you can imagine, the psychological repercussions of the experience were serious. In addition to reports of nightmares, insomnia, and readjustment difficulties, nearly all of the men are said to have suffered from *posttraumatic stress disorder,* further discussed in Chapter 13 (Chambers, 2015, October 13; NPR Staff, 2011, August 8; Tobar, 2014, July 7). Even so, the story of Los 33 gives us many reasons to be hopeful. During their time underground, the miners banded together and helped each other survive. As miner Víctor Zamora puts it, "You see the capacity of human beings to be sensitive in critical moments, how a kind of love is born, a bond [cariño], a brotherhood within a moment of danger" (Tobar, 2014, p. 289). Above ground, rescue workers toiled around the clock to bring Los 33 home; wives, mothers, fathers, siblings, cousins, and friends dropped everything and moved to the Atacama Desert to await the men's return; and strangers all over the world followed the story's every turn, shedding tears when they finally watched the miners emerge from the ground. Our capacity for suffering is deep, but so is our well of empathy.

What's In It for You?

The story of the miners, and all the stories in this book, illustrate the most important lesson we hope to impart in the pages to come: Psychology matters to all of us. It matters to 33 miners trapped underground, and it matters to you, a college student trying to survive and thrive in the 21st century (see **Table 0.3**). What you learn in the upcoming chapters can help you become a more successful student, professional, friend, partner, parent, brother, or sister—a better citizen of the world.

TABLE 0.3 21ST-CENTURY SKILLS

21st-Century Skill	How to Develop It
In order to support a family or enjoy a middle-class existence, you need education beyond high school—a minimum of college or technical training.	You have already taken care of this yourself—by choosing to attend college.
You need to master the basics of traditional education—math, science, language, and arts. Even in today's culture of text messaging and emojis, students still need to know how to correspond in a professional manner—for example, writing an e-mail without grammar and punctuation errors.	To assist you in achieving this mastery, the key resources are your instructors and the assigned texts. This book was designed for smooth and easy reading. Being a strong reader is a prerequisite for succeeding in today's information-dense atmosphere.
Regurgitating information on tests is not enough. You must be able to retain and apply the knowledge to real-world scenarios.	Your instructor will be essential in this regard, helping you see how psychology relates to real life. To complement your instructor's efforts, each chapter features several *Put Your Heads Together* exercises prompting you and your classmates to apply material and generate new ideas in small groups. Active learning is also fostered through *Try This* exercises and the online, immersive learning activity *Your Scientific World.*
Your ability to succeed hinges on certain competencies, among them "the ability to think critically about information, solve novel problems" and "communicate and collaborate" (Jerald, 2009, p. 23).	Your instructor will provide many opportunities for critical thinking. The text reinforces this effort with the following features: *Think Critically, Put Your Heads Together,* and *Try This.*
The ideal way to learn competencies like critical thinking is by integrating them into the larger curriculum; for effective learning, you need context.	Throughout the course, your instructor will point out conceptual relationships among different content areas. The *Connections* features do the same. Strategically placed in the margins, these summaries highlight relationships between topics presented in the current chapter and those presented in earlier chapters. *Connections* illuminate some of the "big picture" themes in psychology.

To thrive in today's world, you need what educational experts refer to as "21st-century skills." The five skills listed here, summarized from Jerald (2009), will help you thrive in an increasingly "complex, competitive, knowledge-based, information-age, technology-driven economy and society" (Hidden Curriculum, 2014, August 26, para. 3). Taking an introductory psychology course will help you cultivate these essential skills.

Now let's take a minute and home in on that first category: How can knowledge of psychology empower you as a student?

Explain how studying psychology can help you achieve your academic goals.

CAN PSYCHOLOGY HELP YOU BECOME A BETTER STUDENT? Psychological research has taught us quite a lot about learning, helping identify which study strategies are most effective. Consider, for example, the idea that testing enhances learning (often referred to as the "testing effect"). Research shows that we remember material better *after* we have been tested on it (Batsell, Perry, Hanley, & Hostetter, 2017). Ideally, tests should be given often. Students generally perform better in a course, and specifically on the final exam, when given ample opportunities to check for understanding and practice retrieving information (Foss & Pirozzolo, 2017). But testing needn't be restricted to high-stakes exams and stressful pop quizzes. As you will see, we have built assessment into the book by using end-of-section *Show What You Know* and end-of-chapter *Test Prep* questions that reward you for reading carefully, thinking critically, and applying concepts. Answers to the questions in both features are provided at the back of the book, in Appendix C. For more examples of how psychological research directs us toward effective study tools, see **Table 0.4** and **Infographic 0.1.**

Research also suggests that students learn and remember material better when they see how it applies to personal experience, world events, and cultural phenomena (Kember, Ho, & Hong, 2008; Roberson, 2013, September). For example, you might be more interested in learning about depression if you could see how it relates to a familiar everyday activity, like using social media. Does frequent use of Instagram, Twitter, and Facebook increase the risk of suffering from depression? Psychology research is likely to provide some answers, or at least clues about whether a relationship exists, and you might pay more attention to the findings if you saw how they could apply to your life.

Psychology also tells us that active learning exercises increase students' understanding and retention of material. The *Put Your Heads Together* features appearing in every chapter prompt you to apply material and generate new ideas in small groups. (Note, these activities will only be fully useful if you have read the material beforehand.) You can also take advantage of the *Try This* exercises scattered throughout the chapters, which ask you to apply key concepts by performing simple activities. These are typically fast, easy-to-do, and designed to reinforce chapter content.

Apply This ↓

TABLE 0.4 STUDY SMART (AND OFTEN)

Technique	What to Do
Survey	Skim the material to determine what may be useful to you: review questions, learning objectives, chapter summaries. Identify main ideas and concepts.
Question	Note any questions that arise after your survey. Create an outline to help organize your study based on the questions you generate.
Read	Read through your chapter, ask questions, and take notes on the content. Remember, studying is not the same as reading.
Recall	Go over the material you have read in your mind. Identify key facts and concepts. Discuss how other material supports the key facts and concepts.
Review	Reread the material, and include additional material to enhance your notes. "Teach" the material to someone else.
Individualize the process	Break down the reading into small sections you can read, recall, and review effectively.
Space your study	Build in breaks and spread the study sessions over time.
Minimize distractions	Focus on the task at hand; multitasking while studying diverts attention, resulting in more time spent learning the material.
Test frequently	Test yourself frequently. Low-stakes feedback provides an opportunity to learn the material and retain it longer. Work together—collaborative study can be quite effective.
Sleep	Get enough rest. Good sleep helps us learn new material and retain it.

Listed here are some practical tips for remembering information you learn in your classes. This advice is largely based on research presented in Chapter 6. Information from Al Firdaus (2012); Roediger, Putnam, & Smith (2011); Rohrer & Taylor (2006).

You've Got the Power

If you have looked at Table 0.4, you have a sense of which study strategies work, but have you devised a specific course of action? Psychologists recommend that you take stock of all available resources and then map out a study plan (Chen, Chavez, Ong, & Gunderson, 2017). It's one thing to know what resources are available, but it is just as important to decide how and when you will use them.

What's Your Plan?

To succeed in college, you must identify a set of valuable study strategies. Which of the following tools will help you learn the material and prepare for exams? Check all that apply:

- Attend classes.
- Read assigned material before class. ← *Record questions to bring to class.*
- Ask questions in class and actively participate in learning activities.
- Review the syllabus regularly.
- Plan ahead for assignments. ← *e.g., create a schedule for your study plan, use instructor-provided templates*
- Take notes on key points discussed in class.
- Write summaries of major sections.
- Complete **Show What You Know** questions.
- Discuss material with other students. ← *e.g., in-class activities, study groups*
- Use chapter learning objectives to test your understanding.
- Do the **Try This** exercises on your own.
- Read the **Connections** to review how the new material relates to previous material.
- Meet with instructor.
- Use resources provided by instructor. ← *e.g., PowerPoints, LaunchPad, LearningCurve, study guides*
- Use Internet resources to complement material. ← *e.g., APA Style guides, instructor-recommended websites*
- Complete **Test Prep** questions.
- Review **Infographics.**
- Review lecture notes.
- Make a concept map.
- Use college-wide resources. ← *e.g., reference librarians, tutoring centers*
- Take breaks.
- Get enough sleep.
- Eat a balanced diet.

Planning Pays Off

Introductory statistics students were asked to think about which resources they would find useful and how they would employ them prior to exam time. The blue bars in the graph represent students who did not complete the exercise (control group), while the red bars represent those who did (experimental group). Throughout the semester, students in the experimental group reflected more on their learning; they reported using resources more successfully; and their course grades were higher by about 3.5–4.5%, or one third of a letter grade (Chen et al., 2017).

Graph data from Chen, P., Chavez, O., Ong, D. C., & Gunderson, B. (2017). Strategic resource use for learning: A self-administered intervention that guides self-reflection on effective resource use enhances academic performance. *Psychological Science, 28*, 774–785.

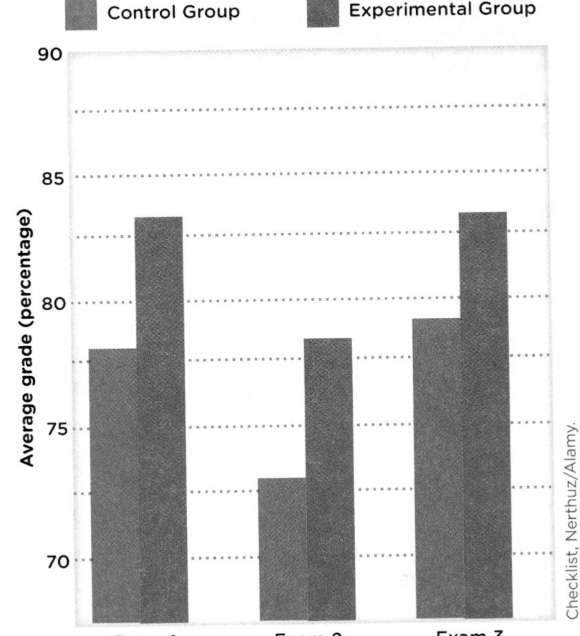

Checklist, Nerthuz/Alamy.

Put Your Heads Together

Working in groups, **A**) identify resources in your textbook, class, and college that will help you learn and be successful. **B**) List the resources you plan to use. **C**) Discuss how you would create a chart to keep track of assignment due dates, plan your work schedule, and monitor your progress in the course.

HOW CAN WE HELP YOU? It goes without saying, keep up with your assigned reading and your experience in class will be richer and more rewarding. As you make your way through each chapter, pay attention to the learning objectives (LOs), which serve as benchmarks for gauging your understanding of each section (see Figure 0.1). You can also use learning objectives to pace yourself as a reader. In other words, read from one learning objective to the next, instead of trying to read the entire chapter in one sitting. For added reinforcement, we have tied the learning objectives to the end-of-chapter *Summary, Show What You Know,* and *Test Prep* questions. Beginning in Chapter 1, you will see **Connections** features strategically placed in the margins **(Figure 0.4)**. These brief summaries complement what many instructors do in the classroom—point out relationships between topics presented in the current chapter and those presented in earlier chapters. Every chapter also features an *Online Video Profile* to provide a more personal connection with the profile subject. Both components of the video profile, "In Their Own Words" and "You Asked, They Answered," are available for free online. Finally, for those of you with access to LaunchPad, make sure you take advantage of the LearningCurve adaptive quizzing system with personalized study plans.

FIGURE 0.4
What Is a Connection?

CONNECTIONS

Connections point out conceptual links between chapters. For example, while reading **Chapter 1**, you will see several *Connections* in the margins explaining how the current discussion relates to concepts introduced in **Chapter 0**. Further into the book, you will come across *Connections* linking back to more and more chapters. Keep an eye out for those red arrows!

Getting Your Bang for the Buck

LO 5 **Describe how an understanding of psychology can foster career success.**

Approximately 1.5 million students enroll in introductory psychology courses every year (Landrum, 2016; Landrum & Gurung, 2013). Some will pursue psychology careers, but most will explore other academic disciplines or technical fields. Whatever path you choose, we guarantee that the material presented in this class will have some relevance. Throughout the book, we will point out how psychology relates to various career areas. We will also highlight skills required to succeed in a competitive, technology-driven world (Jerald, 2009; Strawser & McCormick, 2017). If you are skeptical about the utility of these skills, consider this study: Pollsters asked over 1,300 recruiters from more than 600 companies what qualifications they seek in college grads. They found strategic thinking, creative problem solving, leadership, and communication to be among the most desired skills across various careers (Levy & Rodkin, 2015). Whether you are interested in nursing, business, art, computer science, or agriculture, keep reading . . . this book is designed to help you.

Beyond the Book:
Watch the Video
SCIENTIFIC AMERICAN
PRESENTING PSYCHOLOGY
http://qrs.ly/oe4qsgr

Here We Go

With this introduction, you should have a general sense of what psychology is (and isn't), why the discipline matters to all of us, and how to get the most out of this course. As you make your way through these pages, you will come across five recurring themes: nature and nurture, culture, gender, positive psychology, and psychology in the workplace. Take a moment and familiarize yourself with them before you delve into the chapters (**Table 0.5**).

Are you ready to begin your journey through *Scientific American: Presenting Psychology*? Open your mind. It could be a life-changing ride.

TABLE 0.5 LOOK FOR THESE

Theme	Key Question	What to Look for
Nature and nurture	How do heredity and environment interact to influence behavior and mental processes?	Genes, heredity, environment, instincts, reflexes, adaptation, upbringing, peers, parents
Culture	How does culture shape behavior and mental processes?	Diversity, ethnicity, cultural context, cross-cultural factors, ethnocentrism, in-group, out-group
Gender	How does gender impact behavior and mental processes?	Gender differences, gender roles, gender stereotypes, gender bias, social roles, masculinity, femininity
Positive psychology	What is positive about human beings?	Strengths, optimal behavior, happiness, well-being, achievement, self-confidence, self-actualization, human potential
Psychology in the workplace	How does psychology relate to workplace behaviors and environment?	Connections between psychology and professional activities

Throughout this textbook, you will come across five recurring topics: nature and nurture, culture, gender, positive psychology, and psychology in the workplace. These are not only important issues in psychology; they are relevant to you as a student and as a person living in the 21st century.

CHAPTER 1

Fran Polito/Getty Images.

Introduction to the Science of Psychology

What Is Psychology and How Did It Begin?

PARALLEL LIVES December 15, 2012: It was a cold and rainy day in London, England. Twenty-five-year-old Anaïs Bordier was in a fabric shop, browsing materials for her upcoming fashion show. Born and raised in the suburbs of Paris, France, Anaïs had come to London to study fashion design at the prestigious arts and design college Central Saint Martins.

"Bzzzt, bzzzt!" Thoughts of design portfolios and fabric swatches were suddenly interrupted by Anaïs' cell phone. One of her friends had posted an image on her Facebook wall. Anaïs caught a glimpse of the post, which appeared to be a photo of her own face, but she couldn't figure out where it came from because the Internet connection was slow. "[For] 30–35 minutes, I couldn't look at what was happening on my phone, and I could see people commenting on it," Anaïs recalls. "It was driving me crazy."

"I Was Like Whaaaa???"
The original wall post by Anaïs' friend Kelsang showing the French student's American look-alike in a YouTube video (left). Anaïs and all her friends were astounded by the resemblance. (For comparison, see the profile photo of Anaïs to the right.) A few months later, Kelsang found the mystery woman in yet another video, a trailer for the movie *21 & Over*. Her name was Samantha Futerman, and she was an American actress born on the exact same day as Anaïs! "It's a bit as if another world suddenly opened," Anaïs says, "like a parallel world that you never thought existed." Left: Twinsters (2015). Small Package Films. Right: Anais Bordier.

Anaïs finally got home and made a beeline for her laptop. The Facebook post generating so much buzz was a screen grab from a YouTube video—a close-up of a girl looking over her shoulder and smiling coyly. She looked EXACTLY like Anaïs. Heart racing, Anaïs clicked on the video link, which led to a short comedy piece called "High School Virgin" produced by an American actor popularly known as KevJumba. The girl in the video was a mirror image of Anaïs, and with the exception of her American accent, she sounded identical, too.

Anaïs felt her blood pressure drop. She could not move her body, yet her mind was moving a million miles an hour. Could this American girl be a long-lost identical twin? Impossible. According to Anaïs' birth records, she was a single baby born to an unwed mother in Busan, South Korea. After spending three months in foster care, baby Anaïs had been sent to France to live with her adoptive parents, Jacques and Patricia Bordier.

If the American look-alike wasn't a twin, perhaps she could be a cousin, a younger sister, a half-sister? Maybe Anaïs' friends were just playing tricks on her; after all, some of them were pretty good at editing videos. As all these thoughts darted through her mind, Anaïs kept circling back to the identical twin possibility. "The idea kept coming," Anaïs recalls, "and then [the] other part of my brain was saying, no, you're crazy."

A couple of months (and many Internet searches) later, Anaïs and her friends discovered the mystery girl in another online video: the trailer for a major Hollywood production called *21 & Over*. Anaïs immediately searched the online list of cast members, spotted her look-alike, and clicked on her profile. The young woman's name was Samantha Futerman, and she was born on November 19, 1987 . . . the same date as Anaïs.

Sam and Anaïs, In Their Own Words

http://qrs.ly/2r77rvp

Macmillan Learning.

Note: The story of Anaïs Bordier and Samantha Futerman is based on personal communications with them, as well as the book they co-authored with Lisa Pulitzer, *Separated@Birth*, and the documentary film *Twinsters*. Unless otherwise specified, quotations attributed to Anaïs Bordier, Samantha Futerman, and Dr. Nancy L. Segal are personal communications.

This Is Psychology

On a superficial level, the young actress Samantha Futerman appeared to be Anaïs' identical twin. Her facial features, voice, and physique were virtually the same. Of course, there is much more to a person than a physical body. Anaïs wondered if her look-alike shared similar attitudes, preferences, and behaviors. Did Samantha Futerman have the same offbeat sense of humor and explosive, rolling laugh? Did she surround herself with the same type of smart and creative friends, and was she a glutton for fried chicken and afternoon naps? When it came to Samantha's psychological characteristics—those related to her behavior and mental processes—Anaïs was totally in the dark.

LO 1 Describe the scope of psychology.

By now, you probably realize that psychology has something to do with how people think and act, but let's establish a more precise definition: **Psychology** is the scientific study of behavior and mental processes. Gasping, smiling, and laughing are observable behaviors Anaïs might have displayed when she saw Samantha on YouTube; all these activities are potential research topics in psychology. Anaïs' mental processes included thoughts (*Where was Samantha born? Was she adopted as well?*) and emotions (apprehension or excitement about discovering a long-lost twin). While these thoughts and emotions are not directly observable, they, too, are valid research topics in psychology.

Psychology is a broad field that includes many perspectives and subfields. The American Psychological Association (APA), one of psychology's major professional organizations, has over 50 divisions representing various subdisciplines and areas of interest (APA, n.d.-e). The Association for Psychological Science (APS), another major professional organization in the field, publishes a list of over 100 different societies, organizations, and agencies with some affiliation to the field of psychology (APS, n.d.). In fact, each chapter in this textbook covers a broad subtopic representing one of psychology's major subfields.

As scientists, **psychologists** can conduct two major types of research, *basic* and *applied*. Basic research, which often occurs in university laboratories, focuses on collecting data to support (or refute) theories. The goal of basic research is not to find solutions to specific problems, but rather to gather knowledge for the sake of knowledge. General explorations of human memory, sensory abilities, and responses to trauma are examples of basic research. Applied research, on the other hand, focuses on changing behaviors and outcomes, and often leads to real-world applications, such as specific behavioral interventions for children with autism, or innovative keyboard layouts that improve typing performance. Applied research may incorporate findings from basic research, but it is often conducted in natural settings outside the laboratory.

What's the End Game?

The answer to this question varies according to subfield, but there are four main goals: to describe, explain, predict, and change behavior. These goals lay the foundation for the scientific approach and the research designs used to carry out experiments in psychology. Let's take a closer look at each one.

LO 2 Summarize the goals of the discipline of psychology.

DESCRIBE Goal 1 is to describe or report what is observed. Imagine that a psychologist wants to *describe* the use of mindfulness meditation in elementary schools. What kind of study would she conduct? To start, she would need access to students

psychology The scientific study of behavior and mental processes.

psychologists Scientists who study behavior and mental processes.

at elementary schools willing to implement meditation programs. She might assess the students' academic performance, social adjustment, and physical health before starting the program. She could monitor the participants over time, conducting more assessments at a later date. Eventually, the psychologist would present her observations in a scientific article published in a respected journal.

"Let's Meditate, Class"
Elementary school students meditate during gym class. Could this improve their mental health? A small, preliminary study of sixth graders found that students who practiced mindfulness meditation in school had a "reduced risk of developing suicidal ideation and thoughts of self-harm compared to the controls" (Britton et al., 2014, para. 58). In Baltimore, one elementary school has been replacing detentions with trips to a "Mindful Moment Room," where students take deep breaths and reflect on the incident that brought them there. In the three years since the meditation room was introduced, not a single student has been suspended. Compare that to four suspensions in the prior year (Bloom, 2016, November 8). Hill Street Studios/Getty Images.

EXPLAIN Goal 2 is to organize and make sense of research observations. Suppose the psychologist finds that the students receive fewer detentions and suspensions after the mindfulness meditation program is implemented; this observation may prompt her to explore factors that could influence student conduct. Searching the scientific literature for clues, she might come across studies of people who experienced positive behavioral changes following meditation—for example, residents at an assisted living facility. If she determined that the changes were associated with meditation, this could help *explain* the students' improved behavior, though she still would have to conduct a controlled experiment to identify a causal relationship between meditation and student behavior in school.

PREDICT Goal 3 is to predict behaviors or outcomes on the basis of observed patterns. If the researcher determined that the decreased detention and suspension rates resulted from mindfulness meditation, then she could *predict* that meditation in another setting (such as a correctional institution) might lead to the same outcome.

CHANGE Goal 4 is to use research findings to modify or change behavior. This refers to how we can *apply* the findings of psychological research to change and direct behaviors in a beneficial way. Perhaps the researcher could use her findings to help schools implement meditation in their curricula.

CONNECTION ESTABLISHED February 21, 2013: Samantha Futerman was in Los Angeles getting ready for the red-carpet premiere of *21 & Over*. A Twitter notification appeared on her phone: "Hey Sam, my friend Anaïs sent you a message on FB, check it out ☺ (it might be in the spam box)" (Bordier, Futerman, & Pulitzer, 2014, p. 17). Sam did not recognize the sender of this message, nor did she know anyone named Anaïs. Being an actress, she was wary of social media stalkers, but something about this message sparked her curiosity. She opened Facebook and found a friend request from Anaïs Bordier, a 25-year-old woman living in London whose face appeared to be an exact duplicate of her own. A knot tightening in her stomach, Sam accepted Anaïs' friend request and opened up her message:

> Hey, my name is Anaïs, I am French and live in London. About 2 months ago, my friend was watching one of your videos with Kevjumba on youtube, and he saw you and thought we looked really similar . . . like VERY REALLY SIMILAR. . . . I checked more of your videos (which are hilarious) and then came upon the "how it feels to be adopted" . . . and discovered you were adopted too. (Bordier et al., 2014, p. 13)

Sam stared at her phone, stunned and mystified. Anaïs Bordier, a complete stranger living halfway around the world, had begun to dismantle her life story with a single Facebook message. This notion of being a twin completely contradicted what Sam had learned about her past. According to her papers, she was a single

You Asked, Sam and Anaïs Answer

http://qrs.ly/2r77rvp

What is the best part about having an identical twin?

Love at First Skype
Six days after making contact on Facebook, Sam (left) and Anaïs had their first face-to-face conversation on Skype. They began at about 12:30 A.M. Paris time and continued until almost 4:00 A.M. "Speaking to Anaïs on Skype was unreal. I mean we had to be twins," Sam recalls in the book she coauthored with Anais, *Separated@Birth* (Bordier et al., 2014, p. 102). "There was no reason to be scared anymore," Anaïs writes. "Even though I didn't have absolute proof, I had found my sister" (p. 100). Twinsters (2015). Small Package Films.

POP . . . POP . . . POP!
A drawing by Anaïs, illustrating the "pop" language she and Sam created a few weeks after they connected online. In the beginning, they would say "pop" to reference an incoming text message on WhatsApp, but soon they began using "pop" to replace verbs, pronouns, and other parts of speech. "It can be anything," Sam explains. "We call each other Pop. . . . Are you popping? . . . He's a pop." How is it that Sam and Anaïs can communicate so much with one simple word? Identical twins have almost identical genes, which might explain why they think in such similar ways. Twinsters (2015). Small Package Films.

baby born to a mother in Busan, South Korea, and adopted a few months later by Judd and Jackie Futerman of New Jersey.

Sam began to scour Anaïs' Facebook photos, discovering more parallels: Anaïs had freckles on her nose (uncommon among Koreans); she wore the same kind of goofy animal costumes for Halloween; and comments from friends hinted that she had some of the same personality quirks. The physical resemblance was breathtaking. "I thought she could be my reflection in a mirror," Sam recalls. "It was beyond comprehension" (Bordier et al., 2014, p. 32).

It would take three months for Sam and Anaïs to finally meet in person, but thanks to Facebook, Skype, and WhatsApp (an international texting application), they would already be extremely close. Communicating daily, Sam and Anaïs began to uncover a mountain of shared characteristics and preferences—more evidence that they were twins. For example, both women brush their teeth somewhat obsessively and hate the feeling of shower curtains touching their skin. When faced with a problem, both Sam and Anaïs tend to wallow in it for a bit, or as Sam puts it, "torpedo ourselves into a hole." But after a good snooze, the world looks brighter and the problem seems more manageable.

Of course, Sam and Anaïs are not carbon copies of one another. An obvious physical difference is the color of their skin (Sam is tanner from surfing in the California sun). As for psychological disparities, they seem to differ in their experience of emotional stress. "Depending on what it is, I can just shake it off, but it will kind of live with [Anaïs] a little bit more," says Sam, who attributes this coping style to her experience growing up with two older brothers. When Sam felt stressed or upset, her brothers would often tell her to "get over it" and find something to do. Anaïs was an only child, so she did not "benefit" from this type of sibling interaction.

What Are Psychology's Roots?

You have now learned about the scope and goals of psychology. Soon, you will explore the basics of psychological research: how psychologists use a scientific approach, the many types of studies they conduct, and the ethical standards that guide them through the process. But first, let's take a trip back in time and meet the people whose philosophies, insights, and research findings molded psychology into the vibrant science it is today.

LO 3 Identify the people who helped establish psychology as a discipline, and describe their contributions.

The origins of psychology lie in fields as diverse as philosophy and physiology. In ancient Greece, the great philosopher Plato (427–347 BCE) believed that truth and knowledge exist in the soul before birth; that is, humans are born with some degree of innate knowledge. Plato raised an important issue psychologists still contemplate: the contribution of *nature* in the human capacity for thinking.

One of Plato's most renowned students, Aristotle (384 –322 BCE), went on to challenge his mentor's basic teachings. Aristotle believed that we know reality through our perceptions, and we learn through our sensory experiences, an approach now commonly referred to as *empiricism.* Aristotle has been credited with laying the foundation for a scientific approach to answering questions, including those pertaining to psychological concepts such as emotion, sensation, and perception (Slife, 1990; Thorne & Henley, 2005). Ultimately, because he believed knowledge is the result of our experiences, Aristotle paved the way for scientists to study the world through their observations.

This notion that experience, or **nurture,** plays an all-important role in how we acquire knowledge contradicts Plato's belief that it is inborn, or in our **nature.** Today, psychologists agree that both nature *and* nurture, that is, inherited biological factors and forces in the environment, are important. Current research explores the contribution of each through studies of heredity and environmental factors.

NATURE AND NURTURE Let's suppose Sam and Anaïs are identical twins. How could you use nature and nurture to explain their similarities and differences? At conception, identical twins share 100% of their genes (the units of heredity passed from parents to children), so they are equivalent in their nature (Abdellaoui et al., 2015; McRae, Visscher, Montgomery, & Martin, 2015). But growing up in separate households means they differ in their nurture; that is, they are subject to distinct sets of environmental forces. Thus, the similarities observed between identical twins are likely to be influenced by their common nature, while differences are apt to be linked to their unique upbringing and life experiences, or nurture.

Same Species, Really? Would you believe that these two butterflies belong to the same species? The wing markings and color differ because they were born in different seasons and therefore exposed to distinct environmental pressures (Hey, 2009). A testament to the power of nurture. Courtesy Fred Nighout, Duke University, North Carolina, USA.

Because identical twins are equal in nature but not necessarily in nurture, they can tell us a lot about the relative contributions of these two forces. For example, identical twins—even those raised apart—tend to be very close on measures of intelligence (Bouchard, Lykken, McGue, Segal, & Tellegen, 1990; Shakeshaft et al., 2015). This suggests that genes (nature) can play a major role in determining intellectual ability (Sniekers et al., 2017).

Twin research is not just important to twins; it has implications for all of us. Suppose one identical twin develops cancer but his twin does not. That means that something in the environment likely set off the disease process. If we can figure out what the trigger is, then we can all benefit from that knowledge (Segal, 1999; Winerman, 2015). Studies of identical twins and fraternal twins (who, like non-twin siblings, share approximately 50% of their genes) have helped psychologists untangle the roles of nature and nurture for a variety of areas, including

nurture The environmental factors that shape behaviors, personality, and other characteristics.

nature The inherited biological factors that shape behaviors, personality, and other characteristics.

intelligence (Chapter 7), sexual orientation (Chapter 9), aspects of personality (Chapter 10), and psychological disorders (Chapter 13). We will revisit the nature and nurture theme throughout the book, but for now let's get back to our discussion of history.

DESCARTES If Aristotle placed great confidence in human perception, French philosopher René Descartes (day-KART; 1596–1650) practically discounted it. Famous for saying, "I think, therefore, I am," Descartes believed that most everything else was uncertain, including what he saw with his own eyes. He proposed that the body is like a tangible machine, whereas the mind has no physical substance. The body and mind interact as two separate entities, a view known as *dualism,* and Descartes (and many others) wondered how they were connected. Descartes' work allowed for a more scientific approach to examining thoughts, emotions, and other topics previously believed to be beyond the scope of study.

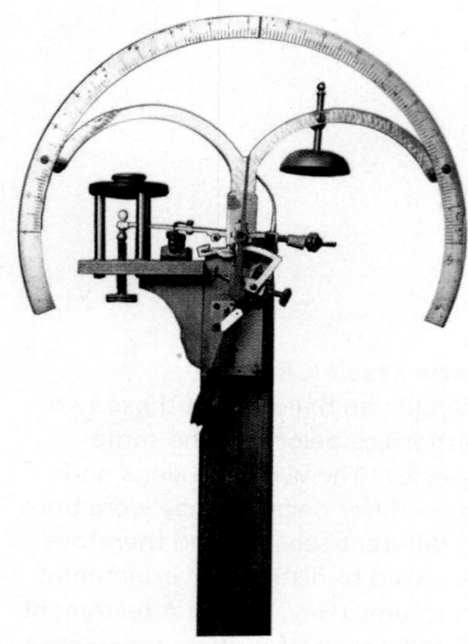

Wundt Measures the Mind
In 1861 Wilhelm Wundt conducted an experiment on reaction time, which was a turning point in the field of psychology. Using a pendulum that hit a bell upon reaching its outer limits, Wundt demonstrated a 10th of a second delay between a person hearing the bell and noting the position of the pendulum (and vice versa). It was during that very brief period that a mental process occurred. Finally, activities of the mind could be measured (Thorne & Henley, 2005). The Drs. Nicolas and Dorothy Cummings Center for the History of Psychology, The University of Akron.

Psychology Is Born

Thus far, the only people in our presentation of psychology's history have been philosophers. *Where are all the psychologists?* you may be wondering. The answer is simple: There were no psychologists until 1879. That was the year Wilhelm Wundt (VILL-helm Vundt; 1832–1920) founded the first psychology laboratory, at the University of Leipzig in Germany, and for this he generally is considered the "father of psychology." Equipped with its own laboratory, research team, and meticulous accounts of experiments, psychology finally became a discipline in its own right (Landrum, 2016).

The overall aim of Wundt's early experiments was to measure psychological processes through **introspection,** a method used to examine one's own conscious activities. For Wundt, introspection involved effortful reflection on the sensations, feelings, and images experienced in response to a stimulus, followed by reports that were *objective,* meaning free of opinions, beliefs, expectations, and values. In order to ensure reliable data, Wundt required all his participants to complete 10,000 "introspective observations" prior to starting data collection. His participants were asked to make quantitative judgments about physical stimuli—how strong they were, how long they lasted, and so on (Boring, 1953; Schultz & Schultz, 2016).

STRUCTURALISM British-born psychologist Edward Titchener (TITCH-e-ner; 1867–1927), who was a student of Wundt, developed a movement in psychology known as **structuralism.** In 1893 Titchener set up a laboratory at Cornell University in Ithaca, New York, where he conducted introspection experiments aimed at determining the structure and "atoms" (most basic elements) of the mind. Titchener's participants, also extremely well trained, were asked to describe the elements of their current consciousness. In contrast to Wundt's focus on *objective,* quantitative reports of conscious experiences, Titchener's participants provided detailed reports of their *subjective* (unique or personal) experiences (Hothersall, 2004; Schultz & Schultz, 2016). Structuralism did not last past Titchener's lifetime. Nevertheless, Titchener demonstrated that psychological studies could be conducted through observation and measurement, and many psychologists are still interested in exploring subjective experiences.

introspection The examination of one's own conscious activities.

structuralism An early school of psychology that used introspection to determine the structure and most basic elements of the mind.

FUNCTIONALISM In the mid-1870s, William James (1842–1910) offered the first psychology classes in the United States, at Harvard University. Eleven years later, James received a $300 grant for laboratory equipment. Wundt was given a small research grant that same year, an indication that both of these founding psychologists were being recognized by their institutions (Harper, 1950). James had little interest in pursuing the experimental psychology practiced by Wundt and other Europeans (Gundlach, 2018); instead, he was inspired by the work of British naturalist Charles Darwin (1809–1882). Studying the elements of introspection was not a worthwhile endeavor, James believed, because consciousness is an ever-changing "stream" of thoughts. Consciousness cannot be studied by looking for fixed or static elements, because they don't exist, or so he reasoned. But James believed consciousness does serve a function, and it is important to study the purpose of thoughts, feelings, and behaviors, and how they help us adapt to the environment. This focus on purpose and adaptation in psychological research is the overarching theme of **functionalism.** Although it didn't endure as a separate field of psychology, functionalism still made an impact by influencing educational psychology, studies of emotion, and comparative studies of animal behavior (Benjamin, 2007; Schultz & Schultz, 2016).

Breaking Ground
Margaret Floy Washburn is perhaps most famous for becoming the first woman psychologist to earn a PhD, but her scholarly contributions must not be underestimated. Her book *The Animal Mind: A Textbook of Comparative Psychology* (1908), which drew on her extensive research with animals, had an enduring impact on the field (APA, 2013b; Washburn, 2010). Macmillan Learning.

WOMEN WHO BROKE THROUGH THE CEILING Like most sciences, psychology began as a "boys' club," with men earning the degrees, teaching the classes, and running the labs. There were, however, a few women, as competent and inquiring as their male counterparts, who beat down the club doors long before women were formally invited. One of William James' students, Mary Whiton Calkins (1863–1930), completed all the requirements for a PhD at Harvard, but was not allowed to graduate from the then all-male college because she was a woman. Nonetheless, she persevered with her work on memory and personality and established her own laboratory at Wellesley College, eventually becoming the first female president of the American Psychological Association in 1905 (Milar, 2016). If you are wondering, the first woman to earn a PhD in psychology was Margaret Floy Washburn (1871–1939), a student of Titchener. Her degree, granted in 1894, came from Cornell University, which—unlike Harvard—allowed women to earn doctorates at the time.

Mamie Phipps Clark (1917–1983) was the first Black woman to be awarded a PhD in psychology from Columbia University. Her work, which she conducted with her husband Kenneth Bancroft Clark, examined the impact of prejudice and discrimination on child development. Their research played an important role in the 1954 Supreme Court decision making segregation in public schools unlawful (Milar, 2016). Although Clark's husband held a faculty position at City University of New York, she was never allowed to teach there. Instead, she found a job analyzing research data and eventually became executive director of the Northside Center for Child Development in upper Manhattan (Pickren & Burchett, 2014).

For the Children
The work of Mamie Phipps Clark (left) raised awareness about the unique psychological issues affecting African American and other minority children. She and her husband founded Harlem's Northside Center for Child Development, an organization that continues to provide psychological and educational support to children in the community. Cecil Beaton/Getty Images.

Thanks to trailblazers such as Calkins, Washburn, and Clark, the field of psychology is no longer dominated by men. Since 2006, the number of women earning doctorates in psychology has increased by almost 21%. These days, women comprise approximately 71% of students earning these advanced degrees in psychology (National Science Foundation, 2018). Do you think this imbalance could cause problems in the field?

functionalism An early school of psychology that focused on the function of thought processes, feelings, and behaviors and how they help us adapt to the environment.

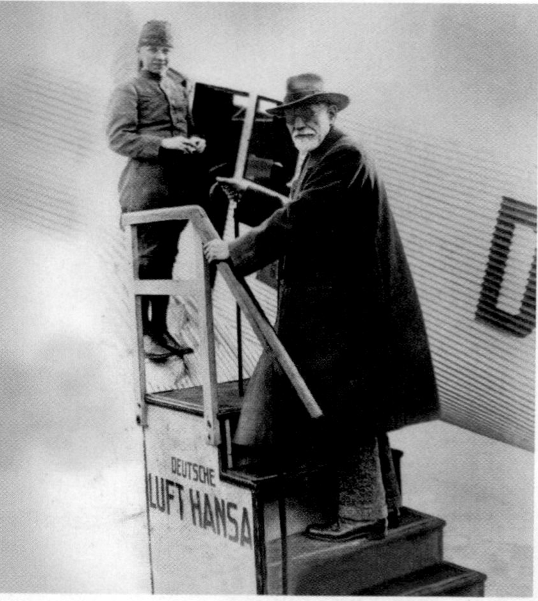

Freud Takes Off
Psychology's most famous icon boards his first airplane in 1928, years after psychoanalysis had gotten off the ground in Europe and America. Freudian ideas are still alive and well, though people often overestimate their importance in psychology. About 90% of American Psychological Association members do not practice psychoanalysis, and most science-minded psychologists have distanced themselves from Freudian notions because they are not supported by solid experimental data (Stanovich, 2013; Hobson, 2006). ASSOCIATED PRESS.

Psychology's Evolution: An Overview

LO 4 List and summarize the major perspectives in psychology.

Some of the early schools of thought surrounding psychology had a lasting impact and others seemed to fade. Nevertheless, they all contributed to the growth of the young science. (See the **Psychology's Roots** infographic on the inside front cover.) Now let's explore the major perspectives in contemporary psychology, all of which shed light on the complex nature of human behavior.

PSYCHOANALYTIC Toward the end of the 19th century, while many early psychologists were busy investigating the "normal" functioning of the mind (in experimental psychology), Austrian physician Sigmund Freud (1856–1939) focused much of his attention on the "abnormal" aspects. Freud believed that behavior and personality are influenced by conflicts between one's inner desires (often sexual and aggressive in nature) and the expectations of society—clashes that primarily occur unconsciously or outside of awareness (Gay, 1988; Chapter 10). This **psychoanalytic perspective** suggests that personality development is heavily influenced by processes that are set into motion early in life and result from interactions with caregivers (Chapter 10). Freud also pioneered psychoanalysis, a new approach to psychotherapy, or "talk therapy" (Chapter 14). Although Freud's name is famous, few people understand that his theories lack solid scientific support, a phenomenon termed the "Freud Problem" (Griggs & Christopher, 2016; Stanovich, 2013).

BEHAVIORAL As Freud worked on his new theories of the unconscious mind, Ivan Pavlov (1849–1936), a Russian physiologist, was busy studying canine digestion. During the course of his research, Pavlov got sidetracked by an intriguing phenomenon. The dogs in his study had learned to salivate in response to stimuli or events in the environment, a type of learning that eventually became known as *classical conditioning* (Chapter 5). Building on Pavlov's conditioning experiments, American psychologist John B. Watson (1878–1958) established **behaviorism,** which viewed psychology as the scientific study of behaviors that could be seen and/or measured. Consciousness, sensations, feelings, and the unconscious were not suitable topics of study, according to Watson.

Carrying on the behaviorist approach to psychology, American psychologist B. F. Skinner (1904 –1990) studied the relationship between behaviors and their consequences. Skinner's research focused on *operant conditioning,* a type of learning that occurs when behaviors are rewarded or punished (Chapter 5). Skinner acknowledged that mental processes such as memory and emotion might exist, but they are not topics to be studied in psychology. To ensure that psychology was a science, he insisted on studying behaviors that could be observed and documented.

The **behavioral perspective** promoted by Watson and Skinner suggests that behaviors and personality are primarily determined by learning. People tend to repeat behaviors that lead to desirable consequences, and discontinue behaviors with undesirable consequences. According to this view, personalities are largely shaped by forces in the environment—that is, *nurture.* But twin studies suggest that *nature* also plays a pivotal role; the genes we inherit from our biological parents can have an important influence on the people we become (Polderman et al., 2015). You will witness the power of nature in the story of Anaïs and Sam.

psychoanalytic perspective An approach developed by Freud suggesting that behavior and personality are shaped by unconscious conflicts.

behaviorism The scientific study of observable behavior.

behavioral perspective An approach suggesting that behavior is primarily learned through associations, reinforcers, and observation.

HUMANISTIC American psychologists such as Carl Rogers (1902–1987) and Abraham Maslow (1908–1970) took psychology in yet another direction. These founders of **humanistic psychology** were critical of the way psychoanalysis and behaviorism suggested that people have little control over their lives. The humanistic perspective proposes that human nature is essentially positive, and that people are naturally inclined to grow and change for the better (Chapter 10) (Maslow, 1943; Rogers, 1961). Reflecting on the history of psychology, we cannot help but notice that new developments are often reactions to what came before. The rise of humanism was, in some ways, a rebellion against the rigidity of psychoanalysis and behaviorism.

COGNITIVE During the two-decade prime of *behaviorism* (1930–1950), many psychologists only studied observable behavior. Yet prior to behaviorism, psychologists had emphasized the study of thoughts and emotions. In the 1950s, a new force in psychology brought these unobservable elements back into focus. This renewed interest in the study of mental processes falls under the field of *cognitive psychology* (Wertheimer, 2012), and American George Miller's (1920–2012) research on memory is considered an important catalyst for this cognitive revolution (Chapter 6). The **cognitive perspective** examines mental processes that direct behavior, focusing on concepts such as thinking, memory, and language. The *cognitive neuroscience* perspective, in particular, explores physiological explanations for mental processes, searching for connections between behavior and the human nervous system, especially the brain. With the development of brain-scanning technologies, cognitive neuroscience has flourished, interfacing with fields such as medicine, computer science, and psychology.

EVOLUTIONARY According to the **evolutionary perspective,** behaviors and mental processes are shaped by the forces of evolution. This perspective is based on Charles Darwin's theory of evolution by *natural selection.* Darwin observed great variability in the characteristics of humans and other organisms. He believed these traits were shaped by **natural selection,** the process through which inherited traits in a given population either increase in frequency because they are adaptive, or decrease in frequency because they are maladaptive. Humans have many adaptive traits and behaviors that appear to have evolved through natural selection. David Buss, currently a professor of psychology at the University of Texas at Austin, is one of the founders of evolutionary psychology. He and others have used the evolutionary perspective to explain a variety of personality traits, intelligence, and behaviors like risk-taking (Buss & Penke, 2015; Schultz & Schultz, 2016).

BIOLOGICAL The **biological perspective** uses knowledge about underlying physiology to explain behavior and mental processes. Psychologists who take this approach explore how biological factors, such as hormones, genes, and brain activity, influence behavior and cognition. Researchers study a diverse array of biological factors in relation to twins—everything from the genetic basis of physical fitness to the influence of hormones on the structure of children's brains (Brouwer et al., 2015; Schutte, Nederend, Hudziak, de Geus, & Bartels, 2016). Chapter 2 provides a foundation for understanding this perspective as well as the field of *neuroscience,* which refers to the study of the brain and nervous system.

SOCIOCULTURAL The **sociocultural perspective** emphasizes the importance of social and cultural factors. Russian psychologist Lev Vygotsky (1896–1934) proposed that we should examine how these forces impact the cognitive development of children (Chapter 8), asserting that parents, teachers, and peers play a critical role in how a child gains knowledge and skills (Hagan, 2016).

May the Biggest Beak Win
In a population of finches, some have little beaks that can only crack open small, soft seeds; others have big beaks that can open big seeds; and still others fall somewhere in between. During times of food scarcity (such as a drought), the big-beaked birds are more likely to survive and reproduce because they have a greater variety of seeds to choose from. Looking at the finch population during this period, you will see more birds being born with bigger beaks. It's natural selection right before your eyes (Grant, 1991). David Hosking/Science Source.

humanistic psychology An approach suggesting that human nature is by and large positive, and the human direction is toward growth.

cognitive perspective An approach examining the mental processes that direct behavior.

evolutionary perspective An approach that uses knowledge about evolutionary forces, such as natural selection, to understand behavior.

natural selection The process through which inherited traits in a given population either increase in frequency because they are adaptive or decrease in frequency because they are maladaptive.

biological perspective An approach that uses knowledge about underlying physiology to explain behavior and mental processes.

sociocultural perspective An approach examining how social interactions and culture influence behavior and mental processes.

Culture Matters
A group of Flower Hmong women shop for fabric in Vietnam. In many Asian markets, the customer is expected to bargain with the seller. How does this compare to shopping in the United States, where prices are pre-established? When it comes to studying human thoughts and behavior, understanding cultural context is key. GRANT ROONEY PREMIUM/Alamy Stock Photo.

In the past, researchers often assumed that the findings of their studies were applicable to people of all ethnic and cultural backgrounds. Then in the 1980s, cross-cultural research began to reveal that Western research participants are not always representative of people from other cultures. Even groups within a culture can influence behavior and mental processes; thus, we need to take into account these various settings and subcultures.

BIOPSYCHOSOCIAL Psychologists use the **biopsychosocial perspective** to explain behavior; in other words, they examine the biological, psychological, and sociocultural factors influencing behavior (Beauchamp & Anderson, 2010). This perspective is used by scientists in many fields, from psychologists studying the mental health of men (McDermott, Schwartz, & Rislin, 2016) to physicians treating patients with sickle-cell disease (Crosby, Quinn, & Kalinyak, 2015).

Put Your Heads Together

A) Identify a movie or television show that is familiar to all members of your group. **B)** Pick a scene that shows a character exhibiting inappropriate or risky behavior. **C)** Try to explain the behavior using at least two of the perspectives of psychology.

COMBINING THE PERSPECTIVES You can see that the field of psychology abounds with diversity. With so many perspectives (**Table 1.1**), how do we know which one is the most useful for accomplishing psychology's goals? Human behavior is complex

TABLE 1.1 CURRENT PERSPECTIVES IN PSYCHOLOGY

Perspective	Main Idea	Questions Psychologists Ask
Psychoanalytic	Underlying conflicts influence behavior.	How do unconscious conflicts affect decisions and behavior?
Behavioral	Behavior is learned primarily through associations, reinforcers, and observation.	How does learning shape behavior?
Humanistic	Humans are naturally inclined to grow in a positive direction.	How do choice and self-determination influence behavior?
Cognitive	Behavior is driven by cognitive processes.	How do thinking, memory, and language direct behavior?
Evolutionary	Humans have evolved characteristics that help them adapt to the environment, increasing their chances of surviving and reproducing.	How does natural selection influence thoughts, emotions, and behaviors?
Biological	Behavior and mental processes arise from physiological activity.	How do biological factors, such as hormones, genes, anatomy, and brain structures, influence behavior and mental processes?
Sociocultural	Other people, as well as the broader cultural context, influence behavior and mental processes.	How do interactions with other people and cultural factors shape behaviors and attitudes?
Biopsychosocial	Behavior and mental processes are shaped by a complex interplay of biological, psychological, and sociocultural factors.	How do the interactions of biology, psychology, and culture influence thoughts, emotions, and behaviors?

Psychologists draw on a variety of theories in their research and practice. Listed here are the dominant theoretical perspectives, all of which reappear many times in this textbook. Human behaviors are often best understood when viewed through more than one lens.

and requires an integrated approach—using the findings of multiple perspectives—to explain its origins. Many psychologists pick and choose among the various approaches to explain and understand a given phenomenon. In some cases, creating a theoretical *model* helps clarify a complex set of observations. Models often enable us to form mental pictures of what we seek to understand.

Now let's shift our focus away from these abstract concepts and onto practical matters. How do psychologists go about conducting research? Like all scientists, they follow the steps of the *scientific method*.

show what you know

1. The goal of ______________ is to gather knowledge for the sake of knowledge, whereas the goal of ______________ is to change behaviors and outcomes.

2. A college dean wants to increase student retention by instituting more formal study groups. She contacts members of the psychology department, who design a program to encourage students to study together. This program falls under which of the main goals of psychology?
   a. describe
   b. explain
   c. predict
   d. change

3. William James suggested that it is important to study the purpose of thoughts, feelings, and behaviors and how they help us adapt to the environment. This focus on purpose and adaptation in psychological research is the theme of:
   a. natural selection.
   b. functionalism.
   c. structuralism.
   d. psychology.

4. We have presented eight perspectives in this section. Describe how two of them are similar. Pick two other perspectives and explain how they differ.

✓ CHECK YOUR ANSWERS IN APPENDIX C.

How Do Psychologists Do Research?

The Scientific Method

LO 5 Describe how psychologists use the scientific method.

The **scientific method** is the process scientists use to conduct research (see **INFOGRAPHIC 1.1** on the next page). The goal of the scientific method is to provide empirical evidence, or data from systematic observations or experiments. This evidence is often used to support or refute a **hypothesis** (hi-POTH-uh-sis), which is a statement used to test a prediction about the outcome of a study. An **experiment** is a controlled procedure involving scientific observations and/or manipulations by the researcher to influence participants' thinking, emotions, or behaviors. In the scientific method, an observation must be objective, or outside the influence of personal opinions and expectations. Humans are prone to errors in thinking, but the scientific method helps to minimize their impact. Now let's examine the five basic steps of the scientific method.

STEP 1: DEVELOP A QUESTION The scientific method typically begins when a researcher observes something interesting in the environment and comes up with a research question. For example, twin researcher Dr. Nancy L. Segal got the idea for her first twin study at a child's birthday party. She noticed a pair of fraternal twins working on a puzzle together, fighting over it like mad, and wondered, would identical twins cooperate better than fraternal twins? Her curiosity also stemmed from years of studying behavioral genetics and evolutionary theory—the work of scientists who had come before her. Reading books and articles written by scientists is an excellent way to generate ideas for new studies. The infographic **How to Read a Scientific Article** (on the inside front cover) explains how to find and read a journal article—skills that will help you in psychology and many other classes. It also shows you how to cite a journal article using the APA style established by the American Psychological Association (APA, 2010b).

biopsychosocial perspective Explains behavior through the interaction of biological, psychological, and sociocultural factors.

scientific method The process scientists use to conduct research, which includes a continuing cycle of exploration, critical thinking, and systematic observation.

hypothesis A statement that can be used to test a prediction.

experiment A controlled procedure that involves careful examination through the use of scientific observation and/or manipulation of variables (measurable characteristics).

The Scientific Method

Psychologists use the scientific method to conduct research. The scientific method allows researchers to collect empirical (objective) evidence by following a sequence of carefully executed steps. In this infographic, you can trace the steps of an actual research project performed by psychologists who were interested in the effect of interruptions on reading comprehension (Foroughi, Werner, Barragán, & Boehm-Davis, 2015). Notice that the process is cyclical in nature. Answering one research question often leads researchers to develop additional questions, and the process begins again.

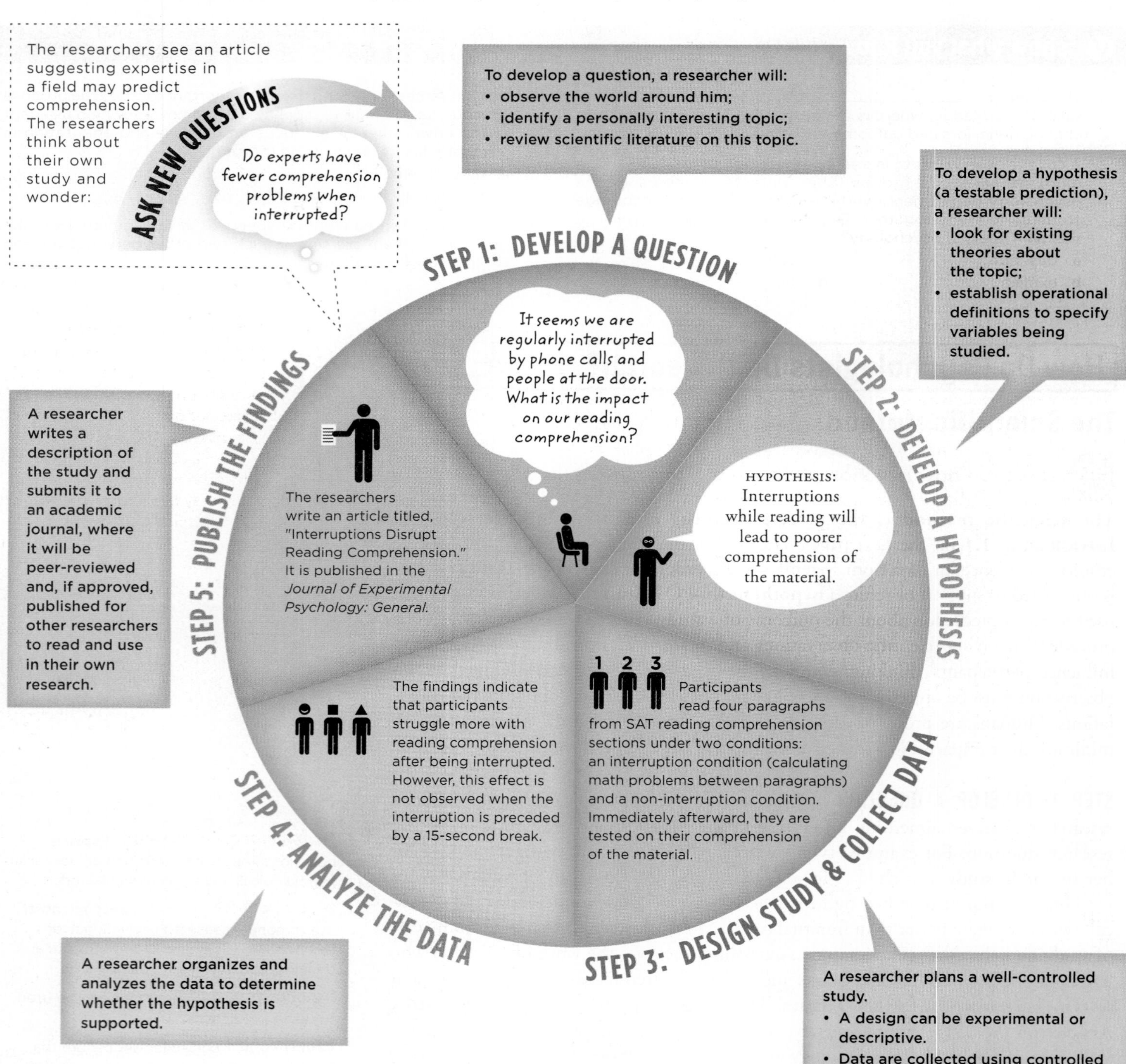

The researchers see an article suggesting expertise in a field may predict comprehension. The researchers think about their own study and wonder:
ASK NEW QUESTIONS
Do experts have fewer comprehension problems when interrupted?
To develop a question, a researcher will:
• observe the world around him;
• identify a personally interesting topic;
• review scientific literature on this topic.
To develop a hypothesis (a testable prediction), a researcher will:
• look for existing theories about the topic;
• establish operational definitions to specify variables being studied.
STEP 1: DEVELOP A QUESTION
It seems we are regularly interrupted by phone calls and people at the door. What is the impact on our reading comprehension?
STEP 2: DEVELOP A HYPOTHESIS
HYPOTHESIS: Interruptions while reading will lead to poorer comprehension of the material.
STEP 5: PUBLISH THE FINDINGS
A researcher writes a description of the study and submits it to an academic journal, where it will be peer-reviewed and, if approved, published for other researchers to read and use in their own research.
The researchers write an article titled, "Interruptions Disrupt Reading Comprehension." It is published in the *Journal of Experimental Psychology: General.*
1 2 3
Participants read four paragraphs from SAT reading comprehension sections under two conditions: an interruption condition (calculating math problems between paragraphs) and a non-interruption condition. Immediately afterward, they are tested on their comprehension of the material.
The findings indicate that participants struggle more with reading comprehension after being interrupted. However, this effect is not observed when the interruption is preceded by a 15-second break.
STEP 4: ANALYZE THE DATA
STEP 3: DESIGN STUDY & COLLECT DATA
A researcher organizes and analyzes the data to determine whether the hypothesis is supported.
A researcher plans a well-controlled study.
• A design can be experimental or descriptive.
• Data are collected using controlled measurement techniques.

Put Your Heads Together

In your group, **A)** brainstorm areas of research that might involve twins. **B)** Connect to an online database through your college or public library. **C)** Search for journal articles, refining your search with appropriate key terms. **D)** Using APA style, create a reference list including at least two of the articles your team found.

STEP 2: DEVELOP A HYPOTHESIS Once a research question has been developed, the next step is to formulate a hypothesis, the statement used to test predictions about a study's outcome. The data collected by the experimenter will either support or refute the hypothesis. Dr. Segal's hypothesis was essentially the following: *When given a joint task, identical twins will cooperate more and compete less than fraternal twins.* Hypotheses can be difficult to generate for studies on new and unexplored topics, because researchers may not have fully developed expectations for the outcome; in these situations, a general prediction may take the place of a formal hypothesis. Researchers cannot just guess when they develop their hypotheses. They must carefully review research and consider relevant psychological perspectives. What perspective do you think influenced Dr. Segal's hypothesis?

While developing research questions and hypotheses, researchers should always be on the lookout for information that could offer explanations for the phenomenon they are studying. Dr. Segal based her hypothesis on behavioral genetics and evolutionary theory. **Theories** synthesize observations in order to explain phenomena, and they can be used to make predictions that can then be tested through research. Many people believe scientific theories are nothing more than unverified guesses or hunches, but they are mistaken (Stanovich, 2013). A theory is a well-established body of principles that should rest on a sturdy foundation of scientific evidence. Evolution is a prime example of a theory that has been mistaken for an ongoing scientific controversy. Thanks to inaccurate portrayals in the media, frequently involving opinions by nonscientists, many people believe evolution is an active area of "debate." In reality, evolution is a theory supported by the overwhelming majority of scientists, including psychologists.

So Much Data
Neuroscientist Narayanan "Bobby" Kasthuri of Argonne National Laboratory is trying to create a complete 3D map of the human brain, one that shows all 100 billion neurons—and all 100 trillion (or more) of the connections between them! If Kasthuri and his colleagues manage to collect all the data needed to generate this map, they may be dealing with the biggest data set scientists have ever confronted (Lerner, 2016, March 16; Moran, 2015, February 23). Argonne National Laboratory.

STEP 3: DESIGN STUDY AND COLLECT DATA Once a hypothesis has been developed, the researcher designs an experiment to test it and then collects the data. Dr. Segal's study involved videotaping sets of identical and fraternal twin children working together on a puzzle. Once the instructions were given ("Complete the puzzle together"), the pairs of twin children were free to solve the puzzle as they wished (Segal, 1984, p. 94). Later, looking at the videos, Dr. Segal and her colleagues rated the twins using a variety of "indices of cooperative behavior." For example, the researchers observed if the twins were equally involved, how often they handed each other puzzle pieces, whether they physically leaned on one another, pushed, or hit. They even tallied up the number of facial expressions each twin displayed (for example, sadness, surprise, and pride).

Researchers must establish **operational definitions** that specify the precise manner in which the characteristics of interest are defined and measured. A good operational definition helps others understand how to perform an observation or take a measurement. In the example above, Dr. Segal operationally defined cooperative behavior based on how often twins worked together, accepted each other's help, or smiled at each other.

theory Synthesizes observations in order to explain phenomena and guide predictions to be tested through research.

operational definition The precise manner in which a variable of interest is defined and measured.

Variable	Record Number	Columns	Format
FAMILYID	1	3–7	Numeric
FROMWHO	1	9–12	Numeric
WHICHATT	1	14–17	Numeric
INT_T_	1	19–24	Numeric
INT_S_	1	26–31	Numeric
CON_T_	1	33–38	Numeric
CON_S_	1	40–46	Numeric
PERS	1	48–52	Numeric
GLOB	1	54–58	Numeric
STA_C_	1	60–64	Numeric
STA_O_	1	66–70	Numeric
BARR	1	72–76	Numeric
BREW	2	1–5	Numeric

FIGURE 1.1
Raw Data
The information in this figure comes from a data file. Until the researcher analyzes the data, these numbers will have little meaning.

Gathering data must be done in a very controlled fashion to ensure there are no errors, which could arise from recording problems or from unknown environmental factors. Suppose a researcher is studying how identical twins react to frustrating situations. He could collect information by talking with them for several hours, but his impressions may differ from those of another researcher doing the same thing. A more objective approach would be to administer a personality test with a standard set of questions (true/false, multiple choice, circle the number) and an automated scoring system. The results of such a test do not depend on the researchers' biases or expectations, and will be the same no matter who administers it.

STEP 4: ANALYZE THE DATA Now that the data are collected, they need to be analyzed, or organized in a meaningful way. As **Figure 1.1** demonstrates, "raw" data are not very useful. In order to make sense of all these numbers, one must use statistical methods. *Descriptive statistics* are used to organize and present data, often through tables, graphs, and charts. *Inferential statistics*, on the other hand, go beyond simply describing the data set, allowing researchers to make inferences and determine the probability of events occurring in the future (for a more in-depth look at statistics, see Appendix A).

Following the data analysis, the researcher must ask several questions: Did the results support the hypothesis? Were the predictions met? In Dr. Segal's case, the results did support her hypothesis: "The identical twins were more cooperative on almost every index that I used," she says. "My conclusion was that yes, identical genes do contribute to the greater cooperation observed between partners." Even if results support a hypothesis, the researcher will reevaluate her hypotheses in light of her findings. For example, she might ask herself if the results are consistent with previous studies, or whether they add support to a particular theory.

STEP 5: PUBLISH THE FINDINGS Once the data have been analyzed and the hypothesis tested, it's time to share findings with other researchers who might be able to build on the work. This typically involves writing a scientific article and submitting it to a scholarly, peer-reviewed journal. Journal editors send these submitted manuscripts to subject-matter experts, or peer reviewers, who carefully read them and make recommendations for publishing, revising, or rejecting the articles altogether.

The peer-review process is notoriously meticulous, and it helps provide us with more certainty that research findings can be trusted. When looking for research to support your presentations or papers, try to use a search engine that allows you to filter out published research that has not been peer-reviewed. Although the Internet is an amazing tool for gathering information, a search engine like Google Scholar casts a wide net, and some of the articles it lists are of questionable **origin and quality**.

CONNECTIONS
In **Chapter 0,** we discussed the importance of considering the source and quality of information before accepting it as valid. This is an important component of critical thinking. *Connections* like this are scattered throughout the textbook, helping you see the relationships between topics discussed in the current chapter and those presented in earlier chapters.

Unfortunately, the peer-review method is not foolproof. There have been cases of fabricated data slipping past the scrutiny of peer reviewers. About once a day an article is retracted, the result of plagiarism, data meddling, and other forms of inappropriate behavior, and retractions occur more often in top journals than in lower-profile ones (Marcus & Oransky, 2015, May 22). Such misconduct can have serious consequences for the general public. Case in point: the confusion over the safety of routine childhood vaccines. In the late 1990s, researchers published a study suggesting that vaccination against infectious diseases caused autism (Wakefield et al., 1998). The findings sparked panic among parents, some of whom shunned the shots, putting their children at risk for life-threatening infections such as measles. The study turned out to be fraudulent and the reported findings were deceptive, but it took 12 years for journal editors to retract the article (Editors of *The Lancet,* 2010). One reason for this long delay was that researchers had to investigate all the accusations of wrongdoing and data fabrication (Godlee, Smith, & Marcovitch, 2011). The investigation included interviews with the parents of the children discussed in the study, which ultimately led to the conclusion that the information in the published account was inaccurate (Deer, 2011).

Misguided Marchers?
People gather in front of the Capitol building to protest the use of mercury-containing vaccines, apparently because they believe these vaccines cause autism or other adverse outcomes. Childhood vaccinations do carry a risk of mild side effects and serious (but very unusual) allergic reactions, but studies have repeatedly shown there is no link between vaccines and autism (CDC, 2017, October 6). Nevertheless, some parents cling to this misconception, which stems from a widely publicized but problematic study published in a peer-reviewed journal two decades ago. Chris Maddaloni/Newscom/CQ/Roll Call/Washington DC USA.

Since the publication of that flawed research, several high-quality studies have found no credible support for the autism-vaccine hypothesis (Honda, Shimizu, & Rutter, 2005; Jain et al., 2015; Madsen et al., 2002). Still, the publicity given to the original article continues to cast a shadow: Some parents refuse vaccines for their children, with serious consequences for the community. Measles outbreaks involving unvaccinated children have occurred in various parts of the United States in recent years, putting children at risk for death and lasting disabilities (Chen, 2014, June 26; Mele, 2017, May 5; Palmer, 2015, January 26).

Publishing an article is a crucial step in the scientific process because it allows other researchers to **replicate** an experiment, which might mean repeating it with other participants or altering some of the procedures. This repetition is necessary to ensure that the initial findings were not just a fluke or the result of a poorly designed experiment. The more a study is replicated and produces similar findings, the more confidence we can have in those findings. In the case of Wakefield's fraudulent autism study, other researchers tried to replicate the research for over 10 years, but could never establish a relationship between autism and vaccines (Godlee et al., 2011). This fact alone made the Wakefield findings highly suspect.

ASK NEW QUESTIONS Although the goal is to increase our knowledge, most studies generate more questions than they answer, and here lies the beauty of the scientific process. The results of one scientific study raise a host of new questions, and those questions lead to new hypotheses, new studies, and yet another collection of questions. New results also prompt researchers to rethink theories, as even the most established theories can be scrutinized and re-explored. You can see the cyclical nature of the scientific method illustrated in Infographic 1.1.

CRITICAL THINKING This continuing cycle of exploration uses *critical thinking* at every step. **Critical thinking** is the process of weighing various pieces of evidence, synthesizing them, and evaluating and determining the contributions of each; it is a type of thinking that is disciplined, clear, rational, and open to the consideration of new ideas. For a review of critical thinking, revisit Chapter 0 and see **INFOGRAPHIC 1.2** on the next page.

replicate To repeat an experiment, generally with a new sample and/or other changes to the procedures, the goal of which is to provide further support for the findings of the first study.

critical thinking The process of weighing various pieces of evidence, synthesizing them, and evaluating and determining the contributions of each; disciplined thinking that is clear, rational, open-minded, and informed by evidence.

INFOGRAPHIC 1.2

Critical Thinking

What is critical thinking and why is it important? Being a critical thinker means carefully evaluating pieces of evidence, synthesizing them, and determining how they fit into the "big picture." Critical thinkers maintain a healthy dose of skepticism, but they are also able to adjust their thinking if presented with contradictory evidence. Consider the issue of global warming: Do you think it's real, and are human beings causing it?

97% **of world's leading climate scientists** believe that greenhouse gas emissions generated by human activities, such as burning gasoline and coal, are driving the warming trend (Benestad et al., 2016).

Government officials consider human-caused climate change an

"urgent and growing threat to our national security,"

and warn of higher temperatures, rising sea levels, floods, droughts, and other natural disasters—events that could threaten agricultural productivity, set the stage for new disease outbreaks, and trigger conflicts (U.S. Department of Defense, 2015, July 23, p. 3).

Yet many people are not too worried about global warming, perhaps because they don't grasp the severity of the problem:

(American Psychological Association, 2015c)

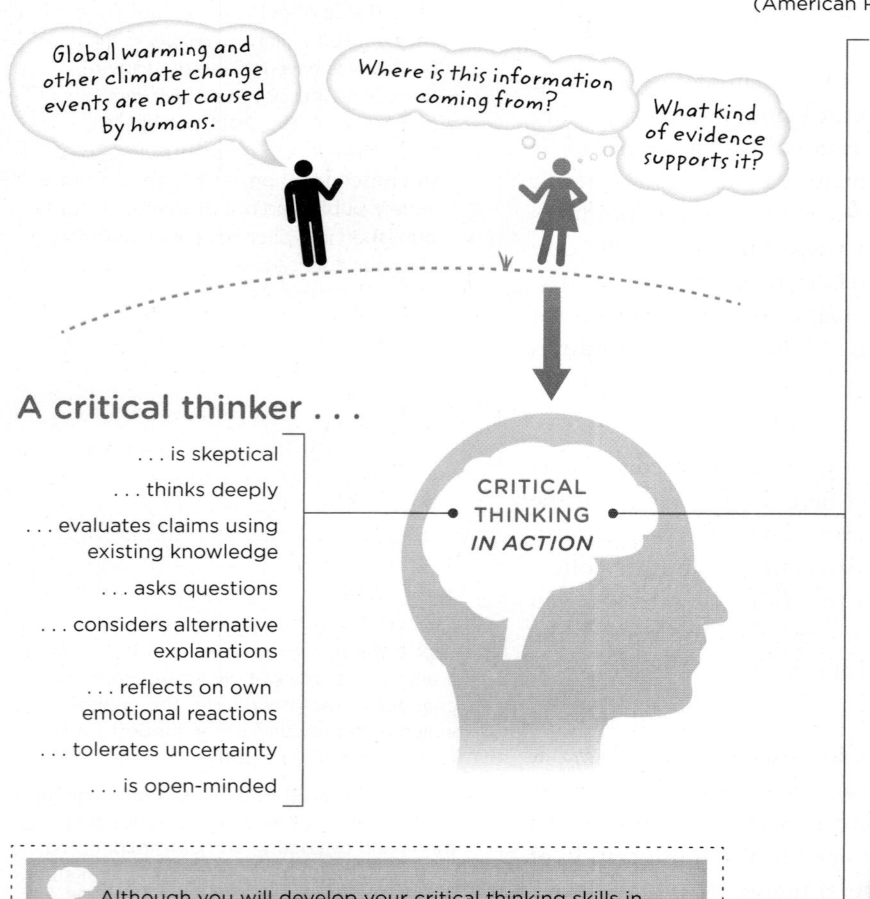

Global warming and other climate change events are not caused by humans.
Where is this information coming from?
What kind of evidence supports it?
CRITICAL THINKING IN ACTION

A critical thinker . . .

. . . is skeptical

. . . thinks deeply

. . . evaluates claims using existing knowledge

. . . asks questions

. . . considers alternative explanations

. . . reflects on own emotional reactions

. . . tolerates uncertainty

. . . is open-minded

Although you will develop your critical thinking skills in psychology class, they can be used in other contexts, from resolving everyday dilemmas, such as, "Why did I get such a mediocre grade after studying so hard?" to understanding global crises such as climate change.

GO TO THE SOURCE: ASK CRITICAL QUESTIONS

Who wrote the article?
- What is the professional background of the author(s)?

Where was it published?
- Is it peer-reviewed, open-source, or popular press?

What are the study's findings?
- Do the findings support the hypothesis?
- Are there limitations cited?
- What other variables might have influenced the outcome?

What were the methods used to conduct the study?
- How big was the sample?
- How did researchers collect data?

Has the study been replicated?
- Have other studies reported the same results?
- Have other studies tried different samples?

Credits: Thermometer, dencg/Shutterstock; Globe, adike/Shutterstock.

Research Basics

ENTER THE PSYCHOLOGIST Soon after making contact, Sam and Anaïs began contemplating the idea of creating a movie to capture their extraordinary story and share it with others. They knew the constant presence of a film crew would be a complete invasion of privacy, but it seemed worth the sacrifice. Their documentary film would be titled *Twinsters* ("twin" + "sisters"). Sam would be a producer, and the other crewmembers would be her trusted friends and colleagues from the film industry. The team immediately began preparing for what would become the film's climax: the first tangible, human-to-human meeting of Sam and Anaïs. It would take place in London, on May 14, two days before Anaïs' spring fashion show.

To raise money for the movie, Sam and her friends posted a proposal on the funding platform Kickstarter. Through Kickstarter, they caught the attention of twin expert Dr. Nancy L. Segal (introduced on p. 11). When Dr. Segal learned about Sam and Anaïs, she immediately wondered if they had taken a DNA test to prove they were identical twins. "When I found out that they had not done that, I was very worried," Dr. Segal explains. Even though Sam and Anaïs had the same birthdates and shared many physical characteristics and behaviors, there was still the remote possibility that they were unrelated look-alikes. Dr. Segal had seen similar cases end in profound disappointment. As she puts it, "You need the biological proof."

Dr. Segal reached out to Sam and Anaïs, and they began discussing the idea of participating in research, a proposition that was both exciting and unsettling. "It was kind of stepping into the unknown," Sam says. "What are you going to find out about us that we don't want to know?!" Sam and Anaïs took the DNA tests, which affirmed what they already knew in their hearts . . . they were indeed identical twins! They also underwent a variety of tests organized by Dr. Segal and her colleagues at California State University, Fullerton. These tests focused on physical characteristics like height, weight, and hand preference, and psychological factors such as job satisfaction, self-esteem, personality traits, and cognitive abilities—all *variables* commonly studied by psychologists.

You Asked, Sam and Anaïs Answer

http://qrs.ly/2r77rvp

Do you have similar boyfriends?

Proof Is in the DNA
Sam (left) and Anaïs on Skype, collecting DNA samples with cheek swabs. DNA (deoxyribonucleic acid) is the genetic material we inherit from our parents, and identical twins have almost the same DNA sequences ("almost" because, although identical twins have duplicate DNA at conception, small genetic changes can occur throughout life). After collecting the samples, Sam and Anaïs sent them to a laboratory, and the results of the analysis confirmed that they are indeed identical twins! Twinsters (2015). Small Package Films.

VARIABLES Measurable characteristics that vary, or change, over time or across individuals are called **variables.** In chemistry, a variable might be temperature, mass, or volume. In psychological experiments, a variable could be any human or animal characteristic—reaction times, problem-solving approaches, aggressive behaviors—you name it. Once the variables for a study are chosen, researchers must create operational definitions with precise descriptions and manners of measurement.

The study of Sam and Anaïs revealed "striking similarities" across a variety of variables, including measures of job satisfaction, and certain mental abilities and personality traits. It also unearthed fascinating differences; for example, Anaïs scored higher on most of the tests measuring visual-spatial skills—not a surprise to Dr. Segal and her colleague Franchesca Cortez, who say this finding is "consistent with the idea that fashion designers benefit from good visual skills" (Segal & Cortez, 2014, p. 103). Meanwhile, Sam did better on some tests measuring memory, which could be a result of her experience memorizing lines for acting roles and waiting on tables (Segal & Cortez, 2014). "It really would stress me out," says Sam, recalling her days running between tables. "I would have nightmares . . . I would wake up and be like, 'I didn't bring his ketchup!'"

variables Measurable characteristics that can vary over time or across people.

Power of Nurture
(left to right) Sam's brother Andrew, Sam, Sam's brother Matt, and Anaïs. Personality assessments suggest that Sam is more extroverted than her twin sister (Segal & Cortez, 2014). Is this because Sam grew up with two older brothers, while Anaïs was an only child?
Small Package Films.

LO 6 Distinguish between a random sample and a representative sample.

POPULATION AND SAMPLE How do researchers decide who should participate in their studies? It depends on the **population,** or overall group, the researcher wants to examine. If the population is large (all college students in the United States, for example), then the researcher selects a subset of that population called a **sample.**

There are many methods for choosing a sample. One way is to pick a **random sample,** that is, theoretically any member of the designated population has an equal chance of being selected to participate in the study. A researcher forming a random sample of high school seniors might try to gain access to SAT or ACT databases and then randomly select students from lists compiled by those test companies. Similarly, if your doctor orders a blood test, the lab doesn't remove all your blood to run these tests; it takes a small sample.

Think about the problems that may occur if a sample is not random. Suppose a researcher is trying to assess attitudes about undocumented workers living in the United States, but the only place she recruits participants is Los Angeles, California, which (along with New York and Houston) has the biggest population of undocumented immigrants (Passel & Cohen, 2017, February 9). How might this bias her findings? Los Angeles residents do not constitute a **representative sample,** or group of people with characteristics similar to those of the population of interest (in this case, the entire U.S. population).

It is important for researchers to choose representative samples, because this allows them to generalize their findings, or apply information from a sample to the population at large. Let's say that 44% of the respondents in the study on attitudes toward undocumented workers believe current immigration laws are acceptable. If the sample is similar enough to the overall U.S. population, then the researcher may be able to infer that this finding from the sample is representative: "Approximately 44% of people in the United States believe that current immigration laws are acceptable."

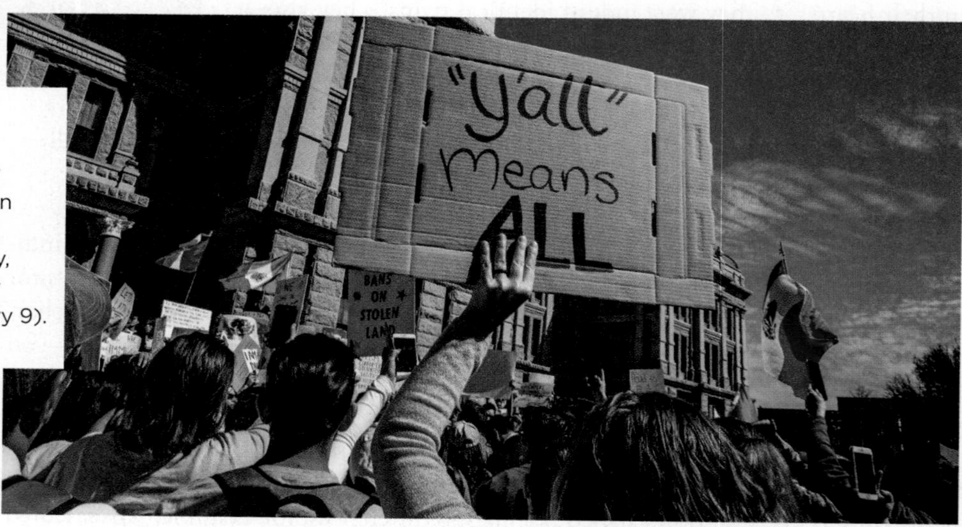

Representative Sample?
A group in Austin, Texas, protests the Trump administration's immigration policies in February 2017. If a researcher aims to understand American attitudes about Trump's immigration stance, she would be foolish to limit her study to a single city, because immigrant populations vary significantly across the country (Passel & Cohen, 2017, February 9).
Drew Anthony Smith/Getty Images.

population All members of an identified group about which a researcher is interested.

sample A subset of a population chosen for inclusion in an experiment.

random sample A subset of the population chosen through a procedure that ensures all members of the population have an equal chance of being selected to participate in the study.

representative sample A subgroup of a population selected so that its members have characteristics similar to those of the population of interest.

Put Your Heads Together

In your group, answer the following questions: **A)** What is the difference between a representative sample and a random sample? **B)** Why is it so important to have a representative sample? **C)** What can happen if a sample is not representative? **D)** If a researcher is planning to study attitudes about undocumented workers, what characteristics should be considered when picking a sample that is representative of the larger population?

The topics we have touched on thus far—variables, operational definitions, and samples—apply to psychology research in general. You will see how these concepts are relevant to studies presented in the upcoming sections when we explore the three major categories of research design: descriptive, correlational, and experimental.

show what you know

1. A research group is interested in studying college students' attitudes about the legalization of marijuana. The group randomly selects students from across the nation, trying to pick a ______________ that closely reflects the characteristics of American college students.
   a. variable
   b. hypothesis
   c. representative sample
   d. representative population
2. Researchers must establish ______________ that specify the precise manner in which the characteristics of interest are defined and measured.
3. Why might it be problematic to make inferences from small samples to large populations?

✓ CHECK YOUR ANSWERS IN APPENDIX C.

Descriptive and Correlational Methods

LO 7 Recognize the forms of descriptive research.

Suppose a researcher wants to compare the types of body language identical twins like Sam and Anaïs exhibit in social situations. This is a great topic for **descriptive research,** a type of investigation psychologists use to explore a phenomenon. Descriptive research is primarily concerned with describing, and is useful for studying new or unexplored topics when researchers might not have specific expectations about outcomes. This method provides clues about the causes of behaviors, but it *cannot* reveal cause-and-effect relationships, a point we will revisit later in the chapter. Now let's explore the major forms of descriptive research.

Please Wash Your Hands
Studies suggest that women are more conscientious than men about washing their hands in restrooms (Humphreys, Fitzpatick, & Harvey, 2015). In one naturalistic observation study, researchers sat quietly inside bathroom stalls on a university campus, using stopwatches to measure how long people spent using the facilities (as determined by flushing sounds of toilets and urinals) and washing their hands. They found that most men and women washed their hands after using the toilet, but almost half of the men failed to clean their hands after using urinals (Berry, Mitteer, & Fournier, 2015). Do you think more men would have washed their hands if they knew they were being observed? Jutta Klee/Getty Images.

Naturalistic Observation

Naturalistic observation refers to the systematic observation of participants in their natural environments. And when we say "natural environments," we don't necessarily mean the "wild." It could be an office, a preschool, or even a dorm room or family home. In one naturalistic study, researchers videotaped interactions between 30 couples in their homes. The goal of the study was to determine which partner (husband or wife) received more social support, how that support was initiated (through requests or offers), and what type of support was provided (practical or emotional). The researchers found that husbands were more likely to provide support to their wives, and that the support was usually practical as opposed to emotional (helping get the kids ready for school, as opposed to offering words of comfort, for example). They also found that wives were more inclined to ask for help, perhaps because they were "taxed with an objectively greater share of the domestic workload" and therefore found themselves in a "position of enlisting assistance" (Wang & Repetti, 2016, p. 8).

NATURALLY, IT'S A CHALLENGE As with any type of research, naturalistic observation centers around variables, and those variables must be pinned down with operational definitions. Let's say a researcher is interested in studying aggressiveness among toddlers: an intriguing topic given that research has demonstrated aggression can present itself in infancy (Hay, 2017). At the beginning of the study, the researcher would need to operationally define aggression, including detailed descriptions of specific behaviors that illustrate it. Then she might create a checklist

descriptive research Research methods that describe and explore behaviors, but with findings that cannot definitively state cause-and-effect relationships.

naturalistic observation A type of descriptive research that studies participants in their natural environment through systematic observation.

of aggressive behaviors like screeching and pushing, and a coding system to help keep track of them.

Naturalistic observation allows psychologists to observe participants going about their business in their normal environments, without the disruptions of artificial laboratory settings. Perhaps the most important requirement of naturalistic observation is that researchers must not disturb the participants or their environment. That way, participants won't change their normal behaviors, particularly those that the researchers wish to observe. Some problems arise with this arrangement, however. Natural environments are cluttered with a variety of unwanted variables, and removing them can alter the natural state of affairs the researchers are striving to maintain. And because the variables in natural environments are so hard to control, researchers may have trouble replicating findings. Suppose the researcher opted to study the behavior of toddlers playing with Legos at day care. In this natural setting, she would not be able to control who played and when; whoever showed up at the Lego table would become a participant in her study.

OBSERVER BIAS How can we be sure observers will do a good job recording behaviors? A researcher who has never been around toddlers might pay attention to very different aspects of play behaviors than a researcher who has six children of his own. One way to avoid such problems is to include multiple observers and then determine how similarly they record the behaviors. If the observers don't execute this task in the same way, there may be **observer bias,** which refers to errors introduced as a result of an observer's value system, expectations, attitudes, and so forth.

Case Study

Another type of descriptive research method is the **case study,** a detailed examination of an individual or small group, often using multiple avenues to gather information. The process might include in-depth interviews with the person being studied and her friends, family, and coworkers, and questionnaires about medical history, career, and mental health. The goal of a case study is to provide a wealth of information from a variety of resources. Case studies are invaluable for studying rare events, like the reunion of identical twins born in South Korea and reared on different continents. They can provide valuable information we can't get anywhere else. This research method also helps guide the design of studies on relatively underexplored topics (Stanovich, 2013), such as the health and behavior of an astronaut on a space mission compared to his identical twin back on Earth (Gushanas, 2015, April 14). Unlike naturalistic observation, where the researcher assumes the role of detached spectator, the case study may require complete immersion in the participant's environment. How do you think this might impact the researcher's observations and the conclusions of the study?

No matter how colorful or thought-provoking a case study may be, it cannot be used to support or refute a hypothesis (Stanovich, 2013). Hypothesis testing involves drawing comparisons between different conditions (Stanovich, 2013), and because the subject of a case study represents a sample of one, comparisons are impossible. Like other types of descriptive research, this method is useful for furthering the development of theories, but it cannot identify the causes of behaviors and events.

The "Jim Twins"
One of the most fascinating case studies in the history of twin research is that of the "Jim Twins." Identical twins Jim Springer and Jim Lewis were separated shortly after birth and reunited at age 39. When the Jims finally met, they discovered some jaw-dropping similarities: Both were named "James" by their adoptive parents and gravitated toward math and carpentry as kids. Each man had a dog named "Toy," a first wife named "Linda," and a second wife named "Betty." They even smoked the same cigarettes (Salems), drove the same type of blue Chevy, and traveled to the same vacation spot in Florida (Leo, 1987, January 12; Rawson, 1979, May 7; Segal, 2012). Photo Courtesy: Dr. Nancy L. Segal.

observer bias Errors in the recording of observations, the result of a researcher's value system, expectations, or attitudes.

case study A type of descriptive research that closely examines an individual or small group.

Case studies are isolated examples, so be wary of using them to make generalizations. Suppose you are trying to examine how parent–child interactions at home might relate to preschoolers' transitions during morning drop-off. What would happen if you limited your research to a case study of a family with two working parents and 10 children? The dynamics of this family may not be representative of those in other families. We should not make sweeping generalizations based on our observations of a single person or group.

Survey Method

One of the fastest ways to collect descriptive data is the **survey method,** which relies on questionnaires or interviews. A survey is basically a series of questions that can be administered on paper, in face-to-face interviews, or via smartphone, tablet, and other digital devices. Your college might send out surveys to gauge student attitudes about new online classes and e-books (using questions such as, "How often do you encounter technical difficulties with your online courses?" or "How would you rate your overall satisfaction with an assigned e-book?"). The benefit of the survey method is that you can gather data from numerous people in a short period of time. Surveys can be used alone or in conjunction with other research methods.

WORDING AND HONESTY Like any research design, the survey method has its limitations. The wording of survey questions can lead to biases in responses (see **Figure 1.2** below for an example). A question with a positive or negative spin may sway a participant's response one way or the other: Do you prefer a half-full glass of soda or a half-empty glass of soda?

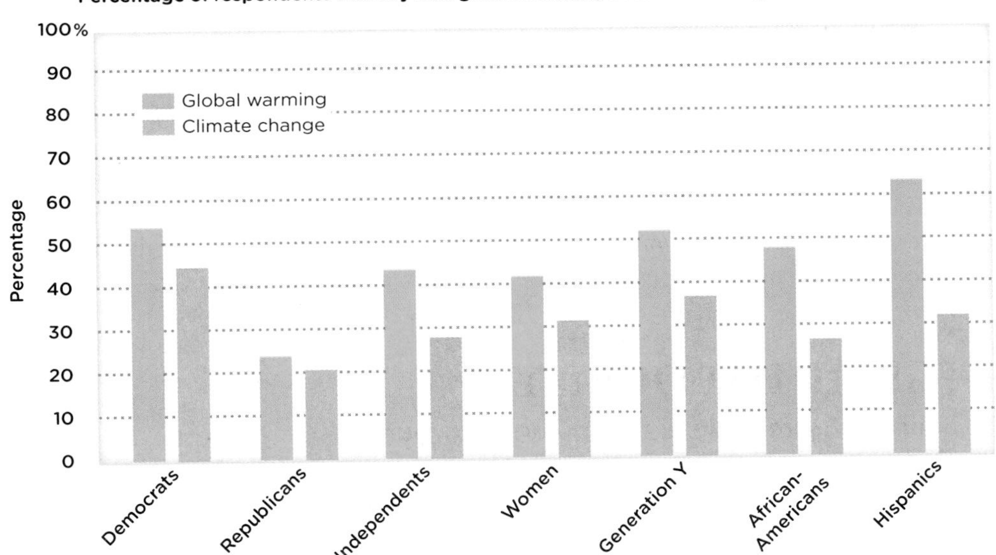

FIGURE 1.2

It Depends How You Ask

What do *global warming* and *climate change* mean to you? To compare the impact of these two phrases, researchers surveyed a representative sample of U.S. adults. About half of the participants answered a series of questions about *global warming*, while the other half answered the exact same questions about *climate change*. In the example above, we can see how differently people reacted to these variations in wording: "How much do you think *global warming* will harm your family?" versus "How much do you think *climate change* will harm your family?" (Leiserowitz et al., 2014, p. 18). Apparently, *global warming* sets off more alarm bells than *climate change,* and this influences the way people answer questions about this issue.

survey method A type of descriptive research that uses questionnaires or interviews to gather data.

More importantly, survey participants are not always forthright in their responses, particularly when they have to admit to things they are uncomfortable discussing face-to-face. In short, people lie. In one study, male and female college students were asked questions about cheating in relationships. When it appeared their responses were being analyzed by a lie detector, men and women were equally likely to provide honest answers about their cheating behaviors. But when they believed their self-reports were anonymous, the men were more likely to be honest than the women (Fisher & Brunell, 2014). People often exhibit a desire not to reveal attitudes or behaviors that are embarrassing or deal with sensitive topics, and it is not always easy to determine if this bias toward *social desirability* has influenced self-reports (Moshagen, Hilbig, Erdfelder, & Moritz, 2014; Tourangeau & Yan, 2007). This may lead to an inaccurate representation of participants' attitudes and beliefs. Researchers in the field recommend collecting information anonymously if possible, noting the irony that infidelity "is rooted in deceit and thus inimical [contrary] to the truth that science seeks to illuminate" (Fincham & May, 2017, p. 73).

SKIMMING THE SURFACE Another disadvantage of the survey method is that it tends to skim the surface of people's beliefs or attitudes, failing to uncover *why* people respond the way they do. Ask 1,000 people if they *intend* to exercise regularly, and you might get a substantial number of affirmative responses. But *yes* might mean something quite different from one person to the next ("Yes, it crosses my mind, but I can never go through with it" versus "Yes, I have a specific plan, and I have been able to follow through"). To obtain more precise responses, researchers conducting surveys often ask people to respond to statements using a scale that indicates the degree to which they agree or disagree (for example, a 5-point scale ranging from *strongly agree* to *strongly disagree*), or the degree to which they have had an experience (for example, a 5-point scale ranging from *never* to *almost always*).

A SAMPLING PROBLEM Another common challenge is obtaining a representative sample. Many surveys fail to do so because their *response rates* fall short of ideal. If a researcher sends out 100 surveys to potential participants and only 20 people return them, how can we be sure that the answers of the 20 responders reflect those of the entire group? Without a representative sample, we cannot generalize the survey findings. What steps might you take to ensure a representative sample in the survey research described next?

From the SCIENTIFIC pages of AMERICAN

DIGITAL HYPOCRISY

To limit kids' screen time, try unplugging yourself.

In a world where we are constantly tweeting, texting, Googling and checking e-mail, technology addiction is a real concern for today's kids. Yet parents are often unable to unplug from their own digital devices, research suggests. A recent national survey conducted by Common Sense Media, which included nearly 1,800 parents of children aged eight to 18, found that parents spend an average of nine hours and 22 minutes every day in front of various screens—including smartphones, tablets, computers and televisions. Of those, nearly eight hours are for personal use, not work. (The survey included people from a wide range of socioeconomic classes and fields, who may or may not use computers at their job all day.)

Perhaps even more surprising is that 78 percent of parents surveyed believe they are good role models for how to use digital technology. Multimedia are designed to be engaging and habit-forming, so we do not even realize how much time we spend when we heed the siren call of our devices, says Catherine Steiner-Adair, a clinical psychologist and author of *The Big Disconnect* (HarperCollins, 2013).

This can be a double whammy for children, who not only feel that their parents are ignoring them or do not find them as engaging as the screen but who also learn to mimic their parents' behavior, Steiner-Adair notes. Studies show that greater use of technology among tweens and teens correlates with shorter attention spans, a preference for digital time over physical activity and worse performance in school. Toddlers and infants also have a harder time learning emotional and nonverbal cues because their parents constantly have what psychologists call "still face phenomenon" from concentrating on mobile devices.

The good news, however, is that if parents use screen time for shared activities with a child—watching a movie or playing an educational game together, for example—it can enhance the child's learning. According to the survey, 94 percent of parents recognize that technology can be used to support their children's education. The key is to limit and track kids' time with technology and set rules for themselves, too. Modeling healthy media habits can start with something as simple as making the family dinner table a device-free zone. **Knvul Sheikh. Reproduced with permission.** ■

Correlations: Is There a Relationship?

LO 8 Describe the correlational method and identify its limitations.

When researchers collect data on many variables, it can be useful to determine if these variables are related to each other in some way. The **correlational method** examines relationships among variables and assists researchers in making predictions. A **correlation** represents a relationship or link between variables (**INFOGRAPHIC 1.3** on the next page). For example, there is a correlation between the amount of time parents spend reading books to their children, and the number of vocabulary words the children know. The more the parents read, the more words their children learn (Pace, Luo, Hirsh-Palek, & Glinkoff, 2017). This is an example of a positive correlation. As one variable increases, so does the other. A negative correlation, on the other hand, means that as one variable goes up, the other goes down (an inverse or negative relationship). An example might be the quantity of time college students spend using their smartphones, and their performance in school. As phone usage increases, academic performance decreases (Samaha & Hawi, 2016). You have probably noticed correlations between variables in your own life. Increase the hours you devote to studying, and you will likely see your grades go up (a positive correlation). The more you go shopping, the less money you have in the bank (a negative correlation).

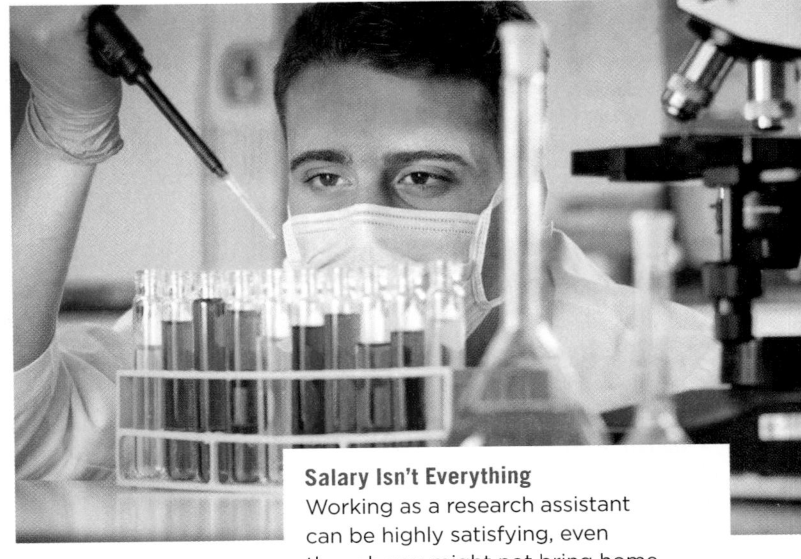

Salary Isn't Everything
Working as a research assistant can be highly satisfying, even though you might not bring home a huge paycheck (Griswold, 2013, December 27). An analysis of 92 studies found a correlation coefficient (*r*) of .15 between salary and job satisfaction (Judge, Piccolo, Podsakoff, Shaw, & Rich, 2010). Remember, the closer *r* is to 0.00, the weaker the relationship. LL28/Getty Images.

CORRELATION COEFFICIENT Some variables are tightly linked, others weakly associated, and still others not related at all. Lucky for researchers, there is one number that indicates the relationship's strength and direction (positive or negative): a statistical measure called the **correlation coefficient**, which is symbolized as *r*. Correlation coefficients range from +1.00 to −1.00, with positive numbers indicating a positive relationship between variables and negative numbers indicating an inverse (negative) relationship between variables. The closer *r* is to +1.00 or to −1.00, the stronger the relationship. The closer *r* is to 0.00, the weaker the relationship. When the correlation coefficient is very close to zero, there may be no relationship at all between the variables. For example, consider the variables of shoe size and intelligence. Are adults with bigger (or smaller) feet more intelligent? Probably not; there

synonyms

correlation coefficient Pearson's correlation coefficient

correlational method A type of descriptive research examining the relationships among variables.

correlation An association or relationship between two (or more) variables.

correlation coefficient The statistical measure (symbolized as *r*) that indicates the strength and direction of the relationship between two variables.

The Correlation Coefficient: What's in a Number?

A correlation indicates a relationship between two variables, such as the amount of time you spend studying and the grade you get on a test. This relationship is often indicated using a correlation coefficient, symbolized as r. To interpret the relationship using a correlation coefficient (r), ask yourself two questions:

(1) What is the *direction* of the relationship?

(2) What is the *strength* of the relationship?

A *scatterplot* helps us see what the relationship looks like.

And remember, a correlation between two variables does not necessarily mean that one variable caused the change in the other variable.

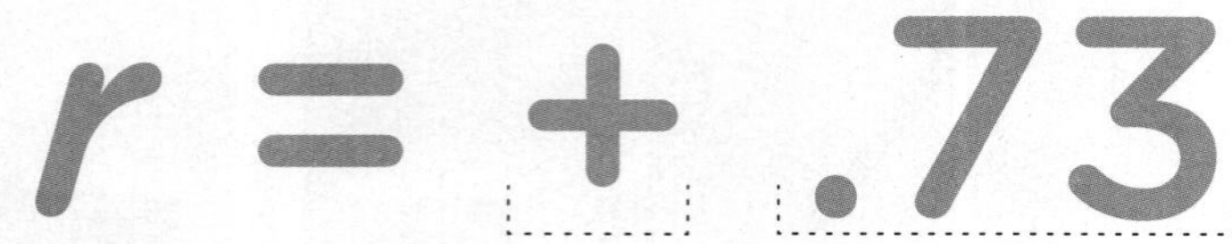

What Is the Direction of the Correlation?

- ***positive* (+) correlation** as one variable increases, the other also increases
- ***negative* (–) correlation** as one variable increases, the other decreases (an inverse relationship)

Example: +.73 is a positive number, showing a **positive correlation.** As hours spent studying increase, test grades also increase.

What Is the Strength of the Correlation?

strength ranges from +1.00 to –1.00

- a value close to +1.00 or –1.00 is a **strong** correlation
- a value close to 0.00 is a **weak** correlation

Example: +.73 is close to 1.00. This shows a **strong correlation** between hours spent studying and test grades.

BEWARE of the potential **Third Variable**

Correlation does not indicate that one variable *causes* a change in the other. A **third variable** may have influenced the results.

Example: Although time spent studying and exam grades are strongly and positively correlated, attendance is another variable. Students who attend classes regularly tend to spend more hours studying. Likewise, students who attend classes regularly know what to expect on the test and are therefore likely to get better grades.

What does the correlation **look** like?

Using a scatterplot, we can express the relationship between two variables. One variable is labeled on the horizontal axis, and the second variable is labeled on the vertical axis. Each dot represents one participant's scores on the two variables. Notice how the shape of the graph changes depending on the direction and strength of the relationship between the variables.

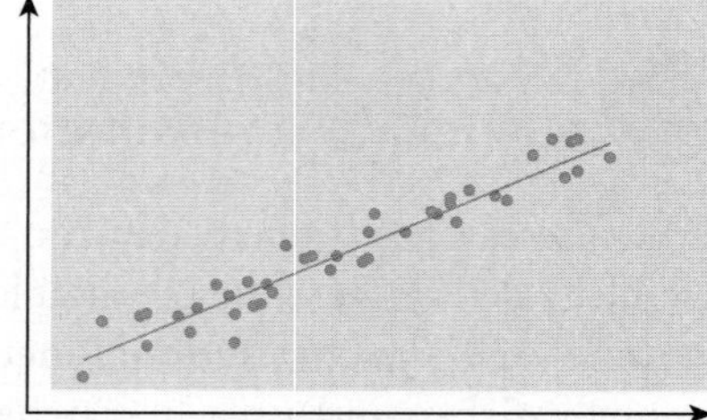

example:
+.73 (strong positive correlation)

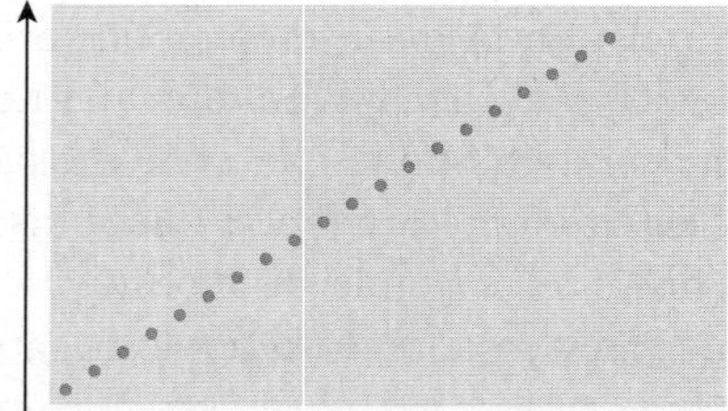

perfect positive correlation (+1.00)

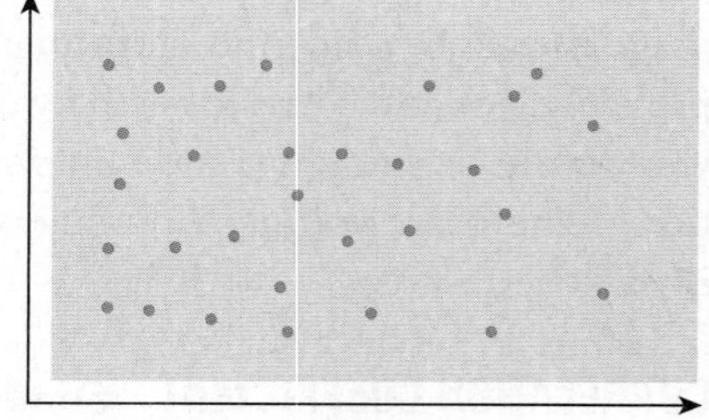

no relationship (0.00)

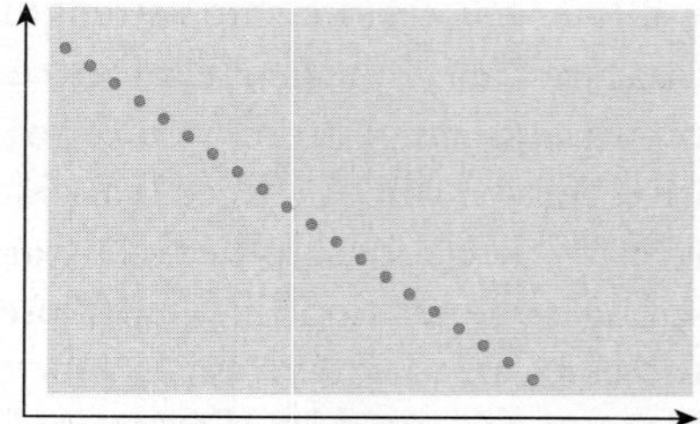

perfect negative correlation (–1.00)

would be no link between these two variables, so the correlation coefficient between them (the *r* value) is around zero. Take a look at Infographic 1.3 to see how correlation coefficients are portrayed on graphs called *scatterplots.*

THIRD VARIABLE Even if there is a very strong correlation between two variables, this does not indicate a causal link exists between them. No matter how high the *r* value is or how logical the relationship seems, it does not *prove* a cause-and-effect connection. Consider this link: As shoe size increases in children, so do reading scores. Does that mean shoe size causes reading scores to go up? Or how about the positive relationship between exposure to violence in media and aggressive behavior reported by some researchers? It's easy to jump to the conclusion that the exposure causes the aggression (Bushman et al., 2016). But it's possible that some other variable is influencing both exposure to media violence and aggressive behavior. Can you think of any additional variables that might "cause" increases or decreases in aggression? One possibility is parenting behaviors; parents who limit and monitor their children's exposure to violent media seem to have children who exhibit less aggressive behavior (Bushman et al., 2016). When parents actively discuss the portrayal of media violence with their children, aggression tends to decrease as well (Coyne, 2016). Parenting style therefore would be considered a **third variable**, some unaccounted for characteristic of the participants or their environment that explains the changes in the two other variables (parent involvement influences both exposure to violence and aggressive behaviors). When you observe strong links between variables, consider other factors that could be related to both.

synonyms
third variable third factor

Now let's consider the direction of the relationship between variables. With a positive correlation between exposure to violent media and aggressive behavior, you might have assumed that exposure leads to aggression. The more violent video games a child plays, the more aggressive he is. But could it be that aggressive children are more likely to be attracted to violent video games in the first place? If this is the case, then aggressive tendencies influence the amount of time spent using violent media, not the other way around. The direction of the relationship (*directionality*) matters. In the case of exposure to violent media and aggressive behaviors, the causal direction can go both ways (Coyne, 2016).

Although correlational and descriptive methods can't identify the causes of behaviors, both *can* provide clues to what underlies behaviors, and thus serve as valuable tools when other types of studies are unethical or impossible to conduct. (For example, researchers couldn't ethically manipulate real-world variables like exposure to violence.) Moreover, descriptive research can produce fascinating results. In some cases, these findings may guide important government decisions; just consider the following example.

ACROSS THE WORLD

THE HAPPIEST PLACES ON THE PLANET Where in the world do the happiest people reside, and what is their secret to contentment? According to the *World Happiness Report,* published by the United Nations Sustainable Development Solutions Network, Earth's happiest people live in Finland (**Figure 1.3** on the next page). The runners-up are Norway, Denmark, and Iceland, while the United States claims 18th place on the list of 156 countries. The unhappiest spots include several nations in Africa, as well as Syria, Yemen, and Haiti (Helliwell, Layard, & Sachs, 2018).

AND THE WINNER IS . . . FINLAND!

Why are some populations happier than others? One key factor is social support; people tend to be happier when they cultivate deep and meaningful relationships. Latin America provides an excellent example of this phenomenon. Many countries in

third variable An unaccounted for characteristic of participants or the environment that explains changes in the variables of interest.

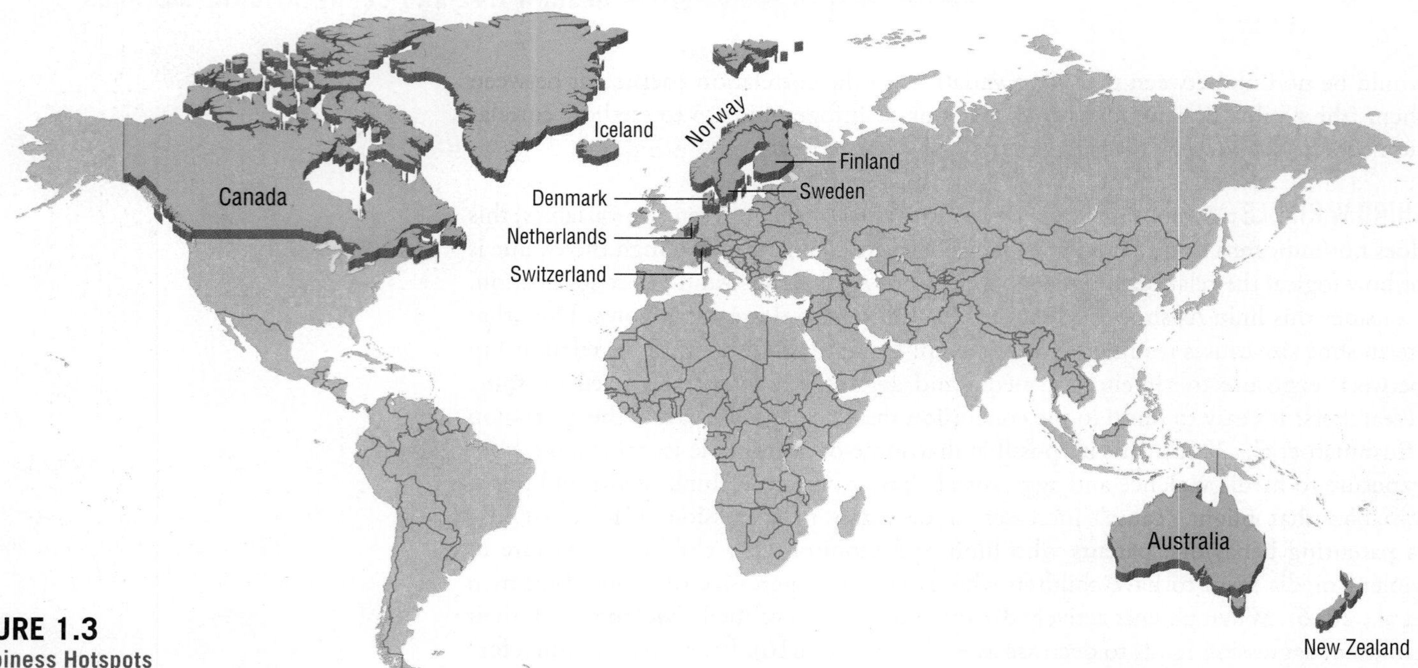

FIGURE 1.3
Happiness Hotspots
Highlighted on this map are the 10 happiest countries in the world. Five of them—Finland, Norway, Denmark, Iceland, and Sweden—are Nordic countries. Why do you think people in this Northern European region are so content? (Information from Helliwell et al., 2018.)

the region are plagued by poverty, crime, corruption, and other problems that tend to reduce "life satisfaction," yet happiness ratings are generally quite high. This is partly due to "the abundance and quality of close, warm, and genuine interpersonal relations" between family members and friends. The case of Latin America "clearly shows that there is more to life than income" (Helliwell et al., 2018, p. 140).

The *World Happiness Report* is a great example of descriptive research, but what is the point of studying this topic? Happiness is associated with *sustainable development,* or development that "meets the needs of the present without compromising the ability of future generations to meet their own needs" (Helliwell, Layard, & Sachs, 2015; United Nations, General Assembly, 1987, August 4, p. 54). Sustainable development is about making economic progress, but also protecting the environment and the social needs of citizens. When these goals are balanced, human happiness and well-being are likely to increase. Some governments are beginning to appreciate this relationship, and now use happiness data in making policy decisions (Helliwell et al., 2015).

show what you know

1. Descriptive research is primarily useful for studying:
   a. operational definitions.
   b. observer bias.
   c. new or unexplored topics.
   d. visual-spatial skills.
2. If a researcher finds a positive correlation between smartphone use and absenteeism from work, why can't she say that phone use causes absenteeism?
3. A researcher interested in studying the behaviors of parents dropping off children at preschool trained teachers to use a stopwatch to record how long it took a caregiver to enter and leave the classroom. This approach to collecting data is referred to as ______________.

✓ CHECK YOUR ANSWERS IN APPENDIX C.

The Experimental Method

TOGETHER AT LAST May 14, 2013 would be the most important day in the lives of Samantha Futerman and Anaïs Bordier. These young women, who shared a womb and came into the world together, would finally be reunited after 25 years of living on separate continents.

Sam and the *Twinsters* crew landed at London's Heathrow Airport, collected their luggage, and headed straight to the apartment they had rented. Shortly after they arrived, a few of Anaïs' friends came over, and everyone began to wait for Anaïs and her mother to show up. Sam, surging with adrenaline, did not know what to do with herself; she was scared, excited, wanting to hide. Then she heard it: a laugh coming from behind the door. It sounded just like her own, but it was Anaïs.

"I entered the room, and there was Sam," Anaïs recalls. "Neither of us knew what to do next, so we just stood in the middle of the room, staring at each other, like two tiny dogs sniffing each other out" (Bordier et al., 2014, p. 151). The twins watched each other in amazement, averting eye contact and periodically erupting in nervous laughter. At one point, Anaïs reached over to poke Sam, as if to see if she was real. "You don't know the person but you know her very well because you can read her perfectly," Anaïs explains. "It's the strangest thing."

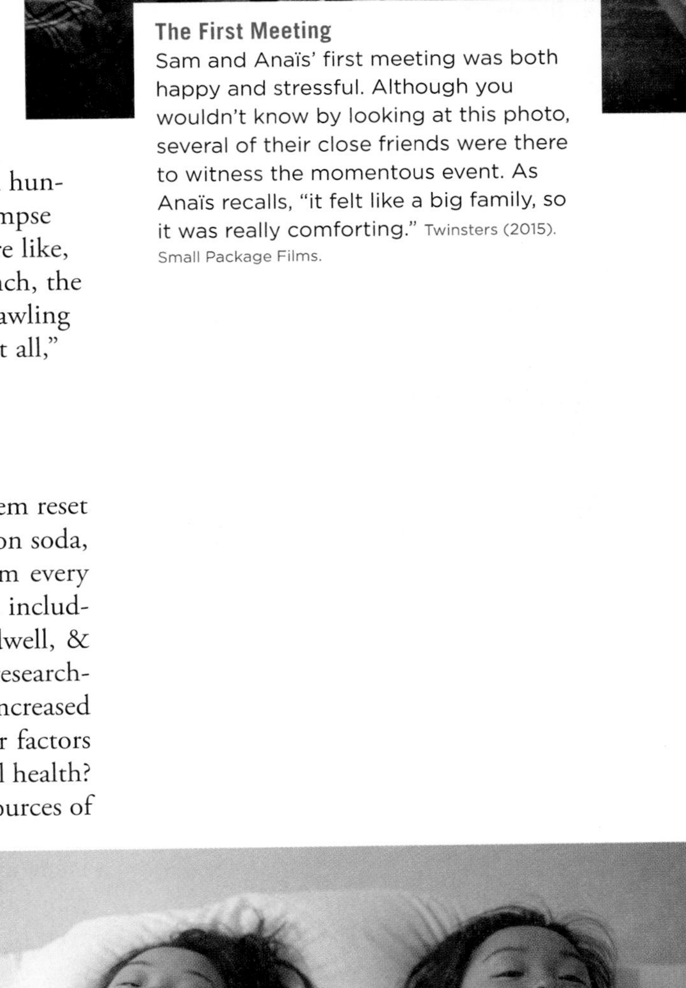

The First Meeting
Sam and Anaïs' first meeting was both happy and stressful. Although you wouldn't know by looking at this photo, several of their close friends were there to witness the momentous event. As Anaïs recalls, "it felt like a big family, so it was really comforting." Twinsters (2015). Small Package Films.

After about 45 minutes, the whole group was emotionally exhausted and hungry. As they made their way toward a restaurant, Sam and Anaïs caught a glimpse of their reflection in a storefront window. "We both kind of stopped and were like, 'that is so weird,'" Sam recalls. "I'll never forget that moment." Following lunch, the twins returned to the apartment and took a nap together. Was it awkward crawling into bed and falling asleep with a person they had just met? "Not awkward at all," says Anaïs. "It took like two seconds."

Control Is the Goal

Napping is what Sam and Anaïs do when they feel overwhelmed. It helps them reset and recharge. Many people use caffeine to achieve the same effect; they rely on soda, coffee, or energy drinks to clear away the mental fog that descends on them every afternoon. Research has linked low to moderate caffeine intake with benefits, including improved attention and mood, and increased alertness (McLellan, Caldwell, & Lieberman, 2016; Wilhelmus et al., 2017). Suppose you are interested in researching the relationship between caffeine and one of these variables—let's say increased attention. How could you isolate the effects of caffeine when so many other factors could potentially affect attention, such as nutrition, sleep habits, and physical health? There is a research method that allows you to monitor these other possible sources of interference: the experimental method.

LO 9 Explain how the experimental method can establish cause and effect.

At last, we arrive at the type of research method that can uncover causes of behaviors and events. Unlike the descriptive and correlational studies discussed earlier, the **experimental method** can tell us about cause and effect, because it aims to ensure that every variable except those being manipulated by the researcher is held constant, or controlled (see **Infographic 1.4** on page 30).

So how does the experimental method allow us to control variables and thus identify cause-and-effect relationships? The researchers assign participants to two or more groups that they try to make equivalent with respect to all variables, with one key exception: the treatment or manipulation being studied. If the groups differ on the measure of interest following this treatment or manipulation, we can say with confidence that the experimental manipulation caused that change. This approach allows researchers to observe the variable of interest without interference from other variables.

Twinsters (2015). Small Package Films.

experimental method A type of research that manipulates a variable of interest (independent variable) to uncover cause-and-effect relationships.

You Asked, Sam and Anaïs Answer

http://qrs.ly/2r77rvp

Did you connect immediately? How long was the process?

Let's examine how you might design a study using the experimental method to investigate how a moderate dose of caffeine impacts attention. Your hypothesis is the following: *Participants given a moderate does of caffeine will perform better on a task that requires increased attention compared to participants given a sugar pill.* To test this hypothesis, you need to put together a group of participants who are very similar in age, educational background, physical health, and other variables that might affect their ability to stay attentive. Next, you divide the participants into two groups: one that receives caffeine supplements and another that gets a sugar pill. After participants take the treatment or placebo for a designated amount of time (two weeks, for example), you compare the two groups' performance on the same tasks measuring attention. If the group receiving the caffeine supplements performs better, then you can attribute that difference to caffeine. This may sound straightforward, but there are still some critical concepts you need to understand.

RANDOM ASSIGNMENT Assigning participants to groups is a crucial step of the experimental method. Fail to divide participants in the correct way and your whole study is compromised. For this reason, researchers use **random assignment** to ensure that participants have an equal chance of being assigned to any of the groups. Randomly choosing which treatment the participants receive reduces the possibility that some other variable (a characteristic of the participants, such as age or sensitivity to caffeine) will influence the findings. You may have noticed some similarities between random assignment and "random sample" introduced earlier in the chapter. Here's the difference: Random sampling is used at the onset of a study to gather participants from a larger population. Random assignment comes into play later, when you are assigning participants to different groups. You can flip a coin, roll dice, or use a computer to generate numbers, but the goal of random assignment is always the same: to ensure that the groups are roughly equal on all characteristics. If the groups are lopsided with respect to some variable, the results may be affected. Getting back to your study on caffeine supplements and attention, imagine that you assigned all the teenage participants to one group and all the middle-age participants to the other. Might age influence the results of a test measuring attention? Perhaps. Random assignment helps reduce some of the interference resulting from such characteristics.

Cartoonstock.

"Well, I guess we're the control group."

EXPERIMENTAL AND CONTROL GROUPS Let's assume you did use random assignment to divvy your participants into two groups. One will receive the treatment (a daily dose of caffeine), and the other will receive no treatment at all (they will, however, be handed a sugar pill that looks identical to the caffeine supplement). Those who get the treatment (the real caffeine supplements) comprise the **experimental group**, and those who get the sugar pill (no treatment) are members of the **control group.** (We explain the need for the fake treatment in a moment.)

INDEPENDENT AND DEPENDENT VARIABLES Let's restate a point we already made earlier in the section, this time using some new vocabulary terms: The only difference between the experimental and control groups should be the variable the researchers are manipulating—in this case, caffeine intake. The different treatment each of the two groups receives is called the **independent variable (IV)**, because it is the one variable the researchers are deliberately changing (in this case, some participants get caffeine, others a sugar pill). This is a critical point, and it's worth restating: In the experimental method, the independent variable is the variable that the researcher is manipulating. Because of the complex nature of human behavior, there may be more than one independent variable in a given experiment.

synonyms

experimental group treatment group

independent variable explanatory variable

random assignment The process of appointing study participants to the experimental or control groups, ensuring that every person has an equal chance of being assigned to either.

experimental group The members of an experiment who are exposed to the treatment variable or manipulation by the researcher; represents the treatment group.

control group The participants in an experiment who are not exposed to the treatment variable; this is the comparison group.

independent variable (IV) In the experimental method, the variable manipulated by the researcher to determine its effect on the dependent variable.

The **dependent variable (DV)** is the characteristic or response the researchers are observing or measuring. In our hypothetical study, the dependent variable is the participants' performance on attention tasks. Just remember, the independent variable is what the researchers are manipulating, and the dependent variable is what they are measuring as a result of that manipulation. In other words, researchers are trying to determine whether the dependent variable (in this case, performance on the attention tasks) "depends" on the independent variable (caffeine supplement or sugar pill).

synonyms
dependent variable response variable

EXTRANEOUS VARIABLES When planning experiments, researchers must take steps to ensure that **extraneous variables** are not allowed to interfere with their measures. Extraneous variables are characteristics of the environment or participants that potentially interfere with the outcome of the research. While conducting your study of caffeine supplements, you discover that three of the participants are particularly sensitive to caffeine; even small doses make it very difficult for them to sleep at night. Their resulting sleep deprivation can definitely influence performance on attention tasks. Unfortunately, you failed to consider this very important variable in your research design, and thus it is an extraneous variable.

In some cases, extraneous variables can *confound* the results of an experiment. A **confounding variable** is a type of extraneous variable that changes in sync with the independent variable, making it very difficult to discern which variable—the independent variable or the confounding variable—is causing changes in the dependent variable. Imagine you test the participants in your study in a very nice lab setting, but because the lab can only hold half the participants at a time, you decide to collect data from the experimental group in the morning and the control group in the afternoon. But some research suggests that the impact of caffeine depends on the time of day it is administered (Sherman, Buckley, & Baena, 2016). When comparing the two groups' performance on attention tasks, you can't be sure whether differences result from the caffeine supplements, or some other variable(s) related to the time of day that the data were collected. These other variables could be confounding variables.

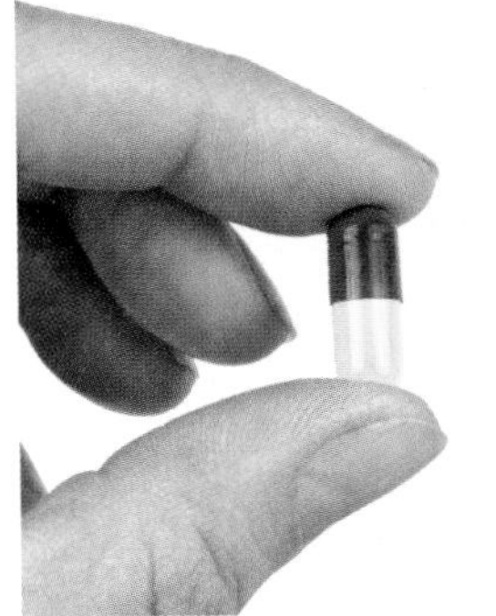
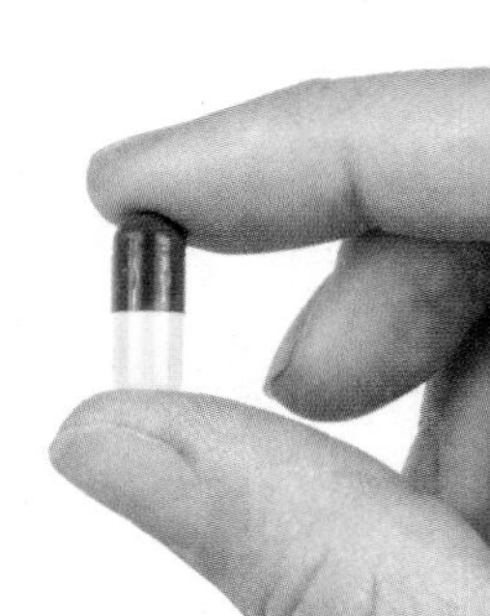

Looks Real
One of these pills contains an active ingredient; the other is a placebo. In placebo-controlled drug trials, researchers give some participants drugs and others placebos. People taking the placebos often experience effects that are similar to those reported by participants taking the actual drug. Cordelia Molloy/Science Source.

The good news is that we can take steps to minimize the influence of extraneous variables. This is called *controlling* a variable. As we mentioned earlier, random assignment to the treatment and control groups can help to lessen the impact of such variables. In the caffeine study, that would mean ensuring that both groups have approximately the same number of participants who are sensitive to caffeine (can't sleep well after using it). Or, you could just eliminate the caffeine-sensitive participants from your sample. Another way to minimize extraneous variables is to treat experimental and control groups exactly the same; for example, giving them attention tests at the same time and location.

If you succeed in holding all variables constant except the independent variable, then you can make a statement about cause and effect. Let's say your study does uncover differences between the experimental and control groups on attention tasks. It is relatively safe to attribute that disparity to the independent variable. In other words, you can presume that the caffeine supplements caused the superior performance of the experimental group.

DOUBLE-BLIND STUDY Deception can sometimes be useful in scientific research. One way researchers use deception is by conducting a *single-blind study* in which participants do not know what treatment they are receiving. An even stronger experimental design is a **double-blind study,** an experiment in which neither the participants nor the researchers working directly with those participants know

dependent variable (DV) In the experimental method, the characteristic or response that is measured to determine the effect of the researcher's manipulation.

extraneous variable A characteristic of participants or the environment that could unexpectedly influence the outcome of a study.

confounding variable A type of extraneous variable that changes in sync with the independent variable, making it difficult to discern which one is causing changes in the dependent variable.

double-blind study Type of study in which neither the researchers who are administering the independent variable nor the participants know what type of treatment is being given.

The Experimental Method: Are You in Control?

The experimental method is the type of research that can tell us about causes and effects. It is different from descriptive studies in that key aspects of the experiment—participants, variables, and study implementation—are tightly controlled. The experiment typically includes at least two groups—an experimental group and a control group. This allows the researcher to isolate the effects of manipulating a single variable, called the independent variable.

Imagine you want to know if laws that ban texting while driving are worthwhile. Does texting really *cause* more accidents? Perhaps texting is merely correlated with higher accident rates in certain populations, such as college students, because college students are both more likely to text and more likely to have accidents. In order to find out, you have to perform an experiment.

INDEPENDENT VARIABLE

The variable that researchers deliberately manipulate.

Example: The independent variable is texting while driving.

- **Experimental group** drives through obstacle course while texting.
- **Control group** drives through obstacle course without texting.

DEPENDENT VARIABLE

The variable measured as an outcome of manipulation of the independent variable.

Example: The dependent variable is the number of accidents (objects hit in obstacle course).

EXTRANEOUS VARIABLE

An unforeseen factor or characteristic that could interfere with the outcome.

Example: Some participants have more driving experience than others. Without controlling the amount of driving experience, we can't be certain the independent variable caused more accidents.

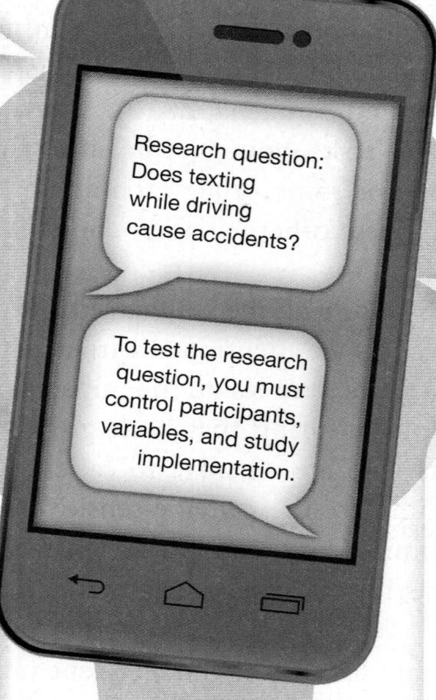

Research question: Does texting while driving cause accidents?
To test the research question, you must control participants, variables, and study implementation.

REPRESENTATIVE SAMPLE

Subset of the population chosen to reflect population of interest.

Example: Participants must be college students. Other groups might be affected differently by the independent variable.

RANDOM SAMPLE

Method used to ensure participants do not introduce unexpected bias.

Example: Researchers recruit participants by randomly selecting students from the college directory.

STUDY IMPLEMENTATION

RANDOM ASSIGNMENT

Process by which researcher randomly assigns participants to experimental or control group.

Example: Experimenter flips coin to determine participant's group.

EXPERIMENTER BIAS

Researchers' expectations and unintentional behaviors can unwittingly change the outcome of a study.

Example: Without thinking, researcher says "good luck" to one group. This might unintentionally cause them to try harder.

Researchers control for these effects by using a double-blind study in which neither researcher nor participant knows what group participants are assigned to.

who is getting the real treatment and who is getting the pretend treatment. In our example, neither the person administering the pills nor the participants would know who was receiving the caffeine supplement and who was receiving the sugar pill. Keeping participants in the dark is relatively easy; just make sure the treatment and sugar pill look the same from the outside (the caffeine supplement and sugar pill look identical). Blinding the researchers is a little trickier but can be accomplished with the help of clever assistants who make it appear that all participants are getting the same treatment.

Smart Horse, or Biased Humans? "Clever Hans," pictured here with his trainer Wilhelm von Osten, was a horse that appeared to be capable of counting, solving math problems, and a host of other cognitive tasks. When prompted with a question, Hans would signal the right answer by tapping his hooves. But as it turned out, Hans was just a brilliant reader of human behavior: By looking at the person asking questions, Hans could tell when he was about to tap on the correct answer. If the person did not know the answer, or if Hans was wearing blinders, his amazing problem-solving ability was no longer apparent (Pfungst, 1911; Samhita & Gross, 2013). The case of "Clever Hans" illustrates experimenter bias, or the tendency for the experimenter's views or expectations to color the results of the study (Rosenthal, 1965). akg-images/The Image Works.

THINKING IS BELIEVING There are some very compelling reasons for making a study double-blind. Prior research tells us that the expectations of participants can influence results. If someone hands you a cup of decaf coffee and says it is regular, you may feel energized after drinking it because you *think* it is caffeinated. Similarly, if someone gives you a sugar pill but tells you it is real medicine, you might end up feeling better simply because this is what you expect will happen. Apparently, thinking is believing. When people are given a fake pill or other inactive "treatment," known as a **placebo** (pluh-SEE-bo), they often get better even though the contents of the pill are inert. The power of this *placebo effect* may depend partly on social context. In one study, participants experienced greater improvement when the person delivering their placebo displayed warmth and competence (Howe, Goyer, & Crum, 2017). Remarkably, the placebo effect has been shown to ease pain, anxiety, depression, and even symptoms of Parkinson's disease. And although placebos are not able to shrink the size of tumors, they can help with some of the side effects of treatment, such as pain, fatigue, and nausea (Kaptchuk & Miller, 2015).

EXPERIMENTER BIAS We've discussed the rationale for keeping participants in the dark, but why is it necessary to keep the researchers clueless as well? Researchers' expectations can influence the outcome of a study, a phenomenon known as **experimenter bias**. A researcher may unwittingly color a study's outcome through subtle verbal and/or nonverbal communication with the participants, conveying hopes or beliefs about the experiment's results (Nichols & Edlund, 2015). Saying something like "I really have high hopes for this medicine" might influence participants' reactions to the treatment. The researcher's value system may also impact the results in barely noticeable but very important ways. Beliefs and attitudes can shape the way a researcher frames questions, tests hypotheses, or interprets findings (Rosenthal, 2002b).

synonyms

experimenter bias experimenter effect, researcher expectancy effect

Congratulations! You have now learned the nuts and bolts of the experimental method, one of psychology's greatest myth-debunking, knowledge-gathering tools. Using this method in a controlled laboratory environment has huge benefits; you have greater control over who participates in the study, more freedom to manipulate variables, and the ability to draw comparisons between groups that differ only with respect to your target variables. The experimental method also stands out in its ability to establish cause and effect. But like any scientific approach, this method has some drawbacks. Laboratory settings are inherently unnatural and therefore cannot always paint an accurate picture of behaviors that would occur in a natural setting. Remember, when people know they are being observed, their behavior changes. Other weaknesses of the experimental method include cost (it's expensive to maintain a laboratory) and time (collecting data in a laboratory setting can be much slower than, say, sending out a survey).

placebo An inert substance given to members of the control group; the fake treatment has no benefit, but is administered as if it did.

experimenter bias Researchers' expectations that influence the outcome of a study.

TABLE 1.2 RESEARCH METHODS: ADVANTAGES AND DRAWBACKS

Research Method	Advantages	Disadvantages
Descriptive	Good for tackling new research questions and studying phenomena in natural environments.	Very little control; increased experimenter/participant bias; cannot determine cause and effect.
Correlational	Shows whether two variables are related; useful when an experimental method is not possible.	Directionality and third-variable problems; cannot determine cause and effect.
Experimental	Can determine cause and effect; increased control over variables.	Results may not generalize beyond lab setting; potential for extraneous variables.

How does a researcher choose which method to use? It depends on the research question. Each approach has advantages and disadvantages.

Table 1.2 gives an overview of some of the advantages and disadvantages of the research methods we have described.

Now it's time to test our understanding of the experimental method with the help of a sprightly yellow square named SpongeBob.

DIDN'T SEE THAT COMING

SPONGEBOB ON THE BRAIN A little television won't hurt a child, will it? Kids' programs are interspersed with lessons on colors, words, and numbers, and only run for periods of 20 to 30 minutes. It seems reasonable to assume that little snippets of TV can't possibly have any measurable effect.

When it comes to the rapidly developing juvenile brain, it's probably not safe to assume anything. Consider the following controlled experiment examining the cognitive changes observed in preschool children after just 9 minutes of exposure to a talking yellow sponge zipping across a television screen.

TURNING YOUNG BRAINS TO "SPONGE"?

The research participants were sixty 4-year-olds, most of whom came from White, upper-middle-class households. Researchers randomly assigned the children to one of three conditions: watching the extremely fast-paced cartoon *SpongeBob SquarePants,* viewing an educational program, or drawing with crayons and markers. Following 9 minutes of the assigned activities, the children took a series of four commonly used tests to assess their executive function—the collection of brain processes involved in self-control, decision making, problem solving, and other higher-level functions. The results were shocking: Children in the SpongeBob group performed considerably worse than those in the other groups (Lillard & Peterson, 2011). Just 9 minutes of SpongeBob produced a temporary lapse in cognitive function.

How do we know that this was not the result of a different variable, such as some children's preexisting attentional issues or television-watching habits at home? Those factors were accounted for in the study. In the experimental method, researchers hold nearly all variables constant except the one they want to manipulate—the 9-minute activity, in this case. This is the independent variable (IV). That way, the researchers can be somewhat confident that changes in the IV are driving changes in the dependent variable (DV)—performance on the cognitive tests.

What aspect of the cartoon caused these effects? The researchers hypothesized it had something to do with the show's "fantastical events and fast pacing" (Lillard & Peterson, 2011, p. 648), and a subsequent study suggests that the fantastical content may be the problem. Shows that are highly fantastical, or involve "physically

Sponge Brain
No one expects cartoons to make kids smarter, but can they hurt them? One study suggests that preschool children watching just 9 minutes of the high-energy, ultra-stimulating kids' show *SpongeBob SquarePants* experience a temporary dip in cognitive function. HANDOUT/KRT/Newscom.

impossible events" (for example, cartoon characters that magically change shape or disappear in poofs of smoke), seem to compromise short-term executive function in a way that non-fantastical shows do not. The negative impact of fantasy is even apparent with slow-paced programs like *Little Einsteins* and "educational" shows such as *Martha Speaks* (Lillard, Drell, Richey, Boguszewski, & Smith, 2015). Researchers have yet to determine how fantastical television affects the developing brain, but stay tuned for future studies.

Is the Research Ethical?

LO 10 Demonstrate an understanding of research ethics.

Conducting psychological research carries an enormous ethical responsibility. Psychologists do not examine dinosaur fossils or atomic particles. They study humans and other living creatures who experience pain, fear, and other complex feelings, and it is their professional duty to treat them with dignity and respect.

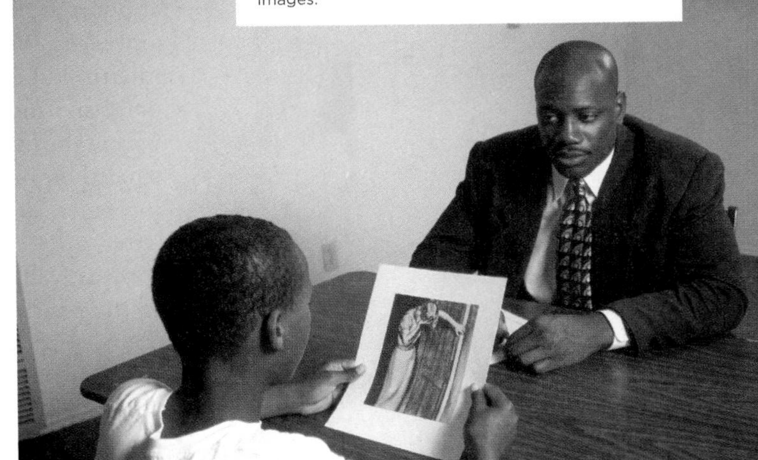

A Lofty Responsibility
A psychologist administers the Thematic Apperception Test to a child. (You will learn about this projective personality test in Chapter 10.) Conducting research on minors involves additional ethical considerations, and informed consent must be obtained from parents or legal guardians. Lewis J. Merrim/Getty Images.

In Chapter 11, you will learn about some of the most famous and ethically questionable studies in the history of psychology. These studies would never be approved today, as psychologists have established specific guidelines to help ensure ethical behavior in their field. Professional organizations such as the American Psychological Association (APA), the Association for Psychological Science (APS), and the British Psychological Society (BPS) provide written guidelines their members agree to follow. These guidelines attempt to ensure the ethical treatment of research participants, both human and animal. (Keep in mind that notions of "ethical treatment" are highly variable; not everyone agrees with the codes established by these organizations.) The guidelines encourage psychologists to do no harm; safeguard the welfare of humans and animals in their research; know their responsibilities to society and community; maintain accuracy in research, teaching, and practice; and respect human dignity, among other things (APA, 2010a).

WHOSE WORDS ARE THESE? One important way that psychologists share information is through scientific journal articles. Along with this sharing comes an ethical responsibility to give credit where credit is due. Let's take a look at how APA style supports the fair use of other people's work.

Put Your Heads Together

In your group, discuss the meaning of fair use and explain how it differs from plagiarism. **A)** Pick any short paragraph in this chapter and copy it, word-for-word, at the top of a piece of paper. **B)** Copy the paragraph again, but this time include quotation marks at its beginning and end, and use APA style to cite the authors' last names, year of publication, and page number from the textbook. **C)** Paraphrase the content of the paragraph in your own words, and use APA style to cite the authors' last names and year of publication. **D)** Which of the paragraphs would be plagiarism and which would be fair use? Why is it important to cite other people's work, and how do the APA guidelines make it obvious whose words are being used?

CONFIDENTIALITY An important component of ethical treatment is confidentiality. Researchers must take steps to protect research data from misuse or theft. Psychologists who offer therapy services are obligated to keep client and therapy session information confidential; in fact, they are required to safeguard this information in their offices. Confidentiality enables clients to speak freely about deeply personal issues. It ensures that research participants feel protected when they share sensitive information (about sexual or controversial matters, for example), because they may rest assured researchers will keep it safe.

There are some occasions when psychologists are legally required to break confidentiality: for example, when a client is a danger to self or others (including the psychologist); in cases of abuse, neglect, or domestic violence; or when the psychologist is given a court order (APA, n.d.-m). At the client's request, psychologists may also share confidential information with an organization, physician, or legally authorized individual. Additionally, psychologists may share a limited amount of information in order to receive payment for services, but only the "minimum that is necessary" (APA, 2017a, para. 4.05).

INFORMED CONSENT AND DEBRIEFING Ethical treatment also involves sharing information. Researchers have a duty to tell participants as much as they can about a study's purpose and procedures; they do this through *informed consent* and *debriefing*. Suppose a researcher has chosen a population of interest and identified her sample. Before enlisting these people as participants and collecting data, she must make certain that they are comfortable with their involvement. Through **informed consent,** participants acknowledge that they understand what their participation will entail, including any possible harm that could result. Informed consent is a critical part of Dr. Segal's twin studies. "You prepare a letter, and you have to keep a copy yourself, and give [the participants] a signed copy as well," she explains. "It lays out everything they will be doing, what some of their benefits are, what some of the risks might be, and that you will ensure them confidentiality. You don't give away hypotheses, but you speak about the research in a more general way because you don't want to bias the findings. It's kind of like your contract with them, and they're also free to withdraw from the study or refuse to do something at any point." Informed consent is a participant's way of saying, "I understand my role in this study, and I am okay with it." It's also the researcher's way of ensuring that participants know what they are getting into.

Following a study, there is a second step of disclosure called **debriefing.** In a debriefing session, researchers provide participants with useful information about the study; in some cases, this means revealing any deception or manipulation used—information that couldn't be shared beforehand. Remember that deception is a key part of the double-blind study (neither participants nor researchers know which group is getting the treatment and which is receiving the placebo). Other types of psychological research require deception as well. Reading this book, you will learn about experiments in which participants were initially unaware of the study's purpose. In some cases, researchers purposely lied to participants, either because it was part of the manipulation, or because they needed to conceal the study's objective until the debriefing phase. It is important to note that no one is or should ever be forced to become a research participant. Involvement is completely voluntary, and participants can drop out at any time. And remember, all experiments on humans and animals must be approved by an **Institutional Review Board (IRB)** to ensure the highest degree of ethical standards.

synonyms

Institutional Review Board (IRB) reviewing committee, Animal Welfare Committee, Independent Ethics Committee, Ethical Review Board

informed consent Acknowledgment from study participants that they understand what their participation will entail.

debriefing Sharing information with participants after their involvement in a study has ended, including the purpose of the research and any deception used.

Institutional Review Board (IRB) A committee that reviews research proposals to protect the rights and welfare of all participants.

Apply This ↓

DON'T BELIEVE EVERYTHING YOU READ

As you venture deeper into the study of psychology, you may find yourself becoming increasingly skeptical of media reports on psychological research. We encourage a healthy dose of skepticism. Although many news stories on scientific findings are accurate and balanced, others are flawed and overhyped. Look at these headlines about a 2017 study investigating the relationship between screen time and language development in toddlers:

"Tablets and smartphones damage toddlers' speech development."
(Snapton, 2017, May 4)

"The scary reason you need to limit your child's screen time ASAP."
(Jung, n.d.)

"Your iPhone could really mess up your baby."
(Brown, 2017, May 4)

It sounds as if screen time is *causing* speech problems in children. We must have a cause-and-effect relationship, right? Wrong. The following is a rough description of the research, which was presented at the 2017 Pediatric Academic Societies Meeting in San Francisco. The study focused on approximately 1,000 children ages 6–24 months. The parents reported the amount of time their kids spent playing on iPhones, tablets, and other handheld devices, and filled out a questionnaire aimed at assessing their children's language development. Upon reviewing the data, the researchers determined there was a link between screen time and problems with speech (Ma, van den Heuvel, Maguire, Parkin, & Birken, 2017).

Provocative as these findings may be, they do not allow us to conclude that using smartphones and tablets causes speech delays in toddlers. Isn't it possible that some third variable is causing both increased screen time and speech delays? Parents who spend less time talking and interacting with their children (activities that promote speech development) may be more inclined to use "digital babysitters." Thus, the lack of interaction with parents may be causing the speech delays, and perhaps these less-involved parents are more lenient when it comes to screen time. Another factor to consider is the direction of causation. When we see headlines like those above, we tend to assume that screen time is causing speech delays. But what if the reverse is true, that is, speech delays are causing increased screen time? Perhaps speech-delayed children are more drawn to digital entertainment because it provides stimulation without challenging them to use words and communicate?

The take-home message: If a news report claims that *X causes Y,* don't automatically assume that the media has it right. In this case, the research has only demonstrated a correlation between variables, not a cause-and-effect relationship.

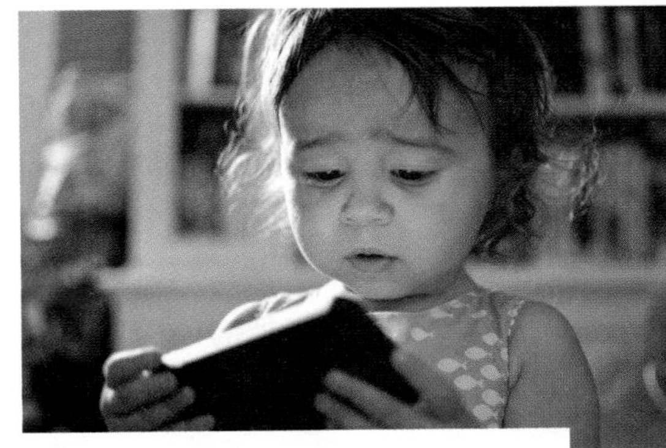

Overhyped Associations
In 2017 researchers presented a study revealing a correlation between toddler speech delays and the use of handheld devices like iPhones and iPads (Ma et al., 2017). The findings could easily be interpreted as "screen time leads to speech delays," but this is a reckless conclusion. Think of all the other variables that might impact language development: parenting style, exposure to television, nutrition, interactions with siblings, and many more. Fran Polito/Getty Images.

Scientists debate whether humans are causing global warming

False Balance in the Media
If 97% of climate scientists agree that humans are causing global warming, and only 3% disagree, why do news outlets sometimes present this issue as a "debate" between two individuals? By giving equal attention to the two viewpoints, the media promotes the misconception that scientists are split 50-50 on the issue. We call this "false balance."

show what you know

1. Following a study involving a double-blind procedure with a treatment and a placebo, a researcher met with each participant individually to discuss important information about the study. This is known as:
   a. informed consent.
   b. debriefing.
   c. deception.
   d. naturalistic observation.

2. Describe what a double-blind study is and explain why deception is necessary in this case.

✓ CHECK YOUR ANSWERS IN APPENDIX C.

Researcher on the Red Carpet
Dr. Segal (left) and Sam smile for the cameras at the Los Angeles premiere of *Twinsters*. Dr. Segal has spent her career studying and writing about twins. Her most recent books are *Twin Mythconceptions: False Beliefs, Fables, and Facts about Twins* and *Accidental Brothers: The Story of Exchanged Twins and the Power of Nature and Nurture*. Angela Weiss/Getty Images.

"ANYTHING IS POSSIBLE" The momentous meeting of Sam and Anaïs marked the beginning of a new journey for the twins and their families. Sam's parents embraced Anaïs as a second daughter, and Anaïs' parents did the same with Sam. After spending time together in London, the families continued getting to know each other through e-mail and text messaging. Anaïs and her parents celebrated Thanksgiving with Sam's family in New Jersey, and the twins celebrated their 26th birthday with Anaïs' parents in France. As Anaïs says, "We really see our family as one huge one living in America and one in France."

As for their biological relatives in Korea, Sam and Anaïs have not been able to establish contact. According to the adoption agency, their biological mother denies ever having twins or giving up her children for adoption. As Sam explains, there is a devastating stigma associated with giving birth to a child out of wedlock in South Korea. "The children, as well as the mothers, are basically outcasts, forced from the family and ostracized by family, peers, employers, and anyone who knows their situation" (Bordier et al., 2014, p. 35). Although Sam and Anaïs were deeply saddened by their birth mother's response, they do not harbor resentment. She gave them life, and she gave them each other, and for that they feel tremendous gratitude.

One of the hardest parts about reuniting with a long-lost twin is resuming everyday life without her by your side, says Sam. In the beginning, the twins saw one another every 2–3 months, meeting in places like Paris, Los Angeles, and Seoul, South Korea. This past year, they haven't seen much of each other, but they continue to talk every day. "We're constantly texting or video chatting," says Sam. "If anything is going on with either of us, we're always talking." When Sam imagines what life would be like if she never connected with Anaïs, she sees a version of herself that is more self-absorbed. "I would have been so focused on my career, acting, and pushing myself . . . and it would have been all about me," she says. "Now I have this amazing human across the world that I'm always thinking about and always worrying about."

For Anaïs, finding Sam has made her feel complete in a way she never did before. "I definitely was missing something. I don't know if it was from being adopted or from being separated from Sam," says Anaïs. "I feel complete now." When Anaïs looks at Sam, it's almost like observing herself from the outside. She sees a smart, funny, and charismatic young woman. Appreciating Sam's beautiful qualities has given her newfound confidence: "I feel like now anything is possible, thanks to Sam."

positive psychology An approach that focuses on the positive aspects of human beings, seeking to understand their strengths and uncover the roots of happiness, creativity, humor, and so on.

THINK POSITIVE

INTRODUCING POSITIVE PSYCHOLOGY Sam and Anaïs are wonderful examples of people who opt to see the brighter side of life. Instead of lamenting the fact that they spent 25 years apart, they rejoice in being united, anticipate good things to come, and want to help other twins and adoptees.

The twin's viewpoint is somewhat analogous to the *positive psychology* movement in the study of human behaviors and mental processes. **Positive psychology** is a relatively new approach that studies the positive aspects of human nature—happiness, creativity, love, and all that is best about people (Seligman & Csikszentmihalyi, 2000). Historically, psychologists have tended to focus on the abnormal and maladaptive patterns of human behavior. Positive psychology does not deny the existence of these darker elements; it just directs the spotlight elsewhere. Positive psychologists explore the upside of personal experiences, traits, and institutions. They believe that humans "strive to lead meaningful, happy, and good lives" (Donaldson, Dollwet, & Rao, 2015, p. 185). In this sense, positive psychology is similar to the humanistic perspective. In fact, the early work of the humanists helped set the stage for the current field of positive psychology (Friedman, 2014; Robbins, 2008). Many positive psychology studies have focused on well-being and optimal functioning (Donaldson et al., 2015), producing results with immediate relevance to everyday life. For example, evidence suggests that people who have a positive outlook tend to have better mental and physical health than their less optimistic peers (Catalino & Fredrickson, 2011; Huffman et al., 2016; Levi & Bavishi, 2016).

HAPPINESS, CREATIVITY, LOVE, AND ALL THAT IS BEST ABOUT PEOPLE

Throughout this book, you will read about people whose lives seem to exemplify the power of this optimistic approach. Each chapter introduces you to one or more individuals who have faced challenges with courage and optimism, keeping their heads high when all hope seemed to be lost. Learning about these men and women has been a humbling experience for the authors. Their stories inspire us to be more thoughtful, compassionate, and fearless in our lives. We hope they move you in the same way. As you make your way through these chapters, look for the positive messages that can be found in all types of psychological research. Open your mind, and keep reading!

Sister Love
Sam and Anaïs on a trip to South Korea. Now that the twins have found each other, they want to help others. Sam and fellow actress Jenna Ushkowitz (also a Korean adoptee) founded Kindred, a nonprofit foundation that provides support and resources for adoptees and their families (Kindred, n.d.). Anaïs, now a designer for the fine leather company Jean Rousseau, hopes to create an educational foundation for orphans and adopted children in Korea, Cambodia, or other countries. Twinsters (2015). Small Package Films.

YOUR SCIENTIFIC WORLD is a new application-based feature appearing in every chapter. In these online activities, you will take on role-playing scenarios that encourage you to think critically and apply your knowledge of psychological science to solve a real world problem. For example: Do you often share posts on social media? This chapter's activity will help you understand why it's important to think critically and evaluate sources for accuracy before sharing them online. You can access Your Scientific World activities in LaunchPad. Have fun!

SUMMARY OF CONCEPTS

LO 1 **Describe the scope of psychology. (p. 2)**

Psychologists are scientists who work in a variety of fields, studying behavior and mental processes. They conduct two major types of research. Basic research focuses on collecting data to support or refute theories, gathering knowledge for the sake of knowledge. Applied research focuses on changing behaviors and outcomes, often leading to real-world applications.

LO 2 Summarize the goals of the discipline of psychology. (p. 2)

The goals of psychology are to describe, explain, predict, and change behavior. These goals lay the foundation for the scientific approach and the research designs used to carry out experiments in psychology.

LO 3 Identify the people who helped establish psychology as a discipline, and describe their contributions. (p. 5)

The roots of psychology lie in disciplines such as philosophy and physiology. Early philosophers established the foundation for some of the longstanding debates in psychology (nature and nurture). In 1879 psychology was officially founded when Wundt created the first psychology laboratory. Titchener established structuralism to study the elements of the mind. James offered the first psychology class in the United States and developed functionalism.

LO 4 List and summarize the major perspectives in psychology. (p. 8)

Psychologists use different perspectives to understand and study topics in the field. Each perspective provides a different vantage point for uncovering the complex nature of human behavior. See Table 1.1 (p. 10) for descriptions of each of these perspectives.

LO 5 Describe how psychologists use the scientific method. (p. 11)

Psychologists use the scientific method to produce empirical evidence based on systematic observation or experiments. The scientific method includes five basic steps: develop a question, formulate a hypothesis, collect data, analyze data, and publish the findings. The scientific method is a continuing cycle of exploration, which uses critical thinking at each step in the process, and asks new questions along the way.

LO 6 Distinguish between a random sample and a representative sample. (p. 18)

A population includes all members of a group a researcher is interested in exploring. If it is a large population, then the researcher will select a subset, called a sample. With a random sample, all members of a population have an equal chance of being selected to participate in a study. Random sampling increases the likelihood of achieving a representative sample, or one that accurately reflects the population of interest.

LO 7 Recognize the forms of descriptive research. (p. 19)

Descriptive research is a type of investigation used to describe and explore a phenomenon. It is especially useful for studying new or unexplored topics, when researchers might not have specific expectations about outcomes. Descriptive research methods include naturalistic observation, case studies, and the survey method.

LO 8 Describe the correlational method and identify its limitations. (p. 23)

The correlational method examines relationships among variables. Variables can be positively correlated (as one variable goes up, the other goes up), negatively correlated (as one variable goes up, the other goes down), or not at all related. While useful for illuminating links between variables and helping researchers make predictions, the correlational method cannot determine cause and effect. Even a very strong correlation between two variables does not indicate a causal link, as there might be a third variable influencing them both.

LO 9 Explain how the experimental method can establish cause and effect. (p. 27)

The experimental method is a type of research that can uncover cause-and-effect relationships between independent and dependent variables. A well-designed experiment holds everything constant, except for the variables being manipulated by the researcher. If the groups of participants differ on the measure of interest, we can say with confidence that the experimental manipulation caused that change.

LO 10 Demonstrate an understanding of research ethics. (p. 33)

Researchers must follow guidelines to ensure the ethical treatment of research participants. These guidelines encourage psychologists to do no harm; safeguard the welfare of humans and animals in their research; know their responsibilities to society and community; maintain accuracy in research, teaching, and practice; and respect human dignity.

KEY TERMS

behavioral perspective, p. 8
behaviorism, p. 8
biological perspective, p. 9
biopsychosocial perspective, p. 10
case study, p. 20
cognitive perspective, p. 9
confounding variable, p. 29
control group, p. 28
correlation, p. 23
correlation coefficient, p. 23
correlational method, p. 23
critical thinking, p. 15
debriefing, p. 34
dependent variable (DV), p. 29
descriptive research, p. 19
double-blind study, p. 29
evolutionary perspective, p. 9
experiment, p. 11
experimental group, p. 28
experimental method, p. 27
experimenter bias, p. 31
extraneous variable, p. 29
functionalism, p. 7
humanistic psychology, p. 9
hypothesis, p. 11

independent variable (IV), p. 28
informed consent, p. 34
Institutional Review Board (IRB), p. 34
introspection, p. 6
natural selection, p. 9
naturalistic observation, p. 19
nature, p. 5
nurture, p. 5
observer bias, p. 20
operational definition, p. 13
placebo, p. 31
population, p. 18
positive psychology, p. 37
psychoanalytic perspective, p. 8
psychologists, p. 2
psychology, p. 2
random assignment, p. 28
random sample, p. 18
replicate, p. 15
representative sample, p. 18
sample, p. 18
scientific method, p. 11
sociocultural perspective, p. 9
structuralism, p. 6
survey method, p. 21
theory, p. 13
third variable, p. 25
variables, p. 17

TEST PREP ARE YOU READY?

1. Experts at a large university were asked to devise and evaluate a campaign to reduce binge drinking. Using findings from prior research, they created a program to curb binge drinking among students. This is an example of:
- **a.** basic research.
- **b.** applied research.
- **c.** naturalistic observation.
- **d.** case studies.

2. An instructor in the psychology department assigns a project requiring students to read several journal articles on a controversial topic. They are then required to weigh various pieces of evidence from the articles, synthesize the information, and determine how the various findings contribute to understanding the topic. This process is known as:
- **a.** empiricism.
- **b.** critical thinking.
- **c.** basic research.
- **d.** applied research.

3. The Greek philosopher Plato believed that truth and knowledge exist in the soul before birth and that humans have innate knowledge. This positions supports:
- **a.** empiricism.
- **b.** the nurture side of the nature–nurture issue.
- **c.** the nature side of the nature–nurture issue.
- **d.** dualism.

4. _____________ suggests that human nature is by and large positive.
- **a.** Natural selection
- **b.** Psychoanalysis
- **c.** Structuralism
- **d.** Humanistic psychology

5. The goal of _____________ is to provide empirical evidence or data based on systematic observation or experimentation.
- **a.** operational definitions
- **b.** critical thinking
- **c.** the scientific method
- **d.** a hypothesis

6. A psychologist studying identical twins was interested in their leadership qualities and educational backgrounds. These characteristics are generally referred to as:
- **a.** operational definitions.
- **b.** hypotheses.
- **c.** variables.
- **d.** empiricism.

7. One way to pick a random sample is to make sure every member of the population has:
- **a.** no extraneous variables.
- **b.** no confounding variables.
- **c.** an equal chance of having a characteristic in common.
- **d.** an equal chance of being picked to participate.

8. A researcher interested in learning more about the effect of separating identical twins shortly after birth might use Sam and Anaïs as a(n) _____________, which is a type of descriptive research invaluable for studying rare events.
- **a.** experiment
- **b.** case study
- **c.** naturalistic observation
- **d.** correlational study

9. With a(n) _____________ study, neither the researchers nor the participants know who is getting the treatment or who is getting the placebo.
- **a.** double-blind
- **b.** experimental
- **c.** correlational
- **d.** blind

10. A researcher forming a _____________ of high school seniors might select participants using a comprehensive database of all seniors in the United States, as all members of the population would have an equal chance of being selected for the study.
- **a.** control group
- **b.** experimental group
- **c.** natural selection
- **d.** random sample

11. Describe the goals of psychology and give an example of each.

12. A researcher is planning to conduct a study on aggression and exposure to media violence. What can she do to ensure the ethical treatment of the children in her study?

13. Use the perspectives of psychology to explain the similarities between Sam and Anaïs.

14. Find an article in the popular media that presents variables as having cause-and-effect relationships, but that is really a correlational study.

15. Reread the feature on the SpongeBob study. How does it establish a cause-and-effect relationship between watching the cartoon and changes in cognitive function? If you were to replicate the study, what would you do to change or improve it?

✓ CHECK YOUR ANSWERS IN APPENDIX C.

Go to **LaunchPad** or **Achieve: Read & Practice** to test your understanding with **LearningCurve**.

CHAPTER

2

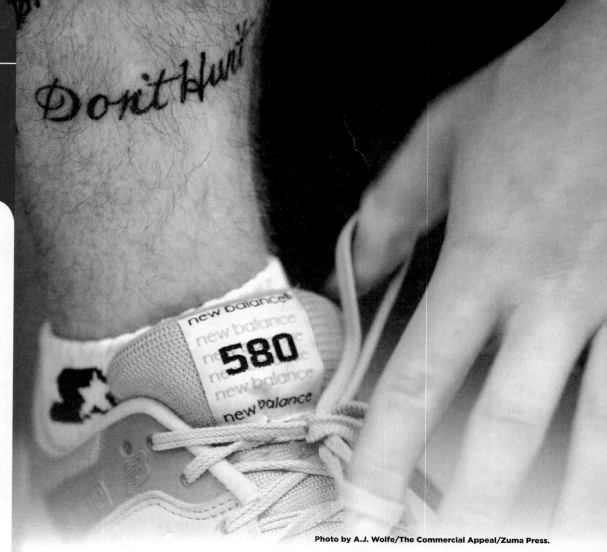

Photo by A.J. Wolfe/The Commercial Appeal/Zuma Press.

Biology and Behavior

Introducing the Brain

IN THE LINE OF FIRE It was November 9, 2004, and U.S. Marine Brandon Burns was surrounded on all sides by gunfire. The enemy was everywhere, in the buildings, streets, and alleyways of Fallujah. "I was in the deepest part of the city [and] there was chaos," remembers Brandon. At age 19, Brandon was on the front lines in the Iraq War, fighting in the battle of Fallujah.

"I was on top of the Humvee automatic grenade launcher shooting round after round," Brandon recalls. Suddenly, there was darkness. A bullet from an enemy sniper had pierced Brandon's helmet and skull, and ricocheted through the back left side of his brain. Bleeding and unconscious, Brandon was rushed from Fallujah to Baghdad. Medics had to resuscitate him on five separate occasions during that ambulance ride. Brandon explains, "Five times I died."

Ready for Duty
Brandon Burns poses for a photo at the Marine Corps Recruit Depot in Parris Island, South Carolina, in the fall of 2003. The following year, he was shot by an enemy sniper in the battle of Fallujah. Laura Burns.

Front Lines
At the age of 17, Brandon signed up to join the Marines. Two years later, he found himself engaged in some of the most rigorous urban combat of the Iraq War (Filkins, 2004, November 21).
Corbis Wire/Corbis.

From Baghdad, Brandon was transferred to a hospital in Germany. Doctors concluded that some parts of his brain were no longer viable. "They removed part of my skull and dug out the injured part of my brain," and now, Brandon says, "one third of my brain is gone."

A Complex Communication Network

Imagine you were Brandon and lost a sizable chunk of your brain. How would it impact your life? Would you be the same person as before? Your brain houses your thoughts, emotions, and personality, and orchestrates your behavior. It files away all your memories and dark secrets, and is involved in your every move, from the beat of your heart to the blink of your eye.

Scientists suspect the human brain is "the most complex entity in the known universe" (Huang & Luo, 2015, p. 42). This squishy, pinkish organ is definitely the most important component of your *nervous system*—a communication network that conveys messages throughout your body, using electrical and chemical processes. In this chapter, you will learn all about the human nervous system, which includes the brain, spinal cord, and nerves.

The brain is home to somewhere between 86 and 100 billion nerve cells (Herculano-Houzel, 2012; Huang & Luo, 2015). And since a typical nerve cell can communicate with thousands of others, the total number of links among them has been estimated by some researchers to be about 100 trillion (10^{14}) (Huang & Luo, 2015). This intricate, ever-adapting web of connections gives us the power to think and feel in ways that are different from—and vastly more complex than—the thinking and feeling capacities of most other organisms.

Consider the many tasks your brain is juggling at this very moment. As you scan the words on this page, your brain helps control the tiny muscles moving your eyes back and forth as well as the larger muscles in your neck and torso that keep you sitting upright. Light-sensitive cells in the back of your eyes relay signals, using electricity and chemicals, to various brain regions that transform the black marks on this page into words, sentences, and ideas for you to remember. And all the while, your brain is processing sounds and smells, and working with other nerve cells in your body to make sure your heart keeps pumping, your lungs keep breathing, and your glands and organs keep releasing hormones properly.

Note: Quotations attributed to Brandon Burns, Laura Burns, and Christina Santhouse are personal communications.

From Bumps to Brain Scans

LO 1 Define neuroscience and biological psychology and explain how they contribute to our understanding of behavior.

Brandon's injury resulted in a significant loss of his brain tissue. Remarkably, not only did he survive, but he can still talk about what occurred, think about the events, and feel emotions related to the injury. How exactly does his brain orchestrate all these complex functions, especially after severe trauma? And how does a noninjured brain carry out such processes? Scientists have developed a decent understanding of how individual brain cells communicate with each other, but they have yet to provide definitive answers to "big questions" about the brain and other parts of the nervous system, such as "How do we think?" and "What is consciousness?" This is why the brain may be regarded as the "last frontier of scientific inquiry" (Huang & Lo, 2015, p. 44). **Neuroscience,** the study of the brain and nervous system, draws on disciplines as diverse as medicine, engineering, computer science, and our personal favorite—psychology. The subfield of psychology concerned with understanding how the brain and other biological systems influence human behavior is called **biological psychology**, which brings us to the **goal of this chapter**: to examine how biology influences our behavior.

synonyms

biological psychology biopsychology, psychobiology, neuropsychology, physiological psychology, behavioral neuroscience

CONNECTIONS

In **Chapter 1,** we presented the four major goals of psychology, which are to describe, explain, predict, and change behavior. These four goals guide psychologists as they investigate how biology influences behavior. As you read through this chapter, try to keep these goals in mind.

LO 2 Compare and contrast tools scientists use to study the brain.

Brandon underwent many brain scans before and after his surgeries, which allowed doctors to get a detailed look inside his head without lifting a scalpel. But had Brandon lived in a different era, brain scans would not have been an option. Before there were technologies to study the brain, people could only speculate about what was going on beneath the skull of a living person. One theory was that bumps on the skull revealed characteristics about an individual. Judging the topography of a person's head was a core part of **phrenology,** the now discredited **brain "science"** that achieved enormous popularity at the beginning of the 19th century through its founder, German neuroanatomist Franz Joseph Gall (1757–1828). Another early approach to studying the brain was

CONNECTIONS

If phrenology were practiced today, we would consider it a pseudoscience, or an activity that resembles science but is not supported by objective evidence. See **Chapters 0 and 1** to learn more about pseudoscience and critical thinking.

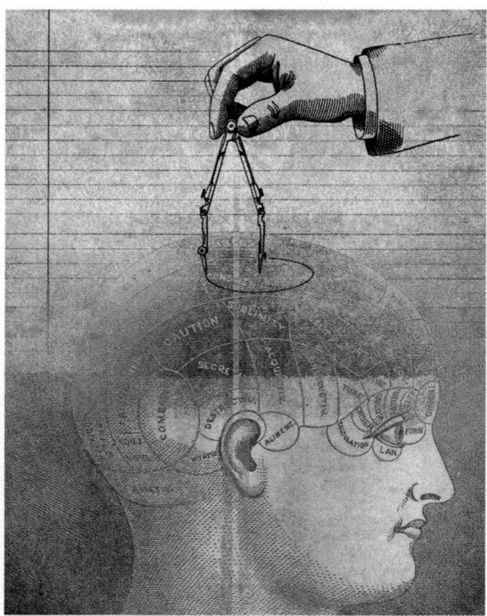

All in Your Head

Are you a secretive person? How high is your self-esteem? The answers to these questions lie on the surface of the skull, or so claimed the phrenologists, such as the one depicted in this 1886 illustration (right). The phrenological map (left) shows the locations of brain "organs" thought to be responsible for various psychological traits. The now-discredited brain "science" of phrenology achieved enormous popularity at the beginning of the 19th century through its founder Franz Joseph Gall. Left: Roy Scott/Getty Images. Right: Image Asset Management Ltd/Superstock.

neuroscience The study of the brain and nervous system.

biological psychology The branch of psychology that focuses on how the brain and other biological systems influence human behavior.

phrenology An early approach to explaining the functions of the brain by trying to link the physical structure of the skull with a variety of characteristics.

Ways to Study the Living Brain

In the past, scientists were limited in their ability to study the brain. Most of what they learned came from performing surgeries, often on cadavers. Today, imaging and recording technologies enable us to investigate the structure and function of the living brain. CAT and MRI techniques provide static pictures of brain structures, while functional imaging and recording techniques allow us to see the relationship between brain activity and specific mental functions. Functional technologies can also be used to diagnose injuries and diseases earlier than techniques that look at structure.

New technologies are continually being developed, allowing us to study the brain in ways we couldn't imagine just a few years ago.

Looking at Brain STRUCTURE

COMPUTERIZED AXIAL TOMOGRAPHY (CAT)

Using X-rays, a scanner creates multiple cross-sectional images of the brain. Here, we see the brain from the top at the level of the ventricles, which form the butterfly-shaped dark spaces in the center.

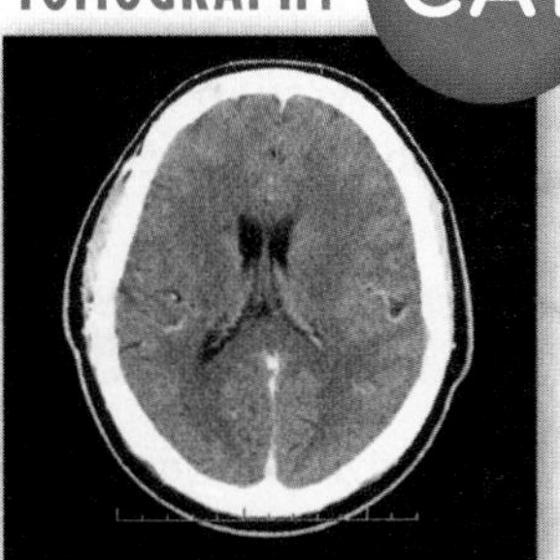

MAGNETIC RESONANCE IMAGING (MRI)

An MRI machine's powerful magnets create a magnetic field that passes through the brain. A computer analyzes the electromagnetic response, creating cross-sectional images similar to those produced by CAT, but with superior detail.

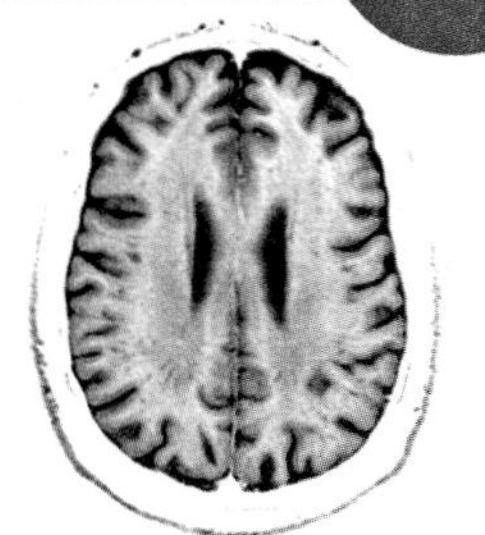

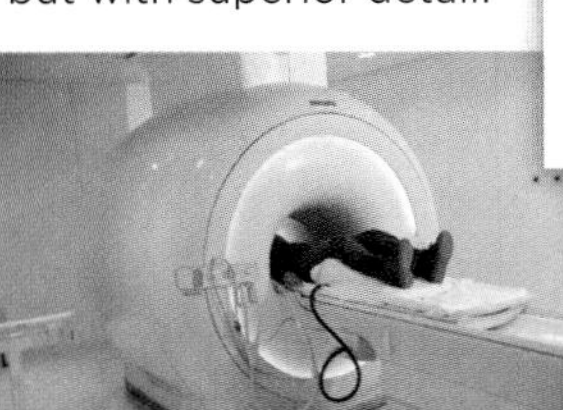

Watching Brain FUNCTION

(EEG) ELECTROENCEPHALOGRAM

Electrodes placed on the scalp record electrical activity from the area directly below. When the recorded traces are lined up, as in the computer readout seen here, we can see the scope of functional response across the brain's outer layer.

(PET) POSITRON EMISSION TOMOGRAPHY

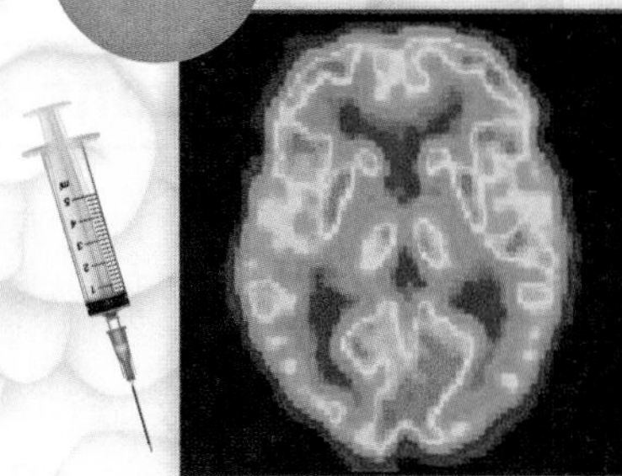

A radioactively labeled substance called a tracer is injected into the bloodstream and tracked while the participant performs a task. A computer then creates 3-D images showing degrees of brain activity. Areas with the most activity appear in red.

(fMRI) FUNCTIONAL MAGNETIC RESONANCE IMAGING

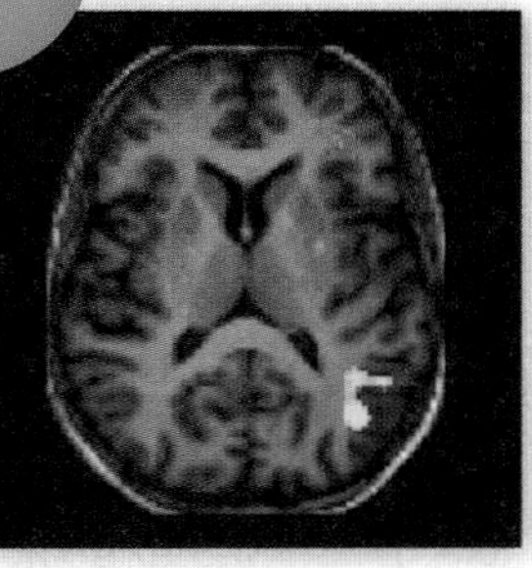

The flow of oxygen-rich blood increases to areas of the brain that are active during a task. fMRI uses powerful magnets to track changes in blood-oxygen levels. Like PET, this produces measurements of activity throughout the brain.

What's Next? Making Connections

The intricate pathways of myelinated axons in the brain can't be seen in the imaging techniques shown here. But new technologies like diffusion spectrum imaging (DSI), which tracks the diffusion of water molecules through brain tissue, are being used to map neural connections. The resulting images show a complex information superhighway, with different colors indicating directions of travel.

CAT: Southern Illinois University/Science Source. MRI (brain): Living Art Enterprises, LLC/Science Source. MRI (person in MRI machine): Arno Massee/Science Source. EEG: Science Source. Woman with EEG electrodes: AJPhoto/Science Source. PET scan: National Institute on Aging/Science Source. Syringe: istockphoto/thinkstock. DSI scan: Laboratory of Neuro Imaging at UCLA and Martinos Center for Biomedical Imaging at MGH, Consortium of the Human Connectome Project. fMRI: ISM/Phototake. Background image of brain: PASIEKA/SCIENCE PHOTO LIBRARY.

Admissible in Court?
A growing number of attorneys are submitting brain scans as legal evidence in court (Stix, 2014, May/June). In a criminal case, for example, a defense attorney might use a brain scan to demonstrate that the client has a psychological disturbance. But many judges are reluctant to accept this type of evidence; they believe neuroscience needs more time to mature (Davis, 2015, October 20). AP Photo/The Paducha Sun, John Wright.

through *ablation,* a technique used by French physiologist Pierre Flourens (1794–1867) that involved destroying parts of a living animal's brain and then determining whether some functioning was lost thereafter. Scientists also learned about the brain by studying people with existing brain damage. Despite their limitations, these early methodologies advanced the idea that areas of the brain might have particular functions. The notion that specific brain regions are in charge of certain activities is known as *localization of function.*

The last century, and particularly the last few decades, have witnessed an explosion of technologies for studying the nervous system (see **INFOGRAPHIC 2.1** on page 43). Such advances have made it possible to observe the brain as it sleeps, reads a book, or even tells lies (Horikawa, Tamaki, Miyawaki, & Kamitani, 2013; Hsu, Jacobs, Altmann, & Conrad, 2015; Jiang et al., 2015). With emerging technologies such as *optogenetics,* researchers can essentially create "on" and "off" switches for individual brain cells, and observe what happens when they manipulate the activity of those cells (Max-Planck-Gesellschaft, 2015; Park et al., 2017).

Now that we have learned how scientists study the brain, let's familiarize ourselves with some of the basic knowledge they have acquired.

show what you know

1. Positron emission tomography ____________, whereas computerized axial tomography ____________.
   a. records electrical activity from cortical areas; uses X-rays to create cross-sectional images
   b. records electrical activity from cortical area; tracks changes of radioactive substances
   c. tracks changes of radioactive substances; uses X-rays to create cross-sectional images
   d. creates cross-sectional images with a magnet; tracks changes in blood-oxygen levels

2. A researcher studying the impact of Brandon's brain injury might work in the field of ____________, or the study of the brain and nervous system.

✓ CHECK YOUR ANSWERS IN APPENDIX C.

Neurons and Neural Communication

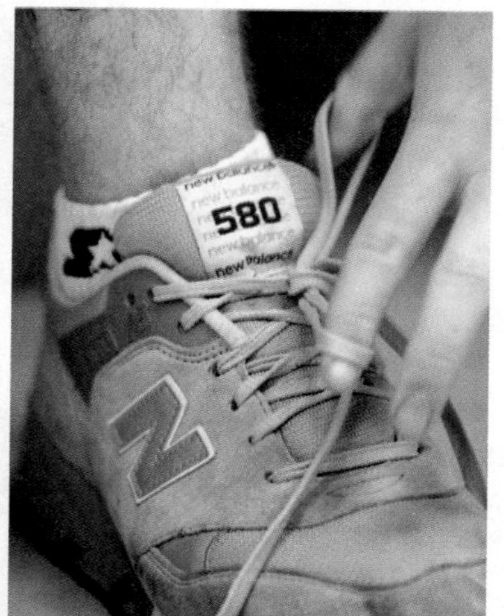

One-Handed
Brandon ties his shoelaces with his left hand. His traumatic brain injury occurred on the left side of his brain, causing paralysis and loss of sensation on the right side of his body. Photo by A. J. Wolfe/The Commercial Appeal/Zuma Press.

THE AWAKENING Two weeks after the shooting, Brandon finally awoke from his coma. He could not move or feel the right side of his body, and he had lost the ability to use language. There were so many things he wanted to say to his family, but when he opened his mouth, the only sound that came out was "ugh." Weeks went by before Brandon uttered his first word: "no." That was all he could say for months, even when he was dying to say "yes."

Apart from the paralysis to his right side and his difficulty with language, Brandon's other abilities appeared to be intact. He could remember people, places, and objects, and he reported no trouble hearing, smelling, or tasting. And although Brandon was not as outgoing and self-assured as before, he hadn't changed much overall. What was occurring in Brandon's nervous system that enabled him to function after such a serious injury? The same process that makes it possible for you to pick up your textbook, read these words, and decipher their meaning: activities of nerve cells, also known as *neurons.*

What Do You Really Need to Know About Neurons?

LO 3 Label the parts of a neuron and describe an action potential.

THE STRUCTURE OF A TYPICAL NEURON **Neurons** are specialized cells that communicate with each other through electrical and chemical signals. They are the building blocks of the brain, spinal cord, and nerves. A typical neuron has three basic parts: a cell body, dendrites, and an axon (see **INFOGRAPHIC 2.2** on p. 46). The **cell body** of a neuron contains the standard components found in most human cells, including structures that nourish the cell and a nucleus containing **genetic material** (for more on this, see Chapter 8 on human development). Extending from the cell body are many **dendrites** (DEN-drites), which are tiny, branchlike fibers that receive messages from sending neurons. Also projecting from the cell body is a long, skinny, tube-like structure called an **axon,** which sends signals away from the cell body. A neuron generally has one axon with branches ending in ***axon terminals***. It is through these axon terminals that messages are sent to other neurons. Many axons are surrounded by a **myelin sheath** (MY-el-in sheeth), a fatty substance that insulates the activities occurring within, speeding the transmission of neural messages down the axon. The **synapse** (SIN-aps) is where the axon terminal of a sending neuron meets a dendrite of a neuron or other type of cell receiving its signal (Infographic 2.2). The tiny space separating them is called the ***synaptic gap***, and it is only about 0.000127 millimeters (mm) wide. For comparison, a single sheet of printer paper is 0.1 mm thick (the equivalent of about 788 synaptic gaps combined).

synonyms

cell body soma

axon terminals axon buds, synaptic knobs, terminal buttons, terminal buds

synaptic gap synaptic cleft

CONNECTIONS

In **Chapter 1,** we discussed deoxyribonucleic acid (DNA), which is the genetic material we inherit from our parents. Here we note that it is present in the cell body of a neuron.

HOLDING IT TOGETHER: GLIAL CELLS Neurons transmit information up and down the body, and they need a little support and nurturing to get the job done. This is where the **glial cells** (GLEE-ul) come into play. Glial cells, which far outnumber neurons (Jäkel & Dimou, 2017), hold neurons together and maintain the structure of the nervous system. (*Glia* means "glue" in Greek.) Yet, glial cells do much more than simply keep things together. For example, after Brandon's injury, *microglia cells* defended his brain from infection and inflammation (Jäkel & Dimou, 2017; Streit, 2000), and *astrocyte cells* restored the barrier between brain and blood (Burda, Bernstein, & Sofroniew, 2016; Gruber, 2009). Glial cells also support communication between neurons, strengthen synapses, and create the myelin sheath that envelops axons (Araque & Navarrete, 2010; Underwood, 2016).

Glia to the Rescue A scanning electron micrograph shows neurons (green) and glia (orange). Glial cells serve as the "glue" of the nervous system, providing cohesion and support for the neurons. Thomas Deerinck, NCMIR/Science Source.

What Language Do Neurons Speak?

Neurons have unique properties that allow them to communicate with other cells. But what information do they convey? In essence, the message is simple: "I have been activated." Neurons are activated in response to other neurons, which can be stimulated by receptors attached to your skin, muscles, and other organs. The ongoing communication that occurs among groups of neurons underlies your every sensation, thought, emotion, and behavior.

RESTING POTENTIAL A neuron is surrounded by and filled with a fluid containing particles (*ions*) that have electrical charge (Infographic 2.2). Some ions have a negative charge; others have a positive charge. The neuron is encased in a membrane that is *selectively permeable,* allowing only some of the ions to pass in and out of

neurons Specialized cells of the nervous system that transmit electrical and chemical signals in the body; nerve cells.

cell body The region of the neuron that includes structures that nourish the cell, and a nucleus containing DNA.

dendrites Tiny, branchlike fibers extending from the cell body that receive messages from other neurons and send information in the direction of the cell body.

axon Skinny tube-like structure of a neuron that extends from the cell body, and that sends messages to other neurons through its axon terminals.

myelin sheath Fatty substance that insulates the axon and speeds the transmission of neural messages.

synapse The tiny gap between the axon terminal of one axon and a dendrite of a neighboring neuron; junction between neurons where communication occurs.

glial cells Cells that support, nourish, and protect neurons; some produce myelin that covers axons.

Communication Within Neurons

Neural communication involves different processes *within* and *between* neurons. In this infographic, we follow the electrical action that conveys messages *within* the neuron, from one end to the other.

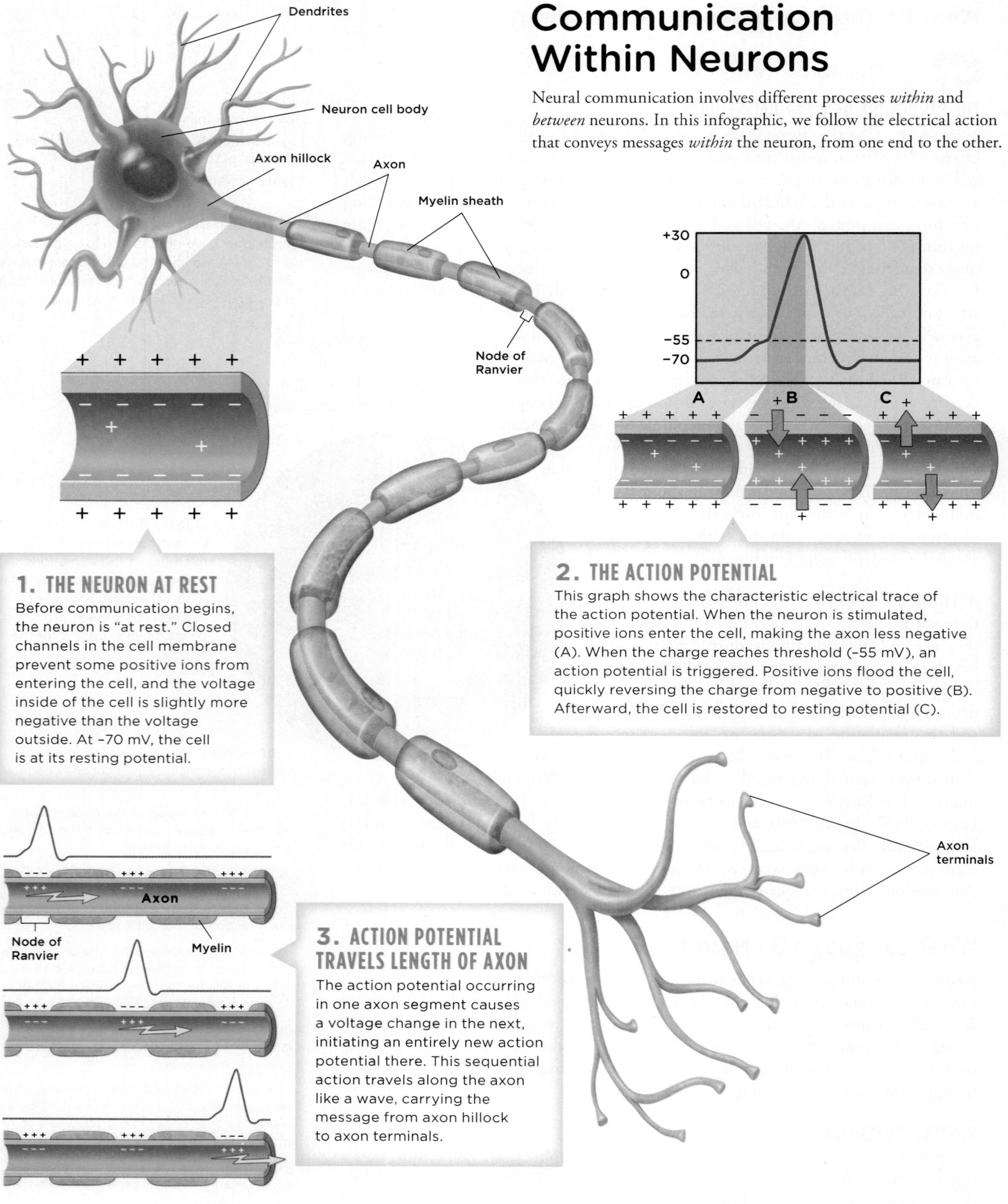

1. THE NEURON AT REST

Before communication begins, the neuron is "at rest." Closed channels in the cell membrane prevent some positive ions from entering the cell, and the voltage inside of the cell is slightly more negative than the voltage outside. At –70 mV, the cell is at its resting potential.

2. THE ACTION POTENTIAL

This graph shows the characteristic electrical trace of the action potential. When the neuron is stimulated, positive ions enter the cell, making the axon less negative (A). When the charge reaches threshold (–55 mV), an action potential is triggered. Positive ions flood the cell, quickly reversing the charge from negative to positive (B). Afterward, the cell is restored to resting potential (C).

3. ACTION POTENTIAL TRAVELS LENGTH OF AXON

The action potential occurring in one axon segment causes a voltage change in the next, initiating an entirely new action potential there. This sequential action travels along the axon like a wave, carrying the message from axon hillock to axon terminals.

its channels. The difference between the number of negative and positive charges being held back by the membrane produces *potential energy.* You can think of the membrane as playing the same role as a gate at the top of a hydroelectric dam. The dam holds back the water until the gate opens. This water has the potential to do work (the higher the dam, the more work the water can do). We call this ability to do work the potential energy of the water relative to the river below. The **resting potential** represents the *electrical potential* of a neuron "at rest," and its value is −70 millivolts (mV). For comparison, the voltage of a AA battery is 1,500 mV. Now let's look at what happens when a neuron stops "resting" and goes into "action" (Infographic 2.2).

ACTION POTENTIAL Although particles on the outside of the neuron are being pulled toward the membrane, they cannot move into the cell until the neuron is stimulated by neighboring cells. When this happens, channels in the neuron's membrane start to open up, starting at the dendrites. The influx of positive particles at the beginning of the axon causes a change in the voltage, going from −70 mV to the ***threshold potential*** of −55 mV. This triggers the channels to open in the first segment of the axon, allowing an influx of more positive ions. The voltage there rises rapidly, increasing from −55 mV to +30 mV. This spike in voltage, which passes through the axon of a neuron, is called an **action potential**.

What happens after this sudden jump in voltage? The solutions inside and outside this first segment of the axon come back into balance, and resting potential is reestablished. Now this segment is in its "natural" state, and ready to do more work. Meanwhile, the firing of the first segment of the axon has produced changes that cause the voltage of the second segment to reach the threshold potential (−55 mV), which leads to a spike of voltage there (+30 mV). This process repeats through each segment of the axon, like a row of dominos tumbling down; an axon segment fires, while the prior segment returns to its resting potential, all along the length of the axon to its end, always traveling in the same direction toward the axon terminal. Each action potential takes about 1 millisecond (ms) to complete, and a typical neuron can fire several hundred times per second. The action potentials constantly occurring in billions of neurons form the basis for all our thoughts, feelings, and behaviors.

synonyms
threshold potential stimulus threshold
action potential spike potential

EXCITATORY AND INHIBITORY SIGNALS What triggers a neuron to fire an action potential? The message begins at the dendrites. Neighboring cells deliver chemical messages, prompting channels in the dendrites to open up. These sending cells can be neurons or other types of cells that communicate with neurons, but we will assume they are neurons for the sake of simplicity. If enough sending neurons signal the receiving neuron to pass along the message, their combined signal becomes *excitatory* and the neuron fires. However, not all neighboring neurons send an excitatory signal. Some deliver an *inhibitory* signal, instructing the neuron not to fire. For an action potential to occur, excitatory signals must exceed inhibitory signals. Let's return to the top of the dam—imagine thousands of people yelling at the person in charge of the gate, some shouting "Open it!" and others screaming "Don't open it!" If enough of them are in favor, the gatekeeper will open the gate.

ALL-OR-NONE Action potentials are **all-or-none:** They either happen or they don't, and their strength remains the same regardless of the conditions. So how does a neuron convey the strength of a stimulus? By (1) firing more often and (2) delivering its message to more neurons. Consider a loud scream and a quiet whisper. The loud scream is a stronger stimulus, so it causes more *sensory neurons* to fire than the quiet whisper. The loud scream also prompts each neuron to fire more often.

resting potential The electrical potential of a cell "at rest"; the state of a cell when it is not activated.

action potential The spike in voltage that passes through the axon of a neuron, the purpose of which is to convey information.

all-or-none A neuron either fires or does not fire; action potentials are always the same strength.

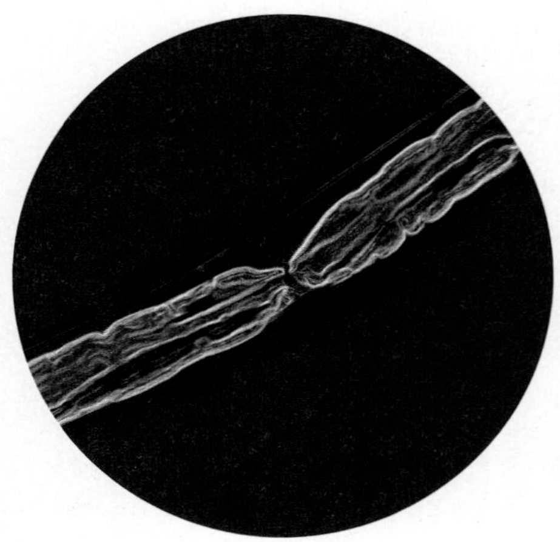

So Fast
Action potentials may travel as fast as 268 miles per hour (mph) through a myelinated axon, compared to only 1.1 to 4.5 mph in an unmyelinated axon (Susuki, 2010). Myelin is a fatty substance that envelops and insulates the axon, facilitating faster transmission of the impulse. The action potential "skips" over the segments of myelin, hopping from one node of Ranvier to the next (see the small space in the center), instead of traversing the entire length of the axon.
Jean-Claude Revy, ISM/Phototake.

ROLE OF MYELIN SHEATH The firing of a neuron is facilitated by the myelin sheath, which insulates and protects the tiny voltage changes occurring inside the axon. Myelin is a good insulator, but the axon is not entirely enclosed with myelin (you can see the segments of myelination in the photograph to the left). The action potential seems to "jump" from segment to segment, instead of traversing the entire axon in one continuous movement, accelerating transmission of the signal. Unmyelinated axons have slower transmission speeds because the signal must make its way down the entire length of the axon. Myelination damage from diseases such as multiple sclerosis can lead to many symptoms, including fatigue, trouble with vision, and cognitive disabilities (Brownlee, Hardy, Fazekas, & Miller, 2017; Calabrese et al., 2015).

LO 4 Illustrate how neurons communicate with each other.

COMMUNICATION BETWEEN NEURONS Neurons communicate with each other via chemicals called **neurotransmitters** (see **INFOGRAPHIC 2.3**). An action potential moves down the axon, eventually reaching the axon terminal. The action potential causes *vesicles* (small fluid-filled sacs) in the axon terminal to unload neurotransmitters into the synapse. The majority of these neurotransmitters drift across the synaptic gap and come into contact with **receptor sites** of the receiving neuron's dendrites. Just as it takes the right key to unlock a door, the neurotransmitter must fit a corresponding receptor site to convey its message. When the neurotransmitters latch onto the receptors, gates in the receiving neuron's membrane fly open, ushering in positively charged particles and thus restarting the cycle of the action potential in the receiving neuron (if the threshold is met).

What happens to the neurotransmitters once they have conveyed their message? Neurotransmitters that latch onto receptors may be reabsorbed by the sending axon terminal in a process known as **reuptake**. Those that are not reabsorbed may drift out of the synapse through a process called diffusion. This is how the synapse is cleared of neurotransmitters in preparation for the next release of chemical messengers.

How Do Neurotransmitters Influence Our Behavior?

LO 5 Describe specific neurotransmitters and summarize how their activity affects human behavior.

Researchers have identified approximately 100 different types of neurotransmitters, with many more yet to be discovered. Neurotransmitters secreted by one neuron may influence the activity of neighboring neurons, which can affect the regulation of mood, appetite, muscles, organs, arousal, and a variety of other functions (see **Table 2.1** on p. 50). Now let's take a closer look at some specific neurotransmitters, starting with the first one discovered, *acetylcholine*.

ACETYLCHOLINE Acetylcholine is a neurotransmitter that relays messages from neurons to muscles, thus enabling movement. Any time you move some part of your body, whether dancing your fingers across a keypad or bouncing your head to one of your favorite songs, you have, in part, acetylcholine to thank. Too much acetylcholine leads to muscle spasms; too little causes paralysis. Acetylcholine is also involved in memory; low levels in the brain have been linked to Alzheimer's disease, which can lead to problems of memory, language, and thinking (Bishara, Sauer, & Taylor, 2015; Johannsson, Snaedal, Johannesson, Gudmundsson, & Johnsen, 2015). Normal acetylcholine activity can be disrupted by snake and black widow spider bites, as well as food poisoning (Duregotti et al., 2015).

neurotransmitters Chemical messengers that neurons use to communicate at the synapse.

receptor sites Locations on the receiving neuron's dendrites where neurotransmitters attach.

reuptake Process by which neurotransmitters are reabsorbed by the sending axon terminal.

Communication Between Neurons

Messages travel within a neuron using electrical signals. But communication *between* neurons depends on the movement of chemicals—neurotransmitters. Though they all work in the same way, there are many different types of neurotransmitters, each linked to unique effects on behavior. However, drugs and other substances, known as *agonists* and *antagonists,* can alter this process of communication between neurons by boosting or blocking normal neurotransmitter activity.

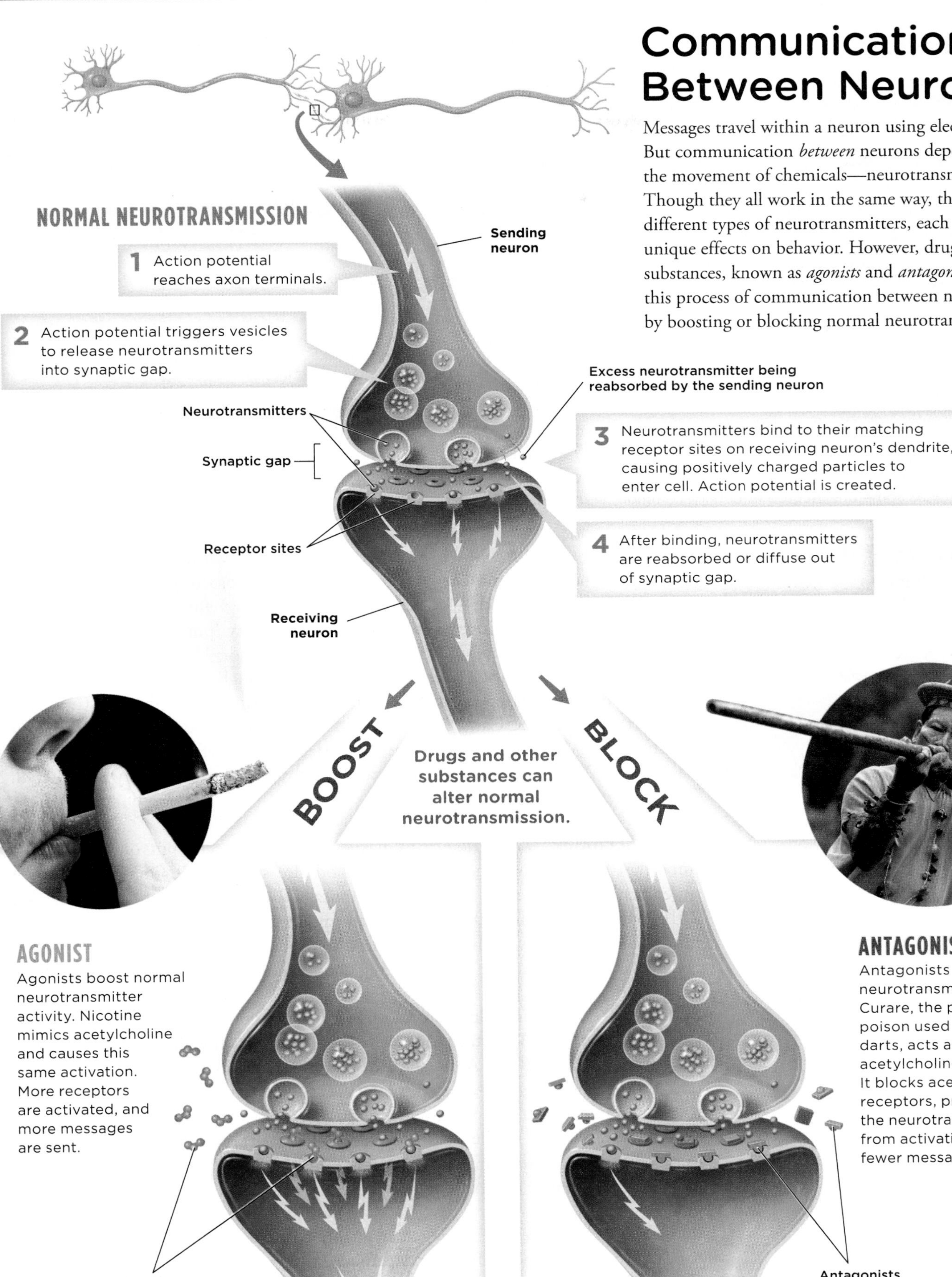
NORMAL NEUROTRANSMISSION
1 Action potential reaches axon terminals.
2 Action potential triggers vesicles to release neurotransmitters into synaptic gap.
Sending neuron
Excess neurotransmitter being reabsorbed by the sending neuron
Neurotransmitters
Synaptic gap
3 Neurotransmitters bind to their matching receptor sites on receiving neuron's dendrite, causing positively charged particles to enter cell. Action potential is created.
Receptor sites
4 After binding, neurotransmitters are reabsorbed or diffuse out of synaptic gap.
Receiving neuron
BOOST
BLOCK
Drugs and other substances can alter normal neurotransmission.
AGONIST
Agonists boost normal neurotransmitter activity. Nicotine mimics acetylcholine and causes this same activation. More receptors are activated, and more messages are sent.
Agonists
ANTAGONIST
Antagonists block normal neurotransmitter activity. Curare, the paralyzing poison used on blowgun darts, acts as an acetylcholine antagonist. It blocks acetylcholine receptors, preventing the neurotransmitter from activating them, so fewer messages are sent.
Antagonists

Credits: Person smoking: wavebreakmedia/Shutterstock. Blowgun: Terra/Corbis.

TABLE 2.1 SURPRISING EFFECTS OF NEUROTRANSMITTERS

Neurotransmitter	Function	Did You Know?
Acetylcholine	Muscle movement, memory, arousal, attention	The anti-wrinkle treatment Botox paralyzes the facial muscles by preventing activity of acetylcholine, which would normally enable muscle movement (Ghose, 2014, August 18; Sinha, Hurakadli, & Yadav, 2015).
Dopamine	Coordination of muscle movement, attention, pleasure	The same dopamine circuits involved in drug addiction may also be implicated in overeating and food addiction (Hauck, Wei, Schulte, Meule, & Ellrott, 2017).
GABA	Inhibits communication between neurons	Anti-anxiety drugs, such as Valium and Xanax, work by enhancing the effects of GABA (Drexler et al., 2013).
Glutamate	Promotes communication between neurons	Glutamate is a close chemical relative to the savory food additive monosodium glutamate, or MSG. Some people believe that consuming MSG causes brain damage, but such claims are not supported by solid scientific data (Hamzelou, 2015, January 26).
Serotonin	Mood, appetite, aggression, sleep	Physical exercise may boost serotonin activity in the brain, leading to improved mood and decreased symptoms of depression (Heijnen, Hommel, Kibele, & Colzato, 2015; Wipfli, Landers, Nagoshi, & Ringenbach, 2011).

Every thought, behavior, and emotion you have ever experienced can be traced to neurotransmitter activity in the nervous system. This table outlines some unexpected effects of common neurotransmitters.

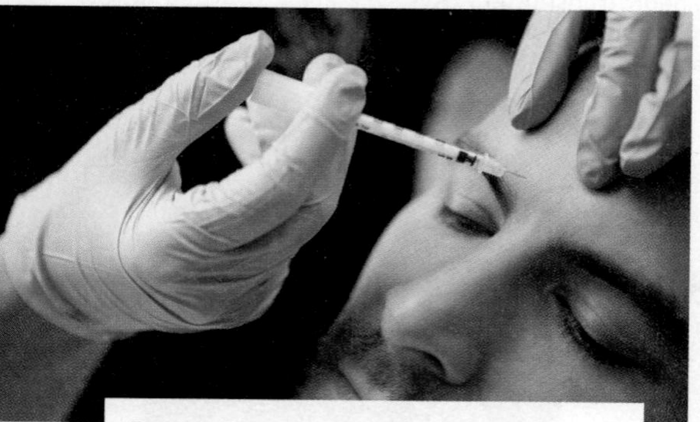

Botox—Not Just for Wrinkles
You've probably heard of the anti-wrinkle treatment *Botox,* which works by inhibiting the muscle activity leading to wrinkles, but did you know that this substance is also effective for treating chronic migraines? Botulinum neurotoxin is a food-borne poison that blocks the release of acetylcholine. This neurotoxin, dubbed the "most poisonous substance known to man," has more than "100 potential medical applications" (Gooriah & Ahmed, 2015, para. 1). Monkey Business Images/Shutterstock.

synonyms
norepinephrine noradrenaline

GLUTAMATE AND GABA Much of the communication within the nervous system involves two neurotransmitters: *glutamate* and *GABA* (short for gamma-aminobutyric acid). Glutamate is an excitatory neurotransmitter, so its main job is to kick neurons into action (make them fire), whereas GABA is inhibitory (puts the brakes on firing). Glutamate plays a central role in learning and memory (André, Güntürkün, & Manahan-Vaughan, 2015; Mukherjee & Manahan-Vaughan, 2013), and its under-activity is theorized to be involved in some symptoms of schizophrenia (Catts, Lai, Weickert, Weickert, & Catts, 2016; Javitt & Sweet, 2015). As an inhibitory neurotransmitter, GABA plays a role in controlling sleep and wakefulness (Vanini, Lydic, & Baghdoyan, 2012) as well as behaviors associated with fear and anxiety (Botta et al., 2015; Füzesi & Bains, 2015).

NOREPINEPHRINE ***Norepinephrine*** has a variety of effects, but one of its most important functions is to help prepare the body for stressful situations. In the brain, norepinephrine is involved in regulating arousal and sleep (Mitchell & Weinshenker, 2010; Moore & Depue, 2016). It plays an important role in maintaining attention, but in some situations, high levels may lead to overarousal and hypervigilance, which could dramatically interfere with thinking and attention (Moore & Depue, 2016).

SEROTONIN Serotonin helps control appetite, aggression, and mood, and regulates sleep and breathing. Abnormally low serotonin activity is thought to drive depression (Moore & Depue, 2016). Antidepressants called selective serotonin reuptake inhibitors (SSRIs), including Prozac and Zoloft, boost the effects of this "feel good" neurotransmitter (Chapter 14). Normally, neurotransmitters that do not connect with receptor sites can be reabsorbed by the sending axon terminal in the reuptake process. SSRIs work to prevent this reabsorption. The longer serotonin is in the synapse, the more time it has to attach to a receptor and exert its effects.

DOPAMINE *Dopamine* plays a key role in attention, learning through reinforcement, and regulating body movements. Irregular dopamine activity is suspected to underlie certain psychological disorders, namely schizophrenia and depression (Grace, 2016; Chapter 13). This neurotransmitter has been implicated in the abuse of certain substances, including stimulants like cocaine and amphetamines (Nutt, Lingford-Hughes, Erritzoe, & Stokes, 2015).

Repeated use of drugs overstimulates and impairs functioning of the neurons in the brain's "pleasure" circuit, theoretically making it more difficult to enjoy non-drug-related activities.

ENDORPHINS *Endorphins* are a group of naturally produced opioids (substances that minimize the perception of pain; see Chapter 4 for information on opioid drugs) that regulate the secretion of other neurotransmitters. The term endorphin is derived from the words "endogenous," meaning it is created within, and "morphine." Released in response to pain, endorphins block pain receptor sites. Brisk exercise increases their production, reducing the experience of pain and elevating mood.

Agonists and Antagonists

Drugs and other substances influence behavior by interfering at the level of the synapse (Chapters 4 and 14). Certain substances mimic neurotransmitters, while others block neurotransmitter action. *Agonists* increase the normal activity of a neurotransmitter (whether its signal is excitatory or inhibitory) and *antagonists* reduce the activity of a neurotransmitter (Infographic 2.3).

Apply This ↓

WHERE'S MY MORNING ANTAGONIST?

Did you jump-start your day with a mug of coffee, an energy drink, or a cup of tea? Caffeine perks you up at the crack of dawn or jolts you from a midafternoon daze by manipulating your nervous system. One way caffeine works is by blocking the receptors for a neurotransmitter called *adenosine;* it is an adenosine antagonist. When adenosine latches onto receptors, it reduces neural activity (making neurons less likely to fire), and this tends to make you feel drowsy. Caffeine resembles adenosine enough that it can dock onto the same receptors ("posing" as adenosine). With caffeine occupying its receptors, adenosine can no longer exert its calming effect (Clark & Landolt, 2017; Julien, Advokat, & Comaty, 2014). The result: More neurons fire and you feel full of energy. After several days of reduced sleep, the right dose of caffeine can help maintain reaction time, attentiveness, and reasoning skills (Kamimori et al., 2015). This drug may even boost your ability to form long-term memories (Borota et al., 2014). The effects of caffeine do not stop at the brain. As anyone who has enjoyed a double latte or a Red Bull can testify, caffeine also kicks the body into high gear; some research suggests it may enhance stamina in endurance exercise (Hodgson, Randell, & Jeukendrup, 2013).

CAFFEINE CAN ENHANCE REACTION TIME, STAMINA, AND REASONING SKILLS.

As stimulating as these findings may be, interpret them with caution. The performance benefits of caffeine may be, in part, due to the placebo effect; simply *believing* you ingested caffeine may be enough to get your body to do more work (Saunders et al., 2016). And although moderate use of caffeinated sports drinks may enhance performance during short bursts of exercise, these products contain ingredients that have not been well studied, and they are generally not good for rehydrating (Mora-Rodriguez & Pallarés, 2014). Caffeine also has a tendency to intrude on sleep. According to a review of 58 studies, using caffeine can make it harder to fall asleep, reduce total sleep time, and interfere with the deep stages of sleep that help you feel refreshed in the morning (Clark & Landolt, 2017). Continued use can lead to irritability, exhaustion, and headaches if you reduce your consumption (Chawla, 2017, April 12; Chapter 4). For some people (pregnant women, children, and those with certain health conditions), caffeine use should be limited or avoided entirely (Medline Plus, 2015, April 25).

amenic181/Getty Images.

Now sit back, relax, and sip on a beverage, caffeinated or not. It's time to examine the nervous system running through your arms, legs, fingers, toes—and everywhere else.

show what you know

1. Many axons are surrounded by a _______________, which is a fatty substance that insulates the axon.
2. _______________ are released into the _______________ when an action potential reaches the axon terminal.
   a. Sodium ions; synapse
   b. Neurotransmitters; synapse
   c. Potassium ions; cell membrane
   d. Neurotransmitters; sodium gates
3. Describe how three neurotransmitters impact your daily behavior.

✓ CHECK YOUR ANSWERS IN APPENDIX C.

The Brain Can't Do It Alone

Like any complex system, the brain needs a supporting infrastructure to carry out its directives and relay essential information from the outside world. Running up and down your spine and branching throughout your body is a network of neurons that connects your brain to the rest of you. As **Figure 2.1** illustrates, the **central nervous system (CNS)** consists of the brain and spinal cord, while the **peripheral nervous system (PNS)** comprises all the neurons that are not in

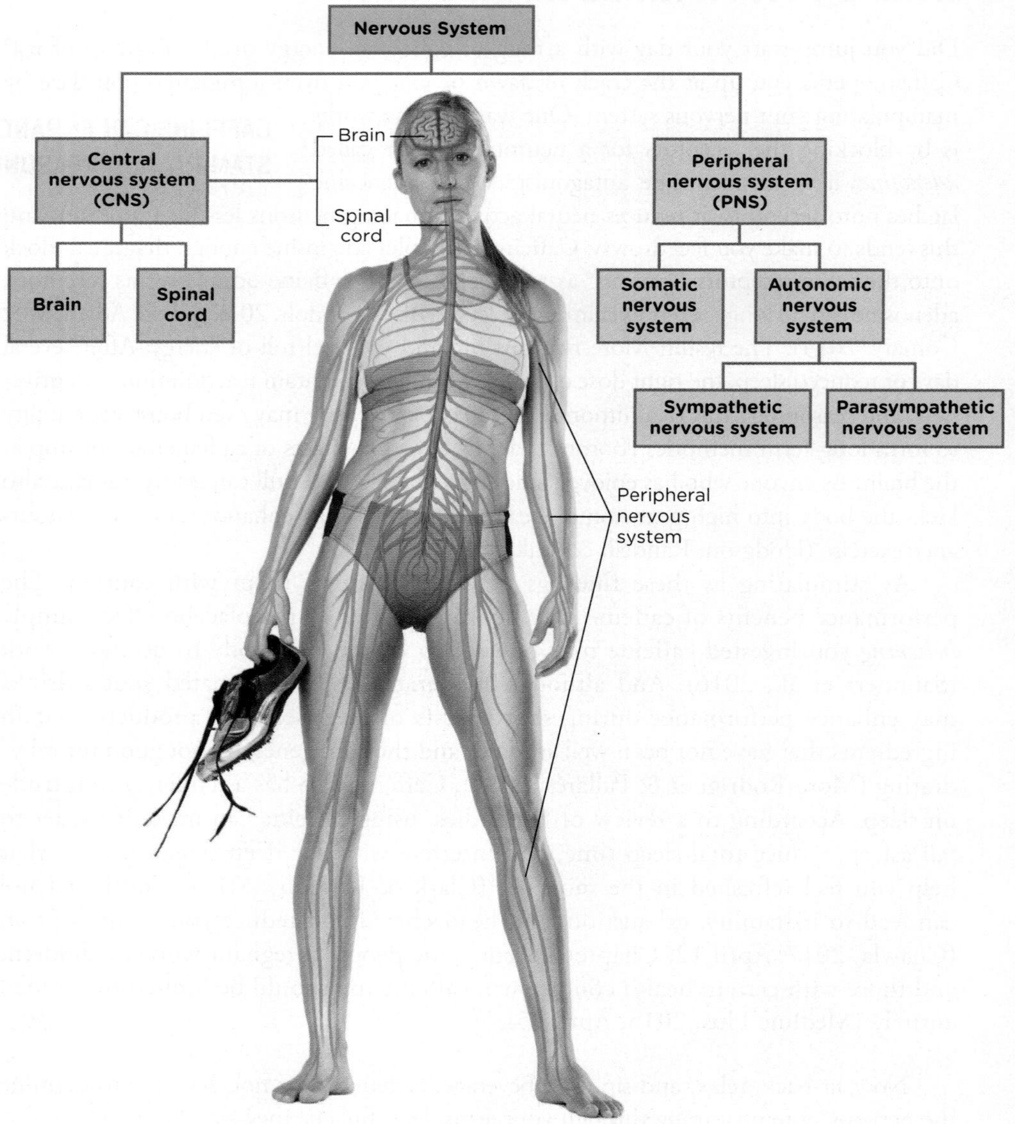

FIGURE 2.1
Overview of the Nervous System
The nervous system is made up of the central nervous system, which includes the brain and spinal cord, and the peripheral nervous system. Photo: moodboard/Alamy.

central nervous system (CNS) A major component of the human nervous system that includes the brain and spinal cord.

peripheral nervous system (PNS) The part of the nervous system that connects the central nervous system to the rest of the body.

spinal cord The bundle of neurons that allows communication between the brain and peripheral nervous system.

sensory neurons Neurons that receive information from the sensory systems and convey it to the brain for further processing.

motor neurons Neurons that transmit information from the central nervous system to the muscles and glands.

interneurons Neurons that reside exclusively in the brain and spinal cord; act as a bridge connecting sensory and motor neurons.

the central nervous system. The peripheral nervous system connects the central nervous system with the body's muscles, glands, and organs, and it can be divided into two branches: the *somatic nervous system* and *autonomic nervous system.*

The Spinal Cord and Simple Reflexes

Brandon suffered a devastating brain injury that temporarily immobilized half of his body. The paralysis could have affected his entire body if the bullet had pierced his **spinal cord**. This bundle of neurons provides a communication pathway between the brain and peripheral nervous system. The spinal cord has two major responsibilities: (1) receiving information from the body and sending it to the brain; and (2) taking information from the brain and sending it to the body. If this pathway is blocked, commands from the brain cannot reach the muscles responsible for making you walk, talk, and pour yourself a glass of orange juice. Likewise, the skin and other parts of the body have no way of communicating sensory information to the brain, like "Ooh, that burner is hot," or "Oh, this massage feels good."

LO 6 Explain how the central and peripheral nervous systems connect.

TYPES OF NEURONS How do the brain and spinal cord, which make up the central nervous system, communicate with the rest of the body through the peripheral nervous system? In essence, there are three types of neurons participating in this back-and-forth communication. **Sensory neurons** receive information about the environment from the sensory systems and convey this information to the brain for processing. **Motor neurons** carry information from the central nervous system to various parts of the body, causing muscles to contract and glands to release chemicals. **Interneurons**, which reside exclusively in the brain and spinal cord, act as bridges connecting sensory and motor neurons. By gathering and processing sensory input from multiple neurons, interneurons facilitate the nervous system's most complex operations, from solving equations to creating lifelong memories. They are also involved in a relatively simple operation, the reflex.

synonyms
sensory neurons afferent neurons
motor neurons efferent neurons
interneurons association neurons, relay neurons

THE REFLEX ARC Have you ever touched a burning hot pan? You probably withdrew your hand before you even had a chance to think about it. This ultrafast response to a painful stimulus is known as a reflex (see **Figure 2.2** on next page). Touching the hot pan activates a communication pathway that begins with the sensory neurons, travels through interneurons in the spinal cord, and ends with motor

See Ian Move His Hands

http://qrs.ly/9u7827n

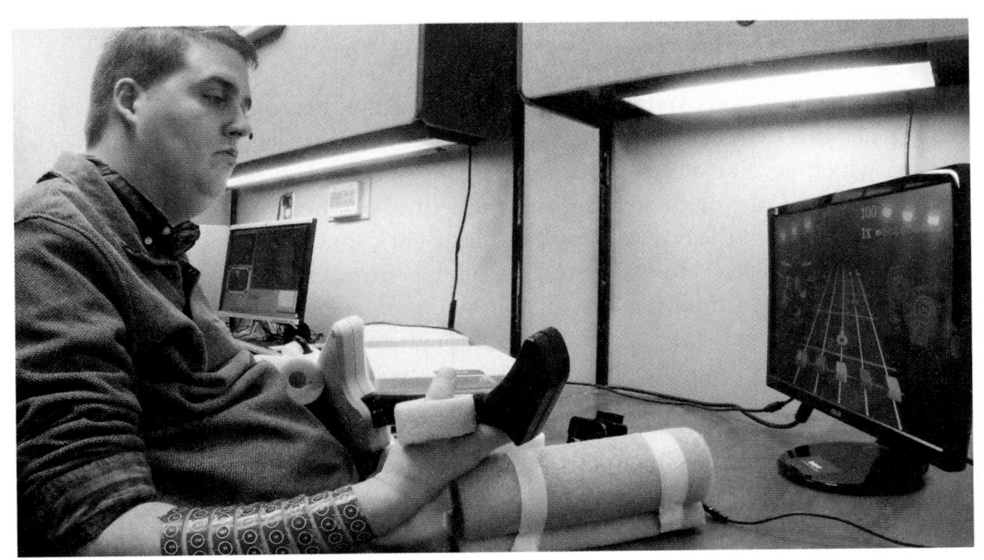

Breakthrough Technology
A tragic diving accident left Ian Burkhart with paralysis in all four limbs, but thanks to a groundbreaking technology developed at The Ohio State University, he can now manipulate objects with his fingers and wrists. The "brain-computer interface" essentially reads his thoughts about hand movements and turns those thoughts into action by electrically stimulating his arm. Here, Ian uses the interface to play Guitar Hero. The technology acts as a simplified version of the spinal cord, receiving commands from the brain and conveying that message to muscles in the body (Bouton et al., 2016). The ultimate goal is to take the technology out of the lab and into homes and workplaces, allowing people suffering from paralysis to achieve a new form of independence.

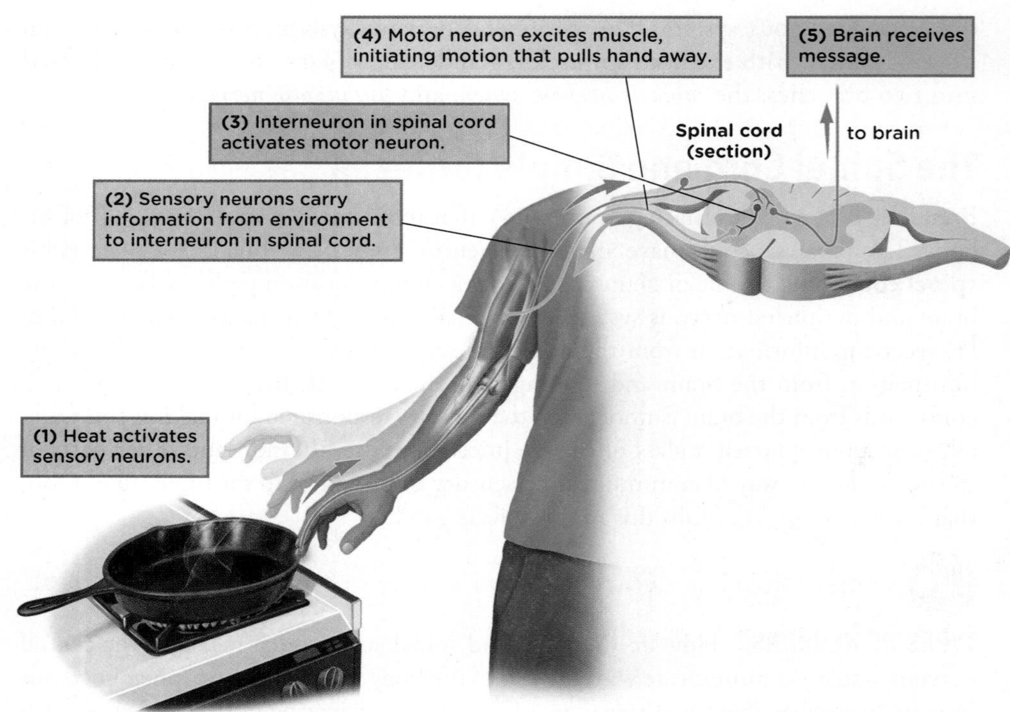
(4) Motor neuron excites muscle, initiating motion that pulls hand away.
(5) Brain receives message.
(3) Interneuron in spinal cord activates motor neuron.
Spinal cord (section)
to brain
(2) Sensory neurons carry information from environment to interneuron in spinal cord.
(1) Heat activates sensory neurons.

FIGURE 2.2
The Spinal Cord and Reflex Arc
Without any input from the brain, the spinal cord neurons are capable of creating some simple reflexive behavior. While this reflex is occurring, sensory neurons also send messages to the brain, letting it know what has happened. Let's break this pain reflex into steps: (1) Your hand touches the hot pan, activating sensory receptors, which cause the sensory neurons to carry a signal from your hand to the spinal cord. (2) In the spinal cord, the signal from the sensory neurons is received by interneurons. (3) The interneurons quickly activate motor neurons and instruct them to respond. (4) The motor neurons then command your muscles to contract, causing your hand to withdraw quickly.

neurons that cause movement. Amazingly, the brain is not involved in this initial reaction. A sensory neuron has a rendezvous with an interneuron in the spinal cord, which then commands a motor neuron to react—no brain required. We refer to this process, in which a stimulus causes an involuntary response, as a **reflex arc**.

Eventually, your brain does process the event; otherwise, you would have no clue it happened. You become consciously aware of your reaction *after* it has occurred (*My hand just pulled back; that pan was hot!*). Although many sensory and motor neurons are involved in this reaction, it happens very quickly, hopefully in time to reduce injury in cases when the reflex arc involves pain. Why do you think the reflex arc evolved? In other words, how might this reflex promote human survival over evolutionary time?

The Peripheral Nervous System

LO 7

Describe the organization and function of the peripheral nervous system.

The peripheral nervous system (PNS) includes all the neurons that are not in the central nervous system. These neurons are bundled together in collections called **nerves**, which act like electrical cables carrying signals from place to place. Nerves of the peripheral nervous system inform the central nervous system about the body's environment—both the exterior (for example, sights, sounds, and tastes) and interior (for example, heart rate, blood pressure, and temperature). The central nervous system, in turn, makes sense of all this information and then responds by dispatching orders to the muscles, glands, and other tissues through the nerves of the peripheral nervous system. As mentioned earlier, the PNS has two functional branches: the *somatic nervous system* and *autonomic nervous system*.

THE SOMATIC NERVOUS SYSTEM The **somatic nervous system** includes sensory nerves and motor nerves. (*Somatic* means "related to the body.") The sensory nerves

synonyms

reflex arc spinal reflex

reflex arc An automatic response to a sensory stimulus, such as the "knee-jerk" reaction; a simple pathway of communication from sensory neurons through interneurons in the spinal cord back out through motor neurons.

nerves Bundles of neurons that carry information to and from the central nervous system; provide communication between the central nervous system and the muscles, glands, and sensory receptors.

somatic nervous system The branch of the peripheral nervous system that includes sensory nerves and motor nerves; gathers information from sensory receptors and controls the skeletal muscles responsible for voluntary movement.

autonomic nervous system The branch of the peripheral nervous system that controls involuntary processes within the body, such as contractions in the digestive tract and activity of glands.

sympathetic nervous system The division of the autonomic nervous system that mobilizes the "fight-or-flight" response to stressful or crisis situations.

gather information from sensory receptors and send it to the central nervous system. The motor nerves receive information from the central nervous system and relay it to the muscles. The somatic nervous system controls the skeletal muscles involved in *voluntary* movements, like picking up a pencil or climbing into bed. It also receives sensory information from the skin and other tissues, providing the brain with constant feedback about temperature, pressure, pain, and other stimuli.

THE AUTONOMIC NERVOUS SYSTEM Meanwhile, the **autonomic nervous system** (au-te-NOM-ic) is working behind the scenes, regulating *involuntary* activity, such as the pumping of the heart, the expansion and contraction of blood vessels, and digestion. Most of the activities supervised by the somatic nervous system are voluntary (within your conscious control and awareness), whereas processes directed by the autonomic nervous system tend to be involuntary (automatic) and outside of awareness.

The autonomic nervous system has two divisions that help us respond to and recover from stressful situations (**Figure 2.3**). The **sympathetic nervous system** initiates what is often referred to as the "fight-or-flight" response, which prepares the body to deal with a crisis. When faced with a stressful situation, the sympathetic nervous system preps the body for action by increasing heart rate and respiration, and by slowing digestion and other maintenance functions. Earlier, we mentioned that caffeine makes you feel physically energized. This is because it activates the fight-or-flight response (Flueck et al., 2016).

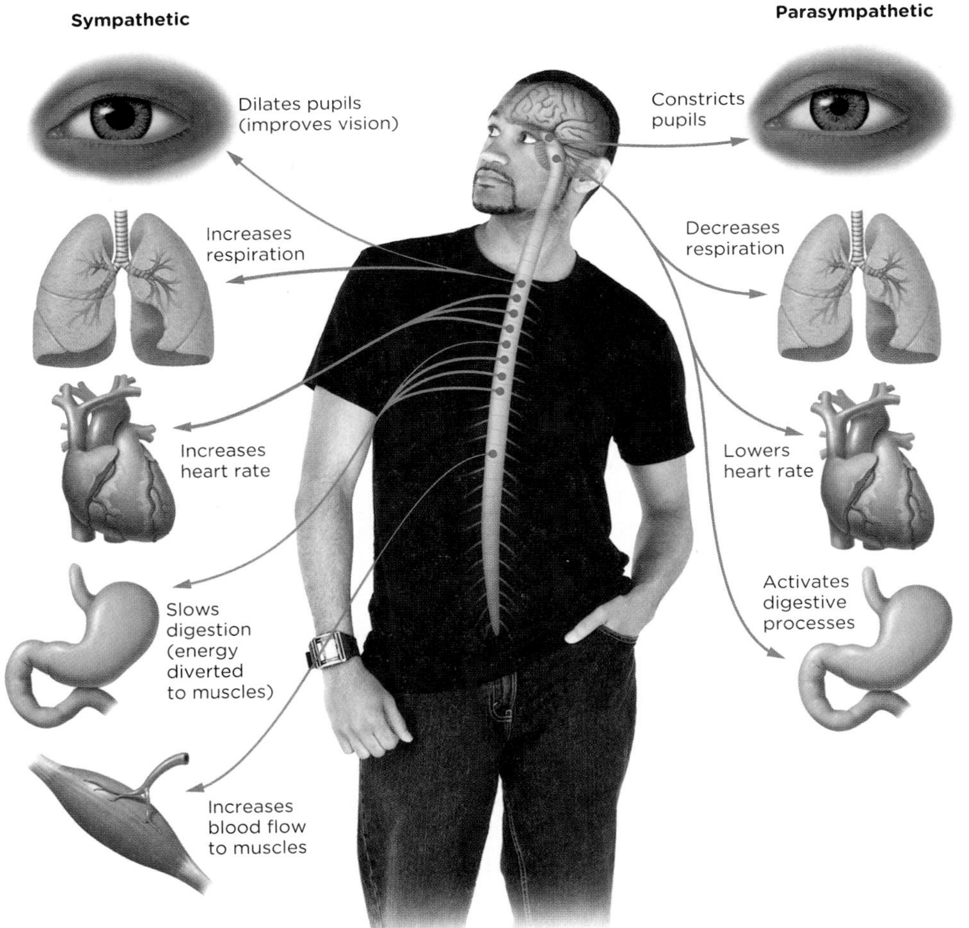

FIGURE 2.3
The Sympathetic and Parasympathetic Nervous Systems
The autonomic nervous system has two divisions, the sympathetic and parasympathetic nervous systems. In a stressful situation, the sympathetic nervous system initiates the "fight-or-flight" response. The parasympathetic nervous system calms the body when the stressful situation has passed. Photo: PhotoObjects.net/Thinkstock/Getty Images.

The fight-or-flight response would certainly come in handy if fleeing predators were part of your day-to-day life (as it may have been for our primitive ancestors), but you probably are not often chased by wild animals. You may, however, notice your heart racing and your breathing rate increase during other types of anxiety-producing situations—going on a first date, taking a test, or speaking in front of an audience. You have your sympathetic nervous system to thank for these effects (Chapter 12).

The **parasympathetic nervous system**, on the other hand, oversees the "rest-and-digest" process, which basically works to bring the body back to a noncrisis mode. When a crisis has ended, the parasympathetic nervous system reverses the activity initiated by the sympathetic system (for example, lowering heart rate and respiration, increasing digestion). The two systems work together, balancing the activities of these primarily involuntary processes. Sometimes they even have a common goal. For example, parasympathetic stimulation increases blood flow to the penis to create an erection, but it is the sympathetic system that causes ejaculation (Reynard, Brewster, & Biers, 2013). The parasympathetic and sympathetic systems allow us to fight or flee when necessary, and calm down when danger has passed.

The Endocrine System

How do you think 19-year-old Brandon Burns felt during the battle of Fallujah? There he was, right in the middle of one of the war's bloodiest battles. The sound of gunfire rang through the air; bullets zipped past his helmet; people were dying all around; his life could have ended at any moment. We cannot begin to imagine what thoughts and feelings Brandon had at this time, but one thing seems certain: He was under a great deal of stress.

When faced with imminent danger, the sympathetic nervous system responds almost instantaneously. Activity in the brain triggers the release of neurotransmitters that cause increases in heart rate, breathing rate, and metabolism—changes that will come in handy if you need to flee or defend yourself. But the nervous system does not act alone. The *endocrine system* is also hard at work, releasing stress hormones, such as *cortisol,* which prompt similar physiological changes.

LO 8 Summarize how the endocrine system influences behavior and physiological processes.

The **endocrine system** (EN-doe-krin) is a communication system that uses glands, rather than neurons, to send messages (**Figure 2.4**). These messages are conveyed by **hormones,** chemicals produced by the glands and released into the bloodstream. There are many types of hormones; some promote aggression and mood swings; others influence growth, alertness, cognition, and appetite. Like neurotransmitters, hormones are chemical messengers that affect many processes and behaviors. In fact, some chemicals, such as norepinephrine, can act as both neurotransmitters and hormones depending on where they are released. Neurotransmitters are unloaded into the synapse, whereas hormones are secreted into the bloodstream by endocrine glands stationed around the body.

When neurotransmitters are released into a synapse, their effects can be almost instantaneous. Hormones usually make long voyages to far-away targets by way of the bloodstream, creating a relatively delayed but usually longer-lasting impact. A neural impulse can travel over 250 mph, much faster than messages sent via hormones, which take minutes (if not longer) to arrive where they are going. However, the messages sent via hormones are more widely spread because they are delivered through the bloodstream.

parasympathetic nervous system The division of the autonomic nervous system that orchestrates the "rest-and-digest" response to bring the body back to a noncrisis mode.

endocrine system The communication system that uses glands to convey messages by releasing hormones into the bloodstream.

hormones Chemical messengers released into the bloodstream that influence mood, cognition, appetite, and many other processes and behaviors.

If the endocrine system had a chief executive officer, it would be the **pituitary gland,** a gland about the size of a pencil eraser located in the center of the brain, just under the *hypothalamus* (a structure we will explore later). Controlled by the hypothalamus, the pituitary gland, also known as the master gland, influences all the other glands, as well as promoting growth through the secretion of hormones.

The **thyroid gland** regulates the rate of metabolism by secreting *thyroxin,* and the **adrenal glands** (uh-DREEN-ul) are involved in stress responses and maintenance of salt balance. Other endocrine glands and organs directed by the pituitary include the pineal gland, which secretes melatonin (controls sleep–wake cycles); the pancreas, which secretes insulin (regulates blood sugar); and the ovaries and testes, which secrete sex hormones (cause differences in male and female development). Together, these glands and organs can impact: (1) growth and sex characteristics, (2) regulation of some of the basic body processes, and (3) responses to emergencies. Just as our behaviors are influenced by neurotransmitters we can't see and action potentials we can't feel, the hormones secreted by the endocrine system are also hard at work behind the scenes.

Now that we have discovered how information moves through the body via electrical and chemical signals, let's turn our attention toward the part of the nervous system that integrates this activity, creating a unified and meaningful experience. Time to explore the brain.

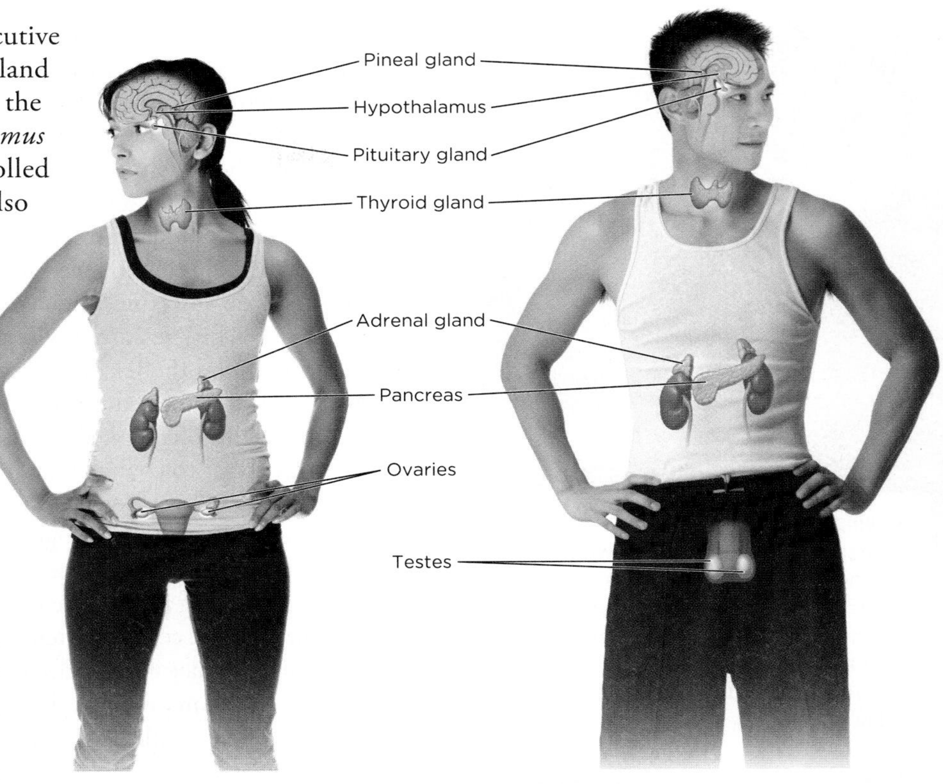

FIGURE 2.4
The Endocrine System
This system of glands conveys messages throughout the body by secreting hormones directly into the bloodstream.
Photos: (left, face) Hemera/Thinkstock/Getty Images; (left, body) © Yuri Arcurs/Alamy; (right) Asiaselects/Getty Images.

show what you know

1. The ____________ regulates involuntary activity, such as the pumping of the heart, the expansion and contraction of blood vessels, and digestion.
   a. reflex arc
   b. spinal cord
   c. autonomic nervous system
   d. somatic nervous system
2. The ____________ gland, located in the center of the brain, just under the hypothalamus, is in charge of the endocrine system.
3. As you recall, Brandon's brain injury led to paralysis on the right side of his body. What do you think would happen if a doctor tapped on his right knee—would he experience a reflex?

✓ CHECK YOUR ANSWERS IN APPENDIX C.

The Amazing Brain

THE GIRL WITH HALF A BRAIN As Brandon Burns began his long journey to recovery, a 17-year-old girl in Bristol, Pennsylvania, was enjoying a particularly successful senior year of high school. Christina Santhouse was an honor roll student for the fourth year in a row, and she had been named captain of the varsity bowling team. But these accomplishments did not come so easily. It took Christina twice

pituitary gland The small endocrine gland located in the center of the brain just under the hypothalamus; known as the master gland.

thyroid gland Endocrine gland that regulates the rate of metabolism by secreting thyroxin.

adrenal glands Endocrine glands involved in responses to stress as well as the regulation of salt balance.

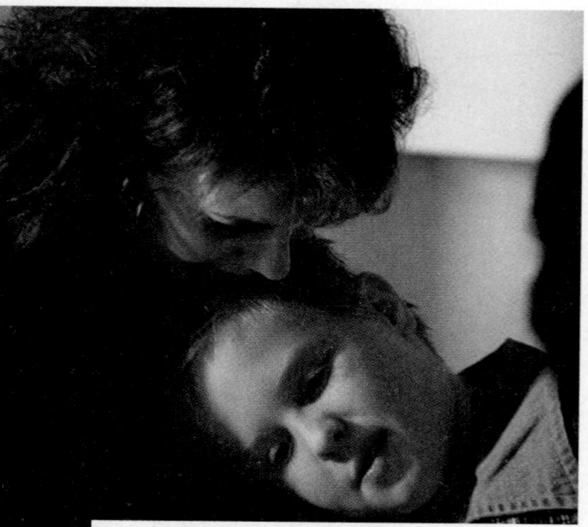

Staying Strong
Christina Santhouse relaxes with her mother at Johns Hopkins, where she had a dramatic brain surgery known as a hemispherectomy. Prior to the operation, Christina experienced hundreds of seizures a day. William Johnson.

as much time as classmates to do homework assignments because her brain needed extra time to process information. She had to invent a new bowling technique because the left side of her body was partially paralyzed, and she was constantly aware of being "different" from the other kids at school. Christina wasn't simply different from her classmates, however. She was extraordinary because she managed to do everything they did (and more) with nearly half of her brain missing.

Christina's remarkable story began when she was 7 years old. She was a vibrant, healthy child who loved soccer and playing outside with friends. Barring an occasional ear infection, she basically never got sick—that is, until the day she suffered her first seizure. It was the summer of 1995 and Christina's family was vacationing on the Jersey Shore. While playing in a swimming pool with her cousins, Christina hopped onto the deck to chase a ball and noticed that something wasn't quite right. She looked down and saw her left ankle twitching uncontrollably. Her life was about to change dramatically.

As the days and weeks wore on, the tremors in Christina's ankle moved up her left side and eventually spread throughout her body. In time, she was having seizures every 3 to 5 minutes. Doctors suspected she had Rasmussen's encephalitis, a rare disease that causes severe swelling in one side of the brain, impairing movement and thinking and causing seizures that come as often as every few minutes (Varadkar et al., 2014).

Christina, In Her Own Words

http://qrs.ly/c65a583

Macmillan Learning.

Christina and her mother decided to seek treatment at The Johns Hopkins Hospital in Baltimore, the premiere center for treating children with seizure disorders. They met with Dr. John Freeman, a pediatric neurologist and an expert in *hemispherectomy,* a surgery to remove nearly half of the brain. A rare and last-resort operation, the hemispherectomy is only performed on patients suffering from severe seizures that can't be controlled in other ways. After examining Christina, Dr. Freeman made the same diagnosis of her condition—Rasmussen's encephalitis—and indicated that the seizures would get worse, and they would get worse fast. He recommended a hemispherectomy and told Christina (and her mother) to let him know when she had reached her limit with the seizures. Then they would go ahead with the operation.

Why did Dr. Freeman recommend this drastic surgery to remove nearly half of Christina's brain? And what side of the brain did he suggest removing? Before addressing these important questions, we need to develop a general sense of the brain's geography. 

The Two Hemispheres

LO 9 Describe the two brain hemispheres and how they communicate.

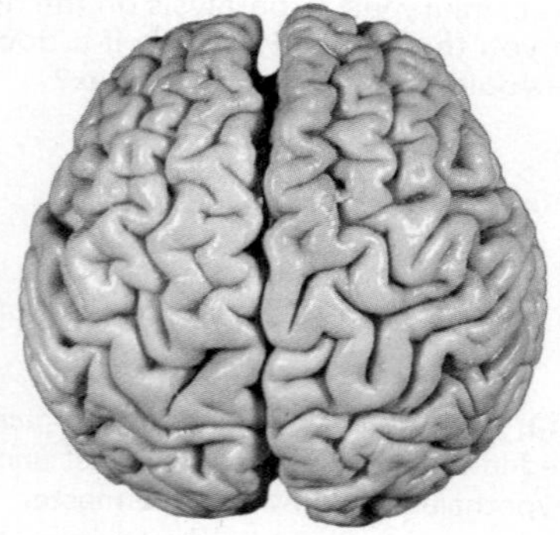

Two Hemispheres
The cerebrum looks like a walnut with its two wrinkled halves. Regions of the left and right hemispheres specialize in different activities, but the two sides of the brain are constantly communicating and collaborating. Science Source.

If you look at a photo or an illustration of the brain, you will see a walnut-shaped wrinkled structure—this is the **cerebrum** (Latin for "brain"), the largest and most conspicuous part of the brain. The cerebrum includes virtually all parts of the brain except the brainstem structures, which you will learn about later. Like a walnut, the cerebrum has two distinct halves, or *hemispheres.* Looking at the brain from above, you can see a deep groove running from the front of the head to the back, dividing it into the right cerebral hemisphere and the left cerebral hemisphere. The hemispheres may look like mirror images of one another, with similar structures on the left and right; but they are not perfectly symmetrical, nor do they have identical jobs. The two hemispheres are linked by a bundle of nerve fibers known as the **corpus callosum** (KOR-pus kuh-LOW-sum). Through the corpus callosum, the left and right sides of the brain communicate and work together to process information. Generally speaking, the right hemisphere controls the left side of the body, and the left hemisphere controls the right. This explains why Brandon, who was shot on the *left* side of his head, suffered paralysis and loss of sensation on the *right* half of his body. Christina's situation is roughly the opposite. Rasmussen's encephalitis struck the *right* side of her brain, which explains why her *left* ankle started twitching at the pool and why all her subsequent seizures affected the left side of her body. This is why Dr. Freeman recommended the removal of her right hemisphere.

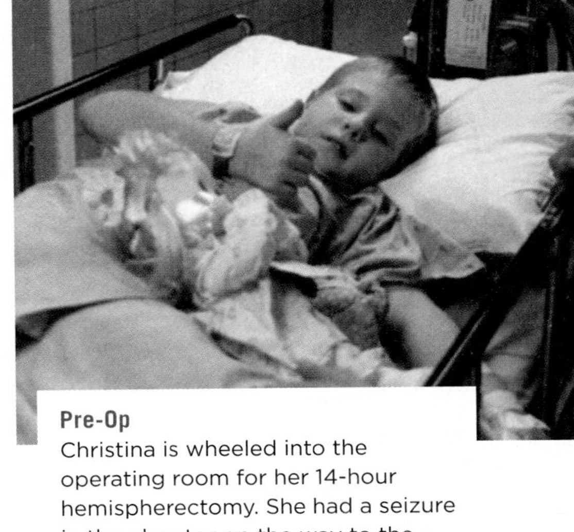

Pre-Op
Christina is wheeled into the operating room for her 14-hour hemispherectomy. She had a seizure in the elevator on the way to the surgery. William Johnson.

CHRISTINA MAKES THE DECISION Within 2 months, Christina's seizures were occurring every 3 minutes, hundreds of times a day. She was unable to play soccer or go outside during school recess, and she sat on a beanbag chair in class so she wouldn't hurt herself when overcome with a seizure. "I couldn't do anything anymore," Christina says. "I wasn't enjoying my life."

In February 1996 the doctors at Johns Hopkins removed the right hemisphere of Christina's brain. The operation lasted some 14 hours. When Christina emerged from the marathon surgery, her head was pounding with pain. "I remember screaming and asking for medicine," she recalls. The migraines persisted for months but eventually tapered off, and ultimately the surgery served its purpose: Christina no longer experienced debilitating seizures.

The Split-Brain Operation

Removing nearly half of a brain may sound barbaric, but hemispherectomies have proven to be effective for eliminating and reducing seizures, with success rates from multiple studies ranging from 54% to 90% (Lew, 2014). In a study from the Cleveland Clinic, 83% of hemispherectomy patients could walk independently nearly 13 years after surgery. Meanwhile, 70% possessed good spoken language skills, and 42% were able to read satisfactorily (Moosa et al., 2013).

Hemispherectomies are only used for cases that do not respond to drugs and other interventions, and are characterized by seizures originating in one hemisphere (Lew, 2014). Another less extreme, last-resort surgery for drug-resistant seizures is the **split-brain operation**, which essentially disconnects the right and left hemispheres. Normally, the two hemispheres communicate through the corpus callosum. But this same band of nerve fibers can also serve as a passageway for the electrical storms responsible for seizures. With the split-brain operation, the corpus callosum is severed so that these storms can no longer pass freely between the hemispheres (Wolman, 2012, March 15).

synonyms
split-brain operation callosotomy

LO 10 Define lateralization and explain what the split-brain experiments reveal about the right and left hemispheres.

STUDYING THE SPLIT BRAIN In addition to helping many patients with severe, drug-resistant epilepsy (Abou-Khalil, 2010), split-brain operations have provided researchers with an excellent opportunity to explore the specialization of the hemispheres. Before we start to look at this research, you need to understand how visual information is processed. Each eye receives visual sensations, but information presented in the right visual field is processed in the left hemisphere, and information presented in the left visual field is processed in the right hemisphere.

Equipped with this knowledge, American neuropsychologist Roger Sperry and his student Michael Gazzaniga conducted groundbreaking research on epilepsy patients who had undergone split-brain operations to alleviate their seizures. Not only did Sperry

cerebrum The largest part of the brain, includes virtually all parts of the brain except brainstem structures; has two distinct hemispheres.

corpus callosum The thick band of nerve fibers connecting the right and left cerebral hemispheres; principal structure for information shared between the two hemispheres.

split-brain operation A rare procedure used to disconnect the right and left hemispheres by cutting the corpus callosum.

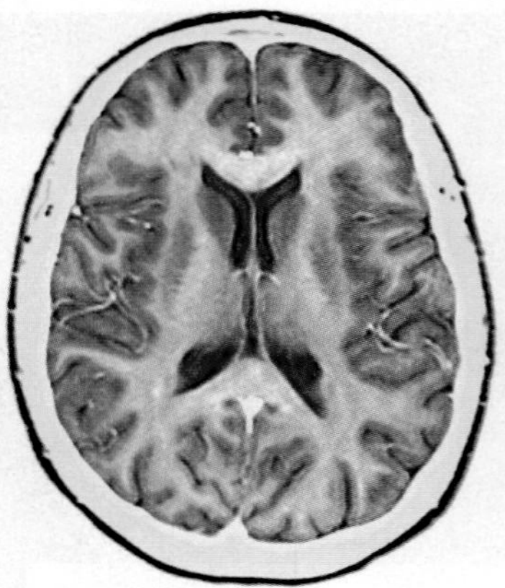

Hemispherectomy
On the left is an MRI scan of a brain with both hemispheres intact. The scan on the right shows the brain of a person who has undergone a hemispherectomy. The green area, once occupied by the removed hemisphere, is now filled with cerebrospinal fluid. Medical body Scans/Science Source.

and Gazzaniga's "split-brain" participants experience fewer seizures, they had surprisingly normal cognitive abilities and showed no obvious changes in "temperament, personality, or general intelligence" as a result of their surgeries (Gazzaniga, 1967, p. 24). But under certain circumstances, the researchers observed, they behaved as though they had two separate brains (Gazzaniga, 1967, 1998; **Figure 2.5**).

Because the hemispheres are disconnected through the surgery, researchers can study each hemisphere separately to explore its own unique capabilities (or specializations). Imagine that researchers flashed an image (let's say an apple) on the right side of a screen, ensuring that it would be processed by the brain's *left* hemisphere. The split-brain participant could articulate what she had seen (*I saw an apple*). If, however, the apple appeared on the left side of the screen (processed by the *right* hemisphere), she would claim she saw nothing. But when asked to identify the image in a nonverbal way (pointing or touching with her left hand), she could do this without a problem (Gazzaniga, 1967, 1998).

LATERALIZATION The split-brain experiments offered an elegant demonstration of **lateralization**, the tendency for the left and right hemispheres to excel in certain activities. When images are flashed in the right visual field, the information is sent to the left side of the brain, which excels in language processing. This explains why the split-brain participants were able to articulate the image they had seen on the right side of the screen. Images appearing in the left visual field are sent to the right side of the brain, which excels at visual-spatial tasks but is generally not responsible for processing language. Thus, the participants were tongue-tied when asked to report what they had seen on the left side of the screen. They could, however, reach out and point

FIGURE 2.5
The Split-Brain Experiment
An example of a "split-brain" experiment is shown below.

I see an apple.
I don't see anything.

Information presented in right visual field is sent to the left hemisphere where language processing occurs. Participant can speak the answer.

Information presented in left visual field is sent to the right hemisphere. Participant can't use language to say what he was shown.

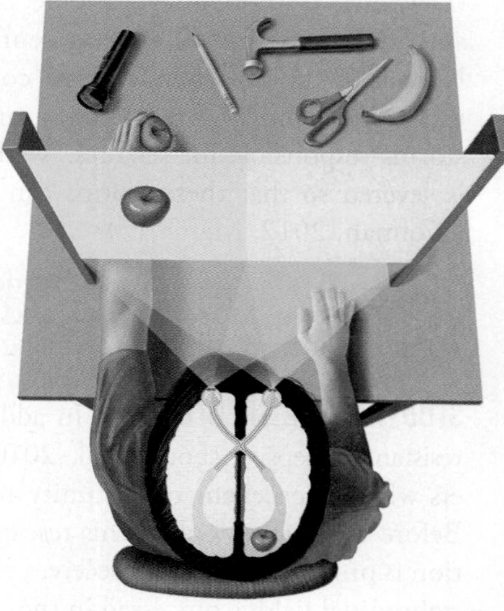

Touch the object matching the image on the screen.

The participant can touch the correct object even if he can't say what has been projected in his left visual field. The participant uses his left hand, which is controlled by the right hemisphere, where the visual information has been processed.

to it using their left hand, which is controlled by the right hemisphere (Gazzaniga, 1998; Gazzaniga, Bogen, & Sperry, 1965).

The split-brain studies revealed that the left hemisphere plays a crucial role in language processing and the right hemisphere in managing visual-spatial tasks. These are only generalizations, however. While there are clear differences in the way the hemispheres process information (and the speed at which they do it), they can also process the same types of information. In a split-brain individual, communication between the hemispheres is limited. This is *not* the case for someone with an intact corpus callosum. The hemispheres are constantly integrating and sharing all types of information (Lilienfeld, Lynn, Ruscio, & Beyerstein, 2011; Pinto et al., 2017). Next time you hear someone claim that certain personality and cognitive characteristics are associated with being "left-brained" or "right-brained," ask him to identify research to back it up (Nielsen, Zielinski, Ferguson, Lainhart, & Anderson, 2013; Schmerling, August, 2017), because there is no evidence for this strict dividing line between right and left-brain activities. Similarly, beware of catchy sales pitches for products designed to increase your "logical and analytical" left-brain thinking or to help you tap into the "creative" right brain (Staub, 2016). This way of thinking is oversimplified. Keep this in mind while reading the upcoming sections on specialization in the left and right sides of the brain. The two hemispheres may have certain areas of expertise, but they work as a team to create your experience of the world.

Speak Again
Brandon works on his pronunciation in front of a mirror during a speech therapy session at the Memphis VA hospital. You can see the extent of his injury on the left side of his head. Upon awaking from his coma, Brandon could not articulate a single word. Today, he can hold his own in complex conversations. Photo by A. J. Wolfe/The Commercial Appeal/Zuma Press.

Roles of the Left and the Right

Armed with this new knowledge of the split-brain experiments, let's return our focus to Brandon. Brandon's injury occurred on the left side of his brain, devastating his ability to use language. Before the battle of Fallujah, he had breezed through Western novels at breakneck speeds. After his injury, even the simplest sentence baffled him. Words on a page looked like nothing more than black lines and curls. Brandon remembers, "It was like a puzzle that I couldn't figure out." Brandon's difficulties with language are fairly typical for someone with a brain injury to the left hemisphere, because regions of the left hemisphere tend to predominate in language. This is not true for everyone, however. The left hemisphere handles language processing in around 95% to 99% of people who are right-handed, but only in about 70% of those who are left-handed (Corballis, 2014).

LO 11 Identify areas in the brain responsible for language production and comprehension.

LANGUAGE PRODUCTION AND COMPREHENSION Evidence for the "language on the left" notion appeared as early as 1861, when a French surgeon named Pierre Paul Broca (1824–1880) encountered two patients who had, for all practical purposes, lost the ability to talk. One of the patients could only say the word "tan," and the other had an oral vocabulary of five words. When Broca later performed autopsies on the men, he found that both had sustained damage to the same area on the side of the left frontal lobe (right around the temple; see **Figure 2.6** on next page). Over the years, Broca identified several other speech-impaired patients with damage to the same area, a region now called **Broca's area** (BRO-kuz) (Greenblatt, Dagi, & Epstein, 1997; Wickens, 2015), which is involved in speech production.

Around the same time Broca was doing his research, a German doctor named Karl Wernicke (1848–1905) pinpointed a different place in the left hemisphere

lateralization The idea that each cerebral hemisphere processes certain types of information and excels in certain activities.

Broca's area A region of the cortex that is critical for speech production.

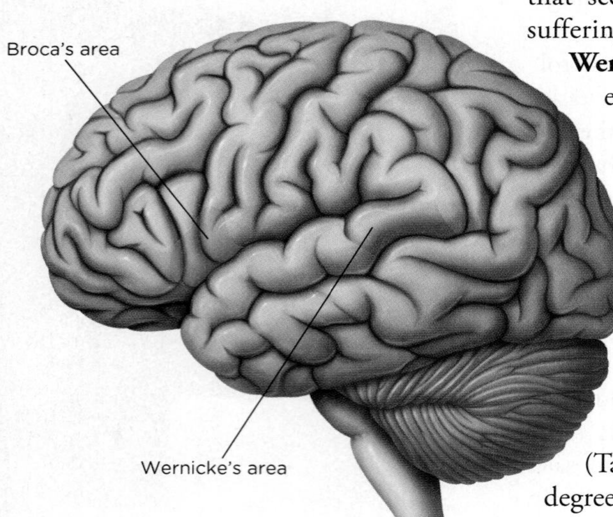

FIGURE 2.6
Language Areas of the Brain
For most people, the left hemisphere controls language. Broca's area plays a critical role in language production, and Wernicke's area in language comprehension.

that seemed to control speech comprehension. Wernicke noticed that patients suffering damage to a small tract of tissue in the left temporal lobe, now called **Wernicke's area** (VAIR-nick-uhz), struggled to make sense of what others were saying. Wernicke's area is the brain's headquarters for language comprehension (Wickens, 2015).

Broca's and Wernicke's work, along with other early findings, highlighted the left hemisphere's critical role in language. Scientists initially suspected that Broca's area was responsible for speech creation and Wernicke's area for comprehension, but it is now clear that language processing is far more complicated (Berwick, Friederici, Chomsky, & Bolhuis, 2013). These areas may perform additional functions, such as processing music and interpreting hand gestures (Schlaug, 2015; Xu, Gannon, Emmorey, Smith, & Braun, 2009), and they cooperate with multiple brain regions to allow us to produce and understand language (Tate, Herbet, Moritz-Gasser, Tate, & Duffau, 2014). Furthermore, a certain degree of speech processing appears to occur in the right hemisphere, and some researchers propose that other parts of the brain may also be involved in generating speech (Tate et al., 2014).

THE ROLE OF THE RIGHT We know that the left hemisphere tends to dominate in language processing, but where does the right hemisphere excel? Research suggests that the right hemisphere surpasses the left when it comes to identifying mirror images and spatial relationships, and mentally rotating images (Gazzaniga, 2005). The right side of the brain also appears to specialize in understanding abstract and humorous use of language (Coulson & Van Petten, 2007), and is somewhat better at following conversations that change topic (Dapretto, Lee, & Caplan, 2005). This hemisphere also plays a key role in recognizing faces and processing information about the faces of people who are chewing or exhibiting emotional expressions (De Winter et al., 2015; Kanwisher, McDermott, & Chun, 1997; Rossion, 2014). And while the left hemisphere seems to focus on creating hypotheses and exploring causality, the right hemisphere appears more involved in evaluating hypotheses, and rejecting those that lack supporting evidence (Marinsek, Turner, Gazzaniga, & Miller, 2014).

You Asked, Christina Answers

http://qrs.ly/c65a583

What kind of therapy did you have and for how long?

Put Your Heads Together

In your groups, discuss the following: **A**) How is a split-brain operation different from a hemispherectomy? **B**) If you were faced with a hypothetical decision to undergo a hemispherectomy, which half of your brain would you choose to have removed and why? **C**) What functions might you lose as a result?

CHRISTINA WAKES UP When Christina was wheeled out of surgery, her mother approached, grabbed hold of her right hand, and asked her to squeeze. Christina squeezed, demonstrating that she could understand and respond to language. Remember, she still had her left hemisphere.

Losing the right side of her brain did come at a cost, however. We know that Christina suffers partial paralysis on the left side of her body; this makes sense, because the right hemisphere controls movement and sensation on the left. We also know that it took Christina extra time to do her schoolwork. But if you ask Christina whether she has significant difficulty with any of the "right-brain" tasks described earlier, her answer will be no.

Wernicke's area A region of the cortex that plays a pivotal role in language comprehension.

In addition to making the honor roll and leading the bowling team, Christina managed to get her driver's license (even though some of her doctors said she never would), graduate from high school, and go to college. These accomplishments are the result of Christina's steadfast determination, but also a testament to the brain's amazing ability to heal and regenerate. 

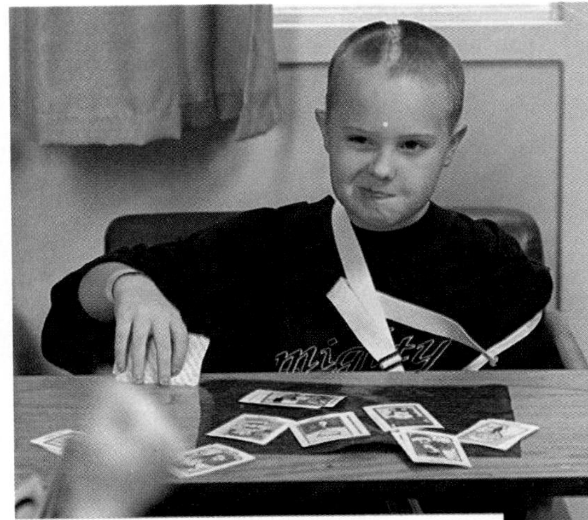

Brain Games
Christina's dramatic recovery was facilitated by physical, occupational, vision, and speech therapy. "The more therapy," says Christina, "the better chance of recovery." William Johnson.

Neuroplasticity

LO 12 Define neuroplasticity and recognize when it is evident in the brain.

The brain undergoes constant alteration in response to experiences, and is capable of some degree of physical adaptation and repair. Its ability to heal, grow new connections, and make do with what is available is a characteristic we refer to as **neuroplasticity.** New connections are constantly forming between neurons, and unused ones are fading away. Vast networks of neurons have the ability to reorganize in order to adapt to the environment and an organism's ever-changing needs, a quality particularly evident in the young. After brain injuries, younger children have better outcomes than adults; their brains show more plasticity, although this depends somewhat on the type of injury (Johnston, 2009; Su, Veeravagu, & Grant, 2016).

As you learned from Christina's example, the remarkable plasticity of the young brain is also evident in hemispherectomy patients. Even after the loss of an entire left hemisphere (the primary location for language processing), speech abilities may be retained, although some impact is inevitable. The younger the patient, the better the outcome; however, factors such as language delays prior to surgery and ongoing seizures after surgery can impact further language development (Choi, 2008, March; Moosa et al., 2013).

In one study, researchers **removed the eyes**  of newborn opossums and found that brain tissues normally destined to become visual processing centers took a developmental turn. Instead, they became areas that specialized in processing other types of sensory stimuli, such as sounds and touch (Karlen, Kahn, & Krubitzer, 2006). The same appears to happen in humans. Brain scans reveal that when visually impaired individuals learn to read Braille early in life, a region of the brain that normally specializes in handling visual information becomes activated. This suggests that visual processing centers are being used for another purpose—processing touch sensations (Burton, 2003; Lazzouni & Lepore, 2014; Liu et al., 2007).

CONNECTIONS
In **Chapter 1,** we described the guidelines psychologists use to ensure the ethical treatment of humans and animals. In order to conduct the experiment described here, the researchers had to get pre-approval from an ethics board. The board determined that the animals would be treated humanely and that the proposed research necessitated this surgery.

STEM CELLS Scientists once thought that people were born with all the neurons they would ever have. Brain cells might die, but no new ones would crop up to replace them. Thanks to research beginning in the 1990s, that dismal notion has been turned on its head (Sailor, Schinder, & Lledo, 2017). In the last few decades, studies with animals and humans have shown that some areas of the brain are capable of generating new neurons, a process known as **neurogenesis,** which might be tied to learning and creating new memories (Eriksson et al., 1998; Gould, Beylin, Tanapat, Reeves, & Shors, 1999; Jessberger & Gage, 2014). A recent study suggests that neurogenesis occurs in the hippocampus during childhood, but probably not into adulthood (Sorrells et al., 2018).

The cells responsible for churning out these new neurons are known as **stem cells,** and they are quite a hot topic in biomedical research. Scientists hope to harness these little cell factories to repair tissue that has been damaged or destroyed. Imagine that you could use stem cells to bring back all the neurons that Brandon lost from his injury or replace those that Christina lost to surgery.

neuroplasticity The brain's ability to heal, grow new connections, and reorganize in order to adapt to the environment.

neurogenesis The generation of new neurons in the brain.

stem cells Cells responsible for producing new neurons.

Cure All?
Because stem cells can differentiate into any type of cell in the body, they have great therapeutic potential. The cells pictured here are derived from a human embryo, but stem cells also reside in various adult tissues such as the brain and bone marrow. Professor Mlodrag Stojkovic/Science Source.

Cultivating new brain tissue is just one potential application of stem cell science. These cellular cure-alls might also be used to alleviate the symptoms of Parkinson's disease, or replenish neurons of the spine, enabling people with spinal cord injuries to regain movement. Both have already been accomplished in mice, and some clinical trials are underway for stem cell therapy targeting Parkinson's and restoring function after spinal cord injury (Kegel, 2017, April; Keirstead et al., 2005; Schroeder, Kepler, & Vaccaro, 2016; Wernig et al., 2008). Although embryonic stem cells can be used for such purposes, some stem cells can be found in tissues of the adult body, such as the brain and bone marrow. There has been great hope that "adult-born neurons" might be used to repair injured brain tissue, but a growing body of evidence suggests it may be beyond their capability. Still, researchers have not given up, and studies are ongoing (Lois & Kelsch, 2014; Peretto & Bonfanti, 2015).

The Cortex: A Peek Beneath the Skull

Imagine you were one of the surgeons performing Christina's hemispherectomy. What exactly would you see when you peeled away the scalp and cut an opening into the skull? Before seeing the brain, you would come upon a layer of three thin membranes, the *meninges,* which envelop and protect the brain and spinal cord (see **Infographic 2.4**). Perhaps you have heard of meningitis, a potentially life-threatening condition in which the meninges become inflamed as a result of an infection. The meninges are bathed in a clear watery substance called cerebrospinal fluid, which offers additional cushioning and helps transport nutrients and waste in and out of the central nervous system. Once you peeled back the meninges, you would behold the pink cerebrum.

As Christina's surgeon, your main task would be to remove part of the cerebrum's outermost layer, the **cerebral cortex** (suh-REE-brul). The cerebral cortex processes information and is the layer of cells surrounding nearly all the other brain structures. You'll remember our earlier comment that the cerebrum looks like a wrinkled walnut. This is because the cortex is scrunched up and folded onto itself to fit inside a small space (the skull). This outermost section of the brain is also the part that is "newest," or most recently evolved compared to the "older" structures closer to its core. We know this because researchers have compared the brains of humans with other primates. The structures we share with our primate relatives are considered more primitive, or less evolved, than the structures unique to humans.

LO 13 Identify the lobes of the cortex and explain their functions.

The cortex overlying each hemisphere is separated into different sections, or lobes. The major function of the **frontal lobes** is to organize information among the other lobes of the brain. The frontal lobes also direct higher-level cognitive functions, such as thinking, perception, and impulse control. The **parietal lobes** (puh-RY-uh-tul) receive and process sensory information like touch, pressure, temperature, and spatial orientation. Visual information goes to the **occipital lobes** (ok-SIP-i-tul) for processing, and hearing and language comprehension are largely handled by the **temporal lobes.** We'll have more to say about the lobes as we discuss each in turn below (see **Table 2.2** on page 68).

cerebral cortex The wrinkled outermost layer of the cerebrum, responsible for higher mental functions, such as decision making, language, and processing visual information.

frontal lobes The area of the cortex that organizes information among the other lobes of the brain and is responsible for cognitive functions, such as thinking, perception, and impulse control.

parietal lobes The area of the cortex that receives and processes sensory information such as touch, pressure, temperature, and spatial orientation.

occipital lobes The area of the cortex in the back of the head that processes visual information.

temporal lobes The area of the cortex that processes auditory stimuli and language.

The Lobes: Up Close and Personal

Prior to her hemispherectomy, Christina was extroverted, easygoing, and full of energy. "I had absolutely no worries," she says, recalling her pre-Rasmussen's days.

Getting Into the Brain

Finding Personality in the Brain

In 1848 an accidental blast drove a 3-foot iron bar through the head of railroad worker Phineas Gage. He survived, but his personality was markedly changed. Previously described as having a "well-balanced" mind, post-injury Gage was prone to angry outbursts and profanity (Harlow, 1868, 1869, as cited in Macmillan, 2000).

Phineas Gage holding the iron bar that injured him.

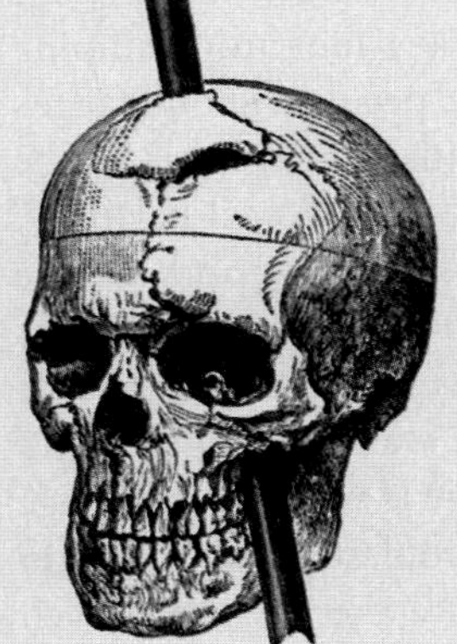

Using measurements from his fractured skull, scientists have been able to estimate where the damage occurred (Ratiu, Talos, Haker, Lieberman, & Everett, 2004; Van Horn et al., 2012). Cases like this have helped psychologists understand the role of different structures in the brain.

Getting TO the Brain

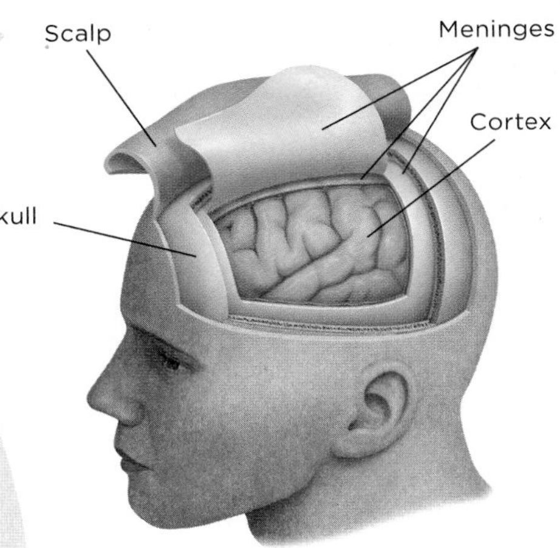

In order to study the brain, we must get to it first. Peel away the scalp and cut away the bony skull, and you will find still more layers of protection. Three thin membranes—the meninges—provide a barrier to both physical injury and infection. Bypass them, and the outermost layer of the brain, the cortex, is revealed.

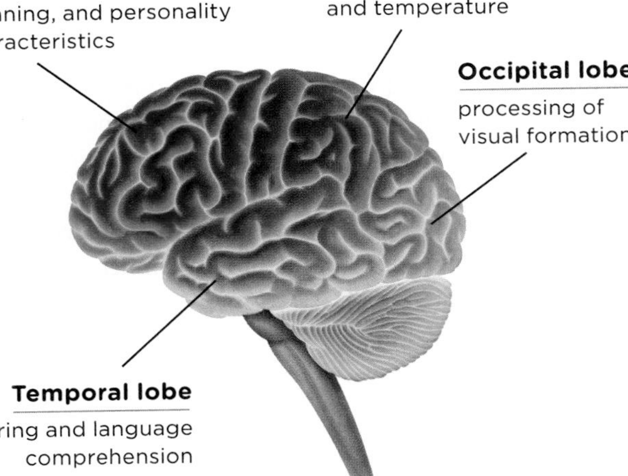

Lobes of the Brain

This drawing shows the left hemisphere of the brain. Each hemisphere is divided into lobes, which are associated with certain functions.

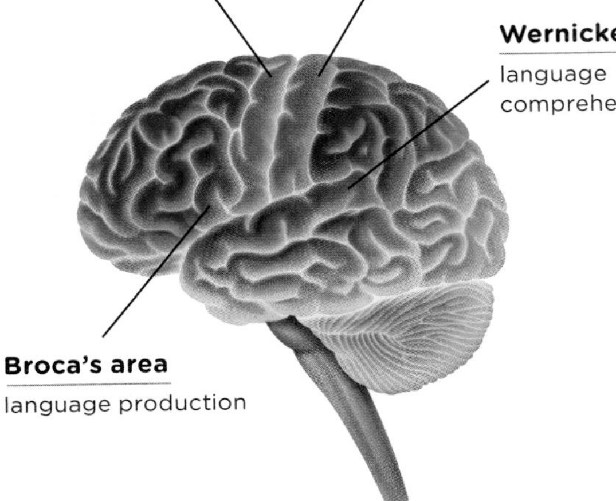

Specialized Areas of the Brain

Unlike the lobes, which are associated with many functions, some areas of the brain have one specialized function.

Phineas Gage photo: Warren Anatomical Museum in the Francis A. Countway Library of Medicine. Gift of Jack and Beverly Wilgus.

Enjoying Life
Christina, as a teenager, walking her dog. The left side of her body is partially paralyzed, but her gait is quite natural. She wears a device on her left leg that activates her nerves, causing her muscles to contract at the appropriate time. William Johnson.

After her operation, Christina became more introverted and passive. She felt more emotionally unsettled. "You go into surgery one person," she says, "and you come out another."

The transformation of Christina's personality may be a result of many factors, including the stress of dealing with a serious disease, undergoing a major surgery, and readjusting to life with disabilities. But it could also have something to do with the fact that she lost a considerable amount of brain tissue, including her right frontal lobe. Networks of neurons in the frontal lobes are involved in processing emotions, making plans, controlling impulses, and carrying out a vast array of mental tasks that each person does in a unique way (Williams, Suchy, & Kraybill, 2010). The frontal lobes play a key role in the development of personality and many of its characteristics (Forbes et al., 2014; Stuss & Alexander, 2000). A striking illustration of this phenomenon involves an unlucky railroad foreman, Phineas Gage.

PHINEAS GAGE AND THE FRONTAL LOBES The year was 1848, and Phineas Gage was working on the railroad. An accidental explosion sent a 3-foot iron tamping rod clear through his frontal lobes (Infographic 2.4). What's peculiar about Gage's accident (besides the fact that he was walking and talking just hours later) is the extreme transformation it caused. Before the accident, Gage was a well-balanced, diligent worker whom his supervisors referred to as their "most efficient and capable foreman" (Harlow, 1848, as cited in Neylan, 1999, p. 280). After the accident, he was unreliable, unpleasant, and downright vulgar. His character was so altered that people acquainted with him before and after the accident claimed he was "no longer Gage" (Harlow, 1848, as cited in Neylan, 1999, p. 280). However, there is evidence that Gage recovered to some degree, illustrating again the remarkable neuroplasticity of the brain (Griggs, 2015a). He spent almost 8 years working as a horse caretaker and stagecoach driver after the accident (Harlow, 1968, 1969, as cited in Macmillan, 2000).

The only good thing about Gage's horrible accident, it seems, is that it illuminated the importance of the frontal lobes in defining personality characteristics.

CARTOONS AND THE MOTOR CORTEX Toward the rear of the frontal lobes is a strip of the brain known as the **motor cortex**, which works with other areas to plan and execute voluntary movements (Infographic 2.4). North American neurosurgeon Wilder Penfield (1891–1976) conducted research to create a map showing which points along the motor cortex corresponded to the various parts of the body (Penfield & Boldrey, 1937). Penfield's map is often represented by the "homunculus" (huh-MUN-kyuh-lus; Latin for "little man") cartoon, a distorted image of a human being with huge lips and hands and a tiny torso (**Figure 2.7**). The size of each body part in the figure roughly reflects the amount of cortex devoted to it, which explains why parts requiring extremely fine-tuned motor control (the mouth and hands) are gigantic in comparison to other body parts.

CONNECTIONS

In **Chapter 1,** we discussed the importance of having a representative sample and the potential problems with using case studies to make generalizations about the population. Comparing Einstein (a single participant) to the control group could be considered a type of case study, and may be problematic on both counts.

ALBERT EINSTEIN AND THE PARIETAL LOBES Directly behind the frontal lobes on the crown of your head are the parietal lobes (Infographic 2.4). The parietal lobes help orient the body in space, are involved in tactile processing (for example, interpreting sensations related to touch, such as pain and pressure), and may play a role in mathematical reasoning associated with spatial cognition (Desco et al., 2011; Grabner et al., 2007; Wolpert, Goodbody, & Husain, 1998). A study published in 1999 **compared the brain of Albert Einstein** to a control group of 35 brain specimens from men who had donated their bodies for use

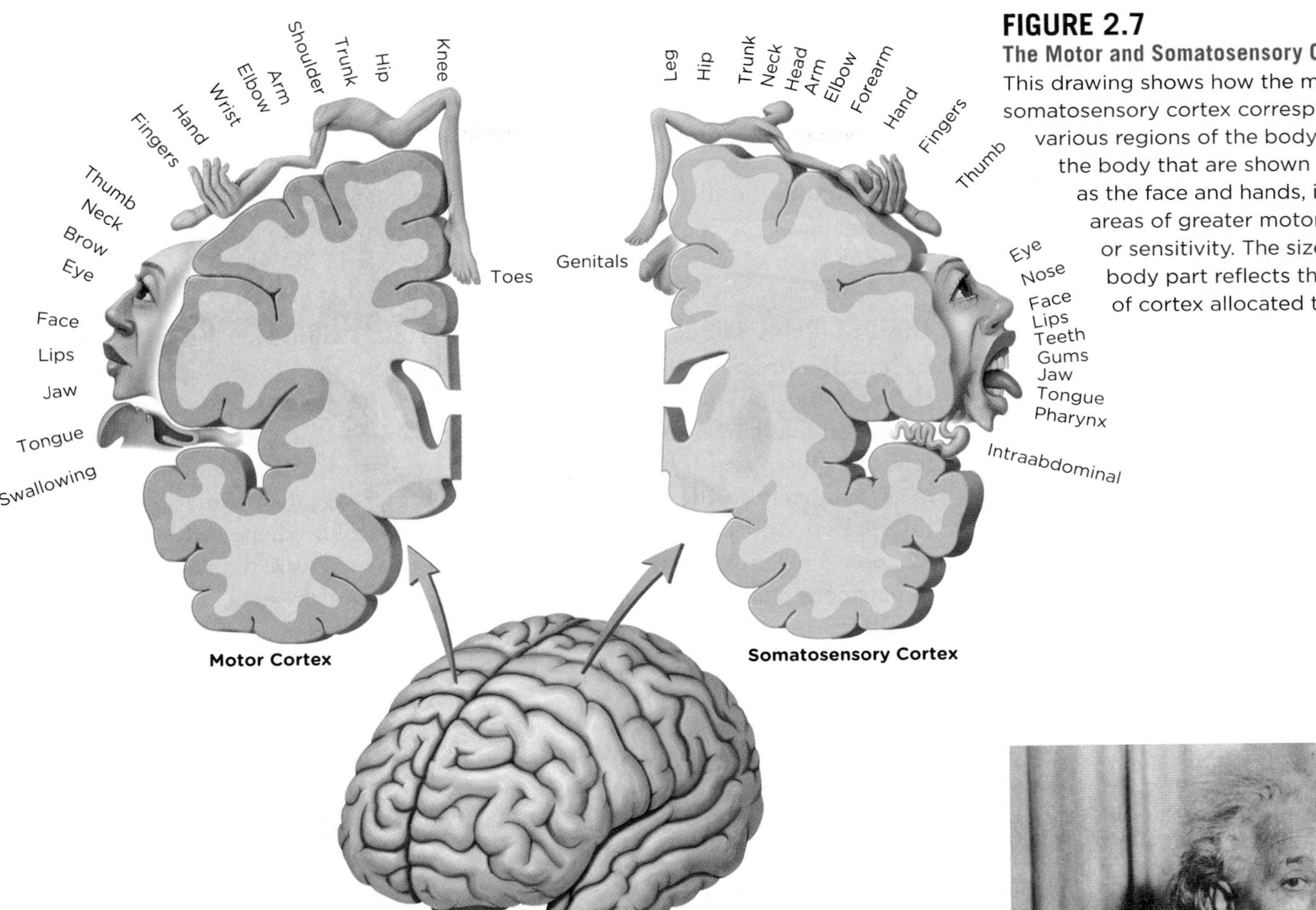

FIGURE 2.7
The Motor and Somatosensory Cortex
This drawing shows how the motor and somatosensory cortex correspond to the various regions of the body. Parts of the body that are shown larger, such as the face and hands, indicate areas of greater motor control or sensitivity. The size of each body part reflects the amount of cortex allocated to it.

in research. Prior to their deaths, these men had normal cognitive functioning, average intelligence, and no mental health issues. The researchers reported that Einstein's brain did not exceed the average brain weight of the control group, but a region of his parietal lobe believed to be important for visual–spatial processing was 15% larger. They proposed that the differences in that specific region of Einstein's parietal lobe may have been linked to his "exceptional intellect" in areas of visual-spatial cognition and mathematical thinking (Witelson, Kigar, & Harvey, 1999). We are left to wonder how Einstein's experiences (nurture) molded the structure of his brain; for example, his long history playing the violin may have contributed to a "large 'knob'-shaped fold" in the part of his cortex responsible for movement of his left hand (Chen, Chen, Zeng, Zhou, & Hou, 2014).

Superbrain
A postmortem examination of Albert Einstein's brain revealed his "extraordinary prefrontal cortex" (Falk, Lepore, & Noe, 2012, p. 1). The irregularities in Einstein's parietal lobes may explain some of his spectacular mathematical and visual-spatial abilities (Witelson et al., 1999; Falk et al., 2012). Could it be that Einstein's mathematical activities caused changes to his parietal lobes? Keystone/Getty Images.

PENFIELD AND THE SOMATOSENSORY CORTEX The parietal lobes are home to the **somatosensory cortex,** a strip of brain running parallel to the motor cortex, which receives and integrates sensory information from all over the body (pain and temperature signals, for example). Penfield, the neurosurgeon mentioned earlier, also created a map for the somatosensory cortex similar to that of the motor cortex (Penfield & Boldrey, 1937; Figure 2.7). As you might expect, the most sensitive areas of the body like the face and tongue are oversized on the homunculus, whereas less sensitive areas, such as the forearm and the calf, are smaller.

motor cortex A band of tissue toward the rear of the frontal lobes that works with other brain regions to plan and execute voluntary movements.

somatosensory cortex A band of tissue running parallel to the motor cortex that receives and integrates sensory information from all over the body.

Seeing Stars
If you have ever been struck or fallen on the back of the head, you may recall perceiving bright blobs or dots floating by. The occipital lobes at the rear of the brain are home to the visual processing centers. Repeated blows to the head may lead to the development of chronic traumatic encephalopathy (CTE). For more on CTE, see Chapters 6 and 7.
Toshifumi Kitamura/Getty Images.

THE TEMPORAL LOBES AND THE AUDITORY CORTEX Below the parietal lobes, on the sides of your head, are the temporal lobes, which process auditory stimuli, recognize visual objects, especially faces, and play a key role in language comprehension and memory (Hickok & Poeppel, 2000; Infographic 2.4). The temporal lobes are home to the *auditory cortex,* which receives information from the ears and allows us to "hear" sounds. Studies of primate vocalizations suggest that the ability to recognize language has evolved over time and is processed within the temporal lobes (Scott, Blank, Rosen, & Wise, 2000; Squire, Stark, & Clark, 2004).

THE OCCIPITAL LOBES AND THE PRIMARY VISUAL CORTEX Visual information is initially processed in the occipital lobes, in the lower back of the head (Infographic 2.4). If you have ever suffered a severe blow to the rear of your head, you may remember "seeing stars," probably because activity in the occipital lobes was disrupted (hopefully only for a few seconds). It is here, where the optic nerve connects to the *primary visual cortex,* that visual information is received, interpreted, and processed (for example, about color, shape, and motion). (See Chapter 3 for more on the visual process.) If this area were damaged, severe visual impairment could occur—even in a person with healthy eyes. Yet, the individual would still be able to "see" vivid *mental* images (Bridge, Harrold, Holmes, Stokes, & Kennard, 2012).

TABLE 2.2 REGIONS OF THE CORTEX

Structure	Function and Importance
Association areas	Integrate information from all over the brain; allow us to learn, have abstract thoughts, and carry out complex behaviors.
Broca's area	Involved in speech production; helps us generate speech.
Corpus callosum	Connects the hemispheres; allows the left and right sides of the brain to communicate and work together to process information.
Frontal lobes	Organize information among the other lobes of the brain; responsible for higher-level cognitive functions, such as thinking, perception, and impulse control.
Left cerebral hemisphere	Controls the right side of the body; excels in language processing.
Motor cortex	Plans and executes voluntary movements; allows us to move our body.
Occipital lobes	Process visual information; help us see.
Parietal lobes	Receive and process sensory information; orient the body in space.
Primary visual cortex	Receives and interprets visual information; allows us to "see" vivid mental images.
Right cerebral hemisphere	Controls the left side of the body; excels in visual-spatial tasks.
Somatosensory cortex	Receives and integrates sensory information from the body; for example, helps us determine if the touch we feel is pleasurable or painful.
Temporal lobes	Comprehension of hearing and language; process auditory stimuli; recognize visual objects; key role in language comprehension and memory.
Wernicke's area	Controls language comprehension; enables us to make sense of what is being said.

The cortex, or outermost layer of the brain, can be divided into functionally significant areas.

Describe the association areas and identify their functions.

THE ASSOCIATION AREAS In addition to the different lobes described above, the cortex contains **association areas** whose role is to integrate information from all over the brain. The association areas are located in all four lobes; however, they are much harder to pinpoint than the motor and sensory areas. These areas allow us to learn (just as you're doing now), to have abstract thoughts (for example, 2 + 2 = 4), and to carry out complex behaviors like texting and tweeting. The language-processing hubs we learned about earlier, *Broca's area* and *Wernicke's area,* are association areas that play a role in the production and comprehension of speech. In humans, the vast majority of the brain's cortex is dedicated to the association areas.

synonyms

association areas intrinsic processing areas

SOCIAL MEDIA AND PSYCHOLOGY

FACEBOOK IN THE BRAIN A major theme of this chapter is localization of function, the idea that certain areas of the brain tend to specialize in performing certain tasks. When we say "tasks," we mean just about any activity you can imagine, from riding a bicycle to managing friend networks on Facebook.

FACEBOOK FRIENDS: A GRAY MATTER

The average number of Facebook "friends" is 338, but the friend tally varies significantly from one person to the next, ranging from zero to 5,000, the maximum allowed by Facebook (Facebook Help Center, 2015; Pew Research Center, 2014, February 3). What does a Facebook friend number reveal about a person—job networking skills, offline popularity, time wasted at work? According to one preliminary study, friend volume may reflect something about the brain of the user.

Using MRI technology, researchers studied the brain structures of a sample of Facebook users. They discovered a correlation between the number of Facebook friends and the density of gray matter (the primary tissue of the cerebral cortex) in areas of the brain important for social interaction. One of those regions, the *superior temporal sulcus,* is thought to be important for detecting socially meaningful movements such as hand gestures and eye shifts. Another, known as the *entorhinal cortex,* appears to play a key role in matching faces to names, a critical skill for Facebookers (Kanai, Bahrami, Roylance, & Rees, 2012). As anyone with a few hundred friends can testify, keeping track of all those names and faces can be challenging.

We should point out that this study is correlational. So it cannot reveal whether the number of friends causes changes in brain structure, or whether the characteristics of the brain structures determine the number of friends. Perhaps some other variable is responsible for both. While there remain many unknowns, one thing seems certain: Social media provides psychologists with a whole new laboratory for studying the brain and social behavior. There is no shortage of data: "Each day, people send one billion posts to Facebook, tweet 400 million messages through Twitter, upload 12 years' worth of videos to YouTube, and make 300,000 edits to Wikipedia" (Meshi, Tamir, & Heekeren, 2015, p. 771).

You Asked, Christina Answers

http://qrs.ly/c65a583

How does your condition affect your confidence and social life?

Put Your Heads Together

This section introduced the lobes of the cortex and their associated functions. In your group, come up with two strategies to remember the lobes of the cortex and their functions.

We have now explored the brain's outer layer, or cortex, where a variety of high-level processes occur. Thanks to your cortex, you can read maps, calculate your monthly budget, learn new languages, and plan your daily life. What happens to the precious cortex as you age?

association areas Regions of the cortex that integrate information from all over the brain, allowing us to learn, think in abstract terms, and carry out other intellectual tasks.

"SUPER AGERS" HAVE BRAINS THAT LOOK YOUNG

Older adults who perform like young people on tests of memory have a shrink-resistant cortex.

As we get older, we start to think a little bit more slowly, we are less able to multitask, and our ability to remember things gets a little wobblier. This cognitive transformation is linked to a steady, widespread thinning of the cortex, the brain's outermost layer. Yet the change is not inevitable. So-called super agers retain their good memory and thicker cortex as they age, a recent study suggests.

Researchers believe that studying what makes super agers different could help unlock the secrets to healthy brain aging and improve our understanding of what happens when that process goes awry. "Looking at successful aging could provide us with biomarkers for predicting resilience and for things that might go wrong in people with age-related diseases like Alzheimer's and dementia," says study co-author Alexandra Touroutoglou, a neuroscientist at Harvard Medical School.

Touroutoglou and her team gave standard recall tests to a group of 40 participants between the ages of 60 and 80 and 41 participants aged 18 to 35. Among the older participants, 17 performed as well as or better than adults four to five decades younger. When the researchers looked at MRI scans of the super agers' brains, they found that their brains not only functioned more like young brains, they also looked very similar.

Two brain networks in particular seemed to be protected from shrinking: the default mode network, which helps to store and recall new information, and the salience network, which is associated with directing attention and identifying important details. In fact, the thicker these regions were, the better the super agers' memory was.

The results, which were published in . . . the *Journal of Neuroscience,* corroborate previous research that shows these regions are critical communication hubs in the brain. The findings do not explain why super agers have these thicker cortical regions, although most likely it is a combination of genetic factors and a healthy way of life. If confirmed by other studies, the discovery of shrink-resistant brain regions in super agers could provide a target for future research on aging-related brain changes, says Emily Rogalski, a cognitive neuroscientist at Northwestern University who also studies super agers but was not involved in the new study. She notes that "we will be better able to investigate the cellular, molecular and genetic mechanisms that keep superagers' cortices thicker" and their minds shipshape. **Knvul Sheikh. Reproduced with** ■

show what you know

1. The left hemisphere excels in language and the right hemisphere excels in visual-spatial tasks. This specialization of the two hemispheres is known as:
   a. split-brain.
   b. callosotomy.
   c. hemispherectomy.
   d. lateralization.

2. A man involved in a car accident suffered severe brain trauma. Following the accident, he had difficulty producing speech, even though he could understand what people were saying. It is very likely he had suffered damage to the left frontal lobe in a part of the brain referred to as:
   a. Wernicke's area.
   b. Broca's area.
   c. the visual field.
   d. the corpus callosum.

3. How do the two brain hemispheres communicate? How does this change after a split-brain operation?

4. The brain is constantly undergoing alterations in response to experiences, and is capable of a certain degree of physical adaptation and repair. This ability is known as:
   a. neuroplasticity.
   b. phrenology.
   c. ablation.
   d. lateralization.

5. The major function of the _______________ is to organize information among the other lobes of the brain.
   a. parietal lobes
   b. frontal lobes
   c. corpus callosum
   d. temporal lobes

6. Briefly describe the lobes of the cortex and their associated functions.

✓ CHECK YOUR ANSWERS IN APPENDIX C.

Let's Dig a Little Deeper

Now that we have surveyed the brain's outer terrain, identifying some of the hotspots for language and other higher cognitive functions, let's dig deeper and examine some of its structures (see **Table 2.3** on page 73).

Drama Central: The Limbic System

LO 15 Distinguish the structures and functions of the limbic system.

Buried beneath the cortex is the **limbic system,** a group of interconnected structures that play an important role in our experiences of emotion, motivation, and memory. It also fuels our most basic drives, such as hunger, sex, and aggression. The limbic system includes the *hippocampus, amygdala, thalamus,* and *hypothalamus* (**Figure 2.8**).

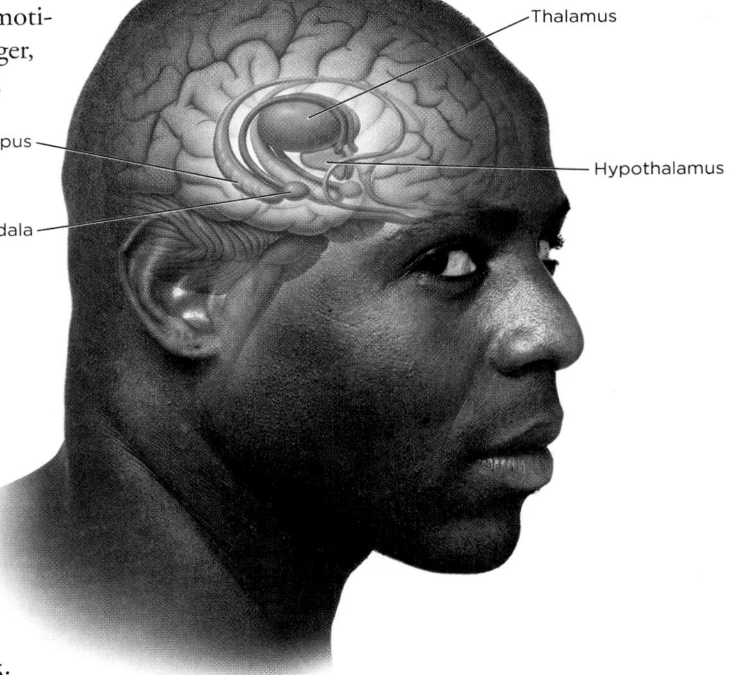

FIGURE 2.8
The Limbic System
The limbic system fuels basic drives and processes emotions and memories. Photo: Stockbyte/Getty Images.

HIPPOCAMPUS The largest structure in the limbic system is a pair of C-shaped structures called the hippocampus. The **hippocampus** is primarily responsible for processing and forming new memories from experiences, but it is not where memories are permanently stored (see Chapter 6 on memory; Eichenbaum, 2004). Given its key role in memory, it may come as no surprise that the hippocampus is one of the brain areas affected by Alzheimer's disease (Henneman et al., 2009; Hsu et al., 2015). On the brighter side of things, the hippocampus is also one of the few places in the brain known to generate new neurons throughout life (Eriksson et al., 1998; Tate et al., 2014; Sailor et al., 2017).

AMYGDALA Another structure of the limbic system is the **amygdala** (uh-MIG-duh-la), which processes aggression and basic emotions such as fear, and the memories associated with them (Janak & Tye, 2015; Kluver & Bucy, 1939). Having spent many months in a war zone, Brandon encountered more than his fair share of fear-provoking experiences. On one occasion, he was riding at nearly 60 mph in a Humvee that spun out of control and almost flipped over. "My heart was beating faster than ever before," Brandon recalls. In dangerous situations like this, the amygdala is activated and the nervous system orchestrates a whole-body response (racing heart, sweaty palms, and the like), as well as an emotional reaction (fear).

Life-threatening situations are not only common in war; they occasionally occur in everyday life. When faced with a potentially dangerous scenario, the brain must determine whether a real threat exists. In such cases, the amygdala shares information with areas in the frontal lobes to make this assessment (Likhtik, Stujenske, Topiwala, Harris, & Gordon, 2014). Once a situation is deemed safe, the frontal lobes give the amygdala an "all clear" signal and fear diminishes. Like many parts of the nervous system, the amygdala has structural divisions that seem to play different roles; in assessing the threat of a situation, some structures come into play immediately (reflexive behavior occurs), while others react slightly later as attention is focused on the threat (voluntary behavior results). The speed of our fear reactions depends on these types of "dual routes" (de Gelder, Hortensius, & Tamietto, 2012; see Chapter 9). The amygdala also helps us to perceive and experience a wide range of positive emotions, with processing speed depending on the intensity of the emotion (Bonnet et al., 2015).

THALAMUS Seated at the center of the limbic system is the **thalamus** (THAL-uh-muss), whose job is to process and relay information to the appropriate parts of the cortex.

limbic system A collection of structures that regulates emotions and basic drives like hunger, and aids in the creation of memories.

hippocampus A pair of structures located in the limbic system; primarily responsible for creating new memories.

amygdala A pair of almond-shaped structures in the limbic system that processes aggression and basic emotions such as fear, as well as associated memories.

thalamus A structure in the limbic system that processes and relays sensory information to the appropriate areas of the cortex.

For example, the great majority of the data picked up by the sensory systems pass through the thalamus before moving on to the cortex for processing (Mitchell, 2014b). You might think of the thalamus as an air traffic control tower guiding incoming aircraft; when pilots communicate with the tower, the controllers direct their routes or tell them what runway to use.

HYPOTHALAMUS Just below the thalamus is the **hypothalamus** (hi-po-THAL-uh-muss; *hypo* means "under" in Greek), which keeps the body's systems in a steady state, making sure variables like blood pressure, body temperature, and fluid/electrolyte balance remain within a healthy range. When faced with an emergency, the hypothalamus and endocrine system work together to help us cope with perceived threats (Chapter 12). The hypothalamus is also involved in regulating sleep–wake cycles (Saper, Scammell, & Lu, 2005; Xu et al., 2015), sexual arousal, and appetite (Hurley & Johnson, 2014). For example, neurons from the digestive system send signals to the hypothalamus (such as "stomach is empty"), which then sends signals to higher regions of the brain (such as "it's time to eat"). But deciding what and when to eat does not always come down to being hungry or full. Other brain areas are involved in eating decisions and can override the hypothalamus, driving you to polish off the french fries or scarf down that chocolate bar even when you are not that hungry.

What Roles Do the Brainstem and Cerebellum Play?

The brain is made up of structures responsible for processes as complex as rebuilding a car's engine or selecting the right classes for a degree program. But delve deeper and you will find structures that control more primitive functions.

Distinguish the structures and functions of the brainstem and cerebellum.

COMPONENTS OF THE BRAINSTEM The brain's ancient core consists of a stalklike trio of structures called the *brainstem* (**Figure 2.9**). The brainstem, which includes the midbrain, pons, and medulla, extends from the spinal cord to the *forebrain*, which is the largest part of the brain and includes the cerebral cortex and the limbic system, discussed above.

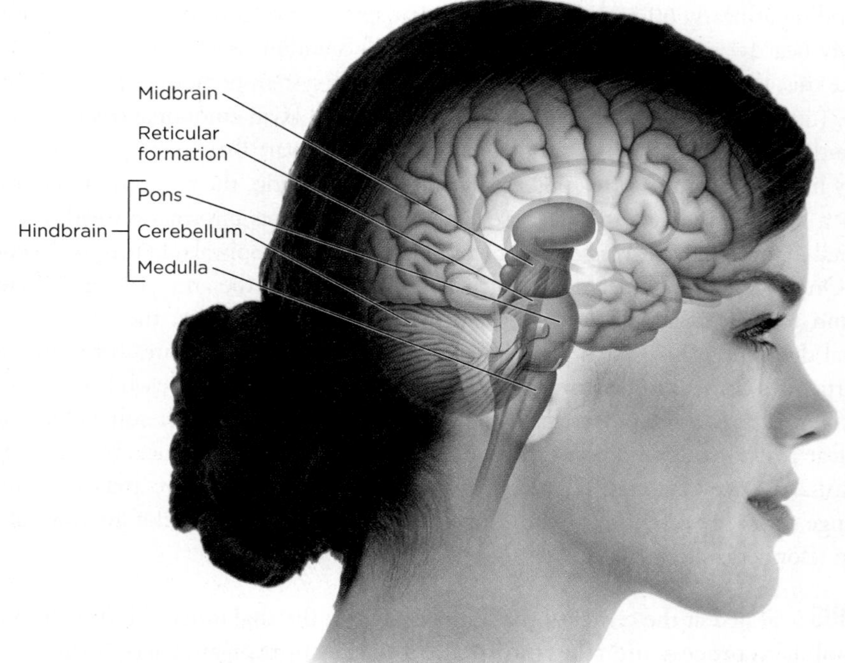

FIGURE 2.9
The Brainstem and Cerebellum
Located beneath the structures of the limbic system, the brainstem includes the midbrain, pons, and medulla. These structures are involved in arousal, movement, and life-sustaining processes. The cerebellum is important for muscle coordination and balance and, when paired with the pons and medulla, makes up the hindbrain. Photo: Onoky/Corbis.

TABLE 2.3 BELOW THE CORTEX: STRUCTURES TO KNOW

Structure	Function and Importance
Amygdala	Processes aggression and basic emotions like fear, and the memories associated with them.
Cerebellum	Involved in muscle coordination and balance.
Forebrain	The largest part of the brain that includes the cerebral cortex and limbic system.
Hindbrain	Responsible for fundamental life-sustaining processes.
Hippocampus	Primarily responsible for processing and forming new memories from experiences.
Hypothalamus	Keeps the body's systems in a steady state.
Limbic system	Group of interconnected structures that play a role in our experiences of emotion, motivation, and memory; fuels basic drives, such as hunger, sex, and aggression.
Medulla	Oversees functions such as breathing and heart rate.
Midbrain	Plays a role in levels of arousal; home to neurons that help generate movement patterns in response to sensory input.
Pons	Helps regulate sleep-wake cycles and coordinates movement between the right and left sides of the body.
Reticular formation	Responsible for levels of arousal and our ability to selectively attend to important incoming sensory data.
Thalamus	Processes and relays sensory information to the cortex.

Tucked below the cortex are brain structures with a variety of different functions. Make sure you are familiar with these key regions.

The top portion of the brainstem is known as the **midbrain**, and although there is some disagreement about which brain structures belong to the midbrain, most agree it plays a role in levels of arousal. The midbrain is also home to neurons that help generate movement patterns in response to sensory input (Stein, Stanford, & Rowland, 2009). For example, if someone shouted "Look out!," neurons in your midbrain would play a role when you flinch. Also located in the midbrain is part of the **reticular formation**, an intricate web of neurons that is responsible for levels of arousal—whether you are awake, dozing off, or somewhere in between. The reticular formation also helps you selectively attend to important information and ignore what's irrelevant, by sifting through sensory data on its way to the cortex. Imagine how overwhelmed you would feel by all the sights, sounds, tastes, smells, and physical sensations in your environment if you didn't have a reticular formation to help you discriminate between information that is important (the sound of a honking car horn) and that which is trivial (the sound of a dog barking in the distance).

The **hindbrain** includes areas of the brain responsible for fundamental life-sustaining processes. The **pons**, which helps regulate sleep–wake cycles and coordinates movement between the right and left sides of the body, is an important structure of the hindbrain. The pons sits atop the **medulla** (muh-DUL-uh), a structure that oversees some of the body's most vital functions, including breathing and heart rate maintenance (Broadbelt, Paterson, Rivera, Trachtenberg, & Kinney, 2010).

CEREBELLUM Behind the brainstem, just above the nape of the neck, sits the orange-sized **cerebellum** (sehr-uh-BELL-um). (Latin for "little brain," the cerebellum looks like a mini-version of the whole brain.) Centuries ago, scientists found that removing parts of the cerebellum from animals caused them to stagger, fall, and act clumsy. Although the cerebellum is best known for its importance in muscle coordination and balance, researchers are exploring how this "little brain" influences higher cognitive processes in the "big brain," such as abstract reasoning and language production (Fine, Ionita, & Lohr, 2002; Mariën et al., 2014).

synonyms

reticular formation reticular activating system

hypothalamus A small structure located below the thalamus that maintains a constant internal environment within a healthy range; helps regulate sleep-wake cycles, sexual behavior, and appetite.

midbrain The part of the brainstem involved in levels of arousal; responsible for generating movement patterns in response to sensory input.

reticular formation A network of neurons running through the midbrain that controls levels of arousal and quickly analyzes sensory information on its way to the cortex.

hindbrain Includes areas of the brain responsible for fundamental life-sustaining processes.

pons A hindbrain structure that helps regulate sleep-wake cycles and coordinate movement between the right and left sides of the body.

medulla A structure that oversees vital functions, including breathing, digestion, and heart rate.

cerebellum A structure located behind the brainstem that is responsible for muscle coordination and balance; Latin for "little brain."

Put Your Heads Together

Now that you are almost finished reading this chapter, you probably realize how hard your brain works 24/7, often in ways beyond your awareness. In your group, **A)** choose an important activity that you would like to examine (for example, giving a presentation in class, going on a first date) and discuss how specific structures of the **B)** limbic system, **C)** brainstem, and **D)** cerebellum may be involved.

show what you know

1. The specific brain structure that processes basic emotions, such as fear and aggression and the memories associated with them, is the ________________.
2. The primary role of the thalamus is to:
   a. relay sensory information.
   b. keep the body's systems in a steady state.
   c. generate movement patterns in response to sensory input.
   d. regulate sleep-wake cycles.
3. The structure located behind the brainstem that is responsible for muscle coordination and balance is the ________________.

✓ CHECK YOUR ANSWERS IN APPENDIX C.

WHERE ARE THEY NOW? You may be wondering what became of Brandon Burns and Christina Santhouse. Three years after returning from Iraq, Brandon married a young woman named Laura who has witnessed his dramatic recovery. When Laura first met Brandon, he had a lot of trouble communicating his thoughts. His sentences were choppy; he often omitted words and spoke in a flat and emotionless tone. "His speech was very delayed, very slow," Laura recalls. Now he is able to use more humor and emotion, articulate his thoughts in lengthy, complex sentences; read a book; and write for his website. Much of Brandon's time is spent caring for his three young children. He also works in a church ministry and in that capacity has traveled to numerous countries, including Haiti, Kenya, and Honduras.

As for Christina, she continues to reach for the stars—and grab them. After studying speech-language pathology at Misericordia University in Dallas, Pennsylvania, for 5 years (and making the dean's list nearly every semester), Christina graduated with both a bachelor's and master's degree. But those years were not smooth sailing.

Life Is Good
Three years after his traumatic brain injury, Brandon celebrated his marriage to Laura. The couple now has three children. Laura Burns.

Hard at Work
With her master's degree in speech-language pathology, Christina now works full time in Pennsylvania's public school system. Bucks County Courier Times/Calkins Media, Inc.

Christina remembers the department chairman telling her that she wouldn't be able to handle the rigors of the program. According to Christina, on graduation day, that same chairman presented her with the department's Outstanding Achievement Award. "People often don't expect too much from people with disabilities," she says.

Today, Christina works as a full-time speech–language pathologist in Pennsylvania's public school system, helping elementary schoolchildren overcome their difficulties with stuttering, articulation, and other speech problems. She is also a member of the local school district's Brain STEPS team, which supports students who are transitioning back into school following brain injuries. "Hopefully, I have opened some doors for other people with disabilities," Christina offers. "There were never doors open for me; I've had to bang them down."

You Asked, Christina Answers

http://qrs.ly/c65a583

Which medical professional had the biggest impact on your recovery?

THINK POSITIVE

THE VERSATILE BRAIN Brandon and Christina provide breathtaking illustrations of neuroplasticity—the brain's ability to heal, grow new connections, and make do with what is available. These amazing changes can occur under a variety of circumstances—after a stroke, in the face of blindness, and even adapting to motherhood (Convento, Russo, Zigiotto, & Bolognini, 2016; Hasson, Andric, Atilgan, & Collignon, 2016; Kim, Strathearn, & Swain, 2016). Your brain can change, too. Every time you acquire knowledge or learn a new skill, whether it's cooking Pad Thai or plucking out melodies on a guitar, new networks of communication are sprouting between your neurons (Barss, Pearcey, & Zehr, 2016; Vaquero et al., 2016). Expose yourself to new information and activities, and your brain will continue to develop and adapt. There is no limit to the amount you can learn!

YOUR BRAIN CAN CHANGE, TOO

The stories of Brandon and Christina also highlight the importance of maintaining hope, even in the face of stress and daunting obstacles (Abel, Hayes, Henley, & Kuyken, 2016; Brady et al., 2016). There were many times Brandon and Christina could have lost hope and wallowed in self-pity, but instead they decided to fight. So, too, did the neuropsychologists, physical therapists, occupational therapists, speech pathologists, and other professionals who assisted in their rehabilitation. The recoveries of Brandon and Christina bear testimony to the awesome tenacity of the human spirit.

CAREER CONNECTIONS

NEUROSCIENCE Now that you have finished the chapter, you may be wondering how this material will be useful in your career. If your field of choice is psychology, the connection is obvious, but what if you plan to pursue a career in nursing, business, social work, education, or some other non-psychology field? Researchers have confirmed that "students' brains continuously adapt to the environments where they live and work, including school, home, workplaces, community centers, and so forth" (Hinton, Fischer, & Glennon, 2012, p. 3). Our interactions with our environments literally shape the "architecture of the brain" (p. 3). What does this mean for you as a student? Engagement and participation are crucial to learning; active participation and hands-on experiences, both in and outside of the classroom, are key (Hinton et al., 2012). Whether you are interested in a traditional academic track or a technical education, remember to be an active learner; the neural networks in your brain will be stronger, and you will be more prepared for your career.

ACTIVE PARTICIPATION IS KEY TO EFFECTIVE LEARNING AND CAREER SUCCESS

YOUR SCIENTIFIC WORLD is a new application-based feature appearing in every chapter. In these online activities, you will take on role-playing scenarios that encourage you to think critically and apply your knowledge of psychological science to solve a real world problem. For example: What is it like to live with a brain injury? Step inside a rehabilitation center and learn how brain injuries impact daily functioning. You can access Your Scientific World activities in LaunchPad. Have fun!

SUMMARY OF CONCEPTS

LO 1 Define neuroscience and biological psychology and explain how they contribute to our understanding of behavior. (p. 42)

Neuroscience is the study of the nervous system and the brain, and it overlaps with a variety of disciplines and research areas. Biological psychology is a subfield of psychology focusing on how the brain and other biological systems influence behavior.

LO 2 Compare and contrast tools scientists use to study the brain. (p. 42)

Researchers use a variety of technologies to study the brain. An electroencephalogram (EEG) detects electrical impulses in the brain. Computerized axial tomography (CAT) uses X-rays to create many cross-sectional images of the brain. Magnetic resonance imaging (MRI) uses a magnet and pulses of radio waves to produce more detailed cross-sectional images; both MRI and CAT scans only reveal the structure of the brain. Positron emission tomography (PET) uses radioactivity to track glucose consumption to construct a map of the brain. Functional magnetic resonance imaging (fMRI) captures changes in brain activity by tracking patterns of blood flow.

LO 3 Label the parts of a neuron and describe an action potential. (p. 45)

A typical neuron has three basic parts: a cell body, dendrites, and an axon. The dendrites receive messages from other neurons, and branches at the end of the axon send messages to neighboring neurons. These messages are electrical and chemical in nature. An action potential is the electrical signal that moves down the axon, causing a neuron to send chemical messages across the synapse. Action potentials are all-or-none, meaning they either fire or do not fire.

LO 4 Illustrate how neurons communicate with each other. (p. 48)

Neurons communicate with each other via chemicals called neurotransmitters. An action potential moves down the axon to the axon terminal, where neurotransmitters are released. Most of the neurotransmitters released into the synapse drift across the gap and come into contact with receptor sites of the receiving neuron's dendrites.

LO 5 Describe specific neurotransmitters and summarize how their activity affects human behavior. (p. 48)

Neurotransmitters are chemical messengers that neurons use to communicate. There are many types of neurotransmitters, including acetylcholine, glutamate, GABA, norepinephrine, serotonin, dopamine, and endorphins, and each has its own type of receptor site. Neurotransmitters can influence mood, cognition, behavior, and many other processes.

LO 6 Explain how the central and peripheral nervous systems connect. (p. 53)

The brain and spinal cord make up the central nervous system (CNS), which communicates with the rest of the body through the peripheral nervous system (PNS). There are three types of neurons participating in this back-and-forth communication: Motor neurons carry information from the CNS to various parts of the body such as muscles and glands; sensory neurons relay data from the sensory systems (for example, eyes and ears) to the CNS for processing; and interneurons, which reside exclusively in the CNS, act as bridges connecting sensory and motor neurons. Interneurons mediate the nervous system's most complex operations, including sensory processing, memory, thoughts, and emotions.

LO 7 Describe the organization and function of the peripheral nervous system. (p. 54)

The peripheral nervous system is divided into two branches: the somatic nervous system and the autonomic nervous system. The somatic nervous system controls the skeletal muscles that enable voluntary movement. The autonomic nervous system regulates the body's involuntary processes and has two divisions: the sympathetic nervous system, which initiates the fight-or-flight response, and the parasympathetic nervous system, which oversees the rest-and-digest processes.

LO 8 **Summarize how the endocrine system influences behavior and physiological processes. (p. 56)**

Closely connected with the nervous system, the endocrine system uses glands to send messages around the body. These messages are conveyed by hormones—chemicals released into the bloodstream that can cause aggression and mood swings, and influence growth and alertness, among other things.

LO 9 **Describe the two brain hemispheres and how they communicate. (p. 58)**

The cerebrum includes virtually all parts of the brain except for the primitive brainstem structures. It is divided into two hemispheres: the right cerebral hemisphere and left cerebral hemisphere. The left hemisphere controls most of the movement and sensation on the right side of the body. The right hemisphere controls most of the movement and sensation on the left side of the body. Connecting the two hemispheres is the corpus callosum, a band of fibers that enables them to communicate.

LO 10 **Define lateralization and explain what the split-brain experiments reveal about the right and left hemispheres. (p. 59)**

Researchers have gleaned valuable knowledge about the brain hemispheres from experiments on split-brain patients—people whose hemispheres have been surgically disconnected. Under certain experimental conditions, people who have had the split-brain operation act as if they have two separate brains. By observing the brain hemispheres operating independent of one another, researchers have discovered that each hemisphere excels in certain activities, a phenomenon known as lateralization. Generally, the left hemisphere excels in language and the right hemisphere excels in visual-spatial tasks.

LO 11 **Identify areas in the brain responsible for language production and comprehension. (p. 61)**

Several areas in the brain are responsible for language processing. Located on the side of the left frontal lobe is Broca's area, which is primarily responsible for speech production. Located in the left temporal lobe is Wernicke's area, which is primarily responsible for language comprehension.

LO 12 **Define neuroplasticity and recognize when it is evident in the brain. (p. 63)**

Neuroplasticity is the ability of the brain to form new connections between neurons and adapt to changing circumstances. Networks of neurons, particularly in the young, can reorganize to adapt to the environment and an organism's ever-changing needs.

LO 13 **Identify the lobes of the cortex and explain their functions. (p. 64)**

The outermost layer of the cerebrum is the cerebral cortex. The cortex is separated into different sections called lobes. The major function of the frontal lobes is to organize information among the other lobes of the brain. The frontal lobes are also responsible for higher-level cognitive functions, such as thinking and personality characteristics. The parietal lobes receive and process sensory information such as touch, pressure, temperature, and spatial orientation. Visual information goes to the occipital lobes for processing. The temporal lobes are primarily responsible for hearing and language comprehension.

LO 14 **Describe the association areas and identify their functions. (p. 69)**

The association areas in the cortex integrate information from all over the brain, allowing us to learn, have abstract thoughts, and carry out complex behaviors.

LO 15 **Distinguish the structures and functions of the limbic system. (p. 71)**

The limbic system is a group of interconnected structures that play an important role in our emotions and memories. The limbic system includes the hippocampus, amygdala, thalamus, and hypothalamus. In addition to processing emotions and memories, the limbic system fuels our most basic drives, including hunger, sex, and aggression.

LO 16 **Distinguish the structures and functions of the brainstem and cerebellum. (p. 72)**

The brain's ancient core consists of a stalklike trio of structures called the brainstem, which includes the midbrain, pons, and medulla. The brainstem extends from the spinal cord to the forebrain, which is the largest part of the brain that includes the cerebral cortex and limbic system. Located at the top of the brainstem is the midbrain, which most agree plays a role in levels of arousal. The hindbrain includes areas responsible for fundamental life-sustaining processes. Behind the brainstem is the cerebellum, which is responsible for muscle coordination and balance.

KEY TERMS

action potential, p. 47
adrenal glands, p. 57
all-or-none, p. 47
amygdala, p. 71
association areas, p. 69
autonomic nervous system, p. 55
axon, p. 45
biological psychology, p. 42
Broca's area, p. 61
cell body, p. 45
central nervous system (CNS), p. 52
cerebellum, p. 73
cerebral cortex, p. 64
cerebrum, p. 58
corpus callosum, p. 58
dendrites, p. 45
endocrine system, p. 56
frontal lobes, p. 64
glial cells, p. 45
hindbrain, p. 73
hippocampus, p. 71
hormones, p. 56
hypothalamus, p. 72
interneurons, p. 53
lateralization, p. 60
limbic system, p. 71
medulla, p. 73
midbrain, p. 73
motor cortex, p. 66
motor neurons, p. 53
myelin sheath, p. 45
nerves, p. 54
neurogenesis, p. 63
neurons, p. 45
neuroplasticity, p. 63
neuroscience, p. 42
neurotransmitters, p. 48
occipital lobes, p. 64
parasympathetic nervous system, p. 56
parietal lobes, p. 64
peripheral nervous system (PNS), p. 52
phrenology, p. 42
pituitary gland, p. 57
pons, p. 73
receptor sites, p. 48
reflex arc, p. 54
resting potential, p. 47
reticular formation, p. 73
reuptake, p. 48
sensory neurons, p. 53
somatic nervous system, p. 54
somatosensory cortex, p. 67
spinal cord, p. 53
split-brain operation, p. 59
stem cells, p. 63
sympathetic nervous system, p. 55
synapse, p. 45
temporal lobes, p. 64
thalamus, p. 71
thyroid gland, p. 57
Wernicke's area, p. 62

TEST PREP **ARE YOU READY?**

1. A typical neuron has three basic parts. The ____________ contains a nucleus with genetic material, the ____________ receive messages from sending neurons, and the ____________ send messages to other neurons.
a. cell body; dendrites; axon terminals
b. cell body; axon; dendrites
c. dendrites; axon; myelin sheath
d. dendrites; axon terminals; myelin sheath

2. Match each neurotransmitter on the left with its primary role(s) on the right.

____ 1. acetylcholine	a. reduction of pain
____ 2. glutamate	b. learning, memory
____ 3. endorphins	c. movement
____ 4. serotonin	d. mood, aggression, appetite

3. A neuroscientist studying the brain and spinal cord would describe her general area of interest as the:
a. central nervous system.
b. peripheral nervous system.
c. autonomic nervous system.
d. neurons.

4. A serious diving accident can result in damage to the ____________, which is responsible for receiving information from the body and sending it to the brain, and for sending information from the brain to the body.
a. corpus callosum
b. spinal cord
c. reflex arc
d. somatic nervous system

5. After Brandon returned from a frightening situation in a war zone, his ____________ reacts with a "rest-and-digest" process.
a. reflex arc
b. myelin sheath
c. somatic nervous system
d. parasympathetic nervous system

6. Lately, your friend has been prone to mood swings and aggressive behavior. The doctor has pinpointed a problem in his ____________, which is a communication system that uses ____________ to convey messages via hormones.
a. endocrine system; action potentials
b. endocrine system; glands
c. central nervous system; glands
d. central nervous system; peripheral nervous system

7. Which of the following statements is correct regarding the function of the right hemisphere in comparison to the left hemisphere?
a. The right hemisphere is less competent handling visual tasks.
b. The right hemisphere is more competent handling visual tasks.
c. The left hemisphere is more competent judging if lines are oriented similarly.
d. The right hemisphere is more competent with speech production.

8. The ____________ is a group of interconnected structures that process emotions, memories, and basic drives.
a. left hemisphere
b. limbic system
c. corpus callosum
d. superior temporal sulcus

9. Match each structure on the left with its principal function on the right:

____ 1. association areas	a. three thin membranes protect brain
____ 2. temporal lobes	b. integration of information from all over brain
____ 3. meninges	c. hearing and language comprehension
____ 4. occipital lobes	d. receive sensory information, such as touch
____ 5. parietal lobes	e. process visual information

10. The ______________ is located in the midbrain and is responsible for levels of arousal and your ability to selectively attend to important stimuli.
    a. cerebellum
    b. thalamus
    c. hippocampus
    d. reticular formation

11. What is neuroplasticity? Give an example of when it is evident.

12. The "knee-jerk" reaction that occurs when a doctor taps your knee with a rubber hammer provides a good example of a reflex arc. Describe this involuntary reaction and then draw your own diagram to show the reflex arc associated with it.

13. Compare and contrast the body's two major chemical messengers.

14. The research conducted by Sperry and Gazzaniga examined the effects of surgeries that severed the corpus callosum. Describe what these split-brain experiments tell us about the lateralization of the hemispheres of the brain and how they communicate.

15. We described a handful of tools scientists use to study the brain. Compare their functions.

✓ CHECK YOUR ANSWERS IN APPENDIX C.

Go to **LaunchPad** or **Achieve: Read & Practice** to test your understanding with **LearningCurve**.

CHAPTER

3

Clive Brunskill/Getty Images.

Sensation and Perception

An Introduction to Sensation and Perception

THE JAZZ SINGER A warm spotlight shines upon jazz singer Mandy Harvey. She begins strumming her ukulele, fingers moving with delicate confidence, head bobbing to the beat. A piano joins in, and Mandy begins to sing. Her voice is clear and sweet perfection, and her lyrics tell the story of an internal struggle. The song, *Try,* is about accepting yourself and not being afraid to *try,* that is, take chances, perhaps fall on your face, and get up and move forward. As Mandy explained at one of her concerts, *Try* is about believing "what's within me is stronger than what's in my way" (No Barriers, 2015, 2:02). No one exemplifies this mantra better than Mandy herself.

Mandy has been deaf since her freshman year of college. That was more than a decade ago, and today she is living a dream most would consider inconceivable. With four albums to her name and a repertoire of original songs, Mandy is living proof that music can still be created and enjoyed after hearing loss. On a broader level, she shows all of us that good things come to those who dream big and confront their fears of failure. You can see this message resonating with her audience; look closely and you will likely observe a few lips trembling and eyes watering.

Mandy's band performs at all types of venues, from cozy jazz lounges to grand settings like the Kennedy Center in Washington, D.C. While singing, Mandy translates her lyrics to sign language, but this is the only clue that she is deaf. Her pitch, timing, and execution are virtually flawless. How does she do it?

Where Does Sensation End and Perception Begin?

Mandy has had hearing problems since she was a baby, but she didn't face profound hearing loss until the age of 18, and thus has two decades of musical memories to draw upon. The sound of middle C still rings in her brain, and she knows how it feels to move up and down the scale, or change keys. "I remember music that I sang when I was four," Mandy says, "so once I learn a song, it's very difficult for me to forget it." But memories alone are not enough to stay in sync with a band of musicians. For this, Mandy relies on other *sensations*—what she sees and feels—to compensate for what she cannot hear.

Music That Touches the Soul
At least half of the music Mandy Harvey performs is original material; the other half consists of rearranged jazz numbers, 60s music, and an occasional pop song like Cold Play's "Yellow." Her favorite songs tend to be those with poetic lyrics and "genuine emotion." Macmillan Learning.

LO 1 Define sensation and perception and explain how they are different.

SENSATION VERSUS PERCEPTION The subject of this chapter is sensation and perception, the absorbing and deciphering of information from the environment. **Sensation** is the process by which receptors in our sensory organs (located in the eyes, ears, nose, mouth, skin, and other tissues) receive and detect stimuli. **Perception** is the process through which information about these stimuli is organized, interpreted, and transformed into something meaningful. Sensation is hearing a loud, shrill tone; perception is recognizing it as the warning sound of a fire alarm. Sensation and perception work together to provide a coherent experience of the world around you and inside you, and they often occur without your effort or awareness.

Mandy, In Her Own Words

http://qrs.ly/jh7829i

Macmillan Learning.

Psychologists frequently characterize the processing of sensory information as *bottom-up* or *top-down*. **Bottom-up processing** occurs when the brain collects basic information about incoming stimuli and prepares it for further interpretation. **Top-down processing** generally involves the next step, using past experiences and knowledge to understand and pay attention to sensory information. Bottom-up processing is what cameras and video recorders do best—collect data without any expectations. Top-down processing is where humans excel. For example, if your cell phone signal momentarily breaks up, you can't hear every word the other person is saying. Thanks to top-down processing, you can often fill in the gaps and make sense of what you are hearing using your familiarity with language. Using both types of processing, the brain constructs a representation of the world based on what you have learned and experienced in the past. This depiction is not always accurate, however. Both bottom-up and top-down processing can lead us astray in our interpretations of ambiguous figures, and the resulting errors may have serious consequences. Just think what might happen if a doctor failed to detect a hemorrhage (bleed) on a patient's brain scan, or mistook a normal anatomical variation for a breast mass. Sometimes radiologists have to make a diagnosis using ambiguous X-ray images (Buckle, Udawatta, & Straus, 2013).

Sensory systems collect information from inside and outside your body and transform it into your impressions of the world. But how are beams of light turned into an image of a fiery orange sunrise, and chemical sensations converted into the taste of a sweet strawberry? It all starts with *transduction*.

Note: Quotations attributed to Mandy Harvey are personal communications.

synonyms

bottom-up processing data-based processing

top-down processing knowledge-based processing

sensation The process by which sensory organs in the eyes, ears, nose, mouth, skin, and other tissues receive and detect stimuli.

perception The organization and interpretation of sensory stimuli by the brain.

bottom-up processing Taking basic information about incoming sensory stimuli and processing it for further interpretation.

top-down processing Drawing on past experiences and knowledge to understand and interpret sensory information.

LO 2 Define transduction and explain how it relates to sensation.

TRANSDUCTION Sensation begins when your sensory systems receive input from the environment. Each sensory system is designed to respond to stimuli of a certain kind. Light waves and sound waves accost your eyes and ears, heat waves bathe your skin, molecules of different chemical compositions float into your nostrils and descend upon your tongue, and physical objects press against your body. But none of these stimuli can have an impact on your brain unless they are translated into a language it understands: **electrical and chemical signals.** This is the job of the specialized sensory cells located in the back of your eyes, the caverns of your ears and nose, the spongy surface of your tongue and within your skin, muscle, and other tissues. The process of transforming sensory stimuli into the electrical and chemical signals of neurons is called **transduction**. **Neural signals** are then processed by the central nervous system, resulting in what we experience as *sensations* (*seeing* a person's face or *smelling* smoke).

CONNECTIONS

In **Chapter 2,** we described how neurons work together to shape our experiences. Information moves through the body via electrical and chemical processes, including action potentials traveling along the neuron's axon and neurotransmitters released at the synapse. In this chapter, we see how this activity ultimately is translated into sensation and perception.

CONNECTIONS

As discussed in **Chapter 2,** neurons (also called nerve cells) are the building blocks of the nervous system. The brain and the spinal cord make up the central nervous system. The peripheral nervous system includes the somatic and autonomic branches of the nervous system. Here, we see how our central nervous system enables us to experience sensations.

For sensations to be useful, we must assign meaning to them: "That face belongs to my girlfriend," or "I smell smoke; there must be a fire." And even though we describe and explain sensation and perception as two distinct events, there is no physical boundary in the brain marking the end of sensation and the beginning of perception. The processing of stimuli into sensations and perceptions happens quickly and automatically.

How do these concepts figure into *psychology,* the scientific study of behavior and mental processes? Sensation and perception are the starting points for every psychological activity you can imagine, from reading this book to creating snaps on Snapchat. Through careful and systematic observation, psychologists are continually discovering ways that sensation and perception affect our thoughts, emotions, and behaviors.

Sensation: It Just Depends

Studying sensation means studying human beings, who are complex and variable. Not everyone is born with the same collection of stimulus-detecting equipment. Some people have eyes that see 20/20; others have been wearing glasses since they were toddlers. There is even variation within a given individual. The ability to detect faint stimuli, for instance, depends on your state of mind and body (such as how preoccupied or bored you happen to be, how stressed you feel, or whether you've had your morning cup of coffee).

Sensory Blending
Singer-songwriter Pharrell Williams says he sees colors when he listens to music (NPR, 2013, December 31). Williams is describing *synesthesia,* a "rare experience where one property of a stimulus evokes a second experience not associated with the first" (Banissy, Jonas, & Kadosh, 2014, para. 1). With synesthesia, the senses seem to blend; for example, the word "Tuesday" might taste like bacon, or the letter "Y" may smell like pine trees. Kevin Winter/WireImage/Getty Images.

Such fluctuations in sensing ability can have profound consequences in situations that demand high levels of attention. Think about the enormous responsibility taken on by lifeguards, for example. These men and women are expected to prevent drownings and injuries at beaches and pools, yet they must contend with visual challenges like glare, interpret ambiguous behaviors (*Are those joyous yelps or terrified screams?*), and maintain constant attention even when they are hot, bored, or experiencing strong emotions (Lanagan-Leitzel, 2012; Lanagan-Leitzel, Skow, & Moore, 2015). Their brains are juggling multiple tasks, so their attention is divided. Research suggests that only around 2% of people can multitask flawlessly. This may be due, in part, to their ability to efficiently handle simultaneous cognitive tasks (Medeiros-Ward, Watson, & Strayer, 2015). The rest of us are limited in our ability to attend to the environment, especially when focusing on more than one demanding task (Medeiros-Ward et al., 2015; Watson & Strayer, 2010).

With handheld technology so widely available, resisting the urge to multitask is growing more and more difficult. In certain situations, our safety might hinge on the ability to restrain ourselves. Some experts suggest we approach texting and driving the same way we have treated drinking and driving. One company is developing a *textalyzer* that would enable law enforcement officials to determine if someone has been texting and driving, just as a *breathalyzer* can detect alcohol (Richtel, 2016, April 27).

Describe and differentiate between absolute thresholds and difference thresholds.

ABSOLUTE THRESHOLDS Even if we have no intention of multitasking, our sensory systems are prone to interferences from outside and within. This tendency makes it challenging for psychologists to measure sensory abilities, though they have been successful in many respects. For example, researchers have established various types of sensory *thresholds,* which are the lowest levels of stimulation people can detect. Of particular interest to psychologists are **absolute thresholds**, defined as the weakest stimuli that can be detected 50% of the time. The absolute threshold commonly cited for vision, for instance, is the equivalent of being able to see the flame of one candle, in the dark of night, 30 miles away 50% of the time (**Figure 3.1**; Galanter, 1962).

SENSORY ADAPTATION Absolute thresholds are important, but there is more to sensation than noting the presence of a stimulus. Have you ever put on deodorant or cologne and wondered if its scent was too strong, but within a few minutes you no longer notice it? Or perhaps you have jumped into an ice-cold swimming pool, and after 10 minutes you are oblivious to the frigid water. Our sensory receptors become less sensitive to constant stimuli through **sensory adaptation**, a natural lessening of awareness of unchanging conditions. This process allows us to focus instead on critical changes in our environment—a skill that has proven invaluable for **survival.** For example, sounds that are repeated or continuous are most likely not dangerous, so we learn to ignore them—we become *habituated* after multiple exposures.

CONNECTIONS

In **Chapter 1,** we presented the evolutionary perspective. Here, it is used to explain how sensory adaptation has evolved. By ignoring unchanging stimuli, we are better prepared to detect changes in the environment. For our ancestors, picking up new information often meant the difference between life and death.

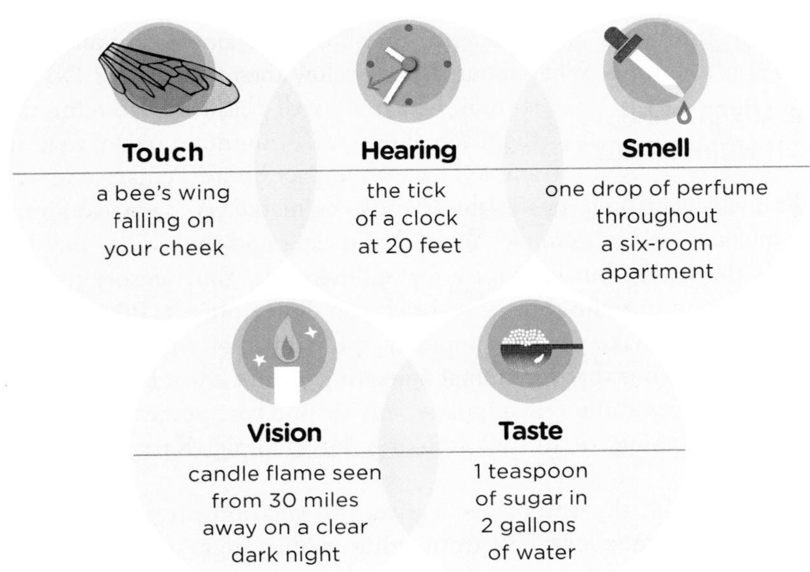

FIGURE 3.1
Absolute Thresholds
Absolute thresholds are the weakest stimuli that can be detected 50% of the time. Listed here are absolute thresholds for each of the five senses. Information from Galanter, 1962.

transduction The process of transforming stimuli into neural signals.

absolute thresholds The weakest stimuli that can be detected 50% of the time.

sensory adaptation The process through which sensory receptors become less sensitive to constant stimuli.

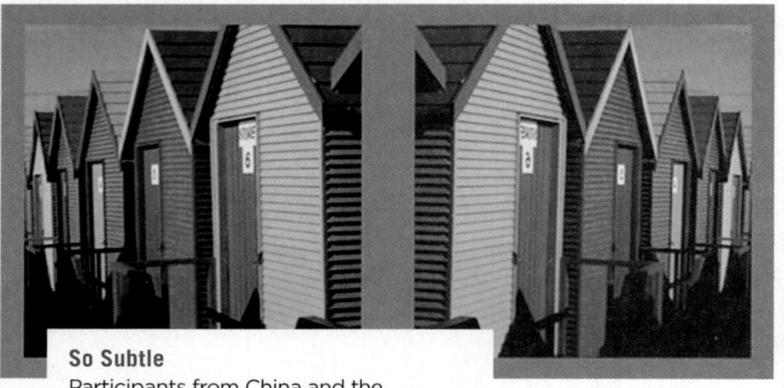

So Subtle
Participants from China and the Netherlands were asked to choose the darker image. Can you tell there's a difference in brightness? The difference threshold, or just noticeable difference, is the minimum difference between two stimuli noticed 50% of the time. For Chinese and Dutch participants, the just noticeable difference was the same "for most images" (Qin, Ge, Yin, Xia, & Heynderickx, 2010, p. 25), which suggests that this aspect of sensation and perception might not be influenced by cultural factors. Republished with permission of Qin, S., Ge, S., Yin, H., Xia, J., & Heynderickx, I. From *Displays*, 31, 25–34 (2010); permission conveyed through Copyright Clearance Center, Inc.

This allows us to be alert to novel stimuli, like the snap of a twig, which may be associated with a new threat in the immediate vicinity (for more on habituation, see Chapter 5).

DIFFERENCE THRESHOLDS Suppose a friend asks you to turn down the volume of your music. How much does the sound level need to drop in order for her to notice? There is a certain *change in volume* that will catch her attention, but what is it? Early psychologists asked similar questions; they wanted to know *how different* sounds and other stimuli must be in order for someone to notice their difference. Through careful experimentation, they established various **difference thresholds**, or the minimum differences between two stimuli noticed 50% of the time. For example, imagine you are holding a 5-pound weight. If ½ a pound is added, you would most likely notice that change. If, however, you were holding a 50-pound weight, adding ½ a pound would not be noticeable. The bigger the original weight, the greater the difference needs to be.

During the 1800s, German physiologist Ernst Weber (1795–1878) proposed that difference thresholds are based on ratios. The *just noticeable difference* for weight is 2%; that is, the proportion of added weight needed for you to feel the difference 50% of the time. **Weber's law** states that *ratios,* not raw number values, determine difference thresholds, and each sense has its own Weber ratio. To detect a difference between two stimuli at least 50% of the time, the intensity of two lights must differ by 8%, the weight of objects lifted must differ by 2%, the intensity of sounds must differ by 4%, the taste of salt must differ by 8%, and the strength of electric shocks must differ by 1% (Poulton, 1967; Teghtsoonian, 1971). As the size of the stimulus increases, the bigger the difference must be to be detected.

Apply This ↓

HOW POWERFUL ARE SUBLIMINAL INFLUENCES?

The absolute thresholds and difference thresholds pertain to stimuli that we can detect 50% of the time. What about stimuli below these thresholds? Do *subliminal* stimuli, which are well below our absolute thresholds (light too dim to see, or sounds too faint to hear, for example), have an impact on us? Perhaps you have heard of "subliminal advertising," or stealthy attempts by marketers to woo you into buying their products. Here's an example: You're in a theater and the words "Buy Popcorn!" flash across the screen, but only for a few milliseconds. Your sensory receptors may detect this fleeting stimulus, but it's so brief, you don't notice it. **Urban myth** suggests subliminal ads can make you buy popcorn, soft drinks, or whatever happens to be advertised. The truth is that subliminal marketing cannot affect behavior in this way. Subliminal messages cannot manipulate you to purchase something you had not planned on purchasing, or to quit smoking, for example (Karremans, Stroebe, & Claus, 2006).

SUBLIMINAL ADVERTISING . . . DOES IT WORK OR NOT?

CONNECTIONS
In **Chapters 0** and **1,** we discussed critical thinking. The claim that subliminal advertising can make us buy unwanted items is an example of "misinformation" about human behavior. With critical thinking, we determine if there is scientific evidence to support a claim, including those conveyed in urban myths.

That being said, the brain does register information presented at an unconscious or nonconscious level. Neuroimaging studies suggest that neural activity is evident in response to the "subliminal presentation" of stimuli (Axelrod, Bar, Rees, & Yovel, 2014; Kouider & Dehaene, 2007). These subliminal messages may be able to influence fleeting moods through *priming,* which occurs when memories are awakened by cues in the environment (Chapter 6). Priming occurs without our awareness. One study found that if you subliminally expose people to ugly scenes (for example, pictures of dead bodies or buckets of snakes) for

difference thresholds The minimum differences between two stimuli that can be noticed 50% of the time.

Weber's law States that each of the senses has its own constant ratio determining difference thresholds.

signal detection theory Explains how internal and external factors influence our ability to detect weak signals in the environment.

several milliseconds (thus "priming" them), they then will rate a neutral picture of a woman's face as less likable than when exposed to feel-good subliminal images, such as pictures of kittens and bridal couples (Krosnick, Betz, Jussim, & Lynn, 1992).

Thus far, we have focused on the stimulus itself. But what about other environmental factors, such as background stimuli competing for the observer's attention, or internal factors like the observer's state of mind—how do these variables affect one's sensing capacity?

SIGNAL DETECTION THEORY Our ability to detect weak stimuli in the environment is based on many factors, including the intensity of the stimulus, the presence of interfering stimuli, and our psychological state (how alert we are, for example). **Signal detection theory** draws together all these pieces, based on the idea that "noise" from our environment can interfere with our ability to detect weak signals. The noise could be from internal factors, including how tired you are, when you last ate, your expectations about the importance of success, your motivation, and so on. Noise could also be from external variables, such as the light level in the room and dust in the air.

Signal detection theory is useful in a variety of real-world situations. In one study, researchers used this theory to explain how nurses make decisions about patient safety. The study called attention to "missed signals," that is, medical errors resulting from noise interfering with nurses' ability to hear alarm monitors and identify patient signs and symptoms (Despins, Scott-Cawiezell, & Rouder, 2010).

In settings like this, the ability to sense and perceive may have life or death implications. But how does each of the senses collect and process information? Let's start by exploring vision.

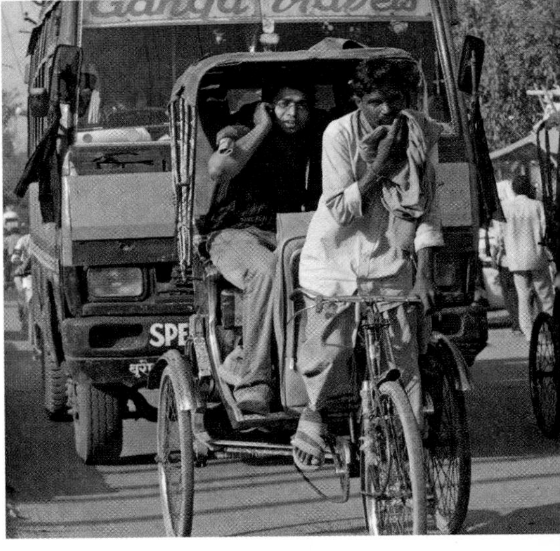

Is That My Phone?
It's difficult to detect the sound of a cell phone ringing in a noisy, chaotic environment. Complicating matters further, some of us occasionally "feel" our phones vibrating in our pockets, even when there is no call, message, or notification. Phantom Phone Signals (PPS) are very common, especially among avid cell phone users (Tanis, Buekeboom, Hartmann, & Vermeulen, 2015). Paul Springett C/Alamy.

✓ show what you know

1. Information received by sensory receptors is organized, interpreted, and assigned meaning through the process of:
   a. perception.
   b. transduction.
   c. sensation.
   d. signal detection.
2. Transduction is the process of transforming stimuli into neural signals. Identify some stimuli that are currently being transformed into neural signals you experience as sensations.
3. Someone at work brought in fresh flowers. You notice the odor immediately, but within minutes you can barely detect it. This reduced sensitivity results from the process of:
   a. sensation.
   b. transduction.
   c. perception.
   d. sensory adaptation.

✓ CHECK YOUR ANSWERS IN APPENDIX C.

Vision

HOW DOES SHE DO IT? Mandy has near perfect pitch, a stunning ability given that she cannot hear the notes coming out of her mouth. "Certain areas of your throat, you can tell if you're hitting [a note] or not." But every once in a while, Mandy explains, she finds herself slightly off key. "If I'm singing not quite right, in my brain I'm like, *this doesn't feel right*. I'm not sure exactly where I'm wrong, but I know that I'm not right."

In these situations, Mandy may rely on her fellow musicians to adjust their key to match hers. "It's the benefit of having really great musicians back you up," Mandy says. "So you never really fall flat on your face; you only kind of stub your face a little." Other times, Mandy changes her key to match the band's. If she's singing a quarter step too low,

Showing Their Love
Mandy's fans shower her in "deaf applause," the visual equivalent of clapping. Courtesy Mandy Harvey.

for example, the pianist might signal with his hands, "move up." Throughout the performance, Mandy and the other musicians continue communicating with visual cues, bobbing their heads to maintain rhythm and using eye contact to signal transitions. "Every musician looks at me when it's my turn to go in and sing . . . and I look at them when they're about to solo," Mandy says. At the end of the show, the crowd claps and cheers, and some show their appreciation with "deaf applause," raising their hands and shaking them.

The silent communication occurring between Mandy, her musicians, and the fans is made possible by a remarkable communication system running from the eyes to the brain. How does the visual system work? To tackle this question, we must have a basic understanding of light and color.

You Asked, Mandy Answers

http://qrs.ly/jh7829i

Can you still "hear" music in your head?

Light and Color

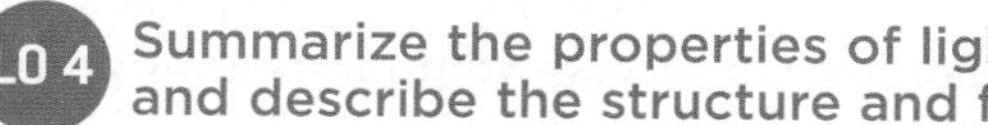

LO 4 Summarize the properties of light and color, and describe the structure and function of the eye.

When Mandy sees fans erupt in deaf applause, she is not seeing their actual hands; she is sensing light waves bouncing off those hands and entering her eyes. The eyes do not sense faces, objects, or scenery. They detect light. But what exactly *is* light? Light is an electromagnetic energy wave, composed of fluctuating electric and magnetic fields zooming from place to place at a very fast rate. And when we say "fast," we mean from Atlanta to Los Angeles in a tenth of a second. Electromagnetic energy waves are everywhere all the time, zipping past your head, and bouncing off your nose. As you can see in **Figure 3.2**, light that is visible to humans falls along a spectrum, or range, of electromagnetic energy.

WAVELENGTH The various types of electromagnetic energy can be distinguished by their **wavelength**, which is the distance from one wave hump to the next (like the distance between the crests of waves rolling in the ocean; Figure 3.2). Gamma rays have short wavelengths and are located on the far left of the spectrum. At the opposite extreme (far right of the spectrum) are the long radio waves. The light humans can see falls in the middle of the spectrum, between 400 and 700 nanometers (nm) or billionths of a meter (Brown & Wald, 1964). Wavelength plays a key role in determining the colors humans and animals can detect.

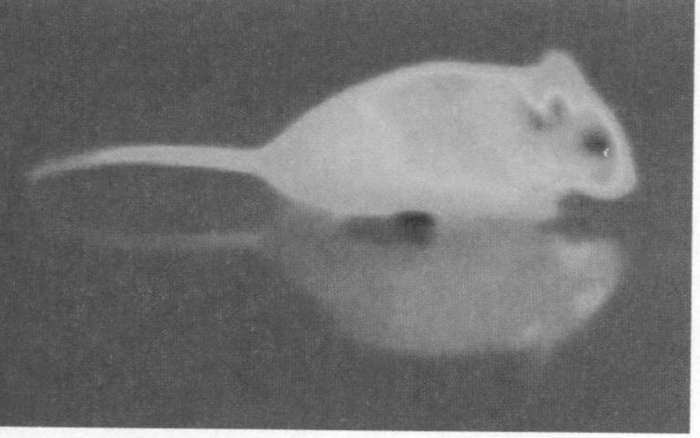

I "See" You
This is what you might perceive if you were a snake searching for dinner in the dark. The western diamondback rattlesnake has facial sensors that detect infrared radiation from warm-blooded prey. Scientists have yet to determine exactly how the heat waves are transduced into neural signals, but the process depends on specialized channels in nerve fibers of the snake's face (Gracheva et al., 2010). Julius Lab at UCSF.

THE COLORS WE SEE Although dogs only see the world in blues, yellows, and grays, humans and other primates can detect a wider spectrum of colors, including reds and oranges (Pongrácz, Ujvári, Faragó, Miklósi, & Péter, 2017). The ability to see reds and oranges may be an adaptation to spot ripe fruits against the green backdrop of leaves, and facilitate memorization and recognition of objects (Hofmann & Palczewski, 2015; Melin et al., 2014). Other creatures can see "colors" that we can't. Snakes can detect infrared light radiating from their prey, and birds evaluate potential mates by sensing ultraviolet (UV) waves reflected by feathers (Bennett, Cuthill, Partridge, & Maier, 1996; Gracheva et al., 2010; Lind & Delhey, 2015).

FEATURES OF COLOR The colors you see result from light reflecting off objects and reaching your eyes. Every color can be described according to three features: hue, brightness, and saturation. The first feature, **hue**, is what we commonly refer to as "color" (blue jeans have a blue hue). Hue is determined by the wavelength reflecting off an object: Violet has the shortest wavelength in the visible spectrum (400 nm), and red has the longest (700 nm). The *brightness* of a color represents a continuum from

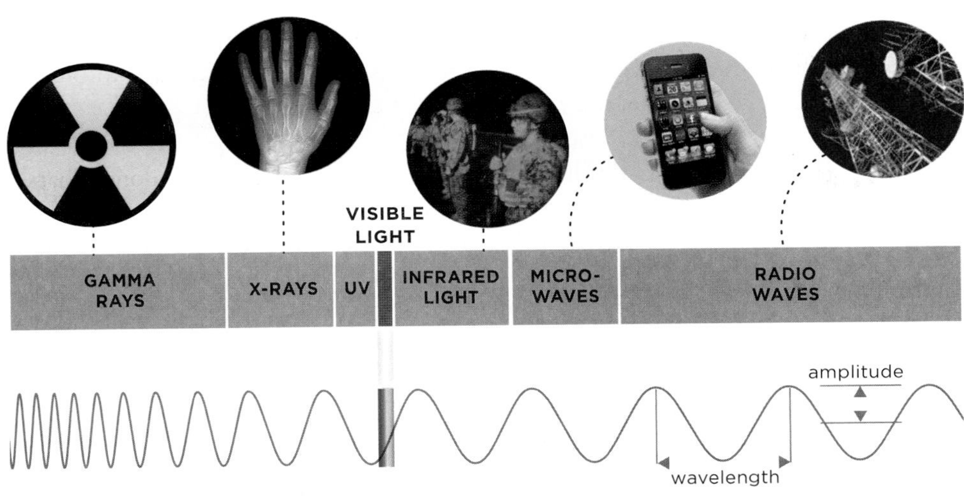

FIGURE 3.2
The Electromagnetic Spectrum and Visible Light
We use electromagnetic energy for a variety of purposes, from warming our dinners to carrying on digital conversations. Only a small part of the electromagnetic spectrum can be detected by the human visual system. Visible light wavelengths range from approximately 400 to 700 nanometers. Radioactive symbol, Thinkstock/Getty Images; X-ray hand, AJ Photo/Science Source; Marines, Lance Cpl. Tucker S. Wolf. U.S. Marine Corps; Hand holding phone, Rob Bartee/Alamy; Radio tower, TERADAT SANTIVIVUT/Getty Images.

intense to dim. Brightness depends on wave height, or **amplitude**, the distance from midpoint to peak (or from midpoint to trough; Figure 3.2). **Saturation**, or color purity, is determined by uniformity of wavelength. Saturated colors are made up of the same wavelengths. Objects we see as pure violet, for instance, are reflecting only 400-nm light waves. We can "pollute" the violet light by mixing it with other wavelengths, resulting in a less saturated, pale lavender. Most colors in the environment are not pure. The pigments in the blue lipstick of Lupita Nyong'o (right) probably reflect a mixture of wavelengths around 475 nm, rather than pure 475-nm blue. Combinations of the three basic features—hue, brightness, and saturation—can produce an infinite number of colors; our eyes are just not sensitive enough to tell them all apart. Findings vary, but some researchers estimate that humans can detect approximately 2.3 million colors (Linhares, Pinto, & Nascimento, 2008; Masaoka, Berns, Fairchild, & Moghareh Abed, 2013). But remember, the colors we perceive do not actually exist in the world around us. Rather, they are the product of (1) the properties of the object and the wavelengths of light it reflects, and (2) the brain's interpretation of that light. When any of these factors change, so do the colors we see. The eyes take light energy and transform it into neural code for the brain to interpret. The exquisite specificity of this code allows us to distinguish between electric blue and cobalt, lime green and chartreuse. All this is made possible by the eye's remarkable biology.

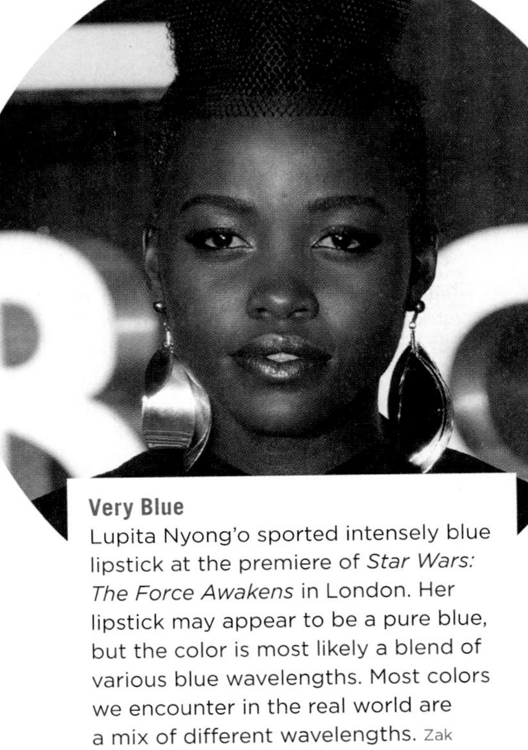

Very Blue
Lupita Nyong'o sported intensely blue lipstick at the premiere of *Star Wars: The Force Awakens* in London. Her lipstick may appear to be a pure blue, but the color is most likely a blend of various blue wavelengths. Most colors we encounter in the real world are a mix of different wavelengths. Zak Hussein/Getty Images.

You Won't Believe Your Eyes

The human eye is an engineering marvel (see **INFOGRAPHIC 3.1** on page 89). When you look in the mirror, you see only a fraction of each eye; the rest is hidden inside your head. Let's explore this biological wonder, starting from the outside, and working our way toward the brain.

THE CORNEA The surface of the eye looks wet and glassy. This clear outer layer over the colored portion of the eye is called the **cornea**, and it has two important jobs: (1) shielding the eye from damage by dust, bacteria, or even a poke, and

wavelength The distance between wave peaks (or troughs).

hue The color of an object, determined by the wavelength of light it reflects.

amplitude The height of a wave; distance from midpoint to peak, or from midpoint to trough.

saturation Color purity.

cornea The clear, outer layer of the eye that shields it from damage and focuses incoming light waves.

(2) focusing incoming light waves. About 65–75% of the focusing ability of the eye comes from the cornea, which is why imperfections in its shape can lead to blurred vision (National Eye Institute, n.d.).

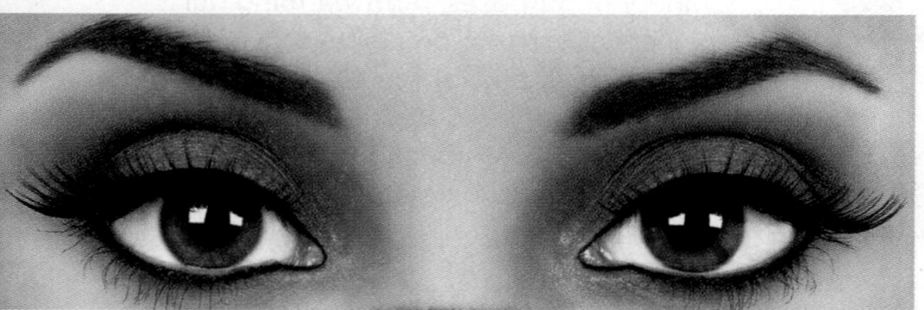

Sexy Pupils
When looking at someone she finds attractive, a woman's pupils dilate—especially during the most fertile time of her monthly cycle. For men, there is a strong link between their genital arousal and the dilation of their pupils (Laeng & Falkenberg, 2007; Rieger et al., 2015). Stephanie Zieber/Shutterstock

THE IRIS AND THE PUPIL Directly behind the cornea is the donut-shaped **iris**. When you say someone has velvety brown eyes, you are really talking about the color of her irises. The black hole in the center of the iris is called the *pupil*. In dim lighting, the muscles of the iris relax, widening the pupil to allow more light inside the eye. In bright sunlight, the iris muscles squeeze, constricting the pupil to limit the amount of light. Interestingly, the pupils also constrict when people look at photographs of the sun (Binda, Pereverzeva, & Murray, 2013).

THE LENS AND ACCOMMODATION Behind the pupil is the lens, a tough, transparent structure that is similar in size and shape to an "M&M's candy" (Mayo Clinic, 2014, October 17). Like the cornea, the lens specializes in focusing incoming light, but it can also change shape in order to adjust to images near and far, a process called **accommodation**. If you take your eyes off this page and look across the room, faraway objects immediately come into focus because your lens changes shape. As we age, the lens begins to stiffen, a condition called *presbyopia,* impairing our ability to focus on up-close images. Most people develop some degree of presbyopia between 40 and 65 years of age (Mayo Clinic, 2014, October 17).

The Retina

After passing through the cornea, pupil, and lens, light waves travel through the eyeball's jellylike filling and land on the **retina**, a carpet of neurons covering the back wall of the eye. The retina is responsible for the *transduction* of light energy into neural activity; that is, sensing light and relaying a **message to the brain**. Without the retina, vision is impossible.

CONNECTIONS
In **Chapter 2,** we noted that neurons are activated in response to sensations. In the case of vision, sensation begins when photoreceptors in the retina transduce light into neural signals. This causes a chain reaction in neurons of the visual pathway, which convey the message to the brain.

LO 5 Describe the function of rods and cones.

PHOTORECEPTORS AND OTHER NEURONS The retina is home to millions of specialized neurons called **photoreceptors**, which absorb light energy and turn it into electrical and chemical signals for the brain to process. Two types of photoreceptors are located in the retina: *rods* and *cones,* which get their names from their characteristic shapes. **Rods** are extremely sensitive, firing in response to even a single *photon,* the smallest possible packet of light, although 50 photons is the absolute threshold for people to detect light through their rods (Hofmann & Palczewski, 2015; Rieke & Baylor, 1998). If rods were all we had, the world would look something like an old black-and-white movie. **Cones** enable us to enjoy a visual experience more akin to HDTV. In addition to providing color vision, cones allow us to see fine details, such as the small print on the back of a gift card.

Rods and cones are just the beginning of a complex neural signaling process that ultimately leads to a visual experience in the brain (Infographic 3.1). Near the rods and cones are *bipolar cells,* another specialized type of neuron, located approximately in the middle of the retina. When a rod or cone is stimulated by light energy, it conveys its signal to nearby bipolar cells. These, in turn, convey their signal to *ganglion cells,* yet another type of neuron, located toward the front of the retina. Axons of the ganglion cells bundle together in the **optic nerve**, which is like an electrical cable (one extending from each eye) connecting the retina to

iris The muscle responsible for changing the size of the pupil.

accommodation The process by which the lens changes shape in order to focus on objects near and far.

retina The layer of the eye containing photoreceptor cells, which transduce light energy into neural activity.

photoreceptors Specialized cells in the retina that absorb light energy and turn it into electrical and chemical signals for the brain to process.

rods Photoreceptors that enable us to see in dim lighting; not sensitive to color, but useful for night vision.

cones Photoreceptors that enable us to sense color and minute details.

optic nerve The bundle of axons from ganglion cells leading to the visual cortex.

Seeing

"Seeing" involves more than simply looking at an object. Vision is a complex process in which light waves entering the eye are directed toward the retina, where they are transduced into messages the brain can understand. Flaws in the clear outer layer of the eye, the cornea, are primarily to blame for so many people (about a third of the American population) needing glasses or contact lenses (National Eye Institute, n.d.-a). LASIK eye surgery, a popular alternative to corrective lenses, uses a laser to reshape the cornea so that it can focus light properly.

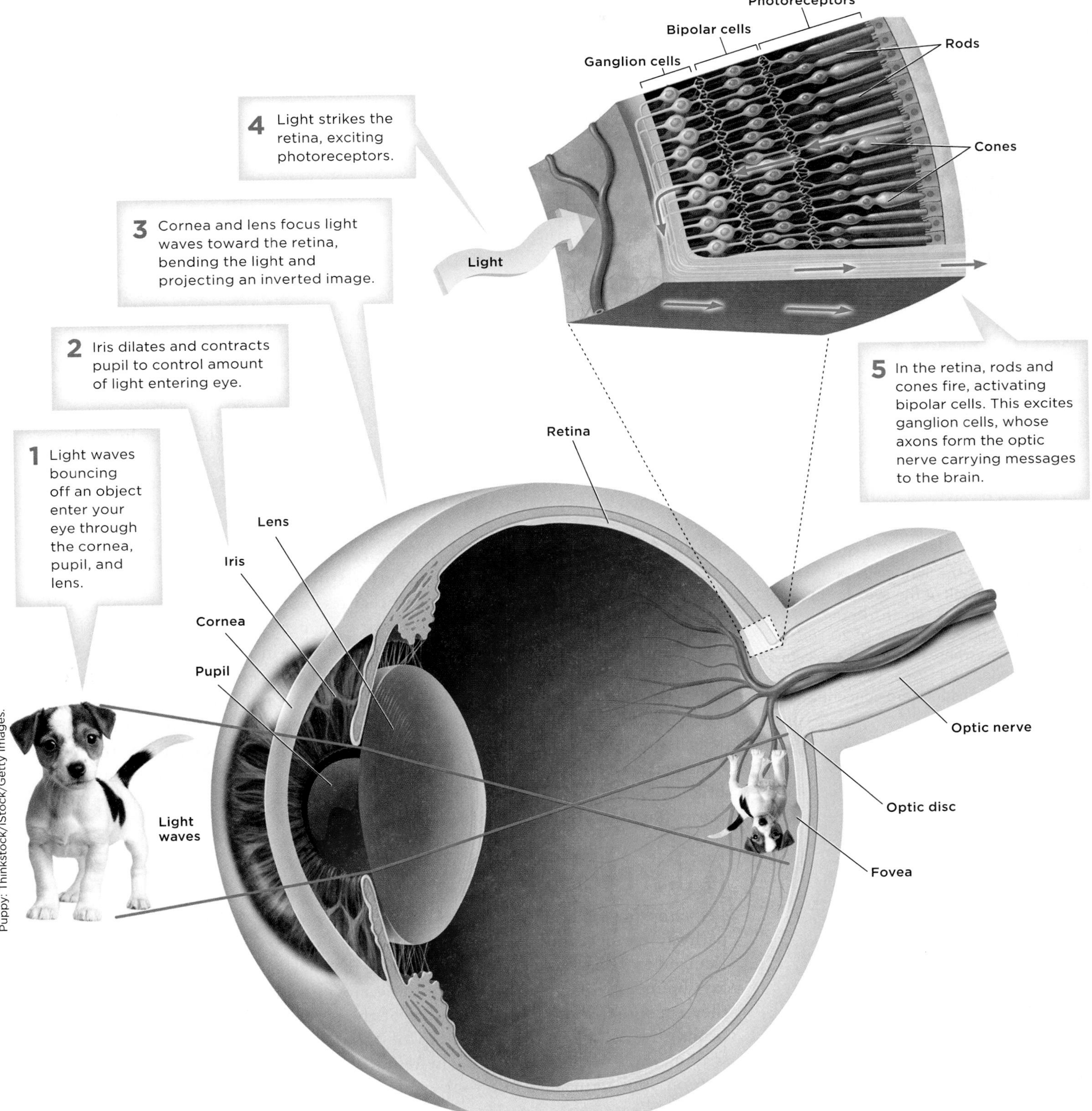
Photoreceptors
Bipolar cells
Ganglion cells
Rods
Cones
Light
4 Light strikes the retina, exciting photoreceptors.
3 Cornea and lens focus light waves toward the retina, bending the light and projecting an inverted image.
2 Iris dilates and contracts pupil to control amount of light entering eye.
1 Light waves bouncing off an object enter your eye through the cornea, pupil, and lens.
5 In the retina, rods and cones fire, activating bipolar cells. This excites ganglion cells, whose axons form the optic nerve carrying messages to the brain.
Retina
Lens
Iris
Cornea
Pupil
Light waves
Optic nerve
Optic disc
Fovea

Puppy: Thinkstock/iStock/Getty Images.

the brain. The optic nerve exits the retina at the *optic disc,* causing a **blind spot**, since this area lacks rods and cones. You can find your blind spot by following the instructions in the Try This below.

try this Holding your book at arm's length, close your right eye and stare at the orange with your left eye. Slowly bring the book closer to your face. The apple on the left will disappear when light from that picture falls on your blind spot.

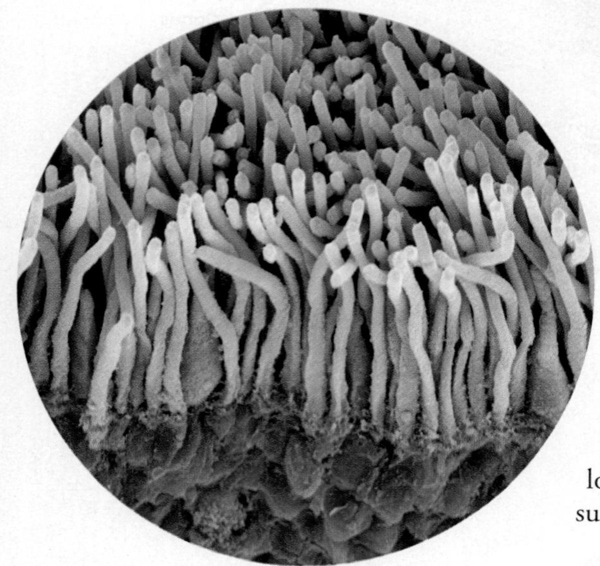

Rods and Cones
You can see why the light-sensing neurons in the back of the eye are called rods (tan) and cones (green). Rods outnumber cones by a factor of 20 and are found everywhere in the retina except the centrally located fovea. This is where the color-sensing cones are concentrated.
Steve Gschmeissner/Science Source.

THE FOVEA The retina in each eye is home to some 120 million rods and 6 million cones (Amesbury & Schallhorn, 2003; Luo & da Cruz, 2014). Rods are found everywhere in the retina, except in the optic disc and in a tiny central spot called the *fovea.* Cones are packed most densely in the fovea, but are also sprinkled through the rest of the retina. When you need to study something in precise detail (like the tiny serial number on the back of a laptop), hold it under a bright light and stare at it straight-on. The cones in the fovea excel at sensing detail and operate best in ample light. But if you want to get a look at something in dim light, focus your gaze slightly to its side, stimulating the super-light-sensitive rods outside the fovea.

DARK AND LIGHT ADAPTATION The eye has an amazing ability to adjust to drastic fluctuations in light levels. This process starts with the pupil, which rapidly shrinks and expands in response to light changes, and then continues with the rods and cones, which need more time to adjust to changes in lighting. When you walk into a dark movie theater, you can barely see an inch in front of your face. After a few minutes, your eyes start to adjust to the dark in a process called **dark adaptation**, which takes about 8 minutes for cones and 30 minutes for rods (Hecht & Mandelbaum, 1938; Klaver, Wolfs, Vingerling, Hoffman, & de Jong, 1998; Wolfe & Ali, 2015). When you *leave* the theater, the eyes also adjust. With **light adaptation**, the pupil constricts to reduce the amount of light flooding the retina, and the rods and cones become less sensitive to light. Light adaptation occurs relatively quickly, lasting at most 10 minutes (Ludel, 1978).

Is That Oprah Over There?

Let's stop for a moment and examine how information flows through the visual pathway (Infographic 3.1). Suppose you are looking at Oprah Winfrey's face. Remember, you're actually seeing the light that her face reflects. Normally, light rays bouncing off Oprah would continue moving along a straight-line path, but they encounter the bulging curvature of the cornea covering your pupil, which bends them. Rays entering the top of the cornea bend downward and those striking the base bend upward. The result is an inverted, or flip-flopped, projection on your retina. It's like your eye is a movie theater, the retina is its screen,

blind spot A hole in the visual field caused by the optic disc (the location where the optic nerve exits the retina).

dark adaptation Ability of the eyes to adjust to dark after exposure to bright light.

light adaptation Ability of the eyes to adjust to light after being in the dark.

and the feature film being played is *Your World, Turned Upside Down* (Kornheiser, 1976; Ramachandran & Rogers-Ramachandran, 2008; Stratton, 1896). The neurons of the retina respond to the stimulus; signals are sent from the photoreceptor cells to the bipolar cells, which then signal the ganglion cells that bundle into the optic nerves.

The optic nerves (one from each eye) intersect at a place in the brain called the *optic chiasm* (see Figure 4.1 on page 128). From there, information coming from each eye gets split, with about half traveling to the same-side thalamus and half going to the opposite-side thalamus. **Interneurons** then shuttle the data to the *visual cortex,* located in the occipital lobes in the back of your head. Neurons in the visual cortex called **feature detectors** specialize in detecting specific features of your visual experience, such as angles, lines, and movements. How these features are pieced together into a unified visual experience (*I see Oprah Winfrey!*) is complex. Researchers have proposed that visual processing begins in the visual cortex, where teams of cells respond to specifically oriented lines (as opposed to just pixel-like spots of light), and then continues in other parts of the cortex, where information from both eyes is integrated (Hubel & Wiesel, 1979, September). Scientists have now identified at least 30 different areas in the brains of humans and other primates that play a role in visual processing (Ramachandran & Rogers-Ramachandran, 2009). Remember, the biological processes occurring inside the eyes and brain underlie every visual experience you have.

CONNECTIONS

In **Chapter 2,** we explained how interneurons of the central nervous system (the brain and spinal cord) receive and process signals from sensory neurons. Interneurons play a vital role in the movement of data from sensory receptors to the brain.

What Color Do You See?

Although we have discussed various features of color, we have not yet explained how waves of electromagnetic energy relate to the colors we see. How does the brain know red from maroon, green from turquoise, yellow from amber? Two theories attempt to explain human color vision: the *trichromatic theory* and *opponent-process theory.* You need to understand both because they address different aspects of the phenomenon.

LO 6 Compare and contrast the theories of color vision.

TRICHROMATIC THEORY Proposed in the 1800s by Thomas Young (an English physician–scientist) and expanded upon decades later by Hermann von Helmholtz (a Prussian physicist), the **trichromatic theory** (try-kroh-MAT-ic) suggests that color vision results from the activity of three different cone types: red, green, and blue. Red cones are excited by electromagnetic energy with wavelengths in the red range (about 620–700 nm); green cones fire in response to electromagnetic energy with wavelengths in the green realm (500–575 nm); and blue cones are activated by electromagnetic energy with wavelengths corresponding to blues (about 450–490 nm; Mollon, 1982).

So how is it that we can detect millions of colors when our cones are only sensitive to red, green, and blue? According to the trichromatic theory, the brain identifies a precise hue by calculating patterns of excitement among the three cone populations. When you look at a yellow banana, for example, both the red and green cones fire, but not the blue ones. The brain interprets this pattern of red and green activation as "yellow." Thus, the brain makes its color calculations based on the relative activity of the three cone types.

COLOR DEFICIENCY AND COLOR BLINDNESS Loss or damage to one or more of the cone types leads to *color deficiency,* more commonly known as "color blindness." These terms are often used interchangeably, but true color blindness is extremely rare. Sometimes color blindness is accompanied by extreme sensitivity to light and

All Together It Makes White
When red, blue, and green light wavelengths are combined in equal proportions, they produce white light. This may seem counterintuitive, because most of us have learned that mixing different-colored paints yields some variation of brown (not white). The rules of light mixing differ from those of paints and other pigmented substances. Peter Hermes Furian/Shutterstock.

feature detectors Neurons in the visual cortex specialized in detecting specific features of the visual experience, such as angles, lines, and movements.

trichromatic theory The perception of color is the result of three types of cones, each sensitive to wavelengths in the red, green, or blue spectrums.

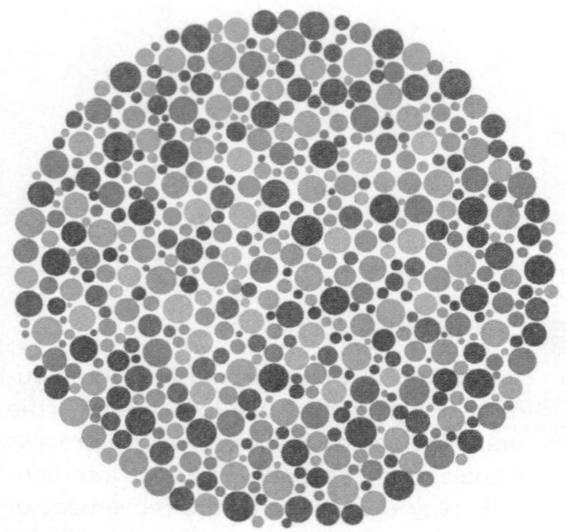

See It?
If you cannot make out the number 45 in this Ishihara color plate, then you might have a red-green color deficiency, the most common variation of "color blindness." Red-green deficiency results from a problem with the red or green cones. There are also smartphone apps designed to evaluate color vision, but these tests vary in sensitivity and may not be as reliable as the traditionally used Ishihara color plates (Sorkin et al., 2016). Science & Society Picture Library/Getty Images.

poor vision for detail, both resulting from deficient or missing cones (Kohl, Jägle, & Wissinger, 2013; Tränkner et al., 2004). Most people with color deficiencies have trouble distinguishing between red and green because they are lacking in red or green cones, but they can see other colors very well. If you can't see the number shown in the Ishihara color plate to the left, then you may have a red–green deficiency (Wong, 2011).

Put Your Heads Together

In 2015 the New York Jets and Buffalo Bills met to play their regularly scheduled game. The Jets wore uniforms that were completely green, and the Bills wore uniforms that were completely red. In your groups, use the trichromatic theory to explain why distinguishing between the teams was difficult for people with red-green color blindness (see photos below). **A**) Write a definition of the trichromatic theory in your own words. **B**) Summarize your group's explanation. **C**) Describe other situations when people with red-green color blindness might have difficulty.

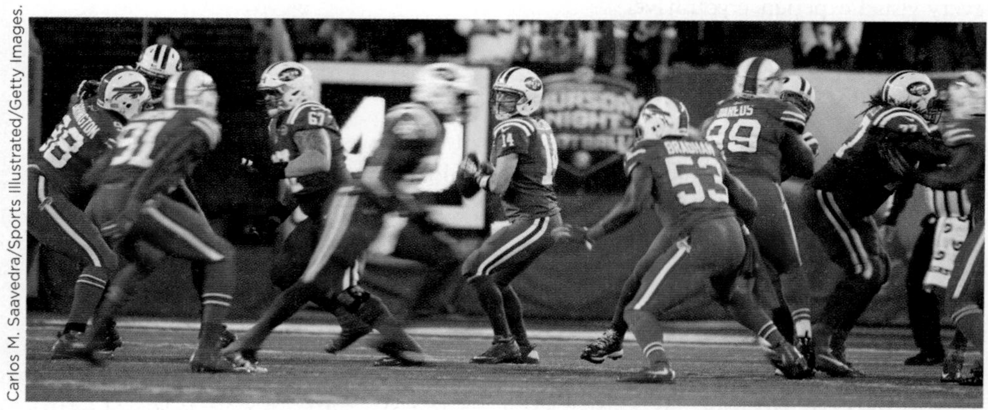

Carlos M. Saavedra/Sports Illustrated/Getty Images.

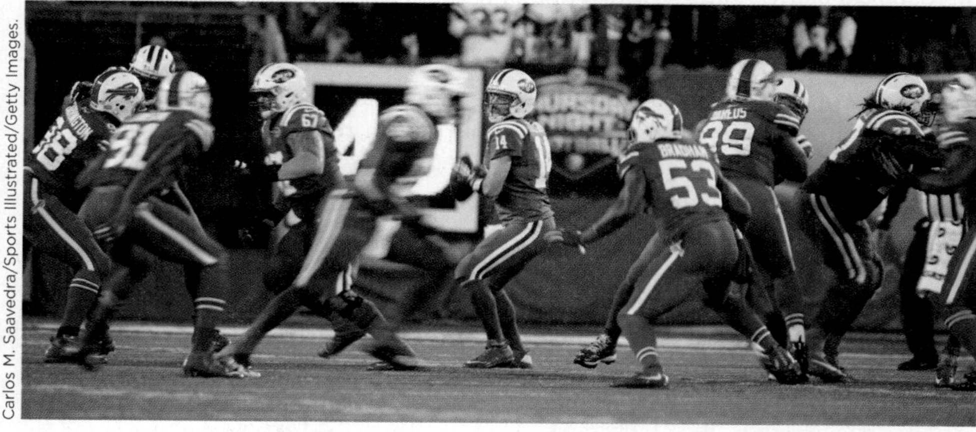

Carlos M. Saavedra/Sports Illustrated/Getty Images.

afterimage An image that appears to linger in the visual field after its stimulus, or source, is removed.

opponent-process theory Perception of color derives from a special group of neurons that respond to opponent colors (red-green, blue-yellow).

Ample research backs up the trichromatic theory, but there are some color-related phenomena it cannot explain. A prime example is the *afterimage effect*. An **afterimage** is an *image* that appears to linger in your visual field *after* its stimulus, or source, is gone. See for yourself in the Try This on the next page.

Fix your eyes on the black cross in the center of the image below. After 30 seconds, shift your gaze to the blank white area to the left. What colors do you see now?

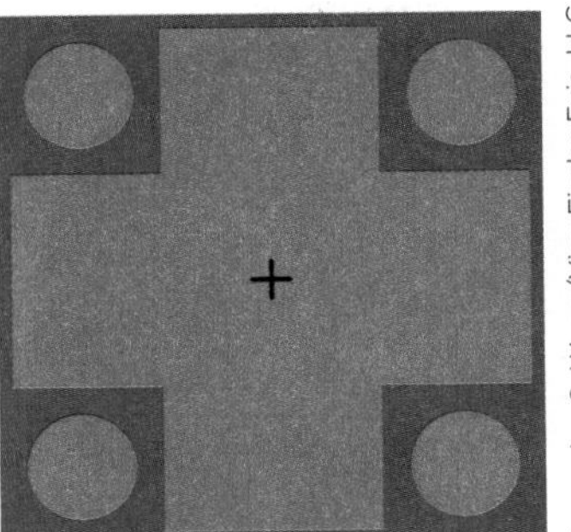

Jacquelyn S. Wong/ViewFinder Exis, LLC.

OPPONENT-PROCESS THEORY German physiologist Ewald Hering (1834–1918) realized that the trichromatic theory could not explain the afterimage effect and thus developed the **opponent-process theory** of color vision. Hering proposed that in addition to the color-sensitive cones, a special group of neurons responds to opponent colors—pairs of colors such as red–green and blue–yellow that cannot be perceived simultaneously (there is no such thing as reddish-green or bluish-yellow light). For example, one neuron in an opponent pair fires when you look at red, but is inhibited when you see green. Meanwhile, the other neuron gets excited by green but turned off by red. If you spend enough time staring at the red and blue picture in the Try This above, the neurons excited by these colors become exhausted and stop responding. When you shift your gaze to the white surface (white reflects all colors), the opponent neurons fire in response to the green and yellow, and you end up seeing a green and yellow afterimage. Research has provided strong support for the opponent-process theory, identifying particular types of neurons in a region of the thalamus (DeValois & DeValois, 1975; Jameson & Hurvich, 1989).

As it turns out, we need both the trichromatic and opponent-process theories to explain different aspects of color vision. Color perception occurs both in the light-sensing cones in the retina and in the opponent cells serving the brain. This ability is not based on processing at a single point along the visual pathway, or even one area of the brain (Rentzeperis, Nikolaev, Kiper, & van Leeuwen, 2014; Solomon & Lennie, 2007).

Vision is a highly complex sensory system. The same could be said of hearing, the subject of the next section. Let's find out how the auditory system takes sound waves and translates them into clapping thunder, buzzing mosquitos, and screeching tires.

show what you know

1. Hue is determined by the ______________ of the light reflecting off an object.
2. Explain the two major theories of color vision.
3. It's dark in your house, and you are struggling to see what time it is without turning on the light. You notice that if you turn your gaze slightly to the side of your watch, you can make out the large numbers. The ability to see these large details in the dark is due to your:
   a. presbyopia.
   b. optic disc.
   c. cones.
   d. rods.

✓ CHECK YOUR ANSWERS IN APPENDIX C.

Hearing

A Time of Mourning
"I've had hearing issues my entire life," says Mandy, whose early auditory problems stemmed from deformed Eustachian tubes. These tubes, which run from the middle ear to the throat, normally regulate pressure in the middle ear. Mandy's were shaped in a way that allowed extreme pressure buildup, often leading to very painful eardrum ruptures. But the problems associated with her Eustachian tubes were just the beginning. "My main, deep hearing loss was when I was 18, 19 years old." Mandy Harvey.

WHEN FEAR BECOMES REALITY In the fall of 2006, Mandy began to pursue her lifelong dream of becoming a musician. She enrolled at Colorado State University, and started working toward a degree in vocal music education. But a few weeks into the semester, the voices of her professors began to sound faint and distant, and she had trouble discerning musical pitches and tones. Within nine months, her world had fallen silent.

"To describe it really as anything other than watching myself die, I don't feel has enough weight to it," Mandy recalls in an interview with the BBC (BBC News, 2017, May 12, 0:48). Up until then, Mandy's life had revolved around music. She spent her childhood listening to soulful songs of the 1960s and 70s, singing in choirs, and dreaming of becoming a choir director. "I wanted to be able to direct voices and [create] cool stories, and make people feel things," says Mandy. Now that seemed impossible.

After about a year of pain and mourning, something miraculous happened. It was an ordinary day, and Mandy's dad asked her to jam with him on the guitar. They played for a while, and then he asked her to learn a new song—a request she found ridiculous—but she decided to humor him anyway. Using a guitar tuner to teach herself the notes, Mandy spent 8 hours learning One Republic's "Come Home." When she performed it for her father, she nailed every note.

Eventually, Mandy tried singing at a local jazz club's open mic night. The idea of giving a solo performance was beyond nerve-racking (Mandy describes herself as "extremely introverted" and "shy"), but she summoned the courage. "I realized after losing my hearing, which was my biggest fear my entire life, what's the worst that can happen?" Mandy says. "I've already survived that, so I can survive this. If they don't like it, they don't like it." The next week Mandy came back and sang more songs; the following week, she did a longer set; and soon the club was a weekly gig. "Then I started having my own concerts at other venues, and then I made my first album," Mandy says. These days, fans can't get enough of Mandy Harvey. In 2017 Mandy captivated people around the world with her performances on *America's Got Talent,* and in 2018, she embarked on a national tour.

She Blew Them Away
Mandy performs in the 2017 finals of NBC's reality show *America's Got Talent.* In her first performance on the show, the crowd was already on its feet clapping and giving deaf applause midway through the song. Even the notoriously surly judge Simon Cowell was beside himself. Following the performance, he walked on stage, hugged Mandy, and said: "I've done this a long time. That was one of the most amazing things I've ever seen and heard" (America's Got Talent, 2017, June 6, 4:43). Courtesy Mandy Harvey.

Listen, Hear

LO 7 Summarize how sound waves are converted into the sensation of hearing.

To understand how Mandy lost her sense of hearing, or **audition**, we need to learn how the ears receive sound waves from the environment and translate them into the electrical and chemical language of neurons. And to get a handle on that process, we need to know a little something about *sound waves:* rhythmic vibrations of molecules that travel through air and other materials, such as water, metal, and wood.

SOUND WAVES Every sound wave begins with a vibration. That could mean a pulsating loudspeaker, a quivering guitar string, or vocal chords fluttering in your throat. When an object vibrates, it sends a pressure disturbance through the molecules of the surrounding medium (usually air). Imagine a very quiet environment, such as the inside

TABLE 3.1 WAVES AND MORE WAVES

Wave Characteristic	Rhyme
Vision involves light waves bouncing off objects; the eyes detect light.	If you don't have light, you don't have sight.
Brightness depends on the amplitude, or height, of the light wave.	The taller the height, the brighter the light.
Loudness is based on the amplitude, or height, of a sound wave.	The taller the mound, the louder the sound.
Pitch is based on the frequency of sound waves; higher-pitched sounds have higher frequency.	Faster peaks mean higher squeaks.
Pitch is based on the frequency of sound waves; lower-pitched sounds have lower frequency.	Waves moving slow make pitch sound low.

Light waves and sound waves are detected and then transformed into our sensory and perceptual experiences. Here are a few rhymes that might help you remember their specific characteristics.

of a parked car, where the air molecules are fairly evenly distributed. Now turn on the radio, and the membrane of the amplified speaker immediately bulges outward, pushing air molecules out of its way. As the speaker rhythmically pushes back and forth, it sends *cycles* of high-pressure waves (with particles "bunched up") and low-pressure waves (with particles "spread out") rippling through the air (Ludel, 1978). It's important to note that air molecules are not being transmitted from the car speaker to your ears; only the sound wave travels over that distance.

Now that we have established what sound waves are—alternating zones of high and low pressure moving through the environment—let's address the immense variation in sound quality. Sounds can be differentiated by *loudness, pitch,* and *timbre.*

LOUDNESS *Loudness* is determined by the amplitude, or height, of a sound wave. A kitten purring generates low-amplitude sound waves; a jet engine generates high-amplitude sound waves. Sound intensity is measured in decibels (dB), with 0 dB being the absolute threshold for human hearing (the weakest sound that can be detected 50% of the time). Meanwhile, 60 dB is the approximate level of normal conversation. Noises at 140 dB can be instantly harmful to hearing (Liberman, 2015). But you needn't stand next to a 140-dB jet engine to sustain hearing loss. Prolonged exposure to moderately loud sounds such as gas-powered lawn mowers (around 90 dB) and music at some rock concerts (110–120 dB) can also cause damage (**INFOGRAPHIC 3.2** on the next page).

PITCH The **pitch** of a sound describes how high or low it is. An example of a high-pitched sound is a flute at its highest notes; a low-pitched sound is a tuba at its lowest notes. Pitch is based on wave **frequency**. We measure frequency with a unit called the *hertz* (Hz), which indicates the number of wave peaks passing a given point in 1 second. If you are hearing a 200-Hz sound wave, then theoretically 200 waves enter your ear per second. A higher-pitched sound will have higher frequency waves; the time between the "bunched up" particles and the "spread out" particles will be less than that for a lower-pitched sound. Humans can detect frequencies ranging from about 20 Hz to 20,000 Hz. For comparison, bats can detect sound frequencies from 2,000 Hz to 110,000 Hz, well beyond the range of humans. Beluga whales can sense frequencies from about 100 Hz to 123,000 Hz and mice from 1,000 Hz to 91,000 Hz (Strain, 2003). If you are having trouble remembering how frequency and other wave properties correspond to the qualities of light and sound stimuli, **Table 3.1** (above) offers some useful rhymes.

You Asked, Mandy Answers

http://qrs.ly/jh7829i

If you could get your hearing back, would you do it?

synonyms
loudness volume

audition The sense of hearing.

pitch The degree to which a sound is high or low, determined by the frequency of its sound wave.

frequency The number of sound waves passing a given point per unit of time; higher frequency is perceived as higher pitch, and lower frequency is perceived as lower pitch.

Can You Hear Me Now?

Hearing is a process in which stimuli (sound waves) are mechanically converted to vibrations that are transduced to neural messages. If one part of this complicated system is compromised, hearing loss results.

1 The pinna funnels sound waves into the auditory canal, focusing them toward the eardrum.

2 Vibrations of the eardrum cause malleus to push incus, which moves stapes, which presses on oval window, amplifying waves.

3 Pressure on oval window causes fluid in cochlea to vibrate.

4 Vibrating fluid in cochlea bends hair cells on basilar membrane, triggering action potentials in the auditory nerve.

5 Auditory nerve carries signals to auditory cortex in brain, where sounds are given meaning.

Pinna
Auditory canal
Ear drum
Malleus
Incus
Stapes
Oval window
Cochlea
INNER EAR
MIDDLE EAR
OUTER EAR
To auditory cortex in brain
Hair cells
Basilar membrane
Oval window
Cochlea

Decibels and Damage

The intensity of a sound stimulus is measured in decibels (dB). The absolute threshold for human hearing—the softest sound a human can hear—is 0 dB. Loud noises, such as the 140 dB produced by a jet engine, cause immediate damage that leads to hearing loss. Chronic exposure to moderately loud noise, such as traffic or an MP3 player near maximum volume, can also cause damage (Keith, Michaud, & Chiu, 2008).

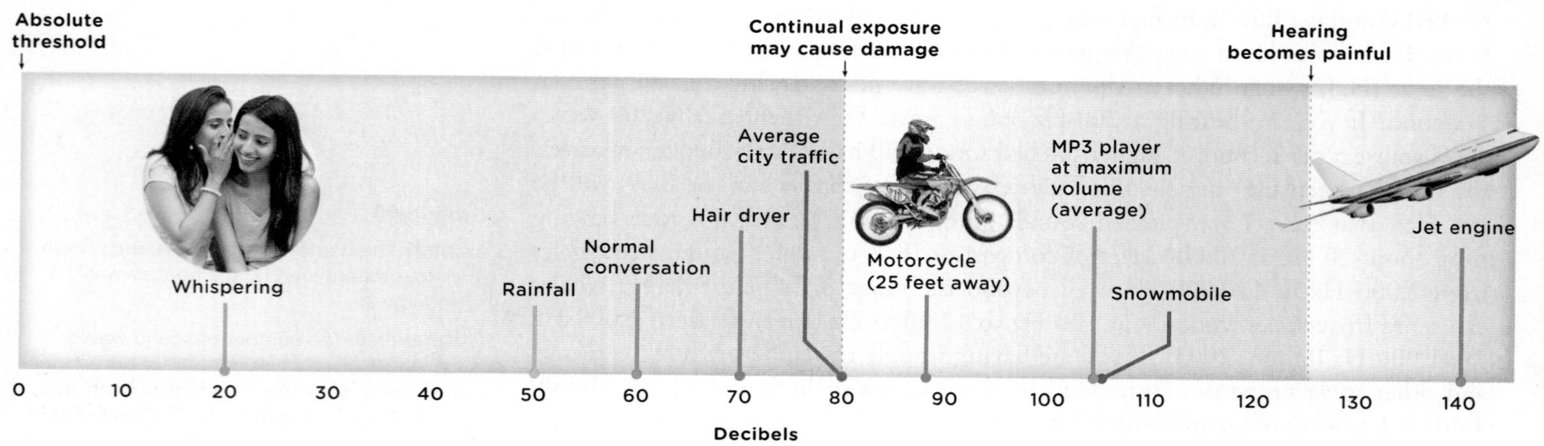

TIMBRE How is it possible that two sounds with similar loudness and pitch (Mandy Harvey and Beyoncé belting the same note at the same volume) can sound so different to us? The answer to this question lies in their *timbre* (TAM-ber; Patil, Pressnitzer, Shamma, & Elhilali, 2012). Most everyday sounds—people's voices, traffic noises, humming air conditioners—consist of more than one wave frequency. In some cases, one frequency dominates, and we perceive it as the pitch of the sound. Let's say Mandy sings a middle C note, which has a frequency of 282 Hz. As she hits that note, her vocal chords also produce softer accompanying frequencies, which may be higher or lower than 282 Hz. These additional frequencies, and the way they fluctuate across time, are referred to as timbre (Patil et al., 2012). Timbre is what makes Mandy's voice sound different from that of Beyoncé, or any person, singing the same note at the same volume. Thanks to the brain's interpretation of timbre, we can identify a person without seeing who it is!

All Ears

Now that we have outlined the basic properties of sound, let's learn how the ears transform sound waves into the language of the brain. Your ears are extraordinarily efficient at what they do—transducing the physical motion of sound waves into the electrical and chemical signals of the nervous system (see Infographic 3.2).

FROM SOUND WAVE TO BONE MOVEMENTS What exactly happens when a sound wave reaches your ear? First, it is ushered inside by the ear's funnel-like structure. Then it sweeps down the auditory canal, a tunnel leading to a delicate membrane called the eardrum, which separates the outer ear from the middle ear. The impact of the sound wave bouncing against the eardrum sets off a chain reaction through the three tiny bones in the middle ear: the malleus (hammer), incus (anvil), and stapes (stirrup). The malleus pushes the incus; the incus moves the stapes; and the stapes presses on a membrane called the *oval window* leading to the ear's deepest cavern, the inner ear (Luers & Hüttenbrink, 2016). It is in this cavern that transduction occurs.

Inspiring Leader
When Claudia Gordon lost the ability to hear at 8 years old, she thought she was "the only deaf person in the world" (Baggetto, 2010, para. 5). Gordon eventually became a leader in the deaf community and in society at large, serving in the Obama administration as public engagement advisor for the disability community. SourceAmerica.

FROM MOVING BONES TO MOVING FLUID The primary component of the inner ear is the **cochlea** (KOHK-lee-uh), a snail-shaped structure filled with liquid. The entire length of the cochlea is lined with the *basilar membrane,* which contains about 16,000 hair cells. These hair cells are the receptor cells for sound waves that have been transformed into liquid waves. Recall that the sound waves enter your ear from the outside world, causing the eardrum to vibrate, which sets off a chain reaction in the middle ear bones. As the last bone in this chain (the stapes) pushes on the oval window, the fluid inside the cochlea vibrates, causing the hair cells to bend. Below the base of the hair cells are dendrites of neurons whose axons form the *auditory nerve* (Ludel, 1978). If a vibration is strong enough in the cochlear fluid, the bending of the hair cells causes these nearby neurons to fire. Signals from the auditory nerve pass through various processing hubs in the brain, including the thalamus, and eventually wind up in the auditory cortex, where sounds are given meaning.

If any part of this pathway is compromised, hearing problems may arise. Mandy says that the profound hearing loss she experienced in college resulted from deterioration of the auditory nerve; this damage is associated with a connective tissue disorder called Ehlers–Danlos syndrome, Type III. According to one study, hearing loss is not uncommon among people with Ehlers–Danlos syndrome (Weir, Hatch, Muus, Wallace, & Meyer, 2016). Mandy suffers from a

cochlea Fluid-filled, snail-shaped organ of the inner ear lined with the basilar membrane.

variety of other symptoms as well, including chronic pain and hypermobile joints. "All of my joints pop out of socket. . . . I dislocate my shoulders and my fingers all the time," says Mandy. "Your body is in a constant state of pain. You just kind of deal with it."

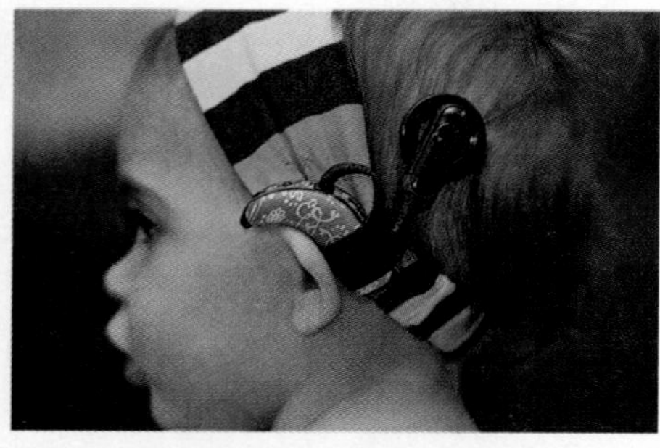

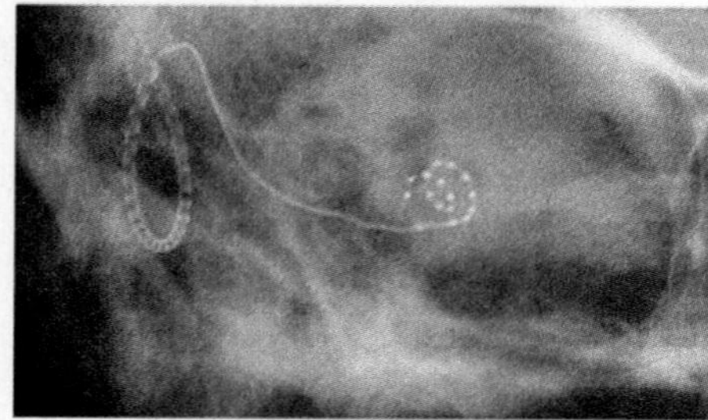

FIGURE 3.3
Cochlear Implants
Cochlear implants enable hearing by circumventing damaged parts of the inner ear. An external microphone gathers sound, which is organized by a speech processor. Internally, an implanted receiver converts this signal into electrical impulses that directly stimulate the auditory nerve. The X-ray on the bottom shows the cochlear implant's electrode array coiling into the cochlea, directly reaching nerve fibers leading to the auditory nerve.
Top: Debbie Noda/Modesto Bee/ZUMA Press/Newscom. Bottom: © ISM/Phototake—All rights reserved.

CAN HEARING BE RECOVERED? For some people with hearing loss, medical technologies can help restore hearing. You are probably familiar with *hearing aids,* devices worn on the ears that increase the amplitude of incoming sound waves (making them louder) so the hair cells in the inner ear can better detect the vibrations. If the hair cells are no longer functioning, a hearing aid won't help, but scientists are trying to develop drug treatments to regenerate hair cells, and they have produced promising results in studies of nonhuman mammals (McLean et al., 2017). Another way to address the problem of damaged hair cells is by using cochlear implants. These so-called "bionic ears" pick up sound waves from the environment with a microphone and turn them into electrical impulses that stimulate the auditory nerve, much as the cochlea would do were it functioning properly (**Figure 3.3**). From there, the auditory nerve transmits electrical signals to the brain, where they are "heard," or interpreted as human voices, hip-hop beats, and dog barks. But note that "hearing" with a cochlear implant is not exactly the same as hearing with two ears. Voices may sound computerized or Mickey Mouse–like (Oakley, 2012, May 30).

How Is Pitch Processed?

We know how sound waves are transformed into auditory sensations, but how does the brain know the difference between the yap of a Chihuahua and the deep bark of a rottweiler, or the whine of a dentist's drill and the rumble of thunder? In other words, how do we distinguish between sound waves of high and low frequencies? There are two complementary theories that explain how the brain processes pitch.

LO 8 Illustrate how we sense different pitches of sound.

PLACE THEORY According to **place theory**, the location of neural activity along the cochlea allows us to differentiate the pitches of high-frequency sounds. Hair cells toward the oval-window end of the basilar membrane vibrate more when exposed to higher-frequency sounds. Hair cells toward the opposite end of the basilar membrane vibrate more in response to lower-frequency sounds. The brain determines the pitch of high-frequency sounds by judging where along the basilar membrane neural signals originate. Place theory works well for explaining higher-pitch sounds (4,000–20,000 Hz), but not so well for lower-pitch sounds—specifically those with frequencies below 4,000 Hz. This is because lower-frequency sounds produce vibrations that are more dispersed along the basilar membrane, with less precise locations of movement.

FREQUENCY THEORY To understand how humans sense lower pitches (from 20–400 Hz), we can use the **frequency theory**, which suggests that the frequency of neural impulses matches that of the incoming sound waves. The entire basilar membrane vibrates at the same frequency as the incoming sound wave, causing the hair cells to be activated at that frequency, too. Nearby neurons fire at that same frequency, sending signals through the auditory nerve at this rate. If the sound wave has a frequency of 200 Hz, the basilar membrane vibrates at 200 Hz, and the neurons in the auditory nerve fire at this rate as well.

place theory States that pitch corresponds to the location of the vibrating hair cells along the cochlea.

frequency theory States that pitch is determined by the vibrating frequency of the sound wave, basilar membrane, and associated neural impulses.

volley principle States that the perception of pitches between 400 Hz and 4,000 Hz is made possible by neurons working together to fire in volleys.

Neurons, however, can only fire so fast, the maximum rate being about 1,000 times per second. How does the frequency theory explain how we hear sounds higher than 1,000 Hz? According to the **volley principle**, neurons can "work" together so that their combined firing may exceed 1,000 times per second. Imagine a hockey team practicing for a tournament. The coach challenges the players to fire shots on goal at the fastest rate possible. The team members get together and decide to work in small groups, alternating shots on the goal. The first group skates and shoots, and as they skate away and return to the back of the line, the next group takes their shots. Each time a group is finished shooting on the goal, the next group is ready to shoot. Groups of neurons work in a similar way, firing together in *volleys;* as one group finishes firing and is "**recovering**," the next group fires. The frequency of the combined firing of all neuron groups results in one's perception of pitch.

We have now examined what occurs in a hearing system working at an optimal level. But many of us have auditory functioning that is far from perfect.

CONNECTIONS

In **Chapter 2,** we described how neurons must recover after they fire; each neuron must return to its resting potential. During this period, they cannot fire, that is, they are "recovering." Without the ability to *volley,* the range of human hearing would be greatly reduced.

I Can't Hear You

In the United States, nearly half of people over age 65 and a quarter of those between 55 and 64 have hearing problems (Mayo Clinic, 2015, September 3). Everyone experiences some degree of hearing loss as they age, primarily resulting from normal wear and tear of the delicate hair cells. Damage to the hair cells or the auditory nerve leads to *sensorineural deafness.* In contrast, *conduction hearing impairment* results from damage to the eardrum or the middle-ear bones that transmit sound waves to the cochlea.

But it's not just older adults who ought to be concerned. One large study found that about 20%, or 1 in 5, of American teenagers suffer from some degree of hearing loss (Shargorodsky, Curhan, Curhan, & Eavey, 2010). Worldwide, some 1.1 billion young people are considered to be at risk of damage to their hearing because of their "unsafe listening practices" (World Health Organization [WHO], 2015, p. 1). Exposure to loud sounds, such as music played at a high volume through earbuds, may contribute (Infographic 3.2). Keep in mind (and remind your friends) that hearing loss often occurs gradually and goes unnoticed for some time. But the damage is permanent, and its impact on communication and relationships can be life-changing (Portnuff, 2016).

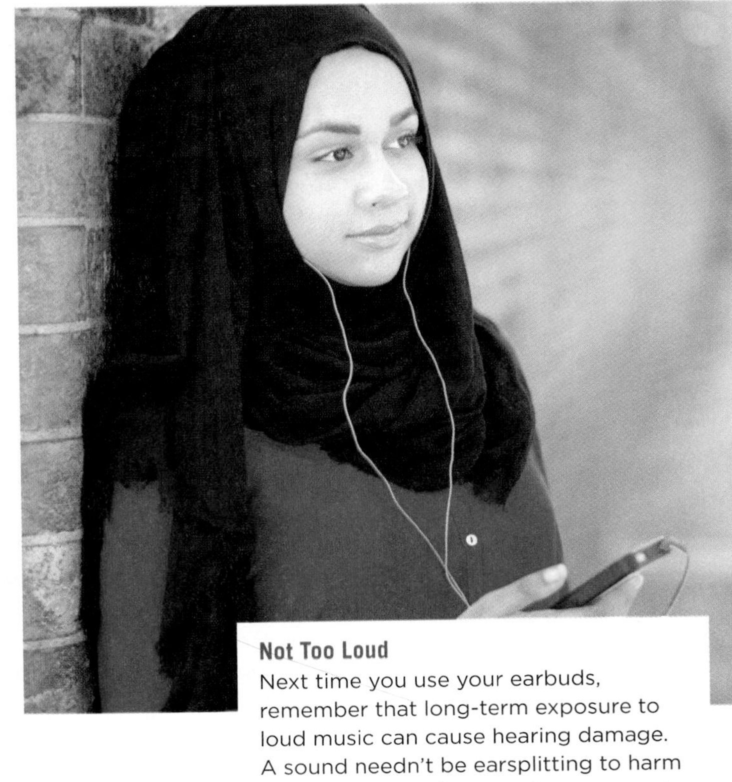

Not Too Loud
Next time you use your earbuds, remember that long-term exposure to loud music can cause hearing damage. A sound needn't be earsplitting to harm your delicate auditory system. Nick Daly/Getty Images.

show what you know

1. The ______________ of a sound is based on the frequency of its waves.
   a. pitch
   b. timbre
   c. amplitude
   d. purity

2. When the stapes pushes on the oval window, the fluid in the cochlea vibrates. This causes the hair cells to bend and nearby nerve cells to fire. This process is known as:
   a. the volley principle.
   b. transduction.
   c. the frequency theory.
   d. audition.

3. A researcher studying the location of neural activity in the cochlea finds that hair cells nearest the oval window vibrate more in response to high-frequency sounds. Explain how this supports the place theory of pitch perception.

✓ CHECK YOUR ANSWERS IN APPENDIX C.

Smell, Taste, Touch

When Mandy lost her hearing, she began to rely more on her other senses to gather information from the environment. "I think everything else heightened a bit," Mandy explains. "I definitely taste things stronger and smell things stronger, but I've been purposely paying more attention." Mandy's enhanced smell and taste are likely the result of **changes in her brain**. After losing one sensory system, the brain reorganizes itself to adapt (Reichert & Schöpf, 2017). "If one sense is lost, the areas of the brain normally devoted to handling that sensory information do not go unused—they get rewired and put to work processing other senses" (Bates, 2012, September 18, para. 2).

CONNECTIONS

In **Chapter 2,** we introduced the concept of neuroplasticity, which refers to the ability of the brain to heal, grow new connections, and make do with what's available. Here, we suggest that Mandy's increased use of other senses is made possible by the plasticity of her nervous system.

Smell: Nosing Around

LO 9 Describe the process of olfaction.

Many people take **olfaction** (ohl-FAK-shun)—the sense of smell—for granted. But such individuals might think twice if they actually understood how losing olfaction would affect their lives. People with the rare condition of *anosmia* are unable to perceive odors. They cannot smell smoke in a burning building or a gas leak from a stove. Nor can they savor the complex palates of pesto, curry, chocolate, or coffee. Because, without smell, food doesn't taste as good.

A CHEMICAL SENSE Olfaction and taste are called chemical senses because they involve sensing chemicals in the environment. For olfaction, those chemicals are odor molecules riding currents of air. For taste, they are flavor molecules surfing on waves of saliva. Odor molecules, which are emitted by a variety of sources (for example, spices, fruits, flowers, bacteria, and skin), make their way into the nose by hitchhiking on currents of air flowing into the nostrils or through the mouth. About 3 inches into the nostrils is a patch of tissue called the *olfactory epithelium.* Around the size of a typical postage stamp, the olfactory epithelium is home to millions of olfactory receptor neurons that provide tiny docking sites, or receptors, for odor molecules (much as a lock acts as a docking site for a key; **Figure 3.4**). When enough odor molecules attach to an **olfactory receptor neuron, it fires.** This is how *transduction* occurs in the chemical sense of olfaction.

CONNECTIONS

In **Chapter 2,** we discussed the properties that allow neurons to communicate. When enough sending neurons signal a receiving neuron to pass along its message, their combined signal becomes excitatory and the neuron fires. Similarly, if enough odor molecules bind to an olfactory receptor neuron, an action potential occurs.

WHAT'S UP WITH THAT SMELL? Olfactory receptor neurons project into a part of the brain called the *olfactory bulb,* where they converge in clusters called *glomeruli* (Figure 3.4). From there, signals are passed along to higher brain centers, including the hippocampus, amygdala, and olfactory cortex (Firestein, 2001; Seubert, Freiherr, Djordjevic, & Lundström, 2013). The other sensory systems relay information through the thalamus before it goes to higher brain centers, but not the olfactory system; its wiring is on a fast track to the olfactory cortex. There is another reason smell is special. Olfactory receptor neurons are one of the few types of neurons that regenerate. Once an olfactory receptor neuron is born, it does its job for a minimum of 30 days, then dies and is replaced (Brann & Firestein, 2014; Schiffman, 1997).

Humans have about 350 different *types* of odor receptors, and some researchers estimate that we theoretically could distinguish over 1 trillion smells (Bushdid, Magnasco, Vosshall, & Keller, 2014). Each receptor type recognizes several odors, and each odor activates several receptors; a given scent creates a telltale pattern of neural activity that the brain recognizes as lemon, garlic, or smelly feet. The types of receptors and the degree to which they are activated enable the brain to identify the odor

olfaction The sense of smell.

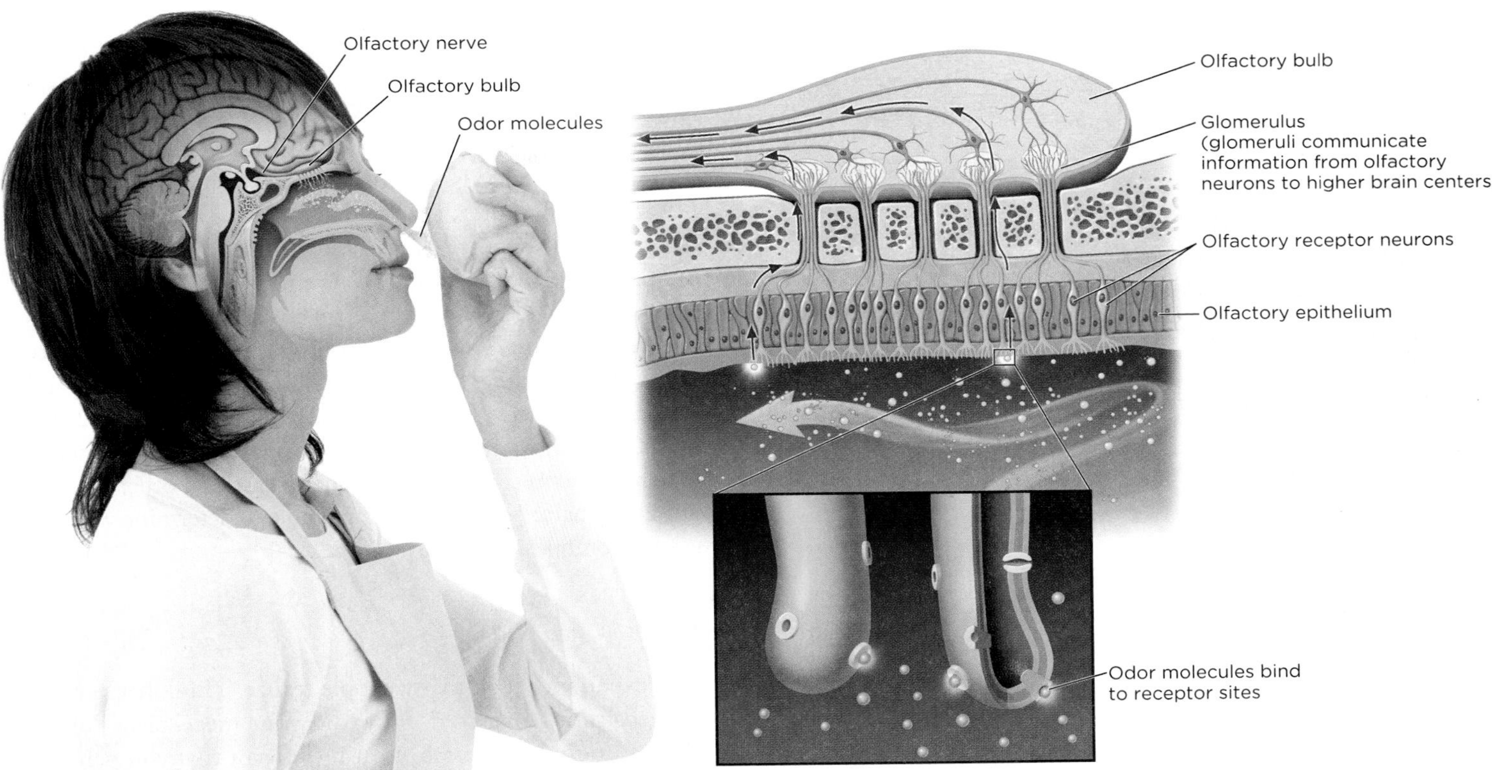

FIGURE 3.4
Olfaction
When enough odor molecules attach to an olfactory receptor neuron, it fires, sending a message to the olfactory bulb in the brain. From there, the signal is sent to higher brain centers. Photo: Collage Photography/Veer.

(Firestein, 2001). Not surprisingly, we are much better at picking up on faint human odor "footprints" (the unique scents of people) than smells coming from inanimate objects (Pazzaglia, 2015).

Scents have a powerful influence on human behaviors and mental processes. Minutes after birth, babies use the scent of their mother's breast to guide them toward the nipple, and they quickly learn to discriminate her milk from someone else's (Makin & Porter, 1989; Marin, Rapisardi, & Tani, 2015; Porter & Winberg, 1999). For adults, scents can trigger emotions (positive and negative) and measurable physiological reactions (Kadohisa, 2013). Odors of burning and vomit bring about disgust (Glass, Lingg, & Heuberger, 2015), while the scent of rose oil seems to dampen the stress response, perhaps by interfering with activity in the hypothalamic–pituitary–adrenal system (Chapter 12; Fukada, Kano, Miyoshi, Komaki, & Watanabe, 2012).

The relationship between olfaction and sexual behavior has long intrigued researchers, and evidence suggests that scent plays an important role in romantic attraction (Gangestad & Haselton, 2015; Griskevicius, Haselton, & Ackerman, 2015; Pazzaglia, 2015). Some researchers even suspect that humans, like animals, communicate via odor molecules called *pheromones* (Tan & Goldman, 2015; Wyatt, 2015).

DIDN'T SEE THAT COMING

SEXY SMELLS? Animals of all different kinds use pheromones to communicate with members of the same species. Rats, for example, release pheromones to mark territory and warn other rats of danger, and female elephants invite males to mate by secreting a pheromone in their urine (Tirindelli, Dibattista, Pifferi, & Menini, 2009).

THEIR ARMPITS SMELLED ENTICING.

Scent of a Woman
Model Alyssa Bishop is one of the many women who have embraced their colorfully dyed armpit hair. Some men are following this trend as well (Johnson, 2017, May 28). Hair or no hair, the armpits are thought to be a potential source of pheromones—chemical signals that can trigger hormonal changes and other effects in members of the same species. JEREMY KORESKI/The New York Times.

Humans may unconsciously communicate through pheromones released into the air by glands in the armpits, breasts, lips, and other parts of the body (Wyatt, 2015). Researchers have found that smelling female armpit and genital secretions affects male testosterone levels (Cerda-Molina, Hernández-López, de la O, Chavira-Ramírez, & Mondragón-Ceballos, 2013; Miller & Maner, 2010). Such findings have sparked great excitement in the media and popular culture. (Perhaps you have heard of "pheromone parties," where people try to find the perfect mates by smelling each other's sweaty T-shirts.) Yet experts do not agree which chemicals are the best human pheromone candidates, and how those substances should be investigated (Liberles, 2015; Wyatt, 2015). Until researchers start using "rigorous methods already proven successful in pheromone research on other species" (Wyatt, 2015, para. 1), it may be impossible to determine whether human pheromones exist.

Taste: Just Eat It

Eating is more of an olfactory experience than many people realize. Think back to the last time your nose was clogged from a bad cold. How did your meals taste? When you chew, odors from food float up into your nose, creating a flavor that you perceive as "taste," when it's really smell. If this mouth–nose link is blocked, there is no difference between apples and onions, Sprite and Coke, or wine and cooled coffee (Herz, 2007). Don't believe us? Then Try This.

try this Tie on a blindfold, squeeze your nostrils, and ask a friend to hand you a wedge of apple and a wedge of onion, both on toothpicks so that you can't feel their texture. Now bite into both. Without your nose, you probably can't tell the difference (Rosenblum, 2010).

LO 10 Identify the structures involved in taste and describe how they work.

TASTY CHEMICALS If the nose is so crucial for flavor appreciation, then what role does the mouth play? Receptors in the mouth are sensitive to five basic but very important tastes: *sweet, salty, sour, bitter,* and *umami*. You are likely familiar with all of them, except perhaps umami, which is a savory taste found in seaweed, aged cheeses, protein-rich foods, mushrooms, and monosodium glutamate (MSG; Chandrashekar, Hoon, Ryba, & Zuker, 2006; Singh, Hummel, Gerber, Landis, & Iannilli, 2015). We call the ability to detect these stimuli our sense of taste, or **gustation** (guh-STAY-shun; **Figure 3.5**).

Stick out your tongue, and what do you see in the mirror? All those little bumps are called *papillae,* and they are home to some 2,000 to 4,000 taste buds (PubMed Health, 2016, August 17). Jutting from each of these buds are 50 to 100 taste receptor cells, and it is onto these cells that food molecules bind (similar to the lock-and-key mechanism of an odor molecule binding to a receptor in the nose). These taste receptor cells are also found in the roof of the mouth and the lining of the cheeks.

As you bite into a juicy orange and begin to chew, chemicals from the orange (sour acid and sweet sugar) are released into your saliva, where they dissolve and

gustation The sense of taste.

bathe the taste buds throughout your mouth. The chemicals find their way to matching receptors and latch on, sparking action potentials in **sensory neurons**, another example of *transduction*. Signals are next sent through sensory neurons to the thalamus, and then on to higher brain centers for processing.

Receptors for taste are constantly being replenished, but their life span is only about 8 to 12 days (Feng, Huang, & Wang, 2013). If they didn't regenerate, you would be in trouble every time you burned your tongue sipping hot coffee or soup. Even so, by age 20, you have already lost half of the taste receptors you had at birth. As the years go by, their turnover rate becomes slower and slower, making it harder to appreciate the basic taste sensations, but not necessarily reducing eating pleasure or appetite (Arganini & Sinesio, 2015; Feng et al., 2013; Kaneda et al., 2000). Drinking alcohol and smoking worsen the problem by impairing the ability of receptors to receive food molecules. Losing taste is unfortunate, and it may take away from life's simple pleasures, but it's probably not going to kill you—at least not if you are a modern human. We can't be so sure about our primitive ancestors.

CONNECTIONS

In **Chapter 2,** we explained that sensory neurons receive information from the sensory systems and send it to the brain. With gustation, the sensory neurons send information about taste. Once processed in the brain, information is sent back through motor neurons signaling you to take another bite!

EVOLUTION, CULTURE, AND TASTE The ability to taste has been essential to the survival of our species. Tastes push us toward foods we need and away from those that could harm us. We gravitate toward sweet, calorie-rich foods for their life-sustaining energy—an adaptive trait if you are a primitive human foraging in trees and bushes, not so adaptive if you are a modern human looking for something to eat at the food court. We are also drawn to salty foods, which tend to contain valuable minerals, and to umami, which signals the presence of proteins essential for cellular health and growth. Bitter and sour tastes we tend to avoid, on the other hand. This also gives us an evolutionary edge because poisonous plants or rancid foods are often bitter or sour. Our *absolute threshold* for bitter is lower than the threshold for sweet. Can you see how this is advantageous? Some people, known as "supertasters," are extremely sensitive to bitterness and other tastes and thus can be characterized as "picky eaters," though food preferences

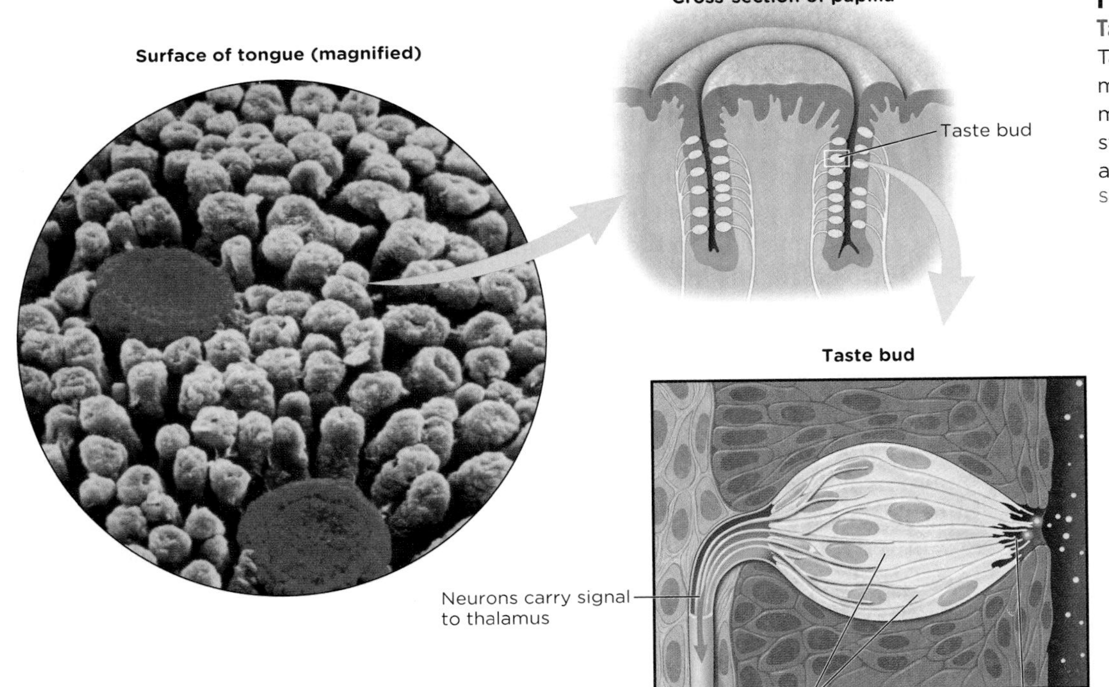

FIGURE 3.5
Tasting
Taste buds located in the papillae are made up of receptor cells that communicate signals to the brain when stimulated by chemicals from food and other substances. Photo: Omikron/Science Source.

are also influenced by families and culture (Catanzaro, Chesbro, & Velkey, 2013; Hayes & Keast, 2011; Rupp, 2014, September 30). Not every picky eater is a supertaster, however; sometimes so-called picky eaters simply prefer doughnuts to kale or carrots. Culture can determine what makes a food "good." For example, most people from Western cultures are not enticed by sea cucumbers and goose intestine. Yet these dishes are considered gourmet delicacies in Chinese culture, mainly because of their unique textures (Greenwood, 2016, January 26). Would you want to taste them?

A Sixth Taste?
Scientists have long suspected there is a sixth taste in addition to the five already identified (sweet, salty, sour, bitter, and umami). Now, strong evidence of this sixth taste exists: Researchers call it *oleogustus*, or "the unique taste of fat" (Running, Craig, & Mattes, 2015, p. 1). Rusty Hill/Getty Images.

Every person experiences taste in a unique way. You like cilantro; your friend thinks it tastes like bath soap. Taste preferences may begin developing before birth, as flavors consumed by a pregnant woman pass into amniotic fluid and are swallowed by the fetus. For example, babies who were exposed to carrot or garlic flavors in the womb (through their mothers' consumption of carrot juice or garlic pills) seem more tolerant of those flavors in their food and breast milk (Mennella, Coren, Jagnow, & Beauchamp, 2001; Underwood, 2014). It's not clear how these early-established taste preferences impact lifelong eating choices, but understanding how they develop could be useful for encouraging healthy habits in children (Underwood, 2014).

We have made some major headway in this chapter, examining four of the major sensory systems: vision, hearing, smell, and taste. Now it is time to get a feel for a fifth sense: touch.

Touch: Can You Feel It?

If you sat down with Mandy at a jazz club, coffee house, or anywhere that has music playing in the background, you might be surprised to see her bobbing her head or tapping her fingers. How does she move in time with music she can't hear? Mandy is constantly aware of vibrations; she feels them in the floor, table, whatever she may be touching. This ability is essential when it comes to staying in sync with fellow musicians. "I perform with my shoes off so I can feel the drum through the floor," Mandy explains. "You designate different parts of your body to paying attention to different things." To feel each instrument in different parts of her body, Mandy relies on touch receptors, many of which dwell in the skin.

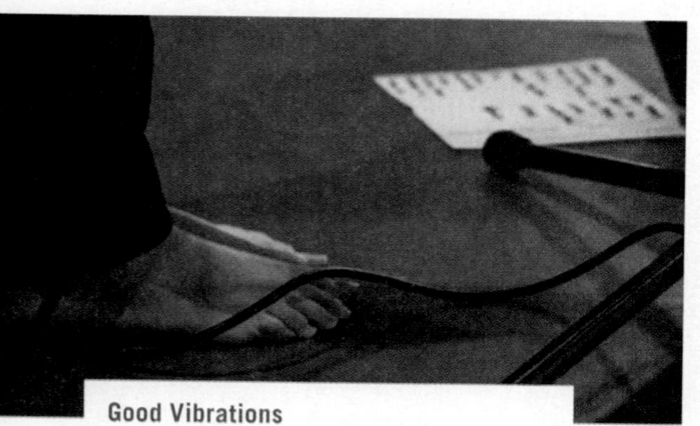

Good Vibrations
Mandy stands on the stage barefoot so she can feel the rhythm of the other instruments coming through the floor. She also uses her sense of touch to gauge how loud she is singing, placing her foot on a monitor that produces vibrations in response to her voice. "I can put my foot on it, and feel that I'm making a rumble, and then I can judge, based off of how loud that rumble is . . . how loud I'm singing," Mandy explains. Courtesy Mandy Harvey.

Take a moment to appreciate your vast *epidermis,* the outer layer of your skin. Every moment of the day, receptors in the skin gather information about the environment. Among them are *thermoreceptors* that sense hot or cold, *Pacinian corpuscles* that detect vibrations, and *Meissner's corpuscles* sensitive to the slightest touch, like a snowflake landing on your nose (Bandell, Macpherson, & Patapoutian, 2007; Zimmerman, Bai, & Ginty, 2014; **Figure 3.6**).

Pain: It Hurts

Not all touch sensations are as pleasant as the tickle of a snowflake. Touch receptors can also communicate signals that are interpreted as pain. *Nociceptive pain* is caused by heat, cold, chemicals, and pressure. *Nociceptors* that respond to these stimuli are primarily housed in the skin, but they also are found in muscles and internal organs.

In very rare cases, a baby is born without the ability to feel pain. Children with this type of genetic disorder may face a greater risk of serious injury (Genetics Home Reference, 2017, July 13). When scrapes and cuts are not felt, they may not receive the necessary protection and treatment. The "ouch" that results from the stub of a toe or the prick of a needle tells us to stop what we are doing and tend to our wounds. Let's find out how this protective mechanism works.

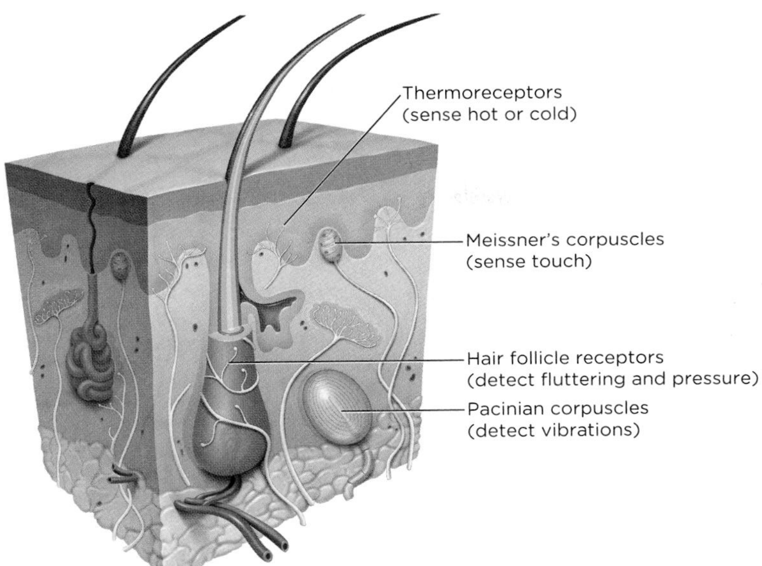

FIGURE 3.6
Touch
The sensation of touch begins with our skin, which houses a variety of receptors including those shown here.

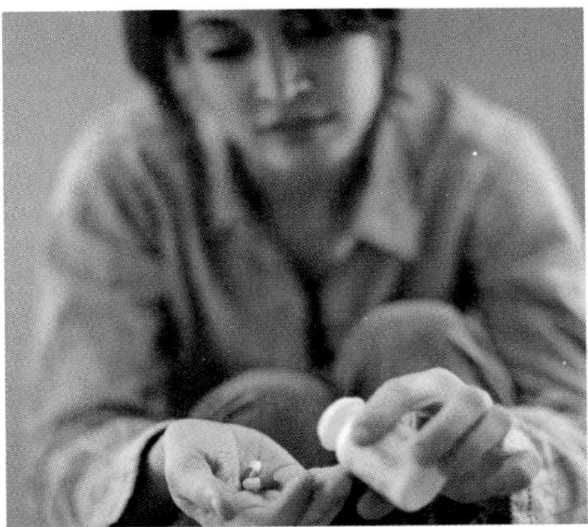

Problems with Painkillers
Acetaminophen is a painkilling and fever-reducing drug found in many over-the-counter medications, notably Tylenol. Nearly 1 in 4 Americans takes acetaminophen on a weekly basis, but are they aware of its psychological effects? Taking acetaminophen can diminish one's capacity to empathize with, or "feel," another person's pain (Mischkowski, Crocker, & Way, 2016). How do you think this side effect might impact social interactions? Ray Kachatorian/Getty Images.

TWO PATHWAYS FOR PAIN Thanks to the elaborate system of nerves running up and down our bodies, we are able to experience unpleasant, yet very necessary, sensations of pain. *Fast nerve fibers,* made up of large, **myelinated neurons**, are responsible for quickly conveying information about pain in the skin and muscles, generally experienced as a stinging feeling in a specific location. If you stub your toe, your fast nerve fibers enable you to sense a painful sting where the impact occurred. *Slow nerve fibers,* made up of smaller, unmyelinated neurons, are responsible for conveying information about dull aching pain that is not necessarily concentrated in a specific region. The diffuse pain that follows the initial sting of the stubbed toe results from activity in the slow nerve fibers.

CONNECTIONS
In **Chapter 2,** we explained how a myelin sheath insulates the axon and speeds the transmission of neural messages. The myelin covering the fast nerve fibers allows them to convey pain information more rapidly than the slow, unmyelinated nerve fibers.

The axons of the fast and slow nerve fibers band into nerves on their way to the spinal cord and brain (**Figure 3.7** on the next page). The fast nerve pathway alerts the brain's reticular formation that something important has happened. The sensory information then goes to the thalamus and on to the somatosensory cortex, where it is processed further (for example, indicating where it hurts most). The slow nerve pathway starts out in the same direction, with processing occurring in the brainstem, hypothalamus, thalamus, and limbic system.

LO 11 Explain how the biopsychosocial perspective helps us understand pain.

IT'S COMPLICATED Understanding the **mechanisms of pain** at the neural level is important, but biology alone cannot explain how we perceive pain and why people experience it so differently. How can the same flu shot cause intense pain in one person but mere discomfort in another? As with most complex topics in psychology, pain is best understood using a multilevel method, such as the biopsychosocial perspective. Chronic pain, for example, can be explained by biological factors (the neurological pathways involved), psychological factors (distress, thoughts), and social factors (social support, or lack thereof; Sutherland, 2017). Prior experiences, environmental factors, and cultural expectations all influence how pain is processed (Gatchel, Haggard, Thomas, & Howard, 2013; Gatchell & Maddrey, 2004).

CONNECTIONS
In **Chapter 2,** we discussed the pain reflex, which occurs when we automatically respond to a painful stimulus before becoming conscious of it. Here, we describe the process by which pain is brought into our conscious awareness.

Even within the same individual, pain sensitivity can ebb and flow, and this is partly due to psychological factors (Gatchel et al., 2007; Gatchel, Haggard, Thomas, & Howard 2013; Raichle, Hanley, Jensen, & Cardenas, 2007). Negative feelings such

FIGURE 3.7

Fast and Slow Pain Pathways

When you stub your toe, two kinds of pain messages can be communicated to your brain. Your first perception of pain may be a sharp, clear feeling where the impact occurred. The message quickly travels through your spinal cord to your brain, signaling arousal and alerting you to react. Slow nerve fibers also travel through your spinal cord to carry messages about the pain that lingers after the initial injury, often generating an emotional response.

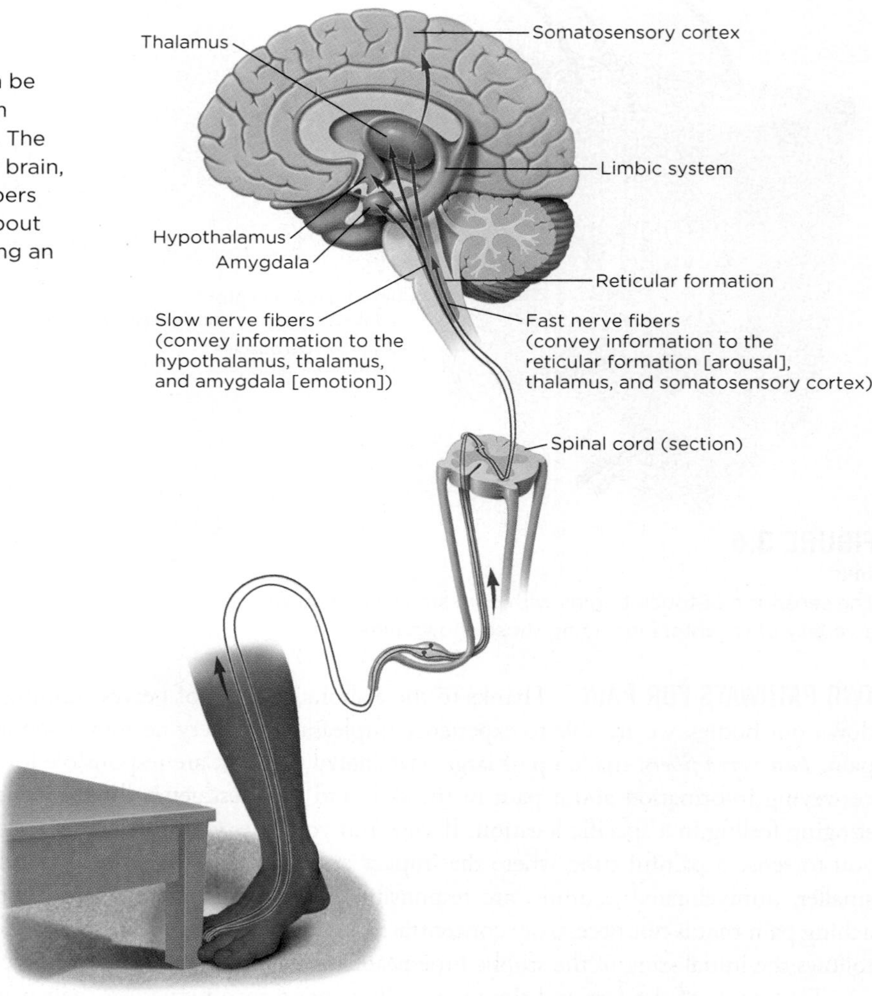

as fear and anxiety can amplify pain, whereas laughter and distraction can soften it by redirecting attention. Certain types of stressors (like running a marathon or giving birth) trigger the release of **endorphins**, which block the transmission of pain signals to the brain and spinal cord, possibly through the inhibition of a neurotransmitter called *substance P* (Rosenkranz, 2007).

CONNECTIONS

In **Chapter 2,** we reported that endorphins are naturally produced opioids that regulate the secretion of other neurotransmitters. Here, we see how they are involved in the experience of pain.

To understand how psychological and social factors influence the experience of pain, we turn to the *gate-control theory*.

OPEN THE GATES . . . NO, CLOSE THE GATES! According to the **gate-control theory**, a collection of *gates* is involved in shuttling information about pain between the brain and the rest of the body. The opening and closing of these gates depend on an interaction of biopsychosocial factors (Melzack & Wall, 1965). Returning to your stubbed toe, recall that pain signals from the injury area traveled up your spinal cord and to your brain. After receiving and interpreting the pain information, the brain sends a signal back down through the spinal cord, instructing the "gates" in the neurological pain pathways to open or close. Depending on psychological and social factors, the gates may open to increase the experience of pain, or close to decrease it. In situations where it's important to keep going in spite of an injury (athletes in competitions, soldiers in danger), the gates might be instructed to close. But when feeling intense pain has value (during an illness, when your body needs to rest), the gates may be instructed to remain open. Signals to shut the gates do not always come from the brain; they can also come from the body (Melzack, 1993, 2008).

gate-control theory Suggests that the perception of pain will either increase or decrease through the interaction of biopsychosocial factors; signals are sent to open or close "gates" that control the neurological pathways for pain.

kinesthesia Sensory system that conveys information about body position and movement.

proprioceptors Specialized nerve endings primarily located in the muscles and joints that provide information about body location and orientation.

vestibular sense The sense of balance and equilibrium.

PHANTOM LIMB PAIN Pain is a complex psychological phenomenon, dependent on many factors beyond the initial stimulus—so complex that a stimulus may not even be necessary. Sometimes people who have had an arm or leg amputated feel like they are experiencing intense pain in the limb they have lost. Phantom limb pain occurs in 50–80% of amputees, who may report burning, tingling, intense pain, cramping, and other sensations that seem to come from the missing limb (Ramachandran & Brang, 2009; Ramchandran & Hauser, 2010; Rosenblum, 2010). Researchers are still trying to determine what causes phantom limb pain, but they have proposed a variety of plausible mechanisms, ranging from changes in the structure of neurons to reorganization of the brain in response to sensations felt in different locations in the body (Flor, Nikolajsen, & Jensen, 2006; Makin, Scholz, Slater, Johansen-Berg, & Tracey, 2015).

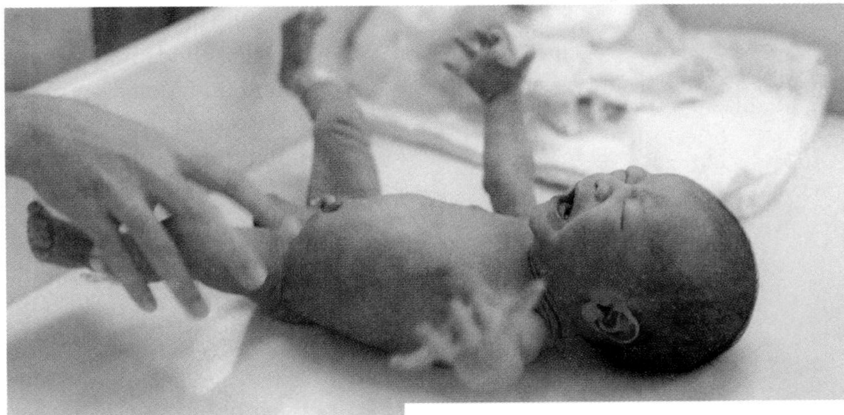

Babies Feel It, Too
Until the 1980s, doctors thought newborns were incapable of feeling pain, and these tiny babies were given no painkilling drugs for unpleasant procedures such as circumcision and needle pricks (Bellieni, Alagna & Buonocore, 2013; Costandi, 2017, May 4). With the help of functional magnetic resonance imaging (fMRI), researchers have demonstrated that the brain activity associated with pain is "extremely similar" for infants and adults, suggesting that babies suffer just like other people (Goksan et al., 2015). RPT.Family/Shutterstock.

Your Body in Space

LO 12 Illustrate how we sense the position and movement of our bodies.

You may have thought "touch" was the fifth and final sense, but there is more to sensation and perception than the traditional five categories. What sense allows Mandy to weave through crowds of people without bumping shoulders or tripping over feet? And how does she know where to put her fingers on the ukulele without looking? For these abilities, she can thank her *kinesthetic* and *vestibular* senses.

Closely related to touch, the kinesthetic sense, or **kinesthesia** (kin-ehs-THEE-zhuh), gives us feedback about our body position and movement. Kinesthesia endows us with the coordination we need to walk gracefully, dance The Floss, and put on our clothes without looking in the mirror. This knowledge of body location and orientation is made possible by specialized nerve endings called **proprioceptors** (PRO-pree-oh-sep-turz), which are primarily located in the muscles and joints. Proprioceptors monitor changes in the position of body parts and the tension in muscles. When proprioception is impaired, our ability to perform physical tasks like holding a book or opening a door is compromised.

The **vestibular sense** (veh-STIB-u-ler) helps the body maintain balance as it deals with the effects of gravity, movement, and position. This system comprises fluid-filled

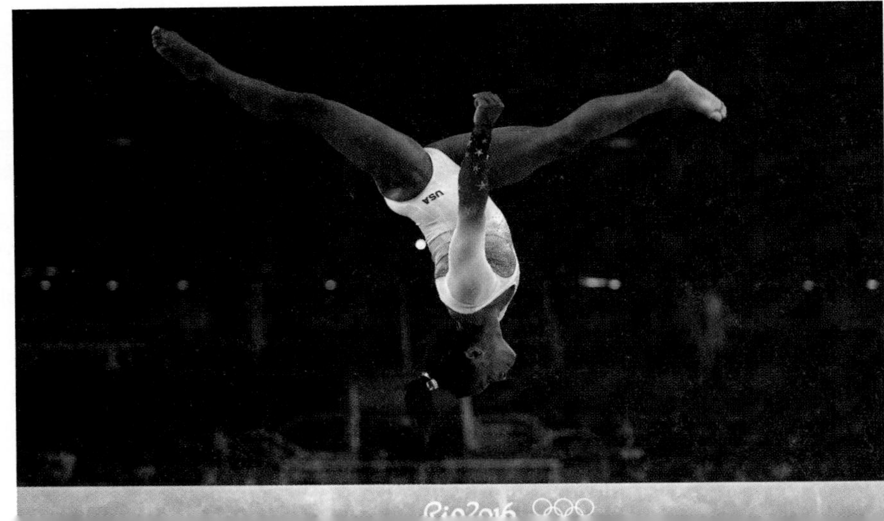

How Is It Possible?
Without her sense of kinesthesia, gymnast Simone Biles could not have performed this stunning feat on the balance beam during the 2016 Summer Olympics in Rio. Kinesthesia enables us to know our body position and movement. Clive Brunskill/Getty Images.

organs in the inner ear: the *semicircular canals* and nearby *vestibular sacs.* When the head tilts, fluid moves the hairlike receptors in these structures, causing neurons to fire, and initiating a signal that travels to the cerebellum. Motion sickness, which many people experience on boats and roller coasters, can be caused by conflicting information coming from the eyes and vestibular system. This is known as the *sensory conflict theory* (Johnson, 2005; Lackner, 2014).

Put Your Heads Together

Take a moment to appreciate the sensory systems that allow you to know and adapt to the surrounding world. In your group, discuss **A)** how you would function without vision, hearing, smell, taste, and touch, and **B)** what steps you can take to preserve them (**Table 3.2**). **C)** What sense would be the most challenging to live without? Why?

Apply This ↓

TABLE 3.2 PROTECTING YOUR SENSES

Sense	Simple Steps to Guard Against Damage
Vision	Don't smoke. Wear sunglasses and a hat in the sun. Both smoking and sun exposure heighten your risk of developing cataracts and other eye diseases. Put on protective eye gear when doing work or playing sports that could endanger your eyes (mowing the lawn or playing baseball, for example); 90% of eye injuries can be avoided by wearing the right eye gear (American Academy of Ophthalmology, 2014a, b, & c).
Hearing	Listen to iPods and other media players at or below half volume while wearing headphones instead of earbuds. Wear earplugs or earmuffs when using leaf-blowers, power tools, and other loud devices (American Speech-Language-Hearing Association, n.d.). If the sound level seems too high at your workplace, talk to your employer; you are legally entitled to a working environment that is safe for your ears (Occupational Safety & Health Administration, n.d.).
Smell	Two of the leading causes of olfactory loss are head trauma and upper respiratory infections like the common cold and sinus infections (Keller & Malaspina, 2013; Temmel et al., 2002). Diminish your chances of serious head injuries by buckling your seatbelt, wearing a bike helmet, and using protective headgear for contact sports. Significantly reduce your exposure to respiratory viruses with regular hand washing.
Taste	Don't smoke. Nicotine may change the structure and function of the tongue's papillae, which could explain why most smokers have decreased sensitivity to taste (Pavlos et al., 2009). Smoking also impairs olfaction (Katotomichelakis et al., 2007), and therefore dampens the appreciation of flavors.
Touch	Touch receptors are located in the skin and throughout the body, so protecting your sense of touch means taking good care of your body in general. Spinal cord or brain injuries can lead to widespread loss of sensation, so take commonsense precautions like buckling your seatbelt and wearing protective headgear for biking, football, construction work, and so on.

Here are just a few tips for protecting your senses. These measures should be considered in addition to regular medical checkups, such as annual eye exams.

✔ show what you know

1. Chemicals from food are released in saliva, where they bathe taste buds. The chemicals find matching receptors and latch on, sparking action potentials. This is an example of:
   a. olfaction.
   b. transduction.
   c. sensory adaptation.
   d. thermoreceptors.

2. List five things you are currently doing that involve the use of kinesthesia.

3. A young woman consulted her physician about severe back pain. In order to help her understand pain perception, the doctor recommended she consider ____________, which suggests that a variety of biopsychosocial factors can interact to amplify or diminish pain perception.
   a. the theory of evolution
   b. an absolute threshold
   c. the gate-control theory
   d. gustation

✔ CHECK YOUR ANSWERS IN APPENDIX C.

Perception: Is It All in Your Head?

We have learned how the sensory systems absorb information and transform it into the electrical and chemical language of neurons. Now let's look more closely at the next step: *perception,* which draws from experience to organize and interpret sensory information, turning it into something meaningful. Perhaps the most important lesson you will learn in this section is that *perception is far from foolproof.* We don't see, hear, smell, taste, or feel the world exactly as it is, but as our brains judge it to be. If you're not convinced, consider the following experiment.

From the SCIENTIFIC AMERICAN pages of

SLO-MO MADE HIM DO IT

Watching video in slow motion can lead us to believe actions are more intentional.

When a football player clocks an opponent on the field, it often does not look so bad—until we see it in slow motion. Suddenly, a clean, fair tackle becomes a dirty play, premeditated to maim (as any bar full of indignant fans will loudly confirm). But why? . . .

Researchers designed experiments based on a place where slow-motion video comes up a lot: the courtroom. They asked subjects to imagine themselves as jurors and watch a video of a convenience store robbery and shooting, either in slow motion or in real time. Those who watched the slow-motion video reported thinking the robber had more time to act and was acting with greater intent. The effect persisted even when the researchers displayed a timer on the screen to emphasize exactly how much time was passing, and it was reduced yet still present when subjects watched a combination of real-time and slow-motion videos of the crime (as they might in an actual courtroom). . . .

One possible explanation for this slo-mo effect stems from our sense of time, which author Benjamin Converse, a psychologist at the University of Virginia, describes as "quite malleable." He explains that when we watch footage in slow motion, we cannot help but assume that because we as viewers have more time to think through the events as they unfold, the same holds true for the people in the video.

Converse adds that we often accept video as the absolute truth, even when it has been manipulated. "There are a million things that go into how the video is recorded in the first place and an equal number of variables that go into playback," he says.

Currently there are no consistent guidelines about using slow-motion video in legal settings, yet whether or not an action is deemed intentional can have a considerable impact on the severity of a suspect's sentence. "We're rapidly reaching a stage in which almost every trial that has a question about somebody's actions is going to be accompanied by a video of some sort," says study co-author Zachary Burns, a psychologist at the University of San Francisco. "But I think we do need to understand what the limitations are." **Catherine Caruso. Reproduced with permission.**

Did He Mean to Do That?
Soccer players Cristiano Ronaldo (left) and Viktor Vasin compete for the ball during the 2017 FIFA Confederations Cup. Are these rivals pushing each other on purpose, or just trying to get to the soccer ball? If you were to watch this interaction unfold in slow motion, you may be more likely to interpret their behavior as deliberate ("I'm going to push this guy out of my way!"). Researchers have found that "viewing an action in slow motion, compared with regular speed, can cause viewers to perceive an action as more intentional" (Caruso, Burns, & Converse, 2016, p. 9250). AFP Contributor/Getty Images.

Perception Deception

Were you surprised to learn that viewing an event in slow motion can alter your perception of what occurred? Our perceptual systems are vulnerable to external and internal interference, and thus "what you see is not always what you get." One of the best ways to reveal distortions in perceptual processes

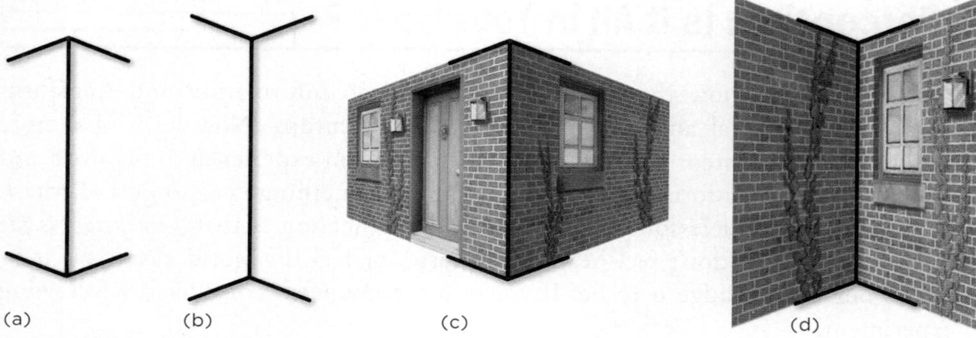

FIGURE 3.8
The Müller–Lyer Illusion
Which line looks longer? All are, in fact, the same length. Visual depth cues cause you to perceive that (b) and (d) are longer because they appear farther away.

is to study illusions. An **illusion** is a perception that is incongruent with actual sensory data, conveying an inaccurate representation of reality (see **Infographic 3.3**). When perception is working "incorrectly," we can examine top-down processing and how past experience influences our interpretation of incoming information (Carbon, 2014). If a clock stops ticking, you can open it up to see what's wrong and better understand how it works. Illusions serve a similar purpose. Let's examine some.

Look at the Müller–Lyer illusion in **Figure 3.8**. Lines (b) and (d) appear to be longer, but, in fact, all four lines (a–d) are equal in length. Why does this illusion occur? Our experiences looking at buildings tell us that the corner presented in line (c) is nearer because it is jutting toward us. The corner presented in line (d) seems to be farther because it is jutting away. Two objects that are the same size but different distances from the eye will not project identical images on the retina; the farther object will project a smaller image. People living in "carpentered worlds" (that is, surrounded by structures constructed with corners, angles, and straight lines, as opposed to more "traditional" settings) are more likely to be tricked by this illusion because of their experience seeing manufactured structures. People in more traditional settings, without all the hard edges and straight lines, are less likely to fall prey to such an illusion (Segall, Campbell, & Herskovits, 1968). However, more recent research suggests that the "processing mechanisms" involved in illusions may be hardwired (Gandhi, Kalia, Ganesh, & Sinha, 2015). In what started as a humanitarian effort to help Indian children who are blind, neuroscientist Pawan Sinha and colleagues found that illusions were perceived by children and adolescents immediately following surgery to restore sight (Chatterjee, 2015). This suggests that their vulnerability to illusions was not dependent on their environments.

See Her Move?
The tennis player and her racquet seem to be moving because their images appear in rapid succession. Stroboscopic motion is an example of a visual illusion. Master1305/Shutterstock.

Another visual illusion is *stroboscopic motion,* the appearance of motion produced when a sequence of still images is shown in rapid succession. (Think of drawing stick figures on the edges of book pages and then flipping the pages to see your figure "move.") The brain interprets this as movement. Although illusions provide clues about how perception works, they cannot explain everything. Let's look at principles of perceptual organization, which provide guidelines on how we perceive our surroundings.

The Whole Is Greater

LO 13 Identify the principles of perceptual organization.

Many turn to the Gestalt (guh-SHTAHLT) psychologists, who were active in Germany in the late 1800s and early 1900s, to understand how perception works. Observing the tendency for perception to be organized and complete, they concluded that the brain naturally organizes stimuli in their entirety rather than

illusion A perception that is inconsistent with sensory data.

Perceptual Illusions

What we see, hear, taste, touch, smell, and feel may seem very real, but perceptions are not always accurate representations of reality. The brain's perceptual systems are prone to errors and distortions. Studying illusions, like those shown here, we can detect and better understand the brain's misinterpretations of visual input.

Moon illusion

Have you ever noticed that the moon can appear much larger when it's on the horizon versus high in the sky? Don't let perceptual errors trump logic: You know the moon does not change size! Researchers have yet to agree upon a definitive explanation for this illusion, but many suspect it has something to do with the surrounding environment (Weidner et al., 2014). Seeing the moon along with trees and other objects at different distances may influence our perception of the moon's size.

Ponzo illusion

Which of the two red bars is longer? Neither! They are identical. When you see two lines converging in the distance, your brain perceives them as getting farther away. Line A appears farther away. It seems longer because the images of the two lines projected onto the retina are the same size, but we interpret the farther line as being bigger. The Ponzo illusion demonstrates how we judge an object's size based on its context.

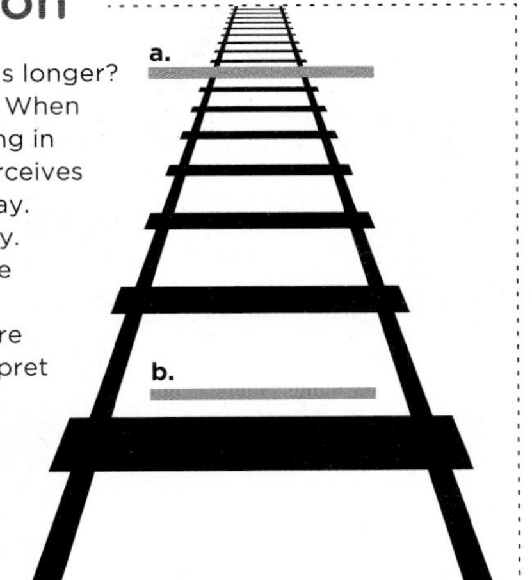

Ames room illusion

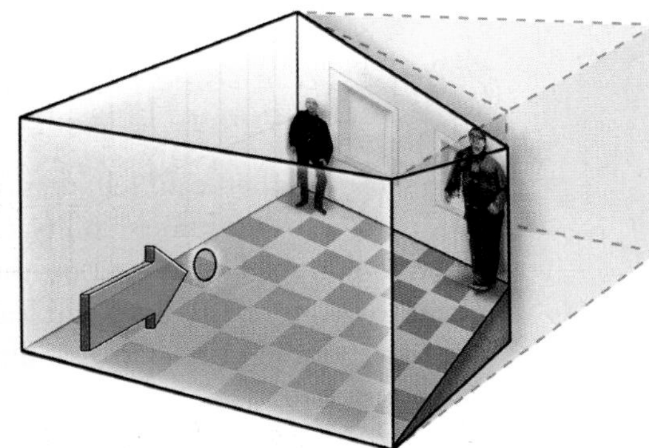

Would you believe that the two people in this room (left) are approximately the same height? The woman on the right appears about twice as big, because the room isn't rectangular! The Ames room is actually trapezoidal (see diagram on the right), but, as the image on the left shows, this is not apparent when it is viewed through a peephole with one eye.

The Shepard Tables illusion

Look carefully at these two tables. Is one longer than the other? If you compare their measurements with your fingers or a piece of paper, you will see that both the length and width are identical.

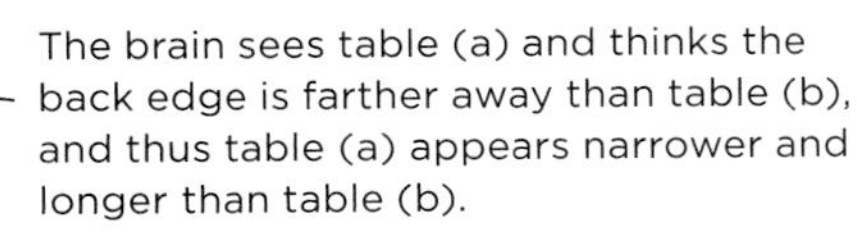

The brain sees table (a) and thinks the back edge is farther away than table (b), and thus table (a) appears narrower and longer than table (b).

a.

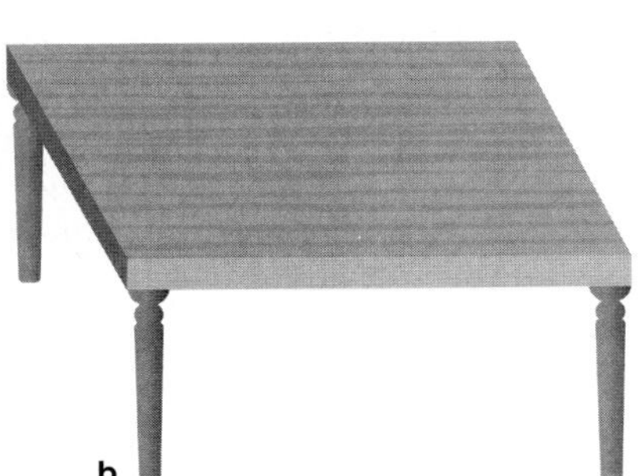

Credits: Moon: Patrick Foto/Getty Images; people in Ames room: Michael Doolittle/Alamy.

perceiving parts and pieces. In other words, "the whole is entirely different from a mere sum; it is prior to its parts" (Wertheimer, 2014, p. 131). **Gestalt** means "whole" or "form" in German. The Gestalt psychologists, and others who followed, studied principles that explain how the brain perceives objects in the environment as wholes or groups (see **Infographic 3.4**).

One central idea illuminated by the Gestalt psychologists is the **figure-ground** principle (Fowlkes, Martin, & Malik, 2007). As you focus your attention on a figure, for example the vase in Infographic 3.4, all other features drop into the background. If, however, you direct your gaze onto the faces, the vase falls into the background with everything else. The figure and ground continually change as you shift your focus. Other gestalt organizational principles include:

- ***Proximity:*** Objects close to each other are perceived as a group.
- ***Similarity:*** Objects similar in shape or color are perceived as a group.
- ***Connectedness:*** Objects that are connected are perceived as a group.
- ***Closure:*** Gaps tend to be filled in if something isn't complete.
- ***Continuity:*** Parts tend to be perceived as members of a group if they head in the same direction.

Although these organizational principles have been demonstrated for vision, it is important to note that they apply to the other senses as well. Imagine a mother who can discern her child's voice amid the clamor of a busy playground: Her child's voice is the figure and the other noises are the ground.

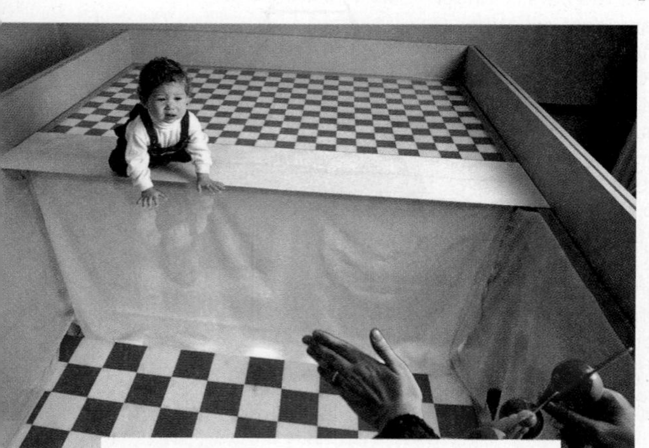

Whoa, Baby
A baby appears distressed when he encounters the visual cliff, a supportive glass surface positioned over a drop-off, or "cliff." Most babies will not proceed, even when coaxed by a trusted caregiver. This finding suggests that depth perception is already in place by the time a child is crawling (Gibson & Walk, 1960). Mark Richards/Photo Edit.

Depth Perception

LO 14 Describe some of the visual cues used in depth perception.

That same mother can tell that the slide extends from the front of the jungle gym, thanks to her brain's ability to pick up on cues about depth. How can a two-dimensional image projected on the retina be perceived in three dimensions? There appear to be inborn abilities and learned cues for perceiving depth and distance. Let's start by examining the inborn ability to recognize depth and its potential for danger. Watch out, baby!

THE VISUAL CLIFF In order to determine whether **depth perception** is innate or learned, researchers studied the behavior of babies approaching a "visual cliff" (see photo above), a flat glass surface with a checkered tablecloth-like pattern directly underneath that gives the illusion of a drop-off (Gibson & Walk, 1960). The researchers placed infants ages 6 to 14 months at the edge of the glass. At the other end of the glass were the babies' mothers, coaxing them to crawl over. For the most part, the children refused to move toward what they perceived to be a drop-off, suggesting that the perception of depth was innate. Without ever having explored the edge of an actual abyss, these infants seemed to realize it should be avoided. The original studies also included a variety of nonhuman animals, starting with rats, and then one-day-old chicks, newborn kids and lambs—and all of them avoided the visual cliff (Rodkey, 2015).

BINOCULAR CUES Some cues for perceiving depth are the result of information gathered by both eyes. **Binocular cues** provide information from the right and left eyes to help judge depth and distance. For example, **convergence** is the brain's interpretation of tension in the muscles that direct where both eyes focus. If an object

gestalt The natural tendency for the brain to organize stimuli into a whole, rather than perceiving the parts and pieces.

figure-ground A central principle of Gestalt psychology, involving the shifting of focus; as attention is focused on one object, all other features drop or recede into the background.

depth perception The ability to perceive three-dimensional objects and judge distances.

binocular cues Information gathered from both eyes to help judge depth and distance.

convergence A binocular cue used to judge distance and depth based on the tension of the muscles that direct where the eyes are focusing.

Gestalt Organizing Principles: The Whole Is Greater

The Gestalt psychologists identified principles that explain how the brain naturally organizes sensory information into meaningful wholes rather than distinct parts and pieces. These principles help you navigate the world by allowing you to see, for example, that the path you are walking on continues on the other side of an intersection. Gestalt principles also help you make sense of the information presented in your textbooks. Let's look at how this works.

figure-ground

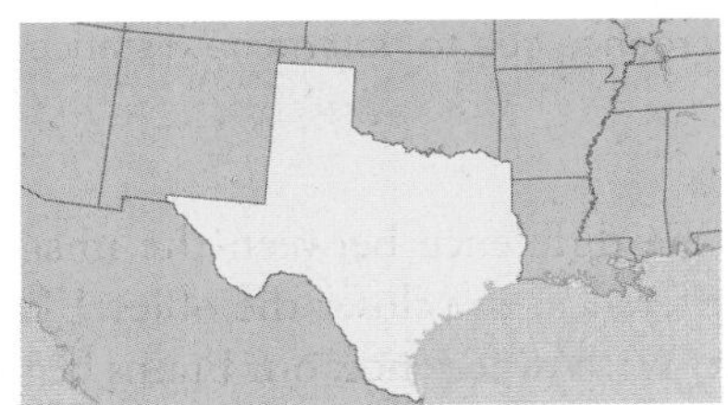

We tend to perceive visual stimuli as figures existing on a background. On this map, one area becomes the focus, while the rest functions as background.

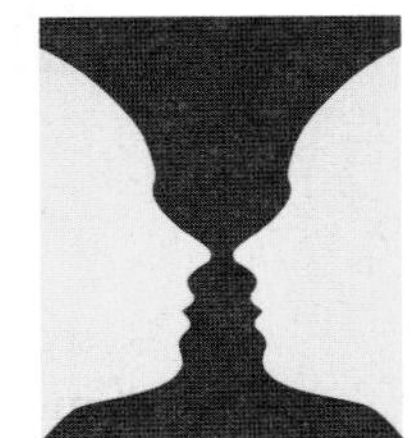

Some stimuli, such as this classic figure-ground vase, are *reversible figures*. You see something different depending on whether you focus on the yellow or the black portion.

LAW OF proximity

We tend to perceive objects that are near each other as a unit. This set of dots is perceived as three groups rather than six separate columns or 36 individual dots.

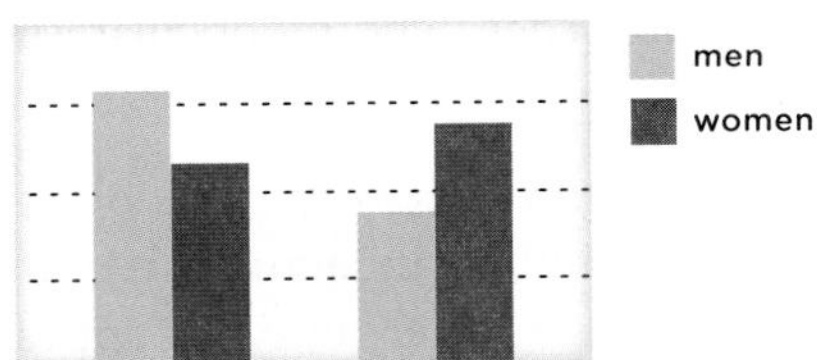

Proximity helps us read graphs like this one. We understand that bars close together should be compared.

LAW OF similarity

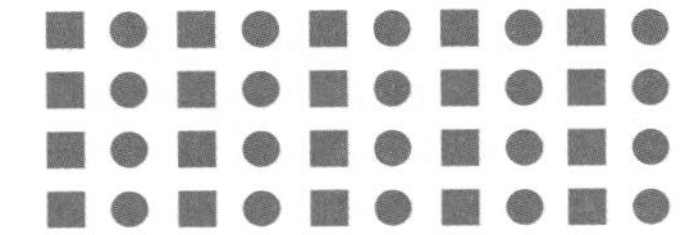

We see objects as a group if they share features such as color or shape. In this example, we perceive eight vertical columns rather than four rows of alternating squares and dots.

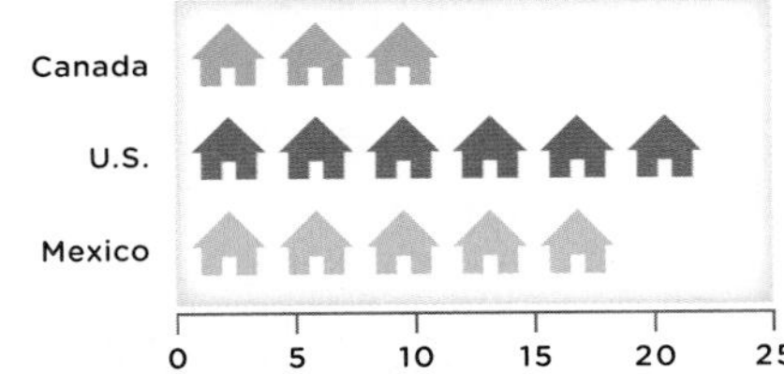

Similarity helps us read color-coded charts and graphs. We understand the graph above as having horizontal bars because we naturally group the similarly colored icons.

LAW OF connectedness

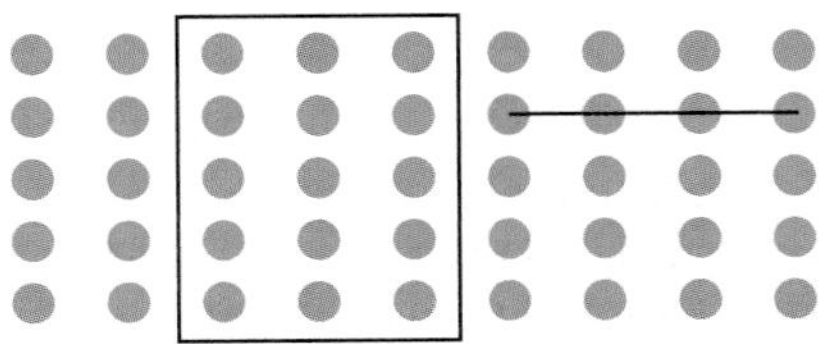

We tend to see objects as a group if there is something that connects them. In this group of dots, the ones enclosed in or connected by lines appear related even though all dots are the same.

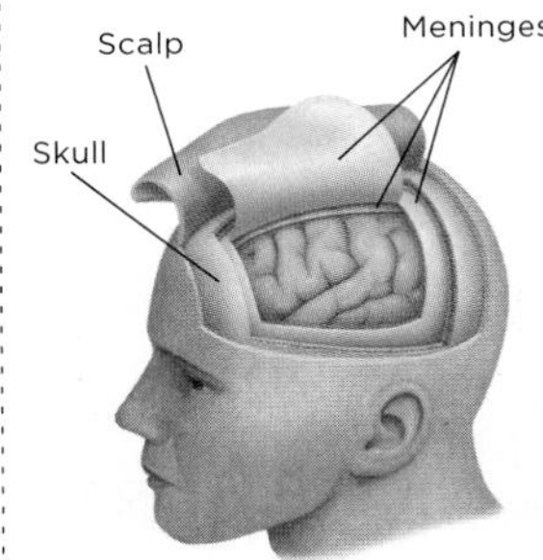

In a textbook figure, connectedness helps us understand what is being labeled.

LAW OF closure

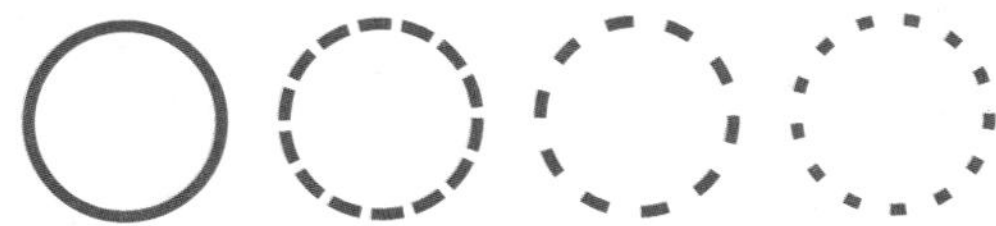

We tend to fill in incomplete parts of a line or figure. In this example, we perceive a circle even when the line is broken.

Closure allows us to read letters and images that are interrupted. We can read this letter even though it is made up of unconnected lines.

LAW OF continuity

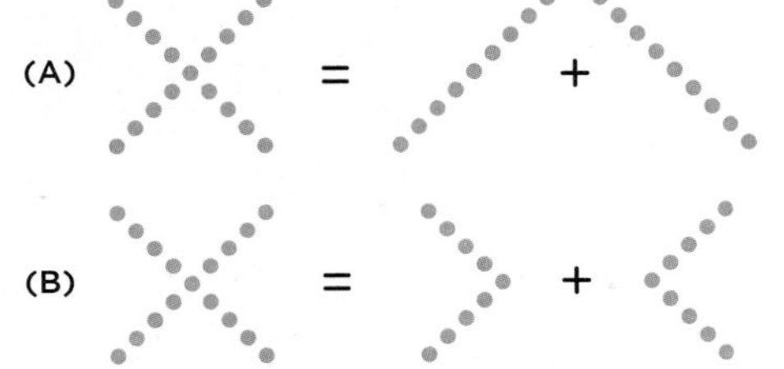

We perceive groups where objects appear to be going in the same direction. In this example, we perceive the figure as made up of two continuous lines that intersect (A) rather than two angles that are brought together (B).

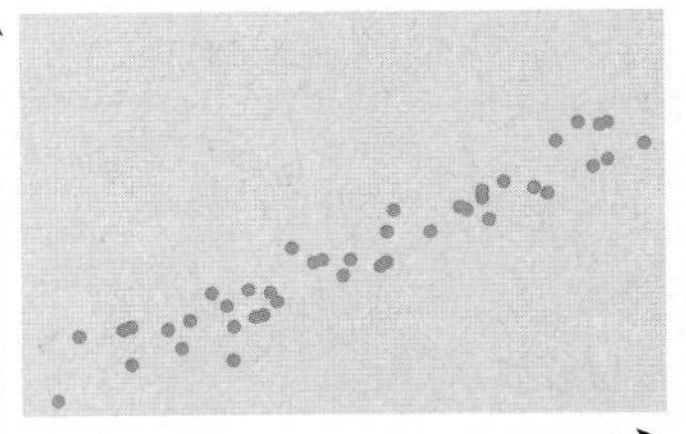

Continuity helps us read graphs like this scatterplot, where we perceive the overall pattern.

is close, there is more muscular tension (as the muscles turn our eyes inward toward our nose), and the object is perceived as near. This perception of distance is based on experience; throughout life, we have learned that muscular tension correlates with the proximity of the object: The more tension we experience, the closer the object. Take a moment to feel that tension.

Point your finger up to the ceiling, arm straight, with both eyes open. Now slowly bring your finger close to your nose. Can you feel tension and strain in your eye muscles? Your brain uses this type of convergence cue to determine distance.

synonyms

retinal disparity binocular disparity

Another binocular cue is **retinal disparity**, the difference between the images seen by the right and left eyes. The greater the difference, the closer the object. The more similar the two images, the farther the object. With experience, our brains begin using these image disparities to judge distance. You can experience retinal disparity at work in the following exercise.

try this Hold your index finger about 4 inches in front of your face pointing up to the ceiling. Quickly open your right eye as you are closing your left eye, alternating this activity for a few seconds; it should appear as if your finger is jumping back and forth. Repeat this procedure with your finger out at arm's length. Does the image seem to jump as much?

MONOCULAR CUES Judgments about depth and distance can also be infomed by **monocular cues**, which do not necessitate the use of both eyes. An artist who paints pictures can transform a white canvas into a three-dimensional perceptual experience by using techniques that take advantage of monocular cues. The monocular cues include the following:

- ***Relative Size***—If two objects are similar in actual size, but one is farther away, it appears to be smaller. We interpret the larger object as being closer.
- ***Linear Perspective***—When two lines start off parallel, then come together, where they converge appears farther away than where they are parallel.
- ***Interposition***—When one object is in front of another, it partially blocks the view of the other object, and this partially blocked object appears more distant.
- ***Texture Gradient***—When objects are closer, it is easier to see their texture. As they get farther away, the texture becomes less visible. The more apparent the texture, the closer the object appears.

Monocular Cues
You can gauge the distance and depth in this photo with at least four types of monocular cues: (1) People who are farther away look smaller (relative size). (2) The two sides of the street start out parallel but converge as distance increases (linear perspective). (3) The trees in the front block those that are behind (interposition). (4) Textures are more apparent for closer objects (texture gradient). Corbis Wire/Corbis.

Motion Parallax
As you walk along a busy street, nearby objects appear to move by faster than objects faraway. This monocular cue, known as motion parallax, also helps with depth perception when you are sitting still and objects in the environment are moving around you (for example, cars driving past at different distances). Martin Botvidsson/Getty Images.

Once a Rectangle, Always a Rectangle
How do you know that all these doors are the same size and shape? The images projected onto your retina suggest that the opened doors are narrower, nonrectangular shapes. Your brain, however, knows from experience that all the opened doors are identical rectangles. This phenomenon is referred to as shape constancy. Image Source/Getty Images.

Put Your Heads Together

A) Look for examples of the six gestalt organizational principles and at least four monocular cues in your classroom. B) Team up with a classmate and compare your results.

Is That What I Think It Is?

All these perceptual skills are great—if you are standing still—but the world around us is constantly moving. How do our perceptual systems adapt to changes? We possess the ability to perceive objects as having stable properties, although our environments are always changing. **Perceptual constancy** refers to the tendency to perceive objects as maintaining their shape, size, and color even when the angle, lighting, and distance change. A door is shaped like a rectangle, but when it opens, the image projected on our retina is not a rectangle. Yet, we still perceive the door as having a rectangular shape. This is called **shape constancy**. As you gaze on cars and trucks from the window of an airplane, they may look like bugs scurrying around, but you know some are as big as elephants because your perceptual toolkit includes **size constancy**. Through experience, we get to know the size of everyday objects and perceive them accordingly, regardless of whether they are far or near. Similarly, **color constancy** allows us to see the world in stable colors, even when the sensory data arriving at our photoreceptors change. A bright red backpack appears bright red outside in the sunshine or inside a house. The light waves bouncing off the backpack have changed, but your understanding of the color has not been altered.

What Color Are They?
Believe it or not, there are no red pixels in this image, just gray and green hues (Kircher, 2017, February 28). The strawberries look red as a result of color constancy; we see the world in stable colors, even when the sensory data arriving at our photoreceptors are variable. Akiyoshi Kitaoka.

Although examples of these organizational tendencies occur with robust regularity, some of them are not necessarily universal. Certain studies suggest that children *learn* to perceive size constancy. For example, their ability to estimate the size of distant objects improves by around 9 years old, in step with cognitive development, such as their reasoning abilities (Granrud, 2009; Kavšek & Granrud, 2012).

Learning also plays a role in the phenomenon of **perceptual set—**the tendency to perceive stimuli in a specific manner based on past experiences and expectations. If someone handed you a picture of two women and said, "This is a mother with her daughter," you would be more likely to rate them as looking alike than if you

retinal disparity A binocular cue that uses the difference between the images the two eyes see to determine the distance of objects.

monocular cues Depth and distance cues that require the use of only one eye.

perceptual constancy The tendency to perceive objects in our environment as stable in terms of shape, size, and color, regardless of changes in the sensory data received.

shape constancy An object is perceived as maintaining its shape, regardless of the image projected on the retina.

size constancy An object is perceived as maintaining its size, regardless of the image projected on the retina.

color constancy Objects are perceived as maintaining their color, even with changing sensory data.

perceptual set The tendency to perceive stimuli in a specific manner based on past experiences and expectations.

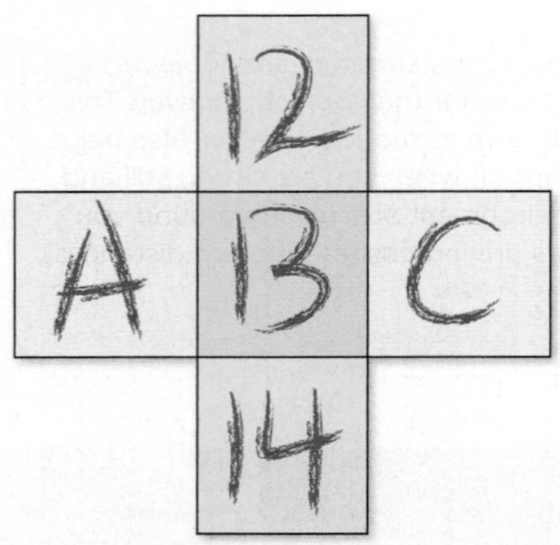

Letters or Numbers?
Look in the green square. What do you see? That depends on whether you viewed the symbol as belonging to a row of letters (A B C) or a column of numbers (12 13 14). Perceptions are shaped by the context in which a stimulus occurs, and our expectations about that stimulus.

had been given the exact same picture and told, "These women are unrelated." Indeed, research shows that people who believe they are looking at photos of parent–child pairs are more likely to rate the members as looking similar than those who believe the pairs are unrelated, even when everyone is looking at all the same images (Oda, Matsumoto-Oda, & Kurashima, 2005). In short, we tend to see what we are looking for.

Perceptual sets are molded by the context of the moment. If you hear the word "sects" in a TV news report about feuding religious groups, you are unlikely to think the reporter is saying "sex" even though "sects" and "sex" sound the same. Similarly, if you see a baby swaddled in a blue blanket, you are probably more likely to assume it's a boy than a girl. Would you believe that people are more inclined to attribute high-pitched cries to female infants, even though there are no measurable pitch differences between the cries of boy and girl babies (Reby, Levréro, Gustafsson, & Mathevon, 2016)?

Although our perceptual sets may not always lead to the right conclusions, they do help us organize the vast amount of information flooding our senses. But can perception exist in the absence of sensation? In other words, is it possible to perceive something without seeing, hearing, smelling, tasting, or feeling it? Some would say "yes."

You Asked, Mandy Answers

http://qrs.ly/jh7829i

How do you know if you are singing the right notes?

Extrasensory Perception: Where's the Evidence?

Have you ever had a dream that actually came to pass? Perhaps you have heard of psychics who claim that they can read people's "auras" and decipher their thoughts. **Extrasensory perception (ESP)** is this purported ability to obtain information about the world without any sensory stimuli. The study of these kinds of phenomena is called **parapsychology**.

THINK CRITICALLY

CAN YOU PREDICT THE FUTURE? ESP, psychic powers—call it what you will, there is no scientific evidence to support its existence (Farha, 2007; Wiseman & Watt, 2006). Nevertheless, a handful of respected researchers have published research suggesting it exists. In 2011 Cornell University's Daryl Bem set off a firestorm of controversy with a journal article offering evidence for ESP. The article, which reported nine experiments involving some 1,000 participants, suggested that human beings have the ability to predict the future (Bem, 2011). When examining this work, other psychologists discovered flaws in Bem's statistical analysis and tried without success to **replicate** his results (Ritchie, Wiseman, & French, 2012; Wagenmakers, Wetzels, Borsboom, & van der Maas, 2011).

THERE IS NO SCIENTIFIC EVIDENCE TO SUPPORT ITS EXISTENCE

CONNECTIONS
This effort to replicate ESP research relates to what we discussed in **Chapter 1**. Replication is a key step in the scientific method: The more a study is replicated with similar findings, the more confidence we can have in those findings. If similar results cannot be reproduced using the same methods, then the original findings may have resulted from chance or experimenter bias.

Despite ESP's lack of scientific credibility, many people remain firm believers. Most often, their "evidence" comes in the form of personal anecdotes. Aunt Tilly predicted she was going to win the lottery based on a dream she had one night, and when she did win, it was "proof" of her ESP abilities. This is an example of what psychologists might call an *illusory correlation*, an apparent link between variables that are not closely related at all. Aunt Tilly dreamed she won the lottery, but so did 1,000 other people around the country, and they didn't win—what about that evidence? Although some may find the idea of ESP compelling, you should be very skeptical about it, because there are no reliable data to back up its existence (Farha, 2007; Rouder & Morey, 2011).

extrasensory perception (ESP) The purported ability to obtain information about the world without any sensory stimuli.

parapsychology The study of extrasensory perception.

"Serious Goose Bumps"
When Mandy was in high school, she had an "absolutely amazing" choral teacher. "He was able to manipulate everything to create such a beautiful story arc that you would get serious goose bumps," says Mandy. "You would almost want to cry." Today, Mandy is doing for other people what her choral director did for her—making them feel deep emotion with her music. Courtesy Mandy Harvey.

NOTHING STANDS IN HER WAY Looking back on her life, Mandy is thankful for everything that happened—even the devastating loss of her hearing. "The whole experience itself has changed who I am," Mandy says. "As a musician, I would adore being able to listen to music again, but I wouldn't trade the experience, and everything that I've learned, for any of it. . . . I've grown so much as a person." As for the future, Mandy wants to continue making music, performing, and spreading her message. She recently published her first book, *Sensing the Rhythm: Finding My Voice in a World Without Sound*. Even in the face of chronic pain and hearing impairment, Mandy continues to spread hope and inspiration around the world.

show what you know

1. ______________ means the "whole" or "form" in German.
2. One binocular cue called ______________ is based on the brain's interpretation of the tension in muscles of the eyes.
   a. convergence
   b. retinal disparity
   c. interposition
   d. relative size
3. Using what you have learned so far in the textbook, how would you try to convince a friend that extrasensory perception does not exist?

✓ CHECK YOUR ANSWERS IN APPENDIX C.

YOUR SCIENTIFIC WORLD is a new application-based feature appearing in every chapter. In these online activities, you will take on role-playing scenarios that encourage you to think critically and apply your knowledge of psychological science to solve a real world problem. For example: Do you have color blindness? If not, can you imagine what it would be like to experience color blindness? This activity will help you understand how the world appears to someone with red-green color deficiency and familiarize you with the components of the visual system. You can access Your Scientific World activities in LaunchPad. Have fun!

SUMMARY OF CONCEPTS

LO 1 Define sensation and perception and explain how they are different. (p. 81)

Sensation is the manner in which physical stimuli are received and detected. Perception is the process of giving meaning to sensations. Bottom-up processing describes how the brain takes in basic sensory information and processes it. Top-down processing uses past experiences and knowledge in order to understand sensory information.

LO 2 Define transduction and explain how it relates to sensation. (p. 82)

Sensory organs receive stimuli from the environment (for example, sound waves, light energy). Transduction is the transformation of stimuli into electrical and chemical signals. The neural signals are then processed by the central nervous system, resulting in what we consciously experience as sensations.

LO 3 Describe and differentiate between absolute thresholds and difference thresholds. (p. 83)

One of the important goals of studying sensation and perception is to determine absolute thresholds, the weakest stimuli that can be detected 50% of the time. Difference thresholds indicate the minimum difference between two stimuli noticed 50% of the time. According to Weber's law, certain ratios determine these difference thresholds. The ability to detect weak signals in the environment is based on many factors.

LO 4 **Summarize the properties of light and color, and describe the structure and function of the eye. (p. 86)**

The eyes do not sense faces, objects, or scenery; they detect light, which is a form of electromagnetic energy. The light we see (visible light) comprises one small portion of the electromagnetic spectrum. The color, or hue, of visible light is determined by its wavelength. Colors also can be characterized by brightness (intensity) and saturation (purity). When light first enters the eye, it passes through a glassy outer layer known as the cornea. Then it travels through a hole called the pupil, followed by the lens. Both the cornea and lens focus the incoming light waves, and the lens can change shape in order to adjust to objects near and far. Finally, the light reaches the retina, where it is transduced into neural activity.

LO 5 **Describe the function of rods and cones. (p. 88)**

Rods are photoreceptors in the retina that are extremely sensitive to light and enable us to see in dim lighting. Rods do not provide the sensation of color. Cones, also in the retina, are responsible for our sensation of color and our ability to see the details of objects. Cones are not used when ambient light is low. Cones are concentrated in the fovea.

LO 6 **Compare and contrast the theories of color vision. (p. 91)**

The trichromatic theory of color vision suggests there are three types of cones, each sensitive to particular wavelengths in the red, green, and blue spectrums. The three types of cones fire in response to different electromagnetic wavelengths. The opponent-process theory of color vision suggests that in addition to the color-sensitive cones, we also have neurons that respond differently to opponent colors (for example, red–green, blue–yellow).

LO 7 **Summarize how sound waves are converted into the sensation of hearing. (p. 94)**

Audition is the term used for the sense of hearing. When we hear, we are sensing sound waves. When the oval window vibrates, it causes the fluid in the cochlea (a fluid-filled, snail-shaped organ of the inner ear) to move. The cochlea is lined with the basilar membrane, which contains hair cells. When the fluid moves, the hairs lining the basilar membrane bend in response, which cause the nerve cells nearby to fire. Neural messages are sent through the auditory nerve to the auditory cortex via the thalamus.

LO 8 **Illustrate how we sense different pitches of sound. (p. 98)**

Place theory suggests that the location of neural activity along the cochlea allows us to sense different pitches of high-frequency sounds. Frequency theory suggests that the frequency of the neural impulses determines the experience of pitch. Frequency theory explains how we perceive the pitch of sounds from 20 Hz to 400 Hz. The volley principle explains our perception of pitches between 400 Hz and 4,000 Hz. Place theory explains perception of pitches from 4,000 Hz to 20,000 Hz.

LO 9 **Describe the process of olfaction. (p. 100)**

The chemical sense referred to as olfaction provides the sensation of smell. Molecules from odor-emitting objects in our environments make their way into our nostrils up through the nose or mouth. The olfactory epithelium is home to millions of olfactory receptor neurons, which provide receptors for odor molecules. When enough odor molecules bind to the receptor neuron, a signal is sent to the brain.

LO 10 **Identify the structures involved in taste and describe how they work. (p. 102)**

Gustation is the sense of taste. The receptor cells for taste are located in the taste buds, which are located on the tongue, the roof of the mouth, and the lining of the cheeks. Each taste bud contains 50 to 100 taste receptor cells; food molecules bind onto these cells. Taste is essential to the survival of species, as it pushes organisms toward needed foods and away from harmful ones.

LO 11 **Explain how the biopsychosocial perspective helps us understand pain. (p. 105)**

The biopsychosocial perspective explains the perception of pain by exploring biological, psychological, and social factors. This multilevel method examines how these factors play a role in the experience of pain. According to the gate-control theory, a person's perception of pain can increase or decrease depending on how the brain interprets pain signals. Neural activity makes its way to the brain, where it is processed. The brain is capable of blocking pain by sending a message through the interneurons to "close the gate" so the pain won't be felt.

LO 12 **Illustrate how we sense the position and movement of our bodies. (p. 107)**

Kinesthesia gives us feedback about the position and movement of the body. We know how our body parts are oriented in space because of specialized nerve endings called proprioceptors, which are primarily located in the muscles and joints. Our proprioceptors monitor changes in the position of body parts and the tension in our muscles. The vestibular sense helps us deal with the effects of gravity, movement, and body position to keep us balanced.

LO 13 **Identify the principles of perceptual organization. (p. 110)**

Gestalt psychologists sought to explain how the human mind organizes stimuli from the environment. They realized the whole is greater than the sum of its parts, meaning the brain naturally organizes stimuli as a whole rather than parts and pieces. Gestalt indicates a tendency for human perception to be organized and complete. Gestalt organizational principles include proximity, similarity, connectedness, closure, and continuity.

LO 14 **Describe some of the visual cues used in depth perception. (p. 112)**

Depth perception appears partially to be an innate ability. Babies in the visual cliff experiment, for example, refuse to move toward what they perceive to be a drop-off. Binocular cues provide information from the right and left eyes to help judge depth and distance. Monocular cues can be used by either eye alone and also help judge depth and distance.

KEY TERMS

absolute thresholds, p. 83
accommodation, p. 88
afterimage, p. 92
amplitude, p. 87
audition, p. 94
binocular cues, p. 112
blind spot, p. 90
bottom-up processing, p. 81
cochlea, p. 97
color constancy, p. 115
cones, p. 88
convergence, p. 112
cornea, p. 87
dark adaptation, p. 90
depth perception, p. 112
difference thresholds, p. 84
extrasensory perception (ESP), p. 116
feature detectors, p. 91
figure-ground, p. 112
frequency, p. 95
frequency theory, p. 98
gate-control theory, p. 106
gestalt, p. 112
gustation, p. 102
hue, p. 86
illusion, p. 110
iris, p. 88
kinesthesia, p. 107
light adaptation, p. 90
monocular cues, p. 114
olfaction, p. 100
opponent-process theory, p. 93
optic nerve, p. 88
parapsychology, p. 116
perception, p. 81
perceptual constancy, p. 115
perceptual set, p. 115
photoreceptors, p. 88
pitch, p. 95
place theory, p. 98
proprioceptors, p. 107
retina, p. 88
retinal disparity, p. 114
rods, p. 88
saturation, p. 87
sensation, p. 81
sensory adaptation, p. 83
shape constancy, p. 115
signal detection theory, p. 85
size constancy, p. 115
top-down processing, p. 81
transduction, p. 82
trichromatic theory, p. 91
vestibular sense, p. 107
volley principle, p. 99
wavelength, p. 86
Weber's law, p. 84

TEST PREP ARE YOU READY?

1. Stimuli are detected through the process called:
   a. perception.
   b. bottom-up processing.
   c. sensation.
   d. top-down processing.

2. The sound waves transmitted through the earbuds in your iPod lead to vibrations in the fluid in your cochlea. This activity causes the hair cells to bend, which causes nearby nerve cells to fire. This process of transforming stimuli into electrical and chemical signals of neurons is:
   a. transduction.
   b. perception.
   c. top-down processing.
   d. convergence.

3. While rollerblading outside, you get something in your eye. As the day goes on, your eye still feels irritated. It is possible you've scratched your ____________, which is the transparent outer layer, the function of which is to protect the eye and help focus light waves.
   a. lens
   b. retina
   c. iris
   d. cornea

4. In color vision, the opponent-process theory was developed to explain the ____________, which could not be explained by the ____________ theory.
   a. afterimage effect; trichromatic
   b. blind spot; place
   c. feature detectors; trichromatic
   d. color deficiencies; frequency

5. Frequency theory of pitch perception suggests it is the number of ____________ that allows us to perceive differences in pitch.
   a. sound waves greater than 1,000 Hz
   b. the timbre
   c. neural impulses firing
   d. the amplitude

6. The wiring of the olfactory system is unique, because other sensory systems relay data through the ____________ before information is passed along to higher brain centers, but this is not the case for olfactory information.
   a. thalamus
   b. cerebellum
   c. reticular formation
   d. basilar membrane

7. We are aware of our body position in space because of specialized nerve endings called ____________, primarily located in the joints and muscles.
   a. proprioceptors
   b. Meissner's corpuscles
   c. Pacinian corpuscles
   d. nociceptors

8. Hector is staring at the small print on the back of a credit card. Which of the following is he using to detect the fine details?
   a. proximity
   b. rods
   c. proprioceptors
   d. cones

9. One of the gestalt organizational principles suggests that objects close to each other are perceived as a group. This is known as:
   a. continuity.
   b. closure.
   c. similarity.
   d. proximity.

10. When two objects are similar in actual size and one of these objects is farther away than the other, the object at a distance appears to be smaller than the closer object. This is a monocular cue called:
    a. linear perspective.
    b. interposition.
    c. relative size.
    d. texture gradient.

11. Use the evolutionary perspective of psychology to explain the importance of any two aspects of human taste.

12. How is extrasensory perception different from the perception of subliminal stimuli?

13. The transformation of a sound wave into the experience of something heard follows a complicated path. To better understand the process, draw a diagram starting with a sound in the environment and ending with the sound heard by an individual.

14. Why does placing ice on a sore shoulder stop the pain?

15. Describe the difference between absolute threshold and difference threshold.

✓ CHECK YOUR ANSWERS IN APPENDIX C.

Go to **LaunchPad** or **Achieve: Read & Practice** to test your understanding with **LearningCurve**.

CHAPTER

4

Westend61/Getty Images.

Consciousness

An Introduction to Consciousness

FRONT ROW SEAT TO CONSCIOUSNESS Everyday that Dr. Divya Chander walks through the doors of the hospital, she assumes a tremendous responsibility: keeping people alive and comfortable as they are sliced, prodded, and stitched back together by surgeons. Dr. Chander is an anesthesiologist, a medical doctor whose primary responsibility is to oversee a patient's vital functions and manage pain before, during, and after surgery. Using powerful drugs that manipulate the nervous system, she makes sure a patient's heart rate, blood pressure, and other critical processes remain in a safe range. She also administers drugs that block pain, paralyze muscles, and prevent memory formation (temporarily, of course). "I am very, very privileged that, as an anesthesiologist, I have access to these drugs that I use on a regular basis in order to make [patients'] lives better, to make surgery possible for them," Dr. Chander explains. Working as an anesthesiologist also affords Dr. Chander a unique opportunity to observe the brain as it falls into a deeper-than-sleep state, unaware of the outside world, then emerges from the darkness, awake and alert. In other words, she has the ability to study human brains as they pass through various levels of *consciousness.*

Note: Quotations attributed to Dr. Divya Chander and Matt Utesch are personal communications.

What Is Consciousness?

LO 1 Define consciousness.

Consciousness is a concept that can be difficult to pinpoint. Psychologist G. William Farthing offers a good starting point: *Consciousness* is "the subjective state of being currently aware of something either within oneself or outside of oneself" (1992, p. 6). Thus, **consciousness** might be described as a state of being aware of oneself, one's thoughts, and/or the environment. According to this definition of subjective awareness, one can be asleep and still be aware (Farthing, 1992). Take this example: You are dreaming about a siren blaring and you wake up to discover it is your alarm clock; you were clearly asleep but aware at the same time, as the sound registered in your brain. This ability to register a sound while asleep helps us be vigilant about dangers day and night. For our primitive **ancestors**, this might have meant hearing a predator rustling in the bushes, and for modern people, detecting the "BEEP" of a fire alarm or smoke detector. Researchers have conducted numerous studies to determine what factors influence the likelihood of a person waking up to different types of sounds—factors such as age, gender, level of sleep deprivation, hearing ability, and sleep stage (Moinuddin, Bruck, & Shi, 2017; Thomas & Bruck, 2010). This is the type of research conducted by human factors psychologists, who study the relationship between machines and conscious processes, among other things.

"Sometimes people think that when you lose consciousness, or you go to sleep, that your brain is less active," explains Dr. Chander. "In some dimensions it is less active," she notes, "[but] a better characterization might be that it's less functionally connected to itself." In other words, there is less communication occurring between different parts of the brain. As a person lies on the operating table, in a "less conscious" state, the brain also seems to be doing fewer calculations, processing less information. "When I say 'less conscious,' I do literally mean that because I do think it's an entire spectrum," Dr. Chander explains. "There isn't just 'unconscious' and 'conscious.' There are varied depths of consciousness."

Exploring Inner Space
As a child, Dr. Divya Chander dreamed of becoming a neuroscientist and an astronaut. She went on to earn both an MD and a PhD in neuroscience and now practices anesthesiology. As for the astronaut dream, it nearly became reality when she made it to the final round of NASA's astronaut selection. Dr. Chander still aspires to become a space explorer, but for now her exploration centers on what you might call "inner space"—uncovering the mysteries of consciousness. Macmillan Learning, photo by Norbert von der Groeben.

CONNECTIONS

In **Chapter 1**, we introduced the evolutionary perspective. The adaptive trait to remain aware even while asleep has evolved through natural selection, allowing our ancestors to defend against predators and deal with other dangerous situations.

A DELICATE BALANCE For a patient undergoing major surgery, the goal is to decrease the level of consciousness to a point where pain is no longer felt and awareness of the outside world dissipates. But the anesthesiologist must be careful; giving too much anesthetic can suppress vital functions and kill a person. (Music legend Michael Jackson died from an overdose of the commonly used anesthetic propofol, which he was misusing as a sleep aid.) To reduce consciousness and keep patients safe, the anesthesiologist must give just the right combination, and proper dosage, of anesthetic drugs. To keep her patients in this safe zone, Dr. Chander constantly monitors their brain activity with an electroencephalogram (EEG), which picks up electrical signals from the brain's surface (the cortex) and displays this information on a screen. Looking at the EEG monitor, Dr. Chander can determine a patient's depth of anesthesia, or the degree to which the drugs have induced a "hypnotic state," or changed his level of consciousness. Changes in wave frequency tell her when a patient is becoming "light" (getting close to waking up), "deep" (in a profound slumber, deeper than sleep), and even when he is receiving a particular drug.

Dr. Chander is unusual in this respect; most anesthesiologists are not trained to read an EEG with this level of precision (in addition to her medical degree, Dr. Chander has a PhD in neuroscience). Instead, they rely on other, less direct, indicators of consciousness, such as **blood pressure** and heart rate. This approach actually works very well because the amount of anesthetic needed to suppress

CONNECTIONS

Anesthetic drugs can lower blood pressure and heart rate by suppressing the sympathetic nervous system. In **Chapter 2,** we discussed how the sympathetic nervous system orchestrates the "fight-or-flight" response, prepping the body to respond to stressful situations. Surgery would certainly qualify as a stressful situation.

consciousness The state of being aware of oneself, one's thoughts, and/or the environment; includes various levels of conscious awareness.

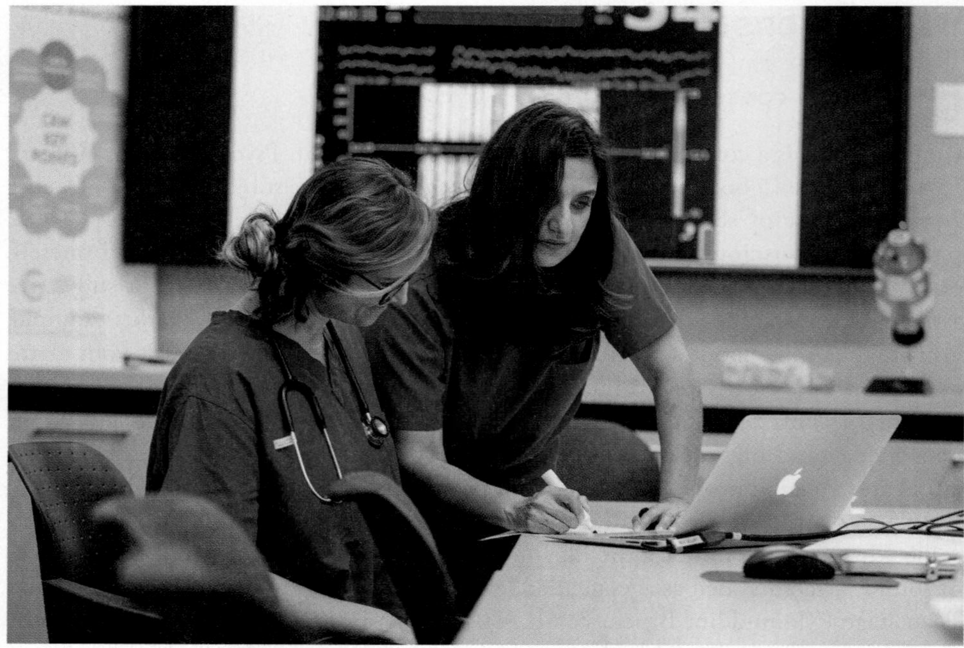

See It in the EEG
Dr. Chander and a colleague review an electroencephalogram (EEG), the technology she uses to monitor her patients' level of consciousness. By observing the changes in wave frequency, she can tell if the patient is in a deep unconscious state, approaching wakefulness, or somewhere in between. Macmillan Learning, photo by Norbert von der Groeben.

blood pressure, heart rate, and movement is greater than that required to suppress consciousness (Aranake, Mashour, & Avidan, 2013). But Dr. Chander's ability to read raw EEG data, and her deep knowledge of neuroscience, put her in an ideal position to track her patients' levels of consciousness.

Studying Consciousness

Without modern technologies such as EEG, early psychologists were very limited in their ability to conduct research on consciousness. But that didn't stop them from trying. **Wilhelm Wundt and his student Edward Titchener** founded psychology as a science based on exploring consciousness and its contents. Another early psychologist, William James, regarded consciousness as a "stream" that provides a sense of moment-to-moment continuity (James, 1890/1983). Think about how this "stream" of thoughts is constantly rushing through your head. An e-mail from a friend appears in your inbox, jogging your memory of the birthday party she threw last month, and that reminds you that tomorrow is your *mother's* birthday (better not forget that). You notice your shoe is untied, think about your homework, and remember the credit card bill you need to pay, all within a matter of seconds. Thoughts interweave and overtake each other like currents of flowing water; sometimes they are linked by topic, emotion, or events, but other times they don't seem to be connected by anything other than your stream of consciousness.

CONNECTIONS
In **Chapter 1,** we discussed the contributions of these early psychologists. Wundt founded the first psychology laboratory, edited the first psychological journal, and used experimentation to measure psychological processes. Titchener was particularly interested in examining consciousness and the "atoms" of the mind.

Although psychology started with the introspective study of consciousness, American psychologists John Watson, B. F. Skinner, and other behaviorists insisted that the science of psychology should restrict itself to the study of observable behaviors. This attitude persisted until the 1950s and 60s, when psychology underwent a revolution of sorts. Researchers began to direct their focus back on the unseen mechanisms of the mind. **Cognitive psychology,** the scientific study of conscious and unconscious mental processes such as thinking, problem solving, and language, emerged as a major subfield. Today, understanding consciousness is an important goal of psychology, and science remains the key to investigating its mysteries.

cognitive psychology The scientific study of mental processes such as thinking, problem solving, and language.

In her neuroscience research, Dr. Chander has employed a cutting-edge technology called *optogenetics,* which uses genetics and light sources to control the activities of individual neurons (Zhao, 2017). With optogenetics, researchers can activate or deactivate neurons or groups of neurons and see how it affects animals' behavior (Deisseroth, 2015). This technology helps Dr. Chander search for groups of neurons that may act as "on" or "off" switches for different states of consciousness (asleep versus awake, for example).

Technologies like optogenetics and functional magnetic resonance imaging (fMRI) have added to our growing knowledge base (Reichert et al., 2014; Song & Knöpfel, 2016), yet barriers to studying consciousness remain. One is that consciousness is **subjective**, pertaining only to the individual who experiences it. Thus, some have argued it is impossible to *objectively* study another's conscious experience (Blackmore, 2005; Farthing, 1992). To make matters more complicated, consciousness changes from moment to moment. Right now you are concentrating on these words, but in a few seconds you might be thinking of something else or slip into light sleep. In spite of these challenges, researchers around the world are inching closer to understanding consciousness by studying it from many perspectives. Welcome to the world of consciousness and its many shades of gray.

CONNECTIONS

In **Chapter 1**, we presented the concept of objective reports, which are free of opinions, beliefs, expectations, and values. Here, we note that descriptions of consciousness are more subjective in nature, and do not lend themselves to objective reporting.

Are You Paying Attention?

There are many elements of conscious experience, including desire, thought, language, sensation, perception, and knowledge of self. Memory is also involved, as conscious experiences usually involve the retrieval of memories. Let's look at what this means, for example, when you go shopping online. As you navigate from page to page, you recognize visual images (*That's the PayPal home page*), you read to yourself (*Shipping and handling fees not included*), and you may even have emotional reactions (*I paid much more than that in the store!*)—all of this is part of your consciousness, your stream of thought.

Explain how automatic processing relates to consciousness.

AUTOMATIC PROCESSING Stop reading and listen. Do you hear background sounds you didn't notice before—a soft breeze rustling through the curtains, a clock ticking? You may not have picked up on these sounds, because you were not paying attention to them, but your brain was monitoring all this activity. In describing consciousness, psychologists often distinguish between cognitive processes that occur *automatically* (without effort, awareness, or control) and those that

Do You Multitask?
When you sit down to prepare for an exam, do you truly study, or are you periodically texting, checking social media, and watching YouTube videos? A recent study of 441 college students uncovered a not-so-surprising relationship between exam performance and multitasking with different types of digital media, such as Facebook, Instagram, text messaging, and e-mail. Students who used no more than two forms of digital media while preparing for an exam performed "significantly better" than those who juggled seven or more (Patterson, 2017). Sidekick/Getty Images.

TABLE 4.1 BE SMART ABOUT MULTITASKING

Problem	Solution
You think you can drive safely while using your phone, because you can text and talk without even looking at the screen.	If you're like the overwhelming majority of drivers (97.5%, according to one study), you cannot drive safely while using a cell phone (Watson & Strayer, 2010). This is even the case when you use Bluetooth and other hands-free technologies (National Safety Council, n.d.). The only safe way to use a phone when behind the wheel is to pull completely off the road.
Sometimes you can't resist checking Instagram and Facebook during study sessions.	Intersperse your study sessions with "media breaks." For example, allow yourself 5 minutes of screen time for every 1 hour of studying. This is much better than constantly switching your focus between studying and media, because every little adjustment requires added time (Carrier, Rosena, Cheeverb, & Lima, 2015).
You know you shouldn't text during class, but you must respond to a time-sensitive message before the lecture is over.	If you must text during class, and you know your instructor will permit this, choose a strategic time to do so. Rather than replying instantly, wait until your instructor has finished expressing a thought or explaining a concept (Carrier et al., 2015).
You know it's rude, but you can't help glancing at your phone during face-to-face conversations.	Put away your phone or turn down the volume during face-to-face conversations, especially with the people you love. Snubbing someone with your phone ("phubbing") can cause conflict in romantic relationships, which may lead to lower levels of "life satisfaction" (Roberts & David, 2016). Phubbing may also undermine your relationships with people at work (Roberts & David, 2017).

Multitasking with technology cannot always be avoided. But with strategies like these, you can avoid some of the negative effects of juggling media with other tasks.

CONNECTIONS In **Chapter 3**, we introduced the concept of *sensory adaptation,* the tendency to become less sensitive to and less aware of constant stimuli after a period of time. This better prepares us to detect changes in the environment, which can signal important activities that require our attention. Here, we see how this can occur through automatic processing.

occur with effort, awareness, and control. **Our sensory systems** absorb an enormous amount of information, and the brain must quickly determine what requires immediate attention, what can be ignored, and what can be processed and stored for later use. This **automatic processing** allows information to be collected and saved (at least temporarily) with little or no conscious effort (McCarthy & Skowronski, 2011; Schmidt-Daffy, 2011). Without automatic processing, we would be overwhelmed with incoming sensory data.

Automatic processing can also refer to the involuntary cognitive activity guiding some behaviors. Do you remember the last time you walked a familiar route, checking your phone and daydreaming the entire time? Somehow you arrived at your destination without noticing much about your surroundings. You were aware enough to complete complex tasks, but not enough to realize you were doing so. This type of multitasking is commonplace, although the great majority of people have difficulty trying to accomplish more than one demanding task at the same time (Medeiros-Ward, Watson, & Strayer, 2015). See **Table 4.1** for solutions to some multitasking problems.

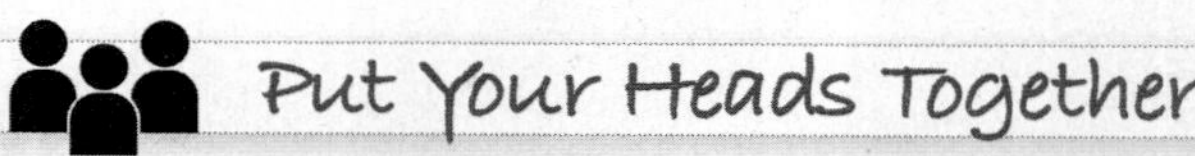

In your group, discuss and record examples of **A**) when multitasking is advantageous to you, and **B**) when multitasking could be risky or problematic.

automatic processing Collection and sometimes storage of information without conscious effort or awareness.

Although unconscious processes direct various behaviors, we can also make conscious and controlled decisions about where to focus our attention. While walking to class, you might focus intently on a conversation you just had with your friend or an exam you will take in an hour. In these cases, we deliberately direct our attention.

LO 3 Describe how we narrow our focus through selective attention.

SELECTIVE ATTENTION Although we have access to a vast amount of information in our internal and external environments, we can only focus our attention on a small portion at one time. This narrow focus on specific stimuli is known as **selective attention.** Talking to someone in a crowded room, you are able to block out the chatter and noise around you and immerse yourself in the conversation. This efficient use of selective attention is known as the *cocktail-party effect,* and it occurs when the brain is responsive to some "speech streams" while ignoring others (Golumbic et al., 2013; Koch, Lawo, Fels, & Vorländer, 2011). Many factors can impact selective attention. Studies suggest it may be influenced by emotions. Anger, for example, increases our ability to selectively attend to something or someone (Finucane, 2011). We also get better at ignoring distractions as we age (Couperus, 2011). This tendency to focus on specific stimuli does not mean we fail to detect everything else; remember, the brain is constantly gathering data through automatic processing.

With so much data competing for our attention, what determines where we direct our focus? Humans are highly sensitive to abrupt, unexpected changes in the environment, and to stimuli that are unfamiliar, rewarding, or especially strong (Bourgeois, Neveu, & Vuilleumier, 2016; Daffner et al., 2007; Parmentier & Andrés, 2010). Meanwhile, we tend to ignore continuous input, like unimportant background stimuli. Imagine you are studying in a busy courtyard. You are aware it is bustling with activity, but you fail to pay attention to every person—until something changes (someone yells or starts running). Then your attention might be directed to that specific event.

INATTENTIONAL BLINDNESS Selective attention is great if you need to study for a psychology test while people around you are talking, but it can also cause you to miss important events—even when you are looking right at them. Suppose you are worried about being late for an important appointment, and the address of the building has slipped your mind. As you walk toward a busy intersection, your preoccupation with street numbers momentarily steals your attention away from signs of danger, like a car turning right on red without stopping. This "looking without seeing" is known as *inattentional blindness*, and it can have serious consequences (Hyman, 2016; Mack, 2003).

Ulric Neisser illustrated just how blind we can be to objects directly in our line of vision. In one of his studies, participants were instructed to watch a video of men passing a basketball from one person to another (Neisser, 1979; Neisser & Becklen, 1975). As the participants diligently followed the basketball with their eyes, counting each pass, a partially transparent woman holding an umbrella was superimposed walking across the court. Only 21% of the participants even noticed the woman (Most et al., 2001; Simons, 2010); the others had been too fixated on counting the basketball passes to see her (Mack, 2003). Even experts can fall prey to this phenomenon. When researchers embedded an image of a gorilla on a CAT scan of a lung, 20 of 24 expert radiologists failed to detect the gorilla (Drew, Vo, & Wolfe, 2013). Since "looking without seeing" seems to be a common experience, it likely serves an

What Umbrella?
In an elegant demonstration of inattentional blindness, researchers asked participants to watch a video of men passing around a basketball. As the participants kept careful tabs on the players' passes, a semi-transparent image of a woman with an umbrella appeared among them. Only 21% of the participants (1 out of 5) even noticed; the others had been focusing their attention elsewhere (Most et al., 2001).

selective attention The ability to focus awareness on a small segment of information that is available through our sensory systems.

important purpose. When might it be useful to ignore some stimuli while paying attention to others?

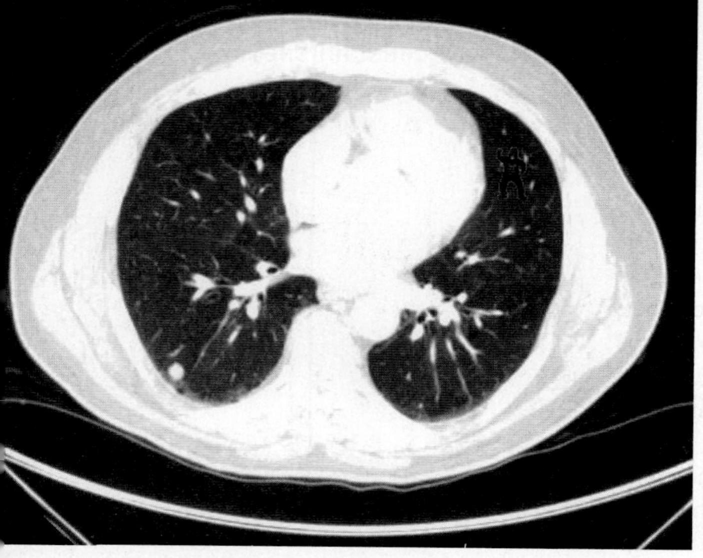

Is That a Gorilla in My Lung?
Look on the upper right side of this lung scan. Do you see a gorilla? Researchers showed this image to a group of radiologists, medical professionals who specialize in reading computerized axial tomography (CAT) scans like this. A whopping 83% did not notice the gorilla, even though it was 48 times bigger than the lung nodules they identify on a regular basis (Drew, Vo, & Wolfe, 2013). A beautiful illustration of inattentional blindness. Trafton Drew.

LEVELS OF CONSCIOUSNESS People often equate consciousness with being awake and alert, and unconsciousness with being passed out or comatose. But as Dr. Chander suggested earlier, the distinction is not so clear. There are different *levels of consciousness,* including wakefulness, sleepiness, dreaming, as well as drug-induced, hypnotic, and meditative states. One way to define these levels of consciousness is to determine how much control you have over your awareness. When focusing intently on a task (using a sharp knife), you have great control over your awareness, but that control diminishes as you daydream. Sometimes we can identify what causes a change in the level or state of consciousness. Psychologists typically delineate between *waking consciousness* and *altered states of consciousness* that may result from drugs, alcohol, or hypnosis—all topics covered in this chapter.

Wherever your attention is focused at this moment, that is your conscious experience—but there are times when attention essentially shuts down. What's going on when we lie in bed motionless, lost in a peaceful slumber? Sleep, fascinating sleep, is the subject of our next section.

show what you know

1. While studying for an exam, your sensory systems absorb a huge amount of information from your surroundings, most of which escapes your awareness. Because of ______________, you generally do not get overwhelmed with incoming sensory data.
   a. human factors
   b. automatic processing
   c. subjective awareness
   d. inattentional blindness

2. Inattentional blindness is the tendency to "look without seeing." Given what you know about selective attention, how would you advise someone to avoid inattentional blindness?

3. ______________ can be described as the state of being aware of oneself, one's thoughts, and/or the environment.

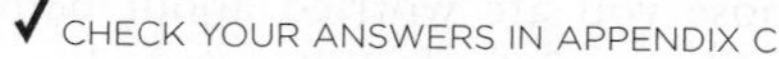

✓ CHECK YOUR ANSWERS IN APPENDIX C.

Sleep

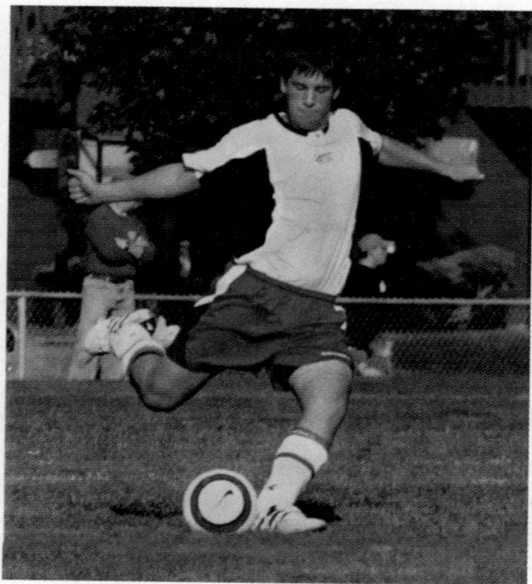

Sleep Troubles
Matt Utesch was active and full of energy as a child, but come sophomore year in high school, he periodically fell asleep throughout the day. Matt was beginning to experience the symptoms of a serious sleep disorder. Courtesy Matthew Utesch.

ASLEEP AT THE WHEEL Matt Utesch was a kid with a lot of energy. He played basketball, ran cross-country, and competed in one of the nation's top-ranking private soccer leagues. But everything changed during Matt's sophomore year of high school. At first it seemed like nothing serious, just a little nap here and there. But eventually, Matt was dozing off in every class except physical education. Most of his teachers assumed he was exhausted from late-night partying. Nobody, not even Matt's doctor, suspected he had a serious medical condition—until the accident happened.

The summer before junior year, Matt was driving his truck home from work. One moment he was rolling along the street at a safe distance from other cars, and the next he was ramming into a brown Saturn that had slowed to make a left turn. What had transpired in the interim? Matt had fallen asleep. He slammed on the brake pedal, but it was too late; the two vehicles collided. Unharmed, Matt leaped out of his truck and ran to check on the other driver—a woman who, as he remembers, "was totally out of it." Her backrest had broken, and her back had nearly broken along with it. A few weeks after the accident, Matt went to the woman's home to bring her flowers. She invited him inside, and they sat down and began to chat. Then, right in the midst of their conversation, Matt fell asleep.

We've Got Rhythm

Worms, monkeys, kangaroos. They all do it. "Virtually all animals, including insects, nematodes, scorpions, spiders, and vertebrates, show some form of sleep, or at least sleep-like states" (Libourel & Herrel, 2016, p. 836). There are animals that require plenty of sleep—bats and opossums sleep 18 to 20 hours a day—and those that need barely any—elephants and giraffes get by on 3 or 4 hours (Siegel, 2005). Sleep needs vary greatly among people, but the National Sleep Foundation recommends adults get between 7 and 9 hours per night (Hirshkowitz et al., 2015). Do the math and that translates to about a third of the day, and therefore a third of your *life*. Clearly, sleep serves some important function, but what is it? And how does it relate to consciousness? How can sleep go so wrong, as happened for Matt? Before tackling these questions, let's get a handle on the basics.

Matt, In His Own Words
http://qrs.ly/mx5a5ag

Macmillan Learning.

 Identify how circadian rhythm relates to sleep.

CIRCADIAN RHYTHM Have you ever noticed that you often get sleepy in the middle of the afternoon? Even if you had a good sleep the night before, you inevitably begin feeling tired in the early afternoon; it's like clockwork. That's because it is clockwork. Many things your body does, including sleep, are regulated by a biological clock. Body temperature rises during the day, reaching its maximum in the early evening. Growth hormone is released at night, and the stress hormone cortisol soars in the morning, reaching levels 10 to 20 times higher than at night (Wright, 2002). Many physiological functions follow predictable daily patterns, affecting behaviors, alertness, and activity levels. Such patterns roughly follow the 24-hour cycle of daylight and darkness; they follow a **circadian rhythm** (ser-KAY-dee-an; Bedrosian, Fonken, & Nelson, 2016).

In the circadian rhythm for sleep and wakefulness, there are two times when the desire for sleep hits hardest. The first is between 2:00 and 6:00 A.M., the same window of time when most car accidents caused by sleepiness occur (Horne, 2006). The second, less intense desire for sleep strikes mid-afternoon, between 2:00 and 4:00 P.M. (Lohr, 2015, September/October), when many college students have trouble keeping their eyes open in class (Mitler & Miller, 1996; Mizuno, 2014). This is a time when many, but not all, people nap.

Not all biological rhythms are circadian, or daily. Some occur over longer time intervals (monthly menstruation), and others cycle much faster (90-minute sleep cycles, to be discussed shortly). Many animals migrate or hibernate during certain seasons and mate according to a yearly pattern. Biological clocks are everywhere in nature, acting as day planners for organisms as basic as bacteria and slime mold (Wright, 2002; Summa & Turek, 2015, February).

Animal Sleep
Crocodiles snooze keeping one eye cracked open most of the time; horses can sleep standing up (although they also lay down to sleep); and some birds appear to doze mid-flight (Kelly, Peters, Tisdale, & Lesku, 2015; U.S. Fish & Wildlife Service, 2006).
Westend61/Getty Images.

SUPRACHIASMATIC NUCLEUS Where in the human body do these inner clocks and calendars dwell? Miniclocks are found in cells all over your body, but a master clock is nestled deep within the **hypothalamus**, a brain structure whose activities revolve around maintaining homeostasis, or balance, in the body's systems. This master of clocks, known as the *suprachiasmatic nucleus (SCN),* actually consists of two clusters, each no bigger than an ant, totaling around 20,000 neurons (Bedrosian et al., 2016; Forger & Peskin, 2003; Wright, 2002). The SCN plays a role in our circadian rhythm by communicating with other areas of the hypothalamus, which regulates daily patterns of hunger and temperature, and the reticular formation, which regulates alertness and sleepiness (**Figure 4.1** on the next page).

CONNECTIONS
In **Chapter 2**, we explained the functions of the hypothalamus. For example, it maintains blood pressure, temperature, and electrolyte balance. It also is involved in regulating sleep-wake cycles, sexual arousal, and appetite.

circadian rhythm The daily patterns roughly following the 24-hour cycle of daylight and darkness; a 24-hour cycle of physiological and behavioral functioning.

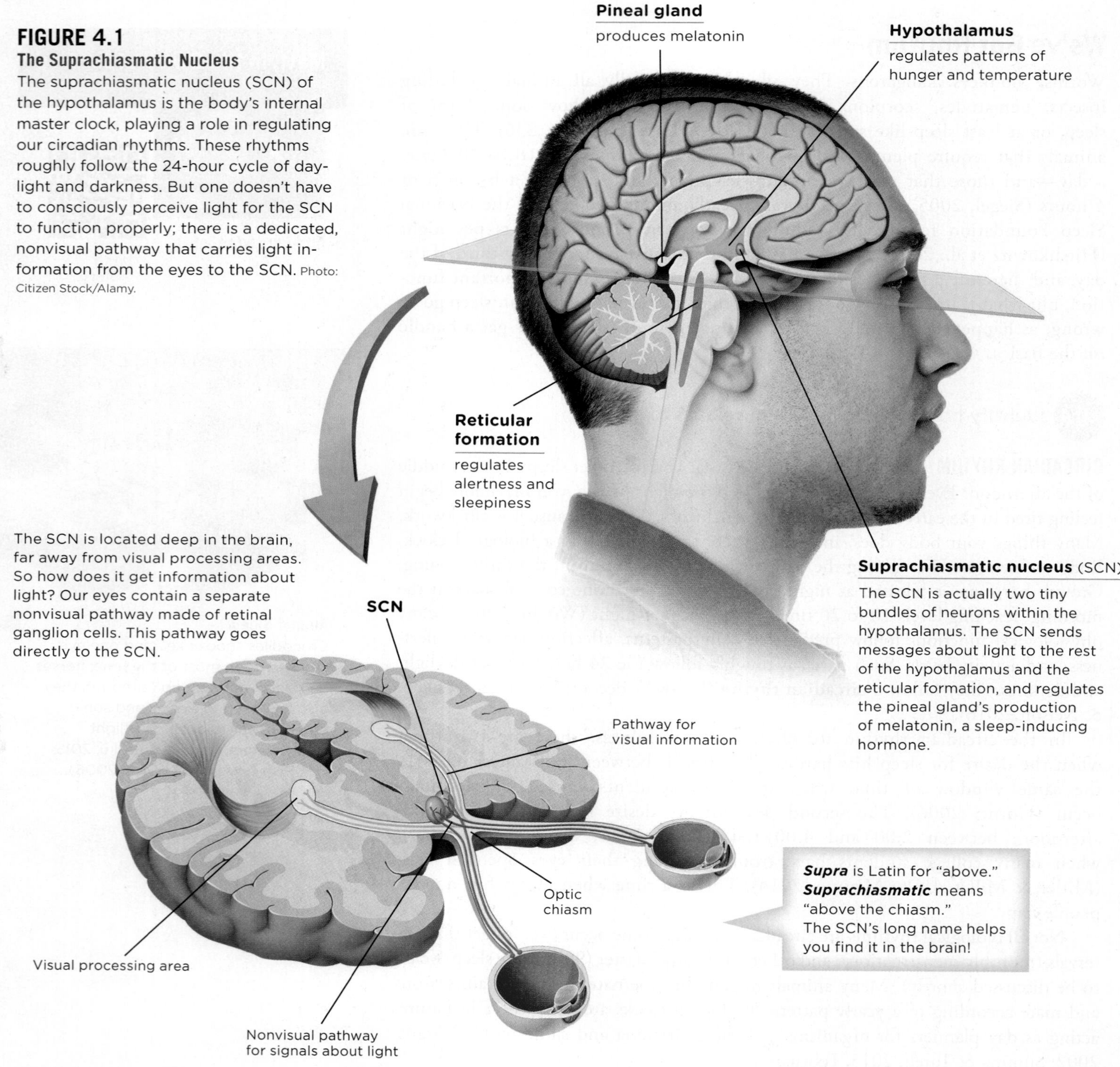
Pineal gland
produces melatonin
Hypothalamus
regulates patterns of hunger and temperature
Reticular formation
regulates alertness and sleepiness
Suprachiasmatic nucleus (SCN)
The SCN is actually two tiny bundles of neurons within the hypothalamus. The SCN sends messages about light to the rest of the hypothalamus and the reticular formation, and regulates the pineal gland's production of melatonin, a sleep-inducing hormone.
The SCN is located deep in the brain, far away from visual processing areas. So how does it get information about light? Our eyes contain a separate nonvisual pathway made of retinal ganglion cells. This pathway goes directly to the SCN.
SCN
Pathway for visual information
Optic chiasm
Visual processing area
Nonvisual pathway for signals about light
Supra is Latin for "above." *Suprachiasmatic* means "above the chiasm." The SCN's long name helps you find it in the brain!

FIGURE 4.1
The Suprachiasmatic Nucleus
The suprachiasmatic nucleus (SCN) of the hypothalamus is the body's internal master clock, playing a role in regulating our circadian rhythms. These rhythms roughly follow the 24-hour cycle of day-light and darkness. But one doesn't have to consciously perceive light for the SCN to function properly; there is a dedicated, nonvisual pathway that carries light information from the eyes to the SCN. Photo: Citizen Stock/Alamy.

CONNECTIONS

In **Chapter 2,** we presented the endocrine system, a communication system that uses glands to convey messages within the body. The messages are delivered by hormones, which are chemicals released in the bloodstream. The pineal gland, a part of the endocrine system, secretes melatonin, a hormone involved in sleep-wake cycles.

One way the SCN keeps you on schedule is by indirectly communicating with the **pineal gland** to regulate the release of *melatonin,* a hormone that promotes sleep (Bedrosian et al., 2016). In dark conditions, the clock commands the pineal gland to produce melatonin, making it easier to sleep. When light hits the eye, melatonin secretion slows down. So if you want to sleep, turn down the lights, and let the melatonin get to work. And when we say "lights," we are referring to all sources, including the screens of your favorite devices.

DIDN'T SEE THAT COMING

ARE SCREENS RUINING YOUR RHYTHM? Many Americans use smartphones, tablets, and computers within 1 hour of bedtime, often to the detriment of their sleep (Bedrosian et al., 2016). The blue light wavelengths emitted by LEDs (light-emitting diodes) may suppress melatonin (Galbraith, 2015, April 7; Wood, Rea, Plitnick, & Figueiro, 2013). The brighter the light and the closer the device to the eye, the greater the impact (Galbraith, 2015, April 7).

How can we take this knowledge gleaned from research and use it to improve our sleep quality? The National Sleep Foundation (2016) suggests removing electronics from the bedroom a minimum of 1 hour before sleep. If you feel compelled to check your e-mail close to bedtime, be quick and turn down the backlight, which gives off blue wavelengths (Galbraith, 2015, April 7). You can further reduce your exposure by turning on a blue light filter (for example, "Night Shift" on an iPhone or "Night Mode" on an Android). You may even consider lighting your home with bulbs designed to work with your circadian rhythm, providing a lit environment that matches the time of day (Kaysen, 2017, February 10).

PROTECT YOUR CLOCK

Want to Sleep Tight? Cut Out the Blue Light
The blue light emitted by LED screens of smartphones, computers, and other electronics may suppress the sleep hormone melatonin, and thereby disrupt sleep–wake cycles. Sam Diephuis/Getty Images.

LARKS AND OWLS Everyone has their own unique clock, which helps explain why some of us are "morning people" or so-called larks, and others are "night owls," a distinction known as *chronotypes*. If you are a lark, you roll out of bed feeling energized and alert, accomplish a lot in the morning, but grow weary as the day drags on. If you're an owl, you tend to wake up late, feel most energized later in the day or evening, and go to bed late (Ferrante et al., 2015). These types of circadian rhythms impact peak performance in athletes (Facer-Childs & Brandstaetter, 2015) and schedules among working people. A common job-related stereotype associated with chronotypes is "morning bias," or the tendency to view workers with later start times as less conscientious than their early-starting colleagues. Supervisors (especially those who are larks themselves) can be influenced by this morning bias, rating their "owl" employees as "lower performers" (Yam, Fehr, & Barnes, 2014).

Put Your Heads Together

College students are often portrayed as owls, but is this just a stereotype? In your group, **A**) discuss factors in the college environment that influence sleep–wake cycles. **B**) Using the experimental method, design a study to explore one of these factors, making sure to include an independent and dependent variable. **C**) Decide what variables you would have to control for to make sure the groups are similar to each other.

JET LAG AND SHIFT WORK Whether you are a lark or an owl, your biological clock is likely to become confused when you travel across time zones. Your clock does not immediately reset to match the new time. The physical and mental consequences of the delayed adjustment, known as ***jet lag***, may include difficulty concentrating, headaches, and gastrointestinal distress. The symptoms may be more disruptive when flying from west to east due to loss of time immediately upon landing (the time is later at the new destination). Fortunately, the biological clock can readjust by about 1 or 2 hours each day, eventually falling into step with the schedule of the new environment (Cunha & Stöppler, 2016, June 6). To minimize jet lag, you should get as much sleep as possible before traveling, avoid

synonyms
jet lag desynchronisis

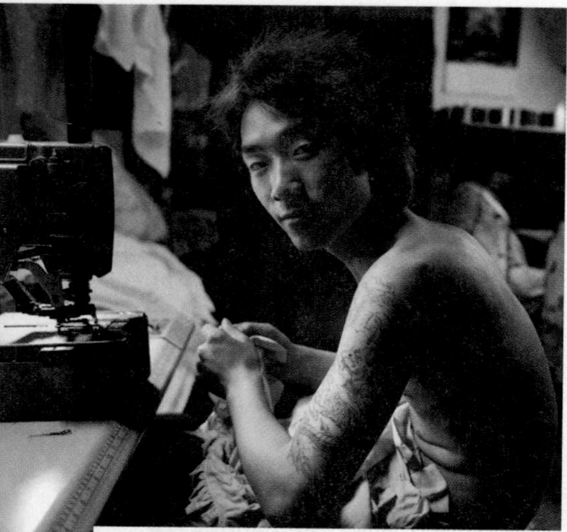

Night Shift
A young man works at a garment factory in China's Guangdong Province. Factory workers are among the many employees who endure shift work, which disrupts circadian rhythms. Minimizing these disturbances can be difficult, but regular exercise and close monitoring of light exposure can help. During work hours, light levels should be high, but at bedtime, darkness is key (Bedrosian et al., 2016; Harvard Medical School, 2007). China Photos/Getty Images.

caffeine and alcohol during the trip, and shift your sleep schedule ahead of time so that it's more aligned with the time zone of your destination (Weingarten & Collop, 2013).

Jet lag is frustrating, but it's only temporary. Imagine plodding through life with a case of jet lag you just can't shake. This is the tough reality for some of the world's shift workers—firefighters, nurses, miners, power plant operators, and other professionals who work while the rest of the world is snuggled under the covers. Shift workers represent about 20% of the workforce in the United States and other developed countries, or 1 in 5 people who are employed (Di Lorenzo et al., 2003; Wright, Bogan, & Wyatt, 2013). Some work rotating shifts, which means they are constantly going to bed and waking up at different times; others consistently work the overnight shift, so their sleep–wake cycles are permanently out-of-step with the light and dark cycles of the earth. Constantly fighting the clock takes a heavy toll on the mind and body. An irregular sleep schedule may lead to symptoms of *insomnia,* or difficulty falling asleep and sleeping soundly. Insomnia resulting from shift work can lead to mood disorders, diabetes, and other chronic diseases (Baron & Reid, 2014; Bedrosian et al., 2016; Wright et al., 2013). Shift workers also face an elevated risk of becoming overweight, and of developing stomach ulcers and heart disease (Baron & Reid, 2014; Monk & Buysse, 2013). Many people use over-the-counter melatonin supplements to reduce jetlag and treat symptoms of insomnia, but there are questions about the quality of these products, as well as their efficacy across individuals (Erland & Saxena, 2017; Grigg-Damberger & Ianakiefa, 2017).

The Stages of Sleep

LO 5 Summarize the stages of sleep.

Have you ever watched someone sleeping? The person looks blissfully tranquil: body still, face relaxed, chest rising and falling like a lazy ocean wave. Don't be fooled. Underneath the body's quiet front is a very active brain, as revealed by an electroencephalogram (EEG). If you could look at an EEG readout of your brain at this very moment, you would probably see a series of tiny, short spikes in rapid-fire succession. These high-frequency brain waves are called **beta waves,** and they appear when you are solving a math problem, reading a book, or any time you are alert (**Infographic 4.1** on page 133). Researchers call this Stage W, indicating a "waking state," and it can range from being fully alert to slightly drowsy (Berry et al., 2016). Now let's say you climb into bed, close your eyes, and relax. As you become more and more drowsy, the EEG would likely begin showing **alpha waves,** which are lower in frequency than beta waves (Cantero, Atienza, Salas, & Gómez, 1999; Silber et al., 2007). At some point, you drift into a different level of consciousness known as sleep.

NON-REM SLEEP A normal sleeper begins the night in **non-rapid eye movement (non-REM),** or nondreaming, sleep, which has three stages (Berry et al., 2016; Infographic 4.1). The first and lightest is Stage N1, also known as "light sleep." During Stage N1, muscles go limp and body temperature starts to fall. The eyeballs may move gently beneath the lids. If you looked at an EEG of a person in Stage N1, you would likely see **theta waves,** which are lower in frequency than both alpha and beta waves. This is the type of sleep many people deny having. Example: Your friend begins to snooze while watching TV, so you nudge her and say, "Wake up!" but she swears she wasn't asleep. It is also during this initial phase of sleep that *hallucinations,* or imaginary sensations, can occur. Do you ever see

synonyms
non-REM NREM

beta waves Brain waves that indicate an alert, awake state.

alpha waves Brain waves that indicate a relaxed, drowsy state.

non-rapid eye movement (non-REM) The nondreaming sleep that occurs during sleep Stages N1 to N3.

theta waves Brain waves that indicate light sleep.

blotches of color or bizarre floating images as you drift off to sleep? Or perhaps you have felt a sensation of falling and then jerked your arms or legs in response? False perceptions that occur during the limbo between wakefulness and sleep are called *hypnagogic hallucinations* (hip-nuh-GOJ-ik), and they are no cause for concern—in most cases. More on this when we return to Matt's story.

After a few minutes in Stage N1, you move on to the next phase of non-REM sleep, called Stage N2, which is slightly deeper than Stage N1. Evidence of theta waves continues showing up on the EEG, along with little bursts of electrical activity called *sleep spindles* and large waves called *K-complexes* appearing every 2 minutes or so. Researchers suspect that sleep spindles are associated with indicators of intelligence and the formation of memories (Fogel & Smith, 2011; Laventure et al., 2016). Studies suggest K-complexes are involved in processes as diverse as memory formation and regulation of the cardiovascular system (Caporro et al., 2012; de Zambotti et al., 2016).

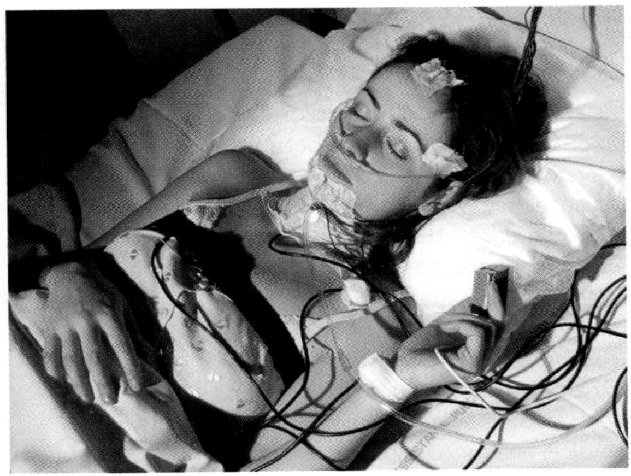

Sleep Waves
A sleep study participant undergoes an EEG test. Electrodes attached to her head pick up electrical activity from her brain, which is transformed into a series of spikes on a computer screen. Through careful study of EEG data, researchers have come to understand the various stages of sleep. Garo/Phanie/Superstock.

After passing through Stages N1 and N2, the sleeper descends into Stage N3 sleep, when it can be most difficult to awaken someone. Stage N3 is considered slow-wave sleep, because it is characterized by low-frequency **delta waves.** Waking a person from slow-wave sleep is not easy. Most of us feel groggy, disoriented, and downright irritated when jarred from a slow-wave slumber. This is also the peak time for the secretion of growth hormone, which helps build tissue and promotes growth in children, making them taller and stronger (Backeljauw & Hwa, 2016).

REM SLEEP You don't stay in deep sleep for the remainder of the night. After about 40 minutes of Stage N3 sleep, you return to the lighter stage of N2 sleep. Then, instead of waking up, you enter Stage R, or **rapid eye movement (REM)** sleep. During REM sleep, the eyes often dart around, even though they are closed (hence the name "rapid eye movement" sleep). The brain is very active, with EEG recordings showing faster and shorter waves similar to those of someone wide awake. Pulse and breathing rate fluctuate, and blood flow to the genitals increases, which explains why people frequently wake up in a state of sexual arousal. When roused from REM, sleepers often report having vivid, illogical dreams. Another name for REM sleep is *paradoxical sleep,* because the body is essentially paralyzed, but the brain is astir with activity. During this sleep stage, certain neurons in the brainstem control the voluntary muscles, keeping most of the body still. This prevents us from acting out our dreams.

SLEEP ARCHITECTURE Congratulations. You have just completed one sleep cycle, working your way through Stages N1, N2, and N3 of non-REM sleep and ending with a dream-packed episode of REM. Each of these cycles lasts about 90 minutes, and the average adult loops through five of them per night. The composition of these 90-minute cycles changes over the course of a sleep session. During the first two cycles, a considerable amount of time is devoted to the deep sleep Stage N3. Halfway through the night, however, Stage N3 vanishes. Meanwhile, the REM periods become progressively longer, with the first REM episode lasting only 5 to 10 minutes, and the final one lasting nearly a half-hour (Siegel, 2005). Therefore, we pack in most of our non-REM sleep early in the night and most of the dreaming toward the end; and the sleep stage we spend the most time in—nearly half the night—is Stage N2 (Epstein & Mardon, 2007).

The make-up of our sleep cycles, or *sleep architecture,* changes throughout life. Infants spend almost half of their sleep in REM periods (Skeldon, Derks, & Dijk, 2016).

delta waves Brain waves that indicate a deep sleep.

rapid eye movement (REM) The stage of sleep associated with dreaming; sleep characterized by bursts of eye movements, with brain activity similar to that of a waking state, but with a lack of muscle tone.

Why Do We Nap?
As many as 50% of college students nap a minimum of once a week. Some are shift workers and need to catch up on lost sleep; others nap because they do not sleep well at night, or because they hope it gives them a cognitive boost. There are also those who nap for emotional reasons (to deal with depression or boredom, for example). Napping for emotional reasons has been consistently linked to negative outcomes, including "poor sleep, psychological functioning, and physical health" (Duggan, McDevitt, Whitehurst, & Mednick, 2016, p. 12).
Art Phaneuf/Alamy stockphoto.

Older people spend far less time in REM sleep and the deeply refreshing stages of non-REM sleep (N3). Instead, they experience longer periods of light sleep (Stages N1 and N2), which can be interrupted easily by noises and movements (Cirelli, 2012; Ohayon, Carskadon, Guilleminault, & Vitiello, 2004; Scullin & Bliwise, 2015).

How many hours of shut-eye do people need each night? It depends on their age. Newborns should be sleeping 14 to 17 hours per day, toddlers 11 to 14 hours, school-aged children 9 to 11 hours, and teens 8 to 10 hours (National Sleep Foundation, n.d.). As mentioned earlier, adults should be getting 7 to 9 hours, but does this actually occur?

From the SCIENTIFIC pages of AMERICAN

WHO GETS THE MOST SLEEP?

Researchers at the University of Michigan used a free smartphone app to collect bedtime and wake-time data from 8,000 people in 128 countries. No big surprise: most people fail to get the solid eight hours that experts often recommend. Folks in Singapore average the least sleep, and the Dutch get the most. Other findings:

- Women average 30 minutes more snooze time than men.
- Middle-aged men get the least shut-eye.
- Bedtime, not wake time, makes the biggest difference in how much sleep you ultimately get.

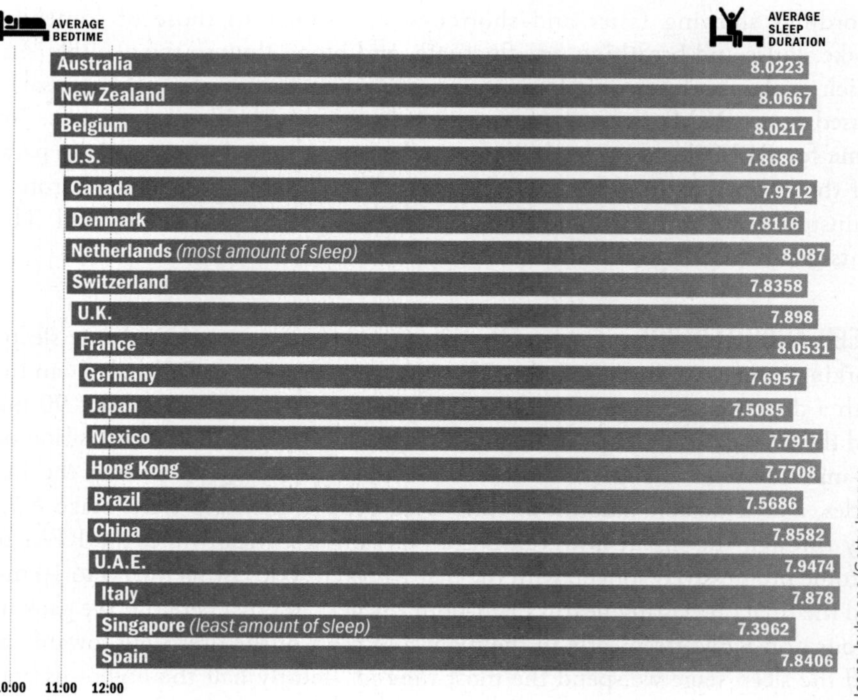

Icons, bubaone/Getty Images.

Sleep

Looking in on a sleep study, you'll see that the brain is actually very active during sleep, cycling through non-REM stages and ending in REM sleep approximately five times during the night. Transitions between stages are clearly visible as shifts in EEG patterns.

Graphs illustrating the human sleep cycle typically present an 8-hour time span, as shown below. But this doesn't tell the whole story of sleep. The amount of time spent sleeping and the content of our sleep change across the life span. Currently, only two thirds of U.S. adults get the recommended minimum of 7 hours per night (Liu, Wheaton, et al., 2016).

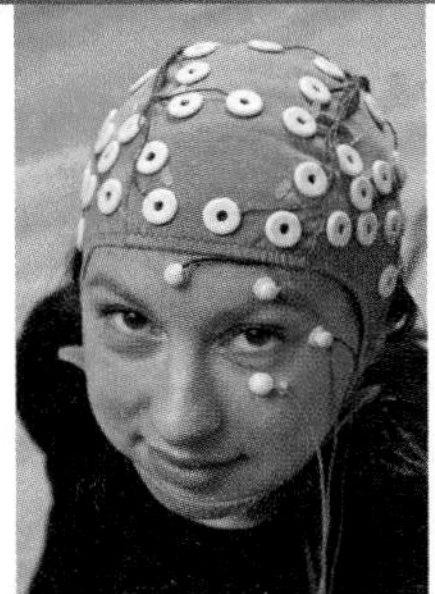

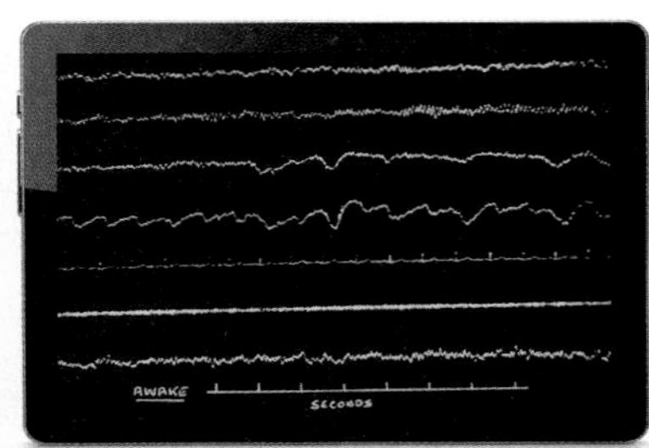

This sleep study participant wears electrodes that will measure her brain waves and body movements during sleep.

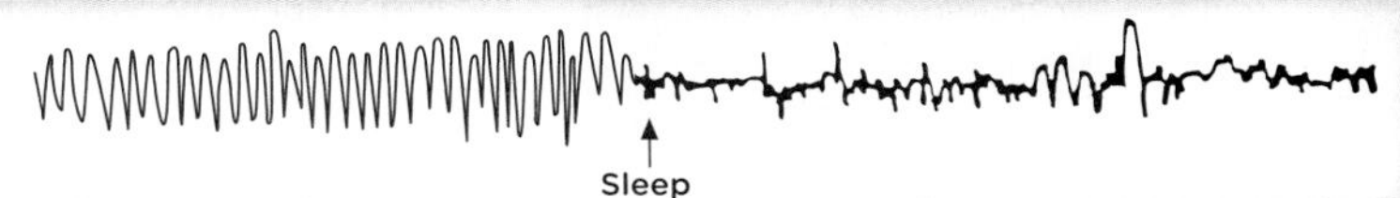

Looking at brain waves allows us to trace a person's stage of sleep. Here, we can see a clear shift from waking to sleeping patterns.
(FROM DEMENT & VAUGHAN, 1999.)

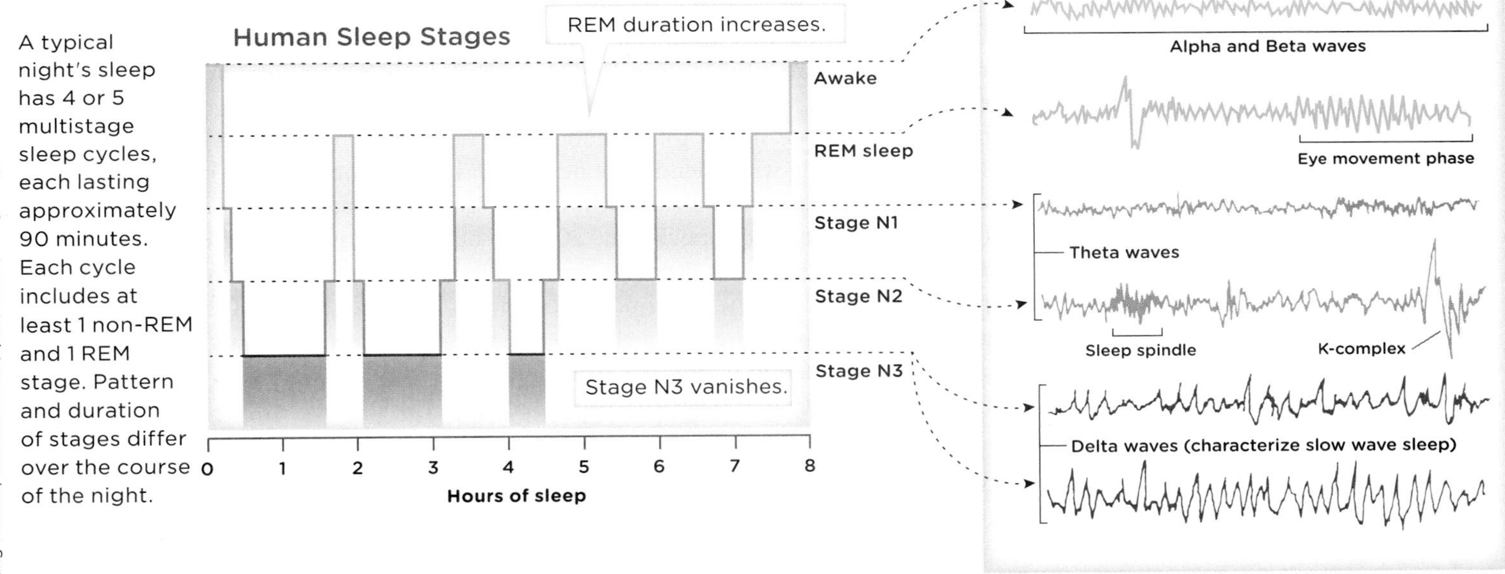

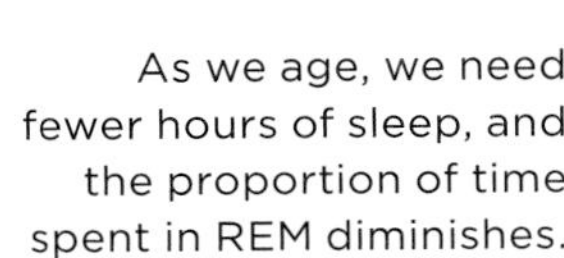

A typical night's sleep has 4 or 5 multistage sleep cycles, each lasting approximately 90 minutes. Each cycle includes at least 1 non-REM and 1 REM stage. Pattern and duration of stages differ over the course of the night.

REM duration increases.

As we age, we need fewer hours of sleep, and the proportion of time spent in REM diminishes.

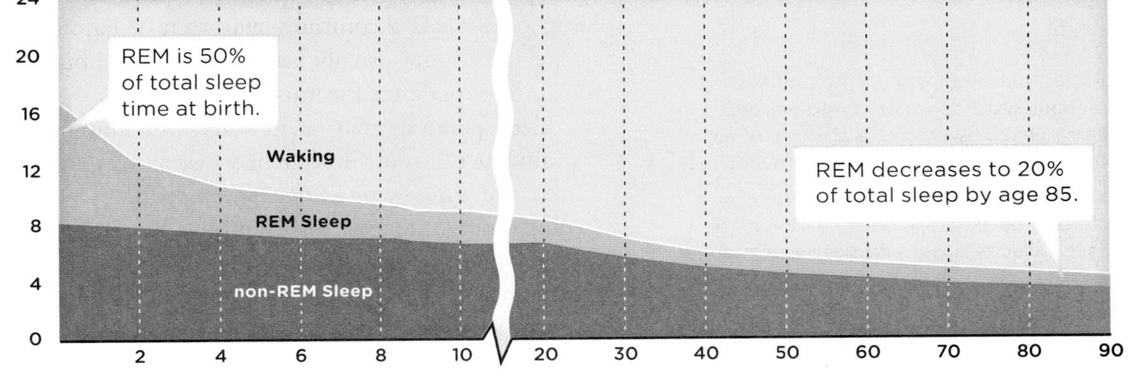

REM is 50% of total sleep time at birth.

REM decreases to 20% of total sleep by age 85.
2 4 6 8 10 20 30 40 50 60 70 80 90
Age in years

Did She Have Narcolepsy?
Harriet Tubman is famous for helping hundreds of people escape slavery through the Underground Railroad. But few people know that Tubman suffered from symptoms of narcolepsy. Her sleep problems began after an incident that occurred when she was still a slave: An overseer struck her in the head as punishment for protesting the beating of a fellow slave (Michals, 2015; Poole, 2016, April 20).
UniversalImagesGroup/Getty Images.

Have Trouble Sleeping?

LO 6 Recognize various sleep disorders and their symptoms.

PROBLEM IDENTIFIED: NARCOLEPSY Shortly after the car accident, Matt was diagnosed with **narcolepsy,** a neurological disorder characterized by excessive daytime sleepiness and other sleep-related disturbances. The most striking symptoms of narcolepsy include the "irrepressible need to sleep, lapsing into sleep, or napping occurring within the same day" (American Psychiatric Association, 2013, p. 372). With narcolepsy, sleepiness can strike anytime, anywhere—during a job interview, while riding a bicycle, or in the midst of a passionate kiss. One time Matt fell asleep while making a sandwich. When he awoke, he was still holding a slice of meat in his hand.

People with narcolepsy may be alert when they first wake up, but they feel extremely tired for a good portion of the day, and may periodically lapse into sleep (National Institute of Neurological Disorders and Stroke, 2017, May 9). "Sleep attacks" can occur several times a day. Most are measured in seconds or minutes, and they often progress into longer naps (Genetics Home Reference, 2017, July). By the time Matt was a junior in high school, his uncontrollable naps were striking upward of 20 to 30 times a day.

CATAPLEXY And that wasn't all. Matt developed another debilitating symptom of narcolepsy: *cataplexy,* an abrupt loss of strength or muscle tone that occurs when a person is awake. During a severe cataplectic attack, some muscles go limp, and the body may collapse slowly to the floor like a rag doll. One moment Matt would be standing laughing with friends; the next he was splayed on the floor unable to move. Cataplexy attacks come on suddenly, usually during periods of emotional excitement (American Psychiatric Association, 2013). The effects usually wear off quickly, but some attacks can render a person immobilized for minutes. Cataplexy may completely disable the body, but it produces no loss in awareness. Even during the worst attack, Matt remained completely aware. He could hear people talking about him, sometimes snickering in amusement. "Kids can be cruel," Matt says. By junior year, he was having 60 to 100 cataplexy attacks a day.

SLEEP PARALYSIS AND HYPNAGOGIC HALLUCINATIONS Matt also developed two other common narcolepsy symptoms: sleep paralysis and hypnagogic hallucinations. *Sleep paralysis* is a temporary paralysis that strikes just before falling asleep or upon waking (American Psychiatric Association, 2013). Picture yourself lying in bed, awake and fully aware yet unable to roll over, climb out of bed, or even wiggle a toe. Sleep paralysis is a common symptom of narcolepsy, but it can also strike ordinary sleepers. Episodes usually last a few seconds, but some go on for several minutes—a terrifying experience for most people.

Sleep paralysis may seem scary, but now imagine seeing bloodthirsty vampires standing at the foot of your bed just as you are about to fall asleep. Earlier we discussed the *hypnagogic hallucinations* people can experience during Stage N1 sleep (seeing strange images, for example). But not all hypnagogic hallucinations involve harmless blobs. They can also be realistic visions of axe murderers or space aliens trying to abduct you (McNally & Clancy, 2005). Matt had a recurring hallucination of a man with a butcher knife racing through his doorway, jumping onto his bed, and stabbing him in the chest. Upon awakening, Matt would often quiz his mother with a question like, "When is my birthday?" He wanted to verify she was real. Like sleep

obstructive sleep apnea hypopnea A serious disturbance of non-REM sleep characterized by complete absence of air flow (apnea) or reduced air flow (hypopnea).

narcolepsy A neurological disorder characterized by excessive daytime sleepiness, which includes lapses into sleep and napping.

REM sleep behavior disorder A sleep disturbance in which the mechanism responsible for paralyzing the body during REM sleep does not function, resulting in the acting out of dreams.

paralysis, vivid hypnagogic hallucinations can occur in people without narcolepsy, too. Shift work, insomnia, and sleeping face up are all factors that appear to heighten one's risk (Cheyne, 2002; McNally & Clancy, 2005).

LIVING WITH NARCOLEPSY Throughout junior year, Matt took various medications to control his narcolepsy, but his symptoms persisted. Narcolepsy was beginning to interfere with virtually every aspect of his life. It was during this time that Matt realized who his true friends were. "The people that stuck with me [then] are still my close friends now," he says. Matt's loyal buddies learned to recognize the warning signs of his cataplexy (for example, when he suddenly stands still and closes his eyes) and did everything possible to keep him safe, grabbing hold of his body and slowly lowering him to the ground. His buddies had his back—literally.

Approximately 1 in 2,500 people suffers from narcolepsy (Ohayon, 2011). This disorder is believed to result from the loss of a specific type of neuron that helps regulate sleep–wake patterns (Lecendreux et al., 2017). Normally, the boundaries separating sleep and wakefulness are relatively clear—you are awake, in REM sleep, or in non-REM sleep. The symptoms of narcolepsy may be explained by occurrences of REM sleep in the midst of wakefulness (Attarian, Schenck, & Mahowald, 2000). In other words, REM sleep occurs in the wrong place, at the wrong time.

You Asked, Matt Answers

http://qrs.ly/mx5a5ag

In hindsight, did you notice any changes that may have foreshadowed the onset of narcolepsy?

REM SLEEP BEHAVIOR DISORDER Narcolepsy is just one of many sleep disorders (**Table 4.2** on page 137). There is also **REM sleep behavior disorder,** characterized by "repeated episodes of arousal often associated with vocalizations and/or complex motor behaviors arising from REM sleep" (American Psychiatric Association, 2013, p. 408). For people with REM sleep behavior disorder, something has gone awry with the brainstem mechanism responsible for paralyzing their bodies during REM sleep. Therefore, they are able to move around, get out of bed, and act out their dreams (Peever, Luppi, & Montplaisir, 2014). This is not a good thing, since often their dreams tend to be unusually violent and action-packed, involving fights with wild animals and other attackers (Fantini, Corona, Clerici, & Ferini-Strambi, 2005). According to some research, up to 65% of REM sleep behavior disorder sufferers have injured either themselves or their bedmates at one point or another. Scrapes, cuts, and bruises are common, and traumatic brain injuries have also been reported (American Psychiatric Association, 2013; Aurora et al., 2010). REM sleep behavior disorder primarily affects older men (age 50 and up) and frequently foreshadows the development of serious neurodegenerative disorders—conditions such as Parkinson's disease and dementia, which are associated with the gradual decline and death of neurons (Boeve et al., 2007; Fantini et al., 2005; Postuma et al., 2009; Peever et al., 2014).

When Apnea Turns Tragic
About a year after the release of *Star Wars: The Force Awakens,* actor Carrie Fisher ("Princess Leia") died of "sleep apnea and other undetermined factors" (County of Los Angeles, Department of Medical Examiner-Coroner, 2017, p. 4). The coroner found evidence of cocaine, heroin, and ecstasy (MDMA) in Fisher's body, but it remains unclear if and how these drugs might have contributed to her death. Mike Marsland/WireImage/Getty Images.

BREATHING-RELATED SLEEP DISORDERS **Obstructive sleep apnea hypopnea** (hi-POP-nee-uh) is relatively common, affecting about 1 in 5 adults, according to a review of research spanning two decades (Franklin & Lindberg, 2015). As the name indicates, this condition is characterized by a complete absence of airflow (apnea) or reduced air flow (hypopnea). During normal sleep, the airway remains open, allowing air to flow in and out of the lungs. With obstructive sleep apnea, the upper throat muscles go limp, allowing the upper airway to close (American Psychiatric Association, 2013). Breathing stops for 10 seconds or more, causing blood oxygen levels to drop (Chung & Elsaid, 2009; Teodorescu et al., 2015). The brain responds by commanding the body to *wake up and breathe!* The sleeper wakes up and gasps for air, sometimes with a noisy nasal sound, and then drifts back to sleep. This process can repeat itself several hundred times per night, preventing a person from experiencing the deep stages of sleep so crucial for feeling reenergized in the morning. Most people have no memory of the repeated awakenings and wonder why they feel so exhausted during the day; they are completely unaware that they suffer from this serious sleep disorder. Obstructive sleep apnea hypopnea is more common among men than women and is more prevalent in people who are obese, and in women after menopause. This condition is linked to increased risk of death in elderly people, traffic accidents, and reduced quality of life, as well as elevated blood pressure, which increases the risk of cardiovascular disease (American Psychiatric Association, 2013).

INSOMNIA About a third of adults say they suffer from symptoms of **insomnia,** and 6% to 10% meet the diagnostic criteria for *insomnia disorder* (American Psychiatric Association, 2013; Mai & Buysse, 2008; Roth, 2007). People with insomnia may have trouble falling asleep, remaining asleep, or getting high-quality sleep; they may arise in the middle of the night or wake up too early, and then have difficulty falling back to sleep. This poor-quality sleep can lead to daytime sleepiness and difficulty with cognitive tasks (American Psychiatric Association, 2013). Insomnia can result in mood changes, memory problems, difficulty with coordination, and physical injuries (Kessler et al., 2012; Pavlovich-Danis & Patterson, 2006). To a certain degree, insomnia is inherited (Van Someren et al., 2015), but its symptoms can be triggered by many factors, including the stress of a new job, college studies, depression, anxiety, jet lag, shift work, aging, drug use, and chronic pain.

You Asked, Matt Answers

http://qrs.ly/mx5a5ag

What kind of physician did you visit in order to be diagnosed with narcolepsy?

OTHER SLEEP DISTURBANCES Have you ever found yourself feeling around in the dark of night, wondering where you are and how you got there? This scenario may sound familiar to those who have experienced ***sleepwalking***, a common disturbance that occurs during non-REM sleep (typically Stage N3). A quarter of all children will experience at least one sleepwalking incident, and it seems to run in families (Licis, Desruisseau, Yamada, Duntley, & Gurnett, 2011; Petit et al., 2015). Sleepwalkers may be spotted sitting up in bed, walking around with their eyes wide open, and speaking gibberish. (Note that this garbled speech is different from *sleep talking,* which can occur in either REM or non-REM sleep, and is not considered a sleep disturbance.) Sleepwalkers can accomplish a variety of tasks, such as opening doors, going to the bathroom, and getting dressed, but they may have "limited recall" of these events upon awakening (American Psychiatric Association, 2013). Most sleepwalking episodes are not related to dreaming, and contrary to urban myth, waking a sleepwalker will not cause sudden death or injury. What's dangerous is leaving the car keys in the ignition, as sleepwalkers have been known to wander into the streets and even to attempt driving (American Psychiatric Association, 2013).

synonyms
sleepwalking somnambulism
sleep terrors night terrors

Sleep terrors are non-REM sleep disturbances primarily affecting children. A child experiencing a sleep terror may sit up in bed, stare fearfully at nothing, and scream. Parents may find the child crying hysterically, breathing rapidly, and sweating. No matter what they say or do, the child remains inconsolable. Fortunately, sleep terrors only last a few minutes, and most children outgrow them. Generally, sleep terrors are forgotten by morning (American Psychiatric Association, 2013).

Nightmares are frightening dreams that occur in REM sleep. And unlike sleep terrors, nightmares can often be recalled in vivid detail. Research suggests that people who frequently experience nightmares are "more susceptible to daily stressors" and may suffer from other problems like depression and insomnia (Hochard, Heym, & Townsend, 2016, p. 47; Nadorff, Nadorff, & Germain, 2015). In some cases, nightmares have no apparent cause. In other cases, they may be related to issues such as posttraumatic stress disorder (PTSD; see Chapter 13), substance abuse, and anxiety. Unless they suffer from REM sleep behavior disorder, people generally do not "act out" their nightmares (American Psychiatric Association, 2013). Given what you know about REM sleep, why do you think this is the case?

insomnia Sleep disturbance characterized by an inability to fall asleep or stay asleep, impacting both the quality and quantity of sleep.

sleep terrors A disturbance of non-REM sleep, generally occurring in children; characterized by screaming, staring fearfully, and usually no memory of the episode the following morning.

nightmares Frightening dreams that occur during REM sleep.

TABLE 4.2 SLEEP DISTURBANCES

Sleep Disturbance	Definition	Characteristics
Narcolepsy	Neurological disorder characterized by excessive daytime sleepiness, which includes lapses into sleep and napping.	Irrepressible need to sleep; daytime napping; cataplexy; sleep paralysis; hypnagogic hallucinations.
REM Sleep Behavior Disorder	The mechanism responsible for paralysis during REM does not function, resulting in the acting out of dreams.	Dreamers vocalize and act out dreams; violent and active dreams are common; upon awakening, the dream is remembered; risk of injury to self and sleep partners.
Obstructive Sleep Apnea Hypopnea	Serious disturbance characterized by a complete absence of air flow (apnea) or reduced air flow (hypopnea).	Upper throat muscles go limp; airway closes; breathing stops for 10 seconds or longer; sleeper awakens, gasping for air.
Insomnia	Inability to fall asleep or stay asleep.	Poor sleep quantity or quality; tendency to wake up too early; difficulty falling back to sleep; not feeling refreshed after a night's sleep.
Sleepwalking	Disturbance of non-REM sleep characterized by complex motor behavior during sleep.	Expressionless face; open eyes; sleeper may sit up in bed, walk around, or speak gibberish; upon awakening, has limited recall.
Sleep Terrors	Disturbance of non-REM sleep generally occurring in children.	Screaming, inconsolable child; usually no memory of the episode the next day.

Problems can arise during both REM and non-REM sleep. This table outlines some of the most common sleep disturbances and their defining characteristics.

Losing Sleep?

Matt's worst struggle with narcolepsy stretched through the last two years of high school. During this time, he was averaging 20 to 30 naps a day. You might think that someone who falls asleep so often would at least feel well rested while awake. Not the case. Matt had trouble sleeping at night, and it was taking a heavy toll on his ability to think clearly. He remembers nodding off at the wheel a few times but continuing to drive, reassuring himself that everything was fine. He forgot about homework assignments and couldn't recall simple things people told him. Matt was experiencing two of the most common symptoms of sleep deprivation: impaired judgment and lapses in memory (Goel, Rao, Durmer, & Dinges, 2009, September).

"Wake up, Tom. You're having the American dream again."

Peter Steiner/The New Yorker Collection/www.cartoonbank.com.

SLEEP DEPRIVATION What happens to humans and animals when they don't sleep at all? Laboratory studies show that sleep deprivation kills rats faster than starvation (Rechtschaffen & Bergmann, 1995; Siegel, 2005). In humans, sleep deprivation leads to rapid deterioration of mental and physical well-being. Stay awake for 48 consecutive hours and you can expect your memory, attention, reaction time, and decision making to suffer noticeably (Goel et al., 2009, September; Van Someren et al., 2015). Sleepy people find it especially challenging to accomplish tasks that are monotonous and boring. They may have trouble focusing on a single activity, like keeping their eyes on the road while driving (Lim & Dinges, 2010). Using driving simulators and tests to measure alertness, hand–eye coordination, and other factors, researchers report that getting behind the wheel while sleepy is similar to driving drunk. Staying awake for just 17 to 19 consecutive hours, which many of us do regularly, produces the same effect as having a blood alcohol content (BAC) of 0.05%, the legal limit

Sleep Culture
A rickshaw driver snoozes in the bright sun. Afternoon siestas are common in countries such as India and Spain, but atypical in the United States (Randall, 2012, September 22). Cultural norms regarding sleep vary significantly around the world. Christine Welman/Alamy.

in many countries. Driving under these circumstances is dangerous (Watson et al., 2015; Williamson & Feyer, 2000). Sleep loss also makes you more prone to *microsleeps,* or uncontrollable mini-naps lasting several seconds—enough time to miss a traffic light turning red. Staying awake for several days at a time produces a host of disabling effects related to speech, thinking, mood swings, and hallucinations (Gulevich, Dement, & Johnson, 1966). The current world record is 11 days, according to experimental data (Gillin, 2002, March 25). Can you imagine how you would feel after 11 days and nights with no sleep?

We have discussed short-term sleep deprivation, but what happens when you fail to get enough sleep night-upon-night for weeks, months, or years? People with chronic sleep deprivation face a greater risk of developing health problems—both minor illnesses like colds and serious ailments like heart disease, diabetes, and cancer (Luyster, Strollo, Zee, & Walsh, 2012; Prather, Janicki-Deverts, Hall, & Cohen, 2015; Tobaldini et al., 2016). Many researchers suspect the obesity epidemic plaguing Western countries is linked to chronic sleep deprivation. Skimping on sleep appears to disrupt appetite-regulating hormones, which may lead to excessive hunger and overeating (Van Someren et al., 2015; Willyard, 2008).

REM SLEEP DEPRIVATION So far, we have only covered sleep loss in general. What happens if a certain type of sleep—REM, for instance—is compromised? Preliminary research suggests depriving people of REM sleep can cause emotional overreactions to threatening situations (Rosales-Lagarde et al., 2012). REM sleep deprivation can also lead to **REM rebound,** an increased amount of time spent in REM sleep when one finally gets an opportunity to sleep in peace.

WHY DO WE SLEEP? The purpose of sleep has yet to be conclusively identified (Assefa, Diaz-Abad, Wickwire, & Scharf, 2015). Drawing from sleep deprivation studies and other types of experiments, researchers have constructed various theories to explain why we spend so much time sleeping. **Table 4.3** describes some of the main theories.

Whatever the purpose of sleep, there is no denying its importance. After a couple of sleepless nights, we are grumpy, clumsy, and unable to think straight. Most of us know that sleep is important, but we don't always practice the best bedtime habits—or even know what they are. Let's explore some behaviors and assumptions to avoid.

TABLE 4.3 THEORIES OF SLEEP

Theory	Description	A Closer Look
Restorative	Sleep allows for growth and repair of the body and brain.	Growth hormone is secreted during non-REM sleep, and protein production ramps up in the brain during REM. Sleep is a time for rest and replenishment of neurotransmitters, especially those important for attention and memory (Borbély, Daan, Wirz-Justice, & Deboer, 2016; Hobson, 1989).
Evolutionary	Sleep serves adaptive function; evolved as it helped survival.	Dark environments were unsafe for our primitive ancestors; humans have poor night vision compared to animals hunting at night, so it was adaptive to avoid moving around. The development of circadian rhythms driving nighttime sleep served an important evolutionary purpose (Barton & Capellini, 2016).
Consolidation	Sleep aids in the consolidation or formation of memories and learning (Tononi & Cirelli, 2014).	Similar patterns of brain activity are observed during learning and post-learning sleep. Without sleep, our ability to form complex memories, and thus learn difficult concepts, is hampered (Farthing, 1992). Studies show that areas of the brain excited during learning tasks are reawakened during non-REM sleep (Diekelmann & Born, 2010; Maquet, 2000).

We spend approximately a third of our lives sleeping, yet the precise purpose of sleep is still to be established. Listed here are three of the dominant theories.

Apply This ↓

TABLE 4.4 HOW TO GET A GOOD NIGHT'S SLEEP

What to Do	Reason
Get on a schedule.	The body operates according to daily cycles, or circadian rhythms. Putting your body and brain on a regular schedule—going to bed and waking up at roughly the same time every day—is critical.
Set the stage for sleep.	Turn down the lights, turn off your phone, and slip into soft pajamas. Do everything possible to create a quiet, dark, and comfortable sleeping environment.
Watch eating, drinking, and smoking.	Beware of foods that create heartburn, and avoid excessive use of alcohol, caffeine, and nicotine, especially late in the day. Be careful not to drink too much coffee, especially closer to bedtime, as this may lead to further sleep disruption (Drake, Roehrs, Shambroom, & Roth, 2013).
Move it or lose it.	Exercise is associated with better sleep, but not right before bed. Generally speaking, exercise at the proper time promotes slow-wave sleep, the type that makes you feel bright-eyed and bushy-tailed in the morning (Driver & Taylor, 2000; Youngstedt & Kline, 2006; Uchida et al., 2012). Exercising 2 to 3 hours before bed can actually prevent good sleep.

If you frequently wake up feeling groggy and unrestored, here are several simple measures you can take to improve the quality of your sleep. Source: NIH (2012).

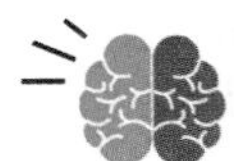

THINK CRITICALLY

6 SLEEP MYTHS

HAVE YOU FALLEN FOR ANY OF THEM?

- **Drinking alcohol helps you sleep better:** Alcohol helps people fall asleep, but it undermines sleep quality and may cause night awakenings (Ebrahim, Shapiro, Williams, & Fenwick, 2013).
- **Yawning means you are exhausted:** Unlikely. Yawning appears to be related to temperature, and functions to help keep the brain cool (Massen, Dusch, Eldakar, & Gallup, 2014).
- **Everyone needs 8 hours of sleep each night:** Experts recommend we get more than 7 hours of sleep each night (Watson et al., 2015), but sleep needs can range greatly from person to person. Some people do fine with 6 hours; others genuinely need 9 or 10 (Schoenborn et al., 2013).
- **You can catch up on days or weeks of sleep loss with one night of "super-sleep":** Settling a sleep debt is not easy. You may feel refreshed upon waking from 10 hours of "recovery" sleep, but the effects of sleep debt will likely creep up later on (Cohen et al., 2010).
- **Pressing snooze is a good way to catch a few more minutes of rest:** Because we need more than a few minutes of sleep to feel rested, hitting snooze is a good indication that you are not getting enough sleep (Oexman, 2013, May 5).
- **Sleep aids are totally safe:** When taken according to prescription, sleep aids are relatively safe and effective, although they do not guarantee a normal night of sleep. That being said, research has linked some of these medications to an increased risk of death (Kripke, 2015; Parsaik et al., 2016), as well as an increased risk of sleep eating, sleep sex, and "driving while not fully awake" (U.S. Food and Drug Administration, n.d., para. 5).

Now that we have busted some sleep-related myths, you may be wondering how you can improve your nightly shut-eye. For some helpful hints, see **Table 4.4** at the top of this page.

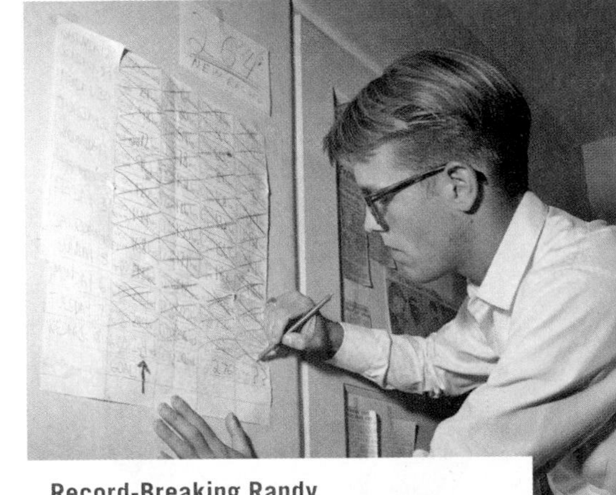

Record-Breaking Randy
A half-century ago, 17-year-old Randy Gardner set the record for the longest documented period of self-imposed sleep deprivation. With the help and encouragement of two friends, and no caffeine or stimulants of any sort, the young man went 11 consecutive days without snoozing (Gulevich et al., 1966). San Diego History Center.

REM rebound An increased amount of time spent in REM after sleep deprivation.

show what you know

1. Many physiological functions follow predictable daily patterns, affecting behaviors and activity levels. Such patterns roughly follow the 24-hour cycle of a(n) ________________.
2. In which of the following stages of sleep do adults spend the most time at night?
   a. Stage N1
   b. Stage N2
   c. Stage N3
   d. Stage W
3. Narcolepsy is a neurological disorder characterized by excessive daytime sleepiness and other sleep-related disturbances such as ________________, which refers to an abrupt loss of muscle tone that occurs when a person is awake.

✓ CHECK YOUR ANSWERS IN APPENDIX C.

Dreams

REM is a particularly active sleep stage, characterized by fast and irregular brain waves. During REM, anything is possible. We can soar through the clouds, kiss superheroes, and ride roller coasters with frogs. Time to explore the world of dreaming.

SLEEP, SLEEP, GO AWAY Just 2 months before graduating from high school, Matt began taking a new medication that vastly improved the quality of his nighttime sleep. He also began strategic power napping, setting aside time in his schedule to go somewhere peaceful and fall asleep for 15 to 30 minutes. "Power naps are probably the greatest thing a person with narcolepsy can do," Matt insists. The naps helped eliminate the daytime sleepiness, effectively preempting all those unplanned naps that had fragmented his days. Matt also worked diligently to create structure in his life, setting a predictable rhythm of going to bed, taking medication, going to bed again, waking up in the morning, attending class, taking a nap, and so on.

Today, Matt is a college graduate and working professional, and his narcolepsy is under control. All his major symptoms—the spontaneous naps, cataplexy, sleep paralysis, and hypnagogic hallucinations—have faded. "Now if I fall asleep, it's because I choose to," Matt says. "Most people don't even know I have narcolepsy."

When Matt goes to sleep at night, he no longer imagines people coming to murder him. In dreams, he soars through the skies like Superman, barreling into outer space to visit the planets. "All my dreams are now pleasant," says Matt, "[and] it's a lot nicer being able to fly than being stabbed by a butcher knife." Onward and upward, like Superman. 

Under Control
After a few very challenging years, Matt developed effective strategies for managing his narcolepsy. In addition to using a medication that helps him sleep more soundly at night, Matt takes strategic power naps and sticks to a regular bedtime and wake-up schedule.
Courtesy Matthew Utesch.

What Are Dreams?

LO 7 Summarize the theories of why we dream.

People have contemplated the significance of dreams for millennia, and scholars have developed many intriguing theories to explain them. Let's explore some of the most prominent ones.

PSYCHOANALYSIS AND DREAMS The first comprehensive theory of dreaming was developed by the father of psychoanalysis, Sigmund Freud. In 1900 Freud laid out his theory in his now-classic *The Interpretation of Dreams,* proposing that dreams were a form of "wish fulfillment," or a playing out of unconscious desires. As Freud saw it, many of the desires expressed in dreams conflict with the expectations of society and would produce great anxiety in a dreamer if she were aware of them. In dreams, these desires are disguised so they can be experienced without danger of discovery. Freud believed dreams have two levels of content: *manifest* and *latent.*

Manifest content, the apparent meaning of a dream, refers to the events occurring in the dream—what you remember when you wake up. **Latent content** is the hidden meaning of a dream, and can provide a window into unconscious conflicts and desires. During therapy sessions, psychoanalysts look deeper than the actual story line of a dream, using its latent content to uncover what's occurring unconsciously. Critics of Freud's approach to dream analysis would note that it is not grounded in scientific evidence (Domhoff, 2017a). What's more, there are an infinite number of ways to interpret any dream, and all of them are impossible to prove wrong.

ACTIVATION–SYNTHESIS MODEL In contrast to Freud's theory, the **activation–synthesis model** suggests that dreams have no meaning whatsoever (Hobson & McCarley, 1977). During REM sleep, the motor areas of the brain are inhibited (remember, the body is paralyzed), but sensory areas of the brain hum with a great deal of neural activity. According to the activation–synthesis model, we create meaning in response to this sensory excitement, even though it is only random chatter among neurons (Hobson & Pace-Schott, 2002). Our creative minds make up stories to match this activity, and these stories are our dreams. Have your ever felt like you were floating or flying in a dream? This is because your brain is trying to make sense of neural activity coming from the **vestibular system**. If the vestibular system is active while we are lying still, the brain may interpret this as floating or flying. Earlier we noted that REM sleep deprivation can impact daily functioning and lead to REM rebound. This suggests that we need REM sleep, even if it is associated with apparently meaningless neural activity.

CONNECTIONS

In **Chapter 3**, we noted that the vestibular system is responsible for our balance. Here we see how the brain tries to make sense of random neural activity occurring in areas of the cortex that receive information from the vestibular system.

NEUROCOGNITIVE THEORY OF DREAMS The neurocognitive theory of dreams proposes there is a high degree of similarity between thinking when we are awake and the cognitive activity of dreaming. In fact, most dream content resembles "waking thought" in terms of "personal concerns" and how we view ourselves and others (Domhoff, 2017b). Stated differently, "Both of these states [being awake and dreaming] are dealing with the same psychological issues to a large extent" (Domhoff, 2001, p. 26).

According to the neurocognitive theory, there is a network of neurons essential for dreaming (and perhaps daydreaming, too) in areas of the limbic system and forebrain (Domhoff, 2001; Domhoff & Fox, 2015). People with damage to these brain areas either do not have dreams, or their dreams are not normal (they lack visual imagery, for example). This finding provides support for the neurocognitive theory of dreams. Another line of supporting evidence comes from studies of children. Before about 13 to 15 years of age, children report dreams that are less vivid and story-oriented than those of adults. Certain brain developments must occur before a child experiences the cognitive activities that allow her to dream like an adult.

Unlike Freud, who proposed that the content of dreams has special meaning, neurocognitive theorists suggest that dreams result from the same type of cognition we experience when awake. In fact, dreams may be a mere consequence of evolution: "It is most likely that dreams are the accidental by-product of two great evolutionary adaptations, sleep and consciousness" (Domhoff, 2001, p. 15). Dreams may also result from another cognitive process: memory consolidation. Studies suggest that sleep facilitates the formation of memories (Murkar, Smith, Dale, & Miller, 2014).

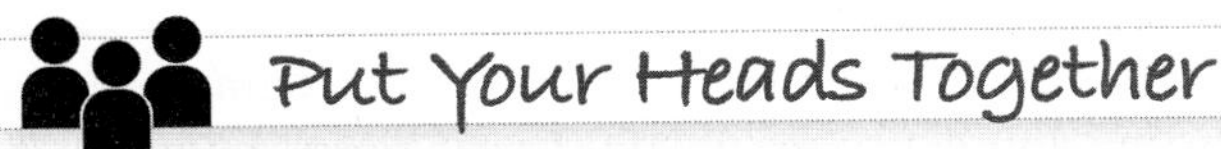

In your groups, review Table 1.1 on p. 10 of Chapter 1. Use at least two of the perspectives to explain why we dream. Write down your responses.

manifest content The apparent meaning of a dream; the remembered story line of a dream.

latent content The hidden meaning of a dream, often concealed by the manifest content of the dream.

activation–synthesis model The theory proposing that humans respond to random neural activity while in REM sleep as if it has meaning.

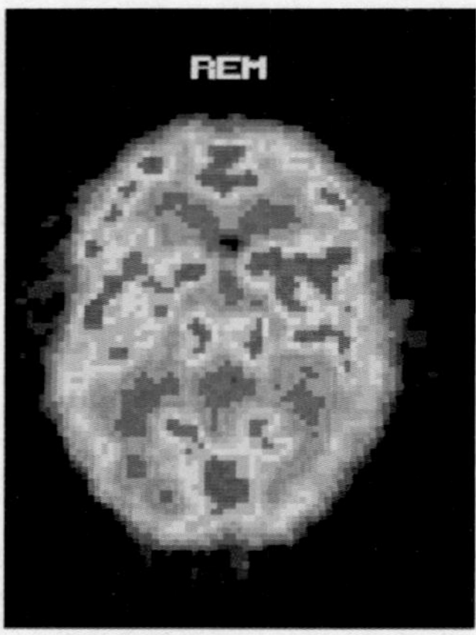

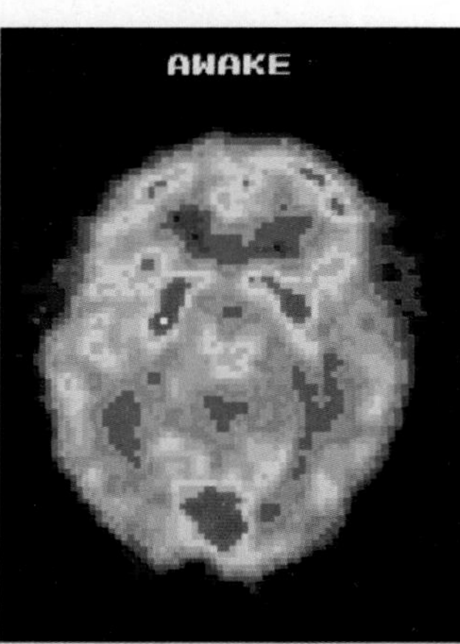

Dreaming Brain
PET scans reveal the high levels of brain activity during REM sleep (left) and wakefulness (right). During REM, the brain is abuzz with excitement. (This is especially true of the sensory areas.) According to the activation-synthesis model, dreams may result when the brain tries to make sense of all this neural activity. Hank Morgan/Science Source.

Dream a Little Dream

Most dreams feature ordinary, everyday scenarios like driving a car or sitting in class. The content of dreams tends to be repetitive and is frequently in line with our activities, emotions, and thoughts during wakeful hours. Life experiences that get incorporated into our dreams tend to be emotional (Malinowski & Horton, 2014), and dream content is relatively consistent across cultures. For example, studies suggest that the most common dream themes among people from China and Germany (very different cultures) involve teachers, school, flying, being chased, and eating delicious foods (Mathes, Schredl, & Göritz, 2014; Yu, 2015). Some people report that they don't dream, but it's more likely they simply fail to remember their dreams (Yu, 2014). If awakened during a dream, one is more likely to recall it at that moment than if asked to remember it at lunchtime.

Most dreaming takes place during REM sleep and is jam-packed with rich sensory details and narrative. Dreams also occur during non-REM sleep, but they are reported less frequently (Siclari et al., 2017). The average person starts dreaming about 90 minutes into sleep, then goes on to have about four to six dreams during the night. Add up the time and you get a total of about 1 to 2 hours of dreaming per night.

Have you ever realized that you are in the middle of a dream? A *lucid dream* is one that you are aware of having, and research suggests that about half of us have had one, and almost a fourth of us have them monthly (Gackenbach & LaBerge, 1988; Saunders, Roe, Smith, & Clegg, 2016). There are two parts to a lucid dream: the dream itself and the awareness that you are dreaming. Some suggest lucid dreaming is actually a way to direct the content of dreams (Gavie & Revonsuo, 2010), but this claim is difficult to "verify objectively" since dreams cannot be experienced by an outsider (LaBerge, 2014).

Fantastical, funny, or frightening, dreams represent a distinct state of consciousness, a fluid, ever-changing entity. Now it's time to explore how consciousness transforms when chemicals are introduced into our bodies, or when we undergo hypnosis. On to the altered states. . . .

show what you know

1. According to the ______________, dreams have no meaning whatsoever. Instead, the brain is responding to random neural activity as if it had meaning.
   a. psychoanalytic perspective
   b. neurocognitive theory
   c. activation-synthesis model
   d. evolutionary perspective
2. What kinds of neural activity occur in the brain when you dream?
3. Freud believed dreams have two levels. The ______________ refers to the apparent meaning of the dream, whereas the ______________ refers to the hidden meaning.

✓ CHECK YOUR ANSWERS IN APPENDIX C.

What Are Altered States?

UNDER THE KNIFE You wake in the morning with a dull pain around your belly button. By the time you get to your 10:00 A.M. class, the pain is sharper and has migrated to your lower right abdomen, so you head to the local emergency room. Doctors diagnose you with appendicitis, an inflammation of the appendix often caused by infection (and potentially fatal, if allowed to progress too far). You need an emergency operation to remove your appendix. You've never had surgery, and the prospect of "going under" is making you very nervous: *I hate needles—do I have to have an IV? What if I wake up in excruciating pain? What if I never wake up?*

Dr. Chander, introduced at the start of the chapter, is your anesthesiologist. She is there to keep you safe and comfortable throughout the process; she also may be able to ease your anxiety by connecting with you on a human level. "The most important thing, in addition to assessing what their surgical and anesthetic risk is, is to form that quick bond, and rapport with that patient," Dr. Chander explains. "If you're an anesthesiologist that can really connect to humans . . . you can really make a difference in someone's life," she adds. "I think you can impact their entire healing process by taking away a lot of their fear in the beginning."

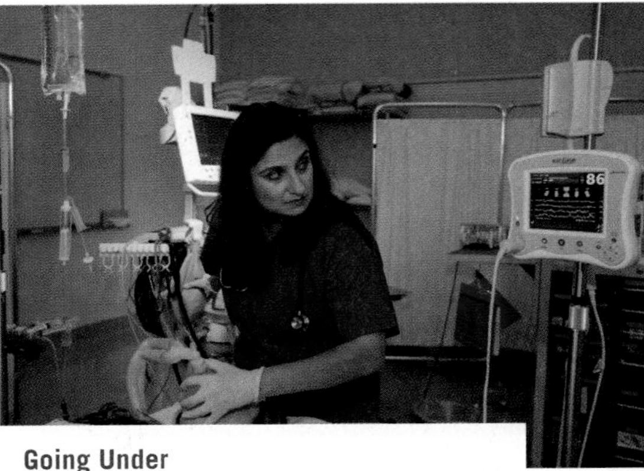

Going Under
Dr. Chander uses various drugs to lull her surgical patients into a deeper-than-sleep state. She may administer a gas, such as nitrous oxide, or a volatile liquid, such as sevoflurane, through a mask (as demonstrated here). In other instances, she delivers drugs through injection. Macmillan Learning, photo by Norbert von der Groeben.

After taking notes on your medical history and examining your heart, lungs, and airways, Dr. Chander explains the procedure you are about to undergo. When you're ready, she starts an IV, delivering a drug such as Versed (midazolam) to ease your anxiety and interfere with your ability to form new memories for the next 20 minutes or so. Why the need for this temporary memory block? The moments before surgery are terrifying; some patients tremble and cry in anticipation. But everyone is different. A small number of Dr. Chander's patients refuse the Versed because they want to remember their presurgery experience.

The Versed kicks in; you start to feel relaxed and sleepy; and before you know it, you're in the operating room, hooked up to all sorts of tubes and monitors. Dr. Chander lulls you into unconsciousness with a drug called propofol, and blunts your perception of pain with a powerful narcotic such as fentanyl. She also paralyzes your muscles with drugs such as rocuronium or vecuronium, whose effects are readily reversible. These drugs are modern derivatives of curare, an arrowhead poison used by South American natives. Curare works by blocking the activity of the neurotransmitter **acetylcholine**, which stimulates muscle contractions in the body. But curare does not cross into the brain, and therefore it does not have the power to transport you to another level of consciousness (Czarnowski, Bailey, & Bal, 2007).

CONNECTIONS

In **Chapter 2**, we described neurotransmitters and the role they play in the nervous system. Acetylcholine is a neurotransmitter that relays messages from motor neurons to muscles, enabling movement. Too little acetylcholine causes paralysis. Here, we see how drugs can block the normal activity of acetylcholine, causing the paralysis useful during surgery.

A few minutes ago, you were awake, sensing, perceiving, thinking, and talking. Now you see nothing, hear nothing, feel nothing. It's like you are gone. The anesthetics Dr. Chander used to produce these effects are called *psychoactive drugs*. 

Psychoactive Drugs: From Caffeine to Heroin

LO 8 Define psychoactive drugs.

Psychoactive drugs cause changes in psychological activities such as sensation, perception, attention, judgment, memory, self-control, emotion, thinking, and behavior—all of which are associated with our conscious experiences. You don't have to visit a hospital to have a psychoactive drug experience. Mind-altering drugs are everywhere—in the coffee shop around the corner, at the liquor store down the street, and probably in your own kitchen. About 85% of people in the United States (aged 2 and older) drink at least one *caffeine*-containing beverage per day—typically coffee, but also soda, tea, and energy drinks (Mitchell, Knight, Hockenberry, Teplansky, & Hartman, 2014). Trailing behind caffeine are *alcohol* (around 70% of adults

psychoactive drugs Substances that can cause changes in psychological activities such as sensation, perception, attention, judgment, memory, self-control, emotion, thinking, and behavior; substances that cause changes in conscious experiences.

Vaping
Use of traditional cigarettes is decreasing among teens, while e-cigarettes are rapidly gaining popularity. Introduced in 2007, these battery-powered devices, also known as "e-hookahs" and "vape-pens," are now the most popular tobacco products used by young people. E-cigarettes infuse the lungs with nicotine and formaldehyde (both carcinogens) and other potentially hazardous chemicals (U.S. Department of Health and Human Services, 2016).
Stanton j Stephens/Image Source/Getty Images.

report drinking alcohol in the previous year) and *nicotine* (approximately 15% smoke cigarettes). Both of these substances present serious health risks (Centers for Disease Control and Prevention, n.d.; National Institute on Alcohol Abuse and Alcoholism, n.d.). Another huge category of psychoactive drugs is prescription medications—drugs for pain relief, depression, insomnia, and just about any ailment you can imagine. Don't forget the illicit, or illegal, drugs like LSD and Ecstasy. In one study, 10.6% of Americans aged 12 and older reported they had used illegal drugs over the past month (Center for Behavioral Health Statistics and Quality, 2017). It's important to note that both legal and illegal drugs can be misused. Later in the chapter, we will discuss "substance use disorder," the continued use of a drug despite significant problems associated with "cognitive, behavioral, and physiological symptoms" (American Psychiatric Association, 2013, p. 483).

Psychoactive drugs alter consciousness in an untold number of ways. They can rev you up, slow you down, release your inhibitions, and convince you that the universe is on the verge of collapse. We will discuss the three major categories of psychoactive drugs—depressants, stimulants, and hallucinogens—but keep in mind that some drugs fall into more than one group.

Depressants

LO 9 Identify several depressants and stimulants and know their effects.

In the operating room, Dr. Chander relies heavily on a group of psychoactive drugs that *suppress* certain kinds of activity in the central nervous system (CNS), or slow things down. They are known as ***sedative-hypnotics*** or, more broadly, **depressants**. In the example above, you learned how she used Versed to ease anxiety. Versed is a benzodiazepine—a type of depressant that has a calming, sleep-inducing effect. Other examples of benzodiazepines are Valium (diazepam) and Xanax (alprazolam), used to treat anxiety disorders. "The date-rape drug" Rohypnol (flunitrazepam), also known as "roofies," is a benzodiazepine legally manufactured in other countries, but banned in the United States (Talbert, 2014). Sex predators have been known to slip the pills, which are flavorless and sometimes colorless, into their victims' alcoholic drinks—a potentially deadly combination. Rohypnol can cause confusion, amnesia, physical weakness, and sometimes loss of consciousness, preventing victims from defending themselves or remembering the details of a sexual assault (NIDA Blog Team, 2015, March 16). A growing number of Americans have been overusing and misusing benzodiazepines in recent years, but because so much attention has been focused on the opioid epidemic (soon to be discussed), this problem has been somewhat ignored (Lembke, Papac, & Humphreys, 2018).

synonyms
sedative-hypnotics tranquilizers
depressants downers
barbiturate yellow jackets, pink ladies, goof balls, reds, rainbows

BARBITURATES Once a patient is in the operating room and ready for surgery, Dr. Chander puts him "to sleep," a process called *induction.* In the past, anesthesiologists might have induced patients with a type of depressant called a **barbiturate** (bar-BICH-er-it), which also has a calming or sleep-inducing effect. In low doses, barbiturates cause many of the same effects as alcohol—relaxation, lowering of spirits, or alternatively, aggression (Julien, Advokat, & Comaty, 2014)—which may explain why they have become popular among recreational users. But these substances are addictive and extremely dangerous when taken in excess or mixed with other drugs. If barbiturates are taken with alcohol, for example, the muscles of the diaphragm may relax to the point of suffocation (**Infographic 4.2**).

depressants A class of psychoactive drugs that *depress* or slow down activity in the central nervous system.

barbiturate Depressant drug that decreases neural activity and reduces anxiety; a type of sedative.

INFOGRAPHIC 4.2

The Dangers of Drugs in Combination

Taking multiple drugs simultaneously can lead to unintended and potentially fatal consequences because of how they work in the brain. Drugs can modify neurotransmission by increasing or decreasing the chemical activity. When two drugs work on the same system, their effects can be additive, greatly increasing the risk of overdose. For example, alcohol and barbiturates both bind to GABA receptors. GABA's inhibitory action has a sedating effect, which is a good thing when you need to relax. But too much GABA will relax physiological processes to the point where unconscious, life-sustaining activities shut down, causing you to stop breathing and die.

In the United States, alcohol use leads to nearly 5 million emergency room visits per year. Combined use of alcohol and other drugs is more likely to result in hospital admissions (White, Slater, Ng, Hingson, & Breslow, 2018).

NORMAL GABA ACTIVITY

GABA
Alcohol
Barbiturate
Action potential
Sending neuron
GABA receptor
Receiving neuron
GABA message communicated

GABA activation, which calms nervous system activity, is essential for proper functioning of the central nervous system. Without GABA, nerve cells fire too frequently.

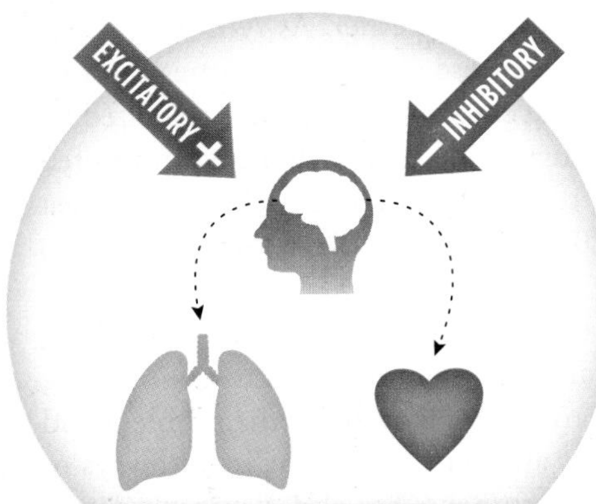

When systems are functioning normally, GABA's inhibitory signals perfectly balance excitatory signals in the central nervous system (CNS). This results in regular breathing and heart rate.

ALCOHOL

Alcohol activates the same receptors, increasing GABA's activity.

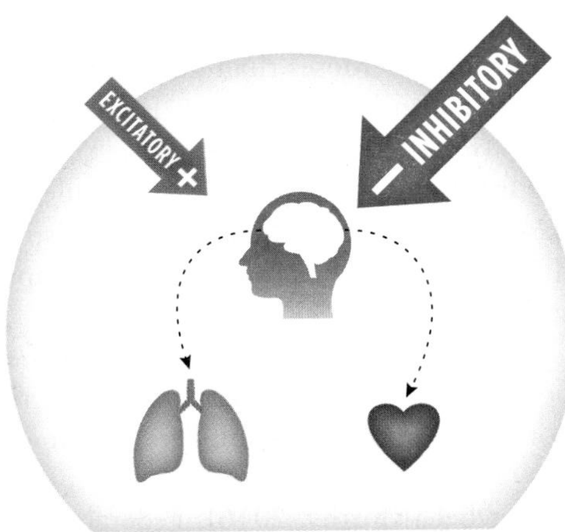

When alcohol increases GABA's inhibitory signals, excitatory and inhibitory signals in the CNS are out of balance. Along with increased relaxation, heart and breathing rates decrease. Increasing levels of alcohol could eventually lead to stupor and coma.

ALCOHOL + BARBITURATE

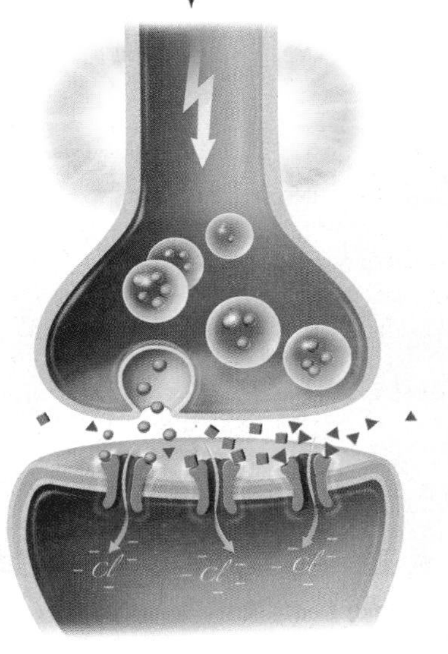

Barbiturates bind to and activate GABA receptors too, creating even more GABA-related inhibition.

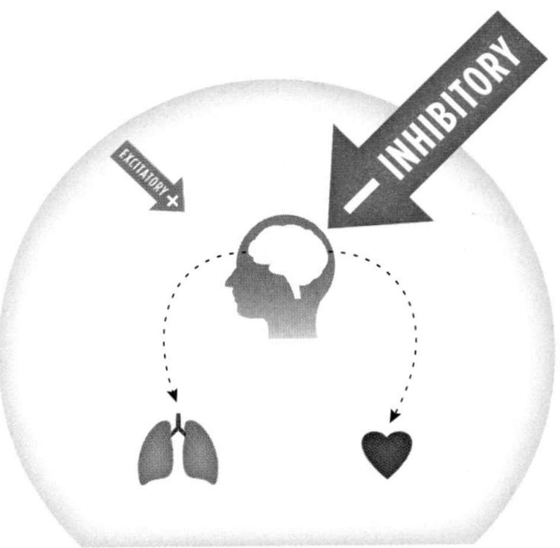

Together, alcohol and barbiturates further unbalance excitatory and inhibitory signals, suppressing heart rate and the impulse to breathe.

OPIOIDS Putting a patient to sleep is not enough to prepare him for a major surgery; he also needs drugs that combat pain. Even when a patient is out cold on the operating table, his brain receives pain impulses, and pain during surgery can lead to greater pain during recovery. "When the surgeon is cutting, it causes trauma to the body whether or not you're consciously perceiving it," explains Dr. Chander. "If you don't block pain receptors up front, you could have significant pain afterwards, sometimes lasting well beyond the period of healing from the surgery. We call this conversion from acute to chronic pain." With this in mind, Dr. Chander may use an opioid, a drug that minimizes the brain's perception of pain, induces drowsiness and euphoria, and slows breathing (Julien et al., 2014). "Opioid" is an umbrella term for a large group of similarly acting drugs, some found in nature (morphine, derived from the poppy plant) and others synthesized by humans (methadone, concocted in laboratories). There are two types of naturally occurring opioids: the endorphins produced by your body, and the **opiates** found in the opium poppy. Morphine is used to alleviate pain in medical settings; it also serves as the raw material for making the street drug heroin, which enters the brain more quickly and has 3 times the strength (Julien et al., 2014).

Overdose Death Toll
A woman marches during Overdose Awareness Day in the summer of 2017. The number one cause of death among Americans below age 50 is drug overdose (Katz, 2017, June 5). Some people are reluctant to call 911 when they suspect a friend is suffering from an overdose because they fear criminal repercussions for their own drug activities. But most states offer these individuals protection through Good Samaritan or 911 drug immunity laws, which "generally provide immunity from arrest, charge or prosecution for certain controlled substance possession and paraphernalia offenses" (National Conference of State Legislatures, 2017, June 5, para. 8). Spencer Platt/Getty Images News/Getty Images.

THINK CRITICALLY

AMERICA'S OPIOID EPIDEMIC Fifteen years ago, heroin use in the United States was relatively rare. Since then, the number of adults who have used this dangerous drug has jumped "almost 5-fold," from 0.33% to 1.6% (Martins et al., 2017, p. E5). What is behind this massive increase? One important factor is overuse of opioid painkillers such as Vicodin (hydrocodone) and OxyContin (oxycodone) (Barnett, Olenski, & Jena, 2017). Doctors prescribe these drugs for pain, but some patients get hooked and then turn to heroin as an alternative. Imagine a patient arriving at the emergency room and complaining of severe pain; the doctor writes a prescription for an opioid painkiller, and the patient (or perhaps a friend or family member of the patient) becomes dependent on it. Unable to obtain a new prescription, the person turns to another opioid available on the street: heroin.

"THE WORST DRUG OVERDOSE EPIDEMIC IN AMERICAN HISTORY"

Misuse of opioids and other drugs causes 175 deaths per day in the United States (Mitchell, 2018, January 29). To put this in perspective, more Americans are dying from drug overdoses than gun murders and car crashes together. As *New York Times* reporter Josh Katz observes, "It's the worst drug overdose epidemic in American history" (Katz, 2017, April 14, para. 5). This overdose epidemic has been accelerated by the misuse of fentanyl, a powerful anesthetic drug that should only be administered in a medical setting. When fentanyl is illegally manufactured and packaged in street drugs, the effects can be deadly (Compton, 2017, June 30). What can be done to stem the crisis?

For starters, doctors (and dentists) need to be extremely careful about prescribing opioids. For their part, patients should think carefully when it comes to taking these potentially addictive painkillers. The medical community is aware of the problem and has taken steps to curb unnecessary prescriptions and pursue alternative pathways to pain relief (Murthy, 2016). Federal and state governments are also clamping down, and the number of opioid prescriptions has declined in recent years (Goodnough, 2017, July 6). At the community level, people need to understand that opioid abuse can signal a "disease" that needs treatment—not a sign of personal weakness or failure. As the American College of Physicians (ACP) recommends, "Substance use

opiates A class of psychoactive drugs that cause a sense of euphoria; a drug that imitates the endorphins naturally produced in the brain.

Do you know someone who might have a problem with opioids or other drugs?

Do something before the situation spirals into tragedy. Help is available 24-7 through the **National Health Helpline: 1-800-662-HELP (4357)**. You can also find a nearby treatment facility through SAMHSA's Behavioral Health Treatment Services Locator: https://findtreatment.samhsa.gov.

FIGURE 4.2
You Might Save a Life

disorder is a chronic medical condition and should be managed as such" (Crowley, Kirschner, Dunn, & Bornstein, 2017, p. 734). The ACP also emphasizes the value of offering treatment in place of criminal punishment for people with substance use disorders who have been caught selling or using drugs (Crowley et al., 2017). Finally, we all need to be on heightened alert for signs of trouble (**Figure 4.2**). Do you know what an opioid overdose looks like? If you have the slightest suspicion that someone is suffering from a drug overdose, call 911 immediately. Be on the lookout for three signs in particular, which the World Health Organization calls the "opioid overdose triad": (1) pinpoint pupils (unusually small pupils), (2) unconsciousness, and (3) difficulty breathing (WHO, 2014, November).

Death by Fraternity Hazing? Nineteen-year-old Timothy Piazza had a blood alcohol level between .26 and .36% the night he sustained fatal brain trauma at a Penn State fraternity house. After participating in a binge-drinking activity for Beta Theta Pi pledges, Piazza tumbled down the basement stairs and lost consciousness. Surveillance footage shows Piazza's frat "brothers" lugging him up the stairs, placing him on a couch, dousing him with beer, and throwing a shoe at his head. At other points in the night, Piazza appears alone, writhing on the floor (apparently in pain), meandering through the house, and falling several more times. Fraternity members waited 12 hours to call 911, and many of them have faced criminal charges associated with Piazza's death (Ganim, Grinberg, & Welch, 2017, June 13; Turpin, 2017, June 14). Joe Hermitt/AP Images.

ALCOHOL AND BINGE DRINKING Alcohol is the most commonly used depressant in the United States. Around 33% of adults and 22% of high-school seniors report that they have engaged in *binge drinking* (consuming four or more drinks for women and five or more for men, on one occasion) at least one time in the last month (Hingson, Zha, & White, 2017; Patrick & Schulenberg, 2014). Many people think binge drinking is fun, but they might change their minds if they reviewed the research. Studies have linked binge drinking to poor grades, low self-esteem, and behavior problems in adolescents (Patrick & Schulenberg, 2014). Even worse, binge drinking may lead to accidental injury and death: "Of the nearly 90,000 people who die from alcohol each year, more than half, or 50,000, die from injuries and overdoses associated with high blood alcohol levels," notes George F. Koob, director of the National Institute on Alcohol Abuse and Alcoholism (National Institutes of Health, 2017, May 17, para. 2). Think getting wasted is sexy? Consider this: Too much alcohol impairs sexual performance, particularly for men, who may have trouble obtaining and sustaining an erection.

You don't have to binge drink in order to have an alcohol problem. Some people cannot get through the day without a midday drink; others need alcohol to unwind or fall asleep. The point is there are many forms of alcohol misuse. About 8.5% of the adult population in the United States (nearly 1 in 10 people) struggle with alcohol dependence or some other type of drinking problem (American Psychiatric Association, 2013; Grant et al., 2004).

ALCOHOL IN THE BODY Let's stop for a minute and examine how alcohol influences consciousness (**Figure 4.3** on the next page). People sometimes say they feel "high" when they drink. How can such a statement be true when alcohol is a *depressant,* a drug that slows down activity in the central nervous system? Alcohol alters the effects of GABA, a neurotransmitter that dampens activity in certain brain networks, including those that regulate social inhibition. By interfering with GABA, alcohol loosens inhibitions, which can lead to feelings of euphoria and may cause

FIGURE 4.3
Blood Alcohol Concentration (BAC)
The effects of one drink—a 12-oz bottle of beer, 4-oz glass of wine, or 1-oz shot of hard liquor—vary depending on weight, ethnicity, gender, and other factors. Across most of the United States, a BAC of .08 is the legal limit for driving. But even at lower levels, our coordination and focus may be impaired. Information from CDC (2017); University of Notre Dame (n.d.). Photos: (left & center) Danny Smythe/Shutterstock; (right) Elitsa/Thinkstock.

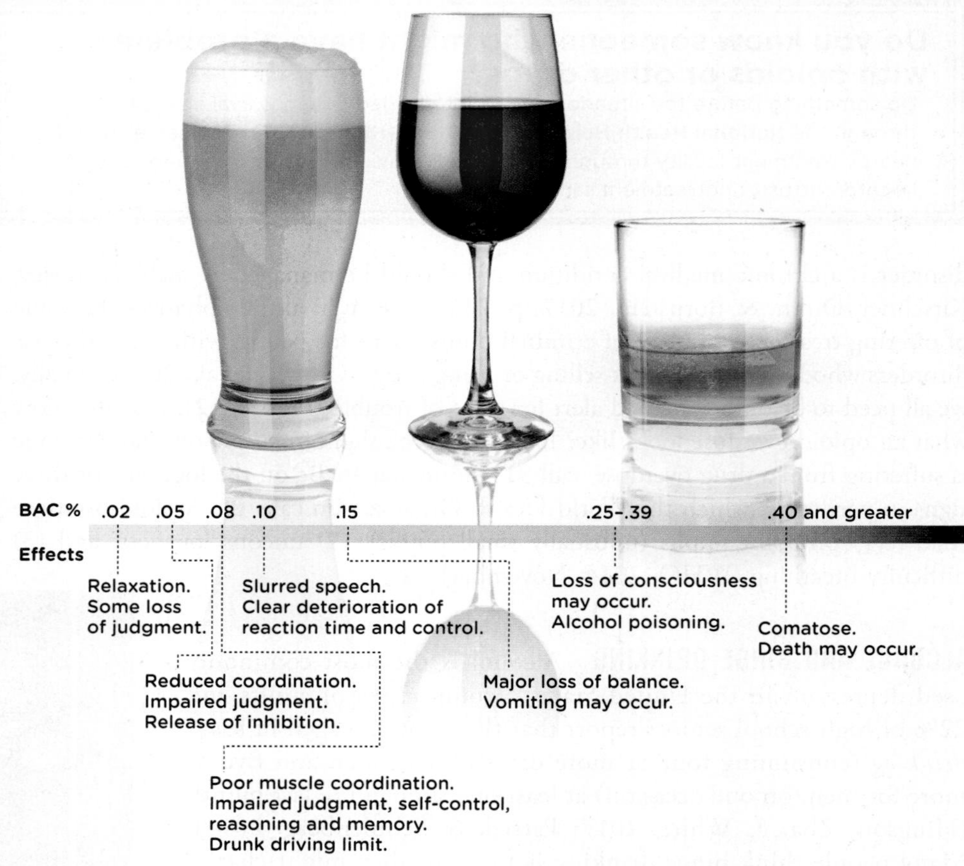
BAC %
.02
.05
.08
.10
.15
.25-.39
.40 and greater
Effects
Relaxation. Some loss of judgment.
Reduced coordination. Impaired judgment. Release of inhibition.
Poor muscle coordination. Impaired judgment, self-control, reasoning and memory. Drunk driving limit.
Slurred speech. Clear deterioration of reaction time and control.
Major loss of balance. Vomiting may occur.
Loss of consciousness may occur. Alcohol poisoning.
Comatose. Death may occur.

people to do things they regret the next morning. Drinking affects other processes, such as reaction time, balance, attention span, memory, speech, and involuntary life-sustaining activities like breathing (Howland et al., 2010; McKinney & Coyle, 2006). Drink enough, and these vital functions will shut down entirely, leading to coma and even death (Infographic 4.2).

The female body seems to be less efficient at breaking down (metabolizing) alcohol. Women achieve higher blood alcohol levels (and thus a significantly stronger "buzz") than men who have consumed equal amounts. Why? Some research suggests that men have more of an alcohol-metabolizing enzyme in their stomachs, which means they start to break down alcohol almost immediately after ingestion (Baraona et al., 2001). However, it is still not entirely clear why men and women metabolize alcohol differently; it may be related to hormonal differences (Erol & Karphyak, 2015).

HERE'S TO YOUR HEALTH? Light alcohol consumption by adults—one to two drinks a day—may boost cardiovascular health, although some of the observed benefits may be specific to red wine (American Heart Association, 2015). However, excessive drinking is associated with a host of health problems, including malnourishment, cirrhosis of the liver, and *Wernicke–Korsakoff syndrome,* whose symptoms include confusion and memory problems. Overuse of alcohol has also been linked to heart disease, various types of cancer, tens of thousands of yearly traffic deaths, and *fetal-alcohol syndrome* in children whose mothers drank during pregnancy. Would you believe that 1 in 10 deaths of "working-age" Americans (ages 20 to 64) results from overuse of alcohol (Stahre, Roeber, Kanny, Brewer, & Zhang, 2014)? Looking at the overall impact of alcohol consumption across the world, the risks outweigh the

- Having your friends or relatives express concern
- Being annoyed when people criticize your drinking behavior
- Feeling guilty about your drinking behavior
- Thinking you should drink less but being unable to do so
- Needing a morning drink as an "eye-opener" or to relieve a hangover
- Not fulfilling responsibilities at work, home, or school because of drinking
- Engaging in dangerous behavior (like driving under the influence)
- Having legal or social problems due to drinking

FIGURE 4.4
Warning Signs of Problematic Drinking
The presence of one or more of these warning signs could indicate a developing problem with alcohol. Information from: APA (2012, March); NIH, National Institute on Alcohol Abuse and Alcoholism (2013).

benefits (Rehm, Shield, Roerecke, & Gmel, 2016). The warning signs of problematic drinking are presented in **Figure 4.4**.

Stimulants

Not all drugs used in anesthesia are depressants. Did you know that some doctors use cocaine as a local anesthetic for sinus surgeries (Dwyer, Sowerby, & Rotenberg, 2016)? Cocaine is a **stimulant**—a drug that increases neural activity in the central nervous system (CNS), producing heightened alertness, energy, elevated mood, and other effects (Julien et al., 2014). When applied topically, however, cocaine has a numbing effect.

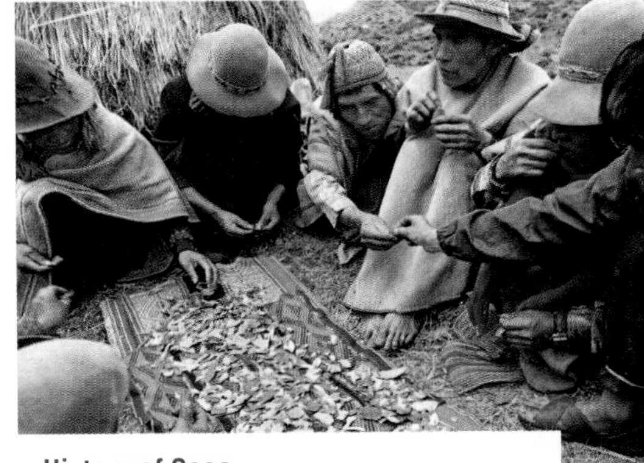

History of Coca
Villagers in Peru chew coca leaves, which contain less than 1% cocaine. For thousands of years, people in South America's Andean regions have been chewing coca leaves to increase energy, reduce hunger, and fight altitude sickness (Morales Ayma, 2009, March 13). In 1860, a German chemist named Albert Niemann extracted an active part of the coca leaf and dubbed it "cocaine" (Julien et al., 2014; Keys, 1945). Within a few decades, doctors were using cocaine for anesthesia, Sigmund Freud was giving it to patients (and himself), and Coca-Cola was putting it in soda (Keys, 1945; Musto, 1991). Kazuyoshi Nomachi/Corbis Documentary/Getty Images.

COCAINE Cocaine is illegal in the United States and most other countries, but it has been a popular recreational drug for many decades. Depending on the form in which it is prepared (powder, rocks, and so on), it can be snorted, injected, or smoked. The sense of energy, euphoria, and other alterations of consciousness that cocaine induces after entering the bloodstream and infiltrating the brain last anywhere from a few minutes to an hour, depending on how it is delivered. Cocaine produces a rush of enjoyment and excitement by amplifying the effects of the brain's pleasure-producing neurotransmitter dopamine. This high comes at a steep price. People who use cocaine risk suffering a seizure, stroke, or heart attack, even if they are young and healthy (National Institute on Drug Abuse [NIDA], 2016, June). It is also extremely addictive. Many users find they can never quite duplicate the high they experienced the first time, so they take increasingly higher doses. As they develop a physical need for the drug, they increase their risk of effects such as anxiety, insomnia, and schizophrenia-like psychosis (Julien et al., 2014).

Cocaine use grew rampant in the 1980s. That was the decade that *crack*—an ultra-potent (and ultra-cheap) crystalline form of cocaine—began to ravage America's urban areas. Although cocaine use is still a major problem, another stimulant—methamphetamine—has come to rival it.

METHAMPHETAMINE *Methamphetamine* belongs to a family of stimulants called the **amphetamines** (am-FET-uh-meens). In the 1930s and 40s, doctors used amphetamines to treat medical conditions as diverse as excessive hiccups and hypotension (unusually low blood pressure; Julien et al., 2014). During World War II, soldiers and factory workers used methamphetamine to increase energy and boost performance (Lineberry & Bostwick, 2006). Ridiculously cheap, easy to make, and capable of producing a euphoric high lasting many hours, methamphetamine stimulates the release of dopamine, causing a surge in energy and alertness similar to a cocaine high. Users often "binge and crash" repeatedly after the high has worn off (NIDA, 2017, February). Chronic meth use alters the brain, causing harm at

synonyms
methamphetamine meth, crystal meth, crank
amphetamines speed, uppers, bennies

stimulants A class of drugs that increase neural activity in the central nervous system.

amphetamines Stimulant drugs; methamphetamine is an example of a drug in this class.

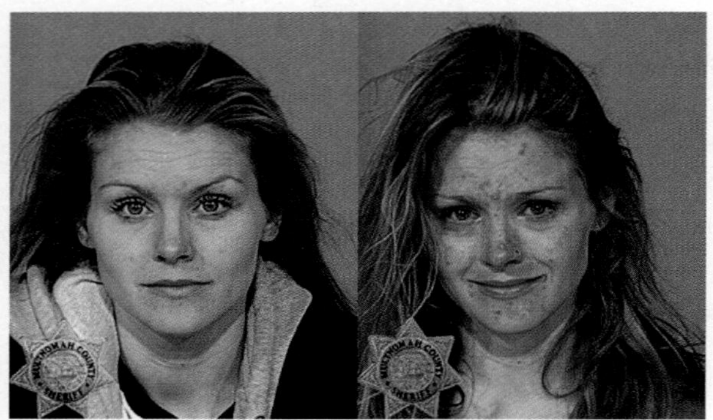

This Is Your Face on Meth
Would you believe this dramatic physical transformation occurred in just 8 months? Methamphetamine ravages the body, the brain, and one's overall appearance. Some meth users have lingering symptoms: Imagine experiencing horrific tactile hallucinations that cause you to believe bugs are crawling underneath your skin, and in response you tear your skin to the bone in order to kill them. Multnomah County Sheriff's Office/Barcroft USA/Getty Images.

the neuronal level. This damage, which is linked to cognitive problems, is "greater and more widespread" in the brains of teenagers (Lyoo et al., 2015). Other consequences of meth use include severe weight loss, tooth decay ("meth mouth"), frequent skin scratching (causing skin lesions), paranoia, and violent behavior (National Institute on Drug Abuse, 2017, February).

CAFFEINE Most people have not experimented with illegal stimulants like cocaine and meth, but many are regular users of caffeine. We usually associate caffeine with beverages like coffee, but this pick-me-up drug also lurks in places you wouldn't expect, such as over-the-counter cough medicines, chocolate, and energy bars. Caffeine works by interfering with the action of the neurotransmitter adenosine. Under normal conditions, adenosine exerts a calming effect by blocking the activity of other neurotransmitters (McLellan, Caldwell, & Lieberman, 2016). Caffeine resembles adenosine enough that it can dock onto the same receptors ("posing" as adenosine). With caffeine occupying its receptors, adenosine can no longer exert its calming effect (Clark & Landolt, 2017; Julien, Advokat, & Comaty, 2014). Thus, caffeine makes you feel physically and mentally wired.

Moderate caffeine use (up to four cups of coffee per day) has been associated with increased alertness, enhanced recall ability, elevated mood, and greater endurance during physical exercise (McLellan et al., 2016). Some studies have also linked moderate long-term consumption with lower rates of depression and suicide, and reduced cognitive decline with aging (Lara, 2010; Rosso, Mossey & Lippa, 2008). But just because researchers find a **link** between caffeine and positive health outcomes, we should not conclude that caffeine is responsible. We need to remember that correlation does not prove causation. What's more, too much caffeine can make your heart race, your hands tremble, and your mood turn irritable. It takes several hours for your body to metabolize caffeine, so a late afternoon mocha latte may still be in your system as you lie in bed at midnight counting sheep—with no luck.

CONNECTIONS
In **Chapter 1**, we emphasized that correlation does not prove causation. Here, we need to be cautious about making too strong a statement about coffee causing positive health outcomes, because third variables could be involved in increased caffeine consumption and better health.

One final note of warning: Be wary of energy drinks, some of which contain three times as much caffeine as soda (Marczinski, Fillmore, Maloney, & Stamates, 2017). Although they might help you get through a long night of studying, the high level of caffeine, sugar, and other stimulants can lead to a variety of problems like "rapid heartbeat, insomnia, increased blood pressure and even death" (Kim & Anagondahalli, 2017, p. 898). Perhaps even more concerning is the combination of alcohol and energy drinks, particularly when driving is involved. People who consume beverages containing both alcohol and energy drinks are more likely to think they are sufficiently sober to drive than those who drink the same amount of alcohol without the mixer. This bears repeating: "Alcohol consumers should be warned that the use of energy drink mixers with alcohol could lead to a false sense of security in one's ability to drive after drinking" (Marczinski, Stamates, & Maloney, 2018, p. 147).

TOBACCO What do you think is the number one cause of premature death worldwide—AIDS, illegal drugs, road accidents, murder . . . suicide? None of the above (**Figure 4.5**). Tobacco causes more deaths than any of these other factors combined (CDC, 2017, May 15). This is because smoking is associated with a variety of ailments, including cancer (many types, not just lung cancer), heart disease, lung disease, and others you might not expect, such as kidney failure (Carter et al., 2015). Cigarette smoking causes over 480,000 "premature deaths" every year in the United States (CDC, 2015c).

Despite these harrowing statistics, about 15% of adults in the United States continue to light up (Jamal et al., 2016). Cigarettes and other tobacco products contain a highly addictive stimulant called *nicotine,* which sparks the release of epinephrine

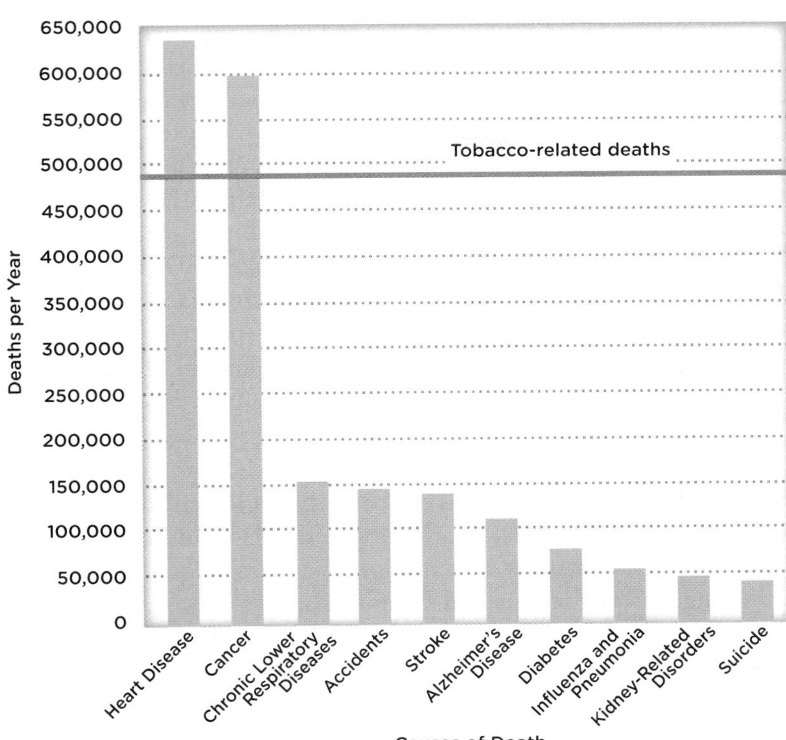

FIGURE 4.5
Leading Causes of Death in the United States
The leading killers in this country—heart disease, cancer, and chronic lower respiratory diseases—are largely driven by smoking. Tobacco exposure is behind nearly half a million deaths every year. Data from Kochanek et al., (2011); CDC (2017). Photo: David J. Green—Lifestyle/Alamy.

and norepinephrine. Nicotine use appears to be associated with activity in the same brain area activated by cocaine, another drug that is extremely difficult to give up (Pich et al., 1997; Zhang, Dong, Doyon, & Dani, 2012). Around 90% of those who quit smoking relapse within 6 months (Nonnemaker et al., 2011), suggesting that relapse is a normal experience when quitting, not a sign of failure.

Smoking is not just a problem for the smoker. It impacts spouses, children, friends, and anyone who is exposed to the ***secondhand smoke***. Secondhand smoke is particularly dangerous for children, whose developing tissues are highly vulnerable (Chapter 8). By smoking, parents increase their infant's risk for sudden infant death syndrome (SIDS). They also make their children vulnerable to a host of illnesses, including respiratory infections, asthma, and bronchitis (CDC, 2017, January). Secondhand smoke contributes to 41,000 deaths in nonsmokers and 400 infant deaths every year in the United States (Homa et al., 2015), and according to the Centers for Disease Control and Prevention (2017), "There is no risk-free level of exposure" (para. 3).

synonyms
secondhand smoke passive smoke
hallucinogens psychedelic drugs

Hallucinogens, Club Drugs, and Marijuana

LO 10 Discuss how hallucinogens alter consciousness.

We have learned how various depressants and stimulants are used in anesthesia. Believe it or not, there is also a place for **hallucinogens** (huh-LOO-suh-nuh-gens)—drugs that produce hallucinations (sights, sounds, odors, or other sensations of things that are not actually present), altered moods, and distorted perception and thought. Phencyclidine (PCP or *angel dust*) and ketamine (*Special K*) are sometimes referred to as *psychedelic anesthetics* because they were developed to block pain and memory in surgical patients during the 1950s and 60s (Julien et al., 2014). PCP is highly addictive and extremely dangerous. Because users cannot feel normal pain signals, they run the risk of unintentionally harming or killing themselves. Long-term use can lead to depression and memory impairment. Doctors stopped giving PCP to patients long ago; its effect was just too erratic.

hallucinogens A group of psychoactive drugs that can produce hallucinations, distorted sensory experiences, alterations of mood, and distorted thinking.

You Asked, Matt Answers

http://qrs.ly/mx5a5ag

What sorts of medications help to control narcolepsy?

Ketamine, on the other hand, continues to be used in hospitals across the country. Unlike many of the depressants used in anesthesia, which can reduce respiratory drive to the point of death (hence the need for the breathing tube and ventilator), ketamine causes less interference with breathing and respiratory reflexes. "Ketamine is an amazing drug for preventing pain," Dr. Chander says. "It's great to use in trauma. You can give it in the muscle, especially if somebody can't start an IV . . . and help them go to sleep that way," she adds. "But used in medicinal ways, or even for recreational purposes, it can have long-lasting effects, much like LSD, a structurally analogous drug, which can cause later flashbacks. Ketamine can in fact induce lasting plastic changes in the brain. Some of these changes can be positive. Interestingly, researchers are finding that ketamine may contribute antidepressant effects through different brain networks than the ones that provide analgesia (pain relief). The drug is being investigated further for this."

LSD The most well-known hallucinogen is probably **lysergic acid diethylamide (LSD**; lih-SER-jic; die-eth-ul-AM-ide)—the odorless, tasteless, and colorless substance that produces extreme changes in sensation and perception. People using LSD may report seeing "far out" colors and visions of spirals and other geometric forms. Some experience a crossover of sensations, such as "tasting sound" or "hearing colors." Emotions run wild and bleed into one another. The person "tripping" can quickly flip between depression and joy, excitement and terror (Julien et al., 2014). Trapped on this sensory and emotional roller coaster, some people panic and injure themselves. Others believe that LSD opens their minds, offers new insights, and expands their consciousness. The outcome of a "trip" depends a great deal on the environment and people who are there. LSD is rarely overused, and its reported use has remained at an all-time low, although there is some evidence LSD use has increased substantially among 18- to 25-year olds in the past few years (Johnston, O'Malley, Bachman, & Schulenberg, 2012; Substance Abuse and Mental Health Services Administration [SAMHSA], 2017). Long-term use may be associated with depression and other psychological problems, including flashbacks that can occur weeks, months, or years after taking the drug. LSD flashbacks may be triggered by fatigue, stress, and illness (Centre for Addiction and Mental Health, 2010; Friedman, 2017, February 13).

synonyms
methylenedioxymethamphetamine
E, X, Ecstasy, Molly

MDMA In addition to the traditional hallucinogens, there are quite a few "club drugs," or synthetic "designer drugs," used at parties, raves, and dance venues. Among the most popular is **methylenedioxymethamphetamine** (MDMA; meth-ul-een-die-ox-ee-meth-am-FET-uh-meen), commonly known as *Ecstasy* (de Wit, Gorka, & Phan, 2015; Roberts, Jones, & Montgomery, 2016). An Ecstasy trip might bring on feelings of euphoria, love, openness, heightened energy, and floating sensations. The drug also has "unusual sociability-enhancing effects," meaning it can increase self-reports of positive social feelings and interpersonal behaviors that benefit others, such as cooperation and generosity (Kamilar-Britt & Bedi, 2015). But Ecstasy can also cause a host of troubling changes in the body, including decreased appetite, lockjaw, blurred vision, dizziness, heightened anxiety, rapid heart rate, and dehydration (Gordon, 2001, July 5; Noller, 2009; Parrott, 2004, 2015).

CONNECTIONS

In **Chapter 2**, we reported that serotonin is critical for the regulation of mood, appetite, aggression, and automatic behaviors like sleep. Here, we see how the use of Ecstasy can alter levels of this neurotransmitter.

Ecstasy triggers a sudden increase of **serotonin** activity in the brain, followed by a temporary depletion of serotonin (Klugman & Gruzelier, 2003; Roberts et al., 2016). The growing consensus is that even light-to-moderate Ecstasy use can handicap the brain's memory system, and heavy use may impair higher-level functions, such as shifting attention and planning for the future (Klugman & Gruzelier, 2003; Parrott, 2015; Roberts et al., 2016). Studies also suggest that Ecstasy users are more likely to experience symptoms of depression (Guillot, 2007; Parrott, 2015).

MARIJUANA Weed, herb, reefer, chronic, 420—call it what you will. ***Marijuana*** is the most widely used illegal drug in the United States (NIDA, 2016, October), and when we say "illegal," we are referring to the federal level. The U.S. government has marijuana listed as a Schedule I drug, indicating that it has "no currently accepted medical use and a high potential for abuse" (Drug Enforcement Administration, n.d., para. 3), but 29 states have now passed laws permitting its use for medical purposes, and eight states allow its recreational use.

synonyms

marijuana Mary Jane, M.J., grass, reefer, weed, pot, ganja, hemp

Marijuana comes from the hemp plant, *Cannabis sativa,* which has long been used as—surprise—an anesthetic (Keys, 1945). These days, doctors prescribe cannabis and its chemical derivatives to treat chronic pain, nausea from chemotherapy, and some symptoms of multiple sclerosis, and there is "conclusive or substantial evidence" that such treatments are effective (National Academies of Sciences, Engineering, and Medicine, 2017, January, para. 4). Outside of a medical context, marijuana use poses significant risks, especially for teenagers. It may harm the brain's neurons, and this damage may be linked to increased impulsivity (acting without thinking), particularly among adolescents (Gruber, Dahlgren, Sagar, Gönenç & Lukas, 2014; Weir, 2015, November). Studies suggest that marijuana use can lead to memory impairment, and deficits in attention and learning (Harvey, Sellman, Porter, & Frampton, 2007; Kleber & DuPont, 2012). There is also solid scientific support linking marijuana use to increased risk of car crashes and low birth weight in babies whose mothers used the drug during pregnancy (National Academies of Sciences, Engineering, and Medicine, January, 2017).

Dangerous Habit
A man lies on the sidewalk in New York City, apparently unconscious after using synthetic marijuana. Use of this drug, also called "Spice" or "K2," may lead to a variety of undesirable outcomes, including paranoia, violent behavior, seizures, dangerous increases in blood pressure, and sometimes death (National Institute on Drug Abuse, 2018, February).
Spencer Platt/Getty Images.

Marijuana contains **tetrahydrocannabinol (THC**; te-truh-high-druh-kuh-NAB-uh-nawl), which toys with consciousness in a variety of ways, making it hard to classify the drug in a single category (for example, depressant, stimulant, or hallucinogen). In addition to altering pain perception, THC can induce mild euphoria, and create intense sensory experiences and distortions of time. At higher doses, THC may cause hallucinations and delusions (Murray, Morrison, Henquet, & Di Forti, 2007). It's important to recognize that not all products called "marijuana" contain THC. A relatively new group of psychoactive drugs collectively known as "synthetic marijuana" target the same receptors as THC, but they do not come from the hemp plant, or any plant for that matter. Instead, they are prepared with synthetic chemicals and can be smoked, vaped, or inhaled (National Institute on Drug Abuse, 2018, February).

Now that we have discussed the major categories of drugs (**INFOGRAPHIC 4.3** on the next page), let's explore what it means to become dependent on them.

Overuse and Dependence

We often joke about being "addicted" to our coffee or soda, but do we understand what this really means? In spite of frequent references to *addiction* in everyday conversations, the term has been omitted from the American Psychiatric Association's diagnostic manual due to its "uncertain definition and potentially negative connotation" (American Psychiatric Association, 2013, p. 485). Instead, the manual refers to "substance use disorder." Historically, both laypeople and professionals have used the term addiction to refer to the urges people experience for using a drug or engaging in an activity to such an extent that it interferes with their functioning or is dangerous. This could mean a gambling habit that depletes your bank account, a sexual appetite that destroys your marriage, or perhaps even a social media fixation that prevents you from holding down a job.

lysergic acid diethylamide (LSD) A synthetically produced, odorless, tasteless, and colorless hallucinogen that is very potent; produces extreme changes in sensations and perceptions.

methylenedioxymethamphetamine (MDMA) A synthetic drug that produces a combination of stimulant and hallucinogenic effects.

tetrahydrocannabinol (THC) The active ingredient of marijuana.

Psychoactive Drugs

Recreational use of psychoactive drugs is not only dangerous. It can have disastrous personal and financial consequences for users, families, and society as a whole. Summarized below are some common effects and negative outcomes seen with drugs belonging to three broad categories: depressants, stimulants, and hallucinogens. Note that responses can vary from person to person.

What are some possible consequences?

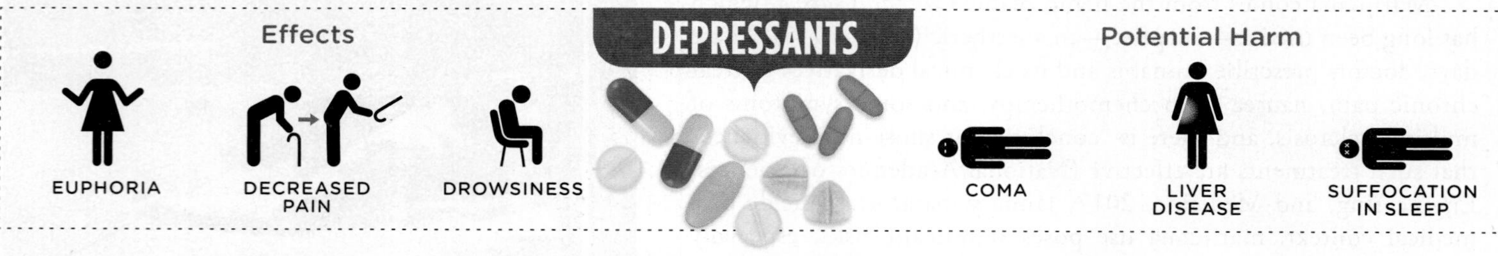

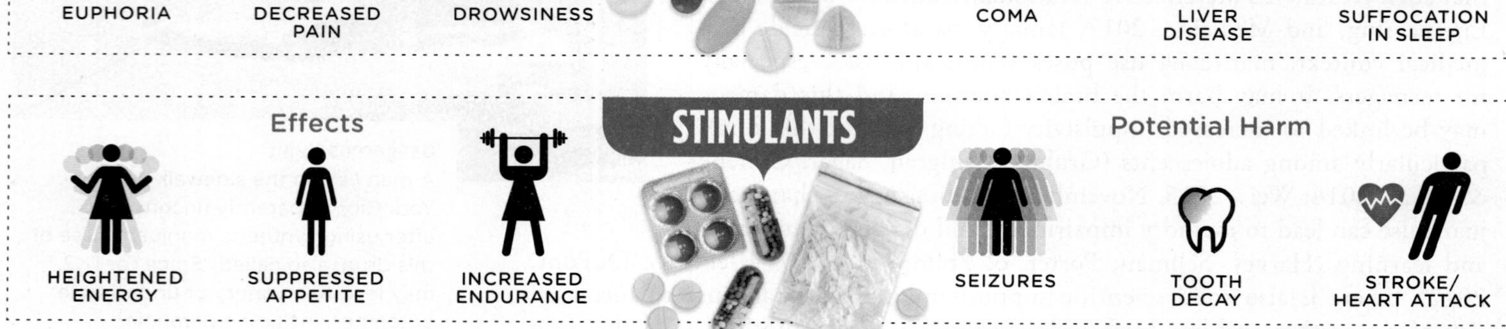

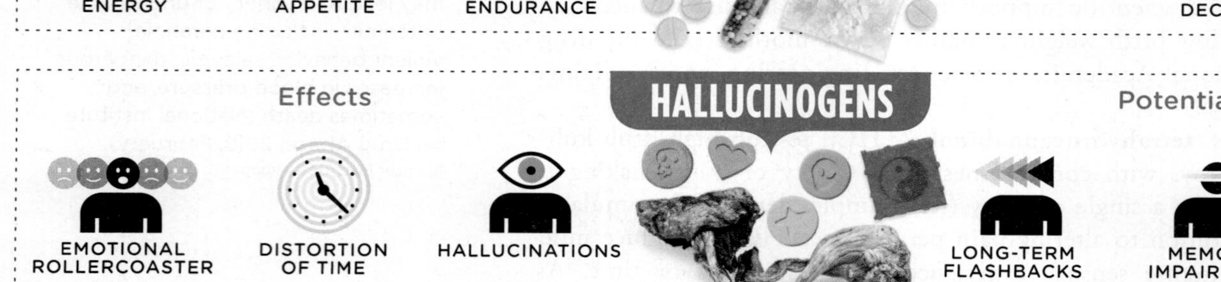

A Country in Crisis: The Opioid Epidemic

The United States is experiencing an unprecedented epidemic of opioid misuse.
BELOW Various government statistics on the opioid epidemic.
RIGHT Number of deaths by type of opioid and altogether.

The Opioid Epidemic in the U.S. in 2016/2017

11.4 million people misused prescription opioids
2 million people misused prescription opioids for the first time
42,249 people died from overdosing on opioids
2.1 million people had opioid use disorder
886,000 people used heroin
17,087 deaths attributed to overdosing on commonly prescribed opioids
19,413 deaths attributed to overdosing on non-methadone synthetic opioids
81,000 people used heroin for the first time
15,469 deaths attributed to overdosing on heroin

Data from Assistant Secretary for Public Affairs (ASPA), U.S. Department of Health and Human Services (2017).

Overdose Deaths Involving Opioids, by Type of Opioid, United States, 2000–2016

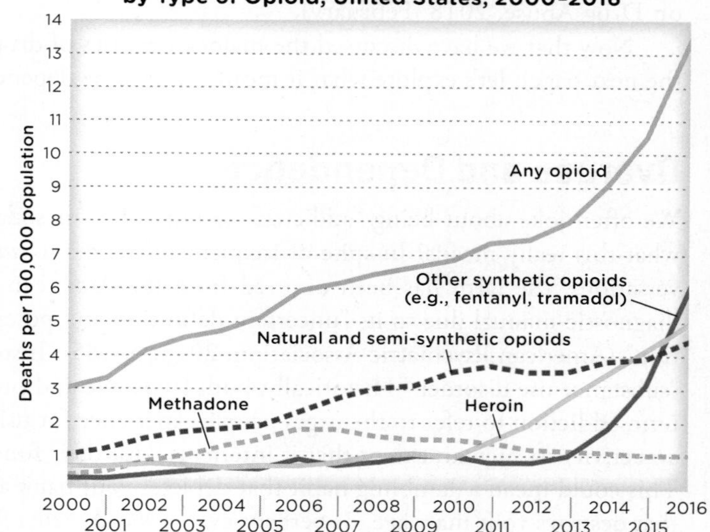

Data from CDC/NCHS, National Vital Statistics System, Mortality (2016).

Photo credits: Depressants: Red/White pill: Paket/Shutterstock, Colorful Pills: Againstar/Shutterstock; Stimulants: Red Pills: Sergiy Tryapitsyn/Alamy, Colorful Pills: Againstar/Shutterstock, Triff/Shutterstock, Bag of Methamphetamine: Daniel Kaesler/EyeEm/Getty Images; Hallucinogens: Ecstasy Tablets: Portokalis/Alamy, Mushroom: Atomazul/Alamy, Acid Tab: nigel dodds/Alamy.

SOCIAL MEDIA AND PSYCHOLOGY

CAN'T GET ENOUGH Is it difficult for you to sit through a movie without posting a new selfie on Instagram? Are you constantly looking at your Facebook News Feed in between work e-mails? Do you sleep with your iPhone? If you answered "yes" to any of the above, you are not alone. People around the world, from India to the United States, are getting hooked on social media—so hooked in some cases that they are getting treatment for social media or Internet "addiction" (Kessler, 2016, January 8; Saikia, 2017, April 19).

THE URGE TO USE MEDIA WAS HARDER TO RESIST THAN SEX, SPENDING MONEY, ALCOHOL. . . .

Facebook and Twitter may be habit forming, but you would think these sites might be easier to resist than, say, coffee or cigarettes. Such is not the case, according to one study. With the help of smartphones, researchers kept tabs on the daily desires of 205 young adults and found the urge to use media was harder to resist than sex, spending money, alcohol, coffee, or cigarettes (Hofmann, Vohs, & Baumeister, 2012). Subsequent research has highlighted the "addictive potential" of social media for certain individuals (Müller et al., 2016), and some scholars have examined ways to understand and diagnose the problem (van den Eijnden, Lemmens, & Valkenburg, 2016; van Rooij, Ferguson, van de Mheen, & Schoenmakers, 2017). However, the latest edition of the American Psychiatric Association's (2013) diagnostic manual does not include any such thing as a social media disorder. Will this diagnosis appear in a future edition? Stay tuned. . . .

Unhealthy use of social media is a critical problem, but it's relatively new and not well understood. Drug dependence, on the other hand, is a longstanding and extensively studied phenomenon. Let's explore how dependence can occur in both body and mind.

LO 11 Explain how physiological and psychological dependence differ.

WHAT IS DEPENDENCE? Substance use can be fueled by both *physiological* and *psychological* dependence. **Physiological dependence** means the body no longer functions normally without continued use of the drug (see **Figure 4.6**). Want to know if

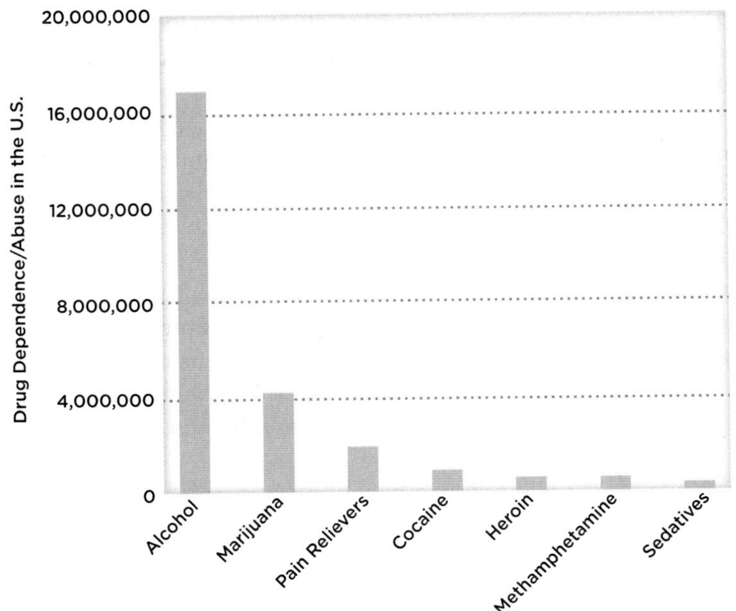

FIGURE 4.6
Drug Dependence in the United States
This graph shows the number of people experiencing drug dependence/abuse in the United States. As you can see, alcohol tops the list, followed by marijuana, and then pain relievers such as Vicodin and Oxycontin. The sedatives category includes benzodiazepines and barbiturates, which are powerful nervous system depressants. Data from National Institute on Drug Abuse (2012); Center for Behavioral Health Statistics and Quality (2015).

physiological dependence With constant use of some psychoactive drugs, the body no longer functions normally without the drug.

TABLE 4.5 PSYCHOACTIVE DRUGS

Substance	Classification and Effects	Potential Harm
Alcohol	Depressant; disinhibition, feeling "high"	coma, death
Barbiturates	Depressant; decreased neural activity, relaxation, possible aggression	loss of consciousness, coma, death
Caffeine	Stimulant; alertness, enhanced recall, elevated mood, endurance	heart racing, trembling, insomnia
Cocaine	Stimulant; energy, euphoria, rush of pleasure	heart attack, stroke, anxiety, psychosis
Heroin	Depressant; pleasure-inducing, reduces pain, rush of euphoria and relaxation	boils on the skin, hepatitis, liver disease, spontaneous abortion
LSD	Hallucinogen; extreme changes in sensation and perception, emotional roller coaster	depression, long-term flashbacks, other psychological problems
Marijuana	Properties of stimulants, depressants, and hallucinogens; stimulates appetite, suppresses nausea, relaxation, mild euphoria, distortion of time, intense sensory experiences	respiratory problems, immune system suppression, cancer, memory impairment, deficits in attention and learning
MDMA	Properties of stimulants and hallucinogens; euphoria, heightened energy, anxiety, and depersonalization	blurred vision, dizziness, rapid heart rate, dehydration, heat stroke, seizures, cardiac arrest, and death
Methamphetamine	Stimulant; energy, alertness, increases sex drive, suppresses appetite	lasting memory and movement problems, severe weight loss, tooth decay, psychosis, sudden death
Opioids	Depressant; blocks pain, induces drowsiness, euphoria, slows down breathing	respiratory problems during sleep, falls, constipation, sexual problems, death
Tobacco	Stimulant; relaxed, alert, more tolerant of pain	cancer, emphysema, heart disease, stroke, reduction in life span

Psychoactive drugs carry serious risks. Listed here are their effects and the potential harm that can result from their use.

you are physiologically dependent on your morning cup of Joe? Try removing it from your routine for a few days and see if you get a headache or feel fatigued. If your answers are yes and yes, odds are that you have experienced *withdrawal,* a sign of physiological dependence. **Withdrawal** is the constellation of symptoms that surface when a drug is removed or withheld from the body, and it's not always as mild as a headache and fatigue. If a person who is physiologically dependent on alcohol suddenly stops drinking, she may suffer from **delirium tremens (DTs),** withdrawal symptoms that include sweating, restlessness, hallucinations, severe tremors, seizures, and even death. Withdrawal symptoms disappear when you take the drug again, and this of course makes you more likely to continue using it. (The removal of the unpleasant symptoms acts as negative reinforcement for taking the drug, a process you can learn about in Chapter 5.) In this way, withdrawal powers the overuse cycle.

Another sign of physiological dependence is **tolerance.** Persistent use of alcohol and other drugs alters the chemistry of the brain and body. Over time, your system adapts to the drug and therefore needs more and more to re-create its original effect. If it once took you 2 beers to unwind, but now takes you 4, then tolerance has probably set in. Tolerance increases the risk for accidental overdose, because more drug is needed to obtain the desired effect.

Psychological dependence is indicated by a host of problematic symptoms distinct from tolerance and withdrawal. It is a strong urge or craving, not a physical need to continue using the substance. Individuals with psychological dependence believe, for example, they need the drug because it will increase their emotional or mental

withdrawal With constant use of some psychoactive drugs, the body becomes dependent and then reacts when the drug is withheld; a sign of physiological dependence.

delirium tremens (DTs) Withdrawal symptoms that can occur when a person who is physiologically dependent on alcohol suddenly stops drinking; can include sweating, restlessness, hallucinations, severe tremors, and seizures.

tolerance With constant use of some psychoactive drugs, the body requires more and more of the drug to create the original effect; a sign of physiological dependence.

psychological dependence With constant use of some psychoactive drugs, a strong desire or need to continue using the substance occurs without the evidence of tolerance or withdrawal symptoms.

well-being. The "pleasant" effects of a drug can act as positive reinforcement for taking it, and this can lead to repeated use (Chapter 5). In some cases, environmental cues can facilitate psychological dependence. Suppose a smoker develops a habit of smoking while talking on the phone. If the phone rings, she immediately reaches for her cigarettes and lighter. Her smoking behavior has become linked to cues associated with using the phone (Bold, Yoon, Chapman, & McCarthy, 2013).

Psychologists and psychiatrists use specific criteria for identifying substance use disorders. These disorders are maladaptive and cause significant impairment or distress to the user and/or his family. Consequences may include problems at work or school, neglect of children or household duties, physically dangerous behaviors, and so forth (American Psychiatric Association, 2013).

Depressants, stimulants, hallucinogens, marijuana—every drug we have discussed, and every drug imaginable—must physically enter the body in order to alter activity in the brain. Some are inhaled, others snorted or injected directly into the veins, but they all alter the user's state of consciousness (**Table 4.5**). But is it possible to enter an altered state of consciousness without using a substance? It is time to explore hypnosis.

Mesmerizing
A 19th-century doctor attempts to heal a patient using the hypnotic techniques created by Franz Mesmer in the 1770s. Mesmer believed that every person was surrounded by a magnetic field, or "animal magnetism," that could be summoned for therapeutic purposes (Wobst, 2007). The word "mesmerize" derives from Mesmer's name. Jean-Loup Charmet/Science Source.

Hypnosis

Describe hypnosis and explain how it works.

What would it be like to undergo hypnosis? The hypnotist would probably talk to you in a calm, quiet voice, running through a list of suggestions on how to relax. She may suggest that your eyelids are starting to droop and that you need to yawn. Feeling tired, you may breathe slower and feel your arms grow heavy. Experienced hypnotists can perform an induction in less than a minute, especially if they know the individual being hypnotized.

The term *hypnosis* comes from the Greek root word for "sleep," but hypnosis is by no means the equivalent of sleep. Most would agree **hypnosis** is an altered state of consciousness allowing for changes in perceptions and behaviors, which result from suggestions made by a hypnotist. "Changes in perceptions and behaviors" can mean a lot of things, of course, and there is some debate about what hypnosis is. Before going any further, let's be clear about what hypnosis *isn't.*

...BELIEVE IT...OR NOT

FALSE CLAIMS ABOUT HYPNOSIS Popular conceptions of hypnosis often clash with scientists' understanding of the phenomenon. Let's take a look at some examples:

- **People can be hypnotized without consent:** You cannot force someone to be hypnotized; they must be willing.

NO ONE CAN FORCE YOU TO BECOME HYPNOTIZED

- **Hypnotized people will act against their own will:** Stage hypnotists seem to make people walk like chickens or miscount their fingers, but these are things they may be willing to do when not hypnotized.
- **Hypnotized people can exhibit "superhuman" strength:** Hypnotized or not, people have the same physical capabilities (Druckman & Bjork, 1994). Stage hypnotists often choose stunts that hypnotized performers could achieve under non-hypnotized circumstances.
- **Hypnosis helps people retrieve lost memories:** Studies find that hypnosis may actually promote the formation of false memories and one's confidence in those memories (Kihlstrom, 1985).

hypnosis An altered state of consciousness allowing for changes in perceptions and behaviors, which result from suggestions made by a hypnotist.

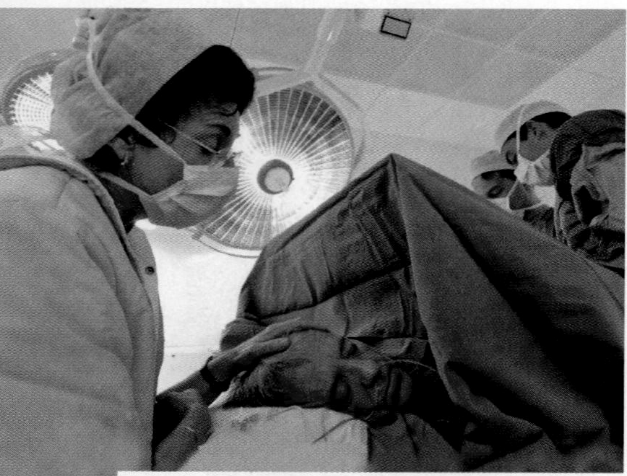

Hypnosis for Pain
A doctor in Belgium performs hypnosis on a patient undergoing a painful procedure. For those who are receptive to hypnosis, this approach may complement the use of anesthesia by reducing pain and anxiety (Häuser, Hagl, Schmierer, & Hansen, 2016). Universal Images Group/Getty Images.

- **Hypnotized people experience age regression. In other words, they act childlike:** Hypnotized people may indeed act immaturely, but the underlying cognitive activity is that of an adult (Nash, 2001).
- **Hypnosis induces long-term amnesia:** Hypnosis cannot make you forget your first day of kindergarten or your wedding. Short-term amnesia is possible if the hypnotist specifically suggests that something will be forgotten after the hypnosis wears off.

Now that some misconceptions about hypnosis have been cleared up, let's focus on what we know. Researchers propose that the following characteristics are evident in a hypnotized person: (1) ability to focus intently, ignoring all extraneous stimuli; (2) heightened imagination; (3) an unresisting and receptive attitude; (4) decreased pain awareness; and (5) high responsivity to suggestions (Hoeft et al., 2012; Kosslyn, Thompson, Costantini-Ferrando, Alpert, & Spiegel, 2000; Silva & Kirsch, 1992).

Does hypnosis have any real-life applications? With some limited success, hypnosis has been used therapeutically to treat phobias and commercially to help people stop smoking or lose weight (Green, 1999; Kraft, 2012). Some have found that hypnotherapy can help people confront fears of going to the dentist (Butler, 2015). Hypnosis has also been used on children, to alleviate chronic pain, insomnia, and anxiety related to routine medical procedures (Adinolfi & Gava, 2013). When used in conjunction with traditional therapies, hypnosis may help in the treatment of tension headaches (Shahkhase, Gharaei, Fathi, Yaghoobi, & Bayazi, 2014). Some research suggests that hypnosis can ease the pain associated with childbirth and surgery, reducing the need for painkillers (Cyna, McAuliffe, & Andrew, 2004; Wobst, 2007). However, other research indicates that hypnosis does not reduce the use of painkillers during labor and childbirth (Cyna et al., 2013; Wemer, Uldbjerg, Zachariae, Rosen, & Nohr, 2013).

HYPNOSIS AND THE MIND People in a hypnotic state sometimes report having sensory experiences that deviate from reality. For example, they may see or hear things that are not there. In a classic experiment, participants were asked to place one hand in ice-cold water. If they felt pain, they were supposed to press a button with the other hand. Because these participants were hypnotized to believe that they wouldn't experience pain, they did not report any pain. Yet, they did press the button (Hilgard, Morgan, & Macdonald, 1975). This suggests a "divided consciousness." That is, part of our consciousness is always aware, even when we are hypnotized and instructed to feel no pain. People in a hypnotic state can also experience temporary blindness and deafness.

Studies using positron emission tomography (PET) suggest that hypnosis induces changes in the brain that might explain this diminished pain perception (Faymonville et al., 2000; Rainville, Duncan, Price, Carrier, & Bushnell, 1997, August 15). The perception of pain is complex, and "virtually all of the brain areas involved in the processing of pain have been shown to be impacted by hypnosis" (Jensen et al., 2015, p. 41). Hypnosis and other relaxation techniques, such as meditation (Chapter 12), can indeed reduce anxiety and pain.

Fade to Black

It is time to conclude our discussion of consciousness, but first let's run through some of the big picture concepts you should take away from this chapter. Consciousness refers to a state of arousal (wakefulness) and awareness that has many gradations and dimensions. During sleep, awareness decreases, but it does not fade entirely (remember that alarm clock that becomes part of your dream about a wailing siren). Sleep has many stages, but the two main forms are non-REM and REM. Dreams may serve a purpose, but they also may be nothing more than your brain's interpretation of neurons signaling in the night. You learned from Dr. Chander that anesthetic drugs can profoundly alter consciousness. The same is true of drugs used outside of medical supervision; legal or not, many drugs can lead to dependence, health problems, and death. Finally, there is hypnosis. Although somewhat controversial and misunderstood, hypnosis appears to induce an altered state of consciousness and may have useful therapeutic applications.

Put Your Heads Together

In your group, **A)** discuss the most surprising thing you learned from reading this chapter on consciousness, and **B)** make a list of what you found most useful. **C)** How might these useful concepts be important in your career?

show what you know

1. Match the drug in the left column with an outcome on the right:
   ____ 1. depressant — a. blocks pain
   ____ 2. opioid — b. slows down activity in the CNS
   ____ 3. alcohol — c. increases activity in the CNS
   ____ 4. cocaine — d. cirrhosis of the liver
2. An acquaintance described an odorless, tasteless, and colorless substance he took many years ago. He discussed a variety of changes to his sensations and perceptions, including seeing colors and spirals. It is likely he had taken which of the following hallucinogens?
   a. alcohol
   b. marijuana
   c. LSD
   d. cocaine
3. Dr. Chander uses a range of ______________ to inhibit memories of surgery and change levels of consciousness.
4. Given what you have learned about physiological and psychological dependence, how would you determine if someone had a physiological versus a psychological dependence?

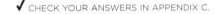

✓ CHECK YOUR ANSWERS IN APPENDIX C.

YOUR SCIENTIFIC WORLD is a new application-based feature appearing in every chapter. In these online activities, you will take on role-playing scenarios that encourage you to think critically and apply your knowledge of psychological science to solve a real world problem. For example: Have you ever struggled with sleep? Visit a sleep center and participate in a sleep study to better understand sleep disorders, sleep stages, and healthy sleep habits. You can access Your Scientific World activities in LaunchPad. Have fun!

SUMMARY OF CONCEPTS

LO 1 Define consciousness. (p. 121)

Consciousness might be described as a state of being aware of oneself, one's thoughts, and/or the environment. There are various levels of consciousness, including wakefulness, sleepiness, drug-induced states, dreaming, hypnotic states, and meditative states.

LO 2 Explain how automatic processing relates to consciousness. (p. 123)

Our sensory systems absorb large amounts of information, and we cannot be consciously aware of all of it. Without our awareness, the brain determines what is important, what requires immediate attention, and what can be processed and stored for later use if necessary.

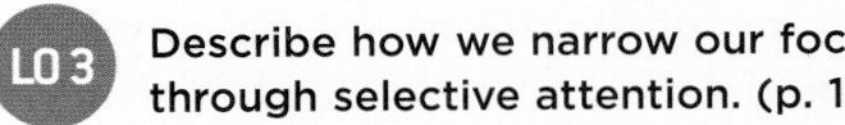

LO 3 Describe how we narrow our focus through selective attention. (p. 125)

We can only direct our attention toward a small portion of information that is available to us. This narrow focus on specific stimuli is referred to as selective attention. Humans are highly sensitive to abrupt, unexpected changes in the environment, and to stimuli that are unfamiliar, rewarding, or especially strong.

LO 4 Identify how circadian rhythm relates to sleep. (p. 127)

Predictable daily patterns influence our behaviors, alertness, and activity levels in a cyclical fashion. These circadian rhythms in our physiological functioning roughly follow the 24-hour cycle of daylight and darkness. In the circadian rhythm for sleep and wakefulness, there are two times when the desire for sleep hits hardest. The first occurs in the early hours of the morning, between about 2:00 to 6:00 A.M., and the second, less intense desire for sleep strikes midafternoon, around 2:00 or 3:00 P.M.

LO 5 Summarize the stages of sleep. (p. 130)

Sleep begins in non-rapid eye movement (non-REM), or nondreaming sleep, which has three stages. The lightest is Stage N1; this is the time during which imaginary sensations can occur. Stage N1 lasts only a few minutes before Stage N2 begins. At this point, it is more difficult to rouse the sleeper before she drifts even further into Stage N3, also known as slow-wave sleep. The sleeper then works her way back up to Stage N2. And instead of waking up, she enters the R Stage, known as rapid eye movement (REM) sleep. During this stage, closed eyes dart around, and brain activity changes. People awakened from REM sleep often report having vivid dreams. Each cycle, from Stage N1 through REM, lasts about 90 minutes, and the average adult loops through five complete cycles per night. The composition of these cycles changes as the night progresses.

LO 6 Recognize various sleep disorders and their symptoms. (p. 134)

Narcolepsy is a neurological disorder characterized by excessive daytime sleepiness and other sleep-related disturbances. REM sleep behavior disorder occurs when the mechanism responsible for paralyzing the body during REM sleep does not function properly. As a result, the individual is able to move around and act out dreams. Obstructive sleep apnea hypopnea is a serious disturbance of non-REM sleep characterized by periodic interruptions in breathing. The upper throat muscles go limp, allowing the airway to close. The sleeper awakens and gasps for air, then drifts back to sleep. Insomnia is the inability to fall asleep or stay asleep. People with insomnia report poor quantity or quality of sleep, and some may complain about waking up too early and being unable to fall back to sleep.

LO 7 Summarize the theories of why we dream. (p. 140)

Freud believed that dreams were a playing out of unconscious desires. Manifest content, the apparent meaning of the dream, refers to the events of the dream. Latent content is the hidden meaning of the dream, and can provide a window into unconscious conflicts and desires. The activation–synthesis model suggests that dreams have no meaning whatsoever: We respond to random neural activity of the sleeping brain as if it has meaning. Neurocognitive theory suggests there is a network of neurons in the brain necessary for dreaming to occur. According to this theory, dreams are the result of how sleep and consciousness have evolved in humans.

LO 8 Define psychoactive drugs. (p. 143)

Psychoactive drugs can cause changes in psychological activities, such as sensation, perception, attention, judgment, memory, self-control, emotion, thinking, and behavior. These drugs alter consciousness in an untold number of ways. They can, for example, depress activity in the central nervous system (CNS), produce hallucinations, or cause a sense of euphoria.

LO 9 Identify several depressants and stimulants and know their effects. (p. 144)

Depressants decrease activity in the central nervous system (CNS). These include barbiturates, opioids, and alcohol. Stimulants increase activity in the CNS, producing effects such as heightened alertness, energy, and mood. These include cocaine, amphetamines, methamphetamine, caffeine, and nicotine.

LO 10 Discuss how hallucinogens alter consciousness. (p. 151)

Hallucinogens produce hallucinations, altered moods, and distorted perception and thought. The most well-known is lysergic acid diethylamide (LSD). This odorless, tasteless, and colorless substance often produces extreme changes in sensation and perception. Others are the "club drugs," or synthetic "designer drugs." Methylenedioxymethamphetamine (MDMA) is a synthetic drug that produces a combination of stimulant and hallucinogenic effects. The most widely used illegal drug in the United States is marijuana ("illegal," meaning at the federal level, as many states have legalized the drug for medicinal and/or recreational use). At high doses, its tetrahydrocannabinol (THC) can induce mild euphoria and create intense sensory experiences.

LO 11 Explain how physiological and psychological dependence differ. (p. 155)

With continued use of some psychoactive drugs, the body may become dependent. Signs of this physiological dependence include tolerance and withdrawal. Psychological dependence is indicated by a host of problematic symptoms distinct from tolerance and withdrawal. It is an urge or craving, not a physical need. People with psychological dependence believe they need the drug because it increases their emotional or mental well-being.

LO 12 Describe hypnosis and explain how it works. (p. 157)

An altered state of consciousness allowing for changes in perceptions and behaviors, which result from suggestions made by a hypnotist. Hypnosis has been used to treat phobias, and during childbirth and surgery to reduce pain. One theory suggests that with hypnosis there is a "divided consciousness," that is, part of our consciousness is always aware, even when we are hypnotized.

KEY TERMS

activation–synthesis model, p. 141
alpha waves, p. 130
amphetamines, p. 149
automatic processing, p. 124
barbiturate, p. 144
beta waves, p. 130
circadian rhythm, p. 127
cognitive psychology, p. 122
consciousness, p. 121
delirium tremens (DTs), p. 156
delta waves, p. 131
depressants, p. 144
hallucinogens, p. 151
hypnosis, p. 157
insomnia, p. 136
latent content, p. 141
lysergic acid diethylamide (LSD), p. 152
manifest content, p. 141
methylenedioxymethamphetamine (MDMA), p. 152
narcolepsy, p. 134
nightmares, p. 136
non-rapid eye movement (non-REM), p. 130
obstructive sleep apnea hypopnea, p. 135
opiates, p. 146
physiological dependence, p. 155
psychoactive drugs, p. 143
psychological dependence, p. 156
rapid eye movement (REM), p. 131
REM rebound, p. 138
REM sleep behavior disorder, p. 135
selective attention, p. 125
sleep terrors, p. 136
stimulant, p. 149
tetrahydrocannabinol (THC), p. 153
theta waves, p. 130
tolerance, p. 156
withdrawal, p. 156

TEST PREP ARE YOU READY?

1. A great deal of information is available in our internal and external environments, but we can only focus on a small portion of it. This narrow focus on specific stimuli is known as:
   a. stream of consciousness.
   b. selective attention.
   c. waking consciousness.
   d. manifest content.

2. The daily patterns of our physiological functioning, such as changes in body temperature, roughly follow the 24-hour cycle of daylight and darkness. These patterns are driven by our:
   a. psychological dependence.
   b. need for sleep.
   c. levels of consciousness.
   d. circadian rhythm.

3. Shift workers may experience problems with their sleep–wake cycles, sometimes resulting in ____________, which refers to difficulty falling asleep and sleeping soundly.
   a. insomnia
   b. cataplexy
   c. narcolepsy
   d. hypnagogic hallucinations

4. Lysergic acid diethylamide (LSD) is classified as a ____________, as it can produce altered moods and distorted perceptions and thoughts.
   a. depressant
   b. hallucinogen
   c. microsleep
   d. circadian rhythm

5. During the stage of sleep known as ____________, brain activity looks similar to that of someone who is wide awake.
   a. microsleep
   b. sleep spindles
   c. non-REM sleep
   d. REM sleep

6. According to Sigmund Freud's theory, dreams are a form of:
   a. REM rebound.
   b. wish fulfillment.
   c. microsleep.
   d. withdrawal.

7. ____________ such as caffeine, alcohol, and hallucinogens can cause changes in sensation, perception, attention, judgment, and other psychological activities.
   a. Tranquilizers
   b. Depressants
   c. Psychoactive drugs
   d. Stimulants

8. Methamphetamine stimulates the release of the brain's pleasure-producing neurotransmitter ____________, causing a surge in energy and alertness.
   a. dopamine
   b. serotonin
   c. acetylcholine
   d. adenosine

9. Which of the following statements about hypnosis is TRUE?
   a. People can be hypnotized against their will.
   b. People can have superhuman strength under hypnosis.
   c. Short-term amnesia can occur if the hypnotist suggests something will be forgotten.
   d. People can retrieve lost memories when in a hypnotic state.

10. Drug use can be fueled by dependence. ____________ dependence means the body no longer functions normally without the drug, and one sign of this type of dependence is ____________, as indicated by the symptoms that occur when the drug is withheld.
    a. Psychological; tolerance
    b. Physiological; substance abuse
    c. Physiological; withdrawal
    d. Psychological; withdrawal

11. Give an example showing that you are still conscious when asleep.

12. Describe automatic processing, and give two reasons why it is important.

13. Interns and residents in hospitals sometimes work 48-hour shifts. Why wouldn't you want a doctor to care for you at the end of her 48-hour shift?

14. Name and describe four different sleep disturbances. Differentiate them by describing their characteristics.

15. Give four examples of drugs that people may use legally on a daily basis.

✓ CHECK YOUR ANSWERS IN APPENDIX C.

Go to **LaunchPad** or **Achieve: Read & Practice** to test your understanding with **LearningCurve**.

CHAPTER 5

Richard Levine/Alamy.

Learning

An Introduction to Learning

BEFORE HE WAS THE DOG WHISPERER December 23, 1990: Cesar Millan had made up his mind; it was time to leave Mexico and start a new life in America. He was 21 years old, spoke no English, and had exactly $100 in his pocket. Since the age of 13, Cesar had dreamed of becoming the greatest dog trainer in the world. Now he was ready to pursue that goal, even if it meant saying goodbye to everything he knew and cherished—his family, his homeland, and his culture (Millan & Peltier, 2006).

From his home in Mazatlán, Cesar traveled to the dangerous border city of Tijuana, where he met a human smuggler who said he would get him into the United States for a fee of—you guessed it—$100. Trudging over muddy terrain, darting across a busy freeway, and hiding in a frigid trench of water, Cesar stuck with the smuggler. When he finally reached San Diego, he was "dripping wet, filthy, thirsty, [and] hungry." But, as Cesar recalls in his book *Cesar's Way,* "I was the happiest man in the world" (Millan & Peltier, 2006, p. 39).

For more than a month, Cesar slept under a freeway and lived on hotdogs from 7-Eleven (Partisan Pictures, 2012). Technically, he was "homeless," but he didn't feel like a drifter. "I never felt lost," Cesar recalls, "I always knew what I wanted." Cesar got a job at a pet-grooming parlor in San Diego and eventually moved to Los Angeles, where he worked as a kennel boy, a limousine washer, and a self-employed dog trainer. His dog-training business was based in Inglewood, a city just south of Los Angeles with a strong gang

Dog's Best Friend
Young Cesar Millan walking a pack of large and powerful dogs. Early on, Cesar knew he wanted to devote his life to dogs. He remembers himself as a 13-year-old asking his mother, "Mom, you think I can be the best dog trainer in the world?" She responded, "You can do whatever you want" (NPR, 2014, March 30). Eight years later, at the age of 21, Cesar arrived in the United States with no money, no acquaintances, and virtually no knowledge of English. But he had a dream, and that was more powerful than anything. Gregg Cobarr/WireImage/Getty Images.

presence and many dogs trained to protect and fight (Fine, 2013, February 7; Lopez, 2012, March 18; Millan & Peltier, 2006). Capable of pacifying even the fiercest of dogs, Cesar could be seen strolling through the city with a pack of Rottweilers and pit bulls—off leash (Millan, n.d.)! Word spread about the "Mexican guy who has a magical way with dogs" (Millan & Peltier, 2006, p. 50), and Cesar accumulated more and more clients. The *Los Angeles Times* got wind of Cesar's work and profiled him in 2002, sparking the interest of several television producers (Levine, 2002, September 25).

Fast-forward to 2018. Cesar Millan is now a U.S. citizen and perhaps the most famous dog expert on the planet. His résumé includes nine seasons of the Emmy-nominated reality television series *Dog Whisperer with Cesar Millan* (broadcast in more than 100 countries), along with other TV series such as *Cesar 911*. A best-selling author, Cesar travels the world giving seminars in auditoriums packed with thousands of eager listeners. Fans flood his website with comments, some of them desperate ("HEY Ceser! I really need HELP! I have a 10 month old pit mix. . . ."), others adoring ("Dear Cesar, keep doing what you're doing. . . . You've got a believer in me and millions of others"; Millan, n.d.).

How do you explain Cesar's rise from poverty to superstardom? Clearly, he is hardworking, motivated, and has an innate gift for understanding dogs. But Cesar's life, and the lives of countless dogs and their owners, have also been shaped by *learning*.

Top Dog
The world's most famous dog expert doesn't train dogs—he trains people. "I'm training humans to understand how dogs react, how dogs behave, what is their communication, and what makes them happy," Cesar explains. It's all about bringing balance to dogs' lives and promoting more fulfilling relationships between dogs and their owners. Mathew Imaging/FilmMagic for Academy of Television Arts and Sciences/Getty Images.

What Is Learning?

LO 1 Define learning.

Psychologists define **learning** as a relatively enduring change in behavior or thinking that results from experiences. Studies suggest that learning can begin before we are even born—fetuses can hear voices and learn basic speech sounds from inside the womb. This becomes apparent immediately following birth when they are able to distinguish among vowels used in their native language (Moon, Lagercrantz, & Kuhl, 2013; Partanen et al., 2013). Learning occurs every day, and may continue until our dying breath.

learning A relatively enduring change in behavior or thinking that results from experiences.

Note: Unless otherwise specified, quotations attributed to Cesar Millan are personal communications.

CONNECTIONS

In **Chapter 3**, we discussed sensory adaptation, which is the tendency to become less aware of constant stimuli. Becoming habituated to sensory input keeps us alert to changes in the environment.

Cesar, In His Own Words
http://qrs.ly/la7829l

Macmillan Learning.

The ability to learn is not unique to humans. Dogs can learn to dance salsa (Goldman, 2012, December 13) and fruit flies can be trained to avoid smells associated with electrical shocks (Dissel, Melnattur, & Shaw, 2015). Female elk are so good at learning to elude people with rifles and bows that they are "almost invulnerable to human hunters" after reaching 9 or 10 years of age (Thurfjell, Ciuti, & Boyce, 2017, para. 1).

One of the most basic forms of learning is called **habituation** (huh-bich-oo-EY-shun). Habituation occurs when an organism **reduces its response** to a recurring **stimulus** (an event or object that generally leads to a change in behavior). Initially, an animal might respond to a stimulus, but that response may diminish with repeated exposures (assuming the stimulus is not threatening). Essentially, an organism learns about a stimulus and becomes less responsive to it. This type of learning is apparent in a wide range of living beings, from humans to sea slugs to baby chickens. When 3-day-old chicks are exposed to a loud sound, they automatically freeze. But if the loud sound is repeated, even just 5 times, the newborn chicks become habituated to it and carry on with what they were doing (Chiandetti & Turatto, 2017).

Reading this chapter, you will learn about many important animal studies. Animals can be useful models for studying and understanding human behavior, including how we learn. The use of animals also sidesteps many of the ethical dilemmas that arise with human research. It's generally considered okay to keep rats, cats, and birds in cages to ensure control over experimental variables (as long as they are otherwise treated **humanely**), but locking up people in laboratories would obviously be unacceptable.

CONNECTIONS

In **Chapter 1**, we discussed Institutional Review Boards, which must approve all research with human participants and animal subjects to ensure safe and humane procedures.

This chapter focuses on three major types of learning: classical conditioning, operant conditioning, and observational learning. As you make your way through each section, you will begin to realize that learning is very much about creating associations. Through *classical conditioning,* we associate two different stimuli: for example, the sound of a buzzer and the arrival of food. In *operant conditioning,* we make connections between our behaviors and their consequences: for example, through rewards and punishments. With *observational learning,* we learn by watching and imitating other people, establishing a closer link between our behavior and the behavior of others.

Learning allows us to grow and change, and it is critical for achieving our goals. Let's see how learning has shaped the life and work of Cesar Millan.

Serving His Country
Special Agent L. A. Bykowsky works with Gavin in an explosives-detecting exercise. During his five years with the Bureau of Alcohol, Tobacco, Firearms and Explosives (ATF), Gavin helped ensure the safety of people attending Super Bowls and NASCAR races; then he went on a mission in Iraq, where his problems with noises seemed to begin (Millan & Peltier, 2010). AP Photo/Wilfredo Lee.

PATRIOT WITH A PROBLEM Every year around July 4th, animal shelters around the country report a surge in the number of runaway dogs and other pets (Hanson, 2017, July 1). The banging and popping of fireworks are so terrifying to some dogs, they flee their homes to escape the sounds. A dog that fears fireworks or thunder is nothing out of the ordinary. But what if the animal went into panic mode every time he heard the beep of a microwave, cell phone, or elevator? This was the sad reality for Gavin, a sweet Labrador retriever who worked as a bomb-sniffing dog for the Bureau of Alcohol, Tobacco, Firearms and Explosives (ATF).

When Cesar first met Gavin, the yellow Lab had already retired from the ATF, but his work experiences had left a mark. While on a tour in the Iraq War, Gavin had witnessed several loud explosions. Whenever an explosion occurred, "he quivered and shook," but then was able to carry on with his duties, according to his handler, Special Agent L. A. Bykowsky (Millan & Peltier, 2010, p. 58). Gavin may have been able to hold it together in Iraq, but the experience had a profound impact on him. Shortly after returning to his home in Florida, Gavin lived through two consecutive hurricanes (Millan & Peltier, 2010), which "just took him [through] the roof," according to Cesar. As a result of these experiences, Gavin became hypersensitive to many different sounds. Any beeping noise would trigger his fear response: the sound of a voicemail ringtone might cause uncontrollable shaking.

How did Gavin come to associate harmless, everyday sounds with danger? To answer this question, we need to travel back in time and visit the lab of an aspiring Russian scientist: Ivan Pavlov.

show what you know

1. ________________ is a relatively enduring change in behavior and thinking resulting from experiences.

2. Learning is often described as the creation of associations, or links, for example, between a behavior and its consequences. List some associations you have made this week.

✓ CHECK YOUR ANSWERS IN APPENDIX C.

Classical Conditioning

Russian physiologist Ivan Pavlov spent the 1890s studying the digestive system of dogs at Russia's Imperial Institute of Experimental Medicine, where about 100 people worked in his laboratory (Todes, 2014; Watson, 1968). Many of his early experiments involved measuring how much dogs salivate in response to food. At first, the dogs salivated as expected, but as the experiment progressed, they began **salivating** at the mere sight or sound of the lab assistant arriving to feed them. Pavlov realized that the dogs' "psyche," or personality, and their "thoughts about food" were interfering with the collection of objective data on their digestion (Todes, 2014, p. 158). In other words, some unobservable activities were affecting their physiology, making it difficult for the researchers to study digestion as an isolated phenomenon. The dog was associating the sound of footsteps or the sight of a bowl with the arrival of food; it had linked certain sights and sounds with eating. Intrigued by his discovery, Pavlov shifted the focus of his research, investigating the dogs' salivation in these types of scenarios (Fancher & Rutherford, 2012; Todes, 2014).

CONNECTIONS

A dog naturally begins to salivate when exposed to the smell of food, even before tasting it. This is an involuntary response of the autonomic nervous system, which we explored in **Chapter 2**. Dogs do not normally salivate at the sound of footsteps, however. This response is a *learned* behavior, as the dog salivates without tasting or smelling food.

Mouth-Watering Science

LO 2 Explain what Pavlov's studies teach us about classical conditioning.

Beginning in the early 1900s, Pavlov conducted numerous studies examining the link between stimulus (food) and response (salivation). The behaviors Pavlov studied were involuntary (reflexive), meaning they occurred automatically (Pavlov, 1906). The connection between food and salivation is innate and universal (all dogs salivate in response to food). However, the link between salivation and non-food stimuli is learned (for instance, dogs don't automatically salivate in response to the sound of footsteps, they *learn* to do it). Any time a new, nonuniversal link between a stimulus and a response is established (footsteps and salivation), a type of learning called *conditioning* has occurred.

Many of Pavlov's studies had the same basic format (**INFOGRAPHIC 5.1** on page 168). Prior to the experiment, the dog had a tube surgically inserted into its cheek so researchers could determine exactly how much saliva it was producing. Once the dog had recovered from the surgery, it was placed alone in a soundproof room and outfitted with equipment to keep it from moving around. Because Pavlov was interested in exploring the link between a stimulus and the dog's response, he had to pick a stimulus that was **more controlled** than the sound of someone walking into a room. Pavlov used

CONNECTIONS

In **Chapter 1**, we discussed the importance of control in the experimental method. Here, if the sound of footsteps is the stimulus, then Pavlov would need to control the number of steps taken and the type of shoes worn to ensure the stimulus was identical across trials. Otherwise, he would be introducing extraneous variables, or characteristics that interfere with the research outcome, making it difficult to determine what caused the dog to salivate.

habituation A basic form of learning evident when an organism does not respond as strongly or as often to an event following multiple exposures to it.

stimulus An event or object that generally leads to a response.

What Is a Metronome?
Pavlov conditioned his dogs to salivate in response to auditory stimuli, such as buzzers and ticking metronomes. A metronome is a device that musicians often use to maintain tempo. This "old-fashioned" metronome has a wind-up knob and a pendulum that ticks at various speed settings. Modern metronomes are digital and often come with additional features such as adjustable volume. Perhaps Pavlov could have used these new features to test different aspects of classical conditioning.
Galina Ermolaeva/Dreamstime.com.

a variety of stimuli, including flashing lights and sounds produced by metronomes and buzzers, which normally have nothing to do with food or salivation. In other words, they are neutral stimuli in relation to feeding and responses to food.

On numerous occasions during an experimental trial, Pavlov and his assistants presented a dog with a stimulus—the sound of a buzzer, for instance—and then moments later gave the dog a piece of meat. Each time the buzzer was sounded, the assistant would wait a couple of seconds and then give the dog meat. All the while, the dog's saliva was being measured, drop by drop. After repeated pairings, the dog began to link the buzzer with the meat. It would salivate in response to the sound alone, with *no* meat present, evidence that learning had occurred. The dog had *learned* to associate the buzzer with food.

What Do You Need to Know?

LO 3 Identify the differences between the US, UR, CS, and CR.

Now that you know Pavlov's basic research procedure, it is important to learn the **specific concepts and terminology** psychologists use to describe what is happening (**Table 5.1**).

synonyms
classical conditioning Pavlovian conditioning, respondent conditioning

CONNECTIONS
In **Chapter 1**, we discussed operational definitions, which are the precise ways in which characteristics of interest are defined and measured. Earlier, we described the research in everyday language, but here we are providing operational definitions for the procedures of the study.

COMING TO TERMS The pairings of the buzzer with the meat occur during the process of **acquisition,** or initial learning phase. Before the experiment begins, the sound of the buzzer is a **neutral stimulus (NS)**—something in the environment that does not normally cause a relevant automatic response. In this case, that automatic response is salivation; dogs do not normally salivate when they hear a buzzer. But through experience, they learn to link this neutral stimulus (the buzzer sound) with another stimulus (food) that normally prompts salivation. This type of learning is called **classical conditioning**, and it is evident when an originally neutral stimulus (NS) triggers an involuntary response, such as salivation, eye blinks, and other types of reflexive behaviors.

At the start of a trial, before a dog is conditioned or has learned anything about the neutral stimulus (NS), it salivates when it smells or receives food, in this case meat. The meat is considered an **unconditioned stimulus (US)** because it triggers an automatic response. Salivating in response to food is an **unconditioned response (UR)** because it doesn't require any learning; the dog just does it involuntarily. To reiterate, the smell or taste of meat (US) elicits the automatic response of salivation (the UR). After conditioning has occurred, the dog responds to the buzzer almost as if it were food. The buzzer, previously a neutral stimulus (NS), has now become a **conditioned stimulus (CS)** because it prompts the dog to salivate. When salivation occurs in response to the buzzer, it is a learned behavior; we call it a **conditioned response (CR)**. When trying to figure out the proper label for the response, ask yourself what caused it: Was it the food or the buzzer? Knowing this will help you determine whether it is conditioned (learned) or unconditioned (not learned).

Now that you have a general understanding of classical conditioning, let's have some fun with it. Imagine you wanted to play a Pavlovian prank on an unsuspecting friend.

acquisition The initial learning phase in both classical and operant conditioning.

neutral stimulus (NS) A stimulus that does not cause a relevant automatic or reflexive response.

classical conditioning Learning process in which two stimuli become associated with each other; when an originally neutral stimulus is conditioned to elicit an involuntary response.

unconditioned stimulus (US) A stimulus that automatically triggers an involuntary response without any learning needed.

unconditioned response (UR) A reflexive, involuntary response to an unconditioned stimulus.

conditioned stimulus (CS) A previously neutral stimulus that an organism learns to associate with an unconditioned stimulus.

conditioned response (CR) A learned response to a conditioned stimulus.

stimulus generalization The tendency for stimuli similar to the conditioned stimulus to elicit the conditioned response.

TABLE 5.1 CLASSICAL CONDITIONING: STIMULUS AND RESPONSE

Stimulus	Response	Dog and Buzzer
Neutral stimulus (NS) does not cause an automatic response.	No relevant response to NS.	Buzzer (NS) initially does not cause dog to salivate.
Unconditioned stimulus (US) causes *unlearned* response.	**Unconditioned response (UR)** is automatic and is triggered by US.	Meat is always a US (the dog never has to learn how to respond to it). Dog's salivation is initially a UR to meat.
Conditioned stimulus (CS) causes *learned* response. Always different from US.	**Conditioned response (CR)** is learned from pairing with US.	Buzzer (CS) causes dog to salivate (CR).

Here are some of the terms used in classical conditioning. Remember, unconditioned means unlearned, conditioned means learned, stimulus is something that occurs in the environment, response is how the learner reacts.

All you would need is a phone and some Sour Patch Kids (sour candy). Personalize your alert tone with a unique sound (twinkle). Then, every time you get a notification ("twinkle, twinkle!"), hand your friend a Sour Patch Kid. The twinkle sound is initially a neutral stimulus (NS), and the candy is an unconditioned stimulus (US), because it causes salivation (an unconditioned response). With repeated pairings of the "twinkle, twinkle!" and the candy, your friend will begin to associate the neutral stimulus (twinkle sound) and the unconditioned stimulus (candy). After this conditioning has occurred, the twinkle sound becomes a conditioned stimulus (CS) that has the power to produce a conditioned response (salivation)—and your friend may wonder why your phone is making his mouth water!

Office Pranks
In Season 3 of NBC's *The Office,* "Jim" played by John Krasinski (right) plays a classical conditioning trick on his coworker "Dwight" played by Rainn Wilson (left). Every time Jim's computer makes the reboot sound, Jim hands Dwight an Altoids breath mint. After several pairings of the reboot sound and the mint, Dwight automatically reaches out his hand in anticipation of the mint. "What are you doing?" asks Jim. Looking confused, Dwight replies, "My mouth tastes so bad all of the sudden" (Williams & Whittingham, 2007, 0:53–1:03). NBC/Photofest.

LO 4 Recognize and give examples of stimulus generalization and stimulus discrimination.

GENERALIZATION AND DISCRIMINATION What would happen if your friend heard a similar-sounding notification coming from someone else's phone? If he salivates, he is displaying **stimulus generalization,** which is the tendency for stimuli similar to the conditioned stimulus (CS) to elicit the conditioned response (CR). Once an association is forged between a conditioned stimulus (CS) and a conditioned response (CR), the learner often responds to similar stimuli as if they were the original CS. When Pavlov's dogs learned to salivate in response to a metronome ticking at 90 beats per minute, they also salivated when the metronome ticked a little faster (100 beats per minute) or slower (80 beats per minute; Hothersall, 2004). Their response was generalized to metronome speeds ranging from 80 to 100 beats per minute.

If a new stimulus is significantly different from the conditioned stimulus (CS), stimulus generalization may not occur. Suppose Pavlov's dogs learned to salivate in response to a high-pitched sound. If these dogs were exposed to lower-pitched sounds, they may not salivate. If so, they would be demonstrating **stimulus discrimination,** the ability to distinguish between a particular conditioned stimulus (CS) and other stimuli **sufficiently different** from it. Getting back to your cell-phone prank, if your friend does not salivate in response to a notification sound from someone else's phone, he is displaying stimulus discrimination.

CONNECTIONS
In **Chapter 3**, we introduced the concept of difference threshold, the minimum difference between two stimuli noticed 50% of the time. Here, we see that difference thresholds can play a role in stimulus discrimination. The difference between the conditioned stimulus and the comparison stimuli must be greater than the difference threshold.

EXTINCTION Once the dogs associate the buzzer sound with meat, can they ever listen to the sound without salivating? The answer is yes—if they are repeatedly exposed to the buzzer without the meat to follow. Present the conditioned stimulus (CS)

stimulus discrimination The ability to differentiate between a conditioned stimulus and other stimuli sufficiently different from it.

Learning Through Classical Conditioning

During his experiments with dogs, Ivan Pavlov noticed them salivating before food was even presented. Somehow the dogs had learned to associate the lab assistant's approaching footsteps with eating. This observation led to Pavlov's discovery of classical conditioning, in which we learn to associate a neutral stimulus with an unconditioned stimulus that produces an automatic, natural response. The crucial stage of this process involves repeated pairings of the two stimuli.

PAVLOV'S EXPERIMENT

Before conditioning

Dog salivates automatically when food is presented.

Unconditioned stimulus → Unconditioned response (salivates)

Buzzer means nothing to dog, so there is no response.

Neutral stimulus (buzzer sound) — No response

During conditioning

In the process of conditioning, buzzer is repeatedly sounded right before dog receives food. Over time, dog learns that buzzer signals arrival of food.

Neutral stimulus (buzzer sound) + Unconditioned stimulus = Unconditioned response (salivates)

repeated over time

After conditioning

Dog has now learned to associate buzzer with food and will begin salivating when buzzer sounds.

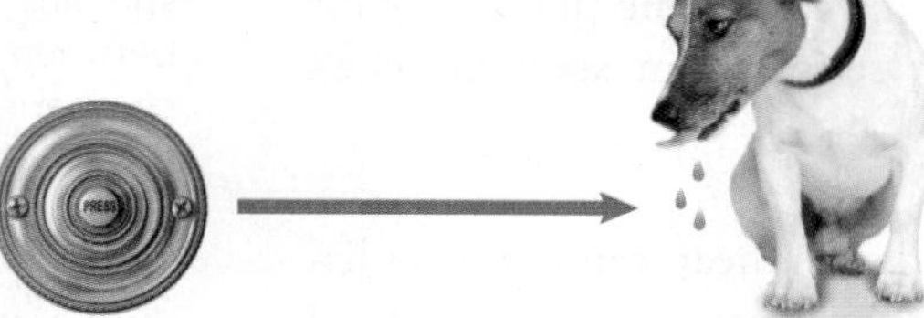

Conditioned stimulus (buzzer sound) → Conditioned response (salivates)

HAVE YOU BEEN CONDITIONED?

Before conditioning

Neutral stimulus — No response

Unconditioned stimulus → Unconditioned response (stomach growls)

During conditioning

Neutral stimulus + Unconditioned stimulus

Unconditioned response (stomach growls)

repeated over time

After conditioning

Conditioned stimulus → Conditioned response (stomach growls)

Classical conditioning is an involuntary form of learning that happens every day. Does your stomach rumble when you see the McDonald's "golden arches"? Just like Pavlov's dogs, we learn through repeated pairings to associate neutral stimuli (the golden arches) with food (french fries). Once this association is formed, the sight of the golden arches can be enough to get our stomachs rumbling.

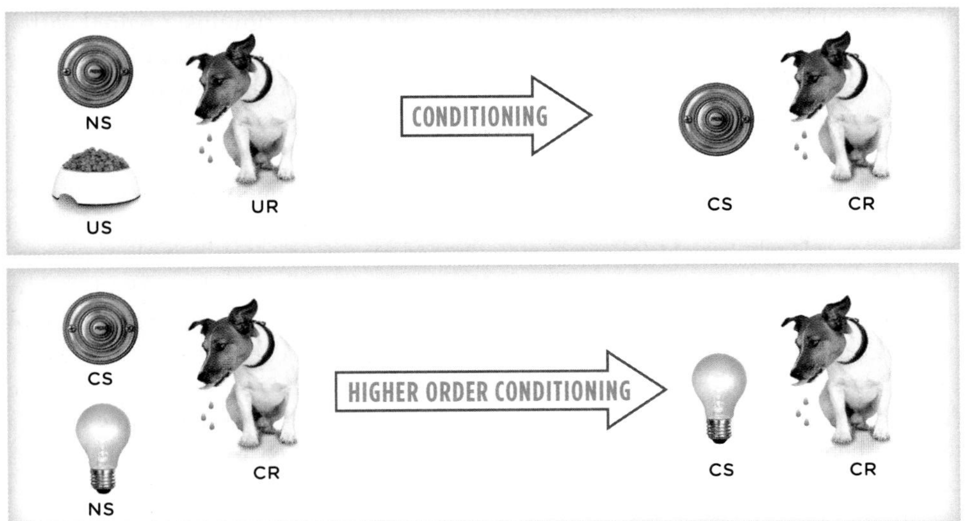

FIGURE 5.1
Higher Order Conditioning
Once an association has been made through classical conditioning, the conditioned stimulus (CS) can be used to learn new associations. When a conditioned stimulus (CS), such as a buzzer that now triggers salivation, is repeatedly paired with a neutral stimulus (NS), such as a flashing light, the dog will learn to salivate in response to the light—without food ever being present! These multiple layers of learning help us understand how humans form associations between many different stimuli. Jack Russell terrier and bowl: Thinkstock/Getty Images. Light bulb: Denphumi/Shutterstock. Buzzer: Paul Fleet/Shutterstock.

in the absence of the unconditioned stimulus (US), over and over, and the conditioned response (CR) decreases and eventually disappears in a process called **extinction.** In general, if dogs are repeatedly exposed to a conditioned stimulus (for example, a metronome or buzzer) without any tasty treats to follow, they produce progressively less saliva in response to the stimulus and, eventually, none at all (Watson, 1968).

SPONTANEOUS RECOVERY With extinction, the connection is not necessarily gone forever. After conditioning a dog to associate the buzzer with meat, Pavlov (1927/1960) stopped presenting the meat, and the association was extinguished (the dog didn't salivate in response to the buzzer). Two hours later, Pavlov reintroduced the buzzer (earlier a conditioned stimulus) and the dog salivated. This reappearance of the conditioned response (CR) following its extinction is called **spontaneous recovery.** The dog had not "forgotten" the association when the pairing was extinguished. Rather, the conditioned response (CR) was suppressed when the dog was not being exposed to the unconditioned stimulus (US). Let's return to your friend whose mouth waters when he hears that twinkle alert. His conditioned response (salivation) might be extinguished if several days go by and you don't give him candy when your phone makes the "twinkle" sound. However, spontaneous recovery may occur at some point in the future, causing him to salivate in response to that twinkle once again (the conditioned stimulus).

HIGHER ORDER CONDITIONING Is it possible to add another layer to the conditioning process? Absolutely, as we can create a link between a second neutral stimulus (NS) and a previously acquired conditioned stimulus (CS). Suppose the sound of the buzzer has become a conditioned stimulus (CS) for the dog. Now the researcher adds a new neutral stimulus (NS), such as a light flashing, every time the dog hears the buzzer. After pairing the buzzer and the light (without the meat anywhere in sight or smell), the light becomes associated with the sound and the dog begins to salivate in response to seeing the light alone. This is called **higher order conditioning** (**Figure 5.1**). With repeated pairings of the conditioned stimulus (buzzer) and a new neutral stimulus (the light), the second neutral stimulus becomes a conditioned stimulus as well. When all is said and done, both stimuli (the buzzer and the light) have gone from being neutral stimuli to conditioned stimuli, and either of them can elicit the conditioned response (salivation).

extinction In classical conditioning, the process by which the conditioned response decreases after repeated exposure to the conditioned stimulus in the absence of the unconditioned stimulus; in operant conditioning, the disappearance of a learned behavior through the removal of its reinforcer.

spontaneous recovery The reappearance of a conditioned response following its extinction.

higher order conditioning With repeated pairings of a conditioned stimulus and a second neutral stimulus, that second neutral stimulus becomes a conditioned stimulus as well.

Note that in higher order conditioning, the second neutral stimulus is paired with a conditioned stimulus instead of being paired with the original unconditioned stimulus (Pavlov, 1927/1960). In our example, the light is associated with the buzzer, not the food directly.

CONNECTIONS

In **Chapter 1**, we described the scientific method and its dependence on *objective* observation. This approach requires us to observe and record free from personal opinion or expectations. We are all prone to biases, but the scientific method helps minimize their effects. Pavlov was among the first to insist that behavior must be studied objectively.

Why is Pavlov's work important? He paved the way for a new generation of psychologists who considered behavior to be a topic of **objective**, scientific study. Like many scientists who would follow, Pavlov focused on the objective recording of measurable behaviors, in this case counting the exact number of saliva drops produced by the dogs. His work transformed our understanding of learning and our approach to psychological research.

We launched the discussion of classical conditioning with the story of Gavin, the ATF dog. Let's apply the principles of classical conditioning to imagine how Gavin's unusual behaviors developed, and discover how Cesar helped this yellow Lab overcome his fear.

You Asked, Cesar Answers

http://qrs.ly/la7829l

Has there ever been a dog you couldn't help?

FROM IVAN PAVLOV TO CESAR MILLAN An explosion is an alarming event. Think of the sound it emits as an unconditioned stimulus (US) that can elicit a physiological fear response of shaking (the unconditioned response). Somewhere along the line, Gavin likely heard another sound paired with explosions—perhaps the faint popping sound of faraway artillery fire. (It doesn't seem too farfetched that one would hear artillery fire and explosions in the same general location.) After repeated pairings of the popping of distant artillery fire (the neutral stimulus) and the explosion sound (the unconditioned stimulus), Gavin came to associate these two stimuli. The sound of distant artillery fire became a conditioned stimulus (CS) that could elicit the conditioned response (CR) of shaking. Following this acquisition phase, the sound of artillery fire evoked the same physiological response (shaking) as an explosion.

So what does all this have to do with Gavin's fear of beeping microwaves, cell phones, and elevators? Again, we can only speculate because we weren't there to observe Gavin in Iraq. But supposing he was conditioned to fear the sound of artillery fire, then it's possible that this fear became generalized to other rhythmic, mechanical sounds, such as beeping cell phones and elevators. Through *stimulus generalization,* these sounds began to evoke a *conditioned response* (CR) of fearful trembling as well.

Cesar brought Gavin to the Dog Psychology Center in Santa Clarita, California, where he was well received by the dogs in Cesar's pack. "As I've seen hundreds of times, a pack of dogs can do more rehab in a few hours than I can do alone in a few days," Cesar writes in his book *Cesar's Rules* (Millan & Peltier, 2010, p. 59). Spending time with Cesar and his pack helped Gavin relax, but he still exhibited the fear response when he heard beeping elevators and other sounds. How could this apparent classically conditioned response be extinguished?

Calm in the Water
According to Cesar, being in the water brings out the instinctual side of most dogs, connecting them with nature and making them feel calm. To help Gavin the ATF dog overcome his fear of everyday noises (the conditioned stimulus), Cesar paired the disturbing sounds with activities that were relaxing and pleasurable for Gavin.
MPH/Emery Sumner JV.

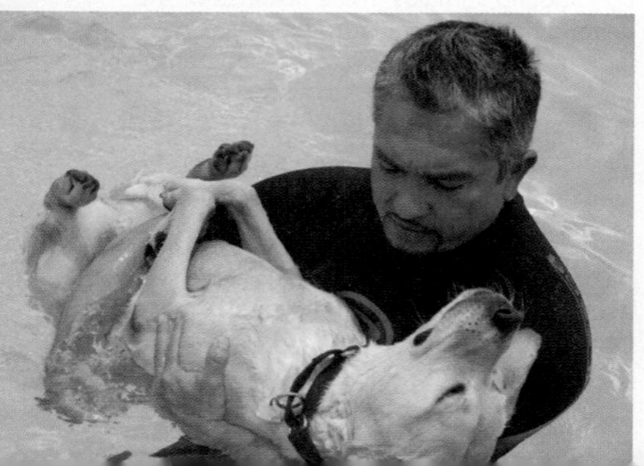

One option would be to pair a new response with the unconditioned stimulus (US) or the conditioned stimulus (CS). Cesar took this approach, and it worked wonders. To help Gavin overcome his fear of everyday loud noises (conditioned stimulus), Cesar combined those sounds with something distracting. For example, he would create a loud noise just as he presented Gavin with his favorite food (carrots). To reduce Gavin's fear of truly frightening sounds like thunder, fireworks, and explosions (unconditioned stimulus), Cesar placed him in a virtual reality environment. As Gavin walked on a treadmill (an activity that appeared to relax him), Cesar exposed him to the sounds he feared most (not all at once, but in small steps). Eventually, Gavin's fear response diminished and he could visit a firing range without "shutting down" and shaking (Millan & Peltier, 2010). In Chapter 14, we present similar techniques used by therapists to help human clients struggling with anxiety and fear. 

We've learned how classical conditioning can cause a variety of reflexive responses, including salivation (Pavlov's dogs) and shaking (Gavin). Would you believe that this form of learning can also make you feel nauseous?

Yuck: Conditioned Taste Aversion

LO 5 Summarize how classical conditioning is dependent on the biology of the organism.

Have you ever experienced food poisoning? After falling ill from something, whether it was uncooked chicken or unrefrigerated mayonnaise, you probably steered clear of that particular food for a while. This is an example of **conditioned taste aversion,** a powerful form of classical conditioning that occurs when an organism learns to associate a specific food or drink with illness. Often, it only takes a single pairing between a food and a bad feeling—that is, one-trial learning—for an organism to change its behavior. Imagine a grizzly bear that avoids poisonous berries after vomiting from eating them. In this case, the unconditioned stimulus (US) is the poison in the berries; the unconditioned response (UR) is the vomiting caused by the poison. After acquisition, the conditioned stimulus (CS) would be the sight or smell of the berries, and the conditioned response (CR) would be a nauseous feeling. The bear would likely steer clear of the berries in the future.

Avoiding foods that induce sickness has **adaptive value,** meaning it helps organisms survive, upping the odds they will reproduce and pass their genes along to the next generation. According to the **evolutionary perspective**, humans and other animals have a powerful drive to ensure that they and their offspring reach reproductive age, so it's critical to steer clear of tastes that have been associated with illness.

CONNECTIONS

In **Chapter 1**, we introduced the evolutionary perspective, which suggests that behaviors and traits are shaped by natural selection. Here, this perspective helps clarify why some types of learning are so powerful. In the case of conditioned taste aversion, species gain an evolutionary advantage through quick and efficient learning about poisonous foods.

How might conditioned taste aversion impact you? Suppose you eat a hot dog a few hours before coming down with a stomach virus. The hot dog isn't responsible for your illness—and you may be aware of this—but the slightest taste of one can make you feel sick, even after you have recovered. In fact, just thinking about a hot dog might make you nauseous. Physical experiences like this can be so strong they override our common sense.

Identify the neutral stimulus (NS), unconditioned stimulus (US), unconditioned response (UR), conditioned stimulus (CS), and conditioned response (CR) in the hot dog scenario.

✓CHECK YOUR ANSWERS IN APPENDIX C.

RATS WITH BELLYACHES American psychologist John Garcia (1917–2012) and his colleagues demonstrated conditioned taste aversion in their well-known research on laboratory rats (Garcia, Ervin, & Koelling, 1966). In one study, Garcia and his colleagues provided the animals with flavored water followed by injections of a drug that upset their stomachs. The animals rejected that

conditioned taste aversion A form of classical conditioning that occurs when an organism learns to associate the taste of a particular food or drink with illness.

adaptive value The degree to which a trait or behavior helps an organism survive.

flavored drink thereafter. This is clearly adaptive, because nausea often results from ingesting food that is poisonous or spoiled. An animal is more likely to survive and reproduce if it can recognize and shun the tastes of dangerous substances. Garcia's research highlights the importance of **biological preparedness,** the predisposition or inclination of animals (and people) to form certain kinds of associations through classical conditioning. Conditioned taste aversion is a powerful form of learning. Would you believe it can be harnessed to save the lives of endangered species?

DIDN'T SEE THAT COMING

RESCUING ANIMALS WITH CLASSICAL CONDITIONING An animal is in trouble in Australia: A large lizard called the "floodplain goanna" is threatened by a non-native "cane toad" that is invading its tropical habitat. Cane toads may look delicious (at least to the goannas), but they pack a lethal dose of poison, killing the unlucky lizards that try to feast on them. In areas of cane toad invasion, goanna populations have plummeted, with death estimates exceeding 90% (Ujvari & Madsen, 2009; Ward-Fear, Pearson, Brown, Rangers, & Shine, 2016).

ATTACK OF THE KILLER TOADS

How could you use conditioned taste aversion to **protect these lizards** from looming toad invasions? Remember that conditioned taste aversion occurs when an organism rejects a food or drink after consuming it and becoming very sick. To condition the goannas to avoid the toxic toads, you must teach them to associate these amphibians with nausea. You could do this by feeding them baby cane toads. Unlike their parents, these youngsters pack a "sublethal" dose of poison—enough to induce nausea, but not enough to cause death. After the unpleasant training with the baby toads, the goannas should avoid eating the more dangerous adult toads. Researchers from the University of Sydney used this approach, and the results are promising. Goannas subjected to conditioned taste aversion prior to a toad invasion were less likely than their unconditioned comrades to eat the killer toads and die (Ward-Fear et al., 2016).

CONNECTIONS

In **Chapter 1**, we introduced two types of research. Basic research is focused on gathering knowledge for the sake of knowledge. Applied research focuses on changing behaviors and outcomes, often leading to real-world applications. Here, we see how classical conditioning principles are applied to help save wildlife.

Similar approaches are being tried across the world. In Africa, ranchers often kill lions for preying upon cattle (Platt, 2015, June 24). But researchers have shown that the big cats can learn to avoid beef through conditioned taste aversion (Platt, 2011, December 27). In California, researchers have worked to protect an endangered bird by feeding its predator bird eggs that contain vomit-inducing chemicals (Oskin, 2013, May 17). As you see, lessons learned by psychologists working in a lab can have far-reaching applications.

Learning to the Rescue
Australia's large lizard species, the floodplain goanna (held by University of Sydney researcher Dr. Georgia Ward-Fear) is threatened by the introduction of an invasive species known as the cane toad (right). The goannas eat the toads, which carry a lethal dose of poison, but they can learn to avoid this toxic prey through conditioned taste aversion (Ward-Fear et al., 2016). Left: Courtesy Dr. David Pearson. Right: Chris Mattison/FLPA/Science Source.

Lessons from Little Albert

LO 6 Describe the Little Albert study and explain how fear can be learned.

So far, we have focused on the classical conditioning of physical responses—salivation, shaking, and nausea. Now let's look at how classical conditioning can influence emotions. A **conditioned emotional response** occurs when a neutral stimulus is paired with an emotional reaction.

The classic case study of "Little Albert," conducted by John B. Watson (1878–1958) and Rosalie Rayner (1898–1935), provides a famous illustration of conditioned emotional response (Watson & Rayner, 1920). Little Albert was around 9 months old when first tested by Watson and Rayner (Griggs, 2015d; Powell, Digdon, Harris, & Smithson, 2014). Initially, he had no fear of rats; in fact, he was rather intrigued by the white critters and sometimes reached out to touch them. But all this changed when Albert was about 11 months old; that's when the researchers began banging a hammer against a steel bar whenever he reached for the rat (Harris, 1979). Each time the researchers paired the loud noise (an unconditioned stimulus) and the appearance of the rat (a neutral stimulus), Albert responded in fear (the unconditioned response). After only seven pairings, he began to fear rats and generalized this fear to other furry objects, including a sealskin coat and a rabbit (Harris, 1979). The sight of the rat went from being a neutral stimulus (NS) to a conditioned stimulus (CS), and Albert's fear of the rat was a conditioned response (CR).

Nobody knows exactly what happened to Little Albert after he participated in Watson and Rayner's research. Some psychologists believe Little Albert's true identity is still unknown (Powell, 2010; Reese, 2010). Others have proposed Little Albert was Douglas Merritte, who had a neurological condition called hydrocephalus and died at age 6 (Beck & Irons, 2011; Beck, Levinson, & Irons, 2009; Fridlund, Beck, Goldie, & Irons, 2012). Still others suggest Little Albert was a healthy baby named William Albert Barger, who lived until 2007 (Bartlett, 2014; Digdon, Powell, & Harris, 2014; Powell et al., 2014). We may never know the true identity of Little Albert or the long-term effects of his conditioning through this unethical study. Watson and Rayner (1920) discussed how they might have reduced Little Albert's fear of rats (for example, giving him candy while presenting the rat), but they were never able to provide him with such treatment (Griggs, 2014a).

The Little Albert study would never happen today. Contemporary psychologists conduct research according to stringent ethical guidelines, and instilling terror in a baby would not be accepted or allowed at research institutions.

Bang! Baby Is Scared
"Little Albert" was a baby who developed a fear of rats through his participation in an ethically questionable experiment conducted by John B. Watson and Rosalie Rayner (Watson & Rayner, 1920). Watson and Rayner repeatedly showed the child a rat while terrifying him with a loud banging sound. Albert quickly learned to associate the sight of the rat with the scary noise, and his resulting fear of rats is known as a conditioned emotional response. The Drs. Nicholas and Dorothy Cummings Center for the History of Psychology, The University of Akron.

Do You Buy It?

Classical conditioning affects you in ways you may not realize. Think about how you feel when you see one of your favorite actors or sports heroes appearing in an advertisement. Cover Girl makeup looks pretty appealing on the face of Zendaya, and who can resist Under Armor gear worn by Yankees slugger Aaron Judge? In one study, researchers had some participants view images of sports events paired with famous athletes, while others viewed the same events without celebrity endorsement. As you might expect, participants exposed to celebrity endorsement developed more favorable attitudes toward the events (Chen, Lin, & Hsiao, 2012). Through classical conditioning, the sports events had become associated with the famous people.

biological preparedness The tendency for animals to be predisposed or inclined to form certain kinds of associations through classical conditioning.

conditioned emotional response An emotional reaction acquired through classical conditioning; process by which an emotional reaction becomes associated with a previously neutral stimulus.

Does Sexy Sell?
Research suggests that advertisements may instill attitudes toward brands through classical conditioning (Chen, Chang, Besherat, & Baack, 2013; Grossman & Till, 1998), but how do these attitudes affect sales? Now, that is a question worth researching. Richard Levine/Alamy.

Advertisements can instill emotions and attitudes toward product brands, and these classically conditioned responses may linger as long as 3 weeks (Chen, Chang, Besherat, & Baack, 2013; Grossman & Till, 1998). Have any of your recent purchases been influenced by such ads? Do you think you are susceptible to classical conditioning? We would venture to say that we all are (**Table 5.2**).

This does not mean that classical conditioning can force you to go out and spend money on items you otherwise would not buy. If it did lead to changes in purchasing behavior, the implications could be far-reaching. Imagine, for example, that consumers made decisions based on medical advice offered by celebrities, instead of health professionals (Hoffman & Tan, 2013).

Remember that classical conditioning is a type of learning related to involuntary behaviors: physiological reactions such as salivation and nausea, emotional responses like fear, and attitudes like those we develop toward product brands. If classical conditioning is primarily concerned with involuntary behaviors, then how do we acquire the countless behaviors within our control? Voluntary behaviors are often learned through *operant conditioning*.

TABLE 5.2 REAL-LIFE EXAMPLES OF CLASSICAL CONDITIONING

Type	Neutral Stimulus (NS) and Unconditioned Stimulus (US)	Expected Response
Advertising	Repeated pairing of products such as cars (NS) with sexually provocative images (US)	Automatic response to sexual image is arousal (UR); pairing leads to a similar response (CR) to the product (CS).
Fears	Pairing of a dog lunging (US) at you, and the street where the dog lives (NS)	Automatic response to the dog lunging at you is fear (UR); pairing leads to similar response of fear (CR) to the street (CS) where the dog lives.
Fetishes	Repeated pairings of originally nonsexual objects like shoes (NS) and sexual activity (US)	Automatic response to sexual activity is sexual arousal (UR); pairing leads to sexual arousal (CR) in response to the objects (CS).
Romance	Repeated pairings of a cologne (NS) with a passionate embrace (US)	Automatic response to the embrace is sexual arousal (UR); pairing leads to sexual arousal (CR) in response to the cologne (CS).
Pet behavior	Repeated pairings of an electric can opener sound (NS) and the serving of food (US)	Automatic response to food is the dog/cat's salivation (UR); pairing leads to salivation (CR) in response to the sound of the can opener (CS).
Startle reaction	Repeated pairings of the toilet flushing (NS) with the sudden rise in water temperature in the shower (US)	Automatic response to the sensation of scalding water is jumping back (UR); pairing causes the person showering to jump back (CR) in response to the sound of the toilet flushing (CS).

The implications of classical conditioning extend far beyond salivating dogs. Here are just a few examples illustrating its widespread relevance.

show what you know

1. The dogs in Pavlov's early experiments began to salivate at the sound of the lab assistant's footsteps. Through the process of learning, the dogs were ______________ to link certain sights and sounds with eating.
2. After eating a hamburger tainted with salmonella (which causes food poisoning), you cannot smell or taste one without feeling nauseous. Which of the following is the unconditioned stimulus?
   a. salmonella
   b. nausea
   c. hamburgers
   d. the hamburger vendor
3. Watson and Rayner used classical conditioning to instill fear in Little Albert. Create a diagram of the neutral stimulus, unconditioned stimulus, unconditioned response, conditioned stimulus, and conditioned response in their experiment. In what way does Little Albert show stimulus generalization?
4. Because of ______________, animals and people are predisposed to form associations that increase their chances of survival.

✔ CHECK YOUR ANSWERS IN APPENDIX C.

Operant Conditioning

WE'VE GOT DOG PROBLEMS Cesar spent much of his early life on his grandfather's cattle ranch in Ixpalino, a small town in Sinaloa, Mexico. He loved being around the ranch animals, especially the dogs. They lived in a pack of about 5 to 7 members, slept outside, and hunted wild animals. Cesar's family depended on the dogs to herd cattle and guard the property, but also gave them plenty of "free time" to splash around in the creek and play. The ranch dogs organized their activities as a pack, as wolves do in nature, and their needs for daily exercise were satisfied (Fine, 2013, February 7; Millan & Peltier, 2006).

When Cesar arrived in the United States, he encountered quite a different type of dog. In America, dogs dined on gourmet biscuits, slept on memory foam mattresses, and got their hair blown dry at doggie salons. Cesar began to realize that many owners didn't understand their dogs' needs or know how to communicate with them. The dogs were suffering from an untold number of "issues," including anxiety, aggression, and hyperactivity (Millan & Peltier, 2006). In order to "fix" the dogs' misbehaviors, Cesar would have to teach their human owners a few things. As Cesar often says, "I rehabilitate dogs, and I train people" (Millan, 2013, March 26, para. 3).

What methods does Cesar use? We can't possibly cover the myriad approaches he employs, but we can explore how *operant conditioning* impacts his work.

Consequences Matter

Whether pleasant or unpleasant, the consequences of a behavior influence future actions. Think about the many effects of Cesar's hard work. Helping people understand and connect with their dogs is a positive consequence: "When I show them how the brain of a dog works, when I show them what makes a dog happy, when I show them how dogs communicate, and how we can communicate with [dogs]," Cesar explains, "then [I] see people understanding." This is a rewarding experience for Cesar, one that makes him more likely to continue his work. Imagine what would happen if all of Cesar's human clients ignored his advice and continued with their bad habits. How do you think this consequence would influence Cesar's future behaviors—would he be more or less likely to continue his work rehabilitating dogs and training people?

Describe Thorndike's law of effect.

THORNDIKE AND HIS CATS One of the first scientists to objectively study how consequences affect behavior was American psychologist Edward Thorndike (1874–1949). Thorndike's early research focused on chicks and other animals, which he sometimes kept in his apartment (Hothersall, 2004). The research with chicks was only a starting point, as Thorndike's most famous studies involved cats. One of his experimental setups involved putting a cat in a latched cage called a "puzzle box" and planting enticing pieces of fish outside the door. When first placed in the box, the cat would scratch and paw around randomly, but after a while, just by chance, it would pop the latch, causing the door to release. The cat would then escape the cage to devour the fish (**Figure 5.2** on the next page). The next time the cat was put in the box, it would repeat this random activity, scratching and pawing with no particular direction. And again, just by chance, the cat would pop the door latch and escape to eat the fish. Each time the cat was returned to the box, the number of random activities decreased until eventually it was able to break free almost immediately (Thorndike, 1898).

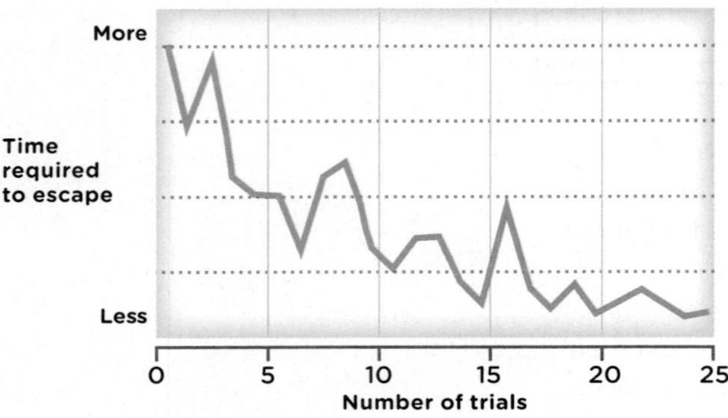

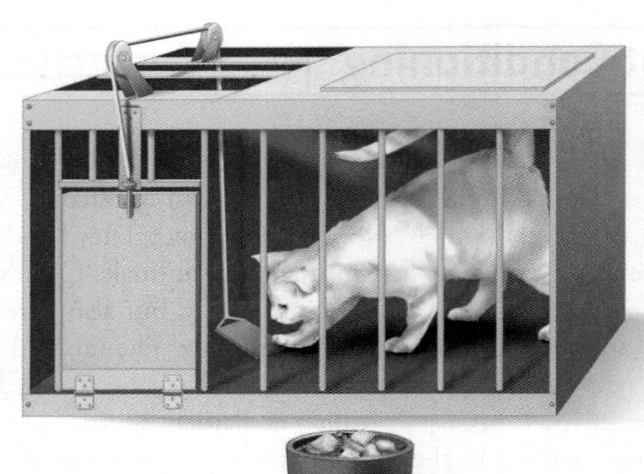

FIGURE 5.2
Puzzle Box
Early psychologist Edward Thorndike conducted his well-known cat experiments using "puzzle boxes" like the one shown here. At the start of the experiment, Thorndike's cats pawed around haphazardly until they managed to unlatch the door and then eat the fish treats placed outside. As the trials wore on, the felines learned to free themselves more quickly. After several trials, the amount of time needed to escape the box dropped significantly (see the graph above). Information from Thorndike (1898).

Radical Behaviorist
American psychologist Burrhus Frederic Skinner, or simply B. F. Skinner, is one of the most influential psychologists of all time. Skinner believed that every thought, emotion, and behavior (basically anything psychological) is shaped by factors in the environment. Using animal chambers known as "Skinner boxes," he conducted carefully controlled experiments on animal behavior. Nina Leen/The LIFE Picture Collection/Getty Images.

The cat's behavior, Thorndike reasoned, could be explained by the **law of effect,** which says that a behavior (opening the latch) is more likely to happen again when followed by a pleasurable outcome (delicious fish). Behaviors that lead to pleasurable results will be repeated, while behaviors that don't lead to pleasurable results (or are followed by something unpleasant) will not be repeated. The law of effect applies broadly, not just to cats. When was the last time your behavior changed as a result of a pleasurable outcome?

Most contemporary psychologists would call the pieces of fish in Thorndike's experiments **reinforcers,** because these treats increased the likelihood that the preceding behavior (escaping the cage) would occur again. Reinforcers are events or stimuli that follow behaviors, and they increase the chances of those behaviors being repeated. Examples of reinforcers that might impact human behavior include praise, hugs, good grades, enjoyable food, and attention. Through the process of **reinforcement,** target behaviors become more frequent. A dog given a treat for sitting is more likely to obey the "sit" command in the future. An Instagram user who is reinforced with a lot of "likes" is more inclined to continue posting photos and videos.

SKINNER AND BEHAVIORISM Reinforcers are a key component of **operant conditioning,** a type of learning whereby people or animals come to associate their voluntary actions with consequences. B. F. Skinner coined the term *operant conditioning,* and its meaning is fairly simple. The term operant "emphasizes the fact that the behavior *operates* on the environment to generate consequences" and in "operant conditioning we 'strengthen' an operant in the sense of making a response more probable . . . or more frequent" (Skinner, 1953, p. 65). Some of the earliest and most influential research on operant conditioning came from Skinner's lab. His research followed the principles of *behaviorism,* the scientific study of observable behavior. Behaviorists believe that psychology can only be considered a "true science" if it restricts itself to the study of behaviors that can be seen and documented. And although mental processes such as memory and emotion may not be observable, Skinner and other behaviorists have proposed that all behaviors, thoughts, and emotions are shaped by factors in the external environment. In other words, they are learned.

law of effect Thorndike's principle stating that behaviors are more likely to be repeated when followed by pleasurable outcomes, and less likely to be repeated when followed by unpleasant outcomes.

reinforcers Events, stimuli, and other consequences that increase the likelihood of a behavior reoccurring.

reinforcement Process of increasing the frequency of behaviors with consequences.

operant conditioning Learning that occurs when voluntary actions become associated with their consequences.

Trouble with the Moos
Cesar works with the three bichons frises owned by Takis Stathoulis and his wife Joanne. The dogs were notorious for their obnoxious barking and hyperactivity. Takis unwittingly reinforced their bad behaviors with his approving body language and verbal feedback (Furtado, 2014).

REINFORCING BAD BEHAVIOR Have you ever wondered why some dogs are annoyingly hyper? You know, the ones who greet you on their hind legs, jumping and pawing as they pant and slobber in your face. Most dogs that act this way are not getting enough exercise (Millan, 2013). But other factors, including misdirected reinforcement, can contribute to the problem as well.

Consider the case of Takis Stathoulis and his three fluffy white bichons frises, who appeared in the first season of *Cesar 911.* The three little fluffballs, collectively known as "The Moos," were extremely loud and high-strung. Every time Takis walked into the restaurant he owns (Frisco's in Long Beach, California), the Moos would accost customers and bark in their faces. Takis did nothing to stop them; actually, he reinforced their behaviors by smiling, patting them, and emanating the same type of boisterous energy (Furtado, 2014). "Dog lovers, they have a tendency to reinforce excited behavior," explains Cesar, "and that's where it gets tricky." Here, we see how reinforcement can perpetuate undesirable behaviors.

Types of Reinforcement

Like most people who have achieved a high level of success and fame, Cesar has accumulated a fair number of critics. They question his "antiquated view of dominance hierarchies," suggesting that his discipline-before-affection approach is misguided (Derr, 2016, March 9, para. 2), and contend that his self-taught approach "ignores 80 years of research in animal behavior" (Breeden, n.d., para 35). Some claim he is too physical with the animals, forcing them into submission with vibrating collars and foot taps to the area above the hind leg (Grossman, 2012, June 9; Hanna, 2012, October 27). Cesar has defended himself by saying he reserves these techniques for "red zone" dogs—those that pose a threat to other animals and/or people and therefore may be at risk for being euthanized. "My mission has always been to save dogs—especially troubled and abandoned dogs," he said in an interview with the *Daily Mail.* "I've dedicated my life to this" (Barber, 2012, October 27, para. 4).

We are not interested in taking sides here, but it is surprising how little attention Cesar receives for using nonforceful approaches. Watch Cesar closely, and you'll see that he employs quite a bit of *positive reinforcement.*

You Asked, Cesar Answers

http://qrs.ly/la78291

Can some of your techniques be used on humans?

LO 8 Explain how positive and negative reinforcement differ.

POSITIVE REINFORCEMENT Earlier, we explained that a reinforcer is a consequence that increases the likelihood of a behavior being repeated. *Any* stimulus, pleasant or unpleasant, is considered a reinforcer if it eventually increases the behavior that immediately precedes it. In the process of **positive reinforcement,** reinforcers are presented (added) following the target behavior, and they are generally pleasant (**Infographic 5.2** on page 180). The fish treats that Thorndike's cats received for escaping the puzzle box were positive reinforcers. They were pleasurable; they were added following the desired behavior; and they increased the frequency of that desired behavior.

What reinforcers does Cesar employ in dog rehabilitation? Sometimes it's not as obvious as a dog biscuit or bone. Before giving reinforcement, Cesar explains, you have to help your dog feel calm and happy, and that requires exercise and mental stimulation. Once the dog reaches that relaxed state, you can reinforce it with affection. For some dogs, playtime

positive reinforcement The process by which reinforcers are added or presented following a target behavior, increasing the likelihood of it occurring again.

is a powerful positive reinforcer. Remember Gavin, the ATF agent with the classically conditioned response to certain noises? After Gavin completed his sessions in the virtual reality environment, Cesar would reward him with "a vigorous play period," which often meant a dip in the pool (Millan & Peltier, 2010, p. 63).

Dogs offer positive reinforcement to humans as well; you just have to be perceptive enough to notice. Consider this example from Cesar: "Your dog wants to go outside and pee. He sits by the door. You open the door. The dog walks out, but as he passes by you, he looks up at you for a moment and makes eye contact. He just rewarded you" (Millan & Peltier, 2010, p. 121). Why is eye contact reinforcing? When you gaze into your dog's eyes, both you and the dog experience a release of the hormone *oxytocin,* which plays a key role in social bonding. Oxytocin increases "social reward" and enhances attachment between infants and their mothers, and between sexual partners. Eye contact is just one way dogs and humans have established mutually reinforcing relationships during the course of evolution (MacLean & Hare, 2015; Nagasawa et al., 2015).

But take note: Not all positive reinforcers are pleasant. In this case, "positive" means that something has been added. For example, if a child is starved for attention, then any kind of attention (including a reprimand) might act as a positive reinforcer. Every time the child misbehaves, she gets reprimanded, and reprimanding is a form of attention, which the child craves. The addition of this seemingly unpleasant stimulus increases the likelihood of the misbehavior occurring again. Thus, it serves as a positive reinforcer.

Reinforced Through Social Media Healthy living apps such as MyFitnessPal and PumpUp enable users to share their exercise accomplishments and get feedback from friends and family members. Can the reinforcing power of social media be harnessed to promote exercise and other health-related behaviors, such as HIV testing and responsible use of prescription drugs? Studies have yielded promising results, but further research is needed (Centola, 2010; Maher et al., 2014; Smith, 2016; July 13). Courtesy Jack Stone.

NEGATIVE REINFORCEMENT We have now learned that behaviors can be increased or strengthened by the addition of a stimulus (positive reinforcement). We can also increase a behavior through **negative reinforcement**, or removing something unpleasant immediately following a behavior. Skinner demonstrated how negative reinforcement could be used to influence the behavior of rats. He placed them in special cages with floors that delivered a continuous mild electric current—except when they pushed on a lever. At the start of the experiment, the animals would scamper around the floors to escape the electric current, but every once in a while, they would accidentally hit the lever and turn it off. Eventually, they learned to associate pushing the lever with the removal of the unpleasant stimulus (a mild shock). After several trials, the rats would push the lever immediately, reducing the amount of time they were exposed to the current.

synonyms

negative reinforcement omission training

Think about some examples of negative reinforcement in your own life. Have you ever started driving before putting on your seat belt? If so, you likely heard an annoying beeping sound. In order to stop the beeping (an unpleasant stimulus), you buckle up (the desired behavior). Automakers have cleverly used negative reinforcement to increase seat belt use. We are more inclined to buckle up right away (an increase in the desired behavior) because we have learned that it stops the beeping. Another example is giving in to a dog that constantly begs for treats. The begging (an unpleasant stimulus) stops the moment the dog is given a treat, a pattern that increases your treat-giving behavior. Meanwhile, the dog's begging behavior is being strengthened through positive reinforcement; the dog has learned that the more it begs, the more treats it receives.

Notice that with negative reinforcement, the desired behaviors increase in order to remove an unwanted stimulus. Let's say a dog is barking on and off all day—an undesirable sound for most owners and any neighbors within earshot. If the dog is a high-energy Australian shepherd whose biggest need is exercise, then the owner would be wise to take her dog for a spin around the park. In doing so, she performs a desired behavior herself (walking for exercise). The removal of the annoying stimulus (dog barking) increases a desirable behavior in the owner (exercising). Thus, the owner's exercise is negatively reinforced by the removal of the dog's barking. Keep in mind that the goal of positive *and* negative reinforcement is to increase a desired behavior.

negative reinforcement The removal of an unpleasant stimulus following a target behavior, which increases the likelihood of it occurring again.

Put Your Heads Together

Imagine you have an elderly relative who is hard-of-hearing, but won't admit it. Team up with classmates and **A)** design a positive reinforcement system to encourage him to use hearing aids, and **B)** explain how you could use negative reinforcement to increase this behavior.

LO 9 Distinguish between primary and secondary reinforcers.

PRIMARY AND SECONDARY REINFORCERS There are two major categories of reinforcers: primary and secondary. The food Thorndike used to reward his cats is considered a **primary reinforcer,** because it satisfies a biological need. Food, water, and physical contact are considered primary reinforcers (for both animals and people) because they meet essential requirements. **Secondary reinforcers** do not satisfy biological needs, but often derive their power from their connection with primary reinforcers. Although money is not a primary reinforcer, we know from experience that it gives us access to primary reinforcers, such as food and a safe place to live. Thus, money is a secondary reinforcer. Good grades might also be considered secondary reinforcers, because doing well in school leads to job opportunities, which provide money to pay for food and other necessities.

You might think that animals would always favor primary reinforcers over secondary reinforcers, but this is not necessarily true. In one small study, researchers found evidence that many dogs prefer praise and affection (secondary reinforcers) over food rewards (primary reinforcers). "For most dogs, social reinforcement is at least as effective as food—and probably healthier too" (Cook, Prichard, Spivak, & Berns, 2016, p. 1860).

"Trophy Culture?"
In decades past, trophies and medals were only awarded to top teams and players. These days, everyone is a winner, as children often receive these rewards for simply participating. Some people claim that "participation trophies" fail to prepare kids for today's competitive world and send the wrong message: "Losing is okay" (Berdan, 2016, October 6; Flaherty, 2017, May 27). Others value the idea of reinforcing children for their effort, regardless of how skilled or successful they may be (Powers, 2015, August 28).
Rana Faure/Getty Images.

Shaping and Successive Approximations

LO 10 Explain shaping and the method of successive approximations.

Using reinforcers and building on the work of Thorndike and Watson, Skinner demonstrated, among other things, that rats can learn to push levers and pigeons can learn to bowl (Peterson, 2004). Animals cannot immediately perform such complex tasks, but they can learn through **successive approximations,** the use of reinforcers to change behaviors through small steps toward a desired behavior (see Infographic 5.2). In the photo on page 176, you can see that Skinner placed animals in chambers, or ***Skinner boxes,*** which could be outfitted with food dispensers the animals could activate (by pecking a target or pushing on a lever, for instance) and recording equipment to monitor these behaviors. Such boxes allowed Skinner to conduct carefully controlled experiments, measuring activity with precision and advancing the scientific and systematic study of behavior.

Some of Skinner's most incredible results occurred through **shaping,** a process in which a person observes the behaviors of another organism (an animal, for example) and provides reinforcers if the organism performs at a required level (Peterson, 2000). Through shaping by successive approximations, Skinner taught a rat to "play basketball" (dropping a marble through a hole) and pigeons to "bowl" (nudging a ball down a miniature alley).

Let's nail down this concept using the bowling pigeons example. Skinner's first task was to break the bowling lessons into activities the birds could accomplish. Next, he began delivering reinforcers (usually food) for behaviors that came closer and closer to achieving the desired goal—bowling a strike! Choosing the right increments for the behaviors was crucial. If his expectations started too high, the pigeons would never receive

synonyms

secondary reinforcers conditioned reinforcers

Skinner boxes operant chambers

primary reinforcer A reinforcer that satisfies a biological need; innate reinforcer.

secondary reinforcer Reinforcers that do not satisfy biological needs but often gain power through their association with primary reinforcers.

successive approximations A method that uses reinforcers to condition a series of small steps that gradually approach the target behavior.

shaping Process by which a person observes the behaviors of another organism, providing reinforcers if the organism performs at a required level.

Learning Through Operant Conditioning

Operant conditioning is a type of learning in which we associate our voluntary actions with the consequences of those actions. For example, a pigeon naturally pecks things. But if every time the pigeon pecks a ball, it is given a *reinforcer,* the pigeon will soon learn to peck the ball more frequently.

B. F. Skinner showed that operant conditioning could do more than elicit simple, isolated actions. He taught pigeons to "bowl" and play "tennis" with the help of *shaping*; that is, he observed their behaviors and provided reinforcers when they performed at a required level. Today, shaping is used routinely by parents, teachers, coaches, and employers to train all kinds of complex behaviors.

SKINNER'S EXPERIMENT: TRAIN A PIGEON TO PLAY TENNIS

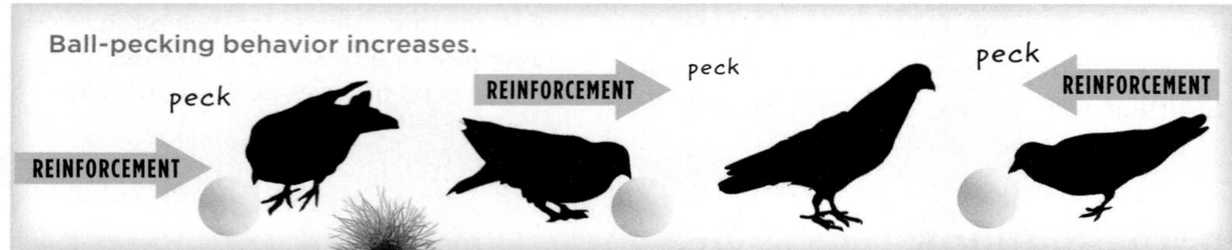

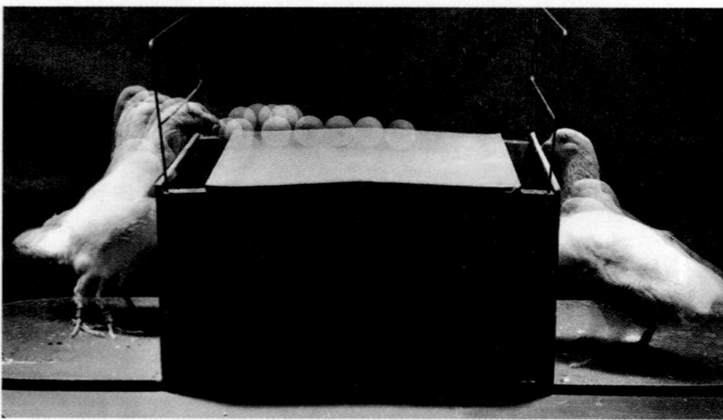

After behavior has been shaped through reinforcement, the pigeon has learned to play tennis.

HAVE YOU BEEN TRAINED?

Not every child is born loving the healthy foods his parent offers. But shaping can help a child learn to eat his vegetables. Over a period of time, reinforcement is given for behaviors that are closer and closer to this goal. Can you think of anything that would be a reward for eating vegetables? Praise or the excitement of a contest may work in this way.

1
Child refuses to eat vegetables.
2
YES!
Reinforced for touching fork
3
GOOD JOB!
Now, reinforced for touching vegetables
4
After behavior has been shaped through reinforcement, the child has learned to eat his vegetables.

Credits: Collection of four raw grains (broomcorn millet, wheat, rye, and sunflower seeds), Le Do/Shutterstock; Gray dove on a white background, photomaster/Shutterstock; Ping pong, Africa Studio/Shutterstock; Greek salad, Shutterstock; Boy with salad, istock/Thinkstock; Two pigeons play a version of ping pong, Yale Joel/Time & Life Pictures/

any reinforcers. If his expectations were too low, the pigeons would get reinforcers for everything they did. Either way, they would be unable to make the critical connection between the desired behavior and the reward. Every time the animals did something that brought them a step closer to completing the desired behavior, they would get a reinforcer. The first reward might be given for simply looking at the ball; the second, for bending down and touching it; and the third, for nudging the ball with their beaks. By the end of the experiment, the pigeons were driving balls down miniature alleys, knocking down pins with a swipe of the beak (Peterson, 2004).

It is amazing that pigeons can learn to bowl with reinforcement! Is there anything operant conditioning can't accomplish?

THINK CRITICALLY

CHICKENS CAN'T PLAY BASEBALL Rats can be conditioned to press levers; pigeons can be trained to bowl; and—believe it or not—chickens can learn to dance and play the piano (Breland & Breland, 1951). Keller Breland (1915–1965) and Marian Breland (1920–2001), a pair of Skinner's students, managed to train 6,000 animals not only to boogie but also to vacuum, dine at a table, and play sports and musical instruments (Breland & Breland, 1961). But as hard as they tried, the Brelands could not coax a chicken to play baseball.

BASEBALL? NO. PIANO? YES.

Here's what happened: The Brelands placed a chicken in a cage next to a scaled down "baseball field," where it had access to a loop attached to a baseball bat. With a forceful yank of the loop, the chicken might swing the bat hard enough to send the ball into the outfield, causing a food reward to be delivered at the other end of the cage. Off the bird would go, running toward its meal dispenser like a baseball player sprinting to first base—or so the routine was supposed to go. But as soon as the Brelands took away the cage, the chicken behaved nothing like a baseball player; instead, it madly chased and pecked at the ball (Breland & Breland, 1961).

How did the Brelands explain the chicken's behavior? They believed that the birds were demonstrating **instinctive drift,** the tendency for instinct to undermine conditioned behaviors. A chicken's pecking, for example, is an instinctive food-getting behavior. Although it's useful for opening seeds and killing insects (Breland & Breland, 1961), pecking won't help the bird get to first base. Animal behavior can be shaped by forces in the environment (nurture), but instinct (nature) may interfere with the process. 

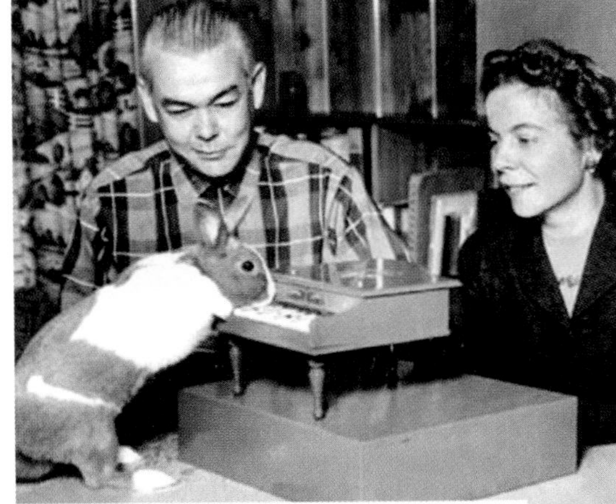

Musical Bunny
Keller and Marian Breland observe one of their animal performers at the IQ Zoo in Hot Springs, Arkansas, circa 1960. Using the operant conditioning concepts they learned from B. F. Skinner, the Brelands trained ducks to play guitars, raccoons to shoot basketballs, and chickens to tell fortunes. But their animal "students" did not always cooperate; sometimes their instincts interfered with the conditioning process (Bihm, Gillaspy, Lammers, & Huffman, 2010). The Central Arkansas Library System/Courtesy of Bob Bailey.

Continuous or Partial?

Now that we have a basic understanding of what reinforcement can—and cannot—accomplish, let's explore the various ways it can be delivered.

LO 11 Describe continuous reinforcement and partial reinforcement.

CONTINUOUS REINFORCEMENT When it comes to teaching new behaviors to dogs, people, and other organisms, most psychologists would agree that positive reinforcement is extremely effective. Let's say you are teaching a puppy to "sit." You begin the process by giving her a treat every time she obeys the "sit" command. Rewarding the pup in this manner is called **continuous reinforcement,** because the reinforcer is presented every time the desired behavior occurs. Continuous reinforcement can be used in a variety of settings: a child getting praise every time he does the dishes; a salesperson receiving a bonus every time she makes a sale. You get the commonality: reinforcement every time the behavior occurs.

instinctive drift The tendency for animals to revert to instinctual behaviors after a behavior pattern has been learned.

continuous reinforcement A schedule of reinforcement in which every target behavior is reinforced.

PARTIAL REINFORCEMENT Continuous reinforcement is ideal for establishing new behaviors during the acquisition phase, but delivering reinforcers intermittently generally works better for maintaining behaviors. We call this approach **partial reinforcement.**

synonyms
partial reinforcement intermittent reinforcement

As often occurs in scientific research, Skinner stumbled on this idea by chance. Late one Friday afternoon, Skinner realized he was running low on the food pellets he used as reinforcers for his laboratory animals. If he continued rewarding the animals on a continuous basis, the pellets would run out before the end of the weekend. So, he decided only to reinforce some of the desired behaviors (Skinner, 1956, 1976). The new strategy worked like a charm. The animals kept performing the desired behaviors, even though they weren't given reinforcers every time.

Earlier we offered examples of continuous reinforcement, but we could also apply partial reinforcement in these scenarios: A dog receives a treat every other time it sits on command; a child is praised for doing the dishes only once in a while; and a salesperson gets a bonus for every third sale. The reinforcer is not given every time the behavior is observed, only on some occasions.

"Uber" Reinforcemnt
Why do so many Uber drivers work painfully long shifts? Partial reinforcement may be driving their behavior. With fares constantly fluctuating, drivers can never be certain when they are going to meet their earnings goals. Eventually, they will reach a certain target; it's just not clear when (Shahani, 2017, June 9).
QUIQUE GARCIA/Getty Images.

The amazing thing about partial reinforcement is that it happens to all of us, in an infinite number of settings, and we might never know how many times we have been partially reinforced for any particular behavior. Common to all these partial reinforcement situations is that the target behavior is exhibited, but the reinforcer is not supplied each time it occurs.

PARTIAL REINFORCEMENT EFFECT Behaviors acquired or maintained through partial, rather than continuous, reinforcement are often resistant to extinction. Psychologists call this phenomenon the **partial reinforcement effect.** When Skinner's pigeons learned to peck at a target through partial reinforcement, they would repeat this behavior up to 10,000 times without receiving any food (Skinner, 1953). According to Skinner, "Nothing of this sort is ever obtained after continuous reinforcement" (p. 99). The same seems to be true with humans. In one study from the mid-1950s, researchers observed college students playing slot machines. Some of the slot machines provided continuous reinforcement, delivering pretend coins every time students pulled their levers. Other slot machines provided partial reinforcement, dispensing coins only some of the time. After the students played eight rounds, all the machines stopped giving coins. Without any coins to reinforce them, the students stopped pulling the levers—but not at the same time. Those who had received coins with every lever pull gave up more quickly than did those rewarded intermittently. In other words, lever-pulling behavior took longer to extinguish when established through partial reinforcement (Lewis & Duncan, 1956).

Timing Is Everything: Reinforcement Schedules

Name the schedules of reinforcement and give examples of each.

Skinner identified various ways to administer partial reinforcement, or *partial reinforcement schedules*. Skinner used four schedules of partial reinforcement: fixed-ratio, variable-ratio, fixed-interval, and variable-interval (**Infographic 5.3** on page 184).

FIXED-RATIO SCHEDULE If reinforcement is delivered in a **fixed-ratio schedule,** the subject must exhibit a preset number of desired responses or behaviors before a reinforcer is given. A pigeon in a Skinner box, for example, must peck a spot five times in order to score a delicious pellet. Generally, the fixed-ratio schedule produces a high response rate, but with a characteristic dip immediately following the reinforcement. (The pigeons rest briefly after being reinforced.) Some instructors use the fixed-ratio

partial reinforcement A schedule of reinforcement in which target behaviors are reinforced intermittently, not continuously.

partial reinforcement effect The tendency for behaviors acquired through intermittent reinforcement to be more resistant to extinction than those acquired through continuous reinforcement.

fixed-ratio schedule A schedule in which the subject must exhibit a predetermined number of desired behaviors before a reinforcer is given.

schedule to reinforce attendance. For example, treats are provided when all students show up on time for three classes in a row.

VARIABLE-RATIO SCHEDULE In a **variable-ratio schedule,** the subject must exhibit a specific number of desired responses or behaviors before a reinforcer is given, but the number changes across trials (fluctuating around a precalculated average). If the goal is to train a pigeon to peck a spot on a target, a variable-ratio schedule could be used as follows: Trial 1, the pigeon gets a pellet after pecking the spot twice; Trial 2, the pigeon gets a pellet after pecking the spot once; Trial 3, the pigeon gets a pellet after pecking the spot three times; and so on. Here's another example: To encourage on-time attendance, an instructor provides treats after several classes in a row, but students don't know if it will be on the third class, the second class, or the fifth class. This variable-ratio schedule tends to produce a high response rate. And because of its unpredictability, this schedule tends to establish behaviors that are difficult to extinguish.

FIXED-INTERVAL SCHEDULE Sometimes it's important to focus on the interval of time between reinforcers, rather than the number of desired responses. In a **fixed-interval schedule,** a reinforcer is given for the first target behavior occurring after a specific time interval. If a pigeon is on a fixed-interval schedule of 30 seconds, it can peck away at the target once the interval starts, but it will only get a reinforcer following its first response after the 30 seconds have ended. With this schedule, the target behavior tends to increase as each time interval comes to an end. The pigeon pecks the spot more often when the time nears 30 seconds. Do you want to increase your focus while studying? Reinforce yourself with a treat after each hour you work without digital distractions.

VARIABLE-INTERVAL SCHEDULE In a **variable-interval schedule,** the reinforcer comes after an unpredictable period of time has passed. Training a pigeon to peck a target on this schedule might look something like this: Trial 1, the pigeon gets a pellet after 41 seconds; Trial 2, the pigeon gets a pellet after 43 seconds; Trial 3, the pigeon gets a pellet after 40 seconds; and so on. As with the fixed-interval schedule, the pigeon is rewarded for the first response it makes after the time interval has passed (but in this case, the length varies from trial to trial). The variable-interval schedule tends to encourage steady patterns of behavior. Want to increase your study group's focus? Reinforce them with a treat following 45 minutes of steady work, and then maybe another treat after 30 minutes. Keep them guessing!

Put Your Heads Together

Imagine you are teaching math to seventh-grade students. In your groups, **A**) explain how you would use each of the four reinforcement schedules to increase the time students study for quizzes; **B**) describe how each schedule might affect student behavior; and **C**) predict the problems that could arise with each schedule.

So far, we have learned about increasing behaviors through reinforcement, but sometimes we need to *decrease* behaviors. Let's turn our attention to techniques used for this purpose.

In the Doghouse: Punishment

In contrast to reinforcement, which makes a behavior more likely to recur, the goal of **punishment** is to decrease or stop a behavior. Punishment works by instilling an association between a behavior and some unwanted consequence

variable-ratio schedule A schedule in which the number of desired behaviors that must occur before a reinforcer is given changes across trials and is based on an average number of behaviors to be reinforced.

fixed-interval schedule A schedule in which the reinforcer comes after a preestablished interval of time; the behavior is only reinforced after the given interval is over.

variable-interval schedule A schedule in which a behavior is reinforced after an interval of time, but the length of the interval changes from trial to trial.

punishment The application of a consequence that decreases the likelihood of a behavior recurring.

Schedules of Reinforcement

Continuous reinforcement is ideal for establishing new behaviors. But once learned, a behavior is best maintained through partial reinforcement. Partial reinforcement can be delivered according to four schedules: fixed-ratio, variable-ratio, fixed-interval and variable-interval.

TIMING IS EVERYTHING

Fixed-Ratio
Subject must exhibit a predetermined number of desired responses before a reinforcer is given.

Variable-Ratio

peck peck peck — reinforcement with food pellet on 3rd peck — REINFORCEMENT

peck peck peck peck peck peck peck peck — reinforcement with food pellet on 8th peck — REINFORCEMENT

peck peck peck peck — reinforcement with food pellet on 4th peck — REINFORCEMENT

Variable-Ratio
Reinforcement is unpredictable, that is, the number of desired responses that must occur before a reinforcer is given changes across trials and is based on an average number of responses to be reinforced.

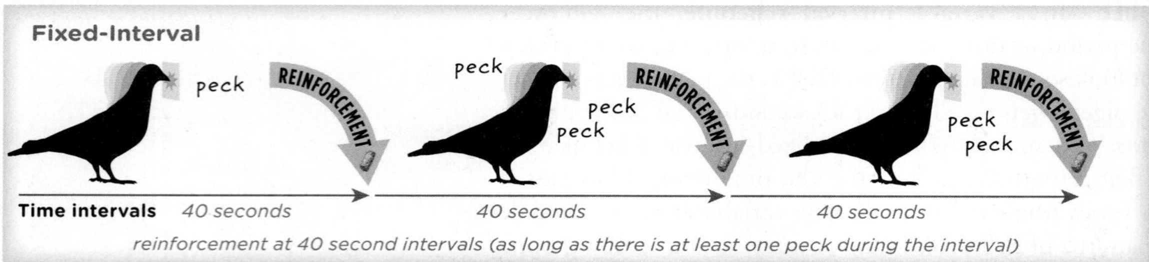

Fixed-Interval
The reinforcer comes after a preestablished interval of time; the target response is only reinforced after the given time period is over.

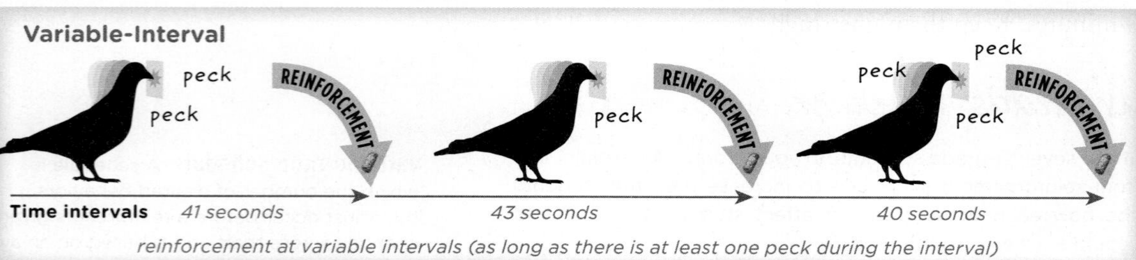

Variable-Interval
Reinforcement follows the first target response after the time interval has elapsed. The length of the time interval changes from trial to trial.

Credits: Pigeon in clock, nilovsergey/Shutterstock; Clock, Bildagentur Zoonar GmbH/Shutterstock.

Which schedule of reinforcement matches each of the following examples? Choose from **fixed-ratio**, **variable-ratio**, **fixed-interval**, and **variable-interval**.

1. Checking the clock more frequently as the time for your favorite television show approaches is an example of______________.
2. You listen intently to your favorite radio show because they will randomly select times throughout the day for listeners to call in to win free tickets to a concert. This is an example of______________.
3. Finding it difficult to walk away from the slot machine because you think the next pull will be a winner is an example of______________.
4. You consistently submit your chapter summaries to your instructor because you can earn 5 points for every 4 summaries submitted. This is an example of______________.

Answers 1. fixed-interval, 2. variable-interval, 3. variable-ratio, 4. fixed-ratio (for example, between stealing and jail, or misbehaving and loss of screen time). Punishment isn't always effective, as people are sometimes willing to accept unpleasant consequences to get something they really want.

WHAT KIND OF PUNISHMENT? There are two major categories of punishment: positive and negative (**INFOGRAPHIC 5.4** on page 187). With **positive punishment,** something aversive or disagreeable is applied following a certain behavior. For example, getting a traffic ticket for rolling through a stop sign is a positive punishment. The unpleasant experience of getting a citation tends to decrease your behavior of running the stop sign.

Negative punishment also aims to reduce behaviors, but it involves taking away something pleasant or valuable. People who drive drunk run the risk of negative punishment, as their driver's license may be taken away. Show up late for class, and you may suffer the negative punishment of missing that day's lecture altogether, as many instructors lock the door at the beginning of class. Their goal is to decrease the unwanted behavior of arriving late.

Think about the last time you tried using punishment to reduce unwanted behavior. Perhaps you scolded your cat for jumping on the counter, or ignored a friend when she let you down. If you are a parent or caregiver of a young child, you may have tried to reign in misbehavior with various types of punishment—taking away toys, screen time, or dessert, or perhaps giving a time out. Some parents use a controversial form of positive punishment known as spanking.

WHAT SCIENCE REALLY SAYS ABOUT SPANKING

From the SCIENTIFIC AMERICAN pages of

Does this punishment cause behavioral problems, or are troubled kids more likely to be spanked?

To spank or not to spank? This age-old parenting question elicits fierce debate among parents, psychologists and pediatricians. Surveys suggest that nearly half of U.S. parents have spanked their children as a disciplinary tactic, but many experts argue that this form of punishment—hitting a child on the bottom with an open hand—increases the risk that kids will develop emotional and behavioral problems. Other scientists counter that research on the issue is fraught with problems, making it impossible to draw definitive conclusions. A new meta-analysis speaks to several of the most contentious points in the debate and concludes that spanking does pose risks, but differences of opinion persist.

In the meta-analysis, researchers Elizabeth Gershoff and Andrew Grogan-Kaylor of the University of Texas at Austin and the University of Michigan, respectively, evaluated 75 published studies on the relation between spanking by parents and various behavioral, emotional, cognitive and physical outcomes among their kids. They found that spanking was associated with 13 out of a total of 17 negative outcomes they assessed, including increased aggression, behavioral and mental health problems, and reduced cognitive ability and self-esteem.

This was not simply an attempt to synthesize studies—Gershoff and Grogan-Kaylor also wanted to address two concerns often raised about the body of research linking spanking to childhood problems. The first is that much of it has evaluated the effects of physical punishment in general, without homing in on the effects of spanking specifically—and because physical punishment can include tactics such as hitting with objects, pinching and biting, this "lumping problem" may ultimately exaggerate spanking's risks. The second concern is that many published studies are "cross sectional," which means that they evaluate the effects of spanking by collecting data at a single point in time, making determinations of cause and effect difficult.

positive punishment The addition of something unpleasant following an unwanted behavior, with the intention of decreasing that behavior.

negative punishment The removal of something desirable following an unwanted behavior, with the intention of decreasing that behavior.

Time-Out
Sending a child to a corner for a "time-out" is an example of negative punishment because it involves removing something (the privilege to play) in order to decrease a behavior. Some experts advise against time-outs, saying that it makes children feel rejected, angry, and ashamed at a time when they really need help finding constructive ways to deal with a problem (Coulson, 2016, October 20; Lamia, 2016, June 25). Other psychologists contend that a blanket ban of time-outs is not the best approach for defiant toddlers, who can benefit from both reasoning and occasional time-outs or time-out forewarnings (Larzelere, 2016, October 31). RonTech2000/Getty Images.

A cross-sectional study might, for instance, find that aggressive 10-year-olds were more likely than docile 10-year-olds to have been spanked as toddlers, but that does not mean that spanking made them aggressive. They may have been spanked because they were acting out back then, too.

To confront these issues, Gershoff and Grogan-Kaylor did several things. First, they limited their meta-analysis to studies that evaluated the effects of spanking, slapping and hitting children without the use of objects and found that spanking is still associated with negative outcomes. They also compared the results from cross-sectional studies with results from longitudinal studies, which track the kids' behavior over time and are better able to tease out cause and effect. Gershoff and Grogan-Kaylor found that spanking is associated with negative outcomes in both types of studies, which strengthens the argument that spanking poses risks.

Yet some researchers remain skeptical. Studies suggest, for instance, that the effects of spanking can differ depending on the circumstances. Two studies have found no associations between spanking and mental health problems among kids who were spanked less than once or twice a month; other research has shown that spanking has much less of a negative effect on preschool kids than on infants and adolescents. So the conclusion from the meta-analysis that spanking itself is dangerous might be overly simplistic. "I think it's irresponsible to make exclusive statements one way or another," says Christopher Ferguson, a psychologist at Stetson University in Florida.

And then there is the chicken-or-egg question: Are kids spanked because they act out, or do they act out because they are spanked—or both? Ferguson tried to control for the effects of preexisting child behavior in a 2013 meta-analysis he published of the longitudinal studies on this issue; when he did, the relation between spanking and mental health problems was much smaller than it had appeared without these controls in place. As a further demonstration of the importance of careful statistical controls, Robert Larzelere, a psychologist at Oklahoma State University, and his colleagues reported in a 2010 study that grounding and also psychotherapy are linked just as strongly to bad behavior as spanking is but that all the associations disappear once controls are used.

Still, a number of individual studies have found associations between spanking and negative outcomes, even after controlling for preexisting behaviors. Thus, Gershoff says that in spite of the lingering controversy, the safest approach parents can take is not to spank their kids. "Studies continue to find that spanking predicts negative behavior changes—there are no studies showing that kids improve," she says. In other words, not a shred of data suggests spanking actually helps kids become better adjusted—and with the large body of work suggesting it might do harm, why take the chance? **Melinda Wenner Moyer. Reproduced with permission.**

Put Your Heads Together

There are now 52 countries that ban spanking and other forms of corporal (physical) punishment of children (Global Initiative to End All Corporal Punishment of Children, n.d.). In your groups, **A**) discuss whether the United States should follow suit, and **B**) provide evidence to support your position.

Learning: Punishment and Reinforcement

Behavior: *Driving Fast*

Do you want to increase this behavior?

YES!
It's Nascar! You have to drive faster than anyone else to win.
We will apply a reinforcer to **increase** the behavior.

Negative Reinforcement

You don't like working in the family auto-body shop. Your family says you can work fewer hours if you win the next race. **Taking away** unwanted work increases the speeding behavior.

Positive Reinforcement

You win a trophy and a cash prize for going fast at the race. **Adding** desirable rewards increases your speeding behavior.

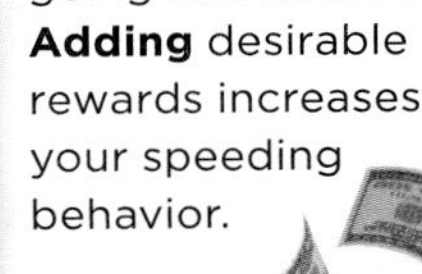

NO!
We're not at the racetrack! Speeding is dangerous and against the law.
We will apply a punishment to **decrease** the behavior.

Negative Punishment

The police officer confiscates your license. **Taking away** something desirable decreases your speeding behavior.

Positive Punishment

The police officer gives you a citation. **Adding** something undesirable decreases your speeding behavior.

Which process matches each of the following examples?
Choose from **positive reinforcement**, **negative reinforcement**, **positive punishment**, and **negative punishment**.

1. Carlos' parents grounded him the last time he stayed out past his curfew, so tonight he came home right on time.
2. Jinhee spent an entire week helping an elderly neighbor clean out her basement after a flood. The local newspaper caught wind of the story and ran it as an inspiring front-page headline. Jinhee enjoyed the attention and decided to organize a neighborhood work group.
3. The trash stinks, so Sheri takes it out.
4. Gabriel's assistant had a bad habit of showing up late for work, so Gabriel docked his pay.
5. During food drives, the basketball team offers to wash your car for free if you donate six items or more to the local homeless shelter.
6. Claire received a stern lecture for texting in class. She doesn't want to hear that again, so now she turns off her phone when she enters the classroom.

Answers 1. negative punishment, 2. positive reinforcement, 3. negative reinforcement, 4. negative punishment, 5. positive reinforcement, 6. positive punishment

Credits: Red and green sports cars, lenka/Fotolia LLC; Police officer writing a ticket, © Lisa F. Young - Fotolia.com; Flags, freesoulproduction/Shutterstock; Green Traffic Light, Thinkstock; Red Traffic Light, Thinkstock; Wrench, Thinkstock; Green highway sign isolated, Thinkstock; Speed limit road sign with post and different numbers, © Thomaspajot/Dreamstime.com; Red flashing light on a white background, © Fotovika/Dreamstime.com; Trophy, Stockbyte/Thinkstock; Falling money, istockphoto/Thinkstock; Vector design set of racing flags, freesoulproduction/Shutterstock.

LO 13 Explain how punishment differs from reinforcement.

PUNISHMENT VERSUS REINFORCEMENT Punishment and reinforcement are two concepts that students often find difficult to distinguish (**Table 5.3**; also see Infographic 5.4). Remember that punishment (positive or negative) is designed to decrease the behavior that it follows, whereas reinforcement (positive or negative) aims to increase the behavior. If all the positives and negatives are confusing you, just think in terms of math: Positive always means adding something, and negative means taking it away. Punishment can be positive, which means the addition of something viewed as unpleasant ("Because you made a mess of your room, you have to clean the toilets!"), or negative, which involves the removal of something viewed as pleasant or valuable ("Because you made a mess of your room, no ice cream for you!").

CAREER CONNECTIONS

REINFORCEMENT IS GOLDEN Reinforcement is one of the most effective ways to change behaviors, but many people fail to take full advantage of its power. Would you believe that 37% of business managers report that they *never* offer positive reinforcement? Yet this type of input is key to maintaining good work relationships. Managers who offer positive reinforcement are actually perceived as more effective than those who offer mere criticism (Zenger & Folkman, 2017, May 2). What's more, workers tend to be more engaged when supervisors emphasize their strengths rather than homing in on their weaknesses (Fessler, 2017, June 22; Harter, & Adkinds, 2015, April 8).

EFFECTIVE MANAGERS USE POSITIVE REINFORCEMENT

Put Your Heads Together

In your current or past jobs, you have probably offered feedback to colleagues or received it from your boss. In your groups, **A**) discuss some scenarios in which you were compelled to give constructive feedback to a colleague who was struggling to learn a new skill, or **B**) describe a situation when you were the recipient of such input. Was the feedback well received? Was it effective? Which type of feedback was most effective? Why?

TABLE 5.3 REINFORCEMENT VERSUS PUNISHMENT

Term	Defined	Goal	Example
Positive reinforcement	Addition of a pleasant stimulus following a target behavior	Increase desired behavior	Students who complete an online course 15 days before the end of semester receive 10 points of extra credit.
Negative reinforcement	Removal of an unpleasant stimulus following a target behavior	Increase desired behavior	Students with perfect attendance do not have to take weekly quizzes.
Positive punishment	Addition of something unpleasant following an unwanted behavior	Decrease undesired behavior	Students who are late to class more than two times have to write an extra paper.
Negative punishment	Removal of something pleasant following an unwanted behavior	Decrease undesired behavior	Students late to class on exam day are not allowed to use their notes when taking the exam.

The positive and negative forms of reinforcement and punishment are easy to confuse. Here are some concrete definitions, goals, and examples to help you sort them out.

Let's Compare

Operant and classical conditioning share many common principles (**Table 5.4**). For example, both types of learning involve forming associations: In classical conditioning, the learner links different stimuli; in operant conditioning, the learner connects behavior to consequences (reinforcement and punishment). Another commonality is the acquisition phase. Just as Pavlov's dogs acquired their conditioned response through a series of pairings, Thorndike's cats learned to escape the puzzle boxes over multiple trials. In both cases, acquisition occurred gradually.

As with classical conditioning, behaviors acquired through operant conditioning are subject to extinction and spontaneous recovery—that is, they may fade in the absence of reinforcers and then reappear after a rest period. A rat in a Skinner box eventually gives up pushing on a lever if it stops receiving reinforcers. But that same lever-pushing behavior can make a sudden comeback through spontaneous recovery. After a rest period, the rat returns to his box and reverts to his old lever-pushing ways.

Stimulus generalization and discrimination also occur in operant conditioning. If a rat is conditioned to push a particular type of lever, it may push a variety of other lever types similar in shape, size, and color (stimulus generalization). But that same rat may not push a button; it can differentiate between a button and a lever (stimulus discrimination). For another example of stimulus discrimination, we look to a study on turtles. Using positive reinforcers (morsels of meat), researchers showed that these animals can learn to discriminate among black, white, and gray paddles (Leighty et al., 2013).

TABLE 5.4 CONDITIONING BASICS

Concept	Classical Conditioning	Operant Conditioning
The association	Links different stimuli, often through repeated pairings	Links behaviors with consequences, often through repeated pairings
Response	Involuntary behavior	Voluntary behavior
Acquisition	The initial learning phase	The initial learning phase
Extinction	The disappearance of a conditioned response after repeated exposure to the conditioned stimulus in the absence of the unconditioned stimulus	The disappearance of a learned behavior through the removal of its reinforcer
Spontaneous recovery	The reappearance of the conditioned response following its extinction	The reappearance of a behavior following its extinction

These fundamental learning concepts apply to both classical and operant conditioning.

Let's Contrast

Students sometimes have trouble differentiating classical and operant conditioning (**Figure 5.3** on the next page). Let's examine their key differences. In classical conditioning, learned behaviors are involuntary, or reflexive. Gavin the ATF agent could not directly control his shaking any more than Pavlov's dogs could decide when to salivate. Operant conditioning, on the other hand, concerns voluntary behavior. Cesar had power over his decision to work with problem dogs, just as Skinner's pigeons had control over their beaks. In short, classical conditioning is an involuntary form of learning, whereas operant conditioning requires active effort.

Another important distinction is the way behaviors are strengthened. In classical conditioning, behaviors become more established with repeated pairings of stimuli.

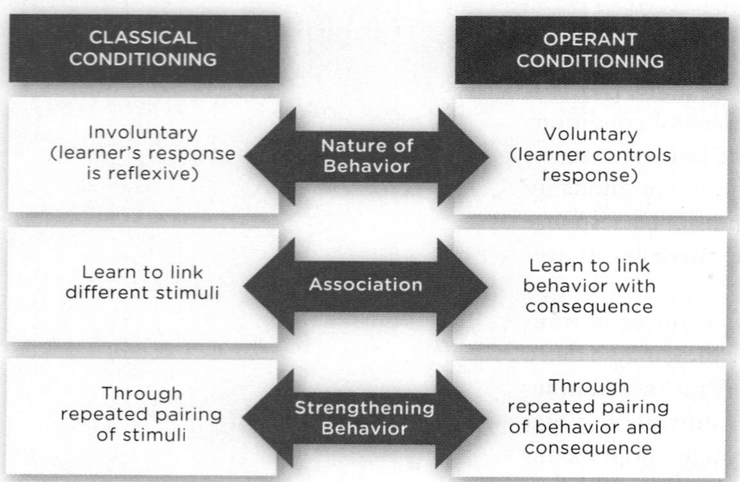

FIGURE 5.3
Differences Between Classical and Operant Conditioning

The more Pavlov's dogs were exposed to the pairing of food and the buzzer sound, the greater the chances they would salivate in response to the buzzer alone. With operant conditioning, behaviors are also strengthened by repeated pairings, but the connection is between a behavior and its consequences. Reinforcers strengthen the behavior; punishment weakens it. The more benefits (reinforcers) Cesar accrues by working with people and dogs, the greater the likelihood he will continue cultivating his career.

Often, classical conditioning and operant conditioning occur simultaneously. A baby learns that he gets fed when he cries; getting formula or breast milk reinforces the crying behavior (operant conditioning). At the same time, the baby learns to associate formula or breast milk with the appearance of the bottle or breast; the moment he sees either, he begins salivating in anticipation of being fed (classical conditioning).

Classical and operant conditioning are not the only ways we learn. Here is a question to get you thinking about the next type of learning we will cover: How do you know how to peel a banana, trim your fingernails, and throw a Frisbee? Somebody must have shown you.

show what you know

1. Thorndike proposed the ______________, which states that behaviors are more likely to be repeated when they are followed by pleasurable outcomes.

2. Students given prizes for passing math tests improve their math scores, but they also begin studying harder for spelling tests as a result of this reinforcement. Their increased studying of spelling is an example of:
   a. classical conditioning.
   b. an unconditioned response.
   c. an unconditioned stimulus.
   d. stimulus generalization.

3. When a student disrupts class, the teacher writes her name on the board. For the rest of the week, the student does not act up. The teacher used ______________ to decrease the child's disruptive behaviors.
   a. positive punishment
   b. negative punishment
   c. positive reinforcement
   d. negative reinforcement

4. Think about a behavior you would like to change (either yours or someone else's). Devise a schedule of reinforcement using positive and negative reinforcement to change that behavior. Also contemplate how you might use successive approximations. What primary and secondary reinforcers would you use?

5. How do continuous and partial reinforcement differ?

✓ CHECK YOUR ANSWERS IN APPENDIX C.

On the Ranch
Left to right: Cesar's mother, grandmother, sister, cousin, grandfather, and Cesar on the family farm in Ixpalino. Many of the behaviors Cesar learned in childhood came from observing role models on the family farm. His mother, for example, always worked hard and never complained about not having enough food or money. Courtesy Cesar's Way Inc.

Observational Learning and Cognition

CESAR'S ROLE MODELS Growing up in Mexico, Cesar loved watching reruns of the dog shows *Lassie* and *The Adventures of Rin Tin Tin* from the 1950s and 60s. The dogs in these shows performed incredible physical and intellectual feats—behaviors young Cesar imagined were typical of all American dogs. Once in the United States, Cesar began searching for someone who could teach him the art of American dog training. "You have to look for somebody with wisdom," he says. "That's what kept me going."

But Cesar would eventually discover that his most important teachers were back in Mexico, and he had already learned from them. His grandfather Teodoro had taught him what it means to be pack leader, and how to interact effectively with dogs. He didn't talk much, but he demonstrated behaviors that Cesar could observe and imitate. "Never work against Mother Nature," Teodoro would say, or "You have to be calm." Then, after stating these tenets, Teodoro would execute them, and the dogs would trot after him and perform desired behaviors.

The ranch dogs also served as role models for young Cesar. "From the time I was very little, I found joy in dogs simply by observing them" (Millan & Peltier, 2006, p. 25). Cesar spent hours studying how the dogs interacted, and adopted some of these behaviors himself. If you watch Cesar meet a dog for the first time, you'll see he demonstrates "no talk, no touch, no eye contact" (Millan & Peltier, 2006, p. 46). This is exactly how dogs greet one another with respect.

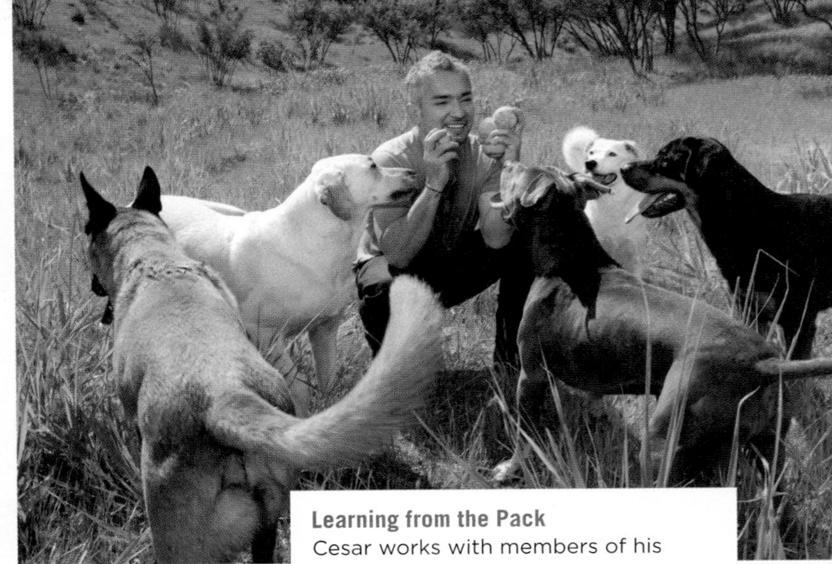

Learning from the Pack
Cesar works with members of his pack at the Dog Psychology Center in Santa Clarita, California. His dogs are excellent role models for troubled dogs that come to the Center for rehabilitation. As he explains, "Dogs are great at copying behavior—that's one of the many ways in which they learn from one another when they are pups" (Millan & Peltier, 2010, p. 15). Courtesy Cesar's Way Inc.

Cesar's grandfather and the ranch dogs served as **models**, demonstrating behaviors that could be observed and imitated. We call this process **observational learning**, as it results from watching the behavior of others. According to Bandura (1986), observational learning is more likely to occur when learners: (1) pay attention to the model; (2) remember what they observed (Bahrick, Gogate, & Ruiz, 2002); (3) are capable of performing the observed behavior; and (4) are motivated to demonstrate the behavior.

What specific skills have you developed through observational learning? If you have ever used a "how to" video on YouTube (for example, "how to unclog a drain" or "how to make a man bun"), you were probably watching and imitating a model. Or, perhaps someone has shown you how to change a flat tire, prepare an omelet, or perform CPR. All these skills can be acquired with the help of observational learning. What about table manners—remember how you learned those?

synonyms
observational learning social learning

MIND YOUR MANNERS Travelers, be advised: Eating etiquette can greatly differ from one culture to the next. Something as simple as eating with your left hand, which is commonplace in the United States, is considered unsanitary in India and the Middle East (Boscamp, 2013, July 11). In Afghanistan and Korea, people sit down on the floor to eat a meal (Leontovich, 2016), but this is rarely done in France or Italy. Mexicans often eat with their hands, while Chileans use utensils for almost everything, including french fries! Burping, generally viewed as ill-mannered in the United States, is interpreted as a sign of contentment in China (Boscamp, 2013, July 11). When you are traveling, use observational learning to pick up on the table manners of the country you are visiting.

LOOK BEFORE YOU EAT

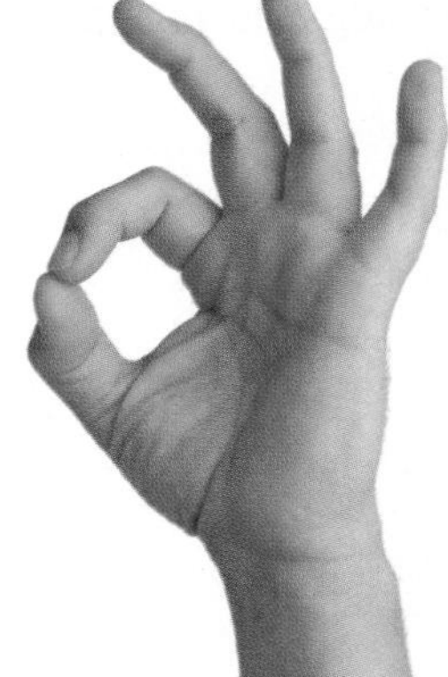

Not "Okay" Everywhere
If you grew up in the United States, you probably picked up the "okay" hand gesture by watching and imitating others (observational learning). If you grew up in Brazil, you likely learned *not* to use this gesture because it is considered rude and obscene. Tetra Images/Getty Images.

Monkey See, Monkey Do

LO 14 Summarize what Bandura's classic Bobo doll study teaches us about learning.

Just as observational learning can lead to positive outcomes (Cesar adopting the ways of his grandfather, or children learning manners), it can also breed undesirable behaviors. The classic Bobo doll experiment by American psychologist Albert Bandura and his colleagues reveals just how fast children can adopt aggressive ways they see modeled by adults, as well as exhibit their own novel aggressive responses (Bandura, Ross, & Ross, 1961). In one of Bandura's studies, 76 preschool children were placed in a room one at a time with an adult. Some of the children were paired with an adult who acted

model The individual or character whose behavior is being imitated.

observational learning Learning that occurs as a result of watching the behavior of others.

The Bobo Assault
Preschool children in Albert Bandura's famous Bobo doll experiment performed shocking displays of aggression after seeing such behaviors modeled by adults. The children were more likely to copy models who were rewarded for their aggressive behavior and less likely to mimic those who were punished (Bandura, 1986). Dr. Albert Bandura.

aggressively toward a 5-foot-tall inflatable Bobo doll—punching it in the nose, hitting its head with a mallet, kicking it around the room, and yelling phrases such as "Sock him in the nose" and "Pow!" The other children in the study were paired with an adult who played with toys peacefully (Bandura et al., 1961).

At the end of the experiment, all the children were given an opportunity to play with a Bobo doll themselves. Those who had observed adults attacking and shouting were much more likely to do the same. Boys were more likely than girls to mimic physical aggression, especially if they had observed it modeled by men. And boys and girls were about equally likely to imitate verbal aggression (Bandura et al., 1961).

You Asked, Cesar Answers

http://qrs.ly/la7829l

What kind of dogs did you have growing up?

try this Identify the independent variable and dependent variable in the experiment by Bandura and colleagues. What might you change if you were to replicate this experiment?

✓ CHECK YOUR ANSWERS IN APPENDIX C.

VIOLENCE IN THE MEDIA Psychologists have followed up on Bandura's research with studies investigating how children are influenced by violence they see on television, the Internet, and in movies and video games. One study conducted in New Zealand followed over 1,000 children from as early as birth until they were around 26 years old. The results were alarming: The more television the children watched, the more likely they were to exhibit antisocial behaviors as young adults. Interestingly, this association was not dependent on program content (Robertson, McAnally, & Hancox, 2013). Another study of over 5,000 fifth graders found strong associations between physical aggression and exposure to violent music, video games, and TV. The researchers concluded that media violence was just as strongly linked to physical aggression as other well-known factors, such as neighborhood and domestic violence (Coker et al., 2015, January/February).

However, an association between violent media content and aggressive behavior is not necessarily evidence for a cause-and-effect relationship. There are other factors that could influence both television viewing and aggression (Gentile, Reimer, Nathanson, Walsh, & Eisenmann, 2014; Huesmann, Moise-Titus, Podolski, & Eron, 2003). For example, if a parent is emotionally neglectful and places a child in front of the television all day, the child may eventually imitate some of the aggression she sees on TV. At the same time, the child may resent the parent for ignoring her, and this resentment could lead to aggression. But how do you know which of these factors—

television exposure or parenting approach—is more important in the development of aggressive tendencies? This is an active area of psychological research, but experts agree that exposure to media violence is one of the factors that may lead to aggression in children (American Psychological Association, 2013c; Beresin, 2015; Coyne, 2016). The American Academy of Pediatrics sums it up nicely: "Extensive research evidence indicates that media violence can contribute to aggressive behavior, desensitization to violence, nightmares, and fear of being harmed" (American Academy of Pediatrics, 2009, p. 1495).

How can parents and caregivers deal with this problem? One approach is to limit the amount of time children spend with electronic media. The American Academy of Pediatrics recommends minimal screen time for children under the age of 2, a maximum of 1 hour per day for preschoolers, and parental supervision for all age groups (American Academy of Pediatrics, 2016a & b). Unfortunately, children and their parents have not followed these guidelines. The average American child spends 7 hours per day watching TV, and using tablets, cell phones, and other electronic media (American Academy of Pediatrics, n.d.). Instead of focusing on total screen time, some researchers suggest we direct our attention toward media content, and try to reduce exposure to violence and increase exposure to prosocial behaviors (Christakis et al., 2013; McCarthy, 2013). And don't underestimate the benefits of sending children outdoors to play, which improves their sleep, health, and social well-being (Alexander, Frohlich, & Fusco, 2014; Xu, Wen, Hardy, & Rissel, 2016).

Some types of screen time can be beneficial for families, however. Video-chatting enables people to stay in close contact with family and friends who live thousands of miles away. For young children participating in these chats, the American Academy of Pediatrics (2016a) recommends parental participation and supervision.

Sunny Days
The prosocial behaviors demonstrated by *Sesame Street* friends such as Elmo and Big Bird (and sometimes even Oscar the Grouch!) appear to have a meaningful impact on child viewers. In fact, *Sesame Street* is the only show specifically mentioned in the American Academy of Pediatrics (2016a) policy statement on Media and Young Minds: "Well-designed television programs, such as *Sesame Street*, can improve cognitive, literacy, and social outcomes for children 3 to 5 years of age" (p. 2). Hulton Archive/Getty Images.

LEARNING TO BE NICE **Prosocial behaviors** are actions that are kind, generous, and beneficial to others. Children can easily pick up these positive behaviors by observing models, and TV shows like *Sesame Street* may be effective in this regard (Cole, Labin, & del Rocio Galarza, 2008). In one study, researchers had parents change the television shows their preschoolers were viewing, substituting "aggression-laden programming" with "high quality prosocial and educational programming" (Christakis et al., 2013, p. 431). When assessed 6 and 12 months after the intervention, the children who had switched to prosocial/educational programming showed more behavioral improvement than those in the control group. This effect was more pronounced for boys from low-income households (Christakis et al., 2013). Perhaps the prosocial messages of shows like *Dora the Explorer* and *Super Why* had made a difference.

Whistling Ape
Bonnie the orangutan seems to have learned whistling by copying workers at the Smithsonian National Zoological Park in Washington, D.C. Her musical skill is the result of observational learning (Stone, 2009; Wich et al., 2009). Jennifer Zoon/Courtesy of Smithsonian's National Zoological Park.

Put Your Heads Together

A camp director wants to teach campers to come quickly when the dinner bell rings. Team up and discuss **A)** how she could use operant conditioning and observational learning to accomplish this, **B)** why classical conditioning may not be an appropriate technique here, and **C)** what kind of classically conditioned behavior campers might acquire without even realizing it.

Latent Learning

Earlier, we pointed out that Cesar focuses on rehabilitating dogs and training people. When did his unique philosophy take form? When Cesar began working at a dog-training facility in Los Angeles, he awed the other workers with his ability to placate out-of-control dogs. His approach was simple: If he noticed a dog was afraid or on edge,

prosocial behaviors Actions that are kind, generous, and beneficial to others.

You Won't Believe This Story
When Rachel Kauffman first encountered this white German shepherd at a Tennessee animal shelter, he was gaunt and withdrawn. Rachel took the dog home, named him "Hank," and became his temporary foster mother. After 6 days with Rachel, Hank was placed in an official foster home 11 miles away, but it seems he had no intention of staying. Hank broke out of the house and appeared at Rachel's doorstep 2 days later. He hasn't left since (Fawal, 2015, November 23). How did Hank find his way back to Rachel? Just like rats and humans, dogs have the ability to form cognitive maps, which help them navigate from place to place (Bensky, Gosling, & Sinn, 2013). Mark Weber/The Commercial Appeal via ZUMA Wire.

he would quietly open the door, avoid eye contact, turn his back, and allow the dog to come to him. "Unconsciously, I was beginning to apply the dog psychology I had learned from my years observing dogs on my grandfather's farm," Cesar writes. "I was interacting with the dogs the way they interacted with one another" (Millan & Peltier, 2006, p. 47). Could this be an example of *latent learning?*

LO 15 Describe latent learning and explain how cognition is involved in learning.

Latent learning occurs without awareness and regardless of reinforcement, and is not evident until there is a need to use it. You experience latent learning all the time. For example, any time you explore a new park, neighborhood, or shopping mall, you are unconsciously gathering data from your senses—sights, sounds, smells, touch, and perhaps even taste if you stop for a bite to eat.

RATS THAT KNOW WHERE TO GO American psychologist Edward Tolman and his colleague C. H. Honzik demonstrated latent learning in rats in their classic 1930 maze experiment (**Figure 5.4**). The researchers took three groups of rats and let them run free in mazes for several days. One group received food for reaching the goal boxes in their mazes; a second group received no reinforcement; and a third group received nothing until the 11th day of the experiment, when they, too, received food after finding the goal box. As you might expect, rats getting the treats from the onset solved the mazes more quickly as the days wore on. Meanwhile, their unrewarded compatriots wandered through the twists and turns. But on Day 11 when the researchers started to give treats to the third group of rats, their behavior changed markedly. After just one round of treats, the rats were scurrying through the mazes and scooping up the food as if they had been rewarded throughout the experiment (Tolman & Honzik, 1930). They had apparently been learning, even when there was no reinforcement for doing so—or in simpler terms, learning just for the sake of learning.

A MAP THAT CANNOT BE SEEN Like Tolman's rats, we remember locations, objects, and details of our surroundings without realizing it, and bring this information together in a mental layout (Lynch, 1960). The representations we form through latent learning are called **cognitive maps.** People vary in their ability to form these

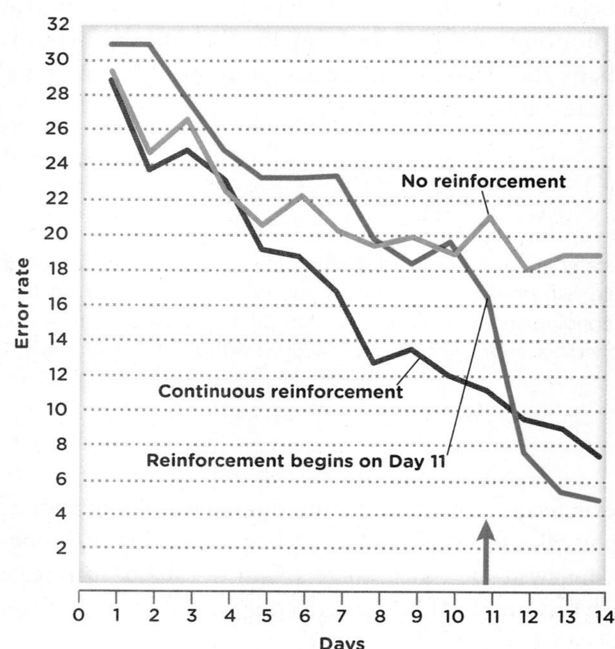

FIGURE 5.4
Latent Learning
In a classic experiment, groups of rats learned how to navigate a maze at remarkably different rates. Rats in a group receiving reinforcement from Day 1 (the green line on the graph) initially had the lowest rate of errors and were able to work their way through the maze more quickly than the other groups. But when another group began to receive reinforcement for the first time on Day 11, their error rate dropped immediately. This shows that the rats were learning the basic structure of the maze even when they weren't being reinforced. Information from Tolman (1948).

latent learning Learning that occurs without awareness and regardless of reinforcement, and is not evident until needed.

cognitive map A mental representation of physical space.

cognitive maps, as some are better than others at remembering details of the physical environment (Weisberg & Newcombe, 2016).

Studies on latent learning and cognitive maps focus on the cognitive processes underlying behavior, and their findings suggest that learning can occur in the absence of reinforcement. This emphasis on cognition conflicts with the strict form of behaviorism endorsed by Skinner and some other 20th-century psychologists. Many other studies have challenged the behaviorist notion that all behaviors and mental processes are determined by forces in the environment. For example, German psychologist Wolfgang Köhler (1887–1967) found evidence that chimpanzees are capable of thinking through a problem before taking action. Köhler designed an experiment in which chimps were presented with out-of-reach bananas, and showed that the animals were able to plan a variety of banana-fetching strategies, including stacking crates for climbing (1925). Here, the chimps displayed *insight,* a sudden coming together of awareness of a situation, leading to the solution of a problem (Chapter 7). Like latent learning, insight can occur in the absence of reinforcement.

Today, most psychologists agree that both observable, measurable behaviors and internal cognitive processes such as insight are necessary and complementary elements of learning. Environmental factors have a powerful influence on behavior, as Pavlov, Skinner, and others discovered, but every action can be traced to activity in the brain. Understanding how cognitive processes translate to behaviors remains one of the great challenges facing psychologists.

Discovering the Brain's "GPS"
John O'Keefe (left), May-Britt Moser, and Edvard Moser won the 2014 Nobel Prize in Physiology or Medicine for discovering the "place cells" and "grid cells" in the brain that allow us to form cognitive maps of our surroundings (Vogel, 2014, October 6). AP Photo/TT News Agency, Anders Wiklund.

The time has come to wrap up this chapter on learning, but first, let's take one more opportunity to learn something from Cesar Millan. Imagine you could sit down and talk with Cesar. What advice might he offer about lifelong learning and career goals?

THINK POSITIVE

YOU ARE A VALUABLE MEMBER OF THE PACK Each of us plays a unique and important role in society, or the "human pack," as Cesar might describe it. "Once you find your place in the pack," says Cesar, "you serve a big purpose." Some of us are leaders, others are not, but every pack member has equal value.

FIND YOUR PASSION AND NEVER STOP LEARNING

What would Cesar say to those of us still struggling to find our place in the world? It may sound like a platitude, but find your passion, figure out what makes you happy, and pursue a path that allows you to nurture it. "Once you find your passion, you don't think you're working," Cesar says. Indeed, research suggests that people who are satisfied at work often feel more satisfied in their personal lives (Allen & McCarthy, 2016). If you ever find yourself lost, focus your energy on learning. "I think [that] listening is more powerful than anything else," Cesar explains. "When you're lost, when you're sad, you have to ask questions." In other words, seeking answers and learning should be continuous, lifelong activities.

28 Years Later
Cesar enjoys the company of his right-hand dog Junior. It has now been almost three decades since this celebrated dog expert illegally crossed the border into the United States. And although he became a U.S. citizen in 2009, Cesar really views himself as a citizen of the world. "I belong to a worldwide community of people who love dogs," he writes. "This is my pack" (Millan, 2013, p. 12). Vincent Sandoval/WireImage/Getty Images.

show what you know

1. You want to learn how to play basketball, so you watch videos of Steph Curry demonstrating skills and executing plays. If your game improves as a result, this would be considered an example of:
   a. observational learning.
   b. association.
   c. prosocial behavior.
   d. your cognitive map.

2. Bandura's Bobo doll study shows us that observational learning results in a wide variety of learned behaviors. Describe several types of behaviors you have learned by observing others.

3. Although Skinner believed that reinforcement is the cause of learning, there is robust evidence that reinforcement is not always necessary. This comes from experiments studying:
   a. positive reinforcement.
   b. negative reinforcement.
   c. latent learning.
   d. stimulus generalization.

✓ CHECK YOUR ANSWERS IN APPENDIX C.

YOUR SCIENTIFIC WORLD is a new application-based feature appearing in every chapter. In these online activities, you will take on role-playing scenarios that encourage you to think critically and apply your knowledge of psychological science to solve a real-world problem. For example: How does an ordinary dog learn to be a therapy animal? In this activity, you will explore how the principles of classical and operant conditioning can be used to train therapy dogs. You can access Your Scientific World activities in LaunchPad. Have fun!

SUMMARY OF CONCEPTS

LO 1 Define learning. (p. 163)

Learning is a relatively enduring change in behavior or thinking that results from experiences. Organisms as simple as fruit flies and as complex as humans have the ability to learn. Learning is about creating associations. Sometimes we associate two different stimuli (classical conditioning). Other times we make connections between our behaviors and their consequences (operant conditioning). We can also learn by watching and imitating others (observational learning), creating a link between our behavior and the behavior of others.

LO 2 Explain what Pavlov's studies teach us about classical conditioning. (p. 165)

The dogs in Pavlov's studies learned to link food to various stimuli, such as flashing lights and buzzer sounds, that normally have nothing to do with food or salivation. Once such a link was formed, the dogs would salivate in response to the stimulus alone, even with no food present. An originally neutral stimulus (a buzzer sound, for example) triggered an involuntary response (salivation). We call this type of learning classical conditioning.

LO 3 Identify the differences between the US, UR, CS, and CR. (p. 166)

In classical conditioning, a neutral stimulus (NS) is something in the environment that does not normally cause a relevant automatic response. This neutral stimulus (NS) is repeatedly paired with an unconditioned stimulus (US) that triggers an unconditioned response (UR). During this process of acquisition, the neutral stimulus (NS) becomes a conditioned stimulus (CS) that elicits a conditioned response (CR). In Pavlov's experiment with dogs, the neutral stimulus (NS) might have been the sound of a buzzer; the unconditioned stimulus (US) was the meat; and the unconditioned response (UR) was the dog's salivation. After repeated pairings with the meat, the buzzer (originally a neutral stimulus) became a conditioned stimulus (CS), eliciting the conditioned response (CR) of salivation, a learned behavior.

LO 4 Recognize and give examples of stimulus generalization and stimulus discrimination. (p. 167)

Once conditioning has occurred, and the conditioned stimulus (CS) elicits the conditioned response (CR), the learner may respond to similar stimuli as if they were the original CS. This is called stimulus generalization. For example, someone who has been bitten by a small dog and reacts with fear to all dogs, big and small, demonstrates stimulus generalization. Stimulus discrimination is the ability to differentiate between a particular conditioned stimulus (CS) and other stimuli sufficiently different from it. Someone who was bitten by a small dog may be afraid of small dogs, but not large dogs, thus demonstrating stimulus discrimination.

LO 5 Summarize how classical conditioning is dependent on the biology of the organism. (p. 171)

Animals and people show biological preparedness, meaning they are predisposed to learn associations that have adaptive value. For example, a conditioned taste aversion is a form of classical conditioning that occurs when an organism learns to associate the taste of a particular food or drink with illness. Avoiding foods that induce sickness increases the odds the organism will survive and reproduce, passing its genes along to the next generation.

LO 6 Describe the Little Albert study and explain how fear can be learned. (p. 173)

The case study of Little Albert illustrates conditioned emotional response (fear in Little Albert's case) acquired via classical conditioning. When Little Albert heard a loud bang (an unconditioned stimulus), he responded in fear (an unconditioned response). Through conditioning, the sight of a rat became paired with the loud noise and went from being a neutral stimulus to a conditioned stimulus (CS). Little Albert's fear of the rat was a conditioned response (CR).

LO 7 **Describe Thorndike's law of effect. (p. 175)**

Thorndike's law of effect states that a behavior is more likely to reoccur when followed by a pleasurable outcome. For the cats in Thorndike's puzzle boxes, the behavior was breaking free and the pleasurable outcome was a piece of fish waiting outside the door. Over time, the cats escaped faster and faster, until eventually they were breaking free almost immediately. The pieces of fish in Thorndike's experiments served as reinforcers, because they increased the frequency of the preceding behavior (escaping the box). Reinforcers are a key component of operant conditioning, a type of learning wherein people or animals come to associate their voluntary actions with consequences.

LO 8 **Explain how positive and negative reinforcement differ. (p. 177)**

Positive reinforcement occurs when target behaviors are followed by rewards and other reinforcers. The addition of reinforcers (typically pleasant stimuli) increases the likelihood of the behavior recurring. Behaviors can also increase in response to negative reinforcement, or the removal of something unpleasant immediately following the behavior. Both positive and negative reinforcement increase desired behaviors.

LO 9 **Distinguish between primary and secondary reinforcers. (p. 179)**

Primary reinforcers satisfy biological needs. Food, water, and physical contact are considered primary reinforcers. Secondary reinforcers do not satisfy biological needs, but often derive their power from their connection with primary reinforcers. Money is an example of a secondary reinforcer; we know from experience that it gives us access to primary reinforcers, such as food and a safe place to live.

Explain shaping and the method of successive approximations. (p. 179)

Building on Thorndike's law of effect and Watson's approach to research, Skinner used shaping through successive approximations (small steps leading to a desired behavior) with pigeons and other animals. With shaping, a person observes the behaviors of animals, providing reinforcers when they perform at a required level. Animal behavior can be shaped by forces in the environment, but instinct may interfere with the process. This instinctive drift is the tendency for instinct to undermine conditioned behaviors.

Describe continuous reinforcement and partial reinforcement. (p. 181)

Reinforcers can be delivered on a constant basis (continuous reinforcement) or intermittently (partial reinforcement). Continuous reinforcement is generally more effective for establishing a behavior. However, behaviors learned through partial reinforcement are generally more resistant to extinction (the partial reinforcement effect).

Name the schedules of reinforcement and give examples of each. (p. 182)

In a fixed-ratio schedule, reinforcement follows a pre-set number of desired responses or behaviors. In a variable-ratio schedule, reinforcement follows a certain number of desired responses or behaviors, but the number changes across trials (fluctuating around a precalculated average). In a fixed-interval schedule, reinforcement comes after a preestablished interval of time; the response or behavior is only reinforced after the given interval passes. In a variable-interval schedule, reinforcement comes after an interval of time passes, but the length of the interval changes from trial to trial.

Explain how punishment differs from reinforcement. (p. 188)

In contrast to reinforcement, which makes a behavior more likely to recur, the goal of punishment is to decrease a behavior. Punishment decreases a behavior by instilling an association between a behavior and some unwanted consequence (for example, between stealing and going to jail, or between misbehaving and loss of screen time). Negative reinforcement strengthens a behavior that it follows by removing something aversive or disagreeable.

Summarize what Bandura's classic Bobo doll study teaches us about learning. (p. 191)

Observational learning can occur when we watch a model demonstrate a behavior. Albert Bandura's classic Bobo doll experiment showed that children readily imitate aggression when they see it modeled by adults. Studies suggest that children may be inclined to mimic aggressive behaviors seen in TV shows, movies, video games, and on the Internet. Observation of prosocial behaviors, on the other hand, can encourage kindness, generosity, and other forms of behavior that benefit others.

Describe latent learning and explain how cognition is involved in learning. (p. 194)

Latent learning occurs without awareness and regardless of reinforcement. Edward Tolman showed that rats could learn to navigate mazes even when given no reinforcement. Their learning only became apparent when it was needed. Latent learning is evident in our ability to form cognitive maps, or mental representations of our physical surroundings. Studies on latent learning and cognitive maps focus on the cognitive processes underlying behavior.

KEY TERMS

acquisition, p. 166
adaptive value, p. 171
biological preparedness, p. 172
classical conditioning, p. 166
cognitive map, p. 194
conditioned emotional response, p. 173
conditioned response (CR), p. 166
conditioned stimulus (CS), p. 166
conditioned taste aversion, p. 171
continuous reinforcement, p. 181
extinction, p. 169
fixed-interval schedule, p. 183
fixed-ratio schedule, p. 182
habituation, p. 164
higher order conditioning, p. 169
instinctive drift, p. 181
latent learning, p. 194
law of effect, p. 176
learning, p. 163
model, p. 191
negative punishment, p. 185
negative reinforcement, p. 178
neutral stimulus (NS), p. 166
observational learning, p. 191
operant conditioning, p. 176
partial reinforcement, p. 182
partial reinforcement effect, p. 182
positive punishment, p. 185
positive reinforcement, p. 177
primary reinforcer, p. 179
prosocial behaviors, p. 193
punishment, p. 183
reinforcement, p. 176
reinforcers, p. 176
secondary reinforcer, p. 179
shaping, p. 179
spontaneous recovery, p. 169
stimulus, p. 164
stimulus discrimination, p. 167
stimulus generalization, p. 167
successive approximations, p. 179
unconditioned response (UR), p. 166
unconditioned stimulus (US), p. 166
variable-interval schedule, p. 183
variable-ratio schedule, p. 183

TEST PREP ARE YOU READY?

1. One basic form of learning is ____________, which is evident when an organism does not respond as strongly or as often following multiple exposures to a stimulus.
   a. insight
   b. habituation
   c. classical conditioning
   d. operant conditioning

2. Even turtles can learn through operant conditioning, as evidenced by their:
   a. innate urge to get food.
   b. reaction to an unconditioned stimulus.
   c. responses to positive reinforcement.
   d. reactions to predators.

3. Behaviors learned through classical conditioning are ____________, whereas those learned through operant conditioning are ____________.
   a. involuntary; voluntary
   b. voluntary; involuntary
   c. voluntary; innate
   d. involuntary; innate

4. Every time you open the pantry where dog food is stored, your dog starts to salivate. His reaction is a(n):
   a. unconditioned response.
   b. conditioned response.
   c. stimulus discrimination.
   d. reaction based on observational learning.

5. Little Albert was a baby who originally had no fear of rats. In an experiment conducted by Watson and Rayner, Albert was classically conditioned to fear white rats through the pairing of a loud noise with exposure to a rat. His resulting fear is an example of a(n):
   a. unconditioned stimulus.
   b. operant conditioning.
   c. conditioned emotional response.
   d. biological preparedness.

6. ____________ indicates that if a behavior is followed by a pleasurable outcome, it likely will be repeated.
   a. Latent learning
   b. Classical conditioning
   c. Biological preparedness
   d. The law of effect

7. Which of the following is an example of negative reinforcement?
   a. working hard to get an A on a paper
   b. a child getting more computer time when he finishes his homework
   c. a dog whining in the morning, leading an owner to wake up and take it outside
   d. getting a speeding ticket and then not exceeding the speed limit afterward

8. A child is reprimanded for misbehaving, but then she seems to misbehave even more! This indicates that reprimanding her was:
   a. negative punishment.
   b. positive reinforcement.
   c. positive punishment.
   d. an unconditioned response.

9. In Bandura's Bobo doll study, children who saw an adult punching and shouting at the doll:
   a. were more likely to display aggressive behavior.
   b. were less likely to display aggressive behavior.
   c. did not play with the Bobo doll at all.
   d. began to cry when they saw the adult acting aggressively.

10. Rats allowed to explore a maze without getting reinforcers until the 11th day of the experiment subsequently navigated the maze as if they had been given reinforcers throughout the entire experiment. Their behavior is evidence of:
    a. latent learning.
    b. observational learning.
    c. classical conditioning.
    d. operant conditioning.

11. What is the difference between stimulus generalization and stimulus discrimination?

12. Give an example showing how you have applied shaping and partial reinforcement to change your behavior. Which schedule of reinforcement do you think you used?

13. What is the difference between primary reinforcers and secondary reinforcers? Give an example of each and explain how they might be used to change a behavior.

14. How are punishment and negative reinforcement different? Give examples of negative reinforcement, positive punishment, and negative punishment and explain how they aim to change behavior.

15. Describe conditioned taste aversion and provide an example. Identify the neutral stimulus, unconditioned stimulus, unconditioned response, conditioned stimulus, and conditioned response.

✓ CHECK YOUR ANSWERS IN APPENDIX C.

Go to **LaunchPad** or **Achieve: Read & Practice** to test your understanding with **LearningCurve**.

CHAPTER 6

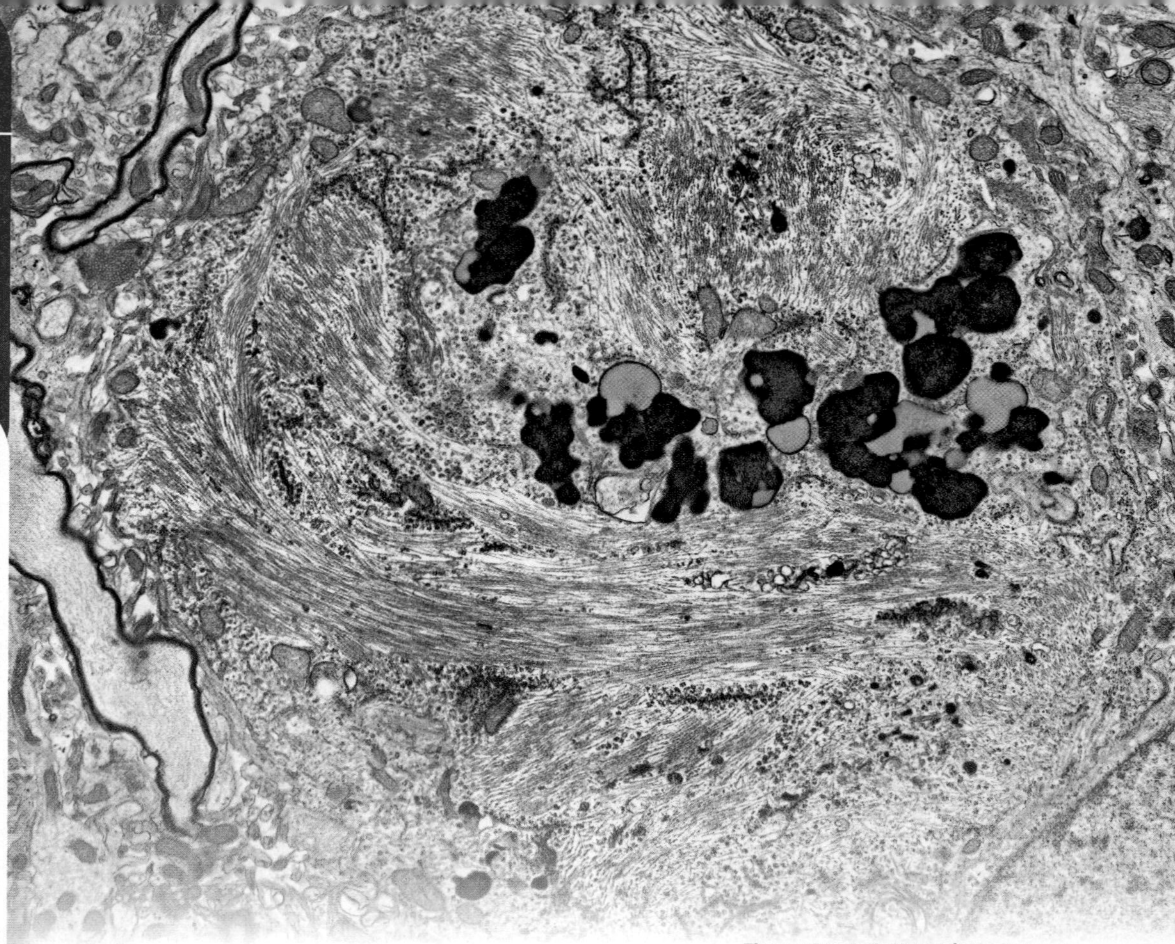

Thomas Deerinck, NCMIR/Science Source.

Memory

What Is Memory?

MEMORY BREAKDOWN Monday, March 25, 1985: Deborah Wearing awoke in a sweat-soaked bed. Her husband Clive had been up all night perspiring, vomiting, and with a high fever. He said that he had a "constant, terrible" headache, like a "band" of pain tightening around his head (Wearing, 2005, p. 27). The symptoms worsened over the next few days, but the two doctors caring for Clive reassured Deborah that it was just a bad case of the flu. By Wednesday, Clive had spent three nights awake with the pain. Confused and disoriented, he turned to Deborah and said, "Er, er, darling. . . . I can't . . . think of your name" (p. 31).

The doctor arrived a couple of hours later, reassured Deborah that her husband's confusion was merely the result of sleep deprivation, and prescribed sleeping pills. Deborah came home later that day, expecting to find her husband in bed. But no Clive.

The Conductor
In 1985 conductor Clive Wearing (pictured here with his wife Deborah) developed a brain infection—viral encephalitis—that nearly took his life. Clive recovered physically, but his memory was never the same. Ros Drinkwater/Alamy.

She shouted out his name. No answer, just a heap of pajamas. After the police had conducted an extensive search, Clive was found when a taxi driver dropped him off at a local police station; he had gotten into the cab and couldn't remember his address (Wearing, 2005). Clive returned to his flat (which he did not recognize as home), rested, and took in fluids. His fever dropped, and it appeared that he was improving. But when he awoke Friday morning, his confusion was so severe he could not identify the toilet among the various fixtures in his bathroom. As Deborah placed urgent calls to the doctor, Clive began to drift away. He lost consciousness and was rushed to the hospital in an ambulance (Wearing, 2005; Wilson & Wearing, 1995).

Clive and Deborah, In Their Own Words
http://qrs.ly/8m5a5d1

Jiri Rezac/Polaris/Newscom

Prior to this illness, Clive Wearing had enjoyed a fabulous career in music. As the director of the London Lassus Ensemble, he spent his days leading singers and instrumentalists through the emotionally complex music of his favorite composer, Orlande de Lassus. A renowned expert on Renaissance music, Clive produced music for the prestigious British Broadcasting Corporation (BBC), including that which aired on the wedding day of Prince Charles and Lady Diana Spencer (Sacks, 2007, September 24; Wilson, Baddeley, & Kapur, 1995; Wilson, Kopelman, & Kapur, 2008). But Clive's work—and his whole life—tumbled into chaos when a virus that normally causes blisters on the mouth invaded his brain.

Millions of people carry herpes simplex virus type 1 (HSV-1). Usually, it causes unsightly cold sores in the mouth and on the face. (There is also HSV-2, more commonly associated with genital herpes.) But for a small minority of the adult population—approximately 1 in 500,000 annually—the virus invades the central nervous system and causes a life-threatening infection called *encephalitis* (Anderson, 2017, August 23). Left untreated, herpes encephalitis causes death in over 70% of its victims. Most who survive have lasting brain damage and neurological deficits (Sabah, Mulcahy, & Zeman, 2012; Sili, Kaya, Mert, & HSV Encephalitis Study Group, 2014).

Although Deborah saw to it that Clive received early medical attention, having two doctors visit the house day and night for nearly a week, these physicians mistook his condition for the flu with meningitis-like symptoms (Wilson & Wearing, 1995). Misdiagnosis is common with herpes encephalitis (even to this day), as its symptoms resemble those of other conditions, including the flu, meningitis, a stroke, and epilepsy (Sabah et al., 2012). When Clive and Deborah arrived at the hospital on the sixth day of his illness, they waited another 11 hours just to get a proper diagnosis (Wearing, 2005; Wilson & Wearing, 1995).

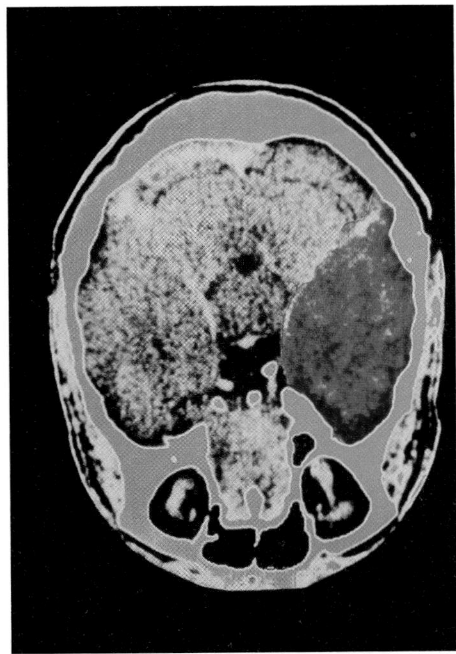
Encephalitis
The red area in this computerized axial tomography (CAT) scan reveals inflammation in the temporal lobe. The cause of this swelling is herpes simplex virus, the same virus responsible for Clive's illness. Many people carry this virus (it causes cold sores), but herpes encephalitis is rare, affecting approximately 1 in 500,000 people annually (Anderson, 2017, August 23). Even with treatment, this brain infection usually leaves its victims with neurological deficits (Anderson, 2016, June 15). Airelle-Joubert/Science Source.

Clive survived, but the damage to his brain was extensive and profound. And though Clive could still sing and play the keyboard (and spent much of the day doing so), he was unable to continue working as a conductor and music producer (D. Wearing, personal communication, June 18, 2013; Wilson & Wearing, 1995). In fact, he could barely get through day-to-day life. In the early stages of recovery, simple activities like eating baffled him. He ate the menu and attempted to spread cottage cheese on his bread, apparently mistaking it for butter. He confused basic concepts such as "scarf" and "umbrella," and shaved his eyebrows and nose (Wearing, 2005; Wilson & Wearing, 1995).

In the months following his illness, Clive was overcome with the feeling of just awakening. His senses were functioning properly, but every sight, sound, odor, taste, and feeling registered for just a moment, and then vanished. As Deborah described it, Clive saw the world anew with every blink of his eye (Wearing, 2005). The world must have seemed like a whirlwind of sensations, always changing. Desperate to make sense of it all, Clive would pose the same questions time and again: "How long have I been ill?" he would ask Deborah and the hospital staff members looking

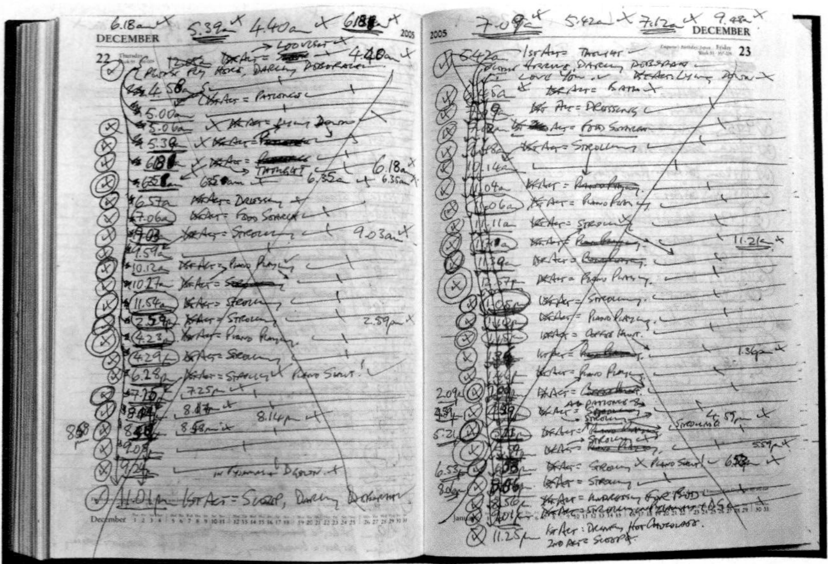

The Diary
Looking at a page from Clive's diary, you can see the fragmented nature of his thought process. He writes an entry, forgets it within seconds, and then returns to the page to start over, often writing the same thing. Encephalitis damaged many areas of Clive's brain, including the hippocampus (crucial for learning and memory), so he can no longer recall what is happening from moment to moment. Jiri Rezac/Polaris/Newscom.

after him. "How long's it been?" (Wearing, 2005, p. 181). For much of the first decade following his illness, Clive repeated the same few phrases almost continuously in his conversations with people. "I haven't heard anything, seen anything, touched anything, smelled anything," he would say. "It's just like being dead" (p. 160).

The depth of Clive's impairment is revealed in his diary, where he wrote essentially the same entries all day long. On August 25, 1985, he wrote, "I woke at 8:50 A.M. and baught [sic] a copy of *The Observer,*" which is then crossed out and followed by "I woke at 9:00 A.M. I had already bought a copy of *The Observer.*" The next line reads, "This (officially) confirms that I awoke at 9:05 A.M. this morning" (Wearing, 2005, p. 182). Having forgotten all previous entries, Clive reported throughout the day that he had just become conscious. His recollection of writing in his journal—along with every experience in his life—came and went in a flash. The herpes virus had ravaged his memory system.

The story of Clive Wearing launches our journey through *memory.* You may be wondering why we chose to start this chapter with the story of a person whose memory system failed. When it comes to understanding complex cognitive processes, sometimes it helps to examine what happens when elements of the system are not working properly. And when we say "working properly," we do not mean working perfectly. Unlike a smartphone camera, which captures, stores, and reproduces events with high fidelity, the human memory system is vulnerable to errors and distortions. By the time you finish this chapter, you may find yourself questioning some of the memories you once considered absolute truths.

Encoding, Storage, and Retrieval

LO 1 Define memory.

In everyday conversations, "memory" refers to anything remembered ("I remember my 14th birthday" or "I recall our trip to the beach"). In psychology, **memory** refers to the brain processes involved in the encoding (collection), storage, and retrieval of information. Scientists have proposed many theories and models to explain how the brain processes, or works on, data en route to becoming memories. As you learn about some of these theories and models, keep in mind that none are perfect. Rather than labeling one as *right* and another as *wrong,* most psychologists embrace a combination of approaches, considering their strengths and weaknesses.

CONNECTIONS
In **Chapter 2,** we described the electrical and chemical processes involved in communication between neurons. We also reported that the human brain contains billions of cells interlinked by trillions of connections.

memory Brain processes involved in the encoding, storage, and retrieval of information.

One often-used model likens the brain's memory system to a computer. Think about how a computer operates: It receives data from external sources, like your fingers typing on the keyboard, and **converts that data** into a code it can manipulate. Once this is accomplished, the information can be saved on a hard drive or in the cloud so you can open up the documents, GIFs, and other data files you need. The brain's memory system accomplishes similar tasks, but it is very different from a computer. Communication among neurons in the brain is more complicated than signals running between electrical components in a circuit. And unlike a computer, which maintains your files exactly how you last saved them, memories are subject to modifications over time, and this means they may be somewhat different each time you access them. Finally, the brain has seemingly unlimited storage capabilities, and the ability to process many types of information, both consciously and unconsciously.

We don't completely understand how a functioning memory system works, but there is basic agreement on its general processes, particularly *encoding, storage,* and *retrieval.*

LO 2 Describe the processes of encoding, storage, and retrieval.

CONNECTIONS

In **Chapters 2** and **3**, we described how sensory information is taken in by sensory receptors and transduced; that is, transformed into neural activity. Here, we explore what happens *after* transduction, when information is processed in the memory system.

ENCODING During the course of a day, you are bombarded with input from all of your senses and internal data in the form of thoughts and emotions. Some of that information you will remember, but the majority will not be retained for long. Most psychologists agree that information enters the memory system through a process called **encoding.** Imagine you are getting your hair cut. Sitting in the chair, you smell hair products, feel a comb running over your scalp, and hear the sounds of voices and snipping scissors. The stimuli associated with the event are taken in by your senses and then **converted to neural activity** that travels to the brain. The information is processed, and from this point it can take one of two paths: Either it enters the memory system (it is encoded to be stored for a longer period of time) or it slips away.

STORAGE For information that is successfully encoded, the next step is **storage.** Storage is exactly what it sounds like: preserving information for possible recollection in the future. Before Clive Wearing fell ill, his memory was excellent. His brain was able to encode and store a variety of events and learned skills. Following his bout with encephalitis, however, his ability for long-term storage of new memories was destroyed—he could no longer retain new information for more than seconds at a time.

RETRIEVAL After information is stored, how do we access it? Perhaps you still have a memory of your first-grade teacher's face, but can you remember his or her name? This process of coming up with stored information (*Ms. Ventura! Mr. Kopitz!*) is called **retrieval.** Sometimes information is encoded and stored in memory but cannot be retrieved. Have you ever felt that a person's name or a certain vocabulary word was just sitting "on the tip of your tongue"? Chances are you were struggling from a retrieval failure, which we discuss later in this chapter.

Lion of a Memory
Saroo Brierley at the Berlin premiere of *Lion,* the Oscar-nominated film that tells his amazing story. Brierley was just 5 years old when he lost contact with his family in India. After getting separated from his older brother at a train station, Brierley boarded a train to Kolkata (previously Calcutta), 1,000 miles from home. He survived on the streets for weeks, ended up in an orphanage, and was adopted by a couple in Tasmania, Australia. Two decades later, Brierley used Google Earth and his memory of landmarks to find his way back home, where he reunited with his biological family (Dunlop, 2017, January 19; NPR Staff, 2014, June 22). People Picture/Norbert Kesten/REX/Shutterstock.

How Deep Are Your Memories?

Now that we understand the three major processes involved in memory—encoding, storage, and retrieval—let's focus on how deeply information is processed. To what degree does incoming data get worked on, and how does that affect the memory's staying power? According to the *levels of processing* framework, there are different depths of information processing ranging from shallow to deep (Craik & Lockhart, 1972; **Figure 6.1** on the next page). Shallow-level processing is primarily concerned with physical features (structural), such as the brightness or shape of an object, or the number of letters in a word, and generally results in short-lived memories. Deeper-level processing relies on characteristics related to patterns, like rhymes (phonemic) and meaning (semantic), and generally results in longer-lasting and easier-to-retrieve memories. So when you give little attention to data entering your sensory system, shallow processing occurs, resulting in more

encoding The process through which information enters our memory system.

storage The process of preserving information for possible recollection in the future.

retrieval The process of accessing information encoded and stored in memory.

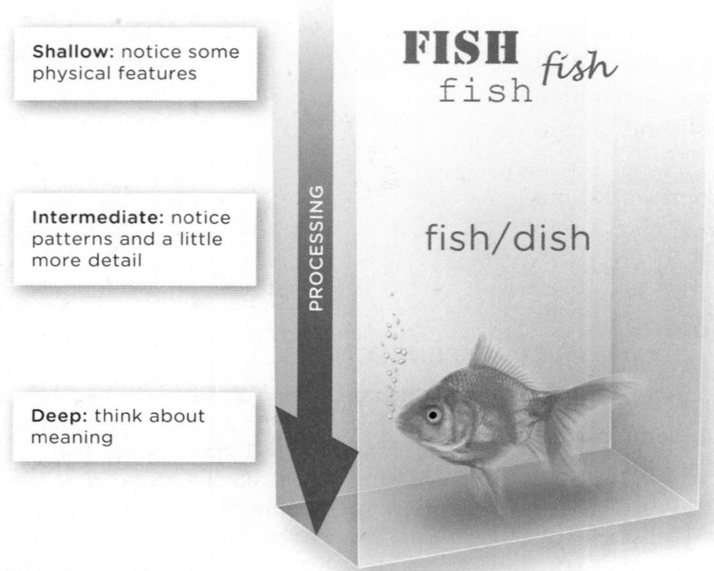

FIGURE 6.1
The Levels of Processing Framework
Information can be processed along a continuum from shallow to deep, affecting the probability of recall. Shallow processing, in which only certain details like the physical appearance of a word might be noticed, results in brief memories that may not be recalled later. We are better able to recall information we process at a deep level, thinking about meaning and tying it to memories we already have.
Goldfish: Gunnar Pippel/Shutterstock.

transient memories. If you really contemplate incoming information and relate it to memories you already have, deeper processing occurs, and the new memories are more likely to persist (Craik & Tulving, 1975; Francis & Gutiérrez, 2012; Newell & Andrews, 2004).

Fergus Craik and Endel Tulving explored levels of processing in their classic 1975 study. After presenting college students with various words, the researchers asked them yes or no questions, prompting them to think about and encode the words at three different levels: shallow, intermediate, and deep. The shallow questions required the students to study the appearance of the word: "Is the word in capital letters?" The intermediate-level questions related to the sound of the word: "Does the word rhyme with 'weight'?" And finally, the deep questions challenged students to consider the word's meaning: "Is the word a type of fish?" When the researchers surprised the students with a test to see which words they remembered without any cues or clues, the students were best able to recall words whose meaning they had thought about (Craik & Tulving, 1975). The take-home message: Deep thinking helps create stronger memories (Dunlosky, Rawson, Marsh, Nathan, & Willingham, 2013; Foos & Goolkasian, 2008).

The levels of processing model helps us understand why testing, which often requires you to connect new and old information, can improve memory and further your success in school. Research strongly supports the idea that "testing improves learning," as long as the stakes are low (Dunlosky et al., 2013). The *Show What You Know* and *Test Prep* resources in this textbook are designed to take advantage of this *testing effect*. Repeated testing results in a variety of benefits: better information retention, identification of areas needing more study, and increased self-motivated studying (Roediger, Putnam, & Smith, 2011). Speaking of testing, why not take a moment and show what you know?

✔ show what you know

1. ______________ is the process whereby information enters the memory system.
   - a. Retrieval
   - b. Encoding
   - c. Communication
   - d. Spatial memory

2. Give some examples of shallow processing versus deep processing as it relates to studying.

3. ______________ refers to the information your brain collects, stores, and may use at a later time.

✔ CHECK YOUR ANSWERS IN APPENDIX C.

Stages of Memory

Because memory is so complex, psychologists use several models to explain how it works. Among the most influential is the ***information-processing model*** first developed by Richard Atkinson and Richard Shiffrin. This model conceptualizes memory as a *flow of information* through a series of stages: *sensory memory, short-term memory,* and *long-term memory* (**Figure 6.2**) (Anderson, 1971; Atkinson & Shiffrin, 1968, January 31; Wood & Pennington, 1973).

synonyms
information-processing model modal model of memory

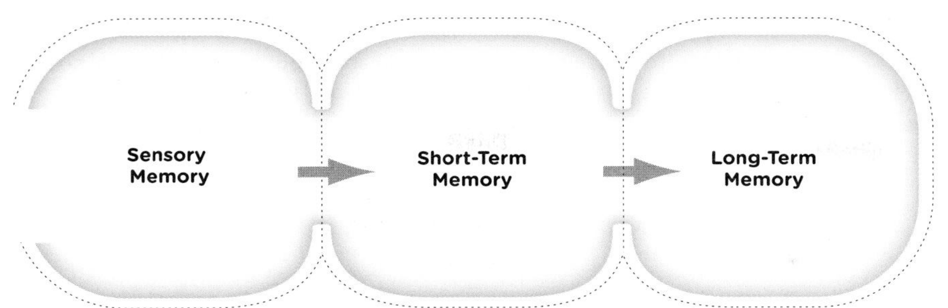

FIGURE 6.2
The Information-Processing Model

The Information-Processing Model

LO 3 Explain the stages of memory described by the information-processing model.

According to the information-processing model, each stage of memory has a certain type of storage with distinct capabilities: **Sensory memory** can hold vast amounts of sensory stimuli for a sliver of time, **short-term memory** can temporarily maintain and process limited information for longer periods (about 30 seconds, if there are no distractions), and **long-term memory** has almost unlimited capacity and can hold onto information indefinitely. In the sections that follow, we will flesh out these concepts of sensory, short-term, and long-term memory, which are incorporated in most memory models.

synonyms
sensory memory sensory register

The information-processing model is a valuable tool for learning about and researching memory, but like any scientific model, it has flaws. Some critics doubt that a clear boundary exists between *short-term* and *long-term* memory (Baddeley, 1995). Others argue that this "pipeline" model is too simplistic a representation because information does not necessarily flow through the memory system in a straight-line path (Cowan, 1988). Despite its weaknesses, the information-processing model remains an essential tool for explaining how memory works.

Sensory Memory

LO 4 Describe sensory memory.

Think of all the information streaming through your sensory channels at this very moment. Your eyes may be focused on this sentence, but you are also collecting data through your peripheral vision. You may be hearing noises (voices in the distance), smelling odors (the scent of lotion or deodorant you applied earlier today), tasting foods (if you are snacking), and even feeling things (shoes gently squeezing your feet). Many of these sensory stimuli never catch your attention, but some are being registered in your sensory memory, the first stage of the information-processing model. The bulk of information entering sensory memory comes and goes like images flitting by in a movie. A few things catch your attention—the beautiful eyes of Gal Gadot, the sound of her voice, and perhaps the color of her shirt—but not much more before the frame switches and you're looking at another image. Information floods our sensory memory through multiple channels—what we see enters through one channel, what we taste through another, and so on.

sensory memory A stage of memory that captures near-exact copies of vast amounts of sensory stimuli for a very brief period of time.

short-term memory A stage of memory that temporarily maintains and processes a limited amount of information.

long-term memory A stage of memory with essentially unlimited capacity and the ability to store information indefinitely.

try this Stare at the photo of the monkey and then shut your eyes for several seconds. Did you see the image in your mind's eye and, if so, how long did this iconic memory last?

Georgegid/Shutterstock.com.

"MORE IS SEEN THAN CAN BE REMEMBERED" The visual impressions in our sensory memory, also known as **iconic memory,** are photograph-like in their accuracy but dissolve in less than a second. To explore how the brain processes data entering the visual channel, Harvard graduate student George Sperling (1960) set up a screen that flashed multiple rows of letters for one-twentieth of a second, and then asked participants to report what they saw. When an *array* of letters (for example, three rows of four letters) was flashed briefly, he found that, on average, the participants only reported four letters. Were the participants able to store only one row at a time, or did they store all the rows, but just not long enough to recite them before they were forgotten?

Sperling suspected that "more is seen than can be remembered" (1960, p. 1), so he again briefly flashed an array of letters with all rows visible. But instead of having the participants report what they remembered from all the rows, he asked them to report what they remembered from just one row at a time (**Figure 6.3**). In this version of the study, the participants doubled their performance, recalling approximately 76% of the letters regardless of which row they were assigned (Sperling, 1960). Sperling's research suggests that the visual impressions in our sensory memory dissolve quickly. Given the short duration of iconic memory, can you predict what would happen if there were a delay before participants had to report what they saw?

FIGURE 6.3
How Fast It Fades
How do we know how long iconic memory lasts? George Sperling developed a creative way to measure how quickly iconic memories fade from awareness. Participants were shown an array of letters and were asked to recall one row. They performed well when recalling that one row, but couldn't recall other letters: Their sensory memory had faded (Sperling, 1960). This technique is still used today to study fleeting sensory memories.

K Z R A
Q B T P
S G N Y

Letters flash on screen, then disappear.

High Tone
Medium Tone
Low Tone

A tone sounds. Participants report only the row associated with that tone.

Participants can report row associated with tone, but no other row. All letters initially registered in their sensory memory, but the iconic memory dissolves before more letters can be reported.

Almost Photographic
After one helicopter fight over Mexico City, artist/architect Stephen Wiltshire is able to produce this cityscape from memory. "Wiltshire's drawings are so accurate that even small details, such as the number of columns or windows on individual buildings are faithfully reproduced in images that encompass many city blocks, even whole cities" (Martin, 2013, pp. R732–R733). Wiltshire, who has autism, appears to possess *eidetic imagery*, meaning he can "see" an image or object sometimes long after it has been removed from sight, describing its parts with amazing specificity. Anadolu Agency/Getty Images.

EIDETIC IMAGERY Perhaps you have heard friends talk about someone who claims to have a "photographic memory" that can record and store images with the accuracy of a camera, but is there scientific evidence to back up such an assertion? Not at this time (Gordon, 2013, January 1; MacLeod, Jonker, & James, 2013). According to some reports, though, researchers have documented a phenomenon that comes fairly close to photographic memory. It's called *eidetic imagery* (ahy-DET-ik), and those who have this rare ability can "see" an image or object sometimes long after it has been removed from sight, describing its parts with amazing specificity. For example, architect Stephen Wiltshire is an *autistic savant,* who reportedly can create detailed and accurate drawings of entire "cityscapes after a single helicopter ride" (Martin, 2013, p. R732). This ability seems to occur primarily in children, with some suggesting this type of memory is lost as the brain grows and develops (Ko, 2015; Searleman, 2007, March 12).

ECHOIC MEMORY Exact copies of the sounds we hear linger longer than visual impressions; **echoic memory** (eh-KOH-ik) can last from about 1 to 10 seconds (Lu, Williamson, & Kaufman, 1992; Peterson, Meagher, & Ellsbury, 1970). Even if you are not aware of it, your auditory system is detecting stimuli and storing them in echoic memory for a brief moment. In this way, you don't have to pay attention to every incoming sound. Perhaps you have had the following experience: During class, your instructor notices a classmate daydreaming: "Olivia, could you please restate the question for us?" Her mind was indeed wandering, but amazingly she can recall the instructor's last sentence, responding, "You asked us if brain scans should be allowed as evidence in courtrooms." For this, Olivia can thank her echoic memory.

Although brief, sensory memory is critical for memory formation. Without it, how would information enter the memory system in the first place? The bulk of research has focused on iconic and echoic memories, but memories can also be rich in smells, tastes, and touch. Data received from all of the senses are held momentarily in sensory memory. Most of this information disappears in a flash, but items that capture your attention can move into the second stage in the information-processing model proposed by Atkinson and Shiffrin (1968): short-term memory.

Short-Term Memory

Summarize short-term memory.

The amount of time information is maintained and processed in short-term memory depends on how much you are distracted by other cognitive activities, but the duration can be about 30 seconds (Atkinson & Shiffrin, 1968). You can stretch short-term memory further with **maintenance rehearsal**, a technique of repeating what you want to remember over and over in your mind. Using maintenance rehearsal, you can theoretically hold onto information as long as you desire. This strategy comes in handy when you need to remember a series of numbers or letters (for example, phone numbers or zip codes). Imagine the following: While strolling down the street, you witness a hit-and-run accident. A truck runs a red light, smashes into a car, and then speeds away. As the truck zooms off, you manage to catch a glimpse of the license plate number, but how will you remember it long enough before reaching the 911 operator? If you're like most people, you will say the plate number to yourself over and over, either aloud or in your mind, using maintenance rehearsal.

synonyms
maintenance rehearsal rote rehearsal

iconic memory Visual impressions that are photograph-like in their accuracy but dissolve in less than a second; a form of sensory memory.

echoic memory Exact copies of the sounds we hear; a form of sensory memory.

maintenance rehearsal Technique of repeating information to be remembered, increasing the length of time it can be held in short-term memory.

CONNECTIONS

In **Chapter 4,** we discussed the limited capacity of human attention. At any given point in time, there are only so many items you can attend to and thus move into your memory system. Thus, we see how memory is related to attention.

However, maintenance rehearsal does not work so well if you are **distracted.** In a classic study examining the duration of short-term memory, most participants were unable to recall three-letter combinations beyond 18 seconds while performing another task (Peterson & Peterson, 1959; **Figure 6.4**). The task (counting backward by 3s) interfered with their natural inclination to mentally repeat the letter combinations; in other words, they were limited in their ability to use maintenance rehearsal. This study reveals that short-term memory has a limited capacity. Remember this if you text during class or watch Netflix while studying; in order to remember what you *should be* concentrating on, you need to give it your full attention.

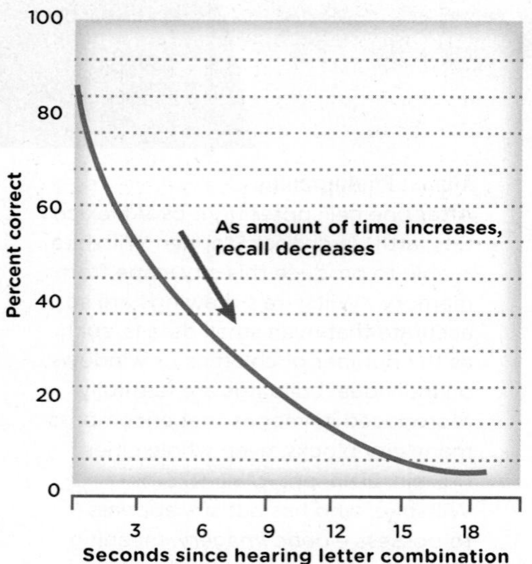

FIGURE 6.4
Duration of Short-Term Memory
Distraction can reduce the amount of time information remains in short-term memory. When performing a distracting cognitive task, most people were unable to recall a letter combination beyond 18 seconds.

LO 6 Give examples of how we can use chunking to improve our memory span.

With maintenance rehearsal, you try to remember numbers, letters, or other items by repeating them over and over in your mind. But how many items can we realistically hold in our short-term memory at one time? Using a task called the Digit Span Test (**Figure 6.5**), cognitive psychologist George Miller (1956) determined that most people can retain only five to nine digits: He called this the "magical number seven, plus or minus two." Indeed, researchers following up on this discovery have found that most people can only attend to about five to nine *items* at one time (Cowan, Chen, & Rouder, 2004; Cowan, Nugent, & Elliott, 2000). But what exactly constitutes an item? Must it be a single-digit number? Not necessarily; we can expand short-term memory by packing more information into the items to be remembered. Consider this example: Your friend has just gotten a new phone number, which she rattles off as the elevator door closes between you. How are you going to remember her number long enough to create a new entry in your cell phone? You could try memorizing all 10 digits in a row (8935550172), but a better strategy is to break the number into more manageable pieces (893-555-0172). Here, you are using **chunking,** Miller's (1956) name for grouping numbers, letters, or other types of information into recognizable "chunks," or units of information (Cowan, 2015).

Put Your Heads Together

Short-term memory can only hold so much, but we can push the limit by chunking. In your group, discuss some ways you use chunking in everyday life. Write down at least three examples your group identifies.

The fact that short-term memory is actively processing information and has a flexible storage capacity suggests that it may be more than just a temporary holding place for information. Indeed, many psychologists believe that short-term memory is hard at work.

2390
45791
340982
0128957
93781256
501298347

FIGURE 6.5
Digit Span Test
The Digit Span Test is a simple way to assess memory. Participants are asked to listen to a string of numbers and then repeat them. The string of numbers grows longer as the test progresses. Ask a friend to give you this test and see how many numbers you can remember.

Working Memory

LO 7 Describe working memory and its relationship to short-term memory.

Updated versions of the information-processing model include a concept known as **working memory** (Baddeley, 2012; Baddeley & Hitch, 1974), which refers to what is *going on* in short-term memory. Working memory is the active processing through which we maintain and manipulate information in the memory system. Let's use an analogy of a "bakery" and what goes on inside it. Short-term memory is the bakery, that is, the place that hosts your current thoughts and whatever your brain

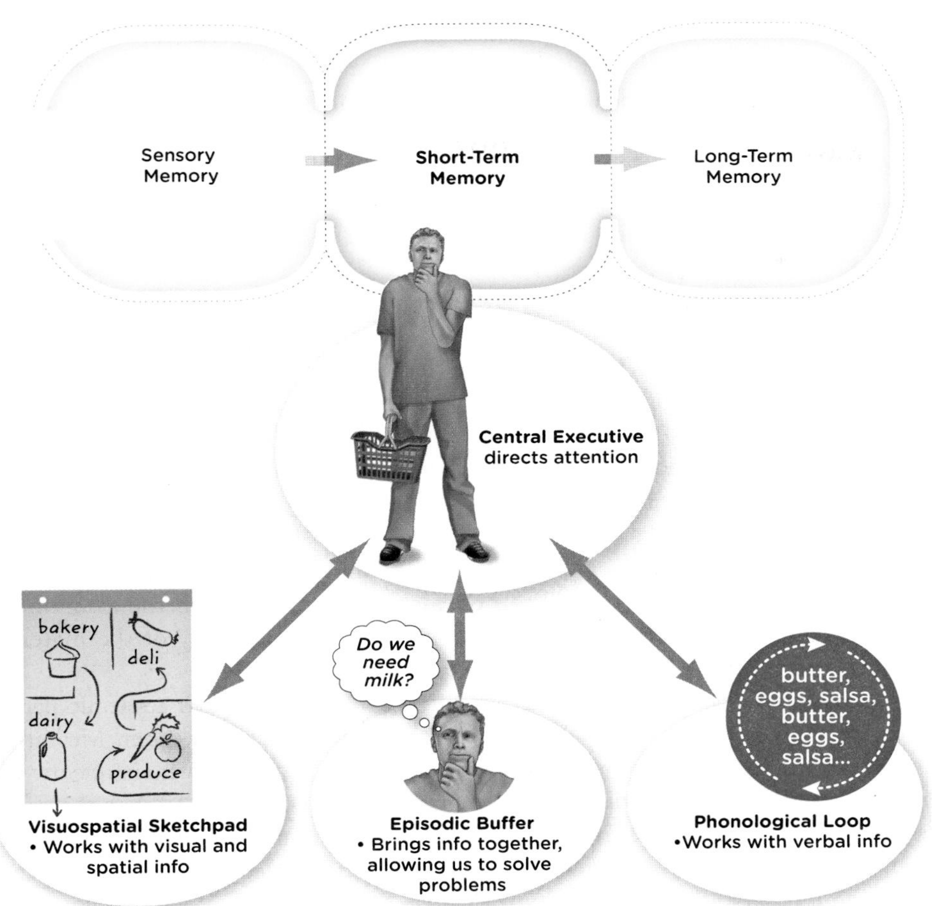

FIGURE 6.6
Working Memory
Working memory represents the active processing occurring in short-term memory. Overseeing the big picture is the central executive, which directs attention and integrates processing among three subsystems: the phonological loop, visuospatial sketchpad, and episodic buffer. To see how this model works, imagine you have stopped by the supermarket to pick up groceries. You rehearse the shopping list with your phonological loop, produce a mental layout of the store with your visuospatial sketchpad, and use the episodic buffer to access long-term memories and determine whether you need any additional items. Tying together all these activities is the central executive.

is working on at this very moment. Working memory is what's going on inside the bakery—making bread, cakes, and pastries—or in the case of the brain, processing information. Some psychologists use the terms short-term and working memory interchangeably. For our purposes, we will identify "short-term memory" as a stage in the original information-processing model as well as the "location" where information is temporarily held, and "working memory" as the activities or processing occurring within.

According to the model of working memory originally proposed by psychologists Alan Baddeley and Graham Hitch (1974; Baddeley, 2012), the purpose of working memory is to actively maintain information, and thus enable complex cognitive tasks. To accomplish this, working memory has four components: the phonological loop, visuospatial sketchpad, central executive, and episodic buffer (Baddeley, 2002; **Figure 6.6**).

The *phonological loop* is responsible for working with verbal information for brief periods of time; when exposed to verbal stimuli, we "hear" an immediate corollary in our mind. This component of working memory is what we use, for example, when we are reading or trying to remember what someone said. The *visuospatial sketchpad* is where visual and spatial data are briefly stored and manipulated, including information about your surroundings and where things are in relation to you and to each other. This working memory component allows you to close your eyes and reach for the coffee mug you just set down (Baddeley, 1999, 2006). The *episodic buffer* is the part of working memory where information from the phonological loop, visuospatial sketchpad, and long-term memory can be brought together temporarily, under the direction of the central executive (Baddeley, 2000). It enables us to assign meaning to past events, solve problems, and make plans for the future.

chunking Grouping numbers, letters, or other items into recognizable subsets as a strategy for increasing the quantity of information that can be maintained in short-term memory.

working memory The active processing of information in short-term memory; the maintenance and manipulation of information in the memory system.

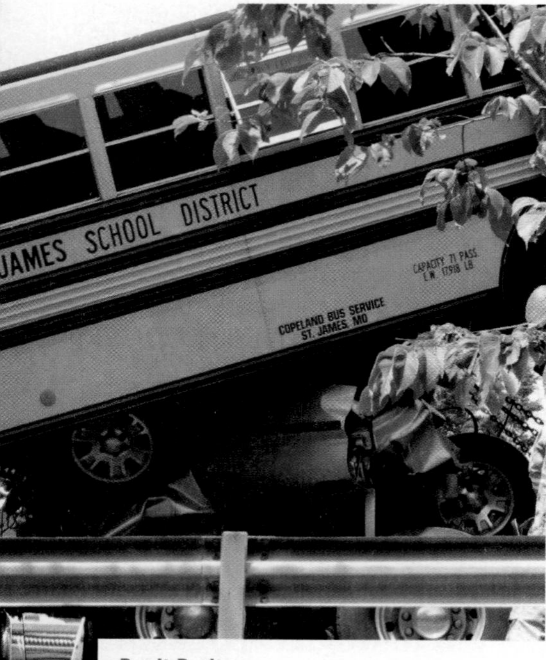

Don't Do It
Media multitasking doesn't just threaten your academic performance; it can endanger your life, too. Picture this crumpled car next time you consider using your smartphone behind the wheel. Texting while driving increases the likelihood of crashing by four times (National Safety Council, 2015), and studies show that using a cell phone impairs driving to the same degree as drunkenness (Strayer & Watson, 2012, March). Jeff Roberson/AP Images.

The *central executive* has responsibilities similar to those of the chief executive in any organization—it directs attention, makes plans, and coordinates activities (Baddeley, 2002). Part of its role is to determine what information is important, and to guide our consciousness. Why is it that we cannot actually text, eat, and safely drive all at once? Like a juggler, the central executive can only catch and toss one ball at a time. We may think we are doing all three tasks at once, but we are really just swapping the activities in and out at a fast pace. Keep this in mind the next time you sit down to study.

SOCIAL MEDIA AND PSYCHOLOGY

MULTITASKING: YOUR MEMORY'S WORST ENEMY? It's Sunday evening, and you need to catch up on the reading for your psychology class. You find a quiet place and open your textbook. But just as you are getting into the psychology groove, you feel a vibration inside your pocket—your cell phone. Could it be a text, a new Snap, a reply to your latest tweet? You can't resist checking. You return to your studies, but social media notifications continue every 5 or 10 minutes, pulling your attention away from psychology. By the evening's end, you do manage to get through the assignment, but how have all these digital distractions affected your memory of the material? Definitely not for the better.

THIS IS YOUR GPA ON FACEBOOK

Various studies have linked media multitasking with diminished academic performance (Hawi & Samaha, 2016; Junco, 2015; Karpinski, Kirschner, Ozer, Mellott, & Ochwo, 2013). One group of researchers found that college students who frequently text and use Facebook while studying have lower grade point averages (GPAs) than those who do not (Junco & Cotten, 2012). Another research team found that teenagers who commonly multitask with media perform worse on math and English achievement tests than those who multitask less (Cain, Leonard, Gabrieli, & Finn, 2016). Many of these studies are **correlational**, making it difficult to untangle cause-and-effect relationships. Does media multitasking make it harder to remember material and thus lead to inferior academic performance, or do lower-achieving students simply have a more difficult time resisting the lure of Twitter, Snapchat, and Instagram? Perhaps students with lower GPAs spend more time on social media (Michikyan, Subrahmanyam, & Dennis, 2015).

CONNECTIONS
In **Chapter 1,** we discussed negative correlations, or the inverse link between two variables. Here, we see that as time spent using Facebook goes up, GPA goes down. But correlation does not prove causation; perhaps people with lower GPAs have less interest in studying, and thus more time to socialize. Or, maybe there is a third factor, such as the ability to manage time effectively, influencing both variables.

What does this mean for you? If you're multitasking with media, you are likely missing important information from lectures and readings. Just having a computer in the classroom may be a distraction, even if you are not multitasking. One study found that "students who took notes on laptops performed worse on conceptual questions than students who took notes longhand" (Mueller & Oppenheimer, 2014, p. 1159). Some professors think laptops should not be allowed during lectures, except for students who have disabilities (McMurtrie, 2017, November 27). Where do you stand on this issue?

Put Your Heads Together

With a partner, **A**) choose an activity that requires your attention (for example, texting each other the names of TV show characters; taking turns naming meals you've eaten this month). **B**) As you perform this task, try to memorize the 40 key terms listed at the end of the chapter. **C**) After 5 minutes, close your textbook and write the key terms (in order) on a blank sheet of paper. **D**) Discuss how multitasking affected your maintenance rehearsal of the key terms.

As you know, short-term memory is limited in its capacity and duration, and working memory has its limitations as well. So how do we maintain so much information over the years? What aspect of memory makes it possible to recall thousands of words, names, facts, and lyrics to our favorite songs? Enter long-term memory.

Long-Term Memory

Items that enter short-term memory have two possible fates: Either they fade away or they move into *long-term memory* (**Figure 6.7** on the next page). Just think about how much information is stashed away in your long-term memory: funny jokes, images of faces, multiplication tables, storylines from books and movies, and so many words—around 10,000 to 11,000 word families (such as "smile," "smiled," "smiling") for English-speaking college students (Treffers-Daller & Milton, 2013). Could it be that long-term memory has an endless holding capacity? It may be impossible to answer this question, but for all practical purposes long-term memory has no limits. Some memories stored there, such as street names from your childhood, may be available for a lifetime (Reber, 2010, May/June; Schmidt, Peeck, Paas, & van Breukelen, 2000).

LO 8 Describe long-term memory.

Long-term memory can be described in a variety of ways, but psychologists often distinguish between two categories: explicit and implicit. **Explicit memory** is the type of memory you are aware of having and can consciously express in words, or declare. **Implicit memory** is a memory of something you know or know how to do, which may be automatic, unconscious, and difficult to bring to awareness and express.

synonyms
explicit memory declarative memory
implicit memory nondeclarative memory

EXPLICIT MEMORY Endel Tulving (1972) proposed there are two forms of explicit memory: semantic and episodic. **Semantic memory** pertains to general facts about the world (*the Earth is located in the Milky Way; the United States holds presidential elections every four years; the brain has two hemispheres*). But there is also a type of memory you can call your own. Your first experience riding a bike, the time you got lost in the supermarket, the sandwich you ate yesterday—all these personal memories are part of your **episodic memory** (ep-uh-SOD-ik). You can think of episodic memory as the record of memorable experiences, or "episodes," in your life, including when and where they occurred (Tulving, 1985).

FLASHBULB MEMORIES Often, our most vivid episodic memories are associated with intense emotion. Think about an emotionally charged experience from your past: learning about a terrorist attack, getting news that someone you love has been in an accident, or hearing that your favorite sports team has won a historic championship. If recollecting these moments feels like watching a 4-D movie, you might be experiencing what psychologists call a **flashbulb memory,** a detailed account of circumstances surrounding an emotionally significant or shocking, sometimes historic, event (Brown & Kulik, 1977). With flashbulb memories, you often recall the precise moment you learned of an event—where you were, who or what source relayed the news, how it made you feel, what you did next, and other random details about the experience (Brown & Kulik, 1977). Perhaps you have a flashbulb memory of hearing about the horrific massacre at Marjory Stoneman Douglas High School in Parkland, Florida, in 2018, or learning that Donald Trump won the 2016 presidential election; you recall whom you were with, what you were drinking and eating, what music was playing. Flashbulb memories are experienced across cultures, but the content of those memories may differ (Gandolphe & El Haj, 2017). For example, people in Chicago might have a vivid memory of the Cubs finally winning the 2016 World Series. Meanwhile, people in France are likely to have flashbulb memories of their team winning the 2018 World Cup. Note that a flashbulb memory is a specific type of episodic memory of experiences associated with *learning about* an event rather than "firsthand memories" of *experiencing* the event (Hirst & Phelps, 2016).

explicit memory A type of memory you are aware of having and can consciously express in words or declare, including memories of facts and experiences.

implicit memory A memory of something you know or know how to do, which may be automatic, unconscious, and difficult to bring to awareness and express.

semantic memory The memory of information theoretically available to anyone, which pertains to general facts about the world; a type of explicit memory.

episodic memory The record of memorable experiences or "episodes," including when and where an experience occurred; a type of explicit memory.

flashbulb memory A detailed account of circumstances surrounding an emotionally significant or shocking, sometimes historic, event.

FIGURE 6.7
Long-Term Memory

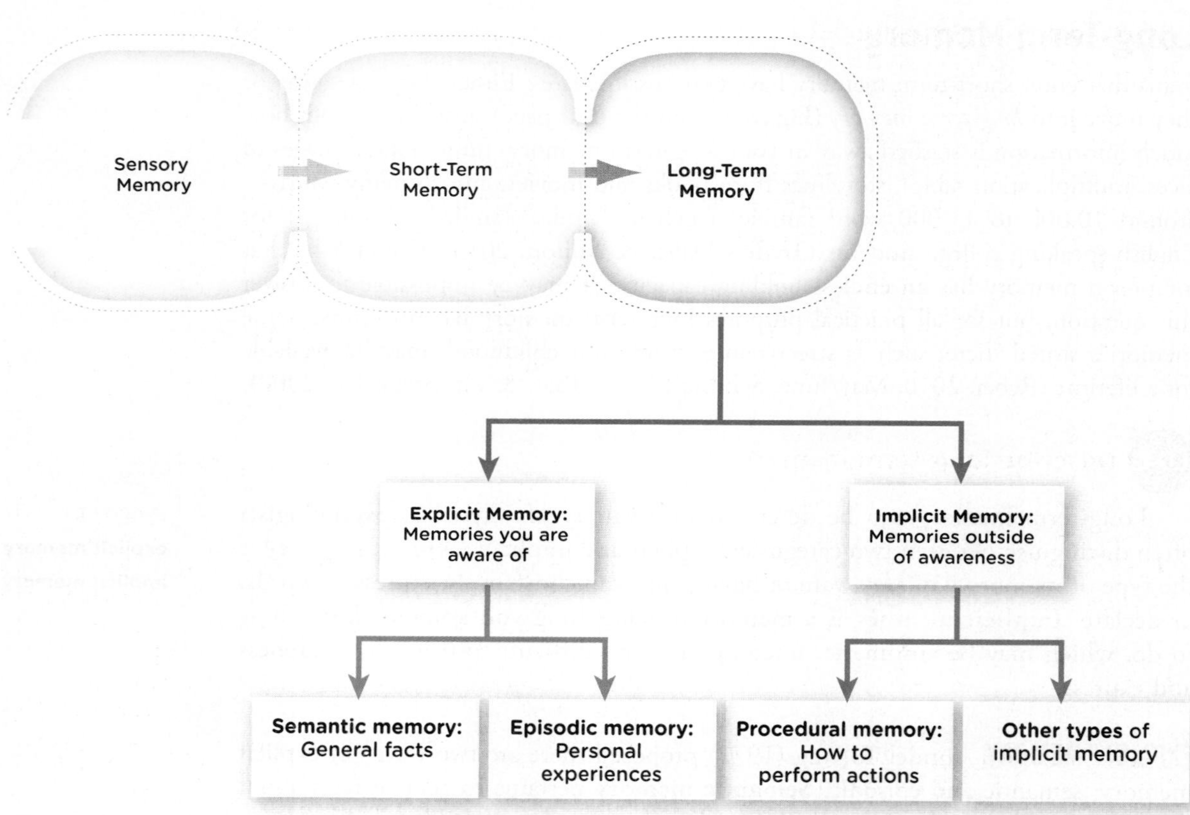

Effortless
Following his bout with encephalitis in 1985, Clive could still read music and play the piano, demonstrating that his procedural memory was not destroyed. Researchers documented a similar phenomenon in a professional cello player who battled herpes encephalitis in 2005 (Vennard, 2011, November 21).
Jiri Rezac/Polaris/Newscom.

Because flashbulb memories seem so strong, vivid, and rich in detail, we often place great confidence in them, but research suggests that these memories can be inaccurate or lack specific details (Hirst et al., 2015; Neisser, 1991). And as you will learn later in this chapter, such errors are not uncommon.

IMPLICIT MEMORY Unlike explicit memory, which can easily flow into conscious thought, implicit memory is difficult to bring into awareness and express. It is a memory for something you know or know how to do, which might be automatic or unconscious. Many of the physical activities we take for granted, such as playing an instrument, driving a car, and dribbling a basketball, use a special type of implicit memory called **procedural memory,** that is, the memory of how to carry out an activity without conscious control or attention. After his illness, Clive Wearing could still pick up a piece of music and play it on the piano. He had no recollection of learning to sight-read or play, yet he could execute these skills like the professional he had always been (Vennard, 2011, November 21). Therefore, Clive's procedural memory was still working.

Memories acquired through classical conditioning are also implicit. Let's say you enjoy eating food at McDonald's and the very sight of the golden arches makes you salivate like one of **Pavlov's dogs**. Somewhere along the line, you formed a memory linking the appearance of that restaurant to juicy hamburgers and salty fries, but the association does not require your conscious awareness (Cowan, 1988). It is implicit.

CONNECTIONS

In **Chapter 5,** we introduced the concept of classical conditioning, which occurs when an originally neutral stimulus elicits an involuntary response, such as salivation, eye blinks, and other types of reflex reactions. Here, we can see how closely linked learning and memory are.

What's the Best Way to Make Memories?

How does the process of moving data into the memory system lead to the creation of memories? Some activities work well for keeping information in short-term memory (maintenance rehearsal, for example). Others involve moving information from short-term memory to long-term memory.

USE MNEMONICS Have you ever relied on the *first-letter technique* to remember the order of operations in math (Please Excuse My Dear Aunt Sally)? Or, perhaps you have used an *acronym,* such as ROY G BIV, to remember the colors of the rainbow (**Figure 6.8**)? These are **mnemonic** (nih-MON-ik) devices, or techniques for improving memory. Chunking, which we discussed earlier, is another mnemonic device. So, too, is the *method of loci* (LOH-sahy, meaning "places"), which involves placing items to be remembered along a mental journey. Just pick a familiar route—through your favorite restaurant, college campus, even your body parts—and mentally place things you need to remember at points along the way. The method of loci works very well for memorizing lists, especially if you practice often. **INFOGRAPHIC 6.1** on the next page presents mnemonics and other strategies that can enhance the retention of material as you study.

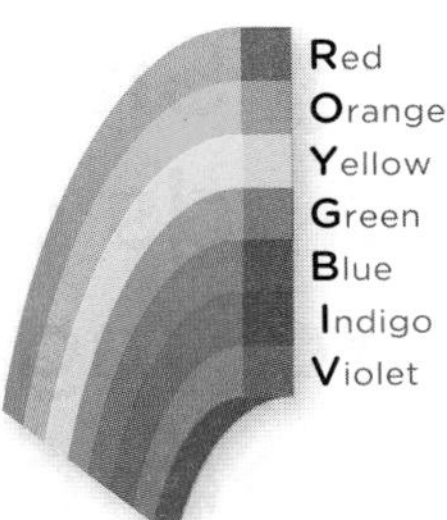

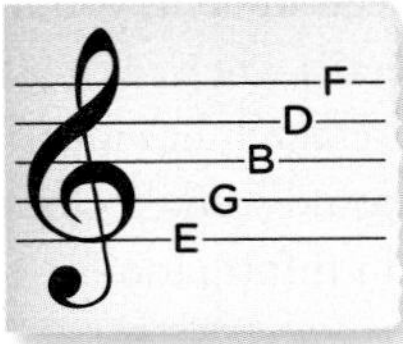

FIGURE 6.8
Mnemonics
Mnemonics enable us to translate information into a form that is easier to remember. For example, the common acronym ROY G BIV helps us remember the order of the seven colors in the rainbow. And when music students have trouble remembering the notes on the lines of the treble clef (EGBDF), they often rely on the first-letter technique, creating a sentence out of words beginning with these letters: *Every Good Boy Deserves Fudge.*

HOW MUCH EFFORT? Earlier we noted that stronger memories result when you think about information on a deep level. This requires **effortful processing,** which involves the encoding and storage of information with conscious effort or awareness. Some types of effortful processing, such as maintenance rehearsal, are useful for extending the amount of time you can hold onto information in short-term memory. Others employ patterns and meaning to encode information for longer storage. Your decisions to use (or not use) effortful processing may impact your academic achievement and ability to solve everyday problems. But you might not always choose the effortful path, particularly if you believe the "cost" is too high and the effort feels "aversive" (Westbrook & Braver, 2015). For example, your psychology writing assignment is so cognitively taxing that you decide it's not worth the effort; instead you spend your time creating a new photo album on Facebook. Choosing whether to use effortful processing takes effort, putting a strain on working memory, which has limited resources (Boureau, Sokol-Hessner, & Daw, 2015). What can a student do to facilitate effortful processing? Work in a quiet room, keep cell phones out of sight, sit at the front of the classroom, and keep your eye on a clock so you can use your time wisely (Duckworth, Gendler, & Gross, 2016).

Effortful processing is evident in **elaborative rehearsal,** the method of connecting incoming information to knowledge in long-term memory. The method of loci involves this type of deeper processing (elaborative rehearsal) because it requires that you take new information and put it in the familiar framework of a place you know. By picturing the journey and the objects-to-be-remembered in your minds' eye, you also take advantage of *visualization,* another effective encoding strategy.

SPACING IS KEY One strategy you should avoid is "cramming" when trying to learn new material. This type of **massed practice** refers to learning sessions that occur generally within the same day, "back-to-back or in relatively close succession" (Dunlosky et al., 2013, p. 36). A more effective approach is **distributed practice**, or spreading study sessions over the course of many days. When researchers asked students to learn a new mathematical skill, they found that participants who practiced the new skill in two sessions (separated by a week) did better on a practice test (4 weeks later) than those who spent the same amount of time practicing in one session (Pashler, Rohrer, Cepeda, & Carpenter, 2007). Similarly, students who reviewed material from a natural science class 8 days after the original lectures did better on final exams than those who reviewed the material 1 day after the lectures (Kapler, Weston, & Wiseheart, 2015).

synonyms
distributed practice spacing effect

procedural memory The unconscious memory of how to carry out a variety of skills and activities; a type of implicit memory.

mnemonic Technique to improve memory.

effortful processing The encoding and storage of information with conscious effort or awareness.

elaborative rehearsal The method of connecting incoming information to knowledge in long-term memory; a deep level of encoding.

massed practice Studying for long periods of time without breaks.

distributed practice Spreading out study sessions over time with breaks in between.

Put Your Heads Together

In your groups, **A)** discuss your daily routines. **B)** Create a weekly calendar showing when and how much time you devote to each study session. **C)** How might you adjust your schedule to take full advantage of distributed practice?

Study Smarter: Methods of Improving Your Memory

As a college student, you must be able to remember many details when taking an exam. Lucky for you, research has identified several memory strategies and study techniques that can help you retain information.

start studying

Recall details

Mnemonics translate information into a more easily remembered form.

Acronyms and first-letter technique
It's easier to remember a short phrase than a string of information.

Chunking
It's easier to remember a few chunks than a long string.

8935550172
893-555-0172

Method of loci
It's easier to remember information when you deliberately link it to locations along a familiar route.

Organize information

Hierarchical structures organize information into a meaningful system. The process of organizing aids encoding and, once encoded, the information is easier to recall.

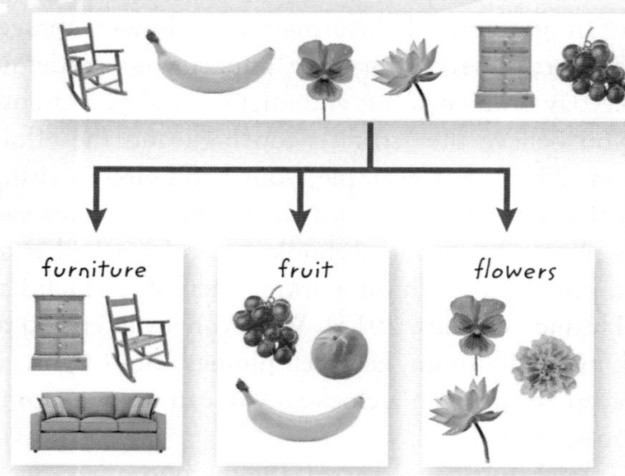

Make connections

Elaborative rehearsal is deep processing that boosts transfer to long-term memory by connecting new information to older memories.

Give yourself time

Distributed practice creates better memory than study crammed into a single session.

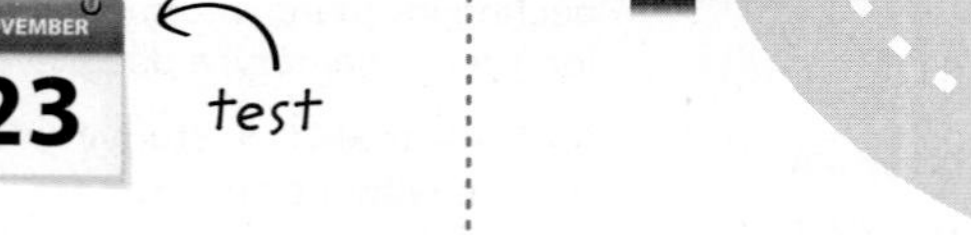

Get some rest

Sleep, or even wakeful resting after study, allows newly learned material to be encoded better.

ZZZ

Credits: Single lotus flower, fanedison/Shutterstock; Pine chest of drawers, Paul Maguire/Shutterstock; Pansy, AndreyKlepikov/Shutterstock; Green sofa, Shutterstock; Marigold, Alexander Mozymov/Shutterstock; City map with labels, Laralova/Shutterstock; Vintage wooden rocking chair, eurobanks/Shutterstock; Red grape, HeinzTeh/Shutterstock; Peach, Nattika/Shutterstock; November calendar icon, DVARG/Shutterstock; Banana, Tatiana Popova/Shutterstock; Portrait of teenage girl with hand on chin, BLOOMimage/Getty Images; Shutterstock; Marigold: Alexander Mozymov/Shutterstock; High education (student with chemical models and chemical formula on the blackboard), zorani/Getty Images.

GET SOME SLEEP We have touched on many strategies for boosting memory, but if we could leave you with one final piece of advice, it would be to *sleep*. Exactly how **sleep** promotes memory is still not completely understood, but there is no question that good sleep makes for better processing of memories (Diekelmann & Born, 2010; Marshall & Born, 2007; Rasch & Born, 2013). Even periods of "wakeful resting" can be of benefit (Schlichting & Bäuml, 2017). In one study, participants who experienced a 15-minute period of sitting in a dark quiet room displayed better retention of newly learned material than those who played a game for 15 minutes. Wakeful resting seems to allow newly learned material to be encoded better, and thus retained in memory longer (Dewar, Alber, Butler, Cowan, & Della Sala, 2012). Of course, it takes more than rest to succeed; you need to be able to analyze, apply, and synthesize material, not just remember it.

CONNECTIONS

In **Chapter 4,** we discussed how sleep and dreams relate to memory. For example, researchers suspect that sleep spindles are associated with memory consolidation, and some theorists emphasize the importance of REM sleep in this process.

"Wow, that's a lot to remember," you may be saying. Hopefully, you can retain it with the help of some of the mnemonic devices we have presented. You might also take a wakeful resting break in preparation for the next section, which focuses on memory retrieval.

show what you know

1. According to the information-processing model, our short-term memory can hold onto information for up to about ________________ if we are not distracted by something else.
   a. 10 seconds
   b. 30 seconds
   c. 45 seconds
   d. 60 seconds

2. As you enter the airport, you try to remember the location of the baggage claim area. You remember the last time you picked up your friend at this airport, and using your visuospatial sketchpad, realize the area is to your left. This ability demonstrates the use of your:
   a. sensory memory.
   b. working memory.
   c. phonological loop.
   d. flashbulb memory.

3. If you are trying to memorize a long password, you could use ________________, by grouping the numbers and symbols into recognizable units of information.

4. Develop a mnemonic device to help you memorize the following terms from this section: sensory memory, long-term memory, explicit memory, semantic memory, episodic memory, flashbulb memory, implicit memory, and procedural memory.

✓ CHECK YOUR ANSWERS IN APPENDIX C.

Retrieval and Forgetting

Have you ever heard the saying "An elephant never forgets"? Granted, this might be somewhat of an overstatement, but as far as animals go, elephants do have remarkable memories. Consider the story of two elephants that briefly worked together in the circus and then were separated for 23 years. When they re-encountered one another at an elephant sanctuary in Tennessee, the two animals started to inspect each other's trunk scars and "bellowed" in excitement: The long-lost friends had recognized one another (Ritchie, 2009, January 12)! An elephant's memory—and yours, too—is only as good as its ability to retrieve stored memories.

Friends Forever
Elephants Jenny and Shirley remembered each other after being separated for 23 years. Reunited at the Elephant Sanctuary in Hohenwald, Tennessee, they examined one another's trunks and hollered with joy (Ritchie, 2009, January 12). Courtesy of Carolyn Buckley, www.carolbuckley.com.

What strategies do you use to help yourself retrieve important information? If you are using conventional approaches, such as wearing a rubber band on your wrist or making a "to do" list, you may want to consider thinking a bit more outside the box.

From the SCIENTIFIC pages of AMERICAN

STOP SENDING YOURSELF REMINDER E-MAILS

A physical object is a more effective way to jog your memory.

Is your home littered with sticky notes telling you to mail that birthday card or pay that parking fine? Are your desk and computer similarly festooned with paper or digital reminders? Chances are, they are not very effective. Recent research suggests there is a better way: put an unusual object in a spot where it will catch your eye at the right moment.

"There are so many virtuous things we want to do that we don't follow through on," says behavioral scientist Todd Rogers of the Harvard Kennedy School of Government. Rogers ran a series of experiments to test what makes a reminder effective, the results of which were published in . . . *Psychological Science*. In one experiment, participants who said they wanted the researchers to donate a dollar to charity were told to indicate that choice by remembering to pick up a paper clip on their way out of the laboratory. Those who were told to look for a small elephant statue near the paper clips were more likely to follow through. Subsequent experiments showed that the reminder object worked better when it was unusual or unique in its context (for instance, the only stuffed animal on the desk). A reminder picture on a computer screen worked in the same way.

For a reminder to succeed, Rogers says, it has to capture your attention at the moment when you can focus on the task. A string around your finger is always there, so it fails to cue you at the right time. Written reminders may be found at the right time and place, but they are often not distinct from the many other papers around us. If instead you place, say, a plush alien by your door and think, "I will remember to mail that card when I see the alien," you may be more likely to complete the task. **Sara Chodosh.** ■

Can Bieber Retrieve?
Singer/songwriter Justin Bieber performs in Seattle, Washington, during his Purpose World Tour in 2016. Like all of us, Bieber is vulnerable to occasional retrieval failures. He famously forgot the lyrics to his own song "Despacito" while performing at a New York nightclub in 2017. "I don't know the words, so I say Dorito," he reportedly sang in place of the Spanish lyrics he once nailed at the recording studio (Izadi, 2017, July 27, para. 31). What kind of retrieval cues might have helped Bieber remember the words? Mat Hayward/Getty Images.

What Can You Retrieve?

Anything that jogs your memory, be it a plush alien or a cell phone alarm, is called a **retrieval cue**—a stimulus that helps you retrieve stored information that is difficult to access (Tulving & Osler, 1968). Let's say you were trying to remember the researcher who created the working memory model. If we gave you the first letter of his last name, *B,* would that help you? If your mind jumped to "Baddeley" (the correct answer), then *B* served as your retrieval cue. You undoubtedly create your own retrieval cues. When you take notes, for example, you don't copy everything you are reading; you write down enough information (the cue) to help you later retrieve what you are trying to learn. Or when you save a photo on your computer, the name of the file ("SanFran2014" or "NOLA2017") might serve as a retrieval cue to help you recall where and when it was taken. Remember, "a good external cue can sustain memory retrieval in the face of considerable forgetting" (Tullis & Benjamin, 2015, p. 922).

Even Clive Wearing showed evidence of using retrieval cues. For instance, Clive spent 7 years of his life at St. Mary's Hospital in Paddington, London, yet had no conscious memory of living there. And, according to his wife Deborah, Clive was "completely devoid" of knowledge of his own location (D. Wearing, personal communication, June 25, 2013). But if Deborah prompted him with the words "St. Mary's," he would chime back, "Paddington," oblivious to its connection (Wearing, 2005, p. 188). In this instance, the retrieval cue in Clive's environment (the sound of the word "St. Mary's") was **priming** his memory of the hospital name.

But how can priming occur in a person with severe amnesia? Priming is made possible by *implicit memory,* the type of memory that is often unconscious and

retrieval cues Stimuli that help in the retrieval of stored information that is difficult to access.

priming The stimulation of memories as a result of retrieval cues in the environment.

difficult to express. Although Clive's conscious, *explicit* memory is diminished, his *implicit* memory still functions. He could not articulate, or "declare," the name of the hospital, but that does not mean that the previously known word combination had vanished from his memory system.

RECALL AND RECOGNITION Unfortunately, we don't always have retrieval cues to help us. Sometimes we must rely on pure **recall,** the process of retrieving information held in long-term memory without the help of retrieval cues. Recall is what you depend on when you answer fill-in-the-blank or short-answer essay questions on exams. Say you are given the following prompt: "What are the three processes involved in memory?" You must come up with the answer from scratch and recall they are *encoding, storage,* and *retrieval.*

Now let's say you are faced with a multiple-choice question: "One proven way to help you retain information is: (a) distributed practice, (b) massed practice, or (c) cramming." Answering this question relies on **recognition,** the process of matching incoming data to information stored in long-term memory. Recognition is generally a lot easier than recall because the information is right before your eyes; you just have to identify it (*Hey, I've seen that before*). Recall, on the other hand, requires you to come up with information on your own.

SERIAL POSITION EFFECT Recall and recognition come into play outside of school as well. Just think about the last time someone asked you to pick up some items at the store. In order to find the requested goods, you had to recognize them (*There's the ketchup*), but even before that you had to recall them—a much harder task if they are not written down. The ability to recall items from a list depends on where they fall in the list, a phenomenon psychologists call the **serial position effect** (**Figure 6.9**). When given a list of words to memorize, research participants are better able to remember items at the beginning of the list, which is known as the **primacy effect,** as well as items at the end, which is called the **recency effect** (Deese & Kaufman, 1957; Kelley, Neath, & Surprenant, 2015; Murdock, 1962).

Imagine you are on your way to the store to buy supplies for a dinner party, but your cell phone battery is about to die. Your phone rings; it's your housemate asking you to pick up the following items: napkins, paper towels, dish soap, butter, laundry soap, paper plates, sparkling water, ice cream, plastic spoons, bread, pickles, and flowers. Without any way to write down this list, your performance may hinge on the serial position effect. In all likelihood (and if you don't use mnemonics), you will return home with napkins, paper towels, and a bottle of dish soap (due to the primacy effect), as well as bread, pickles, and flowers (due to the recency effect); the items in the middle will more likely be forgotten. Similarly, items are more "popular" when listed at the beginning or end of a menu, as opposed to the middle, presumably due to the serial position effect; they pop into your head more easily when you are ordering your meal (Bar-Hillel, 2015).

FIGURE 6.9
The Serial Position Effect
Items at the beginning and end of a list are more likely to be recalled.

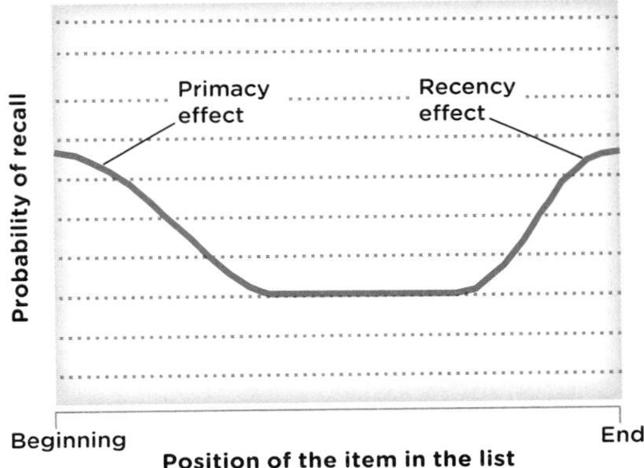

recall The process of retrieving information held in long-term memory without the help of explicit retrieval cues.

recognition The process of matching incoming data to information stored in long-term memory.

serial position effect The ability to recall items in a list depends on where they are in the series.

primacy effect The tendency to remember items at the beginning of a list.

recency effect The tendency to remember items at the end of a list.

ACROSS THE WORLD

MEMORY AND CULTURE Culture is another factor that may influence what types of information people are able to retrieve. For example, if you ask people from the United States and China to recount some life memories, you may detect some interesting cultural themes in their reports. Research suggests that Chinese people are more likely than Americans to remember social and historical occurrences and focus their memories on other people. Americans, on the other hand, tend to recall events as they relate to their individual actions and emotions (Wang, 2016; Wang & Conway, 2004). Why is this so?

MEMORIES OF WE, OR MEMORIES OF ME?

It may have something to do with the fact that China—like many countries in Asia, Africa, and Latin America—has a *collectivist* culture, whereas the United States is more *individualistic.* People in collectivist societies tend to prioritize the needs of family and community over those of the individual. Individualistic cultures are more "me" oriented, or focused on autonomy and independence. Thus it makes sense that people from the collectivist culture of China would have more community-oriented memories than Americans.

The Encoding Specificity Principle

Now that we have touched on some of the ways cultural context can influence memory, let's explore context in a more general sense. How does your environment—both internal and external—impact your ability to retrieve memories?

LO 9 Illustrate how encoding specificity relates to retrieval cues.

CONTEXT IS EVERYTHING Have you ever noticed that old memories tend to emerge from out of nowhere when you return to the places where they were created? Dining at a restaurant you once frequented with an ex-boyfriend or girlfriend probably sparks memories of romantic moments (or perhaps a bitter argument) you had there. Going to a high school reunion might bring back memories of football games, dances, and classrooms not recalled in years. How does returning to the birthplace of a memory help bring it to mind? Places where memories are created often abound with retrieval cues—sights, sounds, tastes, smells, and feelings present at the time of encoding. When it comes to retrieving memories, context matters.

In a classic study, participants learned lists of words under two conditions: (1) underwater (using scuba gear) and (2) on dry land (Godden & Baddeley, 1975). Then they were tested for recall in both conditions: If they learned the list underwater, they were tested underwater and on dry ground; if they learned the list on dry ground, they were tested on dry ground and underwater. As it turned out, participants were better at retrieving words when the learning and recall occurred in the same location (**Figure 6.10**). If they learned the words underwater, they had an easier time recalling them underwater. Similarly, words learned on land were easier to recall on land. Here, we have an example of *context-dependent memory;* memories are more accessible when encoding and retrieval occur in similar contexts.

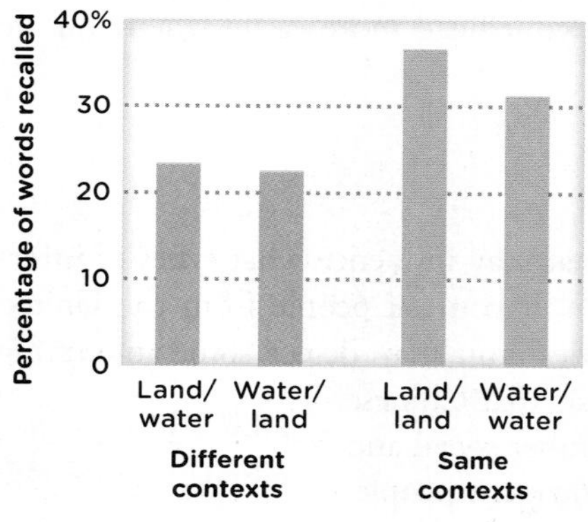

FIGURE 6.10
Diving into Memory Research
Researchers asked participants to learn a list of words in two contexts, underwater and on dry land. The participants had an easier time recalling words when learning and recall happened in the same setting: learning underwater and recalling underwater, or learning on dry land and recalling on dry land. Information from Godden and Baddeley (1975). Photo: Sergey Dubrov/Shutterstock.

Context-dependent memory is part of a broader phenomenon conveyed by the **encoding specificity principle,** which states that memories are more easily recalled when the context and cues at the time of encoding are similar to those at the time of retrieval (Smith, Glenberg, & Bjork, 1978; Tulving & Thomson, 1973). There is even evidence that summoning a memory for an event reactivates the same brain areas that became excited during the event itself (Danker & Anderson, 2010). This suggests that the activity in your brain at the time of encoding is similar to that at retrieval, and researchers using **fMRIs** have found support for this (Gottfried, Smith, Rugg, & Dolan, 2004).

CONNECTIONS

In **Chapter 2,** we presented a variety of technologies used to explore the brain. fMRI captures changes in brain activity by revealing patterns of blood flow in a particular area. This is a good indicator of how much oxygen is being used as a result of activity there.

Put Your Heads Together

Team up and discuss how you might use the encoding specificity principle to **A**) help you remember people's names; and **B**) improve your retention of course content.

MOODS, INTERNAL STATES, AND MEMORY The encoding specificity principle does not merely apply to the external context. Remembering things is also easier when physiological and psychological conditions, including moods and emotions, are similar at the time of encoding and retrieval. Sometimes memories are best retrieved under such circumstances; we call this *state-dependent memory.* One morning upon awakening, you spot a red cardinal on your window ledge. You forget about the cardinal for the rest of the day—even when you pass the very same window. But come tomorrow morning when you are once again half-awake and groggy, memories of the red bird return. Here, your ability to recall the cardinal is dependent on your internal or physiological state being the same as it was at the time of encoding. Retrieval is also easier when the content of a memory corresponds to our present emotional state, a phenomenon known as *mood congruence* (Bower, Gilligan, & Menteiro, 1981; Drace, Ric, & Desrichard, 2010). If you are in a happy mood, you are more likely to recollect a happy-go-lucky character from a book, but if you are in a sour mood, you are more inclined to remember the character whose bad mood matches yours.

Retrieval Cues
Daenerys Targaryen (played by Emilia Clarke) and Jon Snow (Kit Harington) appear in the 7th season of HBO's *Game of Thrones*. Suppose you enjoy a bowl of microwave popcorn while watching the latest "Thrones" episode. The smell and taste of the popcorn, and all the sensory experiences you have at the time, become entwined with your memory of the show, and therefore can serve as retrieval cues in the future. So, next time you smell buttery popcorn, don't be surprised if an image of these two royals pops into your head. HBO/Photofest.

Memory Savings: Easier the Second Time Around

Retrieval is clearly at work in recall and recognition, the two processes we compared earlier. But there is another, less obvious form of retrieval that occurs in the process of **relearning.** Perhaps you've noticed that you learn material much faster a second time around. Math equations, vocabulary, and grammar rules seem to make more sense if you've been exposed to them before. Some information seems to stick better when we learn it twice (Storm, Bjork, & Bjork, 2008).

CONNECTIONS

As we noted in **Chapter 1,** case studies generally have only one participant. Here, we see that Ebbinghaus, the researcher, was the sole participant. We should exercise caution when interpreting the results of such a study, especially when it comes to making generalizations about the population.

HERMANN EBBINGHAUS The first person to quantify the effect of relearning was Hermann Ebbinghaus (1850–1909), a German psychologist and pioneering researcher of human memory. Ebbinghaus was the **sole participant** in his experiments, so his research actually shed light on *his* memory, although the trends he uncovered in himself seem to apply to human memory in general (Murre & Dros, 2014).

Thorough scientist that he was, Ebbinghaus spent hour upon hour, day after day memorizing lists of "nonsense syllables"—meaningless combinations of vowels and consonants such as DAZ and MIB. Once Ebbinghaus had successfully remembered a list, meaning he could recite it smoothly and confidently, he would put it aside. Later, he would memorize it all over again and calculate how much time he had saved in Round 2, a measure called the "savings score" (Ebbinghaus, 1885/1913).

encoding specificity principle Memories are more easily recalled when the context and cues at the time of encoding are similar to those at the time of retrieval.

relearning Material learned previously is acquired more quickly in subsequent exposures.

Since no one spends all day memorizing nonsense syllables, you may wonder how Ebbinghaus' research and the "savings score" apply to real life. At some point in school, you probably had to memorize a famous speech like Dr. Martin Luther King's "I Have a Dream." Let's say it took you 100 practice sessions to recite the speech flawlessly. Then, a month later, you tried memorizing it again and this only took 50 attempts. Because you cut your learning time in half (from 100 practice sessions to 50), your savings score would be 50%.

Why Do We Forget?

LO 10 Identify and explain some of the reasons why we forget.

In addition to demonstrating the effects of relearning, Ebbinghaus was the first to illustrate just how rapidly memories vanish. Through his experiments with nonsense syllables, Ebbinghaus (1885/1913) found that the bulk of forgetting occurs immediately after learning. If you look at his *curve of forgetting* (**Figure 6.11**), you will see his memory of word lists plunging downward the hour following learning, then leveling off thereafter. Think about how the curve of forgetting applies to you. Some of what you hear in a psychology lecture may disappear from memory as soon as you walk out the door, but what you remember a week later will probably not differ much from what you recall in a month.

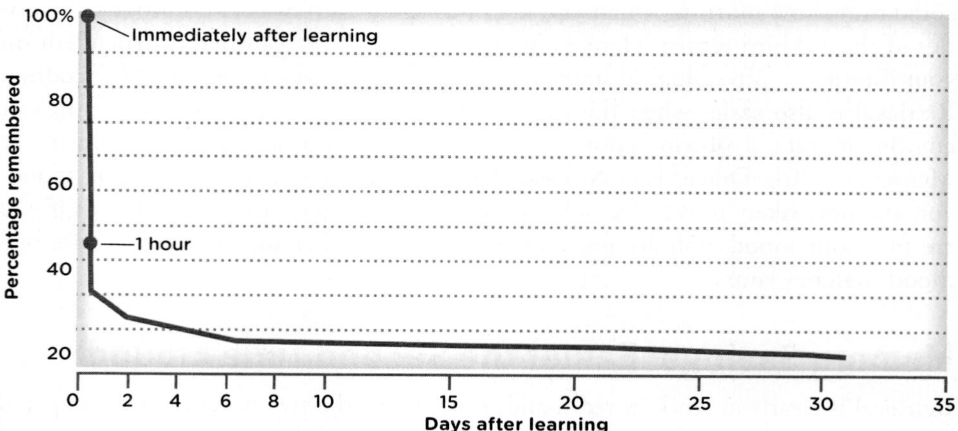

FIGURE 6.11
Ebbinghaus' Curve of Forgetting
Ebbinghaus discovered that most forgetting occurs within 1 hour of learning and then levels off.

try this Are any of these the correct Apple logo?

A B C D

Research from Adam B. Blake and Alan D. Castel, 2015.

ENCODING FAILURE What exactly causes us to forget? That may depend on the type of memory processing—encoding, storage, or retrieval—for which a given instance of memory failure occurs. Sometimes details and events we think we have forgotten were actually never encoded in the first place. Take this example: After a long and stressful day, you stop at the supermarket to pick up some blackberries and dark chocolate. While fumbling through your bag in search of your wallet, you put your keys on the cashier's counter, but because your attention is focused on finding your wallet, you don't even notice where you've placed the keys. Then you pay and walk out the door, only to get to your car wondering where you left your keys! This is an example of *encoding failure* because the data never entered your memory system. You never registered putting your keys on the counter in the first place, so how can you expect to remember where you left them? For a demonstration of encoding failure, take a look at the four images appearing in the Try This. You've looked at the Apple logo countless times, so it should be easy to identify one that's phony, right?

If you're like most people, you identified one of the wrong logos as correct (the real Apple logo is not shown), perhaps because there is no "functional reason" for you to *encode* the logo's visual elements. Or, maybe you have been exposed to the logo so many times that you no longer attend to its details (Blake, Nazarian, & Castel, 2015).

STORAGE FAILURE Memory lapses can also result from *storage failure*. Take a moment and try to remember your schedule from last semester. At one point, you knew this schedule by heart, but it may have slipped your mind because all your classes have now changed. Many memories decay over time, but as we have previously indicated, there is plenty of evidence that we can store a vast fund of information, sometimes for very long periods. Such memories might include the name of the street where you grew up (Schmidt et al., 2000), grades in college (Bahrick, Hall, & Da Costa, 2008), and factual knowledge from college courses (Conway, Cohen, & Stanhope, 1991). However, these types of memories are subject to a variety of inaccuracies and distortions, and tapping into them is not always easy.

RETRIEVAL FAILURE Sometimes we know that we have knowledge of something but just can't pull it out of storage, or retrieve it. The name of that college classmate or that new blockbuster movie, it's just sitting on the tip of your tongue but it won't slide off! This simple *retrieval failure* is called the *tip-of-the-tongue phenomenon.* Most of us have this feeling about once a week, but luckily we are able to retrieve the elusive phrase approximately 50% of the time (James & Burke, 2000; Schwartz, 2012). Often, we can correctly guess the first letter of the word or how many syllables it has (Hanley & Chapman, 2008). Studies suggest that the tip-of-the-tongue phenomenon becomes more common with age (Brown & Nix, 1996).

Can You Name Them All? Sometimes a name we are trying to remember feels so close, yet we cannot quite pull it out of storage. This feeling of near-retrieval is known as the tip-of-the-tongue phenomenon, and it happens frequently when we try to recall the names of celebrities. Kate Hudson: Steve Granitz/Getty Images. Dwayne Johnson: David Livingston/Getty Images. Lisa Ling: Jason LaVeris/FilmMagic/Getty Images.

PROACTIVE INTERFERENCE You now know that forgetting can stem from problems in encoding and storage. And the tip-of-the-tongue phenomenon tells us that it can also result from glitches in retrieval. Studies also show that retrieval is influenced, or in some cases blocked, by information we learn before and after a memory is made. We refer to this process as *interference* (Waugh & Norman, 1965). If you have studied more than one foreign language, you have probably experienced interference. Suppose you take Spanish in middle school, and then begin studying Italian in college. As you try to learn Italian, you may find Spanish words creeping into your mind and confusing you; this is an example of **proactive interference,** the tendency for information learned in the past to interfere with the retrieval of

proactive interference The tendency for information learned in the past to interfere with the retrieval of new material.

FIGURE 6.12
Proactive and Retroactive Interference

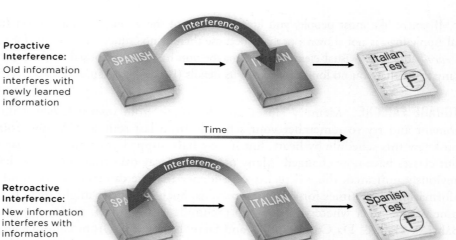

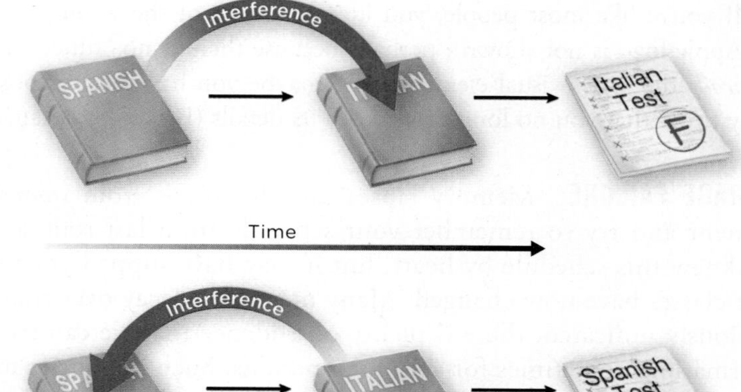
Proactive Interference:
Old information interferes with newly learned information
Interference
SPANISH
Italian Test
F
Time
Retroactive Interference:
New information interferes with information learned in the past
Interference
ITALIAN
Spanish Test
F

new material. People who learn to play a second musical instrument experience the same problem; the fingering of the old instrument interferes with the retrieval of new fingering.

RETROACTIVE INTERFERENCE Now let's say you are going on a trip to Mexico and need to use the Spanish you learned back in middle school. As you approach a vendor in an outdoor market in Costa Maya, you may become frustrated when the only words that come to mind are *ciao bello* and *buongiorno* (Italian for "hello handsome" and "good day"), when you really are searching for phrases with the same meaning in Español. Here, recently learned information interferes with the retrieval of things learned in the past. We call this **retroactive interference.** This type of interference can also impact the musician; when she switches back to her original instrument, the fingering techniques she uses to play the new instrument interfere with her old techniques. Thus, proactive interference results from knowledge acquired in the past and retroactive interference is caused by information learned recently (**Figure 6.12**).

Now that we have discussed the many ways you can forget, let's turn our attention in the opposite direction. What would happen if you couldn't forget—that is, you remembered almost everything?

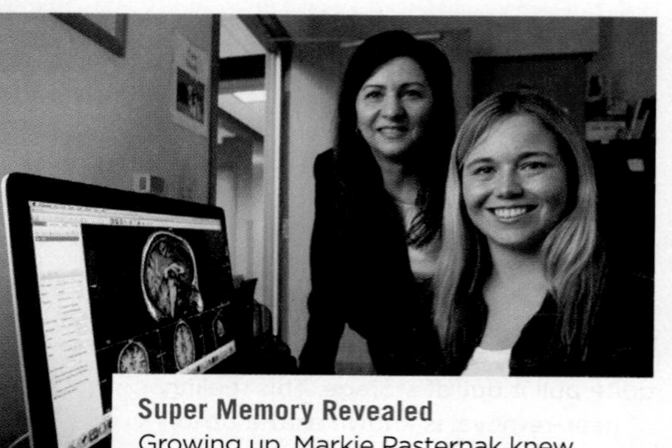

Super Memory Revealed
Growing up, Markie Pasternak knew there was something unusual about her memory; she could remember every day of her life in astounding detail beginning at age 11. But it wasn't until college that Markie discovered her gift had a scientific name: *highly superior autobiographical memory* (HSAM). Here, Markie (right) appears with her psychology professor from Marquette University, Dr. Kristy Nielson, who helped her identify her remarkable ability. Markie is currently a graduate student at Indiana University, Bloomington. Michael Sears/Milwaukee Journal Sentinel.

DIDN'T SEE THAT COMING

HIGHLY SUPERIOR AUTOBIOGRAPHICAL MEMORY About two decades ago, researchers became aware of a rare form of super memory, which has come to be called *highly superior autobiographic memory,* or HSAM (McGaugh & LePort, 2014). People with HSAM have an inherent ability to "retain and retrieve vast amounts of public and autobiographical events," without trying (LePort et al., 2012, p. 13). They can recall what they experienced and learned every single day, going back many years. If you ever encounter someone with HSAM (unlikely, as there are only about 60 documented cases in the world; McRobbie, 2017, February 8), pick a date—let's say August 17, 2008. Right away, she will know it was Sunday, and she will probably remember this was the day that Michael Phelps won his 8th gold medal in Beijing, a record for a single Olympics. Additionally, she will be able to describe several autobiographic details—the skinny vanilla latte she drank on the

"I CAN LITERALLY REMEMBER EVERYTHING."

retroactive interference The tendency for recently learned information to interfere with the retrieval of things learned in the past.

Quotations attributed to Markie Pasternak are personal communications.

way to work, a phone call from her grandmother, watching a *Meet the Press* interview with Condoleezza Rice.

People with HSAM can remember almost every day of their lives, often beginning at some point in middle childhood (Patihis, 2016). For 24-year-old Markie Pasternak, it began on February 13, 2005, when she was in fifth grade. "I can literally remember everything since this one day," recalls Markie, whose HSAM has been confirmed by researchers at the University of California, Irvine, where the phenomenon was first identified. Markie feels blessed to have memory superpowers, but she notes there are some drawbacks. For example, the tendency to get lost in intense recollection can interfere with other cognitive activities. If presented with a retrieval cue (an odor, for instance), Markie may fall into an episode of "hardcore reminiscing" that feels like another state of consciousness, similar to hypnosis. Just one whiff of the perfume "Sensual Amber" by Bath & Body Works can transport her back to the ninth grade and awaken thoughts and emotions she had at specific moments. "I can picture all my classes," says Markie. "I can picture my friends, I can even feel my heart flutter for the guy that I liked at that time." Snapping out of a deep memory can take a minute or two, so you can imagine how it might get in the way of academic and professional endeavors—even for a highly successful graduate student like Markie. Could there be some advantages to forgetting? The research certainly suggests there are. Forgetting allows you to focus on items that need your attention, and it clears the way for new memories (Williams, Hong, Kang, Carlisle, & Woodman, 2013; Wimber, Alink, Charest, Kriegeskorte, & Anderson, 2015).

What's It Like to Have HSAM?
http://qrs.ly/ey79m5q

Can Memories Be Trusted?

Interestingly, people with HSAM can remember what they had for lunch a decade ago, but when asked to remember a word list, they make a similar number of errors as members of a control group (Patihis et al., 2013). Like the rest of us, these individuals can suffer from "memory distortions." You see, memories are not **reliable records** of reality. They are *malleable* (that is, capable of being changed or reshaped by various influences) and constantly updated and revised, like a wiki. We can see how this occurs with a little help from Elizabeth Loftus.

CONNECTIONS

In **Chapter 1,** we introduced the concepts of expectations and bias, and their potential to produce inaccuracies in thinking and research. Here, we describe the ways in which our memories can fail. As accurate as our thoughts and memories may seem, we must be aware that they are vulnerable to error.

LO 11 Explain how the malleability of memory influences the recall of events.

A renowned psychologist and law professor, Loftus has been studying memory and its reliability for the last four decades. During the course of her career, she has been an expert witness in over 200 trials. The main focus of her work is a problem you have probably pondered at some point in life: How is it that two people can have different memories of the exact same event?

MEMORY RECONSTRUCTED Loftus suggests that we should not expect our accounts of the past to be identical to those of other people. Nor should we assume that our own memories remain unchanged over time. Instead, she and others propose a *reconstructionist* model of memory "in which memories are understood as creative blendings of fact and fiction" (Loftus & Ketcham, 1994, p. 5). Over the course of time, memories can fade, and because they are permeable, they become more vulnerable to the invasion of new information. In other words, your memory of some event might include revisions to what really happened, based on knowledge, opinions, and information you have acquired since the event occurred. Episodic memories are not exact duplicates of past events (recent or distant).

Comedy or Reality?
Alec Baldwin and Kate McKinnon (top) impersonate then-presidential candidates Donald Trump and Hillary Clinton in *Saturday Night Live's* 2016 "Debate Cold Open" skit (photo from actual Trump/Clinton debate below). Did Donald Trump bring up the Monica Lewinsky scandal during the real presidential debate, or was that just Baldwin doing an impersonation of Trump on *Saturday Night Live*? Sometimes, we unknowingly edit our memories, incorporating bits and pieces of information learned after the fact. Top: NBC/Photofest. Bottom: PAUL J. RICHARDS/Getty Images.

Suppose you watch a debate between two presidential candidates on live television. A few days later, you see that same debate parodied on *Saturday Night Live.* Then a few weeks later, you try to remember the details of the actual debate—the topics discussed, the phrases used by the candidates, the clothes they wore. In your effort to recall the real event, you may very well incorporate some elements of the *Saturday Night Live* skit (for example, words or expressions used by the candidates). The memories we make are not precise depictions of reality, but representations of the world as we perceive it. With the passage of time, we lose bits and pieces of a memory, and unknowingly replace them with new information.

THE MISINFORMATION EFFECT If you witnessed a car accident, how accurately would you remember it? Elizabeth Loftus and John Palmer (1974) tested the reliability of people's memories for such an event in a classic experiment. After showing participants a short film clip of a multiple-car accident, Loftus and Palmer quizzed them about what they had seen. They asked some participants, "About how fast were the cars going when they *smashed* into each other?" Replacing the word "smashed" with "hit," they asked others, "About how fast were the cars going when they *hit* each other?" Can you guess which version resulted in the highest estimates of speed? If you guessed "smashed," you are correct.

One week later, the researchers asked the participants to recall the details of the accident, including whether they had seen any broken glass in the film. Although no broken glass appears, the researchers predicted there would be some "yes" answers from participants who had initially been asked about the speed of the cars that "smashed" into each other. Their predictions were correct. Participants who had heard the word "smashed" apparently incorporated a faster speed in their memories, and were more likely to report having seen broken glass. Participants who had not heard the word "smashed" seemed to have a more accurate memory of the filmed car collision. The researchers concluded that memories can change in response to new information, and specifically that the participants' recollections were altered by the wording of a questionnaire (Loftus & Palmer, 1974). This research suggests that eyewitness accounts of accidents, crimes, and other important events might be altered by factors that come into play *after* the event occurs. Because memories are malleable, the wording of questions can change the way events are recalled, and care must be taken when questioning people about the past, whether it's in a therapist's office, social service agency, or police station.

History Facts, or Film "Facts"?
Colonel Winnant (played by James D'Arcy, left) and Commander Bolton (Kenneth Branagh) in the Oscar-winning film *Dunkirk*. Hollywood doesn't always get the facts right, and viewers sometimes incorporate movie fallacies into their memories of historical events (Butler, Zaromb, Lyle, & Roediger, 2009; Zacks, 2015, February 13). This tendency for memories to become distorted in response to new and misleading information is called the misinformation effect. Even a movie like *Dunkirk,* which historians applaud for its accurate portrayal of the facts, contains slight misrepresentations. For example, the film features the fictional character Commander Bolton (Alexander, 2017, July 20). Will some moviegoers mistakenly "remember" learning about Commander Bolton in a history book? Pictorial Press Ltd/Alamy stock photo.

Researchers have since conducted numerous studies on the **misinformation effect,** or the tendency for new and misleading information to distort one's memory of an incident. Studies with a variety of participants have resulted in their "remembering" a stop sign that was really a yield sign, a screwdriver that was really a hammer, and a barn that did not actually exist (Loftus, 2005). Prosecutors often tell people who have witnessed crimes not to speak to each other, and with good reason. Suppose two people witnessed an elderly woman being robbed. One eyewitness remembers seeing a bearded man wearing a blue jacket swiping the woman's purse. The other noticed the blue jacket but *not* the beard. If, however, the two eyewitnesses exchange stories of what they saw, the second eyewitness may unknowingly incorporate the beard into his "memory." Information learned after the event (that is, the "fact" that the thief had a beard) can get mixed up with memories of that event (Loftus, 2005; Loftus, Miller, & Burns, 1978). If we can instill this type of "false" information into a "true" memory, do you suppose it is possible to give people memories for events that never happened? Indeed, it is.

Memory Sketches
Comparing the two police sketches (left) and the more accurate drawing by sketch artist Jeanne Boylan (right), you see how renderings of the same individual can be dramatically different, even though all three were based on eyewitness information. Police sketches are based on the memories of eyewitnesses, each of whom has a unique—and potentially erroneous—memory of the suspect.
COMPOSITE BY NATE CAPLIN/KRT/Newscom.

Can Memories Be . . . Fake?

LO 12 Define and explain the significance of rich false memory.

Elizabeth Loftus knows firsthand what it is like to have a memory implanted. Tragically, her mother drowned when she was 14 years old. For 30 years, she believed that someone else had found her mother's body in a swimming pool. But in the middle of her uncle's 90th birthday party, he told her that she, Elizabeth, had found her mother's body. Loftus initially denied any memory of this horrifying experience, but as the days passed, she began to "recall" the event, including images of the pool, her mother's body, and numerous police cars arriving at the scene. These images continued to build for several days, until she received a call from her brother who told her that her uncle had been wrong, and that all the other relatives agreed Elizabeth was not the one who found her mother. According to Loftus, "All it took was a suggestion, casually planted" (Loftus & Ketcham, 1994, p. 40), and she was able to create a memory of an event she never witnessed. Following this experience, Loftus began to study **rich false memories,** that is, "wholly false memories" characterized by "the subjective feeling that one is experiencing a genuine recollection, replete with sensory details, and even expressed with confidence and emotion, even though the event never happened" (Loftus & Bernstein, 2005, p. 101).

Would you believe that about 25% of participants in rich false memory studies are able to "remember" an event that never happened? Using the "lost in the mall" technique, Loftus and Pickrell (1995) showed just how these imaginary memories take form. The researchers recruited a pair of family members (for example, parent–child or sibling–sibling) and told them they would be participating in a study on memory. With the help of one member of the pair (the "relative"), the researchers recorded three true events from the pair's shared past and created a plausible story of a trip to a shopping mall that never happened. Then they asked the true "participant" to recall as many details as possible about each of the four events (remember, only three of the events were real), which were presented in a book provided by the researchers. If the participant could not remember any details from an event, he was instructed to write, "I do not remember this." In the "lost in the mall" story, the participant was told that he had been separated from the family in a shopping mall around the age of 5. According to the story, the participant began to cry, but was eventually helped by an elderly woman and was reunited with his family. Mind you, the "lost in the mall" episode was pure fiction, but it was made to seem real through the help of the participant's relative (who was working with the researchers). Following a series

misinformation effect The tendency for new and misleading information obtained after an incident to distort one's memory of it.

rich false memories Recollections of events that never occurred, which are expressed with emotions and confidence and include details.

False Memories
Would you believe that looking at photo-shopped pictures can lead to the creation of false memories? In one study, researchers discovered that participants could "remember" hot air balloon rides they never took after looking at doctored photos of themselves as children on balloon rides. The researchers speculate that a photo "helps subjects to imagine details about the event that they later confuse with reality" (Garry & Gerrie, 2005, p. 321). Mike Sonnenberg/Getty Images.

of interviews, the researchers concluded that 29% of the participants were able to "recall" either part or all of the fabricated "lost in the mall" experience (Loftus & Pickrell, 1995). These findings may seem shocking (they certainly caused a great uproar in the field), but keep in mind that a large majority of the participants did not "remember" the fabricated event (Hyman, Husband, & Billings, 1995; Loftus & Pickrell, 1995). Still, we must be vigilant in "educating people about the malleability of memory" (Scoboria et al., 2017, p.160).

Repressed Memories?

Given what you learned from the "lost in the mall" study, do you think it's possible that false memories can be planted during psychotherapy? Imagine a clinical psychologist or psychiatrist who firmly believes that her client was sexually abused as a child. The client has no memory of abuse, but the therapist is convinced that the abuse occurred and that the traumatic memory for it has been *repressed*, or unconsciously pushed below the threshold of awareness (see Chapter 10). Using unproven methods such as **hypnosis** and dream analysis, the therapist "helps" the client resurrect a "memory" of the abuse (that presumably never occurred). Angry and hurt, the client then confronts the "abuser," who happens to be a close relative, and forever damages the relationship. Believe it or not, this scenario is very plausible. Consider these true stories picked from a long list:

- With the help of a psychiatrist, Nadean Cool came to believe that she was a victim of sexual abuse, a former member of a satanic cult, and a baby killer. She later claimed these to be false memories brought about in therapy (Loftus, 1997).
- Under the influence of prescription drugs and persuasive therapists, Lynn Price Gondolf became convinced her parents molested her during childhood. Three years after accusing her parents of such abuse, she concluded the accusation was a mistake (Loftus & Ketcham, 1994).
- Laura Pasley "walked into her Texas therapist's office with one problem, bulimia, and walked out with another, incest" (Loftus, 1994, p. 44).

CONNECTIONS

In **Chapter 4,** we described hypnosis as an altered state of consciousness that allows for changes in perceptions and behavior, resulting from suggestions made by the hypnotist. Here, we discuss the use of hypnosis in a therapeutic setting; the hypnotist is a therapist trying to help a client "remember" an abuse that the therapist believes has been repressed.

In the history of psychology, few topics have stirred up as much controversy as repressed memories (Brewin & Andrews, 2014; Patihis, Ho, Tingen, Lilienfeld, & Loftus, 2014; Patihis, Lilienfeld, Ho, & Loftus, 2014). Some psychologists believe that painful memories can indeed be repressed and recovered years or decades later, but levels of skepticism vary considerably (Knapp & VandeCreek, 2000; Patihis, Ho, et al., 2014). The majority would agree that the studies supporting the existence of repressed memories have many shortcomings (Piper, Lillevik, & Kritzer, 2008). Although childhood sexual abuse is shockingly common, with approximately 18% of girls and 8% of boys being affected worldwide (Stoltenborgh, Bakermans-Kranenburg, Alink, & IJzendoorn, 2015), there is not solid evidence that these traumas are repressed. Even if they were, many believe retrieved memories of them would likely be inaccurate (Patihis, Ho, et al., 2014; Roediger & Bergman, 1998). Trauma survivors often face quite a different challenge—letting go of painful memories that continue to haunt them. (See posttraumatic stress disorder in Chapter 13.)

The American Psychological Association (APA) and other authoritative mental health organizations have investigated the repressed memory issue at length. In 1998 the APA issued a statement offering its main conclusions, summarized below:

- Sexual abuse of children is very common and often unrecognized, and the repressed memory debate should not detract attention from this important issue.
- Most victims of sexual abuse have at least some memory of the abuse.
- Memories of past abuses can be forgotten and remembered at a later time.

- People sometimes do create false memories of experiences they never had.
- We still do not completely understand how accurate and flawed memories of childhood abuse are formed (APA, 1998).

Keep these points in mind next time you hear the term "repressed memory" tossed around in television talk shows, Internet posts, or casual conversations. You are now prepared with scientific knowledge to evaluate claims about repressed memories, so weigh all the evidence and ask critical questions. If you or someone you know is dealing with issues related to abuse, seek help from a licensed psychotherapist (APA, n.d.-o).

CAREER CONNECTIONS

MEMORY AND THE LAW You have just learned how malleable, or changeable, memory can be. How might this knowledge be useful in your future career? Suppose you are an attorney or investigator and you are interviewing someone who witnessed a crime. How do you know that person's memory of the event can be trusted? If your goal is to obtain accurate information, you better ask questions right away. People who witness crimes are often asked to rate their confidence in identifying a suspect. This "eyewitness confidence" is linked to the accuracy of the account—but only when the confidence level is assessed "at the time of the initial identification," that is, when suspects are viewed in a lineup (Wixted, Mickes, Clark, Gronlund, & Roediger, 2015, p. 515). Simply stated, if the eyewitness has a high level of confidence in identifying a suspect *shortly after the crime,* her identification is more accurate (Wixted & Mickes, 2017).

"THEY RECALLED . . . INTERACTIONS WITH THE POLICE THAT NEVER HAPPENED."

When the eyewitness is a child, obtaining an accurate account can be challenging. To minimize the number of inaccurate responses, interviewers should structure questions carefully and understand rewards and punishments from the perspective of a child (Sparling, Wilder, Kondash, Boyle, & Compton, 2011). Asking children to close their eyes increases the accuracy of the testimony (Vredeveldt, Baddeley, & Hitch, 2014), but relying solely on their accounts has contributed to many cases of mistaken identity. Finally, the presence of a person in a uniform appears to put added pressure on child eyewitnesses, resulting in more guessing and inaccurate recall (Lowenstein, Blank, & Sauer, 2010).

The interrogation of people at any age can lead to life-changing consequences. Following a series of interviews using suggestive memory-retrieval methods, 70% of the young adults participating in one study generated rich false memories of criminal behavior they had *not* committed during adolescence. They recalled incidents involving theft and assault, including interactions with the police that never happened (Shaw & Porter, 2015)! The implication is that some interrogation techniques can lead to false recall and confession of crimes that were not committed. A person can believe he committed a crime that never happened, falsely confess to it, and then be wrongly convicted (Porter & Baker, 2015).

Innocent
February 2016: Vanessa Gathers leaves a Brooklyn courthouse after her 1998 manslaughter conviction was overturned. Gathers served 10 years in prison after a detective manipulated her into giving a false confession (Nir, 2016, February 23). AP Photo/Seth Wenig.

Put Your Heads Together

Understanding that memories are malleable is important for people in all types of career settings. In your groups, describe other workplace scenarios where this knowledge may be useful (for instance, social work, nursing, business).

Before you read on, take a minute and allow the words of Elizabeth Loftus to sink in: "Think of your mind as a bowl filled with clear water. Now imagine each memory as a teaspoon of milk stirred into the water. Every adult mind holds thousands of these murky memories. . . . Who among us would dare to disentangle the water from the milk?" (Loftus & Ketcham, 1994, pp. 3–4). What is the basis for all this murkiness? It's time to explore the biological roots of memory.

show what you know

1. Your uncle claims he attended a school play in which your role was the "Cowardly Lion." He has described the costume you wore, the lines you mixed up, and even the flowers he gave you. At first you can't remember the play, but eventually you seem to. Your mother insists you were never in that school play, and your uncle wasn't in the country that year, so he couldn't have attended the performance at all. Instead, you have experienced a:
   a. curve of forgetting.
   b. repressed memory.
   c. savings score.
   d. rich false memory.
2. The ______________ refers to the tendency for new and misleading information to distort memories.
3. Loftus and Palmer (1974) conducted an experiment in which the wording of a question (using "smash" versus "hit") significantly influenced participants' recall of the event. What does this suggest about the malleability of memory?

✓ CHECK YOUR ANSWERS IN APPENDIX C.

The Biology of Memory

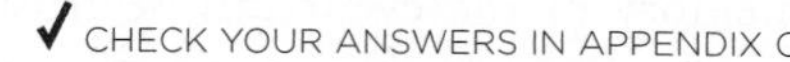

What did you do today? Did you have breakfast, brush your teeth, put your clothes on, drive your car, read an assignment, text a friend? Whatever you did, we are sure of one thing: It required a whole lot of memory. You could not send a text message without knowing how to spell, read, and use a cell phone—all things you had to learn and remember. Likewise, you could not drive without remembering how to unlock your car, start the engine, use the pedals. Memory is involved in virtually everything you do.

Love Triumphs
Clive forgot many things, but not the love he has for his wife. Every time Deborah came to visit, he recognized her but could not recall their last meeting, even if it had happened just minutes before. Hugging, kissing, and sometimes twirling Deborah in the air, he would ask how much time had passed (Wearing, 2005). Jiri Rezac/Polaris/Newscom.

If memory is behind all your daily activities, important processes must be occurring in the brain to make this happen: both on the macro (large) and micro (small) scale. But as we learned from Clive's example, these processes are fragile and can be profoundly disrupted. Exploring the causes of memory failure can help us understand the biological basis of memory.

Amnesia

THE AFTERMATH In the months and years following Clive's illness, researchers administered many tests to assess his cognitive functioning. They found his IQ to be within an average range but his ability to remember past events deeply impaired. When prompted to name as many musical composers as possible in 1 minute, Clive—a man who had devoted his career to the study of music—could only produce four: Mozart, Beethoven, Bach, and Haydn. He denied that dragonflies have wings and claimed he had never heard of John F. Kennedy (Wilson et al., 1995).

Clive was even more disabled when it came to developing new memories. Initially, he could not hold onto incoming information for more than a blink of an eye. If his wife Deborah stepped out of the room for just a few minutes, he would welcome her back as if she had been away for years—embracing, celebrating, sometimes weeping. "How long have I been ill?" he would ask, forgetting the answer and repeating himself within seconds (Wearing, 2005, p. 181).

LO 13 Compare and contrast anterograde and retrograde amnesia.

Amnesia, or memory loss, can result from either a physical or psychological condition. There are different types and degrees of amnesia, ranging from extreme (losing decades of autobiographical memories) to mild (temporarily forgetting people's names after a concussion).

ANTEROGRADE AMNESIA According to researchers, Clive suffers from "a more severe anterograde amnesia than any other patient previously reported" (Wilson et al., 1995, p. 680). **Anterograde amnesia** (ANT-er-oh-grade) is the inability to "lay down" or create new long-term memories (**Figure 6.13**), and it is generally caused by damage to the brain, resulting from surgery, alcohol, head trauma, or illness. Someone with anterograde amnesia cannot form memories of events and experiences that occur following the brain damage; as you can imagine, this inability to lay down new memories makes it hard to remember routine tasks and function in the world. For Clive, his short-term memory still functioned to a certain extent, but he could only absorb and process information for several seconds before it was lost. Every experience was fresh, and every person (with the exception of some he knew well from the past) a total stranger.

RETROGRADE AMNESIA A second type of memory loss is **retrograde amnesia,** an inability to access memories created before damage to the brain occurred (Brandt & Benedict, 1993; Figure 6.13). With retrograde amnesia, a person has difficulty retrieving old memories, though how "old" depends on the extent of brain trauma. People with retrograde amnesia generally remember who they are and the most important events of their earlier lives (Manns, Hopkins, & Squire, 2003; Squire & Wixted, 2011). Remember that *retrograde* refers to the inability to access old memories (think of "retro," meaning in the past, to help you distinguish between the terms), and *anterograde* refers to the inability to create new memories.

Clive suffered from retrograde amnesia in addition to his anterograde amnesia. While he appeared to retain a vague outline of his past (hazy information about his childhood, the fact that he had been a choral scholar at Clare College, Cambridge, and so on), he could not retrieve the names of his children unless prompted. And although Clive's children were all adults when he developed encephalitis, he came out of the illness thinking they were young children. The retrograde amnesia has improved, but only minimally. In 2005, for example, Clive asked his 40-something son what

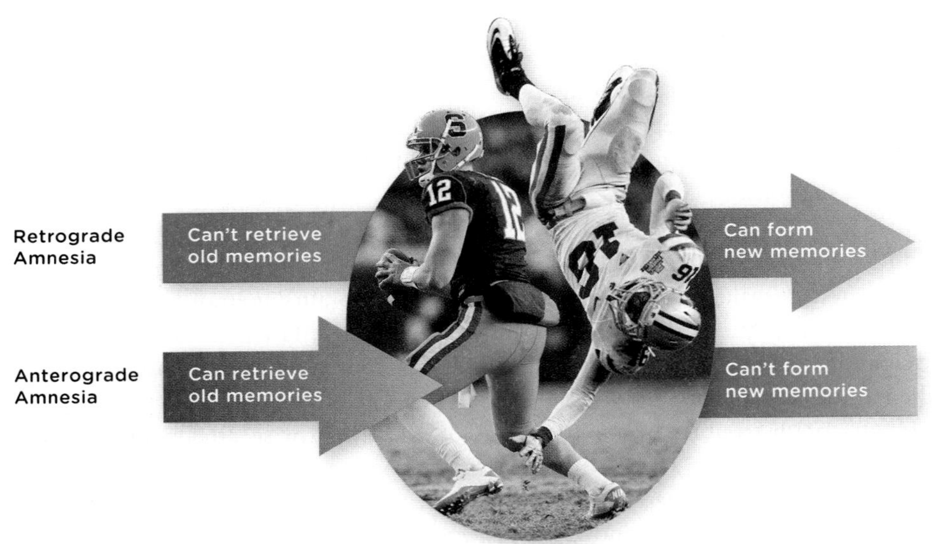

FIGURE 6.13
Retrograde and Anterograde Amnesia
Retro means "before," so retrograde amnesia is the inability to retrieve memories for events that occurred *before* an amnesia-causing injury. *Antero* means "after," so anterograde amnesia is the inability to form memories for events that occur *after* an injury. Photo: Getty Images Sport/Getty Images.

anterograde amnesia A type of memory loss; an inability to create new memories following damage to the brain.

retrograde amnesia A type of memory loss; an inability to access memories formed prior to damage to the brain.

subjects he was studying in grammar school (equivalent to American high school). Nowadays when inquiring about his children, Clive simply asks, "What are they doing?" (D. Wearing, personal communication, June 18 and 25, July 11, 2013).

In spite of the severe retrograde and anterograde amnesia, some of Clive's memory functions continued to operate quite well. At one point, Deborah arranged for Clive to be reunited with the singers from the London Lassus Ensemble, a group he had conducted for more than a decade before his illness. At first, Clive paused and looked at the musicians with uncertainty, but then he raised his hands and began conducting, leading them through the music with precision and grace. Remembering the piece (which he had edited himself), Clive mouthed its words in Latin and employed the same tempo and conducting style he had used in the past (D. Wearing, personal communication, July 11, 2013). After the performance, the musicians left and Clive sat in the empty chapel wondering what had gone on there earlier (Wearing, 2005). When shown a video of himself leading the chorus, he remarked, "I wasn't conscious then" (Wilson et al., 2008). Clive's explicit memory of the event vanished in seconds, but his implicit memory—knowing how to conduct—was intact.

How is it possible that some of Clive's long-term memories were blotted out, while others, such as how to conduct music, remained fairly clear? The evidence suggests that different types of long-term memories have distinct processing routes in the brain. Thus, damage to one area of the brain may impair some types of memory but not others. Let's take a closer look at where memories seem to be stored in the brain.

Memories in the Brain: A Macro Perspective

LO 14 Identify the brain structures involved in memory.

A few years after the onset of Clive's illness, doctors evaluated his brain using an MRI scan. A troubling picture emerged; the virus had destroyed many parts of his brain, notably the **hippocampus**, which plays a vital role in the creation of new memories (Wilson et al., 2008).

CONNECTIONS 

In **Chapter 2,** we described the hippocampus as a pair of curved structures buried deep within the temporal lobes. The hippocampus is primarily responsible for processing and making new memories, but is not where memories are permanently stored. It is also one of the brain areas where neurogenesis, or the creation of new neurons, may occur.

Only in the last 60 years or so have scientists come to appreciate the role of the hippocampus in memory (**INFOGRAPHIC 6.2**). Back in the 1920s, psychologist Karl Lashley set out to find a **memory trace:** the physical spot where memories are etched in the brain, also called an *engram.* Lashley selected a group of rats that had learned the layout of specific mazes, and then made large cuts at different places in their cortices to see how this affected their memory of the mazes. No matter where Lashley sliced, the rats still managed to maneuver their way through the mazes (Costandi, 2009, February 10; Lashley, 1950). These findings led Lashley and other scientists to believe that memory is spread throughout the brain rather than localized in a particular region (Costandi, 2009, February 10; Kandel & Pittenger, 1999). ***Connectionism*** is a model suggesting that memories are distributed throughout the brain in a network of interlinked neurons.

synonyms

connectionism parallel distributed processing (PDP)

THE CASE OF H.M. Henry Molaison (better known as "H.M.") forced scientists to completely reevaluate their understanding of the brain's memory system. From the onset of his amnesia in 1953 until his death in 2008, H.M. served as a research participant for some 100 scientists (Corkin, 2002), making him the most extensively studied amnesic patient.

H.M.'s brain troubles began at the age of 10, a year or so after being knocked unconscious in a bicycle accident. He began to experience seizures, which worsened with age and eventually became so debilitating that he could no longer hold a steady job. Medications could not control his seizures, so at the age of 27, H.M. opted for

memory trace The location where memories are etched in the brain via physiological changes.

INFOGRAPHIC 6.2

Tracking Memory in the Brain

Whether with lab rats or case studies, psychologists have spent decades tracking the location of memory in the brain. What they've found so far should be no surprise: Memory is a complex system involving multiple structures and regions of the brain. Memory is formed, processed, and stored throughout the brain, and different types of memory have different paths. So to find memory in the brain, it helps to know your way around the brain's structures. Remembering the amygdala's role in processing basic emotion, for instance, can help you understand its role in processing the emotional content of memories.

Forming New Memories

In an attempt to control the disabling seizures of a man named Henry Molaison (H.M.), doctors surgically removed portions of his brain, including the hippocampus. The surgery affected H.M.'s memory. He had profound anterograde amnesia: He could tap into old memories, but he could no longer make new explicit memories. However, he could still create implicit memories. Using information gathered about H.M.'s brain, scientists have been able to directly connect the hippocampus to the creation of new explicit memories.

After his death, H.M.'s brain was cut into over 2,000 slices that were preserved and digitized for research.

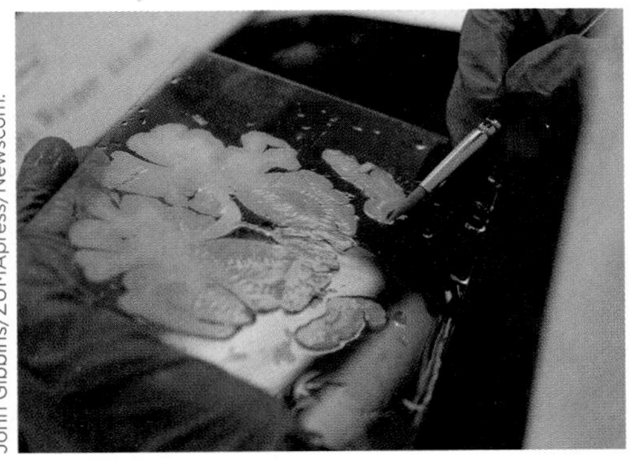

John Gibbins/ZUMApress/Newscom.

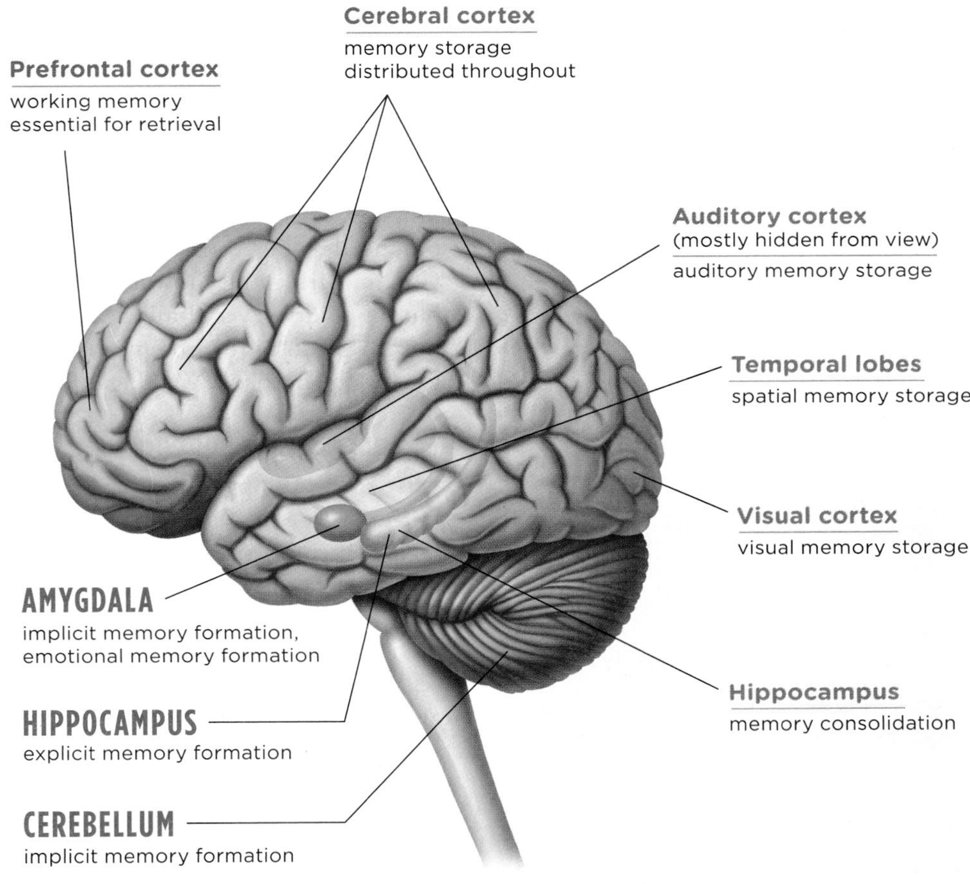

Storing Memories

Through his experiments slicing the cortices of rats that had learned to navigate mazes, Karl Lashley concluded that complex memories are not localized to a particular region in the cortex, but are instead widely distributed. Later research has established the interrelated roles of specific structures in the process of encoding, storing, and retrieving memories.

In a process called *memory consolidation,* which is thought to occur in the hippocampus and cortex, information is moved into long-term storage (Genzel et al., 2017). Research on this topic is ongoing, but some evidence suggests that REM sleep plays a crucial role in memory consolidation (Li, Ma, Yang, & Gan, 2017).

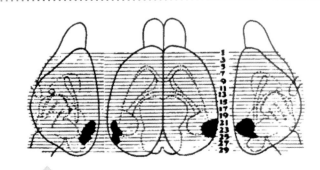

Lashley kept a careful record of the sizes and locations of lesions made in each rat as part of his experiments.

an experimental surgery to remove parts of his brain: the temporal lobes (just beneath the temples), including the hippocampus (Scoville & Milner, 1957).

H.M.'s surgery succeeded in reining in his epilepsy but left his memory in shambles. Upon waking from the operation, he could no longer find his way to the bathroom or recognize the hospital workers caring for him. He played with the same jigsaw puzzles and read the same magazines day after day as if he were seeing them for the first time (Scoville & Milner, 1957). Like Clive, H.M. suffered from profound anterograde amnesia, the inability to encode new long-term memories, and a milder form of retrograde amnesia, trouble retrieving existing memories from storage. Although H.M. had difficulty recalling what occurred during the few years leading up to his surgery (Scoville & Milner, 1957), he did remember events from the more distant past, for example, the 1929 stock market crash and the events of World War II (Carey, 2008, December 4).

H.M. maintained his implicit memory, which he demonstrated in an experiment involving the complex task of tracing a pattern reflected in a mirror. With repeated practice sessions (none of which he remembered), H.M. improved his performance on the drawing task, learning it as well as someone without amnesia (Gabrieli, Corkin, Mickel, & Growdon, 1993). Clive can also acquire new implicit memories, but his ability is very limited. According to Deborah, it took years for Clive to learn how to get to his bedroom in the small community residence where he moved after leaving the hospital (Wearing, 2005).

THE ROLE OF THE HIPPOCAMPUS Imagine you are a scientist trying to figure out what role the hippocampus plays in memory. Consider the facts you know about H.M.: (1) He has virtually no hippocampus; (2) he has lost the ability to make new *explicit* memories, yet can create *implicit* memories; and (3) he can still tap into memories of the distant past. So what do you think the hippocampus does? Evidence suggests that the hippocampus is essential for creating new explicit memories but *not* implicit memories. Researchers have also shown that explicit memories are processed and stored in other parts of the brain, including the temporal lobes and areas of the frontal cortex (García-Lázaro, Ramirez-Carmona, Lara-Romero, & Roldan-Valadez, 2012).

As in H.M.'s case, Clive's ability to form explicit memories is profoundly compromised, largely a result of the destruction of his hippocampus. Yet Clive also struggles with the creation of implicit memories—not surprising given the extensive damage to other regions of his brain, such as the amygdala and temporal lobes (Wilson et al., 2008). See Infographic 6.2 for more information about memory processing in the brain.

So although the hippocampus plays a central role in laying down new memories, it does not appear to serve as their ultimate destination. This process of memory formation, which moves a memory from the hippocampus to other areas of the brain, is called *memory consolidation* (Squire & Bayley, 2007). The consolidation that begins in the hippocampus allows for the long-term storage of memories. According to Kandel and Pittenger (1999): "The final locus of storage of memory is widely assumed to be the cerebral cortex, though this is a difficult assertion to prove" (p. 2041). There is also some evidence that memory formation may be occurring simultaneously in both the hippocampus and the cortex, but little is known about the specific processes (Kitamura et al., 2017). As for retrieval, the hippocampus appears to be in charge of accessing young memories, but then passes on that responsibility to other brain regions as memories grow older (Smith & Squire, 2009).

This idea that the hippocampus is essential for creating explicit memories (as opposed to implicit memories) is supported by what we know about *infantile amnesia,* that is, the inability to remember events from our earliest years. Most adults cannot

Do Forgotten Memories Matter? By the time this child is an adult, he will have will long forgotten his first birthday celebration, so why go to the trouble of throwing a party? The memory of the event may disappear, but something more important sticks for life. As psychologist Dima Amso explains, "Specific memories may be forgotten, but because those memories form the fabric of our identities, knowledge and experiences, they are never truly or completely gone" (Amso, 2017, January/February, para. 5). Rogdy Espinoza Photography/Moment Open/Getty Images.

remember events before the age of 3. Some researchers suggest that it is because the hippocampus and frontal cortex, both important for the creation of long-term explicit memories, are not fully developed in children (Bauer, 2006; Willoughby, Desrocher, Levine, & Rovet, 2012). Simply stated, young children do not construct complete episodic memories of their experiences (Bauer & Larkina, 2014). We are less likely to forget events starting around age 7 because the memories we begin generating are more elaborate and personally relevant. The efficiency of how the memories are formed (more effective neural processes) also make these memories "more impervious to the ravages of forgetting" (Bauer, 2015, p. 225).

The macro level perspective presented in this section allows us to see the "big picture" of memory, but what's going on microscopically? Next we will focus on the important changes occurring in and between neurons.

Memories in the Brain: A Micro Perspective

How does your brain change when you learn a new driving route to school? If we could peer into your skull, we might see a change in your hippocampus. Now imagine what might happen in the brain of a taxicab driver in London, who must memorize the 25,000 streets in the city, including their businesses and landmarks. As one study found, London taxicab drivers with greater time spent on the job had structural changes in some regions of the hippocampus, particularly to an area that processes "spatial knowledge" (Maguire, Woollett, & Spiers, 2006; Rosen, 2014, November 10). Zooming in for a closer look, we might actually see changes at the level of the neuron. If you are looking for a memory imprint, the best place to look is the **synapse**.

CONNECTIONS

In **Chapter 2,** we introduced the synapse: the junction between two neurons. Neurons communicate with each other via chemicals called neurotransmitters, which are released into the synaptic gap. Here, we see how activities at the neural level relate to the formation and maintenance of memories.

LONG-TERM POTENTIATION The more neurons communicate with each other, the better the connections between them. **Long-term potentiation** occurs when sending neurons release neurotransmitters more effectively, and receiving neurons become more sensitive, boosting synaptic strength for days or even weeks (Lynch, 2002; Malenka & Nicoll, 1999; Whitlock, Heynen, Shuler, & Bear, 2006). In other words, long-term potentiation refers to the increased efficiency of neural communication over time, resulting in learning and the formation of memories. As you learn a new skill, for example, the neurons involved begin to communicate more. It might start with a somewhat random firing of neurons, but new and more efficient neural pathways eventually take form. Having trouble visualizing the process? Imagine this: Your college has opened a new campus with an array of brand-new buildings, but it has yet to construct sidewalks connecting them. To go from one building to the next, students have to wade through tall grass and weeds. All the trampling eventually gives way to a system of efficient paths linking the buildings. Long-term potentiation of neural connections occurs in a similar fashion: Over time, communication among neurons improves and strengthens, allowing for the skill to develop and become more natural (Whitlock et al., 2006). The paths represent how a skill, whether tying your shoes or texting, is learned and thus becomes a memory.

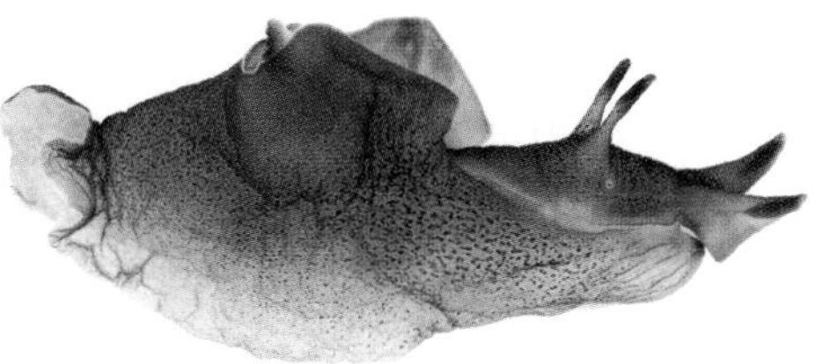

Smart Slug
Studying the neurons of sea slugs, researchers have observed the synaptic changes that underlie memory. Long-term potentiation enables a sea slug to retract its gills in anticipation of being squirted with water. NaturePL/Superstock.

IF A SEA SLUG CAN, SO CAN YOU! Amazingly, we have learned much about long-term potentiation from the sea slug *Aplysia,* which has only about 20,000 neurons (Kandel, 2009)—a little easier to work with than the billions of neurons in a human brain. In addition to having a small number of neurons, the sea slug's synapses are relatively easy to examine at an individual level.

long-term potentiation The increased efficiency of neural communication over time, resulting in learning and the formation of memories.

Studies on sea slugs indicate that long-term potentiation, or increases in synaptic "strength," is associated with learning and memory. **What can a sea slug learn?** They can be classically conditioned to retract their gills in response to being squirted with water, resulting in structural changes to both presynaptic and postsynaptic cells, including changes to connections between neurons (Kandel, 2009)—evidence of long-term potentiation.

CONNECTIONS

In **Chapter 5,** we discussed classical conditioning and how a neutral stimulus can be paired with an unconditioned stimulus, ultimately leading to a conditioned stimulus resulting in a conditioned response. In the case of the sea slug, the squirt of water is the conditioned stimulus and the involuntary response of retracting its gills is the conditioned response.

LO 15 Summarize the symptoms and causes of Alzheimer's disease.

ALZHEIMER'S DISEASE On a less positive note, disruptions in long-term potentiation appear to be at work in *Alzheimer's disease,* a progressive, devastating brain illness that causes cognitive decline, including memory, language, and thinking problems. Alzheimer's affects over 5 million Americans (National Institute on Aging, n.d.). The disease was first discovered by Alois Alzheimer, a German neuropathologist, in the early 1900s. He had a patient with severe memory problems whose autopsy revealed that neurons in her brain had become tangled like the wires of earbud headphones. These *neurofibrillary tangles,* as they came to be called, were eventually shown to result from twisted protein fibers accumulating inside brain cells. In addition to the tangles, the other distinctive sign of Alzheimer's is the presence of *amyloid plaques,* protein clumps that build up between neurons, blocking their lines of communication (Vingtdeux, Davies, Dickson, & Marambaud, 2011).

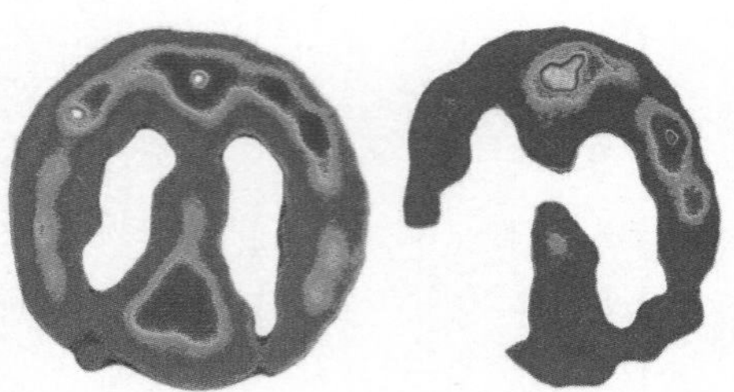

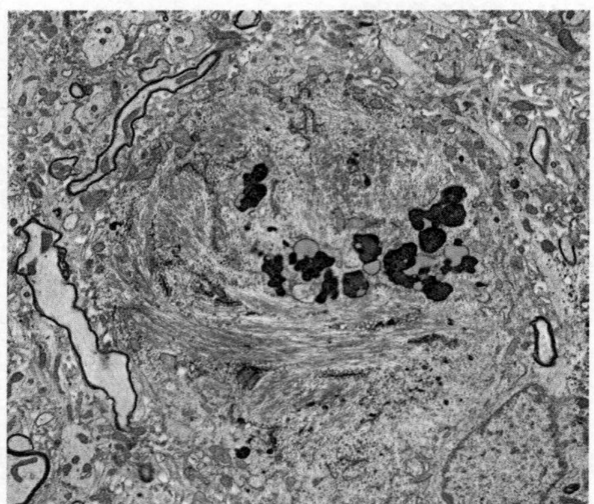

Inside Alzheimer's
The PET scan (top left) depicts the brain of a normal person, while the scan to the right shows that of a person with Alzheimer's. Studies using PET suggest a slowing of brain activity in certain regions of the Alzheimer's brain (Alzheimer's Association, 2013a). The neurofibrillary tangles (bottom image, with tangles in pink) result from twisted protein fibers accumulating inside brain cells. Top: Jessica Wilson/Science Source. Bottom: Thomas Deerinck, NCMIR/Science Source.

While we still don't have a solid understanding of what causes Alzheimer's, we know some forms of the disease are inherited. People who have a first-degree relative (a parent, sibling, or child) with Alzheimer's have a higher risk for developing the disease. Researchers have zeroed in on a specific gene, APOEε4, which seems to predispose people to Alzheimer's (Liu, Kanekiyo, Xu, & Bu, 2013). But we also know that factors such as diet and exercise can influence the development and progression of the disease (Alzheimer's Association, 2013b). Being obese and sedentary can heighten one's risk; in fact, studies suggest that the standard American diet (one that is high in sugar, fats, and processed food, and low in fruits, vegetables, and whole grains) can cause "nutrient deficiency and inflammation that could impact cognition directly" (Graham et al., 2016, p. 2). Even the air we breathe may play a role, as long-term exposure to air pollution has been linked to cognitive decline in older adults (Ailshire & Clarke, 2014; Gatto et al., 2014; Weuve et al., 2012).

No cure for Alzheimer's disease exists, and current treatments focus only on reducing the severity of symptoms rather than correcting the brain damage responsible. But there is also reason to be hopeful. Promising new drugs are coming down the pipeline, and some preliminary evidence suggests that simple lifestyle changes, like becoming more physically active and pursuing intellectually and socially stimulating activities, may actually decrease the speed and severity of cognitive decline (Hertzog, Kramer, Wilson, & Lindenberger, 2009, July/August; Walsh, 2011; Wilson & Bennett, 2003; **Table 6.1**).

CHRONIC TRAUMATIC ENCEPHALOPATHY Similar in some ways to Alzheimer's disease, **chronic traumatic encephalopathy (CTE)** (en-sef-uh-LOP-uh-thee) is distinct in its progression and impact on memory (McKee et al., 2013). CTE is a neurodegenerative disease that leads to atypical deposits of tau protein throughout various regions in the brain as a result of repeated mild traumatic brain injury. This disease affects football players, soccer players, wrestlers, rugby players, boxers, hockey players, lacrosse players, combat war veterans, and many other people who have suffered impacts to the head (Maroon et al., 2015; McKee et al., 2016). Symptoms include

chronic traumatic encephalopathy (CTE) A neurodegenerative disease that leads to atypical deposits of tau protein throughout various regions in the brain as a result of repeated mild traumatic brain injury.

TABLE 6.1 FACTS ABOUT MEMORY LOSS

Category	Facts
Family	There is no definitive way to know whether you or a family member will suffer from a neurocognitive disorder; most cases result from a complex combination of genetic, environmental, and lifestyle factors.
Exercise	Studies of both animals and people have linked physical exercise to a variety of positive changes in the brain, including enhanced blood flow, increased thickness of the cortex, and less age-related deterioration of the hippocampus (Polidori, Nelles, & Pientka, 2010). Research suggests that people who begin exercising in their thirties (and stick with it) experience less cognitive decline than their sedentary peers by the time they reach their forties and fifties (Hertzog, Kramer, Wilson, & Lindenberger, 2009, July/August), although consistent exercise at any age has lasting cognitive benefits (Cotman & Berchtold, 2002; Kramer, Erickson, & Colcombe, 2006).
Intellectual stimulation	Intellectually engaging activities such as reading books and newspapers, writing, drawing, and solving crossword puzzles have been associated with a lower risk of memory loss (Hertzog et al., 2009, July/August; Wang, Karp, Winblad, & Fratiglioni, 2002).
Social activity	Being socially active and hooked into social groups may reduce the risk of developing dementia (Fratiglioni, Paillard-Borg, & Winblad, 2004).

Memory loss needn't be an inevitable part of aging. Here are some facts you should know.

significant memory issues, impulsivity, aggression, insomnia, problems with speech, and depression. CTE is progressive, and symptoms may not appear for months to years following the impact, and can only be diagnosed definitively after death (Kirk, Gilmore, & Wiser, 2013; McKee et al., 2013). Who's at risk and what are some of the more obvious symptoms of CTE? Discover the answers in **INFOGRAPHIC 6.3** on the next page.

As we continue to learn more about CTE, parents must make difficult decisions about the sports they encourage their children to pursue. Studies on football players, in particular, have produced alarming results. One group of researchers examined the brains of 202 deceased football players with experience ranging from high school to the NFL; they found evidence of CTE in 177, or 87%, of those brains (Mez, 2017). Another group concluded that playing football before the age of 12 may lead to greater risk of depression, problems regulating behavior, and other "clinically meaningful impairments" in adulthood. As the researchers pointed out, the brain undergoes critical changes between ages 9 and 12, so the impact of head trauma may have special significance at this stage in life (Alosco et al., 2017).

Approximately 4 million concussions are reported every year as a result of playing sports, but an estimated 50% of all concussions may not be reported. Furthermore, the subconcussive hits (those not hard enough to cause a concussion) may also put athletes at risk for the development of this disease (Harmon et al., 2013). To better understand the impact of CTE, read the story of NFL Hall of Famer Harry Carson in Chapter 7.

Like many topics psychologists study, the biological mechanisms that give rise to memory remain somewhat mysterious. We know we have memories, we know they are formed in the brain, and we know the brain is a physical entity; yet we still don't know exactly how we go from an array of firing neurons to a vivid recollection of your 21st birthday bash, your high school prom, or the image of Justin Timberlake paying tribute to Prince at the Super Bowl halftime show. Studies attempting to test the various theories of memory formation are inconclusive, often generating more questions than answers. But one thing seems certain: Memory researchers face plenty of important work ahead.

Chronic Traumatic Encephalopathy

Chronic traumatic encephalopathy (CTE) is a progressive neurodegenerative disease caused by a single or repeated blow to the head. CTE affects athletes of many types, combat war veterans, and others who experience head trauma (Maroon et al., 2015; McKee et al., 2016). The symptoms, which may not appear for months or years after the injury, include changes to memory, emotions, thinking, and personality. CTE is somewhat similar to other neurodegenerative diseases like Alzheimer's and Parkinson's in that it can impair memory, movement, and the ability to plan and carry out everyday tasks (McKee et al., 2013).

In 2012, after 20 seasons as an NFL player, **Junior Seau** committed suicide at age 43. In the years leading to his death, Seau's family noticed a change in his thinking, personality, and enthusiasm for the game. Impulsive gambling, alcoholism, and violence became the new conversation around the man once known as a beloved philanthropist (Fainaru-Wada, 2013, February 15). Upon his death, his brain showed the hallmarks of CTE (National Institute of Neurological Disorders and Stroke, 2013, January 10).

Retired soccer star **Brandi Chastain** has announced she will donate her brain to research. Chastain believes this will be a bigger legacy than her game-winning shot in the 1999 World Cup. Like many soccer players, Chastain advocates the banning of headers in youth soccer (Branch, 2016, March).

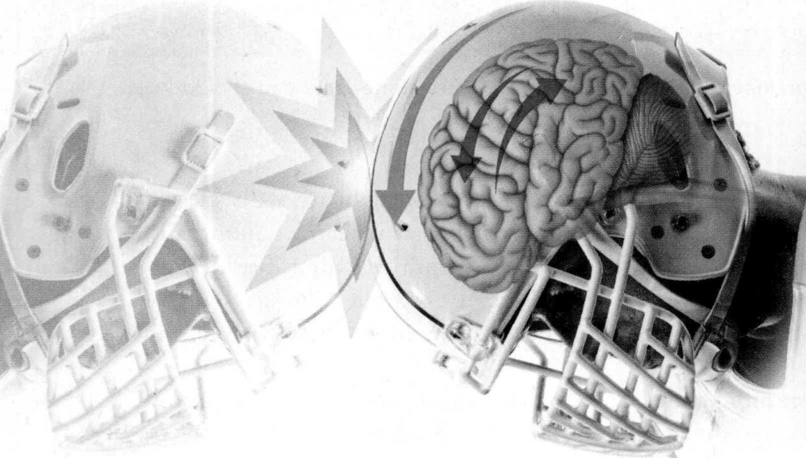

THE PROGRESSION OF CTE

Stage 1

Tau protein accumulates locally in the cortex.

Symptoms: headaches, and difficulty maintaining focus.

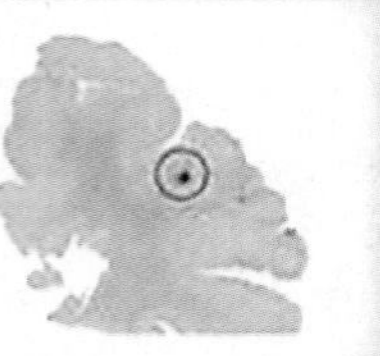

Stage 2

The damage spreads to surrounding areas.

Symptoms: short-term memory impairment, mood swings, depression, explosive temper, and continued headaches and trouble focusing.

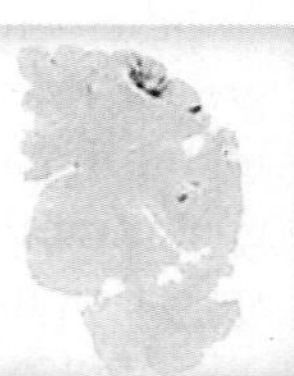

Stage 3

Damage continues to spread, reaching areas such as the hippocampus, amygdala, and brainstem.

Symptoms: memory loss, difficulty planning and carrying out tasks, "visuospatial abnormalities," and ongoing difficulties with mood and attention.

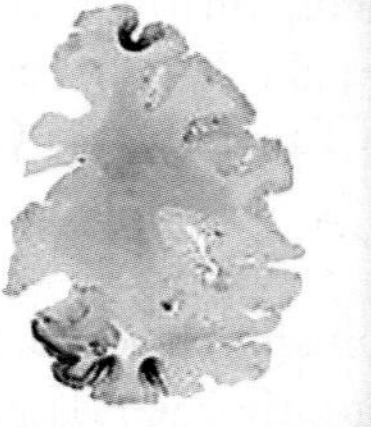

Stage 4

Widespread damage across many regions of the brain, including the medial temporal lobe, hypothalamus, and thalamus.

Symptoms: worsening of existing symptoms, along with language difficulties and paranoia. Severe memory loss.

How does CTE differ from other neurodegenerative diseases such as Alzheimer's? Symptoms associated with CTE typically present around age 40, while those of Alzheimer's generally appear around 60. Changes in thinking, cognition, and personality are common symptoms of CTE, while Alzheimer's is typically associated with memory problems (Frequently Asked Questions, n.d.). However, emerging research suggests that behavioral changes and "neuropsychiatric symptoms" (depression or anxiety, for example) may signal the beginning of the disease process in Alzheimer's patients (Donovan et al., 2014; Ismail, 2016).

Credits: Junior Seau, John W. McDonough/Getty Images; Brandi Chastain, DENIS POROY/AP Images; Football helmet, Beto Chagas/Shutterstock; Brain slices, Dr. Ann McKee.

show what you know

1. ______________ refers to the inability to lay down new long-term memories, generally resulting from damage to the brain.
   a. Anterograde amnesia
   b. Retrograde amnesia
   c. Infantile amnesia
   d. Long-term potentiation

2. The ______________ is a pair of curved structures in the brain that play a central role in memory.
   a. engram
   b. temporal lobe
   c. hippocampus
   d. aplysia

3. ______________ is a progressive, devastating brain illness that causes cognitive decline, including memory, language, and thinking problems. The cause of this illness is unknown, but some forms of it are thought to be inherited.

4. Infantile amnesia makes it difficult for people to remember events that occurred before the age of 3. What is your earliest memory and how old were you when that event occurred?

✓ CHECK YOUR ANSWERS IN APPENDIX C.

FINAL THOUGHTS At this point, you may be wondering what became of Clive Wearing. After living in the hospital for 7 years, Clive moved to a country residence specially designed for people suffering from brain injuries. As he left the hospital, some of the staff members offered him a farewell and said they would miss him. Addressing them with a polite bow, Clive exclaimed, "You're the first people I've seen!" When Deborah would visit Clive in his new home, she found him happy and relaxed, spending much of his time on walks through gardens and the local village (Wearing, 2005, p. 293). In 2002 Clive and Deborah renewed their marriage vows. Clive participated fully in the service, reciting scripture he had memorized during his career as a professional singer decades before (D. Wearing, personal communication, June 10, 2013). After the ceremony, he had no recollection of what had taken place but nevertheless was very happy, laughing and devouring sponge cake (Wearing, 2005).

Onward
Nearly two decades after falling ill, Clive renewed his wedding vows with Deborah. Now in his eighties, Clive lives in a country residence for people suffering from brain injuries (Vennard, 2011, November 21). Jiri Rezac/Polaris/Newscom.

YOUR SCIENTIFIC WORLD is a new application-based feature appearing in every chapter. In these online activities, you will take on role-playing scenarios that encourage you to think critically and apply your knowledge of psychological science to solve a real-world problem. For example: Is pulling an all-nighter a good way to prepare for an exam? How about studying a little each day? In this activity, learn about effective study strategies, mnemonic devices, and other topics related to memory. You can access Your Scientific World activities in LaunchPad. Have fun!

SUMMARY OF CONCEPTS

LO 1 Define memory. (p. 202)

Memory refers to the brain processes involved in the collection, storage, and (in some cases) retrieval of information. Exactly how the brain absorbs information from the outside world and files it for later use is still not completely understood. However, scientists have proposed many theories and constructed various models to help explain how the brain processes, or works on, data on their way to becoming memories.

LO 2 Describe the processes of encoding, storage, and retrieval. (p. 203)

Encoding is the process through which new information enters our memory system. Information is taken in by our senses and converted into neural activity that travels to the brain, and if successfully encoded, it is stored. Storage preserves the information for possible recollection in the future. Retrieval is the process of accessing information stored in memory.

LO 3 Explain the stages of memory described by the information-processing model. (p. 205)

According to the information-processing model, the brain has three types of storage associated with the stages of memory: sensory memory, short-term memory, and long-term memory.

LO 4 Describe sensory memory. (p. 205)

Data picked up by the senses enter sensory memory, where sensations are registered. Here, almost exact copies of our sensations are processed for a very brief moment. Information from the outside world floods our sensory memory through multiple channels. Although this stage of memory is fleeting, it is critical to the creation of memories.

LO 5 Summarize short-term memory. (p. 207)

Short-term memory is the second stage of the original information-processing model. This is where information is temporarily maintained and processed before moving on to long-term memory or leaving the memory system. Short-term memory has a limited capacity; how long and how much it can hold depend on how much you are distracted by other cognitive activities. Through maintenance rehearsal, we can prolong short-term memory.

LO 6 Give examples of how we can use chunking to improve our memory span. (p. 208)

Grouping numbers, letters, or other items into recognizable subsets, or "chunks," is an effective strategy for increasing the amount of information in short-term memory. In addition, chunking can help nudge the same information into long-term memory.

LO 7 Describe working memory and its relationship to short-term memory. (p. 208)

The active processing component of short-term memory, working memory, has four important parts. The phonological loop is responsible for working with verbal information for brief periods of time. The visuospatial sketchpad is where visual and spatial data are briefly stored and manipulated. The central executive directs attention, makes plans, coordinates activities, and determines what information should be ignored. The episodic buffer is where information from the phonological loop, visuospatial sketchpad, and long-term memory can all be brought together temporarily, as directed by the central executive.

LO 8 Describe long-term memory. (p. 211)

Long-term memory is a stage of memory with seemingly unlimited capacity. Long-term memories may be explicit or implicit. Explicit memory is the type of memory you are aware of having and can consciously express, and can be further divided into semantic and episodic memory. Semantic memory pertains to general facts about the world, while episodic memory is your record of the memorable experiences in your life. Implicit memory is for something you know or know how to do, which might be automatic or unconscious, and therefore difficult to articulate.

LO 9 Illustrate how encoding specificity relates to retrieval cues. (p. 218)

Retrieval cues are stimuli that help you retrieve stored information that is difficult to access. The encoding specificity principle states that memories are more easily recalled when the context at the time of encoding is similar to that at the time of retrieval. Thus, the context (external or internal) at the time of encoding and retrieval provides retrieval cues. Priming, recall, and recognition also play a role in the retrieval of stored information.

LO 10 Identify and explain some of the reasons why we forget. (p. 220)

Memory failure may occur during any of the three stages of memory processing: encoding, storage, or retrieval. One example of memory failure is the tip-of-the-tongue phenomenon, which occurs when we cannot retrieve a stored memory.

LO 11 Explain how the malleability of memory influences the recall of events. (p. 223)

Eyewitness accounts are not always reliable because people's memories are imperfect. Memories can change over time, which means we lose bits and pieces of a memory, and unknowingly replace them with new information; this can influence the recall of the event.

LO 12 Define and explain the significance of rich false memory. (p. 225)

Rich false memories are experienced as true recollections of an event that never happened, including details, emotions, and confidence that the event occurred. Some researchers have managed to implant false memories in the minds of participants.

LO 13 Compare and contrast anterograde and retrograde amnesia. (p. 229)

There are varying degrees of amnesia, or memory loss, due to medical or psychological conditions. Anterograde amnesia is the inability to "lay down" or create new long-term memories, and is generally caused by damage to the brain resulting from surgery, alcohol, head trauma, or illness. Retrograde amnesia is an inability to access memories created before damage to the brain occurred.

LO 14 Identify the brain structures involved in memory. (p. 230)

Researchers have identified many brain structures involved in the processing and storage of memory. The hippocampus is essential for creating new explicit memories, as are the temporal lobes and frontal cortex. Other areas, such as the cerebellum and amygdala, are integral in the processing of implicit memories.

LO 15 Summarize the symptoms and causes of Alzheimer's disease. (p. 234)

Alzheimer's disease is a progressive, devastating brain illness that causes various types of cognitive decline, including memory, language, and thinking problems. There are two distinctive signs of Alzheimer's disease: neurofibrillary tangles, which result from twisted protein fibers accumulating inside brain cells, and amyloid plaques, which are protein clumps that build up between neurons, blocking their lines of communication. Although the causes of Alzheimer's are not completely understood, we know some forms of the disease are inherited. Factors such as diet and exercise can also influence the development and progression of the disease. There is no cure for Alzheimer's; current treatments focus on reducing the severity of symptoms rather than correcting the brain damage responsible.

KEY TERMS

anterograde amnesia, p. 229
chronic traumatic encephalopathy (CTE), p. 234
chunking, p. 208
distributed practice, p. 213
echoic memory, p. 207
effortful processing, p. 213
elaborative rehearsal, p. 213
encoding, p. 203
encoding specificity principle, p. 219
episodic memory, p. 211
explicit memory, p. 211
flashbulb memory, p. 211
iconic memory, p. 206
implicit memory, p. 211
long-term memory, p. 205
long-term potentiation, p. 233
maintenance rehearsal, p. 207
massed practice, p. 213
memory, p. 202
memory trace, p. 230
misinformation effect, p. 225
mnemonic, p. 213
primacy effect, p. 217
priming, p. 216
proactive interference, p. 221
procedural memory, p. 212
recall, p. 217
recency effect, p. 217
recognition, p. 217
relearning, p. 219
retrieval, p. 203
retrieval cues, p. 216
retroactive interference, p. 222
retrograde amnesia, p. 229
rich false memories, p. 225
semantic memory, p. 211
sensory memory, p. 205
serial position effect, p. 217
short-term memory, p. 205
storage, p. 203
working memory, p. 208

TEST PREP ARE YOU READY?

1. You try to remember the name of a movie you watched last year, but struggle to recall it. When you do finally remember the film was *Black Panther,* which memory process were you using?
 a. short-term memory
 b. sensory memory
 c. encoding
 d. retrieval

2. Alzheimer's disease is a progressive brain illness that can cause various types of cognitive decline, including memory, language, and thinking problems. Which of the following is a distinctive sign of this disease?
 a. neurofibrillary tangles
 b. encephalitis
 c. herpes simplex virus
 d. epilepsy

3. George Miller reviewed findings from the Digit Span Test and found that short-term memory capacity is between 5 and 9 numbers, that is, the "magical number seven, plus or minus two." However, through the use of ___________, we can improve the span of our short-term memory.
 a. echoic memory
 b. iconic memory
 c. multitasking
 d. chunking

4. Baddeley and colleagues proposed that the purpose of ___________ is to actively maintain information while the mind is performing complex tasks. The phonological loop, visuospatial sketchpad, central executive, and episodic buffer all play a role in this process.
 a. eidetic imagery
 b. working memory
 c. short-term memory
 d. semantic memory

5. In a classic study, Godden and Baddeley asked participants to learn lists of words under two conditions: while underwater and on dry land. Participants were better able to recall the information in the same context in which it was encoded. This finding supports:
 a. the encoding specificity principle.
 b. Baddeley's working memory model.
 c. the serial position effect.
 d. the information-processing model of memory.

6. ___________ causes problems with the retrieval of memories because of information you learned in the past, and ___________ causes problems with retrieval due to recently learned information.
 a. The recency effect; the primacy effect
 b. The primacy effect; the recency effect
 c. Proactive interference; retroactive interference
 d. Retroactive interference; proactive interference

7. According to ___________, memories can fade over time, becoming more vulnerable to new information. Thus, your memory of an event might include revisions of what really happened.
 a. the information-processing model of memory
 b. the levels of processing framework
 c. Baddeley's model of working memory
 d. a reconstructionist model of memory

8. In studies by Loftus and colleagues, around 25% of participants were able to "remember" an event that never happened. This type of ___________ shows us how the malleability of memory can influence recall.
 a. highly superior autobiographic memory
 b. rich false memory
 c. proactive interference
 d. serial position effect

9. Retrograde amnesia is generally caused by some sort of damage to the brain. People with retrograde amnesia generally cannot:
 a. form memories of events that occur following the damage.
 b. access memories of events created before the damage.
 c. form semantic memories following the damage.
 d. use procedural memories.

10. The ___________ is essential for creating new explicit memories, but not implicit memories.
 a. parietal lobe
 b. amygdala
 c. cerebellum
 d. hippocampus

11. A friend says, "My grandmother has terrible short-term memory. She can't remember anything from a couple of hours ago." This statement represents a very common misconception. How would you explain this confusion about short-term memory versus long-term memory?

12. How are iconic memory and echoic memory different?

13. How does working memory differ from short-term memory?

14. Create a mnemonic to help you remember the process of encoding, storage, and retrieval.

15. Imagine you are a teacher creating a list of classroom rules in case of an emergency. If you were expecting your students to remember these rules after reading through them only once, where in the list would you position the most important rules? Why?

✓ CHECK YOUR ANSWERS IN APPENDIX C.

Go to **LaunchPad** or **Achieve: Read & Practice** to test your understanding with **LearningCurve**.

CHAPTER

7

Dave King/Getty Images.

Cognition, Language, and Intelligence

What Is Cognition?

BLEEDING BRAIN December 10, 1996, was the day a blood vessel in Dr. Jill Bolte Taylor's brain began to bleed. At approximately 7:00 A.M., Dr. Taylor awoke to a pain behind her left eye, a stabbing sensation she found similar to the "brain freeze" felt after a hasty gulp of ice cream. It seemed strange for a healthy 37-year-old woman to experience such a terrible headache, but Dr. Taylor was not the type to lounge in bed all day. Pushing through the pain, she got up and climbed onto her cardio-glider. But as soon as she began moving her limbs back and forth, a weird out-of-body sensation took hold. "I felt as though I was observing myself in motion, as in the playback of a memory," Dr. Taylor writes in her book *My Stroke of Insight.* "My fingers, as they grasped onto the handrail, looked like primitive claws" (Taylor, 2006, p. 37).

The Brain Scientist An accomplished neuroanatomist, Dr. Jill Bolte Taylor had devoted her career to studying the brains of others. But one winter morning in 1996, she was given the frightening opportunity to observe her own brain in the midst of a meltdown. AJ Mast/The New York Times/Redux.

The pain, meanwhile, kept hammering away at the left side of her head. She stepped off the cardio-glider and headed toward the bathroom, but her steps seemed plodding, and maintaining balance demanded intense concentration. Finally reaching the shower, Dr. Taylor propped herself against the wall and turned on the faucet, but the sound of the water splashing against the tub was like an earsplitting roar. Her brain was no longer processing sound normally. For the first time that morning, she began to wonder if her brain was in serious trouble (Taylor, 2006).

"What is going on?" she thought. "What is happening in my brain?" (Taylor, 2006, p. 41). If anyone was poised to answer these questions, it was Dr. Taylor. A devoted neuroanatomist, she spent her days studying neurons at a laboratory affiliated with Harvard Medical School. Wading in a dreamlike fog, Dr. Taylor managed to shower and put on clothes. Then, just as she began visualizing the journey to work, her right arm fell limp like a dead fish. It was paralyzed. At that moment she knew: "Oh my gosh, I'm having a stroke! I'm having a stroke!" (p. 44). Then: "Wow this is so cool! . . . How many scientists have the opportunity to study their own brain function and mental deterioration from the inside out?" (p. 44).

Dr. Taylor was indeed having a rare form of stroke caused by a defective linkage between blood vessels in the brain. This faulty connection in the central nervous system, known as an arteriovenous malformation (AVM), is present in a substantial number of people—about 300,000 in the United States alone (around 0.1% of the population). Most individuals born with AVMs are symptomless and unaware of their condition, but about 12% (36,000 people) experience effects ranging from annoying headaches to life-threatening brain bleeds like the one Dr. Taylor was experiencing (National Institute of Neurological Disorders and Stroke, n.d.).

Having a backstage pass to her own stroke was a once-in-a-lifetime learning opportunity for a neuroanatomist, but it was also a serious condition requiring immediate medical attention. Aware of this urgency, Dr. Taylor took a seat by the phone, racking her brain for ideas of how to get help. The usual strategies like calling 911 or knocking on a neighbor's door simply did not cross her mind. As she gazed at the phone keypad, a string of digits materialized in her brain: the phone number of her mother in Indiana. Not wanting to worry her mom, Dr. Taylor sat and waited, hoping that another phone number would come to mind (Taylor, 2006).

Finally, the digits of her work number flickered by. She scrawled them down as fast as she could, but her writing looked like cryptic lines and curves. Fortunately, those lines and curves matched the figures she saw on the phone keypad. Dr. Taylor picked up the receiver and dialed (Taylor, 2006). Her coworker and friend Dr. Stephen Vincent answered immediately, but his words were incomprehensible to Dr. Taylor. "Oh my gosh, he sounds like a golden retriever!" she thought. Mustering all her mental might, she opened her mouth and said, "This is Jill, I need help!" But, her own voice sounded like a golden retriever as well (Taylor, 2006, p. 56; 2008, February). Luckily, Dr. Vincent recognized that the murmurs and cries belonged to his friend Jill, and before long he was driving her to the hospital (Taylor, 2006).

As blood hemorrhaged into Dr. Taylor's brain, she struggled to process sensory information, **tap into memories**, and use language. As she later reflected: "In the course of four hours, I watched my brain completely deteriorate in its ability to process all information" (Taylor, 2008, February). The bleeding was beginning to limit her capacity for cognition. 

Note: Story and quotations from *My Stroke of Insight*, by Jill Bolte Taylor, © 2006 by Jill Bolte Taylor. Used by permission of Viking Penguin, a division of Penguin Group (USA) Inc. Unless otherwise stated, quotations attributed to Harry Carson are personal communications.

Dr. Taylor, In Her Own Words
http://qrs.ly/1v5a5d3

Photo: AJ Mast/The New York Times/Redux.

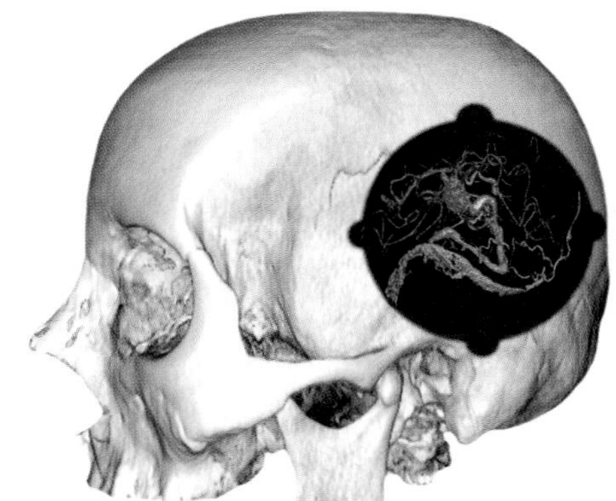

Tangled
The tangled intersection of arteries (red) and veins (blue) is an arteriovenous malformation (AVM), the anatomical abnormality that led to Dr. Taylor's stroke. An AVM is essentially a clump of blood vessels that results when there are no capillaries linking arteries to veins. Sometimes the vessels of an AVM burst under pressure, allowing blood to pool in the brain; this is called a hemorrhagic stroke (National Institute of Neurological Disorders and Stroke, 2017). Medical Body Scans/Science Source.

CONNECTIONS

In **Chapter 6,** we presented the process of retrieval in memory. Dr. Taylor was having difficulty retrieving her memories. We assume that the information she was trying to access had been successfully encoded and stored prior to the stroke.

Cognition. You've probably heard the word tossed around in conversation, and perhaps you know it has something to do with thinking. But what exactly do we mean by cognition, and where does it figure in the vast landscape of psychology?

Cognition Versus Thinking

The study of cognition is deeply rooted in the history of psychology. Early psychologists focused on understanding the mysterious workings of the mind, often using **introspection** (examination of one's own conscious activities) in their studies. With the rise of behaviorism in the 1930s, the emphasis shifted away from internal processes and on to behavior. Researchers shunned the study of thoughts, emotions, and anything they could not observe or measure objectively. In the 1950s, psychologists once again began to probe the mind. Psychology experienced a *cognitive revolution,* and research on thinking and other aspects of cognition has flourished ever since.

CONNECTIONS

In **Chapter 1,** we described how Wundt used introspection to examine psychological responses to stimuli. Titchener used introspection to determine the structure of the mind. These early psychologists paved the way for cognitive psychology, the study of mental processes, and cognitive neuroscience, which explores their physiological basis.

LO 1 Define cognition and explain how it relates to thinking.

Cognition is the mental activity associated with obtaining, converting, and using knowledge. But how is this different from *thinking?* Thinking is a specific type of cognition that requires us to "go beyond" information or to manipulate information to reach a goal. **Thinking** involves transforming information to make a decision, reach a solution, or form a belief (Matlin & Farmer, 2016). Cognition is a broad term that describes mental activity, and thinking is a subset of cognition. Dr. Taylor was clearly experiencing significant impairments in both cognition and **thinking** on the morning of her stroke.

CONNECTIONS

In **Chapters 0** and **1,** we discussed critical thinking, which drives the cycle of scientific exploration. The process involves weighing and synthesizing evidence—thinking clearly, rationally, and with an open mind. Here, we explore thinking more broadly.

THE HOSPITAL At Mount Auburn Hospital, Dr. Taylor had a computerized axial tomography (CAT) scan, which revealed a giant hemorrhage in the left side of her brain. "My left hemisphere was swimming in a pool of blood and my entire brain was swollen in response to the trauma," she recalls (Taylor, 2006, p. 68). Dr. Taylor was rushed by ambulance to Massachusetts General Hospital, which has a neurological intensive care unit. The following day, Dr. Taylor was told that her mother, who went by the name of "G.G.," was on her way. She found the news perplexing (Taylor, 2006). What on Earth was a *mother,* and who or what was a *G.G.?* "Initially, I didn't understand the significance of G.G.—as I had lost the *concept* of what a mother was," she writes (p. 88). When G.G. arrived, she walked over to her daughter's bed and climbed in alongside her. As Dr. Taylor recalls, "She immediately wrapped me up in her arms and I melted into the familiarity of her snuggle" (p. 90).

Bleeding Brain
The red zone on the right of the CAT scan shows a hemorrhage on the left side of the brain. (Note that the patient's left is your right.) In Dr. Taylor's case, the bleeding interfered with activity in Broca's and Wernicke's areas, impairing her ability to produce and understand language. Her frontal lobe function also deteriorated the morning of the stroke, as illustrated by the difficulty she had in devising a coherent strategy to get medical help. Scott Camazine/Science Source.

Can You Grasp This Concept?

LO 2 Demonstrate an understanding of concepts and how they are organized.

Although the touch of G.G. felt familiar, the *concept* of her had slipped away, at least temporarily. What exactly is a concept? We can define **concepts** as mental representations of categories of objects, situations, and ideas that belong together based

cognition The mental activity associated with obtaining, converting, and using knowledge.

thinking Mental activity associated with coming to a decision, reaching a solution, or forming a belief.

concepts Mental representations of categories of objects, situations, and ideas that belong together based on their central features or characteristics.

on their central features (characteristics). The concept of *superhero,* for example, includes a variety of recognizable characteristics, such as supernatural powers, bravery, and a strong desire to protect the innocent. Concepts are a central ingredient of cognitive activity, playing an important role in memory, reasoning, and language (McCaffrey & Machery, 2012; Slaney & Racine, 2011).

Without concepts, we would have a hard time communicating and organizing our thoughts. For example, we all know what a *cat* is. But if the concept *cat* did not exist, we would have to describe many of the characteristics that we expect of a cat whenever one comes up in conversation: "Yesterday I saw the cutest animal—you know, those furry, four-legged creatures with pointy ears and long tails, the ones that say *meow?*" Thanks to our *cat* concept, however, we can simply use the word "cat" as shorthand for all of them ("Yesterday I saw the cutest cat"). Even if you encounter a cat breed you have never seen before (for example, a hairless Sphynx cat), you still know it's a cat. Concepts allow us to organize and synthesize information, and to draw conclusions about specific objects, situations, and ideas that we have never encountered before (Yee & Thompson-Schill, 2016). Imagine how exhausting thinking and talking would be if we did not have concepts to fall back on.

You Asked, Dr. Taylor Answers

http://qrs.ly/1v5a5d3

How did you communicate thoughts and ideas to others when you weren't able to effectively express yourself?

ORGANIZING FURNITURE? One way to understand concepts is to consider how they can be organized in *hierarchies,* or rankings. Generally, psychologists use a three-level concept hierarchy to categorize information. At the top of the hierarchy are *superordinate* concepts. This is the broadest category, encompassing all objects belonging to a concept. In **INFOGRAPHIC 7.1** on page 245, we see the superordinate concept of furniture, a broad group that includes everything from couches to nightstands, at the top of the hierarchy. If we limit our focus to couches only, we are looking at the *midlevel* or basic level of our hierarchy. Narrowing our focus further brings us to the *subordinate-level,* which includes specific types or instances of couches, such as a loveseat, a La-Z-Boy, or that family couch with crumbs between the cushions.

We typically use the midlevel category to identify objects in our everyday experience ("That's a nice couch"). Most children learn the midlevel concepts first, followed by the superordinate and subordinate concepts (Mandler, 2008; Rosch, Mervis, Gray, Johnson, & Boyes-Braem, 1976). Although a child might grasp the meaning of *couch,* she may not understand *furniture* (the superordinate level) or *chaise lounge* (the subordinate level).

Put Your Heads Together

As a team, **A**) pick a superordinate concept that could serve as the top level of a concept hierarchy. **B**) Identify several members of the midlevel and subordinate level of this hierarchy. **C**) How might you use a concept hierarchy when studying?

Reconstructing concept hierarchies was a formidable task for Dr. Taylor, because so many of their layers had been washed away by the hemorrhage. With hard work, optimism, and the help of G.G., she slowly reconstructed concepts as diverse as *alphabet letters* and *tuna salad.* Using children's books, G.G. helped her daughter retrain her brain to read, and by putting together puzzles, Dr. Taylor was able to re-create concepts such as *right side up* and *edge* (Taylor, 2006).

Cool Cats
Perhaps you've never come face to face with a Red Self Longhair (top), a Devon Rex (middle), or a hairless Sphynx (bottom). However, you immediately know they are cats because you have developed a "cat" concept, which specifies the defining features of these animals. Red Self Longhair: Dave King/Getty Images. Devon Rex and Sphynx: Jagodka/Shutterstock.

LO 3 Differentiate between formal concepts and natural concepts.

LOGICAL OR PERSONAL? Concepts can be divided into two major categories: *formal* and *natural.* **Formal concepts** are based on rigid and logical rules (or "features" of a concept). When a child learns that 5 is an odd number because, like all other odd numbers, it cannot be divided evenly by 2 without a remainder, she is developing a simple **formal concept**. An object, idea, or situation must explicitly adhere to strict criteria in order to meet the definition of a particular formal concept. Science uses formal concepts to develop laws, theorems, and rules.

synonyms
formal concepts artificial concepts

CONNECTIONS
In **Chapter 1,** we introduced operational definitions, which specify the precise manner in which a variable is defined and measured. Creating operational definitions for formal concepts is relatively straightforward, because they are already defined by rigid and logical rules. Natural concepts are more challenging, as experts do not always agree on how to define or measure them.

Unlike formal concepts, **natural concepts** are defined by general characteristics and are acquired during the course of our daily lives (Rosch, 1973; Yee & Thompson-Schill, 2016). Examples we have already discussed include *furniture* and *superhero.* Like all natural concepts, these are mental representations of categories formed through each person's unique experience and culture. Your concept of superhero, for example, is likely based on stories you've heard, books you've read, and movies you've seen. There are no universal or fixed rules for what constitutes a superhero, as they are "constantly changing and are inextricably linked to their contexts" (Yee & Thompson-Schill, 2016, p. 1015). Identifying objects that fall into such categories is difficult because their boundaries are imprecise and hard to define; natural concepts don't have the types of rigid rules for identification that formal concepts do (Hampton, 1998).

Unfamiliar Fruits
If we asked you to classify a durian (top) or a rambutan (bottom), you might pause before saying the word "fruit"! This is because durians and rambutans do not closely resemble our typical fruit prototypes, apples and oranges. If we showed you a peach, however, your response might be faster because peaches are more similar to apples and oranges. Top: Mrs_ya/Shutterstock. Bottom: tarapong srichaiyos/Shutterstock.

PROTOTYPES In our daily use of natural concepts, we rely on **prototypes,** the ideal or most representative examples of natural concepts (Mervis & Rosch, 1981). A prototype is the image or definition that quickly comes to mind when you consider a concept. If asked to give an example of a fruit, you would most likely say apple or orange—and *not* rambutan, unless you happen to be from Indonesia, where this sweet fruit is eaten regularly. Infographic 7.1 presents a list of fruits organized from the most frequently suggested prototype (orange) to the least frequently suggested prototype (olive) among a group of American college students (Rosch & Mervis, 1975).

Prototypes help us identify objects and ideas as members of a concept. (*That object looks kind of like an orange; it must be a fruit.*) This process is much easier when the items presented closely resemble our prototypes. If shown an image of a papaya, many people in the United States would take longer to identify it as belonging to the fruit category than if they were shown an image of a peach (which is more similar to the common prototypes of apples and oranges). It would likely take them even longer to identify a durian or rambutan. Let's consider the concept of *hero* (scaling back from superheroes), the subject of much research over the years. The natural concept of hero can be defined by its "most prototypical features," including bravery, moral integrity, conviction, self-sacrifice, honesty, altruism, and determination (Kinsella, Ritchie, & Igou, 2015). But such qualities do not constitute "rigid boundaries" for identifying a hero.

We now know how the brain organizes information into meaningful categories, or concepts. But how is that information represented inside our heads, especially for concepts related to people, places, and things that aren't present? With the help of *mental imagery,* we can imagine how they look, sound, smell, taste, and feel.

formal concepts The mental representations of categories that are created through rigid and logical rules or features.

natural concepts The mental representations of categories resulting from experiences in daily life.

prototype The ideal or most representative example of a natural concept; helps us categorize or identify specific members of a concept.

Picture This

Where is your cell phone right now? Did a picture of your beloved mobile device suddenly materialize in your "mind's eye"? If so, you have just created a *mental image.* Whether contemplating cell phones or daydreaming about celebrities, our brains are constantly whipping up vivid pictures. This cognitive activity often involves manipulating objects in three dimensions.

Concepts and Prototypes

Concepts are used to organize information in a manner that helps us understand things even when we are encountering them for the first time. *Formal concepts,* like "circle," allow us to categorize objects and ideas in a very precise way— something either meets the criteria to be included in that category, or it doesn't. *Natural concepts* develop as a result of our everyday encounters, and vary according to our culture and individual experiences. We tend to use *prototypes,* ideal representations with features we associate most with a category, to identify natural concepts.

formal CONCEPT

Defined by rigid, precise rules

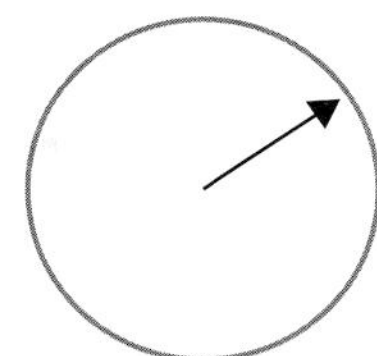

A circle is a two-dimensional shape in which all points are the same distance from its center.

natural CONCEPT

Defined by general characteristics established through everyday encounters

A couch is a large piece of furniture used for sitting.

Concepts can be organized into **HIERARCHIES**

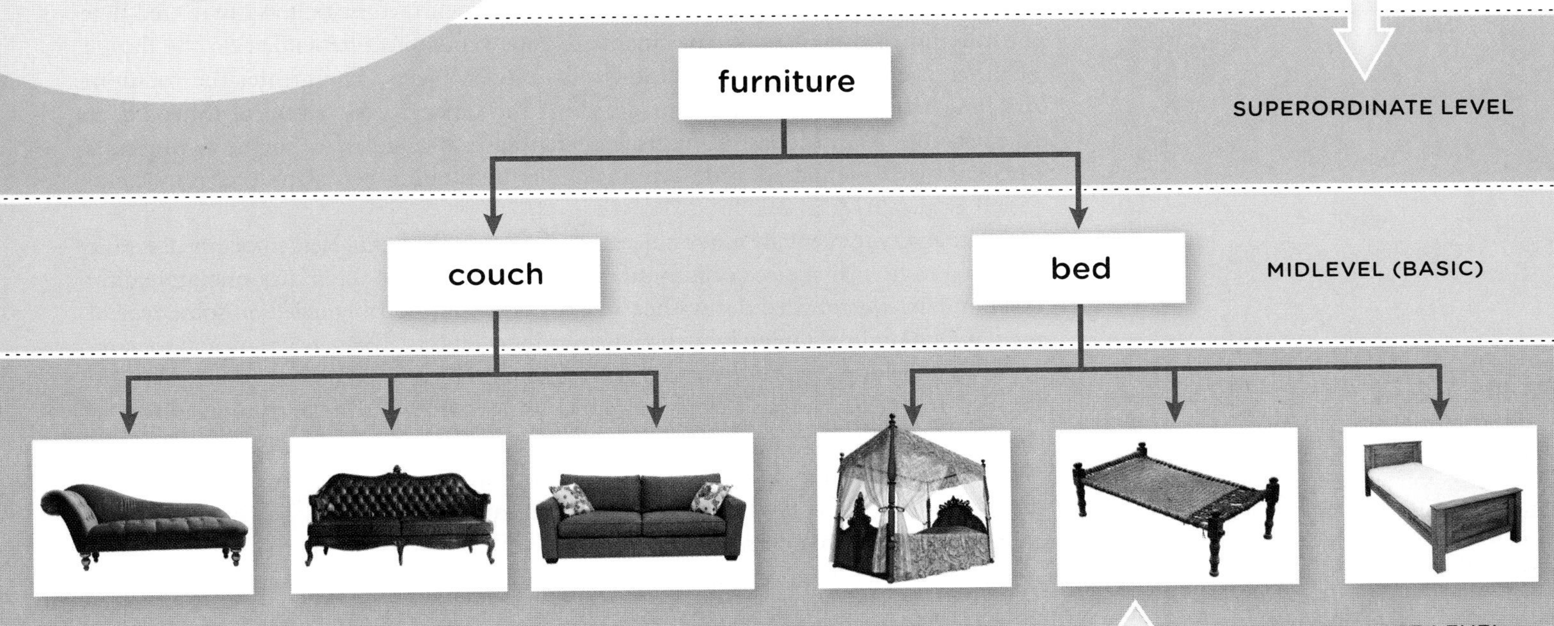

Did you think of this? Maybe not. But if you're from India, the traditional charpai may be your prototype—the first image that comes to mind when someone says "bed." What comes to mind when you think of the concept "fruit"? Researchers studying the development of categories organized a group of items from the most prototypical to the least prototypical (Rosch & Mervis, 1975). How long would it take you to think of an olive?

Credits: Vintage bed, sagir/Shutterstock; Two green olives, Smit/Shutterstock; Ripe pineapple, Alex Staroseltsev/Shutterstock; Ripe orange, Maks Narodenko/Shutterstock; Ripe banana, Tatiana Popova/Shutterstock; Red apple, Valentina Razumova/Shutterstock; Lemon, Viktar Malyshchyts/Shutterstock; Fresh tomato, topseller/Shutterstock; Fresh red strawberry, topseller/Shutterstock; Dried dates, Klimkov Alexey/Shutterstock; Coconut, Viktar Malyshchyts/Shutterstock; Black sofa, luckypic/Shutterstock; Charpoy bedstead cot furniture, © Dinodia/age fotostock; 3D rendering of the canopy bed of Louis XV, Ralf Juergen Kraft/Shutterstock; Red daybed, Eric Jamison/Thinkstock; Upholstered Sofa, AnnaDavy/Thinkstock.

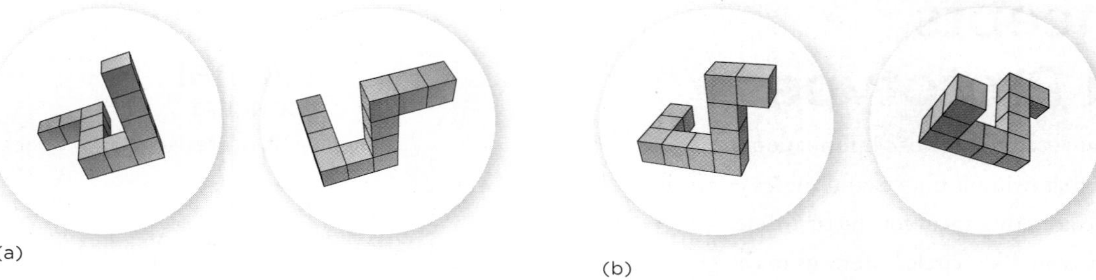

FIGURE 7.1
Manipulating Mental Images
Can you tell which object pair is congruent? In order to determine this, you must hold images of these figures in your mind and mentally manipulate them. (The answer appears at the bottom of this page.)

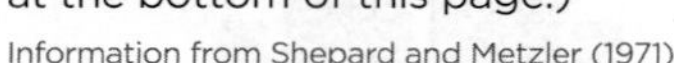

Information from Shepard and Metzler (1971).

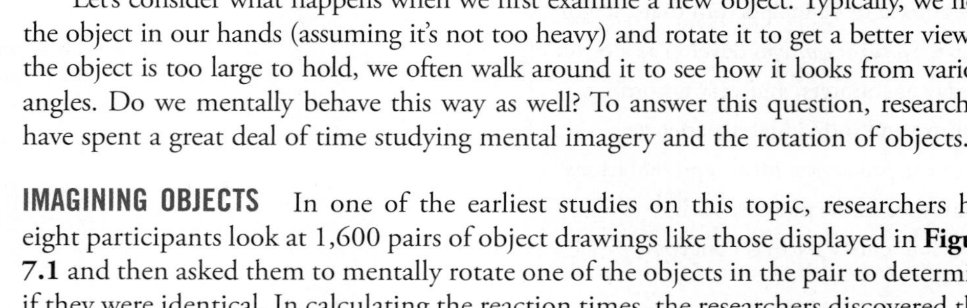

Let's consider what happens when we first examine a new object. Typically, we hold the object in our hands (assuming it's not too heavy) and rotate it to get a better view. If the object is too large to hold, we often walk around it to see how it looks from various angles. Do we mentally behave this way as well? To answer this question, researchers have spent a great deal of time studying mental imagery and the rotation of objects.

IMAGINING OBJECTS In one of the earliest studies on this topic, researchers had eight participants look at 1,600 pairs of object drawings like those displayed in **Figure 7.1** and then asked them to mentally rotate one of the objects in the pair to determine if they were identical. In calculating the reaction times, the researchers discovered that the amount of time it took participants to rotate the object depended on the degree of difference between the orientations of the two objects. The greater the rotation, the longer it took participants to decide if the objects were identical (Shepard & Metzler, 1971). In the last 50 years, research has indicated that "cognitive processes involved with mental rotation are analogous to rotating actual objects physically" (Stieff et al., 2018, p. 2).

The ability to mentally rotate objects can be extremely useful. Remember the last time you tried to fit a large piece of furniture through a doorway or cram just one more dirty bowl into an overcrowded dishwasher. In each case, you probably relied on some type of mental rotation in planning how to maneuver these objects. Teachers use mental rotation activities to help students understand 3-dimensional structures (Chamberlain et al., 2018; Stieff et al., 2018). In organic chemistry, for example, students learn by manipulating concrete and virtual models of molecules. This allows students to "internalize a mental model of these transformations," which helps them use more accurate mental rotation when the models are not physically present (Stull & Hegarty, 2016, p. 521). See **Figure 7.2** for an example of research on mental imagery. And take note: Mental imagery is not always visual. Have you ever imagined the smell or taste of freshly baked chocolate chip cookies? Or, perhaps you have "heard" a song in your head. We use all types of sensory experiences to construct imagery in our minds.

FIGURE 7.2
Scanning Mental Images
In a study on mental imagery, participants were instructed to study a map of a small fictional island. The researchers then asked them to close their eyes and imagine the map, first picturing one object (the hut) and then scanning across their mental image of the map until they "arrived" at a second object (the rock). The researchers found that it took longer for participants to "find" objects on the mental map when the objects were farther apart. As with the scanning of real objects, the amount of time it takes to scan a mental image is relative to the distances between the objects in the image. Information from Kosslyn, Ball, and Reiser (1978).

Every cognitive activity we have discussed thus far, from establishing prototypes of fruit to mentally rotating bowls you are trying to cram into the dishwasher, is made possible by the electrical and chemical activity of billions of neurons. Let's get acquainted with the biology of cognition.

What's Happening in the Brain?

LO 4 Describe the biological processes associated with cognition.

Dr. Taylor's story provides a stark illustration of the following principle: If the brain's biological integrity is compromised, cognition is likely to suffer. The bleeding began in a small region on the left side of Dr. Taylor's cerebral cortex but soon spread across large areas of her brain (Taylor, 2006). Among those affected was her left frontal lobe, which is critical for a broad array of higher-level cognitive

Answer to Figure 7.1: a

functions such as processing emotions, controlling impulses, and making plans. Remember that Dr. Taylor had great difficulty devising a simple plan to save her own life (for example, she was unable to think of calling 911).

The stroke also ravaged brain regions crucial to another element of cognition: language processing. "As the blood interrupted the flow of information transmission between my two language centers (Broca's anteriorly and Wernicke's posteriorly) . . . I could neither create/express language nor understand it," Dr. Taylor recalls (Taylor, 2006, p. 62). **Broca's and Wernicke's areas** work with other parts of the brain to produce speech and comprehend language.

CONNECTIONS

In **Chapter 2,** we described the association areas, which integrate information from all over the brain. Dr. Taylor's stroke impacted her ability to use language, presumably by disrupting the normal activities of two association areas: Broca's area, pivotal for speech production, and Wernicke's area, for language comprehension.

The biology of cognition can also be observed on a micro scale. At the neural level, we can observe the brain's amazing plasticity. Following a stroke, healing and regeneration are associated with greater excitability of neurons, rewiring to take advantage of both hemispheres, increases in dendritic connections, and **increased efficiency** of communication at the synapses (Dobkin, 2005).

CONNECTIONS

In **Chapter 6,** we described how learning and memory are evident at the neural level. Through the process of long-term potentiation, communication between sending and receiving neurons is enhanced. This increased synaptic strength facilitates learning and memory formation, and is apparent in the aftermath of a stroke.

STUDYING COGNITION Reading Dr. Taylor's CAT scans, the doctors were able to see the cause of all these cognitive malfunctions—an enormous hemorrhage on the left side of her brain: "It didn't take someone with a Ph.D. in neuroanatomy to figure out that the huge white hole in the middle of the brain scan didn't belong there!" (Taylor, 2006, p. 68). CAT scans are extremely useful for detecting abnormalities like strokes and tumors, while other technologies focus on cognitive activities, such as mental imagery.

Research suggests that imagery and perception share many of the same neural mechanisms (Ganis et al., 2004; Lisman, 2015). Using positron emission tomography (PET) and functional magnetic resonance imaging (fMRI), researchers have found that the **visual cortex** can be activated by both external stimuli and mental imagery (Ganis, Thompson, & Kosslyn, 2004; Lisman, 2015). In fact, neurons often display similar patterns of activity when a person imagines something or sees it in real life (Lisman, 2015).

CONNECTIONS

In **Chapter 2,** we reported that the visual cortex is the part of the brain where visual information is received, interpreted, and processed. Here, we see that the information processed by the visual cortex does not always arise from visual stimuli.

We have now learned about several key components of cognition. The ability to perform cognitive functions is highly variable, as each of us has a unique collection of talents and deficiencies. Could some cognitive strengths be influenced by our gender?

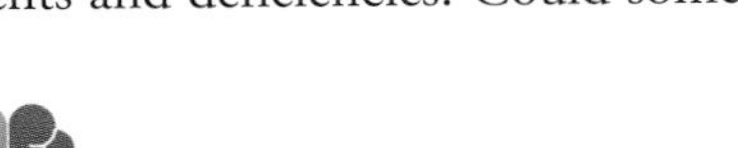

THINK CRITICALLY

DOES GENDER MATTER? Look at the research comparing the cognitive abilities of males and females and you will discover some interesting trends. In childhood and adolescence, for example, girls tend to perform better than boys on tests of verbal ability. Early research indicated these differences were negligible, but more recent evidence suggests they might be significant (Hyde & Linn, 1988; Stoet & Geary, 2013). Males, on the other hand, seem to be more adept at mental rotation tasks, a disparity that appears as early as infancy (Heil, Krüger, Krist, Johnson, & Moore, 2018; Miller & Halpern, 2014; Moore & Johnson, 2008).

WE ARE MORE ALIKE THAN DIFFERENT

Where do such gender disparities arise? Genes, hormones, and sociocultural factors all play a role, but untangling the effects of nature and nurture can be tricky (Goldman, 2017, Spring). Perhaps the most important point to remember is that men and women are far more alike than they are different, not only in cognitive abilities, but across psychological characteristics (Hyde, 2016). What's more, the small number of disparities researchers have uncovered apply to populations—not necessarily individuals. "These findings describe group averages and therefore often have limited relevance to understanding individual men and women. Many men excel in writing tasks and many women excel in mental rotation tasks, even if group averages exist" (Miller & Halpern, 2014, p. 42).

show what you know

1. ______________ is the mental activity linked to obtaining, converting, and using knowledge.

2. If you were to define the ______________ of *hero,* you might suggest that people in this category are characterized by bravery, moral integrity, self-sacrifice, honesty, and determination.
   a. cognition
   b. concept
   c. hierarchy
   d. mental imagery

3. Your instructor explains that the pitch of a sound is defined by the frequency of the sound wave. She is describing a ______________, which is based on rigid rules or features.
   a. prototype
   b. natural concept
   c. formal concept
   d. cognition

4. Give two examples illustrating how biology relates to cognition.

✓ CHECK YOUR ANSWERS IN APPENDIX C.

Problem Solving and Decision Making

THE BIG DILEMMA On Day 3 at the hospital, a team of doctors arrived at Dr. Taylor's bedside to discuss the possibility of performing surgery. One of the doctors, an expert in AVMs (the blood vessel abnormality responsible for her stroke), informed Dr. Taylor that there was a blood clot as big as a "golf ball" on the left side of her brain. Both the clot and the remainder of the AVM needed to be extracted; otherwise, she risked suffering another stroke (Taylor, 2006). But with surgery come risks. Dr. Taylor had a very big problem on her hands, and a very important decision to make: Would she undergo the surgery?

What's the Problem?

Have you ever considered the many problems you encounter and solve every day? Problems crop up when something gets in the way of a goal, like a computer crashing when you are racing to finish a project. They range from mundane (*the printer is jammed*) to potentially overwhelming (*I have a life-threatening brain bleed*). In psychology, **problem solving** refers to the variety of approaches we can use to achieve our goals.

One early model suggests that problem solving proceeds from an initial state (the situation at the start of a problem) to a goal state (the situation when the problem is solved; Matlin & Farmer, 2016; Newell, Shaw, & Simon 1958). How might this model apply to Dr. Taylor? Her *initial state* included a massive blood clot and a troublesome clump of vessels in her left hemisphere. The *goal state* was maximizing her health, both physically and cognitively.

Another crucial component of problem solving is recognizing obstacles that block the paths to a solution (Matlin & Farmer, 2016). Think about a problem you want to solve and identify the initial state, the goal state, and the obstacles in your way. If your initial state is unfinished homework and your goal state is timely completion, the obstacles might include competing responsibilities or something more internal, like sleepiness or lack of motivation.

Solar Solution
Traditional solar panels are large, heavy, and not especially attractive. Tesla, the company known for making electric cars, recognized this problem and developed a brilliant solution: the "Solar Roof." Made from a combination of solar tiles and nonsolar tiles, the Solar Roof captures energy from the sun and turns it into electrical energy you can use for turning on lights, toasting bread, and charging iPads (Tesla, n.d.; *Time* Magazine Staff, 2016, November 17).
Tesla/Newscom/United Press International (UPI)/WASHINGTON/DC/UNITED STATES.

How Do We Solve It?

The first step in problem solving is understanding the problem (see **Infographic 7.2** on page 251). If you can't identify or label a problem, then solving it is going to be difficult. Once you grasp the problem, you must choose one of many available approaches or strategies to tackle it. Which strategy you settle on—and the speed, accuracy, and success of your solution—will depend on many factors, including your reservoir of knowledge, and the amount of time you spend assessing the problem (Ericsson, 2003; Goldstein, 2011). Let's look at some strategies.

problem solving The variety of approaches that can be used to achieve a goal.

 Explain how trial and error and algorithms can be used to solve problems.

TRIAL AND ERROR One common approach to problem solving is **trial and error,** the process of finding a solution through a series of attempts. Mistakes are likely, but you can simply eliminate options that don't work. Let's say you have a HUGE set of keys, but you don't know which one, if any, fits the lock you are trying to open. Using trial and error, you would try the keys, one by one, until you find the right one (assuming the correct key is on the ring). But this approach is only useful in certain circumstances and should be avoided when the stakes are high. Imagine if Dr. Taylor's physicians had used trial and error to choose the procedure she needed. *Let's try this surgery first. If it doesn't work, we'll try a different one next week, and then another the following week.* Trial and error is also not recommended for problems with too many possible solutions. If you have 50 keys, you probably don't want to spend your time trying every single one of them. Besides, there is no guarantee you will arrive at a solution.

64,000 Combos
Forgot your lock combination? Trying to figure it out by trial and error is not an effective strategy, as there are 64,000 possible solutions. Better buy a new lock. Pixel Embargo/Shutterstock.

ALGORITHMS If you're looking for a problem-solving approach that is more of a sure thing, an *algorithm* is probably your best bet. **Algorithms** (AL-guh-rith-umz) use formulas or sets of rules to solve problems. Unlike trial and error, algorithms ensure a solution, as long as you choose the right one and follow all its steps. Have you ever assembled furniture using a manual, followed the instructions on a food package, or installed software with a series of drags and clicks? If so, you were using an algorithm. Sometimes, the steps of an algorithm are not written; you just have to remember them. Suppose you need to calculate a 20% tip. Here's an algorithm that can help: Take the total amount of your bill, move the decimal to the left one space, and multiply by 2. Voila: You've just calculated 20% of the bill.

 Identify different types of heuristics used to solve problems.

HEURISTICS When it comes to solving everyday problems, algorithms may be impractical, time-consuming, or simply unavailable. In these cases, we may turn to **heuristics** (hyoo-RISS-tiks). A heuristic is a problem-solving approach that employs a "rule of thumb" or broad application of a strategy. These shortcuts do not always produce reliable results, but they help us identify and evaluate possible solutions to our problems. Let's say you are cooking rice, but the instructions are unavailable. One good rule of thumb is to use 2 cups of water for every cup of rice. Another heuristic is to put the rice in the pot and add water until it is one thumb-knuckle above the rice. But unlike algorithms, which use formulas and sets of rules, there is no guarantee a heuristic will yield a correct solution.

The advantage of heuristics is that they help shrink the pool of possible solutions to a size that is manageable. Once that is accomplished, trial and error may be useful for identifying the best solution. Suppose a hacker is trying to break into an online bank account with Wells Fargo. She uses a heuristic that combines a commonly used password (123456, password, football) and something from the domain itself (WF), producing passwords such as 123456WF, passwordWF, and footballWF. From there, she uses trial and error and breaks into the account.

One frequently used heuristic is **means–ends analysis,** where "means" refers to the way one reaches the "end," or goal state. With means–ends analysis, the objective is to decrease the distance between the initial state and the goal state. Suppose you are writing a term paper. Once you identify the problem (finding appropriate support for your thesis), you could follow the advice of many instructors and break the problem into a set of *subgoals* or *subproblems*. In this case, your subproblems might be the following: (1) selecting an appropriate database to search for articles; and (2) finding a

trial and error An approach to problem solving that involves finding a solution through a series of attempts and eliminating those that do not work.

algorithm An approach to problem solving using a formula or set of rules that, if followed, ensures a solution.

heuristics Problem-solving approaches that incorporate a rule of thumb or broad application of a strategy.

means–ends analysis Heuristic used to determine how to decrease the distance between a goal and the current status (the means), leading to the solution of a problem (the end).

I Want a Banana
In a classic study, Gestalt psychologist Wolfgang Köhler provided chimpanzees with some out-of-reach bananas and materials that could potentially be used to fetch them. Resourceful chimps they were, building towers of crates and poking at the fruit with sticks. Rather than using trial and error to solve the problem, they seemed to rely on intelligence and insight (Köhler, 1925).

library where you can obtain and read the articles. While tackling these subproblems one by one, you continuously look for ways to decrease the distance from the initial state to the goal state (Matlin & Farmer, 2016).

Put Your Heads Together

You have an appointment on Saturday afternoon, and traffic is really bad! With your group, solve this problem using the following approaches: **A**) trial and error, **B**) an algorithm, and **C**) heuristics. **D**) Decide which of these approaches would work the best in this situation.

INSIGHT Problems can also be solved through **insight,** an understanding that occurs in a sudden stroke of clarity (that oh-so-satisfying "aha!" or "eureka!" moment). Insight can stem from experience solving previous problems, or it can be totally new. It often comes as a pleasant surprise because we are not aware of the mental "work" we did to achieve it.

Sometimes insight happens so suddenly that we find ourselves wondering, *Why did it take me so long to figure that out? The answer seems so obvious now.* Without our conscious awareness, our minds are busy reorganizing the way the problem is represented, and this allows us suddenly and inexplicably to see things in a new light (Sio & Ormerod, 2009). A unique pattern of neural activity appears to accompany insight (as opposed to a more analytical problem-solving approach). Immediately preceding the "aha!" moment, we see increased activation in the frontal and temporal lobes (Kounios & Beeman, 2009). Sometimes the best thing to do is step away from a problem and allow your brain to do this work; the solution may pop into your head unexpectedly (Sio & Ormerod, 2009). Evidence also suggests that fatigue, moderate alcohol consumption, and letting go of complex problem-solving approaches can potentially increase "insight problem solving" (DeCaro, Van Stockum, & Wieth, 2016).

We've Hit a Roadblock

With the capacity for insight, humans can be masterful problem solvers. Still, barriers do arise (Infographic 7.2). One such barrier is **functional fixedness,** which occurs when we can only imagine using familiar objects in their **usual way.** This *fixation* can stop us from finding new, creative uses for objects. Suppose the hem of your pants catches on something and tears. A roll of tape and a stapler are on your desk, and both could be used to "fix" your wardrobe malfunction. But because of functional fixedness, you only view these items in their "usual" capacities. Children have less trouble with functional fixedness because they have not become accustomed to using familiar objects in a fixed way (German & Defeyter, 2000). Yet, the more they observe others using objects, the less likely they are to be innovative. Sometimes observation and classroom experiences can get in the way, leading to "restricted exploration and learning" (Carr, Kendal, & Flynn, 2015, p. 331).

CONNECTIONS
In **Chapter 3,** we described the phenomenon of perceptual set, which is the tendency to perceive stimuli in a specific manner based on past experiences and expectations. With functional fixedness, we can only imagine using objects in their usual way.

Mental sets are another barrier to problem solving. People tend to fall back on strategies they have always used—even if they don't work so well. For example, students often start their first semester of college believing they can succeed in their courses using strategies that worked in high school. But these old methods are often incompatible with the requirements and expectations of college. High school students might get away with finishing assignments during class, but college students? No way! Mental sets can prevent us from seeing other solutions—like starting on assignments as soon as they are given.

Emotional barriers can also get in the way of problem solving. If you are trying to figure out how to fix a dripping faucet and someone is peering over your shoulder saying,

insight An understanding or solution that occurs in a sudden stroke of clarity (the feeling of "aha!").

functional fixedness A barrier to problem solving that occurs when familiar objects can only be imagined to function in their normal or usual way.

Problem Solving

Problem solving involves figuring out how to achieve a goal. Once you understand a problem, you can identify an approach to solving it. A successful approach will help you manage obstacles that come from the problem itself, such as a rigid deadline for an essay you're struggling to write. But sometimes the way we think about a problem can itself be a barrier, preventing us from identifying available approaches.

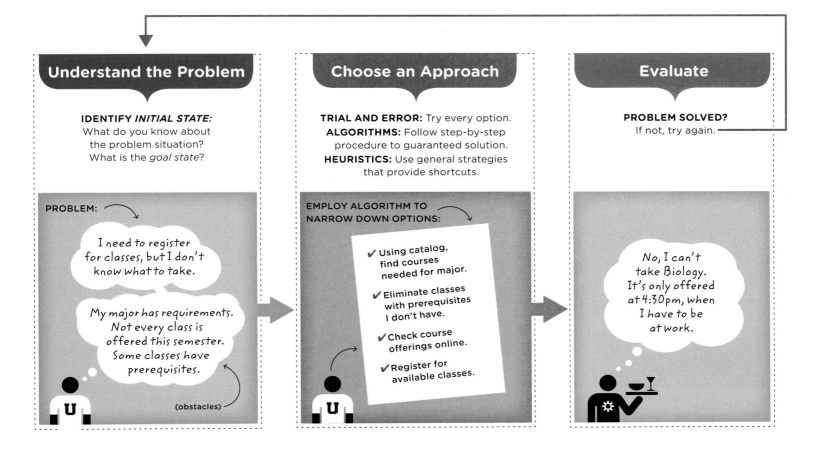

Understand the Problem

IDENTIFY *INITIAL STATE:* What do you know about the problem situation? What is the *goal state*?

PROBLEM:

I need to register for classes, but I don't know what to take.

My major has requirements. Not every class is offered this semester. Some classes have prerequisites.

(obstacles)

U

Choose an Approach

TRIAL AND ERROR: Try every option.
ALGORITHMS: Follow step-by-step procedure to guaranteed solution.
HEURISTICS: Use general strategies that provide shortcuts.

EMPLOY ALGORITHM TO NARROW DOWN OPTIONS:

- ✔ Using catalog, find courses needed for major.
- ✔ Eliminate classes with prerequisites I don't have.
- ✔ Check course offerings online.
- ✔ Register for available classes.

U

Evaluate

PROBLEM SOLVED? If not, try again.

No, I can't take Biology. It's only offered at 4:30pm, when I have to be at work.

Barriers to Problem Solving

Being stuck in a certain way of thinking about a problem can limit what we see as available approaches. For example, our student registering for classes may assume that "classes" must be in-person with an instructor on campus. This assumption prevents the student from investigating more flexible online classes, hybrid classes, or classes that could be transferred from another college.

Sticking with our usual solution strategies is called a *mental set.* To see if you can overcome your mental set, try solving this problem:

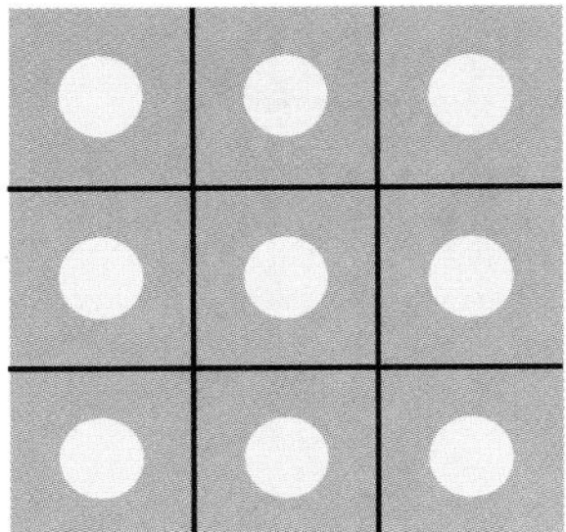

Without lifting your pencil, can you connect all nine dots using only 4 straight lines and without crossing any dot more than once? *(Solution on page 252.)*

Functional fixedness is another barrier in which we can only imagine using familiar objects in their usual way. Say you need to tie two ropes together, but you can't reach them both at the same time. Will functional fixedness keep you from solving this problem? *(Solution on page 252.)*

Credits: Ship ropes with knot, Seregam/Shutterstock; Bushes, 3dmentor/Shutterstock.

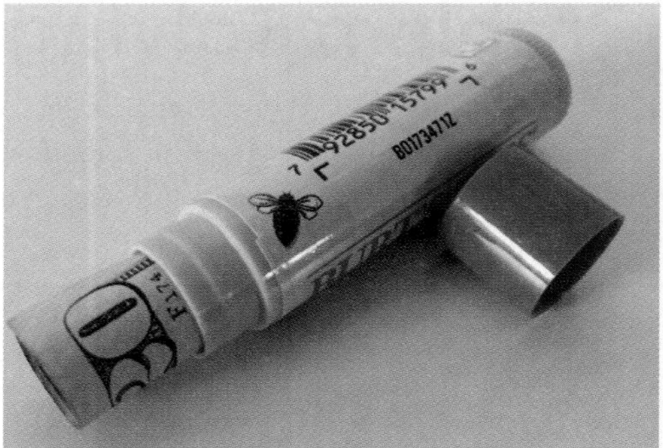

Think Outside the Box
Who knew that money can be hidden in an empty lip balm tube, and that a cell phone camera could be used as a mirror? Sometimes it's hard to imagine using things for unconventional purposes. Our resistance to using familiar objects in new ways is known as functional fixedness, and it can get in the way of problem solving. Left: Coco Ballantyne. Right: Pazargic Liviu/Shutterstock.

"Hurry up! What's taking you so long?," you may feel rushed, anxious, and annoyed. These negative emotions affect your ability to think clearly and creatively. Positive emotions, on the other hand, are thought to promote a "flexible" way of thinking, one that enables quick shifts in attention and strategy in response to changing conditions (Isen, 2008). Keep this in mind next time you help someone solve a problem.

Put Your Heads Together

In your groups, **A)** list the conventional uses of paper clips and pencils, and then **B)** brainstorm as many creative uses as possible. **C)** Discuss the ways that functional fixedness has interfered with your ability to solve problems in the past. **D)** What are other examples of familiar objects that can be used in unconventional ways?

Brightness in Her Spirit
Dr. Taylor poses with her mother G.G. who played an instrumental role in the recovery process. When Dr. Taylor emerged from surgery, G.G. was anxious to know whether her daughter's language-processing abilities were still intact. As soon as Dr. Taylor opened her mouth and spoke, it seemed clear that everything was going to be okay. © My Stroke of Insight, Inc. Photo by Kip May.

Decisions, Decisions

UNDER THE KNIFE With the help of her mother's gentle coaxing, Dr. Taylor made the decision to go through with surgery. On the afternoon of December 27, 1996, she awoke in the recovery room with the left side of her head shaved clean and a 9-inch wound in the shape of a horseshoe (Taylor, 2006). Dr. Taylor had survived the operation, and she didn't feel drained and confused, as you might expect: "Upon awakening, I realized that I felt different now. There was brightness in my spirit again and I felt happy" (p. 112).

"Say something!" demanded G.G. as she approached her daughter's bedside (Taylor, 2006, p. 113). G.G. needed to know that her daughter could still use language. Surgeons had just spent hours poking around her left hemisphere, home to the language-processing regions of Broca's and Wernicke's areas. The surgeons might have inadvertently damaged one of these key regions, compromising her ability to

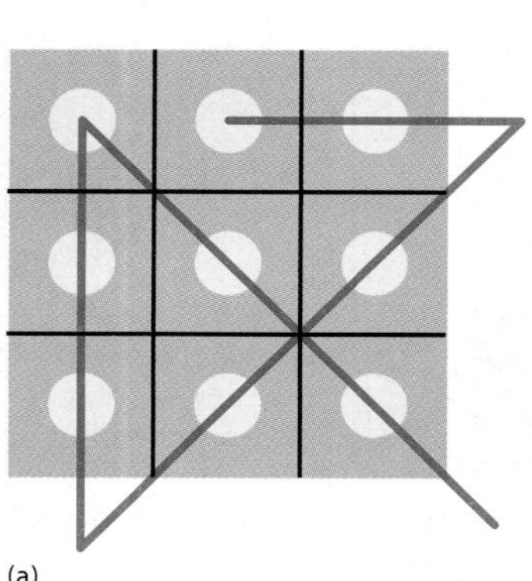

(a)

(b)

FIGURE 7.3
(a) Solution to the Dot Problem in Infographic 7.2
Did your mental set cause you to assume the square implied boundaries? If so, it may not have occurred to you that one could draw lines extending outside the square.
(b) Solution to the Two-Rope Problem in Infographic 7.2
Using a shovel to create a pendulum will allow you to swing the second rope. When it swings near you, you can grab it and hold both ropes at the same time.
Ropes: Seregam/Shutterstock. Bushes: 3dmentor/Shutterstock.

understand or produce words. Dr. Taylor opened her mouth and responded, and she and G.G. both became teary-eyed. The operation appeared to have gone well; Dr. Taylor, it seemed, had made the right decision (Taylor, 2006). 

You Asked, Dr. Taylor Answers

http://qrs.ly/1v5a5d3

Did you fully recover language and cognition after the surgery?

LO 7 Describe the process of decision making and how heuristics can lead us astray.

If problem solving refers to the variety of approaches you can use to achieve a goal, how is it different from decision making? **Decision making** is the cognitive process of choosing from these approaches. Thus, problem solving and decision making can occur together.

Often, decision making involves predicting the future: What is the likelihood that Event A will occur under these circumstances? How about Event B? Some situations lend themselves to accurate guesses: If the Weather Channel predicts a 99% chance of thunderstorms today, you can probably assume it's going to rain. Better bring your umbrella. Other times, predicting the future is like rolling dice—you have almost no way of knowing the outcome. Suppose you are searching for a used car on Craigslist. With no prior knowledge of the cars or their owners (apart from the information they have chosen to post and a few clues you have gathered from your own research), all you can do is hope that you don't end up with a lemon. Choices that hinge on unknowns can be very risky, and we can make the wrong decision.

Predicting the future can be easier with heuristics, but these problem-solving shortcuts can also lead us astray.

Why Do We Make Bad Decisions?

Israeli-American psychologists Daniel Kahneman and Amos Tversky (1937–1996) were among the first to systematically research the errors caused by heuristics. They found that people tend to ignore important information while using heuristics (Kahneman & Tversky, 1996). This is particularly true for the *availability heuristic* and the *representativeness heuristic.*

THE AVAILABILITY HEURISTIC With the **availability heuristic,** we predict the probability of something happening in the future based on how easily we can recall a similar type of event from the past. The availability heuristic is essentially a decision-making strategy that relies on memory. If we can easily recall a certain event, then we tend to base our decisions on the assumption that it can happen again. Many factors make an event more available for recall, including its recency, frequency, familiarity, and vividness. Let's look at each of these qualities.

CONNECTIONS

In **Chapter 6,** we described the recency effect, which is the tendency to remember items more accurately when they appear at the end of a list or series. Here, we discuss the tendency to remember similar events better if they have occurred recently.

Imagine it is the spring of 2017 and you have seen a series of news reports about acts of terrorism in Great Britain: first the Westminster attack, then a bombing at an Ariana Grande concert, followed by attacks on London Bridge and the Finsbury Park Mosque. Every time you look at the news, you see images of people being taken away in ambulances and witnesses describing the horrors of the scene. Because of the *recency* of these events, you may be vulnerable to the availability heuristic and assume that visiting the United Kingdom (UK) puts you at serious risk for being a victim of a terrorist attack. Yet, the likelihood of this occurring is extremely low; in fact, you are far more likely to die in a car crash while vacationing in the UK (Coffey, 2017, June 19). The **recency** of the terror attacks makes them easier to recall, and thus you are more inclined to overestimate the likelihood of their reoccurrence.

The *frequency* of an event also makes it more available for recall. Suppose someone asks you the following: Do more students at your college use Macs or PCs?

decision making The cognitive process of choosing from alternatives that might be used to reach a goal.

availability heuristic A decision-making strategy that predicts the likelihood of something happening based on how easily a similar type of event from the past can be recalled.

Before answering, you would probably think about the number of students you have seen using these computers in the halls, classrooms, and library; the frequency of occurrence influences your estimate. If you happen to be in the graphic design department, you probably see more Macs than PCs. (Macs tend to be popular in art departments.) Limiting your observations to the art department, or any single department, makes for a **sample that is not representative** of the entire college. The availability heuristic leads you to the wrong answer. This heuristic can generate accurate conclusions, but only when based on the appropriate information.

CONNECTIONS In **Chapter 1,** we discussed the importance of using a representative sample when making generalizations about a population. Here, we must be careful that our observations are representative, and not chosen because of their recency, frequency, familiarity, or vividness.

Now consider the *familiarity* of an event. If you and your friends are all avid PC users, you may overestimate the extent to which others use PCs. The more familiar you are with a situation, the more likely you are to predict a similar occurrence in the future.

Finally, the *vividness* of an event can make it more available for recall. Try to conjure up an image of someone winning big at a casino. The prizewinner jumps joyfully in the air, hollering at the top of her lungs, with onlookers clapping in approval. This type of dramatic display never occurs when people lose money; the details of a losing bet would be far more difficult to recall. Because the winning image is more vivid, we are more likely to recall it and thus overestimate the likelihood of a win occurring in our own lives. Memorable imagery leads us to believe that these types of wins happen all the time, when in fact they are very rare. If an event has made a striking impression on you, even a rare occurrence such as an airplane crash, you will be more likely to overestimate the probability of it happening again (Tversky & Kahneman, 1982).

The Psychology of Terrorism
Would you be comfortable walking across London Bridge in the weeks following the terrorist attacks that occurred there? The risk of becoming a casualty in such an attack is remote, but we may overestimate the odds of it occurring if we can easily recall a similar event from the past (a decision-making strategy called the availability heuristic). Worried about being killed by a terrorist in the United States? A far greater threat is distracted driving, which claims well over 3,000 lives per year (National Highway Traffic Safety Administration, 2017, March). Andras Polonyi/EyeEm/Getty Images.

THE REPRESENTATIVENESS HEURISTIC Often, we base decisions on our evaluations of the world around us. With the **representativeness heuristic,** we make quick, effortless judgments about how closely a person or situation fits our preconceived prototype (Lerner, Li, Valdesolo, & Kassam, 2015; Shah & Oppenheimer, 2008). (As mentioned earlier, a prototype is the ideal or most representative example of a natural concept.)

Let's examine how the representativeness heuristic works in practice. Peter is a middle-aged man. He is conservative, an eloquent speaker, thoughtful, and well read. He lives alone in an apartment in the city. Is Peter a truck driver or a poet? Using the representativeness heuristic, most people would guess that Peter is a poet because his description better matches their prototype of a poet. But this approach fails to consider the *base rate,* or prevalence, of these occupations. There are far more truck drivers than poets, suggesting that truck driver is a better guess. The representativeness heuristic can be useful, but not when our prototypes ignore base rates and draw on simplistic stereotypes. As you will learn in Chapter 11, stereotypes are the conclusions or inferences we make about people who are different from us, based on their group membership.

CONFIRMATION AND HINDSIGHT BIAS We can also miss important information through the **confirmation bias,** when we unintentionally look for evidence that upholds our beliefs. People tend to overlook or discount evidence that runs counter to their original views or convictions. For example, you decide to go on a date with someone you are *really* interested in, even though you don't know him very well. You Google stalk him and look on his Facebook page, and immediately connect with a few of his "likes." Focusing on this information (and ignoring all evidence that you might not be compatible), you stop your search and decide to date him. Because of the confirmation bias, we tend to focus on information that supports desirable outcomes (Krizan & Windschitl, 2007; Scherer, Windschitl, O'Rourke, & Smith, 2012).

representativeness heuristic A decision-making strategy that evaluates the degree to which the primary characteristics of a person or situation are similar to our prototype of that type of person or situation.

confirmation bias The tendency to look for evidence that upholds our beliefs and to overlook evidence that runs counter to them.

The **hindsight bias,** or "I knew it all along" feeling, leads us to believe that we could have predicted the outcome of an event. It may seem obvious in retrospect, but that doesn't mean we could have foreseen it. Examples of hindsight bias abound in everyday life. Suppose your instructor returns an exam, and you are surprised to learn that you got a certain question wrong. Now that you're staring at the correct answer, it seems so obvious. But if you really knew it all along, why did you give the wrong answer (Tauer, 2009)? Even practicing physicians fall victim to hindsight bias. When doctors hear about the details of an autopsy and learn about the cause of death, they often believe they could have easily predicted it (Arkes, 2013). In these scenarios, hindsight bias can get in the way of learning and decision making. How do you learn from your mistakes if you cannot identify gaps in your knowledge (Arkes, 2013; Tauer, 2009)?

The Problem with the Problem

We have spent a great deal of time discussing factors that impede the decision maker. But in many situations, some aspect of the problem is to blame.

The **framing effect** demonstrates how the presentation or context of a problem can influence our decision making, often in ways beyond our awareness. Consider the following study: Researchers instructed participants to imagine that they had purchased a $10 ticket to attend a show, but lost their ticket on the way to the theater. Each participant was then asked whether he or she would be willing to pay $10 for another ticket. Only 46% of participants indicated that they would spend another $10 for a new ticket. Participants were next instructed to imagine another situation: This time, they planned to buy a $10 ticket to attend a show, but once they got in the ticket line, they suddenly realized that they had lost one of their $10 bills. Faced with this second scenario, 88% of the participants were willing to fork over the $10. In each case, the participants considered the idea of spending an additional and unexpected $10, but they tended to make different decisions. The circumstances framing these hypothetical scenarios influenced the decisions made, even though the outcomes would have been identical—a net loss of $10 (Kahneman & Tversky, 1984; Tversky & Kahneman, 1981).

The framing effect also **applies to wording.** One study found that people are more likely to prefer ground beef if it is described as "80% lean," as opposed to "20% fat." Although 80% lean and 20% fat describe exactly the same product, these phrases evoke very different responses (Johnson, 1987). Another study demonstrated how the wording of a question can influence people's descriptions of themselves. Researchers prompted college students to describe themselves using one of two questions: "Please

CONNECTIONS

In **Chapter 1,** we presented the survey method, a form of descriptive research that relies on questionnaires and interviews. Here, we see that the wording of questions can influence the way people respond.

hindsight bias The mistaken belief that an outcome could have been predicted easily; the "I knew it all along" feeling.

framing effect Occurs when the wording of questions or the context of a problem influences the outcome of a decision.

take five minutes and write what you *think* about yourself," or "Please take five minutes and write what you *feel* about yourself." The group assigned to the "feel" condition evaluated themselves in a more negative way than the group assigned to the "think" condition. This may be because those in the "feel" condition were focusing on emotions, and the English language has more words to describe negative emotions than positive emotions (Holtgraves, 2015). How might these findings help psychologists create better questionnaires?

Jill Bolte Taylor's story has helped us understand how quickly cognitive functions can deteriorate. But not all changes in cognition and behavior stem from catastrophic events like strokes. Brain injuries can also occur in small increments, accumulating over time. Imagine you spent 21 years playing a game that required slamming your body against 200- to 300-pound men. How would the rapid changes in speed and direction, and the constant banging of your skull, affect the delicate brain inside? Football Hall of Famer Harry Carson is here to tell you.

show what you know

1. It's the first day of class, but you forgot to write down the room number of your psychology class. You decide to stick your head in a random number of rooms until you see the assigned psychology textbook on someone's desk. This problem-solving approach is called:
   a. means-ends analysis.
   b. an algorithm.
   c. trial and error.
   d. heuristics.

2. A(n) ______________ is a problem-solving approach that employs a "rule of thumb."

3. We often predict the probability of an event happening in the future based on how easily we can recall a similar type of event from the past. This is known as the:
   a. framing effect.
   b. confirmation bias.
   c. representativeness heuristic.
   d. availability heuristic.

4. A good friend is terrified of flying. How would you use your knowledge of heuristics to make him feel less afraid?

✓ CHECK YOUR ANSWERS IN APPENDIX C.

The Power of Language

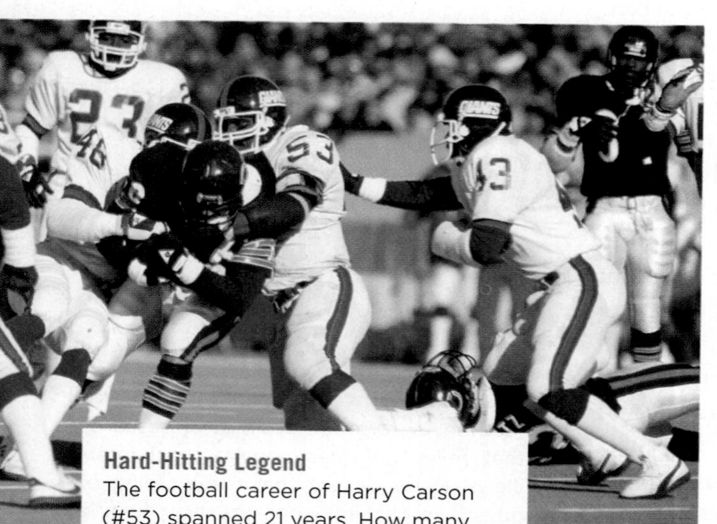
Hard-Hitting Legend
The football career of Harry Carson (#53) spanned 21 years. How many blows to the head do you think he sustained during that time? Using data from a study of collegiate players, which found the number of head impacts per season to be as high as 1,444 (Crisco et al., 2010), we estimate that Harry took as many as 30,000 hits to the head. Jonathan Daniel/Getty Images.

"I SAW STARS" Harry Carson was 14 years old when he first stepped onto the football field. It was August in Florence, South Carolina; the air was warm, moist, and steeped in the scent of freshly cut grass. Wearing 20 pounds of football equipment was uncomfortable, but Harry felt proud having it on, especially the imposing shoulder pads and helmet (Carson, 2011).

During that first practice at Wilson High School, the coaches assigned the players to a man-on-man blocking drill. Young Harry was pitted against "Bubble Gum," a bigger, more experienced player. "As he came off the ball to block me, I could do little to defend myself," Harry recalls in his memoir *Captain for Life*. "He must have blocked me three or four times, and with each block I felt like a rag doll being chewed up by a pit bull" (Carson, 2011, p. 12).

Colliding with Bubble Gum was not only painful; it jarred Harry's brain, causing immediate changes in perception. "I was conscious," Harry recalls, "[but] I saw little stars twinkling before my eyes." Like most players of his time, Harry didn't realize that "seeing stars" or momentarily "blacking out" was a sign of concussion, a brain injury that is not fatal but can have life-changing consequences.

After playing football in high school, Harry went on to become a star lineman and team captain at South Carolina State. Then he achieved what many American boys only dream about—he was drafted into the National Football League (NFL). During his 13-year career with the New York Giants, Harry established himself as one of the greatest middle linebackers in the history of professional football. Eventually, he was inducted into the Pro Football Hall of Fame. But becoming a football legend came at a price.

About halfway through his professional career, Harry starting having migraines, unexplained mood swings, and suicidal thoughts. He also had difficulties with language. During media interviews, he sometimes had trouble processing and responding to reporters' questions. Maybe no one else noticed the problem because Harry did a good job filling in the gaps with expressions like "um" and "you know." But he knew something was wrong.

It was not until his retirement from pro football that Harry began to connect his symptoms with the repeated brain trauma he had sustained on the field. In 1990, two years after he left the NFL, a neuropsychologist diagnosed him with *post-concussion syndrome,* a collection of physical and psychological symptoms that linger after a concussion occurs (Legome, 2016, September 12). "I came to realize that all of this stuff that I was experiencing was a result of the dings, the bell-ringers, the concussions that I sustained as a player," says Harry, who began sharing his story at conferences and in media interviews. "There were people who probably thought I was crazy for even talking about it," he says. "Football players are very proud individuals, and they do not go around talking about being brain damaged."

Chronic Traumatic Encephalopathy (CTE)

Discoverer of CTE
Pathologist Bennet Omalu was the first to identify chronic traumatic encephalopathy (CTE) in the brain of a former football player. Omalu, now a professor at the University of California, Davis, believes that allowing children to play football may one day be considered child abuse. "Someday there will be a district attorney who will prosecute for child abuse [on the football field], and it will succeed," Omalu reportedly said at the New York Press Club in 2017. "It is the definition of child abuse" (Axson, 2017, August 8, para. 5). Pete Marovich/Getty Images.

In 2005, about a decade after Harry began raising awareness about sports-related brain injuries, a groundbreaking scientific report came out in the journal *Neurosurgery.* The study, led by pathologist Bennet Omalu, detailed the extensive brain damage of deceased NFL player Mike Webster (Omalu et al., 2005). It was the first time a retired pro football player had been diagnosed with chronic traumatic encephalopathy (CTE), a neurodegenerative disease caused by repeated head trauma. Since then, researchers have studied the brains of many more football players; a recent analysis led by Dr. Ann McKee found evidence of CTE in 110 out of 111, or 99%, of the NFL players studied (Mez et al., 2017).

One of the telltale signs of CTE is abnormal accumulation of *tau,* a protein also implicated in Alzheimer's disease (McKee et al., 2013; Turner et al., 2013). The symptoms of CTE may include anxiety, depression, explosive anger, suicidal tendencies, and a host of cognitive problems (McKee, Stein et al., 2013; Mez et al., 2017). Advanced cases have been associated with "severe memory loss with dementia" (McKee et al., 2013, p. 59).

The discovery of CTE in professional football players came as no surprise to Harry Carson. In fact, he is relatively confident he suffers from CTE as well: "I don't really worry about it, because I think that, with the information that has already been presented, we all probably have it." The damage Harry sustained cannot be undone, but he doesn't seem bitter or hardened. Instead, he focuses on managing his life in a positive way—eating healthy foods, exercising, and educating others about sports-related brain injuries.

SEE THE WORDS When Harry gets a headache, it often starts on the left side (Kirk & Carson, 2013, September 4). Perhaps it's no coincidence that his pain originates in the brain hemisphere where language processing occurs. As you may recall, Harry periodically struggled with media interviews, taking extra time to digest journalists' questions and articulate his responses. These language roadblocks continued popping up when Harry left the NFL and began a career as a sports commentator. "Once football was over, I went into broadcasting," he says, "and that was something that I failed at horribly because I would lose my train of thought live on the air." There are still times that Harry has difficulty expressing thoughts, but he has developed a cognitive strategy for dealing with it: "Sometimes when I am trying to make the points that I want to make . . . I have to visualize each word that I want to use in my brain before I allow it to leave my lips."

Let's Get Down to Basics

Until something goes wrong, it's easy to take language for granted. Words are so much a part of our daily routines that it's difficult to imagine life without them. How would we conduct Google searches, read CNN headlines, or rant on Twitter if we didn't have words? There would be no such thing as the U.S. Constitution or the Bill of Rights. No Bible, Torah, or Qur'an. You wouldn't be able to say, "I love you" or "What are you thinking about?" Language allows us to explicitly convey complex thoughts and feelings. Some might say it is the very foundation of modern civilization.

"I suppose you want Polly to forget she heard that."

CartoonStock.com

The Bright Side of Swearing?
Foul mouths are offensive, but could they be more trustworthy than clean ones? Using three distinct studies, researchers examined the relationship between profanity and honesty and discovered that "profanity was associated with less lying and deception at the individual level and with higher integrity at the society level" (Feldman, Lian, Kosinski, & Stillwell, 2017, para. 1).
Martha Campbell/cartoonstock.com.

LO 8 Define language and give examples of its basic elements.

Language can be defined as a system for using symbols (words, gestures, and sounds) to think and communicate. These symbols can be spoken, written, and signed. The average English-speaking college student is familiar with around 10,000 to 11,000 word families (groups of related words such as "smile," "smiled," "smiling"; Treffers-Daller & Milton, 2013). What's more, humans are always finding new meanings for old words or inventing new ones. Have you ever heard of a "squib kick," a "pooch punt," or a "flea flicker" (Kostora, 2012, May 16)? All these were created to describe kicks and plays in football.

PHONEMES At the core of all spoken words are **phonemes** (FOH-neemz), the units of sound that serve as basic building blocks for all words (**INFOGRAPHIC 7.3** on page 261). Examples of English phonemes include the sounds made by the letter *t* in the word "tail" and the letter *s* in "sail." Some letters correspond to more than one phoneme. For example, the letter *i* can represent two clearly different phonemes, as in the words "bit" and "bite."

Infants between 6 and 8 months can recognize all phonemes from all languages, but this ability begins to diminish at about 10 months. At this point, babies show the first signs of being "culture-bound listeners" (Kuhl, 2015, p. 67). That is, they have a harder time distinguishing between phonemes of languages they don't normally hear (de Boysson-Bardies, Halle, Sagart, & Durand, 1989; Werker & Tees, 1984). This is why older children and adults have difficultly learning to speak foreign languages without an accent.

If you have children (or plan to have them), it would be a great idea to teach them more than one language very early in life. Not only will their pronunciation sound natural; they may enjoy some cognitive perks, too.

language A system for using symbols to think and communicate.

phonemes The basic building blocks of spoken language.

DIDN'T SEE THAT COMING

THE PERKS OF BEING BILINGUAL Psychologists once thought that the brain was best suited for learning a single language, and that exposing children to more than one language frustrated their intellectual development (Klass, 2011, October 10). Researchers are now uncovering evidence that learning two languages may actually improve a child's communication skills (Fan, Liberman, Keysar, & Kinzler, 2015; Hoff & Core, 2015). What's more, juggling two languages could potentially lead to improved performance on various cognitive tasks (Blom, Boerma, Bosma, Cornips, & Everaert, 2017; Crivello et al., 2016; Westly, 2011, July/August).

DOES IT CLUTTER YOUR BRAIN?

One of the most striking qualities associated with bilingualism is strong executive control, which begins in infancy and carries into adulthood (Bialystok, 2011; Bialystok, Poarch, Luo, & Craik, 2014). As the name implies, executive control is concerned with managing the brain's precious resources, deciding what's important and where to focus attention. How does this advantage arise? Through constant exercise of the brain. People who speak two languages cannot just turn on one language and turn off the other; they are eternally torn between the competing tongues. Resolving this ongoing conflict seems to keep the executive control system very busy and always practicing (Bialystok, 2011).

Of course, there are some challenges associated with this balancing act. Bilingual children must absorb the grammar and vocabulary of two different languages, and this additional learning may cause them to fall behind their monolingual peers—but only with respect to one language. However, the gap narrows over time (Hoff & Core, 2015). Bottom line: The long-term cognitive benefits of learning two languages probably outweigh any drawbacks.

MORPHEMES Representing the next level of language are **morphemes** (MOR-feemz). Morphemes consist of one or more phonemes, and they bring meaning to a language. For example, the word "unimaginable" has three morphemes: *un, imagine,* and *able.* Each morpheme communicates something. Remove just one, and the word takes on a whole new significance. Clipping off *un,* for example, produces the word "imaginable," which means the exact opposite of "unimaginable."

Yoda Syntax
Moments before his death in *Return of the Jedi*, Yoda says to Luke Skywalker, "When gone am I, the last of the Jedi you will be" (Lucasfilm & Marquand, 1983, 43:46). Yoda's syntax is atypical, as most people would order the words like this: "When I am gone, you will be the last Jedi." Lifestyle pictures/Alamy.

GRAMMAR **Grammar** refers to the rules associated with both word and sentence structure (Evans & Green, 2006). It tells us how words are made from sounds, how sentences are formed with words, where to place punctuation, and which word tenses to use. It combines syntax and semantics.

Syntax refers to the collection of rules dictating where words and phrases should be placed. It guides both word choice and word order, providing consistency in sentence organization (Brandone, Salkind, Golinkoff, & Hirsh-Pasek, 2006). We say, "I love you," not "Love you I," because English syntax demands that the words appear in this order. Different languages have different syntaxes. In German, some verbs come at the end of sentences, which is strikingly noticeable to native English speakers learning German.

Semantics represents the rules used to bring meaning to words and sentences. Here are two sentences with different word order (syntax), but the same meaning (semantics): "Jane kicked the ball." "The ball was kicked by Jane." Now, here are two sentences with the same syntax, but slightly different semantics: "Some people enjoy cooking, their families, and their dogs." "Some people enjoy cooking their families and their dogs" (Oxford Royale Academy, 2014, October 15, para. 3). Semantics also refers to the context in which words appear. Consider the meaning of "snap" based

morphemes The fundamental units that bring meaning to language.

grammar The rules associated with word and sentence structure.

syntax The collection of rules concerning where to place words or phrases.

semantics The rules used to bring meaning to words and sentences.

on the context of the following sentences: Can you *snap* your fingers? He got the job done in a *snap*. Don't *snap* at me! Oh *Snap*!

PRAGMATICS Language is used in social interactions, which are governed by certain norms and expectations. **Pragmatics** are the social rules that help organize this activity. We have to learn how to take turns in a conversation, what gestures to use and when, and how to address people according to social standing (Steiner, 2012, September 4; Yule, 1996). When addressing the Queen of Denmark, you would say, "Good day, Your Majesty," but to a friend you might say, "Hey, there."

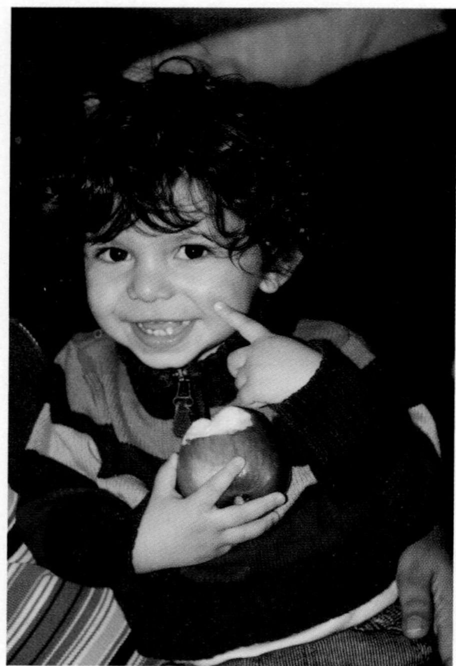

Babble
Deaf babies who are exposed to sign language develop their own version of babbling. Instead of rattling off spoken syllables (*da-da-da* or *ma-ma-ma*) as hearing infants typically do, they babble with their hands, repeating the basic units of sign language (Petitto & Marentette, 1991). Babbling and other stages of language acquisition appear to proceed along the same path for deaf and hearing babies (Emmorey, 2015), suggesting that the ability to learn language is innate. Boaz Rottem/Alamy.

IS IT INNATE? How do we "know" these rules for language? Learning theorists propose that children learn language just like they learn other behaviors, through processes such as reinforcement and modeling (Bandura, 1977; Skinner, 1957). In contrast, linguist Noam Chomsky suggests that humans are born with innate language abilities. Children needn't be taught the basics of language, according to Chomsky (2000); language develops like other organs in the body. Chomsky's position is based on the observation that children possess a much deeper knowledge of language than would be expected if they only learned through experience. This knowledge is not simply the result of hearing and imitating; it is hardwired within the brain. A built-in *language acquisition device* (LAD) accounts for the universality of language development. In fact, researchers have observed this innate capacity for language across cultures and in nonhearing children (Chomsky, 2000; Petitto & Marentette, 1991).

IS IT UNIQUE? Many scientists argue that language, more than any other human ability, truly sets us apart from other species. Animals have evolved complex systems of communication (more on this in a moment), but some features of human language appear to be unique. One such feature is *displacement*—the ability to talk and think about things that are not present at the moment. "I wonder if my instructor is going to give a pop quiz today," you might say to a friend. This statement demonstrates displacement, because it refers to a hypothetical event. Displacement allows us to communicate about the future and the past, and fantasize about things that may or may not exist.

Thinking What We Say?

Explain how language influences thought.

For many years, psychologists have tried to understand the relationship between language and thought. According to the ***linguistic relativity hypothesis*** developed by Benjamin Lee Whorf (1897–1941), the language people speak has an impact on their thinking and perception (1956). For example, the Inuit and other Alaska Natives have many terms that refer to "snow" (in contrast to the single word used in English). This may cause them to perceive and think about snow differently than English speakers. Whorf's hypothesis is not universally accepted, however. Critics suggest that he exaggerated the number of words Alaska Natives have for "snow" and underestimated the number of words in English (Pullum, 1991).

synonyms
linguistic relativity hypothesis linguistic determinism theory, Sapir-Whorf hypothesis

Although language might not *determine* how we perceive and think about the world, it certainly has an influence (Athanasopoulos et al., 2015; Kersten et al., 2010). Consider how the English language tends to use "he" and "his" when gender is unspecified; this use of masculine pronouns often results in people focusing on males when forming mental images (Gastil, 1990; Hegarty & Buechel, 2006). Perhaps you can predict the potential downside of this tendency. Narrowing the focus to male

pragmatics The social rules that help to organize language.

The Building Blocks of Language

Language is made up of a collection of units and rules. These build upon each other to help us think and communicate. At the base are phonemes, which combine to make up morphemes, the smallest unit of language that carries meaning. At the top is displacement, which is the human ability to refer to things that are abstract or hypothetical.

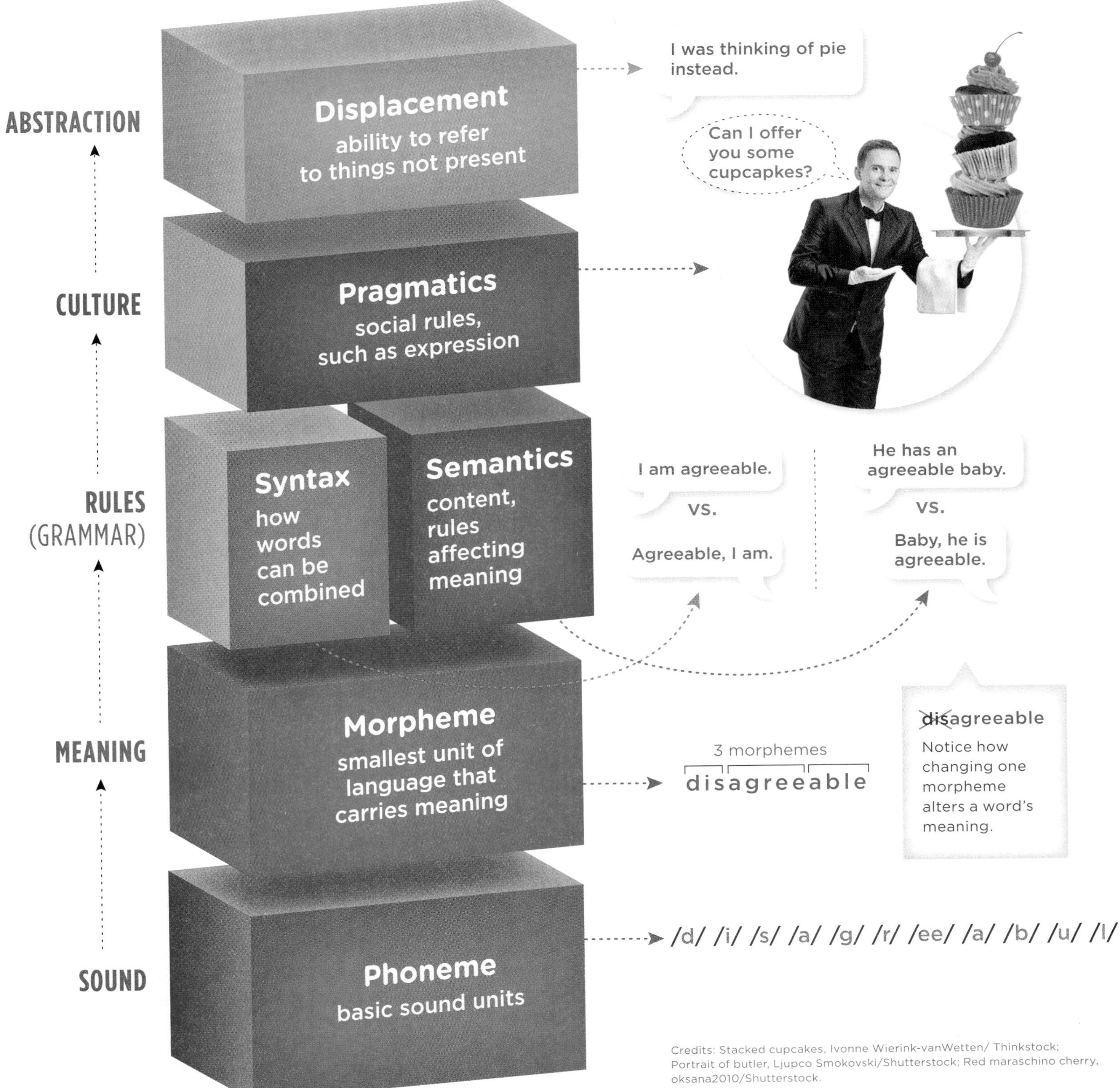
ABSTRACTION
Displacement
ability to refer to things not present
I was thinking of pie instead.
Can I offer you some cupcapkes?
CULTURE
Pragmatics
social rules, such as expression
RULES (GRAMMAR)
Syntax
how words can be combined
Semantics
content, rules affecting meaning
I am agreeable.
vs.
Agreeable, I am.
He has an agreeable baby.
vs.
Baby, he is agreeable.
MEANING
Morpheme
smallest unit of language that carries meaning
3 morphemes
disagreeable
disagreeable
Notice how changing one morpheme alters a word's meaning.
SOUND
Phoneme
basic sound units
/d/ /i/ /s/ /a/ /g/ /r/ /ee/ /a/ /b/ /u/ /l/

Credits: Stacked cupcakes, Ivonne Wierink-vanWetten/ Thinkstock; Portrait of butler, Ljupco Smokovski/Shutterstock; Red maraschino cherry, oksana2010/Shutterstock.

images inevitably promotes gender bias and stereotyping. In one study, researchers exposed Dutch and German schoolchildren to job titles in plural form (an English example being "firefighters") or pairs of the titles in female and male forms ("fireman" and "firewoman"). Children who were exposed to both male and female forms were more confident about their ability to be successful in traditionally male jobs (Vervecken & Hannover, 2015).

Put Your Heads Together

Consider how language influences thinking. In your group, **A)** discuss the implications of using terms like spokes*man*, *man*kind, and *man*made. **B)** What other potential biases can you identify in English words and phrases? **C)** How can we counter their influences?

Human language is special, but animals also display remarkable communication abilities—instinctual (unlearned) behaviors, such as chirping, whistling, tail slapping, and dancing. Is it possible they use language as well?

...BELIEVE IT...OR NOT

DO ANIMALS USE LANGUAGE, TOO? Rico was a border collie in Germany who knew 200 vocabulary words, including the name of a bunny toy, "Kaninchen," and a little Santa Claus named "Weihnachtsmann" (Newsweek, 2004, June 20). When Rico's owners instructed him to fetch a certain toy, he would run into the next room and race back with it in his mouth. So impressive were the dog's skills that a team of researchers decided to make him the focus of a case study. They concluded that Rico was capable of "fast-mapping," the ability to deduce the meaning of a word by hearing someone use it just once (Kaminski, Call, & Fischer, 2004). Rico's accomplishments were eventually eclipsed by those of another border collie, Chaser, who learned 1,022 words (Pilley & Reid, 2011). In addition to her impressive vocabulary, Chaser demonstrated a rudimentary understanding of grammar, distinguishing between commands such as "to ball take Frisbee" and "to Frisbee take ball" (Bower, 2013, May 21, para. 2).

HOT DOG!

Rico and Chaser are not alone in possessing exceptional communication skills. Kanzi the bonobo can create simple phrases with the help of lexigrams, or images that represent words (Jabr, 2017, May 12). Sarah the chimpanzee reportedly learned to read 130 word symbols and connect them into meaningful combinations, such as "Mary give raisin Sarah" (Premack & Premack, 1972, p. 6). And prairie dogs have the ability to warn each other about specific predators; they have one alarm call for a coyote, another for a red-tailed hawk, and yet another for a human. If presented with human "predators" (research assistants) wearing various colored T-shirts, the prairie dogs can create distinct calls for different colors (Jabr, 2017, May 12; Slobodchikoff, Paseka, & Verdolin, 2008).

Sharp Canine
Chaser, with her owner John Pilley. With the help of Pilley and others, this border collie learned to recognize the names of 1,022 objects (Pilley & Reid, 2011). Mark Olencki-Wofford College.

There is no question that animals are capable of sophisticated communication. But does that communication qualify as language? Keep in mind that animals need extensive training to learn and use vocabulary (you don't think Chaser learned 1,022 words on her own, do you?), while human children pick up language through mere exposure. To our knowledge, only people have the ability to express an infinite number of ideas by organizing words in complex grammatical constructs (Pinker, 2003). The way we use phonemes and syntax, for example, gives our language a "remarkable and flexible expressive capacity" not seen in other creatures (Anderson, 2017, p. 343). Humans are also the only species that communicates with written language.

CAREER CONNECTIONS

CAN DYSLEXIA BE AN ASSET? Reading and writing are essential in today's job market, but these abilities do not come easily for everyone. Between 5 and 17.5% of children have dyslexia, or specific reading disability, which may persist for a lifetime (Shaywitz & Shaywitz, 2005). Although people with dyslexia may struggle with reading, spelling, and other activities that rely on phonological processing, this does not mean they cannot thrive in the workforce. Dyslexia affects many successful people, including actor Orlando Bloom, financier Charles Schwab, and Nobel Prize winners Pierre Curie, Archer Martin, and Carol Greider (Allen, 2009, October 30). Some studies suggest that individuals with dyslexia tend to excel in certain types of spatial tasks (Gilger, Allen, & Castillo, 2016; Schneps, Brockmole, Sonnert, & Pomplun, 2012). "Such visual-spatial gifts may be advantageous in jobs requiring three-dimensional thinking such as astrophysics, molecular biology, genetics, engineering, and computer graphics" (Armstrong, 2015, pp. 348–349).

INDIVIDUALS WITH DYSLEXIA TEND TO EXCEL IN CERTAIN TYPES OF SPATIAL TASKS

show what you know

1. ______________ are the basic building blocks of spoken language.
2. According to the linguistic relativity hypothesis, language has distinct effects on:
   a. phonemes.
   b. thinking and perception.
   c. the language acquisition device.
   d. displacement.
3. The Dutch word *gezelligheid* has no one-word counterpart in English. It refers to a cozy type of setting that can be quaint, fun, and intimate. Most languages have these types of untranslatable words. How might this be an advantage for people who are bilingual?

✓ CHECK YOUR ANSWERS IN APPENDIX C.

Intelligence

INTELLIGENT ATHLETES In high school and college, Harry was a defensive lineman, one of the guys who tries to disrupt the opposing team's offense before they can execute their play. When drafted by the Giants, Harry was challenged to learn a new position: middle linebacker. "It was a position that basically, I had to become the leader, the quarterback of the defense," says Harry, who spent many hours taking cognitive tests and meeting with the team psychologist. It was the psychologist's job to determine whether Harry was cognitively fit to play the demanding position of middle linebacker. As history shows, Harry was more than qualified. A fast-thinking problem solver, he proved he could multitask and make sound judgments on the fly. For any given play, he was able to remember what every defensive player was supposed to be doing, and he learned from past experiences, rarely making the same mistake twice. Harry demonstrated a high level of *intelligence*.

Play It Smart
A play diagram illustrates the positions and movements of football players on the field. A defense playbook may contain as many as 300 plays, and members of the defense are expected to learn all of them, according to Harry. "You are ultimately responsible for everything in that book, and if you don't know it, and if you're not able to compete, then you become a liability." Memorizing plays and mentally adjusting when things don't go as planned require a certain level of intelligence. Alex Belomlinsky/Getty Images.

What Is Intelligence?

LO 10 Examine and distinguish among various theories of intelligence.

Generally speaking, **intelligence** is one's innate ability to solve problems, adapt to the environment, and learn from experiences. Intelligence relates to a broad array of psychological processes, including memory, learning, perception, and language, and how it is defined may depend on the variable being measured.

intelligence Innate ability to solve problems, adapt to the environment, and learn from experiences.

TABLE 7.1 GARDNER'S ORIGINAL MULTIPLE INTELLIGENCES

Logical-mathematical	Scientist Mathematician	Sensitivity to, and capacity to discern, logical or numerical patterns; ability to handle long chains of reasoning.
Linguistic	Poet Journalist	Sensitivity to the sounds, rhythms, and meanings of words; sensitivity to the different functions of language.
Musical	Composer Violinist	Abilities to produce and appreciate rhythm, pitch, and timbre; appreciation of the forms of musical expressiveness.
Spatial	Navigator Sculptor	Capacities to perceive the visual-spatial world accurately and to perform transformations on one's initial perceptions.
Bodily-kinesthetic	Dancer Athlete	Abilities to control one's body movements and to handle objects skillfully.
Interpersonal	Therapist Salesman	Capacities to discern and respond appropriately to the moods, temperaments, motivations, and desires of other people.
Intrapersonal	Person with detailed, accurate self-knowledge	Access to one's own feelings and the ability to discriminate among them and draw on them to guide behavior; knowledge of one's own strengths, weaknesses, desires, and intelligences.

Summarized here are Gardner's original seven intelligences, all of which are associated with certain strengths and capabilities.
Reprinted with permission from Gardner and Hatch (1989).

In the United States, intelligence is often associated with "book smarts." Many of us think "intelligent" people are those who score high on tests measuring academic abilities. But intelligence is more complicated than that—so complicated, in fact, that psychologists have yet to agree on its precise parameters. It is not even clear whether intelligence is a single unified entity, or a collection of capabilities.

We do know that intelligence is, to a certain degree, a cultural construct. So although people in the United States tend to equate intelligence with school smarts, this is not the case everywhere in the world. Children living in a village in Kenya on the African continent, for example, grow up using herbal medicine to treat parasitic diseases in themselves and others. Identifying illness and developing treatment strategies are a regular part of life. These children would score much higher on intelligence tests relating to practical knowledge than on those assessing vocabulary (Sternberg, 2004). Even within a single culture, the meaning of intelligence changes across time. "Intelligence" for modern Kenyans may differ from that of their 14th-century ancestors.

As we explore the theories of intelligence below, please keep in mind that intelligence does not always go hand in hand with *intelligent behavior*. People can score high on intelligence measures but exhibit poor judgment. Perhaps you know a straight-A student who is somewhat lacking in common sense?

THE *G*-FACTOR How can we explain differences in intelligence? English psychologist and statistician Charles Spearman (1863–1945) speculated that humans have a **general intelligence** (or ***g*-factor**). This *g*-factor is a singular underlying aptitude or intellectual ability that drives capabilities in many areas, including verbal, spatial, and reasoning competencies. Simply stated, the *g*-factor is the common link.

general intelligence (*g*-factor) A singular underlying aptitude or intellectual ability that drives capabilities in many areas, including verbal, spatial, and reasoning competencies.

triarchic theory of intelligence Sternberg's theory suggesting that humans have varying degrees of analytical, creative, and practical abilities.

MANY TYPES OF INTELLIGENCE? American psychologist Howard Gardner suggests that people have *multiple intelligences* (Gardner, 1999, 2011). He originally proposed seven types of intelligences or "frames of mind": linguistic (verbal), logical-mathematical, spatial, bodily-kinesthetic, musical, intrapersonal, and interpersonal. Take a look at **Table 7.1** and consider how different occupations might be well suited for individuals who excel in Gardner's original seven intelligences. Gardner later added two more intelligences: naturalistic and existential. Naturalistic intelligence primarily refers to the "capacity to categorize objects according to salient similarities and differences among them" and existential intelligence is "the intelligence of big questions" (Visser, Ashton, & Vernon, 2006, p. 491; Gardner, 2003, p. 7).

According to Gardner (2011), partial evidence for multiple intelligences comes from studying people with brain damage. Some mental capabilities are lost, whereas others remain intact, suggesting that they are really distinct categories. Further evidence for multiple intelligences (as opposed to just a *g*-factor) comes from observing people with *savant syndrome.* Individuals with savant syndrome have some area of extreme singular ability (calendar calculations, art, mental arithmetic, and so on; Treffert, 2015). The late Kim Peek, for example, was able to simultaneously read two pages of a book—one with each eye—and memorize nearly all the information it contained. Like the movie character he inspired ("Raymond Babbitt" in the movie *Rain Man*), Peek had extraordinary intellectual abilities (Brogaard & Marlow, 2012, December 11; Treffert, 2015).

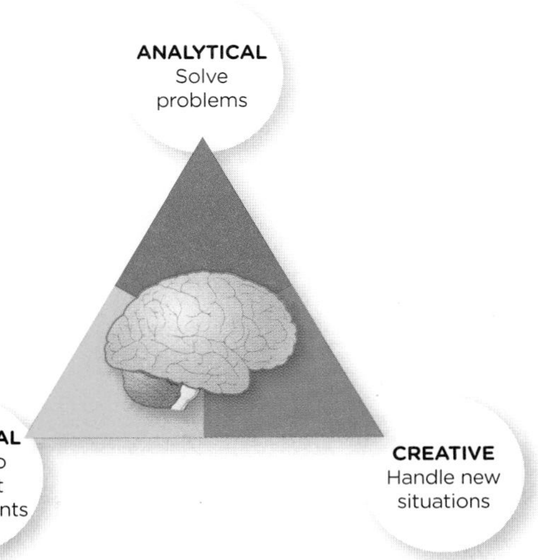

FIGURE 7.4
Sternberg's Triarchic Theory of Intelligence

THREE KINDS OF INTELLIGENCE? Robert Sternberg proposed three kinds of intelligence. Sternberg's (1988) **triarchic theory of intelligence** (trahy-AHR-kik) suggests that humans have varying degrees of analytical, creative, and practical competencies (**Figure 7.4**). *Analytic intelligence* refers to our capacity to solve problems; *creative intelligence* represents the knowledge and skills we use to handle new situations; and *practical intelligence* includes our ability to adjust to different environments.

TABLE 7.2 THEORIES OF INTELLIGENCE

Theory	Summary	Further Questions
Spearman's general intelligence (*g*-factor): There is a general intelligence driving abilities in many areas.	A connection exists among different abilities, such as verbal, spatial, and reasoning competencies.	Given the complexity of the mind, can intelligence really be explained by a single general factor?
Gardner's multiple intelligences: There are nine types of intelligences, each associated with certain strengths and capabilities.	Different "frames of mind" allow humans to succeed.	What differentiates intelligence from skills?
Sternberg's triarchic theory: Humans have varying degrees of analytical, creative, and practical competencies.	Analytic intelligence is the capacity to solve problems; creative intelligence is the knowledge and skills used to handle new situations; and, practical intelligence is the ability to adjust to different environments.	Are each of these areas separate, or do they share something in common (like a *g*-factor)?

Summarized here are the main theories of intelligence and some of the questions they raise.

Clearly, there are many ways to understand intelligence (**Table 7.2**), none of which appear to be categorically "right" or "wrong." The development of these theories, to some degree, was aided by tests of intelligence. What are these tests, and what exactly do they aim to measure?

Measuring Intelligence

LO 11 Describe how intelligence is measured and identify the important characteristics of assessment.

Tests of intelligence ("IQ tests") generally aim to measure **aptitude,** or a person's potential for future learning. On the other hand, measures of **achievement** (tests such as the SAT and ACT) are designed to assess acquired knowledge; that is, what a person has previously learned. The line between aptitude and achievement tests can be blurry; tests are not always one or the other. For example, the SAT is considered an achievement test because it measures knowledge, but acquiring knowledge is somewhat contingent on innate ability. Therefore, the SAT might also qualify as an indirect measure of aptitude. Likewise, aptitude tests may incorporate some level of achievement, or learned content. For example, intelligence tests can be biased in favor of groups of people who have had certain life experiences (exposure to high-quality schools, for example). More on this to come.

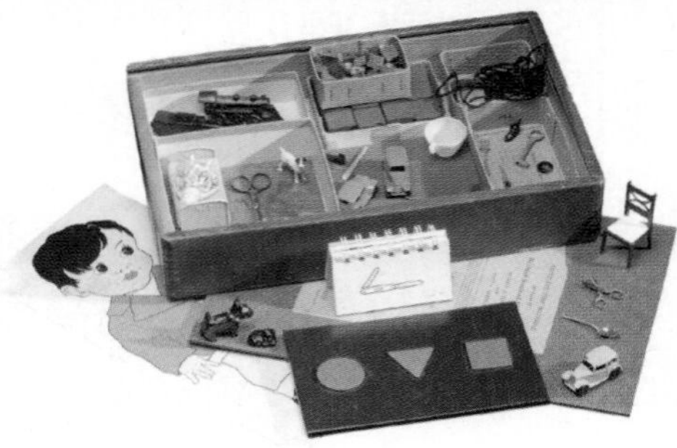

What's Your IQ?
French psychologist Alfred Binet collaborated with one of his students, Théodore Simon, to create a systematic assessment of intelligence. The materials pictured here come from Lewis Terman and Maude Merrill's 1937 version of Binet and Simon's test. Using these materials, the test administrator prompts the test taker with statements such as "Point to the doll's foot," or "What advantages does an airplane have over a car?" (Sattler, 1990). Top: Albert Harlingue/Roger-Viollet/The Image Works. Bottom: Science & Society Picture Library/Getty Images.

HOW DID INTELLIGENCE TESTING BEGIN? Intelligence testing is more than a century old. In 1904 psychologist Alfred Binet (1857–1911) joined a commission of the French government that was looking for a way to predict the performance of schoolchildren (Fancher & Rutherford, 2012; Watson, 1968). Working with one of his students, Théodore Simon (1872–1961), Binet constructed an intelligence assessment consisting of 30 items. These items were designed to be of increasing difficulty, starting with a simple test instructing the child to follow the movement of a lit match, and later asking him to explain how paper and cardboard are different, and to create rhymes with words, for instance (Fancher & Rutherford, 2012).

Binet and Simon assumed that children generally follow the same path of intellectual development. By comparing a child's mental ability with the mental abilities of other children in the same age group, they could determine the child's **mental age (MA).** For example, a 10-year-old boy with average intellectual abilities would perform similarly to other 10-year-old children and thus would have a *mental age* of 10. An intelligent 10-year-old boy would perform better than other 10-year-old children and thus have a mental age that was higher than his chronological age (for example, 12). Similarly, a child who was intellectually delayed would have a mental age that was lower than his chronological age.

Although Binet and Simon's intelligence measure was groundbreaking at the time, it had limitations. Most important, perhaps, was the fact that it could not be used to compare intelligence levels *across* age groups. You can't use mental age to compare the intelligence levels of an 8-year-old girl and a 12-year-old girl, for example. German psychologist William Stern (1871–1938) solved this problem by devising the **intelligence quotient (IQ).** To calculate an IQ score, simply divide a child's mental age by her chronological age and multiply by 100. For example, a 10-year-old with a mental age of 8 would have an IQ score of $(8 \div 10) \times 100 = 80$. When mental age and chronological age are the same, the IQ score is 100. The IQ score allows you to compare, for example, a 10-year-old with children of other ages.

The IQ calculation does not work with adults, however. It wouldn't make sense to give a 60-year-old man who scores the same as a 30-year-old man an IQ score of 50 (that is, $(30 \div 60) \times 100 = 50$). Modern intelligence tests still assign a numerical score (which we continue to refer to as "IQ"), but they no longer use the actual quotient.

THE STANFORD–BINET TEST American psychologist Lewis Terman (1877–1956) revised Stern's work so that Binet's test could be used in the United States, where it came to be known as the Stanford–Binet. Terman (1916) changed some items, added items, developed standards based on American children, and extended the test to include teens and adults. *The Stanford–Binet Intelligence Scales,* now in its fifth edition

aptitude An individual's potential for learning.

achievement Acquired knowledge, or what has been learned.

mental age (MA) A score representing the mental abilities of an individual in relation to others of a similar chronological age.

intelligence quotient (IQ) A score from an intelligence assessment; originally based on mental age divided by chronological age, multiplied by 100.

(Roid, 2003), includes the assessment of verbal and nonverbal abilities (for instance, defining words, tracing paths in a maze). This test generates an overall score for general intelligence as well as scores associated with more specific abilities, such as knowledge, reasoning, visual processing, and working memory (Becker, 2003).

THE WECHSLER TESTS In the late 1930s, American psychologist David Wechsler (1896–1981) began creating intelligence tests for adults (Anastasi & Urbina, 1997). At the time, adults were often given the Stanford–Binet, which was really geared to the daily experiences of school-aged children. The Wechsler Adult Intelligence Scale (WAIS) was published in 1955 and has since been revised numerous times (1981, 1997, 2008), and the newest version (WAIS-5) is being developed. In addition to creating assessments for adults, Wechsler also developed scales for older children (Wechsler Intelligence Scale for Children, WISC–V) and younger children (Wechsler Preschool and Primary Scale of Intelligence, WPPSI–IV).

The Wechsler assessments consist of subtests designed to measure different aspects of intellectual ability. The 10 subtests on the WAIS target four domains of intellectual performance: verbal abilities, perceptual reasoning, working memory, and processing speed. If you take the WAIS–IV, you will receive scores for these four domains, as well as an overall intelligence quotient (IQ) score. Psychologists look for consistency among the domain and subtest scores, as opposed to focusing only on the overall IQ score. A substantial inconsistency could be a sign of a problem, such as a reading or language disability. In the United States, Wechsler tests are now used more frequently than the Stanford–Binet.

Let's Test the Intelligence Tests

As you read about the history of intelligence assessment, did you wonder how effective those early tests were? We hope so, because this would indicate you are thinking critically. Psychologists make great efforts to accurately assess intelligence, focusing on three important characteristics: validity, reliability, and standardization (**Infographic 7.4** on the next page).

HOW VALID IS IT? **Validity** is the degree to which an assessment measures what it intends to measure. A valid intelligence test measures intelligence, and not something else. We can assess the validity of a measure by comparing its results to those of other assessments that measure the factor of interest. We can also determine whether the test predicts future performance on other assessments (a concept known as *predictive validity*). Valid intelligence tests generate scores that are consistent with those of other intelligence tests, and they can predict future performance on tasks related to intellectual ability.

HOW RELIABLE IS IT? Another important characteristic of assessment is **reliability,** the ability of a test to provide consistent, reproducible results. If given repeatedly, a reliable test will continue producing similar scores. Suppose you take an intelligence test today, next month, and five years from now; if the test is reliable, your scores should be consistent. Another way to gauge reliability is by splitting the test in half and then determining whether the findings of the first and second halves agree with each other; we call this *split-half reliability*.

Is it possible for a test to be reliable, but not valid? Absolutely. For this reason, we always have to determine *both* reliability and validity. Imagine a psychologist is using a test that claims to measure intelligence. The test is reliable because it produces similar scores when people are retested, but it's not valid because it actually measures reading level instead of intelligence. In other words, the test reliably measures reading level (achievement), but it does not measure intelligence (aptitude).

validity The degree to which an assessment measures what it intends to measure.

reliability The ability of an assessment to provide consistent, reproducible results.

How Smart Are Intelligence Tests?

Tests that claim to measure intelligence are everywhere—online, in your favorite magazine, at job interviews, and in many elementary and secondary schools. But can all of these tests be trusted? The results of an intelligence test aren't meaningful unless the test is *valid*, *reliable*, and *fair*. But what do those concepts mean, and how can we be sure whether a test is valid, reliable, or fair—let alone all three? Let's take a look.

validity DOES THE TEST MEASURE WHAT IT INTENDS TO MEASURE?

Is a bathroom scale valid for measuring height?

How about a ruler missing its first inch?

A shortened ruler would not be a valid measure because it would provide different results than other rulers.

A valid intelligence test will provide results that:

- ✔ agree with the results of other valid intelligence tests
- ✔ predict performance in an area related to intelligence, such as academic achievement

reliability WILL YOUR SCORE BE CONSISTENT EVERY TIME YOU TAKE THE TEST?

A shortened ruler isn't valid, but it is *reliable* because it will give the same result every time it's used.

A reliable intelligence test will provide results that:

- ✔ are reproducible (produces a similar score if taken a second time)
- ✔ show the first and second halves of the test are consistent with each other

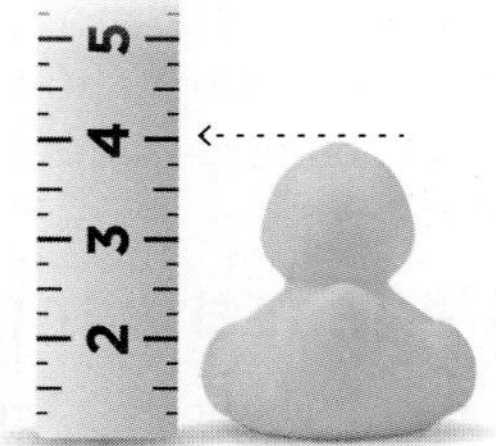

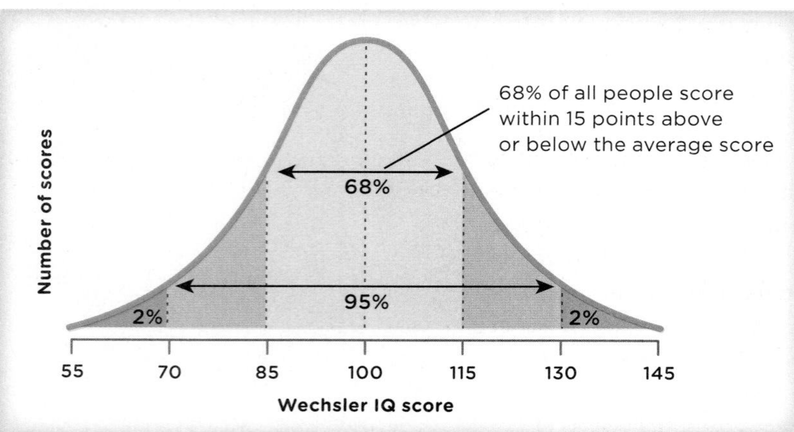

Because most intelligence tests are *standardized,* you can determine how well you have performed in comparison to others. Test scores tend to form a bell-shaped curve—called the normal curve—around the average score. Most people (68%) score within 15 points above or below the average. If the test is reliable, each person's score should stay around the same place on the curve across multiple testings.

fairness IS THE TEST VALID FOR THE GROUP?

An animal weighing 2 stone is likely to be a:

(a) sparrow
(b) small dog
(c) mature lion
(d) blue whale

Unless you live in the United Kingdom, where the imperial system of weights is used, you probably wouldn't know that a stone is approximately 14 pounds, and therefore the correct answer is B. Does this mean that you are less intelligent, or that the test is biased against people without a specific background? A test that is culture-fair is designed to minimize the bias of cultural background.

3 inches

2.286 Chinese Imperial cùn

.1667 cubits

IS IT STANDARDIZED? In addition to being valid and reliable, a good intelligence test provides *standardization*. Perhaps you have taken a test that measured your achievement in a particular area (for example, an ACT or SAT), or an aptitude test to measure your innate abilities (for example, an IQ test). Upon receiving your scores, you may have wondered how you performed in comparison to other people in your class, college, or state. Most aptitude and achievement tests allow you to make these judgments through **standardization.** Test developers achieve standardization by administering a test to a large sample of people and then publishing the average scores, or *norms,* for specified groups. This allows you to compare your score (often as a percentile) with people of the same age, gender, socioeconomic status, or geographic region.

Standardization is also achieved through the use of **standard procedures**, which ensure that no one is given an unfair advantage. Intelligence tests are subject to tight control. The public does not have access to the questions or answers, and all testing must be administered by a professional. Perhaps you have come across IQ tests on the Internet? We don't recommend them, in part because they lack standardization.

CONNECTIONS

In **Chapter 1,** we discussed the importance of operational definitions, which specify the precise manner in which variables are defined and measured. Here, we note that standard procedures are important when administering assessments as well. Data must be collected in a controlled fashion to ensure errors don't arise from unknown environmental factors.

THE NORMAL CURVE Have you ever wondered how many people in the population are really smart? Or perhaps how many people have average intelligence? With results from aptitude tests like the Wechsler and Stanford–Binet, we can graph a **normal curve,** which shows us how scores on intelligence tests are distributed (Infographic 7.4). The normal curve is symmetrical and shaped like a bell. The highest point on the graph represents the average score.

The normal curve shown in Infographic 7.4 portrays the distribution of scores for the Wechsler tests. As you can see, the *mean* or average score is 100. As you follow the horizontal axis, notice that the higher and lower scores occur less and less frequently in the population. A score of 145 or 70 is far less common than a score of 100, for example. The normal curve can be used to make predictions about a variety of traits, including IQ, height, weight, and personality characteristics. (See Appendix A for more information about the normal curve and other statistical concepts.)

synonyms

normal curve normal distribution

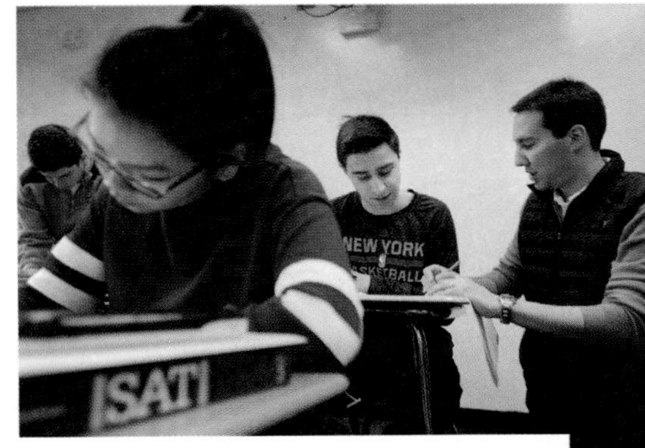

Equal Opportunity?

An SAT prep class in Connecticut. Tests such as the SAT and ACT are supposed to be reliable, valid, and standardized (and thus fair), but do they really level the playing field? Some families can pay for SAT prep classes and private tutors, while others can afford only test prep books, or nothing at all. Associated Press/Brian A. Pounds/APImages.

BUT ARE THEY FAIR? One major concern with intelligence assessments is fairness. Are these tests biased in favor of people of a certain gender, ethnicity, or socioeconomic class? Some evidence suggests they may be. For example, researchers have reported that Black Americans generally have lower scores on cognitive tests than White Americans (Cottrell, Newman, & Roisman, 2015), the average differences between these two groups being about 10 to 15 IQ points (Ceci & Williams, 2009; Dickens & Flynn, 2006). Group differences are also apparent for East Asians, who score around 6 points higher than average White Americans, and Hispanics, who score around 10 points lower than average White Americans (Rushton & Jensen, 2010).

Although researchers disagree about what causes these gaps in IQ scores, they generally agree that there is *no* evidence to support a "genetic hypothesis" across races (Nisbett et al., 2012). In other words, group differences in cognitive test scores do not result from race-wide genetics, but rather environmental factors. Evidence for this environmental influence is strong and points to many factors, including income level, education, and maternal verbal abilities (Cottrell et al., 2015). Socioeconomic status (SES) appears to play a key role. A disproportionate number of minority children grow up in lower SES communities, and therefore are exposed to environmental factors that may be linked to performance on tests of intelligence. For example, children raised in homes with lower SES tend to have more exposure to TV, and less access to books, technology, and adults who are available to read to them. They may also have limited access to quality schools (Hanscombe et al., 2012).

Stress is another factor that may contribute to the IQ gap. Research suggests that Black families, "on average, tend to live in more stressful environments than do" White families (Nisbett et al., 2012, p. 152). Chronic stress can have a negative

standardization Occurs when test developers administer a test to a large sample and then publish the average scores for specified groups.

normal curve Depicts the frequency of values of a variable along a continuum; bell-shaped symmetrical distribution, with the highest point reflecting the average score.

impact on the function of the brain, particularly those areas responsible for attention and memory (**short-term, long-term, and working memory**) (McEwen, 2000).

CONNECTIONS

In **Chapter 6,** we discussed the biology of memory, exploring areas of the brain responsible for memory formation and storage (hippocampus, cerebellum, and amygdala) as well as changes at the level of the neuron (long-term potentiation). Here, we note that stressful environments can impact the functioning of the memory system.

CAN WE EVEN THE PLAYING FIELD? We have discussed some environmental factors that might lead to disparities in IQ scores (maternal qualities, SES, and stressful living conditions). Could the gap in test scores also result from biases of the tests themselves? Early versions of IQ tests exhibited some bias against individuals from rural areas, people of lower socioeconomic status, and African Americans. Bias may result from language, dialect, or the culture of those who have created the tests (Sattler, 1990; Sternberg, 2004).

Psychologists have tried to create **culture-fair intelligence tests,** which aim to measure intelligence without putting people at a disadvantage because of their cultural backgrounds. One way to avoid bias is to create questions that are familiar to people from a variety of cultures. Another approach is to use nonverbal questions. (See the Raven's Progressive Matrices in **Figure 7.5.**) Since intelligence is defined within a culture, and tests are created within a culture, it may be impossible to develop assessments that are truly culture-fair or culture-free (Sternberg, 2004).

Despite their limitations, IQ tests are useful in certain contexts. For example, they can be used to predict academic success. IQ scores, particularly those in the higher and lower ranges, are strongly correlated with performance on SATs, ACTs, and Graduate Record Examinations (GREs), although some researchers have found that self-discipline may be a better predictor of success (Duckworth & Seligman, 2005). Intelligence tests are also helpful for identifying delays in intellectual functioning, or *intellectual disability.*

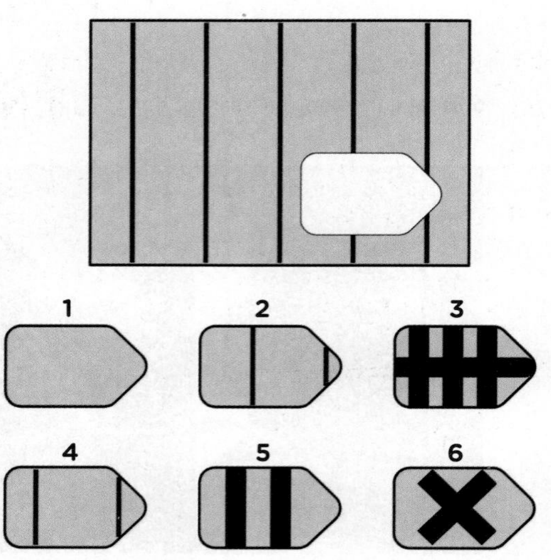

FIGURE 7.5
Nonverbal Intelligence
The Raven's Progressive Matrices test is used to assess components of nonverbal intelligence. For the sample question pictured here, the test taker is required to choose the item that completes the matrix pattern. The correct answer is choice 2. This type of test is generally considered culturally fair, meaning it does not favor certain cultural groups over others. Sample item similar to those found in the Raven's Progressive Matrices (Coloured, Parallel, Sets A, AB, B) (CPM). Copyright © 1998 NCS Pearson, Inc. Reproduced with permission. All rights reserved. "Ravens" and "Raven's Progressive Matrices" are trademarks, in the US and/or other countries, of Pearson Education, Inc. or its affiliates(s).

The Diversity of Human Intelligence

Intellectual disability consists of delays in thinking, intelligence, and social and practical skills that are evident before age 18. This condition is indicated by low IQ scores (below approximately 70 on the Wechsler tests) and adaptive functioning deficits (difficulty living independently and understanding number concepts, money, and hygiene, for example; American Psychiatric Association, 2013). Although intellectual disability is the preferred term, prior to October 5, 2010, references to "mental retardation" existed in many laws and policies (Schalock et al., 2010). On that special day in 2010, President Barack Obama signed Rosa's Law declaring that all earlier references to this phrase be removed from federal, health, education, and labor laws (Ford, Acosta, & Sutcliffe, 2013).

There are many causes of intellectual disability, but we cannot always pinpoint them. According to the American Association on Intellectual and Developmental Disabilities (AAIDD), nearly half of intellectual disability cases have unidentifiable causes (Schalock et al., 2010). Known causes include Down syndrome (an extra chromosome in what would normally be the 21st pair), fetal alcohol syndrome (exposure to alcohol while in utero), and fragile X syndrome (a defect in a gene on the X chromosome leading to reductions in protein needed for development of the brain). There are also known environmental factors, such as lead and mercury poisoning, lack of oxygen at birth, various diseases, and exposure to drugs during fetal development.

At the other end of the intelligence spectrum are the intellectually **gifted,** those who have IQ scores of 130 or above. Above 140, one is considered a "genius." As you might imagine, very few people—about 2% of the population—are classified as gifted. An even smaller proportion falls in the genius range: only 1% of the population (Simonton, 2012, November/December).

culture-fair intelligence tests Assessments designed to minimize cultural bias.

gifted Highly intelligent; defined as having an IQ score of 130 or above.

THE "TERMITES" Lewis Terman (mentioned earlier) was curious to know how gifted children function in adulthood. His work led to the longest-running longitudinal study on genius and giftedness. This study, formerly called the Genetic Studies of Genius, is now called the Terman Study of the Gifted. Terman (1925) monitored 857 boys and 671 girls with IQ scores ranging from 130 to 200. These children (known as "Termites") were well adjusted socially, showed leadership skills, and were physically healthy and attractive (Terman & Oden, 1947). Following the participants into adulthood, the study found that they earned a greater number of academic degrees and achieved more financial success than their nongifted peers (Fancher & Rutherford, 2012; Holahan & Sears, 1995). Compelling as these findings may be, they do not necessarily indicate that high IQ scores guarantee success in all areas of life.

Higher Education for All
A student (left) works with his teacher at Syracuse University (SU), which has an "InclusiveU" program that serves students with intellectual disabilities. Students in InclusiveU take regular college classes, pursue internships, and participate in athletics. "At SU, we celebrate disability because it makes our campus stronger, more diverse, and much more interesting" (Syracuse University, n.d., para. 3). HEATHER AINSWORTH/The New York Times.

LIFE SMARTS The ability to function in everyday life also is influenced by *emotional intelligence* (Goleman, 1995). **Emotional intelligence** is the capacity to perceive, understand, regulate, and use emotions to adapt to social situations. People with emotional intelligence use information about their emotions to direct their behavior in an efficient and creative way (Salovey, Mayer, & Caruso, 2002). They are self-aware and can properly judge how to behave in social situations. A high level of emotional intelligence is indicated by self-control—the ability to manage anger, impulsiveness, and anxiety. Other attributes include empathy, awareness of emotions, and persistent self-motivation. Research suggests that emotional intelligence is related to performance on the job and at school (Joseph, Jin, Newman, & O'Boyle, 2015; MacCann, Fogarty, Zeidner, & Roberts, 2011). Emotional intelligence sounds like a wonderful gift, but can too much of a good thing cause distress?

From the SCIENTIFIC AMERICAN pages of

THE DARK SIDE OF EMOTIONAL INTELLIGENCE

Profound empathy may come at a price.

Recognizing when a friend or colleague feels sad, angry, or surprised is key to getting along with others. But a new study suggests that a knack for eavesdropping on feelings may sometimes come with an extra dose of stress. This and other research challenge the prevailing view that emotional intelligence is uniformly beneficial to its bearer.

In a study published in the September 2016 issue of *Emotion,* psychologists Myriam Bechtoldt and Vanessa Schneider of the Frankfurt School of Finance and Management in Germany asked 166 male university students a series of questions to measure their emotional smarts. For example, they showed the students photographs of people's faces and asked them to what extent feelings such as happiness or disgust were being expressed. The students then had to give job talks in front of judges displaying stern facial expressions. The scientists measured concentrations of the stress hormone cortisol in the students' saliva before and after the talk.

In students who were rated more emotionally intelligent, the stress measures increased more during the experiment and took longer to go back to baseline. The findings suggest that some people may be too emotionally astute for their own good, says Hillary Anger Elfenbein, a professor of organizational behavior at Washington University in St. Louis, who was not involved in the study. "Sometimes you can be so good at something that it causes trouble," she notes.

Indeed, the study adds to previous research hinting at a dark side of emotional intelligence. A study published in 2002 in *Personality and Individual Differences* suggested that emotionally perceptive people might be particularly susceptible to feelings of depression and hopelessness. Furthermore, several studies, including one published in 2013 in *PLOS ONE*, have implied that emotional intelligence can be used to manipulate others for personal gain.

More research is needed to see how exactly the relation between emotional intelligence and stress would play out in women and in people of different ages and education

emotional intelligence The capacity to perceive, understand, regulate, and use emotions to adapt to social situations.

levels. Nevertheless, emotional intelligence is a useful skill to have, as long as you learn to also properly cope with emotions—both others' and your own, says Bechtoldt, a professor of organizational behavior. For example, some sensitive individuals may assume responsibility for other people's sadness or anger, which ultimately stresses them out. Remember, Bechtoldt says, "you are not responsible for how other people feel." **Agata Blaszczak-Boxe.** ■

As you may have observed in your own life, people display varying degrees of emotional intelligence. Where does this diversity in emotional intelligence—or any facet of intelligence—arise? Like most topics in psychology, it comes down to nature and nurture.

Is Intelligence Genetic?

Researching identical and fraternal twins is an excellent way to evaluate the contributions of nature and nurture for virtually any psychological trait. The Minnesota Study of Twins Reared Apart (MISTRA) indicates there are strong correlations between the IQ scores of identical twins—stronger than those between fraternal twins or other siblings. In other words, the closer the genetic relationship (identical twins have identical genes at conception), the greater similarity in IQ scores (Johnson & Bouchard, 2011; McGue, Bouchard, Iacono, & Lykken, 1993; Shakeshaft et al., 2015). In fact, identical twins' IQ scores have correlations as high as .86 (remembering that ±1.00 is a perfect correlation) (**Figure 7.6**). This suggests that genes play a major role in determining intellectual abilities.

The results of these twin studies suggest that intelligence is highly heritable. **Heritability** refers to the degree to which heredity is responsible for a particular characteristic or trait in the population. Many traits, such as eye color and height, are highly heritable. Others, such as manners, are largely determined by the environments in which we are raised (Dickens & Flynn, 2001). Results from twin and adoption studies suggest that heritability for "general cognitive abilities" is about 50% (Plomin & DeFries, 1998; Plomin, DeFries, Knopik, & Niederhiser, 2013). In other words, about half of the variation in intellectual or cognitive ability can be attributed to genetic make-up, and the other half to environment. However, with studies of twins who grow up in the same families, it is impossible to completely

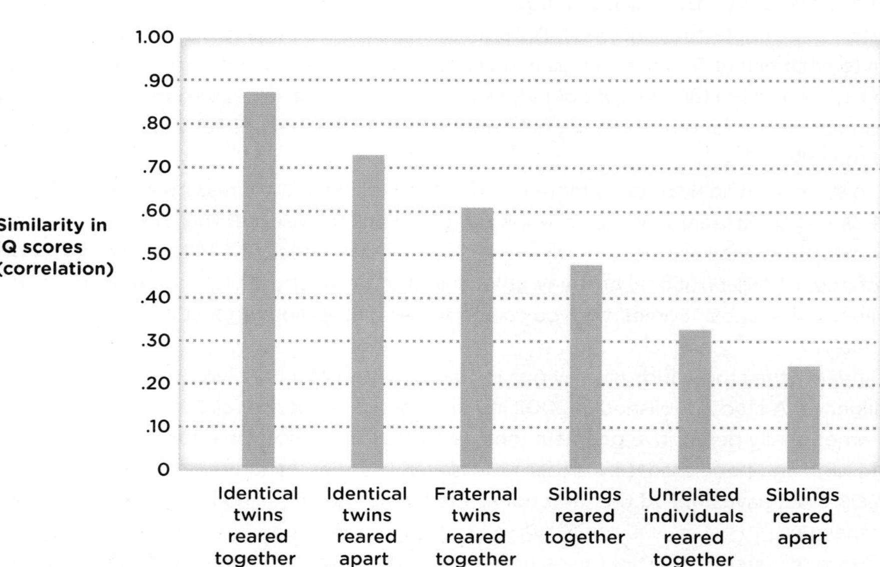

FIGURE 7.6
Nature, Nurture, and Intelligence
The most genetically similar people, identical twins, exhibit the strongest correlation between their scores on IQ tests. This suggests that genes play a major role in determining intelligence. But if identical twins are raised in different environments, the correlation is slightly lower, showing some environmental effect. Information from McGue et al. (1993).

TABLE 7.3 CHARACTERISTICS OF CREATIVITY

Characteristic	Meaning
Originality	The ability to come up with unique solutions when trying to solve a problem
Fluency	The ability to create many potential solutions
Flexibility	The ability to use a variety of problem-solving tactics to arrive at solutions
Knowledge	A sufficient base of ideas and information
Thinking	The ability to see things in new ways, make connections, see patterns
Personality	Characteristics of a risk taker, someone who perseveres and tolerates ambiguity
Intrinsic motivation	Influenced by internal rewards, motivated by the pleasure and challenge of work

Creativity is difficult to measure because it doesn't present itself in a singular or uniform manner. However, these basic characteristics are generally associated with creativity (Baer, 1993; Sternberg, 2006a, 2006b).

isolate the impact of the shared environment (von Stumm & Plomin, 2015). Evidence from direct genetic analyses indicates that between 40% and 51% of the variation in intelligence between individuals is due to "many genes of small effects" (Davies et al., 2011, p. 996).

We should close this discussion with a few important points to remember: (1) Heritability applies to groups of people, not individuals. We cannot say, for example, that an individual's intelligence level is 40% due to genes and 60% the result of environment. We can only make general predictions about groups and how they are influenced by genetic factors (Dickens & Flynn, 2001). (2) Although we see gaps in cognitive test results across groups of people, these differences are not thought to result from genetics. They most likely result from environmental factors, particularly those relating to socioeconomic status (Cottrell et al., 2015). (3) Cognitive abilities run in families, with approximately 40–50% of variation due to genes (Davies et al., 2011).

We have now explored the various approaches to conceptualizing and assessing intelligence. Let's shift our focus to a quality that is associated with intelligence but far more difficult to measure: *creativity.*

Let's Get Creative

Harry never approached football in a conventional way. When he was learning the ropes in his new middle linebacker position with the Giants, the coach provided specific instructions to accomplish his objectives. Harry would execute the task, but not always the way the coach had prescribed. "Everything he tried to get me to do, I did it [backwards], but I got the same or better results," Harry explains. Eventually, the coach gave up and allowed Harry the freedom to think outside the box. He threw up his hands and said, "As long as you get the job done, I can't fault you!"

LO 12 Define creativity and its associated characteristics.

Harry was using creativity to solve problems on the football field, just as you might use creativity to resolve a tricky situation in school or spice up a bland recipe in your kitchen. In a problem-solving scenario, **creativity** is the ability to construct valuable results in innovative ways (**Table 7.3**). Creativity and

heritability The degree to which hereditary factors (genes) are responsible for a particular characteristic observed within a population; the proportion of variation in a characteristic attributed to genetic factors.

creativity In problem solving, the ability to construct valuable results in innovative ways; the ability to generate original ideas.

In this test, you will be asked to consider some common objects. Each object has a common use, which will be stated. You are to list as many as six other uses for which the object or parts of the object could serve.

Example:

Given: A NEWSPAPER (used for reading). You might think of the following other uses for a newspaper.

a. *Start a fire*
b. *Wrap garbage*
c. *Swat flies*
d. *Stuffing to pack boxes*
e. *Line drawers or shelves*
f. *Make a kidnap note*

Notice that all of the uses listed are different from each other and different from the primary use of a newspaper. Each acceptable use must be different from others and from the common use.

FIGURE 7.7
Guilford's Alternate Uses Task
The sample question above is from Guilford's Alternate Uses Task, a revised version of the unusual uses test, which is designed to gauge creativity. Reproduced by special permission of the publisher, MIND GARDEN, Inc., www.mindgarden.com from the *Alternate Uses* by J. P. Guilford, Paul R. Christensen, Philip R Merrifield, & Robert C. Wilson. Copyright 1960 by Sheridan Supply Co. Further reproduction is prohibited without the publisher's written consent.

intelligence are not equivalent, but they are correlated, and a basic level of intelligence is necessary for creativity to flow (Jaarsveld et al., 2015). For example, you need to have a certain level of intelligence to generate original ideas, as opposed to just more ideas (Benedek, Franz, Heene, & Neubauer, 2012; Nusbaum & Silvia, 2011).

DIVERGENT AND CONVERGENT THINKING An important component of creativity is **divergent thinking,** or the ability to devise many solutions to a problem (Baer, 1993). A classic measure of divergent thinking is the *unusual uses test* (Guilford, 1967; Guilford, Christensen, Merrifield, & Wilson, 1960; **Figure 7.7**). A typical prompt would ask a test taker to come up with as many uses for a brick as she can imagine. (What ideas do you have? Paperweight? Shot put? Stepstool?) Remember that we often have difficulty thinking about how to use familiar objects in atypical ways, a result of functional fixedness.

In contrast to divergent thinking, **convergent thinking** focuses on finding a single best solution by converging on the correct answer. Here, we fall back on previous experience and knowledge. This conventional approach to problem solving leads to one solution, but, as we have noted, problems often have multiple solutions.

Creativity comes with many benefits. People with this ability tend to have a broader range of knowledge and interests. They are open to new experiences and often less inhibited in their thoughts and behaviors (Feist, 2004; Simonton, 2000). The good news is that we can become more creative by practicing divergent thinking, taking risks, and looking for unusual connections between ideas (Baer, 1993).

You Asked, Dr. Taylor Answers

http://qrs.ly/1v5a5d3

Did you undergo any psychological treatment during your recuperation?

HAPPY ENDINGS

This chapter may be coming to an end, but the stories Dr. Taylor and Harry Carson continue full speed ahead. It took Dr. Taylor 8 years to recuperate from what she now calls her "stroke of insight." Regaining her physical and cognitive strength required steadfast determination and painstaking effort. "Recovery was a decision I had to make a million times a day," she writes (Taylor, 2006, p. 115). She also had many people cheering her on—family and friends who had faith in her brain's plasticity, or ability to repair and rewire (Taylor, 2006). Today, Dr. Taylor is busy writing a new book and working on various projects aimed at increasing awareness and understanding of the brain, and supporting those recovering from neurological damage (drjilltaylor.com, n.d.).

In 2006 Harry Carson was inducted into the Pro Football Hall of Fame, but he was not in the mood for celebrating. Harry used his enshrinement speech to advocate on behalf of his fellow players: "I would hope that the leaders of the NFL, the future commissioner, and the player[s] association do a much better job of looking out for those individuals. . . . If we made the league what it is, you have to take better care of your own" (Pro Football Hall of Fame, n.d.).

It would take another decade for the NFL to finally admit that head injuries sustained in football are associated with chronic traumatic encephalopathy (CTE; Fainaru, 2016, March 15). Although this represents a positive shift in the discussion about football-related brain injuries, Harry's work is far from done. One of his main goals is to help other NFL retirees see that they are not alone in their struggles with mood swings, cognitive impairment, and other symptoms of traumatic brain injury—and that these challenges can become manageable. Another of his major objectives is to educate parents about the neurological consequences

divergent thinking The ability to devise many solutions to a problem; a component of creativity.

convergent thinking A conventional approach to problem solving that focuses on finding a single best solution to a problem by using previous experience and knowledge.

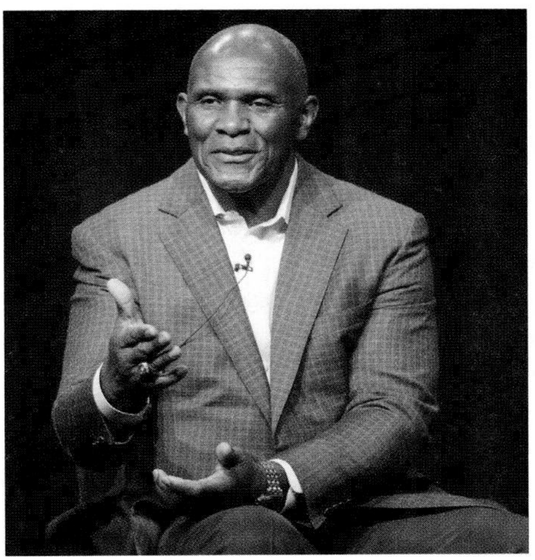

"Captain for Life"
Harry participates in the *League of Denial: The NFL's Concussion Crisis* panel discussion at the 2013 Summer Television Critics Association tour. Since his retirement in 1988, Harry has become a leader and advocate for generations of football players facing the repercussions of brain injury. The title of his memoir, *Captain for Life,* could not be more fitting. Frederick M. Brown/ Getty Images.

New Beginnings
Dr. Taylor currently serves as the national spokesperson for the Harvard Brain Tissue Resource Center, where scientists conduct research on brain tissue from cadavers. It took 8 years for Dr. Taylor to recover from her stroke. © My Stroke of Insight, Inc. Photo by Kip May.

of contact sports in general. Brain injuries may happen in a variety of sports, including soccer, lacrosse, hockey, and horseback riding. As Harry says, "there needs to be a warning to parents to understand that in signing [their] kids up to play ice hockey or football or some other sport where their child might sustain neurological damage, that young person might not be the same after they've been concussed."

✓ show what you know

1. Sternberg believed that intelligence is made up of three types of competencies, including:
   a. linguistic, spatial, musical.
   b. intrapersonal, interpersonal, existential.
   c. analytic, creative, practical.
   d. achievement, triarchic, prototype.
2. Some tests of intelligence are designed to measure ______________, or a person's potential for learning, and other tests are used to assess ______________, or acquired knowledge.
3. Define IQ. How is it derived?
4. An artist friend of yours easily comes up with many solutions when trying to solve problems. This ______________ is one of the defining characteristics of creativity, and it can be measured with the *unusual uses test*.

✓ CHECK YOUR ANSWERS IN APPENDIX C.

YOUR SCIENTIFIC WORLD is a new application-based feature appearing in every chapter. In these online activities, you will take on role-playing scenarios that encourage you to think critically and apply your knowledge of psychological science to solve a real-world problem. For example: Have you ever faced a tough decision? In this activity, you will decide where to live while in college by working through problem solving strategies. You can access Your Scientific World activities in LaunchPad. Have fun!

SUMMARY OF CONCEPTS

LO 1 Define cognition and explain how it relates to thinking. (p. 242)

Cognition is the mental activity associated with obtaining, converting, and using knowledge. Thinking is a specific type of cognition, which involves coming to a decision, reaching a solution, forming a belief, or developing an attitude. Cognition is a broad term that describes mental activity, and thinking is a subset of cognition.

LO 2 Demonstrate an understanding of concepts and how they are organized. (p. 242)

Concepts are mental representations of categories of objects, situations, and ideas that belong together based on their central features (characteristics). Psychologists often use a three-level hierarchy to categorize objects. At the top of the hierarchy is the superordinate category, which encompasses all objects belonging to a concept. Below is the more specific midlevel category, often used to identify objects. At the bottom of the hierarchy is the subordinate level, or most specific category.

Differentiate between formal concepts and natural concepts. (p. 244)

Formal concepts are created through rigid and logical rules (or "features" of a concept). Natural concepts, on the other hand, are acquired through everyday experience. Natural concepts don't have the same types of rigid rules for identification that formal concepts do, and this makes them harder to outline. We organize our worlds with the help of prototypes, the ideal or most representative examples of particular natural concepts.

Describe the biological processes associated with cognition. (p. 246)

The biology of cognition is evident in the brain, both on a micro and macro level. Changes at the level of the neuron, whether through rewiring, heightened excitability, or increased efficiency of synaptic transmission, make it possible to store, retrieve, and manipulate information. The plasticity of the brain enables dramatic recoveries from trauma.

Explain how trial and error and algorithms can be used to solve problems. (p. 249)

Problem solving refers to the variety of approaches used to achieve goals. One approach to problem solving is trial and error, which involves finding a solution through a series of attempts. Algorithms provide a virtually guaranteed solution to a problem by using formulas or sets of rules. Unlike trial and error, algorithms ensure that you will reach a solution if you follow all the steps correctly.

Identify different types of heuristics used to solve problems. (p. 249)

Heuristics are problem-solving approaches that incorporate a rule of thumb or broad application of a strategy. One commonly used heuristic is means–ends analysis, where "means" refers to how to reach the "end," or goal state. With means–ends analysis, the objective is to decrease the distance between the initial state and the goal state.

Describe the process of decision making and how heuristics can lead us astray. (p. 253)

Decision making generally refers to the cognitive process of choosing among various approaches to reach a goal. Using the availability heuristic, we predict the probability of something happening based on how easily we can recall a similar event from the past. If this recall occurs easily, we judge the event as being more likely to occur. With the representativeness heuristic, we evaluate the degree to which the primary characteristics of a person or situation are similar to our prototype.

Define language and give examples of its basic elements. (p. 258)

Language is a system for using symbols to think and communicate. These symbols are words, gestures, or sounds, and there are specific rules for putting them together. Phonemes are the basic building blocks of spoken language. Morphemes consist of one or more phonemes and represent the fundamental units of meaning. Grammar refers to the rules associated with word and sentence structures. It includes both syntax and semantics. Syntax is the collection of rules guiding word choice and word order. Semantics refers to rules used to bring meaning to words and sentences. Pragmatics refers to the social rules for using language.

Explain how language influences thought. (p. 260)

The linguistic relativity hypothesis proposes that language differences lead to disparities in thinking and perception. Most psychologists agree that, although language might not determine thinking and perception, it certainly can influence it.

Examine and distinguish among various theories of intelligence. (p. 263)

Charles Spearman speculated that intelligence consists of a general intelligence (or *g*-factor), which refers to a singular underlying aptitude or intellectual ability. Howard Gardner suggested we have multiple intelligences, proposing nine different types of intelligences or "frames of mind": linguistic (verbal), logical-mathematical, spatial, bodily-kinesthetic, musical, intrapersonal, interpersonal, naturalist, and existential. Robert Sternberg proposed three kinds of intelligences. His triarchic theory of intelligence suggests that humans have varying degrees of analytical, creative, and practical abilities.

LO 11 Describe how intelligence is measured and identify the important characteristics of assessment. (p. 266)

Some tests of intelligence aim to measure aptitude, or a person's potential for learning. Measures of achievement are designed to assess acquired knowledge (what a person has learned). Psychologists must ensure the accurate assessment of intelligence by determining validity, that is, the degree to which the test measures what it intends to measure. Another important characteristic is reliability, the ability of a test to provide consistent, reproducible results. A reliable test, given repeatedly, will result in similar scores.

Define creativity and its associated characteristics. (p. 273)

Creativity is the ability to construct valuable results in innovative ways. Basic components of creativity include divergent thinking, originality, fluency, and flexibility.

KEY TERMS

achievement, p. 266
algorithm, p. 249
aptitude, p. 266
availability heuristic, p. 253
cognition, p. 242
concepts, p. 242
confirmation bias, p. 254
convergent thinking, p. 274
creativity, p. 273
culture-fair intelligence test, p. 270
decision making, p. 253
divergent thinking, p. 274
emotional intelligence, p. 271
formal concepts, p. 244
framing effect, p. 255
functional fixedness, p. 250
general intelligence (*g*-factor), p. 264
gifted, p. 270
grammar, p. 259
heritability, p. 272
heuristics, p. 249
hindsight bias, p. 255
insight, p. 250
intelligence, p. 263
intelligence quotient (IQ), p. 266
language, p. 258
means–ends analysis, p. 249
mental age (MA), p. 266
morphemes, p. 259
natural concepts, p. 244
normal curve, p. 269
phonemes, p. 258
pragmatics, p. 260
problem solving, p. 248
prototypes, p. 244
reliability, p. 267
representativeness heuristic, p. 254
semantics, p. 259
standardization, p. 269
syntax, p. 259
thinking, p. 242
trial and error, p. 249
triarchic theory of intelligence, p. 265
validity, p. 267

TEST PREP ARE YOU READY?

1. ____________ is a mental activity associated with obtaining, converting, and using knowledge, and ____________ means coming to a decision, reaching a solution, or forming a belief.
   a. Thinking; formal concept
   b. Cognition; superordinate concept
   c. Thinking; cognition
   d. Cognition; thinking

2. ____________ are the mental representations of categories of objects, situations, and ideas that share central features or characteristics.
   a. Concepts
   b. Prototypes
   c. Algorithms
   d. Heuristics

3. The boundaries of ____________ are imprecise and hard to define; they do not have rigid rules for identification.
   a. algorithms
   b. heuristics
   c. natural concepts
   d. formal concepts

4. Following a stroke, the neurons in the brain exhibit greater excitability, rewiring occurs, and there is increased efficiency of synaptic connections, all indicating ____________ of the brain.
   a. algorithms
   b. the plasticity
   c. means–ends analysis
   d. the functional fixedness

5. After eating at a restaurant, you try to calculate a 20% tip for the server. Your friend suggests that you take the amount of the bill, move the decimal to the left one space, and multiply by 2. Your friend is using ____________ to solve the problem.
   a. prototypes
   b. a heuristic
   c. trial and error
   d. an algorithm

6. The ____________ suggests that language can affect thinking and perception.
   a. confirmation bias
   b. *g*-factor
   c. triarchic theory
   d. linguistic relativity hypothesis

7. Because of the ____________, we tend to overestimate the likelihood of an event occurring if we can easily recall a similar event from the past.
   a. representativeness heuristic
   b. availability heuristic
   c. additive model
   d. confirmation bias

8. Infants can recognize and distinguish among all ____________ from all languages until about 10 months of age. This is why older children and adults have more difficulty learning to speak a foreign language without an accent.
   a. morphemes
   b. phonemes
   c. words
   d. semantics

9. ____________ is one's innate ability to solve problems, adapt to the environment, and learn from experience.
   a. Heritability
   b. Giftedness
   c. Insight
   d. Intelligence

10. Although there has been a consistent gap in the IQ scores of Black Americans and White Americans, research suggests there is no evidence to support a(n) ____________ across races.
    a. split-half reliability
    b. normal curve
    c. genetic hypothesis
    d. emotional intelligence

11. How are formal and natural concepts different? Give examples of each.

12. Compare the theories of intelligence presented in this chapter.

13. Many people on the Jersey Shore had to leave their homes during Hurricane Irene in 2001. On returning home, they found no significant damage. When told to evacuate for Superstorm Sandy in 2012, many of these same residents did not leave. What heuristic do you think they used?

14. Why are reliability and validity important in test construction? What are the risks associated with an unreliable IQ test? Can you think of any negative consequence of using an IQ test that is not valid?

15. How many uses can you think of for a hammer? Use divergent thinking.

✓ CHECK YOUR ANSWERS IN APPENDIX C.

CHAPTER

8

Courtesy Ericka Harley.

Human Development

Why Study Human Development?

COLLEGE DOWN THE DRAIN? Joan Brown was 18 years old when she became pregnant for the first time. From that point on, she put her personal ambitions on hold and focused on taking care of her family. Joan worked as a waitress, took a job at Kmart, and spent several years at home with her three kids. When her middle child Ericka began preschool, Joan went along with her. She never intended to accompany her daughter to preschool 6 hours a day for the entire year, but if it eased Ericka's anxiety, Joan was willing to do it.

By the time Ericka was 16, the insecurity of her preschool days had vanished. Ericka was now a strong and independent young woman with the ability to accomplish most anything she wanted. "She was very smart, and I saw potential in her," Joan says. "And I knew that she was going to be better than I was, and that's what I always wanted."

Girl with Potential
Ericka Harley was 16 years old and starting her junior year of high school when she found out she was pregnant. Her mother Joan was disappointed to discover that her daughter, an honor-roll student, would soon be a mom; she had hoped Ericka might attend college and enjoy a successful career. Would Ericka ever make it to college? Courtesy Ericka Harley.

But Joan's expectations were shattered one summer day at the doctor's office. Ericka had not been feeling well, though she couldn't quite articulate what was wrong, so Joan took her in for a checkup. When the doctor emerged from the examination room and said, "Ericka wants me to tell you something," Joan knew immediately: "What, she's pregnant?"

The car ride home was very quiet. Joan didn't say much of anything, and she remained withdrawn for a couple days. "I was furious because, you know, you have that talk so many times," Joan recalls. "I figured no college; [it's] gone down the drain."

Joan had reason to be concerned, as the statistics were not in Ericka's favor. Half of all teenage moms don't even graduate from high school by the age of 22. By comparison, 90% of women who don't have babies in their teenage years earn high school diplomas (Centers for Disease Control and Prevention [CDC], 2016a).

Ericka had reached a crossroads, both in her relationship with her mom and in her life. How would she face the challenge of teen pregnancy? What kinds of physical, mental, and social changes would she experience in the months and years ahead? In other words, how would this major life event affect Ericka's *development?* 

Three Categories of Change

LO 1 Define human development.

When psychologists use the word "development," they are referring to the age-related changes that occur in our bodies, minds, and social functioning from conception to death. The goal of **developmental psychology** is to examine these changes. Research in developmental psychology helps us understand the struggles and triumphs of everyday people like Ericka and Joan as they journey through life. Psychologists often focus their studies on "typical" people, as it helps them uncover common themes and variations across the life span.

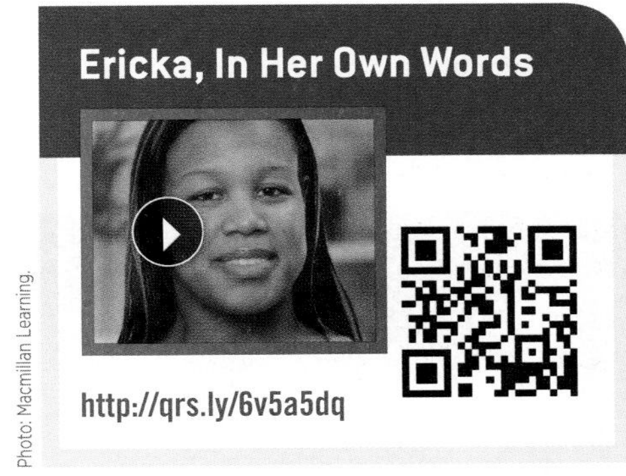

Ericka, In Her Own Words
http://qrs.ly/6v5a5dq

Photo: Macmillan Learning.

This chapter homes in on three major categories of developmental change: physical, cognitive, and socioemotional. *Physical development* begins the moment a sperm unites with an egg, and it continues until we take our final breath. The physical growth experienced by children and teens is referred to as **maturation.** For the most part, the **changes**  associated with maturation progress in a predictable pattern that is biologically driven and universal across cultures and ethnicities. After maturation, physical changes continue, but not necessarily in a positive or growth direction. Some people, for example, experience vision loss as they age, and this requires changes to their everyday activities and goals (Schilling et al., 2016). Changes in memory, problem solving, decision making, language, and intelligence all fall under the umbrella of *cognitive development. Socioemotional development* refers to social behaviors, emotions, and the changes people experience with respect to their relationships, feelings, and overall disposition.

CONNECTIONS

In **Chapter 5,** we described how various types of learning result in changes to behavior. Here, we describe maturation, which also results in behavioral changes. Although some activities like sitting up independently appear to be learned, they are biologically driven and thus the result of maturation.

In this chapter, we draw on the biopsychosocial perspective, which recognizes a variety of forces shaping human development. We consider the intricate interplay of heredity, chemical activity, and hormones (biological factors); learning and personality traits (psychological factors); and family, culture, and media (social factors). Psychologists use the biopsychosocial perspective to understand a wide range of developmental events, from childbirth to characteristics associated with health and well-being throughout the life span (Melchert, 2015; Saxbe, 2017).

Note: Quotations attributed to Ericka Harley and Joan Brown are personal communications.

developmental psychology A field of psychology that examines age-related physical, cognitive, and socioemotional changes across the life span.

maturation Physical growth beginning with conception and ending when the body stops growing.

We Can Sit!
Most babies begin sitting up on their own around 6 months (CDC, 2016e). Sitting upright is one of the milestones of physical development. Maturation tends to follow a predictable pattern, regardless of ethnicity or culture. Mel Yates/Getty Images.

Three Debates

LO 2 Outline the three longstanding discussions in developmental psychology.

Science is, at its core, a work in progress, full of unresolved questions and areas of disagreement. In developmental psychology, longstanding debates and discussions tend to cluster around three major themes: stages and continuity, nature and nurture, and stability and change.

STAGES OR CONTINUITY? Some aspects of development occur in stages with clear beginning and end points, others through a steady, continuous process. Examples of physical changes that may occur in stages include learning to walk and talk, or developing the physical characteristics of a sexually mature adult.

One line of evidence supporting the existence of discrete developmental stages comes to us indirectly through the animal kingdom. Konrad Lorenz (1937) documented the *imprinting* phenomenon, showing that when baby geese hatch, they become attached to the first "moving and sound-emitting object" they see, whether it's their mother or a nearby human (p. 269). Lorenz made sure he was the first moving creature several goslings saw. As a result, the young geese became permanently attached and followed him as soon as they could stand up and walk. But there appeared to be a limited time frame during which this behavioral change (imprinting) occurred. During a **critical period** of development, experiences can lead to new behavior patterns and "irreversible changes" in brain function (Knudsen, 2004). Unlike baby geese, humans do not exhibit dramatic behavioral changes resulting from experiences that occur during critical periods. However, some researchers hypothesize that there are critical periods for the normal development of vision, attachment, and language (Hensch, 2004; Myers, 1987/2014).

He Must Be My Mother
A brood of baby geese follows scientist Konrad Lorenz. The goslings treated Lorenz like a mother because he was the first "moving and sound-emitting" object with whom they had contact (Lorenz, 1937, p. 269). As Lorenz discovered, there appears to be a critical period during which this behavioral change called imprinting occurs. Nina Leen/The LIFE Picture Collection/Getty Images.

While some developmental changes occur in steps, others happen gradually, without clear beginnings and endpoints (McAdams & Olson, 2010). In other words, they are continuous. Observing a toddler making her transition into early childhood, you probably won't be able to pinpoint her shift from the "terrible twos" to a more emotionally self-controlled young child.

critical period Specific time frame in which an organism is sensitive to environmental factors, and certain behaviors and abilities are readily shaped or altered by events or experiences.

NATURE AND NURTURE Psychologists also debate the degree to which heredity (nature) and environment (nurture) influence behavior and development, but few would dispute the important contributions of both (Moore, 2013; Mysterud, 2003). Researchers can study a trait like impulsivity (the tendency to act before thinking) to determine how much it results from hereditary factors and environment. In this particular case, **nature and nurture** both appear to play a substantial role (Anokhin, Grant, Mulligan, & Heath, 2015; Bezdjian, Baker, & Tuvblad, 2011).

CONNECTIONS

In **Chapter 1,** we introduced the concepts of nature and nurture in our discussion of the ancient philosophers. In **Chapter 7,** we introduced the concept of heritability, or the degree to which heredity (nature) is responsible for a particular characteristic. Here, we examine how nature and nurture influence human development.

STABILITY AND CHANGE Yet another debate centers on the degree to which characteristics change across the life span. For example, how stable is personality over time and across situations? Some researchers suggest that personality traits identified early in life can be used to predict behaviors across the life span (Allemand, Steiger, & Hill, 2013; McAdams & Olson, 2010). Others report that personality characteristics change as a result of relationships and other experiences. The way we adapt to aging may also influence personality development (Kandler, Kornadt, Hagemeyer, & Neyer, 2015; Specht, Egloff, & Schmukle, 2011).

Three Designs

Developmental psychologists use a variety of research designs to study differences across age groups and time periods (**INFOGRAPHIC 8.1** on the next page).

LO 3 Identify several research methods used in the study of human development.

A SNAPSHOT IN TIME With the **cross-sectional method,** we can examine people of different ages at a given point in time. For example, researchers used the cross-sectional method to investigate developmental changes in beliefs about theories of intelligence, by dividing their participants into groups according to age and then comparing the beliefs of the different groups across the life span (Gunderson, Hamdan, Sorhagen, & D'Esterre, 2017). One advantage of the cross-sectional method is that it can provide a great deal of information quickly; by studying differences across age groups, we don't have to wait for people to get older. However, this approach doesn't tell us whether differences across age groups result from actual developmental changes or from common experiences within groups, a phenomenon known as the **cohort effect.** Members of each age group, or **cohort**, have lived through similar historical and cultural eras, and these common experiences may be responsible for some disparities across groups. In the study described above, the youngest cohort included first and second graders raised in the era of smartphones, tablets, and other digital technologies. The oldest group, consisting of college students, did not have this exposure to digital technology in early childhood. These different environmental exposures may influence how they view intelligence.

CONNECTIONS

In **Chapter 1,** we described confounding variables as unaccounted factors that change in sync with the independent variable, making it very hard to discern which is causing changes in the dependent variable. Here, we consider how a cohort can act as a confounding variable.

FOLLOWING PEOPLE OVER TIME Researchers can avoid the cohort effect by using the **longitudinal method,** which follows one group of individuals over a period of time. Curious to find out what "lifestyle activities" are associated with age-related cognitive decline, one team of researchers studied individuals over a 12-year period (Small, Dixon, McArdle, & Grimm, 2012). Every couple of years, they administered tests to all participants, assessing, for example, cognitive abilities and health status. The more engaged and socially active participants were, the better their long-term cognitive performance. But longitudinal studies are difficult to conduct because they require a great deal of money, time, and participant investment. Common challenges include attrition (people dropping out of the study) and practice effects (people performing better on measures as they get more "practice").

cross-sectional method A research design that examines people of different ages at a single point in time.

cohort effect The differences across groups that result from common experiences within the groups.

longitudinal method A research design that examines one sample of people over a period of time to determine age-related changes.

Research Methods in Developmental Psychology

Developmental psychologists use several research methods to study changes that occur with age. Imagine you want to know whether using social media helps protect against feelings of loneliness over time. How would you design a study to measure that? Let's compare methods.

Longitudinal

Measure a **single group** at **different points in time**

Example: Researchers follow a sample of participants, interviewing them every decade for a total of three measurements. As they age, participants report lower levels of loneliness than expected. But because the study is longitudinal, we can't eliminate the possibility that this particular group of participants is less lonely because of some historically specific effect.

GROUP 1

2005 2015 2025

BENEFITS
+ Can track age-related changes.

PROBLEMS
- Measured changes could be specific to the particular group of participants.
- Takes a long time, leading some participants to drop out before study is complete.

Cross-sectional

Measure groups of people of **different ages** (for example, 20-, 40-, and 60-year-olds) at a **single point in time**

Example: Researchers interview participants in three different age groups: 20-, 40-, and 60-year-olds. The oldest group reports higher levels of loneliness. But because the study is cross-sectional, we can't be sure if this finding reflects a cohort effect, in which differences may be due to age or to common experiences within the group, as opposed to developmental changes in physical, cognitive, or socioemotional functioning.

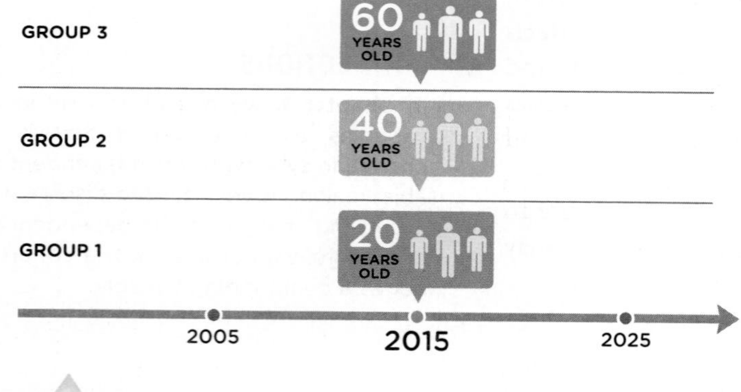

BENEFITS
+ Allows comparison between age groups.
+ Can be completed relatively quickly.

PROBLEMS
- Susceptible to cohort effect.

Cross-sequential

Measure groups of people of **different ages,** following them across **different points in time**

Example: Researchers interview participants from three age groups every decade for a total of three measurements. This results in data showing how social media use and loneliness change within each group as they age.

GROUP 3

GROUP 2

GROUP 1

2005 2015 2025

BENEFITS
+ Shows changes within individuals and between groups.
+ Better addresses cohort effect.

PROBLEMS
- Requires substantial resources and many participants.
- Takes a long time, leading some participants to drop out before study is complete.

BEST OF BOTH WORLDS? The **cross-sequential method,** also used by developmental psychologists, is a mixture of the longitudinal and cross-sectional methods. Participants are divided into groups and followed over time, so researchers can observe changes in individuals as they age *and* identify differences across age groups. Researchers used this approach to explore cognitive decline, assigning participants to 5-year age groups, and then following them for as long as 28 years (Sabia et al., 2017; Singh-Manoux et al., 2012). This method has its own set of drawbacks, however. It is costly and requires many participants, some of whom may drop out before the study is complete.

Put Your Heads Together

The people of Flint, Michigan, were exposed to lead-contaminated drinking water for about one year in 2014–2015. You want to study how exposure to lead impacted the intellectual development of children in the area. Team up and **A**) formulate a hypothesis for your study, and **B**) decide which of the three designs would be best for testing your hypothesis and explain why.

show what you know

1. A 6-month-old infant sits upright on his own, and his parents are delighted that he has reached this physical milestone. This is an example of human ______________, as this change in his behavior is biologically driven.
2. Explain the three longstanding debates in developmental psychology.
3. A researcher asks 300 participants to take a memory test and then compares the results across five different age groups. This researcher is using which of the following methods?
   a. cross-sequential
   b. longitudinal
   c. cross-sectional
   d. biopsychosocial

✓ CHECK YOUR ANSWERS IN APPENDIX C.

Inside the Womb

LIFE GOES ON Ericka suspected she was pregnant weeks before visiting the doctor's office with her mom. "I felt like something was different, but even before the missed period," she recalls. Ericka feared that her mother would not take the news well, and she was right. Joan was indeed angry and disappointed in the beginning, but a talk with her own mother changed her outlook: "I remember having a conversation with my mom," Joan recalls, "and she said, '[Ericka is] not the first, and she won't be the last,' and something just clicked."

From that point on, Joan continued to do what she had always done as a mother—give Ericka unconditional emotional support. She also made it clear that Ericka would be taking full responsibility for herself and her child. Ericka was welcome to live at home, but there would be no complimentary babysitting or financial assistance.

As the pregnancy progressed, Ericka began to experience some of the common symptoms of pregnancy, like changes in eating habits and aversions to certain smells and tastes. She suffered from dizziness and headaches, which triggered a frightening fall down the stairs, and prevented her from attending school. But Ericka, always a bright and motivated student, kept up by doing schoolwork at home.

Meanwhile, she began imagining the little person developing inside of her. "I wondered about everything," Ericka says. "Would she smile like me? Would she act like me? Would she love me back? . . . . I found out at about 5 months that I was having a girl. My heart melted and I was even more in love."

cross-sequential method A research design that examines groups of people of different ages, following them across time.

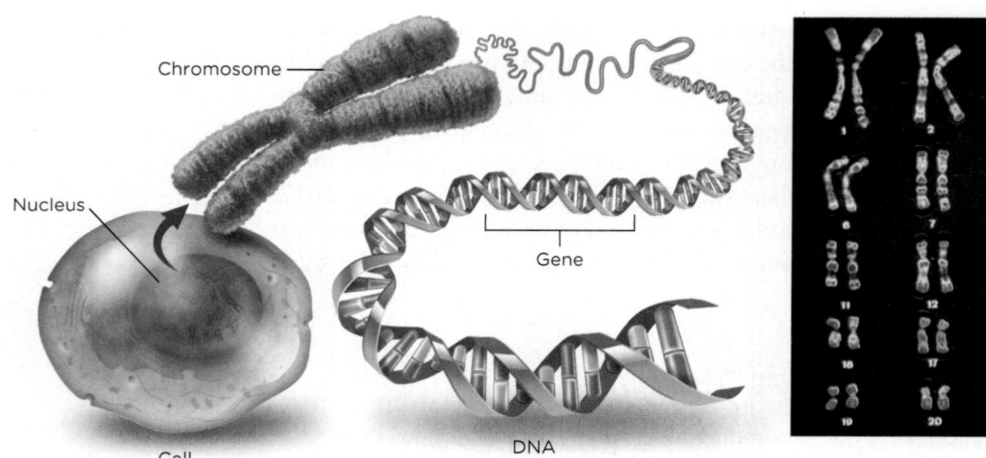

FIGURE 8.1
Chromosomes, DNA, and Genes
Every cell in your body, except red blood cells and sex cells (sperm or egg), contains a full set of chromosomes like that shown in the photo on the far right. These 23 chromosome pairs contain the full blueprint for you as a complete, unique person. The primary component of each chromosome is a single, tightly wound molecule of DNA. Within that DNA are around 20,000 genes (Dolgin, 2017, November 22), each determining specific traits such as hair texture and eye color. Note the sex chromosomes (X and Y) on the lower right, indicating that the sex is male. Photo: CNRI/Science Source.

The qualities Ericka imagined in her baby—the smile, the voice, the sex, and even to some degree the behaviors—would be influenced by the *genes* found in most every cell of the developing baby's body. Let's venture inside the cell and find out where those genes dwell.

What Are Chromosomes and Genes?

Examine the role genes play in our development and identify the biological factors that determine sex.

With the exception of red blood cells, every cell in the human body has a nucleus at its center. Within this nucleus is material containing the blueprint, or plan, for the building of a complete person. This material is coiled tightly into 46 **chromosomes,** the threadlike structures we inherit from our biological parents (23 from our father and 23 from our mother). A chromosome contains one molecule of **deoxyribonucleic acid (DNA).** Looking at the DNA molecule in **Figure 8.1**, you can see a specific section along its length has been identified. This section corresponds to a **gene,** and genes provide the instructions for making proteins. The proteins encoded by genes determine the texture of your hair, the color of your eyes, and some aspects of your personality. Genes influence nearly every dimension of the complex living system known as YOU.

As noted, your chromosomes, and all the genes they contain, come from your biological parents. In the moment of conception, your father's sperm united with your mother's egg to form a **zygote** [ZAHY-goht], a single cell that eventually gave rise to the trillions of cells that now make up your body (Sherwood, 2016).

TWINS In some cases, conception leads to twins or multiples. Identical or **monozygotic twins** develop when one egg is fertilized by one sperm and then splits, forming two separate zygotes with identical sets of 46 chromosomes. Eventually, these zygotes develop into identical twin infants who have the same sex and almost identical features. Fraternal or **dizygotic twins,** on the other hand, result when two eggs are fertilized by two different sperm, leading to two distinct zygotes. This can occur naturally, but assisted reproductive technology may increase the odds of a woman releasing more than one egg (Manninen, 2011). Over the past four decades, the number of twin births in developed countries has "nearly doubled," largely due to medically assisted reproduction (Pison, Monden, & Smits, 2015). Twins and multiples resulting from distinct sperm–egg combinations (that is, not identical) are like other biological siblings; they share around 50% of their genes.

chromosomes Inherited threadlike structures composed of deoxyribonucleic acid (DNA).

deoxyribonucleic acid (DNA) A molecule that provides instructions for the development of an organism.

gene Specified segment of a DNA molecule.

zygote A single cell formed by the union of a sperm and egg.

monozygotic twins Identical twins who develop from one egg inseminated at conception, which then splits into two separate cells.

dizygotic twins Fraternal twins who develop from two eggs inseminated by two sperm, and are as genetically similar as any sibling pair.

SEX CHROMOSOMES Typically, both sperm and egg contain 23 chromosomes, so the resulting zygote has 23 *pairs* of chromosomes, or a total of 46. The 23rd pair of chromosomes, also referred to as the *sex chromosomes,* includes specific instructions for the zygote to develop into a male or female (*XX* for female, and *XY* for male). This genetic sex depends on the father's sperm, which can contribute either an *X* or a *Y* to the 23rd pair (the egg, on the other hand, can only contribute an *X*). If the sperm carries an *X*, the genetic sex is *XX*, and the zygote generally develops into a female. If the sperm carries a *Y*, the genetic sex is *XY*, and the zygote typically develops into a male. This designation of genetic sex is called *sex determination,* and it guides the activity of hormones directing the development of reproductive organs and structures (Ngun, Ghahramani, Sánchez, Bocklandt, & Vilain, 2011).

Genetic sex is established at conception and remains constant throughout life. In a genetic male, the presence of the Y chromosome causes the fetal sex glands (also known as *gonads*) to become testes. If the Y chromosome is not present, as in the case of a genetic female, then the gonads develop into ovaries (Hines, 2011a; Koopman, Sinclair, & Lovell-Badge, 2016). Both the testes and ovaries secrete sex hormones that influence the development of reproductive organs: **Androgens** come from the testes and **estrogens** from the ovaries. **Testosterone,** for example, is an androgen that influences whether male or female genitals develop.

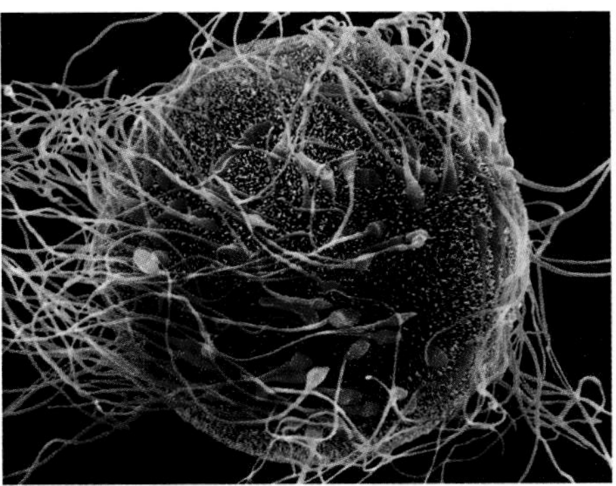

Where Did All the Sperm Go?
Men in Western countries are producing far fewer sperm than they did in past decades. Between 1973 and 2011, sperm counts dropped more than half among men from North America, Europe, Australia, and New Zealand. What's behind the sperm slump? Researchers cite many possible factors, including diet, stress, and exposure to chemicals (Levine et al., 2017). For example, plastic chemicals known as phthalates (found in many everyday products) interfere with normal hormone activity in mammals (Jones et al., 2016; Salam, 2017, August 16). David M. Phillips/Science Source.

DIVERSITY OF SEXUAL DEVELOPMENT Irregularities in genes or hormone activity can lead to differences of sex development (DSD), or the emergence of "physical sex characteristics" that are not typical (APA, 2015b; Topp, 2013). Such disparities result from inherited "conditions in which development of chromosomal, gonadal, or anatomic sex is atypical" (Lee, Houk, Ahmed, & Hughes, 2006, p. e488). According to the American Psychiatric Association (2013, p. 451), **intersexual** refers to having "conflicting or ambiguous biological indicators" of male or female in sexual structures and organs. For example, intersexual development would be apparent in a genetic female (*XX*) or male (*XY*) who has sexual structures and organs that are ambiguous or inconsistent with genetic sex. Around 1% of infants are found to have intersex traits at birth. These individuals might once have been called "hermaphrodites," but this term is outdated, derogatory, and misleading because it refers to the impossible condition of being both fully male and fully female (Vilain, 2008).

LO 5 Discuss how genotype and phenotype relate to development.

GENOTYPE AND PHENOTYPE Remember, almost every cell in your body has 23 chromosome pairs (46 chromosomes total). These chromosomes contain all your genes, collectively known as your **genotype.** Genotypes do not change in response to the environment, but they do interact with the environment. Because so much variability exists in the surrounding world, the outcome of this interaction is not predetermined. The color and appearance of your skin, for example, result from an interplay between your genotype and a variety of environmental factors including sun and wind exposure, age, nutrition, and smoking—all of which can impact how your genes are expressed (Kolb, Whishaw, & Teskey, 2016; Rees, 2003). The product of this interaction is the **phenotype**—a person's observable characteristics. Your phenotype is apparent in your unique physical, psychological, and behavioral characteristics (Plomin, DeFries, Knopik, & Neiderhiser, 2016; Scarr & McCartney, 1983).

You might be wondering what genotypes and phenotypes have to do with psychology. Our genetic make-up influences our behavior, and psychologists are interested in learning how this occurs. Consider schizophrenia, a disabling psychological disorder with symptoms ranging from hallucinations to disorganized thinking (Chapter 13). A large body of evidence suggests that some people have

androgens The male hormones secreted by the testes in males and by the adrenal glands in both males and females.

estrogens The female hormones secreted primarily by the ovaries and by the adrenal glands in both males and females.

testosterone An androgen produced by the testes.

intersexual Having ambiguous or inconsistent biological indicators of male or female in the sexual structures and organs.

genotype An individual's complete collection of genes.

phenotype The observable expression or characteristics of one's genetic inheritance.

CONNECTIONS

In **Chapter 7,** we described heritability as the degree to which heredity is responsible for a particular characteristic. Here, we see that around 60–80% of the population-wide variation in schizophrenia can be attributed to genetic make-up and 20–40% to the environment.

genotypes that predispose them to schizophrenia, with **heritability** rates between 60% and 80% (Cardno & Owen, 2014; Edwards et al., 2016; Matheson, Shepherd, & Carr, 2014). But the expression of the disorder results from a combination of genotype and experience, including diet, stress, toxins, and childhood adversity (Hameed & Lewis, 2016; Zhang & Meaney, 2010). Identical twins, who have the same genotype, may display different phenotypes, including distinct expressions of schizophrenia if they both have developed this disorder. This is because schizophrenia, or any psychological phenomenon, results from complex relationships between genes and environment (Kremen, Panizzon, & Cannon, 2016). Understanding these relationships is the main thrust of **epigenetics,** a field that examines the processes involved in the development of phenotypes.

Have a Peak?
Some traits are determined by the presence of a single, dominant gene. The "widow's peak," or V-shaped hairline, is thought to be one of them (Chiras, 2015). The man on the left must have at least one dominant widow's peak gene, while the one on the right has two recessive straight hairline genes. Left: Johner Images/Getty Images. Right: Dougal Waters/Getty Images.

DOMINANT OR RECESSIVE? Genes are behind just about every human trait you can imagine—from height, to disease susceptibility, to behavior. But remember, you possess two versions of each chromosome (one from mom, one from dad), and therefore two of each gene. Sometimes the genes in a pair are identical (both of them encode dimples, for instance). Other times, the two genes differ, providing dissimilar instructions for development (one encodes dimples, while the other encodes no dimples). Often one gene variant has more influence than the other. This **dominant gene** governs the expression of the inherited characteristic, overpowering the recessive, or subordinate, gene in the pair. A **recessive gene** cannot overcome the influence of a dominant gene. For example, "dimples" are dominant, and "no dimples" are recessive. If one gene encodes for dimples and the other no dimples, then dimples will be expressed. If both genes encode for no dimples, no dimples will be expressed. This all sounds relatively straightforward, but it's not. Psychological traits—and the genetics behind them—are exceedingly complex. Characteristics like intelligence and aggressive tendencies, as well as disorders like schizophrenia, are influenced by multiple genes (a phenomenon known as *polygenic inheritance*), and most of these genes have yet to be identified (Consortium, 2009).

Now that we have a basic handle on genetics, let's shift our attention toward the developmental changes that occur within the womb. How do we get from a single cell to a living breathing human with 10 little fingers and toes, fully functional organ systems, and a brain equipped with 86 to 100 billion neurons (Herculano-Houzel, 2012; Huang & Luo, 2015)? It's time to explore *prenatal development,* the 39–40 weeks between conception and the birth of a full-term baby (Spong, 2013).

From Single Cell to Full-Fledged Person

LO 6 Describe the progression of prenatal development.

Once the zygote is formed, it immediately begins to divide into two cells, then each of those cells divides, and so on. From conception to the end of the 2nd week is the *germinal period,* during which the rapidly dividing zygote implants in the uterine wall. Between weeks 3 and 8, the growing mass of cells is called an **embryo.** The embryo develops in the *amniotic sac,* which is the "bag" of fluids that provides protection. An organ called the *placenta* supplies the embryo with oxygen and nourishment, disposes of waste, and prevents mixing between the mother's and baby's blood. The embryo is connected to the placenta by the *umbilical cord.*

epigenetics A field of study that examines the processes involved in the development of phenotypes.

dominant gene One of a pair of genes that has power over the expression of an inherited characteristic.

recessive gene One of a pair of genes that is overpowered by a dominant gene.

embryo The unborn human from the beginning of the 3rd week of pregnancy, lasting through the 8th week of prenatal development.

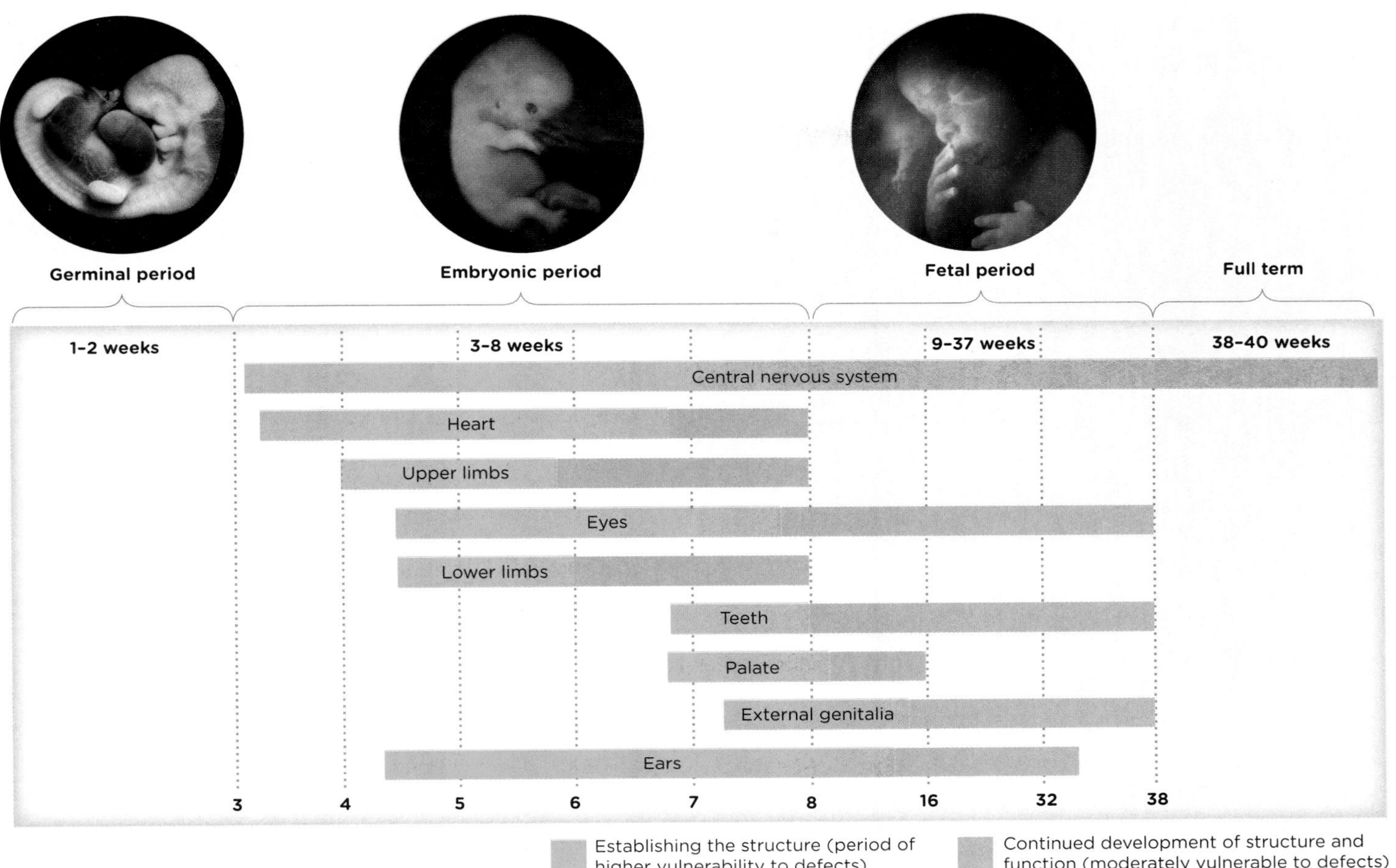

FIGURE 8.2
Prenatal Development and Periods of Critical Growth
During prenatal development, individual structures form and are fine-tuned at different times. As each structure is being established, it is particularly vulnerable to interference. Once their critical periods are complete, the structures are fully formed. Photos: (left) Omikron/Science Source; (center) Anatomical Travelogue/Science Source; (right) Neil Bromhall/Science Source.

Unlike the germinal period, when all cells are identical, the *embryonic period* marks the time when cells differentiate and the major organs and systems begin to form (**Figure 8.2**). This differentiation allows for the heart to begin beating, the arms and legs to grow, and the spinal cord and intestinal system to develop. But less than half of all zygotes actually implant in the uterine wall (Gold, 2005). Of reported pregnancies, nearly 20% end in a miscarriage (Rossen, Ahrens, & Branum, 2017), many of which result from genetic abnormalities of the embryo (Velagaleti & Moore, 2011).

THE WORLD CAN BE TOXIC The embryo may be safely nestled in the amniotic sac, but it is not protected from all environmental dangers. **Teratogens** (tuh-RAT-uh-jenz) are agents that can damage a zygote, embryo, or fetus (**Table 8.1** on the next page). Radiation, viruses, bacteria, chemicals, and drugs are all considered teratogens. The damage depends on the agent, as well as the timing and duration of exposure, and can result in miscarriage, decreased birth weight, heart defects, long-term behavioral problems, and other adverse outcomes (Jamkhande, Chintawar, & Chandak, 2014). One well-known teratogen is alcohol, which can lead to *fetal alcohol spectrum disorders (FASD)*. In particular, **fetal alcohol syndrome (FAS)** is the result of moderate to heavy alcohol use during pregnancy, which can cause delays in normal development, a small head, lower intelligence, and distinct facial characteristics (for example, wide-spaced eyes, flattened nose). Around "10% of women in the general population consume alcohol during pregnancy and one in 67 of these women delivered a child with FAS" (Popova, Lange, Probst, Gmel, & Rehm, 2017, p. e296).

teratogens Environmental agents that can damage the growing zygote, embryo, or fetus.

fetal alcohol syndrome (FAS) Delays in development that result from moderate to heavy alcohol use during pregnancy.

TABLE 8.1 DANGEROUS TERATOGENS

Category	Teratogen	Potential Effects
Drugs	Acne medication (isotretinoin)	Heart defects; neurological, musculoskeletal, and liver issues
	Alcohol	Fetal alcohol syndrome: intellectual disability, poor growth, heart problems, growth delay
	Caffeine	High exposure associated with miscarriage
	Cocaine	Birth defects, miscarriage, placental abruption
	Marijuana	Low birth weight, small skull, tremors
	Nicotine	Malformations, low birth weight, cleft lip or palate, heart defects
Environmental factors	Lead	High exposure linked with miscarriage and stillbirth, intellectual disability
	Mercury	Cerebral palsy, intellectual disability, blindness
	Radiation exposure	Small skull, blindness, spina bifida, cleft palate
Infections	Rubella	Heart disease, small skull, liver issues
	Syphilis	Inflamed joints, rash, swollen liver and spleen
	Toxoplasmosis	Small skull, intellectual disability, malformations of the eye
Maternal disease	Diabetes (insulin-dependent)	Abnormal tissue formation, death, birth defects
	Epilepsy (antiepileptic drugs and seizures)	Miscarriages, spina bifida, heart defects, small skull, cleft lip, cleft palate, developmental delays

From conception until birth, the developing human is nestled deep inside a woman's body, but it remains vulnerable to threats from the outside. Listed here are some common teratogens and their effects. Information from Brent (2004), Huizink (2014), and Jamkhande, Chintawar, & Chandak (2014).

Wondering how much alcohol is safe to drink during pregnancy? None (O'Brien, 2007; Vall, Salat-Batlle, & Garcia-Algar, 2015). "Even low-to-moderate consumption of alcohol crosses the placenta and interferes with the development of the embryo and later the foetus" (Landgren, 2017, p. 353). Alcohol consumption is something we can control, but this is not the case with all teratogens. Simply living near a farm that applies certain pesticides may increase a mother's risk of giving birth to a child with autism, developmental delay, and abnormal brain development (Rauh, 2018; Shelton et al., 2014).

FROM PUMPKIN SEED TO WATERMELON Between 2 months and birth, the growing human is called a **fetus** (Figure 8.2). During the *fetal period,* the developing person grows from the size of a pumpkin seed to a small watermelon, the average birth weight being approximately 7 pounds (by North American standards). It is also during this time that the developing person begins to demonstrate clear **sleep–wake cycles** (Suwanrath & Suntharasaj, 2010). By the end of the fetal period, most systems and structures are fully developed, and the baby is ready for the outside world.

If you step back and contemplate the baby-making phenomenon, it's really quite amazing. But many more exciting developments are in store. Are you ready for some shrieking, babbling, and a little game of peekaboo? Let's move on to infancy and childhood.

CONNECTIONS

In **Chapter 4,** we noted that some physiological activities are driven by a *circadian* rhythm; that is, they roughly follow the 24-hour cycle of daylight and darkness. Here, we can see that daily sleep–wake cycles become evident before birth.

fetus The unborn human from 2 months following conception to birth.

show what you know

1. ______________ are threadlike structures we inherit from our biological mothers and fathers.
   a. Teratogens
   b. Zygotes
   c. Genes
   d. Chromosomes

2. ______________ represents a complete collection of genes, and ______________ represents the observed expression of inherited characteristics.

3. A coworker is in her 6th week of pregnancy. She is excited because during this ______________, her baby is developing a spinal cord and its heart is beginning to beat.
   a. embryonic period
   b. phenotype
   c. germinal period
   d. genotype

✓ CHECK YOUR ANSWERS IN APPENDIX C.

Infants and Children

BABY'S COMING! April, 18, 2006: Ericka was already three days past her due date. Doctors were concerned the baby was growing too big, so they planned to induce labor (use medications to activate contractions of the uterus, and thereby start the birthing process). But just a few hours before Ericka was supposed to be induced, she began feeling strange sensations in her abdomen. Her little girl was coming. Twenty hours and many painful contractions later, Ericka was in the final stages of labor. As she strained to push the baby out, doctors asked if she wanted to feel the baby's head. "I don't want to feel her head. I just want it to be over!" Ericka remembers saying. Within minutes, she was looking into the eyes of her baby girl. "She was just perfect," Ericka recalls. "I couldn't believe how tiny her fingers were, and I counted them, and I touched all of them."

Ericka cried as she watched Joan take the baby in her arms. Then the baby's father held her, and he looked like he might cry, too. It was an emotional moment. After nine months of anticipation, a new little person had finally arrived. They named her Aa'Niyah.

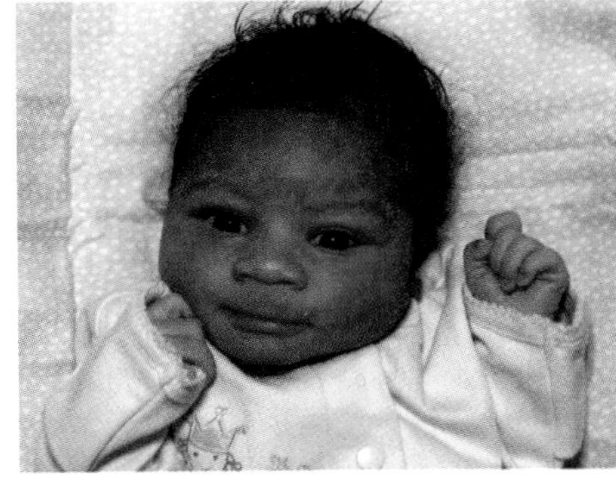

Introducing . . . Aa'Niyah! After 40 weeks and 4 days of anticipation, Aa'Niyah finally arrived. Niyah was full-term, but many babies are born before the typical 39–41 weeks of gestation. In the past (and in many developing nations today), some of these premature babies would not survive outside the womb. Thanks to advances in medicine, the *age of viability* has dropped to approximately 23 weeks in the United States (Seri & Evans, 2008). Courtesy Ericka Harley.

Newborns

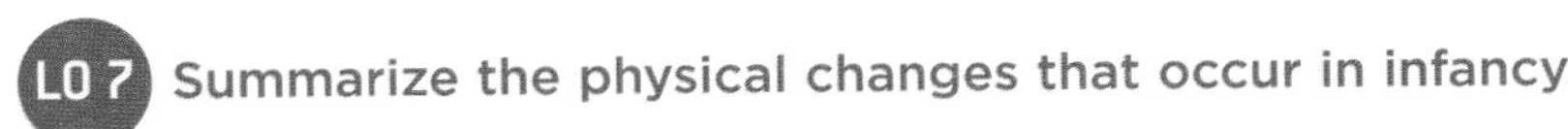

LO 7 Summarize the physical changes that occur in infancy.

At 7 pounds, 13 ounces, Aa'Niyah (affectionately called "Niyah") was within the average weight range for babies born in North America. She was also hungry, and drinking twice the amount of milk as other babies her age, according to Ericka. Unfortunately, breastfeeding was extremely painful because Niyah was born with two teeth ("natal teeth" are rare, affecting 1 in 2,000 to 3,000 babies; National Library of Medicine [NLM], 2016, February 22). But Ericka held out as long as she could, and nursed baby Niyah for the first two weeks—a worthy sacrifice, since breast milk is thought to have important effects on growth and cognitive development (Victora et al., 2016).

NEWBORN SENSES From the moment Niyah was born, she was intensely interested in people. She made a lot of eye contact, listened closely to voices, and responded with her own little noises. Babies come into the world equipped with keen sensory capabilities that seem to be designed for facilitating relationships. They are drawn to people, and prefer to look at human faces over geometric shapes (Salva, Farroni, Regolin, Vallortigara, & Johnson, 2011; Simion & Di Giorgio, 2015). Within hours of birth, these tiny babies can discriminate their mother's voice from those of other women, and they show a preference for her voice (DeCasper & Fifer, 1980; Moon, Zernzach, & Kuhl, 2015). This ability to recognize Mom's voice may actually begin developing in utero (Kisilevsky et al., 2003; Moon et al., 2015). The auditory system is functioning before birth, but it takes time for fluids to dry up so the baby can hear clearly (Hall, Smith, & Popelka, 2004).

Smell and taste are also well developed in newborn infants, who can distinguish the smell of their own mothers' breast milk from that of other women within days of birth (Marin, Rapisardi, & Tani, 2015; Nishitani et al., 2009). Babies prefer sweet tastes, react strongly to sour tastes, and notice certain changes to their mothers' diets because those tastes are present in breast milk. If a mother has eaten something very sweet, for instance, the infant tends to breastfeed longer.

The sense of touch, and thus the ability to feel pain, are evident before birth (Marx & Nagy, 2015). It was once believed that newborns were incapable of experiencing pain, but research suggests otherwise. The brain activity infants and adults display in response to painful stimuli is "extremely similar," suggesting that babies suffer like the rest of us (Goksan et al., 2015).

Vision is the weakest sense in newborns, who have difficulty seeing things outside their immediate vicinity. They see objects most clearly at about 8–14 inches (American Academy of Pediatrics, 2015), which happens to be the approximate distance between the face of the nursing baby and the mother. Eye contact is thought to strengthen the mother-infant relationship. Vision can be blurry for the first few months, one reason being that the **light-sensitive cones** in the eye are still developing (Banks & Salapatek, 1978).

CONNECTIONS

In **Chapter 3,** we described specialized neurons called photoreceptors, which absorb light energy and turn it into chemical and electrical signals for the brain to process. A cone is a type of photoreceptor that enables us to see colors and details. Newborns have blurry eyesight, in part because their cones have not fully developed.

NEWBORN REFLEXES Newborns exhibit several *reflexes,* or automatic responses to stimuli. Some are necessary for survival, while others serve no obvious purpose. Reflexes may fade away in the first weeks and months of life, but many resurface as voluntary movements as the infant grows and develops motor control (Thelen & Fisher, 1982). **Table 8.2** describes several reflexes evident in recently born babies.

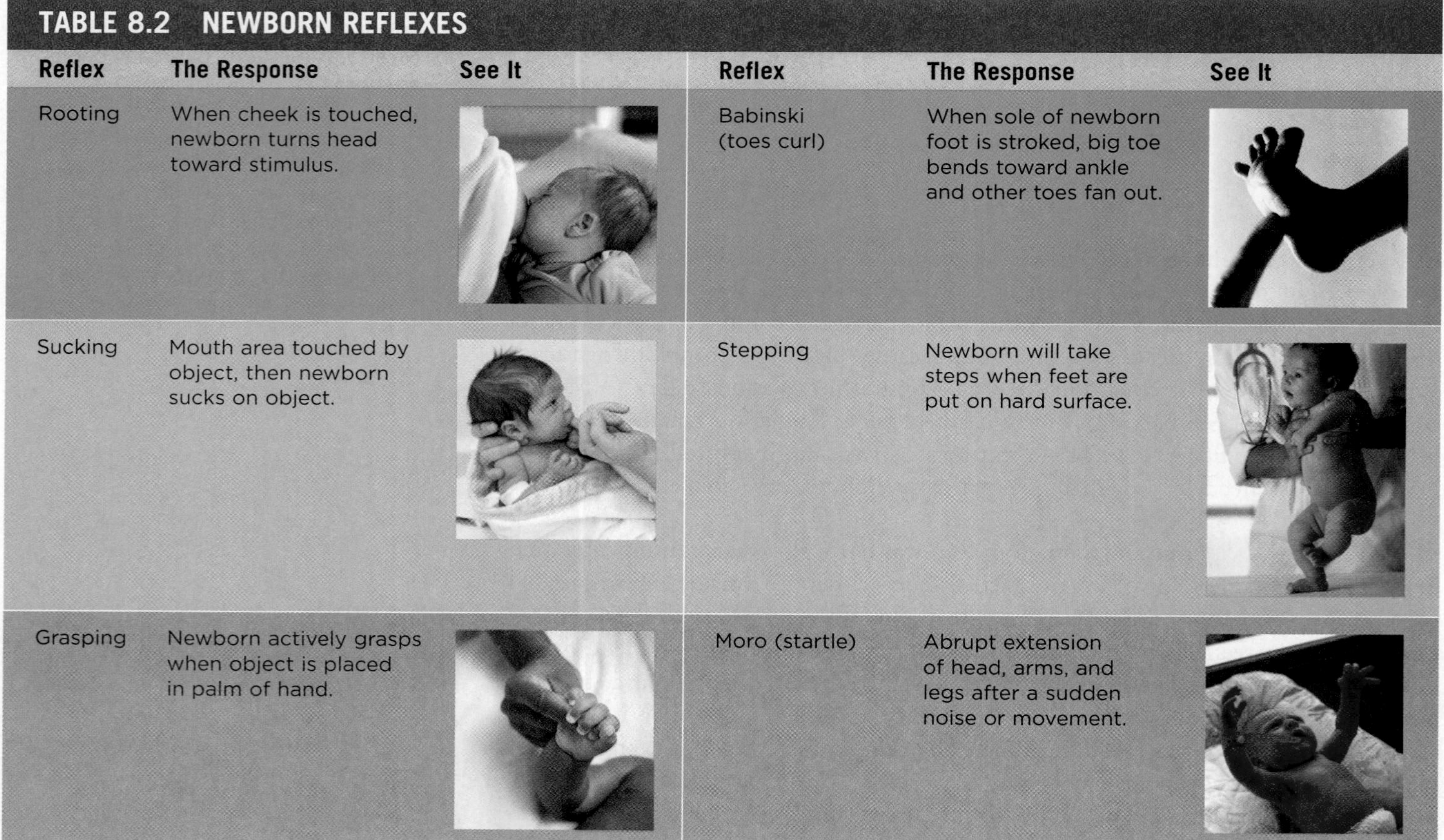

TABLE 8.2 NEWBORN REFLEXES

Reflex	The Response	See It	Reflex	The Response	See It
Rooting	When cheek is touched, newborn turns head toward stimulus.		Babinski (toes curl)	When sole of newborn foot is stroked, big toe bends toward ankle and other toes fan out.	
Sucking	Mouth area touched by object, then newborn sucks on object.		Stepping	Newborn will take steps when feet are put on hard surface.	
Grasping	Newborn actively grasps when object is placed in palm of hand.		Moro (startle)	Abrupt extension of head, arms, and legs after a sudden noise or movement.	

Newborns exhibit various reflexes, or automatic responses to stimuli. Listed here are some of the reflexes first evident at birth.
Information from Zafeiriou (2004). Photos: (Left column, top to bottom) Christine Hanscomb/Science Source; BSIP SA/Alamy Stock Photo; Michelle Gibson/Getty Images. (Right column, top to bottom) Ray Ellis/Science Source; Picture Partners/Alamy; ASTIER/age fotostock.

A newborn spends most of the time eating, sleeping, and crying. But this stage soon gives way to a period that is far more interactive and features some of the most memorable milestones of human development, from waving "bye-bye" to taking those precious first steps. **Infographic 8.2** on the next page details some of the sensory and motor milestones of infancy, and the average ages at which they occur. Although the sequence and timing of these achievements are fairly universal, there can be significant variation from one infant to the next.

What's Going On in the Brain?

The speed of brain development in the womb and immediately after birth is astounding. There are times in fetal development when the brain is producing approximately 250,000 new neurons per minute! The creation of new neurons is mostly complete by the end of the 5th month of fetal development (Kolb & Gibb, 2011). At the time of birth, a baby's brain has approximately 100 billion neurons (Toga et al., 2006)—roughly the same number as that of an adult. Meanwhile, **axons** are growing longer, and more neurons, particularly those involved in motor control, are developing a myelin sheath around their axons. The myelin sheath increases the efficiency of neural communication, which leads to better motor control, enabling a baby to wave and walk.

CONNECTIONS

In **Chapter 2,** we described the structure of a typical neuron, which includes an axon projecting from the cell body. Many axons are surrounded by a myelin sheath, a fatty substance that insulates them. This insulation allows for faster communication within and between neurons. Here, we see how myelination impacts motor development.

MAKING—AND BREAKING—CONNECTIONS As young children interact with the environment, new connections sprout between neurons, but not uniformly throughout the brain. Between ages 3 and 6, for example, the greatest increase in neural connections occurs in the frontal lobes, the area of the brain involved in planning and attention (Thompson et al., 2000; Toga et al., 2006). As more links are established, more associations can be made between different stimuli, and between behavior and consequences. A young person needs to learn quickly, and this process makes it possible. The extraordinary growth in synaptic connections does not last forever, however, as the number of connections decreases by 40% to 50% by the time a child reaches puberty (Thompson et al., 2000; Webb, Monk, & Nelson, 2001). Through the process of *synaptic pruning,* unused synaptic connections are downsized or eliminated, helping increase the efficiency of the brain (Chechik, Meilijson, & Ruppin, 1998; Spear, 2013; Vainchtien et al., 2018).

ENRICHMENT Many aspects of brain development are strongly influenced by experiences and input from the environment. In the 1960s and 1970s, Mark Rosenzweig and his colleagues at the University of California, Berkeley, demonstrated how much environment can influence the development of nonhuman animal brains (Kolb & Whishaw, 1998). They found that rats placed in stimulating environments (furnished with opportunities for exploration and social interaction) experience greater increases

Environment Matters

The children on the left appear to be immersed in an enriched environment, which offers opportunities for physical exercise, social interaction, and other types of stimulating activity that promote positive changes in the brain (Khan & Hillman, 2014; van Praag, Kempermann, & Gage, 2000). Fewer signs of enrichment appear in the photo to the right, which shows children in a Romanian orphanage in the late 1990s.

Left: Rawpixel.com/Shutterstock.com.
Right: Romano Cagnoni/Getty Images.

Infant Brain and Sensorimotor Development

As newborns grow, they progress at an astounding rate in seen and unseen ways. When witnessing babies' new skills, whether it be reaching for a rattle or pulling themselves into a standing position, it's easy to marvel at how far they have come. But what you can't see is the real action. These sensorimotor advancements are only possible because of the incredible brain development happening in the background.

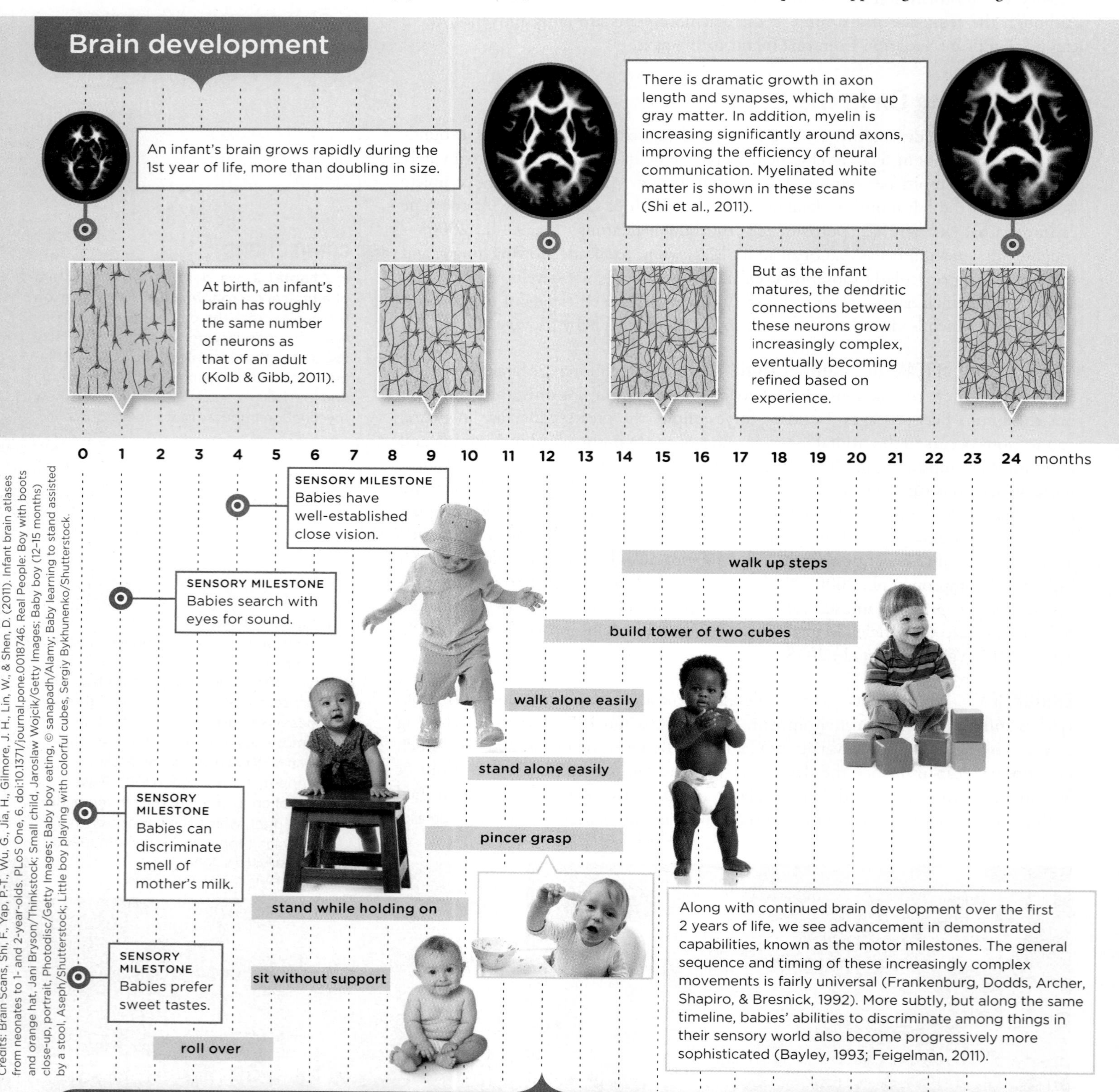

Brain development
An infant's brain grows rapidly during the 1st year of life, more than doubling in size.
There is dramatic growth in axon length and synapses, which make up gray matter. In addition, myelin is increasing significantly around axons, improving the efficiency of neural communication. Myelinated white matter is shown in these scans (Shi et al., 2011).
At birth, an infant's brain has roughly the same number of neurons as that of an adult (Kolb & Gibb, 2011).
But as the infant matures, the dendritic connections between these neurons grow increasingly complex, eventually becoming refined based on experience.
0 1 2 3 4 5 6 7 8 9 10 11 12 13 14 15 16 17 18 19 20 21 22 23 24 months
SENSORY MILESTONE Babies have well-established close vision.
SENSORY MILESTONE Babies search with eyes for sound.
SENSORY MILESTONE Babies can discriminate smell of mother's milk.
SENSORY MILESTONE Babies prefer sweet tastes.
walk up steps
build tower of two cubes
walk alone easily
stand alone easily
pincer grasp
stand while holding on
sit without support
roll over
Along with continued brain development over the first 2 years of life, we see advancement in demonstrated capabilities, known as the motor milestones. The general sequence and timing of these increasingly complex movements is fairly universal (Frankenburg, Dodds, Archer, Shapiro, & Bresnick, 1992). More subtly, but along the same timeline, babies' abilities to discriminate among things in their sensory world also become progressively more sophisticated (Bayley, 1993; Feigelman, 2011).
Motor and Sensory Development

Credits: Brain Scans, Shi, F., Yap, P.-T., Wu, G., Jia, H., Gilmore, J. H., Lin, W., & Shen, D. (2011). Infant brain atlases from neonates to 1- and 2-year-olds. PLoS One, 6. doi:10.1371/journal.pone.0018746. Real People: Boy with boots and orange hat, Jani Bryson/Thinkstock; Small child, Jaroslaw Wojcik/Getty Images; Baby boy (12-15 months) close-up, portrait, Photodisc/Getty Images; Baby boy eating, © sanapadh/Alamy; Baby learning to stand assisted by a stool, Aseph/Shutterstock; Little boy playing with colorful cubes, Sergiy Bykhunenko/Shutterstock.

in brain weight and synaptic connections than those put in nonstimulating environments (Barredo & Deeg, 2009, February 24; Kolb & Whishaw, 1998; Rosenzweig, 1984). Environmental stimulation (or lack thereof) may have a similar impact on infants and children. "Severe deprivation" early in life can lead to startling problems with brain development (Kennedy et al., 2016). For example, babies raised in orphanages that provide minimal care and human interaction not only experience "deficits" in cognitive, social, and physical development; they also face "life-long risks of chronic disorders of mental and physical health" (Kumsta et al., 2016, p. 5).

The Language Explosion

Babies come into the world incapable of using **language**, yet by the age of 6, most have amassed a vocabulary of about 13,000 words—that amounts to about one new word every 2 hours awake (Pinker, 1994). One important component of this learning process is ***infant-directed speech (IDS),*** which is often used by parents and other caregivers. High-pitched and repetitious, infant-directed speech is observed throughout the world (Singh, Nestor, Parikh, & Yull, 2009). Can't you just hear Ericka saying to baby Niyah, "Who's my baby girl?" Infants as young as 5 months pay more attention to people who use infant-directed speech, which allows them to choose "appropriate social partners," or adults who are more likely to provide them with chances to learn and interact (Schachner & Hannon, 2011). When parents use IDS, infants listen (Golinkoff, Can, Soderstrom, & Hirsh-Pasek, 2015; Spinelli, Fasolo, & Mesman, 2017).

CONNECTIONS

In **Chapter 7,** we introduced basic elements of language, such as phonemes, morphemes, and semantics, and explored how language relates to thought. In this chapter, we discuss how language develops.

synonyms

infant-directed speech (IDS) motherese

Infants benefit from a lot of chatter. It turns out that the amount of language spoken in the home correlates with socioeconomic status. Children from high-income families are more likely to have parents who engage them in conversation. Just look at findings from studies of parents of toddlers: 35 words a minute spoken by high-income parents; 20 words a minute spoken by middle-income parents; and 10 words a minute spoken by low-income parents (Hoff, 2003). The consequences of such interactions are apparent, with toddlers from high-income households having an average vocabulary of 766 words, and those from low-income homes only 357 (Hart & Risley, 1995). How might this disparity in exposure impact these same children when they start school (Hirsh-Pasek et al., 2015)? Research suggests that children from lower socioeconomic households begin school already lagging behind in reading, math, and academic achievement in general, all of which might be linked to fewer verbal interactions (Hoff, 2013; Lee & Burkan, 2002).

Benefits of Sign
A baby and a caregiver communicate with sign language. Introducing sign to children as young as 6 months may help them communicate before they use verbal speech (Doherty-Sneddon, 2008). Early use of sign may also provide a verbal advantage down the road when they enter elementary school (Barnes, 2010). Christina Kennedy/Alamy Stock Photo.

LO 8 Outline the universal sequence of language development.

COO, BABBLE, TALK No matter what language infants speak, or who raises them, you can almost be certain they will follow the universal sequence of language development (Chomsky, 2000). At 2 to 3 months, infants typically start to produce vowel-like sounds known as *cooing*. These "oooo" and "ahhh" sounds are often repeated in a joyful manner. Every time Ericka put Niyah down to sleep, she would coo like a songbird in her bassinet. Niyah always made her presence known. Says Ericka, "she was always . . . letting you know she was in the room, making little sounds."

When infants reach 4 to 6 months, they begin to combine consonants and vowels in the *babbling* stage. These sounds are meaningless, but babbling can resemble real language ("ma, ma, ma, ma, ma" *Did you say . . . mama?*). Nonhearing infants also go through this babbling stage, but they move their hands instead of babbling aloud (Petitto & Marentette, 1991). For infants with normal hearing and infants who are deaf, the babbling stage becomes an important foundation for speech production; when infants babble, they are on their way to their first words.

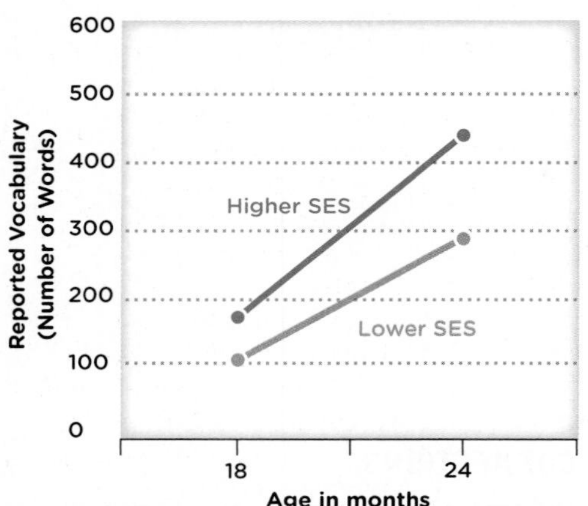

FIGURE 8.3
Language Disparities
In the first few years of life, a child's vocabulary increases dramatically. In one study, parents identified the words understood and spoken by their children (from a list of 680 items). As shown above, the vocabulary gap between children of higher and lower socioeconomic status (SES) widened between 18 and 24 months. Information from Fernald, Marchman, and Weisleder (2014).

Around the one-year mark, infants typically begin to utter their magical first words. Often these are nouns used to convey an entire message, or *holophrase.* Perhaps you have heard an infant say something emphatically, such as "JUICE!" or "UP!" The baby might be trying to say "I am thirsty, could I please have some juice?" or "I want you to pick me up."

At about 18 months, infants start using two-word phrases, or **telegraphic speech.** These brief statements include only the most important words of a sentence, such as nouns, verbs, and adjectives, but no prepositions or articles. "Baby crying" might be a telegraphic sentence meaning the baby at the next table is crying loudly. As children mature, they start to use more complete sentences and increasingly complex grammar. A "vocabulary explosion" tends to occur at about 2 to 3 years of age (McMurray, 2007; **Figure 8.3**). It was around this time that Niyah began asking a lot of questions: "What did you do today? Where are we going? Is this the way to Grandma's house? Why are we buying that?" As Ericka tried to keep pace with Niyah's inquiries, she wondered how this little person came up with such questions. *Why are you asking me that? How do you know to ask me that?* By 5 to 6, most children are fluent in their native language, although their vocabulary does not match that of an adult.

There are two important components of normal language acquisition: (1) physical development, particularly in the language-processing areas of the brain (Chapter 2); and (2) exposure to language. Children who do not observe people using language during the first several years of life fail to develop normal language skills. Evidence for this comes from case studies of people who were deprived of language in childhood (Goldin-Meadow, 1978). One of the most documented—and deeply troubling—cases centers on a young girl known as Genie.

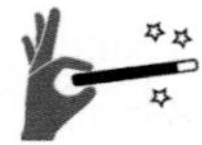

...BELIEVE IT...OR NOT

GENIE THE "FERAL CHILD" In 1970 a social worker in Arcadia, California, discovered a most horrifying case of child neglect and abuse. "Genie," as researchers came to call her, was 13 at the time her situation came to the attention of the authorities, though she barely looked 7. Feeble and emaciated, the child could not even stand up straight. Genie was not capable of chewing food or using a toilet, and she could not articulate a single word (Curtiss, Fromkin, Krashen, Rigler, & Rigler, 1974; PBS, 1997, March 4).

Between the ages of 20 months and 13 years, Genie had been locked away in a dark room, strapped to a potty chair or confined in a cagelike crib. Her father beat her when she made any type of noise. There, Genie stayed for 12 years, alone in silence, deprived of physical activity, sensory stimulation, and affection (Curtiss et al., 1974).

AT AGE 13, SHE COULD NOT EVEN SPEAK

When Genie was taken from her family at age 13, "there was little evidence that she had acquired any language; she did not speak" (Curtiss et al., 1974, p. 127). Researchers tried to build Genie's vocabulary, teaching her basic principles of syntax, and she made considerable gains, eventually speaking meaningful sentences. But some aspects of language, such as the ability to use the passive tense ("The carrot was given to the rabbit") and words like "what" and "which," continued to mystify her (Goldin-Meadow, 1978).

Similar outcomes have been observed in other "feral" children. Consider the example of 6-year-old Danielle Crockett of Florida, discovered by authorities in 2005. Living among cockroaches and excrement in her mother's home, Danielle was starving and unable to speak (DeGregory, 2008, July 31). After being removed from the home and adopted by a loving family, Danielle learned a variety of skills, such as

telegraphic speech Two-word phrases typically used by infants around the age of 18 months.

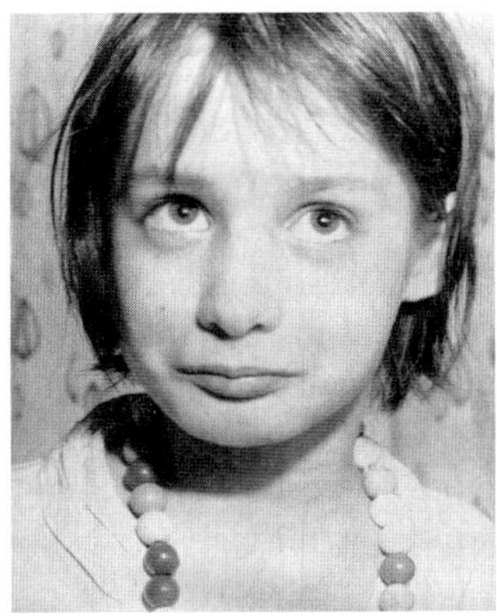

"Modern-Day Genie"?
Genie the "feral child" (left) and Danielle Crockett (now Danielle Lierow) with her adoptive parents and brother. There are many parallels between the cases of Genie and Danielle. Both were found living alone in small rooms, deprived of stimulation and affection, and severely malnourished. At the time of their discovery, they were unable to eat solid foods, use the bathroom, stand upright without assistance, and communicate with language (Curtiss et al., 1974; DeGregory, 2008, July 31). Left: Bettmann/Getty Images. Right: Tampa Bay Times/Melissa Lyttle/The Image Works.

brushing her teeth and using a computer. However, her speech is extremely limited; she can only articulate short phrases such as "I love you" (Owen, 2016, June 22; Times Staff Writer, 2014, June 18).

Why do children like Genie and Danielle have trouble mastering certain linguistic skills—is it because they missed a critical window of development? Some psychologists suggest there is indeed a *critical period* for language acquisition. Critical periods are times during development when "certain capacities are readily shaped or altered by experience," leading to "irreversible changes in brain function" (Knudsen, 2004, p. 1412). Until a certain age, children are highly receptive to learning language, but after that period ends, acquiring a first language that is age-appropriate and "normal" is difficult (Friedmann & Rusou, 2015; Kuhl, Conboy, Padden, Nelson, & Pruitt, 2005). Others propose that language development occurs during *sensitive periods,* which are characterized by substantial, but not necessarily irreversible, changes in the brain (Knudsen, 2004). Perhaps *both* critical and sensitive periods come into play: "Language acquisition is characterized by multiple critical and sensitive periods, with different onsets and offsets and different dynamics" (Werker & Hensch, 2015, p. 175).

You may be wondering what has become of Genie after all these years. Reporters and researchers have attempted to find out where she is and how she is doing, but human services agencies in California have not been forthcoming. Now about 60 years old, Genie "apparently remains in state care" (Carroll, 2016, July 14, para. 8).

At Play with Piaget
Developmental psychologist Jean Piaget (center) works with students in a New York City classroom. Piaget's research focused on school-age children, including his own three, who became participants in some of his studies. Children think differently from adults, Piaget proposed, and they experience cognitive development in distinct stages. Bill Anderson/Science Source.

Lessons from Piaget

LO 9 Discuss the key elements of Piaget's and Vygotsky's theories of cognitive development.

Language is just one domain of cognitive development. How do other processes like memory and problem solving evolve through childhood? Swiss biologist and developmental psychologist Jean Piaget (pee-uh-ZHAY; 1896–1980) was among the first to propose that infants have cognitive abilities.

One important component of cognition, according to Piaget (1936/1952), is the **schema** [SKEE-muh], a collection of ideas that serves as a building block of understanding. Young children create these schemas by learning about functional relationships. The schema "toy," for example, might include any object used for play, such as a doll, truck, or ball. As children mature, so do their schemas, which begin to organize their thinking around more abstract categories, such as "love" (romantic

schema A collection of ideas that represents a basic unit of understanding.

love, love for one's country, and so on). In other words, they expand their schemas in response to experiences.

Piaget (1936/1952) believed humans are biologically driven to advance intellectually, partly because they have an innate need to maintain *cognitive equilibrium,* or a feeling of cognitive balance. Suppose a toddler's schema of house pets only includes small dogs like his own, which he recognizes as having fur, four legs, and a tail. When he sees a very large cat for the first time, he looks to his father and says "puppy," because he notices that it, too, has fur, four legs, and a tail. This is an example of **assimilation;** the child attempts to understand new information (the sight of an unfamiliar small animal) using his already existing knowledge base, or schema (the characteristics of small animals familiar to him). Hearing the mistake, his father responds, "That's a cat, and cats say 'meow.' 'Woof' is what puppies say." This shakes up the child's notion of what a house pet is, causing an uncomfortable sense of *disequilibrium* that motivates him to restore cognitive balance. The new information about this four-legged creature is confusing and it cannot be assimilated. Instead, the child must use **accommodation,** the restructuring of old notions to make a place for new information. In this case, he forms a new schema: *Small furry animals with four legs and a tail that say "meow" are cats.* Both assimilation and accommodation enable great strides in cognitive growth. We assimilate new information to fit into old ways of thinking, and we accommodate old ways of thinking to understand new information.

As noted earlier, psychologists do not always agree on whether development is continuous or occurs in steps. Piaget (1936/1952) proposed that cognitive development occurs in four stages with distinct beginnings and endings **(INFOGRAPHIC 8.3).**

SENSORIMOTOR STAGE From birth to about age 2 is what Piaget called the **sensorimotor stage.** Infants use their sensory and motor activities to explore the surrounding world—crawling around, reaching for things, and handling objects with their mouths, fingers, and toes. It's a nerve-racking process for parents ("Please do *not* put that shoe in your mouth!"), but an important part of cognitive development.

One significant milestone of the sensorimotor stage is **object permanence,** or an infant's realization that objects and people still exist when they are out of sight or touch. While playing with babies, Piaget observed how they react when a toy is hidden under a blanket. Those who had reached the object permanence milestone realized the toy still existed even though it was out of sight; they would actively look for it (Piaget, 1936/1952). Babies who had not reached this stage would continue playing as if nothing were missing.

PREOPERATIONAL STAGE The next stage in Piaget's cognitive development theory is the **preoperational stage,** which occurs between ages 2 and 7. Rather than relying primarily on sensory and motor activities, children in this stage start using language to explore and understand their worlds. They ask questions and use symbolic thinking in their pretend and fantasy play. Dirt and sticks in a bowl might symbolize food for the baby doll. A toy truck becomes a real fire engine rushing to extinguish flames in a burning building. Children in the preoperational stage tend to be somewhat limited by their **egocentrism,** primarily imagining the world from their own perspective (see the Three Mountains task in Infographic 8.3). This egocentrism makes it hard to understand another person's point of view, but it does not necessarily mean children are selfish or spoiled. Egocentrism may dominate during this period, but a *theory of mind* is also developing: Children begin to understand that other people have thoughts, emotions, and perceptions. For example, "an adult knows certain things that they, themselves, do not" (Atance & Caza, 2018, p. 862). Theory of mind is

assimilation Using existing knowledge and ideas to understand new information and experiences.

accommodation A restructuring of old ideas to make a place for new information.

sensorimotor stage Piaget's stage of cognitive development during which infants use their sensory capabilities and motor skills to learn about the surrounding world.

object permanence A milestone of the sensorimotor stage of cognitive development; an infant's realization that objects and people still exist even when out of sight or touch.

preoperational stage Piaget's stage of cognitive development during which children can start to use language to explore and understand their worlds.

egocentrism When a person is only able to imagine the world from his or her own perspective.

Piaget's Theory of Cognitive Development

Jean Piaget proposed that children's cognitive development occurs in stages characterized by particular cognitive abilities. These stages have distinct beginnings and endings.

Formal Operational
Child is now able to think logically and systematically and is capable of hypothetical thinking.

Concrete Operational
Child understands operations and thinks more logically in reference to concrete objects and circumstances.

Preoperational
Child uses symbolic thinking to explore and understand the world. Children at this stage are known for magical thinking and egocentrism.

Sensorimotor
Child uses sensory capabilities and motor activities to learn about the world; develops object permanence.

Piaget's four stages of cognitive development

Sensorimotor birth–2 yrs

Preoperational 2–7 yrs

Concrete Operational 7–11 yrs

Formal Operational 11 yrs and up

How do we assess a child's stage of cognitive development?
Piaget developed techniques to test characteristic capabilities associated with each stage.

Object Permanence test: Does the child realize objects continue to exist when they are hidden? Infants who have developed object permanence will search for an object.

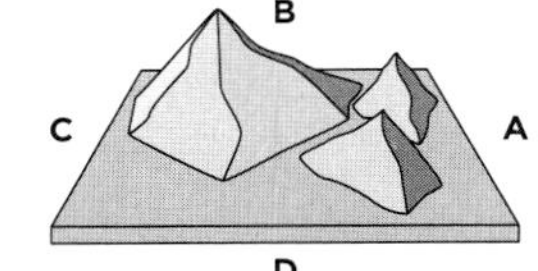

Three Mountains task tests egocentrism. Can the child imagine a perspective different from her own? "What would you see if you were standing at Point B?"

Conservation of Volume test assesses understanding of operations. Does a child understand that the amount of liquid remains constant when it is poured into a container with a different shape?

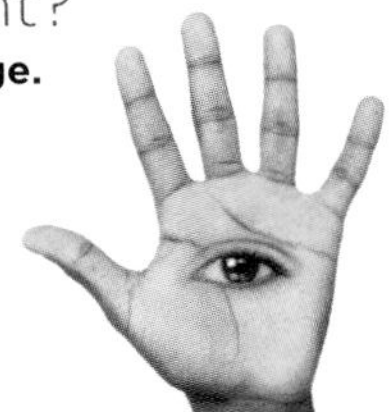

Third Eye task tests formal operational thought. "If you had a third eye, where would you put it?" Children at this stage come up with logical, innovative answers.

FIGURE 8.4
Conservation Tasks
Children in the preoperational stage don't realize that properties like volume and mass stay constant when items are rearranged or reshaped. Tasks like these are used to test children's understanding of conservation.

Type of Conservation Task	Original Presentation	Alteration	Question	Preoperational Child's Answer
Volume	Two equal beakers of liquid	Pour one into a taller, narrower beaker.	Does one beaker have more liquid?	The taller beaker has more liquid.
Mass	Two equal lumps of clay	Roll one lump into a long, hotdog shape.	Does one lump weigh more?	The original lump weighs more.

Hello, Doctor
During the preoperational stage (ages 2–7), many children relish imaginative play. In addition to pretending to be a "baker" in her kitchen, Niyah played the role of the family "doctor," nursing the wounds of grandmothers, aunts, uncles, and, of course, her mom. "She would always fix my boo boos, even if I didn't have any," Ericka says. "She was very nurturing."
Courtesy Ericka Harley.

a "component of social competence" and may impact school readiness (Cavadel & Frye, 2017, p. 2290).

According to Piaget (1936/1952), children in the preoperational stage have not yet mastered *operations,* the logical reasoning processes older children and adults use to understand the world. For example, young children have a difficult time understanding the *reversibility* of some actions and events. They may have trouble comprehending that vanilla ice cream can be refrozen after it melts, but not turned back into sugar, milk, and vanilla. This difficulty with operations is also apparent in errors involving **conservation,** which refers to the unchanging properties of volume, mass, or amount in relation to appearance (**Figure 8.4**). For example, if you take two masses of clay of the same shape and size, and then roll only one of them out into a hotdog shape, a child in this stage may think that the hotdog-shaped clay contains more clay than the undisturbed clump. Or, the child may see that the newly formed clump of clay is skinnier and therefore assume it is smaller. Children in the preoperational stage do not understand that an object stays fundamentally the same, even if it is manipulated or takes on a different appearance.

CONCRETE OPERATIONAL STAGE Around age 7, children enter what Piaget called the **concrete operational stage.** They begin to think more logically, but mainly in reference to concrete objects and circumstances: things that can be seen or touched, or are well defined by strict rules. Children in this stage tend to be less egocentric and can understand the concept of conservation. However, they still have trouble with abstract ideas and hypothetical thinking. For example, a 7-year-old may respond with a blank stare when asked a question such as, "What would you do if you could travel to the future?" or, "If you had to choose between losing your eyebrows or your eyelashes, which would you give up?"

FORMAL OPERATIONAL STAGE At age 11, children enter Piaget's **formal operational stage;** they begin to think more logically and systematically. For example, they can solve problems such as the Third Eye task (Infographic 8.3), which asks children where they would put a third eye, and why. ("I'd put it in the back of my head so that I could see what is going on behind my back.") Such logical abilities do not necessarily develop overnight, and are likely to advance in the pursuit of interests and skills developed on the job. Piaget suggested that not everyone reaches this stage of formal operations. But to succeed in most colleges, this type of logical thinking is essential; students need to use abstract ideas to solve problems.

conservation Refers to the unchanging properties of volume, mass, or amount in relation to appearance.

concrete operational stage Piaget's stage of cognitive development during which children begin to think more logically, but mainly in reference to concrete objects and circumstances.

formal operational stage Piaget's stage of cognitive development during which children begin to think more logically and systematically.

WHAT DO THE CRITICS SAY? Cognitive development may occur in stages with distinct characteristics, as Piaget suggested, but critics contend that transitions between stages are likely gradual, and may not represent complete leaps from one type of thinking to the next. Some believe Piaget's theory underestimates children's cognitive abilities. For example, object permanence may occur sooner than Piaget suggested, depending on factors such as the length of time an object is out of sight (Baillargeon, Spelke, & Wasserman, 1985; Bremner, Slater, & Johnson, 2015). Others question Piaget's assertion that children reach the formal operational stage by 11 to 12 years of age, and that no further delineations can be made between the cognitive abilities of adolescents and adults of various ages.

Lessons from Vygotsky

Another major criticism of Piaget's theory is that it overlooks the social interactions influencing child development. The work of Russian psychologist Lev Vygotsky (vie-GOT-skee) helps fill in some of these gaps. Vygotsky was particularly interested in how social and cultural factors affect a child's cognitive development (Vygotsky, 1934/1962). As he saw it, children are like apprentices to others who are more capable and experienced (Zaretskii, 2009), and those who receive help from older children and adults progress more quickly in their cognitive abilities.

One way to support children's cognitive development is through **scaffolding:** pushing them to go just beyond what they are competent and comfortable doing, but also providing help in a decreasing manner. A parent gives support when necessary, but allows the child to solve problems independently: "Successful scaffolding is like a wave, rising to offer help when needed and receding as the child regains control of the task" (Hammond et al., 2012, p. 275). Instructors often use scaffolding, by having students start with an outline, then requiring a rough draft, and adding complexity to an assignment as the semester progresses.

In order to scaffold effectively, we should consider not only what children know, but also where they are in their current development and what remains to be learned. We must consider a child's **zone of proximal development,** which includes cognitive tasks that can be accomplished alone and those that require guidance and help from others. We should create an environment that provides activities a child can achieve alone, and challenges that can be overcome with help.

Culture and Cognition
A man and a boy thresh rice in the fields of Madagascar. What this child learns and how his cognitive development unfolds are shaped by the circumstances of his environment. Children reared in agricultural societies may acquire different cognitive skill sets than those raised in urban, industrialized settings.
Yvan Travert/Corbis.

Vygotsky also emphasized that learning always occurs in a cultural context. Children across the world have different sets of expected learning outcomes, from raising sheep to weaving blankets to completing a geometry proof. We need to keep these differences in mind when exploring their cognitive development.

Until now, we have focused on physical and cognitive development, but recall we are also interested in *socioemotional* development.

Temperament and Attachment

"BEST BABY EVER" After Niyah was born, Ericka finished high school and began working full-time. "She went to school, she worked, she took care of Niyah, and she took her to the babysitter," says Joan. "She lived in my house, but she took full responsibility for everything." Niyah spent only 2–3 days a month with her father, so Ericka was essentially a single parent. But it was manageable because Niyah was such a good-natured and happy baby. She was, according to Ericka, "the best baby ever."

scaffolding Pushing children to go just beyond what they are competent and comfortable doing, while providing help in a decreasing manner.

zone of proximal development The range of cognitive tasks that can be accomplished alone and those that require the guidance and help of others.

You Asked, Ericka Answers

http://qrs.ly/6v5a5dq

Do you feel that being a single mother affected Aa'Niyah's development?

Ericka was lucky, because not all babies are so easygoing. Niyah began sleeping solid 8-hour stretches when she was just 3 months old, but many newborns wake up crying every 2 hours during the night. They may cry for no obvious reason, or only fall asleep when nursing or riding in a car. Some babies experience *separation anxiety,* which typically peaks at approximately 13 months (Hertenstein & McCullough, 2005). "I don't ever remember there being a situation where she would just not stop crying," Ericka says. Apparently, Niyah was born with a calm and happy *temperament.*

FROM LOW-KEY TO HIGH-STRUNG **Temperament,** which refers to a person's distinct patterns of emotional reactions and behaviors, is apparent across all developmental stages. We begin to see evidence of temperament in the first days of life. "High-reactive" infants exhibit a great deal of distress when exposed to unfamiliar stimuli, such as new sights, sounds, and smells. "Low-reactive" infants do not respond to new stimuli with great distress (Fox, Snidman, Haas, Degnan, & Kagan, 2015; Kagan, 2003). Classification as high- and low-reactive is based on measures of behavior, emotional response, and physiological factors, such as heart rate and blood pressure (Kagan, 1985, 2003).

These different characteristics seem to be innate, as they are apparent from birth and consistent in infants' daily lives (Plomin, DeFries, Knopik, & Neiderhiser, 2013). However, the environment can also shape temperament (Briley & Tucker-Drob, 2014). Factors such as maternal education, neighborhood, and paternal occupation through adolescence can predict characteristics of adult temperament, such as shyness and impulsiveness (Congdon et al., 2012).

Easy, Baby
Most babies can be classified according to one of three fundamental temperaments: About 40% are "easy," meaning they are generally content and follow predictable schedules; approximately 10% are "difficult," or hard to please and irregular in their schedules; and another 15% are "slow to warm up," meaning they struggle with change but eventually adjust. The remaining 35% do not fall into any one category. YinYang/Getty Images.

EASY, DIFFICULT, OR SLOW TO WARM UP? Another way to classify babies is to focus on how easy they are to care for. Researchers have found that the majority of infants can be classified as having one of three fundamental temperaments (Thomas & Chess, 1986). Around 40% are considered "easy" babies; they are easy to care for because they follow regular eating and sleeping schedules. These happy babies can be soothed when upset and don't appear to get rattled by transitions or changes in their environments. "Difficult" babies (around 10%) are more challenging because they don't seem to have a set schedule for eating and sleeping, nor do they deal well with transitions or changes in the environment. Often irritable and unhappy, these babies are far less responsive than their "easy" counterparts to the soothing attempts of caregivers. They also tend to be very active, kicking their legs on the changing table and wiggling around in their strollers. "Slow to warm up" babies (around 15%) are not as irritable (or active) as difficult babies, but they are not fond of change. Give them enough time, however, and they will adapt.

While these temperament categories are useful, it's important to note that 35% of babies share the characteristics of more than one type and therefore are hard to classify. And, no matter what their temperament, babies are sensitive to input from parents and other caregivers. A very important component of that input is physical touch. If you don't believe us, consider the fascinating and harrowing experiment described below.

temperament Characteristic differences in behavioral patterns and emotional reactions that are evident from birth.

MONKEYS LIKE TO KEEP IN TOUCH Harry Harlow, Margaret Harlow, and their colleagues at the University of Wisconsin were among the first to explore the importance of physical touch in an experimental situation (Harlow, Harlow, & Suomi, 1971).

These researchers were initially interested in learning how physical contact affects the development of loving relationships between infants and mothers. Realizing that **such a study** would be difficult to conduct with human infants, they turned to newborn macaque monkeys (Harlow, 1958).

CONNECTIONS

In **Chapter 1,** we discussed the importance of ensuring the ethical treatment of research participants (human and animal). Psychologists must do no harm and safeguard the welfare of participants. Obviously, the Harlows could not take human newborns from their parents to study the importance of physical contact. Many question the ethics of using newborn monkeys in this manner.

Here's how the experiment worked: Infant monkeys were put in cages alone, each with two artificial "surrogate" mothers. One surrogate was outfitted with a soft cloth and heated with a bulb, and thus provided some degree of "contact comfort." The other surrogate mother did not provide such comfort, as she was made of wire mesh with no cloth covering. Both of these surrogates could be set up to feed the infants. In one study, half the infant monkeys received milk from the cloth surrogates and the other half got their milk from the wire surrogates. Regardless of which provided milk, the infant monkeys showed a strong preference for the cloth mother, holding and touching her 15 to 18 hours a day, as opposed to 1 to 2 hours for the wire mother.

Harlow and colleagues also created situations in which they purposefully scared the infant monkeys with a moving toy bear, and found that the great majority of them (around 80%) ran to the cloth mother, regardless of whether she provided milk. In times of fear and uncertainty, these infant monkeys found more comfort in the soft, cloth mothers (Harlow, 1958; Harlow & Zimmerman, 1959). Do you think human children would do the same?

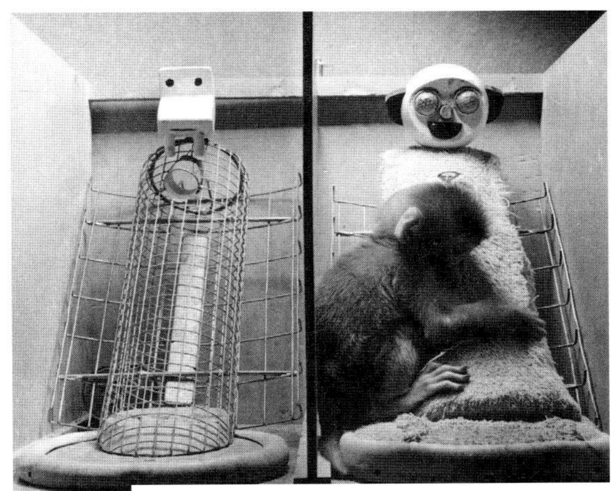

Soft Like Mommy
A baby monkey in a laboratory experiment clings to a furry mother surrogate. Research by Harry and Margaret Harlow and colleagues at the University of Wisconsin showed that physical comfort is important for the socioemotional development of these animals. When given the choice between a wire mesh "mother" that provided milk and a cloth-covered "mother" without milk, most of the monkeys opted to snuggle with the cuddly cloth-covered one (Harlow, 1958). SCIENCE SOURCE/Getty Images.

ATTACHMENT Physical contact plays an important role in **attachment,** or the degree to which an infant feels an emotional connection with primary caregivers. British psychiatrist John Bowlby (1907–1990) was the first to formulate a theory of attachment, proposing that infants naturally form an emotional bond with caregivers (Polat, 2017). Expanding on Bowlby's work, American-Canadian psychologist Mary Ainsworth (1913–1999) studied the attachment styles of infants between 12 and 18 months using a research procedure called the *Strange Situation* (Ainsworth, 1979, 1985; Ainsworth & Bell, 1970; Ainsworth, Blehar, Waters, & Wall, 1978; Van Rosmalen, van der Horst, & Van der Veer, 2016). In one study, (1) a mother and child are in a room alone. (2) A stranger enters, and (3) the mother then exits the room, leaving the child in the unfamiliar environment with the stranger, who tries to interact with the child. (4) The mother returns to the room but leaves again, and then returns once more. At this point, (5) the stranger departs. During this observation, the researchers note the child's anxiety before and after the stranger arrives, willingness to explore the environment, and reaction to the mother's return. Here are three of the response patterns observed:

- **Secure attachment:** The majority of the children were mildly upset when their mothers left the room, but were easily soothed upon her return, quickly returning to play. These children seemed confident that their needs would be met and felt safe exploring their environment, using the caregiver as a *secure base.*
- **Avoidant attachment:** Some of the children displayed no distress when their mothers left, and no signs of wanting to interact with their mothers when they returned. They were happy to play in the room without looking at their mothers or the stranger.
- **Ambivalent:** Children in this group were quite upset and very focused on their mothers, showing signs of wanting to be held, but unable to be soothed. They were angry (often pushing away their mothers) and not interested in returning to play.

attachment The degree to which an infant feels an emotional connection with primary caregivers.

Feeling Secure
A father takes his baby underwater. Infants are more willing to explore their environments when they have caregivers who consistently meet their needs and provide a secure base.
Blend Images - Erik Isakson/Getty Images.

Ideally, parents and caregivers provide a secure base for infants, and are ready to help regulate emotions (soothe or calm) or meet other needs. This makes infants feel comfortable exploring their environments. Ainsworth and colleagues (1978) suggested that development, both physical and psychological, is greatly influenced by the quality of an infant's attachment to caregivers. More recent research indicates that attachment impacts cognition, as children with a secure base have more accurate memories of their experiences in settings like the Strange Situation (Chae et al., 2018).

Early research in this area focused on infants' attachment to their mothers. Subsequent studies suggest that we should examine infants' attachment to multiple individuals (mother, father, caregivers at day care, and close relatives), as well as cross-cultural differences in attachment (Field, 1996; Rothbaum, Weisz, Pott, Miyake, & Morelli, 2000; Vicedo, 2017).

Critics of the Strange Situation method suggest it creates an artificial environment and fails to provide good measures of how infant–mother pairs act naturally (Vicedo, 2017). Some suggest that temperament, not just attachment, predisposes infants to react the way they do in this setting. Those prone to anxiety and uncertainty are more likely to respond negatively (Kagan, 1985).

Attachments are formed early in childhood, but they have implications for a lifetime (Høeg et al., 2018; Lopez, Ramos, & Kim, 2018; Simpson & Rholes, 2010). Some people who experienced ambivalent attachment as infants have been described as exhibiting an "insatiability for closeness" in their adult relationships. Meanwhile, those who had secure attachments are more likely to expect that they are lovable and that others are capable of love (Cassidy, 2001). Infant attachment may even have long-term health consequences. One 32-year longitudinal study found that adults who had been insecurely attached as infants were more likely to report inflammation-based illnesses (for example, asthma, cardiovascular disease, and diabetes) than those with secure attachments (Puig, Englund, Simpson, & Collins, 2013).

Put Your Heads Together

In your group, **A**) list the characteristics of an effective caregiver or parent, and **B**) support this list using the lessons you learned from Vygotsky, Ainsworth, and the Harlow experiments.

Erikson's Psychosocial Stages

LO 10 Explain Erikson's theory of psychosocial development up until puberty.

One of the most influential theories of socioemotional development comes from German-born American psychologist Erik Erikson (1902–1994). According to Erikson, human development is marked by eight psychosocial stages, spanning infancy to old age (**Infographic 8.4;** Erikson & Erikson, 1997). Each of these stages is marked by a developmental task or an emotional crisis that must be handled successfully to allow for healthy psychological growth. The crises, according to Erikson, stem from conflicts between the needs of the individual and expectations of society (Erikson, 1993). Successful resolution of a stage makes it possible to approach the following stage with more tools, while unsuccessful

INFOGRAPHIC 8.4

Erikson's Eight Stages

Psychologist Erik Erikson proposed that human development proceeds through eight psychosocial stages, outlined below. Each stage is marked by a developmental task or an emotional crisis that must be handled successfully to allow for healthy psychological growth (information from Erikson and Erikson, 1997). Critics contend that Erikson's theory does not rest on a solid foundation of scientific evidence, but it provides a useful model for conceptualizing the different phases of human life.

+ POSITIVE RESOLUTION ✖ NEGATIVE RESOLUTION

BIRTH to 1 YEAR)	Trust versus mistrust	+ Trusts others, has faith in others. ✖ Mistrusts others, expects the worst of people.
1 to 3 YEARS	Autonomy versus shame and doubt	+ Learns to be autonomous and independent. ✖ Learns to feel shame and doubt when freedom to explore is restricted.
3 to 6 YEARS	Initiative versus guilt	+ Becomes more responsible, shows the ability to follow through. ✖ Develops guilt and anxiety when unable to handle responsibilities.
6 YEARS to PUBERTY	Industry versus inferiority	+ Feels a sense of accomplishment and increased self-esteem. ✖ Feels inferiority or incompetence, which can later lead to unstable work habits.
PUBERTY to TWENTIES	Ego identity versus role confusion	+ Tries out roles and emerges with a strong sense of values, beliefs, and goals. ✖ Lacks a solid identity, experiences withdrawal, isolation, or continued role confusion.
YOUNG ADULTHOOD (20s to 40s)	Intimacy versus isolation	+ Creates meaningful, deep relationships. ✖ Lives in isolation.
MIDDLE ADULTHOOD (40s to mid-60s)	Generativity versus stagnation	+ Makes a positive impact on the next generation through parenting, community involvement, or work that is valuable and significant. ✖ Experiences boredom, conceit, and selfishness.
LATE ADULTHOOD (mid-60s and older)	Integrity versus despair	+ Feels a sense of accomplishment and satisfaction. ✖ Feels regret and dissatisfaction.

Baby sitting: José Manuel Gelpi Diaz / Alamy, Baby pointing: Amos Morgan/Getty Images, Girl playing doctor: DragonImages/Getty Images, Girl with dog: Lane Oatey/Blue Jean Images/Getty Images, Soccer player: Ljupco Smokovski/Shutterstock, Young couple: LJSphotography / Alamy, Farmer: Iakov Filimonov / Alamy, Elderly couple: Hongqi Zhang / Alamy.

resolution creates difficulties. Let's take a look at the stages associated with infancy and childhood.

- **Trust versus mistrust (birth to 1 year):** In order for infants to learn to trust, caregivers must attend to their needs. If caregivers are not responsive, infants will develop in the direction of mistrust, always expecting the worst of people and the environment.
- **Autonomy versus shame and doubt (1 to 3 years):** If caregivers provide freedom to explore, children learn how to be autonomous and independent. If exploration is restricted and children are punished, they will likely learn to feel shame and doubt.
- **Initiative versus guilt (3 to 6 years):** During this time, children have more opportunities to extend themselves socially. Often they become more responsible and capable of creating and executing plans. If children do not have responsibilities or cannot handle them, they will develop feelings of guilt and anxiety.
- **Industry versus inferiority (6 years to puberty):** Children in this age range are generally engaged in a variety of learning tasks. When successful, they feel a sense of accomplishment, and their self-esteem increases. When unsuccessful, they feel a sense of inferiority or incompetence, theoretically leading to unstable work habits or unemployment later on.

Erikson's theory includes four additional stages (Infographic 8.4), all discussed in the upcoming sections on adolescence and adulthood. Are you ready to venture into these next phases of life?

✓ show what you know

1. The ______________ reflex occurs when you stroke a baby's cheek; she opens her mouth and turns her head toward your hand. The ______________ reflex occurs when you touch the baby's lips; this reflex helps with feeding.
2. When we try to understand new information and experiences by incorporating them into our existing knowledge and ideas, we are using what Piaget called:
   a. the rooting reflex.
   b. schemas.
   c. accommodation.
   d. assimilation.
3. Vygotsky recommended supporting children's cognitive development through ______________, pushing them a little harder while gradually reducing the amount of help you give them.
4. Erikson proposed that socioemotional development comprises eight psychosocial stages that include:
   a. scaffolding.
   b. physical maturation.
   c. developmental tasks or emotional crises.
   d. conservation.
5. What can new parents expect regarding the sequence of their child's language development, and how might they encourage it?

✓ CHECK YOUR ANSWERS IN APPENDIX C.

The Teenage Years

WALKING ON PINS AND NEEDLES Ericka got pregnant with Niyah when she was 16 years old, and it was not something she had planned. Like many teenagers, she was probably living in the moment and not too worried about the long-term consequences of her decisions. The teen years were also a time of rebellion. Although Ericka kept up with her schoolwork and made honor roll each semester, skipping school was one of her favorite escapes. Joan had no idea her daughter was home watching TV during school hours. When the school's automated system called to report the absence, Ericka (home alone) would pick up the phone before it went to voicemail. Then she would erase the school phone number from caller ID. Adolescence also brought out the emotional side of Ericka. Unable to predict what might trigger one of Ericka's angry outbursts, Joan often felt like she was "walking on pins and needles" in her own house. "I don't want to talk about it," Ericka would say defensively, or "I want to go to Grandma's."

You Asked, Ericka Answers

http://qrs.ly/6v5a5dq

Do you wish you would have had a "typical" adolescence?

Behaviors like these are stereotypical of teenagers, or *adolescents*. **Adolescence** refers to the transition period between late childhood and early adulthood, and it can be challenging for both parents and kids.

A Time of Change

Give examples of significant physical changes that occur during adolescence.

Adolescence is a time of dramatic physical growth, comparable to that which occurs during fetal development. The "growth spurt" includes rapid changes in height, weight, and bone growth, and usually begins between ages 9 and 10 for girls and ages 12 and 16 for boys. Sex hormones, which influence this growth and development, are at high levels.

Puberty is the period during which the body changes and becomes sexually mature and able to reproduce. During puberty, the **primary sex characteristics** (reproductive organs) mature; these include the ovaries, uterus, vagina, penis, scrotum, and testes. At the same time, the **secondary sex characteristics** (physical features not associated with reproduction) become more distinct; these include pubic, underarm, and body hair (**Figure 8.5**).

It is during this time that girls experience **menarche** (meh-NAR-key), or the beginning of menstruation. Menarche can occur as early as age 9 or after age 14, but typical onset is around 12 or 13. Boys have their first ejaculation, **spermarche** (sper-MAR-key), during this time period (Ladouceur, 2012), but when it occurs is more difficult to specify, as boys may be reluctant to talk about the event (Mendle, Harden, Brooks-Gunn, & Graber, 2010).

Not everyone goes through puberty at the same time. Researchers have linked the timing of puberty to diet, exercise, and exposure to chemicals such as pesticides

Growing Up Fast
Members of the St. Thomas Boys Choir in Leipzig, Germany, practice a chant in rehearsal. Choir directors are struggling with the fact that young boys' voices are deepening earlier as the years go by. In the mid-1700s, voice changes reportedly occurred in singers aged 17 or 18; these days, the average age is closer to 10 (Mendle & Ferrero, 2012). No one is certain why boys are hitting puberty sooner, but some researchers point to a correlation with an increasing body mass index (Sørensen, Aksglaede, Petersen, & Juul, 2010). Wolfgang Kluge/picture-alliance/dpa/AP Images.

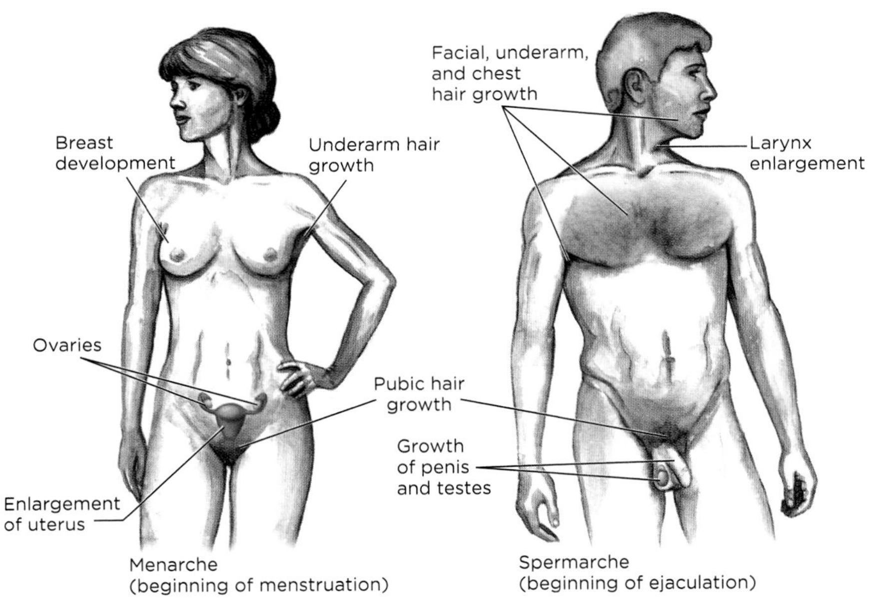

FIGURE 8.5
Physical Changes at Puberty
During puberty, the body changes and becomes sexually mature and able to reproduce. The primary sex characteristics (reproductive organs), including the ovaries, uterus, vagina, penis, scrotum, and testes, mature. Meanwhile, secondary sex characteristics, such as breasts and pubic hair, become more distinct.

adolescence The transition period between late childhood and early adulthood.

puberty The period of development during which the body changes and becomes sexually mature and capable of reproduction.

primary sex characteristics Organs associated with reproduction, including the ovaries, uterus, vagina, penis, scrotum, and testes.

secondary sex characteristics Body characteristics, such as pubic hair, underarm hair, and enlarged breasts, that develop in puberty but are not associated with reproduction.

menarche The point at which menstruation begins.

spermarche A boy's first ejaculation.

(Seltenrich, 2015, October; Windham et al., 2015). Genetics also may play a role, as the timing of puberty for both mother and father may be a "strong influence" on that of their children (Wohlfahrt-Veje et al., 2016, p. 7).

Sexual interest peaks in adolescence, yet the brain is not fully developed; this combination of factors can set the stage for risky sexual behaviors. Over half of new ***sexually transmitted infections*** affect people ages 15–24, yet this group represents only 25% of the sexually active population (CDC, 2017). Sexually transmitted infections are especially risky for adolescents because such infections often go untreated and can lead to a host of problems, including long-term sterility.

synonyms
sexually transmitted infections sexually transmitted diseases

LO 12 Summarize Piaget's description of cognitive changes occurring in adolescence.

WHAT ARE THEY THINKING? Alongside the remarkable physical changes of adolescence are equally remarkable cognitive developments. As noted earlier, children in this age range are better able to understand abstract and hypothetical concepts. This ability indicates that a teenager has entered Piaget's formal operational stage, which begins in adolescence and continues into adulthood. Individuals in this stage begin to use deductive reasoning to draw conclusions and critical thinking to approach arguments. They can reason abstractly, classify ideas, use symbols, and think beyond the current moment.

A specific type of egocentrism emerges in adolescence. Before this age, children can only imagine the world from their own point of view, but during adolescence they start becoming aware of other people's perspectives. Egocentrism is still apparent, however, as adolescents believe that others share their preoccupations and ways of thinking. For example, a teenager who focuses on his appearance may think that others focus on his appearance, too (Elkind, 1967).

This intense focus on the self may contribute to feelings of immortality, which can result in risk-taking behaviors (Elkind, 1967; Lin, 2016). Because adolescents have not had many life experiences, they may fail to consider the long-term consequences of behaviors such as unprotected sex or drug use. Their focus on the present (for example, having fun in the moment) outweighs their ability to assess the potential repercussions (pregnancy or addiction). To help adolescents avoid risky behaviors such as smoking, we might focus on short-term consequences like bad breath when kissing a partner, and long-term dangers such as lung cancer (Lin, 2016; Robbins & Bryan, 2004).

Too Young
A teen inmate sits in her room at a maximum-security juvenile facility in Illinois. As a result of the 2005 *Roper v. Simmons* decision (Borra, 2005), defendants being tried for crimes committed before age 18 are no longer candidates for the death penalty. The U.S. Supreme Court arrived at this decision after carefully weighing evidence submitted by the American Psychological Association (APA) and others, which suggests that the juvenile mind is still developing and vulnerable to impulsivity and poor decision making (APA, 2013b). Chicago Tribune/Getty Images.

ACTING WITHOUT THINKING Characteristics of the adolescent brain are thought to contribute to risk taking. The limbic system, which is responsible for processing emotions and perceiving rewards and punishments, undergoes significant development during adolescence. Meanwhile, more axons are becoming myelinated in the prefrontal cortex, which strengthens connections between neural circuits involved in planning, weighing consequences, and multitasking (Steinberg, 2012). Because the prefrontal cortex develops slower than the limbic system, the adolescent may not foresee the possible consequences of reward-seeking activities. Activity in the limbic system overrides that in the prefrontal cortex, sometimes resulting in poor decisions. Changes to the structure of the brain continue through adolescence, resulting in a fully adult brain between ages 22 and 25, and a decline in risk-taking behaviors (Giedd et al., 2009; Steinberg, 2010, 2012). But take note: Studies on brain structure provide results for groups, so we cannot assume they apply to every individual (Bonnie & Scott, 2013).

Social, Emotional Teens

Adolescence is a time of great socioemotional development. Conflicts may arise as teenagers search for their **identity,** or sense of self based on values, beliefs, and goals. Until this point in development, identity was based primarily on the values and beliefs of parents and caregivers. Adolescents explore who they are by trying out different ideas in a variety of categories, including politics and religion. Then they begin to commit to a particular set of beliefs and attitudes, making decisions to engage in activities related to their evolving identity. However, their commitment may shift back and forth, sometimes on a day-to-day basis (Klimstra et al., 2010). The process of identity formation is, to some degree, influenced by genetics (Markovitch, Luyckx, Klimstra, Abramson, & Knafo-Noam, 2017).

Describe how Erikson explained changes in identity during adolescence.

"I'm Kind of a Big Deal"
Research indicates that young people in Western countries are becoming increasingly narcissistic (Alfano, 2015, June 1; Dingfelder, 2011, February). Those who are narcissistic "feel superior to others, fantasize about personal successes, and believe they deserve special treatment" (Brummelman et al., 2015, p. 3659). What makes young people narcissistic? Mom and Dad may be partly to blame. Some evidence suggests that narcissism is encouraged by parents who view their kids as "more special and more entitled than other children" (p. 3660).
Westend61/Getty Images.

ERIKSON AND ADOLESCENCE Erikson's theory of development addresses this important issue of identity formation (Erikson & Erikson, 1997). From puberty to the twenties is the stage of *ego identity versus role confusion,* which leads to the creation of an adult identity. When teenagers fail to resolve the tasks and crises of the first four stages, they may enter this stage with distrust toward others, and feelings of shame, guilt, and inadequacy (see Infographic 8.4 on p. 303). During this time, the developing person grapples with important life questions: *What career do I want to pursue? What religion (if any) is compatible with my beliefs?* This stage often involves "trying out" different roles. A person who fails to resolve this crisis will not have a solid sense of identity and may experience withdrawal, isolation, or continued role confusion. Resolution, on the other hand, leads to a stronger sense of values, beliefs, and goals.

WHAT PART DO PARENTS PLAY? Generally speaking, parent–adolescent relationships are positive (Paikoff & Brooks-Gunn, 1991), but conflict does increase during early adolescence (Van Doorn, Branje, & Meeus, 2011). Parent–teen struggles often relate to issues of control and parental authority and may revolve around everyday issues such as curfews and chores (Branje, 2018). Parents are routinely faced with decisions that impact the health, safety, and well-being of their children: *Should I allow my child to* **play a contact sport***? How much screen time should I permit each day? Is a midnight curfew too late?* Such dilemmas can spark disagreements between parents and teens, but the turmoil serves an important purpose; it gives teenagers practice dealing with conflict and negotiation in the context of the family (Moed et al., 2015). Fortunately, conflict tends to decline as both parties become more comfortable with the adolescent's growing sense of autonomy and self-reliance (Lichtwarck-Aschoff, Kunnen, & van Geert, 2009; Montemayor, 1983).

CONNECTIONS
In **Chapters 6** and **7,** we discussed chronic traumatic encephalopathy (CTE), a neurodegenerative disease caused by head trauma. Researchers have found that people who play contact sports are at a higher risk for CTE. Parents should consider the risks of CTE before allowing their children to play contact sports.

FRIENDS MATTER During adolescence, friends assume a new level of importance. Some parents express concern about the negative influence of peers, but the friendships formed by teens often support the types of behaviors and beliefs parents encouraged during childhood (McPherson, Smith-Lovin, & Cook, 2001). Adolescents tend to behave more impulsively around peers; their ability to "put the brakes on" may be inhibited by perceived social pressure (Albert, Chein, & Steinberg, 2013). But peers can also have a positive influence, supporting prosocial behaviors like getting good grades and helping others (Roseth, Johnson, & Johnson, 2008; Wentzel, McNamara Barry, & Caldwell, 2004). With the use of smartphones and tablets, these negative and positive influences can be transmitted through digital space.

identity A sense of self based on values, beliefs, and goals.

SOCIAL MEDIA AND PSYCHOLOGY

HAVE TEENS GONE OVERBOARD? Teenagers in the United States spend, on average, a whopping 9 hours using "entertainment media" each day. Television, videos, and music are consumed most frequently, but social media is also popular (Common Sense Media, 2015). How does all this screen time affect their well-being? Let's start with the good news: Evidence suggests that social media can provide a safe medium for self-exploration, and may facilitate friendship building (Uhls, Ellison, & Subrahmanyam, 2017). Interacting through touchscreens may also keep teenagers away from risky activities, like using drugs and alcohol. Researchers have yet to identify a causal relationship, but the rising availability of tablets and smartphones does correlate with a recent trend of decreasing alcohol and drug use (Richtel, 2017, March 13; Twenge & Park, 2017).

"ON THE BRINK OF THE WORST MENTAL-HEALTH CRISIS IN DECADES"

"Addicted" to Smartphones? Before 2007, no one had an iPhone. A decade later, the majority of U.S. teenagers (76%) had them (Piper Jaffray, 2017, Spring). According to one poll, 50% of teenagers believe they are "addicted to their mobile devices" (Common Sense Media, 2016, May, p. 2). Perhaps more disturbing, 28% believe their parents are addicted, and 51% report that they have witnessed their parents using their devices at the wheel (Common Sense Media, 2016, May). Klaus Vedfelt/Getty Images.

But here's the bad news: Overuse of digital technologies has been associated with mental health problems in young people (Flora, 2018; George, Russell, Piontak, & Odgers, 2018). For example, a study of middle and high school students in Canada found a correlation between heavy social media use (over 2 hours per day) and "poor self-rated mental health, psychological distress, suicidal ideation, or unmet need for mental health support" (Sampasa-Kanyinga & Lewis, 2015, p. 383). Using digital technologies to make social comparisons (*Was his senior trip better than mine?*) and gather feedback from others (*Do my friends like my new hairstyle?*) has been associated with depressive symptoms, especially in teens who are unpopular and/or female (Nesi & Prinstein, 2015). Such findings have some experts worried. Psychologist Jean M. Twenge of San Diego State University has been studying generational trends for over two decades, and what she has observed in people raised on the Internet (the cohort she refers to as the "iGen") is unprecedented: "Rates of teen depression and suicide have skyrocketed since 2011. It's not an exaggeration to describe iGen as being on the brink of the worst mental-health crisis in decades. Much of this deterioration can be traced to their phones" (Twenge, 2017, September, para. 10). But this is only one perspective, and studies have yet to identify definitive cause-and-effect relationships between media use, mental health, and other related variables like sleep deprivation (Flora, 2018).

Without definitive answers, what can we do with all this information? As with many things in life, moderation is key (Twenge, 2017, September). Perhaps there is even an ideal degree of moderation—a "Goldilocks" level, if you will.

From the pages of SCIENTIFIC AMERICAN

THE "GOLDILOCKS" LEVEL OF TEEN SCREEN USE

It pays to get the time spent on a device *just right.*

It's a familiar lament: Teenagers are spending all their time on digital devices, and it's wreaking havoc on their physical and mental health. But a study published in January in *Psychological Science* suggests a moderate level of use is not necessarily harmful—and may even be beneficial. The effect on well-being varies depending on the type of medium or device: TV and movies, video games, computers and smartphones, as well as the day of the week (weekday versus weekend). The optimal amount of exposure peaks at around one to two hours daily during the week and longer on weekends.

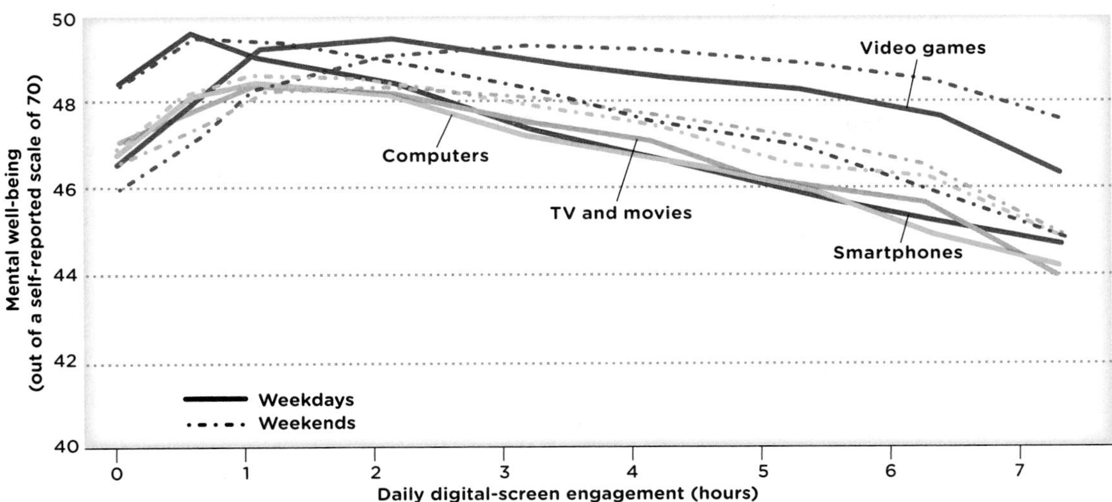

Limiting your teen's screen time is fine, but consider the benefits before you pull the plug entirely. **Tanya Lewis. Reproduced with permission. Copyright © 2017 Scientific American, a division of Nature America, Inc. All rights reserved.**

How Does Morality Develop?

LO 14 Examine Kohlberg's levels of moral development.

We cannot help but wonder how the constant presence of social media impacts morality, another important aspect of socioemotional growth. With so much communication occurring on screens, do we have enough real-world interactions to develop a sense of "right" and "wrong?" If only we could ask Lawrence Kohlberg (1927–1987). Kohlberg proposed there are three levels of moral development occurring sequentially over the life span (**Table 8.3**).

To assess the moral reasoning of his study participants, Kohlberg presented them with a variety of fictional stories. The *Heinz dilemma,* for example, is a story about a man named Heinz trying to save his critically ill wife. Heinz did not have enough money to buy a drug that could save her, so after trying unsuccessfully to borrow money, he finally decided to steal the drug. After learning about Heinz's situation,

TABLE 8.3 KOHLBERG'S STAGES OF MORAL DEVELOPMENT

Level	Age Range	Moral Understanding	What Should Heinz Do?
Preconventional moral reasoning	Young children	Right and wrong are determined by the consequences.	Heinz should not steal the drug because he may go to jail if caught.
Conventional moral reasoning	Emerges around puberty	Right and wrong are informed by the expectations of society and important others, not simply personal consequences. Duty and obedience to authorities define what is right.	Because society says a husband must take care of his wife, Heinz should steal the drugs so that others won't think poorly of him. Or, Heinz should not steal because stealing is against the law.
Postconventional moral reasoning	Adulthood	Right and wrong are determined by the individual's beliefs about morality, which may be inconsistent with society's rules and regulations. Moral behavior is determined by universal principles of justice, equality, and respect for human life.	Heinz should steal the drug because the laws of society fail to consider his unique situation. Or, Heinz should thoughtfully consider all possible options, but ultimately decide that human life overrides societal laws.

Kohlberg believed that people pass through different stages of moral development, described here. Information from Kohlberg & Hersh (1977).

participants were presented with the following questions: "Should the husband have done that? Was it right or wrong?" (Kohlberg, 1981, p. 12). Kohlberg was not really interested in whether his participants thought Heinz should steal the drug; his goal was to determine the moral reasoning behind their answers.

Although Kohlberg described moral development as sequential and universal, he noted that environmental influences and interactions with others (particularly those at a higher level of moral reasoning) support its continued development. Additionally, not everyone progresses through all three levels; a person may get stuck at an early stage and remain there for life.

Put Your Heads Together

In your group, **A**) choose three people in the news whose behaviors exemplify one of Kohlberg's stages of moral development. **B**) Justify your selections with specific examples of those behaviors. **C**) Team up with another group and compare and contrast your results.

NOT A PERFECT THEORY Kohlberg's theory of moral development has certain limitations. American psychologist Carol Gilligan leveled a number of serious critiques, suggesting that the theory did not represent the moral reasoning of women (1982). Gilligan asserted that Kohlberg discounted the importance of caring and responsibility, and that his initial use of all-male samples was partially to blame. Another issue with Kohlberg's theory is that it focuses on the moral reasoning of individuals, and thus primarily applies to Western cultures; in more collectivist cultures, the focus is on the group (Endicott, Bock, & Narvaez, 2003). Kohlberg's theory may be useful for examining and measuring moral reasoning, but not necessarily for making predictions. Research indicates that the ability to predict moral behavior is weak at best (Blasi, 1980; Krebs & Denton, 2005).

What Role Does Gender Play?

LO 15 Define gender and explain how culture plays a role in its development.

One important process that often occurs during childhood and adolescence is the development of gender identity. **Gender** refers to the categories or dimensions of masculinity and femininity based on social, cultural, and psychological characteristics. Men are often expected to be masculine in their "attitudes, feelings, and behaviors," while women are expected to be more feminine (APA, 2015b). But concepts of masculine and feminine vary according to culture, social context, and the individual. The American Psychological Association (APA, 2010, 2012a, 2014a) recommends using the term "sex" when referring to biological status and "gender" for the cultural roles and expectations that distinguish males and females. According to the American Psychiatric Association (2013), "gender" also indicates the public and often legally recognized role a person has as a man or woman, boy or girl. **Gender identity** is the feeling or sense of being either male or female, and compatibility, contentment, and conformity with one's gender (APA, 2015b; Egan & Perry, 2001; Tobin et al., 2010).

LEARNING GENDER ROLES We learn how to behave in gender-conforming ways through the **gender roles** designated by our culture. This understanding of expected male and female behavior is generally demonstrated by age 2 or 3. So, too, is the ability to differentiate between boys and girls, and men and women (Zosuls, Miller, Ruble, Martin, & Fabes, 2011). Let's explore how these gender roles are learned.

gender The dimension of masculinity and femininity based on social, cultural, and psychological characteristics.

gender identity The feeling or sense of being either male or female, and compatibility, contentment, and conformity with one's gender.

gender roles The collection of actions, beliefs, and characteristics that a culture associates with masculinity and femininity.

gender schemas The psychological or mental guidelines that dictate how to be masculine and feminine.

The social-cognitive theory suggests that gender roles can be acquired through **observational learning** (Bussey & Bandura, 1999; Else-Quest, Higgins, Allison, & Morton, 2012; Tenenbaum & Leaper, 2002). We learn from our observations of people around us, particularly those of the same gender. Children also learn and model the behaviors represented in electronic media and books (Kingsbury & Coplan, 2012).

CONNECTIONS

In **Chapter 5,** we described how people and animals learn by observing and imitating a model. Here, we see how observational learning can shape the formation of gender roles.

Operant conditioning is another way gender roles are established. Children often receive reinforcement for behaviors considered gender-appropriate, and punishment (or lack of attention) for those viewed as inappropriate. Parents, caregivers, relatives, and peers reinforce gender-appropriate behavior by smiling, laughing, or encouraging. But when children exhibit gender-inappropriate behavior (a boy playing with a doll, for example), the people in their lives might frown, get worried, or even put a stop to it. Through this combination of **encouragement and discouragement**, a child may learn to conform to society's expectations.

CONNECTIONS

In **Chapter 5,** we discussed operant conditioning, or learning that results from consequences. Here, the positive reinforcer is encouragement, which leads to an increase in a desired behavior. The punishment is discouragement, which reduces the unwanted behavior.

THINKING ABOUT GENDER Children also seem to develop gender roles by actively processing information (Bem, 1981). In other words, they think about the behaviors they observe, including any differences between males and females. Often they watch their parents' behavior and follow suit (Tenenbaum & Leaper, 2002). Using the information they have gathered, children develop a variety of gender-specific rules they believe should be followed—for example, girls help around the house, and boys play with model cars (Martin & Cook, 2018; Yee & Brown, 1994). These rules provide a framework for **gender schemas,** the psychological or mental guidelines that dictate how to be masculine or feminine.

BIOLOGY AND GENDER Clearly, culture and learning influence the development of gender-specific behaviors and interests, but could biology play a role, too? Research on nonhuman primates suggests this is the case (Hines, 2011a). A growing body of literature points to a link between testosterone exposure *in utero* and specific play behaviors (Swan et al., 2010). For example, male and female infants as young as 3 to 8 months demonstrate gender-specific toy preferences that cannot be explained by mere socialization or learning (Hines, 2011b). Research using eye-tracking technology reveals that baby girls spend more time looking at dolls, while boys tend to focus on toy trucks (Alexander, Wilcox, & Woods, 2009). Thus it seems, not all gender-specific behaviors can be attributed to culture and upbringing (Martin & Cook, 2018); this principle is well illustrated by the heartbreaking story of Bruce Reimer.

Monkey Play
A male vervet monkey rolls a toy car on the ground (left), and a female examines a doll (right). When provided with a variety of toys, male vervet monkeys spend more time playing with cars and balls, whereas females are drawn to dolls and pots (Alexander & Hines, 2002). Similar behaviors have been observed in rhesus monkeys (Hassett, Siebert, & Wallen, 2008). These studies suggest a biological basis for the gender-specific toy preferences often observed in human children. Left: MCT/Getty Images. Right: MCT/MCT via Getty Images.

THINK CRITICALLY

THE CASE OF BRUCE REIMER Bruce Reimer and his twin brother were born in 1965. During a circumcision operation at 8 months, Bruce's penis was almost entirely burnt away by electrical equipment used in the procedure. When he was about 2 years old, his parents took the advice of Johns Hopkins psychologist John Money and decided to raise Bruce as a girl (British Broadcasting Corporation [BBC], 2014, September 17).

Just before Bruce's second birthday, doctors removed his testicles and used the tissues to create the beginnings of female genitalia. His parents began calling him Brenda, dressing him like a girl, and encouraging him to engage in stereotypically "girl" activities such as baking and playing with dolls (BBC, 2014, September 17). But Brenda did not adjust so well to her new gender assignment. An outcast at school, she was called cruel names like "caveman" and "gorilla." She brawled with both boys and girls alike, and eventually got kicked out of school (Diamond & Sigmundson, 1997).

HIS PARENTS . . . DECIDED TO RAISE BRUCE AS A GIRL

When Brenda hit puberty, the problem became worse. Despite ongoing psychiatric therapy and estrogen replacement, she could not deny what was in her *nature*—she refused to consider herself female (Diamond & Sigmundson, 1997). Brenda became suicidal, prompting her parents to tell her the truth about the past (BBC, 2014, September 17). At age 14, Brenda changed her name to David, began taking male hormones, and underwent a series of penis construction surgeries (Colapinto, 2000; Diamond & Sigmundson, 1997). At 25, David married and adopted his wife's children, and for some time it appeared he was doing quite well (Diamond & Sigmundson, 1997). But sadly, at the age of 38, he took his own life.

It is important to note that the medical procedures Bruce was subjected to as a child are distinct from gender-affirming surgeries people undergo voluntarily (soon to be discussed). Keep in mind that this is just an isolated case. We should be extremely cautious about making generalizations from case studies, which may or may not be representative of the larger population.

GENDER-ROLE STEREOTYPES The case of Bruce Reimer touches on another important topic: gender-role stereotypes. Growing up, David (who was called "Brenda" at the time) did not enjoy wearing dresses and playing "girl" games. He didn't adhere to the *gender-role stereotypes* assigned to little girls. Gender-role stereotypes, which begin to take hold around age 3, are strong ideas about the nature of males and females—how they should dress, what kinds of games they should like, and so on. Decisions about children's toys, in particular, follow strict gender-role stereotypes (boys play with trucks, girls play with dolls), and any crossing over risks ridicule from peers, sometimes even adults. Gender-role stereotypes are apparent in toy commercials, toy packaging, and pictures in coloring books (Auster & Mansbach, 2012; Fitzpatrick & McPherson, 2010; Kahlenberg & Hein, 2010; Owen & Padron, 2016). They also manifest themselves in academic settings. For example, many girls have negative attitudes about math, which seem to be associated with parents' and teachers' expectations about gender differences in math competencies (Gunderson, Ramirez, Levine, & Beilock, 2012).

Children, especially boys, tend to cling to gender-role stereotypes. You are much more likely to see a girl playing with a "boy toy" than a boy playing with a "girl toy." Society, in turn, is more tolerant of girls who go against gender stereotypes (Weisgram, Fulcher, & Dinella, 2014).

Cosmetics for All
Who says make-up is just for girls? CoverGirl's first male model, James Charles, is breaking down gender role stereotypes and showing the world just how beautiful androgyny can be.
Andreas Branch/Variety/REX/Shutterstock.

ANDROGYNY Those who cross gender-role boundaries and engage in behaviors associated with both genders are said to exhibit **androgyny.** An androgynous person might be nurturing (generally considered a feminine quality) and assertive (generally considered a masculine quality), thereby demonstrating characteristics associated with both genders (Johnson et al., 2006; Wood & Eagly, 2015). But concepts of masculine and feminine—and therefore what constitutes androgyny—are not consistent across cultures. Children in the African nation of Swaziland are dressed androgynously, wearing any color of the rainbow (Bradley, 2011). Meanwhile, American parents frequently dress boy babies in blue and girl babies in pink.

androgyny The tendency to cross gender-role boundaries, exhibiting behaviors associated with both genders.

TRANSGENDER AND TRANSSEXUAL The development of gender identity and the acceptance of gender roles go relatively smoothly for most people. But sometimes societal expectations of being male or female differ from what an individual is feeling inwardly, leading to discontent. At birth, most infants are identified as "boy" or "girl"; this is referred to as a person's *natal gender,* or gender assignment. When natal gender does not feel right, an individual may have *transgender* experiences. According to the American Psychological Association, **transgender** refers to people "whose *gender identity, gender expression,* or behavior does not conform to that typically associated with the sex to which they were assigned at birth" (APA, 2014a, p. 1). Remember that gender identity is the feeling or sense of being either male or female. For a person who is transgender, that sense of identity is incongruent with the gender assignment given at birth. This disparity can be temporary or persistent (American Psychiatric Association, 2013). Almost a million individuals in the United States (around 0.4% of the population) consider themselves transgender (Meerwijk & Sevelius, 2017).

The American Psychological Association (2015b) notes that transitioning "from one gender to another" may involve medical treatments and changes to names, pronouns, hair, and clothing (p. 422). Although the term **transsexual** is not embraced by all, it is used by the American Psychiatric Association (2013) to describe those who undergo "a social transition from male to female or female to male, which in many, but not all, cases also involves a somatic transition by cross-sex hormone treatment and genital surgery" (p. 451). Using "medical intervention" to make this type of transition is also termed *gender affirmation* (APA, 2014a).

Trailblazing for the Trans Community
Danica Roem celebrates her election to the Virginia state legislature on November 7, 2017. A couple months later, Roem became the first openly transgender person to serve in a state legislature (Olivo, 2018, January 10).
Jahi Chikwendiu/The Washington Post via Getty Images.

When Do We Become Adults?

In the United States, the legal age of adulthood is 18 for some activities (voting, military enlistment) and 21 for others (drinking, financial responsibilities). These ages are not consistent across cultures; in some countries, for example, the legal drinking age is as young as 16. The transition into adulthood is often marked by ceremonies and rituals starting as early as age 12—Jewish *bar/bat mitzvahs,* Australian walkabouts, Christian confirmations, and Latin American *quinceañeras,* to name a few.

The line between adolescence and adulthood is becoming somewhat blurred in Western societies, where young people are depending on their families longer and marrying much later (Arnett, 2000; Elliott, Krivickas, Brault, & Kreider, 2012; **Figure 8.6**). Psychologists propose a phase of **emerging adulthood,** which spans

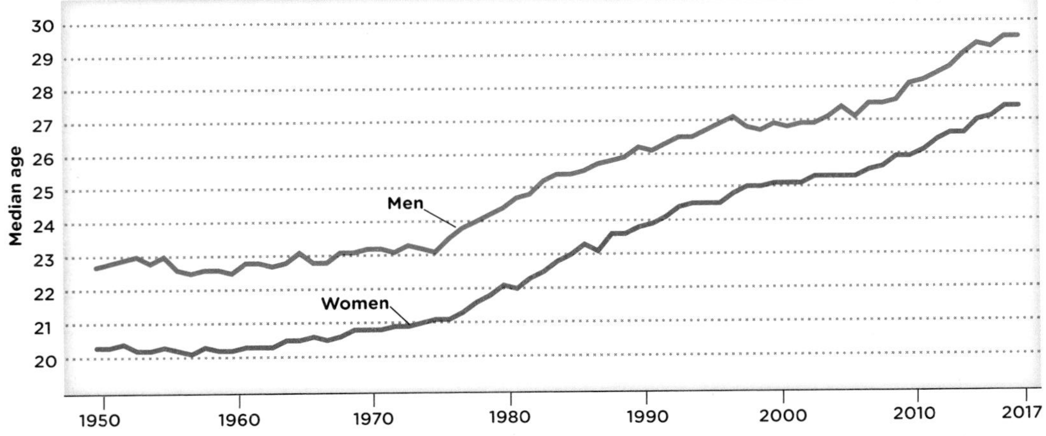

FIGURE 8.6
Age of First Marriage
Many developmental psychologists consider marriage a marker of adulthood because it can represent the first time a person leaves the family home. Since the 1950s and 60s, the median age at which men and women marry for the first time has increased, a trend that appears likely to continue. Information from the U.S. Census Bureau (2017).

transgender Refers to people whose gender identity and expression do not match the gender assigned to them at birth.

transsexual An individual who seeks or undergoes a social transition to the other gender, and who may make changes to his or her body through surgery and medical treatment.

emerging adulthood A phase of life between 18 and 25 years that includes exploration and opportunity.

18 to 25 years of age, and is characterized by exploration and opportunity. The emerging adult has neither the permanent responsibilities of adulthood nor the dependency of adolescence. By this time, most adolescent egocentrism has disappeared, which is apparent in intimate relationships and empathy (Elkind, 1967). One can seek out loving relationships, education, and new world views before settling into the relative permanency of family and career (Arnett, 2000).

CAREER CONNECTIONS

DEVELOPING CAREERS Emerging adulthood is often the time people decide on a profession. Whatever path you choose, knowledge of human development will likely be useful. Are you interested in teaching, social work, speech therapy, or occupational therapy? How about nursing or dental hygiene? If your profession involves working with children, understanding their cognitive, social, and emotional development will be critical. The same goes for jobs oriented toward the elderly; physical therapists, personal attendants, nutritionists, and others who work with older people must have a handle on the complex changes occurring in late adulthood.

KNOWLEDGE OF HUMAN DEVELOPMENT WILL LIKELY BE USEFUL

Developmental psychology may be relevant to career areas you wouldn't expect, like public policy. In the late 1970s, researchers discovered that exposure to lead can create long-term developmental problems in children (Needleman et al., 1979). Congress responded by prohibiting lead-based home paints and, eventually, the sale of leaded gasoline (APA, n.d.-g). Can you think of any other examples showing how knowledge of developmental psychology might provide an advantage for people in legal professions? *Hint:* Consider children testifying in criminal cases, teenagers being tried for crimes, and caregivers being accused of elder abuse.

show what you know

1. The physical features not associated with reproduction, but that become more distinct during adolescence, are known as:
   a. primary sex characteristics.
   b. secondary sex characteristics.
   c. menarche.
   d. puberty.
2. "Helicopter" parents pave the way for their children, troubleshooting problems for them, and attempting to make certain they are always successful. How might this type of parenting impact an adolescent in Erikson's stage of ego identity versus role confusion?
3. ______________ moral reasoning usually is seen in young children, and it focuses on the consequences of behaviors, both good and bad.
4. A 14-year-old has begun to use deductive reasoning to draw conclusions and critical thinking to support her arguments. Her cognitive development is occurring in Piaget's:
   a. formal operational stage.
   b. concrete operational stage.
   c. ego identity versus role confusion stage.
   d. conservation task.
5. A sixth grader states that men are more assertive, logical, and in charge than women. She has learned about this ______________ from sources in her immediate setting and culture.
   a. gender identity
   b. observational learning
   c. gender role
   d. androgyny

✓ CHECK YOUR ANSWERS IN APPENDIX C.

Adulthood

"SHE PROVED ME WRONG." Twelve years ago, when Joan learned of Ericka's pregnancy, she assumed college was no longer an option. But today, Joan is proud to say, "She proved me wrong."

When Niyah was 3 years old, Ericka enrolled at Trinity Washington University in Washington, D.C. Juggling a full-time job and college was not easy, but Ericka "planned out every minute, every hour" to maximize her time with Niyah. In the morning, they would get up early to talk about their day. Then Ericka would drop off Niyah at school, go to work, and pick her up in the late afternoon. After a few more hours of mother–daughter time, Ericka would go to her night classes. In 2011, Ericka earned her associate's degree, and in 2014 she graduated cum laude with her bachelor's degree in business administration.

Ericka proved that she could do it all, and do it all well—motherhood, college, and career. Her accomplishments speak to her own hard work and resolve, and also to the dedicated support of three strong women: her mother Joan, her grandmother Katherine, and a PhD student named Aisha. Ericka met Aisha through her participation in Generation Hope, a non-profit organization devoted to helping teen parents get through college. Like every Generation Hope scholar, Ericka was paired with a mentor (Aisha) who provided financial assistance from her own personal funds and emotional support during college. "She's really helped me to focus on me and what I want," Ericka explains. "My issue has always been being worried about being accepted by other people." With Aisha's guidance, Ericka learned to embrace the person she is, and go after what she wants in life.

Ericka is now married and immersed in young adulthood, a stage of life when many people are forging their identities and laying the groundwork for lifelong relationships. While others her age are still exploring the "Who am I?" type of questions that emerged in adolescence, Ericka already seems to know the answers. "I am pretty confident, and I believe what I believe," Ericka says. "I'm not afraid to express those opinions." Parenthood has a way of making you grow up fast.

Support System
(Left to right, and front) Joan, Ericka, Ericka's mentor Aisha, and Niyah. In addition to Ericka's grandmother, these are the people who helped keep Ericka motivated and inspired throughout college. Ericka considered withdrawing from college at one point, but then she discovered Generation Hope, a non-profit organization devoted to supporting teen parents as they work toward college degrees. In addition to graduating cum laude, Ericka served as president of the Student Government Association and belonged to two honor societies.
Courtesy Ericka Harley.

Whatever you want from life, you are most likely to attain it during the developmental stage known as adulthood. Developmental psychologists have identified various stages of this long period, each corresponding to an approximate age group: *early adulthood* spans the twenties and thirties, *middle adulthood* the forties to mid-sixties, and *late adulthood* everything beyond.

Aging Bodies

LO 16 Name several of the most important physical changes that occur across adulthood.

The most obvious signs of aging tend to be physical in nature. Often you can estimate a person's age just by looking at his hands or facial lines. Understanding physical development is important because it impacts behavior and mental processes.

EARLY ADULTHOOD During early adulthood, we are at the height of our muscular and cardiovascular ability. Other systems have already begun their downhill journey, however. One example is hearing, which often starts to decline as a result of **noise-induced damage** beginning in early adolescence (Niskar et al., 2001; World Health Organization [WHO], 2015). The body is fairly resilient at this stage, but lifestyle choices can have profound health consequences. Heavy drinking, poor eating habits, obesity, lack of exercise, and smoking can make a person look, feel, and function like someone much older. All these factors have been associated with a high risk for cardiovascular disease and premature death in middle adulthood (Hulsegge et al., 2016; Liu et al., 2012).

CONNECTIONS
In **Chapter 3,** we described the causes of hearing impairment. Sensorineural deafness results from damage to the hair cells or auditory nerve. Conduction hearing impairment occurs when the eardrum or middle-ear bones are compromised. Exposure to loud sounds may play a role in hearing impairment that begins in adolescence.

In the late thirties, fertility-related changes occur for both men and women. Female fertility decreases by 6% in the late twenties, 14% in the early thirties, and 31% in the late thirties (Menken, Trussell, & Larsen, 1986; Nelson, Telfer, & Anderson, 2013). Men also experience a fertility dip, but it appears to be gradual and results from fewer and poorer-quality sperm (Sloter et al., 2006). It is not until age 50 that male fertility declines substantially (Kidd, Eskenazi, & Wyrobek, 2001).

Care to Dance?
Dancing is good for the brain. The physical, cognitive, and social stimulation it provides may combat the loss of "white matter integrity" that accompanies aging. White matter consists of axons covered in myelin, and boosting its integrity is "key in preserving cognitive performance necessary for independent functioning in older individuals" (Burzynska et al., 2017, p. 2). Andy Hall/Getty Images.

MIDDLE ADULTHOOD In middle adulthood, the skin wrinkles and sags due to loss of collagen and elastin, and skin spots may appear (Bulpitt, Markowe, & Shipley, 2001). Hair starts to turn gray and may fall out. Hearing loss continues and may be exacerbated by exposure to loud noises (Kujawa & Liberman, 2006). Eyesight may decline. The bones weaken, and osteoporosis can occur (Kaczmarek, 2015). Oh, and did we mention you might shrink? But do not despair. There are measures you can take to slow the aging process occurring in cells throughout your body. Cellular aging has been associated with the shortening of telomeres—DNA and protein structures found at the ends of chromosomes—and some research suggests you can combat telomere shrinkage with simple lifestyle choices. Getting exercise and good sleep, steering clear of cigarettes, and taking steps to reduce stress may help preserve the integrity of telomeres, possibly reducing your risk of age-related ailments (Lina, Epel, & Blackburn, 2012; Ornish et al., 2013; Weintraub, 2017, January 4).

For women, middle adulthood is a time of major physical change. Estrogen production decreases, the uterus shrinks, and menstruation no longer follows a regular pattern. This marks the transition toward **menopause,** the time when ovulation and menstruation cease, and reproduction is no longer possible. Menopausal women can experience hot flashes, sweating, vaginal dryness, and breast tenderness (Kaczmarek, 2015; Newton et al., 2006). These symptoms may sound unpleasant, but many women report a sense of relief following the cessation of their menstrual periods, as well as increased interest in sexual activity (Etaugh, 2008).

Men experience their own constellation of midlife physical changes, sometimes referred to as male menopause or *andropause* (Kaczmarek, 2015). Some suggest calling it *androgen decline,* as there is a reduction in testosterone production, not an end to it (Morales, Heaton, & Carson, 2000). Men in middle adulthood may complain of depression, fatigue, and cognitive difficulties, which might be associated with lower testosterone. But research suggests this link between hormones and behavior is evident in only a tiny proportion of aging men (Pines, 2011).

LATE ADULTHOOD Late adulthood, which begins around 65, is also characterized by the decline of many physical functions. Eye problems, such as cataracts and impaired night vision, are common. Hearing continues on a downhill course, and research suggests age-related hearing loss is linked to cognitive decline. However, the causal relationship between these two factors is unclear, and using hearing aids may help preserve some cognitive functions (Loughrey, Kelly, Kelley, Brennan, & Lawlor, 2018).

Apply This ↓

MOVE IT OR LOSE IT

Some physical decline is inevitable with age, but it is possible to grow old gracefully. One of the best ways to fight aging is to get your body moving. Aerobic exercise improves bone density and muscle strength, and lowers the risk for cardiovascular disease and obesity. It's good for your brain, too. "A single bout of moderate [aerobic] exercise" seems to provide a short-term boost in working memory for adults of various ages (Hogan, Mata, & Carstensen, 2013, para. 1). Maintaining a certain level of day-to-day aerobic activity also appears to make a difference, as older people who are physically active tend to perform better on working memory tasks (Guiney & Machado, 2013). The biological processes underlying these changes are still being investigated (Maass et al., 2016), but animal research suggests that exercise promotes the production of **new neurons** in the hippocampus, a brain structure that plays a central role in memory (Raichlen & Alexander, 2017; **Figure 8.7**). When you take good care of your body, you're also taking care of your mind.

CONNECTIONS
In **Chapter 2,** we discussed neurogenesis, the creation of new neurons that occurs in some areas of the brain. As we age, this production of new neurons seems to be supported by physical exercise.

Aging Minds

What goes on in the brain as we pass through the stages of adulthood, and how do these changes affect our ability to function? Let's explore cognitive development in adulthood.

Identify the most significant cognitive changes that occur across adulthood.

EARLY ADULTHOOD Measures of aptitude, such as intelligence tests, indicate that cognitive ability remains stable from early to middle adulthood (Larsen, Hartmann, & Nyborg, 2008), though processing speed begins to decline (Schaie, 1993). Young adults are theoretically in Piaget's formal operational stage, which means they can think logically and systematically, but some estimate that only 50% of adults ever exhibit formal operational thinking (Arlin, 1975).

MIDDLE AND LATE ADULTHOOD Good news for people in their forties and fifties: Cognitive function does not necessarily fade during this time of life. In fact, longitudinal studies indicate that decreases in cognitive abilities cannot be reliably measured before 60 (Gerstorf, Ram, Hoppmann, Willis, & Schaie, 2011; Schaie, 1993, 2008). There are some exceptions, however. Midlife is a time when information processing and memory can decline, particularly the ability to remember past events (Ren, Wu, Chan, & Yan, 2013).

After the age of 70, cognitive changes are more apparent. The speed with which we acquire new material and create associations decreases (von Stumm & Deary, 2012); working memory, the active processing component of short-term memory that maintains and manipulates information, becomes less efficient (Nagel et al., 2008; Reuter-Lorenz, 2013); and **fluid intelligence,** the ability to think in the abstract and create associations among concepts, has been declining since age 50 (Cornelius & Caspi, 1987).

Not all the changes are bad, however. Older people may not remember everything they learned in school, but their practical abilities seem to grow. Life experiences allow people to develop a more balanced understanding of the world around them, one that only comes with age (Sternberg & Grigorenko, 2005). What's more, **crystallized intelligence,** the knowledge we gain through learning and experience, tends to increase over time (Cornelius & Caspi, 1987).

There's more good news: The Seattle Longitudinal Study has shown that the cognitive performance of today's 70-year-old participants is similar to the performance of 65-year-olds tested 30 years ago (Gerstorf et al., 2011; Schaie, 1993, 2008). What does this finding tell us? From a cognitive abilities perspective, turning 65 does not mean it is time to retire. Processing speed may slow with old age, but older adults are still capable of innovation and awe-inspiring accomplishments (Kennedy, 2017, April 7). Frank Lloyd Wright finished designing New York's Guggenheim Museum when he was 89 years old, and Nelson Mandela became president of South Africa when he was 76.

If you look at intelligence scores from the 1950s, 70s, and 90s, you will see the average intelligence score increasing over the generations. These differences are so impressive that many people taking IQ tests in the 1930s would be considered cognitively delayed by today's standards (Flynn, 2009). We call this global phenomenon the *Flynn effect* (Flynn, 2012). Does this mean that people of today are smarter than those from decades past? Researcher James Flynn (2012) suggests that this is not the case. Intelligence scores are most likely increasing because we confront a larger spectrum of "cognitive problems" than those who came before us. In other words, we now seem to encounter more issues that require abstract thinking.

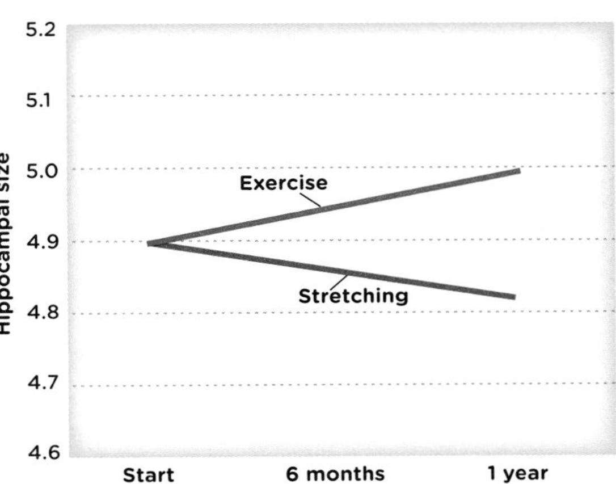

FIGURE 8.7
Exercise to Build Bigger . . . Brains?
To study the effects of exercise on the aging brain, researchers randomly assigned participants to two groups: One group engaged in a program of gentle stretching exercises, and the other began doing more aerobic activity. During the course of the yearlong study, the researchers found typical levels of age-related shrinkage in the hippocampi of the stretching group. However, in the group that exercised more vigorously, not only was age-related deterioration prevented, hippocampal volume actually increased, with corresponding improvements in memory (Erickson et al., 2011). Although the mechanisms are not well understood, "physical exercise can convey a protective effect against cognitive decline in ageing and Alzheimer's disease" (Duzel, van Praag, & Sendtner, 2016, p. 662). Information from Erickson et al. (2011).

menopause The time when a woman no longer ovulates, her menstrual cycle stops, and she is no longer capable of reproduction.

fluid intelligence The ability to think in the abstract and create associations among concepts.

crystallized intelligence Knowledge gained through learning and experience.

Earlier we mentioned that physical exercise provides a cognitive boost. The same appears to be true of mental exercises, such as those required for playing a musical instrument (Hanna-Pladdy & MacKay, 2011). That said, there does appear to be a lot of hype surrounding the "use it or lose it" mantra of aging. The declaration that exercising the brain will stop cognitive decline might be a slight overstatement (Salthouse, 2006). Although there are clear benefits to doing crossword puzzles and reading the newspaper, the evidence is not conclusive that this activity has the same effect it would have on a child, for example. Perhaps the best advice for older people is to keep both brain and body active. People who continue to work, both physically and mentally, and remain in good physical shape are less likely to experience **significant cognitive decline** (Rohwedder & Willis, 2010). They may even live longer, as later retirement has been linked to longer survival (Wu, Odden, Fisher& Stawski, 2016). Thus, if your goal is to maintain a sharp mind as you age, don't just increase your Sudoku playing or reading time. You need to maintain a balanced approach that incorporates a broad range of activities, including those that provide social stimulation.

CONNECTIONS 

Here, we are reminded of an issue presented in **Chapter 1:** We must be careful not to equate correlation with causation. In this case, a decline in cognitive ability may lead to earlier retirement (not the other way around).

Social, Emotional Adults

LO 18 Explain some of the socioemotional changes that occur across adulthood.

Earlier we described Erikson's approach to explaining socioemotional development from infancy through adolescence, noting that unsuccessful resolution of prior stages has implications for the stages that follow (see Infographic 8.4 on p. 303). Here, we will look at the stages associated with adulthood.

- **Intimacy versus isolation (twenties to forties):** During young adulthood, people tend to focus on creating meaningful, deep relationships, and failing at this endeavor may lead to a life of isolation. The focus shifts away from fun-filled first experiences with sex and love to deeper connections. For many, the twenties represent a transition between the "here and now" type of relationships of adolescence to the serious, long-term partnerships of adulthood (Arnett, 2000).
- **Generativity versus stagnation (forties to mid-sixties)**: Moving into middle adulthood, we begin to evaluate our lives. Positive resolution of this stage includes feeling like we have made a real impact on the next generation, through parenting, community involvement, or work that is valuable and significant. Those who cannot resolve this crisis face stagnation, characterized by boredom, conceit, and selfishness.
- **Integrity versus despair (mid-sixties and beyond):** In late adulthood, we look back on life and evaluate how we have done. If previous stages have resulted in positive resolutions, we feel a sense of accomplishment and satisfaction. If not, we feel regret and dissatisfaction.

Golden Years
Late adulthood can be a time of great intellectual, humanitarian, and physical achievement. Ingeborg Syllm-Rapoport (left) was 102 when she earned her doctorate degree; Nelson Mandela (middle) was 76 when he became the first Black president of South Africa; and Katsusuke Yanagisawa (right) was 71 when he climbed Mount Everest. Left: Bodo Marks /AP Images. Center: Per-Anders Pettersson/Getty Images. Right: AP Photo/Kyodo News.

While very important in the field of developmental psychology, Erikson's work has provided more framework than substantive research findings. His theory was based on case studies, with limited supporting evidence. Furthermore, the developmental tasks associated with the eight stages might not be limited to particular time frames. For example, creating an adult identity is not restricted to adolescence, as this stage may resurface at any point in adulthood (Schwartz, 2001).

Now it's time to revisit a topic touched on in earlier sections—something that many people consider the most challenging, yet rewarding, aspect of adult life: parenthood.

Do Parents Create Bullies? Clay Jensen (played by Dylan Minnette) and Hannah Baker (Katherine Langford) in *13 Reasons Why*, a Netflix series that explores bullying and other mental health issues affecting teens. How does bullying arise? Like any psychological phenomenon, bullying behaviors may be related to both nature (genes) and nurture (environment), and an important part of the latter is parenting. In one study, university students answered questions about their parents' past behaviors; their responses suggest that both authoritarian and permissive parenting styles tend to encourage bullying behaviors in children (Luk et al., 2016; Rodriguez, 2016, September 1). Why do you think this is the case? Beth Dubber/Netflix/Kobal/REX/Shutterstock.

The Many Shades of Parenting

Do you ever find yourself watching parent–child interactions in public? Perhaps you have witnessed a mom strapping her screaming baby into a car seat, or a dad chasing a toddler at the grocery store. As you have probably observed, there is a vast spectrum of child-rearing approaches. American psychologist Diana Baumrind has been studying parenting for over four decades, and she has identified four parenting behavioral styles (1966, 1971, 2013). These styles seem to be stable across situations, and are distinguished by levels of warmth, responsiveness, and control (Baumrind, 2013; Maccoby & Martin, 1983).

Parents who insist on rigid boundaries, show little warmth, and expect high control exhibit **authoritarian parenting.** They want things done in a certain way, "because I said so," no questions asked. Authoritarian parents are extremely strict and demonstrate poor communication skills with their children. Their kids, in turn, tend to have lower self-assurance and autonomy, and experience more problems in social settings (Baumrind, 1991). Researchers have found that there are exceptions to this rule, however. In situations where "societal conformance or . . . safety of the child" is vital, "authoritarian parenting is actually more adaptive" (Herzog, Hill-Chapman, Hardy, Wrighten, & El-Khabbaz, 2015, p. 121).

Authoritative parenting may sound similar to authoritarian parenting, but it is very different. Parents who practice authoritative parenting set high expectations, demonstrate a warm attitude, and are responsive to their children's needs. Being supported and respected, children of authoritative parents are responsive to their parents' expectations. They also tend to be self-assured, independent, responsible, and friendly (Baumrind, 1991). There appears to be a positive relationship between the authoritative style and parental education (Anton, Jones, & Youngstrom, 2015).

With **permissive parenting,** the parent demands little of the child and imposes few limitations. These parents are very warm but often make next to no effort to control their children. Ultimately, their children tend to lack self-control, act impulsively, and show little respect for boundaries.

Those who demonstrate **uninvolved parenting** seem indifferent to their children. Emotionally detached, these parents exhibit minimal warmth and devote little time to their kids, apart from taking care of basic needs. Children raised by uninvolved parents tend to exhibit behavioral problems, poor academic performance, and immaturity (Baumrind, 1991).

Keep in mind that the great majority of research on these parenting styles has been conducted in the United States, which should make us wonder how much the findings apply to other countries and cultures (Grusec, Goodnow, & Kuczynski, 2000). Additional factors to consider include the home environment, the child's personality and development, and the unique parent–child relationship. Children with irritable and easygoing dispositions will not exhibit the same reactions to the restrictions imposed by authoritarian parents, for example (Grusec & Goodnow, 1994).

authoritarian parenting A rigid parenting style characterized by strict rules and poor communication skills.

authoritative parenting A parenting style characterized by high expectations, strong support, and respect for children.

permissive parenting A parenting style characterized by low demands of children and few limitations.

uninvolved parenting A parenting style characterized by a parent's indifference to a child, including a lack of emotional involvement.

Growing Old with Grace

When some people think of growing older, they imagine a disabled and frail person sitting in a bathrobe and staring out the window. This stereotype is simply not accurate. As of 2014, fewer than 1% of Americans lived in a nursing home (CDC, 2014). Most older adults in the United States enjoy active, healthy, independent lives. They are involved in their communities, faiths, and social networks, and—contrary to popular belief—a large number have active sex lives (Lindau et al., 2007; Malani, Clark, Solway, Singer, & Kirch, 2018, May). Negative stereotypes are known to be "detrimental" to the physical functioning of elderly people. But researchers have found that **subliminal** exposure to positive age stereotypes can improve physical functioning (Levy, Pilver, Chung, & Slade, 2014).

CONNECTIONS In **Chapter 3,** we discussed subliminal stimuli, which are well beneath absolute thresholds. Even so, subliminal messages are registered by the brain and may influence moods and attitudes. Here, we see how they can lead to changes in physical functioning.

Americans are now living longer than ever, with the average life expectancy of women being 81.2 years and men 76.4 years (Kochanek, Murphy, Xu, J., & Tejada-Vera, 2017, April 3). Many of us dread this "winter of life," but perhaps we should look forward to it; research suggests that happiness generally increases with age (Jeste et al., 2013). Positive emotions become more frequent than negative ones, and emotional stability increases, meaning that we experience fewer extreme mood swings (Carstensen et al., 2011). Stress and anger begin to diminish in early adulthood, and worry becomes less apparent after age 50 (Stone, Schwartz, Broderick, & Deaton, 2010). Why might older people feel happy? Perhaps they no longer care about proving themselves, feel pleased with the outcome of their lives, or have developed a strong sense of emotional equilibrium (Jeste et al., 2013).

Put Your Heads Together

Think of some older people you respect and want to emulate. In your group, **A)** describe some recent accomplishments of these older individuals. **B)** Discuss the factors that you think have led to their successful aging. **C)** How would you define successful aging? **D)** What would you say to someone who harbors negative stereotypes about older people?

You Asked, Ericka Answers

http://qrs.ly/6v5a5dq

How did the death of your grandmother affect you and your views about death?

THE LIFE OF KAT WRIGHT "My grandmother passed away on September 5, 2011," Ericka says. "I really remember it like it was yesterday."

It was Labor Day weekend and the family was hoping to have a cookout at Grandma's house, just as they did every year. But Grandma wasn't feeling well and asked for a small family dinner instead. When Ericka and her relatives arrived, Grandma wanted to stay in bed—unusual for the woman who was the focal point of every family get-together. Eventually, she got up, but her breathing was abnormal. The family called 911, and medical workers came but did not find evidence of any major problem. Ericka wasn't too worried because Grandma had experienced health issues in the past, but she had always recovered.

"Okay Grandma, I'll see you tomorrow," Ericka said on her way out. "I love you." Grandmother told Ericka she loved her, too, and said "goodbye" (odd, because she usually said "see you later"). Later that night, Ericka awoke to the sound of her mom getting ready to go visit Grandma, now in the hospital. Assuming her grandmother would pull through as always, Ericka went back to bed, her mind spinning. She headed for the hospital around 2:00 A.M., but by the time she arrived, Grandma was already gone. "I couldn't like breathe, I couldn't say anything," Ericka recalls. "I knew that one day she would pass away, but I wasn't ready for it."

The death of Katherine Wright had a profound impact on Joan, Ericka, and the whole family. One of the hardest parts of grieving was the sudden loss of everyday contact—the daily phone calls, the frequent visits. Ericka's pregnancy had brought together four generations of women—Katherine, Joan, Ericka, and Niyah—and they were as close as ever. But now their leader was gone. "I remember the first couple months I was really angry at God," Ericka explains. "I felt like, if God loves us, why would he take her away?"

Dying and Death

Ericka eventually came to the realization that having her grandmother for the first 22 years of life had been a great gift, but the anger she felt is relatively typical for a person in mourning. Those who are dying may also experience anger. As psychiatrist Elisabeth Kübler-Ross (2009) observed in the early 1960s, people often have similar reactions when confronted with the news they are dying: stages of denial, anger, bargaining, depression, and acceptance. These stages, Kübler-Ross suggested, are coping mechanisms for dealing with what is to come.

- **Denial:** In the denial stage, people may react to the news with shock and disbelief, perhaps even suggesting the doctors are wrong. Unable to accept the diagnosis, they may seek other medical advice.
- **Anger:** Dying people may feel anger toward others who are healthy, or toward the doctor who does not have the cure. *Why me?* they may wonder, projecting anger and irritability in a seemingly random fashion.
- **Bargaining:** This stage may involve negotiating with God, doctors, or other powerful figures for a way out. Usually, this involves some sort of time frame: *Let me live to see my firstborn get married,* or *Just give me one more month to get my finances in order.*
- **Depression:** There comes a point when dying people can no longer ignore the inevitable. Depression may be due to the symptoms of illness, but it can also result from the overwhelming sense of loss—the loss of the future.
- **Acceptance:** Eventually, dying people accept the finality of their predicament; death is inevitable, and it is coming soon. This stage can deeply impact family and close friends, who, in some respects, may need more support than the person who is dying. According to one oncologist, the timing of acceptance is quite variable. For some people, it occurs moments before death; for others, soon after they learn there is no chance of recovery from their illness (Lyckholm, 2004).

Kübler-Ross was instrumental in bringing attention to the importance of attending to the dying person (Charlton & Verghese, 2010; Kastenbaum & Costa, 1977). The stages she proposed provide a valuable framework for understanding death, but every person responds in a unique way. For some, the stages are overlapping; others don't even experience them (Schneidman, 1973). Also note that this theory has not been thoroughly investigated, and it arose in a Western cultural context. Evidence suggests that people from other cultures have very different perspectives on dying and death.

Celebrating the Dead
A mariachi band plays at a cemetery in Mexico's Michoacan state on Dia de los Muertos, "Day of the Dead." During this holiday, people in Mexico and other parts of Latin America celebrate the lives of the deceased. Music is played, feasts are prepared, and graves are adorned with flowers to welcome back the spirits of relatives who have passed. In this cultural context, death is not something to be feared or dreaded, but rather a part of life that is embraced (National Geographic, 2015). Christian Kober/Corbis.

ACROSS THE WORLD

DEATH IN DIFFERENT CULTURES What does death mean to you? Some of us believe death marks the beginning of a peaceful afterlife. Others see it as a crossing over from one life to another. Still others believe death is like turning off the lights; once you're gone, it's all over.

DEALING WITH DEATH IN DIFFERENT WAYS

Views of death are very much related to religion and culture. A common belief among Indian Hindus, for example, is that one should spend a lifetime preparing for a "good death" (*su-mrtyu*). Often this means dying in old age, after conflicts have been put to rest, family matters settled, and farewells said. To prepare a loved one for a good death, relatives place the person on the floor at home (or on the banks of the Ganges River, if possible) and give her water from the hallowed Ganges. If these and other rituals are not carried out, the dead person's soul may become trapped and the family suffers the consequences: nightmares, infertility, and other forms of misfortune (Firth, 2005). In cultures heavily influenced by Confucianism, family members may care for parents at the end of their lives: "In Korea and Taiwan, dying and death is perceived not as a personal issue, but rather a family issue" (Cheng et al., 2015, p. 4). Imagine a psychologist trying to assist grieving relatives without any knowledge of these beliefs and traditions, or the culture-specific ways people show sympathy and compassion for others (Koopmann-Holm & Tsai, 2014).

THINK POSITIVE

RESILIENT IN THE FACE OF HARDSHIP Ericka may never get completely accustomed to the idea that her grandmother is gone. Sometimes while cooking, Ericka thinks to herself, *I just need to call Grandma and ask how she would make this dish.* But then reality sets in, and she calls Joan to ask what Grandma would do. This is how the whole family deals with the loss—by leaning on each other during times they would normally rely on Grandma. When one person in the family is faced with a dilemma, the other members look at each other and say, "What would Kat Wright do?" This type of social support is important for people who are recovering from the sudden loss of a loved one (Barlé, Wortman, & Latack, 2016).

GETTING THROUGH IT TOGETHER

Sometimes we try to avoid thinking about a person who has died; this may reduce distress temporarily, but a better long-term approach is to confront our feelings of loss (Barlé et al., 2016). Joan and Ericka couldn't stop thinking about Kat Wright if they tried, because of Niyah. Just like Grandma, Niyah sits down at the table with a newspaper, reading articles (especially those on politics) and searching the weekly ads for sales; she loves trivia, crossword puzzles, and making lists; and she's curious about everything. But perhaps most important, Niyah possesses Grandma's special brand of kindness. If a classmate forgets her lunch at home, Niyah will share everything in her lunch bag. When she sees homeless people, she wants to use her own money to buy them food. "She's very compassionate and grateful for what she does have," says Ericka.

Kat Wright Lives On
Ericka's grandmother (left) suddenly passed away at the age of 72, leaving behind a huge family that loved and depended on her. Six years later, Kat Wright is still very much alive in the thoughts and memories of Joan, Ericka, and the rest of the family. She lives on through Niyah, who inherited many of her best qualities, including a seemingly endless capacity for love. As Joan puts it, "We love. We love hard." Left: Ericka Harley. Right: Emily Weiss Photography.

Now, when Ericka reflects on her pregnancy with Niyah, she is nothing but grateful: "Even though it was really unexpected, I think it might have been one of the best things that ever happened." Ericka is in good company, as many young women demonstrate resiliency when faced with the stigma of teen pregnancy. How do these teenage moms achieve successful outcomes? Those who are resilient tend to resist stereotypes about teenage mothers and maintain a positive attitude; they are driven to reach educational goals and willing to put the needs of their children above their own. "Strong social support systems" and quality health care are also important (Solivan, Wallace, Kaplan, & Harville, 2015, p. 352). If we focus on resiliency, we start to see "what is 'right' instead of what is 'wrong'" (p. 354).

show what you know

1. Physical changes during middle adulthood include declines in hearing, eyesight, and height. Which of the following does research suggest can help limit the aging process?
   a. physical exercise
   b. elastin
   c. andropause
   d. collagen

2. As we age, our ______________ intelligence, or ability to think abstractly, decreases, but our knowledge gained through experience, our ______________ intelligence, increases.

3. When faced with death, a person can go through five stages. The final stage is ______________, and sometimes family members need more support during this stage than the dying person.
   a. denial
   b. anger
   c. bargaining
   d. acceptance

4. An aging relative in his mid-seventies is looking back on his life and evaluating what he has accomplished. He feels satisfied with his work, family, and friends. Erikson would say that he has succeeded in solving the crisis of ______________ versus ______________.

✓ CHECK YOUR ANSWERS IN APPENDIX C.

YOUR SCIENTIFIC WORLD is a new application-based feature appearing in every chapter. In these online activities, you will take on role-playing scenarios that encourage you to think critically and apply your knowledge of psychological science to solve a real-world problem. For example: Have you ever considered a career that involves working with children? In this activity, you will play the role of a daycare director. Interacting with children of various ages, you will learn about developmental milestones and different attachment styles. You can access Your Scientific World activities in LaunchPad. Have fun!

SUMMARY OF CONCEPTS

LO 1 Define human development. (p. 279)

Development refers to the changes that occur in physical, cognitive, and socioemotional functioning over the course of the life span. The goal of developmental psychology is to examine these changes, which begin at conception and end at death.

LO 2 Outline the three longstanding discussions in developmental psychology. (p. 280)

In the field of developmental psychology, debates often center on three major themes: stages and continuity; nature and nurture; and stability and change. Each of these themes relates to a basic question: (1) Does development occur in separate or discrete stages, or is it a steady, continuous process? (2) What are the relative roles of heredity and environment in human development? (3) How stable is personality over a lifetime and across situations?

LO 3 Identify several research methods used in the study of human development. (p. 281)

Developmental psychologists use various methods to explore changes across the life span. The cross-sectional method examines people of different ages at one point in time, while the longitudinal method follows one sample of individuals over a certain period. In the cross-sequential method, participants are divided into age groups and followed over time, so researchers can examine developmental changes within individuals and across different age groups.

LO 4 Examine the role genes play in our development and identify the biological factors that determine sex. (p. 284)

All the cells in the human body (except for red blood cells) have a nucleus at their center. Inside this nucleus are chromosomes, which contain genes made of deoxyribonucleic acid (DNA). Genes provide the blueprint for physiological development (and to some degree, psychological development). At conception, the sperm and egg merge to form a zygote, a single cell that eventually gives rise to the trillions of cells that make up a human body. The 23rd pair of chromosomes, also referred to as the sex chromosomes, provides specific instructions for the individual to develop into a female or male. When both members of the 23rd pair are X chromosomes (*XX*), the zygote generally develops into a female. When one member is an X and the other a Y (*XY*), the zygote generally develops into a male.

LO 5 Discuss how genotype and phenotype relate to development. (p. 285)

Genotype refers to an individual's unique collection of genes. These genes are found on the 23 pairs of chromosomes (46 chromosomes in all) located in the nucleus of nearly every cell in the body. Genotype does not change in response to the environment, but it does interact with the environment. The result of this interaction is one's phenotype, or unique set of physical and psychological characteristics.

LO 6 Describe the progression of prenatal development. (p. 286)

At the moment of conception, the mother's egg and the father's sperm come together to form a zygote. The zygote immediately begins to divide into two cells, then each of those cells divides, and so on. During the germinal period (conception to the end of the 2nd week), the rapidly dividing zygote implants in the uterine wall. Between the 3rd and 8th weeks of development, the mass of cells is called an embryo. From 2 months to birth, the growing human is identified as a fetus. The amniotic sac serves as a protective barrier, but harmful environmental agents called teratogens can damage the growing embryo or fetus. Radiation, viruses, bacteria, chemicals, alcohol, and drugs are all considered teratogens.

LO 7 Summarize the physical changes that occur in infancy. (p. 289)

As newborns grow, they experience astounding changes both seen and unseen. We see advancement in demonstrated capabilities, known as the motor milestones, and an increasingly sophisticated ability to discriminate among sensory stimuli. These sensorimotor advances are made possible by dramatic developments in the brain. Neurons rapidly sprout new connections, and this synaptic growth is influenced by experiences and stimulation from the environment.

LO 8 Outline the universal sequence of language development. (p. 293)

At age 2–3 months, infants typically start to produce vowel-like sounds known as cooing. At 4–6 months, they begin to combine consonants and vowels in the babbling stage. First words typically occur around 12 months, followed by two-word telegraphic speech at approximately 18 months. As children mature, they start to use more complete sentences. A "vocabulary explosion" tends to occur around 2 to 3 years of age. Most children are fluent in their native language by age 5 or 6.

LO 9 Discuss the key elements of Piaget's and Vygotsky's theories of cognitive development. (p. 295)

Piaget proposed that an important component of cognition is the schema, the collection of ideas that serves as a building block of understanding. Humans are driven to advance intellectually, partly as a result of an innate need to maintain cognitive equilibrium. With assimilation, we understand new information using an already existing schema. With accommodation, we restructure old notions to make a place for new information. Piaget proposed that cognitive development occurs in four stages: sensorimotor, preoperational, concrete operational, and formal operational. Vygotsky was interested in how social and cultural factors affect cognitive development. One way to help children's cognitive development is through scaffolding, pushing them to go just beyond what they are competent and comfortable doing, but also providing help, when needed, in a decreasing manner.

LO 10 Explain Erikson's theory of psychosocial development up until puberty. (p. 302)

According to Erikson, human development is marked by eight psychosocial stages, spanning infancy to old age. Each stage is marked by a developmental task or an emotional crisis that must be handled successfully to allow for healthy psychological growth. The stages from infancy to puberty are the following: trust versus mistrust, autonomy versus shame and doubt, initiative versus guilt, and industry versus inferiority.

LO 11 Give examples of significant physical changes that occur during adolescence. (p. 305)

The "growth spurt" of adolescence includes rapid changes in height, weight, and bone growth. Sex hormones, which influence this growth and development, are at high levels during this time. Primary sex characteristics (features associated with reproductive organs) and secondary sex characteristics (features not associated with reproductive organs) mature in both boys and girls.

Summarize Piaget's description of cognitive changes occurring in adolescence. (p. 306)

During the formal operational stage of cognitive development, adolescents begin to use deductive reasoning and logic to draw conclusions. A specific type of egocentrism emerges, as adolescents tend to believe that others think the same way they do. Because they have not had a lot of life experiences, teens may not consider the long-term consequences of their behaviors.

Describe how Erikson explained changes in identity during adolescence. (p. 307)

The stage of ego identity versus role confusion occurs during adolescence and is marked by the creation of an adult identity. During this stage, adolescents try out different roles as they attempt to define their values, beliefs, and goals. Successful resolution of this stage results in stronger fundamental values, beliefs, and goals with a firmer sense of identity.

LO 14 Examine Kohlberg's levels of moral development. (p. 309)

Kohlberg proposed there are three levels of moral development occurring sequentially over the life span. Preconventional moral reasoning usually applies to young children and focuses on the personal consequences of behaviors, both good and bad. At puberty, conventional moral reasoning is used, with the determination of right and wrong based on the expectations of society and important others. In postconventional moral reasoning, right and wrong are determined by the individual's beliefs about morality, which may not coincide with society's rules and regulations.

LO 15 Define gender and explain how culture plays a role in its development. (p. 310)

Gender refers to the dimension of masculinity and femininity based on social, cultural, and psychological characteristics. It is often used in reference to the cultural roles that distinguish males and females. We generally learn by observing other people's behavior and by internalizing cultural beliefs about what is appropriate for males and females.

Name several of the most important physical changes that occur across adulthood. (p. 315)

We typically reach our physical peak in early adulthood, and then decline as we approach late adulthood. Gradual changes occur, including hearing and vision loss, wrinkles, graying hair, reduced stamina, and menopause for women. Lifestyle can have a significant impact on health. Heavy drinking, drug use, poor eating habits, and sleep deprivation can make one look, feel, and function like someone much older.

Identify the most significant cognitive changes that occur across adulthood. (p. 317)

Cognitive ability remains stable from early to middle adulthood, but midlife is a time when information processing and memory can decline, particularly the ability to remember past events. Processing speed may slow with old age. Crystallized intelligence refers to the knowledge we gain through experience, and fluid intelligence refers to the ability to think in the abstract and create associations among concepts. Fluid intelligence declines with age, but crystallized intelligence increases.

Explain some of the socioemotional changes that occur across adulthood. (p. 318)

According to Erikson, we face the crisis of intimacy versus isolation during young adulthood; failure to create meaningful, deep relationships may lead to a life of isolation. In middle adulthood, we face the crisis of generativity versus stagnation. Positive resolution of this stage includes feeling like we have made a valuable impact on the next generation. During the crisis of integrity versus despair (late adulthood), we look back on life and evaluate how we have done.

KEY TERMS

accommodation, p. 296
adolescence, p. 305
androgens, p. 285
androgyny, p. 312
assimilation, p. 296
attachment, p. 301
authoritarian parenting, p. 319
authoritative parenting, p. 319
chromosomes, p. 284
cohort effect, p. 281
concrete operational stage, p. 298
conservation, p. 298
critical period, p. 280
cross-sectional method, p. 281
cross-sequential method, p. 283
crystallized intelligence, p. 317
deoxyribonucleic acid (DNA), p. 284
developmental psychology, p. 279
dizygotic twins, p. 284
dominant gene, p. 286
egocentrism, p. 296
embryo, p. 286
emerging adulthood, p. 313
epigenetics, p. 286
estrogens, p. 285
fetal alcohol syndrome (FAS), p. 287
fetus, p. 288
fluid intelligence, p. 317
formal operational stage, p. 298
gender, p. 310
gender identity, p. 310
gender roles, p. 310
gender schemas, p. 311
gene, p. 284
genotype, p. 285
identity, p. 307
intersexual, p. 285
longitudinal method, p. 281
maturation, p. 279
menarche, p. 305
menopause, p. 316
monozygotic twins, p. 284
object permanence, p. 296
permissive parenting, p. 319
phenotype, p. 285
preoperational stage, p. 296
primary sex characteristics, p. 305
puberty, p. 305
recessive gene, p. 286
scaffolding, p. 299
schema, p. 295
secondary sex characteristics, p. 305
sensorimotor stage, p. 296
spermarche, p. 305
telegraphic speech, p. 294
temperament, p. 300
teratogens, p. 287
testosterone, p. 285
transgender, p. 313
transsexual, p. 313
uninvolved parenting, p. 319
zone of proximal development, p. 299
zygote, p. 284

TEST PREP ARE YOU READY?

1. A researcher is interested in studying changes in memory, problem solving, and language across the life span. She chooses a large sample of college seniors and decides to follow them for the next 30 years. This is an example of:
   a. socioemotional development.
   b. longitudinal research.
   c. cross-sectional research.
   d. epigenetics.
2. Ricardo's grandmother has Alzheimer's disease, and he wonders if he will experience a similar future because of his biological connection to her. Which of the following debates in developmental psychology is similar to what Ricardo is contemplating?
   a. stability and change
   b. stages or continuity
   c. critical or sensitive period
   d. nature and nurture
3. DNA molecules include sections corresponding to ________, which encode proteins that determine the texture of hair, color of eyes, and some aspects of personality.
   a. phenotypes
   b. epigenetics
   c. zygotes
   d. genes
4. Your psychology instructor often discusses factors in the environment that can influence how genes are expressed. This topic is a major focus in the field of:
   a. epigenetics.
   b. maturation.
   c. the cohort effect.
   d. prenatal development.
5. Human development is influenced by the interaction of many factors. Brain development, for example, is impacted by biological maturation and experiences in the environment. This is evident in ________, which occurs when unused synaptic connections are eliminated.
   a. myelin
   b. socioemotional development
   c. synaptic pruning
   d. the rooting reflex
6. Vygotsky identified ________ as an approach that helps children learn, providing support when necessary but allowing them to problem-solve as much as possible on their own.
   a. assimilation
   b. scaffolding
   c. phenotype
   d. schema
7. ________ are agents that can damage a growing embryo or fetus.
   a. Phenotypes
   b. Genotypes
   c. Zygotes
   d. Teratogens
8. ________ further develop during adolescence. These changes are associated with the maturation of reproductive organs, such as the ovaries, uterus, penis, and testes.
   a. Gender schemas
   b. Temperaments
   c. Primary sex characteristics
   d. Secondary sex characteristics
9. Adolescents begin thinking more logically and systematically, and start to use deductive reasoning to draw conclusions. They have entered what Piaget referred to as the:
   a. formal operational stage.
   b. postconventional moral reasoning stage.
   c. industry versus inferiority stage.
   d. concrete operational stage.
10. Which of the following represents the universal sequence of language development?
    a. root; babble; coo
    b. babble; coo; first words
    c. coo; babble; first words
    d. coo; root; babble
11. According to Erikson, one of the tasks of adolescence is searching for identity, that is, finding a sense of self based on values, beliefs, and goals. How is identity related to gender? How does culture influence identity?
12. Describe some of the physical changes that occur during adulthood.
13. Draw a diagram that outlines how Erikson's stages of psychosocial development, Piaget's stages of cognitive development, and Kohlberg's stages of moral development fit together on a developmental timeline.
14. Describe and give examples of crystallized intelligence and fluid intelligence. Discuss how these types of intelligence change across the life span.
15. Describe the types of crises that infants, children, and adults face using Erikson's stages of socioemotional development.

✓ CHECK YOUR ANSWERS IN APPENDIX C.

Go to **LaunchPad** or **Achieve: Read & Practice** to test your understanding with **LearningCurve**.

CHAPTER 9

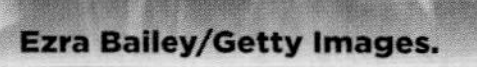

Ezra Bailey/Getty Images.

Ravi Shekhar/Dinodia Photo/AGE Fotostock.

khoa vu/Getty Images.

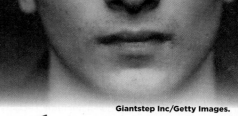

Giantstep Inc/Getty Images.

Motivation and Emotion

Motivation

RIO, AT LAST September 17, 2016: Ivonne Mosquera-Schmidt took her place at the starting line of the 1500-meter race for blind female athletes at the 2016 Paralympics. She had been dreaming of this moment since age 8, and the journey had been long and hard. Just two years before, Ivonne had been diagnosed with cancer for the third time in her life. Sitting in the doctor's office with tears streaming down her face, she had made the vow, "Whatever happens, I have to make it to Rio." Despite the shock, fear, and anger of facing cancer, Ivonne held onto the idea that she was a warrior—a small warrior at 88 pounds—but a warrior no less. "It's not about how big we are," says Ivonne. "It's about how strong we are."

Ivonne has been a fighter all her life. When she was 2 years old, doctors removed both of her eyes to stop the spread of an aggressive cancer. She is completely blind and has no memory of vision, but that hasn't stopped her from doing much of anything. Growing up in New York City, Ivonne used to ride her bicycle across the George Washington Bridge, her father running alongside. She went to school with sighted kids, climbed trees in the park, and studied ballet, tap, and jazz dance (Boccella, 2012, May 6; iminmotion.net, n.d.). A year after earning her undergraduate degree in mathematics from Stanford University, Ivonne took up running. With the help of trainers, guides, and her husband John, she has turned herself into a world-class runner and triathlete, racking up records and titles all over the globe. In Rio, Ivonne showed her warrior strength and did her country proud, earning 6th place in the 1500 meters.

But athletic accomplishments are only part of what makes Ivonne so phenomenal. Did we mention that she speaks four languages, climbs mountains, and has a graduate degree in business? Despite her blindness and repeated battles with cancer, Ivonne has garnered more achievements and life experiences than we can count. How does she do it?

There is little doubt that Ivonne is blessed with intelligence, athletic ability, and other remarkable gifts. But these characteristics are not the only ingredients in the recipe for outstanding achievement: *motivation* is essential, too (Eskreis-Winkler et al., 2016; Reifsteck, Gill, & Labban, 2016).

Paralympian
Ivonne Mosquera-Schmidt (right) and her guide Kyle Wardwell at the 2016 Paralympics in Rio. Representing the United States in the Paralympics is just one of Ivonne's extraordinary athletic feats. In addition to winning two gold medals in the Paratriathlon World Championships, she has won first place in the women's visually impaired category of the Boston Marathon on three occasions, and she holds three American records: in the 1500 meters, 3000 meters, and 5000 meters for totally blind women (iminmotion.net, n.d.).
Lucas Uebel/Getty Images.

What Is Motivation?

LO 1 Define motivation.

Psychologists propose that **motivation** is a stimulus or force that can direct the way we behave, think, and feel. A motivated behavior is guided (has a direction), energized, and persistent. When Ivonne is training, her behavior is *guided* because she sets goals like meeting certain running times, *energized* because she goes after those goals with zeal, and *persistent* because she sticks with her goals even when challenges arise. We exhibit behaviors all the time, but motivated behaviors are different from behaviors that are simply reactions to environmental stimuli.

In this chapter, you will learn about various forms of motivation and theories that attempt to explain them. Keep in mind that human behavior is complex and should be studied in the context of biology, culture, and other environmental factors. Every behavior is likely to have a multitude of causes (Maslow, 1943).

DOES LEARNING PLAY A ROLE? One way to explain motivated behavior is through learning theory. We know that people (not to mention dogs, chickens, and slugs) can *learn* behaviors through classical conditioning, operant conditioning, and observational learning (Chapter 5). Let's take a look at how operant conditioning can help us understand the relationship between learning and motivation. When a behavior is reinforced (with **positive or negative *reinforcers***), an association is established. This association between a behavior and its consequence becomes the **incentive,** or reason, you are motivated to repeat the behavior. Imagine you have been avoiding a particular term paper assignment. You decide to treat yourself to an hour of watching Netflix for every three pages you write. Adding a reinforcer (Netflix) increases your writing behavior; thus, we call it a *positive reinforcer.* The association between the behavior (writing) and the consequence (watching your favorite show) is called the incentive.

CONNECTIONS
In **Chapter 5,** we introduced positive and negative reinforcers, which are stimuli that increase future occurrences of target behaviors. In both cases, the behavior becomes associated with the reinforcer. Here, we see how these associations become incentives.

motivation A stimulus that can direct behavior, thinking, and feeling.

incentive An association established between a behavior and its consequences, which then motivates that behavior.

Note: Quotations attributed to Ivonne Mosquera-Schmidt and Ibrahim Hashi are personal communications.

Ivonne, In Her Own Words
http://qrs.ly/w57829n

Photo: Macmillan Learning.

Before long, you begin to expect this break from work, which motivates you to write. Do you think Ivonne's running behavior was shaped by incentives?

THE POWER OF CHOCOLATE After graduating from college and moving back to New York City, Ivonne started looking for a new activity to get outside and moving. She came across the New York Road Runners Club, which connected her with an organization that supports and trains runners with all types of disabilities. Having no running experience (apart from jogging on a treadmill), Ivonne showed up at a practice one Saturday morning in Central Park and ran 2 miles with one of the running club's guides. The next week she came back for more, and then the next, and the next. During these early practices, Ivonne's teammates promised to buy her hot chocolate whenever she increased her distance. "Every time they would try to get me to run further, they'd say, 'We'll have hot chocolate afterwards!'" Ivonne remembers. "They actually would follow through with their promise!"

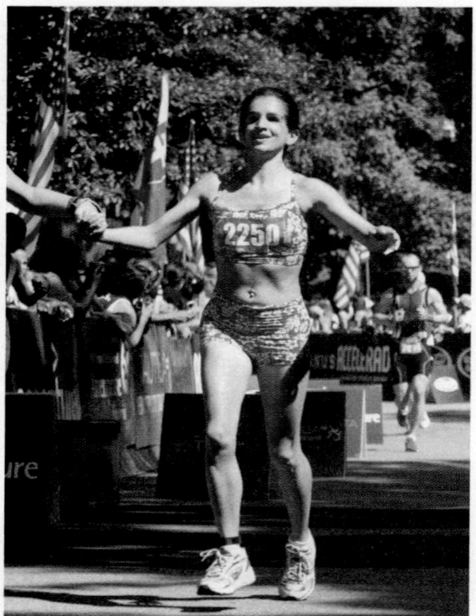

For the Love of Running
Ivonne competes in the 2008 New York City Triathlon. During her early running days, Ivonne's friends reinforced her efforts with hot chocolate. When the incentive to continue a behavior stems from external reinforcers (hot chocolate, in this case), the motivation is extrinsic. These days, Ivonne doesn't need sweet treats to keep her running. Her motivation is more intrinsic in nature; that is, she derives pleasure from the activity itself. Courtesy Ivonne Mosquera-Schmidt.

LO 2 Explain how extrinsic and intrinsic motivation impact behavior.

EXTRINSIC MOTIVATION The idea of getting hot chocolate treats provided Ivonne with an incentive to return to practice again and again. When a learned behavior is motivated by the incentive of external reinforcers in the environment, there is an **extrinsic motivation** to continue that behavior (Deci, Koestner, & Ryan, 1999; Deci, Olafsen, & Ryan, 2017; Ryan & Deci, 2017). In other words, the motivation comes from consequences that exist outside of the person. Bagels and coffee might provide extrinsic motivation for people to attend a boring meeting, grades and diplomas for students to work hard in college. For most of us, money is a powerful form of extrinsic motivation. One final example is avoidance of punishment (Ryan & Deci, 2017). The thought of late fees, traffic tickets, and reprimands from authority figures can provide us with extrinsic motivation to follow rules.

INTRINSIC MOTIVATION Ivonne's motivation to run also originated from inside; she came to love the sense of freedom running gave her, the experience of being in nature, smelling the grass and feeling the breeze, and sharing it with others. When learned behaviors are driven by personal satisfaction, interest in a subject matter, and other variables that exist within a person, **intrinsic motivation** is at work (Deci et al., 1999; Ryan & Deci, 2017). Do you find that reading this textbook is inherently interesting? Do you study it carefully because you enjoy the feeling that comes from mastering the material? If so, your reading behavior stems from intrinsic motivation. The reinforcers originate inside of you (learning feels good and brings you satisfaction), and not from the external environment.

EXTRINSIC VERSUS INTRINSIC What compels you to offer your seat to someone on a bus? Is it because you've been praised for helping others (extrinsic motivation), or because it simply feels good to help someone (intrinsic motivation)? Many behaviors are inspired by a blend of extrinsic and intrinsic motivation. But there do appear to be potential disadvantages to extrinsic motivation, especially when performance (for example, on a presentation) is a factor (Cerasoli, Nicklin, & Ford, 2014; Deci et al., 1999). Researchers have found that using rewards, such as money and marshmallows, to reinforce already interesting activities (like doing puzzles, playing word games, and so on) can lead to a decrease in behaviors that were once intrinsically motivating (Ryan & Deci, 2017). "Tangible rewards—both material rewards, such as pizza

extrinsic motivation The drive or urge to continue a behavior because of external reinforcers.

intrinsic motivation The drive or urge to continue a behavior because of internal reinforcers.

parties for reading books, and symbolic rewards, such as good student awards—are widely advocated by many educators and are used in many classrooms, yet the evidence suggests that these rewards tend to undermine intrinsic motivation" (Deci, Koestner, & Ryan, 2001, p. 15). Recent research suggests the link may not be that simple; extrinsic motivators such as merit-based salary increases do not always erode intrinsic motivation, and the timing of the reward can make a difference (Gerhart & Fang, 2015; Woolley & Fishbach, 2018).

Put Your Heads Together

Imagine you are a psychology instructor and your goal is to motivate students to perform better on exams. Team up and discuss **A**) extrinsic motivation strategies you could implement, and **B**) ways to encourage intrinsic motivation. **C**) Which would be more effective in the long term?

We now have developed a basic understanding of what motivation is; we also have established that motivation may be influenced by learning. Let's take a look at some other major theories of motivation, keeping in mind that each has its strengths and limitations.

Do Humans Have Instincts?

Instinct. You hear that word used all the time in everyday conversation: "Trust your instincts," people might say. "That boxer has a killer instinct," a commentator remarks during a match. But what exactly are instincts, and do humans really have them? **Instincts** are complex behaviors that are fixed, unlearned, and consistent within a species. Because of instinct, honeybees communicate through a "waggle dance," and sea turtles swim to the ocean after they have hatched (Malkemus, 2015). No one teaches the bees to dance or the turtles to swim to the ocean; through evolution, these behaviors appear to be etched into their genetic make-up.

Instincts form the basis of one of the earliest theories of motivation. Inspired in part by Charles Darwin's theory of evolution, early scholars proposed that a variety of instincts motivate human behavior (Krueger & Reckless, 1931; McDougall, 1912). Thousands of human "instincts" were named, among them curiosity, flight, and aggressiveness (Bernard, 1926; Kuo, 1921). Yet there was little evidence they were true instincts—that is, complex behaviors that are fixed, unlearned, and consistent within a species. Only a handful of human activities, among them rooting behavior in newborn infants, might be considered instincts (Chapter 8). But even these are more akin to reflexes than complex activities like honeybee waggle dancing. Although instinct theory faded, some of its themes are apparent in the **evolutionary perspective**. Research suggests that evolutionary forces influence human behavior. For example, emotional responses, such as fear of snakes, heights, and spiders, may have evolved to protect us from danger (Langeslag & van Strien, 2018; Plomin, DeFries, Knopik, & Neiderhiser, 2013).

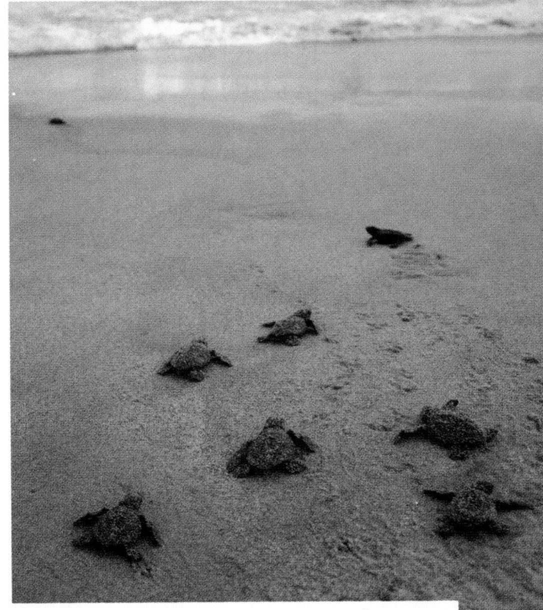

Turtles on a Mission
Baby loggerhead sea turtles instinctually crawl toward the ocean after hatching. When the females reach adulthood, they return to the same beach to lay their own eggs, finding their way "home" with the help of the earth's magnetic field (Brothers & Lohmann, 2015). Elena Tyapkina/Alamy.

CONNECTIONS

In **Chapter 1,** we presented the evolutionary perspective, which suggests that humans have evolved adaptive traits through natural selection. Behaviors that improve the chances of survival and reproduction are most likely to be passed along to offspring, whereas less adaptive behaviors decrease in frequency.

Just Stayin' Alive

LO 3 Describe drive-reduction theory and explain how it relates to motivation.

In order to survive, humans and nonhuman animals must maintain internal conditions, such as temperature and oxygen levels, at a baseline or constant state. **Homeostasis** refers to the way in which our bodies maintain these constant

instincts Complex behaviors that are fixed, unlearned, and consistent within a species.

homeostasis The tendency for bodies to maintain constant states through internal controls.

Spinning for Stimulation?
Fidget spinners are popular among elementary students, but do they really help kids with ADHD stay calm and focused, as advertisers claim? These gadgets might offer just the right amount of stimulation to help some people relax (Isbister, 2017, May 18), but their therapeutic value has not been put to the scientific test (Calfas, 2017, May 11). It's hard to use fidget spinners without looking at them—and this poses a problem when students need to see something their teacher is doing. Alternative toys, such as stress balls and fidget cubes, may satisfy the desire for stimulation without demanding engagement of the eyes (Isbister, 2017, May). Chesnot/Getty Images.

states through internal controls. The **drive-reduction theory** proposes that this biological balancing act (homeostasis) is the basis for motivation (Hull, 1952). In other words, behaviors are driven by the process of fulfilling basic physiological **needs** for nutrients, fluids, oxygen, sleep and so on (see **INFOGRAPHIC 9.1**). Behaviors such as eating, drinking, and sleeping help us meet these physiological needs. If a need is not fulfilled, this creates a **drive,** or state of tension, that pushes us or motivates behaviors to meet the need and restore equilibrium. Once a need is satisfied, the drive is reduced, but not forever. The need inevitably returns, and you feel driven to meet it once again. A good example is hunger. You wake up with an empty stomach, fill it with food, but then find yourself hungry at noon; so you eat lunch, but the hunger returns in the evening, and the cycle continues.

The drive-reduction theory helps us understand how physiological needs can be motivators, but it is less useful for explaining why we buy new clothes, go to college, or drive cars too fast.

LEAPING INTO THE UNKNOWN Ivonne has never been afraid of new experiences. In fact, she has sought out novel and stimulating adventures all her life. "I remember even as a little kid wanting to be on roller skates," she says. "I was always ready to go down the slide, and I had no idea how long the slide was." At age 8, Ivonne was already using the New York City bus system to get from her elementary school to piano lessons. "I would walk over to 5th Avenue and wait for one of the buses," she explains. "I would count my steps from the corner of 81st Street toward 80th Street so that I knew where the bus stop was." To determine when it was safe to move into the crosswalk, Ivonne listened for the sound of cars moving in the same direction she wanted to go. Then she would put her cane out and bravely venture forward. 

Looking for Some Excitement?

New experiences can be frightening. They can also be delightfully exhilarating. Humans are fascinated by novelty, and you see evidence of this innate curiosity in the earliest stages of life. Babies grab, taste, and smell just about everything they can get their hands on; children fearlessly climb trees and playground structures; even adults seek out new experiences, paying loads of money to travel to foreign lands. They also spend hours visiting websites like Wikipedia and YouTube—just to learn about new things.

Why engage in activities that have little, if anything, to do with satisfying basic biological needs? Humans are driven by other types of urges, including the apparent need for stimulation.

LO 4 Explain how arousal theory relates to motivation.

According to **arousal theory,** humans (and perhaps other primates) seek an optimal level of arousal, as not all motivation stems from physical needs. Arousal, or engagement in the world, can be a product of anxiety, surprise, excitement, interest, fear, and many other emotions. Have you ever had an unexplained urge to make simple changes to your daily routines, like taking the stairs instead of the elevator, eating eggs instead of cereal, or styling your hair differently? These behaviors may stem from your need to increase arousal. Optimal arousal is not the same for everyone (Infographic 9.1). Evidence suggests that some people are *sensation seekers;* that is, they appear to seek activities that increase arousal (Zuckerman, 1979, 1994, 2015).

drive-reduction theory Suggests that homeostasis motivates us to meet biological needs.

needs Physiological or psychological requirements that must be maintained at some baseline or constant state.

drive A state of tension that pushes us or motivates behaviors to meet a need.

arousal theory Suggests that humans are motivated to seek an optimal level of arousal, or alertness and engagement in the world.

Theories of Motivation

Motivational forces drive our behaviors, thoughts, and feelings. Psychologists have proposed different theories addressing the needs that create these drives within us. Let's look at the three most prominent theories of motivation. Some theories, like drive-reduction theory, best explain motivation related to physiological needs. Other theories focus on psychological needs, such as the need for an optimum level of stimulation, as described in arousal theory. In his hierarchy of needs, Abraham Maslow combined various drives and proposed that we are motivated to meet some needs before others.

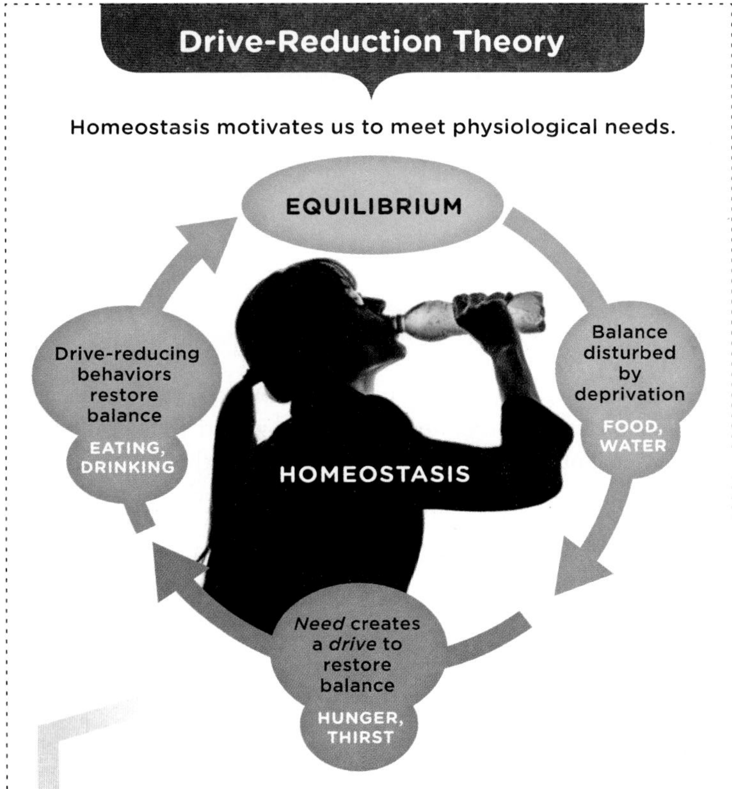
Drive-Reduction Theory
Homeostasis motivates us to meet physiological needs.
EQUILIBRIUM
Balance disturbed by deprivation
FOOD, WATER
Need creates a drive to restore balance
HUNGER, THIRST
Drive-reducing behaviors restore balance
EATING, DRINKING
HOMEOSTASIS

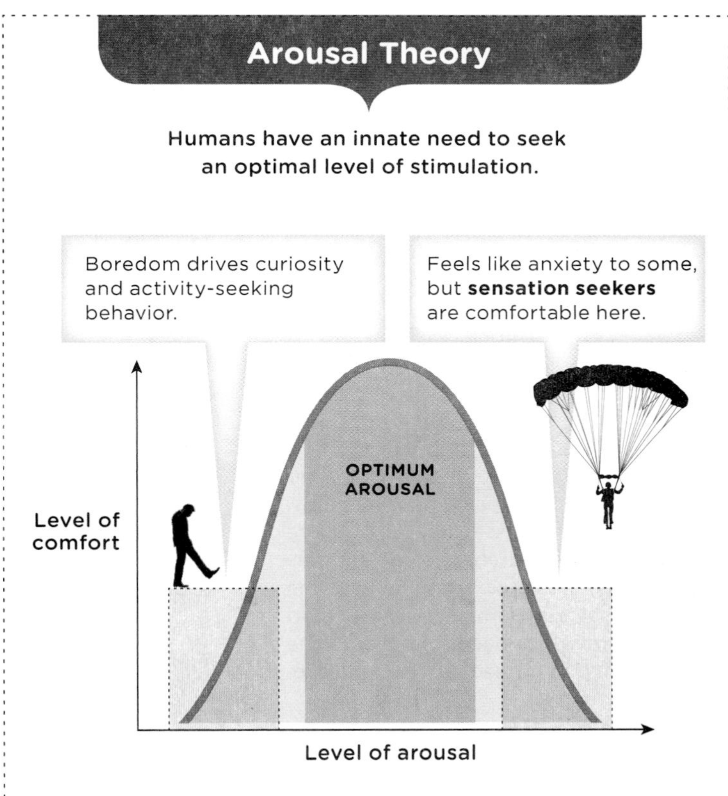
Arousal Theory
Humans have an innate need to seek an optimal level of stimulation.
Boredom drives curiosity and activity-seeking behavior.
Feels like anxiety to some, but sensation seekers are comfortable here.
OPTIMUM AROUSAL
Level of comfort
Level of arousal

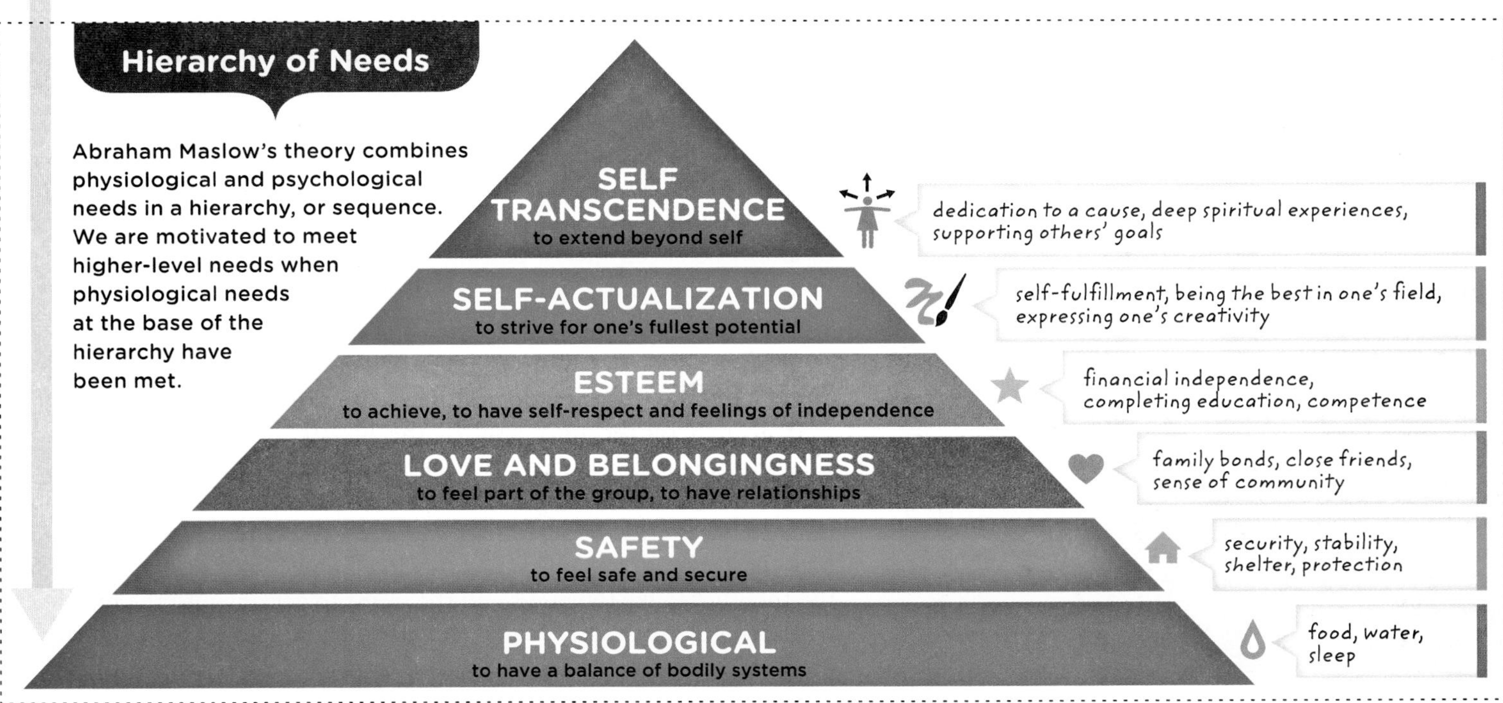
Hierarchy of Needs
Abraham Maslow's theory combines physiological and psychological needs in a hierarchy, or sequence. We are motivated to meet higher-level needs when physiological needs at the base of the hierarchy have been met.
SELF TRANSCENDENCE
to extend beyond self
dedication to a cause, deep spiritual experiences, supporting others' goals
SELF-ACTUALIZATION
to strive for one's fullest potential
self-fulfillment, being the best in one's field, expressing one's creativity
ESTEEM
to achieve, to have self-respect and feelings of independence
financial independence, completing education, competence
LOVE AND BELONGINGNESS
to feel part of the group, to have relationships
family bonds, close friends, sense of community
SAFETY
to feel safe and secure
security, stability, shelter, protection
PHYSIOLOGICAL
to have a balance of bodily systems
food, water, sleep

Credits: Woman with water bottle, OSTILL/iStock/Getty Images; Sad businessman silhouette, ostill/Shutterstock; Skydiver silhouette, vadimmmus/Shutterstock.

CONNECTIONS

In **Chapter 7,** we discussed heritability, the degree to which heredity is responsible for a particular characteristic in a population. The heritability for sensation seeking indicates that 58–67% of population-wide variation can be attributed to genes, and 33–42% to environmental influences.

The **heritability** of this trait appears to be quite high, ranging from 58% to 67% (Zuckerman, 2015). Popularly known as "adrenaline junkies," these individuals relish activities like cliff diving, racing motorcycles, and watching horror movies. Research indicates that sensation seeking can decrease during later adolescence, suggesting that sensation seekers might take more responsible risks as they mature (Lauriola, Panno, Levin, & Lejuez, 2014).

High sensation seeking is not necessarily a bad thing, as it may be associated with a greater tolerance for stressful events (Roberti, 2004). And according to some interpretations of the *Yerkes–Dodson law,* moderate levels of arousal can actually help performance, in rats and humans (Teigen, 1994; Winton, 1987; Yerkes & Dodson, 1908). Suppose you are taking an exam. You don't want to be underaroused because you may fall asleep; nor do you want to be overaroused, as you might have trouble concentrating. You need just the right amount of arousal, somewhere in the moderate range.

Needs and More Needs

LO 5 Outline Maslow's hierarchy of needs.

CONNECTIONS

In **Chapter 1,** we discussed Maslow and his involvement in humanistic psychology. The humanists suggest that people are inclined to grow and change for the better, and this perspective is apparent in the hierarchy of needs. Humans are motivated by the universal tendency to move up the hierarchy and meet needs toward the top.

Have you ever been in a car accident, lived through a hurricane, or witnessed a violent crime? At the time, you probably did *not* think about what show you were going to watch on HBO that night. When physical safety is threatened, everything else tends to take a backseat. This idea that certain needs take priority over others is central to the **hierarchy of needs,** a theory of motivation proposed by Abraham Maslow, a leading figure in the **humanistic movement**. Maslow organized human needs into a hierarchy, often depicted as a pyramid (Infographic 9.1). These needs, which are both biological and psychological in nature, are considered universal and are ordered according to the strength of their associated drives.

PHYSIOLOGICAL NEEDS The most critical needs are situated at the base of the hierarchy and generally take precedence over higher-level needs. These *physiological needs* include requirements for food, water, sleep, and an overall balance of bodily systems. If a life-sustaining need such as fluid intake goes unsatisfied, other needs are placed on hold and the person is motivated to find ways to satisfy it. Maslow suggested that the basic physiological needs of people from most societies are "relatively well gratified" (Maslow, 1943), but this is not always the case. One example is the widespread need for nutrition. The U.S. Department of Agriculture found that 12.3% of American households were "food insecure" in 2016. Food insecurity was evidenced by factors such as "being unable to afford balanced meals, cutting the size of meals, or being hungry because of too little money for food" (Coleman-Jensen, Rabbitt, Gregory, & Singh, 2017, p. vi).

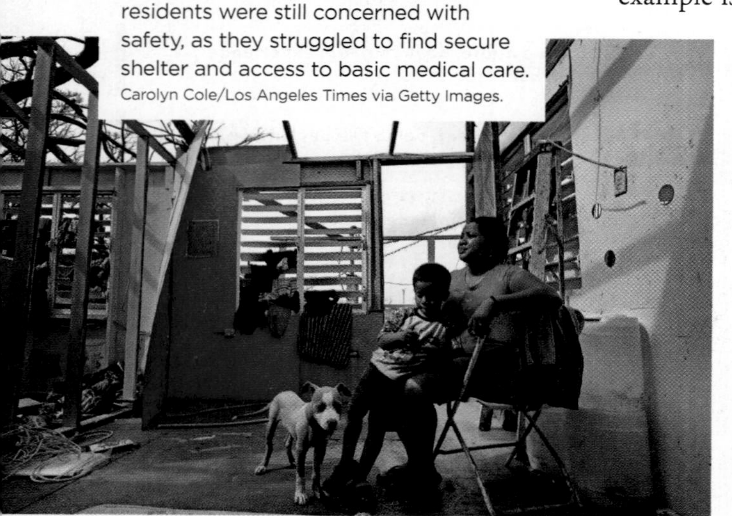

Safety, Ripped Away
A mother and son sit in the remains of their home following Hurricane Maria. When Maria hit Puerto Rico in 2017, people who previously had no trouble meeting their safety needs suddenly found themselves in grave danger. Long after the hurricane passed, many residents were still concerned with safety, as they struggled to find secure shelter and access to basic medical care. Carolyn Cole/Los Angeles Times via Getty Images.

SAFETY NEEDS If physiological needs are satisfied, human behavior is motivated by the next level in the hierarchy: *safety needs.* When baby Ivonne began cancer treatments, she had a safe place to stay in New Jersey, but traveling to New York City for chemotherapy and radiation was treacherous. "[My mother] would have to come from New Jersey by herself without knowing English and traipse through the snow, and take the buses and the trains to get down to the hospital with me," Ivonne says. During this period (the late 1970s), the city's dark subway tunnels were not the safest place for a mother and baby.

In 1979, for example, the subway system saw over 250 felonies per week (Samaha, 2014, August 7).

For many people in the United States, safety is equated with the need for predictability and order: having a steady job, a home in a safe neighborhood, health insurance, and living in a country with a stable economy. What does safety mean for you, and how might it differ from that of someone living in Venezuela, Russia, or Afghanistan?

LOVE AND BELONGINGNESS NEEDS If safety needs are being met, then people will be motivated by *love and belongingness needs.* Maslow suggested this includes the need to avoid loneliness, to feel like part of a group, and to maintain affectionate relationships. As a blind child in the mainstream school system, Ivonne did not always have an easy time fitting in. Her parents could not afford all the material things other kids had, but they provided unconditional love, support, and a strong sense of cultural identity.

What happens when love and belongingness needs go unsatisfied? People who feel disconnected or excluded may demonstrate less prosocial behavior (Twenge, Baumeister, DeWall, Ciarocco, & Bartels, 2007) and act more aggressively and less cooperatively, which only tends to intensify their struggle for social acceptance (DeWall, Baumeister, & Vohs, 2008; Stenseng, Belsky, Skalicka, & Wichstrøm, 2014). Yet, this effect is reduced when the excluded people think about the future and consider the long-term implications of their actions (Balliet & Ferris, 2013). Responses of the excluded person may also depend on characteristics of the excluder. Some evidence suggests that socially isolated people display "less aggression and more prosocial responses" when they are excluded by a "highly attractive" person (Aydin, Agthe, Pfundmair, Frey, & DeWall, 2017, p. 208).

She's Always Been Unstoppable Ivonne (center) with her family. Even in nursery school, Ivonne appeared to be motivated by esteem needs. She was self-directed, confident, and commanded respect from others. Courtesy Ivonne Mosquera-Schmidt.

ESTEEM NEEDS If the first three levels of needs are being met, then the individual might be motivated by *esteem needs,* including the need to be respected by others, to achieve, and to have self-respect and feelings of independence. Fulfilling these needs fosters a sense of confidence and self-worth, both qualities that Ivonne possessed early in life. In nursery school, she was determined to do everything her sighted peers did, from riding a tricycle to pouring her own juice. "I remember those little pitchers and cups like [it] was just yesterday," recalls Ivonne, who insisted on serving herself. "It's me, it's my juice, and I want to pour it!"

You Asked, Ivonne Answers

http://qrs.ly/w57829n

If doctors found a way to restore your vision, would you want to see again?

SELF-ACTUALIZATION When the above-mentioned needs are being met, a person can be motived by what Maslow (1943) called the need for **self-actualization:** "to become more and more what one is, to become everything that one is capable of becoming" (p. 382). This need to self-actualize, or reach one's fullest potential, is at the heart of the humanistic movement: It represents the human tendency toward growth and self-discovery (Chapter 10). For some, self-actualization means becoming the best possible parent; others aim to be outstanding designers or musicians. Ivonne is a prime example of a self-actualizer, because she is always striving to learn and achieve new goals. "Some of my dreams have come true," she says. "I wanted to be in finance, so I found a way to go to business school . . . and I was a financial analyst." Then there are her many physical accomplishments, like climbing Tanzania's Mount Kilimanjaro and competing in over 25 triathlons. "There is always so much more to learn about myself and so much more to learn about the world," she says. "It's like I'm never done."

hierarchy of needs A continuum of needs that are universal and ordered in terms of the strength of their associated drives.

self-actualization The need to be one's best and strive for one's fullest potential.

SELF-TRANSCENDENCE Toward the end of his life, Maslow proposed an additional level in the hierarchy: the need for *self-transcendence.* This need motivates us

Breaking Fast
Iraqi families gather for Iftar, the evening meal eaten after the daytime fast. During the holy month of Ramadan, Muslims deny themselves food, water, tobacco, and chewing gum from dawn to dusk. "As defined in the Qur'an, fasting is a strict practice of deep personal worship in which Muslims seek the highest level of awareness of the Divine" (Ilias, Tayeh, & Pachoundakis, 2016, p. 147). Here, basic needs (food and water) are put on hold for something more transcendent. Johan Spanner/Polaris.

to go beyond our own needs and feel outward connections through "peak experiences" of ecstasy and awe. Fulfilling this need might mean devoting oneself to a humanitarian cause or achieving spiritual enlightenment. Ivonne strives for self-transcendence by bridging the gap between the able-bodied and disabled communities, bringing people together to pursue common passions, such as running and yoga.

EXCEPTIONS TO THE RULE Maslow's hierarchy suggests a certain order of needs, but this sequence is not set in stone. In some cases, people abandon physiological needs to meet a self-actualization need—going on a hunger strike or giving up material possessions, for example. The practice of fasting, which occurs in many faiths, including Islam, Christianity, Hinduism, and Judaism, illustrates how basic physiological needs (food and water) can be placed on hold for a greater purpose (religion). Safety is another basic need often relegated in the pursuit of something more transcendent. Throughout history, soldiers have given their lives fighting for causes like freedom and social justice.

SELF-DETERMINATION THEORY Building on the ideas of Maslow and **Erik Erikson**, researchers Edward Deci and Richard Ryan (2008) proposed the **self-determination theory (SDT),** which suggests that we are born with three universal, fundamental needs that are always driving us in the direction of optimal functioning: competence, relatedness, and autonomy (Stone, Deci, & Ryan, 2009). Competence represents the need to reach our goals through mastery of day-to-day responsibilities (passing an exam, for instance). Relatedness is the need to create meaningful and lasting relationships. We are all intrinsically motivated to establish bonds that allow us to share our deepest thoughts and feelings. Autonomy means managing one's behavior to reach personal goals. Meeting with an academic advisor as you move one step closer to choosing a career is an example of autonomy. When autonomy is threatened (for example, when parents are strict and controlling of their adolescent children), frustration may increase (Van Petegem, Soenens, Vansteenkiste, & Beyers, 2015).

CONNECTIONS

In **Chapter 8,** we introduced Erikson's theory of psychosocial development, which suggests that stages of development are marked by a task or emotional crisis. These crises often touch on issues of competence, relatedness, and autonomy.

NEED FOR ACHIEVEMENT In the early 1930s, Henry Murray proposed that humans are motivated by 20 fundamental needs, one of which has been the subject of extensive research: the **need for achievement (n-Ach).** The n-Ach creates a drive to reach attainable and challenging goals, especially in the face of competition. Researchers suggest that people tend to seek situations that provide opportunities for satisfying this need (McClelland, Atkinson, Clark, & Lowell, 1976). For example, a child who aspires to become a professional basketball player might start training, read books about the sport, and apply for basketball camp scholarships.

NEED FOR POWER Some people are motivated by a **need for power (n-Pow),** or a drive to control and influence others (McClelland et al., 1976). People with this need may project their importance through outward appearances—driving around in luxury cars, wearing flashy designer clothing, and buying expensive houses. Those with high levels of n-Pow enjoy dominating others but hate being dominated themselves; this tendency may correspond to certain types of activity in a part of the brain called the dorsoanterior striatum (Schultheiss & Schiepe-Tiska, 2013).

self-determination theory (SDT) Suggests that humans are born with the needs for competence, relatedness, and autonomy, which are always driving us in the direction of growth and optimal functioning.

need for achievement (n-Ach) A drive to reach attainable and challenging goals, especially in the face of competition.

need for power (n-Pow) A drive to control and influence others.

Put Your Heads Together

In your groups, **A)** pick a media report describing a famous person's behavior. **B)** Apply different theories of motivation to explain their actions.

Whatever your needs may be, there is a good chance you try to fulfill some of them with digital technology. Eighty-six percent of adults under the age of 30 use at least one form of social media (Pew Research Center, 2017, January 12). What needs are they trying to satisfy?

SOCIAL MEDIA AND PSYCHOLOGY

NETWORK NEEDS Like all of us, social media users are driven by the desire for love and belongingness—the third level from the bottom on Maslow's hierarchy. Whether they meet those needs may, to some degree, depend on which activities they choose. Using "image-based platforms" like Instagram and Snapchat, as opposed to "text-based platforms" like Twitter, has been associated with reduced loneliness. Sharing images and videos may create a feeling of intimacy that cannot be attained through tweets and other written communications (Pittman & Reich, 2016). When it comes to Facebook, *active* use (engaging others with messages, comments, and other tools) appears to be more healthy than *passive* use (consuming content created by others). This latter activity, which includes viewing other people's photos and status updates, may lead to feelings of envy, and thereby decrease "affective well-being" (Verduyn et al., 2015). In other words, it diminishes positive emotions. Perhaps you have experienced this firsthand: While browsing through the Facebook and Instagram posts of friends, you get the impression that their lives are more exciting and interesting than your own. But, remember that people often use these platforms to portray themselves in the most flattering ways. Perhaps more importantly, recognize that passively viewing other people's content is unlikely to satisfy your need for love and belongingness. Find a way to connect with friends more directly, online and offline. Comment on a new post, send a message, or make plans to spend time together in person.

FACEBOOK: A CURE FOR LONELINESS?

Unhealthy Relationships?
Texting and social media make it possible to stay in constant touch with loved ones, but digital technology can also abet negative relationship dynamics. Survey data suggest that most teenagers have dated digital stalkers—people who obsessively check in, monitor their whereabouts, or keep tabs on their social media activity, for example. Others say they have been victimized by partners who distribute embarrassing information (Damour, 2017, September 21).
Martin Dimitrov/Getty Images.

show what you know

1. ________ is a stimulus or force that directs the way we behave, think, and feel.
2. When behaviors are driven by internal factors such as interest and personal satisfaction, ________ is involved.
   a. extrinsic motivation
   b. intrinsic motivation
   c. persistence
   d. external consequences
3. According to Maslow, the biological and psychological needs motivating behavior are arranged in a ________.
4. How does drive-reduction theory of motivation differ from arousal theory?

✓ CHECK YOUR ANSWERS IN APPENDIX C.

Sexuality

It's obvious we need food, water, and sleep to survive. But where does sex fit into the needs hierarchy? "Sex may be studied as a purely physiological need," according to Maslow (1943), "[but] ordinarily sexual behavior is multi-determined" (p. 381). In other words, there are many forces motivating us to engage in sexual activity. These include the need for affection and love, and that means "both giving and receiving love" (p. 381). Every person is different, of course. There is tremendous variability in human **sexuality,** a dimension of human nature encompassing everything that makes us sexual beings: sexual activities, attitudes, and behaviors.

sexuality A dimension of human nature encompassing everything that makes us sexual beings: sexual activities, attitudes, and behaviors.

The Birds and the Bees

Describe the human sexual response as identified by Masters and Johnson.

To grasp the complexity of human sexuality, we must understand the basic physiology of the sexual response. Enter William Masters and Virginia Johnson, who studied approximately 10,000 distinct sexual responses of 312 male and 382 female participants (Masters & Johnson, 1966). These researchers were particularly interested in determining the physiological changes that occurred during sexual activities such as masturbation and intercourse. Using a variety of instruments to measure blood flow, body temperature, muscular changes, and heart rate, they discovered that most people experience a similar physiological sexual response, which can result from oral stimulation, manual stimulation, vaginal intercourse, or masturbation. Men and women tend to follow a similar cycle: *excitement, plateau, orgasm,* and *resolution* (**Figure 9.1**). These phases vary in duration for different people.

Sexy Science
In the mid-1950s, William Masters teamed with Virginia Johnson to study the bodily changes that occur during masturbation and sex. Their research was groundbreaking, and it upended many long-held misconceptions about sex. For example, Masters and Johnson found that the length of a man's penis does not determine his ability to give pleasure (Fox, 2013, July 25). Art Phillips/Corbis.

Sexual arousal begins during the *excitement phase,* when physical changes start to become evident. Muscles tense, heartbeat quickens, breathing accelerates, blood pressure rises, and the nipples become firm. In men, the penis becomes erect, the scrotum constricts, and the testes pull up toward the body. In women, the vagina lubricates and the clitoris swells.

Next is the *plateau phase.* There are no clear physiological signs to mark its beginning, but during this time the muscles continue to tense, breathing and heart rate increase, and the genitals start changing color as blood fills the area. The plateau phase is usually short-lived, lasting only a few seconds to minutes.

The shortest phase of the sexual response cycle is the *orgasm phase.* An **orgasm** is a powerful combination of extremely gratifying sensations and a series of rhythmic muscular contractions. When men and women are asked to describe their orgasmic experiences, it is very difficult to differentiate between them. Brain activity observed via PET scans is also quite similar (Georgiadis, Reinders, Paans, Renken, & Kortekaas, 2009; Mah & Binik, 2001), but recent research suggests some patterns of brain activation may differ for men and women during orgasm (Wise, Frangos, & Komisaruk, 2017).

The final phase of the sexual response cycle, according to Masters and Johnson, is the *resolution phase.* This is when bodies return to a relaxed state. Without further sexual arousal, the blood flows out of the genitals, and blood pressure, heart rate, and breathing return to normal. Men lose their erections, the testes move down, and the skin of the scrotum loosens. They also experience a **refractory period,** an interval

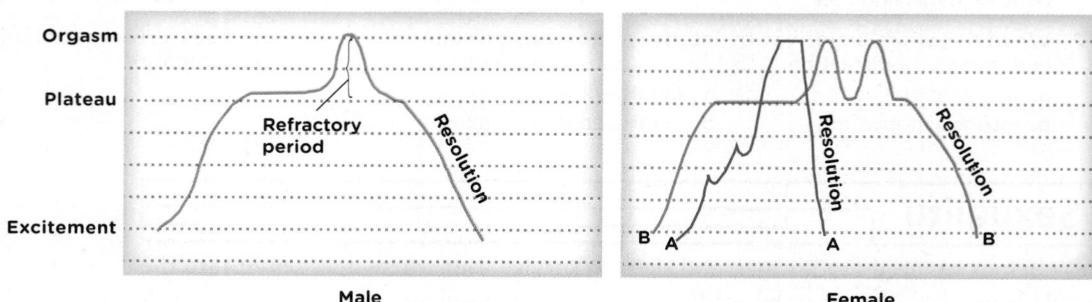

FIGURE 9.1
Masters and Johnson's Human Sexual Response Cycle
In the male sexual response (left), excitement is typically followed by a brief plateau, orgasm, and then a refractory period during which another orgasm is not possible. In the female sexual response (right), there is no refractory period. Orgasm is typically followed by resolution (A) or, if sexual stimulation continues, additional orgasms (B).

during which they cannot attain another orgasm. This can last from minutes to hours, and typically the older a man is, the longer the refractory period lasts. For women, the resolution phase is characterized by a decrease in clitoral swelling and a return to the normal labia color. Women do not experience a refractory period, and if sexual stimulation continues, some are capable of having multiple orgasms.

Armed with this knowledge about the physiology of sex, let's move on to its psychology. How are sexual activities shaped by learning, relationships, and the need to be loved and belong?

Sexual Orientation: It's a Continuum

Define sexual orientation and summarize how it develops.

Sexual orientation refers to "the sex of those to whom one is sexually and romantically attracted" (APA, 2015a, p. 22). This "enduring pattern" of sexual, romantic, and emotional attraction generally involves someone of the same sex, opposite sex, or both sexes (APA, 2008). When attracted to members of the opposite sex, sexual orientation is **heterosexual.** When attracted to members of the same sex, orientation is **homosexual.** When attracted to both sexes, orientation is **bisexual.** Not every individual fits into one of these categories, however. Sexual orientation can be described as a continuum that includes many dimensions of our sexuality, including attraction, desire, emotions, and all the behaviors that result. At one end are people who are "exclusively heterosexual" and at the other end are those considered "exclusively homosexual." Between these two poles is considerable variation (Kinsey, Pomeroy, & Martin, 1948; **Figure 9.2**). Human beings can be "attracted to men, women, both, neither, genderqueer, androgynous or have other gender identities" (APA, 2015a, p. 22).

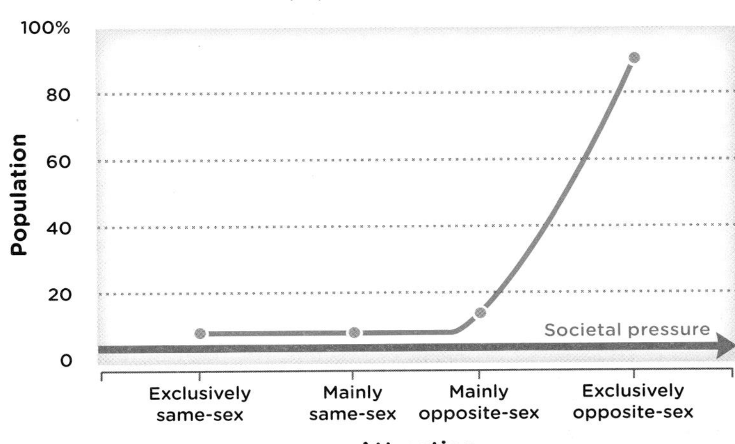

FIGURE 9.2
The Sexual Orientation Continuum
We can think of sexual orientation as a continuum rather than a set of discrete categories. This graph shows the range of orientations that might characterize a population. Information from Epstein (2016).

Those who do not feel sexually attracted to others are referred to as *asexual.* Lack of interest in sex does not necessarily prevent a person from maintaining relationships with spouses, partners, or friends. We can't be sure how many people consider themselves asexual, but estimates range from 0.6% to 5.5% of the population (Crooks & Baur, 2017).

How Does Sexual Orientation Develop?

We are not sure how sexual orientation develops, but many professionals in the field agree it is not a matter of choice. Consistent with this perspective, most people feel they do not have control over whom they find attractive. Research suggests sexual orientation results from an interaction of many biological and environmental factors—nature *and* nurture (APA, 2008; Epstein, 2016).

GENETICS AND SEXUAL ORIENTATION To determine the influence of genes in sexual orientation, we turn to twin studies, which are commonly used to examine the degree to which nature and nurture contribute to psychological traits. Since monozygotic twins share 100% of their genetic make-up at conception, we expect them to share more genetically influenced characteristics than dizygotic twins, who only share about 50% of their genes. In a large study of Swedish twins, researchers reported that monozygotic twins were moderately more likely than dizygotic twins to have the same sexual orientation. They also found that same-sex sexual behavior for monozygotic

orgasm A powerful combination of extremely gratifying sensations and a series of rhythmic muscular contractions.

refractory period An interval of time during which a man cannot attain another orgasm.

sexual orientation A person's enduring sexual attraction to individuals of the same sex, opposite sex, or both sexes; a continuum that includes dimensions of sexuality, attraction, desire, and emotions.

heterosexual Attraction to members of the opposite sex.

homosexual Attraction to members of the same sex.

bisexual Attraction to members of both the same and opposite sex.

twins had heritability estimates around 34–39% for men, and 18–19% for women (Långström, Rahman, Carlström, & Lichtenstein, 2010). Others report heritability estimates ranging from 25% to 50% for men, and "substantially lower" percentages for women (Epstein, 2016). Overall, people are more likely to experience same-sex attraction if they have close relatives who are homosexual, suggesting there is a genetic component for sexual orientation (close relatives share many common genes; Epstein, 2016). These findings highlight two important factors: Heritability of same-sex sexual behavior differs for men and women, and both genes and environment (nature and nurture) contribute to sexual orientation.

THE BIOLOGY OF SEXUAL ORIENTATION The development of sexual orientation may begin before birth. The fetal gonads secrete hormones (estrogen and androgens) that influence reproductive anatomy. The presence of androgens (secreted primarily by the male gonads) may steer the development of sexual orientation toward women. This could potentially lead to heterosexual orientation in men, but homosexual orientation in women (Breedlove, 2017). To explore this possibility, researchers have studied pregnant women with elevated hormone levels (the result of a genetic abnormality or medication). Evidence from these cases suggests that early in utero exposure to high levels of androgens may be associated with "male-typed" development and same-sex attraction in girls (Berenbaum, Blakemore, & Beltz, 2011; Jordan-Young, 2012).

Interestingly, having older brothers in the family seems to be associated with homosexuality in men, a phenomenon known as the *fraternal birth order effect* (Blanchard, 2008, 2014). Why would this be? According to the *maternal immunity hypothesis*, cells from a male fetus are introduced into the mother's circulatory system, triggering an immune response. The mother's immune system produces antibodies that influence the development of the next male fetus she carries, resulting in a variety of changes in neurons that direct the person to "later be attracted to men rather than women" (Blanchard, 2014, p. 851). However, the findings from these studies have not been easy to replicate (Currin, Gibson, & Hubach, 2015; Kishida & Rahman, 2015; Xu & Zheng, 2015).

Despite numerous attempts to identify genetic markers and other biological causes of homosexuality, researchers have had very little success (Dar-Nimrod & Heine, 2011). Some suggest the search for genes underlying same-sex attraction is misguided. Why do we spend time and money seeking biological explanations for a "valid alternative lifestyle" (Jacobs, 2012, p. 393)?

Love and Marriage
Comedian Wanda Sykes (left) and her wife Alex Sykes were married in 2008, when same-sex marriage was banned throughout most of the country (Jordan, 2009, May 13). In 2015 the Supreme Court declared that same-sex marriage should be allowed in all states, a legal shift that seems to parallel the changing attitudes of Americans. Between 2004 and 2017, support for same-sex marriage grew from 42% to 64% (McCarthy, 2017, May 15). Jason LaVeris/FilmMagic/Getty Images.

WHERE'S THE NURTURE? We have discussed the potential role of nature in sexual orientation, but how does nurture fit in? Earlier, we noted that sexual orientation might be understood as a continuum. At one end of the continuum are people who are strictly heterosexual; and at the other end are those who are undeniably homosexual. Many people fall somewhere in the middle of these two extremes. These middle-ground individuals have some flexibility in their orientation, particularly when they are young, and environmental factors (nurture) help determine where they fall on the continuum. Because we live in a *homomisic society*—one that strongly favors heterosexuality—most people in the middle will be pushed toward a heterosexual orientation. Those at either end of the continuum are less likely to be flexible in their orientation, in part due to the strong genetic component of sexual orientation (Epstein, 2016).

While we are on the topic of nurture, we should also note that children raised in same-sex parent households do not appear to be at a disadvantage compared to those from opposite-sex parent households. In fact, one study found that teens raised by lesbian mothers tended to score higher on measures of self-esteem and had fewer behavioral problems than those reared in comparable heterosexual households (Bos, van Gelderen, & Gartrell, 2015; Perrin, Cohen, & Caren, 2013).

A HISTORY OF UNFAIR TREATMENT Although differences in sexual orientation are universal and have been evident throughout recorded history, individuals identified as members of the nonheterosexual minority have been subjected to stereotyping, prejudice, and discrimination. Nonheterosexual people in the United States, for example, have been, and continue to be, subjected to harassment, violence, and unfair practices related to housing and employment. In February 2017 the Department of Justice filed a brief stating that federal law does not shield people against workplace discrimination on the basis of sexual orientation. Administration officials contended that the 1964 Civil Rights Act does not "protect individuals from being fired because they are gay, lesbian or transgender" (Gerstein, 2017, July 27, para. 1).

Radical Research
Alfred Kinsey interviews a subject in his office at the Institute for Sex Research, now the Kinsey Institute. Kinsey began investigating human sexuality in the 1930s, when talking about sex was taboo. He started gathering data with surveys, but then switched to personal interviews, which he believed to be more effective. These interviews often went on for hours and included hundreds of questions (PBS, 2005, January 27).
Wallace Kirkland/Getty Images.

"Normal" Is Relative

It is only natural for us to wonder if what we are doing between the sheets (or elsewhere) is typical or healthy. Is it normal to masturbate? Is it normal to fantasize about sex with strangers? The answers to these types of questions depend somewhat on cultural context. Most of us unknowingly learn *sexual scripts,* or cultural rules that tell us what types of activities are "appropriate" and don't interfere with healthy sexual intimacy. In some cultures, the sexual script suggests that women should have minimal, if any, sexual experience before marriage, but men are expected to explore their sexuality, or "sow their wild oats."

GATHERING SEX DATA Alfred Kinsey and colleagues were among the first to try to scientifically and objectively examine the sexual behavior of Americans (Kinsey, Pomeroy, & Martin, 1948; Kinsey, Pomeroy, Martin, & Gebhard, 1953). Using the survey method, Kinsey and his team collected data on the sexual behaviors of 5,300 White males and 5,940 White females. Their findings were surprising; both men and women masturbated, and participants had experiences with premarital sex, adultery, and sexual activity with someone of the same sex. Perhaps more shocking was the fact that people were willing to talk about their sexual behavior in post–World War II America.

The Kinsey study was groundbreaking in terms of its data content and methodology, which included accuracy checks and assurances of confidentiality. The data continue to serve as a valuable reference for researchers studying how sexual behaviors and attitudes have evolved over time. However, Kinsey's work was not without limitations. For example, Kinsey and colleagues (1948, 1953) failed to obtain a **representative sample** of the population. The sample lacked ethnic diversity, and there was an overrepresentation of well-educated Protestants (Potter, 2006; Wallin, 1949).

CONNECTIONS
In **Chapter 1,** we explained how using representative samples enables us to generalize findings to populations. Here, we see that inferences about sexual behaviors for groups other than White, well-educated Protestants could be problematic, as few members of these groups participated in the Kinsey study.

Subsequent research has been better designed, using samples that are more representative of the population (Herbenick et al., 2010; Michael, Laumann, Kolata, & Gagnon, 1994). "As recently as 2002, the average adult American had sex approximately 64 times a year, but by 2014 that declined to about 53 times a year" (Twenge, Sherman, & Wells, 2017, para. 17). This downward trend is not something to celebrate, because sex may improve well-being. Research suggests that frequency of penile–vaginal intercourse is associated with sexual satisfaction, as well as satisfaction with relationships, mental health, and life in general. Other sexual activities, such as masturbation, may be inversely related to measures of satisfaction (Regnerus & Gordon, 2013).

HOW DO MEN AND WOMEN DIFFER? As stereotypes suggest, men think about sex more often than women (Laumann et al., 1994), and they consistently report a higher frequency of masturbation (Peplau, 2003; see **Table 9.1** on the next page for reported gender differences in frequency of sexual activity). Decades ago in the United States,

TABLE 9.1 WHAT'S GOING ON?

Sexual Activity	Average Frequency in Prior Month for Men	Average Frequency in Prior Month for Women
Penile–vaginal intercourse	5.2	4.8
Oral sex	2.3	1.9
Anal sex	0.10	0.08
Masturbation	4.5	1.5

How often do people engage in different types of sexual activity? Here are the monthly self-reported averages for adult men and women (the average age being 41). Keep in mind that significant variation exists around these averages. Information from Brody and Costa (2009), Table 1, p. 1950.

men tended to be more tolerant than women about casual sex before marriage, and more permissive in their attitudes about extramarital sex (Laumann et al., 1994). But these differences are not apparent in heterosexual teenagers and young adults, as young men and women more commonly engage in "hookups," or "brief uncommitted sexual encounters among individuals who are not romantic partners or dating each other" (Garcia, Reiber, Massey, & Merriwether, 2012, p.161). Hookups, which can be anything from kissing to sexual intercourse, reveal major shifts in the way people view sexual activity.

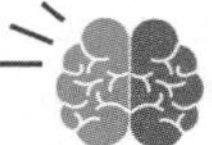

THINK CRITICALLY

SEXT YOU LATER What kinds of environmental factors encourage casual attitudes about sex among young people? Most U.S. teenagers (76%) have iPhones these days (Piper Jaffray, 2017, Spring), and a large number of those young people are using their phones to exchange text messages with sexually explicit words or images. In other words, today's teenagers are doing a lot of *sexting*. One study found that 20% of high school students have used their cell phones to share sexual pictures of themselves, and twice as many have received such images from others (Strassberg, McKinnon, Sustaíta, & Rullo, 2013). Young people who sext are more likely to have sex and take sexual risks, such as having unprotected sex (Olatunde & Balogun, 2017; Rice et al., 2012). Sexting has also led to "criminal and civil legal charges" against minors (Lorang, McNiel, & Binder, 2016), although such cases are uncommon as sexting has become "a psychological and developmental concern rather than a legal risk" (Englander & McCoy, 2018, p. 317).

ARE TEENS WHO SEXT MORE LIKELY TO HAVE SEX?

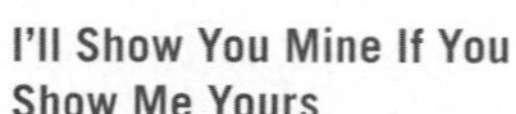

I'll Show You Mine If You Show Me Yours
Media reports often shine the spotlight on adolescent sexting, but adults are the ones who sext the most. Some research suggests that women may be more likely to send sext messages, while men are more apt to be on the receiving end (Klettke, Hallford, & Mellor, 2014). What could be the cause of this gender disparity? spyarm/Shutterstock.

Sexting carries another set of risks for those who are married or in committed relationships. As many people see it, sexting outside a relationship is a genuine form of cheating. And because text messages can be saved and forwarded, they can provide indisputable evidence of philandering. Perhaps you have heard about the sexting scandals associated with golfer Tiger Woods, ex-footballer Brett Favre, or former U.S. Congressman Anthony Weiner?

Now that's a lot of bad news about sexting. Can it also occur in the absence of negative behaviors and outcomes? When sexting is between two consenting adults, it may be completely harmless (provided no infidelity is involved). According to one survey of young adults, sexting was not linked to unsafe sex or psychological problems such as depression and low self-esteem (Gordon-Messer, Bauermeister,

Grodzinski, & Zimmerman, 2013). For some, sexting is just a new variation on flirting; for others, it may fulfill a deeper need, like helping them feel more secure in their romantic attachments (Weisskirch & Delevi, 2011).

Problems with Sex

Sexual dysfunction occurs when there is a "significant disturbance" in the ability to respond sexually or to gain pleasure from sex (APA, 2013). Survey data suggest that 43% of women and 31% of men suffer from some sort of sexual dysfunction (Laumann, Paik, & Rosen, 1999). Temporary difficulties can result from everyday stressors or situational factors, while longer-term problems stem from a variety of issues, including health conditions, beliefs about sex, ignorance about sexual practices, and performance expectations. Let's explore the major categories of sexual dysfunction, keeping in mind that they sometimes overlap.

DESIRE Illness, fatigue, relationship frustration, and other situational factors can lead to temporary problems with desire. In some cases, lack of desire is persistent and distressing. Both men and women can be affected, but women tend to report desire-related problems more frequently (Brotto, 2010; Heiman, 2002).

AROUSAL Problems with arousal occur when the psychological desire to engage in sexual behavior is present, but the body does not cooperate. Men with *erectile disorder* may have trouble getting or maintaining an erection or experience a decrease in rigidity (APA, 2013). Up to 20% of all men report they have occasionally experienced problems with erections (Hock, 2016). Women can also struggle with arousal. *Female sexual interest/arousal disorder* is apparent in reduced interest in sex, lack of initiation of sexual activities, reduced excitement, or decreased genital sensations during sex (APA, 2013).

ORGASM Disorders related to orgasm are yet another category of dysfunction. *Female orgasmic disorder* is diagnosed when a woman is consistently unable to reach orgasm, has reduced orgasmic intensity, or does not reach orgasm quickly enough during sexual activity (APA, 2013). Men who experience frequent delay or inability to ejaculate might have a condition known as *delayed ejaculation* (APA, 2013; Segraves, 2010). With this disorder, the ability to achieve orgasm and ejaculate is inhibited or delayed during partnered sexual activity. Men who have trouble controlling when they ejaculate (particularly during vaginal sex) may suffer from *premature (early) ejaculation* (APA, 2013).

PAIN The final category of sexual dysfunction, painful intercourse, typically affects women. *Genito-pelvic pain/penetration disorder* refers to four types of co-occurring symptoms specific to women: difficulty having intercourse, pain in the genitals or pelvis, fear of pain or vaginal penetration, and tension of the pelvic floor muscles (APA, 2013). Up to 15% of women in North America report frequent pain during intercourse, and issues related to pain are associated with reduced desire and arousal.

Adey Bryant/CartoonStock.com.

"I really think you should see a specialist about your lack of libido Sharon."

Sexually Transmitted Infections

Many people carry **sexually transmitted infections (STIs)**—diseases or illnesses passed on through sexual activity (Workowski & Bolan, 2015; **Table 9.2** on the next page). STIs have many causes, but most are *bacterial* or *viral*. Bacterial infections such as *syphilis, gonorrhea,* and *chlamydia* often clear up with antibiotics. Viral infections like *genital herpes* and *human papillomavirus (HPV)* have no cure, only treatments to reduce symptoms.

sexual dysfunction A significant disturbance in the ability to respond sexually or to gain pleasure from sex.

sexually transmitted infections (STIs) Diseases or illnesses transmitted through sexual activity.

TABLE 9.2 SEXUALLY TRANSMITTED INFECTIONS (STIs)

STI	Symptom	Estimated Annual Prevalence of New Infections in the U.S.
Chlamydia	Women often have no symptoms; men can experience discharge from penis, burning when urinating, and pain/swelling of the testicles.	2.86 million
Gonorrhea	No symptoms may be present in men or women. Men can experience burning when urinating; white, yellow, or green discharge. Women can experience pain/burning when urinating, or vaginal discharge.	820,000
Herpes	Blisters on the genitals, rectum, or mouth; painful sores after blisters break; fever, body aches, and swollen glands can occur.	776,000
Human papillomavirus (HPV)	Genital warts; certain cancers; warts growing in the throat.	14 million
Syphilis	Firm, round sores that first appear where the infection enters the body and can then spread to other parts of the body.	55,400

Sexually transmitted infections (STIs) are extremely common. HPV, for example, is so widespread that nearly all sexually active people become infected with it at one time or another. Information from CDC (2013a; 2015a,b; 2016c,d,f).

Apply This ↓

PROTECT YOURSELF

The more sexual partners you have, the greater your risk of acquiring an STI. But you can lower your risk by communicating with your partner. People who know that their partners have had (or are having) sex with others face a lower risk of acquiring an STI than those who do not know. Why is this so? If you are aware of your partner's activities, you may be more likely to take preventative measures, such as using condoms. Of course, there is always the possibility that your sexual partner (or you) has a disease but doesn't know it. Some people with STIs are asymptomatic, meaning they have no symptoms. Others know they are infected but lie because they are ashamed, in denial, afraid of rejection, or for other reasons. Given all these unknowns, your best bet is to play it safe and use protection.

In the next section, we return our focus to the base of Maslow's pyramid, where life-sustaining drives are represented. We will explore hunger, one of the most powerful motivators of human behavior.

show what you know

1. Masters and Johnson studied physiological changes that accompany sexual activity. Men and women experience a similar sexual response cycle, including the following ordered phases:
   a. excitement, plateau, orgasm, and resolution.
   b. plateau, excitement, orgasm, and relaxation.
   c. excitement, plateau, and orgasm.
   d. excitement, orgasm, and resolution.

2. Having older brothers in the family seems to be associated with same-sex attraction in men, a phenomenon known as the ________________.

✓ CHECK YOUR ANSWERS IN APPENDIX C.

Hunger

"I KNOW HUNGER." Ibrahim Hashi has had enough excitement, fear, and discomfort for a lifetime. While serving with the U.S. Marines, he was deployed on three combat missions—two in Iraq and one in Afghanistan. Those tours gave him a front row seat to the horrors of war. He has seen bodies of the dead, slept on floors littered with cow feces, and heard the screams of a friend who lost both legs to an improvised explosive device (IED). He also knows how it feels to be hungry, truly hungry. During his missions, there were times when food shipments never made it to his unit. "I remember one time we were supposed to get a resupply; the airplane that was going to drop it in got shot at, so they aborted the mission," Ibrahim says. "We just stayed hungry for almost a whole week." As you might imagine, everyone became irritable, and sleep was virtually impossible. "It felt like my stomach was in a knot; it was just empty," Ibrahim recalls. "If you're lucky enough to go to sleep, I guarantee you are going to be dreaming about food . . . . There was no reprieve from the hunger. It was constant." 

Serving His Country
Ibrahim's motivation for joining the military came partly from his parents, who raised him with a strong sense of social responsibility: "You don't take anything for free," Ibrahim says. "For a country that has been so generous to my family and I, for me to just live here and not contribute or give back in any way was unacceptable" (Shams, 2016, December 2, 0:35). Jahi Chikwendiu/The Washington Post via Getty Images.

Hungry Brain, Hungry Body

Have you felt a knot in your stomach, as Ibrahim describes? Perhaps you have noticed your stomach contracting and growling when you haven't eaten for a while. What causes these rumblings, and are they a sign of hunger, or something else?

LO 8 Discuss how the stomach and the hypothalamus make us feel hunger.

THE STOMACH AND BLOOD SUGAR In a classic study, Walter Cannon and A. L. Washburn (1912) sought to answer this question (**Figure 9.3**). Here's a brief synopsis of the experiment: Washburn swallowed an inflatable balloon that could be used to record his stomach contractions. Whenever Washburn felt "hunger pangs," he pushed a button. Using this procedure, the researchers found that stomach contractions and hunger pangs occurred at the same time.

Cannon and Washburn's experiment demonstrates that the stomach plays an important role in hunger, but evidence suggests this is just one small piece of the puzzle. For example, cancer patients who have had their stomachs surgically removed consume normal amounts of food and experience typical levels of satiety, that is, the feeling of being full (Bergh, Sjöstedt, Hellers, Zandian, & Södersten, 2003; Karanicolas et al., 2013). We also must consider the chemicals in the blood, such as glucose, or blood sugar. When glucose levels dip, the stomach and liver send signals to the brain that something must be done about this reduced energy situation. The brain, in turn, initiates a sense of hunger.

FIGURE 9.3
Cannon and Washburn's Classic Study
Washburn swallowed a special balloon attached to a device for monitoring stomach contractions. While the balloon was in place, he pressed a key every time he felt hungry. Comparing the record of key presses against the balloon measurements, Washburn showed that stomach contractions accompany feelings of hunger.

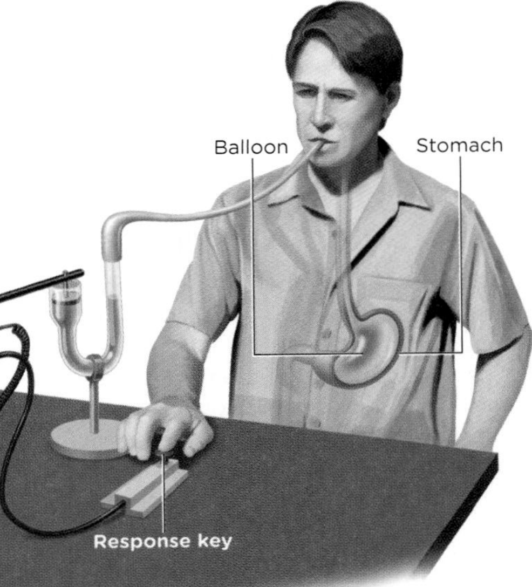

THE HYPOTHALAMUS AND HUNGER Another key player in hunger regulation is the hypothalamus, which can be divided into functionally distinct areas. When the *lateral hypothalamus* is activated, appetite increases. Even well-fed animals will experience a surge in appetite when researchers electrically stimulate this area of the brain. Destroy the lateral hypothalamus, and animals lose interest in food,

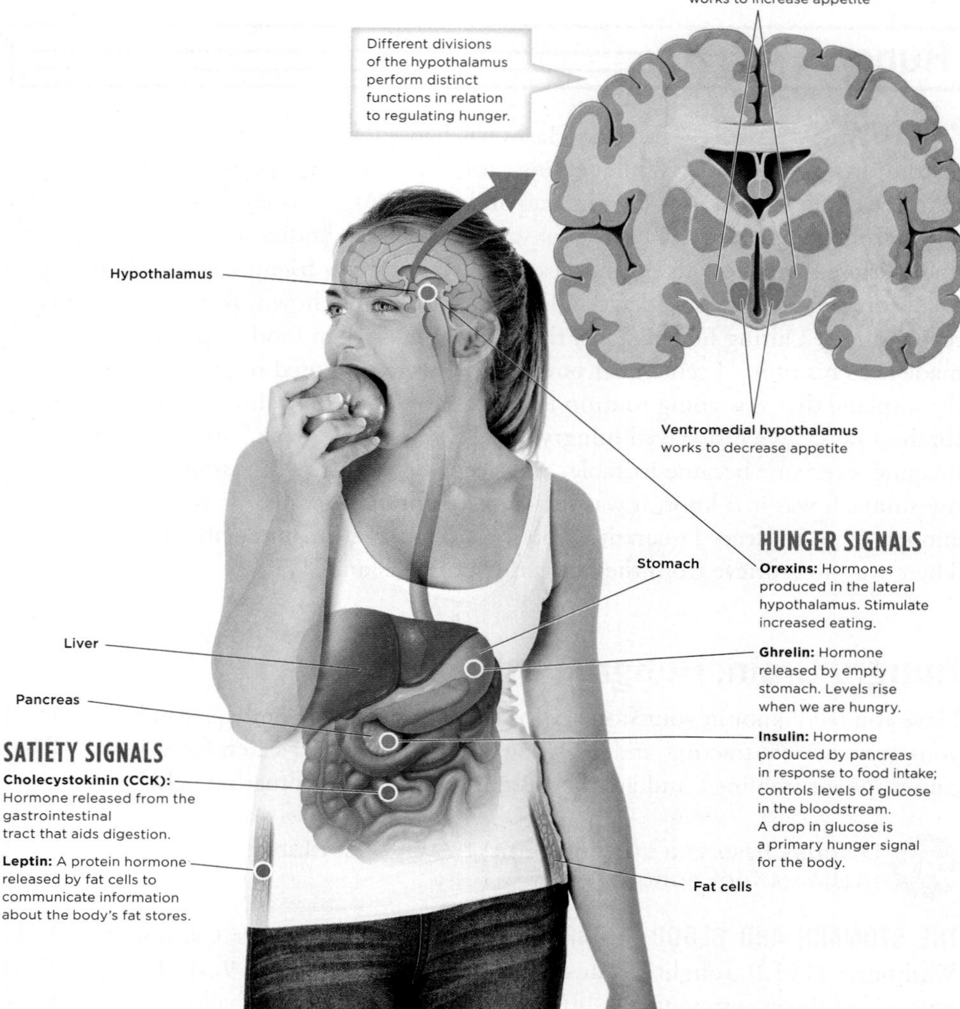
Lateral hypothalamus
works to increase appetite
Different divisions of the hypothalamus perform distinct functions in relation to regulating hunger.
Hypothalamus
Ventromedial hypothalamus
works to decrease appetite
HUNGER SIGNALS
Stomach
Orexins: Hormones produced in the lateral hypothalamus. Stimulate increased eating.
Liver
Ghrelin: Hormone released by empty stomach. Levels rise when we are hungry.
Pancreas
Insulin: Hormone produced by pancreas in response to food intake; controls levels of glucose in the bloodstream. A drop in glucose is a primary hunger signal for the body.
SATIETY SIGNALS
Cholecystokinin (CCK): Hormone released from the gastrointestinal tract that aids digestion.
Leptin: A protein hormone released by fat cells to communicate information about the body's fat stores.
Fat cells

FIGURE 9.4
Hunger Regulation
Feelings of hunger and satisfaction result from a complex communication system linking the brain and body. Hormones from the digestive organs communicate information about satiety and hunger to the hypothalamus, a part of the brain that plays an important role in maintaining homeostasis, or balance, in the body's systems. Separate areas of the hypothalamus then send signals to other parts of the brain, motivating us to increase or decrease eating. Photo: Piotr Marcinski/AGE Fotostock.

even to the point of starvation. Because the lateral hypothalamus plays a role in motivating eating behavior, it helps preserve the balance between energy supply and demand (Leinninger, 2011; Stamatakis et al., 2016).

If the *ventromedial hypothalamus* becomes activated, appetite declines, causing an animal to stop eating. Disable this region of the brain, and the animal will overeat to the point of obesity. The ventromedial hypothalamus receives information about levels of blood glucose and other feeding-related stimuli, as it, too, works to maintain the body's energy balance (Drougard, Fournel, Valet, & Knauf, 2015; King, 2006).

CONNECTIONS

In **Chapter 2,** we described hormones as chemical messengers released into the bloodstream. Hormones do not act as quickly as neurotransmitters, but their messages are more widely spread throughout the body. Here, we see how hormones are involved in communicating information about hunger and feeding behaviors.

The hypothalamus has a variety of sensors that react to information about hunger and food intake. This information is communicated via **hormones** in the bloodstream (**Figure 9.4**). One such hormone is *leptin,* which is secreted by fat cells and plays a role in suppressing hunger. Another is *insulin,* a pancreatic hormone involved in controlling levels of glucose in the bloodstream. With input from these and other hormones, the brain can monitor energy levels and respond accordingly. This complex system enables us to know when we are hungry, full, or somewhere in between.

Let's Have a Meal: Cultural and Social Context

Biology is not the only factor influencing eating habits. We must also consider the social and cultural context. In the United States, social activities, holidays, and work events often revolve around food. We frequently eat on the go, rushing to our next class or meeting, and don't take the time to experience the taste of food. We also tend to match our food intake to those around us, although we may not be aware of their influence (Herman, Roth, & Polivy, 2003; Vartanian, Spanos, Herman, & Polivy, 2015). Gender plays a role in eating habits, too. Using **naturalistic observation**, researchers found that women choose lower-calorie meals or eat less when trying to impress others (Young, Mizzau, Mai, Sirisegaram, & Wilson, 2009; Vartanian, 2015).

CONNECTIONS

In **Chapter 1,** we discussed naturalistic observation, the study of participants in their natural environments. When conducting this type of descriptive research, one must avoid disturbing participants or their environment. Here, we assume the researchers measured and recorded meals without interfering with participants' behaviors.

PORTION DISTORTION Eating decisions are driven by a variety of factors, including social influence, hunger, and satiety (Vartanian, Herman, & Polivy, 2016). But more subtle variables, such as portion size, also come into play. In one study, participants at a movie theater were given free popcorn in medium- or large-sized buckets. Some of the buckets were filled with fresh popcorn, and others contained 14-day-old popcorn. Participants given large buckets consistently ate 33% more than those who received medium-size buckets, regardless of whether the popcorn was fresh or stale. The stale popcorn was described as "soggy" or "terrible," yet the participants still ate more of it when given larger portions (Wansink & Kim, 2005). When we are exposed to images of large food portions, it tends to "recalibrate perceptions of what is a 'normal' serving of that food" (Robinson et al., 2016, p. 32). Remember this the next time you see a food commercial on TV.

Before and After

NBC *Today* weather anchor Al Roker before (left) and after his 2002 gastric bypass surgery. The procedure, which reduces the volume of the stomach and changes the way food is absorbed by the digestive system, helps people lose weight and may lead to improvements in cardiovascular health (Adams et al., 2012; Medline Plus, 2015, March 31). But Roker cautions that surgery is not a magic bullet for people struggling with obesity. "You have to be constantly vigilant," he said in an interview with *Today* (Celizic, 2010, June 7). In other words, exercise and healthy eating are essential even after you have had the procedure.

Left: RJ Capak/WireImage/Getty Images.
Right: Jason LaVeris/FilmMagic/Getty Images.

Obesity

Around the world, a growing number of people struggle with obesity. Approximately 37% of men and 38% of women are overweight or obese—meaning they have a body mass index (BMI) that exceeds 25 or 30, respectively (Albuquerque, Stice, Rodríguez-López, Manco, & Nóbrega, 2015). Adults aren't the only ones battling the bulge; one-third of America's children and teens are overweight, and around 13% of American children are considered obese (Afshin et al., 2017; American Heart Association, 2014b).

HOW MUCH CAN YOU CONTROL? Surprisingly, there is relatively little fluctuation in adult weight over time. According to one theory, we all tend to maintain a stable weight, or **set point,** despite variability in day-to-day exercise and food intake. If you cut back on calories and your weight falls below this set point, metabolism decreases, causing you to gain weight and return to your set point (deShazo, Hall, & Skipworth, 2015). Exceed the set point and metabolism increases, once again moving you back toward your stable weight (deShazo et al., 2015; Keesey & Hirvonen, 1997). The set point acts like a thermostat, helping maintain a consistent weight despite changing conditions.

Some critics of the set point model suggest that it fails to appreciate the importance of social and environmental influences (Stroebe, van Koningsbruggen, Papies, & Aarts, 2013). These theorists suggest we should consider a *settling point,* which is less rigid and might explain how the "set" point can actually change based on the relative amounts of food consumed and energy used. A settling point may also help us understand how body weight can shift to a newly maintained weight, and why so many people are overweight as a result of environmental factors, such as bigger meal portions, calorie-dense foods, and eating during other activities like watching television. This brings us to an important point: If you always have dinner while watching TV or snack before going to sleep, these activities become associated with "hunger." Conditioning is also an important part of emotional eating, or eating

set point The stable weight that is maintained despite variability in exercise and food intake.

You Asked, Ivonne Answers

http://qrs.ly/w57829n

Would you change anything that has happened to you?

because you feel depressed or upset (Bongers, van den Akker, Havermans, & Jansen, 2015).

Whatever your settling point may be, it is partly a result of your genetic make-up. Studies suggest that the heritability of BMI is around 65% (Speakman et al., 2011). Researchers following participants for 25 years reported even higher heritability (84%), and at least one study of monozygotic twins found heritability for fat mass to be as high as 90% (Albuquerque et al., 2015). It seems we are genetically predisposed to stay within a certain weight range.

OVEREATING, SLEEP, AND SCREEN TIME Have you ever noticed how sleep deprivation affects your eating habits? Preliminary research suggests that inadequate sleep is linked to weight problems; in other words, there is a negative correlation between sleep and weight gain. Meanwhile, people who sleep 6 to 8 hours a night have a better chance of losing weight. There is also a positive correlation between screen time (that is, using a tablet, smartphone, computer, or television) and weight gain: As screen time goes up, weight increases. It seems that screen time interferes with making healthy eating choices and getting regular exercise (Buchanan et al., 2016; Elder et al., 2012; Elder, Ammar, & Pile, 2015).

THE SECRET TO SLIMMING DOWN? To lose weight, one must eat less and move more (**Table 9.3**); in other words, use more calories than you are taking in. Our ancestors didn't have to worry about this. Needing energy to sustain themselves, they had no choice but to choose foods rich in calories—an efficient means of survival for them, but not ideal for those of us living in a world of deep dish pizzas, curly fries, and supersize sodas. When experiencing a "famine" (a decrease in the body's habitual caloric intake), our metabolism naturally slows down; we require fewer calories and have a harder time losing weight.

We have now explored many facets of motivation, from basic drives like hunger to more abstract needs for achievement and power. As you may have guessed from the title of this chapter, motivations are intimately tied to emotions. In the sections to come, we will explore the complex world of human emotion.

TABLE 9.3 WEIGHT LOSS: MAKING IT FIT

Strategies	Description
Set realistic goals.	Set goals and expectations that are specific, realistic, and flexible.
Get regular exercise.	Exercising just 30 minutes a day 5 times a week can help with weight loss. Add a variety of physical activities to your daily routines.
Eat regularly and track intake.	Eat on a set schedule to minimize mindless eating. Eat only when hungry, and write down what and how much you consume in a food diary.
Control portions.	Watch your portions. This is the amount you decide to eat. Read labels to determine the recommended serving size.
Drink water.	Eliminate sweetened beverages like soda.
Join a weight loss support group.	Social support helps promote healthier coping strategies and introduces accountability.

Losing weight is not an easy task, but it doesn't have to be painful. Making basic lifestyle changes can have significant benefits.
Information from Kruger, Blanck, and Gillespie (2006).

show what you know

1. Washburn swallowed a balloon to record his stomach contractions. He also pressed a button to record feelings of hunger. The findings indicated that whenever he felt hunger pangs, his:
   a. stomach was contracting.
   b. stomach was still.
   c. blood sugar went up.
   d. ventromedial hypothalamus was active.
2. Describe how the hypothalamus initiates hunger and influences eating behaviors.

✓ CHECK YOUR ANSWERS IN APPENDIX C.

Emotion

FOR HIS FAMILY Ibrahim knew he wanted to join the military at a very young age. Like many people who enter the armed forces, he was motivated by a desire to serve his country. But after the terrorist attacks of September 11, he had another reason to enlist. Prejudice toward Muslims, or Islamophobia, reached record levels in the months following 9/11. According to the Federal Bureau of Investigation (FBI), there were 481 anti-Muslim hate crimes reported in 2001, a 1600% increase from the previous year (FBI Uniform Crime Reports, n.d.; Serrano, 2002, November 26). Aware of this changing cultural climate, Ibrahim enlisted to protect his family from those who might perceive them as un-American. "I went into the military so people could not accuse my parents or any other family members of not having done anything for the United States," Ibrahim says. "I [could] be the example, and they could point to me and say, 'Look that's our son, and he served in the military.'"

Ibrahim's behavior could be understood from a motivational perspective. For example, you might argue that he was operating at one of the most basic levels in Maslow's hierarchy, trying to secure safety needs. But what else might have been driving his decision to join the Marines? Think about how you would *feel* if you saw news reports about murders, assaults, vandalism, and threats targeting your religious or ethnic group. (Perhaps you belong to a group that has been targeted in such a way.) How might *emotions* shape your behaviors?

Courtesy Ibrahim Hashi.

Ibrahim Hashi

What Are Emotions?

Motivation and emotion are tightly intertwined. Emotions can motivate behaviors (helping others when you're feeling happy), and motivation can influence emotions (feeling disappointed you are not motivated to complete an important task). In fact, the words emotion and motive have similar roots. Emotion can be traced to the Latin word *emovere,* which means to "move out, remove, agitate" (Emotion, n.d.), while motive is related to the Latin word *movere,* meaning "to move" (Motive, n.d.). But how do psychologists define emotions?

LO 9 Define emotions and explain how they differ from moods.

An **emotion** is a psychological state that includes a subjective or inner experience. In other words, emotion is intensely personal; we cannot actually feel each other's emotions firsthand. Emotion also has a physiological component; it is not only "in our heads." For example, anger can make you feel hot, anxiety might cause sweaty palms, and sadness may sap your physical energy. Finally, emotion entails a behavioral expression that is often apparent in the face. We scream and run when frightened, gag in disgust, and shed tears of sadness. Think about the last time you felt joyous. What was your inner experience of that joy, how did your body react, and what would someone have noticed about your behavior?

emotion A psychological state that includes a subjective or inner experience, physiological component, and behavioral expression.

We described emotion as a subjective psychological state that includes both physiological and behavioral components. But are these three elements—psychology, physiology, and behavior—equally important, and how do they interact? These types of "big questions" are being explored by people from many fields and perspectives (Davidson, Scherer, & Goldsmith, 2002; Ekman, 2016). In fact, the very definition of emotion is still a subject of academic debate (Coan, 2010; Ekman, 2016).

Most psychologists agree that emotions are different from moods. Emotions tend to be strong, but they generally don't last as long as moods, and they are more likely to have an identifiable cause. An emotion is initiated by a stimulus, and it is more likely than a mood to motivate someone to action. Moods are longer-term emotional states that are less intense than emotions and do not appear to have distinct beginnings or ends (Kemeny & Shestyuk, 2008; Matlin & Farmer, 2016; Oatley, Keltner, & Jenkins, 2006). Here's an example to clarify: Imagine your mood is happy, but a car cuts you off on the highway, creating a negative emotional response like anger. Fortunately, this flash of anger is likely to vanish as quickly as it appeared, and your happy mood persists.

LANGUAGE AND EMOTION Think about all the words you can use to communicate subtle differences in emotions. "I feel *angry* at you" conveys a slightly different meaning than "I feel *resentful* of you," or "I feel *annoyed* by you." Words not only facilitate communication; they also influence our perceptions of emotions, and "perhaps even emotional experiences" (Lindquist, Satpute, & Gendron, 2015, p. 1). Imagine that diamonds were called "doodleboogers"—do you think they would inspire the same emotions as "diamonds"?

The English language includes about 200 words to describe emotions. But does that mean we are capable of feeling only 200 emotions? Probably not. While closely linked, words and emotions are not one and the same. Their relationship has captivated the interest of linguists from fields as different as psychology, anthropology, and evolutionary biology (Majid, 2012).

Rather than focusing on words or labels, scholars typically characterize emotions along different dimensions. American psychologist Carroll Izard (2007) suggests that we can describe emotions according to valence and arousal (**Figure 9.5**). The *valence* of an emotion refers to how pleasant or unpleasant it is. Happiness, joy, and satisfaction are on the pleasant end of the valence dimension; anger and disgust are on the unpleasant end. The *arousal level* of an emotion describes how active, excited, and involved a person is while experiencing the emotion, as opposed to how calm, uninvolved, or passive she may be. With valence and arousal level, we can compare and contrast emotions. Feeling relaxed has a low arousal level and a positive valence. Fear, on the other hand, is characterized by high arousal and negative valence. Let's explore this emotion with a little help from Ibrahim.

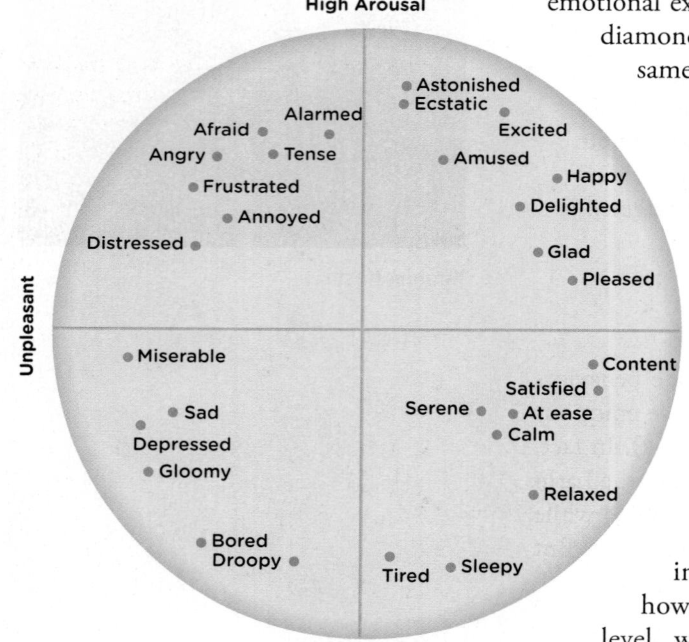

FIGURE 9.5
Dimensions of Emotion
Emotions can be compared and contrasted according to their valence (how pleasant or unpleasant they are) and their arousal level. Copyright © 2005 by the American Psychological Association. Adapted with permission from Lyubomirsky, S., Sheldon, S.M., & Schkade, D. (2005). Pursuing happiness: The architecture of sustainable change. *Review of General Psychology, 9*, 111–131.

"I DON'T EVEN KNOW IF I'M STILL ALIVE." Fortunately for Ibrahim, his first two deployments to Iraq were not extremely violent. He spent much of the time working as an interpreter, translating exchanges between English-speaking military personnel and Arabic-speaking tribal leaders. His 7-month tour in Afghanistan was quite a different story. "My Afghan deployment, my last one, was the most violent," he says. "I definitely felt my life was in danger most of the [time]." It wasn't the combat that scared him: "Training kicks in," he explains. "You're almost a robot during the actual firefight." It was the aftermath that terrified him—seeing the injuries and deaths, and realizing just how close he had come to dying himself.

"I remember this one time, we were on top of a roof in Afghanistan. We were in a firefight all day, pretty much," he explains. "Towards the end of the day, we thought everything was over . . . we're coming down off the roof, we're ready to bed down for the night." As Ibrahim relaxed and sipped water, thinking he was safe, a group of Taliban fighters snuck up on the Marine compound, ready to ambush. Fortunately for Ibrahim, someone detected them: A fighter jet dropped from the sky and did a "gun-run," raining bullets on the enemy. It all happened so fast, and the combined noise of the jet engine and the machine guns was so deafening that no one understood what had happened. Was that the enemy overhead? Were they hit? "At this point, I don't even know if I'm still alive," Ibrahim says. "My body froze. I couldn't move . . . I was breathing so fast, I was starting to get lightheaded, and . . . I could almost feel myself starting to black out."

A Dangerous Time
Ibrahim Hashi during one of his deployments in the Middle East.
Courtesy Ibrahim Hashi.

Feel It in Your Body?

Five minutes later, when Ibrahim realized what had occurred (the fighter jet had saved them), his heart was still pounding and his hands were shaking. His **fight-or-flight** response had taken hold. When faced with a crisis situation, stress hormones are released into the blood; breathing rate increases; the heart pumps faster and harder; blood pressure rises; the liver releases extra glucose into the bloodstream; and blood surges into the large muscles. All these physical changes prepare the body for confronting or fleeing the threat; hence the expression "fight or flight." But fear is not the only emotion that involves dramatic physical changes. Tears pour from the eyes during intense sadness and joy. Anger is associated with sweating, elevated heart rate, and heightened blood flow to the hands, apparently in anticipation of a physical confrontation (Ekman, 2003).

CONNECTIONS

In **Chapter 2,** we explained how the sympathetic nervous system prepares the body to respond to an emergency, whereas the parasympathetic nervous system brings the body back to a noncrisis mode through the "rest-and-digest" process. Here, we see how the autonomic nervous system is involved in physiological experiences of emotion.

List the major theories of emotion and describe how they differ.

Most psychologists agree that emotions and physiology are deeply intertwined, but they have not always agreed on the precise order of events. What happens first: body changes associated with an emotion, or the emotion itself? That's obvious, you may be thinking. Emotions occur first, and then the body responds. American psychologist William James would have begged to differ.

Hot Tempers
Women in Seville, Spain, use a fountain to cool off during a heat wave in the summer of 2017. This scene may look pleasant, but scorching summers can have a negative effect on psychological health. Hot temperatures have been associated with increased aggression, both in laboratory and real-world settings, and researchers suspect that violent crime will increase as global warming continues (Plante & Anderson, 2017, February).
JORGE GUERRERO/Getty Images.

JAMES–LANGE THEORY In the late 1800s, William James and Danish physiologist Carl Lange (1834–1900) independently derived similar explanations for emotion (James, 1890/1983; Lange & James, 1922). The **James–Lange theory of emotion** suggests that a stimulus initiates a physiological reaction (for example, heart pounding, muscles contracting, changes in breathing) and/or a behavioral reaction (crying or striking out) *before* we feel an emotion (**INFOGRAPHIC 9.2** on page 353). Emotions do not cause physiological or behavioral reactions, as common sense might suggest. Instead, "we feel sorry because we cry, angry because we strike, afraid because we tremble" (James, 1890/1983, p. 1066). In other words, changes in the body and behavior pave the way for emotions. Our bodies automatically react to stimuli, and awareness of this physiological response leads to the subjective experience of emotion. As proponents of the James–Lange theory explain, "Feelings are the consequences, not the causes, of emotional behavior and bodily response" (Laird & Lacasse, 2014, p. 32).

How Would You Feel?
A diver comes face-to-face with a crocodile while swimming off the coast of Quintana Roo, Mexico. If you were this unlucky diver, what would you experience first: the emotion of fear, a physiological response (increased heart rate), or a behavioral reaction (flinching)? The Cannon-Bard theory of emotion suggests that all these events would occur simultaneously.
Rodrigo Friscione/Getty Images.

How might the James–Lange theory apply to Ibrahim's experience? It all begins with a stimulus—in this case, the unexpected sound of a jet engine and machine guns overhead. Next occur the physiological reactions (increased heart rate, faster breathing, and so on) and the behavioral responses (freezing, in this case). Finally, the emotion registers. Ibrahim feels fear. Imagine that Ibrahim, for some reason, had no physiological reaction to the sound. Would he still experience the same degree of terror? According to the James–Lange theory, no.

The James–Lange theory suggests that each emotion has a distinct physiological fingerprint. If this were the case, it would be possible to identify an emotion based on a person's physiological/behavioral responses. PET and FMRI scans have confirmed that emotions such as happiness, anger, and fear do indeed have distinct activation patterns in the brain, lending evidence to the James–Lange theory, although there is some overlap among the regions involved (Berthoz, Blair, Le Clec'h, & Martinot, 2002; Damasio et al., 2000; Suardi, Sotgui, Costa, Cauda, & Rusconi, 2016).

Critics contend that the James–Lange theory cannot fully explain emotions because (1) people who are incapable of feeling physiological reactions (as a result of surgery or spinal cord injuries, for example) can still experience emotions; (2) the speed of an emotion is much faster than physiological changes; and (3) when physiological functioning is altered (through a hormone injection, for instance), emotions do not necessarily change (Bard, 1934; Cannon, 1927; Hilgard, 1987). In one experiment, researchers used surgery to stop animals from becoming physiologically aroused, yet the animals continued to exhibit behaviors associated with emotions, such as growling and posturing (Cannon, 1927).

CANNON–BARD THEORY American physiologist Walter Cannon (1871–1945) and his student Philip Bard (1898–1977) were among those who believed the James–Lange theory could not explain all emotions (Bard, 1934; Cannon, 1927). The **Cannon–Bard theory of emotion** suggests that we do not feel emotion as a result of physiological and behavioral reactions; instead, the emotions and the body responses occur *simultaneously* (Infographic 9.2). The starting point of this response is a stimulus in the environment.

James–Lange theory of emotion Suggests that a stimulus initiates the experience of a physiological and/or behavioral reaction, and this reaction leads to the feeling of an emotion.

Cannon–Bard theory of emotion Suggests that environmental stimuli are the starting point for emotions, and physiological or behavioral responses occur at the same time emotions are felt.

Let's use the Cannon–Bard theory and what we know about structures of the brain to understand what happened to Ibrahim. The sudden sound and appearance of the fighter jet activated sensory neurons in his ears, eyes, and perhaps in his skin (through touch receptors detecting the engine's wind). This sensory information passed through the thalamus, where it was split in two directions—one toward the cortex and the other toward the limbic system. Activity in the cortex created Ibrahim's perception of the fighter jet, while his limbic system activated a physiological and behavioral response, causing his heart to race and his breathing to increase. As all of this was happening, he experienced an emotion. The emotion and the physiological reaction occurred simultaneously.

Critics of the Cannon–Bard theory suggest the thalamus might not be capable of carrying out this processing on its own, as other brain areas may contribute (Beebe-Center, 1951; Hunt, 1939). Emotions are processed in many areas of the brain, including the **limbic system**, hypothalamus, and prefrontal cortex (Kolb & Whishaw, 2015; Northoff et al., 2009).

CONNECTIONS

In **Chapter 2,** we introduced the limbic system, a group of interconnected structures that play an important role in emotion, motivation, and memory. It also fuels basic drives, such as hunger, sex, and aggression. The limbic system includes the thalamus, hypothalamus, amygdala, and hippocampus.

How Does Cognition Fit In?

American psychologists Stanley Schachter (1922–1997) and Jerome E. Singer (1934–2010) also took issue with the James–Lange theory, primarily because different emotions do not have distinct and recognizable physiological responses (Schachter & Singer, 1962). They suggested there is a *general* pattern of physiological arousal caused by the sympathetic nervous system, and this pattern is common to a variety of emotions. The **Schachter–Singer theory of emotion** proposes that the experience of emotion is the result of two factors: (1) physiological arousal, *followed by* (2) a cognitive label for this physiological state (the arousal). According to this theory, if you experience physiological arousal but don't know why it has occurred, you will label the arousal and explain your feelings based on your "knowledge" of the environment and previous experiences. Depending on the "cognitive aspects of the situation," you may label the physiological arousal as joy, fear, anxiety, fury, or jealousy (Infographic 9.2).

To test their theory, Schachter and Singer injected participants (male college students) with either epinephrine to mimic physiological reactions of the sympathetic nervous system (such as increased blood pressure, respiration, and heart rate) or a placebo. The participants were left in a room with a "stooge," a confederate secretly working for the researchers, who was either euphoric or angry. When the confederate behaved euphorically, the participants who had been given no explanation for their physiological arousal were more likely to appear happy or report feeling happy. When the confederate behaved angrily, participants were more likely to appear angry or report feeling angry. It was clear that the participants who did not receive an explanation for their physiological arousal could be manipulated to feel either euphoria or anger, depending on the emotion displayed by the confederate. The participants who were accurately informed about side effects did not show signs or report feelings of euphoria or anger. Instead, they attributed their physiological arousal to the side effects clearly explained to them at the beginning of the study (Schachter & Singer, 1962).

Some have criticized the Schachter–Singer theory, suggesting that it overstates the link between physiological arousal and the experience of emotion (Reisenzein, 1983). What's more, studies have shown that people can experience an emotion without labeling it, especially if neural activity sidesteps the cortex and heads straight to the limbic system (Dimberg, Thunberg, & Elmehed, 2000; Lazarus, 1991a). We will discuss this process in the upcoming section on fear.

COGNITIVE APPRAISAL AND EMOTION Rejecting the notion that emotions result from cognitive labels of physiological arousal, American psychologist Richard Lazarus (1984, 1991a) suggested that emotion stems from the way people appraise or interpret the interactions they have. It doesn't matter if we can label an emotion or not; we experience the emotion nonetheless. Emotions such as happiness, anxiety, and shame are universal, and we don't need an agreed upon label or word to experience them. Babies, for example, can feel emotions long before they are able to label them with words.

Schachter–Singer theory of emotion Suggests that the experience of emotion is the result of physiological arousal and a cognitive label for this physiological state.

Lazarus also suggested emotions are adaptive because they help us cope with our surroundings. In a continuous feedback loop, our appraisals or interpretations of the environment change, causing changes in emotions (Folkman & Lazarus, 1985; Lazarus, 1991b). This is the foundation of the **cognitive appraisal approach** to emotion (Infographic 9.2), which suggests that the appraisal causes an emotional reaction. In contrast, the Schachter–Singer theory asserts the arousal comes first and then has to be labeled, leading to the experience of an emotion.

Responding to the cognitive appraisal approach, social psychologist Robert Zajonc (ZI-yunce; 1984) suggested that thinking is not always involved when we experience an emotion. As Zajonc (1980) saw it, emotions can precede thoughts and may even cause them. He also suggested we can experience emotions without interpreting environmental circumstances. Emotion can influence cognition, and cognition can influence emotion.

As you may have noticed, there is substantial disagreement about what role cognition plays in the experience of emotion. The relationship is complex and bidirectional, as thoughts can influence emotions, and emotions can impact memories, perceptions, interpersonal relationships, and physiology (Farb, Chapman, & Anderson, 2013; Forgas, 2008).

Whew! You made it through the theories of emotion—not an easy topic. Now let's see how some of the concepts we have presented relate to real life. You learned that certain physiological changes are likely to occur when a person experiences emotion. Did you know that some technologies are built on this very premise?

...BELIEVE IT...OR NOT

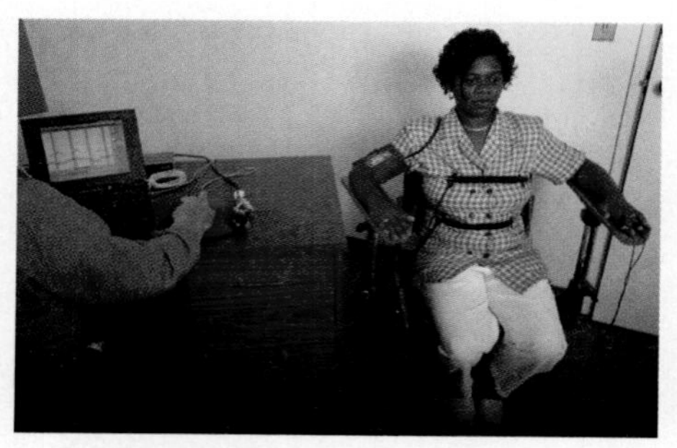

Do Polygraphs Work?
A new recruit undergoes a polygraph, or "lie detector," test at the FBI Academy. The polygraph operates on the premise that emotions are accompanied by measurable physiological changes. However, critics are skeptical of the findings often used to endorse this technology (Nelson & Handler, 2013; Rosky, 2013). Anna Clopet/Getty Images.

JUST HOW ACCURATE ARE POLYGRAPH TESTS? Since its introduction in the early 1900s, the polygraph, or "lie detector," test has been used by government agencies for a variety of purposes, including job screening, crime investigation, and spy identification (Department of Justice, 2006; Nelson, 2014). The FBI (along with many police departments) will not even hire applicants for certain positions unless they undergo a thorough background check, which includes a polygraph (Federal Bureau of Investigation, n.d.). Despite the widespread use of this technology, some scientists have serious doubts about its validity, and emphasize the need to consider the complex interactions of the brain and the body (Palmatier & Rovner, 2015; "True Lies," 2004, April 15).

"SOME SCIENTISTS HAVE SERIOUS DOUBTS ABOUT ITS VALIDITY. . . ."

What is this so-called lie detector and how does it work? The polygraph is a machine that attempts to determine if someone is lying by measuring aspects of physiological arousal presumed to be associated with deceit. When people lie, they often experience changes in breathing rate, blood pressure, and other variables controlled by the autonomic nervous system (Nelson, 2014). By monitoring these variables, the polygraph can theoretically detect when a person is being deceitful.

But here's the problem with this: Biological signs of anxiety do not always go hand-in-hand with deception. There are many other reasons one might experience physiological changes while taking a polygraph, among them "fear, anxiety, anger, and many medical or mental conditions" (Rosky, 2013, p. 2). Some estimates of polygraph accuracy are as high as 90%, but critics contend that studies often cited to justify polygraph use are riddled with methodological problems and have not been subjected to proper peer review (Nelson & Handler, 2013; Rosky, 2013).

cognitive appraisal approach Suggests that the appraisal or interpretation of interactions with surroundings causes an emotional reaction.

INFOGRAPHIC 9.2

Theories of Emotion

Imagine you are swimming and you think you see a shark. Fear pierces your gut, sending your heart racing as you swim frantically to shore. Or is it actually your churning stomach and racing heart that cause you to feel so terrified? And what part, if any, do your thoughts play in this process?

Psychologists have long debated the order in which events lead to emotion. Let's compare four major theories, each proposing a different sequence of events.

Body changes lead to emotions.

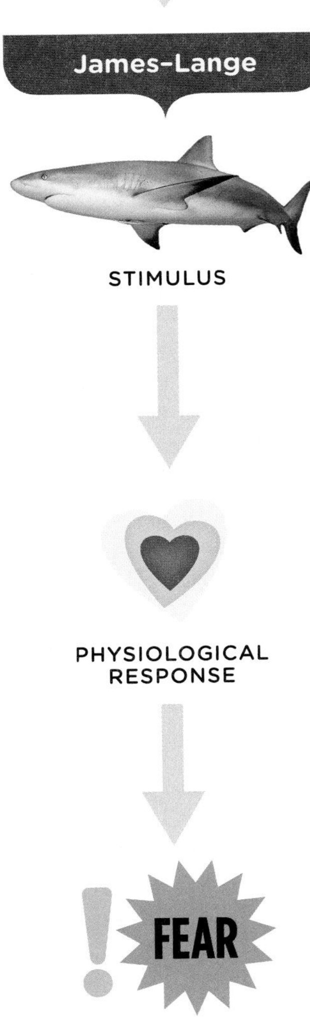

Body changes and emotions happen together.

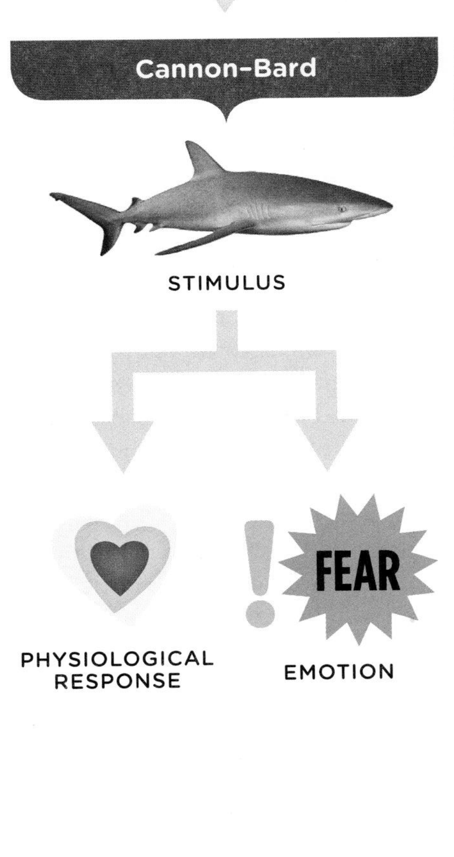

Our thoughts about our body changes lead to emotions.

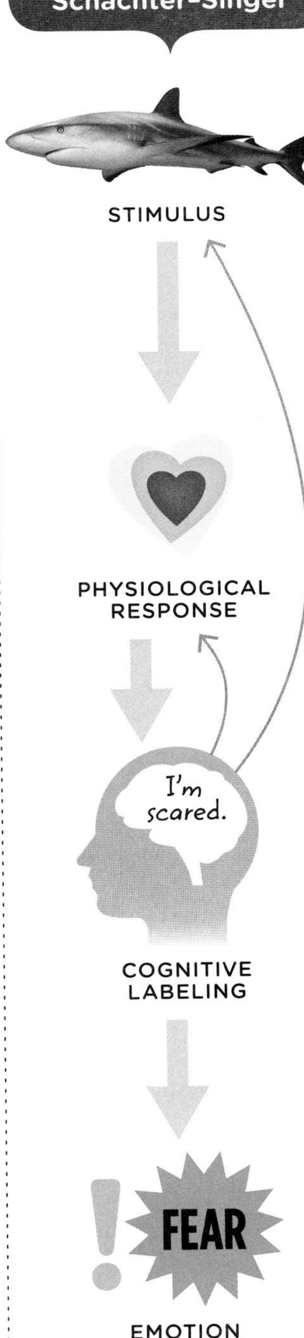

Our thoughts about our situation lead to emotions.

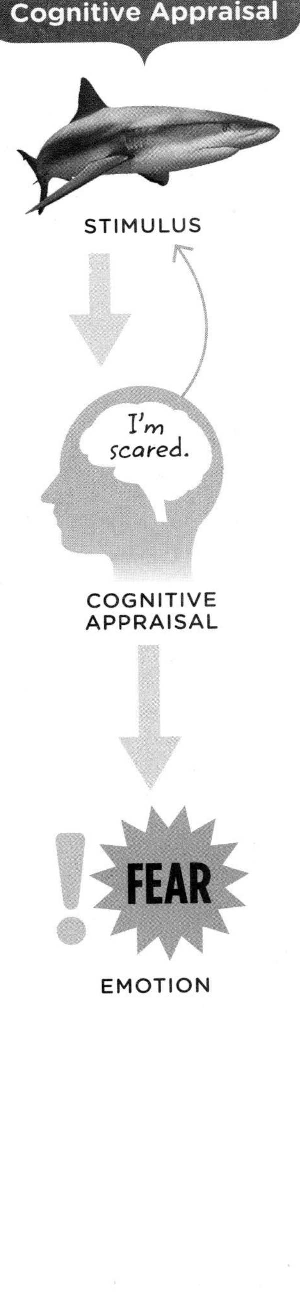

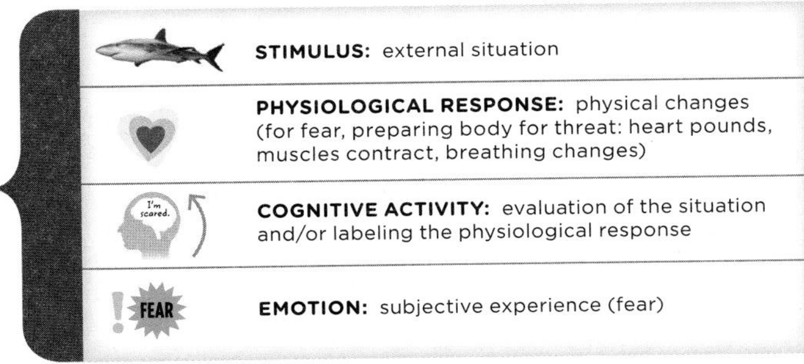

STIMULUS: external situation
PHYSIOLOGICAL RESPONSE: physical changes (for fear, preparing body for threat: heart pounds, muscles contract, breathing changes)
COGNITIVE ACTIVITY: evaluation of the situation and/or labeling the physiological response
FEAR
EMOTION: subjective experience (fear)

Credits: Sharks, Rich Carey/Shutterstock.

Searching for a better approach, some have turned to **fMRI** lie detection, but the accuracy and validity of this technology have also been questioned (Farah, Hutchinson, Phelps, & Wagner, 2014). Neither polygraph nor fMRI evidence is considered admissible in court (Stroud, 2015, February 2), but perhaps this will change as the technology evolves.

CONNECTIONS

In **Chapter 2,** we described how fMRI technology tracks the flow of oxygen-rich blood in the brain, revealing which areas are active. Here, we see how researchers are trying to use this technology to detect lying.

Thus, it appears that current lie detection technologies are not much better than old-fashioned observation. If we rely on body language, facial expressions, and other social cues, our lie-detection accuracy is no more than 60% (Gamer, 2009). Spotting dishonesty may not be our forte, but we are pros at identifying basic emotions like happiness, anger, and fear.

Face Value

Think about the clues you rely on when trying to "read" other people's emotions. Where do you look for signs of anger, sadness, or surprise? It's written all over their face, of course.

"SIR, SOMETHING BAD IS ABOUT TO HAPPEN." To stay safe in wartime, you need to be one step ahead of your enemy. That's why Ibrahim and his platoon mates often seized radios from defeated Taliban fighters and used the devices to eavesdrop on enemy communications. The Marines couldn't understand the Taliban's language, so they relied on allies in the Afghan army to interpret. But sometimes verbal translation wasn't even necessary. Ibrahim remembers a specific instance during a mission in the Musa Qala District in Helmand Province. His Afghan colleague heard something on the radio, and his face immediately transformed. Just by looking at the soldier's face, Ibrahim knew they were in trouble. "Sir, something bad is about to happen," the soldier said. Moments later, their platoon was ambushed.

Misunderstood Emojis
People around the world generally agree upon what constitutes a happy, sad, angry, or frightened facial expression. But when it comes to interpreting emojis, confusion abounds. Part of the problem is that emojis can appear different across platforms; a face that appears to be smiling on a Samsung device may look downright annoyed on an iPhone. Even when people are viewing the exact same emoji (the "grinning face with smiling eyes" shown here), they often don't agree on whether the emotion conveyed is positive, negative, or neither (Miller, 2016, April 5; Miller et al., 2016).
CSP_ikopylov/AGE Fotostock.

Discuss evidence supporting the idea that emotions are universal.

How did human beings become such experts in reading facial expressions? Writing in *The Expression of the Emotions in Man and Animals* (1872/2002), Charles Darwin suggested that this is not a learned ability but rather an innate characteristic that evolved because it promotes survival. Sharing the same facial expressions allows us to communicate critical information, like the presence of danger. If facial expressions are truly innate and universal, then people from all cultures ought to interpret them in the same way. A "happy face" should look much the same all over the world, from the United States to the Pacific island of New Guinea.

EKMAN'S FACES Some five decades ago, American psychologist Paul Ekman traveled to a remote mountain region of New Guinea to study an isolated group of indigenous peoples. Ekman and his colleagues were very careful in selecting their participants, choosing only those who were unfamiliar with *Western facial behaviors*—the signature facial expressions we equate with basic emotions like disgust and sadness. The participants didn't speak English, nor had they watched Western movies, worked for anyone with a Caucasian background, or lived among Westerners. The study went something like this: The researchers told the participants stories conveying emotions such as fear, happiness, and anger. In the story conveying fear, for example, a man is sitting alone in his house with no knife, axe, bow, or any weapon to defend himself. Suddenly, a wild pig appears in his doorway, and he becomes frightened that the pig will bite him. Next, the researchers asked the participants to match the emotion described in

Universal Expressions
A smile in Kenya (top left) means the same thing as a smile in Lithuania (top middle) or India (top right). Facial expressions for other basic emotions such as sadness (middle row) and anger (bottom row) are also strikingly similar across cultures (Ekman & Friesen, 1971).
Top row, left to right: M Lohmann/agefotostock; Wojtek Buss/agefotostock; Design Pics Inc/Alamy Stock Photo. Middle row, left to right: Rieko Honma/Getty Images; Giantstep Inc/Getty Images; Ravi Shekhar/Dinodia Photo/AGE Fotostock. Bottom row, left to right: khoa vu/Getty Images; Kerry Lorimer/Getty Images; Ezra Bailey/Getty Images.

the story to a picture of a person's face (choosing from 6–12 sets of photographs). The results indicated that the same facial expressions represent the same basic emotions across cultures—and this finding has been replicated approximately 200 times (Ekman & Friesen, 1971; Ekman & Keltner, 2014, April 10).

And so it seems, a "happy face" really does look the same to people in the United States and New Guinea. Further evidence for the universal nature of facial expressions is apparent in children born blind; although they have never seen a human face demonstrating emotion, their smiles and frowns are similar to those of sighted children (Galati, Scherer, & Ricci-Bitti, 1997; Matsumoto & Willingham, 2009). Newer research suggests the universal nature of these expressions may not apply to fear and anger, but we shall see if the findings can be replicated (Price, 2016, October 17).

Put Your Heads Together

In your groups, have everyone take out a piece of paper and sketch faces (or emojis) demonstrating happiness, sadness, disgust, anger, surprise, and fear. Compare your faces with others in your group. Describe the similarities. Are there many differences?

ACROSS THE WORLD

WHEN TO REVEAL, WHEN TO CONCEAL Although the expression of some basic emotions appears to be universal, culture acts like a filter, determining the appropriate contexts in which to exhibit them. A culture's **display rules** provide the guidelines for when, how, and where an emotion is expressed. In North America, where individualism prevails, people tend to be fairly expressive. Showing emotion, particularly positive emotions, is socially acceptable. This is less the case in the collectivist (community-oriented) societies of East Asia, where concealing emotions is more the norm. Display rules are taught early in life, as parents

CAN YOU FEEL THE CULTURE?

display rules Framework or guidelines for when, how, and where an emotion is expressed.

show approval or disapproval of children's emotional expressions. For example, Korean and Asian American parents appear more inclined than European American parents to favor "modesty and suppression of children's emotions and to use shaming and love withdrawal to control children" (Louie, Oh, & Lau, 2013, p. 429). Why do collectivist cultures tend to discourage emotional displays? Showing emotions, particularly anger, can threaten the social harmony that is highly valued by their cultures (Louie et al., 2013).

However, we cannot solely attribute variations in display rules to collectivism and individualism because there are key distinctions within these two categories. For example, the United States and Germany (both considered individualistic) appear to have different display rules for contempt and disgust, with Americans more inclined to reveal these emotions (Koopmann-Holm & Matsumoto, 2011). To understand the origins of display rules, we must explore how expressions of *specific* emotions (not emotions in general) are influenced by cultural values (Hareli, Kafetsios, & Hess, 2015; Koopmann-Holm & Matsumoto, 2011).

CAREER CONNECTIONS

SHOW YOUR BENEVOLENCE AT WORK

SHOWING EMOTIONS AT WORK Let's see how research on display rules might help us in a workplace scenario. If you have worked in the service industry, your manager may have told you to treat every customer the same way, and to avoid strong displays of emotion. When it comes to negative emotions like anger and sadness, you would be wise to follow this advice; customers do not respond well to the expression of "malevolent emotions." However, withholding compassion, empathy, and other "benevolent emotions" may be counterproductive. Research suggests that containing these positive emotions may cause employees to come off as "mechanical and superficial" and make customers feel uncomfortable (Yagil, 2015, p. 164). How might this finding help people who rely on tips to support themselves? How about employees whose performance ratings rely on the results of customer satisfaction surveys?

DOES SMILING MAKE YOU HAPPY? As you probably have noticed, facial expressions can have a dramatic impact on social interactions. If you walk into class with an angry frown, people are unlikely to approach you and say "hi." A smile, on the other hand, tends to attract waves and "hellos." Did you ever think about how your facial expressions might affect *you*? Believe it or not, the simple act of smiling can make a person *feel* happier. According to the **facial feedback hypothesis** (Buck, 1980), facial expressions can impact the experience of emotions. If this hypothesis is correct, we should be able to manipulate our emotions with activities like the one described below.

Take a pen and put it between your teeth, keeping your mouth open for about 30 seconds. Consider how you are feeling. Next, hold the pen with your lips, but don't let it touch your teeth, for 30 seconds. Again, consider how you are feeling.

If you are like the participants in a study conducted by Strack, Martin, and Stepper (1988), holding the pen in your teeth should result in your seeing objects and events in your environment as funnier than if you hold the pen with your lips. Why would that be? Take a look at the photo to the left and note how the person holding the pen in his teeth seems to be smiling—the feedback of those smiling muscles leads to a happier mood.

We are now nearing the end of this chapter—and what an emotional one it has been! Before wrapping things up, let's take a closer look at fear and happiness.

Facial Feedback
Holding a pencil between your teeth (top) will probably put you in a better mood than holding it with your lips closed (bottom). This is because the physical act of smiling, which occurs when you place the pencil in your teeth, promotes feelings of happiness. So next time you're feeling low, don't be afraid to flex those smile muscles!
Robert M. Errera.

facial feedback hypothesis The facial expression of an emotion can affect the experience of that emotion.

Types of Emotions

Ibrahim witnessed disturbing sights and sounds in Iraq and Afghanistan, but violence was nothing new to a man who spent some of his formative years in Somalia. After living in the United States until age 8 or 9, Ibrahim spent a few years in his family's homeland, which was mired in civil war. He remembers traveling through the city with his aunt when a firefight broke out between rival factions, just meters away. His aunt ran for her life, leaving Ibrahim to fend for himself as bullets whizzed by his head. Fortunately, Ibrahim escaped the situation unscathed, but how do you think he felt afterwards? *Fear* is the emotion that immediately comes to mind, but there may be others, including *anger* toward his aunt, *disgust* at the sight of blood, *anxiety* about his future safety, and *gratitude* toward those who helped him.

Are such feelings common to all people? Some researchers have proposed that there is a set of "biologically given" emotions, which includes anger, fear, disgust, sadness, and happiness (Coan, 2010). However, some who study facial expressions contend there may be only four patterns of universally recognized emotions—happiness, sadness, surprise/fear, and disgust/anger (Jack, Sun, Delis, Garrod, & Schyns, 2016). Such feelings are considered *basic emotions* because people all over the world experience and express them in similar ways; they appear to be innate and have an underlying neural basis (Izard, 1992).

It is also noteworthy that unpleasant emotions (fear, anger, disgust, and sadness) have survived throughout our evolutionary history, and are more prevalent than positive emotions such as happiness, surprise, and interest (Ekman, 1992; Forgas, 2008; Izard, 2007). This suggests that negative emotions have "adaptive value"; in other words, they may be useful in dangerous situations, like those that demand a fight-or-flight response (Adolphs, 2013; Forgas, 2008; Friedman, Stephens, & Thayer, 2014).

The Biology of Fear

Describe the amygdala's role in the experience of fear.

What's going on in your brain when you feel afraid? With the help of brain-scanning technologies, researchers have zeroed in on an almond-shaped structure in the limbic system (Cheng, Knight, Smith, & Helmstetter, 2006; Pape & Pare, 2010). This structure, known as the amygdala, is central to our experience of fear (Davis & Whalen, 2001; Hariri, Tessitore, Mattay, Fera, & Weinberger, 2002; Méndez-Bértolo et al., 2016). If a person views threatening images, or even looks at an image of a frightened face, the amygdala is activated (Chiao et al., 2008; Laeng et al., 2010; Méndez-Bértolo et al., 2016).

PATHWAYS TO FEAR Any time you are confronted with a fear-provoking situation, the amygdala enables an ultrafast, unconscious response. Sensory information (sights, sounds) entering the thalamus can either go to the cortex for processing, or head straight for the amygdala without stopping at the cortex (LeDoux, 1996, 2000, 2012). The direct path going from the thalamus to the amygdala conveys raw information about the threat, enabling your brain and body to respond to danger without your awareness. Like a panic button, the amygdala issues an alert, summoning other parts of the brain that play a role in the experience of fear (for example, the hypothalamus and medulla), which then alert the sympathetic nervous system. A pathway also goes to the pituitary gland, resulting in the secretion of stress hormones (LeDoux, 2012).

Let's see how this immediate fear response might play out using Ibrahim's example from above. Visual information about the gunfight went directly to his thalamus, and from there to his amygdala, triggering an alarm reaction. His heart and breathing rates increased, preparing him to flee the battle scene. Meanwhile, information sent to the sensory processing centers of his visual cortex resulted in a visual representation of the chaotic scene.

Now suppose it had all been a false alarm; the conflict between the rival factions never escalated to violence, and the fighters dispersed. In this case, Ibrahim's cortex would have alerted the amygdala: "False alarm. The scene is safe." The key thing to note is that it takes longer for neural information to go from the thalamus to the cortex than from the thalamus to the amygdala. This explains why you generally need a moment to calm down: The physiological reaction starts before the false alarm message from the cortex reaches the amygdala (**Infographic 9.3**).

There appears to be an evolutionary advantage to having direct and indirect routes for processing information about potential threats (LeDoux, 2012). The direct route (thalamus to amygdala, causing physiological and emotional reactions) enables us to react quickly to threats for which we are biologically prepared (snakes, spiders, aggressive faces). The other pathway allows us to evaluate more complex threats (such as nuclear weapons, job layoffs) with our cortex, overriding the fast-response pathway when necessary.

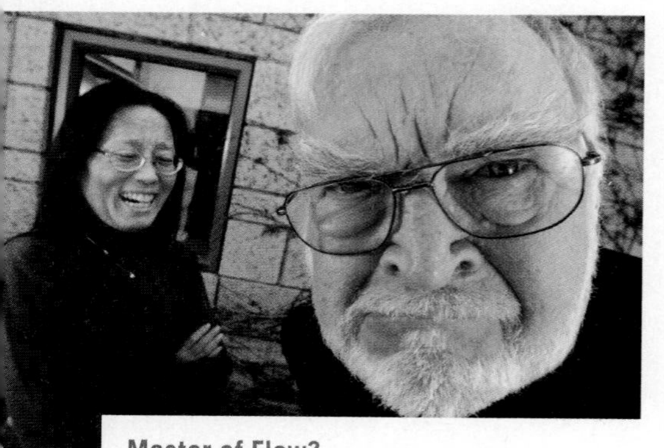

Master of Flow?
Psychologist Mihaly Csikszentmihalyi makes a funny face as his colleague Jeanne Nakamura laughs in the background. Csikszentmihalyi, who is a Distinguished Professor of Psychology and Management at Claremont Graduate University in California, is famous for establishing the concept of flow and furthering our understanding of happiness.
Mel Melcon/Getty Images.

HOW IMPORTANT IS THE AMGDALA? What happens to these automatic responses when the amygdala is not working? Animal studies suggest that damage to the amygdala impairs the fear response (Bliss-Moreau, Bauman, & Amaral, 2011; Phillips & LeDoux, 1992). Similarly, people with a damaged amygdala exhibit weaker-than-normal responses to stimuli that inspire fear or disgust (Buchanan, Tranel, & Adolphs, 2004). They also have difficulty comprehending nonverbal behavior associated with emotion (Adolphs, 2008).

Now it is time to move on to brighter things. What makes you happy, and how might you become more content than you are now?

Happiness

In the very first chapter of this book, we introduced the field of positive psychology, "the study of positive emotions, positive character traits, and enabling institutions" (Seligman & Steen, 2005, p. 410). Rather than focusing on mental illness and abnormal behavior, positive psychology emphasizes human strengths and virtues. The goal is well-being and fulfillment, and that means "satisfaction" with the past, "hope and optimism" for the future, and "flow and happiness" at the current time (Seligman & Csikszentmihalyi, 2000). Let's explore that flow and happiness of the present.

THINK POSITIVE

GOING WITH THE FLOW People often make the mistake of viewing happiness as a goal they will attain at some point in the future, when all of life's pieces fall into place: "Once I start making a lot of money and buy a house, I will be happy," or, "If I just lose 10 pounds, I will finally be content." What they don't realize is that happiness may be within grasp, right here and right now. Sometimes it's just a matter of getting into the "flow."

IS IT THE SECRET TO ACHIEVING HAPPINESS?

Have you ever felt completely absorbed in a challenging task, guided by a focus so intense that everything else, including the past and future, faded from your awareness? Some people call it being "in the zone"; Hungarian-born psychologist Mihaly Csikszentmihalyi (me-High Cheek-sent-me-hi-ee) refers to it as "flow" and considers it a prerequisite for happiness (Csikszentmihalyi, 1999). For flow to occur, you must be engaged in a task

The Anatomy of Fear

You instantly recoil when you spot a snake—then sigh with relief just a moment later when it registers that the snake is a rubber toy. Have you ever wondered why you react with fear when a "threat" turns out to be nothing? Why does it take longer for you to process a threat than react to it? Sensory information (sight, sound) entering the brain travels to the thalamus and is then routed to the cortex for processing. Sensory information can also go directly to the amygdala. In the case of a threat, the amygdala alerts other areas of the brain and the endocrine system instantly without waiting for a conscious command. This enables a response to fear before you are even fully aware of what you are reacting to.

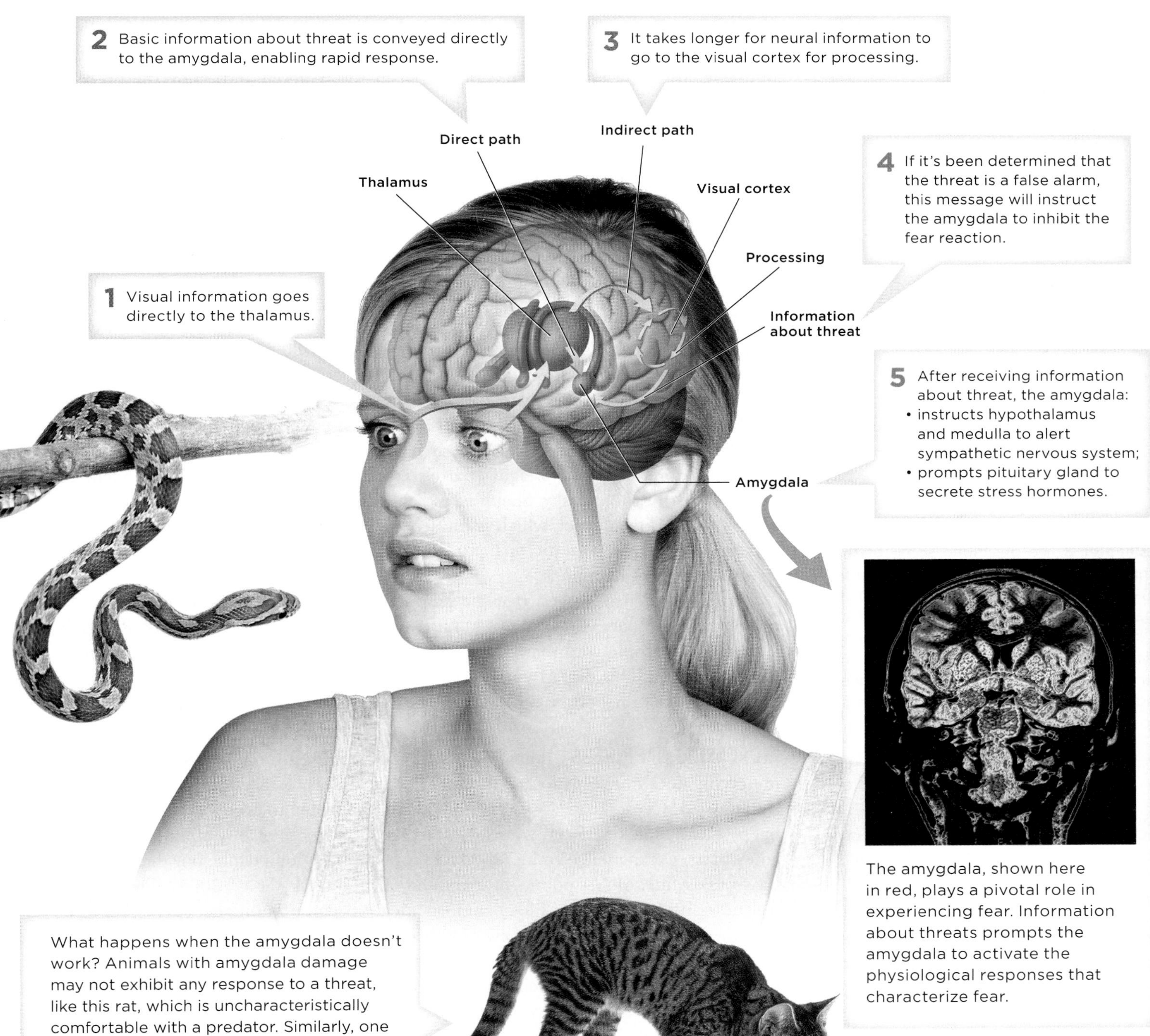
2 Basic information about threat is conveyed directly to the amygdala, enabling rapid response.
3 It takes longer for neural information to go to the visual cortex for processing.
Direct path
Indirect path
Thalamus
Visual cortex
4 If it's been determined that the threat is a false alarm, this message will instruct the amygdala to inhibit the fear reaction.
Processing
1 Visual information goes directly to the thalamus.
Information about threat
5 After receiving information about threat, the amygdala:
• instructs hypothalamus and medulla to alert sympathetic nervous system;
• prompts pituitary gland to secrete stress hormones.
Amygdala

The amygdala, shown here in red, plays a pivotal role in experiencing fear. Information about threats prompts the amygdala to activate the physiological responses that characterize fear.

What happens when the amygdala doesn't work? Animals with amygdala damage may not exhibit any response to a threat, like this rat, which is uncharacteristically comfortable with a predator. Similarly, one study found that people with amygdala damage demonstrated an absence of expected fear behaviors (Feinstein, Adolphs, Damasio, & Tranel, 2011).

Credits: T1 weighted MRI image of the brain demonstrates normal cerebral anatomy, Living Art Enterprises/Science Source; Alarmed woman, Brand New Images/Getty Images; Snake, Eric Isselee/Shutterstock; Mouse, S-F/Shutterstock; Cat, Kitchin & Hurst/Agefotostock.

that is intrinsically rewarding and challenging (but not so challenging that it makes you feel anxious), aware of what you need to accomplish from one minute to the next, and receiving feedback during the process (Csikszentmihalyi, 1975, 1999).

Activities that lend themselves to flow include "fun activities" such as chess, rock climbing, dancing, and composing music, but it can also be achieved during more ordinary tasks associated with work and school (Csikszentmihalyi, 1990; Culbertson, Fullagar, Simmons, & Zhu, 2015). In the classroom, you are most likely to experience flow while performing tasks that afford you some control and require active participation, such as group work and individual assignments (Shernoff, Csikszentmihalyi, Shneider, & Shernoff, 2003). So next time the opportunity arises, try to achieve flow by giving the activity your undivided attention and being fully present in the moment. You may become more interested in the material and enjoy the process. What's more, your positive experience may rub off on those around you, as flow appears to be somewhat contagious (Culbertson et al., 2015). 

Flow is one of the secrets to achieving happiness, and it can be experienced by anyone. However, some of us seem more inclined toward happiness than others. Why is this so?

LO 13 Summarize evidence pointing to the biological basis of happiness.

THE BIOLOGY OF HAPPINESS To what degree do we inherit happiness? Heritability estimates are between 35% and 50%, and as high as 80% in longitudinal studies (Bartels, 2015; Nes, Czajkowski, & Tambs, 2010). In other words, a sizable proportion of the population-wide variation in happiness, life satisfaction, and well-being can be explained by genetic make-up, as opposed to environmental factors.

Research suggests that happiness may have a biologically based "set point" similar to the set point for body weight (Bartels et al., 2010; Cummins, Li, Wooden, & Stokes, 2014; Lyubomirsky, Sheldon, & Schkade, 2005). Happiness tends to fluctuate around this fixed level, which is influenced by genes and related to **temperament**. We may experience periodic ups and downs, but ultimately we move back toward that fixed level of happiness.

CONNECTIONS In **Chapter 8,** we described some of the temperaments exhibited by infants. About 40% can be classified as "easy" babies, meaning they are relatively happy and easy to soothe, follow regular schedules, and quickly adjust to changes in the environment. This early evidence of temperament lends support to the biological basis of happiness discussed here.

Some researchers suggest that the set point theory fails to account for the variety of events that impact well-being over a lifetime. One such event is marriage. Research suggests that people who marry are generally happier than those who remain single throughout life. This disparity appears to result from differences in experience rather than variations in happiness set points (Anusic, Yap, & Lucas, 2014).

INCREASING HAPPINESS That being said, the happiness brought about by positive life events does not seem to last forever (Diener, Lucas, & Scollon, 2006; Mancini, Bonanno, & Clark, 2011). We tend to become **habituated** to events that make us feel happy rather quickly. If you win the lottery, get a new job, or buy a beautiful house, you will likely experience an increased level of happiness for a while, but then go back to your baseline, or "set point," of happiness (Lyubomirsky et al., 2005). Things that feel new and improved or life-changing quickly become mundane, suggesting that happiness will not be found in new possessions or shopping sprees. The implication is that we need to be careful when pursuing happiness as a goal in life, as we don't want to emphasize obtaining a specific outcome (like moving to a house near the ocean) or acquiring a desired object (Lyubomirsky et al., 2005). Rather than trying to become happier, we should be content with what we have (Lyubomirsky, Dickerhoof, Boehm, & Sheldon, 2011).

CONNECTIONS In **Chapter 5,** we presented the concept of habituation, a basic form of learning wherein repeated exposure to an event generally results in a reduced response. Here, we see the same effect can occur with events resulting in happiness. With repeated exposure, we habituate to events that initially elicited happiness.

With this in mind, there are many steps you can take to maximize enjoyment of your life right now (**Infographic 9.4**). Engaging in physical exercise, showing

Pathways to Happiness

When it comes to being happy, there is no "magic bullet," but the latest research suggests we may be able to cultivate positive emotions and well-being through a variety of activities, many of which do not involve spending money. That being said, money does play a role—and it's not so much about how much you have, but how you choose to use it.

YES!
Going to college
Higher levels of education have been linked to greater happiness (Trostel, 2015, October 14).

YES!
Achieving "flow"
While studying, working, or pursuing an interest, allow yourself to become completely absorbed in challenging and rewarding tasks (Csikszentmihalyi, 1999; Culbertson, Fullagar, Simmons, & Zhu, 2015).

NO!
Buying new stuff
Buying new things may provide temporary pleasure, but it is unlikely to increase long-term happiness (Donnelly, Ksendzova, Howell, Vohs, & Baumeister, 2016; Lyubomirsky et al., 2005).

YES!
Prioritizing relationships
Cultivating deep and meaningful relationships with family and friends seems to bolster happiness (Helliwell, Layard, & Sachs, 2018).

YES!
"Buying time"
Paying for timesaving services, such as grocery delivery, is associated with "greater life satisfaction" (Whillans, Dunn, Smeets, Bekkers, & Norton, 2017, p. 1).

NO!
Becoming a millionaire
Salary increases may boost happiness, but "most data suggest that after basic needs have been met, additional income is not associated with increases in well-being" (Mogilner & Norton, 2016, p. 12).

MAYBE
Moving your body
Physically active people are generally happier than their sedentary peers (Lathia, Sandstrom, Mascolo, & Rentfrow, 2017).

YES!
Counting your blessings
Being grateful for what you have may lead to less stress and greater well-being (Emmons & McCullough, 2003; Krejtz, Nezlek, Michnicka, Holas, & Rusanowska, 2016).

MAYBE
Buying experiences
Investing in vacations, restaurant meals, and other activities is more likely to promote "enduring happiness" than purchasing material items (Gilovich & Kumar, 2015).

YES!
Being kind and generous
Whether you are buying a gift or donating to charity, spending money on others is likely to increase your happiness (Dunn, Aknin, & Nortin, 2014; Park et al., 2017).

kindness, and getting involved in activities that benefit others are all linked to increased positive emotions (Lyubomirsky et al., 2011; Lyubomirsky & Layous, 2013; Walsh, 2011). The same can be said for recording positive thoughts and feelings of gratefulness in a journal. In one study, participants were asked to write in a diary each day, identifying what they were most grateful for. The researchers measured well-being and found that the participants in the diary group were better off than those who didn't count their blessings. Members of the diary group were also more likely to report they had helped or offered emotional support to another person (Emmons & McCullough, 2003). As this study shows, "Simple intentional changes in one's thoughts and behaviors can precipitate meaningful increases in happiness" (Lyumbomirsky & Layous, 2013, p. 60).

Spending time with the people we love can also beget happiness. Can you remember the last time you participated in a family tradition?

From the SCIENTIFIC AMERICAN pages of

THE MORE RITUALS THE MERRIER

Family traditions of any type boost enjoyment of gatherings.

Some people go home for the holidays hoping just to survive, burying their attention in their phones or football to avoid conflict with relatives. Yet research now suggests that is the wrong idea. Family rituals—of any form—can save a holiday, making it well worth the effort of getting everyone in the same room.

In a series of studies . . . published in the *Journal of the Association for Consumer Research*, hundreds of online subjects described rituals they performed with their families during Christmas, New Year's Day, and Easter, from tree decoration to egg hunts. Those who said they performed collective rituals, compared with those who said they did not, felt closer to their families, which made the holidays more interesting, which in turn made them more enjoyable. Most surprising, the *types* of rituals they described—family dinners with special foods, religious ceremonies, watching the ball drop in Times Square—did not have a direct bearing on enjoyment. But the *number* of rituals did. Apparently having family rituals makes the holidays better and the more the merrier.

The study could measure only correlations between subjects' responses, leaving causality uncertain—Do rituals increase holiday pleasure, or do people who already enjoy the holidays choose to perform more rituals? Yet enjoyment ratings were higher when given after, versus before, describing rituals, suggesting that simply thinking about rituals can put a warm filter on one's experience. . . . **Matthew Hutson. Reproduced with permission.**

Put Your Heads Together

Can money buy happiness? Team up and **A)** discuss how money influences happiness. **B)** How would your group spend $200 to increase the happiness of each member? **C)** How would you spend $2,000? **D)** Compare your answers with those of other groups.

You Asked, Ivonne Answers

http://qrs.ly/w57829n

What kinds of discrimination have you faced as a blind person?

IN A GOOD PLACE You may be wondering how Ivonne Mosquera-Schmidt and Ibrahim Hashi are doing these days. Ivonne is in a good place, and she attributes that to her faith in God. "Because I have that trust and that sense of hope, I can have peace," she says. "I can be in the moment and I can learn what I need to learn from that moment." When does Ivonne feel happiest? While running, of course! The greatest runs are those that take her through the beautiful outdoors. "My breathing connects me to nature." She explains. "I breathe out, and that's what the plants and trees and everything else take in, and they breathe in and out, and it's kind of this exchange of energy that is so free and open when you're outside."

Ibrahim completed his service with the Marine Corps in 2011, enrolled in American University in Washington, D.C., in 2012, and graduated in 2016. Returning to civilian life was difficult, and it took him a long time to let go of the "super-vigilant, hyper-aware" mindset that once kept him alive in combat. Ibrahim isolated himself, avoiding interactions with people, even family members. During that readjustment period, his only lifeline was friendship with fellow Marines. "Whenever I needed help, I would call them, and if they needed help, they would call me." Like many of his platoon mates, Ibrahim was diagnosed with posttraumatic stress disorder (PTSD; Chapter 13). But eventually he began talking about his experiences, and this helped him heal. "It's not something I hide anymore, and honestly that's been the best thing for me," he says. "Now, within the past year or so, I'm very happy, I'm content with life. . . . What makes me happy is having a good solid network of relationships, of friends and family members and loved ones."

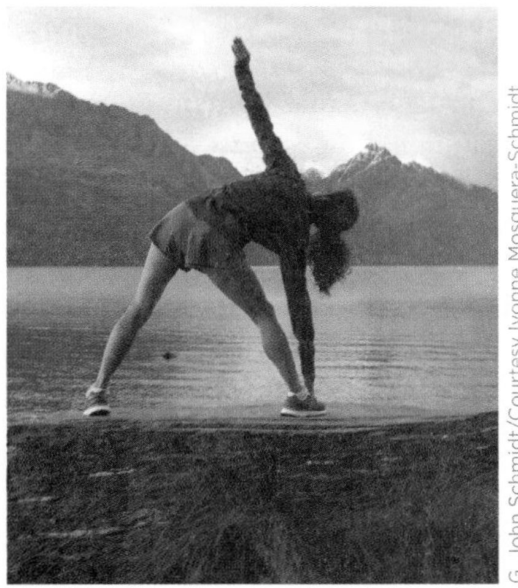

G. John Schmidt/Courtesy Ivonne Mosquera-Schmidt.

Ivonne Mosquera-Schmidt

Courtesy Ibrahim Hashi.

Ibrahim Hashi

show what you know

1. On the way to a wedding, you get mud on your clothing. Describe how your emotion and mood would differ.
2. ______________ of a culture provide a framework for when, how, and where an emotion is expressed.
   a. Beliefs
   b. Display rules
   c. Feedback loops
   d. Appraisals
3. Name two ways that the Cannon-Bard and Schachter-Singer theories of emotion differ.
4. What evidence suggests that emotions are universal?
5. When people view images that are threatening, or when they see images of faces of people who are afraid, the ______________ becomes active.
6. "Happiness has heritability estimates as high as 80%." How would you explain this statement to a fellow student?

✓ CHECK YOUR ANSWERS IN APPENDIX C.

YOUR SCIENTIFIC WORLD is a new application-based feature appearing in every chapter. In these online activities, you will take on role-playing scenarios that encourage you to think critically and apply your knowledge of psychological science to solve a real-world problem. For example: Do you spend a lot of time on social media? Do you ever wonder if all that time online is helping you feel more connected? Explore how your use of social media may—or may not—contribute to your sense of belonging. You can access Your Scientific World activities in LaunchPad. Have fun!

SUMMARY OF CONCEPTS

LO 1 Define motivation. (p. 327)

Motivation is a stimulus that can direct the way we behave, think, and feel. A motivated behavior tends to be guided (has a direction), energized, and persistent. When a behavior is reinforced, an association is established between the behavior and this consequence. With motivated behavior, this association becomes the incentive, or reason, to repeat the behavior.

LO 2 Explain how extrinsic and intrinsic motivation impact behavior. (p. 328)

When a learned behavior is motivated by the incentive of external reinforcers in the environment, there is an extrinsic motivation to continue that behavior. Intrinsic motivation occurs when a learned behavior is motivated by the prospect of internal reinforcers. Performing a behavior because it is inherently interesting or satisfying exemplifies intrinsic motivation; the reinforcers originate from within.

LO 3 **Describe drive-reduction theory and explain how it relates to motivation. (p. 329)**

The drive-reduction theory of motivation suggests that human behaviors are driven by the need to maintain homeostasis—that is, to fulfill basic biological needs for nutrients, fluids, oxygen, and so on. If a need is not fulfilled, this creates a drive, or state of tension, that pushes us or motivates behaviors to meet it. Once a need is satisfied, the drive is reduced, but not forever. The need inevitably returns, and you feel driven to meet it once again.

LO 4 **Explain how arousal theory relates to motivation. (p. 330)**

According to arousal theory, humans seek an optimal level of arousal, or alertness and engagement in the world. What constitutes an optimal level of arousal is variable, and depends on individual differences. Some people seem to be sensation seekers; that is, they seek activities that increase arousal.

LO 5 **Outline Maslow's hierarchy of needs. (p. 332)**

The needs in Maslow's hierarchy, often depicted as a pyramid, are considered universal and are ordered according to the strength of their associated drives. At the base of the hierarchy are physiological needs, which include requirements for food, water, sleep, and overall balance of body systems. Moving up the pyramid are increasingly higher-level needs: safety, love and belongingness, esteem, self-actualization, and self-transcendence. Maslow suggested that basic needs must be met before higher-level needs motivate behavior. In some cases, people abandon their lower-level needs to meet higher-level needs.

LO 6 **Describe the human sexual response as identified by Masters and Johnson. (p. 336)**

The human sexual response is the physiological pattern that occurs during sexual activity. Men and women tend to experience a similar pattern or cycle of excitement, plateau, orgasm, and resolution, but the duration of these phases varies from person to person.

LO 7 **Define sexual orientation and summarize how it develops. (p. 337)**

Sexual orientation is a person's enduring sexual attraction to individuals of the same sex, opposite sex, or both sexes; a continuum that includes dimensions of sexuality, attraction, desire, and emotions. Research has focused on the causes of sexual orientation, but there is no strong evidence pointing to any one factor or factors; it results from an interaction between nature and nurture.

LO 8 **Discuss how the stomach and the hypothalamus make us feel hunger. (p. 343)**

In a classic experiment, researchers confirmed that events in the stomach accompany hunger. When glucose levels dip, the stomach and liver send signals to the hypothalamus. When the lateral hypothalamus is activated, appetite increases. If the ventromedial hypothalamus is activated, appetite declines.

LO 9 **Define emotions and explain how they differ from moods. (p. 347)**

An emotion is a psychological state that includes a subjective or inner experience, physiological component, and behavioral expression. Emotions tend to be strong, but they generally don't last as long as moods. Emotions are more likely to have identifiable causes (as reactions to stimuli), and they are more likely to motivate a person to action. Moods are longer-term emotional states that are less intense, and do not appear to have distinct beginnings or ends.

LO 10 **List the major theories of emotion and describe how they differ. (p. 349)**

The James–Lange theory of emotion suggests that a stimulus initiates a physiological and/or behavioral reaction, and this reaction leads to an emotion. The Cannon–Bard theory of emotion suggests that we do not feel emotion as a result of physiological and behavioral reactions; instead, all these experiences occur simultaneously. The Schachter–Singer theory of emotion suggests that there is a general pattern of physiological arousal caused by the sympathetic nervous system, and this pattern is common to a variety of emotions. The experience of emotion is the result of two factors: (1) physiological arousal and (2) a cognitive label for this physiological state (the arousal). The cognitive appraisal theory suggests that emotion stems from the way people appraise or interpret the interactions they have.

LO 11 **Discuss evidence supporting the idea that emotions are universal. (p. 354)**

Darwin suggested that interpreting facial expressions is not something we learn, but rather an innate ability that evolved because it promotes survival. Sharing the same facial expressions allows for communication. Research on isolated indigenous peoples in New Guinea indicated that the same facial expressions represent the same basic emotions across cultures. In addition, children born deaf and blind have the same types of expressions of emotion (for example, happiness and anger), suggesting the universal nature of such displays.

LO 12 **Describe the amygdala's role in the experience of fear. (p. 357)**

The amygdala is an almond-shaped structure found in the limbic system that appears to be central to our experience of fear. When people view threatening images, or even look at an image of a frightened face, the amygdala is activated. When confronted with a fear-provoking situation, the amygdala enables an ultrafast and unconscious response.

LO 13 **Summarize evidence pointing to the biological basis of happiness. (p. 360)**

Happiness has heritability estimates between 35% and 50%, and as high as 80% in longitudinal studies. There may be a set point for happiness, or level around which our happiness tends to fluctuate. As we strive for personal happiness, we should keep in mind that our set point is strong, and directed by our genes and temperament.

KEY TERMS

arousal theory, p. 330
bisexual, p. 337
Cannon–Bard theory of emotion, p. 350
cognitive appraisal approach, p. 352
display rules, p. 355
drive, p. 330
drive-reduction theory, p. 330
emotion, p. 347
extrinsic motivation, p. 328
facial feedback hypothesis, p. 356
heterosexual, p. 337
hierarchy of needs, p. 332
homeostasis, p. 329
homosexual, p. 337
incentive, p. 327
instincts, p. 329
intrinsic motivation, p. 328
James–Lange theory of emotion, p. 350
motivation, p. 327
need for achievement (n-Ach), p. 334
need for power (n-Pow), p. 334
needs, p. 330
orgasm, p. 336
refractory period, p. 336
Schachter–Singer theory of emotion, p. 351
self-actualization, p. 333
self-determination theory (SDT), p. 334
set point, p. 345
sexual dysfunction, p. 341
sexual orientation, p. 337
sexuality, p. 335
sexually transmitted infections (STIs), p. 341

TEST PREP ARE YOU READY?

1. If a mother wants her son to practice math facts, she could allow him to play games on her tablet when he is done studying. Playing the games eventually will provide ________________ for him to study his math facts.
   a. negative reinforcement
   b. intrinsic motivation
   c. satiety
   d. an incentive

2. The entire week before final exams, the resident advisor (RA) in your dorm provides delicious cookies for students who come to group study sessions in the common room. The RA seems to be using ________________ to encourage students to study together.
   a. extrinsic motivation
   b. intrinsic motivation
   c. negative reinforcement
   d. instincts

3. Human behaviors are driven by the need to maintain homeostasis—that is, to fulfill basic biological needs. If a need is not fulfilled, this creates a state of tension that pushes us to meet it. This describes the ________________ theory.
   a. self-actualization
   b. drive-reduction
   c. cognitive-appraisal
   d. Schachter-Singer

4. Arousal theory suggests that humans seek an optimal level of arousal, but "optimal" is different for each person. Some people are ________________; they appear to seek out activities that increase arousal.
   a. sensation seekers
   b. externally motivated
   c. driven by extrinsic motivation
   d. sympathetic

5. According to Masters and Johnson, sexual arousal begins in the ________________ phase, when physical changes begin to take place.
   a. excitement
   b. plateau
   c. resolution
   d. orgasm

6. Emotion is a psychological state that includes a subjective experience, a physiological component, and a(n):
   a. mood.
   b. drive.
   c. behavioral expression.
   d. incentive.

7. To study the universal nature of emotions, Paul Ekman traveled to New Guinea to explore interpretations of facial expressions. Although unfamiliar with Western facial behaviors, the participants in his study:
   a. could not identify the facial expressions in the photos he showed them.
   b. could identify the facial expressions common across the world.
   c. could understand English.
   d. had no display rules.

8. The Schachter–Singer theory suggests that the experience of emotion results from:
   a. physiological arousal.
   b. cognitive labeling.
   c. physiological arousal and cognitive labeling.
   d. an appraisal of the environment.

9. The ________________ suggests emotion results from the way people appraise or interpret what is going on in the environment, and that emotion does not result from a cognitive label of physiological arousal.
   a. James–Lange theory
   b. cognitive-appraisal approach
   c. Schachter–Singer theory
   d. Cannon–Bard theory

10. A large proportion of population-wide variation in happiness can be explained by genes as opposed to environmental factors. Evidence comes from ________________, which are reported to be between 35% and 50%, and as high as 80%.
    a. display rules
    b. heritability estimates
    c. instincts
    d. feedback loops

11. Explain how twin studies have been used to explore the development of sexual orientation.

12. Describe a situation in which someone's motivation did not follow the order outlined in Maslow's hierarchy of needs.

13. What role do the stomach and hypothalamus play in hunger? How do cultural and social factors influence our eating habits?

14. What role does the amygdala play in the experience of fear? Describe the two pathways that fear-related information can travel in the brain.

15. Explain how you might use set points for body weight or happiness to help someone struggling with weight and/or happiness.

✓ CHECK YOUR ANSWERS IN APPENDIX C.

Go to **LaunchPad** or **Achieve: Read & Practice** to test your understanding with **LearningCurve**.

CHAPTER 10

Jamie Squire/Allsport/Getty Images.

Personality

An Introduction to Personality

WHO IS SAIFA? Sometimes a simple question can change your life. For Sean Saifa Wall, the critical question came in 2007. He was 28 years old and appeared to have his life in order. A graduate of Williams College, Saifa had built an impressive résumé, acquired a desirable job, and amassed a large number of social contacts. But he was tormented on the inside. Unable to make sense of his thoughts, Saifa felt he was losing control, and he worried that something terrible would happen if he didn't seek help: "I was just like, either someone's going to kill me, or I'm going to kill myself."

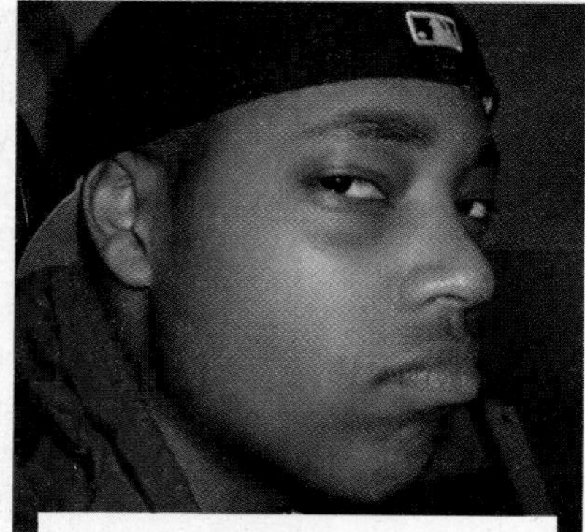

Eyes of Discontent

Sean Saifa Wall was 26 years old when this picture was taken. Looking at this photo today, Saifa sees a young man who is "performing masculinity" to compensate for feelings of insecurity.

Courtesy Sean Saifa Wall.

In a move that may have saved his life, Saifa picked up the phone and made an appointment to talk with a psychotherapist. A few days later, he was sitting on the therapist's couch and beginning to unravel his complicated life story. Apparently, the therapist was perceptive, because during that first appointment, he posed a question that set Saifa's healing process in motion and changed the course of his life: "When did you realize love was not possible?" Saifa broke down and began weeping. "I don't know," he said in between tears. The weeping continued for many sessions.

For years leading to that moment, Saifa had wrestled with feelings of loneliness, isolation, and self-hatred. He tried to fill the void with new relationships and sex, but the emptiness persisted. "I thought that if I just had more sex, that I would eventually be full," Saifa explains. "[But] the more sex I had from all sources (casual sex, relationship sex, pornography), the more miserable and lonely I felt." Saifa's focus on sex was a symptom of something much bigger. "For me, sexual addiction is not about sex," Saifa explains. "Sexual addiction is me dealing with something that is so, so visceral, and so deep. It's such a well of hurt and shame that some places I can't access."

This hurt and shame had prevented Saifa from loving himself, but he went to great lengths to attain approval from others. "I was trying to impress the women I dated," he explains. "I wanted all these material things that I thought would bring me happiness . . . that would bring me more self-esteem, but the more I got these things, the more I realized I wasn't really happy, 'cause I wasn't myself." Like a chameleon, Saifa adjusted his roles and behaviors to please other people. As he explains, "I could be whatever you wanted me to be."

Who was the person beneath that chameleon, and how did he fall into that crater of self-hatred? Perhaps most importantly, did he ever climb out? Let's start with the first question: Who is Sean Saifa Wall?

Saifa, In His Own Words
http://qrs.ly/rx5a5f0

Photo: Macmillan Learning.

What Is Personality?

LO 1 Define personality.

If you ask Saifa to describe himself, he will use words like "vivacious," "loud," "charismatic," "direct," and "empathetic." He might also mention that he has a strong sense of fairness, and always leans in the direction of justice. These attributes have been apparent for much of Saifa's life, and therefore would be considered facets of his *personality*. Generally speaking, **personality** refers to the unique, core set of characteristics that influence the way one thinks, acts, and feels—characteristics many psychologists believe are relatively consistent and enduring throughout the life span and in a variety of settings.

We should point out that personality is not the equivalent of *character*. When people discuss character, they often are referring to qualities of morality or culture-specific ideas about what makes a person "good" or "bad." People who are untrustworthy or make "poor" choices might be described as having a weak character, while those who stand up for what they believe might be said to have a strong character. You may hear that the guy with the blue mohawk or the woman with the multiple body piercings is a "real character." Psychologists try not to make such judgments; our goal is to describe behaviors and personality characteristics objectively. Unlike character, which is essentially a label based on superficial observations, personality is defined by a core set of characteristics that often become evident in infancy.

TEMPERAMENT Certain aspects of adult personality appear to derive from temperament, the distinct patterns of emotional reactions and behaviors observed early in life (Soto & Tackett, 2015). Some infants are easy to calm, others cranky, sociable, or highly reactive. Because various temperaments are evident in infants, they appear to have a genetic basis (Plomin, DeFries, Knopik, & Neiderhiser, 2013). Although behavioral

personality The unique, core set of characteristics that influence the way one thinks, acts, and feels, and that are relatively consistent and enduring throughout the life span.

Note: Unless otherwise specified, quotations attributed to Sean Saifa Wall are personal communications.

CONNECTIONS 

In **Chapter 8,** we described various infant temperaments. Humans are born with certain temperaments, and many of the attending characteristics seem to persist throughout life. Here, we introduce temperament in the context of the development of personality.

patterns associated with **temperament** remain somewhat stable across the life span, they can be molded by the environment (Briley & Tucker-Drob, 2014; Caspi, Roberts, & Shiner, 2005; Soto, 2016). For example, a child born with a calm, easygoing temperament may become more fearful and irritable if her mother is neglectful. However, a child's behavior can also shape parental responses (Van den Akker, Deković, Asscher, & Prinzie, 2014). Although temperament shines through early in life, adult personality does not really take shape until one reaches adulthood. The exact timing of this process is debated, but we can think of temperament as an important, stable aspect of personality (Goldsmith et al., 1987; Soto & Tackett, 2015).

LO 2 Distinguish how the perspectives of psychology explain personality development.

HOW CAN WE EXPLAIN PERSONALITY? Psychologists use a variety of theoretical perspectives to explain the development and expression of personality (**Table 10.1**). None of them are perfect, but they do help accomplish three of psychology's main goals: to describe, explain, and predict behavior. These perspectives have strong ties to their founders, all of whom were influenced by their life experiences and the historical period in which they lived. Sigmund Freud's emphasis on sexuality, for example, was partly a reaction to the prudish Victorian culture into which he was born.

In the next section, we will examine these theories of personality in greater depth, but first let's take a quick detour somewhere fun. How would you describe your sense of humor?

TABLE 10.1 THEORETICAL PERSPECTIVES ON PERSONALITY

Personality Theory	Main Points	Criticisms
Psychoanalytic	Personality develops early in life; we are greatly influenced by unconscious processes (e.g., internal conflicts, aggression, sexual urges).	Ignores importance of current experiences; overemphasis on the unconscious and the role of sexuality in personality; theory based on a biased, nonrepresentative sample; concepts difficult to operationally define and empirically test.
Behavioral	Personality is shaped by interactions with the environment, specifically through learning (operant conditioning and observational learning).	Narrow focus on behavioral processes; ignores influence of unconscious processes and emotional factors.
Humanistic	We are innately good and in control of our destinies; we have a force moving us toward growth.	Concepts difficult to operationally define and empirically test; ignores the negative aspects of human nature.
Social-cognitive	Focuses on social influences and mental processes that affect personality; emphasis on the interaction of environment, cognitive activity, and individual behavior.	Narrow focus on social-cognitive factors; ignores influence of unconscious processes and emotional factors.
Biological	Emphasizes the physiological and genetic influences on personality development; incorporates gene–environment explanations for the emergence of certain characteristics.	Inconsistent findings regarding the stability of the personality dimensions; varying estimates of environmental influences.
Trait	Looks at current traits of the individual to describe personality and predict behaviors.	Underestimates the environmental influences on personality; does not fully explain the foundations of personality.

Psychology uses a variety of theoretical perspectives to explain the development of personality. Listed here are the major theories and some of their key limitations.

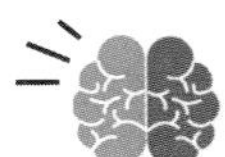

THINK CRITICALLY

THE FUNNY THING ABOUT PERSONALITY Some of us rely on humor to connect with other people, cracking jokes and acting silly for their enjoyment. Others use it as a way to cope with challenges. (We must admit, it does feel good to let loose and laugh when we're feeling overwhelmed.) Both of these styles of humor are considered positive and are inversely correlated with loneliness (Martin, Puhlik-Doris, Larsen, Gray, & Weir, 2003; Schermer et al., 2017). This means that people who have them are less likely to be lonely. There are also negative forms of humor, like ridiculing another person to make yourself look good, or poking fun at yourself in a way that is "excessively self-disparaging" (Martin & Kuiper, 2016, p. 505).

WHERE DID YOU GET THAT SENSE OF HUMOR?

Where do these styles of humor originate? According to one large study conducted in Australia, identical twins (who have nearly identical genes) are more likely to share humor styles than fraternal (nonidentical) twins. In fact, the study suggests that 30–47% of population-wide variation in humor styles can be attributed to genetics (Baughman et al., 2012), and some research indicates an even higher proportion (Martin & Kuiper, 2016; Vernon, Martin, Schermer, Cherkas, & Spector, 2008). But genes aren't everything; environmental factors, such as relationships, may also shape humor. For example, a study of 11- to 13-year-olds found that affiliative humor (the type that strengthens social bonds) can be reinforced by close friends (Hunter, Fox, & Jones, 2016). What do these findings tell you about the roles of nature and nurture in the development of humor styles?

Who Is Funnier?
Comedians Kate McKinnon and Kumail Nanjiani at the 2016 Film Independent Spirit Awards. Have you ever noticed that most famous comedians are men? Perhaps this has something to do with the commonly held—and mistaken—belief that men are funnier than women. In one study, researchers showed participants cartoon captions written by men and women. Participants unknowingly rated men's and women's captions to be equally funny, but they were more likely to credit the funniest captions to male authors (Hooper, Sharpe, & Roberts, 2016). Randall Michelson/Getty Images.

Put Your Heads Together

In your group, **A)** pick a character from a fairy tale, TV show, or movie, and describe some aspects of his or her personality. **B)** Now consider the six theoretical perspectives presented in Table 10.1, and pick at least three of them to explain how these characteristics might have developed.

Nearly 8 billion human beings inhabit this planet, and no two of them have the same personality. Each individual's personality reflects a distinct interplay of inborn characteristics and life experiences. Consider this nature-and-nurture dynamic as you explore the theories of personality in the pages to come. We'll get this discussion going with the help of Saifa.

show what you know

1. ________________ is the unique, core set of characteristics that influence the way one thinks, acts, and feels.
2. Compare three of the theoretical perspectives presented in this section that explain how personality develops.

✓ CHECK YOUR ANSWERS IN APPENDIX C.

Psychoanalytic Theories

BEFORE SAIFA, THERE WAS SUSANNE Saifa was born on December 28, 1978, at Columbia–Presbyterian Hospital in New York City. Unlike most babies, who are readily identified as "boy" or "girl," Saifa had ambiguous genitalia (not clearly male, not clearly female). Doctors assigned him female and instructed his mother to raise him as a girl, indicating that he would "function as such" (Wall, 2015, p. 118). During that era, many psychologists and medical professionals believed that human behaviors were primarily shaped by environmental input, or nurture (Schultz & Schultz, 2016; Segal, 2012). But as you will learn from Saifa's story, nature can sometimes overpower nurture.

CONNECTIONS

In **Chapter 8,** we discussed differences of sex development. People with intersex traits may have internal and external reproductive organs that are not clearly male or female.

Saifa was, and still is, genetically male (*XY*). He has an **intersex trait** called androgen insensitivity syndrome (AIS), characterized by reduced sensitivity to male hormones, or androgens. People with AIS are genetically male, but their bodies do not follow the typical "male" or "female" path of sexual development. Some are designated "male" at birth, others "female." These gender assignments appear to work out for some people (about 75%, according to one study), but a substantial minority feel unsatisfied (Schweizer, Brunner, Handford, & Richter-Appelt, 2014). It is important to note that intersex traits are caused by biological processes, not by psychological, social, or cultural factors.

Saifa was raised as a female named "Susanne," but fulfilling society's gender expectations did not come naturally. His parents accepted his nonconformist approach to girlhood, but within limits. One of Saifa's first memories is from the age of 4 or 5; he was getting ready to visit his grandmother and wanted to wear overalls. But his mom insisted he wear a sundress with spaghetti straps and put his hair in pigtails. Saifa protested and cried, but ended up complying—and feeling miserably out of his element: "I remember being on the train going downtown and just feeling so vulnerable."

Childhood presented other challenges. Saifa grew up in the Bronx during the 1980s, when crack cocaine was devastating urban communities and crime was rampant. He witnessed trauma and suffering not only in his neighborhood, but also within his family: "If we're talking about the most formative experiences I had, if we're talking about between the ages of 0 and 6," Saifa explains, "[It] was seeing my dad drunk, witnessing the domestic violence that took place in the home."

How did these early childhood experiences impact Saifa in the long term, and what role did they play in the development of his personality? If we could pose this question to Sigmund Freud, he would probably say they were critical. Freud believed that childhood is the prime time for personality development, the early years and basic drives being particularly important because they shape our thoughts, emotions, and behaviors in ways beyond our awareness. **Psychoanalysis** refers to Freud's theories about personality, discussed below, as well as his system of psychotherapy and tools for the exploration of the unconscious (see Chapter 14).

Before launching our discussion of Freud, we should point out that his approach is controversial and lacking in scientific support. Freud presented novel and groundbreaking insights on personality development, but his theories are mostly based on isolated case studies that may not be representative of the larger population.

Growing Up Susanne
(Left) Five-year-old Susanne (now Saifa) with friends. "When I was growing up, I felt more connected to boyhood," Saifa explains. "Innately, I felt more masculine, more male [but] externally, what I was presenting to the world based on my body, based on my physical characteristics, was female." Courtesy Sean Saifa Wall.

Does the Mind Have Three Levels?

Sigmund Freud spent the majority of his life in Vienna, Austria. A smart, ambitious young man, Freud attended medical school and became a physician and researcher with a primary interest in physiology and later neurology. Freud loved research, but he soon came to realize that the anti-Semitic culture in which he lived would drastically interfere with his studies (Freud was Jewish). So, instead of pursuing the career he loved, he opened a medical practice in 1881, specializing in clinical neurology. Many of his patients had unexplained or unusual symptoms that seemed related to emotional problems. The basis of these problems, Freud and his colleagues observed, appeared to be sexual in nature, though the patients weren't necessarily aware of this (Freud, 1900/1953). Thus began Freud's lifelong journey to untangle the mysteries of the unconscious mind.

Little Freud
Looking at this photo of Sigmund Freud and his father, Jacob, we can't help but wonder how this father-son relationship influenced the development of the younger Freud's personality. Freud believed that events and conflicts from childhood—particularly those involving parents and other caregivers—have a powerful impact on adult personality.
Imagno/Getty Images.

LO 3 Illustrate Freud's models for describing the mind.

Freud (1900/1953) proposed that the mind has three levels of consciousness—conscious, preconscious, and unconscious—and that mental processes occurring on these levels guide behaviors and shape personality. Everything you are aware of at this moment exists at the *conscious* level, including thoughts, emotions, sensations, and perceptions. At the **preconscious** level are the mental activities outside your current awareness, which can easily drift into the conscious level. (You are studying Freud's theory at this moment, but your mind begins to wander and you start thinking about what you did yesterday.) The **unconscious** level is home to activities outside of your awareness, such as feelings, wishes, thoughts, and urges that are very difficult to bring to awareness without concerted effort and/or therapy. Freud did suggest, however, that some content of the unconscious can enter the conscious level through manipulated and distorted processes beyond a person's control or awareness (more on this shortly). To help patients understand the influence of their unconscious activities, Freud (1900/1953) used a variety of techniques, such as dream interpretation, hypnosis, and free association (Chapters 4 and 14).

CONNECTIONS
In **Chapter 6,** we presented a component of working memory called the episodic buffer, which allows information from long-term memory to reach conscious awareness. Although Freud did not refer to this buffer, the preconscious level includes activities similar to those of the episodic buffer.

This *topographical model* was Freud's earliest attempt to explain the bustling activity occurring within the head (Westen, Gabbard, & Ortigo, 2008). Freud was influenced by German physicist Gustav Fechner's (1801–1887) idea that the great majority of the mind is "hidden below the surface where it is influenced by unobservable forces" (Schultz & Schultz, 2016, p. 290). Many who describe Freud's model compare it to an iceberg: What we see on the surface is just the "tip of the iceberg" (the conscious level), small in comparison to the vast and influential unconscious mind (Schultz & Schultz, 2017; see **Figure 10.1** on the next page).

Id, Ego, and Superego

In addition to the topographical model, Freud proposed a *structural model* describing the "functions or purposes" of the mind's components (Westen et al., 2008, p. 65). As Freud saw it, the human mind is composed of three structures: the *id,* the *ego,* and the *superego.* The battle among these components occurs unconsciously, influencing our thoughts, emotions, and behaviors, and forming our personality (Westen et al., 2008).

THE ID The most primitive structure of the mind is the **id.** Present from birth, the id operates at the unconscious level and is responsible for the biological drives motivating behavior. It also fuels the impulsive, illogical, and infant-like aspects of our thoughts and personality. Freud proposed that the id represents the mind's primary pool of *psychic energy* (Freud, 1923/1961, 1933/1964). Included in that pool is sexual energy, which motivates much of our behavior. The primary goal of the id is to ensure

psychoanalysis Freud's views regarding personality as well as his system of psychotherapy and tools for the exploration of the unconscious.

unconscious According to Freud, the level of consciousness outside of awareness, which is difficult to access without effort or therapy.

id According to Freud, the most primitive structure of the mind, the activities of which occur at the unconscious level and are guided by the pleasure principle.

FIGURE 10.1
Psychoanalytic Description of the Mind

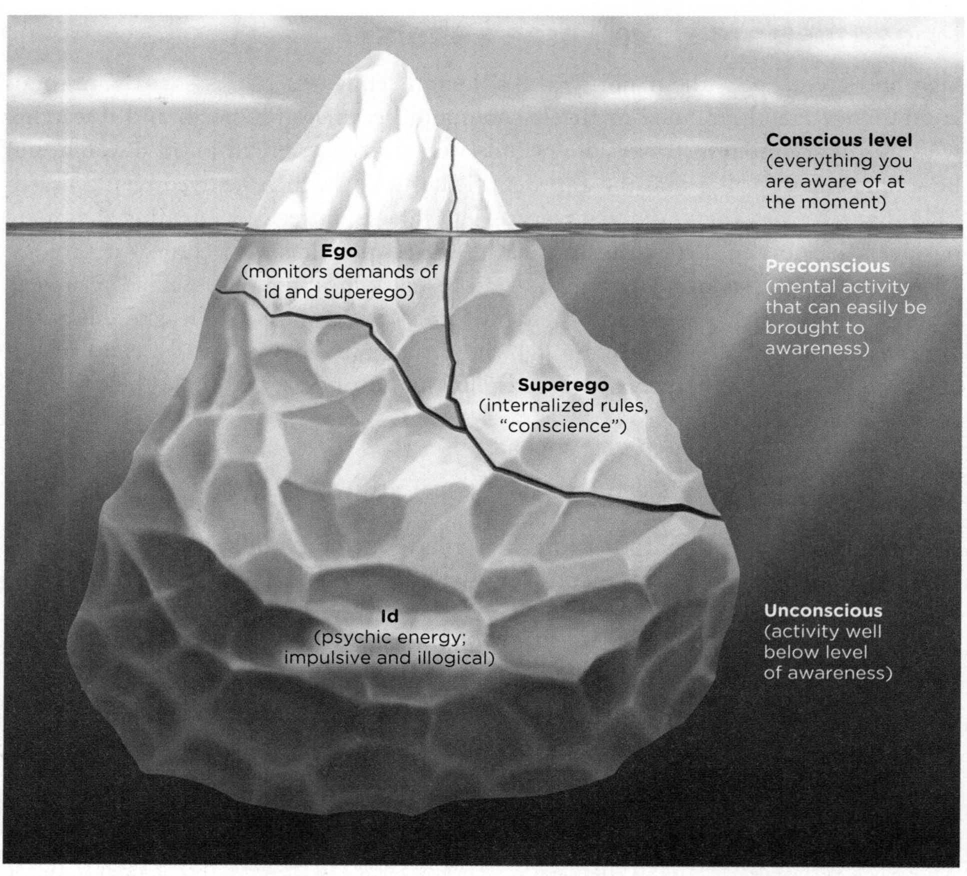

CONNECTIONS

In **Chapter 9,** we discussed the concept of drive reduction, which suggests that unmet needs create tension that motivates behavior. Fulfilling needs reduces tension and helps maintain homeostasis.

that needs are being met, which helps maintain **homeostasis**. The id is not rational, and unfulfilled needs or urges compel it to insist on immediate action. It follows the **pleasure principle,** which guides behavior toward instant gratification—and away from contemplating consequences. The id seeks pleasure and avoids pain.

THE EGO As an infant grows and starts to realize that the desires of the id cannot prevail in all situations, her **ego,** which is not present from birth, begins to develop from the id (Freud, 1933/1964, 1940/1949). The ego manipulates situations, plans for the future, solves problems, and makes decisions to satisfy the needs of the id. The goal is to make sure that the id is not given free rein over behavior, as this would cause problems. Imagine what a busy supermarket would be like if everyone were ruled by their ids. People would ignore societal expectations to stand in line, speak politely, and pay for food; the store would be full of adults having toddler-like tantrums. To negotiate between the id and the environment, the ego follows the **reality principle,** adhering to the rules of the "real" world and delaying gratification as needed (Freud, 1923/1960). The reality principle works through an awareness of potential consequences; the ego can predict what will happen if we act on an urge. We are aware of the ego's activities, although some happen at the preconscious level, and even fewer at the unconscious level (Figure 10.1).

pleasure principle A principle that guides the id, directing behavior toward instant gratification and away from contemplating consequences.

ego According to Freud, the structure of the mind that uses the reality principle to manipulate situations, plan for the future, solve problems, and make decisions.

reality principle A principle that guides the ego as it negotiates between the id and the environment, directing behavior to follow society's rules.

superego According to Freud, the structure of the mind that guides behavior to follow the rules of society, parents, or other authority figures.

THE SUPEREGO The **superego** is the structure of the mind that develops last, guiding behavior to follow the rules of society, parents, or other authority figures (Freud, 1923/1960). The superego begins to form as the toddler starts moving about on his own, coming up against rules and expectations. (*No, you cannot hit your sister! You need to put your toys away.*) The child eventually incorporates the values of others, including ideas about right and wrong, often referred to as the *conscience.* Once the superego is rooted, it serves as a critical internal guide to the values of society so that the child can make "good" choices without reminders from a parent, caregiver, or religious leader. Sometimes, the internal voice of the superego can be harsh and judgmental, and it may set unrealistic standards. For example, married men and women may feel some guilt when they fix their eyes on attractive people who are not their spouses. When this happens, their judgmental superego might say, *What's wrong with you? Are you a cheater?* Some activities of the superego are conscious, but the great majority occur at the preconscious and unconscious levels.

CAUGHT IN THE MIDDLE The ego monitors the demands of both the id and the superego, trying to satisfy both. Think of the energy of the id, pushing to get all desires met instantly. The ego must ensure the id's needs are met in a manner acceptable to the superego, reducing tension as much as possible. But not all urges and desires can be met (sometimes not instantly, sometimes never).

How might this conflict between the id and superego play out in a real-world situation? Imagine you are about to leave for class and you get a text from a friend, inviting you to a movie. You are torn, because you know an exam is coming up and you should not skip today's class. Your id is demanding a movie, some popcorn, and freedom from work. Your superego demands that you go to class so that you will be fully prepared for the exam. Clearly, your ego cannot satisfy both of these demands. Freud (1923/1960) proposed that this sort of struggle is an everyday, recurring experience that the ego cannot always resolve. Sometimes the id triumphs, and the person acts in an infantile, perhaps even destructive, manner. (You give in to the pressures of your friend and your id, and happily decide to skip class.) Occasionally, the superego prevails, and one feels a great deal of remorse or guilt for not living up to some moral ideal. (You skip class, but you feel so guilty you can't enjoy the movie.) Sometimes the anxiety associated with the id-superego conflict, which generally is unconscious, surfaces to the conscious level. The ego then must deal with this anxiety and make it more bearable (perhaps by suggesting that a day off will help you study, because you haven't had any free time all semester).

It Can Happen to Anyone
While speaking at a 2015 fundraiser, then-President Barack Obama reportedly said this: "We should be reforming our criminal justice system in such a way that we are not incarcerating nonviolent offenders in ways that renders them incapable of getting a job after they leave *office*" (Fabian, 2015, June 19, para. 3). Obama meant to say "after they leave *prison*," and he acknowledged his "Freudian slip" to a laughing audience (Fabian, 2015, June 19). A Freudian slip is an unintended word or phrase that accidentally slips off the tongue, shedding light on unconscious thoughts. Jemal Countess/Getty Images.

Defense Mechanisms

If conflicts between the id and superego cannot be resolved and anxiety becomes overwhelming, the ego may turn to **ego defense mechanisms.** According to Freud, ego defense mechanisms distort perceptions and memories of the real world without our awareness.

Freud proposed a variety of defense mechanisms, which were further developed by his daughter, psychoanalyst Anna Freud (1895–1982). As you learn about some of these defense mechanisms in **INFOGRAPHIC 10.1** on the next page, remember these two points: (1) We are often unaware of using them, even if they are brought to our attention, and (2) defense mechanisms are not necessarily a bad thing (Cramer, 2015; Vaillant, 2000). In some cases, distortions are helpful because they can reduce anxiety. However, when conflicts between the id and the superego become overwhelming and the anxiety is too much for the ego, we tend to overuse defense mechanisms. This is when behaviors may turn inappropriate or unhealthy (Cramer, 2000, 2008; Tallandini & Caudek, 2010).

One of the more commonly known defense mechanisms is *repression,* which occurs when the ego moves uncomfortable thoughts, **memories**, or feelings from the conscious to unconscious level. With anxiety-provoking memories, the reality of an event can become distorted to such an extreme that you don't even remember it. The repressed memories do not cease to exist, however, and they may pop up in unexpected forms, influencing behaviors and decisions.

CONNECTIONS
In **Chapter 6,** we discussed the controversy over repressed memories of childhood abuse. Many psychologists question the validity of research supporting the existence of repressed memories. Freud's case studies describing childhood sexual abuse have also been questioned.

ego defense mechanisms Unconscious processes the ego uses to distort perceptions and memories and thereby reduce anxiety created by the id-superego conflict.

Ego Defense Mechanisms

The impulsive demands of the id sometimes conflict with the moralistic demands of the superego, resulting in anxiety. When that anxiety becomes excessive, the ego works to relieve this uncomfortable feeling through the use of defense mechanisms (Freud, 1923/1960). Defense mechanisms give us a way to "defend" against tension and anxiety, but they are not always adaptive, or helpful. Defense mechanisms can be categorized ranging from less adaptive to more adaptive (Vaillant, 1992). Some defense mechanisms are more adaptive as they help us deal with our anxiety in more productive and mature ways.

EGO relieves anxiety by employing a defense mechanism.

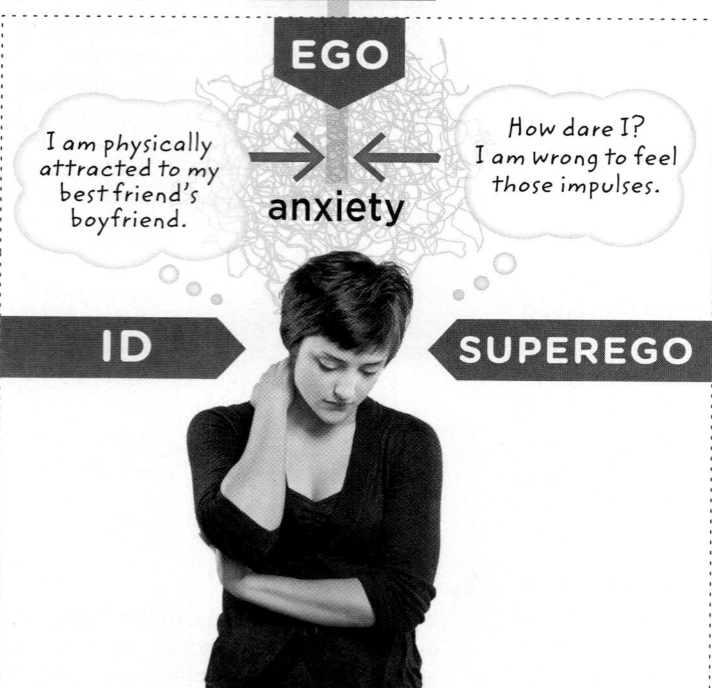
EGO
I am physically attracted to my best friend's boyfriend.
anxiety
How dare I? I am wrong to feel those impulses.
ID
SUPEREGO

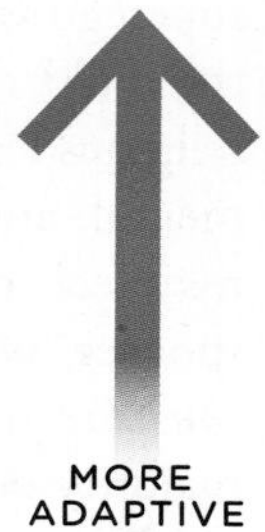
MORE ADAPTIVE

SUBLIMATION

Redirecting unacceptable impulses into acceptable outlets.

Example: Instead of worrying about wanting to date your best friend's boyfriend, you use a dating app to meet other singles.

IDENTIFICATION

Unconsciously modeling our feelings or actions on the behaviors of someone we admire.

Example: Admiring your best friend, and adopting her mannerisms and characteristics.

DISPLACEMENT

Shifting negative feelings and impulses to an acceptable target.

Example: Being rude to someone who's interested in you. "Sorry, I am busy tonight."

REPRESSION

Anxiety-producing information is pushed into the unconscious.

Example: Unconsciously avoiding your friend and her boyfriend in social situations.

RATIONALIZATION

Creating an acceptable excuse for an uncomfortable situation.

Example: "I am a human being. Of course I feel sexually attracted to other people."

PROJECTION

Attributing your own anxiety-provoking thoughts and impulses to someone else.

Example: "What is wrong with Sara? She always seems to be checking out other people's boyfriends."

DENIAL

Refusing to recognize a distressing reality.

Example: "I don't like him. He's just not my type."

LESS ADAPTIVE

* We may get better at dealing with stress and anxiety as we age. In a study comparing the use of defense mechanisms in different age groups, older participants were found to use fewer maladaptive defense mechanisms (Segal, Coolidge, & Mizuno, 2007).

Credits: Smiling couple: Andersen Ross/Blend Images/Getty Images; Sad young woman: Tom Fullum/Getty Images.

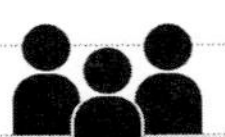

Put Your Heads Together

It's Saturday morning and you have a paper due this week. You could spend the day at the library gathering research and writing the paper, but there is tail-gaiting to do, a football game to watch, and a post-game party to attend. Team up and explain how you might unconsciously justify your decision to avoid the library using at least four ego defense mechanisms.

Stages of Development

LO 4 Summarize Freud's use of psychosexual stages to explain personality.

In addition to his structural and topographical models of the mind, Freud (1905/1953) proposed a *developmental* model to explain how personality is formed through experiences in childhood, with a special emphasis on sexuality. According to Freud, the development of sexuality and personality proceeds through **psychosexual stages,** which all children experience as they mature into adulthood (see **Table 10.2** on the next page). Driving this development is the sexual energy of the id; children are sexual beings starting from birth, indicating there is a strong biological component to personality development. Each psychosexual stage is associated with a specific *erogenous zone,* or area of the body that provides more sexual pleasure than other areas.

Along with each psychosexual stage comes a conflict that the individual must resolve in order to become a well-adjusted adult. If these conflicts are not successfully addressed, one may suffer from a **fixation,** that is, get stuck in that particular stage and fail to progress smoothly through the remaining stages. Freud believed that fixation in a psychosexual stage during the first 5 to 6 years of life can last into adulthood, and this may have a dramatic impact on personality. Let's look at each stage, its erogenous zone and conflicts, and some consequences of fixation.

THE ORAL STAGE The *oral stage* begins at birth and lasts until 1 to 1.5 years old. As the name suggests, the erogenous zone for the oral stage is the mouth; infants derive their greatest pleasure from sucking, chewing, and gumming. According to Freud, the conflict during this stage generally centers on weaning. Infants must stop nursing or using a bottle or pacifier, and the caregiver often decides when it's time. Weaning too early or too late can have long-term consequences for personality development. Freud suggested that oral fixation is associated with certain personality traits and behavior patterns, which might include smoking, nail biting, excessive talking, and increased alcohol consumption.

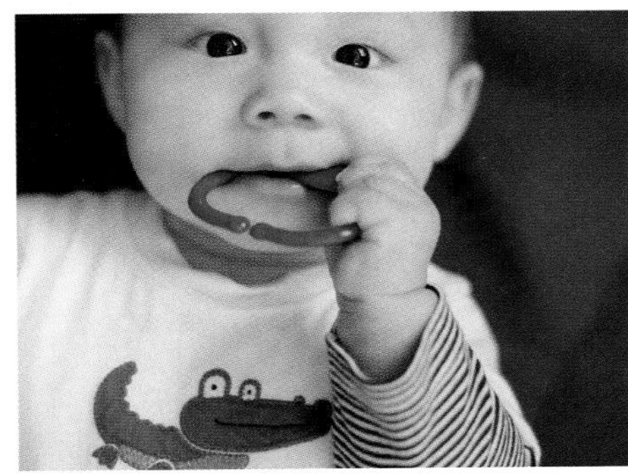

Oral Fixation
The average baby (birth to 18 months) spends 108 minutes per day sucking on a pacifier and another 33 minutes mouthing other objects (Juberg, Alfano, Coughlin, & Thompson, 2001). Freud identified this phase of life with the oral stage of psychosexual development. Natalia Campbell of NC Photography/Getty Images.

THE ANAL STAGE Following the oral stage is the *anal stage,* which lasts until about age 3. The erogenous zone is the anus, and pleasure is derived from eliminating bodily waste and learning to control the process. The conflict during this stage centers on toilet training: The parents want their child to use a toilet, but the child is not necessarily ready. Once again, how caregivers deal with this task may have long-term implications for personality. If a parent is too harsh (growing angry when there are accidents, forcing a child to sit on the toilet until she goes) or too lenient (making excuses for accidents, not really encouraging the child to learn control), the child might grow up with an *anal-retentive* personality (rule-bound, stingy) or an *anal-expulsive* personality (chaotic, destructive).

PHALLIC STAGE Ages 3 to 6 years mark the *phallic stage* (*phallus* means "penis" in Latin). During this period, the erogenous zone is the genitals, and many children begin to discover that self-stimulation is pleasurable. Freud (1923/1960) assigned special importance to the conflict that occurs in the phallic stage.

psychosexual stages According to Freud, the stages of development of sexuality and personality, from birth to adulthood, each of which has an erogenous zone as well as a conflict that must be dealt with.

fixation Being stuck in a particular psychosexual stage of development as a result of unsuccessfully dealing with the conflict characteristic of that stage.

TABLE 10.2 FREUD'S PSYCHOSEXUAL STAGES

Stage	Age	Erogenous Zone	Focus	Type of Conflict	Results of Fixation
Oral	Birth–1½ years	Mouth	Sucking, chewing, and gumming	Weaning	Smoking, drinking, nail biting, excessive talking
Anal	1½–3 years	Anus	Eliminating bodily waste and controlling bodily functions responsible for this process	Toilet training	Being rule-bound, stingy, chaotic, destructive
Phallic	3–6 years	Genitals	Sexual feelings and awareness of self	Self-stimulation	Promiscuity, flirtation, vanity, or overdependence, and a focus on masturbation
Latency Period	6 years–puberty	Period during which children develop mentally, socially, and physically			
Genital	Puberty and beyond	Genitals	Reawakening of sexuality, with focus on relationships	Sexuality and aggression	Inability to thrive in adult activities such as work and love

According to Freud, psychological and sexual development proceeds through distinct stages. Each stage is characterized by a certain pleasure area, or "erogenous zone," and a conflict that must be resolved. If resolution is not achieved, the person may develop a problematic "fixation."

During this time, little boys experience the **Oedipus complex** (ED-uh-puss): They develop a desire to replace their fathers—a normal feeling, according to Freud, but one that leads to jealously because the boy considers his father a rival for his mother's affection. When the boy becomes aware of his attraction to his mother, he realizes his father is a formidable adversary and feels anger toward him. He also begins to fear his powerful father, and worry that he might be punished. Specifically, he fears that his father will castrate him (Freud, 1917/1966). In order to reduce the tension, the boy must identify with and behave like his father, a process known as *identification.* This defense mechanism resolves the Oedipus complex, allowing the boy to take on or internalize the behaviors, mannerisms, morals, and standards of his father. The boy realizes that sexual affection should only be between his father and mother, and the incest taboo develops.

Freud (1923/1960) believed that little girls also experience conflict during this period. Feeling an attraction to their fathers, they become jealous and angry toward their mothers. They also realize that they do not have a penis, which leads to feelings of loss and jealousy, known as *penis envy.* The girl responds with anger, blaming her mother for her missing penis. Realizing she can't have her father, she begins to act like her mother through the process of *identification.* She takes on her mother's behaviors, mannerisms, morals, and standards. Some of Freud's followers labeled this conflict the *Electra complex* (Kilmartin & Dervin, 1997; Schultz & Schultz, 2017).

If children do not resolve the sexual conflicts of the phallic stage, they develop a fixation, which can lead to promiscuity, flirtation, vanity, overdependence, bravado, and an increased focus on masturbation.

Oedipus complex According to Freud, the attraction a boy feels toward his mother, along with the resentment or envy directed toward his father.

LATENCY PERIOD From age 6 to puberty, children remain in a *latency period* (not a "stage" according to Freud's definition, as there is no erogenous zone, conflict, or fixation). During this time, psychosexual development slows and sexual energy is repressed: Although children develop mentally, socially, and physically, their sexual development is on hold. This idea seems to be supported by the fact that most prepubertal children tend to gravitate toward same-sex friends and playmates (Molloy, Gest, Feinberg, & Osgood, 2014).

GENITAL STAGE Following the calm of the latency period, a child's psychosexual development regains speed. The *genital stage* begins at puberty and marks a reawakening of sexuality. The erogenous zone centers on the genitals, but now in association with relationships, as opposed to masturbation. The Oedipus or Electra complex is resolved, and the individual often becomes attracted to partners who resemble the opposite-sex parent (Freud, 1905/1953). Because of the ever-present demands of the *id,* unconscious conflicts persist, including the continual battle against hidden sexual and aggressive urges. If such conflicts are resolved, then it is possible to thrive in adult activities such as work and love.

Who Are the Neo-Freudians?

A DARK PERIOD Young childhood was difficult for Saifa, who faced an ongoing conflict between his innate sense of gender and society's expectations for him as a "girl." But the early years were also a time of great freedom. "When I was like 5, 6, 7, I was the adult that I am now," Saifa says. "I was very uninhibited; I was very loud; I was very free; I was weird."

Life took a dramatic turn when police showed up at his building and took away his father. Saifa, 10 years old, observed the whole event. "That's the last time I saw him alive, [he] was being taken away in handcuffs." While Saifa's mother dealt with the aftermath, Saifa went to live with his sister in North Carolina, where he was relentlessly bullied at his new school. "I think living in North Carolina just really killed my fire as a child," Saifa says. "I was still that quirky, weird, loud kid, but then I was teased, I was bullied, my self-esteem was really low."

A year or two after moving to North Carolina, Saifa began to experience puberty. His voice deepened; he began growing facial hair; and his muscles became more defined—all changes associated with *male* puberty. But Saifa was still a "girl" at this point; recall that he had been assigned female at birth and raised as "Susanne." The masculinization of his body was fueled by testosterone from his undescended testes. (People with androgen insensitivity syndrome [AIS] are born with internal, as opposed to descended, testes.) "I was experiencing this male puberty," Saifa says. "But it felt normal; it felt good."

The male puberty Saifa enjoyed came to an abrupt halt at age 13, when he moved back to New York City and doctors removed his testes. The purpose of the operation was to eliminate the pain he had been feeling in his groin, possibly the result of hernias in his testes. The other reason, doctors told Saifa's mother, was that the internal gonads would likely become cancerous. Following the surgery, Saifa's doctor put him on female hormones, which feminized his face and body. "[The doctors] wanted to create this feminine body that was going against what my body was naturally doing. . . . I was developing with both male and female characteristics, and that's what makes my particular intersex trait so beautiful," Saifa says. "The right to my body was taken away from me."

What's Beneath That Smile? Saifa, 18, poses for his high school graduation photo (top) and a portrait with his older sister. After doctors removed his internal testes, Saifa fell into a deep depression. "I didn't comb my hair, I didn't brush my teeth, I didn't shower," Saifa explains. "It was so bad, I wouldn't even go outside." This depression landed him in therapy, which helped him get back into the world. However, the therapist was not honest with Saifa about the circumstances of his birth. She suggested he was a female born with an underdeveloped uterus and ovaries, and pushed him to adopt a female gender identity. Courtesy Sean Saifa Wall.

According to Freud, personality is largely shaped by early childhood experiences and sexual impulses. Yet, some of the most transformative experiences in Saifa's life—the arrest of his father, the bullying at school, and the surgery to remove his testes—occurred later in life and had little to do with sexual urges. Some theorists would argue that such events are important factors in personality development. We now turn to the neo-Freudians, who agree with Freud on many points, but depart from his intense emphasis on early childhood experiences, aggression, and sexuality.

LO 5 Explain how the neo-Freudians' theories of personality differ from Freud's.

DRIFTING APART Freud's psychoanalytic theory was quite controversial, but he did have a following of students who adapted some central aspects of his theory. Erik Erikson, for example, considered himself a "loyal Freudian," yet he took Freud's ideas in a new direction (Schultz & Schultz, 2017). **Erikson** suggested that psychosocial development occurs throughout life and proceeds through eight stages, each marked by a conflict between the individual's needs and society's expectations. Erikson was not the only one who disagreed with Freud on key points. Those who broke away and developed their own theories are often referred to as neo-Freudians (neo = "new").

CONNECTIONS

In **Chapter 8,** we discussed Erikson's psychosocial stages. Building on the views of Freud, Erikson suggested that every developmental stage is marked by a task or emotional crisis that must be handled successfully for healthy psychological growth.

ALFRED ADLER One of the first followers to forge his own path was a fellow Austrian physician, Alfred Adler (1870–1937), whose theory conflicted with the Freudian notion that personality is primarily shaped by unconscious motivators. As Adler saw it, humans are not just pleasure seekers, but conscious and intentional in their behaviors. We are motivated by the need to feel superior—to grow, overcome challenges, and strive for perfection. This drive originates during childhood, when we realize that we are dependent on and inferior to adults. Whether imagined or real, our sense of inferiority pushes us to compensate, so we cultivate our special gifts and skills. This attempt to balance perceived weaknesses with strengths is not a sign of abnormality, but a natural response.

Adler's theory of *individual psychology* focuses on each person's unique struggle with feelings of inferiority. Unfortunately, not everyone is successful in overcoming feelings of helplessness and dependence, but instead may develop what is known as an *inferiority complex* (Adler, 1927/1994). People with an inferiority complex feel incompetent, vulnerable, and powerless, and cannot achieve their full potential.

Adler was also one of the first to theorize about the psychological repercussions of birth order—that is, how people are affected by their place in the family (first, middle, or youngest child). He believed that firstborn children experience different environmental pressures than youngest and middle children, and these pressures can set the stage for the development of certain personality traits (Ansbacher & Ansbacher, 1956).

...BELIEVE IT...OR NOT

HOW BIRTH ORDER MAY AFFECT YOUR PERSONALITY Firstborns are conscientious and high achieving. They play by the rules, excel in school, and become leaders in the workforce. Youngest children are favored and coddled by their parents, and grow up to be gregarious and rebellious. Middle children tend to get lost in the shuffle, but they learn to be self-sufficient.

DO MIDDLE CHILDREN GET LOST IN THE SHUFFLE?

Have you heard these stereotypes about birth order and personality? How well do they match your personal experience, and do you think they are valid?

If you search the scientific literature, you will indeed find research supporting such claims. According to one analysis of 200 studies, firstborns (as well as only children) are often accomplished and successful; middle children are sociable but tend to lack a sense of belonging; and last-born children are agreeable and rebellious (Eckstein et al., 2010). Other research suggests that later-born children, particularly middle siblings, often go out of their way to help others (Salmon, Cuthbertson, & Figueredo, 2016). These findings are intriguing and often seem consistent with our everyday observations. But historically, birth order studies have been riddled with **confounding variables**, such as family size, and designing studies to circumvent these variables has proven difficult. In 2015 researchers carried out a study that controlled for many of these factors, subduing the longstanding debate. Reviewing studies that include over 20,000 participants, these researchers could not find any connection between birth

CONNECTIONS

In **Chapter 1,** we discussed confounding variables, a type of extraneous variable that changes in sync with an independent variable (IV), making it difficult to discern which variable—the IV or the confounding variable—is causing changes in the dependent variable. Here, family size is a potential confounding variable.

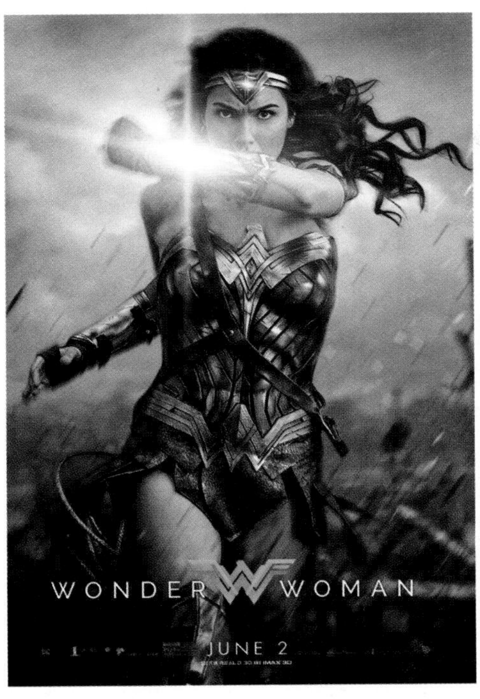

Timeless Heroines
Gal Gadot (left) plays the role of Wonder Woman in the 2017 film *Wonder Woman.* Her strength, bravery, and charisma resemble that of 15th-century French heroine Joan of Arc, portrayed in the poster (right). These heroines have the qualities of a Jungian archetype; the thoughts and feelings they evoke are relatively consistent across time and culture. Left: © Warner Bros. Pictures/Courtesy Everett Collection. Right: V&A Images, London/Art Resource, NY.

order and specific personality characteristics (Bakalar, 2015, October 28; Damian & Roberts, 2015; Rohrer, Egloff, & Schmukle, 2015). And so it seems we can't make assumptions about people based on their birth order.

CARL GUSTAV JUNG Neo-Freudian Carl Gustav Jung (Yoong; 1875–1961) was a Swiss psychiatrist who emphasized growth, self-understanding, and the spiritual aspects of human nature. Jung claimed that Freud viewed the brain as "an appendage to the genital glands" (Westen et al., 2008, p. 66), and proposed that personality development is not limited to childhood, but evolves throughout life. His *analytic psychology* deemphasized biological urges (sex and aggression), and proposed that we are driven by psychological energy (not sexual energy) that promotes growth, insight, and balance (Jung, 1969).

According to Jung, personality is made up of the ego (at the conscious level), a *personal unconscious,* and a *collective unconscious.* The personal unconscious is akin to Freud's notion of the preconscious and the unconscious mind; it contains material that is readily available (easy-to-retrieve memories) and material that is very difficult to access (repressed memories and other anxiety-provoking content). The **collective unconscious** holds the universal experiences of humankind passed from generation to generation—memories that are not easily retrieved without some degree of effort or interpretation. We inherit a variety of primal images, patterns of thought, and storylines. The themes of these **archetypes** (AHR-ki-types) may be found in art, literature, music, dreams, and religions across time, geography, and culture. Some of the consistent archetypes include the nurturing mother, powerful father, innocent child, and brave hero. Archetypes provide a blueprint for responding to objects, people, and situations (Jung, 1969). Jung also proposed that every personality has both feminine and masculine elements, respectively known as the *anima* and *animus,* and both should be acknowledged and appreciated.

KAREN HORNEY Karen Horney (HOR-nahy; 1885–1952) was a German psychoanalyst who immigrated to the United States in the early 1930s. She agreed with Freud that the early years play an important role in shaping adult personality, and that conflict arises between individual desires and the needs of society (Schultz & Schultz, 2017; Tummala-Narra, 2016). But rather than focusing on erogenous zones and psychosexual stages, Horney emphasized the role of social environment, and in particular,

collective unconscious According to Jung, the universal experiences of humankind passed from generation to generation, including memories.

archetypes Primal images, patterns of thoughts, and storylines stored in the collective unconscious, with themes that may be found in art, literature, music, dreams, and religions.

TABLE 10.3 "THE NEO-FREUDIANS"

Alfred Adler

- Rejected Freud's notion that personality is primaily shaped by unconscious processes.
- Alder's *individual psychology* suggests that personality is strongly influenced by the drive to conquer feelings of inferiority.
- Birth order plays a role in personality development.

Carl Gustav Jung

- Agreed with Freud that unconscious processes are critical to personality development, but did not share his focus on sexuality and agression.
- Jung's *analytic psychology* emphasized the importance of growth, self-understanding, and spiritual development over the life span.
- Personality is made up of the ego, the *personal unconscious,* and the *collective unconscious.*

Karen Horney

- Agreed with Freud that childhood is an important time for personality development, but dismissed his sexist approach.
- Relationships between children and caregivers are paramount, and poor parenting can lead to helplessness and isolation, or *basic anxiety.*
- Men have *womb envy,* meaning they envy women's ability to bear and breastfeed children.

Not all of Freud's students completely embraced his approach to understanding the human mind. Alfred Adler, Carl Gustav Jung, Karen Horney, and others branched off on their own theoretical paths. Photos (top to bottom): Imagno/Getty Images; World History Archive/Ann Ronan Collection/AGE Fotostock; Bettmann/Getty Images.

the role of family. She believed that inadequate parenting can create feelings of helplessness and isolation, or *basic anxiety* (Horney, 1945). Horney suggested that people deal with this anxiety using three strategies: moving toward people (looking for affection and acceptance), moving away from people (looking for isolation and self-sufficiency), or moving against people (looking to control others). A balance of these three strategies is important for psychological stability and healthy personality development. A strong critic of Freud's sexist approach to the female psyche, Horney pointed out that women are not jealous of the penis itself, but rather what it represents in terms of power and status in society. Horney (1926/1967) also proposed that boys and men can envy women's ability to bear and breastfeed children (**Table 10.3**).

Freud's Legacy: It's Complicated

Freud's psychoanalytic theory was groundbreaking, and it led to a variety of extensions and permutations through neo-Freudians such as Erikson, Adler, Jung, and Horney. His work is considered among the most important in the field of personality development. It called attention to the existence of infant sexuality at a time when sex was a forbidden topic of conversation, recognized the importance of infancy and early childhood in the unfolding of personality, and appreciated the universal stages of human development. Psychoanalysis helps us understand that the "self has depth; that the complexity of the psyche and of human existence are not an impediment to living a good life, but are the source of our identity" (Strenger, 2015, p. 304).

Despite these key contributions (and some evidence that psychoanalysis works for certain people), many scientists consider Freud's work to be unscientific (Horgan, 2017, March 10). Freud's theories are virtually impossible to prove wrong and can be used to explain most any human behavior (Shea, n.d.), both characteristics of pseudoscience (Chapter 0; Stanovich, 2013). If Freud's theories had been more scientific, perhaps they would have earned him a Nobel Prize in Physiology or Medicine. He was nominated 12 times, but never granted this high honor (Nobelprize.org, 2009, October 9; Shaw, 2016, January 8).

Critics also contend that Freud's psychoanalysis fails to appreciate the importance of development beyond childhood, overemphasizes the role of sexuality, and places too much weight on the unconscious forces guiding behavior. His theory is based on a biased, **nonrepresentative sample** consisting of middle- and upper-class Viennese women and himself. Finally, Freud's theory is male-centered and assumes that women are inferior in their "character development" and should accept their "passive position in a world that is male-dominated" (Tummala-Narra, 2016, p. 18).

CONNECTIONS

In **Chapter 1,** we introduced a form of descriptive research called the case study. Freud's case studies (and all case studies) are based on isolated cases rather than representative samples. Therefore, their findings cannot be generalized to the larger population.

show what you know

1. According to Freud, all children go through ______ stages as they mature into adulthood. If conflicts are not resolved, a child may suffer from a ______.
2. How did the theories of the neo-Freudians differ from Freud's psychoanalytic theory with regard to personality development?
3. Freud's ______ includes three levels: conscious, preconscious, and unconscious.
   a. structural model of the mind
   b. developmental model
   c. individual psychology
   d. topographical model of the mind

✓ CHECK YOUR ANSWERS IN APPENDIX C.

Humanistic, Learning, and Trait Theories

ON A POSITIVE PATH After Saifa's testes were removed and he began taking female hormones, doctors expected (or hoped) he would blossom into a lovely young woman. But as Saifa recalls, "I did not succumb to the pressure to be more feminine, but actually gravitated toward masculinity" (Wall, 2015, p. 118). He excelled in school and eventually became a leader at Williams College, spearheading campus demonstrations against police brutality and anti-gay hate crimes. A few years after graduating, Saifa decided to make the biological and social transition to manhood; he changed his name to Sean Saifa Wall, began taking testosterone, and underwent a double mastectomy.

Saifa had assumed control of his body and his life like never before, yet he could not shake the feelings of loneliness and self-hatred. To do this, he would need to confront a lifetime of trauma, which included the loss of his father—first to prison and then to AIDS—and life-changing medical interventions that occurred before he was old enough to give informed consent. Saifa courageously faced these traumas by going to psychotherapy and enrolling in a 12-step recovery program for sex addiction.

For the last 10 years, Saifa has been on a journey to heal himself and help others. Through his research, writing, and public speaking, he has established himself as an expert on intersex traits. More recently, his focus has shifted to collage art, writing, and advisory work for the Astraea Intersex Fund for Human Rights. "I've definitely been on this journey," Saifa says, "looking outward about how I can change the world around me, but also this inward journey of how I can change the world within me."

Saifa is now approaching 40 and seems to have reached a point of self-acceptance and love. "I still have more work to do and more growing to do, as we all do," he says, "but I can see that I have returned to that child of like 7 who is just in the world . . . totally free."

Every Body Is Beautiful
Saifa advocates for the legal rights of children with intersex traits. "Accepting myself as intersex and advocating for intersex people and children, I really put forward that our bodies are our mosaic," Saifa says. "There is no such thing as a 'normal body'. . . . This variation is what makes us, as a species, beautiful." To learn more about Saifa's advocacy, visit unbornson.com. Courtesy Sean Saifa Wall.

The Brighter Side: Maslow and Rogers

A humanistic theorist might say that Saifa's drive to grow and improve is, and has always been, the main force shaping his personality. Leading humanists such as Abraham Maslow and Carl Rogers believed that people are innately good and in control of their destinies, and these positive aspects of human nature drive the development of personality. This perspective began gaining momentum in the 1960s and 70s in response to the negative, **mechanistic view** of human nature apparent in the psychoanalytic and behaviorist theories. Thus, humanism is often referred to as the *Third Force* in psychology.

CONNECTIONS

The behaviorists, presented in **Chapters 1** and **5,** were only interested in measuring observable behaviors. They suggested that our behaviors are shaped by input from the environment, and thus we are at the mercy of forces beyond our control. The humanists challenged this position.

MASLOW AND PERSONALITY Some consider **Abraham Maslow** to be the "single person most responsible for creating humanistic psychology" (Moss, 2015, p. 13). As a humanist, Maslow believed that psychologists should study human creativity, growth, and healthy functioning, not just mental illness and maladaptive personality traits. He was particularly interested in *self-actualizers,* or people who are continually seeking to reach their fullest potential.

CONNECTIONS

Chapter 9 presents Maslow's hierarchy of needs. According to Maslow, behaviors are motivated by both physiological and psychological needs. These needs are considered universal and are ordered according to the strength of their associated drives. The most critical needs are situated at the base of the hierarchy and generally take precedence over higher-level needs.

Discuss Rogers' view of self-concept, ideal self, and unconditional positive regard.

ROGERS AND PERSONALITY Like Maslow, Carl Rogers had great faith in the essential goodness of people and their ability to make sound choices (Rogers, 1979). This humanistic perspective colored both his theory of personality and his work as a client-centered therapist. According to Rogers, we all have an innate urge to move toward situations and people that will help us grow and away from those that could inhibit growth. This tendency toward self-enhancement begins in infancy and continues throughout life (Murphy & Joseph, 2016). We should trust our ability to find happiness and mental balance, that is, to be *fully functioning,* and strive to actively experience life, according to Rogers. At the same time, we must also be sensitive to the needs of others.

Rogers highlighted the importance of **self-concept,** which refers to knowledge of one's strengths, abilities, behavior patterns, and temperament. Problems arise when the self-concept is *incongruent* with, or does not correspond to, a person's experiences in the world (Rogers, 1959). If a woman believes she is kind and sociable but fails to get along with most people in her life, this incongruence will produce tension and confusion. Rogers also proposed that people often develop an **ideal self,** which is the self-concept they fervently strive to achieve. Problems arise when the ideal self is unattainable or incongruent with the self-concept, a topic we will discuss further in Chapter 14 (Rogers, 1959).

Like Freud, Rogers believed caregivers play a vital role in the development of personality. Ideally, caregivers should show **unconditional positive regard,** or total acceptance of children regardless of their behavior. According to Rogers, people need to feel totally accepted and valued for who they are, not what they do. Caregivers who place too much emphasis on rules, morals, and values, ignoring children's innate goodness, can cause them to experience *conditions of worth.* In other words, children feel worthy of being loved only when they act in accordance with their parents' wishes. When children's behaviors or emotions are judged to be bad or wrong, they feel unworthy and may try hide or repress them. Seeking approval from others, they deny their true selves, and anxiety is ever-present. As caregivers, it is important to show children that we value them all the time, not just when they obey and act the way we want.

You Asked, Saifa Answers

http://qrs.ly/rx5a5f0

Does your social media accurately reflect who you are?

self-concept The knowledge an individual has about his strengths, abilities, behavior patterns, and temperament.

ideal self The self-concept a person strives for and fervently wishes to achieve.

unconditional positive regard According to Rogers, the total acceptance or valuing of a person, regardless of behavior.

Put Your Heads Together

Before meeting with your group, **A)** briefly outline the definitions of self-concept, ideal self, conditions of worth, and unconditional positive regard. **B)** Team up and write a short users' manual for new parents. Provide instructions for how to raise a "fully functioning" child using these principles and any other concepts from humanistic psychology. **C)** Are there situations in which you think unconditional positive regard is not appropriate?

HUMANISTIC THEORIES: WHAT'S THE TAKEAWAY? The humanistic perspective has led to a more positive and balanced view of human nature, influencing approaches to parenting, education, and research. Its legacy is alive and well in the emerging field of **positive psychology**. From psychotherapy to research on human strengths and optimal functioning, we can see the "resurgence" of the humanists' work in the field (DeRobertis, 2016).

CONNECTIONS

In **Chapter 1,** we described positive psychology as a relatively new approach. The humanists' optimism struck the right chord with many psychologists, who wondered why the field was not focusing on human strengths and virtues.

Despite its far-reaching and positive impact, the humanistic approach has limitations. For humanistic and psychoanalytic theories alike, creating operational definitions can be challenging. How can you use the experimental method to test a subjective approach whose concepts are open to interpretation (Schultz & Schultz, 2017)? Imagine submitting a research proposal that included two randomly assigned groups of children: one group whose parents were instructed to show them *unconditional positive regard* and another group whose parents were told to instill *conditions of worth.* The proposal would never amount to a real study, not only because it raises ethical issues, but also because it would be impossible to control the experimental conditions. And while it is important to recognize that humans have great potential to grow and move forward, we should not discount the developmental impact of early experiences. Finally, some have argued that humanism almost ignores the negative aspects of human nature evident in war, greed, abuse, and aggression (Burger, 2015). This may be true, but some humanistic psychologists are "inspired by the challenges" presented by humanity's darker side (Stern, 2016, xi).

In the next section, we will explore how personality is influenced by forces in the outside world. How do you think your interactions with the environment have shaped your personality?

Too Much of a Good Thing?
Sofia Vergara plays the role of Gloria on ABC's *Modern Family*. Gloria appears to demonstrate unconditional positive regard for her son, Manny (middle), played by Rico Rodriguez. But the fact that she "praises everything he does, never criticizing anything" (IMDB, n.d.) may not benefit Manny in the long run. Constantly praising, attempting to boost self-esteem, and withholding criticism can be counterproductive. Some even believe the use of unconditional positive regard is a "narcissist's dream" (Paris, 2014). ABC/Photofest.

Can Personality Be Learned?

NANA LIVES ON More than a decade has passed since Saifa's therapist asked him the crucial question: "When did you realize love was not possible?" Even today, those words strike Saifa in a deep and vulnerable place. But he no longer falls apart—perhaps because he knows that love is possible. There is no doubt he pours love into the world, advocating for the rights of intersex children and others who don't fit neatly into society's male and female gender categories. For those in his close circle, Saifa demonstrates love by cooking and hosting—making sure they are comfortable and happy. He learned these nurturing behaviors from his grandmother, who passed away in 2003.

"One of my role models was my Nana," Saifa says. "She didn't really talk much, she was kind of shy . . . . but she was an amazing cook." Preparing meals and cleaning were the ways she expressed her love. "To speak to her history, she was a domestic worker for most of her life, so that's what she knew," Saifa explains. "She showed her love by doing rather than saying."

LO 7 Use the behavioral perspective to explain personality development.

Saifa's caretaking behaviors have been shaped by years of observational learning—watching and following his role model, Nana. These same behaviors have been strengthened through operant conditioning. When Saifa's friends praise the meals he makes, this provides positive reinforcement for his cooking and nurturing. These learned behaviors follow a predictable pattern, and therefore constitute part of Saifa's personality. According to the behavioral perspective, personality is shaped by a lifetime of learning.

As you may recall, personality is the core set of characteristics that influence the way one thinks, acts, and feels. The behaviorist perspective focuses on just one of those elements: the way a person acts. Behaviorists view personality as a collection of behaviors, all of which have been shaped through learning: Each person "develops under a different or unique set of stimulus conditions and consequently his resulting personality becomes uniquely his own" (Lundin, 1963, p. 265). This perspective offers valuable insights on personality development, but does it overstate the importance of behavior? Critics contend that behaviorism is too simplistic; it ignores everything that is not directly observable and assumes that humans are passive and unaware of what is going on in their internal and external environments.

Believe in Yourself
Nyle DiMarco (left) and Peta Murgatroyd, champions in the 22nd season of ABC's *Dancing With the Stars*. DiMarco, who is deaf, is an actor, model, and social activist who appears to possess a high level of self-efficacy, or belief in his ability to accomplish his goals. As DiMarco said in an interview with *USA Today*, "My message to my deaf community is that we can redefine anything however we want. Anything is re-definable only if we believe and work hard for it" (Jensen, 2016, April 11, para. 7). ABC/Photofest.

LO 8 Summarize Rotter's view of personality.

LOOKING BEYOND BEHAVIOR American psychologist Julian Rotter (1916–2014) was an early social learning theorist, who believed that "personality is the interaction between a person and his or her environment and is dependent on a particular individual's learning experiences and life history" (Strickland, 2014, p. 546). Rotter also suggested that some aspects of personality cannot be directly observed (Rotter, 1990). He proposed several cognitive aspects of personality, including *locus of control* and *expectancy.* Locus of control refers to a pattern of beliefs about where control or responsibility for outcomes resides. People who have an *internal* locus of control believe that the causes of life events generally reside within them, and that they have some control over those causes. These people would say that their career success depends on how hard they work, not on luck, for example (Rotter, 1966). Those with an *external* locus of control generally believe that causes of events reside outside of them; they assign great importance to luck, fate, and other features of the environment, which they cannot control. Getting a job occurs when circumstances are just right and luck is on their side (Rotter, 1966). A person's locus of control refers to beliefs about the self, not about others.

Rotter also explored how personality is influenced by thoughts about the future. **Expectancy** refers to the predictions we make about the outcomes and consequences of our behaviors (**INFOGRAPHIC 10.2**). Suppose you have a bad meal at a restaurant. Your decision to let it go or confront the manager is based on expectancy: Do you believe complaining will lead to a free meal, or do you expect to be treated like a scam artist who doesn't want to pay the bill? In these situations, there is an interaction among expectancies, behaviors, and environmental factors.

expectancy A person's predictions about the consequences or outcomes of behavior.

social-cognitive perspective Suggests that personality results from relationships and other environmental factors (social) and patterns of thinking (cognitive).

LO 9 Discuss how Bandura uses the social-cognitive perspective to explain personality.

BELIEFS, BEHAVIOR, AND ENVIRONMENT Albert Bandura also challenged the behaviorist approach, rejecting the notion that psychologists should only focus on observable behavior (Bandura, 2006). His **social-cognitive perspective** suggests that personality results from reinforcement, relationships, and other environmental factors (social)

The Social-Cognitive Perspective on Personality

Social-cognitive theorists rejected behaviorists' exclusive focus on observable behavior. Acknowledging that personality may be shaped through learning, social-cognitive theorists such as Albert Bandura also emphasized the roles of cognition and environmental influences on behavior. Bandura's theory of reciprocal determinism shows how cognition, behaviors, and the environment all interact to determine our personality.

"Good job!"
Child is praised for reading quietly.
Child receives attention for effort in school.
Child is rewarded for school achievement.

Behaviorists believe personality is the compilation of behaviors shaped through a lifetime of learning. A child who receives reinforcement for studying and effort in school will repeat this behavior, eventually exhibiting the personality characteristic "studious."

cognition

Thinking about behaviors and what they have led to in the past creates expectancies, predictions about what future outcomes will result from a behavior. When we recognize that past efforts to study usually resulted in good grades, we will expect that studying will lead to good grades in the future. Bandura calls this learned expectation of success *self-efficacy.*

I succeed because I am a studious person.

I will apply to college because I can succeed there.

I get good grades when I study, so I will continue to do this.

I am in college, so I know I can handle a busy schedule like other college students.

EXPECTANCIES INFLUENCE BEHAVIOR.

ENVIRONMENT INFLUENCES EXPECTANCIES.

EXPECTANCIES INFLUENCE THE ENVIRONMENT YOU SEEK OUT.

When I study, I get good grades.

PRIOR EXPERIENCES CREATE EXPECTANCIES.

I'm a college student now, so I need to spend more time studying.

ENVIRONMENT INFLUENCES BEHAVIOR.

BEHAVIOR INFLUENCES ENVIRONMENT.

I study hard and am a successful student, so I've chosen to go to college.

behavior

Reinforced behaviors become more consistent over time. When an instructor praises our participation in class, that reinforcement will lead us to participate again. We also learn by observing others' behaviors. If our classmates form a study group that helps them better understand the material, we may learn to adopt that technique.

environment

The environment can include the college you choose, the major you select, the classes you enroll in, and also the culture where you are a student. For example, in Chinese classrooms, struggle is assumed to be part of the learning process. However, in Western classrooms, struggle is often seen as a sign of lower ability (Li, 2005; Schleppenbach, Flevares, Sims, & Perry, 2007). The culture you live in—your environment—can influence how you think about your own skills and behaviors, and how hard you work at something that is difficult for you.

Credits: Graduate: Fuse/Thinkstock/Getty Images; College campus: Jannis Werner (Harvard Images)/Alamy; Student at desk: mocker_bat/iStock/Thinkstock/Getty Images.

It's a Social-Cognitive Thing Psychologist Albert Bandura receives the National Medal of Science in 2016. Bandura asserts that personality is molded by a continual interaction between cognition and social interactions, including observations of other people's behaviors. His approach is known as the social-cognitive perspective. NurPhoto/Getty Images.

and patterns of thinking (cognitive). Our personalities are shaped by experience, and our cognitive abilities and knowledge partly result from interactions with others (Bandura, 1977b, 2006).

Bandura also pointed to the importance of **self-efficacy,** which refers to beliefs about our ability and effectiveness in reaching goals (Bandura, 1977a, 2001). People who exhibit high self-efficacy often achieve greater success at work because they are more likely to be flexible and open to new ideas (Bandura, 2006). Those who demonstrate low self-efficacy generally believe they will not succeed in a particular situation, regardless of their abilities or experience. Beliefs about self-efficacy are influenced by experience and may change across situations. Generally speaking, people who believe they can change and progress are more likely to persevere in difficult situations.

Beliefs play a key role in our ability to make decisions, problem solve, and deal with life's challenges. The environment, in turn, responds to our behaviors. In essence, we have internal forces (beliefs, expectations) directing our behavior, external forces (reinforcers, punishments) responding to those behaviors, and the behaviors themselves influencing our beliefs and the environment. Beliefs, behavior, and environment form a complex system that determines our behavior patterns and personality (Infographic 10.2). Bandura (1978, 1986) refers to this multidirectional interaction as **reciprocal determinism.**

Let's look at an example showing how reciprocal determinism might work. A student harbors a certain belief about herself. (*I am going to graduate with honors.*) This belief influences her behavior (she studies hard and reaches out to instructors), which affects her environment (instructors take note of her enthusiasm and offer support). Her ambition and determination result from an ongoing interaction among cognition, behaviors, and the environment.

SOCIAL-COGNITIVE THEORIES: WHAT'S THE TAKEAWAY? The social-cognitive theorists were among the first to realize that we are not just products of our environments, but dynamic agents capable of altering the environment itself. Personality is shaped by an ongoing interplay of cognitive expectancies, behaviors, and the environment. The focus on research and testable hypotheses provides a clear advantage over the psychoanalytic and humanistic theories. Some argue that these approaches minimize the importance of unconscious processes and emotional influences (Schultz & Schultz, 2017; Westen, 1990), but overall, the inclusion of cognition and social factors offers valuable ways to study and understand personality.

What Are Personality Traits?

Earlier in the chapter, we used some words to describe Saifa's personality—"vivacious," "loud," "charismatic," "direct," and "empathetic." All these might be considered examples of **traits,** the relatively stable properties that describe elements of personality. Unlike the theories presented thus far, which focus on how and why personality develops, the **trait theories** center on describing personality and predicting behaviors.

LO 10 Distinguish trait theories from other personality theories.

ALLPORT IDENTIFIES 4,504 TRAITS One of the first trait theorists was American psychologist Gordon Allport (1897–1967), who compiled a comprehensive list of traits to describe personality. The goal was to operationalize the terminology used in personality research, as researchers need to agree on definitions when studying the

self-efficacy Beliefs one has regarding how effective he or she will be in reaching a goal.

reciprocal determinism According to Bandura, multidirectional interactions among cognition, behaviors, and the environment.

traits The relatively stable properties that describe elements of personality.

trait theories Theories that focus on personality dimensions and their influence on behavior; can be used to predict behaviors.

same topic. (Suppose two psychologists are investigating a trait called "vivacious"; they will have an easier time comparing results if they use the same definition.) Allport and his colleague carefully reviewed *Webster's New International Dictionary* (1925) and identified 17,953 words (among some 400,000 entries) that were "descriptive of personality or personal behavior" (Allport & Odbert, 1936, p. 24). The list contained terms considered personal traits (such as "acrobatical" and "zealous"), temporary states (such as "woozy" and "thrilled"), social evaluations (such as "swine" and "outlandish"), and words that were metaphorical and doubtful (such as "mortal" and "middle-aged"). Most relevant to personality were the personal traits, of which they identified 4,504—a little over 1% of all entries in the dictionary. Surely, this long list could be condensed, reduced, or classified to make it more manageable. Enter Raymond Cattell.

1.	Reserved	⟷	Outgoing
2.	Concrete thinker	⟷	Abstract thinker
3.	Affected by feelings	⟷	Emotionally stable
4.	Submissive	⟷	Dominant
5.	Serious	⟷	Happy-go-lucky
6.	Expedient	⟷	Conscientious
7.	Timid	⟷	Bold
8.	Tough-minded	⟷	Sensitive
9.	Trusting	⟷	Suspicious
10.	Practical	⟷	Imaginative
11.	Forthright	⟷	Shrewd
12.	Self-assured	⟷	Insecure
13.	Conservative	⟷	Experimenting
14.	Group-dependent	⟷	Self-sufficient
15.	Undisciplined	⟷	Controlled
16.	Relaxed	⟷	Tense

FIGURE 10.2
Cattell's 16 Personality Factors
Raymond Cattell produced personality profiles by measuring where people fell along each of these 16 dimensions, or personality factors. The ends of the dimensions represent polar extremes ("reserved" versus "outgoing," for example). Information from Cattell (1973b) and Cattell, Eber, & Tatsuoka (1970).

CATTELL NARROWS THE LIST British-born psychologist Raymond Cattell (1905–1998) proposed grouping the long list of personality traits into two major categories: surface traits and source traits (Cattell, 1950). **Surface traits** are the easily observable personality characteristics commonly used to describe people: *Josie is quiet. Amir is friendly.* **Source traits** are the foundational qualities that give rise to surface traits. For example, "extraversion" is a source trait, and the surface traits it produces may include "warm," "gregarious," and "assertive." There are thousands of surface traits but only a few source traits. Cattell (1950) proposed that source traits are the product of both heredity and environment (nature and nurture), and surface traits are the "combined action of several source traits" (p. 34).

Cattell also condensed the list of surface traits into a much smaller set of 171. Realizing that some of these surface traits would be **correlated**, he used a statistical procedure known as *factor analysis* to group them into a smaller set of dimensions according to common underlying properties. With factor analysis, Cattell was able to produce a list of 16 personality factors. These 16 factors, or personality dimensions, can be considered primary source traits (**Figure 10.2**).

CONNECTIONS
In **Chapter 1,** we described a correlation as a relationship between two variables. Here, we explain factor analysis, which examines the relationships among an entire set of variables.

EYSENCK PROPOSES THREE TRAITS German-born psychologist Hans Eysenck (AHY-sengk; 1916–1997) continued to develop our understanding of source traits, proposing three personality dimensions: introversion–extraversion (E), neuroticism (N), and psychoticism (P) (**Figure 10.3**).

People who are high on the *extraversion* end of the introversion–extraversion (E) dimension tend to display a marked degree of sociability and are outgoing and active with others in their environment. Those on the *introversion* end tend to be quiet and careful and enjoy time alone. Having high *neuroticism* (N) typically goes hand in hand with being restless, moody, and excitable, while low neuroticism means being calm, reliable, and emotionally stable. People high on the *psychoticism* dimension tend to be cold, impersonal, and antisocial, while those at the opposite end of this dimension are warm, caring, and empathetic. (The psychoticism dimension is not related to psychosis, described in Chapter 13.)

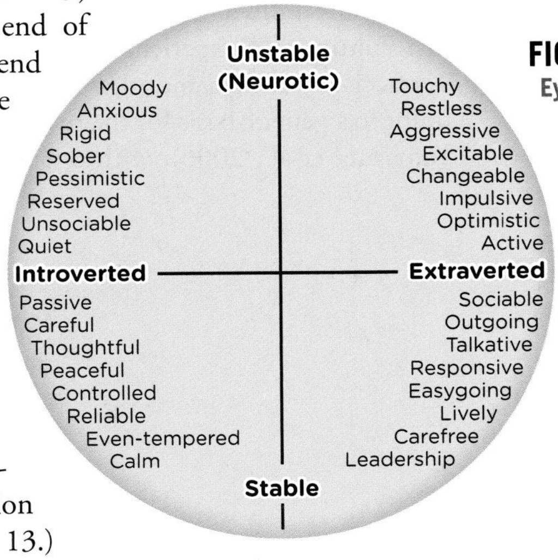

FIGURE 10.3
Eysenck's Dimensions of Personality
Psychologist Hans Eysenck described personality using several dimensions. This figure displays only Eysenck's original dimensions; years later, he proposed an additional dimension called psychoticism. People who score high on the psychoticism trait tend to be impersonal and antisocial. Information from Eysenck & Eysenck (1968). Reproduced from Schultz & Schultz (2013) with permission.

In addition to identifying these dimensions, Eysenck worked diligently to unearth their biological basis. For example, he proposed that there is a direct relationship between behaviors associated with the introversion–extraversion dimension and the reticular formation (Eysenck, 1967).

surface traits Easily observable characteristics that derive from source traits.

source traits Basic underlying or foundational characteristics of personality.

According to Eysenck (1967, 1990), introverted people display higher reactivity in their **reticular formation**. Because they have higher arousal levels, introverts are more likely to react to stimuli, and thus develop certain coping patterns—being more careful or restrained, for example. An extravert has lower levels of arousal, and thus is less reactive to stimuli. Extraverts seek stimulation because their arousal levels are low, so they tend to be more impulsive and outgoing.

CONNECTIONS In **Chapter 2,** we described the reticular formation, a network of neurons responsible for levels of arousal. The reticular formation helps you selectively attend to important information and ignore what's irrelevant, by sifting through sensory data on its way to the cortex. Eysenck suggested that the reticular formation is also associated with the introversion–extraversion dimension of personality.

The theories of Allport, Cattell, and Eysenck paved the way for the trait theories commonly used today. Let's take a look at one of the most popular models.

LO 11 Identify the biological roots of the five-factor model of personality.

THE BIG FIVE The **five-factor model of personality,** also known as the Big Five, is a current trait approach for explaining personality (McCrae, 2011; McCrae & Costa, 1987; McCrae et al., 2013). This model, developed using factor analysis, indicates there are five factors, or dimensions, to describe personality. Although complete consensus on the names for these factors does not exist, trait theorists generally agree on the following labels: (1) openness to experience, (2) conscientiousness, (3) extraversion, (4) agreeableness, and (5) neuroticism (de Raad & Mlačić, 2017; McCrae et al., 2013; McCrae, Scally, Terracciano, Abecasis, & Costa, 2010). Openness is the degree to which a person is willing to try new experiences. Conscientiousness refers to one's attention to detail and organizational tendencies. The extraversion and neuroticism dimensions are similar to those proposed by Eysenck: Extraversion refers to degree of sociability and outgoingness, while neuroticism connotes emotional stability (the extent to which a person is calm, secure, and even tempered). Agreeableness indicates how trusting and easygoing a person is. To remember these factors, students sometimes use the mnemonic OCEAN: Openness, Conscientiousness, Extraversion, Agreeableness, and Neuroticism (**Figure 10.4**).

Empirical support for this model has been established using cross-cultural testing, with people in more than 50 cultures exhibiting these five dimensions (Allik et al., 2017; McCrae et al., 2000, 2005, 2010). The five-factor model of personality "appears to be a universal aspect of human nature" (McCrae et al., 2013, p. 17).

One possible explanation for these cross-cultural similarities is that the five dimensions are biologically based (Allik & McCrae, 2004; McCrae et al., 2000). That is, they are influenced by genes, brain structures, and other biological factors—not just culture and experience (Karwowski & Lebuda, 2016; Riccelli, Toschi, Nigro, Terracciano, & Passamonti, 2017). In fact, three decades of **twin and adoption studies** point to a genetic basis for the five factors (Boomsma et al., 2018; McCrae et al., 2000; Yamagata et al., 2006), with openness to experience showing the greatest degree of

CONNECTIONS **Chapters 1** and **7** describe twin studies, which indicate that genes play an important role in intelligence. Identical twins share 100% of their genes at conception, fraternal twins share about 50% of their genes, and adopted siblings are genetically very different. Comparing personality traits among these siblings can show the relative importance of genes and the environment.

Factor	Low		High
Openness	Conforming Uncreative Practical	⟷	Unconforming Creative Imaginative
Conscientiousness	Unreliable Lazy Spontaneous	⟷	Reliable Ambitious Punctual
Extraversion	Loner Quiet Reserved	⟷	Sociable Talkative Affectionate
Agreeableness	Rude Uncooperative Critical	⟷	Good-natured Trusting Helpful
Neuroticism	Calm Even-tempered Secure	⟷	Emotional Temperamental Worried

FIGURE 10.4
The Five-Factor Model of Personality
The mnemonic OCEAN will help you remember these factors.
Information from McCrae & Costa (1990).

five-factor model of personality A trait approach to explaining personality, including dimensions of openness to experience, conscientiousness, extraversion, agreeableness, and neuroticism; also known as "the Big Five."

TABLE 10.4 HERITABILITY AND THE BIG FIVE

Big Five Personality Dimensions	Heritability
Openness	.61
Conscientiousness	.44
Extraversion	.53
Agreeableness	.41
Neuroticism	.47

Information from Boomsma et al. (2018) and Jang, Livesley, & Vernon (1996).

Impact on Personality
Despite the general stability of inherited personality characteristics, environmental factors such as repeated head trauma can sometimes alter personality. BMX racer Dave Mirra suffered multiple head injuries during his 41 years of life, beginning with a car accident at age 19 and continuing throughout his biking career. This repetitive head trauma may be associated with personality changes his wife observed in the year leading to his suicide: "I started to notice changes in his mood. And then it quickly started to get worse," his wife told ESPN (Roenigk, 2016, May 24, para. 13). After his death, Mirra was diagnosed with chronic traumatic encephalopathy (CTE; Mather, 2016, May 24). Jamie Squire/Allsport/Getty Images.

heritability (McCrae et al., 2000; **Table 10.4**). Some researchers suggest that dog personalities can be described using similar dimensions, such as extraversion and neuroticism (Ley, Bennett, & Coleman, 2008). In fact, animals as diverse as squid and chimpanzees seem to display personality characteristics that are surprisingly similar to those observed in humans (Sinn & Moltschaniwskyj, 2005; Weiss et al., 2017). For example, some squid respond to stimuli "boldly or aggressively," while others act more shyly (Sinn & Moltschaniwskyj, 2005, p. 105). Could some squid be more extraverted than others?

Further evidence for the biological basis of the five factors comes from longitudinal studies, which suggest that these characteristics are generally stable over time, for periods as long as 40 years (Kandler et al., 2010; McCrae et al., 2000, 2013; Terracciano, Costa, & McCrae, 2006). This implies that nature shapes personality more than nurture. Environmental factors do play a role, however, as the five factors may change over the life span (Specht, Egloff, & Schmukle, 2011). As people age, they tend to score higher on agreeableness and lower on neuroticism, openness, extraversion, and conscientiousness. They also seem to become happier and more easygoing as the years go by, displaying more positive attitudes (Marsh, Nagengast, & Morin, 2013). But determining the stability of personality traits is not an easy task. It requires longitudinal research, and that entails following people over many years or decades, as *Scientific American* reports.

From the pages of SCIENTIFIC AMERICAN

ONCE DEPENDABLE, ALWAYS DEPENDABLE?

Some aspects of personality may be subject to change throughout life.

Many studies suggest that our personalities remain fairly stable, even over the course of decades. Yet a small but long-running study finds that traits related to dependability differ substantially between adolescence and late life. The findings raise new questions and highlight the challenges inherent in trying to track a person's defining characteristics over many years.

In the new research, published . . . in *Psychology and Aging,* researchers in the U.K. reached out to a group of 635 77-year-olds from Scotland who had taken part in a study when they were 14. Back then, their teachers had rated them on six personality characteristics related to dependability: self-confidence, perseverance, mood stability, conscientiousness, originality and desire to excel. Some 60 years later a total of 174 participants from the original cohort rated themselves on the same six traits and had a close friend or relative rate them as well.

Lead author Ian Deary, a psychologist at the University of Edinburgh, expected, based on earlier findings, that dependability scores might remain stable over time. In fact, he and his colleagues found no relation between ratings for dependability-related traits over the 63-year span studied. (Deary emphasizes that his findings apply only to these six traits—not overall personality.)

One of the study's strengths is that it covers such a long period, but this characteristic also makes the research challenging. Nate Hudson, a social psychologist at Michigan State University who was not involved in the study, points out that the lack of personality stability could be an artifact of having different people rate the participants. Ideally, the same person would rate a subject's personality at both time points when assessments were made.

In decades-spanning studies, many subjects go missing, die or choose not to participate in follow-up assessments. Deary and his colleagues enrolled only 174 of the original participants, a number that makes it tough to find subtle, but real, correlations in sets of data. "It is difficult to know from their study alone whether there is truly zero stability in personality from age 14 to 77," Hudson says. Deary's work moves the field forward—but more research is needed to get a full picture of how personality evolves throughout a lifetime. **Melinda Wenner Moyer. Reproduced with permission. Copyright © 2017 Scientific American, a division of Nature America, Inc. All rights reserved.**

TRAITS ARE US Personality traits impact your life in ways you may find surprising. Would you believe that creativity—a facet of the personality trait openness—has been linked to longer life span in some men? Apparently, creative thinking stimulates the brain by activating a variety of circuits and helps lower stress, which is good for overall health (Rodriguez, 2012; Turiano, Spiro, & Mroczek, 2012). Another personality trait, conscientiousness, has been associated with certain measures of success, including income level and life satisfaction (Duckworth, Weir, Tsukayama, & Kwok, 2012). Even the personality traits of other people, such as romantic partners, may impact you. One study suggests that marrying a conscientious person could benefit your career; conscientious husbands and wives support their spouses' professional lives by taking care of household chores, and by modeling conscientious behaviors, for example (Solomon & Jackson, 2014). How might such information be useful in everyday life?

HIS TRAITS, HER TRAITS? Men and women appear to differ with respect to the five factors, although there is not total agreement on how. A review of studies from 55 nations reported that, across cultures, women score higher on conscientiousness, extraversion, agreeableness, and neuroticism (Schmitt, Realo, Voracek, & Allik, 2008).

Mountains or Beach?
When given a choice between the mountains and the beach, introverts tend to show a preference for the mountains, while extroverts gravitate toward the beach. Mountains are perceived as quiet places to unwind, and beaches are associated with social activity (Oishi, Talhelm, & Lee, 2015).
Left: Roman Khomlyak/Shutterstock. Right: Vibrant Image Studio/Shutterstock.

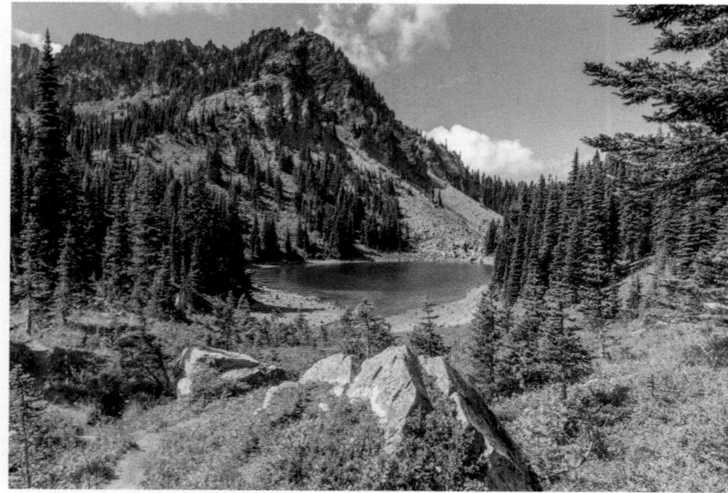

Men, on the other hand, seem to demonstrate greater openness to experience. These disparities are not extreme, however; the variation within groups of males and females is greater than the differences between the two groups. Critics suggest that using such rough measures of personality may conceal some of the true differences between men and women; in order to shed light on such disparities, they suggest investigating models that incorporate 10 to 20 traits rather than just 5 (Del Giudice, Booth, & Irwing, 2012).

Would you have predicted that women score higher on measures of agreeableness and neuroticism? Research suggests that some gender stereotypes do indeed contain a kernel of truth (Costa, Terracciano, & McCrae, 2001; Kajonius, & Johnson, 2018; Terracciano et al., 2005). Let's find out if this is the case for cultural stereotypes as well.

ACROSS THE WORLD

CULTURE OF PERSONALITY Have you heard the old joke about European stereotypes? It goes like this: In heaven, the chefs are French, the mechanics German, the lovers Italian, the police officers British, and the bankers Swiss. In hell, the cooks are British, the police officers German, the mechanics French, the lovers Swiss, and the bankers Italian (Mulvey, 2006, May 15). This joke plays upon what psychologists might call "national stereotypes," or preconceived notions about the personalities of people belonging to certain cultures. Are such stereotypes accurate?

PLEASE LEAVE YOUR STEREOTYPES AT THE BORDER!

To get to the bottom of this question, a group of researchers used personality tests to assess the Big Five traits of nearly 4,000 people from 49 cultures. When they compared the results of the personality tests to national stereotypes, they found no evidence that the stereotypes mirrored reality (Terracciano et al., 2005). Subsequent research supports this conclusion (McCrae et al., 2013). Not only are national stereotypes inaccurate and potentially racist; the type of thinking that drives them may have "far-reaching political consequences" (Sierp & Karner, 2017, para. 3). How do you think these stereotypes might impact relationships between nations, or between host countries and their immigrant communities?

TRAIT THEORIES: WHAT'S THE TAKEAWAY? As you can see from the example above, trait theories have facilitated research that sheds light on issues that might appear unrelated to psychology, like politics. Trait theory research can also lead to new insights on psychological phenomena, including psychological disorders. For example, we can understand personality traits as existing on continuum, with "normal" traits at one end and those associated with disorders at the other (DeYoung, Carey, Krueger, & Ross, 2016). This approach may help combat the stigma associated with mental illness, because it reveals that we all share these traits to some extent.

Like all perspectives in psychology, trait theories have limitations. One major criticism is that they fail to explain the origins of personality. What aspects of personality are innate, and which are environmental? How do unconscious processes, motivations, and development influence personality? Trait theories also tend to underestimate environmental influences on personality. As psychologist Walter Mischel points out, environmental circumstances can affect the way traits manifest themselves (Mischel & Shoda, 1995). A woman who is high on the openness factor may be nonconforming in college, but after she joins the military, her nonconformity assumes a new form. Critics also contend that the samples used in some Big Five cross-cultural studies are not representative. If most of the study participants are college students, for instance, the sample is not necessarily representative of the larger population. Finally, the five-factor model may not apply to all nonindustrialized cultures (Gurven, von Rueden, Massenkoff, Kaplan, & Lero Vie, 2013).

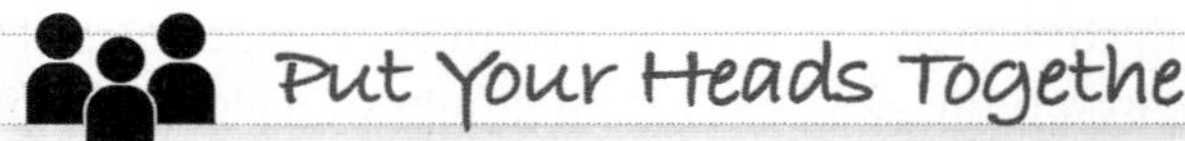

In your group, **A)** discuss the personality traits presented in this section, and what it means when we say that a trait exists "on a continuum." **B)** Choose three of the traits and write a brief scenario involving a fictitious college student who possesses these traits. **C)** Team up with another group and see if you can determine the traits used in each other's case studies.

Time to wrap up our discussion of the trait theories and move on to the intriguing topic of personality assessment. How do psychologists evaluate personality, what do these tests reveal, and can we be confident in the results?

show what you know

1. Total acceptance of children regardless of their behavior is known as:
   - **a.** conditions of worth.
   - **b.** repression.
   - **c.** the real self.
   - **d.** unconditional positive regard.
2. Name the Big Five traits and give one piece of evidence for their biological basis.
3. Julian Rotter proposed several cognitive aspects of personality, including ______, or one's beliefs about where responsibility or control exists.
   - **a.** reinforcement
   - **b.** locus of control
   - **c.** expectancy
   - **d.** reinforcement value
4. Reciprocal determinism refers to a complex multidirectional interaction among beliefs, behavior, and environment. Draw a diagram illustrating how reciprocal determinism explains one of your behavior patterns.
5. The relatively stable properties of personality are:
   - **a.** traits.
   - **b.** expectancies.
   - **c.** reinforcement values.
   - **d.** ego defense mechanisms.
6. According to ______, personality is the compilation of behaviors that have been shaped via reinforcement and other forms of conditioning.

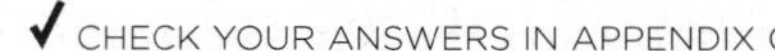
✓ CHECK YOUR ANSWERS IN APPENDIX C.

You Asked, Saifa Answers

http://qrs.ly/rx5a5f0

Has someone shown you unconditional love?

Personality Testing

To assess personality, psychologists rely on both subjective and objective tests. Subjective assessments are based on intuition, clinical judgment, opinion, or interpretation. Objective assessments are free of opinions, personal beliefs, expectations, and values because they are administered and evaluated using standardized procedures. Both approaches have strengths and limitations, which we will explore in the pages to come, but first let's get a handle on the qualities that render these tests effective—reliability and validity.

Are They Reliable, Valid?

LO 12 Explain why reliability and validity are important in personality assessment.

CONNECTIONS 

In **Chapter 7,** we discussed ways to determine the reliability of intelligence tests. In addition to test–retest reliability, we can split a test in half to see if the findings of the two halves agree. This type of reliability can be determined with personality assessment as well.

Reliability can refer to two aspects of an assessment. **Test–retest reliability** is how consistent results are when the same person takes the test more than once: Your scores should not change significantly from today to tomorrow on some measure of your personality. (We wouldn't expect aspects of your personality to change from day to day.) *Interrater reliability* refers to the degree of consistency across people scoring an assessment: With high interrater reliability, results are the same regardless of who scores the test. Validity is the other important quality of a personality test; a valid test is one that measures what it intends to measure. Let's say a psychologist develops an assessment for extraversion. In order for her test to be considered valid, it must yield results that are similar to already established and valid assessments of extraversion. If her test can predict future scores on tasks related to extraversion, this would indicate it has *predictive validity.*

CAREER CONNECTIONS

PERSONALITY TESTS AT WORK Personality assessments are used in many contexts, with profound implications. Psychologists use them to get to know their clients and diagnose mental disorders. Companies may enlist psychologists to administer these tests to job applicants and employees: *Does this person have what it takes to be a manager?* (For more information on these industrial and organizational psychologists, see Appendix B: Careers in Psychology.) Personality tests may also take place in legal settings, as one of many assessments used to evaluate the functioning of parents in custody disputes: *Is the mother depressed? Can she care for this child?* Do you see why it's so important for these tests to be valid and reliable?

In the next section, we will explore the major types of personality assessments used by psychologists: interviews, projective personality tests, and objective personality tests. Many of these are aligned with specific perspectives (psychoanalytic or behavioral, for example), but most psychologists use an integrative approach, drawing on multiple perspectives.

What Brings You Here Today?

Psychologists can gather a great deal of information about clients in face-to-face interviews. An unstructured, or open-ended, interview has no predetermined path, and may begin with a question such as "What brings you here today?" From there, the psychologist may gently direct the conversation in a way that helps uncover aspects of the client's personality. Semi-structured and structured **interviews**, on the other hand, employ specific paths of questioning that hinge on the respondent's answers. This format provides a more systematic means of comparing behaviors across individuals.

CONNECTIONS

When conducting interviews, psychologists must keep in mind that memories are malleable, a concept we discussed in **Chapter 6.** They should avoid posing questions that might lead to the misinformation effect, or the tendency for new or misleading information to distort memories.

One advantage of the interview is that it allows a psychologist to see a client in a relatively natural, realistic setting. Talking with a client face to face, a psychologist can observe facial expressions and body language, which can offer clues about what's going on inside. There are drawbacks, however. Interview subjects may lie to the interviewer (in some cases without even realizing it), spin the facts to misrepresent themselves, or share memories that are distorted or incomplete. Another source of error is the interviewer. Sometimes interviewers unknowingly lead the interview in a particular direction or interpret responses in a way that reinforces their beliefs about personality. Clients can also be influenced by interviewers' nonverbal language. As with surveys, the wording of questions can have a profound influence on the answers obtained. For example, these two questions may elicit incongruent responses: "Are you happy in your marriage?" versus "Are you unhappy in your marriage?"

Tell Me About Yourself
Psychologists assess personality using a variety of tools, including personal interviews. These face-to-face sessions range from open-ended and exploratory to highly structured.
Wavebreakmedia/Getty Images.

What Do *You* See? Projective Tests

LO 13 Define projective personality tests and evaluate their strengths and limitations.

It's a hot summer day and you're lying on the beach, gazing at the clouds. "What do you see?" you ask your friend. "I see the profile of a puppy," she replies. "That's funny," you say. "I see a clump of grapes."

You Asked, Saifa Answers

http://qrs.ly/rx5a5f0

Is there something in your personality that you have tried to change?

How can two people look at the same image and come away with such different impressions? Some would argue that it has a lot to do with personality. The idea that personality influences perception is the premise of **projective personality tests,** which psychologists use to explore characteristics that might not be accessible through interview or observation (**INFOGRAPHIC 10.3**). A person taking a projective test is presented with an ambiguous stimulus and then *projects* meaning onto it. The assumption is that people harbor anxiety and unresolved conflicts, often unconsciously, that may come out in their responses. The goal of the test administrator is to take the manifest content (what the person reports seeing) and try to understand its underlying meaning. Because these tests attempt to gather information indirectly, they are less threatening than other methods, and therefore provoke less resistance.

THE RORSCHACH INKBLOTS The best-known projective personality test is the Rorschach, originally developed by Swiss psychiatrist Hermann Rorschach (1884–1922). Today's psychologists typically use Rorschach inkblots with a comprehensive coding system introduced in the 1970s (Exner, 1980, 1986).

Here is a rough description of how the test is administered: A psychologist hands you a series of cards covered in odd-looking blotches of ink—five black-and-white, five in color. Presenting the cards one by one, the psychologist asks you to report what you see. The images you describe and the details you report will be systematically compared to answers given by other test takers who have known personality characteristics and diagnoses. Do you see bears playing patty cake? Seeing animals in motion might be interpreted as a sign of rashness. Are you concentrating on the black areas? This could suggest a feeling of melancholy or sadness (Lilienfeld et al., 2005).

THE THEMATIC APPERCEPTION TEST (TAT) Developed in the mid-1930s by Henry Murray and his colleagues, the Thematic Apperception Test (TAT) consists of 20 cards showing black-and-white illustrations of ambiguous scenes. Test takers are asked to tell a story about each card. These stories typically include a description of the people pictured, including their emotions and thoughts, an explanation of the events leading up to the scene, and a conclusion to the story. The TAT is based on the premise that test takers project underlying conflicts onto the ambiguous stimuli; the test administrator's job is to unearth those conflicts.

PROJECTIVE PERSONALITY TESTS: WHAT'S THE TAKEAWAY? Perhaps the greatest strength of projective tests is their unstructured format, which allows test takers to speak openly, honestly, and freely. But these tests are time-consuming, and the process of scoring and interpreting their results is somewhat subjective. As noted in prior chapters, humans are prone to a **variety of biases** and cognitive errors that can interfere with their ability to accurately assess people and situations. Test administrators may score differently, and test takers may get inconsistent results when they take the test on different occasions. Thus, projective tests may lack both interrater and test–retest reliability. The comprehensive scoring system for the Rorschach inkblots has resolved some reliability concerns, but the issue of validity remains. Many critics suggest that projective tests are not valid because they do not measure what they claim to measure (Schultz & Schultz, 2017). For these reasons, projective tests should be used cautiously, especially in nonclinical situations such as job interviews.

You may not have Rorschach inkblots at your disposal, but surely you use other tools to size up the personalities of new people. Perhaps you observe the way they interact with others, or how much they tolerate uncertainty, for example. Did it ever occur to you that social media might be a good place to look for clues?

CONNECTIONS

In **Chapters 0** and **7,** we noted that people are prone to the hindsight bias, or the "I knew it all along" feeling. The hindsight bias is just one type of bias that can interfere with personality assessment and other forms of data collection.

projective personality tests Assessments used to explore characteristics that might not be accessible through interview or observation; the test taker is presented with ambiguous stimuli and then projects meaning onto them.

Examining the Unconscious: Projective Personality Tests

The psychoanalytic perspective holds that some aspects of personality exist beneath conscious awareness. Projective personality tests seek to uncover these characteristics. Ideas and anxieties in the unconscious will appear in descriptions of ambiguous stimuli, revealing previously hidden conflicts that the test administrator can evaluate.

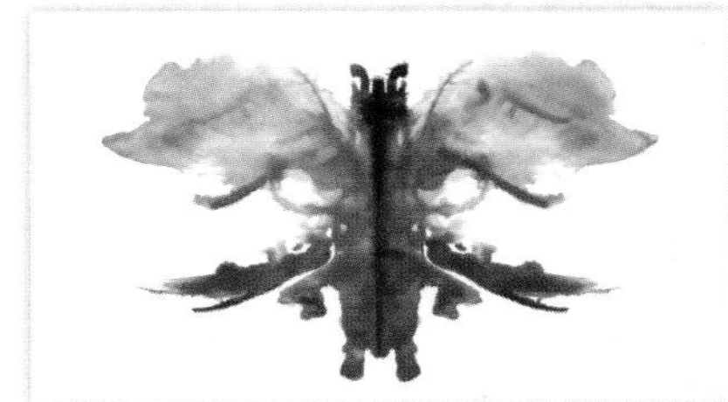

Test administration

The best-known projective tests, the Thematic Apperception Test (TAT) and the Rorschach Inkblot Test, are both conducted in the same way (Lilienfeld, Wood, & Garb, 2005): The test administrator presents a series of picture cards, one at a time, then records the participant's responses. The administrator also notes behaviors such as gestures, tone of voice, and facial expressions.

The standard administration of the TAT presents a selection of 5 to 12 cards. The participant is asked to tell a story for each scene, including what the characters are feeling and how the story might end.

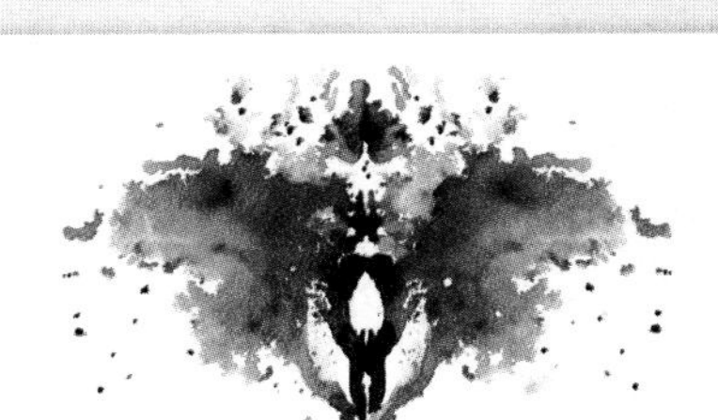

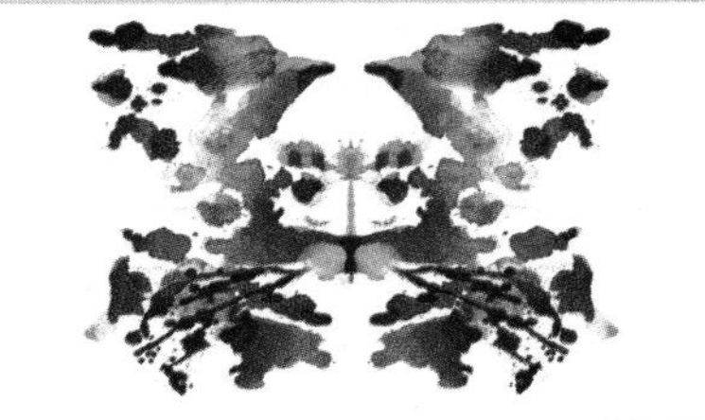

The Rorschach has 10 cards with symmetrical inkblots, 5 in color and 5 in black-and-white. The participant is prompted to give multiple responses for each image, identifying details.

Test Interpretation

To help decrease the influence of administrator bias in interpretation of projective tests, comprehensive systems have been developed to standardize scoring and interpretation of some tests. For the Rorschach Inkblot Test, responses are coded on dimensions such as location (whole inkblot or one detail), themes (unique or consistent), and thought processes (Erdberg, 1990). The use of a comprehensive system allows administrators to compare typical and atypical responses.

PARTICIPANT RESPONSES

"Looks like two people."

"The people are fighting over something."

"Or they're carrying something heavy together."

"Maybe it's one person looking in a mirror."

"I also see a butterfly."

These sample responses are representative of this type of inkblot (Burstein & Loucks, 1989).

EXAMINER RESPONSES

Participant mentions the typical response of two figures.

Suggestion that the people are fighting could indicate issues with aggression or an aggressive personality.

Focus on individuals working together could represent a need for social connection.

However, seeing one person alone could indicate social anxiety.

Now participant switches to a specific part of the image, which could also show that he is uncomfortable thinking about others, perhaps related to introversion.

Credits: Various black and white picture cards depicting an emotional situation, for the Thematic. Apperception Test (TAT), © Spencer Grant/PhotoEdit — All rights reserved; Rorschach Test images: Top right: xpixel/Shutterstock; Center: MadamSaffa/Shutterstock; Bottom right: Alvor/Shutterstock; Left bottom: Golden Shrimp/Shutterstock.

SOCIAL MEDIA AND PSYCHOLOGY

IT'S WRITTEN ALL OVER YOUR FACEBOOK What does your Twitter profile reveal about your personality? According to one study on the Big Five, Twitter users high in conscientiousness tend to select profile photos that convey positive emotions (a picture of themselves smiling); meanwhile, extraverts seem to favor colorful pictures that project youth (photos that make them look younger, or show them with younger people); and those high on openness often skip the headshots and choose artistic photos with high "aesthetic quality" (Liu, Preotiuc-Pietro, Samani, Moghaddam, & Ungar, 2016). As this study suggests, social media profiles can indicate a great deal about the personalities of their owners (Back et al., 2010; Buffardi & Campbell, 2008). This could work to your advantage if the personality traits you hope to project are positive, but not so much if you are narcissistic. Narcissism is a personality trait associated with vanity, self-absorption, and feelings of superiority and entitlement. People who post narcissistic status updates are likely to be perceived as "less likeable, less successful, and less worthy of friendship" (Kauten, Lui, Stary, & Barry, 2015, p. 244). Many narcissistic people flock to Instagram, a photo-sharing platform where they can easily edit photos to promote themselves (Sheldon & Bryant, 2016). What other social media platforms might attract narcissistic individuals?

DO NARCISSISTS FLOCK TO INSTAGRAM?

"But . . . your Facebook profile says you're a vegetarian!"

Dominique Deckmyn/CartoonStock.com.

Objective Tests

Describe objective personality tests and evaluate their strengths and limitations.

Unlike the projective tests, which tend to be open-ended and subjective, *objective personality tests* use a standard set of questions with answer choices (true/false, multiple choice, circle the number) and have clear scoring instructions that are identical for everyone taking the test. Often, the scores are calculated by a computer. These tests are called *objective* because the results are assessed in a standardized way and mostly free of personal bias. In addition to being convenient, objective tests have a solid base of evidence supporting their reliability and validity (Anastasi & Urbina, 1997). Some focus on a particular personality characteristic or trait, such as locus of control; others assess a group of traits like the Big Five. For example, the Big Five Inventory-2 (BFI-2) is a short assessment that is self-administered and designed to be easily understood and completed quickly, reducing testing fatigue in the test taker (Soto & John, 2017).

Personality Tests in the Workplace In addition to running criminal background checks and credit scores, some employers use objective personality assessments to screen job applicants. For example, police departments use assessments such as the MMPI-2-RF to help predict performance on the job (Detrick & Chibnall, 2014; Kaul, 2017, July 17). CSP_mybaitshop/AGE Fotostock.

THE MMPI The most commonly used objective personality test is the Minnesota Multiphasic Personality Inventory (MMPI–2-RF; Ben-Porath, 2012, Butcher & Rouse, 1996). This self-report questionnaire consists of 338 statements with three answer choices: "true," "false," or "cannot say." Examples of these statements include "I often wake up rested and ready to go" and "I want to work as a teacher." Since the original purpose of the MMPI was to identify disorders and abnormal behavior, it included 10 clinical scales (cynicism and antisocial behavior, for example). The assessment also has validity measures, including the Lie Scale and the Defensiveness Scale, to help determine whether test takers are trying to appear more disturbed or healthier than they really are. The MMPI is used in a variety of contexts, including custody disputes, but many feel its application outside of therapeutic settings is inappropriate.

16PF The Sixteen Personality Factor Questionnaire (16PF), originally created by Raymond Cattell and based on his trait theory, consists of 185 questions. The results are used to construct a profile indicating where the respondent falls along the continuum for each of the 16 dimensions (Cattell, 1973a). Looking at **Figure 10.5,** you can see how airline pilots and writers compare on these 16 factors.

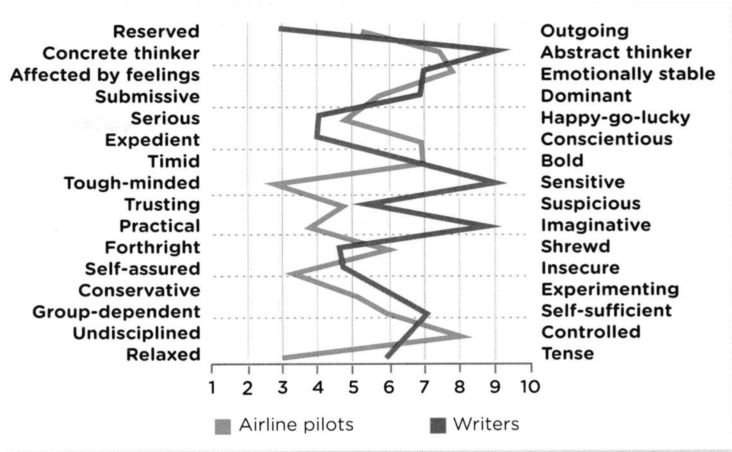

FIGURE 10.5

Example Profiles Generated by the 16PF

On Cattell's 16PF, writers appear to be more reserved, sensitive, and imaginative than airline pilots. Pilots, on the other hand, tend to fall on the tough-minded end of the continuum. Are you surprised that they also appear to be more relaxed?

Information from Cattell (1973b).

MYERS–BRIGGS One very popular objective personality assessment is the Myers–Briggs Type Indicator (MBTI) (Briggs & Myers, 1998). Katherine Briggs and her daughter Isabel Briggs-Myers created this assessment in the 1940s. It designates a personality "type" using the following four dimensions: extraversion (E) versus introversion (I); sensing (S) versus intuiting (N); thinking (T) versus feeling (F); and judgment (J) versus perception (P). For example, someone characterized as ISTP would be introverted, rely on the senses (rather than intuition) to understand the environment, favor logic over emotion, and focus on using perception as opposed to judgment.

Problems arise when assessments incorporate somewhat vague descriptions of personality traits. Some would even liken it to the Barnum effect, which was named after P. T. Barnum (1810–1891), the American showman and founder of the Barnum and Bailey Circus. Barnum was famous for his ability to convince people he could read minds. Essentially, he did this by making generally complimentary and vague statements that could be true about anyone. (*You are creative and work well with others and you sometimes procrastinate, but ultimately you get the job done.*) The MBTI is similar in this respect, providing personality type descriptions that are "generally flattering and sufficiently vague so that most people will accept the statements as true of themselves" (Pittenger, 1993, November, p. 6). Although the MBTI is quite popular, especially in the "corporate world," the supporting research is weak, especially as it relates to job performance, career choices, and other professional matters (Lussier, 2018; Pittenger, 2005). Because test results don't always correlate with job success, the validity of the MBTI is questionable. This assessment can also fall short when it comes to test–retest reliability; a person may take the test twice and end up with different results each time (Hunsley, Lee, & Wood, 2003; Pittenger, 2005).

OBJECTIVE PERSONALITY TESTS: WHAT'S THE TAKEAWAY? We have noted specific criticisms of the MMPI-2-RF and Myers–Briggs tests, but objective assessments have other, more general, drawbacks. Many of these tests include some sort of mechanism for checking the validity of the test taker's answers, but people may still lie, particularly when something personal is at stake, like a job or child custody decision. Social desirability can also influence the results, as test takers may unintentionally answer questions in a way that makes them "look better" to others. Even if test takers try to be honest, self-reports are inevitably biased (can anyone truly see themselves objectively?). Finally, the standardization of these tests may come at a cost, as they have been criticized for lacking flexibility and failing to appreciate the diversity of individual experience. Despite the many criticisms, tests like the MMPI-2-RF are the best tools we have to evaluate personality.

AUTHENTIC AND HONEST You may be wondering why we chose to feature the story of an intersex man in this chapter on personality. Wouldn't Sean Saifa Wall's story be a better fit for one of the chapters that cover gender and sexuality? We don't believe that gender nonconforming people should be confined to discussions of sex and gender. We chose to include Saifa's story here because we were captivated by him, and his rare ability to reflect on his personality development in an authentic and honest way.

show what you know

1. ______________ personality tests present ambiguous stimuli to the test taker. The administrator interprets the responses to uncover underlying personality characteristics.
   a. Objective   c. 16PF
   b. Projective   d. Myers-Briggs

2. A psychologist gives a client several personality tests to help her choose a career path. What might the consequences be if the tests are not valid? How would the client know if the tests were reliable?

3. Critics of objective personality tests report that the ______________ of these tests does not allow for flexibility and fails to consider the diversity of individual experiences.
   a. standardization   c. neuroticism
   b. extraversion   d. factor analysis

✓ CHECK YOUR ANSWERS IN APPENDIX C.

YOUR SCIENTIFIC WORLD is a new application-based feature appearing in every chapter. In these online activities, you will take on role-playing scenarios that encourage you to think critically and apply your knowledge of psychological science to solve a real-world problem. For example: Have you ever taken a personality quiz? This activity allows you to explore your personality traits and consider careers that might be well-suited for your personality. But, how valid and reliable are these assessments? You can access Your Scientific World activities in LaunchPad. Have fun!

SUMMARY OF CONCEPTS

LO 1 Define personality. (p. 367)

Personality refers to the unique, core set of characteristics that influence the way one thinks, acts, and feels—characteristics many psychologists would agree are consistent and enduring throughout the life span.

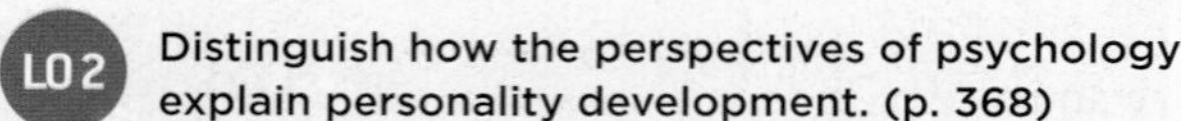

LO 2 Distinguish how the perspectives of psychology explain personality development. (p. 368)

The psychoanalytic perspective suggests that personality development is strongly influenced by early childhood experiences and unconscious conflicts, many of which are sexual or aggressive in nature. The humanistic perspective suggests that humans are innately good and in control of their destinies, and these positive aspects of human nature drive the development of personality. The behavioral perspective explains how reinforcement and other learning processes shape personality. The social-cognitive perspective suggests that personality results from reinforcement, relationships, and other environmental factors (social) and patterns of thinking (cognitive). Trait theories are primarily concerned with describing personality and predicting behavior.

LO 3 Illustrate Freud's models for describing the mind. (p. 371)

Psychoanalysis refers to Freud's views of personality and his system of psychotherapy and tools for exploring the unconscious. According to his topographical model, our personalities and behaviors result from mental processes occurring at three levels: the conscious, preconscious, and unconscious. The structural model of the mind describes the functions of the mind's components. The id is the most primitive component, and its activities occur at the unconscious level. As an infant grows, the ego develops from the id. The ego manipulates situations, plans for the future, solves problems, and makes decisions to satisfy the needs of the id. The superego develops last and guides our behavior to follow the rules of society, parents, or other authority figures.

LO 4 Summarize Freud's use of psychosexual stages to explain personality. (p. 375)

According to Freud, the development of sexuality and personality proceeds through psychosexual stages, which all children experience as they mature into adulthood. Each psychosexual stage is associated with an erogenous zone as well as a conflict that must be dealt with. If the conflict is not successfully resolved, the child may suffer from a fixation and get "stuck" in that particular stage, unable to progress smoothly through the remaining stages. The progression includes the oral stage, anal stage, phallic stage, latency period, and genital stage.

LO 5 Explain how the neo-Freudians' theories of personality differ from Freud's. (p. 378)

Some of Freud's followers disagreed with his intense emphasis on early childhood experiences, aggression, and sexuality, and developed their own theories. Adler proposed that humans are conscious and intentional in their behaviors. Jung suggested that we are driven by a psychological energy (as opposed to sexual energy) that encourages positive growth, self-understanding, and balance. Horney emphasized the role of relationships between children and their caregivers, not erogenous zones and psychosexual stages.

LO 6 Discuss Rogers' view of self-concept, ideal self, and unconditional positive regard. (p. 382)

Rogers suggested that humans have an innate urge to move toward situations and people that provide opportunities for growth, and away from those that inhibit growth. Self-concept is knowledge of one's strengths, abilities, behavior patterns, and temperament. Rogers believed that individuals develop an ideal self, or self-concept they fervently wish to achieve. Ideally, caregivers should show unconditional positive regard, or total acceptance of children regardless of their behavior. People need to feel completely accepted and valued for who they are, not for what they do.

LO 7 Use the behavioral perspective to explain personality development. (p. 384)

According to the behavioral perspective, personality is a collection of behaviors, all of which have been shaped through a lifetime of learning. Some behaviorists use learning principles to explain personality, including those of operant conditioning and observational learning.

LO 8 Summarize Rotter's view of personality. (p. 384)

Rotter suggested that some aspects of personality cannot be directly observed. He believed a key component of personality is locus of control, which is a pattern of beliefs regarding where responsibility or control for an outcome exists. Rotter explored how these beliefs can influence behavior. Expectancy refers to the predictions we make about the consequences or outcomes of our behavior.

LO 9 Discuss how Bandura uses the social-cognitive perspective to explain personality. (p. 384)

Bandura rejected the notion that psychologists should only focus on observable behavior; he realized behavior is determined by cognition as well as reinforcers and other environmental influences. The social-cognitive perspective suggests that personality results from reinforcement, relationships, and other environmental factors (social) and patterns of thinking (cognitive). Bandura refers to this multidirectional interaction among beliefs, behaviors, and the environment as reciprocal determinism.

LO 10 Distinguish trait theories from other personality theories. (p. 386)

Traits are the relatively stable properties that describe elements of personality. The trait theories are different from other personality theories in that they focus less on explaining why and how personality develops, and more on describing personality and predicting behaviors. Allport created a comprehensive list of traits to help operationalize the terminology used in personality research. Cattell grouped the traits into two categories: surface traits and source traits. He used factor analysis to uncover the relationships among surface traits, resulting in 16 personality factors, and developed the Sixteen Personality Factor Questionnaire (16PF) to measure them. Eysenck proposed that we could describe personalities using three dimensions: introversion–extraversion, neuroticism, and psychoticism. He also worked to understand the biological basis of these dimensions.

LO 11 Identify the biological roots of the five-factor model of personality. (p. 388)

The five-factor model of personality, also known as the Big Five, includes the following factors: openness to experience, conscientiousness, extraversion, agreeableness, and neuroticism. These characteristics are stable over time and shaped by genes, brain structures, and other biological factors—not just culture and experience.

LO 12 Explain why reliability and validity are important in personality assessment. (p. 392)

Reliability generally refers to two aspects of a personality assessment: test–retest reliability and interrater reliability. Test–retest reliability is consistency of results when the same person takes a test more than once. Interrater reliability refers to the consistency across people scoring an assessment. Validity refers to the degree to which an assessment measures what it is intended to measure. A valid test must yield results similar to established assessments.

LO 13 Define projective personality tests and evaluate their strengths and limitations. (p. 393)

Projective tests are based on the premise that personality influences perceptions. The test taker is presented with an ambiguous stimulus and then prompted to project meaning onto it. The administrator takes the manifest content (what the person reports seeing) and tries to understand its underlying meaning. Because these tests attempt to gather information indirectly, they are less threatening than other methods, and therefore provoke less resistance. Projective tests are time-consuming, and the process of scoring and interpreting their results is somewhat subjective, which can lead to problems with reliability. Some of the best-known projective tests are the Rorschach Inkblot Test and Thematic Apperception Test (TAT).

Describe objective personality tests and evaluate their strengths and limitations. (p. 396)

Objective personality tests comprise a standard set of questions with answer choices (true/false, multiple choice, circle the number). These tests are called objective because the results are assessed in a standardized way and mostly free of personal bias. But these assessments are not perfect. Test takers may be dishonest or unintentionally answer questions in a way that makes them "look better" (social desirability). Two commonly used objective personality tests are the Minnesota Multiphasic Personality Inventory (MMPI–2) and the Sixteen Personality Factor Questionnaire (16PF).

KEY TERMS

archetypes, p. 379
collective unconscious, p. 379
ego, p. 372
ego defense mechanisms, p. 373
expectancy, p. 384
five-factor model of personality, p. 388
fixation, p. 375
id, p. 371
ideal self, p. 382
Oedipus complex, p. 376
personality, p. 367
pleasure principle, p. 372
projective personality tests, p. 394
psychoanalysis, p. 370
psychosexual stages, p. 375
reality principle, p. 372
reciprocal determinism, p. 386
self-concept, p. 382
self-efficacy, p. 386
social-cognitive perspective, p. 384
source traits, p. 387
superego, p. 372
surface traits, p. 387
traits, p. 386
trait theories, p. 386
unconditional positive regard, p. 382
unconscious, p. 371

TEST PREP ARE YOU READY?

1. The ____________ perspective of personality suggests that personality is shaped by interactions with the environment, specifically through learning.
   a. trait
   b. humanistic
   c. biological
   d. behavioral
2. Freud's topographical model suggests our personalities and behaviors result from:
   a. components of the mind, including the id, ego, and superego.
   b. the reality principle.
   c. the pleasure principle.
   d. mental processes that occur at three levels of consciousness.
3. According to Freud, all children progress through ____________ as they mature into adulthood, but if their progress is not smooth, they may suffer from a ____________.
   a. psychosexual stages; fixation
   b. three levels of consciousness; superego
   c. defense mechanisms; locus of control
   d. erogenous zones; reciprocal determinism
4. Rogers believed that problems can develop when a person's self-concept is ____________ with his experiences in the world.
   a. incongruent
   b. in harmony
   c. self-actualized
   d. conditioned
5. A person high in ____________ strongly believes she will succeed in a particular situation even if she has experienced failure under similar circumstances.
   a. reciprocal determinism
   b. reinforcers
   c. self-efficacy
   d. source traits
6. ____________ refers to the unique, core set of characteristics that influence how we think, act, and feel.
   a. Personality
   b. Ego defense mechanism
   c. Reciprocal determinism
   d. Expectancy
7. Cattell proposed there are 16 personality dimensions that can be considered primary ____________, and these are the product of both nature and nurture.
   a. source traits
   b. conditions of worth
   c. Big Five traits
   d. defense mechanisms
8. Evidence for the biological basis of the five-factor model includes:
   a. the instability of personality characteristics over time.
   b. the stability of personality characteristics over time.
   c. the fact that there are no gender differences in personality characteristics.
   d. the absence of heritability of personality characteristics.
9. ____________ can be determined when someone takes the same personality assessment more than once and the results do not change.
   a. Heritability
   b. Effectiveness
   c. Reliability
   d. Validity
10. The neo-Freudians agree with Freud on many issues, but tend to disagree with which of the following?
    a. his belief in the positive aspects of human nature
    b. his belief in the importance of personality growth throughout life
    c. his intense emphasis on sex and aggression
    d. his notion that caregivers cannot shape personality

11. Think about a friend who is outgoing. How would a behaviorist explain the development of your friend's personality characteristic?

12. How do the humanistic and social-cognitive perspectives of personality differ?

13. Describe the Oedipus complex and Electra complex. How are they different?

14. Consider your current performance in your college courses. Name three causes for your successes that represent an internal locus of control. Name three causes for your successes that represent an external locus of control.

15. Describe the differences between objective and subjective personality assessments.

✓ CHECK YOUR ANSWERS IN APPENDIX C.

Go to **LaunchPad** or **Achieve: Read & Practice** to test your understanding with **LearningCurve**.

CHAPTER

11

Courtesy Alexa Antoni.

Social Psychology

An Introduction to Social Psychology

IS THE SWIPE RIGHT? It was an unusually hot evening in Escondido, California. Twenty-six-year-old Alexa Antoni was sweaty from playing kickball with some teenagers she worked with at San Pasqual Academy, a residential school for foster children. She was already running late for her first date with Dennis Conforti, a 30-year-old Marine she had met through the mobile dating app Tinder. "I almost cancelled because I was so gross and icky," Alexa recalls. Approaching the meeting place, Alexa suddenly felt unsure. It was a small restaurant tucked in between an abandoned car lot and a tire sales place: *Oh my gosh, he's going to kill me!*

Dennis was sitting in the back corner, sipping a drink and listening to the band. The first thing Alexa noticed was how relaxed and happy he appeared. "I remember he wasn't nervous," says Alexa. "It was almost like he was there enjoying it even without me being there, which was refreshing." Dennis dressed nicely, but not in a flashy way, and he had tranquil brown eyes.

The date went well. Alexa appreciated how Dennis was kind to the waitress without being a flirt. He was witty and attractive, and exuded a calm self-confidence. Alexa hoped to see Dennis again and learn more about him. But after a brief text exchange, things just "fizzled out." What was the story with Dennis?

What Is Social Psychology?

As it turned out, Dennis was equally interested in Alexa. "She was smart, beautiful," he recalls. "I really liked her." But in between a full-time job in the Marine Corps, classes at Palomar College, family obligations, and a 4-week-old puppy, Dennis barely had any free time.

Dennis, 30
less than a mile away
Interested in meeting new people to be friends or whatever comes from it. I run, workout, ride, read and usually up for anything adventurous.
Snap: kcco121
165 Friends For Common Connections
We compare your Facebook friends with those of your matches to display any

Alexa, 27
Clinical Therapist
108 miles away
California grown
New York educated
Adventure seeker
Recently relocated
Pretty terrible at using tinder
Old fashioned kind of girl, not interested in hookups :)

The Profile Photos
These are the Tinder profile pictures that helped bring together Dennis (left) and Alexa (right, at left in photo). Courtesy Alexa Antoni.

Not knowing all these details, Alexa could only speculate about the reasons Dennis reacted to her this way. Trying to understand people's actions, thoughts, and feelings in response to others is something we all do on a regular basis. This is also a major area of interest for those who study *social psychology.*

LO 1 Define social psychology and identify how it differs from sociology.

Social psychology is the study of human cognition, emotion, and **behavior in relation to others**. Look carefully, and you will see discussions related to social psychology popping up throughout this book. In Chapter 3, for example, we journeyed into the world of Mandy Harvey, a jazz singer who is completely deaf. How might Mandy's social interactions with band members differ from those of a singer with normal hearing? Then there was Clive Wearing from Chapter 6. How do you suppose Clive's devastating memory loss affects his relationships? Social psychologists strive to answer these types of questions.

CONNECTIONS
The focus of **Chapter 10** is personality, the unique, core set of characteristics that influence the way one thinks, acts, and feels. Studying personality helps us understand behavior patterns in general. Social psychology explores how behaviors are shaped by interactions with other people.

Many times we have emphasized the importance of the biopsycho*social* perspective, which recognizes the biological, psychological, and social factors underlying human behavior. This chapter focuses on the third aspect of that triad: social forces.

HOW IS IT DIFFERENT FROM SOCIOLOGY? Students often ask how social psychology differs from the field of *sociology.* The answer is simple: Social psychology explores the way individuals behave, think, and feel in relation to others and groups (Gollwitzer & Bargh, 2018). Meanwhile, sociology centers on examining the groups themselves—their cultures, societies, and subcultures. A social psychologist studying religion might focus on the relationship between individual congregants and their spiritual leaders. A sociologist would more likely investigate religious practices, rituals, and organizations.

RESEARCH WITH A TWIST Like all psychologists, social psychologists use a variety of research methods, including surveys, naturalistic observation, and the experimental method. But their studies sometimes have an added twist of deception.

social psychology The study of human cognition, emotion, and behavior in relation to others.

Note: Quotations attributed to Julius Achon and Alexa and Dennis Conforti are personal communications.

CONNECTIONS

In **Chapter 1,** we discussed deception in the context of the experimental method. In a double-blind study, neither participants nor researchers administering the treatment know who is getting the placebo and who is receiving the real treatment. Participants are told ahead of time they might receive a placebo.

In some cases, **deception** is necessary because people do not always behave naturally when they know they are being observed. Participants may try to conform to expectations, or do just the opposite—behave in ways they believe will contradict the researchers' predictions. Suppose a team of researchers is studying facial expressions in social settings. If participants know that every glance and grimace is being analyzed, they may feel self-conscious and display atypical facial expressions. Instead of revealing the real focus of their investigation, researchers might lead participants to believe they are studying something else, like problem solving. That way, they can examine the behavior of interest (facial expressions in social settings) more naturally.

CONNECTIONS

In **Chapter 1,** we discussed debriefing, which occurs after the participant's involvement in the study has ended. In a debriefing session, researchers provide participants with useful information about the study—information that couldn't be shared beforehand. Sometimes this means informing participants of any deception or manipulation that was used.

Social psychology studies often involve *confederates,* or people secretly working for the researchers. Playing the role of participants, experimenters, or simply bystanders, confederates say what the researchers tell them to say and do what the researchers tell them to do. They are, unknown to the participants, just part of the researchers' experimental manipulation.

In most cases, the deception is not kept secret forever. Researchers **debrief** their participants at the end of a study, that is, review aspects of the research initially kept under wraps. Even after learning they were deceived, many participants say they would be willing to take part in subsequent psychology experiments (Blatchley & O'Brien, 2007). In one survey concerning medical research, respondents said deception is appropriate as long as there isn't "outright lying" (Pugh, Kahane, Maslen, & Savulescu, 2016). Debriefing is also a time when researchers make sure that participants were not harmed or upset by their involvement in a study. We should note that all psychology research affiliated with colleges and universities must be approved by an Institutional Review Board (IRB) to ensure that no harm will come from participation. This requirement is partly a reaction to early studies involving extreme deception and manipulation—studies that many viewed as dehumanizing and unethical. Psychologists agree that deception is only acceptable if there is no other way to study the topic of interest. We will describe many examples of such research in the upcoming pages, but first let's familiarize ourselves with some basic concepts in social psychology. We'll get started with a little help from Dennis and Alexa.

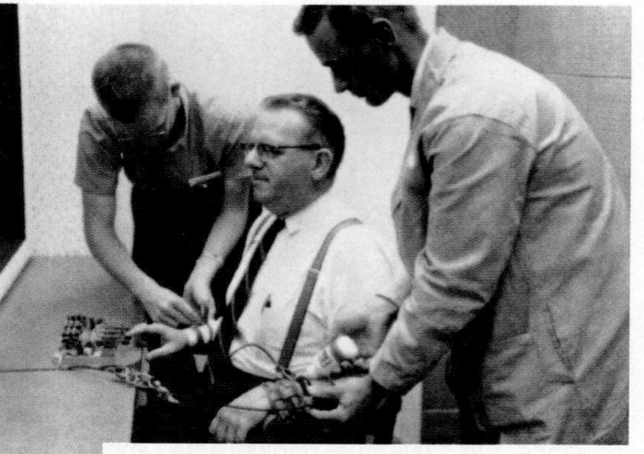

In the Name of Science
A research confederate (center) in Stanley Milgram's classic experiment is strapped to a table and hooked up to electrodes. Participants in this study were led to believe they were administering electrical shocks to the confederate when, in reality, he was just pretending to be shocked. This allowed the researchers to study how far participants would go in applying shocks—without anyone actually being hurt. From the film *Obedience* © 1968 by Stanley Milgram; © renewed 1993 by Alexandra Milgram, and distributed by Alexander Street Press.

DATE TWO: MAKE IT OR BREAK IT About two weeks after their first date, Dennis finally texted Alexa, hoping she wouldn't think he was a total jerk for waiting so long. Alexa responded, but she had already been on another Tinder date with a different person and did not have high expectations for date #2 with Dennis. Their second meeting was a big success, though, and they soon began connecting on a deeper level. "We were able to kind of ask the tough questions," says Dennis, who told Alexa he had been married, and explained some of the reasons for his divorce. Alexa described her motivation for becoming a social worker and helping foster children. "She's just a very kind-hearted person," says Dennis, who was beginning to see the potential for a relationship. He asked Alexa for another dinner date, but this time at his house so she could meet his French bulldog puppy Brutus. This made Alexa feel a bit on edge: "Usually . . . if a guy invites you over they are expecting a lot." 

Why Do People Do the Things They Do?

LO 2 Define social cognition and describe how we use attributions to explain behavior.

Alexa barely knew Dennis, but he seemed like a gentle soul—or perhaps a really good actor. On a conscious level, she was processing all sorts of information she had picked up by observing Dennis, namely through his words and behaviors. There was also some information processing occurring outside of her awareness. It is possible that Dennis reminded her of someone she knew—perhaps a family member—and that sense of familiarity made her more inclined to trust him. Ultimately, she accepted his invitation.

Alexa's decision relied on **social cognition**—the way one thinks about others, attends to social information, and uses this information in life, both consciously and unconsciously. You use **social cognition** all the time, whether you are exchanging knowledge with classmates, working together to understand a difficult concept, or coming to an agreement about something (Baumeister, Maranges, & Vohs, 2018). One critical component of social cognition is the process of making *attributions,* or interpreting the behavior of others.

WHAT ARE ATTRIBUTIONS? As you probably know, the "dating game" typically involves a lot of guesswork about other people's behavior: *Why did Dennis take so long to text? What did Alexa mean by that ?* These kinds of questions have relevance for all human relationships, not just the romantic kind. Just think about how much time you spend wondering why people do the things they do. The "answers" you come up with are called **attributions.** *Why is my friend in such a bad mood?* you ask yourself. Your attribution might be, *Maybe he just got some bad news* or *Perhaps he is hungry.* Attributions are the beliefs we develop to explain human behaviors and characteristics, as well as situations. When psychologists characterize attributions, they use the term *observer* to identify the person making the attribution, and *actor* to identify the person exhibiting a behavior of interest. If Alexa is trying to figure out why Dennis took so long to text, then Alexa is the observer and Dennis is the actor.

TYPES OF ATTRIBUTIONS Psychologists often describe attributions along three dimensions: controllable–uncontrollable, stable–unstable, and internal–external. Let's see how these might apply to attributions relating to Alexa and Dennis:

Controllable–uncontrollable dimension: Alexa was 15 minutes late to her first date with Dennis. If Dennis assumed it was because she got stuck in unavoidable traffic, we would say he was making an uncontrollable attribution. If he assumed that Alexa's lateness resulted from factors within her control, such as how fast she drove or what time she left work, then the attribution would be controllable.

Stable–unstable dimension: According to Alexa, Dennis turned out to be a "pretty good cook." If she inferred that his success in the kitchen stemmed from a longtime interest in cooking, the attribution would be stable—the cause is long-lasting. If she thought it resulted from a short-lived inspiration after watching a recent episode of *Hell's Kitchen,* then her attribution would be unstable—the cause is temporary.

Internal–external dimension: Why did Alexa have bad luck on Tinder before she met Dennis? If Dennis thought it was because most guys on Tinder are creepy, this would be an external attribution, because the cause of the problem resides outside of Alexa. If he believed Alexa was unsuccessful because she was reluctant to explore new relationships, this would be an internal attribution—the cause lies within Alexa.

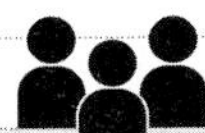

Put Your Heads Together

Suppose you have a classmate who frequently misses class. In your group, explain these absences using **A)** several attributions that are external, uncontrollable, and unstable, and **B)** several attributions that are internal, controllable, and stable. **C)** Consider how your emotional reactions might differ if you think the cause of your classmate's absenteeism is **A)** versus **B)**.

Now that we have explored various types of attributions, let's see how they relate to your life online.

CONNECTIONS

In **Chapter 7,** we defined cognition as the mental activity associated with obtaining, storing, converting, and using knowledge. Thinking is a type of cognition that involves coming to a decision, forming a belief, or developing an attitude. In this section, we examine how we think about social information.

Beware of Smileys
If you want to make a good impression at work, smile at your coworkers. Research suggests that "smiling individuals are perceived as more attractive, sincere, trustworthy, warm, and competent" (Glikson, Cheshin, & van Kleef, 2017, para. 1). But do not assume this principle applies to online communications. Evidence suggests that using smileys in work-related e-mails could make you appear less competent (Glikson et al., 2017).
Top: Tanya Constantine/Getty Images.
Bottom: Rova N/Shutterstock.

social cognition The way people think about others, attend to social information, and use this information in their lives, both consciously and unconsciously.

attributions Beliefs one develops to explain human behaviors and characteristics, as well as situations.

SOCIAL MEDIA AND PSYCHOLOGY

WHAT'S IN A SELFIE? Think about the last time you posted a professional headshot on LinkedIn or a fun photo on Instagram. What was your motivation for doing so? For most of us, the primary goal is to leave a good impression for others—to appear attractive, confident, and likable. To this end, you may take a self-portrait. With a selfie, you can control the angle of the shot to highlight your best features. You can also use "selfie help apps" to make your skin look smoother, your eyes bigger, and your teeth pearly white (Wakeman, 2018, January 15). The problem is that most people viewing your selfie know that you may have manipulated the photo, and this may lead to unfavorable attributions. People in selfies may be perceived as "less open, less socially attractive, less trustworthy, and more narcissistic" than those appearing in photos taken by someone else (Krämer et al., 2017, p. 9). Selfie-enthusiasts, take note: If your goal is to appear "more attractive and likable," you may want to have another person take your picture (Re, Wang, He, & Rule, 2016, p. 594).

PEOPLE MIGHT GET THE WRONG IMPRESSION

Which Angle Is Most Flattering?
If you're taking a selfie, you want to get the best angle. A study on Tinder selfies found that women often position the camera above their face (left), rather than directly in front or below (middle, right). This makes them appear shorter, and perhaps thinner. Men, on the other hand, are more inclined to place the camera below the face, which makes them look taller and more imposing (Sedgewick, Flath, & Elias 2017).
Sedgewick, J. R., Flath, M. E., & Elias, L. J. (2017). Presenting your best self(ie): The influence of gender on vertical orientation of selfies on Tinder. *Frontiers in Psychology, 8*(604). doi:10.3389/fpsyg.2017.00604, https://creativecommons.org/licenses/by/4.0/.

LO 3 Describe several common attribution errors.

Whether online or in person, making attributions about human behavior often involves guesswork. This, of course, leaves plenty of room for error. Let's take a look at four of the most common mistakes (**INFOGRAPHIC 11.1** on page 408).

FUNDAMENTAL ATTRIBUTION ERROR Suppose you are hosting a party tomorrow night. You e-mailed invitations a month ago, and everyone responded except your friend Julia. If you automatically assume Julia failed to reply because she is a little snooty and thinks she's too good for your party, rather than considering situational factors (like the fact that your invitation may have gone straight into her spam folder), then you might be falling prey to the **fundamental attribution error.** Here, the tendency is to favor *dispositional attributions* over *situational attributions.* A **dispositional attribution** is a particular type of internal attribution wherein behaviors are assumed to result from traits or personality characteristics. Here, we are referring to deep-seated, enduring characteristics, as opposed to more transient states, like feeling tired and cranky. A **situational attribution** is an external attribution wherein behaviors are assumed to result from situational factors.

The fundamental attribution error is common; we often assume people's behaviors are caused by personal characteristics (a dispositional attribution) rather than factors in the environment (a situational attribution) (Ross, 1977; Ross, Amabile, & Steinmetz, 1977). This tendency is even evident when people assess the creativity of teams. In some cases, observers attribute a successful product to one member of a group (focusing on his or her disposition), and discount the importance of the teamwork that went into it (Kay, Proudfoot, & Larrick, 2018).

Why do we fall prey to the fundamental attribution error? Perhaps it has something to do with our tendency to make quick decisions about others based on the labels we assign to them. Imagine how dangerous this could be in a medical setting, when doctors and nurses need to make quick choices about treatment. Seeing a patient with slurred speech, difficulty walking, and aggressive behavior, a nurse might assume he is a drunk "alcoholic" and ignore situational factors, such as homelessness and severe dehydration (Levett-Jones et al., 2010). Similarly, a doctor might take one look at a patient and decide he is uncooperative, dirty, and just "another

fundamental attribution error The tendency to overestimate the degree to which the characteristics of an individual are the cause of an event, and to underestimate the involvement of situational factors.

dispositional attribution A belief that some characteristic of an individual is involved in the cause of an event or activity.

situational attribution A belief that some environmental factor is involved in the cause of an event or activity.

homeless hippie," when in fact the patient is on the verge of a diabetic coma (Groopman, 2008, p. 55). Doctors must avoid these automatic responses, and patients and their families should recognize that doctors are not immune to attribution errors. Can you think of any other professionals who make decisions that impact the health and well-being of others? How might the fundamental attribution error lead these individuals astray?

The good news is that we may be able to reduce biases associated with the fundamental attribution error. In one study, researchers showed that single training sessions with educational videos and games can have "significant debiasing effects" on participants (Morewedge et al., 2015).

Why Do We Blame Victims?
Alleged sexual assault victim Rose McGowan takes the stage at the 2017 Women's Convention in Detroit, Michigan. In cases of assault, people may blame victims rather than perpetrators (Correia, Alves, Morais, & Ramos, 2015). The tendency for people to assume that victims "had it coming," or did something to deserve abuse, is an example of the just-world hypothesis. Victim-blaming can deter people from speaking out and seeking justice. Aaron Thornton/Getty Images.

JUST-WORLD HYPOTHESIS Another attribution error associated with biased values and belief systems is the **just-world hypothesis,** which assumes that if people are suffering, they must have done something to deserve it (Rubin & Peplau, 1975). According to this view, the world is a fair place and "bad" things happen for a reason. Thus, when people are "bad," it should be no surprise when things don't go well for them (Riggio & Garcia, 2009). In one study, researchers told a group of participants about a man who was violent toward his wife, slapping and yelling at her. Another group heard about a loving man who gave his wife flowers and frequently made her dinner. Participants who heard about the "bad person" were more likely to predict a bad outcome for him (he will have a "terrible car accident") than those who heard about the "good person" (he will win a "hugely successful business contract"; Callan et al., 2013, p. 35). "Just-world beliefs provide individuals with a conceptual framework for negotiating and making sense of the world, empowering them to navigate through life with confidence in the (illusory) belief that events and outcomes are predictable and therefore within their control" (Strelan, 2018, pp. 22–23).

SELF-SERVING BIAS People who attribute their successes to **internal characteristics** and their failures to environmental factors may be prone to the **self-serving bias.** One of the reasons Dennis was so drawn to Alexa was her apparent *lack* of self-serving bias. She was humble about her academic accomplishments, and she took responsibility for the failures of past relationships. Someone more vulnerable to the self-serving bias might have attributed all her accomplishments to internal characteristics, such as talent, and blamed her relationship woes on external circumstances, like the behavior of ex-boyfriends.

CONNECTIONS
In **Chapter 10,** we discussed locus of control, or patterns of beliefs about where control resides. People with an internal locus of control believe they have control over their lives. Those who fall prey to the self-serving bias appear to have an internal locus of control when it comes to explaining the reasons for their successes.

FALSE CONSENSUS EFFECT When trying to decipher the causes of other people's behaviors, we over-rely on knowledge about ourselves. This can lead to the **false consensus effect,** which is the **tendency to overestimate** the degree to which people think or act like we do (Ross, Greene, & House, 1977). This false consensus effect is evident in our beliefs about everything from celebrities—*Selena Gomez is amazing, right?*—to childhood vaccines—*I don't vaccinate my child, so you shouldn't either* (Bui, 2012; Rabinowitz, Latella, Stern, & Jost, 2016). We seem to make this mistake because we have an overabundance of information about ourselves, and often limited information about others.

CONNECTIONS
In **Chapter 7,** we described the availability heuristic. With this heuristic, we predict the probability of something happening based on how easily we can recall a similar event from the past. The false consensus effect may result partly from our use of the availability heuristic. We rely on information about ourselves because it is easy to recall, and thus overestimate the degree to which other people think and act like we do.

Put Your Heads Together

While driving, a man takes an urgent phone call from his wife. If he crashes into another car while responding, how might an observer explain his actions? In your group, explain the man's behavior using the fundamental attribution error, just-world hypothesis, self-serving bias, and false consensus effect.

just-world hypothesis The tendency to believe the world is a fair place and individuals generally get what they deserve.

self-serving bias The tendency to attribute our successes to personal characteristics and our failures to environmental factors.

false consensus effect The tendency to overestimate the degree to which others think or act like we do.

Errors in Attribution

Attributions are beliefs we develop to explain human behaviors and characteristics, as well as situations. We can explain behaviors in many ways, but social psychologists often compare explanations based on traits or personality characteristics (dispositional attributions) to explanations based on external situations (situational attributions). But as we seek to explain events and behaviors, we tend to make predictable errors, making the wrong assumption about why someone is behaving in a certain way. Let's look at four of the most common types of errors in attribution.

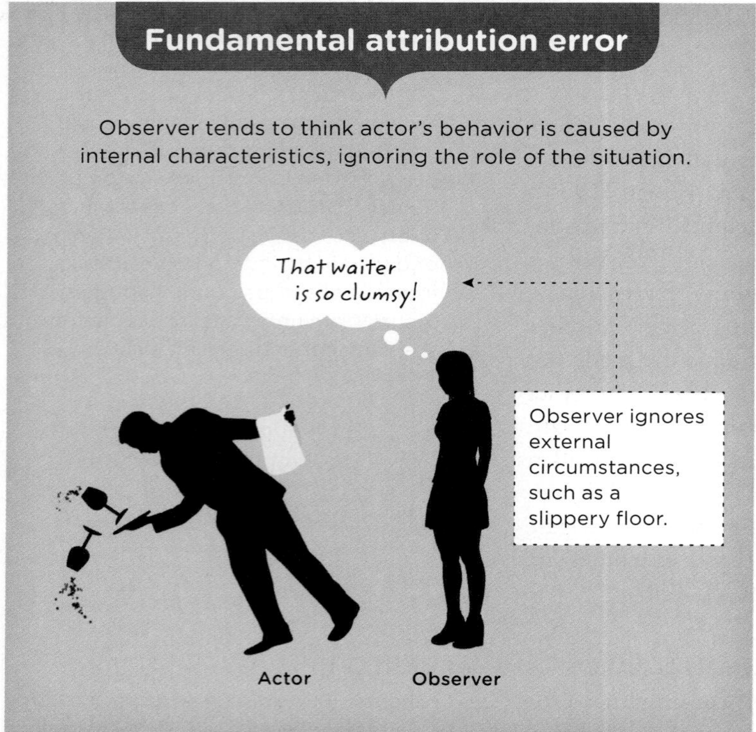

Fundamental attribution error
Observer tends to think actor's behavior is caused by internal characteristics, ignoring the role of the situation.
That waiter is so clumsy!
Observer ignores external circumstances, such as a slippery floor.
Actor
Observer

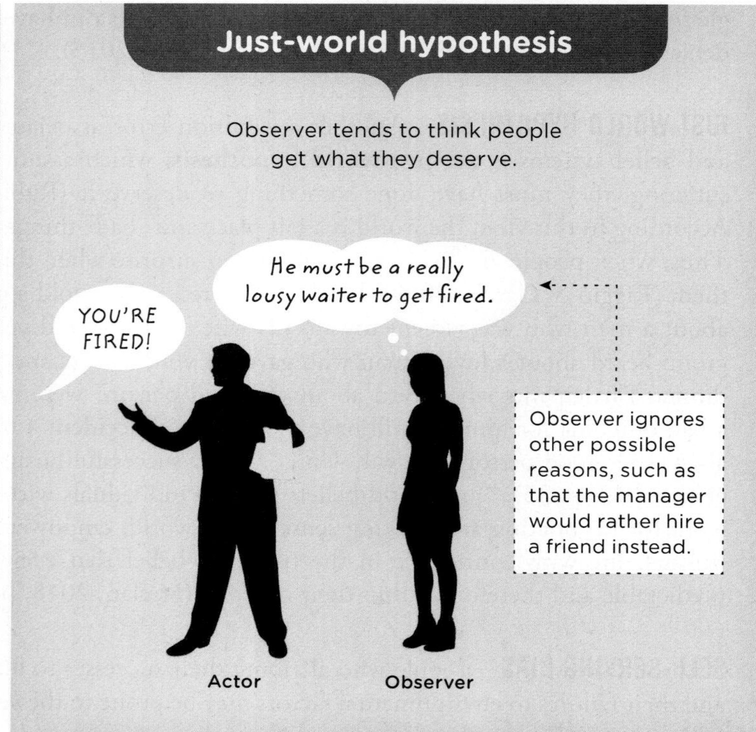

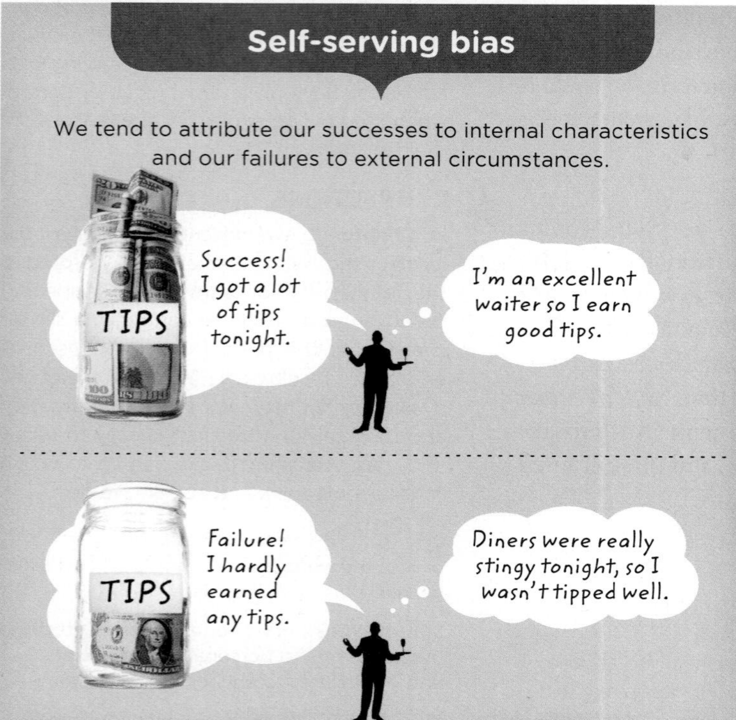

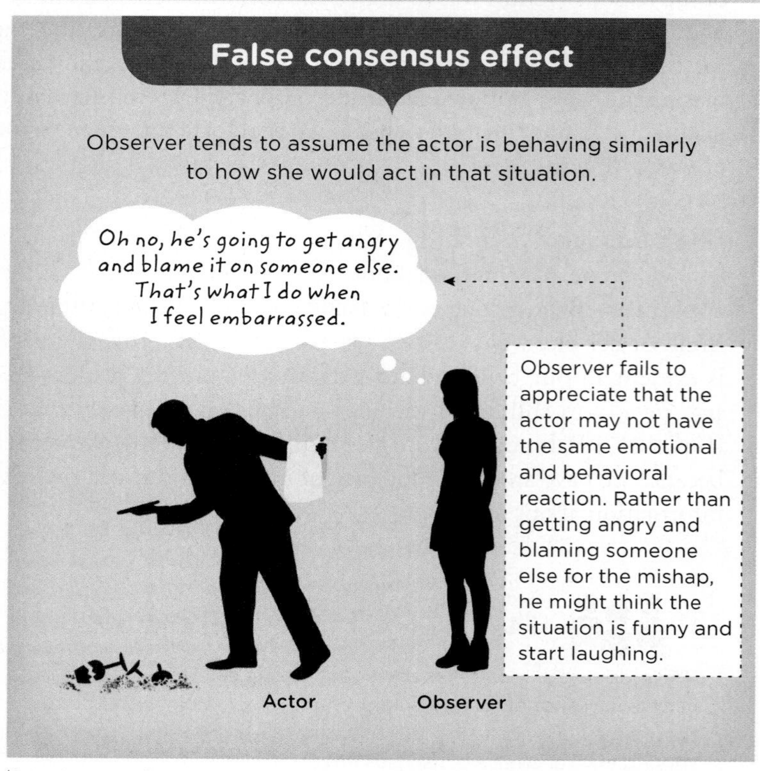

Credits: Waiter silos, © Slobelix/Agefotostock; Glass jars filled with dollar bills, Mike Kemp/Getty Images; Silhouettes of people, Leontura/Getty Images.

Now that we have a grasp of attributions (and the many errors associated with them), let's explore another facet of social cognition: attitudes.

All in the Family?
Children and parents frequently have the same attitudes about politics and social issues. To a certain degree, these similarities can be traced to common personality traits, which are partly inherited (Kandler, Bleidorn, & Riemann, 2012). But attitudes are more strongly influenced by life experiences (Huppertz et al., 2014; Olson, Vernon, Harris, & Jang, 2001).
Adina Tovy-Amsel/Eye Ubiquitous/Getty Images.

What's With the Attitude?

"I AM TOTALLY CRAZY ABOUT THIS GUY" When Alexa arrived at Dennis' house for dinner, her worries evaporated. It was clear he just wanted to make a nice meal and help her relax after a stressful week. "After the third date . . . it kind of took off from there," Alexa recalls. About two months later, Dennis had to go into "the field," or train with the Marines for several days in a remote location. Being out of touch forced Alexa to recognize her feelings: *Oh my gosh, I am totally crazy about this guy.*

When Dennis came home, the couple went to the beach, watched the sun set over the ocean, and had a long talk. They discussed their values and beliefs about raising children, caring for aging parents, and handling finances. "We just ran the gamut of everything you could possibly run into if you continue a relationship," says Alexa. "We [were] either going to come out of this with a really positive future, or . . . break up." By the end of the conversation, Dennis was saying "I love you," and it was clear that they were highly compatible. Alexa and Dennis shared many of the same *attitudes.*

WHAT ARE ATTITUDES? **Attitudes** are the relatively stable thoughts, feelings, and responses we have toward people, situations, ideas, and things (Ajzen, 2001; Wicker, 1969). Psychologists suggest that attitudes are composed of cognitive, affective, and behavioral components (**Figure 11.1** on the next page). The *cognitive* aspect refers to beliefs or ideas: What do you think about federal tax reform? Attitudes may also include an emotional evaluation, which is the *affective* component relating to mood or emotion (Ajzen, 2001). Do you have positive or negative feelings about universal health care? Feelings and beliefs guide the *behavioral* aspect of attitudes, or the way we respond. How will you vote in the next election?

WHERE DO ATTITUDES COME FROM? Your attitudes about marijuana use, gun control, and many other issues are strongly influenced by forces in the environment. They develop through learning processes such as **classical conditioning and observational learning**, and are shaped by social interactions and exposure to books, television, social media, and other communication outlets. Although nurture appears to dominate in this arena, genetic factors play a role in shaping attitudes, too (Hatemi et al., 2014; Hatemi, McDermott, & Eaves, 2015). Studies suggest that **identical twins** have more similar attitudes than fraternal twins on topics such as politics, divorce, voluntary exercise, and reading books (Huppertz et al., 2014; Olson, Vernon, Harris, & Jang, 2001). But as researchers explain, "A single gene or small group of genes does not directly influence ideological preferences" (Hatemi et al., 2014, p. 292). In all probability, attitudes result from an interaction between a large number of genes (perhaps thousands) and a variety of environmental factors. Our genetic predispositions can influence the environments we create for ourselves, which in turn impact our attitudes (Hatemi et al., 2015).

CONNECTIONS
In **Chapter 5,** we described how classical conditioning might instill emotions and influence attitudes toward product brands. Attitudes may also develop through observational learning: We observe the attitudes of family members and friends, and sometimes take them on ourselves.

CONNECTIONS
In **Chapter 7,** we explored the heritability of intelligence. Heritability is the degree to which hereditary factors are responsible for differences in a variety of physical and psychological characteristics in the population. Heritability research often involves comparing identical and fraternal twins, as seen here with the study of attitudes.

CAN ATTITUDES PREDICT BEHAVIOR? Not surprisingly, people are more likely to act on their attitudes when something important is at stake—like money. Imagine your college is holding a meeting to discuss the possibility of increasing student parking fees. What are the chances of your showing up to that meeting if you don't own a car? The greater personal investment you have in an issue, the more likely you are to act (Sivacek & Crano, 1982; Steindl & Jonas, 2015). The strength of an attitude is important, with stronger, more enduring attitudes having a greater impact (Armitage & Christian, 2003; Luttrell, Petty, & Briñol, 2016).

attitudes The relatively stable thoughts, feelings, and responses one has toward people, situations, ideas, and things.

FIGURE 11.1
Attitudes
Attitudes are composed of cognitive, affective, and behavioral components. Cognitive and affective components usually guide the behavioral aspect of an attitude.

Attitude toward personal debt

- **Cognitive component (beliefs and ideas)**: I think it's unwise to carry a large amount of personal debt without a clear plan for repayment.
- **Affective component (emotional evaluation)**: I feel proud when I pay in full for purchases.
- **Behavioral component (the way we respond)**: I pay my credit card bill in full each month. I maintain a minimum balance in my bank account for emergencies. I review my college loan situation regularly.

We now know that attitudes can influence behaviors, but is the opposite true—that is, can behaviors shape attitudes? Read on.

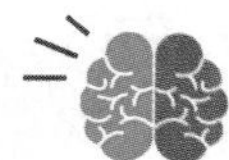

THINK CRITICALLY

SOMETHING DOESN'T FEEL RIGHT Most would agree that cheating on a girlfriend, boyfriend, or spouse is not right. Even so, some people contradict their beliefs by seeking sexual gratification outside their primary relationships. How do you think cheating makes a person feel—relaxed and at peace? Probably not. The tension that results when a behavior (in this case, cheating) clashes with an attitude (cheating is wrong) is known as **cognitive dissonance** (Aronson & Festinger, 1958; Festinger, 1957). One way to reduce cognitive dissonance is to adjust the behavior (stop fooling around). Another approach is to change the attitude to better match the behavior: *Cheating is actually good, because it makes me a better partner.* Such attitude shifts often occur without our awareness.

APPARENTLY, THE BIG BUCKS MADE IT EASIER TO JUSTIFY THEIR LIES

"I Really Should Be Studying"
You know that studying ought to take priority over recreational activities, yet you just can't resist watching the latest episode of *The Big Bang Theory* on CBS. Deciding to watch the show may create some cognitive dissonance, which occurs when your behavior (watching TV) is inconsistent with your belief: *Studying hard leads to good grades.* You could reduce this cognitive dissonance in one of two ways: A) by changing your behavior (turning off the TV and studying), or B) by altering your belief: *I actually study harder when I give myself TV breaks.* ITAR-TASS News Agency/Alamy Stock Photo.

Imagine, for a moment, you are a participant in a classic study on cognitive dissonance (Festinger & Carlsmith, 1959). Researchers have assigned you to a very boring task—placing 12 objects on a tray and then putting them back on a shelf, over and over again for a half-hour. Upon finishing, you spend an additional half-hour twisting 48 pegs ever so slightly, one peg at a time, again and again and again. How would you feel at the end of the hour—fairly bored, right?

Regardless of how you may feel about these activities, you have been paid money to convince someone else that they are a blast: "I had a lot of fun [doing] this task," you say. "It was intriguing, it was exciting. . ." (Festinger & Carlsmith, 1959, p. 205). Unless you like performing repetitive behaviors like a robot, we assume you would feel some degree of cognitive dissonance, or tension resulting from this mismatch between your attitude (*Ugh, this activity is so boring*) and your behavior (saying, "I had so much fun!"). What could you do to reduce the cognitive dissonance? If you're like participants in Festinger and Carlsmith's study, you would probably adjust your attitude to better fit your claims. In other words, you would rate the task as more interesting than it actually was.

But here's the really fascinating part: The participants who were paid more money ($20 versus $1) were less inclined to change their attitudes to match their claim—a sign that they felt less cognitive dissonance. Apparently, the big bucks made it easier to justify their lies. *I said I liked the boring task because I got paid $20, not because I actually liked it.*

cognitive dissonance A state of tension that results when behaviors are inconsistent with attitudes.

We have now learned about cognitive processes that form the foundation of our social existence. Attributions help us make sense of events and behaviors, and attitudes provide continuity in the way we think and feel about the surrounding world. It's time to shift our attention to behavior. How do other people influence the way we act? Are you ready to meet runner extraordinaire Julius Achon?

show what you know

1. ______________ studies individuals in relation to others and groups, whereas ______________ studies the groups themselves, including cultures and societies.
   a. Sociology; social psychology
   b. Social psychology; sociology
   c. Sociology; a confederate
   d. A confederate; social psychology

2. ______________ are beliefs used to explain human behaviors and characteristics, as well as situations.
   a. Attributions
   b. Confederates
   c. Dispositions
   d. Attitudes

3. Because of the fundamental attribution error, we tend to attribute causes of behaviors to the:
   a. characteristics of the situation.
   b. factors involved in the event.
   c. length of the activity.
   d. disposition of the person.

4. Social psychology research occasionally employs some form of deception involving confederates. How is this type of deception different from that used in a double-blind study?

✓ CHECK YOUR ANSWERS IN APPENDIX C.

Social Influence

11 ORPHANS In 1983 a 7-year-old boy in northern Uganda came down with the measles. The child was feverish and coughing. He appeared to be dying. In fact, he did die—or so the local villagers believed. They dug his grave, wrapped him in a burial cloth, and sang him a farewell song. Then, just as they were about to lower the body into the ground, someone heard a sneeze. A few moments later, another sneeze. Could it be? Hastily unwrapping the cloth, the mourners found the child frantically kicking and crying. It's a good thing the boy sneezed that day at his funeral, as the world is a much happier place because he survived. His name is Julius Achon.

Julius grew up in Awake, a village that had no electricity or running water. "Life in Uganda is very tough," says Julius, who spent his childhood sleeping between eight brothers and sisters on the floor of a one-room hut. At age 12, Julius was kidnapped by a government opposition group known as the Lord's Resistance Army (LRA) and forced to become a child soldier. Three months later, he escaped from the rebel camp and, running much of the distance, returned to his village some 100 miles away.

After coming home, Julius began to run competitively. He ran 42 miles barefoot to his first major track meet in the city of Lira. Hours after arriving, Julius was racing—and winning—the 800-, 1,500-, and 3,000-meter races. From that point on, it was one success after another: a stunning victory at the national championships, a scholarship from George Mason University in the United States, a collegiate record in 1996, and participation in the 1996 and 2000 Olympics (Kahn, 2012, January).

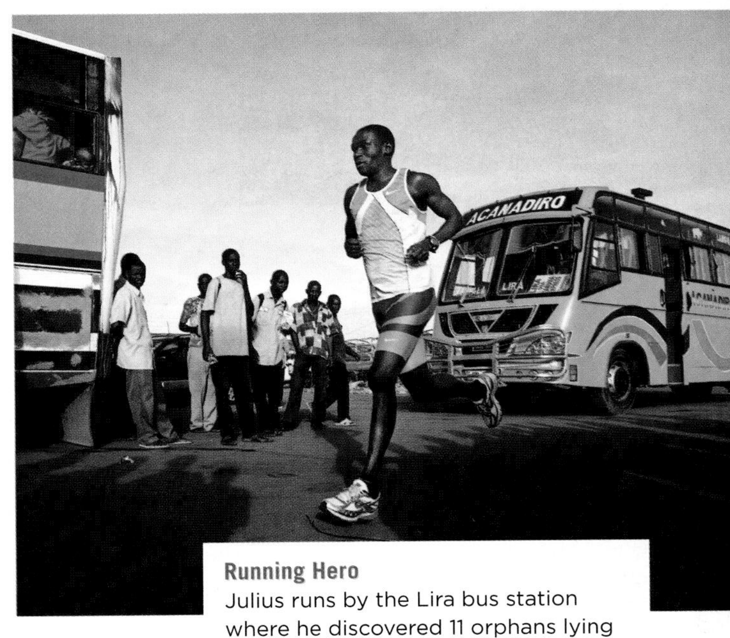

Running Hero
Julius runs by the Lira bus station where he discovered 11 orphans lying under a bus. Charlie Shoemaker.

As awe-inspiring as these accomplishments may be, Julius' greatest achievement had little to do with running. In 2003, while training in Uganda, he came upon a bus station in Lira. "I stopped, and then I saw children lying under the bus," Julius says. One of them stood up and started to beg for money. Then more children emerged, 11 of them in all, some as young as 3. They were thin and dirty, and the little ones wore nothing more than long T-shirts and underwear. "Where are your parents?" Julius remembers asking. One of the children said their parents had been killed. "Can I walk you to my home, you know, to go eat?" Julius asked. The children eagerly agreed and followed him home for a meal of rice, beans, and porridge. What happened next may seem unbelievable, but Julius and his family are extraordinary people. Julius asked his father to shelter the 11 orphans, pledging to help with their living expenses (even though he was barely making ends meet himself). His father, who already had six people living in his one-room home, replied, "Ah, it's no problem." And just like that, Julius and his family adopted 11 children.

Power of Others

Throughout the years Julius was trotting the globe and winning medals, he never forgot about Uganda. He thought of the people back home with empty stomachs and no access to lifesaving medicine, living in constant fear of the LRA. Julius was raised in a family that had always reached out to neighbors in need, and he felt blessed by all the support he had received from outside the family. "I feel I was so loved [by] others," says Julius, referring to the mentors and coaches who had provided him with places to stay, clothes to wear, and family away from home. So when Julius encountered those 11 orphans lying under the bus, he didn't think twice about coming to their rescue. His decision probably had something to do with the positive interactions he had experienced with people in his past.

LO 4 Explain the meaning of social influence and recognize factors associated with persuasion.

Macmillan Learning.

Rarely a day goes by that we do not come into contact with other human beings. The interactions we have with friends, family, and even strangers impact us in ways we may not realize. Psychologists refer to this as **social influence**—how a person is affected by others as evidenced in behaviors, emotions, and cognition. We begin our discussion with a powerful, yet often unspoken, form of social influence: *expectations*.

Think back to your days in elementary school. What kind of student were you—an overachiever, a kid who struggled, or perhaps the class clown? The answer to this question may depend somewhat on the way your teachers perceived you. In a classic study, researchers administered a nonverbal intelligence test to students in a San Francisco elementary school (Rosenthal & Jacobson, 1966, 1968). Then all the teachers were provided with a list of students who were likely to "show surprising gains in intellectual competence" during the next year (Rosenthal, 2002a, p. 841). But the list was fake; the "intellectually competent" kids were just a group selected at random (a good example of how deception is used in social psychology research). About 8 months later, the students were given a second intelligence test. The "surprising gains" children showed greater test score increases than their classmates. Mind you, the only difference between these kids and the rest of the students was teacher expectations. The students who were expected to be superior actually showed superior improvement. Why do you think this happened?

Here, we have a case in which teachers' expectations (based on false information) seemed to transform students' aptitudes and facilitate substantial gains. You might

social influence How a person is affected by others as evidenced in behaviors, emotions, and cognition.

call this a *self-fulfilling prophecy:* "The behavior expected actually came to pass because the expecter expected it" (Rosenthal, 2002a, p. 847). What types of teacher behaviors might explain this self-fulfilling prophecy? The teachers may have inadvertently communicated expectations by demonstrating "warmer socioemotional" attitudes toward the "surprising gains" students; they may have provided them with more material and opportunities; or given them more complex and personalized feedback (Rosenthal, 2002a, 2003). From the student's perspective, teacher behaviors can create a desire to work hard, or they can result in a decline in interest and confidence (Kassin, Fein, & Markus, 2017).

Since this classic study was conducted some 50 years ago, researchers have studied expectations in a variety of classroom settings. Their results demonstrate that teacher expectations do not have the same effect or degree of impact on all students (Jussim & Harber, 2005). They appear to have greater influence on younger children (first and second graders) and those of lower socioeconomic status (Sorhagen, 2013). Expectations also may have a significant effect on second-language students. When teachers consider "language-minority" students to be hard workers, these students "advance in math at the same rates" as their native English-speaking peers (Blanchard & Muller, 2015, p. 262).

Expectations are powerful, but they are just one form of social influence. Let's return to the story of Julius and learn about more deliberate types of influence.

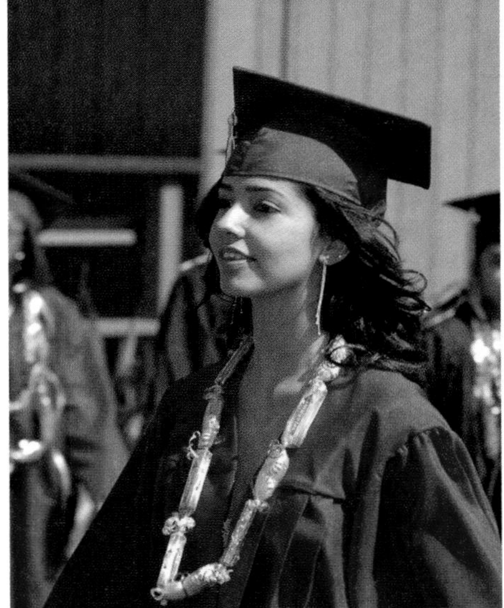

Expectations Pay Off
Liz Farias graduates from Eastside College Preparatory School in East Palo Alto, California. Before the school was founded in 1996, high schoolers from East Palo Alto were bused to schools in other communities, and the majority dropped out before graduating. Eastside raised the expectations for these teenagers, putting every single one of them on a college track. These high expectations, combined with the hard work of students, families, faculty, and staff, have produced impressive results: Every Eastside graduate has attended a four-year college (Eastside College Preparatory School, n.d.).
Courtesy Elizabeth Farias.

Persuasion

When Julius asked his father to shelter and feed the 11 orphans, he was using a form of social influence called **persuasion.** With persuasion, one intentionally tries to make other people change their attitudes and beliefs, which may (or may not) lead to changes in their behaviors. The person doing the persuading does not necessarily have control over those he seeks to persuade. Julius could not force his father to feel sympathy for the orphans.

SOURCE, MESSAGE, AUDIENCE According to American psychologist Carl Hovland (1912–1961), persuasive power is determined by three factors: the source, the message, and the audience (Hovland, Janis, & Kelley, 1953).

The source: People are more likely to be persuaded if the individual or organization sending the message is credible, and credibility may depend on perceived expertise and trustworthiness (Hovland & Weiss, 1951). Physical appearance also matters, as attractive people tend to be more persuasive (Bekk & Spörrle, 2010). This is even true in virtual reality. For example, study participants who faced a survival challenge in a virtual world were more inclined to follow the advice of an attractive avatar (Khan & Sutcliffe, 2014).

The message: Persuasion is more likely if the delivery of the message is logical and to the point (Chaiken & Eagly, 1976). Fear-inducing information can increase persuasion, though it might backfire under certain circumstances (Meczkowski, Dillard, & Shen, 2016). Imagine someone uses this message to encourage teeth-flossing: "If you don't floss daily, you can end up with infected gums, and that infection can spread to your eyes and create total blindness!" If the audience is overly frightened by a message (imagine small children being told to floss . . . or else!), the tension they feel may actually interfere with their ability to process the message (Janis & Feshbach, 1953).

You Asked, Julius Answers

http://qrs.ly/ea5a5ga

How did you persuade your father to take in the 11 orphans?

persuasion Intentionally trying to make people change their attitudes and beliefs, which may lead to changes in their behaviors.

Can Persuasion Bring Us Together? When Black Lives Matter of Greater New York showed up at a pro-Trump rally in Washington D.C., something amazing happened. Rally organizer Tommy Gunn invited the counterprotesters to take the stage (Brooks, 2018, January 21). "It's about freedom of speech," Gunn said. "Whether they disagree or agree with your message is irrelevant . . . you have the right to have the message" (Indicrat, 2017, 0:43-1:02). Representing the counterprotesters, Hawk Newsome took the microphone: "So you ask why there's a Black Lives Matter? Because you can watch a black man die and be choked to death on television, and nothing happened. We need to address that." The crowd booed, but Newsome continued. "We are not anti-cop, we are anti-bad cop. . . . We want our God-given right to freedom, liberty, and the pursuit of happiness" (1:39-3:22). At that point, many audience members were cheering. Did the words of Gunn and Newsome persuade some people on both sides that they were more alike than they realized? Chauncey Alcorn.

The audience: The age of the person being persuaded is important. For example, middle-age adults (40 to 60 years old) are unlikely to be persuaded, whereas children are relatively susceptible (Roberts & DelVecchio, 2000). Another factor is emotional state; when people are happy (and eating tasty food, interestingly enough), they are more likely to be persuaded (Aronson, 2018; Janis, Kaye, & Kirschner, 1965). Mental focus is also key: If your mind is elsewhere, you are less likely to be affected by message content (Petty & Cacioppo, 1986).

ELABORATION LIKELIHOOD MODEL The *elaboration likelihood model* proposes that people are persuaded in different ways. Those who focus on the content of a message, and think critically about it, follow the *central route* to persuasion. Meanwhile, those who pay more attention to "simple, issue-irrelevant cues" such as the credibility or attractiveness of the source rely on the *peripheral route* (Li, Chen, Kotha, & Fisher, 2017, p. 1076; Petty & Cacioppo, 1986). How do we know which route will be used? It depends on the situation. If the people receiving a message are knowledgeable and invested in its outcome, they are more likely to process information along the central route. If they are distracted, lack knowledge about the topic, or do not feel invested in the outcome, the peripheral route is more likely (O'Keefe, 2008).

Following the 2018 massacre at Marjory Stoneman Douglas High School, in Parkland, Florida, where 17 students and staff members lost their lives, the United States has seen an upsurge in calls for tighter gun control (Talbot, 2018, March 12; Wilson, 2018, February 24). A person with strong feelings about gun control (either for or against it) would likely take advantage of central processing when trying to develop a persuasive argument. Consider this statement, written by two prominent scientists: "If the nation is serious about getting firearm-related violence under control, it must rise above its aversion to providing financial support for firearm-related research, and the scientific community will have to expeditiously carry out the needed research" (Leshner & Dzau, 2018, p. 1195). This message—that the United States must invest in firearms research ASAP—would be more persuasive to a person who is knowledgeable and invested in the issue, and thus uses the central processing route. Someone unfamiliar with or indifferent to gun-control policy would more likely be persuaded by the credibility of the source, appearance of the speaker, and so on.

The take-home message is this: If you want to persuade as many people as possible, make sure your arguments are logical *and* you present yourself as credible and attractive. That way you can take advantage of both routes.

Compliance

LO 5 Define compliance and explain some of the techniques used to gain it.

The results of persuasion are internal and related to a change in *attitude* (Key, Edlund, Sagarin, & Bizer, 2009). **Compliance,** on the other hand, occurs when people voluntarily change their *behavior* at the request or direction of another person (or group), who generally does not have any true authority over them. Compliance is evident in changes to "overt behavior" (Key et al., 2009). For example, someone might send an e-mail asking you to fill out a questionnaire. You are not obligated to respond, but perhaps you will comply. Did you know that requests sent by e-mail are less likely to achieve compliance than those made in person? Even so, people tend to place an undue amount of confidence in e-mail requests (Roghanizad & Bohns, 2017).

Surprisingly, compliance often occurs **outside of our awareness**. Suppose you are waiting in line at a copy machine, and a man asks if he can cut in front of you. Do you allow it? Your response may depend on the wording of the request. Researchers studying this very scenario—a person asking for permission to cut in line—have found that compliance is much more likely when the request is accompanied by a reason. Saying, "Excuse me, I have five pages. May I use the [copy] machine?" will not work as well as "Excuse me, I have five pages. May I use the [copy] machine, *because I am in a rush?*" People are more likely to comply with a request that includes a "because" phrase, even if the reasoning is not logical. For example, "*because I am in a rush*" achieves about the same compliance as "*because I have to make copies*" (Langer, Blank, & Chanowitz, 1978, p. 637).

CONNECTIONS

In **Chapter 4,** we discussed automatic processing, cognitive activity that occurs with little or no conscious effort. Automatic processing can guide behaviors, including those associated with compliance.

One way to achieve compliance is the **foot-in-the-door technique,** which occurs when someone makes a small request, followed by a larger request (Freedman & Fraser, 1966). If a college club is trying to enlist students to help with a service project (such as raising money for packages to be sent to soldiers overseas), its members might first stop students in the hallway and ask for help with a smaller task (labeling a couple of donated boxes). If a student responds positively to this small request, then the club members might make a bigger request (to sponsor packages), with the expectation that the student will comply with the second request on the grounds of having said yes to the first request. Why would this technique work?

The reasoning is that if you have already said yes to a small request, you will likely agree to a bigger request in order to remain consistent in your involvement. Your prior participation leads you to believe you are the type of person who gets involved; in other words, your attitude has shifted (Cialdini & Goldstein, 2004; Freedman & Fraser, 1966). So why is such a strategy called *foot-in-the-door?* In the past, salespeople went door to door trying to sell their goods and services, and they often achieved success if they could physically get a "foot in the door," thereby keeping it open and continuing their sales pitch.

Another method for gaining compliance is the **door-in-the-face technique,** which involves making a large, sometimes unreasonable request followed by a smaller request. With this technique, the expectation is that the person will not go along with the large request, but will comply with the smaller request because it may seem minor in comparison. There are numerous reasons people comply under these circumstances, but the main reason seems to be one of *reciprocal concessions.* If the solicitor (the person trying to obtain something) is willing to give up something

compliance Changes in behavior at the request or direction of another person or group, who in general does not have any true authority.

foot-in-the-door technique A compliance technique that involves making a small request first, followed by a larger request.

door-in-the-face technique A compliance technique that involves making a large request first, followed by a smaller request.

(the large request), the person being solicited tends to feel that he, too, should give in and satisfy the smaller request (Cialdini & Goldstein, 2004).

Let's review these concepts using Julius as an example. After meeting the 11 orphans, Julius brought the children home and asked his parents to feed them. Once his parents *complied* with this initial request, Julius made a much larger request—he asked them to shelter the children indefinitely. This is an example of the *foot-in-the-door technique* because Julius first made a modest request ("Will you feed these children?") and then followed up with a larger one ("Will you shelter these children?"). Had these requests been flip-flopped, that is, had Julius only wanted to get the children a meal but first asked his parents to house them, we would call it the *door-in-the-face technique.*

Compliance generally occurs in response to specific requests or instructions: Will you lend me $5? Can you chop these onions? Please hold the door. But social influence needn't be explicit. Sometimes we adapt our behaviors and beliefs simply to fit in with the crowd.

Courageous Non-Conformist
In 2014, 17-year-old Malala Yousafzai (photo held by girl) became the youngest recipient of the Nobel Peace Prize. Yousafzai began her activism at age 11, blogging for the BBC about life under the Taliban in her native Pakistan. Over the next few years, she became an outspoken advocate for girls' education, but her nonconformist stance was not welcomed by all. When Yousafzai was 15, a Taliban gunman entered her school bus and shot her in the head. She recovered from her injuries and has continued her campaign for women's rights, earning the respect and admiration of people around the world (NobelPrize.org, 2014, Kantor, 2014, October 10). RIZWAN TABASSUM/AFP/Getty Images.

Conformity

When Julius came to the United States on a college scholarship in 1995, he was struck by some of the cultural differences he observed between the United States and Uganda—the way people dressed, for example. Women wore considerably less clothing, and men could be seen wearing jeans halfway down their posteriors (the "sagging" pants style). During the decade Julius lived in the United States, he never stopped acting like a Ugandan. Before going out in the evening, he would tuck in his shirt, comb his hair, and make sure his clothes were ironed—and he never wore sagging pants. You might say Julius refused to *conform* to certain aspects of American culture—and resisting conformity is not always easy to do.

LO 6 Identify the factors that influence the likelihood of someone conforming.

FOLLOWING THE CROWD Have you ever found yourself turning to look in the same direction as other people, just because you see them staring at something? We seem to have a commanding urge to do what others are doing, even if it means changing our normal behavior. This tendency to modify our behaviors, attitudes, beliefs, and opinions to match those of others is known as **conformity.** Sometimes we conform to the **norms** or standards of the social environment, like a group of friends or coworkers. Unlike compliance, which occurs in response to an explicit and direct request, conformity is generally unspoken. We often conform because we feel compelled to fit in and **belong**.

CONNECTIONS 

In **Chapter 9,** we described Maslow's hierarchy of needs, which includes the need to belong. If physiological and safety needs are met, we are motivated by the need for love and belongingness, and this can drive us to conform.

It is important to note that conformity is not always a bad thing. We often rely on conformity to ensure the smooth running of day-to-day activities involving groups of people. What would it be like to ride on a bus or subway if nobody conformed to common social rules?

try this Next time you are outside in a crowded area, look up and keep your eyes toward the sky. Do some people change their gazes to match yours, even though there is no other indication that something is happening above?

Heather Shimmin/Shutterstock.com.

conformity The tendency to modify behaviors, attitudes, beliefs, and opinions to match those of others.

norms Standards of the social environment.

CONFORMITY CLOUDS JUDGMENT? In a classic experiment by Solomon Asch, college-student participants were grouped with confederates working for the researchers. Each participant was asked to sit at a table with six confederates (Asch, 1955). Everyone at the table was told to look at two cards; the first marked with one vertical line, the standard line, and the second with three vertical lines of different lengths, marked 1, 2, and 3 (**Figure 11.2**). The group was then instructed to announce, one at a time going around the table, which of the three lines was closest in length to the standard line. The first two rounds went smoothly, with everybody in agreement about which of the three lines matched the standard. But then, in the third round, the first five people (all confederates) offered what was clearly the wrong answer, one after the other (per the researchers' instructions).

Would the real participant (the sixth person to answer) follow suit and conform to the wrong answer, or would he stand his ground and report the correct answer? In roughly 37% of the trials, participants went along with the group and provided the incorrect answer. What's more, 76% of the participants conformed and gave the wrong answer at least once (Asch, 1955, 1956). When members of the **control group** made the same judgments alone in a room, they were correct 99% of the time, confirming that the differences between the standard line and the comparison lines were substantial, and generally not difficult to assess. It is important to note that most participants (95%) refused to conform on at least one occasion, choosing an answer that conflicted with that of the group (Asch, 1956; Griggs, 2015b). Thus, they were capable of thinking and behaving independently. This type of study was later replicated in a variety of cultures, with mostly similar results (Bond & Smith, 1996), a significant achievement given that research published in psychology journals has been reported to be difficult to replicate (De Boeck & Jeon, 2018; Nelson, Simmons, & Simonsohn, 2018).

CONNECTIONS

In **Chapter 1,** we explained that a control group in an experiment is not exposed to the independent variable, or treatment. In this case, the control group is not exposed to confederates giving incorrect answers.

WHY CONFORM? Why did some participants in Asch's study go along with the group and provide incorrect answers? There are three major reasons for conformity. The first is *normative social influence:* Most of us want the approval of others, and this desire for acceptance may influence our behavior. If you are looking for an example of

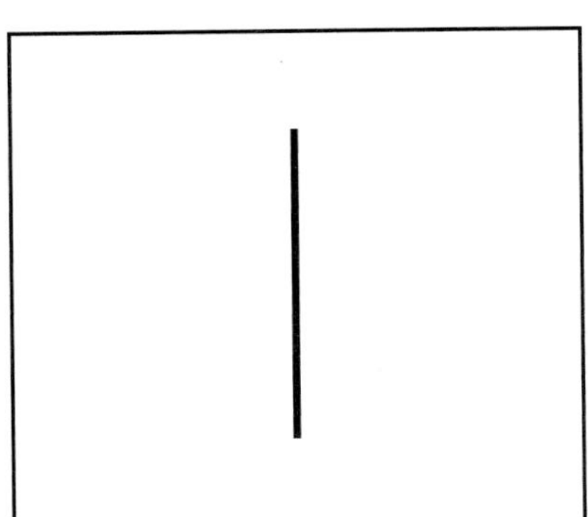

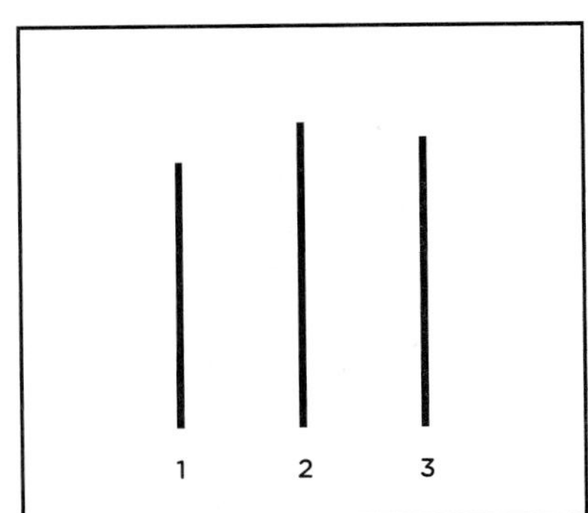

FIGURE 11.2
Asch's Conformity Experiment
Participants in this experiment were asked to look at the lines on two cards and indicate which of the comparison lines was closest in length to the standard line. Imagine you are a participant, like the man wearing glasses in this photo, and everyone else at the table chooses Line 3. Would that influence your answer? If you are like many participants, it would; 76% conformed to the incorrect answer at least once. Photo by William Vandivert/Solomon E. Asch, "Opinions and Social Pressure," *Scientific American*, Nov. 1955, Vol. 193, No. 5, 31–35.

normative social influence, just think back to middle school—perhaps you remember feeling pressure to be like some of your classmates? A second reason for conformity is *informational social influence:* We follow others in order to be correct. Perhaps you have a friend who is very knowledgeable about politics or medicine. When it comes to these topics, you tend to defer to her expertise, look to her for confirmation, and follow her lead. Third, we may conform to others because they belong to a certain *reference group* we respect, admire, or long to join. Conformity is also influenced by situational circumstances (**Figure 11.3**).

FIGURE 11.3
When Do We Conform?
Listed here are some conditions that increase the likelihood of conforming (Aronson, 2012; Asch, 1955) and some that decrease the likelihood (Asch, 1955; Bond & Smith, 1996).

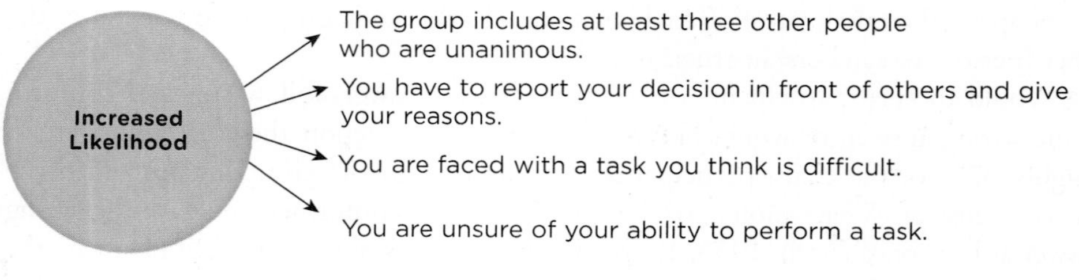

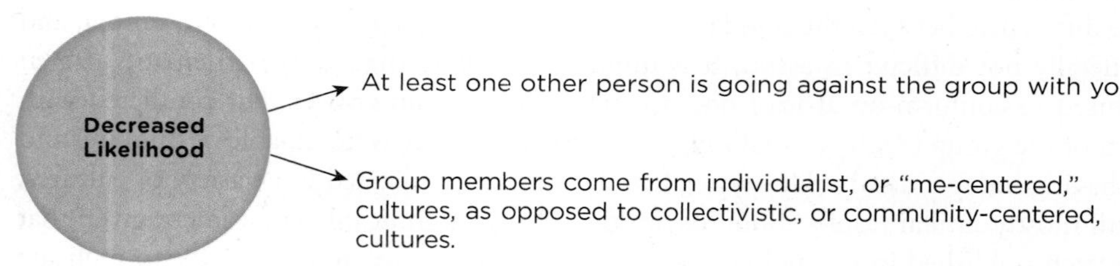

Put Your Heads Together

You are running a fund-raising drive for public television. How would you get people to donate money? Team up and discuss ways to **A**) manipulate attitudes (cognitive, affective, and behavioral components); **B**) use persuasion to get compliance (foot-in-the-door and door-in-the-face); and **C**) encourage conformity.

We have now explored three forms of social influence—persuasion, compliance, and conformity—but there is one yet to cover (**Table 11.1**). Let's take a trip to the darker side and examine the frightening phenomenon of obedience.

TABLE 11.1 CONCEPTS OF SOCIAL INFLUENCE

Concept	Definition	Example
Persuasion	Intentionally trying to make people change their attitudes and beliefs, which may or may not lead to changes in behavior	Trust our product because it contains the purest ingredients.
Compliance	Voluntarily changing behavior at the request or direction of another person or group, who in general does not have any authority over you	Remove your shoes before you walk into the house because you have been asked to do so.
Conformity	The tendency to modify behaviors, attitudes, beliefs, and opinions to match those of others	Remove your shoes before you walk into the house because everyone else does.
Obedience	Changing your behavior because you have been ordered to do so by an authority figure	Follow the detour sign.

Whether or not you realize it, other people constantly shape your thoughts, emotions, and behaviors. Here are some of the key types of social influence.

BOY SOLDIERS During Uganda's two-decade civil war, the Lord's Resistance Army (LRA) is said to have kidnapped some 66,000 youths (Annan, Blattman, & Horton, 2006). While a captive of the LRA, Julius witnessed other boy soldiers assaulting innocent people and stealing property. Sometimes at the end of the day, they would laugh or brag about how many people they had beaten or killed. But these were "normal" boys from the villages, children who never would have behaved this way under regular circumstances. Julius remembers seeing other child soldiers cry alone at night after returning to the camp and reflecting on what they had done.

What drives an ordinary child to commit senseless violence? A psychologist might tell you it has something to do with obedience. 

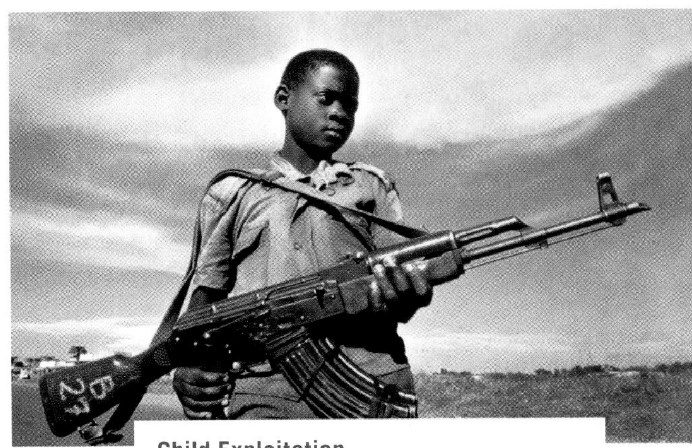

Child Exploitation
A young boy wields a Kalashnikov rifle near Kampala, Uganda. He is among the tens of thousands of children who have been exploited by military groups in Uganda. Julius was just 12 years old when he was abducted by the Lord's Resistance Army (LRA) and forced to fight and plunder on the group's behalf. Dominique Aubert/AFP/Getty Images.

Obedience

LO 7 Describe obedience and explain how Stanley Milgram studied it.

Obedience occurs when we change our behavior, or act in a way we might not normally act, because we have been ordered to do so by an authority figure. In these situations, an imbalance of power exists, and the person with more power (for example, a teacher, police officer, doctor, or boss) generally has an advantage over someone with less power, who is likely to be obedient out of respect, fear, or concern. In some cases, the person in charge demands obedience for the well-being of those less powerful (a father demanding obedience from a child running wildly through a crowded store). Other times, the person wielding power demands obedience for his own benefit (an adult who perpetrates sexual abuses against children).

THIS WILL *SHOCK* YOU: MILGRAM'S STUDY In the 1960s, psychologist Stanley Milgram investigated the extent to which obedience can lead to behaviors that most people would consider unethical. Milgram (1963, 1974) conducted a series of experiments examining how far people would go, particularly in terms of punishing others, when urged to do so by an authority figure. Overall he included 780 participants, only 40 of whom were women (Martin, 2016). The samples included teachers, salespeople, post office workers, engineers, and laborers, representing a wide range of educational backgrounds, from elementary school dropouts to people with graduate degrees. Milgram conducted 24 variations of his experimental method over the course of one year, starting in the summer of 1961 (Martin, 2016). Described here is a basic outline of the method he used.

Upon arriving at Milgram's Yale University laboratory, participants were informed that they would be using punishment as part of a learning experiment (another example of research deception). Then they were asked to draw a slip of paper from a hat. All the slips read "teacher," but the participants were led to believe that the slips read either "teacher" or "learner." Thus, every study participant ended up playing the role of *teacher*, while confederates enlisted by the researchers played that of *learner*. To start, the teacher was asked to sit in the learner's chair so that he could experience a 45-volt shock, just to know what the learner might be feeling. Next, the teacher was instructed to sit at a control panel and led to believe he would be delivering shocks. The panel went from 15 volts to 450 volts, labeled from "slight shock" to "XXX" (**INFOGRAPHIC 11.2** on the next page). The goal, the teacher was told, was for the learner to memorize a set of paired words. Each time the learner made a mistake, the teacher was to administer a shock, and the shock was to increase by 15 volts for every mistake. The learner was located in a separate room, arms strapped to a table and electrodes attached to his wrists, apparently receiving shocks.

obedience Changing behavior because we have been ordered to do so by an authority figure.

Milgram's Shocking Obedience Study

Stanley Milgram's study on obedience and authority was one of the most ground-breaking and surprising experiments in all of social psychology. Milgram wanted to test the extent to which we will follow the orders of an authority figure. Would we follow orders to hurt someone else, even when that person was begging us to stop? Milgram's experiment also raises ethical issues about deception and informed consent.

Participants had to actually think they were shocking another person for the experiment to work. Creating this deception involved the use of confederates (people secretly working for the researchers) whose behaviors and spoken responses were carefully scripted. Milgram found high levels of obedience in his participants—much higher than he and others had predicted at the beginning of the study.

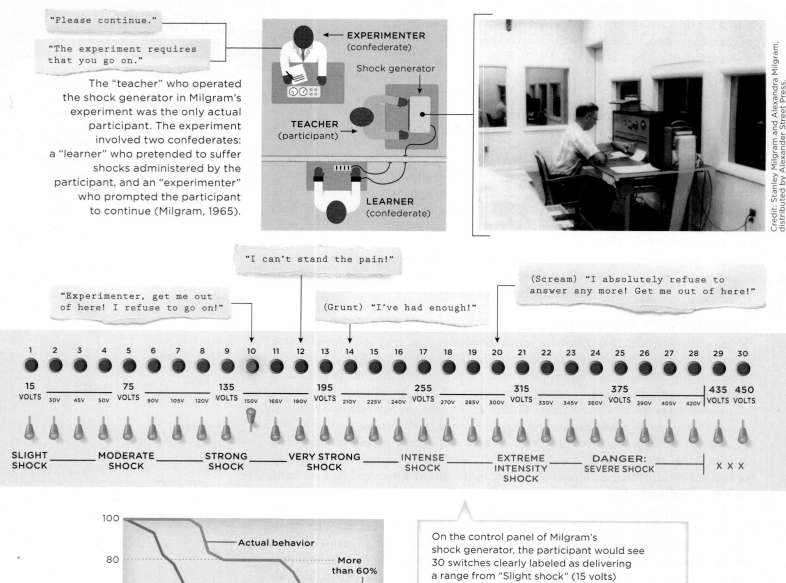

"Please continue."

"The experiment requires that you go on."

The "teacher" who operated the shock generator in Milgram's experiment was the only actual participant. The experiment involved two confederates: a "learner" who pretended to suffer shocks administered by the participant, and an "experimenter" who prompted the participant to continue (Milgram, 1965).

EXPERIMENTER (confederate)

Shock generator

TEACHER (participant)

LEARNER (confederate)

Credit: Stanley Milgram and Alexandra Milgram, distributed by Alexander Street Press.

"Experimenter, get me out of here! I refuse to go on!"

"I can't stand the pain!"

(Grunt) "I've had enough!"

(Scream) "I absolutely refuse to answer any more! Get me out of here!"

1	2	3	4	5	6	7	8	9	10	11	12	13	14	15	16	17	18	19	20	21	22	23	24	25	26	27	28	29	30
15 VOLTS	30V	45V	50V	75 VOLTS	90V	105V	120V	135 VOLTS	150V	165V	180V	195 VOLTS	210V	225V	240V	255 VOLTS	270V	285V	300V	315 VOLTS	330V	345V	360V	375 VOLTS	390V	405V	420V	435 VOLTS	450 VOLTS

SLIGHT SHOCK — MODERATE SHOCK — STRONG SHOCK — VERY STRONG SHOCK — INTENSE SHOCK — EXTREME INTENSITY SHOCK — DANGER: SEVERE SHOCK — X X X

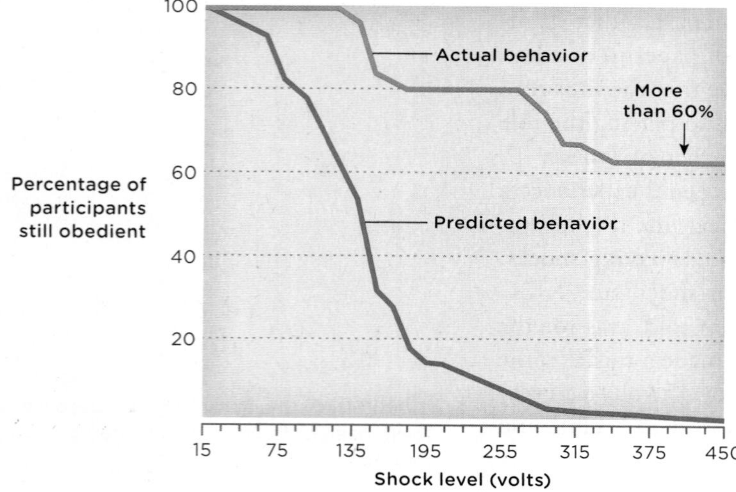

On the control panel of Milgram's shock generator, the participant would see 30 switches clearly labeled as delivering a range from "Slight shock" (15 volts) to "Danger: Severe shock" (375 volts) and beyond. The "learner" produced scripted responses at every level (Milgram, 1963).

Before the experiment, Milgram and a panel of experts predicted most participants would not proceed beyond 150 volts, when the "learner" explicitly demands to end the experiment. In fact, actual results show that most participants obeyed the experimenter's commands all the way to the highest shock level. (Data from Milgram, 1965.)

In reality, the learner (a confederate) did not receive any shocks, but instead followed a script of responses. The learner's behaviors, including the mistakes he made with the word pairs and his reactions to the increasing shock levels (mild complaints, screaming, references to his heart condition, pleas for the experiment to stop, and total silence as if he were unconscious or even dead), were identical for all participants. A researcher in a white lab coat (also a confederate with scripted responses) always remained in the room with the teacher, insisting the experiment proceed if the teacher questioned going any further. Meanwhile, the learner continued with appeals, such as "Experimenter, get me out of here. . . . I refuse to go on" or "I can't stand the pain" (Milgram, 1965, p. 62). The researcher would say to the teacher, "Please continue" and "You have no other choice, you *must* go on" (Milgram, 1963, p. 374).

Troubling Discoveries
A photo of psychologist Stanley Milgram appears on the cover of his biography, *The Man Who Shocked the World: The Life and Legacy of Stanley Milgram* (2004), by Thomas Blass. Milgram's research illuminated the dangers of human obedience. Feeling pressure from authority figures, participants in Milgram's studies were willing to administer what they believed to be painful and life-threatening electric shocks to other human beings (Milgram, 1963). Alexandra Milgram.

How many participants do you think obeyed the researcher and proceeded with the experiment in spite of the learner's desperate pleas? An astounding 60–65% of participants continued to the highest voltage level (Martin, 2016). Most of them showed obvious signs of discomfort (stuttering, sweating, trembling), yet they still obeyed the researcher. One person who witnessed the study reported the following: "I observed a mature and initially poised businessman enter the laboratory smiling and confident. Within 20 minutes he was reduced to a twitching, stuttering wreck, who was rapidly approaching a point of nervous collapse" (Milgram, 1963, p. 377). Even participants who eventually refused to proceed went much further than Milgram or anyone else had predicted—they all used shocks up to at least 300 volts, or "Intense Shock" (Milgram, 1963, 1964; Infographic 11.2).

REPLICATING MILGRAM This type of research has been replicated in the United States and in other countries, and the findings have remained fairly consistent, with 61–90% of participants continuing to the highest level of shock (Aronson, 2018; Blass, 1999; Doliński et al., 2017). Not surprisingly, the criticisms of Milgram's studies were strong (Martin, 2016). Many were concerned that this research went too far with its deception (it would certainly not receive approval from an **Institutional Review Board** today), and some wondered if the participants were harmed by knowing that they theoretically could have killed someone with their choices during the study. Milgram (1964) spent time with participants following the study, and reported that 84% claimed to be "glad" they had participated, while only 1.3% were "sorry." The participants underwent psychiatric evaluations a year later, and none of them were said to "show signs of having been harmed by his experiences" (Milgram, 1964, p. 850). Criticisms of Milgram's research have continued, with some questioning his representation of the "seriously inadequate debriefing process," "extended prodding of participants" to continue the experiment, and "selective nonreporting" of several of his 23 studies (Griggs & Whitehead, 2015, p. 315).

CONNECTIONS
In **Chapter 1,** we reported that professional organizations have specific guidelines to ensure ethical treatment of research participants. They include doing no harm, safeguarding welfare, and respecting human dignity. An Institutional Review Board also ensures the well-being of participants.

Milgram and others followed up on the original study to determine if there are specific factors that increase the likelihood of obedience in such a scenario (Blass, 1991; Burger, 2009; Martin, 2016; Milgram, 1965). All of the following appear to be important: (1) the legitimacy of the authority figure (more legitimate figures gain higher levels of obedience); (2) the physical distance between the authority figure and participant (the shorter the distance, the more obedience); (3) the physical distance between the learner and participant (the greater the distance, the more obedience); and (4) the presence of other teachers (if another confederate acts as an obedient teacher, the participant is more likely to obey as well).

Put Your Heads Together

The experiments conducted by Asch and Milgram show how difficult it is to resist conforming and obeying authority figures. Team up and identify four people who have successfully resisted the urge to conform and/or be obedient.

Milgram's initial motivation for studying obedience came from learning about the horrific events of World War II and the Holocaust, which "could only have been carried out on a massive scale if a very large number of people obeyed orders" (Milgram, 1974, p. 1). His research does seem to support this suggestion, but one ray of hope shines through in his later experiments: When participants saw others refuse to obey, they responded differently. In one follow-up experiment, two additional confederates played the role of teacher. If these confederates showed signs of refusing to obey the authority figure, the participant was far less likely to cooperate. In this type of setting, only 10% of participants were willing to carry on with the learning experiment (Milgram 1974). This suggests that one person can make a difference; when someone stands up for what is right, others will follow that lead.

show what you know

1. Match each definition that follows with its corresponding term below:
   a. how a person is affected by others
   b. intentionally trying to make people change their attitudes
   c. voluntarily changing behavior at the request of someone without authority
   d. asking for a small request, followed by a larger request
   e. the tendency to modify behaviors, attitudes, and beliefs to match those of others

   ____ conformity ____ persuasion ____ social influence
   ____ compliance ____ foot-in-the-door technique

2. ______________ occurs when we change our behavior, or act in a way we might not normally act, because we have been ordered to do so by an authority figure.
   a. Persuasion
   b. Compliance
   c. Conformity
   d. Obedience

3. Describe a situation in which someone successfully resisted the urge to conform.

✓ CHECK YOUR ANSWERS IN APPENDIX C.

Groups and Aggression

Thus far, the primary focus of this chapter has been individuals in social situations. We learned, for example, how people process information about others (social cognition) and how behavior is shaped by interactions with others (social influence). But human beings do not always function as independent units. We often come together in groups that have their own fascinating dynamics.

Better Together?

The most important competition of Julius Achon's career was probably the 1994 World Junior Championships in Portugal. Julius was 17 at the time and representing Uganda. It was his first time traveling in an airplane, wearing running shoes, and racing on a rubber track. No one expected an unknown boy from Uganda to win, but Julius surprised everyone, including himself. Crossing the finish line strides ahead of the others, he almost looked uncertain as he raised his arms in celebration.

Julius ran the 1,500 meters (the equivalent of 0.93 miles) in approximately 3 minutes and 40 seconds. Do you suppose he would have run this fast if he had been alone? Research suggests the answer is no (Worringham & Messick, 1983). In some situations, people perform better when others are observing (Steinmetz, Xu, Fishbach, & Zhang, 2016). This is particularly

Faster Together?
Athletes compete in the 5,000-meter T54 event of the 2016 Paralympics in Rio. Through social facilitation, competitive athletes may help each other perform better. Kyodo via AP Images.

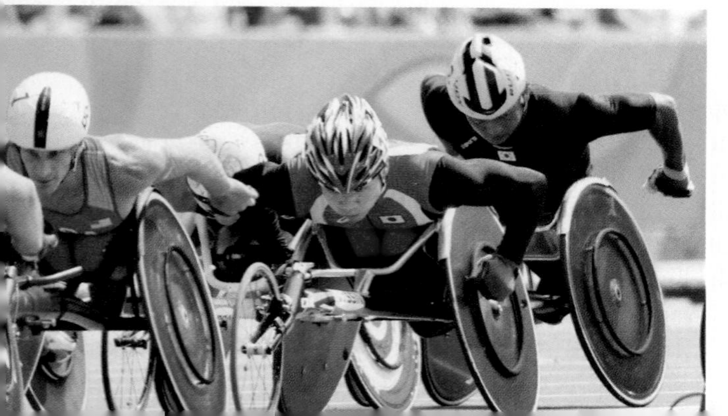

true when the task at hand is uncomplicated (running) and the individual is well prepared. (Runners may spend months training for races.) Thus, **social facilitation** can improve personal performance when the activity is fairly straightforward and the person is adequately prepped.

When Two Heads Are Not Better Than One

Being around other people does not always provide an advantage, however. Learning or performing difficult tasks may actually be harder in the presence of others (Aiello & Douthitt, 2001), and group members may not put forth their best effort. When individual contributions to the group aren't easy to ascertain, **social loafing** may occur (Latané, Williams, & Harkins, 1979). Social loafing is the tendency for people to put forth less than their best effort when individual contributions are too complicated to measure. Social loafing often goes hand-in-hand with **diffusion of responsibility,** or the sharing of responsibilities among all group members. Diffusion of responsibility can lead to feelings of decreased accountability and motivation. If we suspect other group members are slacking, we tend to follow suit in order to keep things equal.

You Asked, Julius Answers

http://qrs.ly/ea5a5ga

Is it difficult for you to return home to Uganda?

Apply This ↓

CUT THE LOAFING

Want some advice on how to reduce social loafing in your workgroups? Even if an instructor doesn't require it, try to get other students in your group to designate and take responsibility for specific tasks. Have group members submit their part of the work to the group before the assignment is due, specify their contributions to the end product, and participate in a group presentation (Jones, 2013; Maiden & Perry, 2011; Voyles, Bailey, & Durik, 2015). If possible, use video conferencing technologies such as Skype or Google Hangouts to work together, as this type of collaboration may encourage group members to do their part. Keep in mind that social loafing is less likely to occur when the assignment is challenging and group members feel they have something special to contribute (Simms & Nichols, 2014). If you do have some "free riders" in your group, don't automatically assume they are lazy or apathetic. Some group members fail to pull their weight because they feel incompetent (perhaps a result of language difficulties), or because they are not "team players" (Barr, Dixon, & Gassenheimer, 2005; Hall & Buzwell, 2012). Communicate with these individuals early in the process, and work with your group to identify a task that each person can perform with confidence and success.

ACROSS THE WORLD

SLACKERS OF THE WEST It turns out that social loafing is more likely to occur in societies where people place a high premium on individuality and autonomy. These *individualistic* societies include the United States, Western Europe, and other parts of the Western world. In more *collectivistic* Eastern cultures, people tend to prioritize community over the individual, and social loafing is less likely to occur (Karau & Williams, 1993; Kerr & Tindale, 2004). Group members from these more community-oriented societies may actually show evidence of working harder (Smrt & Karau, 2011). And unlike their individualistic counterparts, they are less interested in outshining their comrades. Preserving group harmony is more important (Tsaw, Murphy, & Detgen, 2011).

TRAVELING TO EAST ASIA? YOU MAY WANT TO LEAVE YOUR EGO AT HOME

social facilitation The tendency for the presence of others to improve personal performance when the task or event is fairly uncomplicated and a person is adequately prepared.

social loafing The tendency for group members to put forth less than their best effort when individual contributions are too complicated to measure.

diffusion of responsibility The sharing of duties and responsibilities among all group members that can lead to feelings of decreased accountability and motivation.

Nothing in psychology is ever that simple, however. Social loafing may be less common in collectivist cultures, but it certainly happens (Hong, Wyer, & Fong, 2008). And within every "individualistic" or "collectivistic" society are individuals who do not behave according to these generalities (Marcus & Le, 2013).

DEINDIVIDUATION In the last section, we discussed how obedience played a role in the senseless violence carried out by boy soldiers in Uganda. We suspect that the actions of these children also had something to do with *deindividuation.* People in groups sometimes feel a diminished sense of personal responsibility, inhibition, or adherence to social norms. This state of **deindividuation** can occur when group members are not treated as individuals, and thus begin to exhibit a "lack of self-awareness" (Diener, 1979). As members of a group, the boy soldiers may have felt a loss of identity, social responsibility, and ability to discriminate right from wrong.

Research suggests that children are indeed vulnerable to deindividuation. In a classic **study** of trick-or-treaters, psychologist Ed Diener and his colleagues set up an experiment in 27 homes throughout Seattle, Washington. Children arriving at these houses to trick-or-treat were ushered in by a woman (a confederate, of course). She told them they could take *one* piece of candy from a bowl on the table. Next to the bowl of candy was a second bowl full of pennies and nickels. The woman then excused herself, saying she had to get back to work in another room. Unknown to the children, an experimenter was observing their behavior through a peephole, tallying up the amount of candy and/or money they took. The other variable being recorded was the number of children and adults in the hallway; remember, the experimenters never knew how many people would show up when the doorbell rang!

CONNECTIONS

In **Chapter 1,** we discussed a type of descriptive research that involves studying participants in their natural environments. Naturalistic observation requires that researchers do not disturb the participants or their environment. Would Diener's study be considered naturalistic observation?

The findings were fascinating. If a parent was present, the children were well behaved. (Only 8% took more than their allotted piece of candy.) But with no adult present, events unfolded quite differently. Of the children who came through the door **alone** and anonymous (the confederate did not ask for names or other identifying information), 21% took more than they should have. By comparison, 80% of the children who were in a group and anonymous took extra candy and/or money. The condition of being in a group combined with anonymity created a sense of deindividuation (Diener, Fraser, Beaman, & Kelem, 1976).

CONNECTIONS

What motivated the children who were alone? In **Chapter 9,** we discussed various sources of motivation, ranging from instincts to the need for power. These sources of motivation might help explain why some children took more than their fair share of candy when they thought no one was watching.

We have shown how deindividuation occurs in groups of children, but what about adults? This type of behavior has been observed in various settings and with many groups of people. Fans of soccer, football, and other sports have been known to storm playing fields and vandalize property, showing virtually no regard for the safety of others. Internet "trolls" have been observed bullying and harassing people on social media (Craker & March, 2016). Would the fans and trolls act this way if they weren't part of a crowd? We suspect their behaviors have something to do with deindividuation.

As you can see, people sometimes have a tendency to act in rash and extreme ways when surrounded by others. How might this impact decisions in the workplace?

CAREER CONNECTIONS

deindividuation The diminished sense of personal responsibility, inhibition, or adherence to social norms that occurs when group members are not treated as individuals.

BEWARE OF THE RISKY SHIFT Suppose you have $250,000 to spend or save for your company. Will you spend more if you're calling the shots on your own or making a unanimous decision with a committee? Research suggests that people working in groups are more likely to recommend uncertain and risky options than individuals working alone, a phenomenon known as the **risky shift** (Stoner, 1961, 1968). Think about how the risky shift might impact decisions in the fields of finance (*What percentage of the client's portfolio should be allocated to stocks?*), medicine (*Should this patient be sent home or kept in the hospital for observation?*), and engineering (*Should we conduct more safety tests on this self-driving car or move forward with production?*). Whatever profession you pursue, you will likely find yourself making some collaborative decisions—and when you do, beware of the risky shift.

What Fuels Corruption?
Brazilian police officers apprehend a former government official for alleged participation in a massive corruption scandal involving the oil company Petrobras (BBC News, 2017, July 13, para. 8). How does large-scale corruption arise? Research suggests that working together may sometimes foster dishonesty, particularly when members benefit equally. "When facing opposing moral sentiments—to be honest vs. to join forces in collaboration—people often opt for engaging in corrupt collaboration" (Weisel & Shalvi, 2015, p. 10651). HEULER ANDREY/AFP/Getty Images.

MORE PEOPLE, MORE PROBLEMS? As a member of a team, you should also be wary of **group polarization,** or the tendency for a group to take a more extreme stance after deliberations and discussion (Myers & Lamm, 1976). When people with similar beliefs come together, they tend to reinforce each other's positions. Suppose you convene several individuals who strongly support the legalization of marijuana. As they hear others echo their opinions and offer supporting evidence, their original beliefs and positions are reinforced, and the conversation becomes more one-sided. So is group deliberation actually useful? Perhaps not when the members are initially in agreement.

As a group becomes increasingly united, another process known as **groupthink** can occur. This is the tendency for group members to maintain cohesiveness and agreement in their decision making, and fail to consider alternatives and related viewpoints (Janis, 1972; Rose, 2011). Groupthink is thought to have played a role in a variety of disasters, including the sinking of the Titanic in 1912, the explosion of the *Challenger* space shuttle in 1986, the Mount Everest climbing tragedy in 1996, and the U.S. decision to invade Iraq in 2003 (Badie, 2010; Burnette, Pollack, & Forsyth, 2011).

As you can see, groupthink can have life-or-death consequences. So, too, can the bystander effect, another alarming phenomenon that occurs among people in groups.

THE BYSTANDER WHO REFUSED TO STAND BY Before meeting Julius in 2003, the 11 orphans spent their days begging for money. Usually, they ate scraps of food that hotels had poured onto side roads for dogs and cats. At night, they kept each other warm coiled beneath the bus, and they shared food when there was enough to go around. The older children looked after the little ones, making sure they had something to eat. Day after day, the orphans encountered hundreds of passersby. But of all those people, only three or four would typically offer food or money, nothing more—until a thin, muscular man in his mid-twenties appeared wearing the most unusual outfit. Dressed in a sleeveless top (a runner's singlet), short shorts, and fancy sneakers, Julius Achon looked different from any person the orphans had seen before (S. Mugisha, personal communication, March 9, 2012). And he was, of course, different. This man would ultimately ensure the orphans had everything they needed for a chance at a better life—food, clothing, a place to sleep, an education, and a family.

LO 8 Recognize the circumstances that influence the occurrence of the bystander effect.

THE BYSTANDER EFFECT Before meeting Julius, the orphans had been homeless for several months. Why didn't anyone try to rescue them? "Everybody was fearing responsibility," Julius says. In northern Uganda, many people cannot even afford to feed themselves, so they are reluctant to lend a helping hand.

risky shift The tendency for groups to recommend uncertain and risky options.

group polarization The tendency for a group to take a more extreme stance than originally held after deliberations and discussion.

groupthink The tendency for group members to maintain cohesiveness and agreement in their decision making, failing to consider possible alternatives and related viewpoints.

Casualties of the Bystander Effect
Kitty Genovese (left) and Hugo Tale-Yax (right) lived in different eras, but both were victims of brutal assaults and the cold indifference of bystanders in New York City. Genovese and Tale-Yax might have survived if those who heard or saw them in distress had done more to help.
Left: New York Daily News Archive/Getty Images. Right: Christopher Sadowski/Splash News/Newscom.

But perhaps there was another factor at work, one that psychologists call the **bystander effect.** When a person is in trouble, bystanders have the tendency to assume (and perhaps wish) that someone else will help—and therefore they stand by and do nothing, partly a result of the *diffusion of responsibility.* This is particularly true when many other people are present. Strange as it seems, we are more likely to aid a person in distress if no one else is around (Darley & Latané, 1968; Eagly & Crowley, 1986; Latané & Darley, 1968). So when people encountered the orphans begging on the street, they probably assumed somebody else would take care of the problem. *These children must belong to someone; their parents will come back for them.*

The Kitty Genovese attack is perhaps the most famous illustration of the bystander effect. It was March 13, 1964, around 3:15 A.M., when Catherine "Kitty" Genovese arrived home from work in her Queens, New York, neighborhood. As she approached her apartment building, an attacker brutally stabbed her. Kitty screamed for help, but initial reports suggested that no one came to her rescue. The attacker ran away, and Kitty stumbled to her apartment building. But he soon returned, raping and stabbing her to death. *The New York Times* originally reported that 38 neighbors heard her cries for help, witnessed the attack, and did nothing to assist. But the evidence suggests that there were far fewer eyewitnesses (perhaps only a half dozen), and that several people did respond (by screaming out their windows, with at least one person calling the police). What's more, the second attack occurred inside her building, where few people could have witnessed it (Griggs, 2015c; Manning, Levine, & Collins, 2007). The attacker, Winston Moseley, was arrested five days after the attack when, ironically, two bystanders intervened after witnessing him commit a burglary (Kassin, 2017). Moseley was a serial killer and necrophiliac (sexually attracted to corpses). He died in prison in 2016, after spending approximately 52 years behind bars (McFadden, 2016, April 4).

More recently, in April 2010, a homeless man (also in Queens) was left to die after several people walked by him and decided to do nothing. The man, Hugo Tale-Yax, had been trying to help a woman under assault, but the attacker stabbed him in the chest (Livingston, Doyle, & Mangan, 2010, April 25). As many as 25 people walked past Mr. Tale-Yax as he lay on the ground dying, and one even took a cell phone picture of him before walking away. Why didn't they help? Would you help someone in such a situation? The bystander effect also happens online. In one study, only a third of students surveyed reported that they came to the aid of cyberbullying victims (Olenik-Shemesh, Heiman, & Eden, 2015).

A review of the research suggests that things might not be as "bleak" as these events suggest. In extremely dangerous situations, bystanders are actually *more* likely to help even if there is more than one person watching. More dangerous situations are recognized and interpreted quickly as being such, leading to faster intervention and help (Fischer et al., 2011). If we want to increase the likelihood of bystanders getting

bystander effect The tendency for people to avoid getting involved in an emergency they witness because they assume someone else will help.

TABLE 11.2 WHY LEND A HAND?

Why People Help	Explanation
Kin selection	We are more likely to help those who are close relatives, as it might promote the survival of our genes (Gray & Brogdon, 2017; Hamilton, 1964).
Empathy	We assist others to reduce their distress (Batson & Powell, 2003).
Social exchange theory	We help when the benefits of our good deeds outweigh the costs (Cropanzano, Anthony, Daniels, & Hall, 2017; Thibaut & Kelly, 1959).
Reciprocal altruism	We help those whom we believe can return the favor in the future (Brase, 2017; Trivers, 1971).
Mood	We tend to help others when our mood is good, but we also help when our spirits are low, knowing that this behavior can improve our mood (Batson & Powell, 2003; Schnall, Roper, & Fessler, 2010).

Listed here are some of the reasons people assist each other in times of need.

involved in stopping violence, we need to find ways to encourage emotional empathy. This is particularly important for boys, some of whom may need specific training on how to "recognize signs of distress in others" (Menolascino & Jenkins, 2018). Take a look at **Table 11.2** to learn about factors that increase helping behavior.

Aggression

THE ULTIMATE INSULT When Julius attended high school in Uganda's capital city of Kampala, he never told his classmates that he had been kidnapped by the LRA. "I would not tell them, or anybody, that I was a child soldier," he says. Had the other students known, they might have called him a *rebel*—one of the most derogatory terms you can use to describe a person in Uganda. Calling someone a rebel is like saying that individual is worthless. "You're poor; you do not know anything; you're a killer," Julius says. "It's the same pain as in America [when] they used to call Black people 'nigger.' You feel that kind of pain inside you . . . when they call you a 'rebel' within your country."

LO 9 Demonstrate an understanding of aggression and identify some of its causes.

Using racial slurs and hurling threatening insults is a form of *aggression*. Psychologists define **aggression** as intimidating or threatening behavior or attitudes intended to hurt someone. According to the **frustration–aggression hypothesis,** we all can exhibit aggressive behavior when placed in a frustrating situation (Dollard, Miller, Doob, Mowrer, & Sears, 1939). But aggressive tendencies also seem to be rooted in our genes. Studies comparing identical and fraternal twins suggest that aggression runs in families. **Identical twins**, who have nearly all the same genes, are more likely than fraternal twins to share aggressive traits (Bezdjian, Tuvblad, Raine, & Baker, 2011; Porsch et al., 2016). Some research on identical twins suggests that approximately 50–68% of aggressive behavior can be explained by genetic factors (Lubke, McArtor, Boomsma, & Bartels, 2018; DiLalla, 2002; Tackett, Waldman, & Lahey, 2009). Hormones and neurotransmitters also appear to play a role, with high levels of testosterone and low levels of serotonin correlating with aggression (Glenn, Raine, Schug, Gao, & Granger, 2011; Montoya, Terburg, Bos, & van Honk, 2012). Like any psychological phenomenon, aggression results from an interplay of biology and environment.

CONNECTIONS

In previous chapters, we noted that identical twins share 100% of their genetic material at conception, whereas fraternal twins share approximately 50%. Here, we see that identical twins are more likely than fraternal twins to share aggressive traits.

aggression Intimidating or threatening behavior or attitudes intended to hurt someone.

frustration–aggression hypothesis Suggests that aggression may occur in response to frustration.

Expressions of aggression may be influenced by gender. Men tend to show more *direct aggression* (physical displays of aggression such as hitting), while women are more likely to display *relational aggression*—behaviors such as gossip, exclusion, and

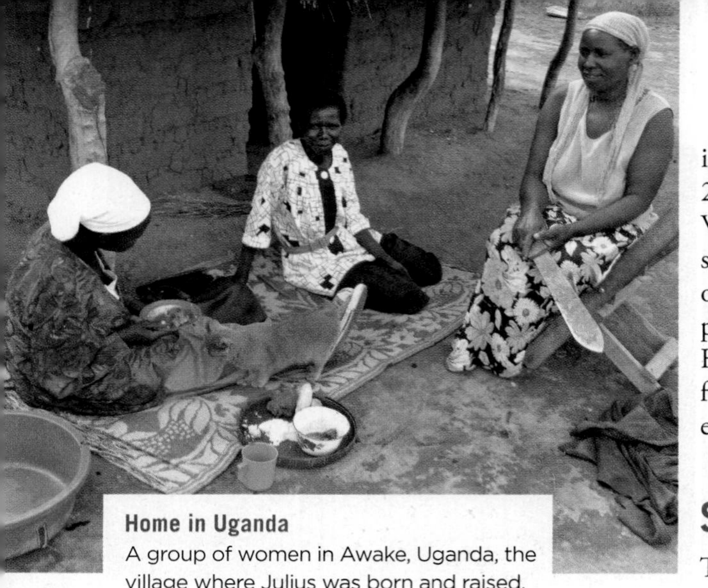

Home in Uganda

A group of women in Awake, Uganda, the village where Julius was born and raised. While living in the United States, Julius sometimes encountered stereotypes about African people. One time, a man approached him and said, "Is it true in Africa people still walk [around] naked?" The message behind this inaccurate stereotype was clearly aggressive; this man judged African people to be primitive and not as advanced as he was.
Courtesy Dr. Julie Gralow.

ignoring, which are indirect and aimed at relationships (Ainsworth & Maner, 2012; Archer & Coyne, 2005; Denson, O'Dean, Blake, & Beames, 2018). Why might women favor relational aggression over direct aggression? One reason, according to the evolutionary perspective, is that females run a greater risk of bodily injury from a physical confrontation (Campbell, 1999). Gender disparities in aggressive behavior typically appear early in life (Denson et al., 2018; Hanish, Sallquist, DiDonato, Fabes, & Martin, 2012, September), and result from a complex interaction of genetics and environmental factors (Brendgen et al., 2005; Lubke et al., 2018).

Stereotypes and Discrimination

Typically, we associate aggression with behavior, but it can also exist in the mind, coloring our *attitudes* about people and things. This is evidenced by the existence of **stereotypes**—the conclusions or inferences we make about people who are different from us, based on their group membership (race, religion, age, or gender, for example). Stereotypes are often negative (*Blondes are airheads*), but they can also be perceived as positive (*Asians are good at math*). Either way, stereotypes can be harmful. The stereotypical college instructor is absentminded, absorbed in thought, and unapproachable. The quintessential motorcycle rider is covered in tattoos, and the teenager with the tongue ring is rebelling against her parents. What do all these stereotypes have in common? They are not objective or grounded in empirical research. Stereotypes typically include a variety of **predicted behaviors** and traits that are rooted in subjective observations and value judgments.

CONNECTIONS

In **Chapter 7,** we described various heuristics, or shortcuts to problem solving. With the representativeness heuristic, we make quick judgments about how closely a person fits our preconceived prototype of a person belonging to a certain group. However, our preconceived ideas are not always accurate, and this can lead to the creation of stereotypes.

LO 10 Recognize how group affiliation influences the development of stereotypes.

GROUPS AND SOCIAL IDENTITY Evolutionary psychologists suggest that stereotypes have allowed human beings to quickly identify the group to which they belong (Liddle, Shackelford, & Weekes-Shackelford, 2012)—an adaptive trait, given that groups provide safety. But because we are inclined to think our group is superior, we may draw incorrect conclusions about members of other groups, or outsiders in general. We tend to see the world in terms of the **in-group** (the group to which we belong, or *us*) and the **out-group** (those outside our group, or *them*). Those in the out-group are particularly vulnerable to becoming scapegoats. A **scapegoat** is the target of negative emotions, beliefs, and behaviors. During periods of major stress (such as an economic crisis), scapegoats are often blamed for undesirable social situations (high unemployment). In the 1930s and 40s, German dictator Adolf Hitler blamed Jewish people for the country's problems, and this scapegoating led to unconscionable treatment of the Jewish population.

Our affiliation with an in-group helps us form a **social identity,** or view of ourselves within a social group, and this process begins at a very young age. But if we only associate with certain crowds, we may be prone to **ethnocentrism,** or seeing the world from the narrow perspective of our own group. This term is often used in reference to cultural groups, yet it can apply to any group (think of football teams, glee clubs, college rivals, or nations). We tend to see our own country or group as the one that is worthy of emulation. This type of group identification can lead to **discrimination,** or showing favoritism or hostility to others because of their group affiliation.

PREJUDICE Discrimination is closely tied to **prejudice,** hostile or negative attitudes toward individuals or groups (**INFOGRAPHIC 11.3**). While some would argue that racial prejudice has declined in the United States over the last half-century,

stereotypes Conclusions or inferences we make about people who are different from us based on their group membership, such as race, religion, age, or gender.

in-group The group to which we belong.

out-group People outside the group to which we belong.

scapegoat A target of negative emotions, beliefs, and behaviors; typically, a member of the out-group who receives blame for an upsetting social situation.

social identity How we view ourselves within our social group.

ethnocentrism Seeing the world only from the perspective of one's own group.

discrimination Showing favoritism or hostility to others because of their affiliation with a group.

prejudice Holding hostile or negative attitudes toward an individual or group.

Thinking About Other People

Stereotypes, Discrimination, and Prejudice

Attitudes are complex and only sometimes related to our behaviors. Like most attitudes, prejudicial attitudes can be connected with our *cognitions* about groups of people (also known as stereotypes), our negative *attitudes* and *feelings* about others (also referred to as prejudice), and our *behaviors* (discriminating against others). Understanding how and when these pieces connect to each other is an important goal of social psychology. Jane Elliott's classic "Blue Eyes/Brown Eyes" exercise helps demonstrate how stereotypes, discrimination, and prejudice may be connected.

Prejudicial attitude toward others

Cognitive component (beliefs and ideas)

We tend to categorize people in terms of the *in-group* (the group to which we belong) and the *out-group* (people different from us in some way). **Stereotypes** are beliefs or assumptions we hold about people, based on perceived differences we think describe members of their group.

Affective component (emotional evaluation)

Prejudice, or feelings of hostility, anger, or discomfort toward members of out-groups.

Social psychologists often use prejudice to refer to both these negative attitudes and the negative feelings tied to them.

Behavioral component (the way we respond)

Discrimination, or treating others differently because of their affiliation with a group. Can include showing hostility or anger to others, or can be more subtle, such as different body language or tone of voice.

Stereotype

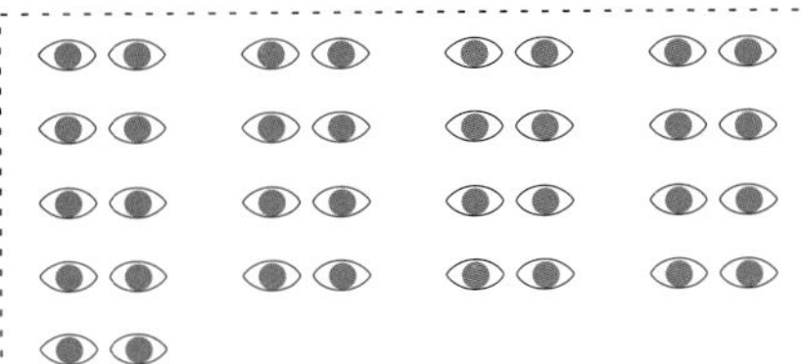

"cleaner, more civilized, smarter"

When Dr. Martin Luther King, Jr., was assassinated in 1968, a teacher named Jane Elliott gave her students a lesson about discrimination. Because no African Americans lived in their Iowa town, she knew students would have trouble understanding what motivated the terrible act. Elliott invited the class to join her in an exercise in which one set of students was segregated into a negatively stereotyped out-group: "Suppose we divided the class into blue-eyed people and brown-eyed people.... [B]rown-eyed people are better than blue-eyed people. They are cleaner . . . more civilized . . . smarter" (Peters, 1971, pp. 20–21).

Prejudice

Prejudice: Brown-eyes dislike blue-eyes, but have to be nice while in class.

Prejudice and Discrimination: Brown-eyes dislike blue-eyes and exclude them from games at recess.

Discrimination: Brown-eyes, who are required to sit at the front of the room, do not sit with blue-eyes, who must sit at the back.

In her exercise, Elliott created a situation in which discrimination initially existed without the presence of actual feelings of hostility or anger. Although prejudice and discrimination often go hand in hand, either condition can exist independently.

Discrimination

During the exercise, a list of rules governed behavior for both groups. For example, only children with brown eyes were allowed to sit at the front of the room near the teacher. The effect of this manufactured discrimination surprised even Elliott. The brown-eyed children quickly became openly hostile toward the blue-eyed children. And "[t]he blue-eyed children were miserable.... [T]heir entire attitudes were those of defeat. Their classroom work regressed sharply from that of the day before" (Peters, 1971, p. 25).

Transcending Prejudice
College student Salim Salim knows what it means to be the target of unpleasant prejudice. As an Iraqi immigrant growing up in Portland, Maine, he encountered classmates with hostile attitudes toward people from the Middle East. "They called me immigrant, terrorist, suicide bomber, and even Osama bin Laden," Salim said in his TEDx Talk. "I was categorized and labeled so much that I was convinced that I didn't belong here" (TedxDirigo, 2015, 2:30, 4:00). Eventually, Salim came to understand that he could transcend categories and labels, and help others do the same. His classmates at Bowdoin College recognized him as a leader, electing him Vice President of Student Affairs. Carly Berlin/Courtesy Salim Salim.

there is considerable evidence that negative attitudes persist. The same is true when it comes to sexual orientation, disabilities, and religious beliefs (Carr, Dweck, & Pauker, 2012; Dovidio, Kawakami, & Gaertner, 2002). Most of us like to believe we are free of prejudice, but it often occurs outside of awareness. *Implicit bias* is a type of unconscious bias that reveals itself through "our behavior toward members of particular social groups, but we remain oblivious to [its] influence" (Banaji & Greenwald, 2013, p. xii). For example, a bank teller may believe she treats every client equally, be they Black, White, Asian, or Hispanic. But a closer look at her behaviors—the warmth she shows in her body language, facial expressions, and subtle choices in wording—may reveal otherwise. Researchers have used a variety of tasks to uncover these unconscious attitudes (Ito et al., 2015), and you can even try some of these tasks online (type key terms like "implicit association test online" into your browser and see what comes up).

How can implicit bias be reduced? We can start by trying to view members of an out-group in a positive light—seeing a "helpful person" or a "wealthy person" as opposed to someone in "that group," for example (Lee, Lindquist, & Payne, 2018; Gonzalez, Steele, & Baron, 2017). When it comes to race, we should remember that labels like Black and White are social categories rather than biological distinctions (Gannon, 2016, February 5). Indeed, some scientists believe that "race is neither a relevant nor accurate way to understand or map human genetic diversity" (Yudell, Roberts, DeSalle, & Tishkoff, 2016, p. 564). Did you know that two people of different races (for example, Black and White) can be more genetically similar than two people of the same race (Witherspoon et al., 2007)?

Evidence suggests that prejudice may diminish when people are forced to work together toward a common goal. In the early 1970s, American psychologist Eliot Aronson and colleagues developed the notion of a *jigsaw classroom*. The teachers created exercises that required all students to complete individual tasks, the results of which would fit together like a jigsaw puzzle. The students began to realize the importance of working cooperatively to reach the desired goal. Ultimately, every contribution was an essential piece of the puzzle, and this resulted in all the students feeling valuable (Aronson, 2015).

STEREOTYPE THREAT Stereotypes, discrimination, and prejudice are conceptually related to **stereotype threat,** a "situational threat" in which a person is aware of negative expectations from others. This leads to a fear of being judged or treated as inferior, and it can actually undermine performance in a specific area associated with the stereotype (Steele, 1997).

African American college students are often the targets of racial stereotypes about poor academic abilities. This can lead to lowered performance on tests designed to measure ability, and to a *disidentification* with the role of student (taking on the attitude *I am not a student*). Interestingly, a person does not have to believe the stereotype is accurate in order to be impacted (Steele, 1997, 2010). One way to counteract this disidentification, which disproportionately impacts male students, is by "building trusting, positive relationships among students and faculty" (McClain & Cokley, 2017, p. 131).

There is a great deal of variation in how people react to stereotype threats (Block, Koch, Liberman, Merriweather, & Roberson, 2011). Some "fend off" the stereotype by working harder to disprove it. Others feel discouraged and respond by getting angry, either overtly or quietly. Still others seem to ignore the threats. These resilient types appear to "bounce back" and grow from the negative experience. When confronted with a stereotype, they redirect their responses to create an environment that is more inclusive and less conducive to stereotyping.

Unfortunately, stereotypes are pervasive in our society. Just contemplate all the positive and negative stereotypes associated with certain lines of work. Lawyers are greedy, truck drivers are overweight, and (dare we say) psychologists are manipulative.

stereotype threat A "situational threat" in which individuals are aware of others' negative expectations, which leads to a fear of being judged or treated as inferior.

Can you think of any negative stereotypes associated with prison guards? As you read the next feature, think about how stereotypes can come to life when people fail to step back and reflect on their behaviors.

...BELIEVE IT...OR NOT

THE STANFORD "PRISON" August 1971: Philip Zimbardo of Stanford University launched what would become one of the most controversial experiments in the history of psychology. Zimbardo and his colleagues carefully selected 24 male college students to play the roles of prisoners and guards in a simulated "prison" setup in the basement of Stanford University's psychology building. The young men chosen for the experiment were deemed "normal-average" by the researchers, who administered several psychological tests (Haney, Banks, & Zimbardo, 1973, p. 90).

"LOOKING BACK, I'M IMPRESSED HOW LITTLE I FELT FOR THEM."

After being "arrested" in their homes by Palo Alto Police officers, the prisoners were searched and booked at a local police station, and then sent to the "prison" at Stanford. The experiment was supposed to last for 2 weeks, but the behavior of some guards and prisoners was so disturbing the researchers abandoned the study after just 6 days (Haney & Zimbardo, 1998). Certain guards became abusive, punishing the prisoners, stripping them naked, and confiscating their mattresses. It seemed as if they had lost sight of the prisoners' humanity, as they ruthlessly wielded their newfound power. As one guard stated, "Looking back, I'm impressed how little I felt for them" (Haney et al., 1973, p. 88). Some prisoners became passive and obedient, accepting the guards' cruel treatment; others were released early due to "extreme emotional depression, crying, rage, and acute anxiety" (p. 81).

How can we explain this fiasco? The guards and prisoners, it seemed, took their assigned **social roles** and ran way too far with them. Social roles are the positions we hold in social groups, and all the associated responsibilities and expectations. These roles guide our behavior in ways we may not even realize.

The prison experiment may have shed light on the power of social roles, but its validity has come under fire. Critics suggest that the participants were merely "acting out their stereotypic images" of guards and prisoners, and behaving in accordance with the researchers' expectations (Banuazizi & Movahedi, 1975, p. 159). As one guard explained decades later, "[Zimbardo] knew what he wanted and then tried to shape the experiment . . . to fit the conclusion that he had already worked out. He wanted to be able to say that . . . people will turn on each other just because they're given a role and given power" (Ratnesar, 2011, July/August, para. 35). Apparently, Zimbardo made his expectations quite clear, instructing the guards to deny the prisoners their "privacy," "freedom," and "individuality" (Zimbardo, 2007). Without this type of guidance from Zimbardo, do you think the study outcome would have been the same? Perhaps not, as "guards" in other prison studies exhibited very different behaviors (Griggs & Whitehead, 2014; Haslam & Reicher, 2012). In the BBC Prison study, for instance, guards were "reluctant to impose their authority"; meanwhile, "prisoners began to mock, challenge, and undermine the guards," and some orchestrated a breakout (Haslam & Reicher, 2012, p. 159).

The Stanford Prison Experiment has been criticized for many reasons, including questionable ethics, bias in selecting participants, and failure to adequately explain why participants responded differently to their assigned roles (Griggs, 2014b). Nevertheless, this study continues to be relevant. In 2004 news broke that American soldiers and intelligence officials at Iraq's Abu Ghraib prison had beaten, sodomized, and forced detainees to commit degrading sexual acts (Hersh, 2004, May 10). The similarities between Abu Ghraib and the Stanford Prison are noteworthy (Zimbardo, 2007).

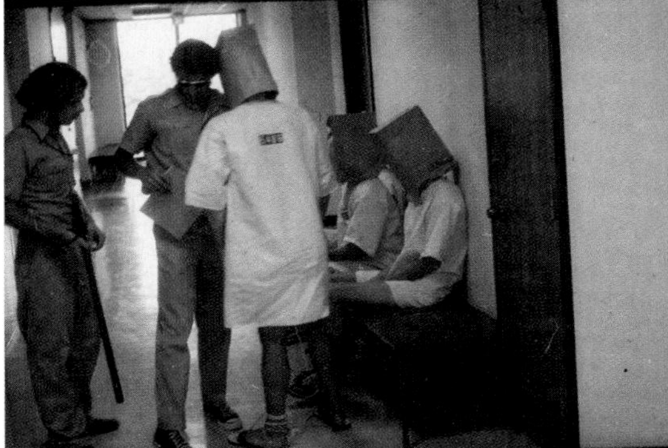

Prison Horrors
(top) Prisoners in Zimbardo's 1971 prison experiment are forced to wear bags over their heads. (bottom) In 2003 an Abu Ghraib detainee lies on the floor attached to a leash. The treatment of prisoners in the "Stanford Prison" and the Abu Ghraib facility were disturbingly similar. In both cases, authority figures threatened, abused, and forced inmates to be naked. Those in charge seemed to derive pleasure from violating and humiliating other human beings (Haney et al., 1973; Hersh, 2004, May 10). Top: Philip G. Zimbardo, Inc. Bottom: AP Photo.

social roles The positions we hold in social groups, and the responsibilities and expectations associated with those roles.

Much of this chapter has focused on negative aspects of human behavior, such as obedience, stereotyping, and discrimination. While we cannot deny the existence of these phenomena, we believe they are overshadowed by the goodness that lies within every one of us.

show what you know

1. ______________ is the tendency for people to stand by and do nothing in an emergency because they assume someone else will step in to help.
   - a. Group polarization
   - b. The risky shift
   - c. The bystander effect
   - d. Deindividuation
2. Name and describe the different displays of aggression exhibited by males and females.
3. Students often have difficulty identifying how the concepts of stereotype, discrimination, and prejudice are related. How would you explain their similarities and differences to a sixth grader?

✓ CHECK YOUR ANSWERS IN APPENDIX C.

Prosocial Behavior, Attraction, and Love

JULIUS MAKES IT HAPPEN We believe that all human beings are capable of *prosocial behavior,* or behavior aimed at benefiting others. An exemplar of this ability is Julius Achon. After meeting the orphans in 2003, Julius kept his promise to assist them, wiring his family $150 a month to cover the cost of food, clothing, and other necessities—even when he and his wife were struggling to stay afloat. For 3 years, Julius was the children's sole source of financial support. Then, in 2007 he formalized his efforts by creating the Achon Uganda Children's Fund (AUCF), a nonprofit organization dedicated to improving the living conditions of children in the rural areas of northern Uganda. Julius currently lives in Uganda, where he oversees the work of the AUCF and represents his home district in the Ugandan Parliament (similar to the Senate in the United States).

As for the 11 orphans, they are flourishing. Most of them have completed high school and gone on to college; one is a nurse at the medical clinic created by the AUCF; and another has become a competitive runner like Julius.

Beautiful Children
Julius runs alongside boys and girls from Uganda's Otuke district, home to the Kristina Acuma Achon Health Center, a medical clinic created by Julius' nonprofit organization, the AUCF. The center is named after Julius' mother, who was shot by the LRA in 2004 and died from her wounds because she lacked access to proper medical care. For more information about Julius and the AUCF, please go to http://achonugandachildren.org, or read *The Boy Who Runs,* a book by John Brant. SAMSON OPUS.

On the Upside

LO 11 Describe altruism.

It feels good to give to others, even when you receive nothing in return. The satisfaction of knowing you made someone feel happier, more secure, or appreciated is enough of a reward. The desire or motivation to help others with no expectation of payback is called **altruism.** *Empathy,* or the ability to recognize and understand another's emotional point of view, is a major component of altruism.

ARE TODDLERS ALTRUISTIC? The seeds of altruism may be planted very early in life. One study found that the vast majority of 18-month-olds would help a researcher obtain an out-of-reach object, assist him in a book-stacking exercise, and open a door for him when his hands were full. The babies only helped when it appeared assistance was needed. They did not lend a hand when the researcher intentionally put the object out of reach, or if he appeared satisfied with the stack of books (Warneken & Tomasello, 2006). Although altruism is apparent in babies, it is "selective from the start." Rather than helping just anyone, they show a preference for those who are familiar and those "who have been kind to them in the past" (Wynn, Bloom, Jordan, Marshall, & Sheskin, 2018, p. 3). Findings from twin studies suggest "considerable heritability" of altruistic tendencies and other prosocial behaviors (Jiang, Chew, & Ebstein, 2013). But as always, we must consider the biopsychosocial perspective, that is, recognize the interaction of genetics, environment, and culture (Knafo & Israel, 2010).

A SECRET TO HAPPINESS? Helping and showing care for others may reduce stress and increase happiness (Cohen, Janicki-Deverts, Turner, & Doyle, 2015; Schwartz, Keyl, Marcum, & Bode, 2009; Schwartz, Meisenhelder, Yunsheng, & Reed, 2003). The gestures don't have to be grand in order to be altruistic or prosocial. Consider the last time you bought coffee for a colleague without being asked, or gave a stranger a quarter to fill his parking meter. Do you recycle, conserve electricity, and take public transportation? These behaviors indicate an awareness of the need to conserve resources for the benefit of all. Promoting sustainability is an indirect, yet very impactful, prosocial endeavor.

Even if you're not the type to reach out to strangers, you probably demonstrate prosocial behavior toward your family and close friends. This giving of yourself allows you to experience the most magical element of human existence: love.

You Asked, Julius Answers

http://qrs.ly/ea5a5ga

What advice would you give to someone interested in charitable work?

The Psychology of Sexiness

TO HAVE AND TO HOLD About eight months after meeting on Tinder, Dennis and Alexa returned to the beach where they first exchanged the words, "I love you." In the middle of goofing around and taking silly pictures, Dennis got down on his knee and pulled out an engagement ring. Alexa was so shocked that she took off running and came back laughing. There to witness the whole moment (in between mouthfuls of sand) was Brutus the French bulldog. It was important for Brutus to be present; after all, his photo was the main reason Alexa responded to Dennis' initial message. A few months later, the couple tied the knot in a cozy beach ceremony, with 50 of their family members and closest friends watching. Since then, marriage has been treating them well. "It is just so fun to have . . . someone to come home to who is excited to hear about all the unimportant details of my day, and to share in my victories and my defeats," Alexa says. Dennis is equally content: "I get to hang out with my best friend."

The Answer is YES!
Alexa and Dennis celebrate their engagement. The proposal caught Alexa completely off guard. "I was really, really excited," Alexa recalls. "For weeks, he had just been saying, 'No, it's not going to happen.'" Dennis had tricked Alexa, which added some humor to the moment. Courtesy Alexa Antoni.

LO 12 Identify the three major factors contributing to interpersonal attraction.

Alexa and Dennis seem to be an ideal match. We suspect their compatibility has something to do with **interpersonal attraction,** the factors that lead us to form friendships or romantic relationships with others. Among the most important are proximity, similarity, and physical attractiveness.

WE'RE CLOSE: PROXIMITY We would guess that the majority of people in your social circle live nearby. **Proximity,** or nearness, plays a significant role in the formation of our relationships. The closer people live geographically, the greater the odds they will meet, spend time together, and establish a bond (Festinger, Schachter, & Back, 1950; Nahemow & Lawton, 1975). One study concluded that sitting in nearby seats and being assigned to the same groups in a college classroom correlates with the development of friendships (Back, Schmukle, & Egloff, 2008). In other words, sitting next to someone in class, or even in the same row, increases the chances you will become friends. Would you agree?

altruism A desire or motivation to help others with no expectation of anything in return.

interpersonal attraction The factors that lead us to form friendships or romantic relationships with others.

proximity Nearness; plays an important role in the formation of relationships.

MERE-EXPOSURE EFFECT Repeated interactions with partners may bring us closer together through the **mere-exposure effect.** In other words, the more we are exposed to people, food, jingles, songs, politics, or music, the more positive our reactions become. For years, researchers have been asking why the mere-exposure effect occurs. The answer is complex, and years of study have been devoted to this topic (Montoya, Horton, Vevea, Citkowicz, & Lauber, 2017). Researchers have also discovered that repeated *negative* exposures may lead to stronger distaste. If a person you frequently encounter has annoying habits or uncouth behavior, negative feelings might develop, even if your initial impression was positive (Cunningham, Shamblen, Barbee, & Ault, 2005). This can be problematic for romantic partners. All those minor irritations you overlooked early in the relationship can evolve into major headaches.

SIMILARITY Perhaps you have heard the saying "birds of a feather flock together." This statement alludes to the concept of *similarity,* another factor that contributes to interpersonal attraction (Moreland & Zajonc, 1982; Morry, Kito, & Ortiz, 2011). We tend to prefer those who share our interests, viewpoints, race, values, and other characteristics. Even age, education, and occupation tend to be similar among those who are close (Brooks & Neville, 2016; Lott & Lott, 1965).

PHYSICAL ATTRACTIVENESS We probably don't need to tell you that *physical attractiveness* plays a major role in interpersonal attraction (Eastwick, Eagly, Finkel, & Johnson, 2011; Lou & Zhang, 2009). Even online, men are more likely to reach out to women they find attractive. Research suggests that profile pictures play a more important role for men when it comes to making initial contact through an online dating site (Eastwick, Luchies, Finkel, & Hunt, 2014). But here is the question: Is beauty really in the eye of the beholder? In other words, do people from different cultures and historical periods have different concepts of beauty? There is some degree of consistency in the way people rate facial attractiveness (Langlois et al., 2000; Sutherland, Liu, Zhang, Oldmeadow, & Young, 2018), with facial symmetry generally considered attractive (Boothroyd, Meins, Vukovic, & Burt, 2014; Grammer & Thornhill, 1994). But certain aspects of beauty do appear to be culturally distinct (Gangestad & Scheyd, 2005). In some parts of the world, people go to great lengths to elongate their necks, increase their height, pierce their bodies, augment their breasts, and enlarge or reduce the size of their waists—just so others within their culture will find them attractive.

Sexy Stubble
Actor Shah Rukh Khan sports a bit of facial hair at the Asian Awards 2015 in London. What do women find most attractive—a face that is cleanly shaven, fully bearded, or somewhere in between? According to research, "heavy stubble" wins the sexiness prize. Full beards, on the other hand, tend to be associated with "parenting ability and healthiness" (Dixson & Brooks, 2013, p. 236). Karwai Tang/Getty Images.

LOOKING GOOD IN THOSE GENES! Why is physical attractiveness so important? Beauty is a sign of health, and healthy people have greater potential for longevity and successful breeding. Consider this evidence: Women are more likely to seek out men with healthy-looking physical characteristics when they are experiencing peak fertility and therefore likely to conceive. Ovulating women tend to look for masculine characteristics that suggest a genetic advantage, such as facial symmetry and social dominance, in order to provide the greatest benefit to offspring (Gangestad & Scheyd, 2005).

BEAUTY PERKS We have discussed beauty in the context of attraction, but how does physical appearance affect other aspects of social existence? Generally speaking, physically attractive people seem to have more opportunities. Beauty is correlated with how much money people make, the type of jobs they have, and overall success (Pfeifer, 2012). Good-looking children and adults are viewed as more intelligent and popular, and are treated better in general (Langlois et al., 2000). Why would this be? From the perspective of evolutionary psychology, these beauty characteristics are good indicators of reproductive potential. Our evaluations of beautiful people may also be

mere-exposure effect The more we are exposed to someone or something, the more positive our reaction to it becomes.

influenced by the *halo effect,* or the tendency to assign excessive importance to one dimension of a person. As early psychologist Edward Thorndike pointed out, people tend to form general impressions early on and then cling to them, even in the absence of supporting evidence, or the presence of contradictory evidence (Aronson, 2018). This may not be the case for everyone, however. Research suggests that "other women may respond with hostility and resentment when exposed to women who are more beautiful than themselves," especially when those attractive women wear makeup (DelPriore, Bradshaw, & Hill, 2018, p. 16). Our initial impressions of people's beauty may lead us to assume they have positive characteristics like superior intelligence, popularity, and desirability—but it also may lead to enmity when we feel others are working too hard to be beautiful.

We know that people are romantically drawn to those who are similar, good-looking, and geographically close, but what other factors may play a role? Read on; we are pretty sure this one is going to surprise you.

From the SCIENTIFIC pages of AMERICAN

IN HUMAN ATTRACTION, YOU ARE WHAT YOU EAT

Women prefer the scent of men who eat diets rich in certain foods—including garlic!

When it comes to your love life, the impact of your diet could go beyond having a few extra pounds around the waist—what you eat may also influence how pleasing your body smells to members of the opposite sex. Scientists have long observed such a link in animal research—female salamanders are attracted to males that eat nutrient-rich diets, for example—and something similar may be true in humans, some preliminary studies suggest.

dlerick/Getty Images.

In a series of experiments published in . . . *Appetite,* 42 men snacked on raw garlic or swallowed garlic capsules, then wore cotton pads under their armpits for 12 hours. The same men also donated pads after wearing them on a garlic-free diet. The pungent samples were later evaluated by 14 women, who collectively rated the body odor of garlic eaters as more pleasant, attractive and masculine compared with that of men who did not ingest any garlic. The men needed to eat at least four cloves or one 1,000-milligram garlic-extract capsule to have a measurable effect. Because garlic enhances levels of antioxidants in the body and kills harmful bacteria, it could change the way our sweat smells, signaling healthiness to potential mates, the researchers hypothesize. "Women may also use cues in body odor to find a partner who can secure quality food," says ethologist Jitka Fialová of Charles University in Prague, the study's lead author.

Garlic is not the only food that might boost a man's sex appeal. For a 2016 study published in *Evolution and Human Behavior,* psychologists at Macquarie University in Sydney, Australia, had several women rate the smell of T-shirts worn by 43 men for 24 hours. The men filled out questionnaires about the foods they ate, and researchers measured the yellowness of the men's skin to gauge their consumption of carotenoids—pigments found in veggies and fruits such as pumpkins, carrots or apricots. Previous studies have found that carotenoid-induced yellowish skin is more visually attractive to potential partners—at least among Caucasians. In this study, the women reported the scent of men who indulged in carotenoid-rich foods to be fruity, sweet and particularly pleasant. These findings, too, could be explained by our evolved skills for finding healthy partners because low plasma carotenoid levels are associated with infection and greater mortality.

So how soon before a date should you pile on the garlic and veggies? Is it really going to sway things your way? And do men find women who eat the same diets as attractive? The jury is still out on these questions. One thing is certain, though—garlic breath is no aphrodisiac, so time your consumption wisely. **Marta Zaraska. Reproduced with permission.**

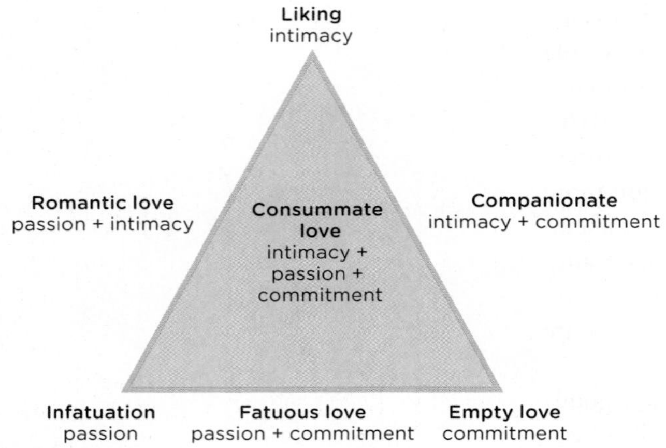

FIGURE 11.4
Sternberg's Triangular Model of Love
Sternberg proposed that there are different kinds of love resulting from a combination of three elements: passion, intimacy, and commitment. The ideal form, consummate love, combines all three elements.
(Information from Sternberg, 1986.)

What Is Love?

In America, we are taught to believe that love is the foundation of marriage. People in Western cultures do tend to marry for love, but this is not the case everywhere. In Harare, Zimbabwe, for example, people might also marry for reasons associated with family needs, such as maintaining alliances and social status (Wojcicki, van der Straten, & Padian, 2010), or for religious reasons (Hallfors et al., 2016). Similarly, many marriages in India and other parts of South Asia are arranged by family members. Love may not be present in the beginning stages of such unions, but it can blossom.

STERNBERG'S THEORY OF LOVE In a pivotal study published in 1986, Robert Sternberg proposed that love is made up of three elements: passion (feelings leading to romance and physical attraction); intimacy (feeling close); and commitment (the recognition of love). He conceptualized these elements as the corners of a triangle (**Figure 11.4**). Love takes many forms, according to Sternberg, and can include any combination of the three elements. Many relationships begin with exhilaration and intense physical attraction, and then evolve into more intimate connections. This is the type of love we often see portrayed in the movies. The combination of connection, passion, care, and intimacy is what Sternberg called **romantic love.** Romantic love is similar to what some psychologists refer to as **passionate love** (also known as "love at first sight"), which is based on zealous emotion, leading to intense longing and sexual attraction (Hatfield, Bensman, & Rapson, 2012). As a relationship grows, intimacy and commitment develop into **companionate love,** or love that consists of profound fondness, camaraderie, understanding, and emotional closeness. Companionate love is typical of a couple that has been together for many years. They become comfortable with each other, routines set in, and passion often fizzles (Aronson, 2018). **Consummate love** (KON-suh-mit) occurs when intimacy and commitment are accompanied by passion. In other words, all three components of the triangle are present.

Research and life experience tell us that relationships inevitably change. Romantic love is generally what drives people to commit to one another (Berscheid, 2010), but the passion of this stage generally decreases over time. Can you think of ways this passion might be rekindled? Companionate love, in contrast, tends to grow over time. As we experience life with a partner, it is companionate love that seems to endear us to one another (Berscheid, 2010).

CONNECTIONS
In **Chapter 3,** we discussed sensory adaptation, which occurs when sensory receptors become less sensitive to constant stimuli. In **Chapter 5,** we presented the concept of habituation, a learning process whereby an organism reduces its response to a recurring stimulus. Humans seem to be attracted to novelty, which might underlie our desire for passion.

IN IT FOR THE LONG HAUL? Couples stay together for many reasons, some better than others. Caryl Rusbult's *investment model of commitment* focuses on the resources at stake in relationships, including finances, possessions, time spent together, and perhaps even children (Rusbult, 1983). According to this model, decisions to stay together or separate are based on happiness with the relationship, ideas of what life would be like without it, and personal investment. Sometimes people stay in unsatisfying or unhealthy relationships because they feel they have too much to lose or no better alternatives (Rusbult & Martz, 1995).

The ability to deal with relationship troubles may depend somewhat on perceptions of what the relationship represents: Do you view your relationship as something that was written in the stars (destined to happen), or more like a long journey you embark upon together? (North, 2014, August 1). "It may be romantic for lovers to think they were made for each other, but it backfires when conflicts arise and reality pokes the bubble of perfect unity" (Lee & Schwarz, 2014, p. 64). A better approach may be to consider your love a journey—one that might have "twists and turns but ultimately [is] moving toward a destination" (p. 64).

romantic love Love that is a combination of connection, concern, care, and intimacy.

passionate love Love that is based on zealous emotion, leading to intense longing and sexual attraction.

companionate love Love that consists of profound fondness, camaraderie, understanding, and emotional closeness.

consummate love Love that combines intimacy, commitment, and passion.

At last, we reach the end of our journey through social psychology. Hopefully you can use what you have learned in your everyday social interactions; research suggests you may be better at it than you realize (Gollwitzer & Bargh, 2018). Be conscious of the attributions you use to explain the behavior of others—are you being objective or falling prey to self-serving bias? Bear in mind that attitudes have a powerful impact on behavior—what types of attitudes do you harbor and how do they impact your everyday decisions? Know that your behaviors are constantly being shaped by your social interactions—both as an individual and as a member of groups. Understand the dangers of prejudice, discrimination, and stereotyping, and know the human suffering caused by aggression. But perhaps most of all, be kind and helpful to others, and allow yourself to experience love.

Young Love
Dennis and Alexa tied the knot on a beautiful beach in San Diego on March 25, 2017. The couple recently moved to Twentynine Palms, a remote desert base in California. "The town is small, the weather is terrible, and we are miles and miles away from the comforts we're used to," says Alexa. "But we are really enjoying the uninterrupted time we get to spend together on what we're calling our 'couples retreat.'" Courtesy Alexa Antoni.

✓ show what you know

1. Julius sent money home every month to help cover the cost of food, clothing, and schooling for the 11 orphaned children. This is a good example of:
   a. the just-world hypothesis.
   b. deindividuation.
   c. individualistic behavior.
   d. prosocial behavior.
2. What are the three major factors that play a role in interpersonal attraction?
   a. social influence; obedience; physical attractiveness
   b. proximity; similarity; physical attractiveness
   c. obedience; proximity; social influence
   d. proximity; love; social influence
3. We described how the investment model of commitment can be used to predict the long-term stability of a romantic relationship. How can you use this same model to predict the long-term stability of friendships, positions at work, or loyalty to institutions?

✓ CHECK YOUR ANSWERS IN APPENDIX C.

YOUR SCIENTIFIC WORLD is a new application-based feature appearing in every chapter. In these online activities, you will take on role-playing scenarios that encourage you to think critically and apply your knowledge of psychological science to solve a real-world problem. For example: Have you ever been persuaded to join a group? In this activity, you'll explore the power of persuasion as you create posters to recruit new members to your campus recycling group. You can access Your Scientific World activities in LaunchPad. Have fun!

SUMMARY OF CONCEPTS

LO 1 Define social psychology and identify how it differs from sociology. (p. 403)

Social psychology is the study of human cognition, emotion, and behavior in relation to others. Social psychology focuses on studying individuals in relation to others and groups, whereas sociology studies the groups themselves—their cultures, societies, and subcultures. Social psychologists use the same general research methods as other psychologists, but their studies sometimes have an added twist of deception. This deception may involve the use of *confederates,* or people secretly working for the researchers. At the end of a study, researchers debrief participants, or review aspects of the research they had previously concealed.

LO 2 Define social cognition and describe how we use attributions to explain behavior. (p. 404)

Social cognition refers to the way we think about others, attend to social information, and use this information in our lives, both consciously and unconsciously. Attributions are the beliefs we develop to explain human behaviors and characteristics, as well as situations. Because attributions rely on whatever information happens to be available (our observations of what people say and do, for example), they are vulnerable to personal bias and inaccuracies.

LO 3 Describe several common attribution errors. (p. 406)

A situational attribution is a type of external attribution wherein behaviors are assumed to result from situational factors.

Dispositional attributions are a type of internal attribution wherein behaviors are thought to result from traits or personality characteristics. Making attributions involves a certain amount of guesswork, and this leaves plenty of room for error. Common mistakes include (1) the fundamental attribution error, where the tendency is to favor dispositional attributions over situational attributions; (2) the just-world hypothesis, the tendency to believe the world is a fair place and individuals generally get what they deserve; and (3) the self-serving bias, the tendency to attribute successes to personal characteristics and failures to environmental factors.

LO 4 Explain the meaning of social influence and recognize factors associated with persuasion. (p. 412)

Social influence refers to the way a person is affected by others, as evidenced in behavior, emotion, and cognition. Expectations are a powerful, yet often unspoken, form of social influence. Research suggests that student performance is impacted by teacher expectations. Persuasion is consciously trying to make people change their attitudes and beliefs, which may (or may not) lead to changes in their behavior. Persuasive power is determined by three factors: the source, the message, and the audience.

LO 5 Define compliance and explain some of the techniques used to gain it. (p. 415)

Compliance occurs when people voluntarily change their behavior at the request or direction of another person (or group), who generally does not have any true authority over them. A common method to gain compliance is the foot-in-the-door technique, which occurs when someone makes a small request, followed by a larger request. Another method is the door-in-the-face technique, which occurs when someone makes a large request, followed by a smaller request.

LO 6 Identify the factors that influence the likelihood of someone conforming. (p. 416)

The tendency to modify behaviors, attitudes, beliefs, and opinions to match those of others is known as conformity. There are three major reasons we conform. Most people want approval, to be liked and accepted by others. This desire, known as normative social influence, can have a significant impact on behaviors. We also conform to be correct, looking to others for confirmation when we are uncertain about something, and then doing as they do. This is known as informational social influence. Finally, we may conform to others because they belong to a certain reference group we respect, admire, or long to join.

Describe obedience and explain how Stanley Milgram studied it. (p. 419)

Obedience occurs when we change our behavior, or act in a way that we might not normally act, because we have been ordered to do so by an authority figure. Milgram conducted a series of studies examining how far people would go when urged by an authority figure to inflict punishment on others. During an early experiment, the goal was for the confederate (*learner*) to memorize a set of paired words. The participant (*teacher*) sat before a control panel for administering electrical "shocks." The teacher was told to administer a shock each time the learner made a mistake, and the shock was to increase by 15 volts for every mistake. An astonishing 60–65% of participants continued to the highest voltage level, and similar findings have been produced in subsequent studies around the world.

Recognize the circumstances that influence the occurrence of the bystander effect. (p. 425)

When a person is in trouble, bystanders tend to assume that someone else will help—and therefore stand by and do nothing, partly because there is a diffusion of responsibility. This bystander effect is more likely to occur when many other people are present. By contrast, individuals are more inclined to aid a person in distress if no one else is around.

Demonstrate an understanding of aggression and identify some of its causes. (p. 427)

Aggression is defined as intimidating or threatening behavior or attitudes intended to hurt someone. Research suggests that aggression has a biological basis. (For instance, high levels of testosterone and low levels of serotonin correlate with increased aggression.) The frustration–aggression hypothesis suggests that we can all show aggressive behavior in frustrating situations.

Recognize how group affiliation influences the development of stereotypes. (p. 428)

We tend to see the world in terms of the in-group (the group to which we belong) and the out-group (those outside our group). Seeing the world from the narrow perspective of our own group may lead to ethnocentrism, which sets the stage for stereotyping and discrimination. Stereotypes are the conclusions or inferences we make about people based on their group membership. Discrimination means showing favoritism or hostility to others because of their affiliation with a group. People who harbor stereotypes are more likely to feel prejudice, that is, hostile or negative attitudes toward individuals or groups.

Describe altruism. (p. 432)

Altruism is a desire or motivation to help others with no expectation of anything in return. Empathy, or the ability to recognize and understand another's emotional perspective, is a major component of altruism. Behavior aimed at benefiting others is known as prosocial behavior.

Identify the three major factors contributing to interpersonal attraction. (p. 433)

Interpersonal attraction leads us to form friendships or romantic relationships. Interpersonal attraction is influenced by three major factors: proximity, similarity, and physical attractiveness. Many relationships begin with exhilaration and intense physical attraction, and then evolve into more intimate connections. The combination of connection, passion, care, and intimacy is romantic love. This is similar to passionate love, or love that is based on zealous emotion, leading to intense longing and sexual attraction. As a relationship grows, intimacy and commitment develop into companionate love, which consists of fondness, camaraderie, understanding, and emotional closeness. Consummate love is evident when intimacy, commitment, and passion are all present.

KEY TERMS

aggression, p. 427
altruism, p. 432
attitudes, p. 409
attributions, p. 405
bystander effect, p. 426
cognitive dissonance, p. 410
companionate love, p. 436
compliance, p. 415
conformity, p. 416
consummate love, p. 436
deindividuation, p. 424
diffusion of responsibility, p. 423
discrimination, p. 428
dispositional attribution, p. 406
door-in-the-face technique, p. 415
ethnocentrism, p. 428
false consensus effect, p. 407
foot-in-the-door technique, p. 415
frustration–aggression hypothesis, p. 427
fundamental attribution error, p. 406
group polarization, p. 425
groupthink, p. 425
in-group, p. 428
interpersonal attraction, p. 433
just-world hypothesis, p. 407
mere-exposure effect, p. 434
norms, p. 416
obedience, p. 419
out-group, p. 428
passionate love, p. 436
persuasion, p. 413
prejudice, p. 428
proximity, p. 433
risky shift, p. 425
romantic love, p. 436
scapegoat, p. 428
self-serving bias, p. 407
situational attribution, p. 406
social cognition, p. 405
social facilitation, p. 423
social identity, p. 428
social influence, p. 412
social loafing, p. 423
social psychology, p. 403
social roles, p. 431
stereotypes, p. 428
stereotype threat, p. 430

TEST PREP ARE YOU READY?

1. Which of the following topics is LEAST likely to be studied by a social psychologist?
a. children's written responses to people with disabilities
b. teachers' reactions to children with disabilities
c. the impact of deafness on social behaviors
d. school board policies regarding support for children with disabilities

2. ______________ refers to the way we think about others, attend to social information, and use this information in our lives.
a. Sociology
b. Social cognition
c. The internal–external dimension
d. The false consensus effect

3. Sometimes we attribute people's behaviors to their traits or personality characteristics, and underestimate the powerful influence of the environment. This is known as:
a. the just-world hypothesis.
b. the false consensus effect.
c. a dispositional attribution.
d. the fundamental attribution error.

4. The desire to help others with no expectation of payback is called:
a. groupthink.
b. deindividuation.
c. altruism.
d. conformity.

5. When it comes to decorating his house, your neighbor seems to follow the lead. If he sees others hanging lights, he immediately does the same. His urge to modify his behaviors to match those of others is known as:
a. conformity.
b. informational social influence.
c. obedience.
d. cognitive dissonance.

6. Changing your behavior at the direction of someone who generally does not have authority over you is known as:
a. obedience.
b. conformity.
c. compliance.
d. normative social influence.

7. A friend believes that suburban teenagers with tongue rings are often troublemakers who are rebelling against their parents. These ______________ are conclusions he has drawn based on his subjective observations and value judgments.
a. norms
b. external attributions
c. situational attributions
d. stereotypes

8. Psychologists define ______________ as intimidating or threatening behavior, or as attitudes intended to hurt someone.
a. prejudice
b. discrimination
c. aggression
d. stereotypes

9. When teachers in a San Francisco elementary school were given a list of students likely to "show surprising gains in intellectual competence" during the next year, those "surprising gain" students achieved greater increases in test scores than their peers. This demonstrates the power of ______________, a form of social influence.
a. cognitive dissonance
b. expectations
c. altruism
d. the mere-exposure effect

10. According to Sternberg, love is made up of three elements:
a. passion, mere exposure, and proximity.
b. proximity, similarity, and passion.
c. romantic love, mere exposure, and similarity.
d. passion, intimacy, and commitment.

11. Social psychology explores the way individuals behave in relation to others and groups, while sociology examines the groups themselves. Give several examples of how these two fields might approach the same overall topic (for example, prosocial behavior of college students versus the impact of social support structures in higher education).

12. Milgram's obedience experiment produced shocking results that are still relevant today. Why is it important to pay attention to your behaviors when operating under the influence of an authority figure?

13. Understanding the bystander effect is critical, particularly when it comes to responding to crises in group settings. How would you explain the bystander effect to others?

14. Identify stereotypes you might harbor about certain groups of people. How did your association with specific groups impact the development of these stereotypes?

15. Think about a close friend or partner and try to determine if—and how—proximity, similarity, and physical attractiveness played a role in your attraction to each other.

✓ CHECK YOUR ANSWERS IN APPENDIX C.

Go to **LaunchPad** or **Achieve: Read & Practice** to test your understanding with **LearningCurve**.

CHAPTER

12

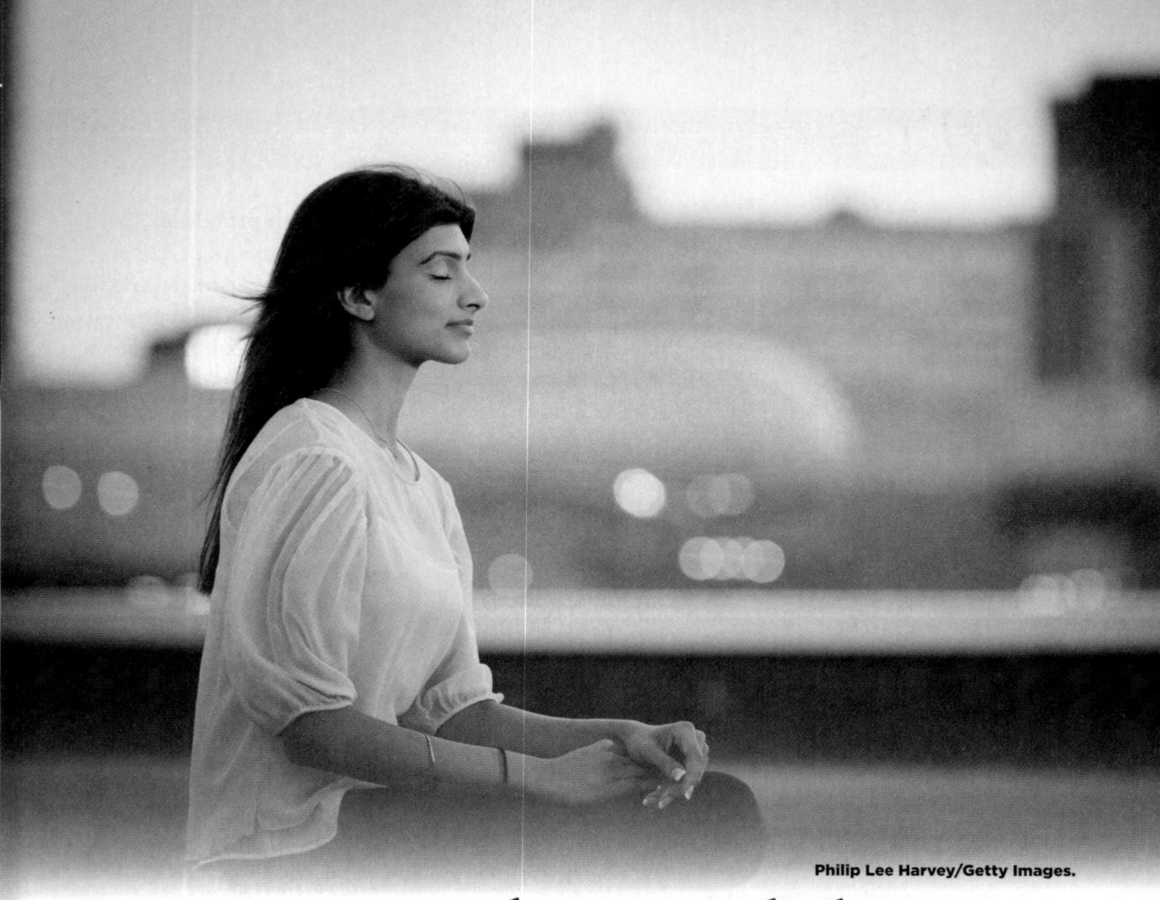

Philip Lee Harvey/Getty Images.

Stress and Health

What Is Stress?

A DAY NOT TO REMEMBER Thursday, October 9, 2014: Christy Sheppard can only recall bits and pieces of that rainy day in Colorado Springs. She remembers leaving her house just before 9:00 A.M., and glancing in the rearview mirror to see if the garage door was closed. Yet, she has no recollection of driving to a local school, getting out of her car, and finding her way to the room where she took a fitness exam administered by the Colorado Springs Police Department. Christy doesn't recall interacting with her fellow officers, or anything about the test itself—not one push-up, sit-up, agility exercise, or shuttle run.

Feeling the Pressure
A 27-year veteran of the Colorado Springs Police Department, Christy Sheppard has taken—and passed—many police fitness exams. Yet, the stakes seemed higher on that testing day in the fall of 2014. "I was worried, being a minority, a female, and a brand new lieutenant," Christy explains. "In my mind I was thinking, *I don't want to be the guy that fails.*" Courtesy of Veronica Garfield Newhoff.

Throughout the morning, Christy kept asking the test administrators the same questions: "How many sit-ups did I do? Did I pass?" The other officers, some of them close friends, found Christy's behavior strange and annoying, but didn't make much of it. After the test, Christy and her friends arranged to meet at a restaurant they had been frequenting for 25 years. She has no recollection of driving there, though she clearly remembers sitting in the parking lot and wondering, *What am I doing here?* That's when she called her husband Ron. "What's today's date?" she asked. Ron told her it was October 9. "Yeah, but what's the day of the week?"

At first, Ron thought Christy was just being funny, but when Christy began repeating herself ("What's today's date? What's the day of the week?"), Ron knew something was wrong. "Where are you?" he asked. "I'm at the Black-eyed Pea," said Christy, beginning to cry. "Why am I at the Black-eyed Pea?"

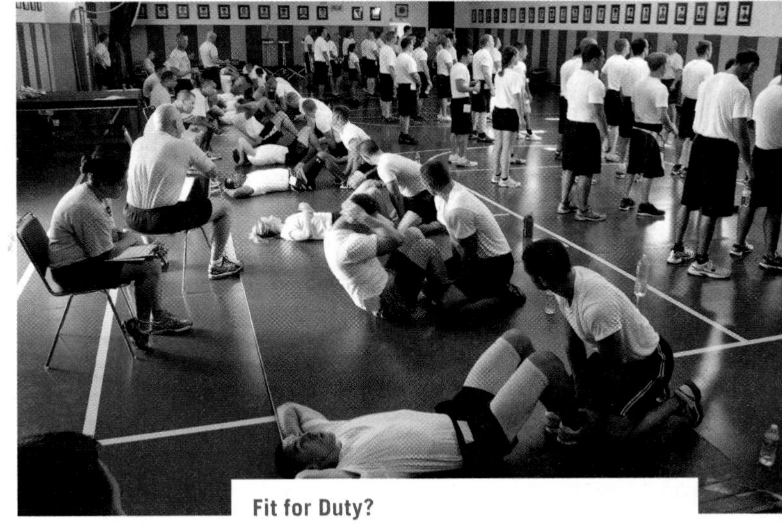

Fit for Duty?
Applicants for the New Jersey State Police take a physical qualification exam. Police officers around the nation must periodically undergo fitness tests to demonstrate they are physically capable of carrying out their duties. The test Christy took included push-ups, sit-ups, an agility test, and a shuttle run known as the Beep Test. Mel Evans/AP Images.

"I'm coming right there," Ron reassured her. "Don't go anywhere." Thinking Christy was having a stroke, Ron called for an ambulance. The emergency medical service (EMS) crew arrived soon after and began assessing her physical and cognitive health. Apart from abnormally high blood pressure, Christy was physically okay, and she could answer general questions like "How many quarters are in two dollars?" Yet, her knowledge of recent events was clearly impaired. In the emergency room, Christy told doctors she was a police sergeant and that her oldest daughter lived at home. She had no memory of being promoted to lieutenant or taking her daughter to college a few months earlier. As Christy explains, "I had completely lost 6 months."

It didn't take long for the neurologist overseeing Christy's case to make a diagnosis: *transient global amnesia,* a mysterious type of memory loss that begins suddenly and lasts no more than 24 hours (Spiegel et al., 2017). People suffering from this rare condition cannot lay down new memories and may have trouble retrieving long-term memories (Romero et al., 2013). Fortunately, transient global amnesia is not a sign of a serious medical condition, and most people fully recover (Mayo Clinic, 2014, July 18). Researchers have yet to nail down the cause, but some evidence suggests that *stress* could be a trigger (Griebe et al., 2015).

Christy, In Her Own Words

http://qrs.ly/wr5a5ff

Photo: Macmillan Learning.

There is no question that Christy was experiencing stress at that point in her life. But what exactly is stress, and how does it arise?

Stressors Are to Blame

LO 1 Define stress and stressors.

We all have an intuitive sense of how stress feels, and many of us are more familiar with it than we would like. Some people report they experience the *feeling* of stress, almost as if stress were an **emotion**. Others describe it as a force that needs to be resisted. An engineer might refer to stress as the application of a force on a target, such as the wing of an airplane, to determine how much load it can handle before breaking (Lazarus, 1993). Do you ever feel you might "break" because the load you bear causes such great strain (**INFOGRAPHIC 12.1** on the next page)?

CONNECTIONS

In **Chapter 9,** we defined emotion as a psychological state that includes a subjective or inner experience. Emotion also has a physiological component and a behavioral expression. Here, we discuss stress responses, which can have an emotional component.

Note: Quotations attributed to Christy Sheppard and Kehlen Kirby are personal communications.

Stressed Out

Periodically, the American Psychological Association (APA) commissions a survey investigating perceived stress among adults in the United States. In addition to measuring attitudes about stress, the survey identifies leading sources of stress and common behaviors used to manage stressors. The resulting picture shows that stress is a significant issue for many people in the United States and that we are not always managing it well (APA, 2016). Even when we acknowledge the importance of stress management and resolve to make positive lifestyle changes, many adults report barriers such as a lack of time or willpower that prevent them from achieving their goals. The good news? Our ability to manage stress appears to improve with age.

4 OUT OF 5 Number of people reporting their **stress level has increased** or **stayed the same in the past year.**

TOP SOURCES OF STRESS

- money **69%**
- work **65%**
- the economy **61%**
- family responsibilities **57%**
- relationships **56%**
- family health problems **52%**

Number experiencing **responses to stress,** including **anger, fatigue,** and **feeling overwhelmed.**

NEARLY 7 IN 10

People with high stress also report poor health behaviors.

Only **30%** of adults with high stress report eating healthy and getting enough sleep.

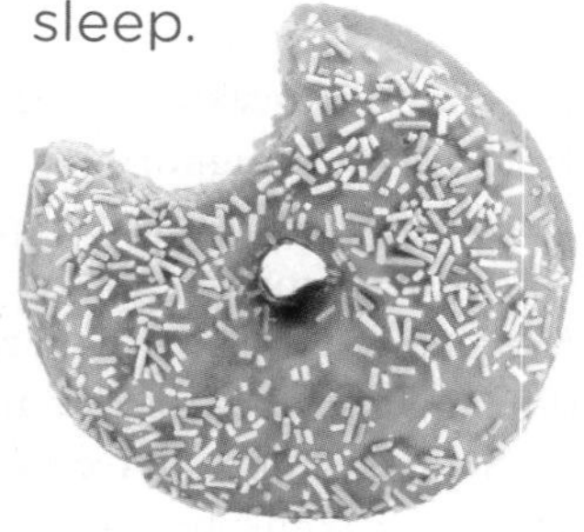

HOW STRESSFUL IS IT?

These are sample items from the College Undergraduate Stress Scale (CUSS), which rates life events according to severity. The more events you experience (particularly severe events with higher ratings), the greater your chances of developing an illness.

Event	Rating
Being raped	100
Death of a close friend	97
Contracting a sexually transmitted infection (other than AIDS)	94
Finals week	90
Flunking a class	89
Financial difficulties	84
Writing a major term paper	83
Talking in front of class	72
Difficulties with a roommate	66
Maintaining a steady dating relationship	55
Commuting to campus or work, or both	54
Getting straight As	51
Falling asleep in class	40

STRESS OVER THE LIFE SPAN

People across all age groups agree that managing stress is very important. However, the ability to manage stress varies with age. Younger adults are more likely to rely on unhealthy behaviors like drinking alcohol and smoking for stress management. Older adults report more success in achieving healthy lifestyle goals such as eating healthy and getting enough sleep. They also report higher rates of religious participation.

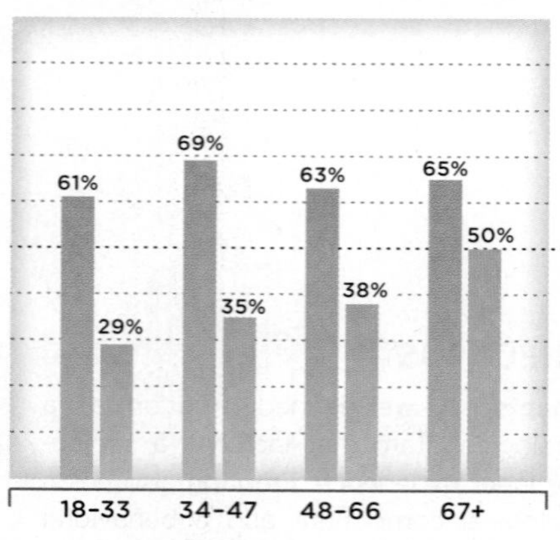

50% Oldest people report highest rate of meeting stress management goals.

Managing stress is very important

Doing a very good job managing stress

All information presented above, except the College Undergraduate Stress Scale, is from APA, 2013c.

Stress is defined as the response to perceived threats or challenges resulting from stimuli or events that cause strain, analogous to the airplane wing bending because of an applied load. For humans, these stimuli, or **stressors,** can cause both psychological and physiological reactions. During Christy's episode of transient global amnesia, she could not remember important facts about her life. She also became uncharacteristically emotional, shedding tears as she sat in the car talking on the phone with her husband. Both the memory loss and the crying might be considered psychological consequences of stress. Christy also had abnormally high blood pressure; this may have been a physiological component of stress. Fortunately for Christy, the condition was only temporary.

As you read this chapter, be careful not to confuse *how we react to stressors* with the *stressors* themselves; stress is the response and stressors are the cause (Harrington, 2013). Hans Selye (ZEL-yeh; 1907–1982), an endocrinologist who studied the impact of **hormones** and stress, proposed that "stress is the nonspecific response of the body to any demand. A stressor is an agent that produces stress at any time" (1976, p. 53).

CONNECTIONS

In **Chapter 2,** we discussed hormones, the chemical messengers of the endocrine system, which travel to their targets via the bloodstream. Hans Selye studied hormones and physiological reactions to stressors. His work describes human behavior from the biological perspective of psychology.

We should note that not all experts agree on the definitions of stress and stressors. Some contend that commonly used definitions are far too broad, and this complicates the collection and interpretation of data (Kagan, 2016). For example, how can you create an operational definition for a "stressor" if researchers use it to describe phenomena as diverse as "a rat restrained in a tube for several hours, a mouse exposed to bright light, and an adolescent bullied by a peer, as well as an adult asked to prepare a speech to be given to strangers" (p. 443)?

Stressors take countless forms. Many of the stressors acting on Christy originate from her job as a police officer. A few months before the fitness test, Christy started working the midnight shift, which begins around 8:00 P.M. and ends at about 6:00 A.M. During those 10-hour nights, Christy and one other lieutenant are the highest-ranking officers on duty; they oversee all police activity in Colorado Springs, a city of almost a half million people.

What are the stressors in your life? Some exist outside of you, like homework assignments, job demands, and credit card bills. Others are more internal, like the *thought* that your partner deceived you or the *realization* that you're not ready for your exam this afternoon. Generally, we experience stress in response to stressors, but there is at least one exception to this rule: People with anxiety disorders can feel intense anxiety in the absence of any apparent stressors (Chapter 13). Which brings us to another point: Stress is very much related to how one perceives the surrounding world.

In many cases, stress results from a *perceived* threat, because what constitutes a threat differs from one person to the next. You might find the idea of undercover police work very threatening; the thought of posing as a drug user and purchasing methamphetamine from a heavily armed dealer seems frightening. Or perhaps you're more like Christy, and you relish this type of challenge. "The undercover work is just fun. It's acting. It's going in some place, acting like someone you're not," Christy says.

PICKING UP THE PIECES Christy's memory recovered within 24 hours, though it took days for her thought processes to return to their normal speed and efficiency. "I just had to sit on my couch, and I couldn't do anything," Christy recalls. "I stayed in my pajamas for a good week." The cause of transient global amnesia remains unknown, but Christy believes her case was triggered by the stressors brought on by police work, and the constant sleep deprivation associated with the midnight shift.

stress The response to perceived threats or challenges resulting from stimuli or events that cause strain.

stressors Stimuli that cause both psychological and physiological reactions.

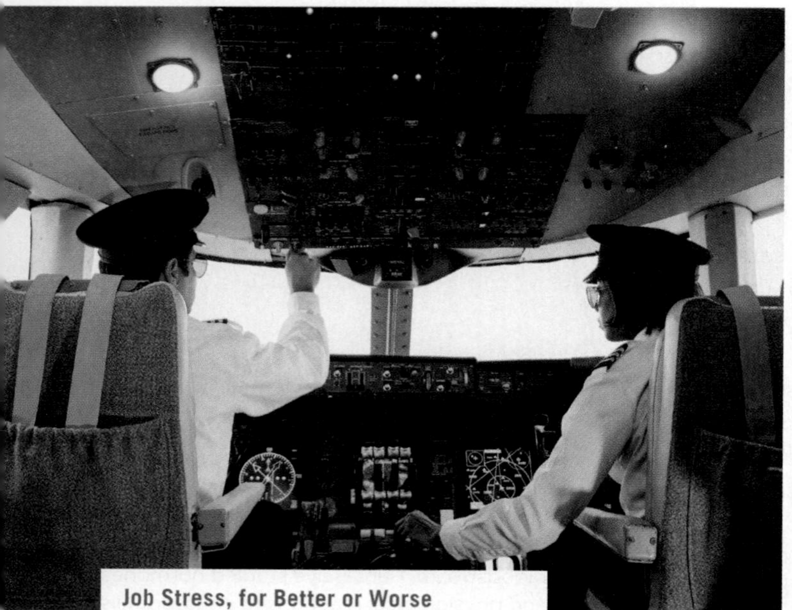

Job Stress, for Better or Worse
Working as an airline pilot may be one of the most stressful occupations, but some former pilots "look back on their careers with fondness and a nearly childlike sense of wonder" (Vanhoenacker, 2016, May 31, para. 6). Is this because pilots and their flight crews have more eustress than distress? Research suggests that work groups experiencing eustress demonstrate more dedication and engagement (Kozusznik, Rodríguez, & Peiró, 2015). Digital Vision/Getty Images.

"We laugh about it now, and talk about the day my marbles rolled down the street," Christy says, "but when I seriously think about it, it was very, very scary." As traumatic as this experience was, Christy bounced back and resumed her job as a police officer. Do you think everyone would have recovered so easily?

EUSTRESS AND DISTRESS Thus far, we have focused on negative stressors and their consequences, but some stressors are positive. For Christy, getting married and having three babies were enjoyable stressors. "You know what else is a positive stressor?" Christy says. "Preparing for a vacation." Every year, Christy and her husband take their three children to a warm and peaceful place, often on a cruise ship or beautiful beach. "I think vacations are important," says Christy, "and I think doing it with your family is important." Getting married, having kids, and planning for vacations are "good" stressors. The stress caused by positive events is called **eustress** (YOO-stress) and can also lead to psychological and physiological reactions. Of course, most people view stress in a negative context. Undesirable or disagreeable occurrences lead to a stress response known as **distress.** This type of stress may occur if you put off studying for your final exam, cram the night before, and show up at the exam sleep-deprived and underprepared.

Now that we have a basic understanding of stress, let's explore various types of stressors and how they impact the mind and body. We'll start big, by focusing on major life events.

Major Life Events

LO 2 Describe the relationship between major life events and illness.

Have you ever considered that life-changing events—both good and bad—can act as stressors? Any event that requires a life adjustment, such as the birth of a child, the death of a spouse, or a change in financial status, can cause a stress reaction (Holmes and Rahe, 1967). What's more, these life-changing events could have a cumulative effect; the more events you experience in a row or within a brief period, the greater the potential for increased stress and negative health outcomes. Recall the analogy of applying a force to an airplane wing. The degree to which the wing bends (or breaks) indicates the strain it is under (Lazarus, 1993). Studies have uncovered associations between certain life events (the forces causing strain) and illnesses (the responses), including heart attacks, leukemia, diabetes, influenza, and psychiatric disorders (Hatch & Dohrenwend, 2007; Rabkin & Struening, 1976; Ridout, Carpenter, & Tyrka, 2016).

SOCIAL READJUSTMENT RATING SCALE Illnesses can be clearly identified and defined, but how do psychologists measure life events? The Social Readjustment Rating Scale (SRRS) was developed to do just that (Holmes & Rahe, 1967). With the SRRS, participants are asked to read through a list of events and experiences, and determine which happened during the previous year and how many times they occurred. A score is then calculated based on the severity ratings of those events and the frequency of their occurrence. An event like the death of a spouse has a greater severity rating than something like a traffic violation. Participants are also asked to report any illnesses or accidents they experienced during the same period. This information is used to

eustress The stress response to agreeable or positive stressors.

distress The stress response to unpleasant and undesirable stressors.

determine if there is a **correlation** between life events and health problems. Researchers have used this model to explore the positive link between these two variables for a variety of populations (Bliese, Edwards, & Sonnentag, 2017; Kobasa, 1979; Slepecky et al., 2017). But remember, a correlation between life events and illness (or any correlation for that matter) is not proof of causality. The possibility always exists that a third variable, such as poverty, may be causing both illnesses and life-changing events. For example, impoverished children tend to have poor nutrition, which impairs physical growth and cognitive development (Storrs, 2017, July 13). They are also more likely to experience stressors (Johnson, Riis, & Noble, 2016; Steele et al., 2016). In this case, poverty is leading to stressful life events *and* poor health outcomes.

CONNECTIONS

In **Chapter 1,** we explained that a positive correlation indicates that as one variable increases, so does the other variable. Here, we see a positive correlation between life events and health problems: The more life events people have experienced, the more health problems they are likely to have.

Since its introduction in the late 1960s, the SRRS has been updated and adapted for specific populations, including college students. Infographic 12.1 shows items from the College Undergraduate Stress Scale (CUSS) developed by Renner and Mackin (1998). Scales like the SRRS and CUSS are useful for uncovering correlations between stress levels and illness, but they are based on self-reports, which are subjective and therefore not always accurate. People tend to forget events over time, or the opposite—they tend to focus more on past events than recent ones (Pachana, Brilleman, & Dobson, 2011). What's more, not all negative life-changing events lead to bad outcomes. Some have even suggested that moderate exposure to stressors makes us stronger, a view described as *stress inoculation.* People with "low to moderate" levels of stress may end up with "better mental health and well-being" and a greater ability to cope with pain than those who either have faced no hardships or have had to handle overwhelming adversity (Seery, 2011).

Put Your Heads Together

Imagine you were tasked with updating the College Undergraduate Stress Scale (CUSS; see Infographic 12.1). With your group, **A**) discuss which items to include in your rating scale. **B**) Gather pilot data by getting students (who are not in your classroom) to complete the CUSS inventory and then asking them to suggest additional events for inclusion in a new inventory. **C**) Team up with other groups to see if you have any new events in common.

It's Nonstop: Chronic Stressors

For some of us, stressors come from balancing school and work, or taking care of children. Others face the chronic stressor of being unemployed (Sumner & Gallagher, 2017), or battling a chronic illness such as diabetes, asthma, or cancer (Sansom-Daly, Peate, Wakefield, Bryant, & Cohn, 2012). Another cause of health-related stress is HIV, which affects nearly 37 million people and their families worldwide (UNAIDS, 2017, July).

CONNECTIONS

In **Chapter 9,** we described various sexually transmitted infections (STIs), diseases that are passed on through sexual activity. There are many types of STIs, but most are caused by viruses or bacteria. Viral STIs such as HIV and herpes do not have cures, only treatments to reduce symptoms.

HIV AND AIDS One of the most feared **sexually transmitted infections (STIs)**, **human immunodeficiency virus (HIV)** is spread through the transfer of bodily fluids, such as blood, semen, vaginal fluid, or breast milk. HIV eventually progresses to **acquired immunodeficiency syndrome (AIDS),** which generally results in a severely compromised immune system and heightened vulnerability to disease. Since the virus was first identified in 1981, it has infected approximately 76 million people, about half of whom have died (UNAIDS, 2017). Worldwide, HIV is a leading cause of death, and sub-Saharan Africa has been hit the hardest (Kendall, 2012, June). Approximately 1.1 million people in the United States have HIV, and about 1 in 7 are not aware they are infected (CDC, 2017, October 11).

human immunodeficiency virus (HIV) A virus transferred via bodily fluids (blood, semen, vaginal fluid, or breast milk) that causes the breakdown of the immune system, eventually resulting in AIDS.

acquired immunodeficiency syndrome (AIDS) This condition, caused by HIV, generally results in a severely compromised immune system, which makes the body vulnerable to other infections.

What comes to mind when you think of stressors linked to HIV? Perhaps you imagine receiving the diagnosis, losing relationships, living with a stigma, or facing the possibility of developing AIDS. Did you think about the cost of treatment? In 2016, only 53% of HIV sufferers around the world were able to obtain therapies (UNAIDS, 2017, July). This inability to access proper medical treatment relates to a stressor that is even more widespread than HIV: poverty.

LO 3 Summarize how poverty, adjusting to a new culture, and daily hassles affect health.

POVERTY Many people in the United States—12.7% of the population—live in poverty. The poverty threshold in the United States is defined as an individual income of less than \$12,486 or less than \$24,755 for a family of four. As of 2016, about 1 in 5 children were living below the poverty level (Semega, Fontenot, & Kollar, 2017, September). People struggling to make ends meet experience numerous stressors, including poor health care and nutrition, noisy living situations, overcrowding, violence, and underfunded schools (Blair & Raver, 2012; Mistry & Wadsworth, 2011; Schickedanz, Dreyer, & Halfon, 2015). The cycle of poverty is difficult to break, so these stressors often persist across generations. The longer people live in poverty, the more exposure they have to stressors, and the greater the likelihood they will become ill (Cheng, Johnson, & Goodman, 2016). And we're not just talking about physical health; the brain pays a price, too.

CONNECTIONS

In **Chapter 7**, we discussed the relationship between poverty and cognitive abilities; studies show that socioeconomic status is associated with scores on intelligence tests. Here, we highlight the link between poverty-related stressors and neurocognitive development.

THINK CRITICALLY

DOES POVERTY CHANGE THE BRAIN? The evidence is undeniable: Growing up poor can leave a lasting psychological imprint. Factors related to low **socioeconomic status (SES)** have been linked to differences in development of cognitive and socioemotional abilities, which can impact performance in school and at work (Blair & Raver, 2015; Javanbakht et al., 2015). "As a group, children in poverty are more likely to experience worse health and more developmental delay, lower achievement, and more behavioral and emotional problems than their more advantaged peers" (Johnson et al., 2016, para. 1). Underlying these disparities are distinct patterns of brain development. For example, scanning technologies reveal that children from lower-SES families have reduced volume in the frontal and parietal cortex as compared to higher-SES children (Kolb & Gibb, 2015). Many poverty-linked variables could be to blame, including poor nutrition, limited exposure to vocabulary words, and stressors such as crowded living conditions. The hippocampus, which is critical for the formation of new memories, seems particularly sensitive to the chronic stress that often goes hand-in-hand with poverty (Johnson et al., 2016). This brain structure tends to be smaller in adults who were raised in low-SES families (Staff et al., 2012). Psychologist Lisa Feldman Barrett sums up the research nicely: "The neuroscience is crystal clear: brains wire themselves to their surroundings. A developing infant brain requires wiring instructions from the world around it. Without proper nourishment, both nutritional and social, that little brain will not develop to its fullest" (Barrett, 2017, June 4, para. 6).

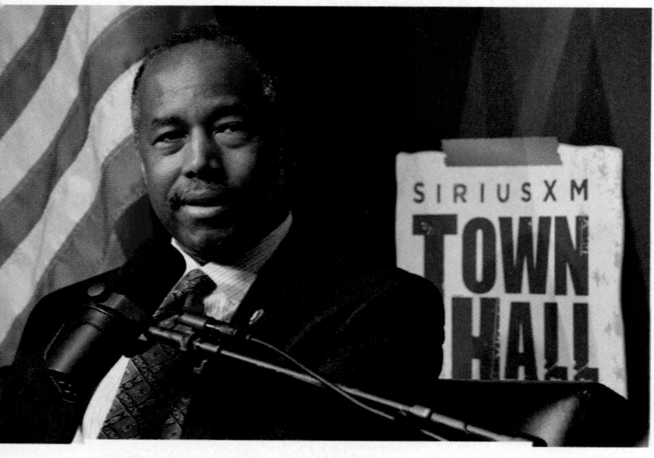

Is Poverty a State of Mind? Secretary of Housing and Urban Development Dr. Ben Carson made headlines when he suggested that poverty is associated with a certain mentality. "You take somebody with the wrong mindset, you can give them everything in the world and they'll work their way back down to the bottom," Dr. Carson reportedly said (Wolfson, 2017, May 30, para. 2). Given what you have read about poverty and brain development, do you agree with this statement?
Larry French/Getty Images.

Put Your Heads Together

In your groups, **A)** discuss why poverty is hard to escape. (*Hint:* List the stressors associated with an income of less than \$24,755 for a family of four.) **B)** Consider how poverty affects the physical health and cognitive abilities of children. **C)** Use at least three of the eight perspectives introduced in Chapter 1 (Table 1.1) to explain the causes of poverty. **D)** What would you say to someone who says that people living in poverty should just "fix" their lives?

You needn't live in poverty to feel stressed out by money. Financial issues can be stressors, whether you are rich, poor, or somewhere in between. Would you believe that money stress can impact the way you experience pain?

FINANCIAL STRESS HURTS, LITERALLY

From the SCIENTIFIC pages of AMERICAN

A recent study links shaky economic outlook and feelings of physical pain.

Few things feel worse than not knowing when your next paycheck is coming. Economic insecurity has been shown to have a whole host of negative effects, including low self-esteem and impaired cognitive functioning. It turns out financial stress can also physically hurt, according to a paper published in . . . *Psychological Science*.

Eileen Chou, a public policy professor at the University of Virginia, and her collaborators began by analyzing a data set of 33,720 U.S. households and found that those with higher levels of unemployment were more likely to purchase over-the-counter painkillers. Then, using a series of experiments, the team discovered that simply thinking about the prospect of financial insecurity was enough to increase pain. For example, people reported feeling almost double the amount of physical pain in their body after recalling a financially unstable time in their life as compared with those who thought about a secure period. In another experiment, university students who were primed to feel anxious about future employment prospects removed their hand from an ice bucket more quickly (showing less pain tolerance) than those who were not. The researchers also found that economic insecurity reduced people's sense of control, which, in turn, increased feelings of pain.

Chou and her colleagues suggest that because of this link between financial insecurity and decreased pain tolerance, the recent recession may have been a factor in fueling the prescription painkiller epidemic. Other experts are cautious about taking the findings that far. "I think the hypothesis [that financial stress causes pain] has a lot of merit, but it would be helpful to see additional rigorous evidence in a real-world environment," says Heather Schofield, an economist at the University of Pennsylvania who was not involved in the study. Given that stress in general is well known to increase feelings of pain, further research is needed to disentangle financial anxiety from other sources of pressure.

ACCULTURATIVE STRESS Another common source of stress is migration. As of 2017, there were 258 million migrants dispersed across the world (United Nations, Department of Economic and Social Affairs, Population Division, 2017). Moving to a new country frequently involves a process of cultural adjustment and adaptation. This **acculturation** can result in changes to language, values, cultural behaviors, and sometimes even national identity (Schwartz et al., 2014). Acculturation is often accompanied by **acculturative stress** (uh-KUHL-chur-a-tiv), or stress associated with adjusting to a new way of life. Perhaps you have experienced acculturative stress; about 1 in 8 people living in the United States was born in another country (Camarota & Zeigler, 2016, October).

In **Chapter 8,** we discussed Piaget's concept of assimilation, a cognitive approach to dealing with new information. A person using assimilation attempts to understand new information using her existing knowledge base. Here, assimilation means letting go of old ways and adopting the customs of a new culture.

People respond to acculturative stress in a variety of ways (Berry, 1997; Kuo, 2014). Some try to **assimilate**, letting go of old ways and adopting those of the new culture. But assimilation can cause problems if family members or friends from the old culture reject the new one, or have trouble assimilating themselves. Other people cling to their roots and remain *separated* from the new culture—an approach that can be problematic if the new culture does not support this type of separation. A combination of these two approaches is *integration,* or holding onto some elements of the old culture but also adopting aspects of the new one.

acculturation The process of cultural adjustment and adaptation, including changes to one's language, values, cultural behaviors, and sometimes national identity.

acculturative stress Stress that occurs when people move to new countries or cultures and must adjust to a new way of life.

Levels of acculturative stress vary greatly from one individual to the next. Why do some people seem to have an easier time adjusting than others?

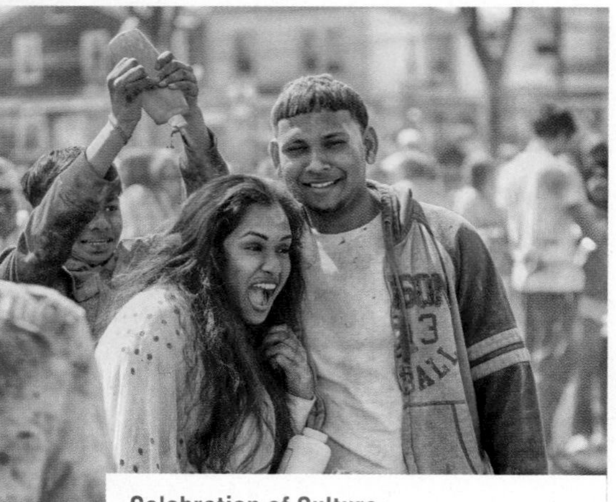

Celebration of Culture
Young people celebrate the Hindu Holi fest in the Richmond Hill neighborhood of Queens, New York. The style of their clothing suggests they have embraced aspects of American culture, but their participation in the festival indicates they have not abandoned their roots. Queens is among the most culturally diverse counties in the United States (Edsall, 2018, April 12). Andy Katz/Pacific Press/Sipa USA/Newscom.

ACROSS THE WORLD

THE STRESS OF STARTING ANEW Imagine trying to get a job, pay your bills, or simply make friends in a world where most everyone speaks a foreign language. If you were new to the United States, speaking English would certainly make life easier. Studies suggest that English proficiency does impact levels of acculturation and acculturative stress among immigrants to North America (Belizaire & Fuertes, 2011; Jia, Gottardo, Chen, Koh, & Pasquarella, 2016). Another important factor is the degree of difference between old and new cultures. Chinese graduate students appear to experience less acculturative stress studying in Hong Kong as opposed to Australia. Presumably, this is because the cultures of China and Hong Kong are more similar (Pan & Wong, 2011). Finally, we cannot forget the unpleasant reality of **discrimination**, which causes great stress for the world's immigrant populations. Common targets of discrimination in the United States are people of Arab and/or South Asian descent. Discrimination against these groups, which appears to have grown after the terrorist attacks of 9/11, may increase acculturative stress, erode psychological well-being, and possibly promote the development of depression (Goforth Oka, Leong, & Denis, 2014; Kaduvettoor-Davidson & Inman, 2013; Tummala-Narra, Alegria, & Chen, 2012).

IMMIGRATION IS STRESSFUL, ESPECIALLY IF YOU DON'T SPEAK THE NEW LANGUAGE

Fortunately, there are ways to combat acculturative stress and cope with the challenges of living in an unfamiliar world. One of the best defenses is **social support,** or assistance from others (Oppedal & Idsoe, 2015; Renner, Laireiter, & Maier, 2012). Here, we are not referring to the type of help provided by gangs and other groups that engage in antisocial behavior. We mean positive types of social support, like that which comes from relationships with family members back home and friends who belong to the new culture (Oppedal & Idsoe, 2015).

CONNECTIONS
As noted in **Chapter 11,** discrimination means showing favoritism or hostility to others because of their group affiliation. Here, we see an example of discrimination toward certain ethnic or cultural groups.

Now that we have described some dramatic stressors like HIV and immigration, let's shift our discussion to more mundane sources of stress. Have you ever wondered how life's little annoyances impact your mind and body?

Hassles, Uplifts, and Conflicts

TORNADO IN MY KITCHEN "Today, I woke up, I went downstairs, walked into my kitchen, and it looks like somebody had a party in there," says Christy. "[They] ate up all this food, and not one person bothered to do any dishes. . . . My kitchen looks like a tornado went off in it." On top of the mess left by her family, Christy cannot get her coffeemaker to function, and the dog is hungry because no one else in the family bothered to feed it.

Functioning on 5 hours of unsatisfying sleep, Christy heads to the police station, where she finds a heap of paperwork sitting on her desk. An officer calls to report that she twisted her ankle and cannot report for duty. Now there is a hole in the schedule, and Christy needs to fix it ASAP; otherwise, there won't be an adequate number of police officers working in the city tonight. Are you feeling stressed yet? Christy certainly is. All these *daily hassles* compound, and she becomes exasperated.

"Monday I woke up at noon and I've been cussing ever since."
Getting 4 to 5 hours of sleep makes Christy feel irritable, moody, and physically exhausted. "Irritable doesn't even cover it," Christy says. "I bet my family wants me to move out!" The constant sleep deprivation also makes it difficult to deal with the daily hassles of home life and police work. Courtesy of Veronica Garfield Newhoff.

WHAT A HASSLE, WHAT A JOY **Daily hassles** are the minor problems or irritants we deal with on a regular basis, such as traffic, financial worries, misplaced keys, messy roommates—a list that does not seem to end. While seemingly minor, these hassles are repetitive and ever-present. It's a good thing that the weight of our daily hassles is counterbalanced by the uplifts in our lives.

Uplifts are positive experiences that have the potential to make us happy. For Christy, it might be a text from her daughter joking about the family dog: "Shasta has gas again!" Think about the last time you smiled; was it in response to an uplift, such as a funny comment on your Instagram post, or a surprise phone call from an old friend? We all experience hassles and uplifts, but how do they interact to affect our health and well-being?

Decades ago, researchers developed a scale of daily hassles and uplifts, and used it to explore the relationship between stress and illness (**Figure 12.1;** DeLongis, Folman, & Lazarus, 1988). They asked participants to read through a list of 53 items that could be either hassles or uplifts, such as meeting deadlines, maintaining a car, interacting with fellow workers, and dealing with the weather. Participants rated these items on a 4-point scale indicating "how much of a hassle" and "how much of an uplift" each was on that particular day. They also asked participants to report any illness, injuries, or symptoms they experienced that same day. What did they find? Over a 6-month period, there was a significant link between hassles and health problems. The more daily stressors the participants reported, the more likely they were to suffer from sore throats, headaches, influenza, back problems, and other health issues. As subsequent research suggests, dealing with daily hassles may increase the risk of catching contagious diseases and could prolong the course of illness (Glaser & Kiecolt-Glaser, 2005). One study found that systolic blood pressure (an important indicator of cardiovascular health) tends to increase when African Americans move into segregated neighborhoods. This may have something to do with the stress associated with having lower-quality schools and fewer "health-promoting resources" like exercise facilities (Kershaw et al., 2017). Apparently, the strain of managing daily hassles can take a toll on health and well-being (DeLongis, Coyne, Dakof, Folkman, & Lazarus, 1982; DeLongis, Folkman, & Lazarus, 1988).

How might you increase the uplifts in your life? Research suggests that people who demonstrate kindness and generosity, and act in ways that benefit others are more likely to experience happiness and other "positive emotions." Thus, by paying it forward, you create uplifts for others and perhaps even yourself: "As people do nice things for others, they may feel greater joy, contentment, and love, which in turn promote greater overall well-being and improve social relationships and [more]" (Nelson, Layous, Cole, & Lyubomirsky, 2016, p. 7).

Hassles		Uplifts
0 1 2 3	Your child(ren)	0 1 2 3
0 1 2 3	Your friend(s)	0 1 2 3
0 1 2 3	Your work load	0 1 2 3
0 1 2 3	Enough money for emergencies	0 1 2 3
0 1 2 3	Financial care for someone who doesn't live with you	0 1 2 3
0 1 2 3	Your drinking	0 1 2 3
0 1 2 3	Your physical appearance	0 1 2 3
0 1 2 3	Political or social issues	0 1 2 3
0 1 2 3	Amount of free time	0 1 2 3
0 1 2 3	Being organized	0 1 2 3

FIGURE 12.1
The Hassles and Uplifts Scale
Research participants were instructed to circle a number rating the degree to which each item was a hassle (left column) and an uplift (right column). Numbers range from 0 ("none or not applicable") to 3 ("a great deal"). The scale includes 53 items, a sample of which is shown here. © 1988 by the American Psychological Association. Adapted with permission from DeLongis, Folkman, & Lazarus (1988).

To Fix—or Not Fix—the Dent
Your auto insurance may cover the cost of fixing a dent, but filing a claim may cause your insurance premium to go up. Do you drive around with an ugly dent, or deal with the higher insurance bills? This is an example of an avoidance–avoidance conflict, because both alternatives are undesirable. Panther Media GmbH/Alamy stockphoto.

FEELING CONFLICTED We have discussed a variety of stressors, from major life events to daily hassles. Conflicts can also serve as stressors. When people think of conflict, they may imagine arguments and fistfights, but conflict can also refer to the discomfort one feels when making tough choices. In an **approach–approach conflict,** you must choose between two or more attractive options. For example, you must pick between two classes you would love to take. An **approach–avoidance conflict** occurs when you face a choice or situation that has both favorable and unfavorable characteristics. You are required to take a biology lab class, and although you like biology, you do not enjoy working with other students in a lab setting. An **avoidance–avoidance conflict** occurs when you face two or more unattractive alternatives. In order to fulfill a requirement, you must choose between two courses that you dread taking.

Now that we have examined different types of stressors, let's explore how the brain and body respond to them.

social support The assistance we acquire from others.

daily hassles Minor and regularly occurring problems that can act as stressors.

uplifts Experiences that are positive and have the potential to make one happy.

approach–approach conflict A type of conflict in which one must choose between two or more options that are attractive.

approach–avoidance conflict A type of conflict that occurs when one faces a choice or situation that has favorable and unfavorable characteristics.

avoidance–avoidance conflict A type of conflict in which one must choose between two or more options that are unattractive.

show what you know

1. _______________ is a response to perceived threats or challenges resulting from stimuli that cause strain.
2. The Social Readjustment Rating Scale (SRRS) was created to measure the severity and frequency of life events. This scale is most often used to examine the link between stressors and:
   a. aging.
   b. levels of eustress.
   c. perceived threats.
   d. illness.
3. _______________ can occur when a person must adjust to life in a new country.
   a. Eustress
   b. Acculturative stress
   c. Uplifts
   d. Correlations
4. List three uplifts and three hassles you experienced over the last three days.

✓ CHECK YOUR ANSWERS IN APPENDIX C.

Stress and Your Health

TROUBLE UNDERCOVER In her 3 decades as a police officer, Christy has faced stressors that are completely unfamiliar to the average person. Imagine knocking on someone's door at 3:00 A.M. and delivering a death notice ("Mrs. X, I regret to inform you . . . "), or discovering a toddler with injuries indicative of child abuse. Such experiences are emotionally disturbing and stressful, but they don't bring on the intense, fear-for-your-life type of stress Christy experienced when her cover was nearly blown in an operation to bust crack-cocaine dealers. Posing as a buyer, Christy walked into a house where a suspected dealer was selling. One of the men in the house gave her a funny look, and she instantly realized that he recognized her as a police officer. Fortunately, the man did not give her away, and Christy escaped the situation unscathed. But we can only imagine what she must have felt at that moment.

Too Stressful? Depends Who You Are An undercover police officer posing as a prostitute (right) is photographed alongside the "john" who attempted to buy her services in Van Nuys, California. Some people, like Christy, appear to be cut out for undercover police work; they enjoy the excitement, bounce back from traumatic experiences, and adapt when things don't go as planned. Others find the stress overwhelming. David Bro/ZUMA Press/Newscom.

Faced with the prospect of being gunned down by a drug dealer, Christy most likely experienced sensations associated with the **fight-or-flight** response, such as increased pulse and breathing rate. A coordinated effort of the sympathetic nervous system and the endocrine system, the fight-or-flight reaction primes the body to respond to danger, either by confronting the threat head on (in Christy's case, defending herself against a physical attack) or escaping (bolting out of the house). Let's take a closer look at this survival mechanism. 

CONNECTIONS We introduced the fight-or-flight response to stressors in **Chapter 2.** The sympathetic nervous system is a division of the autonomic nervous system, which regulates the body's involuntary activity (such as digestion and the beating of the heart). Here, we will learn how this automatic activity may relate to illness.

Fight or Flight

LO 4 Identify the brain and body changes that characterize the fight-or-flight response.

When faced with a threat, portions of the brain, including the hypothalamus, activate the sympathetic nervous system, which leads to the secretion of catecholamines such as epinephrine (adrenaline) and norepinephrine (noradrenaline). These hormones cause increases in heart rate, blood pressure, respiration, and blood flow to the muscles. Meanwhile, digestion slows and the pupils dilate.

Once the emergency has ended, the **parasympathetic system** reverses these processes by reducing heart rate, blood pressure, and so on. If a person is exposed to a threatening situation for long periods of time, the fight-or-flight system remains active.

CONNECTIONS

In **Chapter 2,** we introduced the parasympathetic nervous system, which is responsible for the "rest-and-digest" process following activation of the fight-or-flight response. The parasympathetic nervous system works with the sympathetic nervous system to prepare us for crises and then to calm us when danger has passed.

LO 5 Explain the function of the hypothalamic–pituitary–adrenal (HPA) system.

HYPOTHALAMIC–PITUITARY–ADRENAL SYSTEM Overseeing the sympathetic nervous system's response is the ***hypothalamic–pituitary–adrenal (HPA) system*** (**INFOGRAPHIC 12.2** on the next page). The HPA system helps to maintain balance in the body by directing not only the sympathetic nervous system but also the neuroendocrine and immune systems (Ben-Zvi, Vernon, & Broderick, 2009; Spencer, Emmerzaal, Kozicz, & Andrews, 2015). (The immune system defends the body from bacteria, viruses, and other types of invaders by deploying cells and chemicals to confront these threats.) When a stressful situation arises, the hypothalamus alerts the pituitary gland, prompting it to send signals to the adrenal cortex, which secretes corticosteroids such as cortisol. These hormones summon the immune system to fend off a threat and reduce the amount of energy used for nonessential activities, such as digestion. The HPA system responds to a stressor in the same way it would to a pathogen—by mobilizing a defense response. When stressors are ongoing, the HPA system works overtime. How do you think this affects a person's health?

synonyms

hypothalamic–pituitary–adrenal (HPA) system hypothalamic–pituitary–adrenal axis (HPA axis)

LO 6 Outline the general adaptation syndrome (GAS).

GENERAL ADAPTATION SYNDROME Hans Selye, introduced earlier in the chapter, was one of the first to suggest the human body responds to prolonged stressors in a predictable way (Selye, 1936, 1976). This specific pattern of physiological reactions is called the **general adaptation syndrome (GAS).** The GAS consists of three stages (Infographic 12.2 on the next page). The first is the *alarm stage,* or the body's initial response to a threatening situation, similar to the fight-or-flight response. Arousal increases, and the body prepares to deal with the threat. Next is the *resistance stage.* During this period, the body maintains a high level of arousal (though not as high as that of the *alarm stage*), but decreases its response to new stressors. It simply cannot take on additional threats. According to Selye, this is when some people start to show signs of *diseases of adaptation,* such as hypertension and arthritis (Selye, 1953; Selye & Fortier, 1950). If the threat remains and the person can no longer adapt, the *exhaustion stage* ensues. The body's resources become depleted, resulting in vulnerability to illness, physical exhaustion, and even death.

Selye's Stages
Endocrinologist Hans Selye proposed that the body passes through a predictable sequence of changes in response to stressors. Selye's general adaptation syndrome includes three phases: the alarm stage, the resistance stage, and the exhaustion stage. Corbis.

HEALTH PSYCHOLOGY Selye's work paved the way for researchers to explore the biological, psychological, and social factors that contribute to health and illness. In the 1960s, the field of **health psychology** began to gather momentum. Health psychology seeks to explain how food choices, exercise, social interactions, and living environments affect our predisposition to illness. Research in this field informs public policy and health education, leading to changes in health-related guidelines and the promotion of positive eating and exercise habits. Health psychologists also study the impact of personality factors, coping style, cognitive appraisal, poverty, culture, social support, and religion (**INFOGRAPHIC 12.3** on page 455). Some even seek to understand how stress and health vary across geographic locations.

synonyms

health psychology behavioral medicine

general adaptation syndrome (GAS) A specific pattern of physiological reactions to stressors that includes the alarm stage, resistance stage, and exhaustion stage.

health psychology The study of the biological, psychological, and social factors that contribute to health and illness.

INFOGRAPHIC 12.2

Physiological Responses to Stress

When faced with an emergency, our bodies go through a series of physiological responses that assist us in coping with a stressor. Activation of the *fight-or-flight* response and *hypothalamic–pituitary–adrenal (HPA)* system gives us the energy and resources we need to cope with a temporary stressor. Studying these physiological responses, Hans Selye (1956) found that the sequence follows the same path no matter the stressor. Selye called this sequence the general adaptation syndrome (GAS). He found that when the stressor remains, our bodies can no longer adapt.

GENERAL ADAPTATION SYNDROME (GAS)

In the alarm stage, the short-term responses are activated, giving us the energy to combat a threat. In the resistance stage, resources remain mobilized, and we continue to cope with the stressor. But eventually we enter the exhaustion stage, becoming weak and susceptible to illness, and less able to cope with the stressor (Selye, 1956).

Alarm stage (stress response activated)

Resistance stage (coping with stressor)

Exhaustion stage (reserves diminished)

SHORT-TERM RESPONSES TO STRESS

Amygdala processes information about stressor. If threat is perceived, hypothalamus triggers short-term stress response.

STRESSOR

Hypothalamus

Pituitary gland

FIGHT-OR-FLIGHT SYSTEM

ACTIVATES

Sympathetic Nervous System

SENDS SIGNAL TO

Adrenal Medulla (core of adrenal glands)

RELEASES

Catecholamines epinephrine, norepinephrine

CAUSES

Efficient management of bodily resources so they are available for emergency action:

- increased heart rate
- increased respiration
- increased blood flow to muscles
- digestion slows
- pupils dilate

HYPOTHALAMIC-PITUITARY-ADRENAL (HPA) SYSTEM

ALERTS

Pituitary Gland

SENDS SIGNAL TO

Adrenal Cortex (outside layer of adrenal glands)

RELEASES

Corticosteroids including cortisol

CAUSES

Efficient management of bodily resources; immune system activation

Adrenal glands

kidneys

PROLONGED STRESS

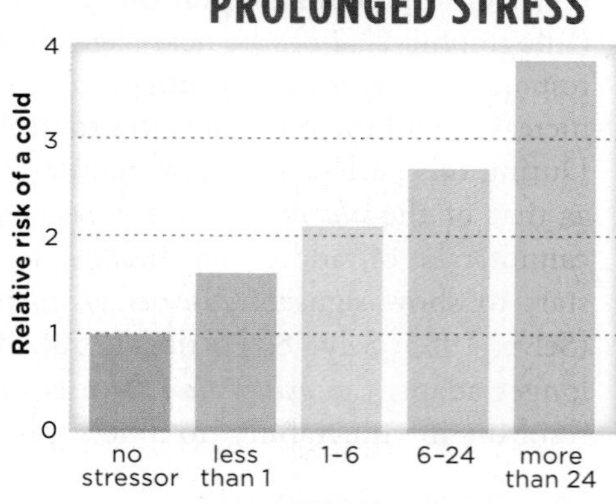

Prolonged stress can cause the immune system to break down. As you can see, the risk of becoming sick is directly related to the duration of a stressor. This effect is seen even when the stressor is not traumatic. Data in this study were collected from people reporting on interpersonal conflicts and problems concerning work (Cohen et al., 1998).

Credits: Chuckmoser/Thinkstock/Getty Images; Alan Bailey/Shutterstock; Colin Anderson/AGE Fotostock.

ACROSS THE WORLD

"BLUE ZONES" Can the place you live contribute to your level of stress and overall health? A group of researchers working with the National Geographic Society set out to identify regions of the world with the highest number of people living over 100 years. These locations came to be called "blue zones" because someone used a blue pen to circle one of them on a map (Buettner, 2015). To qualify as a blue zone, an area had to be inhabited by people reaching old age without health issues such as diabetes, cancer, obesity, and heart trouble. Five areas in the world made the cut: Ikaria, Greece; Okinawa, Japan; Ogliastra Region, Sardinia; Loma Linda, California; and Nicoya Peninsula, Costa Rica (Buettner, 2015). You can learn about the longevity-promoting characteristics of these populations in **Table 12.1**.

"BLUE ZONES" OFFER CLUES ON HOW TO LIVE A LONG AND HEALTHY LIFE

You needn't live in a blue zone to achieve a healthy lifestyle. If you stay physically active, limit stress, eat locally grown foods, and surround yourself with strong social support, you, too, might live to be a centenarian (Daskalopoulou et al., 2017; Govindaraju, Atzmon, & Barzilai, 2015; Poulain, Herm, & Pes, 2013).

TABLE 12.1 LIVING LONGER

Characteristics	Benefits	Applications
Innate movement	You don't have to join a gym or compete in triathlons; every physical activity counts.	Walk to work or to the store, bike to school. Find ways to incorporate natural movement into your daily life.
Finding meaning	Purpose outside of your job makes it easier to wake up each morning; knowing your purpose can extend life expectancy.	Find your motivation for life. What energizes you?
Slow down	Stress affects everyone, but slowing down reduces inflammation that can lead to many age-related illnesses.	Meditate, pray, or nap.
"80% rule"	Helps prevent weight gain and overeating.	Stop eating when you feel 80% full.
Eat more plants	Inexpensive source of complex carbs, fiber, and protein.	Eat lean; make beans and vegetables the bulk of your diet. Limit your intake of meat.
Social support	Healthy friends encourage healthy behaviors.	Surround yourself with people who encourage healthy living and happiness.
Family first	Time spent with grandparents, parents, and a committed life partner can extend life expectancy.	Create strong family ties, and keep loved ones in close proximity.

A long, healthy, low-stress life is possible, especially if you adopt these characteristics, commonly observed in "blue zone" regions of the world. Information from Buettner (2015).

Is Stress Making You Sick?

LO 7 Explain how stressors relate to health problems.

Before we further explore the connection between stress and illness, we must understand how the body deals with illness. Let's take a side trip into introductory biology and learn about the body's main defense against disease—the immune system, comprising the spleen, lymph nodes, and bone marrow (see **Figure 12.2** on the next page). When disease-causing invaders like viruses and bacteria threaten the body, the immune system deploys a special army of white blood cells called **lymphocytes.** Should the intruders get past the skin, white blood cells called *macrophages* ("big eaters") are ready to attack. Macrophages hunt and consume both invaders and worn-out cells of the body. *Natural killer cells* (*NK cells*) target body cells that have been affected by invaders, injecting them with a deadly chemical. NK cells also release a protein that prevents the infection from spreading. In some cases, the body must call on its "special ops" teams: the ***B lymphocytes*** and ***T lymphocytes.*** The B lymphocytes mature in the bone marrow and produce antibodies that chemically inhibit bacteria, while T lymphocytes mature in the thymus and play an integral role in fighting cancer, viruses, and other disease-causing agents that the B lymphocytes have failed to ward off (Matloubain et al., 2004; Straub, 2017). When the body is expending resources to deal with an ongoing stressor, the work of lymphocytes is compromised, and the immune system is less powerful. How do you think this impacts disease susceptibility?

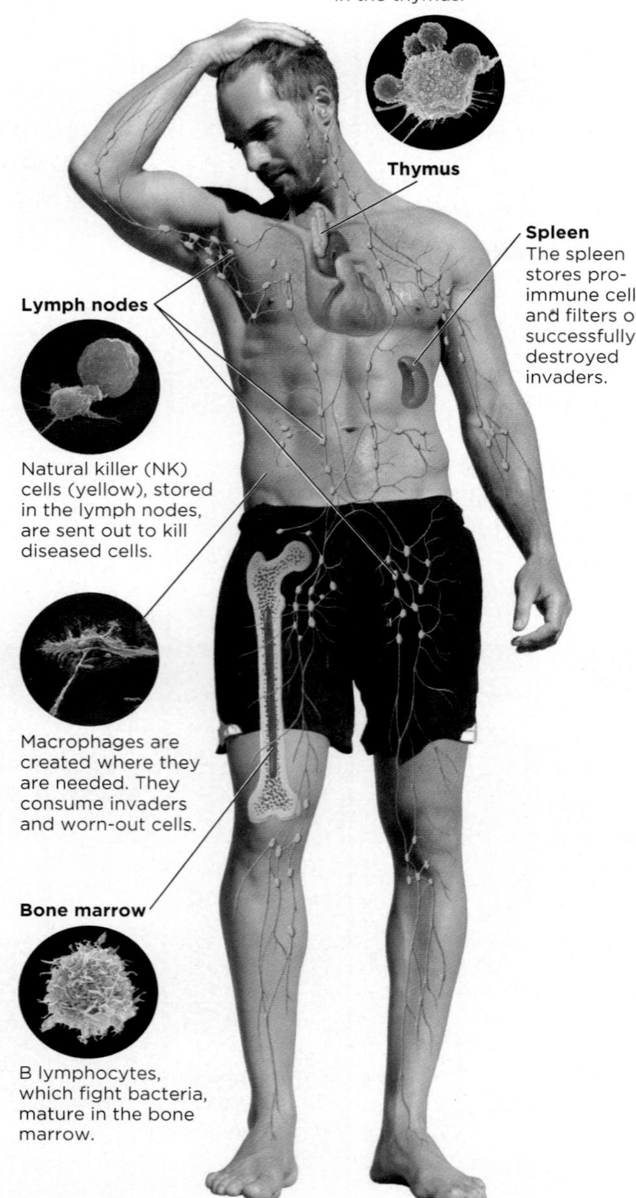

T lymphocytes (pink), which fight viruses, cancer, and other invaders, mature in the thymus.
Thymus
Spleen
The spleen stores pro-immune cells and filters out successfully destroyed invaders.
Lymph nodes
Natural killer (NK) cells (yellow), stored in the lymph nodes, are sent out to kill diseased cells.
Macrophages are created where they are needed. They consume invaders and worn-out cells.
Bone marrow
B lymphocytes, which fight bacteria, mature in the bone marrow.

FIGURE 12.2
The Immune System
Our immunity derives from a complex system involving structures and organs throughout the body that support the work of specialized cell types. Man: B2M Productions/Getty Images; T lymphocytes & B lymphocytes: Steve Gschmeissner/Science Source; Natural killer cells & macrophages: Eye of Science/Science Source.

GASTRIC ULCERS Researchers have long suspected an association between gastric ulcers and stress, but the nature of this link is not entirely clear. For many years, stress was assumed to be the sole culprit, but then researchers began considering other causes of gastric ulcers. They found evidence that the bacterium *H. pylori* plays an important, but not necessarily essential, role. Many factors seem to influence the development of ulcers—among them, tobacco use, family history, and excess gastric acid (Fink, 2011, 2017).

CANCER Cancer has also been associated with stress, both in terms of risk and development. Specifically, stress has been linked to the suppression of T lymphocytes and NK cells, which help monitor immune system reactions to developing tumors (Reiche, Nunes, & Morimoto, 2004; Zingoni et al., 2017).

In the United States and other Western countries, breast cancer is the greatest cancer risk for women. In fact, 1 out of every 8 American women will get invasive breast cancer at some point in her life (Breastcancer.org, 2017, March 10). Is stress to blame for this alarmingly high statistic? A recent study of 106,000 women in the United Kingdom found "no association of breast cancer risk overall with experienced frequency of stress" (Schoemaker et al., 2016, para. 1). Yet those who have breast cancer face a variety of stressors, including physical pain, high treatment costs, and limited sick leave (Andreotti, Root, Ahles, McEwen, & Compas, 2015).

Understanding the relationships between stressors and cancer has been a challenge for researchers. Part of the problem is that studies frequently focus on stressors of different durations. Short- and long-term stressors have distinct effects on the immune system, and thus its ability to combat cancer (Dhabhar, 2014; Segerstrom & Miller, 2004). For short-lived stressors such as midterm exams, public speaking, and other activities lasting between 5 and 100 minutes, the body responds by increasing the number of NK cells and deploying other immune cells where needed. In other words, short-term stressors tend to augment immune functioning. Meanwhile, long-term stressors such as military

synonyms
B lymphocytes B cells
T lymphocytes T cells

lymphocyte Type of white blood cell produced in the bone marrow whose job is to battle enemies such as viruses and bacteria.

INFOGRAPHIC 12.3

Health Psychology

Health psychology is the study of the biological, psychological, and social factors that contribute to health and illness. Using the biopsycho-social perspective, health psychologists examine how a variety of factors, including diet, physical activity, and social relationships, impact our predisposition to illness. One of the primary goals is to increase positive health behaviors and decrease negative ones. Research in this field can benefit the health and well-being of individuals and the community at large through changes to public policy and health education.

Understanding Stress: The Biopsychosocial Perspective

Stress has been linked to a variety of negative health outcomes. The biopsychosocial perspective helps us understand how the interaction among biological, psychological, and social factors contributes to our vulnerability.

BIOLOGY

MORE STRESS: Viruses, bacteria, and other disease-causing organisms invade the body, triggering an immune response and putting a strain on the body's resources.

LESS STRESS: Exercise is one of the best ways to buffer against stress and its negative effects (Milani & Lavie, 2009).

PSYCHOLOGY

OH NO!

MORE STRESS: A perceived lack of control, even in mundane aspects of life, profoundly impacts our ability to manage stress (Pagnini, Bercovitz, & Langer, 2016; Rodin, 1986).

LESS STRESS: Research has shown that mindfulness meditation helps ease anxiety and depression (Goyal et al., 2014).

OM

SOCIAL INTERACTION

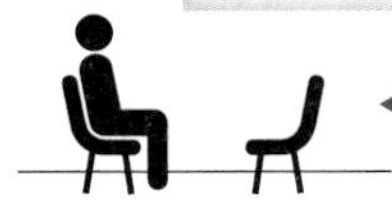

MORE STRESS: Research has shown that feeling judged on one's race, gender, income level, and other factors has a negative impact on physical health and well-being (Clark, DesMeules, Luo, Duncan, & Wielgosz, 2009; Williams & Mohammed, 2009).

LESS STRESS: As a species, human beings are social and benefit from interaction with other humans and even animals (Allen, 2003; John-Henderson, Stellar, Mendoza-Denton, & Francis, 2015).

HEALTH PSYCHOLOGY APPLIED

BIOLOGY
What's in a Color?

PANTONE 448C

With public health in mind, Australia and the United Kingdom have begun requiring cigarette packs to be wrapped in "Opaque Couché" (Pantone 448C), deemed the ugliest color across the globe (Blakemore, 2016, June 9, para. 2). The packaging also features shocking images of smoking-related health consequences. Smoking rates in Australia fell after the new packaging was implemented and tobacco taxes were raised (Australian Department Of Health, 2016, May 27; Blakemore, 2016, June 9).

PSYCHOLOGY
The Power of Thinking "Beyond the Now"

College students who were able to think about and plan for their futures showed an increase in positive health behaviors, such as exercise and conscientious eating habits (Visser & Hirsh, 2014).

SOCIAL INTERACTION
Animal Therapy in Crisis Management

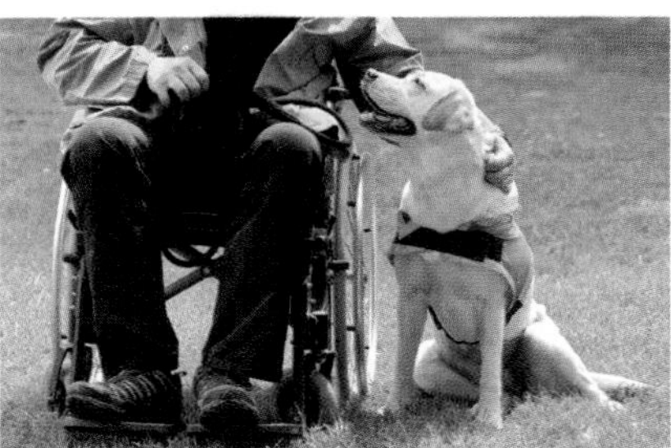

Recognizing how animals can help people manage stress, professionals now use therapy dogs to facilitate coping (Allen, 2003; Associated Press, 2014, May 8; Cunningham & Edelman, 2012, December 17; Fiegl, 2012, December 12).

Credits: Prasit photo/Getty Images; Antonio Gravante/Shutterstock.

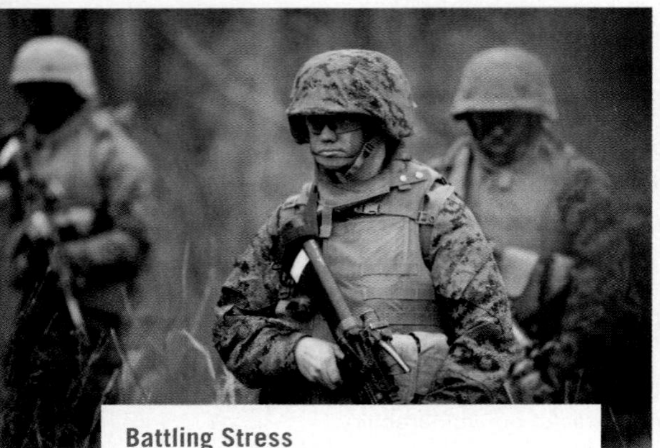

Battling Stress
A group of Marines practice patrolling techniques as part of their combat training. Long-term stressors such as military deployment are associated with declines in activity of NK cells, which help the body fight infections (Dhabhar, 2014). Scott Olson/Getty Images.

deployment or caring for someone with dementia are associated with decreases in NK cells. To appreciate the relationship between stress, immune function, and cancer, we must consider biopsychosocial influences. Factors such as age, medical history, social support, and mental health can impact the link between stressors and cancer (Özkan et al., 2017; Reiche et al., 2004; Segerstrom & Miller, 2004).

HEART DISEASE The same is true for the relationship between stressors and cardiovascular disease. Earthquakes, unhappy marriages, caregiving burdens, and money problems are among the many stressors that may contribute. For people who became unemployed as a result of Hurricane Katrina (a devastating natural disaster that occurred in 2005), the risk of experiencing a "cardiometabolic event" jumped fivefold in the following five years (Joseph, Matthews, & Myers, 2014). The faster people get support to decrease "socioeconomic disruptions" related to a disaster, the better their health outcomes.

What other stressors have been linked to heart disease? "Social-evaluative threats," or concerns about being **judged by others** (about physical appearance or behaviors in a social context, for example), are associated with increases in blood pressure and consequently an elevated risk of heart disease (Smith, Birmingham, & Uchino, 2012). One model suggests that increased job stress can put people at greater risk for developing coronary heart disease, particularly those who perceive a significant degree of job "strain" resulting from high demands, lack of control, and other factors (Ferris, Kline, & Bourdage, 2012).

CONNECTIONS

In **Chapter 11**, we discussed stereotypes, the assumptions we make about people based on their group membership (race, religion, age, or gender, for example). Stereotypes often incorporate some type of judgment. This kind of "social-evaluative threat" can cause stress in the person being stereotyped.

The exact relationship between stressors, high blood pressure, and cardiovascular disease is not totally understood (Straub, 2017). We do know that an increase of fatty deposits, inflammation, and scar tissue within artery walls (a disease known as *atherosclerosis*) is a risk factor for stroke and heart disease (Go et al., 2013). Researchers are not sure exactly how atherosclerosis starts, but one theory suggests that it begins with damage to the inner layer of the artery wall, which may be caused by high blood concentrations of cholesterol and triglycerides, hypertension, and cigarette use. This damage may cause blood flow in an artery to become reduced or blocked, potentially leading to a heart attack or stroke (American Heart Association, 2017).

PSYCHONEUROIMMUNOLOGY We have now discussed some of the effects of short- and long-term stressors. You know that a spurt of cortisol steps up immunity and prepares the body to confront a threat. We discussed how ongoing stress affects one's risk for developing gastric ulcers, cancer, and heart disease, but the list of negative health effects is much longer. According to a meta-analysis of over 300 studies, chronic stressors are associated with problematic immune system responses, which may increase the risk for various illnesses involving inflammation, including asthma, allergies, multiple sclerosis, and rheumatoid arthritis (Segerstrom & Miller, 2004). The exact nature of these relationships has yet to be determined, but researchers are working hard to uncover them, especially for people who are aging and have vulnerable immune systems (Cohen et al., 2001). It is an exciting time for those who specialize in the field of **psychoneuroimmunology** (SI-koh-NUR-oh-IM-mu-NOL-oh-gee), which examines links among psychological factors (such as coping mechanisms and beliefs), the nervous system, and immune functioning (Slavich, 2016).

Substances Don't Help

psychoneuroimmunology The field that studies the relationships among psychological factors, the nervous system, and immune system functioning.

A great way to improve overall health and reduce stress is exercise. Both Christy and her husband Ron (also a law enforcement officer) combat stress with regular workouts. Sometimes they unwind by sharing food and drink with friends. "A good way to deal with stress is laughter, or working out, getting together with your friends, enjoying a good meal," says Christy, who is careful to point out the importance of moderation. Christy and her husband do not drink excessively, but they have seen how **overindulgence of alcohol** can ruin careers. Some people mistakenly view substances as stress relievers. Psychologists explain this type of behavior with the *self-medication hypothesis,* which suggests that people turn to drugs and alcohol to reduce anxiety (Swendsen et al., 2000).

CONNECTIONS

In **Chapter 4,** we described how people use alcohol and other drugs for recreational purposes, and how anesthesiologists rely on drugs to alleviate pain, block memories, and toy with various aspects of consciousness. Here, we discuss how people turn to substances in times of stress.

SMOKING AND STRESS Many smokers rely on cigarettes during times of stress, but does lighting up really help them relax? In one study, participants were forced to abstain from smoking for a half day (a stressful situation for them). When they finally puffed on a cigarette, their mood improved. Yet, smoking did not have this same effect when participants were placed in other stressful situations, like getting ready to deliver a public speech (Perkins, Karelitz, Conklin, Sayette, & Giedgowd, 2010). What do these findings suggest about the relationship between smoking and stress, and what are the long-term implications? There is no simple answer, but continued use of nicotine may interfere with the body's ability to deal with ongoing stressors (Holliday & Gould, 2016). And because it leads to severe health problems, smoking itself may become a stressor for many people and their families.

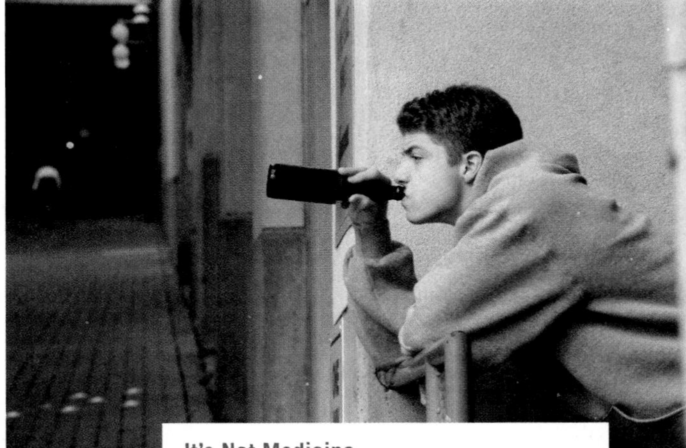

It's Not Medicine
When faced with stressors, we may sleep poorly, eat erratically, and perhaps abuse substances. These behavioral tendencies can lead to significant health problems (Benham, 2010; Ng & Jeffery, 2003). The self-medication approach is not effective. A better strategy might be going to the gym, taking a hike, or doing some deep breathing exercises.
Jill Sabella/Taxi/Getty Images.

Smokers often report that using cigarettes improves their mood, and this is one of the reasons quitting can be so difficult (Lerman & Audrain-McGovern, 2010). How do we get people to kick a habit perceived as so pleasurable? One effective way is to meet them where they are, rather than taking a one-size-fits-all approach (Mahoney, 2010; Prochaska, Velicer, Prochaska, Delucchi, & Hall, 2006). In other words, we should recognize that not all smokers need the same type of help. Some need assistance with smoking only; others engage in additional risky behaviors, like eating high-fat diets or getting too much sun. Meanwhile, smokers who are highly anxious may benefit from high-intensity exercise (Zvolensky et al., 2018). Even if we tailor interventions to address individual needs, the road to recovery may be bumpy. Whether it comes from traditional cigarettes or e-cigarettes (which may serve as a gateway to the traditional variety), nicotine is extremely addictive (Bold et al., 2017; Klein, 2018). Repeated use can lead to **tolerance**; the more you use it, the more you need to achieve the same effect.

CONNECTIONS

In **Chapter 4,** we discussed the concept of tolerance. When we use drugs, such as nicotine, they alter the chemistry of the brain and body. Over time, the body adapts to the drug and therefore needs more and more to create the original effect.

ALCOHOL AND STRESS Alcohol is another drug frequently used to "take the edge off," or counteract, the unpleasant feelings associated with stress. Teenagers, in particular, may rely on alcohol to cope with daily hassles (Bailey & Covell, 2011), which might include insecurities about the way they look and disagreements with family members, teachers, and peers. This is particularly concerning because people who start drinking early in life and have a "greater number of stressful life events [demonstrate] the highest consumption of alcohol in early adulthood" (Stanger, Abaied, & Wagner, 2016, p. 483). Even though teen alcohol use appears to be declining, it remains a significant problem (Schulenberg et al., 2017). We need to help young people find new and healthier ways to handle daily hassles. This means providing more support in schools, and perhaps educating teachers and counselors about the tendency to self-medicate with drugs and alcohol.

Later, we will discuss some positive coping strategies for teens and adults alike, but first let's see how some people seem to thrive under stress.

ADRENALINE JUNKIES Kehlen Kirby sees more pain and suffering in one month than most people do in a lifetime. Working as an emergency medical services (EMS) provider in Pueblo, Colorado, this young man has witnessed the highest highs

Life Saver
Kehlen Kirby has one of the most stressful jobs imaginable—providing emergency medical services to people injured in car accidents, fires, and other traumatic incidents. The constant exposure to pain and suffering helps Kehlen maintain perspective on the hassles of daily life; he doesn't sweat the small stuff. Leslie Nazario/Portraits by Leslie.

and lowest lows of human experience. He has rescued people from flaming car wrecks, treated teenage gang members for gunshot wounds, and watched chain-smokers dying from emphysema yet begging for cigarettes en route to the hospital. In between the sadness and suffering, there are also stories of hope and inspiration, like the time Kehlen and his colleagues delivered a baby on the shoulder of U.S. Route 50.

The reward of alleviating human suffering is "incredible," according to Kehlen. Imagine walking into the home of a diabetic who is lying on the floor, unconscious and surrounded by trembling family members. You insert an IV line into the patient's vein and deliver a dextrose solution that increases blood sugar. In moments, the person is awake as if nothing happened. The family is ecstatic; you have saved their loved one from potential brain damage or death. "People that like to do selfless acts, I think, are made for this job," Kehlen says. And for those who enjoy a challenge, an EMS career will not disappoint. Try working 24 hours in a row, making life-and-death decisions, hoisting heavy bodies, and crouching over patients until your joints burn.

But there appears to be something else drawing people into the EMS profession. You might call it the "adrenaline junkie" factor. (Adrenaline, also called epinephrine, is one of the hormones involved in the "fight-or-flight" response.) Ever since Kehlen was a small boy, he enjoyed a certain amount of risk taking. He was the kid who fearlessly scaled the monkey bars and leaped off the jungle gym, and many of his colleagues claim they were the same way. "All of us probably thought we were 10 feet tall and made of steel," Kehlen says, careful to note that "daring" is not the same as "reckless." One must be calculating when it comes to determining what risks are worth taking.

The adrenaline junkie quality is also apparent in some police officers, according to Christy. An officer patrolling a city beat probably experiences the so-called adrenaline rush at least a few times per week. "When a hot call comes in, anyone worth their salt wants to go," Christy explains. ("Hot call" is anything full of excitement and drama, like a robbery in progress.)

CONNECTIONS
In **Chapter 9,** we introduced arousal theory, which suggests behaviors arise out of the need for stimulation or arousal. Here, we point out that some people seek stressors in order to maintain a satisfying level of arousal.

Is there really some common adrenaline junkie tendency among first responders? **Arousal theory** tells us that humans seek an optimal level of arousal, and what is *optimal* differs from person to person. We also know that first responders are frequently exposed to highly stressful events (Gayton & Lovell, 2012; Lanza, Roysircar, & Rodgers, 2018). Could it be that people like Kehlen and Christy are drawn to these careers because they satisfy a need for arousal? Perhaps, but even adrenaline junkies have their limits. When stress is constant, the body and mind begin to suffer. 

Too Much Cortisol

LO 8 List some consequences of prolonged exposure to the stress hormone cortisol.

Earlier, we discussed the stress hormone cortisol, which plays a key role in mobilizing the body to react to stressful situations. Cortisol is useful if you are responding to immediate danger, like a raging fire or ruthless assailant, but you don't want cortisol levels to remain high for too long.

You Asked, Christy Answers

http://qrs.ly/wr5a5ff

How do you unwind from the daily stresses of work?

CORTISOL AND KIDS Prolonged exposure to cortisol can take a toll on developing brains and bodies. Infants born to mothers subjected to natural disasters, trauma, and other extreme stressors are more likely to be born prematurely, have low birth weights, exhibit behavioral difficulties, and perhaps even show problems with cognitive development (Davis & Sandman, 2010; Levendosky et al., 2016; Tollenaar, Beijers, Jansen, Riksen-Walraven, & De Weerth, 2011). Research has found that conflicts at home can increase cortisol levels in children (Doom et al., 2018). Verbal exchanges such as a child exclaiming, "No! I don't want to!" and parents saying, "You are going to shut your mouth and be quiet!" are exactly the types of exchanges associated with increased cortisol levels. Cortisol activity may help explain why exposure to conflict during childhood is associated with future health problems (Oh et al., 2018; Slatcher & Robles, 2012).

Is She Happy or Mad?
How you interpret this woman's emotional state may depend on your current stress level. In one study, people were more likely to perceive negative emotions in ambiguous facial expressions when their cortisol levels were elevated—the result of a stressor introduced in the experiment (Brown, Raio, & Neta, 2017). drbimages/Getty Images.

CORTISOL AND THE BRAIN Because cortisol enters the brain, it can have substantial effects on cognition and behavior—not only for children but also for adults (Kluen, Agorastos, Wiedemann, & Schwabe, 2017; Wagner et al., 2016; Wirth, 2015). Imagine you are a police officer. During one of your shifts, you come face-to-face with a suspect who may be armed and dangerous. Facing this stressor activates the HPA system, triggering a release of cortisol. In one study, researchers had police officers participate in a realistic simulation of being targeted by shooters. Not only did the officers' cortisol levels rise, but the functioning of their **working memory** decreased, too (Taverniers, Smeets, Van Ruysseveldt, Syroit, & von Grumbkow, 2011). Can you imagine the implications of being in a dangerous situation with impaired working memory?

CONNECTIONS
In **Chapter 6,** we presented the concept of working memory, which refers to the active processing of information in short-term memory. Here, we see how working memory can be impacted by stressors.

Other research suggests that heightened cortisol levels may decrease errors in decision making. When police officers had to make threat-related decisions in a video simulation, they were better able to discern whether an individual was armed when their cortisol levels were high. This accuracy increased when the officer faced a simulation involving a Black suspect, and decreased when the suspect was White. This finding was the same for the White officers and minority officers participating in the study. The researchers concluded that higher cortisol levels, which were caused by the stressful situation, resulted in "heightened vigilance for danger" (Akinola & Mendes, 2012, p. 172). Apparently, the *perceived* threat of Black men was greater, which is consistent with what social psychologists have learned about the conscious and **unconscious reactions** many people have to racial minorities. A meta-analysis of studies concluded that participants engaged in shooting tasks were "quicker to shoot armed Black targets, slower to not shoot unarmed Black targets, and were more likely to have a liberal shooting threshold for Black targets" (Mekawi & Bresin, 2015, p. 128).

CONNECTIONS
In **Chapter 11**, we discussed implicit bias, a type of prejudice we are not aware of having. The officers in this study may not have realized that they respond differently to Black suspects; they might have been acting on implicit bias.

Now that we understand how stressors can impact the body and brain, let's explore how different people tolerate and respond to stress.

✔ show what you know

1. As a police officer, Christy has found herself in life-threatening situations. When faced with danger, Christy's body initially exhibits a fight-or-flight reaction, which is equivalent to the ________ of the general adaptation syndrome.
   a. alarm stage
   b. exhaustion stage
   c. diseases of adaptation
   d. acculturative stress

2. ________ helps maintain balance in the body by overseeing the sympathetic nervous system, as well as the neuroendocrine and immune systems.
   a. The general adaptation syndrome
   b. The exhaustion stage
   c. The hypothalamic-pituitary-adrenal system
   d. Eustress

3. The ________ refers to a specific pattern of physiological reactions observed in response to stressors.

4. Infants of mothers subjected to extreme stressors may be born prematurely, have low birth weights, and exhibit behavioral difficulties. These outcomes result from increased levels of the stress hormone:
   a. *H. pylori.*
   b. lymphocytes.
   c. cortisol.
   d. NK cells.

5. Why are people under stress more likely to get sick?

✔ CHECK YOUR ANSWERS IN APPENDIX C.

Staying Alive
Paramedics care for the victim of an automobile accident. The patient appears to be experiencing a health crisis, but the paramedics face their own set of health risks. Working odd hours, not getting enough exercise, eating poorly, and dealing with the ongoing stressors of paramedic work make staying healthy a challenge. Caiaimage/Trevor Adeline/Getty Images.

CAN YOU DEAL?

AMBULANCE BURNOUT Kehlen has been in the EMS field for nearly a decade, and most of that time he has spent working for a private ambulance company. He estimates that the average ambulance worker lasts about 8 years before quitting to pursue another line of work. What makes this career so hard to endure? The pay is modest, the 24-hour shifts grueling, and the constant exposure to trauma profoundly disturbing. The pressure to perform is enormous, but there is seldom a "thank-you" or recognition for a job well done. Perhaps no other profession involves so much responsibility—combined with so little appreciation. "The ambulance crews, they're kind of like the silent heroes," Kehlen explains. "You work so hard and you don't get any thanks at the end of the day."

Perhaps it's no surprise that the EMS profession has one of the highest rates of *burnout* (Gayton & Lovell, 2012). **Burnout** refers to emotional, mental, and physical fatigue that results from repeated exposure to challenges, leading to reduced motivation, enthusiasm, and performance. People who work in the helping professions, such as mental health professionals, physicians, and child protection workers, are clearly at risk for burnout (Linnerooth, Mrdjenovich, & Moore, 2011; McFadden, Mallett, & Leiter, 2018; Nazir et al., 2018). Some of the factors contributing to burnout include the substantial demands of the job, long work shifts, insufficient support from coworkers and supervisors, and lack of ongoing education. At times burnout is a sign of something worse to come, like substance abuse or thoughts of suicide (Bragard, Dupuis, & Fleet, 2015).

Coping with Stress

Police officers are also susceptible to burnout. To survive and thrive in this career, you must excel under pressure. No wonder over 90% of city police departments in the United States require job applicants to take psychological tests, such as the Minnesota Multiphasic Personality Inventory (MMPI–2-RF; Ben-Porath, 2012; Butcher & Rouse, 1996; Cochrane, Tett, & Vandecreek, 2003). Psychological testing is just one hurdle facing the aspiring police officer; some departments also insist on full-length meetings with a psychologist, and most city agencies require criminal background checks, polygraph (lie detector) tests, and physical fitness assessments. This is on top of about 1,000 hours of training at the police academy (Cochrane et al., 2003). Even after overcoming all the hurdles of the hiring process, some police officers still struggle with stress management (Lanza et al., 2018). In this respect, police work is like any other field; there will always be people who have trouble coping with the stress of their job. As Christy explains, "Officers are just a segment of society. Some people deal with stuff really well, and others, they can't get past it, they can't put it out of their mind."

CONNECTIONS
In **Chapter 9,** we described the cognitive appraisal theory of emotion, which suggests that emotion results from the way people appraise or interpret interactions they have. We appraise events based on their significance, and our subjective appraisal influences our response to stressors.

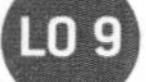

LO 9 Illustrate how appraisal influences coping.

APPRAISAL AND COPING Needless to say, people experience stress in their own unique ways. Psychologist Richard Lazarus (1922–2002) suggested that stress is the result of a person's **appraisal** of a stressor, not necessarily the stressor itself (Folkman & Lazarus, 1985; Lazurs & Folkman, 1984). This viewpoint stands in contrast to Selye's suggestion (noted earlier) that we all react to stressors in a similar manner. **Coping** refers to the cognitive, behavioral, and emotional abilities used to manage something perceived as difficult or challenging. In order to cope, you must appraise the stressor (**INFOGRAPHIC 12.4** on the next page). When making a **primary appraisal,** you determine how an event or situation will affect you: Is it irrelevant, positive, challenging, or harmful? Next, you form a **secondary appraisal,** or decide how to respond, considering what resources are available. If you believe you can cope with virtually any challenge that comes your way, the impact of stress remains low. If you think your coping abilities are poor, the impact of stress will be high. Differences in appraisal help explain why two people can react to the same event in dramatically different ways.

Tend and Befriend
Women at the Kopila Valley Women's Center in Surkhet, Nepal, support each other in their educational and career goals. Many of the women have endured extreme poverty, abuse, and other hardships, but working together gives them strength (BlinkNow, n.d.). During times of stress, women are inclined to "tend and befriend," or direct their energy toward nurturing offspring and developing social relationships. Courtesy of BlinkNow Foundation.

There are two basic types of coping. **Problem-focused coping** means taking a direct approach, confronting a problem head-on. Suppose you are having trouble in a relationship; with problem-focused coping, you might read self-help books or find a counselor. **Emotion-focused coping** involves addressing the emotions that surround a problem, rather than trying to solve it or change the situation. With a troubled relationship, you might think about your feelings, look to friends for support, or exercise to take your mind off it, instead of addressing the problem directly. When emotions interfere with daily functioning or when problems have no solutions (for example, the death of a loved one), emotion-focused coping may be better. However, problem-focused coping is usually more productive in the long run.

Put Your Heads Together

Team up and **A**) explain the meaning of primary and secondary appraisal, as well as problem- and emotion-focused coping. **B**) Follow the steps outlined in Infographic 12.4 using a different stressor.

We all have distinct ways of dealing with stress, and these coping styles appear to be related to our personalities. What's more, personality may have a profound effect on our predispositions to stress-related illness.

LO 10 Describe Type A and Type B personalities and explain how they relate to stress.

TYPE A AND TYPE B PERSONALITIES For decades, researchers have known that people with certain personality types are prone to developing cardiovascular disease. Cardiologists Meyer Friedman (1910–2001) and Ray Rosenman (1920–2013) were among the first to suspect a link between personality type and cardiovascular problems (Friedman & Rosenman, 1974). In particular, they noted that many of the people they treated were intensely focused on time and always in a hurry. These characteristics and other behavior patterns came to be known as **Type A personality.** Someone with a Type A personality is competitive, aggressive, impatient, and often hostile (Diamond, 1982; Smith & Ruiz, 2002). Through numerous studies, Friedman and Rosenman discovered that people with Type A personality were twice as likely to

burnout Emotional, mental, and physical fatigue that results in reduced motivation, enthusiasm, and performance.

coping The cognitive, behavioral, and emotional abilities used to manage something that is perceived as difficult or challenging.

primary appraisal One's initial assessment of a situation to determine its personal impact and whether it is irrelevant, positive, challenging, or harmful.

secondary appraisal An assessment to determine how to respond to a challenging or threatening situation.

problem-focused coping A coping strategy in which a person deals directly with a problem by attempting to solve and address it head-on.

emotion-focused coping A coping strategy in which a person addresses the emotions that surround a problem, as opposed to trying to solve it.

Type A personality A person who exhibits a competitive, aggressive, impatient, and often hostile pattern of behaviors.

The Process of Coping

Coping refers to the cognitive, emotional, and behavioral methods we employ to manage stressful events. But we don't always rely on the same strategies to manage stressors in our lives. Coping is an individual *process* through which we appraise a stressor to determine how it will affect us and how we can respond.

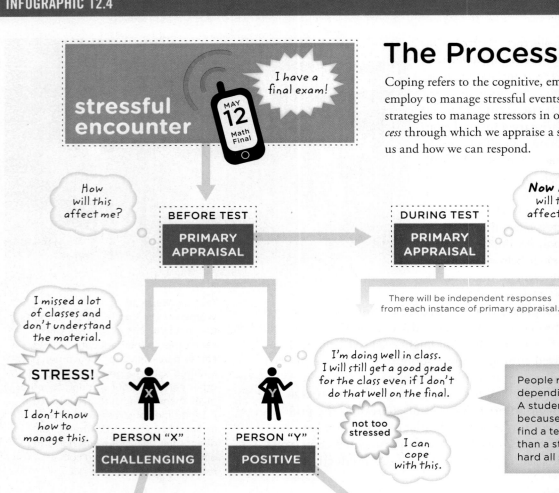

stressful encounter
MAY 12 Math Final
I have a final exam!
How will this affect me?
BEFORE TEST
PRIMARY APPRAISAL
DURING TEST
PRIMARY APPRAISAL
Now how will this affect me?
There will be independent responses from each instance of primary appraisal.
Most stressful events are not static. Therefore, we may appraise them at different stages with different results. For example, you will appraise the challenge of a test differently before you take it, while you are taking it, and after you have taken it but are waiting to receive a grade.
I missed a lot of classes and don't understand the material.
STRESS!
I don't know how to manage this.
X
PERSON "X"
CHALLENGING
Y
PERSON "Y"
POSITIVE
I'm doing well in class. I will still get a good grade for the class even if I don't do that well on the final.
not too stressed
I can cope with this.
People respond differently to stressors depending on how they appraise them. A student who is struggling in a class because she hasn't worked hard may find a test even more challenging than a student who has been working hard all semester.
SECONDARY APPRAISAL
What can I do?
SECONDARY APPRAISAL
What can I do?
Once we know how an event will affect us, we use secondary appraisal to determine our response, taking into consideration what resources are available.
* problem focused
Seek help from friends
I'll get notes from a classmate.
emotion focused
Seek emotional support
I'll feel better after venting.
emotion focused
Mental disengagement
I don't care about this class anyway.
* problem focused
Planning
First I'll take the online self-quiz, then I'll look in my textbook to understand my mistakes.
emotion focused
Emphasize the positive
I feel so much better when I study.
* problem focused
Suppress competing activities
I won't go out this weekend so I can focus on studying.
In response to a stressor, most people use several coping strategies, including both problem-focused and emotion-focused coping. Problem-focused coping involves doing something to deal with the source of stress. People who do not feel they can solve the problem tend to rely more on emotion-focused coping to manage their feelings about the situation.

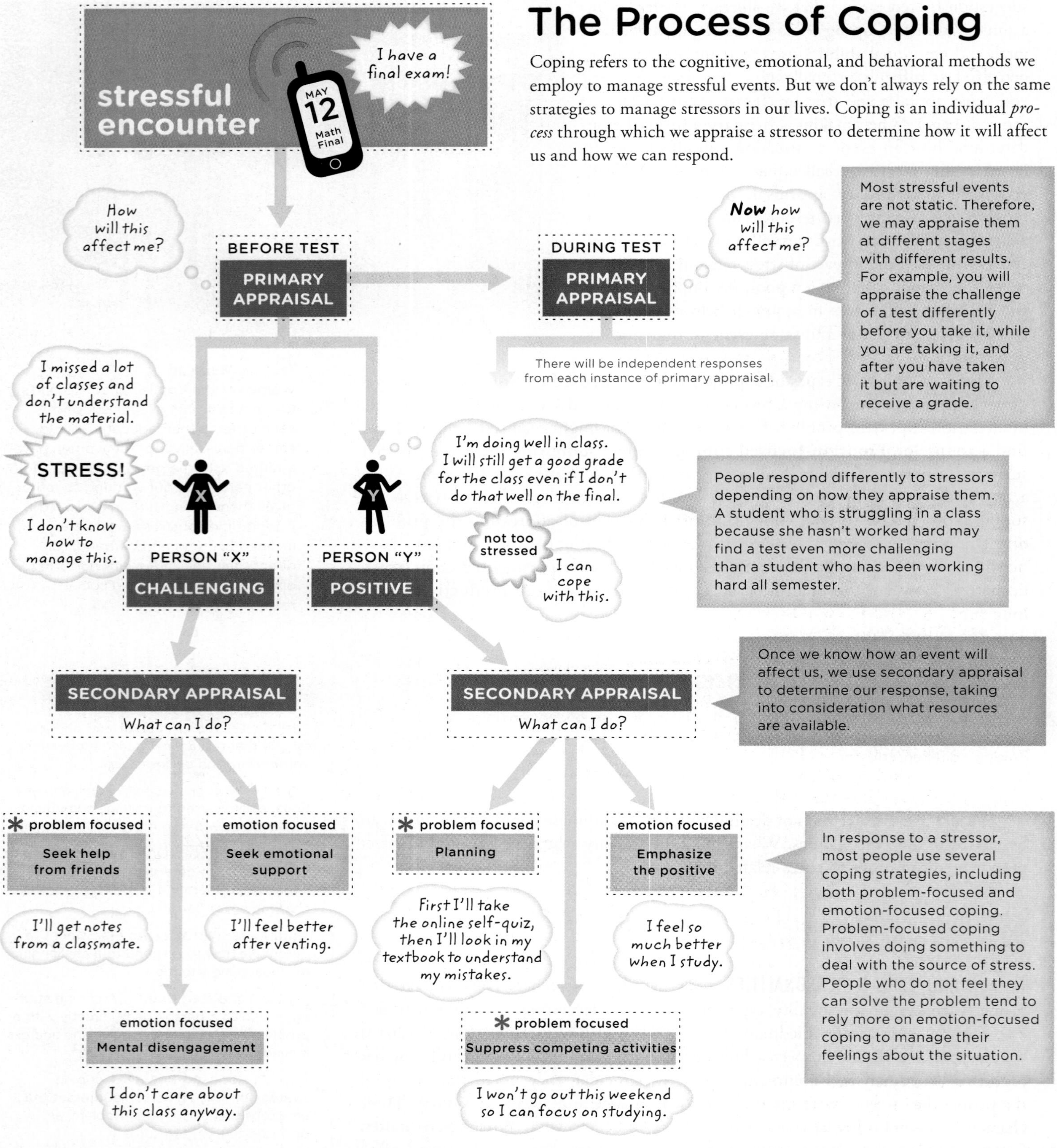

*** Problem-focused coping is usually the most productive.**
Here are some other problem-focused strategies:

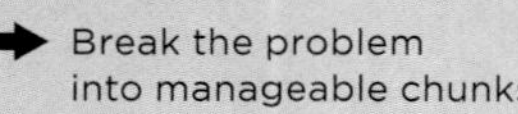

- Restraint (wait to act until all relevant data have come to light)
- Break the problem into manageable chunks

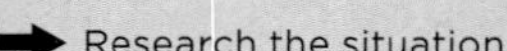

- Research the situation

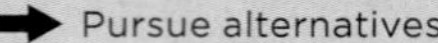

- Pursue alternatives

develop cardiovascular disease as those with **Type B personality.** Individuals with Type B personality are often more relaxed, patient, and nonaggressive (Rosenman et al., 1975). Why would people with Type A personality suffer disproportionately from cardiovascular disease? There are various reasons, but these individuals are more likely to have high blood pressure, an elevated heart rate, and increased levels of stress hormones. They are also prone to more interpersonal problems (for example, arguments, fights, or hostile interactions), which increase the time their bodies are prepared for fight or flight.

Although years of research confirmed the relationship between Type A behavior and heart disease, some researchers reported results that did not support this conclusion, or were unable to replicate the findings (Smith & MacKenzie, 2006). This was partly the result of inconsistent methodologies; for example, some studies used samples with high-risk participants, whereas others included healthy people. As researchers continued to probe the relationship, they found that the component of *hostility* in Type A personality was the strongest predictor of coronary heart disease.

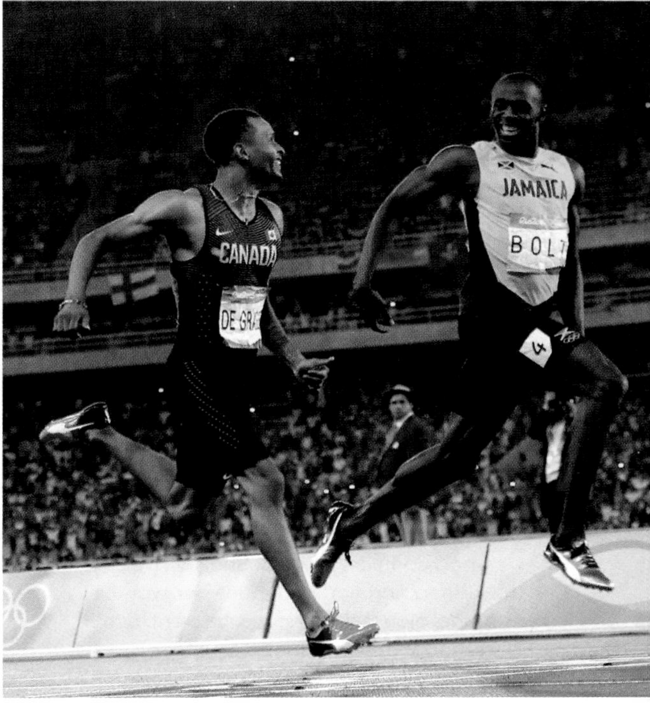

Laid-Back Bolt
The fastest man alive, Usain Bolt (right), may have what psychologists call a Type B personality—he appears to be relaxed and easygoing, even during a race! Here, the Jamaican sprinter exchanges smiles with his competitor, Canadian Andre De Grasse, during the 200-meter semifinal at the 2016 Olympics in Rio de Janeiro (Ng, 2016, August 18). Matt Dunham/AP Images.

TYPE D PERSONALITY Another personality type associated with poor cardiovascular outcomes is the *Type D personality,* where the "D" refers to distress (Denollet & Conraads, 2011). A Type D individual frequently experiences emotions like worry, tension, bad moods, and social inhibition (avoids confronting others and has poor social skills). People who exhibit these Type D qualities and have heart problems are more likely to struggle with their illness. Is this because they tend to avoid dealing with problems directly and fail to take advantage of social support? This is not an effective approach to coping with stressors over time (Martin et al., 2011).

THE THREE Cs OF HARDINESS Clearly, not everyone has the same tolerance for stress (Ganzel, Morris, & Wethington, 2010; Straub, 2017). Some people seem capable of handling intensely stressful situations, such as war and poverty. These individuals appear to have a personality characteristic referred to as **hardiness,** meaning they are very resilient and tend to remain positive when facing a great deal of stress. Kehlen, who considers himself "a very optimistic person," may fit into this category, and findings from one study of Scottish ambulance personnel suggest that EMS workers with this characteristic are less likely to experience burnout (Alexander & Klein, 2001).

Researchers have studied how some business executives seem to withstand the effects of extremely stressful jobs (Kobasa, 1979). Their hardiness appears to be associated with three characteristics: feeling a strong *commitment* to work and personal matters; believing they are in *control* of the events in their lives and not victims of circumstances; and not feeling threatened by *challenges,* but rather seeing them as opportunities for growth. Sometimes the best way to deal with stressors is to embrace them with excitement.

I Am in Control

Psychologists have consistently found that people who believe they have control over their lives and circumstances are less likely to experience the negative impact of stressors than those who do not feel the same control. For a clear illustration of this phenomenon, we turn to a series of studies on nursing home residents (Langer & Rodin, 1976). Residents in a "responsibility-induced" group were allowed to make a variety of choices about their daily activities and their environments.

Type B personality A person who exhibits a relaxed, patient, and nonaggressive pattern of behaviors.

hardiness A personality characteristic indicating an ability to remain resilient and optimistic despite intensely stressful situations.

Documenting War
Lynsey Addario (second from left) poses with fellow photojournalists on March 11, 2011, in Ras Lanuf, Libya. Four days later, Addario was kidnapped along with three colleagues from *The New York Times*. It was the second time Addario had been abducted while covering conflicts abroad. She survived the kidnapping and continues her work as a photojournalist (King & Laurent, 2016, February 6). Addario seems to display a high level of resilience, or the ability to bounce back from stressful experiences. John Moore/Getty Images.

Meanwhile, members of the "comparison" group were not given these kinds of choices; instead, the nursing home staff made all such decisions for them. (The residents were told that the staff was responsible for their happiness and care.) After following the participants for 18 months, the researchers found that members of the responsibility-induced group were more lively, socially engaged, and healthier than those in the comparison group. Perhaps more shocking, twice as many of the residents in the comparison group died during this period (Rodin & Langer, 1977).

Having a sense of personal control may impact disease outcomes and overall health of people across age groups. Cancer patients who exhibit a "helpless attitude" about their disease seem more likely to experience a recurrence of the cancer than those with perceptions of greater control. Why would this be? Women who have had breast cancer and believe they maintain control over their lifestyle, through diet and exercise, are more likely to make proactive changes related to their health (Costanzo, Lutgendorf, & Roeder, 2011). Ultimately, these changes may reduce the risk factors associated with cancer (Simon, 2015, January 16). The same type of relationship is apparent in cardiovascular disease; the less control people feel they have, the greater their risk (Shapiro, Schwartz, & Astin, 1996).

Feelings of control may also have a direct effect on the body; for example, a sense of powerlessness is associated with increases in catecholamines and corticosteroids, both key players in a physiological response to stressors. Some have suggested a causal relationship between feelings of perceived control and immune system function; the greater the sense of control, the better the functioning of the immune system (Shapiro et al., 1996). But these are correlations, and the direction of causality is not clear. Could it be that better immune functioning, and thus better health, might increase one's sense of control?

We must also consider cross-cultural differences. Individual control is emphasized and valued in individualist cultures, but not necessarily in collectivistic cultures, where people look to "powerful others" and "chance factors" to explain events and guide decision making (Cheng, Cheung, Chio, & Chan, 2013).

We Can Do This!
People gather in support of breast cancer research at the Komen South Florida Race for the Cure. Receiving a cancer diagnosis and undergoing cancer treatments are significant stressors, but a patient's capacity to cope can affect her physical and psychological health (Andreotti et al., 2015). Cancer survivors who believe they have control over their health may be inclined to engage in healthy behaviors like exercising and eating well (Costanzo, Lutgendorf, & Roeder, 2011). Ultimately, these behaviors may reduce the risk factors associated with cancer (Simon, 2015, January 16). Richard Graulich/ZUMA Press/Newscom.

LOCUS OF CONTROL Differences in perceived sense of control stem from beliefs about where control resides (Rotter, 1966; Chapter 10). People with an *internal locus of control* generally feel they are in control of life; they believe it is important to take charge and make changes when problems occur. Those with an *external locus of control* generally feel that chance, luck, or fate is responsible for their circumstances; there is no point in trying to change things or make them better. Imagine that a doctor tells a patient he needs to change his lifestyle and start exercising. If the patient has an internal locus of control, he will likely take charge and start walking to work or hitting the gym; he expects his actions will impact his health. If the patient has an external locus of control, he is more apt to think his actions won't make a difference and may not attempt lifestyle changes. In the 1970 British Cohort Study, researchers examined over 11,000 children at age 10, and then assessed their health at age 30. Participants with an internal locus of control, measured at 10 years of age, were less likely to be overweight or obese in adulthood, and had lower levels of psychological problems. They were also less inclined to smoke and more likely to exercise regularly than people with a more external locus of control (Gale, Batty, & Deary, 2008).

Camaraderie
Firefighters climb the notoriously difficult "Incline," a seemingly endless set of stairs up Pikes Peak in Manitou Springs, Colorado. Every year on the morning of September 11, the firefighters walk up the 1-mile path to commemorate those who died in the 9/11 terrorist attacks. The tight-knit community at the firehouse provides Kehlen with friendship, emotional support, and a great deal of stress reduction. Nicole Pritts.

FROM AMBULANCE TO FIREHOUSE Kehlen's original career goal was to become a firefighter, but jobs are extremely hard to secure in this field. Fresh out of high school, Kehlen joined an ambulance crew with the goal of moving on to the firehouse. Seven years later, he reached his destination. Kehlen is now a firefighter paramedic with the Pueblo Fire Department. His job description still includes performing CPR, inserting breathing tubes, and delivering lifesaving medical care. But now he can also be seen handling fire hoses and rushing into 800-degree buildings with 80 pounds of gear.

Compared to an ambulance, the firehouse environment is far more conducive to managing stress. For starters, there is enormous social support. Fellow firefighters are a lot like family members. They eat together, go to sleep together, and wake to the same flashing lights and tones announcing the latest emergency. "The fire department is such a brotherhood," Kehlen says. Spending a third of his life at the firehouse with colleagues, Kehlen has come to know and trust them on a deep level. They discuss the disturbing events they witness and help each other recover emotionally. "If you don't talk about it," says Kehlen, "it's just going to wear on you." Another major benefit of working at the firehouse is having the freedom to exercise, which Kehlen considers a major stress reliever. The firefighters are actually required to work out 1 hour per day during their shifts.

Ambulance work is quite another story. Kehlen and his coworkers were friends, but they didn't share the tight bonds that Kehlen now has with fellow firefighters. And eating healthy and exercising were almost impossible. Ambulance workers don't have the luxury of making a healthy meal in a kitchen. They often have no choice but to drive to the nearest fast-food restaurant and wipe the crumbs off their faces as they race to the next emergency. One of the worst aspects of the job was the lack of exercise. Says Kehlen, "That killed me when I was in the ambulance." 

Tools for Healthy Living

LO 11 Discuss several tools for reducing stress and maintaining health.

Dealing with stressors can be challenging, but you don't have to grin and bear it. There are many ways to manage and reduce stress. Let's take a look at several powerful stress-fighting weapons: good nutrition, physical exercise, and relaxation techniques.

Wash Away the Stress?
Next time you wash dishes, focus on the experience of this activity. Feel the weight of the bowls and plates in your hands, notice the water running over your skin, and take in the clean scent of soap. Be aware of your breathing and stay fully present in the moment—not thinking about something else you'd rather be doing. Turning the everyday chore of dishwashing into a mindful activity may help decrease feelings of nervousness and make you feel inspired (Hanley, Warner, Dehili, Canto, & Garland, 2015). Jonathan Knowles/Getty Images.

Apply This ↓

EVERYDAY STRESS RELIEVERS

NUTRITION Think about the last time you felt stressed. What kinds of food did you crave? Probably not kale salad, whole grains, and walnuts. If you're like most people, you longed for something more along the lines of potato chips and chocolate chip cookies. Unfortunately, stress can lead to poor health choices.

Perhaps you've heard of the "Freshman 15"? The popular assumption that students often put on pounds during their first year of college appears to be more than an urban myth. Weight gain does seem to be a common factor for approximately two thirds of freshmen students, and it has been associated with stress, poor nutrition, inadequate exercise, and alcohol consumption (Vadeboncoeur, Townsend, & Foster, 2015). As the semester progresses, students report choosing unhealthier foods—especially around finals (Wansink, Cao, Saini, Shimizu, & Just, 2013). Weight gain among college freshmen is almost 5 times higher than that of the general population (Vadeboncoeur et al., 2015).

Stress is inevitable, but eating unhealthy food is unlikely to make it disappear. A well-balanced diet is important for long-term health. Reducing sugar and carbs, increasing lean proteins, and eating more vegetables may allow us to live longer (Jankovic et al., 2014). But, good nutrition is just the beginning. If you really want to battle stress, get your heart pumping.

EXERCISE You are feeling the pressure. Exam time is here, and you haven't cracked open a book because you've been so busy at work. The holidays are approaching, you have not purchased a single present, and the list of unread texts is growing by the minute. With so much to do, you feel paralyzed. In these types of situations, the best solution may be to drop to the floor to do some push-ups, or run out the door and take a jog. When you come back, you may feel a new sense of calm. *I can handle this,* you think to yourself. *One thing at a time.*

How does exercise work its magic? Physiologically, we know exercise increases blood flow, activates the autonomic nervous system, and helps initiate the release of several hormones. These physiological reactions help the body defend against potential illnesses, especially those related to stress. Exercise also spurs the release of the body's natural painkilling and pleasure-inducing neurotransmitters, the endorphins (Daenen, Varkey, Kellmann, & Nijs, 2015; Salmon, 2001).

When it comes to choosing an exercise regimen, the tough part is finding an activity that is intense enough to reduce the impact of stress, but sufficiently enjoyable to keep you coming back for more. Research suggests that only 30 minutes of daily exercise is needed to decrease the risk of heart disease, stroke, hypertension, certain types of cancer, and diabetes (Warburton, Charlesworth, Ivey, Nettlefold, & Bredin, 2010), not to mention improve feelings of well-being (Panza, Taylor, Thompson, White, & Pescatello, 2017). Exercise needn't be a chore. Your daily 30 minutes could mean dancing to *Just Dance* on the Wii, going for a bike ride, raking leaves on a beautiful fall day, or shoveling snow. Exercising outdoors improves not only your physical health but your mental health as well (Pasanen, Tyrväinen, & Korpela, 2014).

You Asked, Christy Answers

http://qrs.ly/wr5a5ff

What advice would you give to people who deal with high amounts of stress on a daily basis?

RELAX Exercise is all about getting the body moving, but relaxing the muscles can also relieve stress. "Just relax." We have heard it said a thousand times, but do we really know how to begin? Physician and physiologist Edmund Jacobson (1938) introduced a technique known as *progressive muscle relaxation,* which has since been expanded upon. With this technique, you begin by tensing a muscle group (for example, your toes) for about 10 seconds, and then releasing as you focus on the tension leaving. Next you progress to another muscle group, such as the calves, and then the thighs, buttocks, stomach, shoulders, arms, neck, and so on. After several weeks of practice, you will begin to recognize where you hold tension in your muscles—at least this is the goal. Once you become aware of that tension, you can focus on relaxing those specific muscles without going through the entire process. Progressive muscle relaxation has been shown to defuse anxiety in highly stressed college students. In one study, researchers found that just 20 minutes of progressive muscle relaxation had "significant short-term effects," including decreases in anxiety, blood pressure, and heart rate (Dolbier & Rush, 2012). Participants also reported a feeling of increased control and energy. Inducing this *relaxation response* may also be an effective way to reduce pain (Benson, 2000; Dusek et al., 2008).

You Asked, Christy Answers

http://qrs.ly/wr5a5ff

What was the single most stressful situation in your career?

try this Using a clock or watch to time yourself, breathe in slowly for 5 seconds. Then exhale slowly for 5 seconds. Do this for 1 minute. With each breath, you begin to slow down and relax. The key is to breathe deeply.

BIOFEEDBACK A proven method for managing the physiological responses to stressors is **biofeedback.** This technique builds on learning principles to teach control of seemingly involuntary physiological activity (such as heart rate, blood pressure, and skin temperature). Biofeedback equipment monitors internal responses and provides visual or auditory signals to help a person identify those that are maladaptive (for example, tense shoulder muscles). The person begins by focusing on a signal (a light or tone, for instance) that indicates when a desired response occurs. By controlling this biofeedback indicator, the person learns to maintain the desired response (relaxed shoulders in this example). The ultimate goal is to tap into this technique in real-life scenarios outside of the clinic or lab. Some research suggests biofeedback can decrease the frequency of headaches and chronic pain (Flor & Birbaumer, 1993; Sun-Edelstein & Mauskop, 2011). It appears to be useful for all age groups, including children, adolescents, and the elderly (Morone & Greco, 2007; Palermo, Eccleston, Lewandowski, Williams, & Morley, 2010).

What Goes Around
Volunteers in Chongqing, China, celebrate Father's Day with elderly men in a nursing home. Altruism, or helping others because it feels good, is an excellent stress reliever.
TopPhoto via AP Images.

SOCIAL SUPPORT Dealing with stress is much easier if you have a strong social network. Researchers have found that proactively participating in positive enduring relationships with family, friends, and religious groups can generate a health benefit similar to exercise and not smoking (House, Landis, & Umberson, 1988). People who maintain close, supportive relationships have better overall health (Pietromonaco & Collins, 2017).

You might expect that receiving support is the key to lowering stress, but research suggests that *giving* support also makes a big difference. In a study of older married adults, researchers reported reduced mortality rates for participants who indicated that they helped or supported others, including friends, spouses, relatives, and neighbors. There were no reductions in mortality, however, associated with receiving support from others (Brown, Nesse, Vinokur, & Smith, 2003).

Helping others because it gives you pleasure, and expecting nothing in return, is known as *altruism,* and it appears to be an effective stress reducer and happiness booster (Schwartz, Keyl, Marcum, & Bode, 2009; Schwartz, Meisenhelder, Yunsheng, & Reed, 2003).

biofeedback A technique that involves providing visual or auditory information about biological processes, allowing a person to control physiological activity (for example, heart rate, blood pressure, and skin temperature).

Relax
How does mindfulness meditation impact the brain? The research on meditation is relatively young and problematic in some respects (Stetka, 2017, October 11), but "there is emerging evidence that mindfulness meditation might cause neuroplastic changes in the structure and function of brain regions involved in regulation of attention, emotion and self-awareness" (Tang, Hölzel, & Posner, 2015, p. 10). Philip Lee Harvey/Getty Images.

When we care for others, we generally don't have time to focus on our own problems; we also come to recognize that others may be dealing with more troubling circumstances than we are.

These proactive, stress-reducing behaviors reflect a certain type of attitude. You might call it a positive psychology attitude.

THINK POSITIVE

RIGHT HERE, RIGHT NOW In the very first chapter of this book, we introduced *positive psychology,* "the study of positive emotions, positive character traits, and enabling institutions" (Seligman & Steen, 2005, p. 410). Rather than focusing on mental illness and abnormal behavior, positive psychology emphasizes human strengths and virtues. The goal is well-being and fulfillment, and that means "satisfaction" with the past, "hope and optimism" for the future, and "flow and happiness" at the current time (Seligman & Csikszentmihalyi, 2000, p. 5).

FOCUS ON YOUR BREATHING. . . .

As we wrap up this chapter on stress and health, we encourage you to focus on that third category: flow and happiness in the present. No matter what stressors come your way, try to stay grounded in the here and now. The past is the past, the future is uncertain, but this moment is yours. Finding a way to enjoy the present is one of the best ways to reduce stress. Easier said than done, you may be thinking.

If "being in the moment" does not come naturally, you might try **mindfulness meditation**—the practice of focusing attention on current experiences without passing judgment (Tang, Hölzel, & Posner, 2015; see **Figure 12.3**). Research suggests that "brief mindfulness training can help college students manage their stress in response to the ubiquitous academic and cognitive challenges of college life" (Shearer, Hunt, Chowdhury, & Nicol, 2016, p. 232). This practice may even promote psychological health by reducing depression, stress, and anxiety (Dimidjian et al., 2016; Goldin et al., 2016; Harrington & Dunne, 2015).

FIGURE 12.3
Breathe In, Breathe Out
You don't have to be a Buddhist monk or yoga master to stay in the moment and focus your attention. Practicing meditation may be as easy as following these steps, provided by Diana Winston of the UCLA Mindful Awareness Research Center (Fully Present: The Book, 2010, August 3).

- Sit on a chair or pillow. Keep your back straight but relaxed, close your eyes, and place your hands on your knees or thighs.
- Feel the weight of your body and focus on whatever sensations you are experiencing right now.
- Breathe naturally, and focus on the sensation of inhaling and exhaling; this might mean the rise and fall of your abdomen or chest, or the air entering and exiting your nostrils.
- Continue to focus on breathing, and if a thought enters your mind, try to observe it as if you were a nonjudgmental outsider. Then calmly direct your attention back to the sensation of breathing.
- Continue this practice for 5 minutes.

TO PROTECT, SERVE, AND NOT GET TOO STRESSED If you're wondering how Christy Sheppard and Kehlen Kirby are doing these days, both are thriving in their careers. After spending nearly a year and a half on the night shift, Christy was assigned to the Investigations Division supervising the Technical Investigations Section. She now oversees approximately 30 employees performing a variety of tasks, from administering polygraph examinations to investigating Internet crimes against children and financial crimes such as identity theft and embezzlement. Any case that involves extracting evidence from phones, computers, and other digital devices is within her purview. The new job is demanding and, at times, stressful, but it's much better than working nights. "I am much happier on days," Christy says with a chuckle. "I'm a nicer person!"

mindfulness meditation Being fully present in the moment; focusing attention on the here and now without passing judgment.

Kehlen is currently working at the busiest fire station in Pueblo County. The department responds to over 20,000 calls per year, and that number appears to be growing. "There is some speculation it may be due to the recent legalization of marijuana," says Kehlen, who is now working as an "engineer." One of the most important people in the fire department, the engineer drives the fire truck in addition to carrying out regular firefighting and paramedic responsibilities. As the demand on firefighters increases, the department is "pushing mental health very hard," according to Kehlen. "This is a major nationwide push, but it just emphasizes the amount of stress that EMS personnel have."

Happy at Work
Christy Sheppard (left) and Kehlen Kirby have devoted their careers to keeping the public safe. The work of a first responder can be extremely stressful, but the reward of helping people makes it worthwhile. Left: Macmillan Learning/Photo by Mark Alamo; Right: Code 4 Photography (Kyler Hewes).

✓ show what you know

1. _______________ is apparent when you confront a problem head-on and try to solve it.
   a. Emotion-focused coping
   b. Positive psychology
   c. Support seeking
   d. Problem-focused coping
2. Describe three "tools" for healthy living that you could implement in your own life.
3. Individuals who are more relaxed, patient, and nonaggressive are described as having a:
   a. Type A personality.
   b. Type B personality.
   c. Type C personality.
   d. Type D personality.

✓ CHECK YOUR ANSWERS IN APPENDIX C.

YOUR SCIENTIFIC WORLD is a new application-based feature appearing in every chapter. In these online activities, you will take on role-playing scenarios that encourage you to think critically and apply your knowledge of psychological science to solve a real-world problem. For example: What are the major sources of your stress? Playing the role of a working college student, you will identify a variety of positive and negative stressors and learn skills for managing stress as you juggle the responsibilities of school, work, and home. You can access Your Scientific World activities in LaunchPad. Have fun!

SUMMARY OF CONCEPTS

LO 1 Define stress and stressors. (p. 441)

Stress is the response to perceived threats or challenges resulting from stimuli or events that cause strain, analogous to an airplane wing bending in response to an applied load. For humans, these stimuli, or stressors, can cause both psychological and physiological reactions. We must be careful not to confuse how we react to stressors and the stressors themselves; stress is the response, stressors are the cause.

LO 2 Describe the relationship between major life events and illness. (p. 444)

The Social Readjustment Rating Scale (SRRS) was created to measure the impact of life events. The score is based on the severity and frequency of events. Researchers use the SRRS to examine relationships between life events and health problems. Although correlations exist, they are not necessarily indicative of cause and effect.

LO 3 Summarize how poverty, adjusting to a new culture, and daily hassles affect health. (p. 446)

People living in poverty, moving to a new culture, and dealing with everyday hassles face a number of stressors that increase the likelihood of illness. Unlike major life changes and catastrophes, daily hassles occur on a more constant basis. Moving to a new country is a major life change that can result in acculturative stress; however, integrating the old and new cultures and developing social support help combat the effects. With all the stressors in our lives, we should be grateful for the positive experiences, or uplifts, that can serve to balance them.

LO 4 Identify the brain and body changes that characterize the fight-or-flight response. (p. 450)

When faced with a threatening situation, portions of the brain, including the hypothalamus, activate the sympathetic nervous system, which then leads to the secretion of catecholamines such as epinephrine and norepinephrine. These hormones cause increases in heart rate, blood pressure, respiration, and blood flow to the muscles. At the same time, the digestive system slows and the pupils dilate. These physiological responses prepare us for emergencies.

LO 5 Explain the function of the hypothalamic–pituitary–adrenal (HPA) system. (p. 451)

Overseeing activity in the sympathetic nervous system is the HPA system. When a stressful situation arises, the hypothalamus initiates a cascade of responses by alerting the pituitary gland, which then sends signals to the adrenal cortex, which secretes corticosteroids such as cortisol. These hormones summon the immune system to fight off a threat and reduce the amount of energy used on nonessential activities. When faced with a stressor, the body responds in the same way it would to a pathogen—by mobilizing a defense response.

LO 6 Outline the general adaptation syndrome (GAS). (p. 451)

The human body responds to stressors in a predictable way. The general adaptation syndrome suggests that the body passes through three stages. The first is the alarm stage, or initial response to a threatening situation. Arousal increases, and the body prepares to deal with a threat. Next is the resistance stage; the body maintains a high level of arousal (though not as high as that of the alarm stage) as it deals with a threatening situation. At this point, there is a decreased response to new stressors, and some people start to show signs of diseases of adaptation. Finally, the body enters the exhaustion stage; resources become depleted, resulting in vulnerability to illnesses, physical exhaustion, and even death.

LO 7 Explain how stressors relate to health problems. (p. 453)

When the body is continually mobilizing its resources for fight or flight, the immune system becomes taxed, and the work of the lymphocytes is compromised. During times of stress, people tend to sleep poorly and eat erratically, and may increase their drug and alcohol use, along with other poor behavioral choices. These tendencies can lead to health problems. Stressors have been linked to ulcers, cancer, and cardiovascular disease. The field of psychoneuroimmunology examines links among psychological factors, the nervous system, and immune functioning.

LO 8 List some consequences of prolonged exposure to the stress hormone cortisol. (p. 458)

Cortisol steps up immunity and prepares the body to confront a threat. But when cortisol levels remain high for prolonged periods (which is the case with chronic stressors and threatening situations), the functioning of the immune system may decrease. Elevated cortisol has been associated with premature birth and low birth weight in infants. For workers who have to make on-the-spot safety decisions, high cortisol levels can decrease working memory.

LO 9 Illustrate how appraisal influences coping. (p. 460)

Coping refers to the cognitive, behavioral, and emotional abilities used to manage something perceived as difficult or challenging. We must decide whether an event is irrelevant, positive, challenging, or harmful (primary appraisal) and how we will respond (secondary appraisal). If we determine that we have the ability to cope, then the impact of stress will remain low. We can choose to deal directly with a problem (problem-focused coping), or to address the emotions surrounding the problem (emotion-focused coping).

LO 10 Describe Type A and Type B personalities and explain how they relate to stress. (p. 461)

Personality appears to have a profound effect on coping style and predispositions to stress-related illnesses. People with Type A personalities are competitive, aggressive, impatient, often hostile, and twice as likely to develop cardiovascular disease as people with Type B personalities, who are more relaxed, patient, and nonaggressive. The presence of Type D personality, characterized by emotions such as worry, tension, bad moods, and social inhibition, may be a better predictor of how patients fare when they already have heart disease. People who exhibit a personality characteristic referred to as hardiness seem to be more resilient, optimistic, and better able to handle a great deal of stress.

LO 11 Discuss several tools for reducing stress and maintaining health. (p. 465)

There are many ways to lower the impact of stressors. Exercise, meditation, progressive muscle relaxation, biofeedback, and social support all have positive physical and psychological effects. Caring for and giving to others are also effective ways to reduce the impact of stress.

KEY TERMS

acculturation, p. 447
acculturative stress, p. 447
acquired immunodeficiency syndrome (AIDS), p. 445
approach–approach conflict, p. 449
approach–avoidance conflict, p. 449
avoidance–avoidance conflict, p. 449
biofeedback, p. 467
burnout, p. 460
coping, p. 461
daily hassles, p. 448
distress, p. 444
emotion-focused coping, p. 461
eustress, p. 444
general adaptation syndrome (GAS), p. 451
hardiness, p. 463
health psychology, p. 451
human immunodeficiency virus (HIV), p. 445
lymphocyte, p. 454
mindfulness meditation, p. 468
primary appraisal, p. 461
problem-focused coping, p. 461
psychoneuroimmunology, p. 456
secondary appraisal, p. 461
social support, p. 448
stress, p. 443
stressors, p. 443
Type A personality, p. 461
Type B personality, p. 463
uplifts, p. 449

TEST PREP ARE YOU READY?

1. Stress is the response to perceived threats resulting from stimuli that can cause both psychological and physiological reactions. In this context, these stimuli are known as:
   a. conflicts.
   b. eustress.
   c. assimilation.
   d. stressors.

2. When dealing with chronic stressors, ________ levels remain high, which can lead to a decrease in the functioning of ________.
   a. assimilation; the immune system
   b. cortisol; the immune system
   c. emotional; assimilation
   d. hassle; catecholamines

3. A researcher using the Social Readjustment Rating Scale (SRRS) predicts that the more ________ people have, the greater the potential for increased stress and negative health outcomes.
   a. assimilation
   b. stress inoculation
   c. social support
   d. life-changing events

4. If a threat remains constant, the body enters the ________ of the general adaptation syndrome. Resources become depleted, resulting in a vulnerability to illness, physical exhaustion, and even death.
   a. alarm stage
   b. resistance stage
   c. exhaustion stage
   d. diseases of adaptation stage

5. The hypothalamic–pituitary–adrenal system plays an important role in stress reactions. This system helps to maintain balance in the body by overseeing the neuroendocrine system and ________ while monitoring the immune system.
   a. diseases of adaptation
   b. gastric ulcers
   c. assimilation
   d. sympathetic nervous system

6. Chronic stress can lead to health problems; if the body is constantly mobilizing resources for fight or flight, the work of the lymphocytes is compromised, and the ________ is less powerful.
   a. immune system
   b. *H. pylori*
   c. atherosclerosis
   d. cortisol

7. ________ refers to the cognitive, behavioral, and emotional abilities used to manage a challenging or difficult situation.
   a. Stress
   b. Coping
   c. Altruism
   d. Eustress

8. One of your classmates has been seeing a counselor all semester because of her anxiety. When it's time to take the final exam, she will use what she has learned about ________ to reduce tension in her body.
   a. the hypothalamic–pituitary–adrenal system
   b. macrophages
   c. stress inoculation
   d. progressive muscle relaxation

9. People with ________ are competitive, aggressive, and hostile, and may face an increased risk of developing cardiovascular disease.
   a. Type A personality
   b. Type B personality
   c. Type C personality
   d. Type D personality

10. Last week, you met an exchange student who began to tell you about her life back home. She described times when she had to deal with hunger, war, and living in an orphanage. Yet, she seems so optimistic and resilient. Psychologists would likely suggest her personality includes a characteristic known as:
    a. Type A.
    b. hardiness.
    c. responsibility.
    d. locus of control.

11. When moving to a new country, how might someone use assimilation, separation, or integration to deal with the acculturative stress of this transition?

12. List the many hassles you have faced this past week. Next, list any life events you have experienced in the past 12 months. Consider how all these stressors may have influenced your health and explain what you can do to reduce their impact.

13. Describe a movie or television scene showing a character who appears to respond to a threat with the fight-or-flight response. What evidence suggests this is the case?

14. Give examples of an approach–approach conflict, an approach–avoidance conflict, and an avoidance–avoidance conflict that you have encountered in your own life.

15. Describe an acquaintance who has an internal locus of control, particularly with respect to health-related behaviors. Now describe someone who has an external locus of control, again focusing on health-related behaviors.

CHECK YOUR ANSWERS IN APPENDIX C.

Go to **LaunchPad** or **Achieve: Read & Practice** to test your understanding with **LearningCurve**.

CHAPTER

13

DEA/A. DAGLI ORTI/Getty Images.

Psychological Disorders

An Introduction to Psychological Disorders

WINTER NIGHT It was a clear, cold night in January when 17-year-old Ross Szabo decided to end his life. Nothing bad had happened that day. Ross had woken up, gone to school, played in a basketball game (a victory for his team), and then gone to Friendly's restaurant with his buddies. But for some reason, on that winter night, Ross decided he could no longer take it. Riding home in the car, he gazed out the window at Pennsylvania's snow-blanketed cornfields. An overwhelming sense of calm descended on him.

For the 4 months leading to that moment, Ross had been free-falling into an abyss of sadness. Around other people, he was smiling, joking, acting like a normal teenager. But alone, he was always crying. Ross truly believed his friends and family would be happier without him. *Maybe you're the problem; maybe you'd be doing them a favor by removing the problem,* Ross remembers thinking to himself. "I didn't think I would have a funeral," he says. "I didn't think anyone should care about me."

When Ross got home, he tried calling a friend but was too upset to speak. So he walked into the bathroom and prepared to take his own life. Fortunately, his father intervened and Ross was able to say, "If you don't take me to the hospital right now, I'm going to kill myself." 

Looks Can Be Deceiving
Ross Szabo appears happy in his senior class photo, but beneath his smile is profound pain. This was the year Ross began to have persistent thoughts of death and suicide that nearly drove him to take his own life. Martin Fella/Fella Studios.

What's Normal, What's Not

LO 1 Define psychological disorders and outline the criteria used to identify abnormal behavior.

A year-and-a-half earlier, Ross had been diagnosed with **bipolar disorder,** a condition marked by dramatic mood swings. We all have ups and downs—periods of feeling happy, sad, anxious, or irritable—but the emotional roller coaster of bipolar disorder is something quite different. We will soon explore bipolar disorder in greater detail, but first let's familiarize ourselves with the broader focus of this chapter: *psychological disorders.*

A **psychological disorder** is a set of behavioral, emotional, and cognitive symptoms that are significantly distressing and disabling. These symptoms can interfere with social functioning, work endeavors, and other aspects of life. However, they are not the result of religious or spiritual experiences, or mere departures from cultural norms. And although stressors can trigger symptoms of psychological disorders, these conditions primarily result from disturbances in psychological, biological, and developmental processes (American Psychiatric Association, 2013).

synonyms

psychological disorder mental disorder, mental illness, psychiatric illness, mental disability, mental disease

abnormal psychology experimental psychopathology, clinical psychology

The behaviors and symptoms associated with psychological disorders are not typical in the general population; in other words, they are *abnormal.* The academic field devoted to the study of psychological disorders is generally referred to as ***abnormal psychology***. Researchers and scholars in this field have a variety of backgrounds, including clinical psychology, neuroscience, and psychiatry.

WHAT IS ABNORMAL? Psychologists and other mental health professionals determine if a behavior is abnormal using a variety of criteria (**Table 13.1** on the next page). Perhaps the most straightforward criterion relates to the degree of *typicality*. An atypical behavior is one that is rarely seen, or infrequent. The profound sadness Ross experienced is relatively rare. Most people experience sadness, even deep sadness at times, but suicidal thoughts are unusual. While useful, the typicality criterion is not enough to confirm the existence of a psychological disorder. A child prodigy who learns to play the piano like a virtuoso by age 5 is atypical, but his rare talent does not indicate a psychological disorder. To arrive at a more definitive determination of **abnormal behavior,** mental health professionals commonly rely on three criteria (in addition to typicality): *dysfunction, distress,* and *deviance,* or the "3 Ds" (American Psychiatric Association, 2013; Wakefield, 1992).

Note: Ross Szabo's story is based on our personal communications with Ross Szabo and various passages from the book he coauthored with Melanie Hall: *Behind Happy Faces* (Szabo & Hall, 2007). Unless otherwise specified, quotations attributed to Ross Szabo and Melissa Hopely are personal communications.

bipolar disorder A psychological disorder marked by dramatic swings in mood, ranging from manic episodes to depressive episodes.

psychological disorder A set of behavioral, emotional, and cognitive symptoms that are significantly distressing or disabling in terms of social functioning, work endeavors, and other aspects of life.

abnormal behavior Behavior that is atypical, dysfunctional, distressful, and/or deviant.

Ross, In His Own Words

http://qrs.ly/8z5a5fr

Macmillan Learning.

TABLE 13.1 DEFINING ABNORMAL BEHAVIOR

Criterion	What does it mean?
Typicality	Degree to which behavior is atypical, meaning rarely seen or statistically abnormal
Dysfunction	Degree to which behavior interferes with daily life and relationships
Distress	Degree to which behavior or emotions cause an individual to feel upset or uncomfortable
Deviance	Degree to which behavior is considered outside the standards or rules of society

Psychologists typically identify abnormal behavior using the criteria above.

Deviant, but Not Disordered
Demonstrators in New Delhi, India, mourn the death of a young woman who was viciously raped and beaten by a group of men on a bus. The behavior of these protesters defies social norms and is therefore considered deviant. Yet in this case, deviance is not linked to a mental disorder. HARISH TYAGI/EPA/Newscom.

The first D, *dysfunction,* indicates the degree to which a behavior interferes with daily life and relationships. Ross' depression sometimes rendered him unable to get out of bed; such a behavior certainly has the potential to interfere with daily life. But dysfunction alone does not confirm the presence of a psychological disorder. If you stay up all night to meet a deadline, you might experience temporary dysfunction in memory and attention, but that does not necessarily signal a larger problem. Dysfunctional behaviors are often maladaptive, that is, they go against one's best interests.

The second D is personal *distress.* Feeling regularly upset or uncomfortable because of unwanted behaviors or emotions is another feature of abnormality, and it's not always evident from the outside. Prior to his suicide attempt, Ross appeared to be happy and healthy, but inside he was suffering. Disorders are not always accompanied by distress, however. When Ross experienced the euphoric highs of bipolar disorder, he may not have been distressed at all. People with psychological disorders do not always have the insight to recognize that a problem exists.

The third D is *deviance,* or the degree to which a behavior is considered to be outside the standards or rules of a society. Individuals who are euphoric might talk too loudly in a place of worship where people are expected to be quiet, or become so disinhibited that they walk around naked in a public place. Yet, deviance alone does not necessarily indicate a psychological disorder. Political protesters, for example, may deliberately break **social norms** to make a statement—lying on sidewalks, or setting up camp and sleeping in public places.

CONNECTIONS

In **Chapter 11,** we discussed conformity, the tendency to modify our behaviors, attitudes, beliefs, and opinions to match those of others. Sometimes we conform to the norms or standards of the social environment, like a group of friends or coworkers. The protesters described here are not conforming to social norms.

When evaluating each of the three Ds, mental health professionals also have to consider the degree of risk or danger (both to oneself and others) associated with them. This assessment is often used to determine if a person ought to be admitted to a hospital, or what type of treatment is needed (more on this in Chapter 14).

We should note that conceptions of abnormality and definitions of psychological disorders have changed over the course of history. During the 18th century, some women were said to exhibit a psychological disorder called *hysteria,* linked to "wandering movements of the womb" and characterized by "excessive emotion, irrational speech, paralysis, and convulsions" (Wickens, 2015, p. 245). No such diagnosis exists in today's world. Always remember that the meaning of "abnormal" is relative to historical time.

IT'S A CONTINUUM It's important to understand that anyone can have experiences that resemble symptoms of psychological disorders. This is because there is a continuum for many behaviors and feelings: Those at the ends are generally viewed as abnormal, and those in the middle more normal. Consider the vastly different degrees of sadness. Ross' profound sadness would likely fall at the abnormal end of the continuum; a teary farewell to a close friend who is moving away would be considered a normal reaction in the middle; and someone with limited emotions would be at the other end of the continuum. Bear in mind that notions of normality are not the same throughout the world. As the biopsychosocial model reminds us, we must consider culture and other social influences when trying to understand psychological disorders.

ACROSS THE WORLD

synonyms

cultural syndromes culture-bound syndromes

CONSIDER THE CULTURE Many disorders are universal, meaning they occur throughout the world and have a strong biological foundation. An example is schizophrenia, which has been documented across cultures. There are also ***cultural syndromes*** whose symptoms and attributions (explanations for those symptoms) appear to be unique to particular societies. *Koro,* for example, is an episode of intense anxiety observed in India, China, Thailand, and other Asian countries (Dan, Mondal, Chakraborty, Chaudhuri, & Biswas, 2017). The main feature of *koro* is an unrealistic and intense fear that sexual organs will be pulled into the body, perhaps resulting in death. A man with *koro* might be exceedingly anxious about the idea of his penis disappearing into his abdomen, whereas a woman may fear that her nipples will be pulled into her chest (American Psychiatric Association, 2013). Another example is *susto,* most evident in Mexico, Central America, South America, and Latino populations of the United States. People with *susto* have extreme reactions to frightening situations; they believe their soul has left their body, which results in illness, sadness, lack of motivation, and other symptoms (American Psychiatric Association, 2013).

BUT REMEMBER, EACH INDIVIDUAL IS UNIQUE

Even with universal disorders such as schizophrenia, culture plays an important role in determining how symptoms are interpreted. For example, people living in South Asia are more likely than those in the United States and Canada to attribute symptoms of psychological disorders to supernatural powers, such as "hexes and curses" or "punishment from God" (Knettel, 2016, p. 134). Within the United States, we see evidence of culture shaping people's attitudes and beliefs about psychological disorders. Some research suggests that African Americans have a tendency to view these disorders as a sign of weakness, and may be "very concerned about stigma associated with mental illness" (Ward, Wiltshire, Detry, & Brown, 2013, p. 2). Meanwhile, Asian Americans and Hispanics appear more inclined than other groups to *normalize* the symptoms of psychological disorders, for example, believing that "mental health problems" are a "normal part of life" (Bignall, Jacquez, & Vaughn, 2015, p. 542). Compared to Caucasians, people in these groups may be less likely to think they need mental health services (Breslau et al., 2017).

Keep in mind that these are only cultural generalizations, not rules that apply to every member of the group. Each person is unique, and within each category is immense diversity.

"Social Anxiety"?
In Japan, social anxiety is sometimes manifested through *taijin kyofusho,* "a cultural syndrome characterized by anxiety about and avoidance of interpersonal situations due to the thought, feeling, or conviction that one's appearance and actions in social interactions are inadequate or offensive to others" (American Psychiatric Association, 2013, p. 837). *Taijin kyofusho* is more likely to affect men than women, and has been observed in Korea and other countries outside of Japan (Hofmann & Hinton, 2014). Tokyo Space Club/Corbis/VCG/Getty Images.

Put Your Heads Together

In groups, **A)** identify examples of abnormal behaviors you've seen reported in the news; **B)** show how these behaviors fit the criteria for abnormality listed in Table 13.1; **C)** give examples of some behaviors that might appear deviant, but do not fit the criteria for abnormality; and **D)** identify a behavior that might be considered abnormal in one cultural context, but not another.

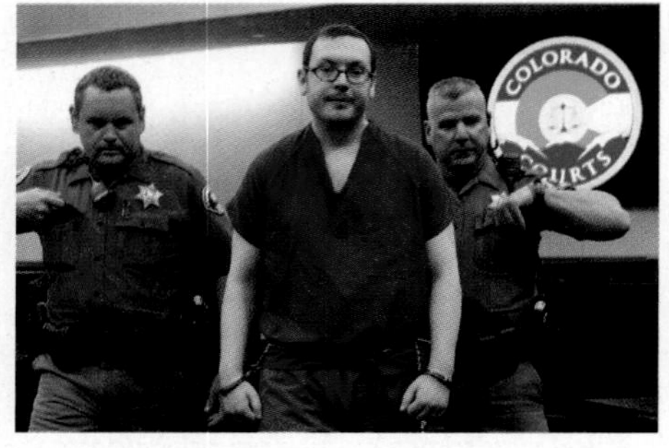

Insanity?
In the summer of 2012, James Holmes walked into a movie theater in Aurora, Colorado, and opened fire on the audience, killing 12 people. Holmes' attorneys entered a plea of insanity; they claimed that he committed the murders while in a psychotic state (Ingold, 2013, September 30). Refusing to accept the insanity plea, jurors determined he should spend the rest of his life in prison (Associated Press, 2015, August 26). REUTERS/RJ Sangosti.

We have learned how psychologists identify abnormality using the criteria of typicality, dysfunction, distress, and deviance. Now let's explore the concept of "insanity" in the judicial system.

THINK CRITICALLY

THE INSANITY PLEA Perhaps you have heard the term "insanity" used in a legal setting. "The defendant got off on an insanity plea," or "The defense failed to demonstrate insanity." What do these statements mean? **Insanity** is a legal determination of the degree to which a person is responsible for his criminal behaviors. Those deemed legally insane are thought to have little or no control over or understanding of their behaviors at the time they committed their crimes. Therefore, they are given psychological treatment in a locked psychiatric facility rather than criminal punishment such as imprisonment or the death penalty. In America, 46 states offer a form of the insanity defense; only Idaho, Kansas, Montana, and Utah do not (Cevallos, 2015, July 17; "The Insanity Defense Among the States," n.d.). **Many people believe** that the insanity defense is frequently used, but it's invoked in only about 1% of cases. Of those cases, just 10–25% of insanity defenses are successful (Torry & Billick, 2010). Among those who avoided prison after entering an insanity plea was John Hinckley Jr., the man who attempted to assassinate President Ronald Reagan in 1981 (PBS, 2014). The insanity plea did not work so well for the man who murdered Kris Kyle, the Navy SEAL whose memoir served as the basis for the Oscar-winning movie *American Sniper*. Kyle's killer, Eddie Ray Routh, is serving life in prison without parole (Payne, Ford, & Morris, 2015, February 25).

IT'S INVOKED IN ONLY ABOUT 1% OF CASES

CONNECTIONS

In **Chapter 7,** we discussed the availability heuristic; we often predict the probability of something happening in the future based on how easily we can recall a similar event from the past. Here, the vividness of a crime and the ensuing trial make the insanity plea more available in our memories, so we tend to overestimate the probability of it happening in the future.

Now that we have learned how psychologists identify abnormality and legal professionals address responsibility, let's explore how it might feel to face a psychological disorder—and the negative judgments that sometimes accompany it.

DISPELLING STIGMA: ROSS FINDS HIS VOICE After being hospitalized, Ross returned to school, where he was greeted with rumors and stares. A couple of his friends stopped spending time with him, perhaps because they were afraid of what they didn't understand. Then one day, a psychologist came to the school to give his annual presentation about helping people with psychological disorders. Most of the students thought the topic was funny and laughed throughout the presentation, but Ross did not find it one bit amusing. After class, he told his teacher that he wanted to give his own presentation. Before long, Ross was standing before his peers, heart pounding and knees wobbling, talking about life with bipolar disorder. The students listened intently, and some approached Ross after class to talk about their own struggles with psychological disorders. By coming forward to share his experiences, Ross dispelled some of his classmates' misconceptions and fears about psychological disorders. He was a real person they knew and liked, and he had a disorder.

You Asked, Ross Answers

http://qrs.ly/8z5a5fr

How do you explain your ability to hide what was going on with your bipolar disorder?

WHAT IS STIGMA? Watching his classmates laugh about people with psychological disorders, Ross bore witness to the *stigma* attached to mental illness. **Stigma** is a negative attitude or opinion about groups of people based on certain characteristics they have. Being the target of stigma may lower self-esteem, impair social functioning, and make a person less likely to seek treatment. Stigma can lead to discrimination, stereotypes, and negative characterizations in general, although researchers are exploring strategies to counteract it (Corrigan & Penn, 2015; Cuttler & Ryckman,

2018). Surely, you have heard people equate psychological disorders with violence, or perhaps you have seen TV shows portraying people with mental illness as wild and aggressive. Reality check: People with psychological disorders are usually *not* violent. Other factors, such as lower socioeconomic status, male gender, and substance abuse, may be better predictors of violence (McAra & McVie, 2016; Stuart, 2003). The criterion of being a danger to oneself or others does determine the necessity of treatment, but given the degree of violence in our society, violent behavior is actually *atypical* of people with serious psychological disorders, and more commonly associated with substance abuse (Arkowitz & Lilienfeld, 2011, July/August; Fazel, Gulati, Linsell, Geddes, & Grann, 2009).

Hollywood Stereotypes
The late Heath Ledger playing the "Joker" in *The Dark Knight* (2008). Ledger described the Joker as a "psychopathic, mass-murdering, schizophrenic clown with zero empathy" (Lyall, 2007, November 4, para. 13). Such characterizations tend to perpetuate stereotypes about people with psychological disorders, most of whom are not violent (Skeem, Kennealy, Monahan, Peterson, & Applebaum 2016). Warner Bros./Photofest.

What can we do to combat stigma? One suggestion is to use "people-first language"; that is, refer to the individual affected by the disorder ("She has been diagnosed with schizophrenia"), rather than defining the person by her disorder ("She is *schizophrenic*"; American Psychological Association, 2010; Granello & Gibbs, 2016). We should also be cautious about using terms such as "crazy" and "insane." When used to describe people, these words are inappropriate, derogatory, and sure indicators of stigma. Another way to reduce stigma is by comparing psychological disorders to medical diseases. We don't ridicule or blame people for having asthma or diabetes, so why would we do this to those suffering from mental illness (Greenstein, 2017, October 11)? Educating others about mental illness is an important avenue for addressing stigma—don't be afraid to share what you've learned about the symptoms and causes of psychological disorders (**INFOGRAPHIC 13.1** on the next page).

CAREER CONNECTIONS

DEVELOPING MENTAL HEALTH LITERACY The material you learn in this chapter may serve as a foundation for ongoing mental health education beyond the classroom. Even if you do not pursue a career in psychology, your future employer may require training in mental health awareness. Nurses, EMS workers, police officers, firefighters, and educators are just a few of the professionals who should be able to recognize and respond to the signs and symptoms of mental health crises. In what other career contexts might this awareness be needed? 

Thus far, our discussion has focused on overarching concepts like abnormal behavior and stigma, which relate to all psychological disorders. Now it's time to shift the discussion to more practical matters: the classification and diagnosis of mental disorders.

CONNECTIONS

In **Chapter 1,** we presented the perspectives that psychologists use to explain the complexities of human behaviors. Because clinicians may have different perspectives, they don't always agree on classification criteria. The diagnostic manual helps to bridge these gaps by providing standard, evidence-based criteria.

Classifying Psychological Disorders

How was Ross diagnosed with bipolar disorder? He consulted with a psychiatrist. But how did this mental health professional come to the conclusion that Ross suffered from bipolar disorder, and not something else? Given the complexity of determining abnormal behavior, it probably comes as no surprise that clinicians have **not always agreed** on what qualifies as a psychological disorder. Yet, over the years, they have developed common criteria and procedures for making reliable diagnoses. These criteria and decision-making procedures are presented in manuals, which are shared across mental health professions, and are based on research findings and clinical observations.

DIAGNOSTIC AND STATISTICAL MANUAL OF MENTAL DISORDERS Think about the last time you were ill and went to a doctor. You probably answered a series of

insanity A legal determination of the degree to which a person is responsible for criminal behaviors.

stigma A negative attitude or opinion about a group of people based on certain traits or characteristics.

Let's Break It Down: Stigma

The stigma of mental illness is pervasive, but with knowledge and determination, we can defeat it. To be effective, we must understand that stigma exists at multiple levels; it is present in our institutions, our communities, and sometimes even our own minds. We can target each of these levels with specific strategies (Corrigan & Al-Khouja, 2018; National Academies of Sciences, Engineering, and Medicine, 2016).

STIGMA

INSTITUTIONAL

Problems

prejudicial laws and policies, unfair hiring practices, housing discrimination, noninclusive cultures

WHAT YOU CAN DO

- Vote for political candidates who support equal opportunity initiatives.
- Write letters to public officials.
- Support businesses with fair employment practices.
- Get involved in government.
- Engage in peaceful protest.

(National Academies of Sciences, Engineering, and Medicine, 2016)

COMMUNITY

Problems

stereotypes, demeaning labels, social exclusion, negative media portrayals of mental illness

WHAT YOU CAN DO

- Talk openly about mental health and treatment.
- Stand up for people with mental disorders.
- If the media reinforces stigma, write a letter to the editor, or start a conversation on social media.
- Use people-first language.
- Show compassion and empathy.

(Cuttler & Ryckman, 2018; Greenstein, 2017, October 11; HarnEnz, 2016, November 14)

SELF-STIGMA

Problems

negative self-stereotypes and shame (both barriers to seeking treatment), low self-esteem, the "why try" attitude associated with undervaluing oneself

WHAT YOU CAN DO

- Seek peer-support.
- Educate yourself about mental health conditions.
- Use empowerment strategies: focus on the positive, surround yourself with supportive people, believe in yourself.
- Practice self-affirmation; attend to your own beliefs and values.

(Greenstein, 2017, October 11; HarnEnz, 2016, November 14; Lannin et al., 2018; National Academies of Sciences, Engineering, and Medicine, 2016) questions about your symptoms. The nurse took your blood pressure and temperature, and the doctor performed a physical exam. Using both subjective and objective findings from the exam, the doctor formulated a diagnosis. Mental health professionals must do the same—make diagnoses based on evidence. In addition to collecting information from interviews and other clinical assessments, psychologists typically rely on manuals to guide their diagnoses. Most mental health professionals in North America use the *Diagnostic and Statistical Manual of Mental Disorders* (*DSM–5;* American Psychiatric Association, 2013). The *DSM* is an evidence-based classification system of mental disorders first developed and published by the American Psychiatric Association (www.psych.org) in 1952. This manual was designed to help ensure accurate and consistent diagnoses based on the observation of symptoms. Although the *DSM* is published by the American Psychiatric Association—different from the American Psychological Association—it is used by psychiatrists, psychologists, social workers, and a variety of other clinicians. The most recent edition of the manual, the *DSM–5,* lists 157 disorders (American Psychiatric Association Division of Research, personal communication, July 26, 2013).

Classifying psychological disorders is useful because it helps therapists develop treatment plans, enables clients to obtain reimbursement from their insurance companies, and facilitates research and communication among professions. But there are some drawbacks, especially for clients, who run the risk of being labeled.

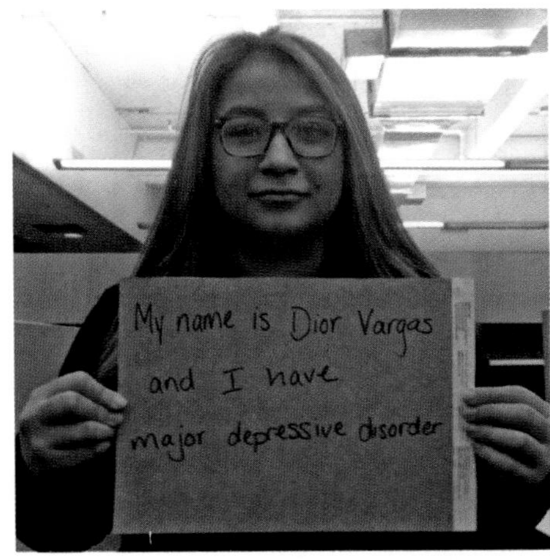

Disorders Do Not Discriminate
Psychological disorders impact people from all different ethnic and cultural backgrounds, yet images of Caucasian people often dominate media portrayals of mental illness. To counter the misconception that mental illness is a "white person's disease," mental health activist Dior Vargas launched the People of Color and Mental Illness Photo Project (DiorVargas.com, n.d.). Dior Vargas.

...BELIEVE IT...OR NOT

A LABEL CAN CHANGE EVERYTHING What do you think would happen if you secretly planted eight "sane" people (with no history of psychological disorders) in American psychiatric hospitals? The hospital employees would immediately identify them as "normal" and send them home . . . right?

In the early 1970s, psychologist David Rosenhan and seven other mentally healthy people managed to get themselves admitted to various psychiatric hospitals by faking auditory hallucinations ("I am hearing voices"), a common symptom of schizophrenia. (Such a feat would be close to impossible today, as psychiatric facilities are too stretched to accommodate the scores of Americans with documented psychological disorders; Raphelson, 2017, November 30; Sisti, Segal, & Emanuel, 2015.) Upon admission, each of these pretend patients, or "pseudopatients," immediately stopped putting on an act and began behaving like their normal selves. But within the walls of a psychiatric hospital, their ordinary behavior assumed a whole new meaning. Staff members who spotted the pseudopatients taking notes concluded it must be a symptom of their psychological disorder. "Patient engaged in writing behavior," nurses wrote of one pseudopatient. "Nervous, Mr. X?" a nurse asked a pseudopatient who had been walking the halls out of sheer boredom (Rosenhan, 1973, p. 253).

NO HOSPITAL STAFF MEMBERS IDENTIFIED THE PSEUDOPATIENTS AS FRAUDS

No hospital staff member identified the pseudopatients as frauds. If anyone had them figured out, it was the other patients in the hospital. "You're not crazy," they would say to the pseudopatients. "You're a journalist, or a professor. You're checking up on the hospital" (Rosenhan, 1973, p. 252). After an average stay of 19 days (the range being 7 to 52 days), the pseudopatients were discharged, but not because doctors recognized their diagnostic errors. The pseudopatients, they determined, had gone into "remission" from their fake disorders. They were released back into society—but not without their labels.

Some critics raised legitimate concerns about the methodology, results, and conclusions of Rosenhan's study (Lando, 1976; Spitzer, 1975). Nevertheless, it shed light on the persistence of labels and stigma.

If eight "sane" people could be diagnosed with serious disorders like schizophrenia, you might be wondering if psychological diagnoses are **reliable or valid**. We've come a long way since 1973, but the diagnosis of psychological disorders remains a challenge, in part because it often relies on self-reports. Evaluating complex behaviors will never be as straightforward as measuring blood pressure or running a test for strep throat.

CONNECTIONS

In **Chapter 10,** we discussed reliability and validity in the context of personality assessment. These concepts are also relevant to classification systems for psychological disorders. We must determine if diagnoses are reliable (providing consistent, reproducible results) and valid (measuring what they intend to measure).

Put Your Heads Together

In your group, discuss the following: **A)** How does being labeled with a psychological disorder affect a person's interactions with family and friends? **B)** Once a label is assigned, can it ever be fully removed? **C)** Describe three ways you can combat the stigmas associated with these labels (see Infographic 13.1).

TABLE 13.2 YEARLY RATES OF PSYCHOLOGICAL DISORDERS

Psychological Disorder	Annual Prevalence
Anxiety disorders	18.1%
Specific phobia	8.7%
Social phobia	6.8%
Disruptive behavior disorders	8.9%
Mood disorders	9.5%
Major depression	6.7%
Substance disorders	3.8%
Any disorder	26.2%

In any given year, many people are diagnosed with a psychological disorder. The numbers here represent annual prevalence: the percentage of the U.S. population affected by a disorder over a year. (Elsewhere, we have referred to lifetime prevalence, which means the percentage of the population affected by a disorder any time in life.) Information from Kessler (2010).

"Abnormal," but Not Uncommon

You probably know someone with bipolar disorder, major depressive disorder, or attention-deficit/hyperactivity disorder (ADHD). Perhaps you have experienced a disorder yourself. Psychological disorders are not uncommon (**Table 13.2**). Findings from a study of approximately 9,000 individuals indicate that around 50% of the population in the United States, at some point in life, experiences symptoms that meet the criteria for a psychological disorder (Kessler, Berglund, et al., 2005; Kessler & Wang, 2008). Yes, you read that correctly; "Nearly half the population meet criteria for a mental disorder in their life. . . ." (Kessler, 2010, p. 60). In fact, some studies suggest that figure is an underestimate (Angst et al., 2016; Schaefer et al., 2017). The lifetime prevalence of disorders varies based on geographic region, with "countries of North and South East Asia in particular returning lower prevalence estimates than countries in other regional groupings" (Steel et al., 2014, p. 490).

A TOUGH ROAD With such high rates of disorders, you can be sure that many people around you are dealing with tough issues. In some cases, psychological disorders lead to greater impairment than chronic medical conditions, yet people with mental ailments are less likely to get treatment (Druss et al., 2009). Further complicating the picture is the fact that many people suffer from more than one psychological disorder at a time, a phenomenon called **comorbidity** (koh-mawr-BID-i-tee). You already know that one psychological disorder can lead to significant impairment; now just imagine how these problems compound for a person coping with more than one disorder. Also keep in mind that various psychological disorders are chronic (a person suffers from them continuously), others have a regular pattern (symptoms appear every winter, for example), and some are temporary.

What Causes Psychological Disorders?

LO 2 Summarize the etiology of psychological disorders.

Throughout this chapter, we will discuss the causal factors, collectively referred to as the *etiology,* underlying psychological disorders. Let's familiarize ourselves with the models commonly used to explain the etiology of mental illness.

comorbidity The occurrence of two or more disorders at the same time.

IT'S IN YOUR BIOLOGY The **medical model** views psychological disorders from a biological standpoint, focusing on genes, neurochemical imbalances, and processes in the brain. This medical approach has had a long and uninterrupted history, as our culture continues to view psychological disorders as illnesses. It is evident in the language used to discuss disorders and treatment: *mental illness, therapy, remission, symptoms, patients,* and *doctors.* Some scholars criticize this approach (Szasz, 2011), in part because it fails to acknowledge how concepts of mental health and illness have changed over time and across cultures (Kawa & Giordano, 2012).

synonyms

medical model biological model

IT'S IN YOUR MIND Another way to understand the etiology of disorders is to focus on psychological factors. Some theories propose that cognitive activities or personality characteristics contribute to the development and maintenance of disorders. Others focus on the ways that **learning** or childhood experiences might lay their foundation. For example, early trauma can increase the risk of suffering from depression, particularly among those who tend to ruminate, or "constantly focus on negative mood and on the possible causes and implications of depressed feelings" (Kim, Jin, Jung, Hahn, & Lee, 2017, p. 2).

CONNECTIONS

In **Chapter 5,** we discussed a variety of theories that explain how behaviors are learned. In this chapter, we see how learning theories help us understand the development of psychological disorders.

IT'S IN YOUR ENVIRONMENT Earlier, we mentioned that culture can shape definitions of "abnormal" and influence the development of psychological disorders. Social factors, like poverty and community support systems, can also play a role in the development and course of these conditions (Lund et al., 2011; Mills, 2015).

THE BIOPSYCHOSOCIAL PERSPECTIVE As we have noted in previous chapters, the best way to understand human behavior is to examine it from a variety of perspectives. The *biopsychosocial perspective* suggests that psychological disorders result from a complex interaction of biological, psychological, and sociocultural factors (**Figure 13.1**). For example, some disorders appear to have a genetic basis, but their symptoms may not be evident until social or psychological factors come into play. We will revisit this concept in the section on schizophrenia, when we explore the *diathesis–stress model.*

Stress Can Be a Trigger
A mother and her daughters rest after crossing the border from Syria to Turkey. Refugees face a host of stressors that may increase their risk for developing symptoms of psychological disorders. Those stressors may include exposure to violence and death, disappearance of family members, lack of employment and educational opportunities, and confinement in refugee camps (Gary & Rubin, 2014; Turrini et al., 2017). Halil Fidan/Anadolu Agency/Getty Images.

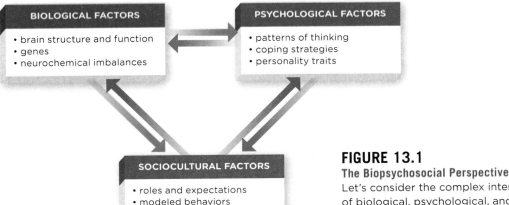

FIGURE 13.1
The Biopsychosocial Perspective
Let's consider the complex interaction of biological, psychological, and sociocultural factors that may contribute to a specific disorder.

Now that we have a general understanding of how psychologists conceptualize psychological disorders, let's delve into specifics. We cannot cover every disorder identified in the *DSM–5,* but we can offer an overview of those commonly discussed in an introductory psychology course.

medical model An approach suggesting that psychological disorders are illnesses that have underlying biological causes.

show what you know

1. Which of the following is a criterion used to define abnormal behavior?
   a. dysfunction
   b. psychopathology
   c. developmental processes
   d. stigma

2. A ______________ is a set of behavioral, emotional, and cognitive symptoms that are significantly distressing and disabling in terms of social functioning, work, and other aspects of life.

3. Describe the models commonly used to explain the etiology of mental illness.

✓ CHECK YOUR ANSWERS IN APPENDIX C.

When Anxiety Is Extreme

UNWELCOME THOUGHTS: MELISSA'S STORY Melissa Hopely was about 5 years old when she began doing "weird things" to combat anxiety: flipping light switches on and off, touching the corners of tables, and running to the kitchen to make sure the oven was turned off. Taken at face value, these behaviors may not seem too strange, but for Melissa they were the first signs of a psychological disorder that eventually pushed her to the edge.

As Melissa grew older, her behaviors became increasingly regimented. She felt compelled to do everything an even number of times. Instead of entering a room once, she would enter or leave twice, four times, perhaps even 20 times—as long as the number was a multiple of 2. Some days she would sit in her bedroom for hours, methodically touching all her possessions twice, then repeating the process again, and again. By performing these rituals, Melissa felt she could prevent her worst fears from becoming reality. What was she so afraid of? Dying, losing all her friends, and becoming homeless were just a few of her worries. It seemed like something dreadful was about to happen, though she couldn't put her finger on what it was. In reality, Melissa had little reason to worry. She had health, intelligence, beauty, and a loving circle of friends and family.

We all experience irrational worries from time to time, but Melissa's had become overwhelming. Where do we draw the line between normal and abnormal? This section focuses on three diagnostic categories associated with excessive anxiety: anxiety disorders, obsessive-compulsive disorders (OCD), and posttraumatic stress disorder (PTSD).

What Was Melissa Battling?
Melissa Hopely was about 3 years old when the photo on the left was taken. Within a couple of years, she would begin to experience the symptoms of a serious mental disorder that would continue into adulthood. Melissa was tormented by a vague feeling that something awful was about to occur. She feared that she would die, lose all her friends, or become homeless—unless she performed certain behaviors to stop these dreaded events from happening. Melissa Hopely.

Anxiety Disorders

LO 3 Define anxiety disorders and demonstrate an understanding of their causes.

Think about the objects or situations that make you feel afraid or uneasy. Maybe you fear creepy crawly insects, slithery snakes, or crowded public spaces. A mild fear of spiders or overcrowded subways is normal, but if you become highly disturbed by the mere thought of them, or if the fear interferes with your everyday functioning, a problem may exist. People who suffer from **anxiety disorders** have extreme anxiety and/or irrational fears that are debilitating and go beyond what is commonly expected in a particular cultural context (American Psychiatric Association, 2013; **Table 13.3**).

TABLE 13.3 ANXIETY DISORDERS

Disorder	Annual Prevalence	Description	Cultural Impact
Separation anxiety disorder	0.9–1.9% in adults; 1.6% in adolescents; 4% in children	Anxiety or fear related to "separation from home or attachment figures" (p. 191)	Cultures vary with respect to the age at which it is appropriate to move from the parental home.
Specific phobia	7–9%	Anxiety about, or fear of, a specific object or situation	Specific phobias vary across cultures.
Social anxiety disorder (social phobia)	7%	Anxiety about, or fear of being in, a social situation that could result in scrutiny by other people	*Taijin kyofusho* (Japan and Korea)
Panic disorder	2–3%	Reoccurring panic attacks that are unexpected and have no apparent cue or trigger	*Trúng gió* (Vietnam); *ataque de nervios* (Latin America); *khyâl* (Cambodia)
Agoraphobia	1.7%	Anxiety or fear about "using public transportation; being in open spaces; being in enclosed places; standing in line or being in a crowd; or being outside of the home" (p. 217)	None listed in *DSM–5*
Generalized anxiety disorder	0.9% in adolescents; 2.9% in adults	Anxiety and worry that are out of proportion to the actual event or situation	Varies by culture

Anxiety disorders are relatively common among both sexes, but they are more apparent in women by an approximate 2:1 ratio.
Information from *DSM–5* (American Psychiatric Association, 2013).

Let's take a look at some of the anxiety disorders identified in the *DSM–5:* panic disorder, specific phobia, agoraphobia, social anxiety disorder, and generalized anxiety disorder.

PANIC DISORDER What should you do if you see somebody trembling and sweating, gasping for breath, or complaining of heart palpitations? If you are concerned it's a heart attack, you may be correct; call 911 immediately if you are not sure. However, a person experiencing a *panic attack* may behave very similarly to someone having a heart attack. A **panic attack** is a sudden, extreme fear or discomfort that escalates quickly, often with no evident cause, and includes symptoms such as increased heart rate, sweating, shortness of breath, chest pain, nausea, lightheadedness, and fear of dying. A diagnosis of **panic disorder** requires such attacks to recur unexpectedly and have no obvious trigger. In addition, the person worries about losing control and having more panic attacks. People with panic disorder often make decisions that are maladaptive, like purposefully avoiding exercise or unfamiliar places in hope of preventing a panic attack.

anxiety disorders A group of psychological disorders associated with extreme anxiety and/or debilitating, irrational fears.

panic attack Sudden, extreme fear or discomfort that escalates quickly, often with no obvious trigger, and includes symptoms such as increased heart rate, sweating, shortness of breath, chest pain, nausea, lightheadedness, and fear of dying.

panic disorder A psychological disorder that includes recurrent, unexpected panic attacks and fear that can cause significant changes in behavior.

No Shame in Anxiety
Zayn Malik is forthright when it comes to discussing his struggle with anxiety. In a statement to his fans, the singer/songwriter announced that he was cancelling a show in the United Kingdom because of anxiety. "I wanted to tell the truth," Malik wrote in a piece for *TIME Magazine*. "Anxiety is nothing to be ashamed of. . . . I know I have fans out there who have been through this kind of thing, too, and I wanted to be honest for their sake" (Malik, 2016, October 31, para. 2).
Ben Gabbe/Getty Images.

Panic disorder affects about 2–3% of the population (American Psychiatric Association, 2013). Research suggests it runs in families, with heritability estimates around 40–48% (Maron, Hettema, & Shlik, 2010; Weber et al., 2012). This means that over 40% of the variation of panic disorder in the *population* can be attributed to genetic factors, and the remaining 60% to environmental factors. In other words, the frequency and distribution of panic disorder across people result from a combination of factors, 40% of which are genetic, and 60% nongenetic. People often assume heritability refers to an individual's risk for a disorder. ("Her panic disorder is 40% the result of her genes, and 60% due to her environment.") This is incorrect. Remember, heritability explains the variation and risk *within a population.*

Women are twice as likely as men to be diagnosed with panic disorder, and this disparity is already apparent by the age of 14 (American Psychiatric Association, 2013; Craske et al., 2010; Weber et al., 2012). Such gender differences appear to result from an interaction between genes and environment (Iurato et al., 2017).

Panic disorder does appear to have a biological cause (American Psychiatric Association, 2013). Researchers have identified specific parts of the brain thought to be involved in panic attacks, including regions of the hypothalamus, which is involved in the **fight-or-flight** response, and its associated structures (Johnson et al., 2010; Wintermann, Kirschbaum, & Petrowski, 2016). Irregularities in the size and shape of the amygdala may help explain dysfunction in the fight-or-flight response, which could be associated with the physical and behavioral symptoms of panic attacks (Yoon et al., 2016).

CONNECTIONS

In **Chapter 2,** we described how the sympathetic division of the autonomic nervous system directs the body's stress response. When a stressful situation arises, the sympathetic nervous system prepares the body to react, causing the heart to beat faster, respiration to increase, and the pupils to dilate.

Some researchers propose that learning—particularly classical conditioning—can play a role in the development of panic disorder (Bouton, Mineka, & Barlow, 2001; Duits et al., 2015). In a panic disorder scenario, the neutral stimulus might be something like a location (a shopping mall), the unconditioned stimulus an unexpected panic attack, and the unconditioned response the fear resulting from the panic attack. After the panic attack is paired with the shopping mall, the mall becomes the conditioned stimulus, such that every time the person thinks of this location, fear results (now the conditioned response).

SPECIFIC PHOBIAS Panic attacks can occur without apparent triggers. This is not the case with a **specific phobia,** which centers on a particular object or situation, such as rats or airplane travel (**Table 13.4**). Most people with phobias do their best to avoid the cause of their fear. If avoidance is not possible, they withstand it, but only with extreme fear and anxiousness.

TABLE 13.4 ARE YOU AFRAID?

Scientific Name	Fear of . . .	Scientific Name	Fear of . . .
Acrophobia	Heights	Epistemophobia	Knowledge
Astraphobia or keraunophobia	Lightning	Gamophobia	Marriage
Brontophobia	Thunder	Ophidiophobia	Snakes
Claustrophobia	Closed spaces	Odontophobia	Dental procedures
Cynophobia	Dogs	Xenophobia	Strangers

The phobias listed above are not specifically included in the *DSM-5,* but they are all associated with the same general response. A person with a specific phobia feels extreme anxiety about a particular object or situation. Fears center on anything from dogs to dental procedures. Information from Reber, Allen, & Reber (2009).

specific phobia A psychological disorder that includes a distinct fear or anxiety in relation to an object or situation.

As with panic disorder, phobias can be explained using the principles of learning (LeBeau et al., 2010; Rofé & Rofé, 2015). Classical conditioning may lead to the acquisition of a fear through the pairing of stimuli. Operant conditioning could maintain the phobia through negative reinforcement; if anxiety (the unpleasant stimulus) is reduced by avoiding a feared object or situation, the avoidance behavior is **negatively reinforced** and thus more likely to recur. Observational learning can also help explain the development of a phobia. Simply watching someone else experience its symptoms could create fear in an observer (Reynolds, Field, & Askew, 2015).

CONNECTIONS

In **Chapter 5,** we discussed negative reinforcement; behaviors increase when they are followed by the removal of something unpleasant. Here, the avoidance behavior takes away the anxious feeling, increasing the likelihood of avoiding the object in the future.

AGORAPHOBIA A person with **agoraphobia** (ag-o-ruh-FOH-bee-uh) feels extremely uneasy in public spaces. This disorder is characterized by a distinct fear or anxiety related to public transportation, open spaces, retail stores, crowds, or being alone and away from home in general. Agoraphobia may also result in "panic-like symptoms," which can be difficult to handle. Typically, people with agoraphobia need another person to accompany them on outings, because they feel they may not be able to cope on their own. They may avoid situations that frighten them, or be overwhelmed with fear when avoidance or escape is not possible.

Did Phobias Evolve?
Humans seem to be biologically predisposed to fear certain threats such as spiders, snakes, and bitter foods (Shackelford & Liddle, 2014; Van Strien, Franken, & Huijding, 2014). From an evolutionary standpoint, such fears would tend to protect us from true danger (a poisonous spider bite, for example). But the link between anxiety and evolution is not always so apparent. It's hard to imagine how an intense fear of being in public, for example, would promote survival. John Crux Photography/Getty Images.

SOCIAL ANXIETY DISORDER According to the *DSM–5,* a person with social anxiety disorder (social phobia) has an "intense" fear of social situations and scrutiny by others. This extreme fear could arise during a speech or presentation, while eating a meal, or simply in conversation. Social anxiety often stems from a preoccupation with offending someone or behaving in a way that reveals one's anxiety, and frequently includes an overestimation of the potential undesirable consequences. The fear is not warranted, however. Being evaluated or even mocked by others is not necessarily dangerous and should not cause debilitating stress.

GENERALIZED ANXIETY DISORDER The anxiety disorders we have discussed thus far relate to specific objects and scenarios. You can predict that a person with agoraphobia will feel distressed walking through a busy college campus, and there is a good chance that someone with social phobia will feel very uncomfortable at a cocktail party. But what about anxiety that is more pervasive, affecting many aspects of life? A person with **generalized anxiety disorder** experiences an excessive amount of worry and anxiety about many activities relating to family, health, school, and other areas (American Psychiatric Association, 2013). This psychological distress is accompanied by physical symptoms such as muscle tension and restlessness. Individuals with generalized anxiety disorder may avoid activities they believe will not go smoothly, spend a great deal of time getting ready for such events, or wait until the very last minute to engage in the anxiety-producing activity.

The development of generalized anxiety disorder is influenced by both nature and nurture. Some affected individuals appear to have a genetic predisposition to developing irregularities in parts of the brain associated with fear, such as the amygdala and hippocampus (Gottschalk & Domschke, 2017; Hettema et al., 2012). Environmental factors such as adversity in childhood and overprotective parents may also play a role (American Psychiatric Association, 2013).

MELISSA'S STRUGGLE We introduced this section with the story of Melissa Hopely, a girl who struggled with anxiety and performed elaborate rituals to alleviate it. Melissa's behavior caused significant distress and dysfunction, which suggests that it was abnormal, but does it match any of the anxiety disorders described above? Her anxiety was not attached to a specific object or situation, so it doesn't appear to be a phobia. Nor was her anxiety widespread and nonspecific,

agoraphobia Extreme fear of situations involving public transportation, open spaces, or other public settings.

generalized anxiety disorder A psychological disorder characterized by an excessive amount of worry and anxiety about activities relating to family, health, school, and other aspects of daily life.

as might be the case with generalized anxiety disorder. Melissa's fears emanated from nagging, dreadful thoughts generated by her own mind. She may not have been struggling with an anxiety disorder per se, but she certainly was experiencing anxiety as a result of some disorder. So what was it?

Fear of Germs
Comedian and television personality Howie Mandel participates in the *America's Got Talent* panel at the NBC Universal Summer Press Day in Westlake Village, California. Mandel, who has spoken publicly about his struggle with obsessive-compulsive disorder (OCD), is known for his signature "fist bump." Receiving people with a fist bump (as opposed to a handshake) allays his worries about catching germs (Hines, 2015, May 27). Frederick M. Brown/Getty Images.

Obsessive-Compulsive Disorder

At age 12, Melissa was diagnosed with **obsessive-compulsive disorder (OCD),** a psychological disorder characterized by unwanted thoughts, or *obsessions,* and repetitive, ritualistic behaviors known as *compulsions.*

LO 4 Summarize the symptoms and causes of obsessive-compulsive disorder.

An **obsession** is a thought, urge, or image that recurs repeatedly, is intrusive and unwelcome, and often causes feelings of intense anxiety and distress. Melissa's recurrent, all-consuming thoughts of disaster and death are examples of obsessions. People with OCD attempt to stop, or at least ignore, their obsessions by engaging in a replacement thought or activity. But this is not always helpful, because the replacement can become a **compulsion,** which is a behavior or "mental act" repeated over and over.

Those who suffer from OCD experience various types of obsessions and compulsions. In many cases, obsessions focus on fears of contamination with germs or dirt, and compulsions revolve around cleaning and sterilizing (Cisler, Brady, Olatunji, & Lohr, 2010). Some OCD sufferers report that they repeatedly wash their hands even after abrasions have formed (Gillan & Robbins, 2014). Other common compulsions are repetitive rituals and checking behaviors. Melissa, for example, developed a compulsion about locking her car. Unlike most people, who lock their cars once and walk away, Melissa felt compelled to lock it twice. Then she would begin to wonder whether the car was really locked, so she would lock it a third time—just in case. But 3 is an odd number, and odd numbers don't sit well with Melissa, so she would lock it a fourth time. When Melissa finally felt comfortable enough to walk away, she had locked her car eight times. And sometimes that was still not enough. OCD compulsions often aim to thwart unwanted situations, and thereby **reduce** anxiety and distress. But the compulsive behaviors of OCD are either "clearly excessive" or not logically related to the event or situation the person is trying to prevent (American Psychiatric Association, 2013).

CONNECTIONS
In **Chapter 5**, we presented the concept of negative reinforcement: Behaviors become more frequent when they are followed by the removal of an unpleasant stimulus. Here, we can see how negative reinforcement drove Melissa's compulsive behavior. The compulsions were not actually preventing unwanted occurrences, but they did lead to a decrease in anxiety, which provided negative reinforcement for her car-locking behavior.

Where do we draw the line between obsessive or compulsive behavior and the diagnosis of a disorder? Remember, behaviors must be significantly distressing or disabling in order to be considered symptoms. The obsessions and compulsions of OCD are very time-consuming (take more than 1 hour a day) and cause a great deal of distress and disruption in daily life. Everyone has odd thoughts and quirky routines, but they don't eat up multiple hours of the day and interfere with school, work, and relationships. That's the key distinction between normal preoccupations and OCD (American Psychiatric Association, 2013). The 12-month prevalence of OCD is estimated to be 1.2% in the United States (American Psychiatric Association, 2013; Ruscio, Stein, Chiu, & Kessler, 2010).

obsessive-compulsive disorder (OCD) A psychological disorder characterized by obsessions and/or compulsions that are time-consuming and cause a great deal of distress.

obsession A thought, an urge, or an image that happens repeatedly, is intrusive and unwelcome, and often causes anxiety and distress.

compulsion A behavior or "mental act" that a person repeats over and over in an effort to reduce anxiety.

THE BIOLOGY OF OCD Evidence suggests that the symptoms of OCD are related to abnormal activity of neurotransmitters. Reduced activity of serotonin is thought to play a role, and additional neurotransmitters are being studied (Bloch, McGuire, Landeros-Weisenberger, Leckman, & Pittenger, 2010; Pittenger et al., 2016). Certain areas of the brain have been implicated, including locations in the basal ganglia, cingulate gyri, and orbital frontal cortex (American Psychiatric Association, 2013; Radua & Mataix-Cols, 2009). Normally, these regions play a role in planning and regulating movement (Rotge et al., 2009).

How do these biological differences arise? There appears to be a genetic basis for OCD. If a first-degree relative (parent, sibling, or offspring who shares about 50% of one's DNA) has an OCD diagnosis, the risk of developing OCD is twice as high as it would be if those close relatives were not affected (American Psychiatric Association, 2013). However, genes do not tell the whole story. The heritability for OCD is around 40%, suggesting that environmental factors also play a substantial role in its development (Pauls, Abramovitch, Rauch, & Geller, 2014).

THE ROLE OF LEARNING To ease her anxiety, Melissa turned to compulsions—repetitive, ritualistic behaviors aimed at relieving or offsetting her obsessions. Because her greatest fears never came to pass, Melissa assumed that her actions had prevented them. *I didn't die because I touched all the things in my room just the right way,* she would think to herself. The more she followed through on her compulsions and saw that her fears never played out, the more convinced she became that her behaviors prevented them. As Melissa put it, "When you feed it, feed it, feed it, it gets stronger."

Melissa's case illustrates how learning can play a role in OCD. Her compulsions were negatively reinforced by the reduction in her fear, and continued to grow stronger through a "negative reinforcement cycle" (Pauls et al., 2014, p. 420). Here, we can draw a parallel with drug addiction. Taking a drug can remove unpleasant withdrawal symptoms, just like carrying out compulsions reduces fear. In both cases, the behavior increases when an unpleasant experience is removed (Abramovitch & McKay, 2016). This learning process is ongoing and potentially very powerful. In one study, researchers monitored 144 people with OCD diagnoses for more than 40 years. The participants' OCD symptoms improved, in some cases with the help of treatment, but almost half continued to show "clinically relevant" symptoms after four decades (Skoog & Skoog, 1999).

Anxiety disorders and OCD result from a complex interplay of genetic and environmental factors, making it difficult to identify their exact triggers. This is not the case with posttraumatic stress disorder (PTSD), which is clearly linked to a "traumatic or stressful event" (American Psychiatric Association, 2013, p. 265).

Gun Violence and PTSD
Survivors of the school shooting in Parkland, Florida, where 17 students and staff members were killed. In the last 5 decades, gun violence has claimed more American lives than all wars in U.S. history added together (Bailey, 2017, October 4; Bauchner et al., 2017). Shooting deaths wreak emotional havoc on family and friends. "Sudden unexpected death of a loved one is the most common traumatic cause of PTSD in the population and mass shooting incidents substantially expand the base population at risk for PTSD" (Shultz, Thoresen, & Galea, 2017, para. 4). John McCall/AP Images.

Posttraumatic Stress Disorder

In order to be diagnosed with **posttraumatic stress disorder (PTSD),** a person must be exposed to or threatened by an event involving death, serious injury, or some form of violence. Someone could develop PTSD after witnessing a violent assault or accident, or upon learning about the traumatic experiences of family members, close friends, or perhaps even strangers. For some people, including firefighters, police officers, and ambulance workers, the exposure to trauma is ongoing. Rates of PTSD among firefighters, for example, may be as high as 37% (Henderson, Van Hasselt, LeDuc, & Couwels, 2016). Another group disproportionately affected is the prison population; in one study, 48% of the inmate sample was diagnosed with PTSD (Briere, Agee, & Dietrich, 2016). For U.S. veterans 21–59 years old, current rates of PTSD are around 8% (Hoge & Warner, 2014). In contrast, an estimated 3.5% to 4% of the general population has received a PTSD diagnosis during the previous 12 months (American Psychiatric Association, 2013; Briere et al., 2016).

posttraumatic stress disorder (PTSD) A psychological disorder characterized by exposure to or being threatened by an event involving death, serious injury, or violence; can include disturbing memories, nightmares, flashbacks, and other distressing symptoms.

Not everyone exposed to trauma will develop PTSD. Over the course of a lifetime, most people will experience an event that qualifies as a "psychological trauma," yet the majority will not meet the diagnostic criteria for PTSD (Bonanno, Westphal, & Mancini, 2011). To be diagnosed, a person must experience at least one of the following symptoms: (1) distressing, disturbing, and spontaneously recurring memories of an event; (2) dreams with content or emotions associated with the event; (3) "dissociative reactions" that include feeling as if the event is happening again (flashbacks); (4) extreme psychological distress when reminded of the event; or (5) obvious physical reactions to cues related to the event (American Psychiatric Association, 2013).

Many people with PTSD try to avoid environmental cues (people, places, or objects) linked to the trauma. Other symptoms include difficulty remembering the details of the event, unrealistic self-expectations, ongoing self-blame, and loss of interest in activities that once were enjoyable. People with PTSD might be irritable or aggressive, lashing out at loved ones for no apparent reason. They may have trouble sleeping and concentrating. *Dissociative symptoms,* which may include distorted perceptions of the world, and the feeling of observing oneself from the outside, are also associated with PTSD (American Psychiatric Association, 2013; Müllerová, Hansen, Contractor, Elhai, & Armour, 2016; Powers, Cross, Fani, & Bradley, 2015).

show what you know

1. Someone with a diagnosis of panic disorder will experience unexpected and recurrent:
   a. comorbidity.
   b. medical illnesses.
   c. panic attacks.
   d. dramatic mood swings.
2. Melissa demonstrated recurrent all-consuming worries. She tried to stop unwanted thoughts with a variety of behaviors that she repeated over and over. These behaviors are known as:
   a. obsessions.
   b. classical conditioning.
   c. panic attacks.
   d. compulsions.
3. Melissa's therapist helped reduce the negative reinforcement of her compulsions by not allowing her to repeatedly check that her car was locked. Explain why such a technique would work.

✓ CHECK YOUR ANSWERS IN APPENDIX C.

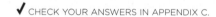

From Depression to Mania

The Importance of Friends
Melissa (right) poses with childhood friend Mary Beth, whom she credits for helping to save her life. The day that Melissa arrived home intending to attempt suicide, Mary Beth recognized her friend's distress and called for help. Thanks to the intervention of friends and family, Melissa received the treatment she needed. Melissa Hopely.

MELISSA'S SECOND DIAGNOSIS Unfortunately for Melissa, receiving a diagnosis and treatment did not solve her problems. "Every day I woke up, I wanted to die," says Melissa, who reached a breaking point during her sophomore year in high school. After a particularly difficult day at school, Melissa returned home with the intention of taking her own life. Luckily, a friend recognized that she was in distress and notified Melissa's family members, who rushed home to find Melissa curled up in a ball in the corner of her room, rocking back and forth and mumbling nonsense. They took Melissa to the hospital, where she finally met people who didn't think she was "crazy." During those 3 days in the psychiatric unit, she explains, "I realized I wasn't my disorder."

While in the hospital, Melissa received a new diagnosis in addition to OCD. Doctors told her that she was suffering from depression. Apparently, the profound sadness and helplessness she had been feeling were symptoms of *major depressive disorder,* one of the depressive disorders described in the *DSM–5.*

Major Depressive Disorder

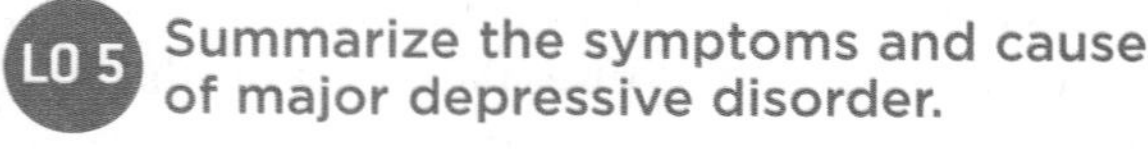

LO 5 Summarize the symptoms and causes of major depressive disorder.

A *major depressive episode* is evident if five or more of the symptoms listed here (1) occur for at least 2 consecutive weeks and represent a change from prior functioning, (2) cause significant distress or impairment, and (3) are not due to a medical or drug-related condition:

- depressed mood, which might result in feeling sad or hopeless;
- reduced pleasure in activities almost all of the time;
- substantial loss or gain in weight, without conscious effort, or changes in appetite;
- sleeping excessively or not sleeping enough;
- feeling tired, drained of energy;
- feeling worthless or extremely guilt-ridden;
- difficulty thinking or concentrating;
- persistent thoughts about death or suicide.

In order to be diagnosed with **major depressive disorder,** a person must have experienced at least one major depressive episode. Some people suffer a single episode, while others battle *recurrent* episodes.

Diagnosing major depressive disorder can be challenging. The clinician must be able to distinguish the symptoms from normal reactions to a "significant loss," such as the death of a loved one. This is not always easy because responses to death often resemble depression. A key distinction is that grief generally decreases with time, and comes in waves associated with memories or reminders of the loss; the sadness associated with a major depressive episode tends to remain steady (American Psychiatric Association, 2013).

Major depressive disorder is one of the most common and devastating psychological disorders. In the United States, the lifetime prevalence is almost 17% (Kessler, Berglund, et al., 2005; Kessler, Petukhova, Sampson, Zaslavsky, & Wittchen, 2012); this means that nearly 1 in 5 Americans experiences a major depressive episode at least once in life. Beginning in adolescence, rates of this disorder are already 1.5 to 3 times higher for females (American Psychiatric Association, 2013). Although this gender disparity reaches its maximum during adolescence, a substantial gap persists in adulthood. Women suffer disproportionally, but "it is important that clinicians do not overlook depression among men" (Salk & Abramson, 2017, p. 808).

Talking About Depression
Rapper Kendrick Lamar performs at the 2016 British Summer Time Festival in London, England. Lamar has touched upon the topic of depression in some of his song lyrics. In a 2015 interview with MTV, he described some of the emotional trauma he experienced as a young person in Compton, California: "Three of my homeboys [one] summertime was murdered, close ones too, not just somebody that I hear about. These [are] people I grew up with. It all, psychologically, it messes your brain up" (Boardman, 2015, April 3, para. 8). If you or someone you know appears to be experiencing depression or suicidal thoughts, do not hesitate to seek help. Call the **National Suicide Prevention Line: 1-800-273-TALK or 1-800-273-8255.**
Samir Hussein/Redferns/Getty Images.

The effects of major depressive disorder extend far beyond the individual. For Americans ages 15 to 44, this condition is a "leading cause" of disability (Greenberg, Fournier, Sisitky, Pike, & Kessler, 2015)—and this means it impacts the productivity of the workforce. In a comprehensive study of major depressive disorder, respondents reported that their symptoms prevented them from going to work or performing day-to-day activities for an average of 35 days a year (Kessler et al., 2003). Stop and think about this statistic—we are talking about a loss of 7 work weeks! Time away from work isn't the only concern. Underperformance at work, also known as "presenteeism," is observed in 13–29% of workers who are depressed (Lerner, Lyson, Sandberg, & Rogers, n.d.).

CULTURE Depression is one of the most common disorders in the world, yet the symptoms experienced, the course of treatment, and the words used to describe it vary from culture to culture. For example, people in China rarely report feeling "sad," but instead focus on physical symptoms, such as dizziness, fatigue, or inner pressure (Kleinman, 2004). In Thailand, depression is commonly expressed through mental and physical symptoms such as headaches, fatigue, daydreaming, social withdrawal, irritation, and forgetfulness (Chirawatkul, Prakhaw, & Chomnirat, 2011). Culture affects the way people experience emotion, and it may even impact rates of depression (Chan, Zhang, Fung, & Hagger, 2015).

major depressive disorder A psychological disorder that includes at least one major depressive episode, with symptoms such as depressed mood, problems with sleep, and loss of energy.

Baby Blues
Model and TV personality Chrissy Teigen feeds her baby in a New York City park. Teigen wrote an essay about her battle with postpartum depression in *Glamour.* "I'm speaking up now because I want people to know it can happen to anybody," Teigen wrote. "I don't want people who have it to feel embarrassed or to feel alone" (Teigen, 2017, para. 25). Approximately 3–6% of women experience depression starting in pregnancy or within weeks or months of giving birth (American Psychiatric Association, 2013). Josiah Kamau/Getty Images.

SUICIDE The recurrent nature of major depressive disorder increases one's risk for suicide and health complications (Knorr et al., 2016; Monroe & Harkness, 2011). Around 9% of adults in 21 countries confirm they have harbored "serious thoughts of suicide" at least once (**Infographic 13.2**), and around 3% have attempted suicide (Borges et al., 2010). Depression is one of many factors that have been linked to suicide; others include substance abuse, medical problems, obstacles to obtaining psychological therapy, and a "family history of child maltreatment" (CDC, 2017, October 3).

What Role Does Biology Play?

Nearly 7% of Americans battle depression in any given year (American Psychiatric Association, 2013; Kessler, Chiu, et al., 2005). What underlies this staggering statistic? There appears to be something biological at work.

ARE GENES INVOLVED? Studies of twins, family pedigrees, and adoptions tell us that major depressive disorder runs in families, with heritability estimates between 37% and 50% (American Psychiatric Association, 2013; Levinson, 2006; Wray et al., 2012). This means that about 37–50% of the variability of major depressive disorder in the population can be attributed to genetic factors. The risk of having this disorder is 2 to 4 times higher if first-degree relatives are affected (American Psychiatric Association, 2013).

DO HORMONES CONTRIBUTE? People with depressive disorders may have high levels of cortisol, a hormone secreted by the adrenal glands (Belmaker & Agam, 2008; Dougherty, Klein, Olino, Dyson, & Rose, 2009). Women sufferers, in particular, appear to be affected by stress-induced brain activity and hormonal fluctuations (Holsen et al., 2011), particularly those associated with pregnancy and childbirth (Schiller, Meltzer-Brody, & Rubinow, 2015). For both women and men, depressive symptoms may link to abnormal activity of the hypothalamic–pituitary–adrenal (HPA) system, which plays an important role in the stress response (American Psychiatric Association, 2013).

WHAT'S GOING ON IN THE BRAIN? Abnormal activity of three neurotransmitters—*norepinephrine, serotonin,* and *dopamine*—may contribute to the development and progression of major depressive disorder. The relationships among these neurotransmitters are complicated, and researchers are still trying to understand their roles (El Mansari et al., 2010; Kambeitz & Howes, 2015; Torrente, Gelenberg, & Vrana, 2012).

Depression also seems to be correlated with specific structural features in the brain (Andrus et al., 2012). One large analysis of brain-imaging studies suggests there are "significant differences in cortical brain structures" in both adolescents and adults with major depressive disorder (Schmaal et al., 2017). Another analysis indicates that people with this disorder (particularly those with "recurrent and early onset") experience a shrinking of the hippocampus (Schmaal et al., 2016, p. 811). Meanwhile, functional magnetic resonance imaging (fMRI) research points to disruptions in neural pathways involved in processing emotions and rewards (American Psychiatric Association, 2013).

Major depressive disorder most likely results from a complex interplay of many neural factors. What's difficult to determine is the causal direction: Do changes in the brain precede the disorder, or does the disorder lead to changes in the brain? In some cases, the former seems to be true: A physical change in the brain triggers the onset of depression.

Suicide in the United States

In recent years, suicide has emerged as a leading cause of death in the United States (Centers for Disease Control and Prevention [CDC], 2018, June 7). American Indian/Alaska Natives have been affected more than any other group, but suicide impacts all ethnicities (Ivey-Stephenson, Crosby, Jack, Haileyesus, & Kresnow-Sedacca, 2017). Researchers examine suicide rates across gender, age, and ethnicity in order to better understand risk factors and to help develop suicide prevention strategies. Let's take a look at what this means—and what you can do if you are concerned a friend or family member might be contemplating suicide.

Suicide rates rose across the US from 1999 to 2016.

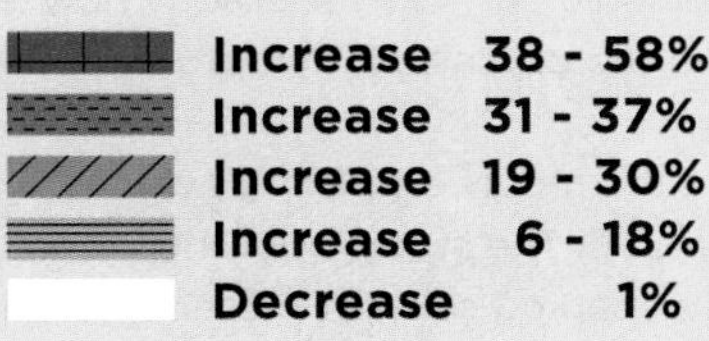

(CDC's National Vital Statistics System; CDC, 2018, June 7).

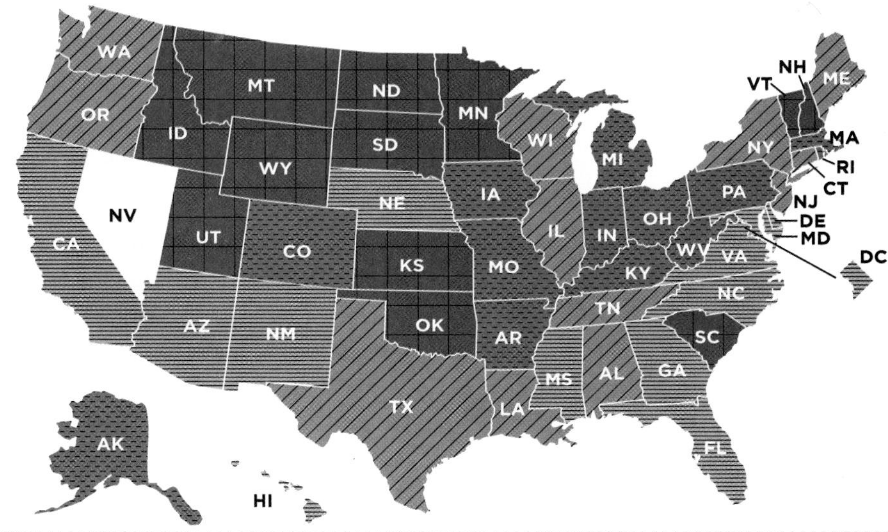

Approximately 4% of U.S. adults think about suicide over the course of a year.

The suicide rate for males is nearly 4 times higher than females.

(National Institute of Mental Health, 2018, May).

In the United States, someone commits suicide every **12 minutes.**

(American Foundation for Suicide Prevention, n.d.).

Suicide is the second leading cause of death for people aged 10–24.

(CDC, National Center for Injury Prevention and Control, 2018, April 18).

Risk factors for suicide include:

- ✔ Previous suicide attempt(s)
- ✔ Family history of suicide or violence
- ✔ Alcohol or drug abuse
- ✔ Physical illness
- ✔ History of depression or other mental illness
- ✔ Feeling alone

(CDC, 2017, October 3).

More than half of those who complete suicide have not been diagnosed with a psychological disorder. "It is possible that mental health conditions or other circumstances could have been present and not diagnosed, known, or reported" (CDC, 2018, June 7, p. 2).

Credit: Young men talking in front of window, Serge/Getty Images.

If you believe a friend may be thinking about suicide:

- Don't be afraid to ask. Talking about suicide will not put the idea in your friend's head. Be direct and ask your friend if he is thinking about hurting himself.
- Listen without being judgmental.
- Never agree to keep someone's thoughts about suicide a secret.
- Encourage your friend to contact a responsible person who can help. This may be a counselor, teacher, or health-care professional. Or call a suicide prevention hotline.
- If your friend admits that she has made a detailed plan or obtained a means of hurting herself, call 911 and stay with her until help arrives.

(CDC, 2018, June 7; Mayo Clinic, 2018, January 31).

NATIONAL SUICIDE PREVENTION LIFELINE: 1-800-273-TALK (8255)
suicidepreventionlifeline.org

Photo is being used for illustrative purposes only; persons depicted in the photos are models.

STRIKING EVIDENCE LINKING FOOTBALL TO BRAIN DISEASE SPARKS CALLS FOR MORE RESEARCH

The biggest study of its kind offers the best evidence to date linking the sport to mood and cognitive impairments.

The controversy began about 10 years ago, when it emerged that the National Football League had first tried to cover up evidence linking repetitive head injuries in players to chronic traumatic encephalopathy (CTE), a progressive neurodegenerative disorder, and then to discredit the scientists doing the work. Since then, evidence supporting this link has grown as an increasing number of players have come forward to report that they are suffering from depression, and some have committed suicide. And yet exactly how repetitive head injuries are linked to CTE development and the psychiatric symptoms associated with it is still a matter of debate.

The largest ever study of its kind has now given the most compelling evidence yet linking repetitive head impacts in football players to CTE. The study, published recently in *JAMA,* has notable limitations, however. It has also sparked calls for more research to measure the impact of head blows on players over the course of a lifetime.

. . . .

In this latest study, the researchers examined the brains of 202 deceased football players, all of which had been donated to a brain bank created to investigate the long-term effects of repetitive head injuries in athletes, military personnel and victims of domestic abuse. They obtained detailed medical histories for all the subjects, measured the volume of their brain and then dissected the organ to look for CTE-related neuropathology.

Of the 202 participants examined in the study, 177 were diagnosed with CTE, based on the previously described pathological characteristics. They had an average of 15 years of experience with the game, at the high school, college or professional level. Their median age of death was 67 years, with the most common causes being neurodegenerative disease (39 percent), cardiovascular disease (19 percent) and suicide (10 percent). The severity of CTE pathologies was associated with the intensity of play, with all the former high school players exhibiting mild CTE pathology and more than half of the former college, semiprofessional and professional players exhibiting severe pathologies.

Behavioral and mood symptoms were common in all the former NFL players diagnosed with CTE, having occurred in almost all the 26 individuals with mild pathology and 75 of the 84 individuals with severe pathology. Other common symptoms included anxiety, depression and impulsivity. Verbal aggression, physical violence, suicidal thoughts and substance abuse had also occurred in the majority of those with mild CTE pathology, but post-traumatic stress disorder was uncommon, occurring in only three cases with mild pathology and nine cases of former players who were more severely affected.

Despite the high proportion of study participants exhibiting CTE pathology, the authors urged caution in interpreting their results. One important limitation of the study is the biased sample—brains that were donated for the specific purpose of examining links between head trauma and CTE. It does not necessarily follow that the frequency of CTE in the wider population of people exposed to repetitive head injuries is as high as that found in the study. Nor is the sample representative of the overall population of football players, most of whom play only on youth or high school teams. . . . **Mo Costandi.** ■

Psychological Factors

Earlier, we mentioned that the heritability of depression is about 37–50%. What about the other 50–63% of the variability? Clearly, biology is not everything. Psychological factors also play a role in the onset and course of major depressive disorder.

LEARNED HELPLESSNESS According to American psychologist Martin Seligman, people often become depressed because they believe they have no control over the

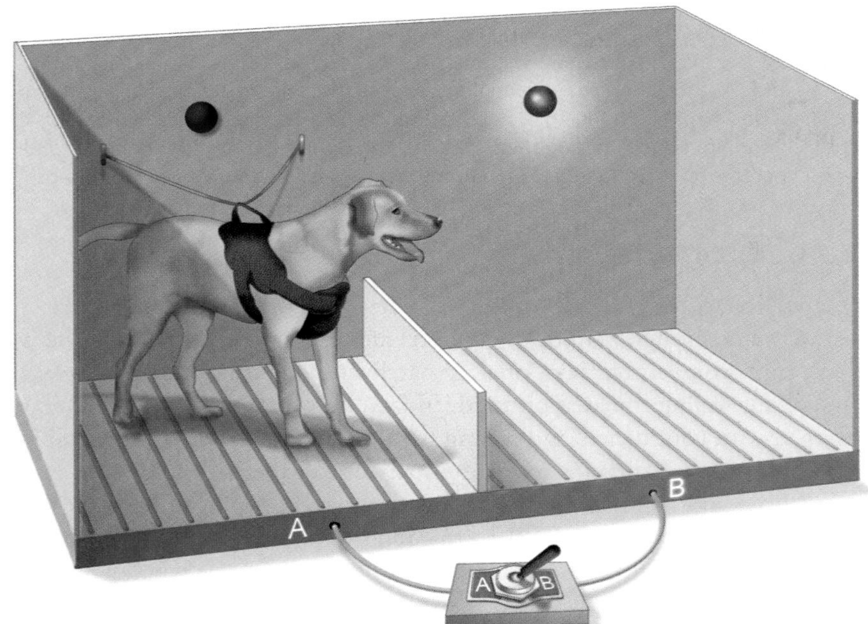

FIGURE 13.2
Seligman's Research on Learned Helplessness
Dogs restrained in a hammock were unable to escape painful shocks administered through an electrical grid on the floor of a specially designed cage called a shuttle box. The dogs soon learned that they were helpless and couldn't control these painful experiences. They did not try to escape by jumping over the barrier even when they were not restrained. The figure here shows the electrical grid activated on side B.

consequences of their behaviors (Overmier & Seligman, 1967; Seligman, 1975; Seligman & Maier, 1967). To demonstrate this **learned helplessness,** Seligman restrained dogs in a hammock and then randomly administered inescapable painful electric shocks to their paws (**Figure 13.2**). The next day, the same dogs were put in another cage where they had the opportunity to escape the shocks, but they did not try. Seligman concluded the dogs had learned they couldn't control this painful situation; they were acting in a depressed manner. He translated this finding to people with major depressive disorder, suggesting that they, too, feel powerless to change things for the better, and therefore become passive and depressed.

NEGATIVE THINKING American psychiatrist Aaron Beck suggests that depression is connected to negative thinking. Depression, according to Beck (1976), is the product of a "cognitive triad"—a negative view of experiences, self, and the future. Here's an example: A student receives a failing grade on an exam, so she begins to think she is a poor student, and that belief leads her to conclude she will fail the course. This self-defeating attitude may actually lead to her failing, reinforcing her belief that she is a poor student, and perhaps evolving into a broader belief that her life is a failure. People with this thinking style are thought to be at risk for developing a deep sense of hopelessness when they experience "negative life events." This "hopelessness depression" can include symptoms such as sadness, suicidal behavior, self-blame, and a low sense of belonging (Fisher, Overholser, Ridley, Braden, & Rosoff, 2015; Liu, Kleiman, Nestor, & Cheek, 2015).

If you aren't convinced that beliefs contribute to depression, consider this: The way people respond to their experience of depression may impact the severity of the disorder. Those who repeatedly focus on this experience are much more likely to remain depressed and perhaps even descend into deeper depression (Eaton et al., 2012; Nolen-Hoeksema, 1991). Women tend to *ruminate* or constantly think about their negative emotions more than men, rather than actively trying to solve their problems (Eaton et al., 2012). We should also note that a correlation between rumination and depression is not the same as a cause-and-effect relationship. Not every negative thinker develops depression, and depression can lead to negative thoughts.

learned helplessness A tendency for people to believe they have no control over the consequences of their behaviors, resulting in passive behavior.

Put Your Heads Together

Team up and **A)** consider the psychological roots of depression, such as learned helplessness and negative thinking, **B)** brainstorm some scenarios in which a person falls prey to the "cognitive triad" of negative thinking, and **C)** discuss how your understanding of this perspective might influence your interactions with someone who is depressed.

Bipolar Disorders

HIGHEST HIGHS, LOWEST LOWS When Ross began battling bipolar disorder, he went through periods of euphoria and excitement. Sometimes he would stay awake for 4 consecutive days, or sleep barely an hour per night for 2 weeks in a row—without feeling the least bit tired. In fact, he was exploding with energy, supercharged with confidence, and feeling high on life. Ideas flashed through his mind so fast that it was difficult to focus on any one of them. "My brain was a television," Ross says, "and someone was just constantly flipping channels." The only way he could ease his mind was by drinking—and we're not talking about a couple of beers or a few shots of vodka, but an entire case or a whole bottle. Ross was using alcohol to drown out his symptoms. 

LO 6 Summarize the symptoms and causes of bipolar disorders.

The extreme energy, euphoria, and confidence Ross felt were most likely the result of **manic episodes,** also known as *mania.* Manic episodes are often characterized by continuous elation that is out of proportion to the situation. A person might show up to work wearing inappropriate, extravagant clothing, talking too fast, and acting like an authority on topics outside his area of expertise. Other features include irritability, very high and sustained levels of energy, and an "expansive" mood, meaning the person feels more powerful than he really is and behaves in a showy or overly confident way. During one of these manic episodes, a person exhibits three or more of the symptoms listed below, which represent deviations from normal behavior (American Psychiatric Association, 2013):

- grandiose or extremely high self-esteem;
- reduced sleep;
- increased talkativeness;
- a "flight of ideas" or the feeling of "racing" thoughts;
- being easily distracted;
- heightened activity at school or work;
- physical agitation;
- displaying poor judgment and engaging in activities that could have serious consequences (risky sexual behavior or excessive shopping sprees, for example).

It is not unusual for a person experiencing a severe manic episode to be hospitalized. Mania is difficult to hide and can be dangerous. One may act out of character, doing things that damage important relationships or jeopardize work, or become violent. Seeking help is unlikely, because mania leads to impaired judgment, feelings of grandiosity, and euphoria. (Why would you seek help if you feel on top of the world?) At these times, the support of others is essential.

There are various types of bipolar disorder. To be diagnosed with *bipolar I disorder,* a person must experience at least one *manic episode,* substantial distress, and great impairment. *Bipolar II disorder* requires at least one major depressive episode, as well as a *hypomanic episode. Hypomania* is associated with some of the same symptoms as a manic episode, but the manic behavior does not last as long and generally does not impair one's ability to function (American Psychiatric Association, 2013; **Table 13.5**).

Battling Bipolar
Demi Lovato takes the stage at the 93.3 FLZ Jingle Ball 2014 in Tampa, Florida. This singer/songwriter is one of millions of Americans living with bipolar disorder, and she has encouraging words for those who share her struggle: "It's possible to live well, feel well, and also find happiness with bipolar disorder or any other mental illness" (Heiser, 2015, May 28, para. 2). Alexander Tamargo/Getty Images for iHeartMedia.

manic episodes States of continuous elation that are out of proportion to the setting, and can include irritability, very high and sustained levels of energy, and an "expansive" mood.

TABLE 13.5 BIPOLAR DISORDERS

Bipolar Disorder	Description	Annual
Bipolar I disorder	Episodes of mania that include an "abnormally, persistently elevated, expansive, or irritable mood and persistently increased activity or energy that is present for most of the day, nearly every day, for a period of at least 1 week" (p. 127). This may be preceded by hypomania or depression.	0.6%
Bipolar II disorder	Repeated major depressive episodes (lasting at least 2 weeks) and "at least one hypomanic episode," which must last for a minimum of 4 days (p. 135).	0.8%

Bipolar I disorder and bipolar II disorder have distinct patterns of highs and lows. Looking at the annual prevalence (yearly occurrence) of these disorders, you can see that they are relatively rare. Information from *DSM-5* (American Psychiatric Association, 2013).

BIPOLAR CYCLING Some people with bipolar disorder cycle between extreme highs and lows of emotion and energy that last for days, weeks, or even months. As mentioned earlier, bouts of mania are often characterized by unusually elevated, irritable, or expansive moods. At the other extreme are feelings of deep sadness, emptiness, and helplessness—the depression pole of bipolar disorder can be as severe as the major depressive episodes described earlier. Periods of mania and depression may be brought on by life changes and stressors, though some research suggests it is only the *first* episode that tends to be triggered by some sort of life event, such as the loss of a job. Subsequent episodes may not be as closely linked to such events (Belmaker, 2004; Malkoff-Schwartz et al., 1998; Weiss et al., 2015).

You Asked, Ross Answers

http://qrs.ly/8z5a5fr

What was the hardest part of having your disorder when you were younger, and what's the hardest part now?

WHO GETS BIPOLAR DISORDER? Bipolar disorder is uncommon. Over the course of a lifetime, about 0.8% of the American population will receive a diagnosis of bipolar I disorder, and 1.1% bipolar II disorder (Merikangas et al., 2007). Men and women have an equal chance of being affected, but men tend to experience earlier onset of symptoms (Altshuler et al., 2010; Kennedy et al., 2005).

Although researchers have yet to determine the cause of bipolar disorder, evidence from twin and adoption studies underscores the importance of genes. If one identical twin is diagnosed with bipolar disorder, there is a 40–70% chance the other twin will have the disorder as well. Among fraternal twins, there is only a 5% chance that the second twin will develop the disorder (Craddock, O'Donovan, & Owen, 2005). The heritability estimates of bipolar disorder are high, falling somewhere between 79% and 90% (Hanford, Nazarov, Hall, & Sassi, 2016). According to the American Psychiatric Association (2013), "A family history of bipolar disorder is one of the strongest and most consistent risk factors for bipolar disorders" (p. 130). Adults who have a first-degree relative with bipolar disorder, on average, have a "10-fold increased risk" for developing the disorder themselves (p. 130).

But nature is not the only force at work in bipolar disorder; nurture plays a role, too. The fact that there is a higher rate of bipolar disorder in high-income countries (1.4%) than in low-income countries (0.7%; American Psychiatric Association, 2013) suggests that environment may act as a catalyst for its development. Additionally, some researchers hypothesize that exposure to viruses, poor nutrition, or stress during fetal development can spark a cascade of biological events that leads to the development of bipolar disorder. The same has been said of another serious disorder: schizophrenia (Carter, 2007; Yolken & Torrey, 1995).

show what you know

1. Li is sleeping too much, feeling tired all the time, and avoiding activities she once enjoyed. Which of the following best describes the disorder Li may be experiencing?
   a. obsessive-compulsive disorder
   b. major depressive disorder
   c. agoraphobia
   d. panic disorder
2. Many factors contribute to the etiology and course of major depressive disorder. Prepare notes for a 3-minute speech you might give on this topic.
3. Ross described going for 4 days straight without sleeping at all, or 2 weeks in a row sleeping only 1 hour per night. He was exploding with energy, supercharged with confidence, and feeling on top of the world. It is likely that Ross was experiencing periods of euphoria and excitement, which can best be described as:
   a. depression.
   b. manic episodes.
   c. panic attacks.
   d. anxiety.
4. Compare the symptoms of bipolar disorder with those of major depressive disorder.

✓ CHECK YOUR ANSWERS IN APPENDIX C.

Schizophrenia and Autism

Schizophrenia: A Complex Disorder

How would it feel to see imaginary figures lurking in your peripheral vision, or to look in the mirror and see an image of your brain decomposing? What if you heard voices and ticking sounds throughout the day, and rarely felt happiness, sadness, or any type of emotion (RACHELSTARLIVE, 2018; Withers & Barnes, 2015, September 11)? These are actual symptoms reported by Rachel Star Withers, who has a disabling psychological disorder called **schizophrenia** (skit-suh-FREH-nee-uh). People with schizophrenia experience **psychosis,** a loss of contact with reality that is severe and chronic.

Living with Schizophrenia
Tens of thousands of YouTube viewers have watched the videos of Rachel Star Withers, a modeling and acting teacher who has schizophrenia. In her videos, Withers talks openly about her struggles with hallucinations, depersonalization (feeling detached from oneself), and other symptoms. She is a successful career woman with inspiring words for those facing schizophrenia and other disorders (NPR, 2016, June 13; Withers & Barnes, 2015, September 11). "[Having schizophrenia] is not a bad thing," Withers tells *Women's Health*. "You're just different, and you have to learn how to manage that and accept it. The world wasn't made for people with mental disorders, but that doesn't mean you can't be in it and have a kickass life" (Withers & Barnes, 2015, September 11, para. 16). Image1st/Courtesy Rachel Star Withers.

LO 7 Recognize the symptoms of schizophrenia.

The hallmark features of schizophrenia are disturbances in thinking, perception, and language (**Table 13.6**). Psychotic symptoms include **delusions,** which are strange or false beliefs that a person maintains even when presented with evidence to the contrary. Common delusional themes are being persecuted by others, spied upon, or ridiculed. Some people have grandiose delusions; they may believe they are extraordinarily talented or famous, for example. Others are convinced that radio reports,

TABLE 13.6 SYMPTOMS OF SCHIZOPHRENIA

Positive Symptoms of Schizophrenia	Negative Symptoms of Schizophrenia
Delusions	Decreased emotional expression
Hallucinations	Lack of motivation
Disorganized speech	Decreased speech production
Grossly disorganized or catatonic behavior	Decreased functioning at work, in social situations, or in self-care
Abnormal motor behavior	Reduced pleasure Lack of interest in interacting with others

Schizophrenia symptoms can be grouped into two main categories: Positive symptoms indicate the presence of excesses or distortions of normal behavior; negative symptoms refer to a reduction in normal behaviors and mental processes. Information from *DSM–5* (American Psychiatric Association, 2013).

schizophrenia A disabling psychological disorder that can include delusions, hallucinations, disorganized speech, and abnormal motor behavior.

psychosis Loss of contact with reality that is severe and chronic.

delusions Strange or false beliefs that a person firmly maintains even when presented with evidence to the contrary.

newspaper headlines, or public announcements are about them. Delusions appear very real to those experiencing them.

People with schizophrenia may also hear voices or see things that are not actually present. This psychotic symptom is known as a **hallucination**—a "perception-like experience" that the individual believes is real, but that is not evident to others. Hallucinations can occur with any of the senses, but auditory hallucinations are most common. Often they manifest as voices commenting on what is happening in the environment, or voices using threatening or judgmental language (American Psychiatric Association, 2013).

The symptoms of schizophrenia are often classified as **positive and negative** (see Table 13.6). **Positive symptoms** are excesses or distortions of normal behavior, and include delusions, hallucinations, and disorganized speech—all of which are generally not observed in people without psychosis. In other words, positive symptoms indicate the *presence* of abnormal behaviors. **Negative symptoms,** on the other hand, refer to the reduction or *absence* of expected behaviors. Common negative symptoms include social withdrawal, diminished speech or speech content, limited emotions, and loss of energy and follow-up (Fusar-Poli et al., 2015; Tandon, Nasrallah, & Keshavan, 2009).

CONNECTIONS

In **Chapter 5,** we noted that the term positive does not always mean "good." Positive punishment means the addition of an aversive stimulus. Positive symptoms refer to additions or excesses, not an evaluation of how "good" the symptoms are. Negative refers to the reduction or absence of behaviors, not an evaluation of how "bad" the symptoms are.

To be diagnosed with schizophrenia, a person must display symptoms for the majority of days in a 1-month period and experience significant dysfunction in work, school, relationships, or personal care for at least 6 months. (And it must be determined that these problems do not result from substance abuse or a serious medical condition.) Using the *DSM-5,* clinicians can rate the presence and severity of symptoms (hallucinations, delusions, disorganized speech, unusual psychomotor behaviors, and negative symptoms).

With estimates ranging from a 0.3–1% lifetime risk, schizophrenia is uncommon (American Psychiatric Association, 2013; Saha, Chant, Welham, & McGrath, 2005). Although men and women appear to face an equal risk (Abel, Drake, & Goldstein, 2010; Saha et al., 2005), the onset of the disorder tends to occur earlier in men, by an average of 3–5 years (Mendrek & Mancini-Marïe, 2016). Males are typically diagnosed during their late teens or early twenties, whereas the peak age for women is the late twenties (American Psychiatric Association, 2013; Gogtay, Vyas, Testa, Wood, & Pantelis, 2011). In most cases, schizophrenia is a lifelong disorder that causes significant disability and a high risk of suicide. The prognosis is worse for earlier onset schizophrenia, but this may be related to the fact that men, who tend to develop symptoms earlier in life, are in poorer condition when first diagnosed (American Psychiatric Association, 2013). Schizophrenia disproportionately affects people of lower socioeconomic classes, but the **causal relationship** remains unclear (Tandon, Keshavan, & Nasrallah, 2008a, 2008b). Having the disorder makes it hard to hold down a job; up to 90% of those affected are unemployed (Evensen et al., 2016).

CONNECTIONS

In **Chapter 1**, we discussed the direction of causality. If there is a correlation between X and Y, it is possible that X is causing Y, or that Y is causing X. In this case, we don't know if lower socioeconomic status increases the risk of developing schizophrenia, or if having schizophrenia leads to lower socioeconomic status.

The Roots of Schizophrenia

Analyze the biopsychosocial factors that contribute to schizophrenia.

Schizophrenia is a complex psychological disorder that results from an interaction of biological, psychological, and social factors, making it difficult to predict who will be affected. For many years, some experts focused the blame on environmental factors, such as unhealthy family dynamics and bad parenting. A common scapegoat was the "schizophrenogenic mother," whose poor parenting style was believed to cause the disorder in her child (Harrington, 2012). Thankfully, this belief has been shattered by our new understanding of the brain. Research on schizophrenia, particularly in the area of genetics, has made great leaps. A large body of evidence now confirms

hallucinations Perception-like experiences that an individual believes are real, but that are not evident to others.

positive symptoms Excesses or distortions of normal behavior; examples are delusions, hallucinations, and disorganized speech.

negative symptoms Behaviors or characteristics that are limited or absent; examples are social withdrawal, diminished speech, limited or no emotions, and loss of energy and follow-up.

that schizophrenia runs in families (Balter, 2017; Schizophrenia Working Group of the Psychiatric Genomics Consortium, 2014). For a dramatic illustration of this phenomenon, we turn to the famous case of the Genain sisters.

...BELIEVE IT...OR NOT

FOUR SISTERS WITH SCHIZOPHRENIA Nora, Iris, Myra, and Hester Genain were identical quadruplets born in 1930. Their mother went to great lengths to treat them equally, and in many ways the children were equals (Mirsky & Quinn, 1988). As babies, they cried in unison and teethed at the same times. As toddlers, they played with the same toys, wore the same dresses, and rode the same tricycles. The little girls were said to be so mentally in sync that they never argued (Quinn, 1963).

LIKE ANY PSYCHOLOGICAL PHENOMENON, SCHIZOPHRENIA IS A PRODUCT OF BOTH NATURE AND NURTURE

Mr. and Mrs. Genain kept the girls isolated. Spending most of their time at home, the quads cultivated few friendships. The Genains may have protected their daughters from the world outside, but they could not shield them from the trouble brewing inside their brains.

The Quads
Identical quadruplets (known under the fictitious surname Genain), each of whom developed symptoms of schizophrenia between the ages of 22 and 24. Schizophrenia is a highly heritable disorder that has been linked to 108 gene areas (Dhindsa & Goldstein, 2016; Schizophrenia Working Group of the Psychiatric Genomics Consortium, 2014). ©AP Images.

At age 22, one of the sisters, Nora, was hospitalized for a psychiatric disorder characterized by hallucinations, delusions, altered speech, and other symptoms. Within months, a second sister, Iris, was admitted to a psychiatric ward as well. She, too, had the symptoms of psychosis. Both Nora and Iris were diagnosed with schizophrenia, and it was only a matter of years before Myra and Hester were diagnosed as well (Mirsky & Quinn, 1988). As you can imagine, the case of the Genain quads has drawn the attention of many scientists. David Rosenthal and his colleagues at the National Institute of Mental Health studied the women when they were in their late twenties and again when they were 51. To protect the quads' identities, Rosenthal assigned them the pseudonyms Nora, Iris, Myra, and Hester, which spell out NIMH, the acronym for the National Institute of Mental Health. *Genain* is also an alias, meaning "dreadful gene" in Greek (Mirsky & Quinn, 1988).

Identical quads have nearly all the same genes, so the Genain case suggests that there is some heritable component to schizophrenia. Yet, each woman experienced the disorder in her own way, highlighting the importance of environmental factors, or nurture. Hester did not receive a diagnosis of schizophrenia until she was in her twenties, but she started to show signs of psychological impairment much earlier than her sisters and was never able to hold down a job or live alone. Myra, however, was employed for the majority of her life and has a family of her own (Mirsky et al., 2000; Mirsky & Quinn, 1988). When researchers interviewed Myra at age 81, she was still living on her own, with some assistance from her son (Mirsky, Bieliauskas, Duncan, & French, 2013). Like any psychological phenomenon, schizophrenia is a product of both nature and nurture.

GENETIC FACTORS Overall, researchers agree that schizophrenia is "highly heritable," with genetic factors accounting for 60–80% of the population-wide risk for developing this disorder (Edwards et al., 2016; Tandon et al., 2008a, 2008b). Much of the evidence derives from twin, family, and adoption studies (**Figure 13.3**). If one identical twin has schizophrenia, the risk of the other twin developing the disorder is approximately 41–65% (Petronis, 2004). Compare that to a mere 2% risk for those whose first cousins have schizophrenia (Tsuang, Stone, & Faraone, 2001). When one parent has the disorder, a person's risk of being diagnosed is 10–15% (Svrakic, Zorumksi, Svrakic, Zwir, & Cloninger, 2013). If both parents have schizophrenia, the risk increases to 27% (Gottesman, Laursen,

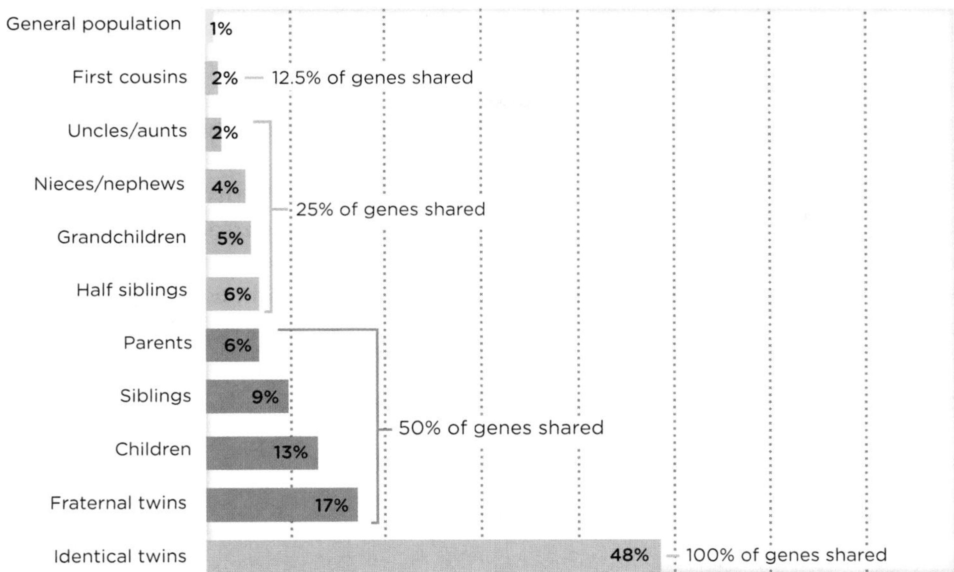

FIGURE 13.3
The Role of Genetics in Schizophrenia
The average lifetime risk of developing schizophrenia for the general population is 1% or lower. However, for someone with a sibling diagnosed with schizophrenia, the lifetime risk increases to 9%. If that sibling is an identical twin, someone with nearly 100% of the same genes, the risk rockets to 48%. This suggests a significant role for genetic factors in the development of schizophrenia (Gottesman, 2001). More recent studies suggest multiple genes are involved (Domenici, 2017).

Bertelsen, & Mortensen, 2010). Keep in mind that schizophrenia is not caused by a single gene, but by a combination of many genes interacting with the environment (Ripke et al., 2014; Svrakic et al., 2013).

DIATHESIS–STRESS MODEL Like other disorders, schizophrenia is best understood from the biopsychosocial perspective. One model that takes this perspective into account is the ***diathesis–stress model,*** where *diathesis* refers to the inherited disposition (to schizophrenia, for example), and *stress* refers to stressors and other factors in the environment (internal and external). Identical twins share 100% of their genetic make-up at conception (diathesis), yet the environment produces different stressors for the twins (only one of them loses a spouse, for example). This helps explain why one twin may develop the disorder, but the other does not. The diathesis–stress model suggests that developing schizophrenia involves a genetic predisposition *and* environmental triggers.

synonyms

diathesis-stress model stress-vulnerability model, constitutional vulnerability

THE BRAIN People with schizophrenia generally experience a thinning of the cortex, leading to enlarged ventricles, the cavities in the brain filled with cerebrospinal fluid. Research also shows that the total volume of the brain is reduced in schizophrenia (Haijma et al., 2013; Tandon et al., 2008a), and that the hippocampus, amygdala, and thalamus tend to be smaller (van Erp et al., 2016). Such abnormalities may relate to problems with cognitive functioning, psychotic symptoms, and sensory changes (Fusar-Poli et al., 2013; Glahn et al., 2008; Matheson, Shepherd, & Carr, 2014). A word of caution when interpreting these findings, however: It is possible that differences in brain structures are not just due to schizophrenia, but may also result from long-term use of medications to control its symptoms (Fusar-Poli et al., 2013; Jaaro-Peled, Ayhan, Pletnikov, & Sawa, 2010).

NEUROTRANSMITTER THEORIES Evidence suggests that abnormal neurotransmitter activity plays a role in schizophrenia. According to the **dopamine hypothesis,** the synthesis, release, and concentrations of dopamine are all elevated in people who

dopamine hypothesis A theory suggesting that the synthesis, release, and concentrations of the neurotransmitter dopamine play a role in schizophrenia.

have been diagnosed with schizophrenia and are suffering from psychosis (van Os & Kapur, 2009). Support for the dopamine hypothesis comes from the successful use of medications that **block the receptor sites for** this neurotransmitter. These drugs reduce the psychotic symptoms of schizophrenia, presumably because they decrease the potential impact of excess dopamine (van Os & Kapur, 2009). Researchers report that both positive and negative symptoms are associated with "dysfunction" in the dopamine system (Kirschner, Aleman, & Kaiser, 2016).

CONNECTIONS

In **Chapter 2,** we discussed activity at the synapse. Neurotransmitters released by the sending neuron must bind to receptor sites on the receiving neuron to relay their message ("fire" or "don't fire"). Medications that block or inhibit the receptor sites on the receiving neuron are referred to as antagonists, and some of these are used to reduce symptoms of schizophrenia.

How do increased levels of dopamine impact the brain? Perhaps by influencing the "reward system." Excess dopamine may make it hard for a person to pay attention to what is rewarding in the environment, or identify which aspects are most salient, or important (van Os & Kapur, 2009). The dopamine hypothesis has evolved over the last several decades, with researchers appreciating the ongoing dynamic between neural activity in the brain and factors in the environment (Edwards et al., 2016; Howes & Kapur, 2009).

ENVIRONMENTAL TRIGGERS AND SCHIZOPHRENIA Complications during pregnancy, such as abnormal growth of the placenta, may increase the risk of developing schizophrenia later in life (Ursini et al., 2018). Some experts suspect that schizophrenia is associated with in utero exposure to a virus, such as **human papilloma virus (HPV).** Pregnant women are vulnerable to several illnesses, including genital and reproductive infections, influenza, and some parasitic diseases, that may increase their babies' risk of developing schizophrenia later in life (Brown & Patterson, 2011; Seidel, 2018). Retrospective evidence (that is, information collected much later) suggests that children of mothers who were exposed to viruses while pregnant are more likely to develop schizophrenia during adolescence. However, research exploring this theory is still ongoing and must be replicated.

CONNECTIONS

In **Chapter 8,** we described teratogens, which are agents that can damage a zygote, embryo, or fetus. HPV is a teratogen that may be linked to the development of schizophrenia, although its impact on the individual may not be evident for many years.

Finally, sociocultural factors may play a minor role in the development and course of schizophrenia. Social stress, childhood adversities, and cannabis abuse have been associated with a slightly increased risk of schizophrenia onset, for example (Balter, 2017; Matheson et al., 2014; Tandon et al., 2008a, 2008b).

As you can see, schizophrenia is a highly complex disorder with a strong genetic component and many possible environmental causes. The same could be said of *autism,* a neurodevelopmental disorder that may share some genetic risk factors with schizophrenia and bipolar disorder (Goes et al., 2016).

Autism

Autism spectrum disorder (ASD) affects 1 in 68 American children (Centers for Disease Control and Prevention, 2016c). This disorder, which is 4 times more common in boys than girls, "is characterized by persistent deficits in social communication and social interaction across multiple contexts" and "restricted, repetitive patterns of behavior, interests, or activities" (American Psychiatric Association, 2013, p. 31). As the name implies, ASD refers to a vast spectrum of symptoms ranging from very mild to debilitating. With proper support, some people with ASD can communicate and function with few obvious deficiencies; others appear to be severely impaired and need a great deal of assistance carrying out daily activities.

CONNECTIONS

In **Chapter 1,** we discussed the publication of flawed research that purported a link between vaccinations and autism. Subsequent studies have found no credible support for the autism-vaccine hypothesis. Still, some parents refuse vaccines for their children, with serious consequences for the community. Here, we present the etiology of autism, suggesting that its causes include genetic and environmental factors.

The causes of ASD are **still under investigation,** but research demonstrates that the disorder runs in families. One large study estimated the heritability of ASD is about 50% (Sandin et al., 2014), the implication being that half of the population-wide variability in this disorder can be attributed to genes. If these findings are accurate, that leaves a lot of room for environment. Some research suggests that infections during pregnancy (those requiring hospitalization of the mother) may heighten a baby's risk for developing ASD by as much as 30% (Lee at al., 2015). Other studies have focused on teratogens, or prenatal exposure to environmental toxins such as pesticides, lead, and methanol (a chemical released into the body during the breakdown of the artificial sweetener aspartame); however, these results are somewhat inconclusive (Arora, 2017; Nevison, 2014; Walton & Monte, 2015). The etiology of this disorder remains a puzzle, and "many cases of ASD are likely to involve complex interactions between genetic and environmental risk factors" (LaSalle, 2013, p. 2).

show what you know

1. Loss of contact with reality is referred to as ______________.
2. A woman with schizophrenia reports hearing voices that tell her she is ugly and worthless. This is an example of a:
   a. hallucination. c. negative symptom.
   b. delusion. d. diathesis.
3. What are some biopsychosocial factors that contribute to the development of schizophrenia?

✓ CHECK YOUR ANSWERS IN APPENDIX C.

Personality, Dissociative, and Eating Disorders

Before reading this chapter, you probably knew something about depression, bipolar disorder, and schizophrenia. But you may have been less familiar with a somewhat common group of disorders relating to personality, which can be very debilitating when it comes to work and interpersonal relationships. Almost 11% of adults in the United States have a *personality disorder* (Clarkin, Meehan, & Lenzenweger, 2015).

Personality Disorders

People with **personality disorders** exhibit "an enduring pattern of inner experience and behavior that deviates markedly from the expectations of the individual's culture, is pervasive and inflexible, has an onset in adolescence or early adulthood, is stable over time, and leads to distress or impairment" (American Psychiatric Association, 2013, p. 645). Specifically, someone with a personality disorder behaves in a way that deviates substantially in the following areas: (1) cognition, including perceptions of self, others, and events; (2) emotional responses; (3) interpersonal functioning; and (4) impulse control. In order to be diagnosed with a personality disorder, one must struggle in at least two of these four categories. In addition, these problems must be resistant to change and have far-reaching consequences for interpersonal relationships.

Like personality traits in general, the core qualities of people with personality disorders (as well as the problems that result) are fairly stable over a lifetime and across situations. When diagnosing this type of disorder, the clinician must focus on troublesome personality traits—and be very careful not to confuse them with problems resulting from developmental changes, culture, drug use, or medical conditions.

The *DSM–5* includes 10 personality disorders. Here, we direct the spotlight onto two that have received considerable research attention: *antisocial personality disorder* and *borderline personality disorder.*

personality disorders A group of psychological disorders that can include impairments in cognition, emotional responses, interpersonal functioning, and impulse control.

LO 9 Differentiate between antisocial and borderline personality disorders.

ANTISOCIAL PERSONALITY DISORDER Many films, including *The Last King of Scotland* and *There Will Be Blood,* feature characters who behave in ways most people find incomprehensible. The qualities of these characters often parallel a diagnosis of **antisocial personality disorder.**

antisocial personality disorder A psychological disorder distinguished by unethical behavior, deceitfulness, impulsivity, irritability, aggressiveness, disregard for others, and lack of remorse.

Antisocial Personality Disorder?
Actor Adam Driver plays "Kylo Ren" in *Star Wars: The Force Awakens.* Both movie fans and psychologists have wondered what psychological disorder this fictitious character may be battling (Langley, 2016, February 10; Plata, 2017, December 19). Does Kylo Ren have antisocial personality disorder? He certainly manipulates, hurts, and uses people in order to gain power, going so far as to kill his own father. Yet (spoiler alert), he seems to display a "speck of empathy" when he decides to spare his mother in *The Last Jedi* (Plata, 2017, December 19, para. 8). Photo 12/Alamy.

People with antisocial personality disorder may seek personal gratification even when it means violating ethical standards and breaking laws. They sometimes lie or con others, and exhibit aggressive, impulsive, or irritable behaviors. These individuals have difficulty feeling empathy, and may not show concern for others or feel remorse upon hurting them. Other common behavior patterns include carelessness in sexual relationships, and the use of intimidation to control others (American Psychiatric Association, 2013). Around 1–4% of American adults are diagnosed with antisocial personality disorder, which is more common in men than women (Lenzenweger, Lane, Loranger, & Kessler, 2007; Werner, Few, & Bucholz, 2015); and, according to some studies, up to 80% of prison inmates have received this diagnosis (Edens, Kelley, Lilienfeld, Skeem, & Douglas, 2015).

How does antisocial personality disorder develop? Heredity appears to play a role, as first-degree biological relatives of people with this disorder are more likely to be affected than those in the general population (American Psychiatric Association, 2013). There is some evidence for family risk factors, but it is unclear how much of this risk is transmitted through genes, and how much results from learning. No single gene has been implicated in the development of antisocial behavior patterns. Like most mental health problems, antisocial personality disorder seems to result from a complex interaction of genes and environment (Ferguson, 2010; Werner et al., 2015).

Is there anything unique about the brain of a person with antisocial personality disorder? Some studies point to irregularities in the frontal lobes. For example, reduced tissue volume in the prefrontal cortex (11% less than expected) is apparent in some men with antisocial personality disorder. This deficit might be linked to reduced morality, and problems with decision making, planning, and developing normal responses to fear and punishment, all potentially associated with antisocial behavior. The fact that the prefrontal cortex plays a role in controlling arousal may explain why people with this disorder tend to seek out stimulation, including aggressive and antisocial activities (Raine, Lencz, Bihrle, LaCasse, & Colletti, 2000). That being said, not everyone with this diagnosis has frontal lobe abnormalities, and the development of this disorder likely involves biological, psychological, and social factors (Paris, 2015).

Mozart's Mystery
Did the great composer suffer from a psychological disorder? Some scholars believe his mood swings were indicative of depression or bipolar disorder, while others speculate he had a personality disorder. Mozart's symptoms included "efforts to avoid real or imagined abandonment, impulsiveness, affective instability due to a marked reactivity of mood . . . a feeling of emptiness, and identity disturbance" (Huguelet & Perroud, 2005, p. 137). What disorder do these characteristics suggest? DEA/A. DAGLI ORTI/Getty Images.

BORDERLINE PERSONALITY DISORDER People with **borderline personality disorder** suffer from feelings of emptiness and an incomplete sense of self. They tend to be emotionally unstable and extremely needy. They may exhibit intense anger, have difficulty controlling their temper, and get into physical fights. When it comes to sexual activity, substance abuse, and spending money, they tend to be impulsive. Recurrent suicide threats or attempts are not uncommon. Developing intimacy may be a struggle, as relationships tend to be unstable, tainted with feelings of mistrust and fear of abandonment. Those with borderline personality disorder may see the world in terms of black and white, rather than different shades of gray. This tendency to perceive extremes may lead a person to become overinvolved or totally withdrawn in relationships (American Psychiatric Association, 2013).

According to the *DSM–5,* individuals with borderline personality disorder experience emotions that are unstable, intense, and inappropriate for the situation at hand. They may feel extreme anxiety and insecurity, concern about being rejected one moment, worry about being too dependent the next. Depressed moods are common, along with feelings of hopelessness, pessimism, and shame. The person may act without thinking and frequently change plans.

Seventy-five percent of people diagnosed with borderline personality disorder are female, and research suggests that some traits associated with this disorder have a genetic component (American Psychiatric Association, 2013). There is also evidence that childhood trauma sets the stage for the development of this condition. A biosocial developmental model has been proposed, indicating an early vulnerability that includes impulsive behavior and increased "emotional sensitivity." If the environment is right, this susceptibility can lead to problems with emotions, behaviors, and cognitive processes (Crowell, Beauchaine, & Linehan, 2009). In addition to the potential contributions of childhood trauma and temperament, overprotective parenting may inhibit a developing child's ability to independently handle "her own emotions" (Sharp & Kim, 2015, p. 3).

All of us have undesirable aspects of our personality, but how do we know if these characteristics indicate the presence of a disorder? Take narcissism, for example. This personality trait is associated with vanity, self-absorption, and feelings of superiority and entitlement. Some have argued that "Generation Me" is more narcissistic than previous generations (Twenge, 2014). Perhaps this is true, but one could also argue that digital media have simply provided more public outlets to channel narcissism. It's always been there, but now it's more in your face. Either way, it is important to understand that not every selfie-obsessed person has a mental disorder.

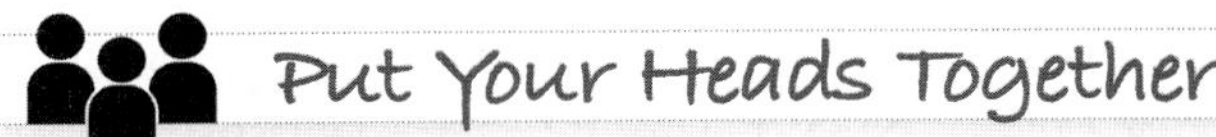

Team up and **A**) review the criteria for identifying a psychological disorder. **B**) How would you distinguish narcissism as a trait from narcissistic personality disorder?

People with personality disorders have traits that are relatively easy to characterize. This is *not* the case for those with dissociative disorders, whose personal identities may be very difficult to pin down.

Dissociative Disorders

LO 10 Identify differences among dissociative disorders.

Dissociative disorders are disturbances in normal psychological functioning that can include problems with memory, identity, consciousness, emotion, perception, and motor control (American Psychiatric Association, 2013). The main feature of these disorders is **dissociation,** or a disturbance in the normally unified experience of psychological functions involved in memory, consciousness, perception, or identity (Spiegel et al., 2011). Dissociation may lead to difficulty recalling personal information (for example, where I live, who I am), or the feeling of being detached from one's body. Here, we focus our discussion on two dissociative disorders: *dissociative amnesia* and *dissociative identity disorder.*

DISSOCIATIVE AMNESIA People suffering from **dissociative amnesia** have difficulty remembering important personal information. In some cases, the amnesia is fixed around a certain event, often one that is traumatic or stressful. Other times, the amnesia spans a lifetime. Those affected typically report a great deal of distress or impairment in work, relationships, and other important areas of life, and put a lot of effort into managing the mundane details of daily existence (Staniloiu & Markowitsch, 2012). Some individuals with dissociative amnesia experience **dissociative fugue** (fyoog), that is, they wander in a confused and disorganized manner (Spiegel et al., 2011).

borderline personality disorder A psychological disorder distinguished by an incomplete sense of self, extreme self-criticism, unstable emotions, and feelings of emptiness.

dissociative disorders Psychological disorders distinguished by disturbances in normal psychological functioning; may include problems with memory, identity, consciousness, perception, and motor control.

dissociation A disturbance in the normally integrated experience of psychological functions involved in memory, consciousness, perception, or identity.

dissociative amnesia A psychological disorder marked by difficulty remembering important personal information and life events.

dissociative fugue A condition in which a person with dissociative amnesia or dissociative identity disorder wanders about in a confused and unexpected manner.

Trance Dance
A young man in São Paulo, Brazil, dances in a trance state during a religious ceremony. Behaviors observed in this type of context may resemble those of dissociative identity disorder, so it is important to differentiate between religious practices and disordered behaviors (Moreira-Almeida, Neto, & Cardeña, 2008). AFP/Getty Images.

DISSOCIATIVE IDENTITY DISORDER Dissociative fugue is also seen in people with **dissociative identity disorder,** once referred to as "multiple personality disorder." This rare condition is characterized by the presence of two or more distinct personalities within the same person (American Psychiatric Association, 2013), and it is considered the most complicated and persistent of the dissociative disorders (Sar, 2011). One of its key features is a lack of connection among behavior, awareness, memory, and cognition. There is often a reported gap in remembering day-to-day events and personal details. These symptoms are not related to substance use or medical issues, and they may cause distress in relationships, work, and other areas of life.

People with dissociative identity disorder have been misrepresented as violent and dangerous in some movies and TV shows, but the film *Frankie & Alice* makes a sincere effort to tell the story of a real person who has lived with this disorder. Set in 1970s Los Angeles, the movie draws upon the experiences of "Frankie Murdoch," a woman who worked as a go-go dancer in this era. Frankie, portrayed by Halle Berry, is dealing with two personalities on top of her own: a white supremacist named "Alice," and a timid little girl named "Genius." All three personalities—Frankie, Alice, and Genius—have distinct accents, mannerisms, and personal histories. Unaware that she is shifting between personalities, Frankie alienates friends and family with her contradictory behaviors; she forgets important events; and she struggles to function in society. Ultimately, Frankie finds a therapist and gains insight on her disorder. As Berry said in an interview, "Frankie manages to find her journey of recovery, to live her life and to eventually achieve a full life" (National Alliance on Mental Illness [NAMI] Film Discussion Guide, n.d., p. 13).

Dissociative identity disorder has been observed all over the world and in many cultures (Dorahy et al., 2014). But, when it comes to understanding dissociative states, clinicians must consider cross-cultural and religious differences. For example, some characteristics associated with dissociative identity disorder seem to present themselves in Brazilian spiritist mediums, and it is important to distinguish between a culturally accepted religious practice and disordered behavior (Delmonte, Lucchetti, Moreira-Almeida, & Farias, 2016; Moreira-Almeida, Neto, & Cardeña, 2008).

WHAT CAUSES DISSOCIATIVE DISORDERS? Historically, there has been a great deal of controversy around the apparent increase in diagnoses of dissociative identity disorder in the United States. One possible explanation is that clinicians have been reinforcing the development of these dissociations. In other words, by suggesting the possibility of alternate personalities or using hypnosis to "recover" lost memories, the clinician "cues" the individual to believe an alternate personality is responsible for behaviors (Lynn, Lilienfeld, Merckelbach, Giesbrecht, & van der Kloet, 2012). However, there is now general agreement that trauma plays a causal role in experiences of dissociation, as do factors like fantasy proneness, suggestibility, and neurological deficits (Dalenberg et al., 2014; Lynn et al., 2014). We should also note that these disorders are often linked to childhood abuse and neglect, war, and terrorism in regions throughout the world (American Psychiatric Association, 2013).

Before reading this chapter, you may not have been familiar with dissociative disorders; this is probably not the case with eating disorders, which have received considerable media attention.

Eating Disorders

LO 11 Outline the characteristics of the major eating disorders.

Eating disorders are serious dysfunctions in eating behavior that can involve restricting food consumption, obsessing over weight or body shape, eating too much, and

dissociative identity disorder A psychological disorder that involves the occurrence of two or more distinct personalities within an individual.

Making Weight
Wrestlers in the 120-kilogram (265-pound) weight class weigh in before a tournament. For some athletes, this pressure to maintain a certain body weight may set the stage for the development of eating disorders. Although eating disorders are often associated with "affluent, middle class, young Caucasian females," a substantial proportion of those affected are male. In fact, eating disorders "have been reported in male patients for as long as they have been reported in females" (Murray et al., 2017, p. 1). Craig Ruttle/AP Images.

purging (American Psychiatric Association, 2013). These disorders usually begin in the early teens and typically affect girls, though boys make up a substantial proportion of cases, specifically those of anorexia nervosa, bulimia nervosa, and binge-eating disorder (Raevuori, Keski-Rahkonen, & Hoek, 2014).

ANOREXIA NERVOSA One of the most commonly known eating disorders is **anorexia nervosa,** which is characterized by self-imposed restrictions on calories needed to maintain a healthy weight. These restrictions lead to extremely low body weight in relation to age, sex, development, and physical health. People with anorexia nervosa have an extreme fear of getting heavier, even though their body weight is very low. They often have a distorted sense of body weight and figure, and fail to realize the "seriousness" of their condition (American Psychiatric Association, 2013). Some women stop getting their menstrual periods, a condition called *amenorrhea* (Mehler & Brown, 2015). Other severe symptoms may include brain damage, multi-organ failure, infertility, and thinning of the bones (NIMH, n.d.-b; Mehler & Brown, 2015). Anorexia is associated with the highest death rate of all psychological disorders (Darcy et al., 2012; Smink, van Hoeken, & Hoek, 2012). Over half the deaths associated with anorexia result from medical complications (Mehler & Brown, 2015), and approximately 20% are suicides (Joy, Kussman, & Nattiv, 2016; Smink et al., 2012). Although anorexia nervosa affects mostly women and adolescent girls, males can also be affected, particularly those involved in wrestling, running, or dancing, who are required to maintain a certain weight.

Distorted Perceptions
People with anorexia nervosa may look in the mirror and behold a version of themselves that others never see. Altered perceptions of body size and shape are common features of this disorder (American Psychiatric Association, 2013). Dan Pearson Photography/Alamy Stock Photo.

BULIMIA NERVOSA Another eating disorder is **bulimia nervosa,** which involves recurrent episodes of binge eating, or consuming large amounts of food in short periods of time (more than most people would eat in the same time frame). While bingeing, the person feels a lack of control and thus engages in purging behaviors to prevent weight gain—for example, self-induced vomiting, misuse of laxatives, fasting, or excessive exercise (American Psychiatric Association, 2013). Like anorexia, bulimia more often affects women and girls, but it can also impact males (Peschel et al., 2016). Bulimia has serious health risks, such as high blood pressure, heart disease, and type 2 diabetes (Haedt-Matt & Keel, 2011). Other symptoms include decaying teeth, damage to the throat, gastrointestinal disorders, and electrolyte imbalance, which can lead to a heart attack (Joy et al., 2016; NIMH, n.d.-b). Research indicates that 23% of deaths associated with bulimia nervosa result from suicide (Joy et al., 2016; Smink et al., 2012).

anorexia nervosa An eating disorder identified by significant weight loss, an intense fear of being overweight, a false sense of body image, and a refusal to eat the proper amount of calories to achieve a healthy weight.

bulimia nervosa An eating disorder characterized by extreme overeating followed by purging, with serious health risks.

BINGE-EATING DISORDER Less commonly known, **binge-eating disorder** is characterized by episodes of excessive food consumption—eating more than most people would in the same amount of time and under similar circumstances (American Psychiatric Association, 2013). As in bulimia, one feels unable to control the bingeing, but the excessive weight control and purging behaviors are not present. Psychological effects could include embarrassment about the quantity of food consumed, depression, and guilt after overeating.

We know that eating disorders occur in America—we see evidence of them on television, in magazines, and in everyday life. But are these disorders also observed in India, South Africa, Egypt, and other parts of the world?

ACROSS THE WORLD

A CROSS-CULTURAL LOOK AT EATING DISORDERS Western concepts of beauty, particularly female beauty, often go hand-in-hand with *thinness*. With all this pressure to be slender, it's no wonder eating disorders like anorexia and bulimia are most commonly diagnosed and treated in Western societies such as the United States (**Table 13.7;** Keel & Klump, 2003; Kolara, Rodriguez, Chams, & Hoek, 2016). Psychologists once believed these conditions were mainly seen in "wealthy, white, educated, young women in industrialized Western nations" (Pike & Dunne, 2015, p. 1). But evidence suggests that eating disorders affect men and women of all colors living in countries around the world, from China to Fiji to Pakistan (Agüera et al., 2017; Gerbasi et al., 2014; Pike & Dunne, 2015).

EATING DISORDERS AFFECT MEN AND WOMEN OF ALL COLORS LIVING IN COUNTRIES AROUND THE WORLD

In recent decades, eating disorders have become increasingly common in non-Western countries. This trend often coincides with industrialization, urbanization, and "media-exposure promoting the Western beauty-ideal" (Smink et al., 2012, p. 412). For women, this Western beauty ideal implies thinness; for men, a muscular physique (Pike & Dunne, 2015). As researchers studying teens in Arab countries explain, "The Western standard of beauty has contributed to the preoccupation with thinness and body image dissatisfaction" (Musaiger et al., 2013, p. 165). This influence may be important, but researchers caution against viewing eating disorders as an "export of Western culture" (Pike & Dunne, 2015, p. 11). These disorders generally result from an interaction between many genetic and environmental factors (Bulik, Kleiman, & Yilmaz, 2016).

TABLE 13.7 TREATMENT OF EATING DISORDERS

Treatment Option	Description
Counseling and psychotherapy	Treatment may involve individual, group, or family counseling, which may focus on nutrition, psychological issues, or thoughts and behaviors surrounding the eating disorder.
Health care and medical monitoring	Many eating disorders result in medical crises. Medical monitoring and care are critical.
Drug therapies	While drugs will not restore normal weight, drug therapies may be useful in treating the mood issues (often anxiety and depression) that can accompany eating disorders.

Effective treatment of eating disorders often involves a combination of approaches tailored to the individual. This strategy tends to be more effective than using a sole treatment option. Information from NIMH (n.d.-b).

binge-eating disorder An eating disorder characterized by episodes of extreme overeating, during which a larger amount of food is consumed than most people would eat in a similar amount of time under similar circumstances.

Put Your Heads Together

The content presented in this chapter has the potential to raise personal issues for students—as we've noted, psychological disorders touch many of our lives. In your group, **A**) discuss the most surprising things you learned about abnormal behaviors and psychological disorders, and **B**) describe how your perspective on mental illness has changed as a result of what you have learned in your psychology class this term.

show what you know

1. Individuals with ________________ are likely to anger easily, feel a sense of emptiness, and maintain intense but unstable relationships.
2. Distress and impairment are two identifiers of abnormal behavior. How would the personality disorders fit these criteria for abnormal behavior?
3. ________________ is characterized by two or more distinct personalities within an individual, and a lack of connection among behavior, awareness, memory, cognition, and other functioning.
4. Bulimia nervosa is an eating disorder characterized by:
   a. restrictions of energy intake.
   b. extreme fear of gaining weight, although one's body weight is extremely low.
   c. a distorted sense of body weight and figure.
   d. extreme overeating followed by purging.

✓ CHECK YOUR ANSWERS IN APPENDIX C.

DEFYING STIGMA: ROSS AND MELISSA LEARN TO THRIVE It took years of hard work for Ross to get on top of his disorder. He quit using alcohol, caffeine, nicotine, and marijuana, and imposed a new structure on his life—waking up and going to sleep at the same time each day, eating regular meals, and exercising. He also started being open and honest in his relationships with friends, family, and his therapist. Most important, he confronted his self-hatred, working hard to identify and appreciate things he liked about himself. "What was missing was me being an active member in my treatment," Ross says, "and doing things outside of treatment [to get better]." After graduating cum laude from American University, Ross became a mental health advocate, giving presentations at high schools and colleges across America. Today, he is busy running his own consulting group, Human Power Project, which designs cutting-edge mental health curricula for middle and high schools. His battle with bipolar disorder is ongoing ("I'm not cured," says Ross), but he continues learning better ways to cope.

You Asked, Ross Answers

http://qrs.ly/8z5a5fr

Are you afraid that you may pass on your disorder to your children and does that impact your desire to have them?

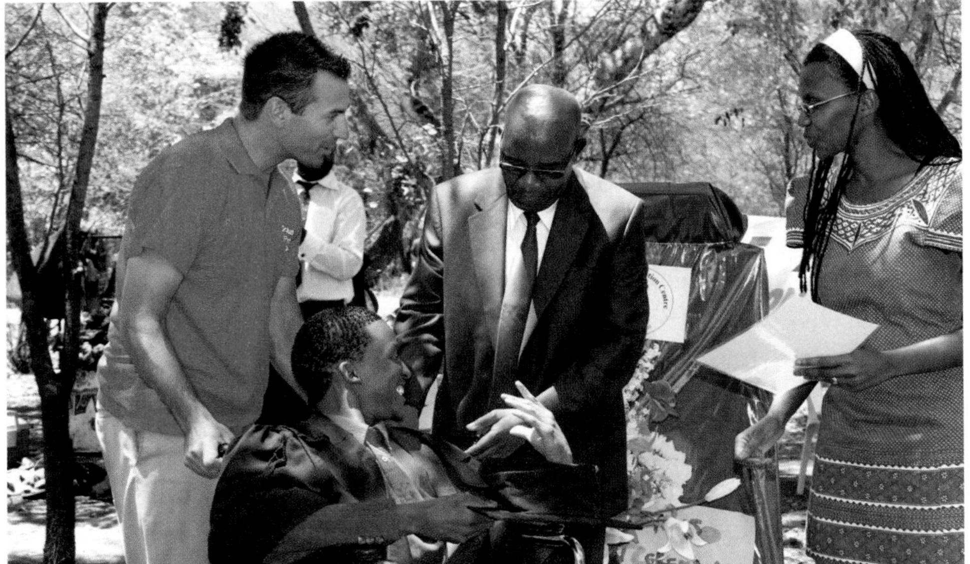

Making a Difference
Ross celebrates graduation day at a center for people with disabilities in Botswana, Africa, where he served in the Peace Corps. After completing his work with the Peace Corps, Ross returned to the United States and founded a consulting group that designs mental health curricula. For more information on Ross' Human Power Project, visit http://humanpowerproject.com. Heidi Pendergast/Ross Szabo.

Voice of Inspiration
As a presenter for the mental health organization Minding Your Mind, Melissa traveled across the country, educating students about mental health issues. She has also published *The People You Meet in Real Life,* which provides first-person accounts of resilient individuals facing a variety of trials and tribulations. The book addresses issues related to mental health, bullying, suicide, cancer, and HIV, sending a message of hope and inspiration. Photo by Ken Alexander.

Shortly after leaving the hospital, Melissa found a therapist who introduced her to cognitive behavioral therapy (CBT), an approach you can learn about in Chapter 14. "He taught me how to live with OCD," says Melissa. "He basically saved my life." Like Ross, Melissa discovered she had a gift for public speaking. She started a mental health awareness group on her college campus, opening a chapter of the national organization Active Minds, and later became a speaker for Minding Your Mind, an organization devoted to educating school communities and families about mental health issues. Melissa is now married and busy caring for her two young children, but she manages to squeeze in public speaking engagements from time to time. Her OCD is still present, but it's under control. Instead of walking through a doorway 20 times, she passes through it twice. And the time she once spent sitting alone in her room meticulously touching objects in sets of 2s, she now spends loving and nurturing her two children, Hope and Parker.

YOUR SCIENTIFIC WORLD is a new application-based feature appearing in every chapter. In these online activities, you will take on role-playing scenarios that encourage you to think critically and apply your knowledge of psychological science to solve a real-world problem. For example: How can you help a friend in need? In this activity, you are trying to support your friend Kris through a difficult time. You want to help Kris, but how do you know if Kris' behavior is abnormal? You can access Your Scientific World activities in LaunchPad. Have fun!

SUMMARY OF CONCEPTS

LO1 Define psychological disorders and outline the criteria used to identify abnormal behavior. (p. 473)

A psychological disorder is a set of behavioral, emotional, and cognitive symptoms that are significantly distressing in terms of social functioning, work endeavors, and other aspects of life. Abnormal behavior falls along a continuum and is based on typicality and the 3 Ds: dysfunction, distress, and deviance. At one end of the continuum are behaviors generally considered normal, while those at the other end are considered abnormal. Conceptions of normal and abnormal are partly determined by culture.

LO2 Summarize the etiology of psychological disorders. (p. 480)

The biopsychosocial perspective provides a model for explaining the causes of psychological disorders, which are complicated and often result from interactions among biological, psychological, and sociocultural factors. Examples of these factors include neurochemical imbalances and genetic predispositions (biological), cognitive activities, personality, and childhood experiences (psychological), and poverty and community support systems (sociocultural).

LO3 Define anxiety disorders and demonstrate an understanding of their causes. (p. 483)

Anxiety disorders are a group of psychological disorders associated with extreme anxiety and/or irrational and debilitating fears. People with panic disorder worry about losing control and having unexpected panic attacks; those with specific phobias fear certain objects or situations; and individuals with agoraphobia are afraid of public transportation, open spaces, retail stores, crowds, or being alone and away from home. Social anxiety disorder (social phobia) is characterized by extreme fear of social situations and scrutiny by others. With generalized anxiety disorder, worries and fears are more widespread, often relating to family, health, school, and other aspects of daily life. Anxiety disorders can develop as a result of environmental factors and genetic predisposition, and are more prevalent in women. They can be culture specific and/or learned.

LO4 Summarize the symptoms and causes of obsessive-compulsive disorder. (p. 486)

Obsessive-compulsive disorder (OCD) includes obsessions and/or compulsions that are very time-consuming (taking more than 1 hour a day) and cause a great deal of distress and disruptions in daily life. An obsession is a thought, urge, or image that occurs repeatedly, is intrusive and unwelcome, and often causes feelings of intense anxiety and distress. Compulsions are behaviors or "mental acts" that a person repeats over and over in an attempt to neutralize obsessions. Sociocultural factors, learning, and biological causes are all involved in the course and maintenance of OCD.

Summarize the symptoms and causes of major depressive disorder. (p. 488)

Symptoms of major depressive disorder include feelings of sadness or hopelessness, reduced pleasure, sleeping excessively or not enough, loss of energy, feelings of worthlessness, or difficulties thinking or concentrating. Symptoms are severe and accompanied by impairment in the ability to perform expected roles. Biological theories suggest the disorder results from a genetic predisposition and irregular activity of neurotransmitters and hormones. Psychological theories focus on feelings of learned helplessness and negative thinking.

Summarize the symptoms and causes of bipolar disorders. (p. 494)

A diagnosis of bipolar I disorder requires that a person experience at least one manic episode, substantial distress, and great impairment. Bipolar II disorder involves at least one major depressive episode as well as a hypomanic episode, which is associated with some of the same symptoms as a manic episode, but is not as severe and does not impair functioning. People with bipolar disorder cycle between extreme highs and lows of emotion and energy that last for days, weeks, or even months.

LO7 Recognize the symptoms of schizophrenia. (p. 496)

Schizophrenia is a disabling disorder that can involve delusions, hallucinations, disorganized speech, abnormal psychomotor behavior, diminished speech, limited emotions, and loss of energy. Delusions are strange and false beliefs that a person maintains even when presented with contradictory evidence. Hallucinations are "perception-like experiences" that the individual believes are real, but that are not evident to others.

LO8 Analyze the biopsychosocial factors that contribute to schizophrenia. (p. 497)

Schizophrenia is a complex psychological disorder that results from biological, psychological, and social factors. Because this disorder stems from an interaction of genes and environment, researchers have a hard time predicting who will be affected. The diathesis–stress model takes these factors into account, with diathesis referring to the inherited disposition, and stress referring to the stressors in the environment (internal and external). Genes, neurotransmitter activity, differences in the brain, and in utero exposure to a virus are all factors that may contribute to the development of schizophrenia.

LO9 Differentiate between antisocial and borderline personality disorders. (p. 501)

People with antisocial personality disorder may seek personal gratification even when it means violating ethics and breaking laws. They sometimes deceive people, and exhibit aggressive, impulsive, or irritable behavior. These individuals lack empathy, and may not show concern for others or feel remorse upon hurting them. Borderline personality disorder is distinguished by an incomplete sense of self and feelings of emptiness. Those affected may exhibit intense anger, have difficulty controlling their temper, and get into physical fights. They can be impulsive, especially where sexual activity, substance abuse, and spending money are concerned. Suicide threats and attempts may occur repeatedly. Both of these personality disorders may result in issues with intimacy and trust.

Identify differences among dissociative disorders. (p. 503)

People suffering from dissociative amnesia seem unable to remember important information about their lives. Dissociative identity disorder, the most complicated and persistent of the dissociative disorders, occurs when an individual experiences two or more distinct personalities. People with either of these disorders may experience dissociative fugue; that is, they wander in a confused and disorganized manner. The commonality in this group of disorders is dissociation, or a disturbance in the normally unified experience of psychological functions involved in memory, consciousness, perception, or identity.

LO 11 Outline the characteristics of the major eating disorders. (p. 504)

Anorexia nervosa is a serious, life-threatening eating disorder characterized by a significantly low body weight in relation to age, sex, development, and physical health; an extreme fear of gaining weight; an altered and distorted sense of body weight and figure; and self-imposed restrictions on calories needed to maintain a healthy weight. Bulimia nervosa is characterized by recurrent episodes of binge eating followed by purging (self-induced vomiting, misuse of laxatives, fasting, or excessive exercise). Binge-eating disorder is characterized by episodes of eating very large amounts of food (more than most people would eat in a similar amount of time under similar circumstances).

KEY TERMS

abnormal behavior, p. 473
agoraphobia, p. 485
anorexia nervosa, p. 505
antisocial personality disorder, p. 501
anxiety disorders, p. 483
binge-eating disorder, p. 506
bipolar disorder, p. 473
borderline personality disorder, p. 502
bulimia nervosa, p. 505
comorbidity, p. 480
compulsion, p. 486
delusions, p. 496
dissociation, p. 503
dissociative amnesia, p. 503
dissociative disorders, p. 503
dissociative fugue, p. 503
dissociative identity disorder, p. 504
dopamine hypothesis, p. 499
generalized anxiety disorder, p. 485
hallucination, p. 497
insanity, p. 476
learned helplessness, p. 493
major depressive disorder, p. 489
manic episodes, p. 494
medical model, p. 481
negative symptoms, p. 497
obsession, p. 486
obsessive-compulsive disorder (OCD), p. 486
panic attack, p. 483
panic disorder, p. 483
personality disorders, p. 501
positive symptoms, p. 497
posttraumatic stress disorder (PTSD), p. 487
psychological disorder, p. 473
psychosis, p. 496
schizophrenia, p. 496
specific phobia, p. 484
stigma, p. 476

TEST PREP ARE YOU READY?

1. A researcher studying psychological disorders from a biological standpoint, focusing on genes, neurochemical imbalances, and problems in the brain, is using an approach known as:
   a. comorbidity.
   b. the medical model.
   c. the diathesis–stress model.
   d. heritability.

2. Melissa experienced recurrent, all-consuming thoughts of disaster and death. These __________ were accompanied by her __________, which included repeating certain behaviors, such as locking her car and entering a room, an even number of times.
   a. obsessions; compulsions
   b. compulsions; obsessions
   c. compulsions; contamination
   d. negative reinforcers; obsessions

3. To help explain the causes of psychological disorders, researchers often use the __________ perspective, which examines the complex interaction of biological, psychological, and sociocultural factors.
   a. medical model
   b. biopsychosocial
   c. etiological
   d. learning

4. A woman is extremely anxious when she is unaccompanied in public. She no longer uses public transportation, refuses to go to the mall, and does not like being away from home. Perhaps she should get evaluated to see if she has which of the following diagnoses?
   a. panic disorder
   b. agoraphobia
   c. social anxiety disorder
   d. specific phobia

5. A neighbor describes a newspaper article she read last night about a man in his twenties who has been known to lie and con others, be aggressive and impulsive, and show little empathy or remorse. These are long-standing traits of his, so it is possible that he has:
   a. borderline personality disorder.
   b. antisocial personality disorder.
   c. dissociative identity disorder.
   d. dissociative amnesia.

6. Rhonda routinely eats large amounts of food that most people could not eat in similar situations or in a similar amount of time. Rhonda often feels an inability to control her eating and frequently eats alone because she is embarrassed by how much she eats. It is likely that Rhonda has a diagnosis of:
   a. anorexia nervosa.
   b. bulimia nervosa.
   c. amenorrhea.
   d. binge-eating disorder.

7. A symptom shared by both major depressive disorder and bipolar disorder is:
   a. hypomania.
   b. manic episodes.
   c. problems associated with sleep.
   d. extremely high self-esteem.

8. A man with schizophrenia has hallucinations and delusions, and seems to be out of touch with reality. A psychologist explains to his mother that her son is experiencing:
   a. mania.
   b. psychosis.
   c. dissociative identity disorder.
   d. hypomania.

9. A woman in your neighborhood develops a reputation for being emotionally unstable, intense, and extremely needy. She also doesn't seem to have a sense of herself and complains of feeling empty. She struggles with intimacy and her relationships are unstable. If these are long-standing traits, which of the following might she be evaluated for?
   a. borderline personality disorder
   b. antisocial personality disorder
   c. bipolar II disorder
   d. major depressive disorder

10. Dissociative identity disorder involves two or more distinct ___________ within an individual.
   a. hypomanic episodes
   b. personalities
   c. panic disorders
   d. psychotic episodes

11. Describe the 3 Ds and give an example of how each may apply to a psychological disorder.

12. What is wrong with the following statement? "My friend is anorexic."

13. How can classical conditioning be used to explain the development of panic disorder?

14. How does negative thinking lead to depression?

15. Briefly summarize the theories of schizophrenia's etiology.

✓ CHECK YOUR ANSWERS IN APPENDIX C.

Go to **LaunchPad** or **Achieve: Read & Practice** to test your understanding with **LearningCurve**.

CHAPTER

14

Thierry Falise/LightRocket via Getty Images.

Treatment of Psychological Disorders

An Introduction to Treatment

VOICES It's a beautiful evening on the Rosebud Indian Reservation in south-central South Dakota. Oceans of prairie grass roll in the wind. The scene could not be more tranquil. But for Chepa,* a young Lakota woman living in this Northern Plains sanctuary, life has been anything but tranquil. For days, Chepa has been tormented by

Breathtaking
The Rosebud Indian Reservation is a vast and beautiful land, but its residents struggle with economic hardship. The poverty rate for American Indians and Alaska Natives is 26.2%, exceeding that of any other racial group in the United States (United States Census Bureau, 2017). Poverty-related stressors can interfere with work, strain personal relationships, and possibly trigger the symptoms of psychological disorders.
Robert VAN DER HILST/Gamma-Rapho via Getty Images.

the voice of a deceased uncle. Hearing voices is nothing unusual in the Lakota spiritual tradition; ancestors visit the living often. But in the case of this young woman, the voice is telling her to kill herself. Chepa has tried to make peace with her uncle's spirit using prayer, pipe ceremony, and other forms of traditional medicine, but he will not be appeased. Increasingly paranoid and withdrawn, Chepa is making her relatives uneasy, so they take her to the home of a trusted neighbor, Dr. Dan Foster. A sun dancer and pipe carrier, Dr. Foster is a respected member of the community. He also happens to be the reservation's lead clinical psychologist.

Upon meeting with Chepa and her family, Dr. Foster realizes that she is having *hallucinations,* **perception-like experiences** she thinks are real, but that are not evident to anyone else. Chepa is also experiencing *delusions,* strange or false beliefs that a person firmly maintains even when presented with evidence to the contrary. And because she is vulnerable to acting on these hallucinations and delusions, she poses a risk to herself, and possibly others. Chepa needs to go to the hospital, and it is Dr. Foster's responsibility to make sure she gets there. "I'm going to make an intervention," Dr. Foster says, "and I'm going to have to do it in a way that's respectful to that person and to the culture, but still respectful to the body of literature and training that I come from as a psychologist."

CONNECTIONS

In **Chapter 3,** we described sensation as the detection of stimuli by sensory organs. Perception is the process through which sensory data are organized, interpreted, and transformed into something meaningful. With hallucinations, the first step does not occur (no apparent physical stimuli).

An ambulance arrives and transports Chepa to the emergency room, where she finds Dr. Foster waiting. He is there to make a diagnosis and develop a treatment plan, but also to provide her with a sense of security, and to do so in the context of a nurturing relationship. "First of all my concern is safety, and secondly my concern is that you realize I am concerned about you," Dr. Foster says. "Whatever it is that we're facing, we are going to make it so that it comes out better than it is right now."

The Sun Dancer

Dr. Dan Foster is the lead clinical psychologist on the Rosebud Reservation. He frequently works with clients suffering from severe emotional trauma, but he maintains a positive outlook. "I feel like the crucible of poverty and pain also is the crucible for transformation," says Dr. Foster, who is a respected member of the Lakota community he serves. Macmillan Learning.

Dr. Foster's observations and assessments point to a complex psychological disorder known as **schizophrenia**. Because Chepa poses an imminent risk to herself, Dr. Foster and his colleagues arrange a transfer to a psychiatric hospital, where she may stay for several days. The medical staff will stabilize her with a drug to help reduce her symptoms, the first of many doses likely to be administered in years to come. When Chepa returns to the reservation, Dr. Foster and his colleagues will offer her treatment designed with her specific needs in mind.

CONNECTIONS

In **Chapter 13,** we reported that schizophrenia is a persistent and debilitating disorder that affects approximately 0.3% to 1% of the population. In this chapter, we will present some approaches to treating people with this diagnosis.

As we learn more about Dr. Foster's work on Rosebud Reservation, be mindful that therapists work with a broad spectrum of psychological issues. Dr. Foster tends to work with people in severe distress, often related to the conditions of extreme poverty that exist on Northern Plains Indian reservations. Some of his clients do not seek therapy, but end up in his care only because friends and relatives intervene. Other therapists spend much of their time helping people with issues such as self-esteem, chronic illness, relationship problems, career challenges, or major life changes like immigration and divorce. Therapy is not just for those with psychological disorders, but for anyone wishing to live a more fulfilling existence.

Dr. Foster, In His Own Words
http://qrs.ly/m65a5fy

Photo: Macmillan Learning.

*The story of Chepa, a Lakota woman with schizophrenia, is hypothetical, but it is based on actual scenarios Dr. Foster has encountered.

Note: Quotations attributed to Dr. Dan Foster and Dr. Nneka Jones Tapia are personal communications.

A Primitive Past

Outline the history of the treatment of psychological disorders.

CONNECTIONS
In **Chapter 13,** we discussed the etiology of psychological disorders. The medical model assumes that disorders have biological causes. The biopsychosocial perspective suggests disorders result from an interaction of biological, psychological, and sociocultural factors.

Psychologists use various **models** to explain abnormal behavior and psychological disorders. As our understanding of disorders has changed over time, so have methods of treatment. Many early attempts to cure mental illness were inhumane and unproven. According to one theory, Stone Age people believed psychological disorders were caused by possession with demons and evil spirits. They may have practiced *trephination,* or drilling of holes in the skull, perhaps to create exit routes for evil spirits (Maher & Maher, 2003). Trephination was used beyond the Stone Age, and some have speculated this "earliest known" surgical procedure was intended to treat "madness, idiocy, moral degeneration, headache, [and used for] the removal of foreign bodies, and the release of pressures, airs, vapours, and humours" (Wickens, 2015, p. 8).

The Reformer
American schoolteacher Dorothea Dix led the nation's "mental hygiene movement," an effort to improve the treatment of people living in institutions. Her advocacy began in the mid-1800s, when people in some mental hospitals were chained, beaten, and locked in cages (Parry, 2006).
National Portrait Gallery, Smithsonian Institution/Art Resource, NY.

ASYLUMS OR PRISONS? A major shift came in the 16th century. Religious groups began creating *asylums,* special places to house and treat people with psychological disorders. However, these asylums were overcrowded and resembled prisons, with inmates chained in dungeonlike cells, starved, and subjected to sweltering heat and frigid cold. During the French Revolution, physician Philippe Pinel (1745–1826) began working in Paris asylums. Horrified by the conditions he observed, Pinel removed the inmates' chains and insisted they be treated more humanely (Frances, 2016; Maher & Maher, 2003). The idea of using "moral treatment," or respect and kindness instead of harsh methods, spread throughout Europe and America (Frances, 2016; Routh & Reisman, 2003). In the mid- to late 1800s, an American schoolteacher named Dorothea Dix (1802–1887) vigorously championed the "mental hygiene movement," a campaign to reform asylums in the United States. Appalled by what she witnessed in American prisons and institutions housing the poor, including the caging of naked inmates, Dix helped establish and upgrade dozens of state mental hospitals (Parry, 2006; Whitaker, 2015). Despite the good intentions of reformers like Pinel and Dix, many institutions eventually deteriorated into overcrowded warehouses for people with psychological disorders.

In the early 1900s, psychiatrists began to realize that mental health problems existed outside asylums—among ordinary, functioning people. Mental health professionals were starting to view mental health as a continuum. Their effort to classify psychological disorders based on symptoms and progression ultimately led to the creation of the first ***Diagnostic and Statistical Manual of Mental Disorders*** in 1952 (*DSM;* American Psychiatric Association, 1952; Pierre, 2012; Shorter, 2015).

CONNECTIONS
In **Chapter 13,** we noted that most mental health professionals in the United States use the *DSM-5.* The *DSM-5* is a classification system designed to help clinicians ensure accurate and consistent diagnoses based on the observation of symptoms. This manual does not include information on treatment.

RETURN TO THE COMMUNITY In the 1950s and 60s, the United States saw a mass exodus of American patients out of institutions and back into the community (**Figure 14.1**). This **deinstitutionalization** was partly the result of a movement to reduce the social isolation of people with psychological disorders and integrate them into society. Deinstitutionalization was also made possible by the introduction of medications that reduced some symptoms of severe psychological disorders (Sisti, Segal, & Emanuel, 2015). Thanks to these new drugs, many people who had previously needed constant care and supervision began caring for themselves and managing their own medications (Harrington, 2012).

deinstitutionalization The mass movement of patients with psychological disorders out of institutions, and the attempt to reintegrate them into the community.

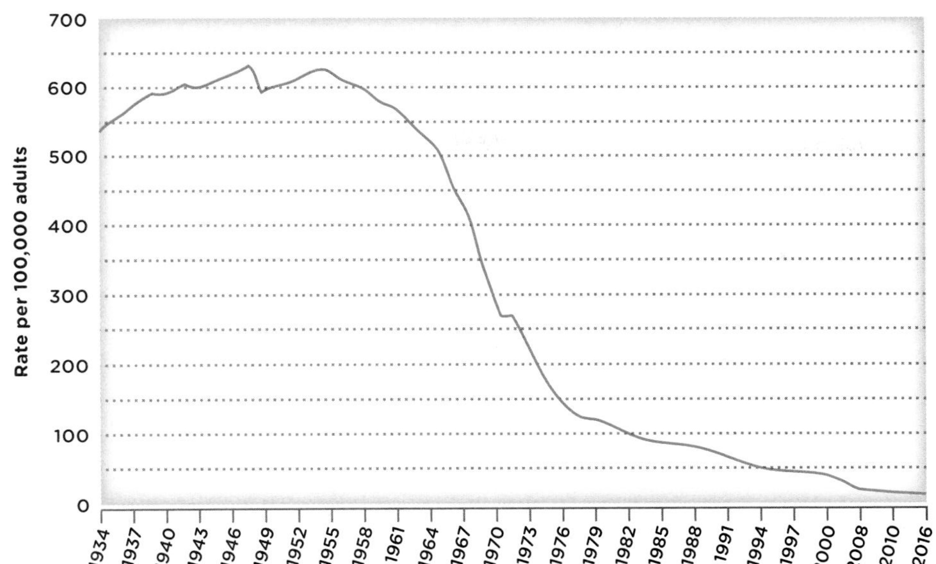

FIGURE 14.1
Deinstitutionalization
Since the 1950s, the rate of institutionalization has declined dramatically. Data from Torrey, Fuller, Geller, Jacobs, & Rogasta (2012) and Fuller, Sinclair, Geller, Quanbeck, & Snook (2016).

Where to Now?

In spite of the deinstitutionalization movement, psychiatric hospitals and institutions continue to play an important role in the treatment of psychological disorders. The scenario involving Dr. Foster and Chepa may be unusual in some respects, but not when it comes to the initiation of treatment. For someone experiencing a dangerous **psychotic episode**, the standard approach includes a stay in a psychiatric facility. Some of these admissions are voluntary; others are not.

CONNECTIONS

In **Chapter 13,** we described psychotic symptoms, such as hallucinations and delusions. Psychotic episodes can be risky for people experiencing them—as well as those nearby. Individuals experiencing psychosis may be admitted to a hospital against their will. Hospitals have procedures in place to ensure that involuntary admissions are ethical.

Typically, a person is ready to leave the hospital after a few days or weeks, but many people in crisis are released after just a few hours, due to the high cost of treatment and financial pressures on hospitals. As critics contend, patients are being "held hostage" by the financial needs of insurance companies and physicians (Decker, 2016a). The length of a hospital stay is often determined by what insurance will cover, rather than what a patient needs, and restricted by the severe shortage of available beds. Many psychiatric facilities simply cannot accommodate the scores of people seeking treatment (Sisti et al., 2015). Approximately 4% of American adults (around 10 million people) suffer from serious and "treatment-resistant psychotic disorders" (often severe schizophrenia or bipolar disorder). These individuals lack insight, often suffer from psychotic symptoms, and can pose a risk to themselves and others, yet the great majority lack access to long-term care (Sisti et al., 2015).

With such a shortage of mental health facilities, where do many people needing treatment end up? A substantial number live on the street. According to the U.S. Department of Housing and Urban Development (2017), about 20% of the homeless population (over 100,000 people) suffers from severe mental illness. A larger number of mentally ill individuals are locked up in jails and prisons, where they have limited access to psychological care (Frances, 2016). But things may be changing, thanks to visionaries like Dr. Nneka Jones Tapia.

JAIL OR MENTAL HOSPITAL? Dr. Jones Tapia is the executive director of the Cook County Jail in Chicago. Home to about 7,500 inmates at any given time, Cook County is the "largest single-site jail in the country" (Cook County Sheriff's Office, n.d., para. 1). According to Dr. Jones Tapia, about 20–24% of the detainees have a history of mental illness or are currently exhibiting symptoms. There is nothing unusual about this statistic, as America's jails and prisons house a huge number of people with psychological disorders. In fact, there are far more people with "serious mental illnesses" living in correctional facilities than in treatment

Inspiring Psychologist
Dr. Nneka Jones Tapia stands in a cell of Chicago's Cook County Jail. Unlike most jail wardens, who have backgrounds in criminal justice, Dr. Jones Tapia is a doctorate-level clinical psychologist (Decker, 2016b). Her training is invaluable in this setting, as mental illness is common in U.S. correctional institutions. For example, a study on state prisons in Iowa found that nearly half of all inmates had been diagnosed with at least one disorder (Al-Rousan, Rubenstein, Sieleni, Deol, & Wallace, 2017). JOSHUA LOTT/The New York Times/Redux.

institutions in this country (Al-Rousan, Rubenstein, Sieleni, Deol, & Wallace, 2017; Torrey et al., 2010).

"We have a crisis at hand right now with the number of individuals with mental illness coming into correctional institutions," says Dr. Jones Tapia, one of the first clinical psychologists to be placed in charge of a U.S. jail. Most correctional facilities are not set up to provide psychological treatment on a large scale (many do not even have a full-time psychologist), but Cook County is setting an inspiring example. With the support of Sheriff Tom Dart and the Cook County Health and Hospitals System, Dr. Jones Tapia has created a comprehensive system for identifying and treating psychological disorders among inmates. Every man and woman admitted to the facility undergoes a psychological assessment performed by a licensed mental health professional. (Mental health screening occurs at other correctional facilities, but is often done by correctional officers or nurses.) The detainee is then assigned to a living arrangement appropriate for his or her level of functioning and, if necessary, a psychological treatment plan. Inmates participate in a variety of mental health programs, including anger management, art therapy, yoga, and meditation. Some of these individuals continue receiving care after they have left jail, as Dr. Jones Tapia and her team have set up two clinics to provide ongoing care to former detainees in need. 

We will learn more about Dr. Jones Tapia and her work in the pages to come, but first let's explore what psychological treatment is all about.

Treatment Today

LO 2 Explain how the main approaches to therapy differ and identify their common goal.

The word "psychotherapy" derives from the Ancient Greek *psychē,* meaning "soul," and *therapeuō,* meaning "to heal" (Brownell, 2010), and there are many ways to go about this healing of the soul. Some therapies promote increased awareness of self and environment: You need to understand the origins of your problems in order to deal with them. Others focus on active steps toward behavioral change: The key to resolving issues is not so much understanding their origins, but changing the thoughts and behaviors directly preceding them. Finally, there are interventions aimed at correcting disorders from a biological standpoint. Such treatments often take the form of medication, and may be combined with other therapies.

These approaches share many common features: The relationship between the client and the treatment provider is critical, as is the hope that things will get better (Feinstein, Heiman, & Yager, 2015; Snyder et al., 2000). They also have a common goal, that is, to reduce symptoms and increase the quality of life.

Therapies can be categorized along three major dimensions (**Infographic 14.1**). The first dimension is the manner of delivery—whether therapy is administered to an *individual* or a *group*. The second dimension is the treatment approach, which can be biomedical or psychological. **Biomedical therapy** refers to drugs and other medical interventions that target the biological basis of a disorder. **Psychotherapy,** or "talk therapy," zeroes in on psychological factors. The third dimension of therapy is the theoretical perspective, or approach. We can group the various approaches into two broad categories: **insight therapies,** which aim to increase awareness of self and environment, and **behavior therapy,** which focuses on behavioral change. As you learn about the many forms of therapy, keep in mind that therapists often incorporate various perspectives (Frances, 2016). In fact, about 25% to 50% of therapists use a

biomedical therapy Drugs and other physical interventions that target the biological processes underlying psychological disorders; primary goal is to reduce symptoms.

psychotherapy "Talk therapy"; a treatment approach in which a client works with a mental health professional to reduce psychological symptoms and improve his or her quality of life.

insight therapies Psychotherapies aimed at increasing awareness of self and environment.

behavior therapy A type of therapy that focuses on behavioral change.

According to some estimates, there exist at least 500 specific types of psychotherapy (Lilienfeld & Arkowitz, 2012, September 1). Therapies can be categorized along three major dimensions: manner of delivery, treatment approach, and theoretical perspective. Here we see where different therapies fall along these dimensions. As many as half of today's therapists use a combined approach (Norcross & Beutler, 2014), intergrating multiple methods. The eclectic or holistic style may incorporate both biomedical and psychological treatments. All therapies share the common goal of reducing symptoms and increasing the quality of life.

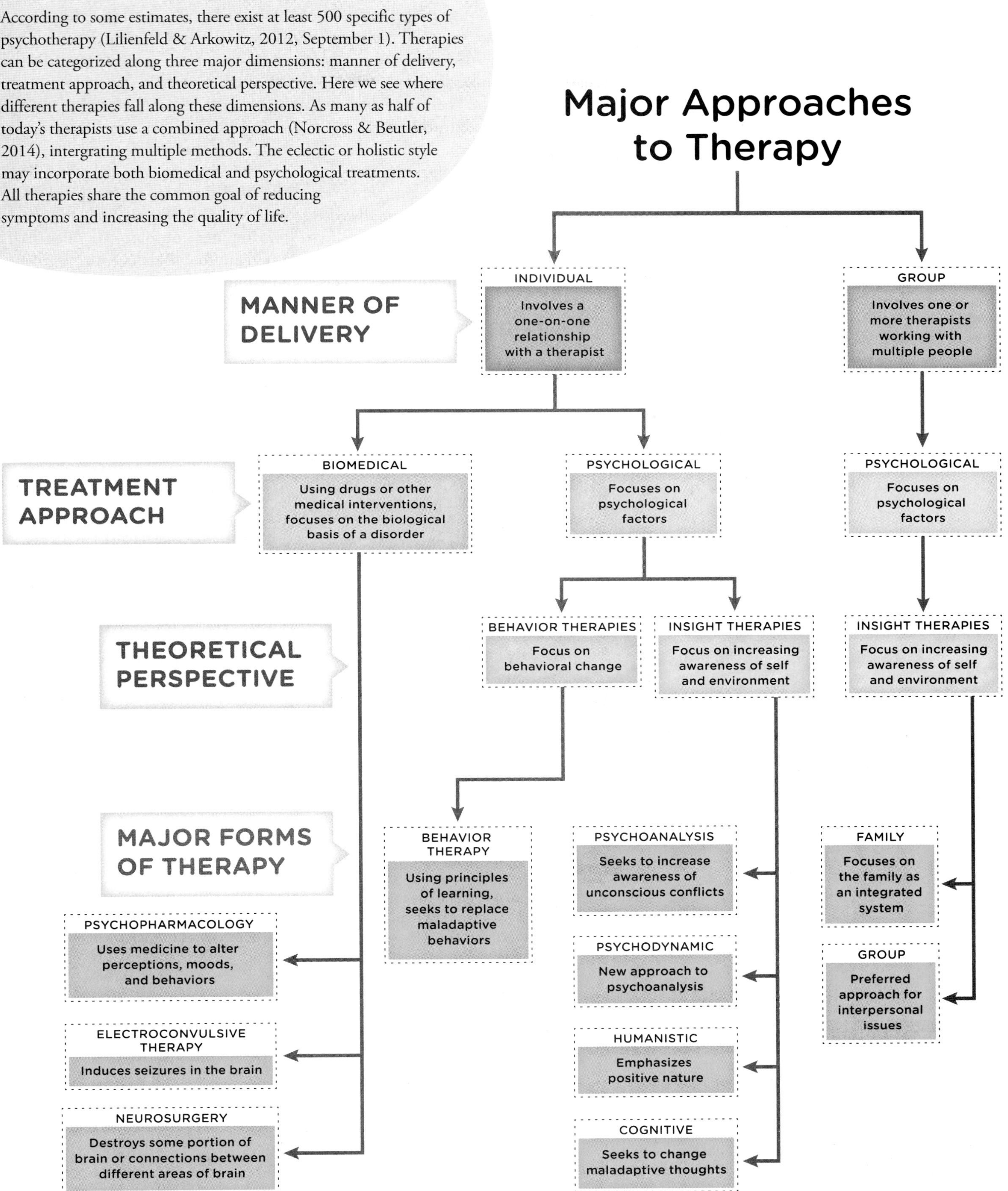

Major Approaches to Therapy
MANNER OF DELIVERY
INDIVIDUAL
Involves a one-on-one relationship with a therapist
GROUP
Involves one or more therapists working with multiple people
TREATMENT APPROACH
BIOMEDICAL
Using drugs or other medical interventions, focuses on the biological basis of a disorder
PSYCHOLOGICAL
Focuses on psychological factors
PSYCHOLOGICAL
Focuses on psychological factors
THEORETICAL PERSPECTIVE
BEHAVIOR THERAPIES
Focus on behavioral change
INSIGHT THERAPIES
Focus on increasing awareness of self and environment
INSIGHT THERAPIES
Focus on increasing awareness of self and environment
MAJOR FORMS OF THERAPY
PSYCHOPHARMACOLOGY
Uses medicine to alter perceptions, moods, and behaviors
ELECTROCONVULSIVE THERAPY
Induces seizures in the brain
NEUROSURGERY
Destroys some portion of brain or connections between different areas of brain
BEHAVIOR THERAPY
Using principles of learning, seeks to replace maladaptive behaviors
PSYCHOANALYSIS
Seeks to increase awareness of unconscious conflicts
PSYCHODYNAMIC
New approach to psychoanalysis
HUMANISTIC
Emphasizes positive nature
COGNITIVE
Seeks to change maladaptive thoughts
FAMILY
Focuses on the family as an integrated system
GROUP
Preferred approach for interpersonal issues

synonyms

eclectic approach to therapy Integrative approach to therapy, holistic approach to therapy

combined approach (Norcross & Beutler, 2014). Even those who are trained in one discipline may integrate multiple methods, tailoring treatment for each client with an **eclectic approach to therapy**. The American Psychological Association (APA) highlights the importance of using **evidence-based practice,** that is, choosing treatment that integrates the "best available" research findings, "clinical expertise," and knowledge of a patient's culture, values, and preferences (APA Presidential Task Force on Evidence-Based Practice, 2006; Bufka & Halfond, 2016).

In addition to describing the various approaches to treatment, we will examine how well they work. *Outcome research,* which evaluates the success of therapies, is a complicated endeavor. First, it is not always easy to pinpoint the meaning of success, or operationalize it. Should we measure self-esteem, happiness, or some other benchmark? Second, it can be difficult for clinicians to remain **free of bias** (both positive and negative) when reporting on the successes and failures of clients. One relatively new and promising approach to measuring success is feedback-informed treatment (FIT). Clients answer questionnaires before and after sessions, and the data are used to determine how well the therapy is working and identify areas that need improvement (DeAngelis, 2018, January). **Table 14.1** describes some of the variables that may impact the success of psychotherapy.

CONNECTIONS

In **Chapter 11,** we discussed the self-serving bias, which is the tendency for people to attribute their successes to internal characteristics and their failures to environmental factors. Clinicians may fall prey to this type of bias, taking credit for their clients' successes but blaming them for failures.

TABLE 14.1 VARIABLES AFFECTING OUTCOMES OF PSYCHOTHERAPY

Variables That *Will* Improve Outcomes	Variables *Likely* to Improve Outcomes	Variables That *Could* Improve Outcomes
Hope	Therapist and client agreement on goals	Genuineness of therapist
Optimistic expectations	Teamwork	Emotional intelligence of therapist
Positive partnerships	Therapist's positive regard	Therapist's ability to mend alliance "ruptures"
Therapist empathy	Positive events in the client's life	Therapist's ability to manage his or her own emotional reactions toward a client

What determines the outcome of psychotherapy? Listed here are several factors that come into play. As you can see, some are more critical than others. Information from Feinstein, Heiman, & Yager (2015).

Put Your Heads Together

Before you team up, **A)** outline the major approaches to therapy discussed in this section. Then in your group, **B)** imagine a man who is terrified of flying, and consider the obstacles he faces getting over his fear. **C)** Explain how one of the approaches to therapy might be used for this individual.

show what you know

1. A therapist writes a letter to the editor in support of more funding for mental health facilities, stating that all therapies share the same goal of reducing ______________ and increasing the quality of life.
   a. symptoms
   b. combined approaches
   c. biomedical therapy
   d. the number of asylums

2. Dorothea Dix championed the ______________, a campaign to reform asylums in America.

3. What were some of the consequences of deinstitutionalization?

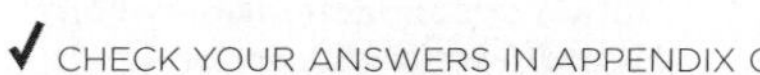
CHECK YOUR ANSWERS IN APPENDIX C.

Insight Therapies

"IMPROVEMENTS, MINOR AS THEY MAY BE" Before becoming the warden at Cook County, Dr. Jones Tapia worked as the jail's staff psychologist, and later as its chief psychologist. It was not easy providing therapy in this setting, because clients tend to come and go without much warning. Unlike prison, where inmates live for years at time, jail is only intended for people who are awaiting trial or serving sentences for less than 365 days. Most inmates at Cook County are awaiting trial, which means they are presumed innocent. Eventually, they will be convicted and sent to prison, or acquitted and released back into the community. "Here, you don't know how much time you have with an individual, and so you want to be careful not to open up wounds that you're unable to close," says Dr. Jones Tapia. For inmates who are ready and willing, the therapist can help them piece together the past and figure out where things went wrong. The goal, according to Dr. Jones Tapia, is to "develop some insight on how they can make some improvements, minor as they may be, but improvements to give them a better outlook on life, and a better trajectory, even if they go to prison."

Developing this type of self-awareness is one of the unifying goals of the insight therapies, which we will now explore.

Taking It to the Couch: Psychoanalysis

LO 3 Describe how psychoanalysis differs from psychodynamic therapy.

When imagining the stereotypical therapy session, many people picture a person reclining on a couch and talking about dreams and childhood memories. Modern-day therapy generally does not resemble this image. But if we could travel back in time to 1930s Vienna, Austria, and sit on Sigmund Freud's sofa, we just might see this stereotype come to life.

FREUD AND THE UNCONSCIOUS Freud (1900/1953) proposed that humans are motivated by animal-like drives that are aggressive and sexual in nature. But acting on these drives is not always compatible with social norms, so they create conflict and get pushed below the surface, or **repressed**. These drives simmer beneath conscious awareness, affecting our moods and behaviors. And when we can no longer keep them at bay, the result may be disordered behavior, as seen with phobias, obsessions, and panic attacks (Solms, 2006, April/May). To help patients deal with these drives, Freud created *psychoanalysis,* the first formal system of psychotherapy. Psychoanalysis attempts to increase awareness of unconscious conflicts, thus making it possible to address and work through them.

Dreams, according to Freud, are a pathway to unconscious thoughts and desires (Freud, 1900/1953). The overt material of a dream (what we remember upon waking) is called the *manifest content,* and it can disguise a deeper meaning, or *latent content.* Because this latent content often consists of uncomfortable issues and desires, it is hidden from awareness (Chapter 4). But with the help of a therapist, it can be unearthed. Freud would often use dreams as a launching pad for **free association,** a therapy technique in which a patient says anything and everything that comes to mind, regardless of how silly, bizarre, or inappropriate it may seem. Freud believed this seemingly directionless train of thought would lead to clues about the patient's

CONNECTIONS

In **Chapter 10,** we introduced the concept of repression, a defense mechanism through which the ego moves anxiety-provoking thoughts, memories, or feelings from the conscious to unconscious level. Here, we will see how psychoanalysis helps uncover some of these unconscious processes.

eclectic approach to therapy Drawing on multiple theories and approaches to tailor treatment for a client.

evidence-based practice Making decisions about treatment that integrate valuable research findings, clinical expertise, and knowledge of a patient's culture, values, and preferences.

free association A psychoanalytic technique in which a patient says anything that comes to mind.

"It's that same dream, where I'm drowning in a bowl of noodles."

Leo Cullum The New Yorker Collection/The Cartoon Bank.

unconscious. Piecing together the hints he gathered from dreams, free association, and other parts of therapy sessions, Freud would identify and make inferences about the unconscious conflicts driving the patient's behavior. He called this investigative work **interpretation.** When the time seemed right, Freud would share his interpretations, increasing his patients' self-awareness and helping them come to terms with conflicts (Freud, 1900/1953).

You might be wondering what behaviors Freud considered signs of unconscious conflict. One indicator is **resistance,** a patient's unwillingness to cooperate in therapy. Examples of resistance might include arriving late or "forgetting" appointments, or becoming angry or agitated when certain topics arise. Resistance is a crucial step in psychoanalysis because it means the discussion might be veering close to something that makes the patient feel uncomfortable or threatened, like a critical memory or conflict causing distress. If resistance occurs, the job of the therapist is to help the patient identify its unconscious roots.

Another sign of unconscious conflict is **transference,** which occurs when patients react to therapists as if they were their parents or other important people from childhood. Suppose a client relates to Dr. Jones Tapia as if she were his mother. The client hated letting his mom down, so he resists telling Dr. Jones Tapia things he suspects would disappoint her. Transference can be a good thing, especially when it illuminates the unconscious conflicts fueling a patient's behaviors (Hoffman, 2009). One of the reasons Freud sat off to the side and out of a patient's sight was to encourage transference. With Freud in this neutral position, patients would have an easier time **projecting** their unconscious conflicts and feelings onto him.

CONNECTIONS

In **Chapter 10,** we presented projective personality tests. These assessments are based on the premise that the test taker will project unconscious conflicts onto the test material. It is up to the therapist to try to uncover these underlying issues. In the context of therapy, a patient may project conflicts onto the therapist.

Goodbye, Couch: Psychodynamic Therapy

Freudian theories have been heavily criticized, and many contemporary psychologists do not identify themselves as psychoanalysts. Still, Freud left an indelible mark on the field of psychology, and his work paved the way for a briefer approach called **psychodynamic therapy.** This newer form of insight therapy has been evolving over the last 30 to 40 years, incorporating many of Freud's core themes, including the idea

The Famous Couch
Freud's psychoanalytic couch appears on display at the Freud Museum in London. All of Freud's patients reclined on this piece of furniture, which is reportedly quite comfortable with its soft cushions and Iranian rug cover (Freud Museum, n.d., para. 4). Freud sat in the chair at the head of the couch, close but not within view of his patient. Bjanka Kadic/Alamy Stock Photo.

interpretation A psychoanalytic technique used to explore unconscious conflicts driving behavior.

resistance A patient's unwillingness to cooperate in therapy; a sign of unconscious conflict.

that personality and behaviors frequently can be traced to unconscious conflicts and experiences from the past.

However, **psychodynamic therapy** breaks from traditional psychoanalysis in important ways. Psychodynamic therapists tend to see clients once a week for several months. (Psychoanalysts may meet with their clients many times a week for years.) And instead of sitting quietly off to the side as the client reclines on a couch, the psychodynamic therapist sits face-to-face with the client, giving feedback and sometimes advice. Frequently, the goal of psychodynamic therapy is to understand and resolve a specific, current problem.

CONNECTIONS

In **Chapter 10,** we introduced the neo-Freudians, who disagreed with Freud's main ideas, including his singular focus on sex and aggression, his negative view of human nature, and his idea that personality is set by the end of childhood. Here, we can see that psychodynamic therapy grew out of discontent with Freud's ideas about treatment.

For many years, psychodynamic therapists treated clients without much evidence to back up their approach (Levy & Ablon, 2010, February 23). More recently, researchers have been testing the effects of psychodynamic therapy with rigorous scientific methods, and their results are encouraging (Leichsenring, Abbass, et al., 2016; Leichsenring, Luyten, et al., 2015; Levy, Hilsenroth, & Owen, 2015). **Randomized controlled trials** suggest that psychodynamic psychotherapy is effective for treating an array of disorders, including depression, panic disorder, and eating disorders (Driessen et al., 2015; Leichsenring & Rabung, 2008; Milrod et al., 2007), and the benefits may last long after treatment has ended (Shedler, 2010).

CONNECTIONS

In **Chapter 1,** we described the experimental method, a research design that can uncover cause-and-effect relationships. Here, we see how this method is used to study therapy outcomes. In randomized controlled trials, participants are randomly assigned to treatment and control groups. The independent variable is the type of treatment, and the dependent variables are measures of their effectiveness.

You Can Do It! Humanistic Therapy

GREATNESS IN ALL OF US Growing up in a small North Carolina town, Dr. Jones Tapia was always aware that her family did not look "perfect" from the outside. "[My father] was arrested for possession of marijuana a few times and spent a considerable amount of my early childhood in prison," she says. "But that did not take away from my sense of family, and it definitely did not negatively impact my relationship with my dad." On the weekends, her mother would prepare food and the whole family would go to the prison for Sunday dinner. "That was our version of normal," says Dr. Jones Tapia, who credits her unyielding optimism to a strong sense of spirituality and the love and support she has received from friends, teachers, and especially her mother and father. "They taught us very early on that, despite what anyone says, despite what our life looks like in the here and now, we can be successful." This sense of hope, along with her extraordinary capacity for empathy, has driven Dr. Jones Tapia's work as a therapist. In many ways, she exemplifies the humanistic perspective of psychology. 

On Her Way
When Dr. Jones Tapia was applying to graduate school, a professor told her she would never make it through her master's program while working full-time. "For me that wasn't an option. I needed to make money," says Dr. Jones Tapia. Fortunately, another professor encouraged and believed in her. "You and I both know that's not true," she remembers him saying. "You have the potential to do whatever you want to do." Not only did Dr. Jones Tapia manage to balance a full-time job with her master's program; she was essentially a straight-A student. Courtesy Dr. Nneka Jones Tapia.

LO 4 Outline the principles and characteristics of humanistic therapy.

For the first half of the 20th century, most psychotherapists leaned on Freud's theoretical framework. But in the 1950s, some psychologists began to question his dark view of human nature and his approach to treating clients. A new perspective began to

transference A type of resistance that occurs when a patient reacts to a therapist as if dealing with parents or other caregivers from childhood.

psychodynamic therapy A type of insight therapy that incorporates core psychoanalytic themes, including the importance of unconscious conflicts and experiences from the past.

CONNECTIONS

In **Chapter 1,** we introduced the field of positive psychology, which draws attention to human strengths and potential for growth. The humanistic perspective was a forerunner to positive psychology. Humanistic therapy recognizes and strives to harness this positive potential.

take shape, one that focused on the positive aspects of human nature. This **humanistic movement** was championed by American psychotherapist Carl Rogers, who believed that human beings are inherently good and inclined toward growth. "It has been my experience that persons have a basically positive direction," he wrote in his widely popular book *On Becoming a Person* (Rogers, 1961, p. 26). Rogers recognized that people have basic biological "demands" for food and sex, but he also saw that we have powerful desires to form close relationships, treat others with warmth and tenderness, and grow and mature as individuals (Rogers, 1961).

With this optimistic spirit, Rogers and others pioneered several types of insight therapy collectively known as **humanistic therapy,** which emphasizes the positive nature of humankind. Unlike psychoanalysis, which tends to focus on the distant past, humanistic therapy concentrates on the present, seeking to identify and address current problems. And rather than digging up unconscious thoughts and feelings, humanistic therapy emphasizes the conscious experience: What's going on in your mind right now?

LO 5 Describe person-centered therapy.

synonyms

person-centered therapy client-centered therapy, Rogerian therapy

PERSON-CENTERED THERAPY Rogers' distinct form of humanistic therapy is known as **person-centered therapy**, and it closely follows his theory of personality. According to Rogers, humans have an innate drive to become fully functioning. We all have a natural tendency toward growth and *self-actualization,* or achieving our full potential. But expectations from family and society can stifle the process. Such external factors often cause an *incongruence,* or a mismatch, between the client's *ideal self* (often involving unrealistic expectations of who she should be) and *real self* (the way the client views herself). One of the main goals of treatment is to reduce the incongruence between these two selves. Person-centered therapy also aims to create a warm and accepting relationship between therapist and client, and to help clients see they have the power to make changes in their lives and follow a path of positive growth.

Person-centered therapy is **nondirective,** meaning the therapist follows the lead of the client. As Rogers once wrote, "It is the *client* who knows what hurts, what directions to go, what problems are crucial, what experiences have been deeply buried" (Rogers, 1961, pp. 11–12). Sitting face-to-face with a client, the therapist's main job is to "be there" for that person through **empathy,** unconditional positive regard, **genuineness,** and **active listening**—all essential components of the therapeutic alliance (**Table 14.2**). This **therapeutic alliance** is based on mutual respect and caring between the therapist and the client, and it provides a safe place for self-exploration.

Part of Rogers' philosophy was his refusal to identify the people he worked with as "patients" (Rogers, 1951). Patients depend on doctors to make decisions for them, or at least give them instructions. In Rogers' mind, it was the patient who had the answers, not the therapist. So he began using the term *client* and eventually settled on the term *person.*

"To me, Rogerian therapy is the essence of good clinical work in a correctional institution," says Dr. Jones Tapia. Detainees are often defined by their alleged crimes, she notes: "If you're accused of a murder, people will see you as a murderer, and people will respond to you as such." To remain as neutral as possible, Dr. Jones Tapia does not try to find out what charges inmates are facing before she meets with them. She also employs unconditional positive regard—total acceptance of a person regardless of his behaviors, beliefs, and words. "Everybody has a story, and it's not meant for me to judge that person based off of whatever reason they are in my custody," says Dr. Jones Tapia. "Many of the detainees that I encounter have had histories of severe

humanistic therapy A type of insight therapy that emphasizes the positive nature of humankind.

person-centered therapy A form of humanistic therapy developed by Rogers; aimed at helping clients achieve their full potential.

nondirective A technique used in person-centered therapy whereby the therapist follows the lead of the client during treatment sessions.

empathy The ability to feel what a person is experiencing by attempting to observe the world through his or her eyes.

genuineness The ability to respond to a client in an authentic way rather than hiding behind a polite or professional mask.

active listening The ability to pick up on the content and emotions behind words in order to understand a client's perspective, often by echoing the main point of what the client says.

therapeutic alliance A warm and accepting client–therapist relationship that serves as a safe place for self-exploration.

TABLE 14.2 BUILDING A THERAPEUTIC ALLIANCE

Components	Description
Empathy	The ability to feel what a client is experiencing; seeing the world through the client's eyes (Rogers, 1951); therapist perceives feelings and experiences from "inside" the client (Rogers, 1961)
Unconditional positive regard	Total acceptance of a client no matter how distasteful the client's behaviors, beliefs, and words may be (see Chapter 10)
Genuineness	Being authentic, responding to a client in a way that is real rather than hiding behind a polite or professional mask; knowing exactly where the therapist stands, allowing the client to feel secure enough to open up (Rogers, 1961)
Active listening	Picking up on the content and emotions behind words in order to understand a client's point of view; reflection, or echoing the main point of what a client says

Humanist Carl Rogers believed it was critical to establish a strong and trusting therapist-client relationship. The key elements of a therapeutic alliance are listed above.

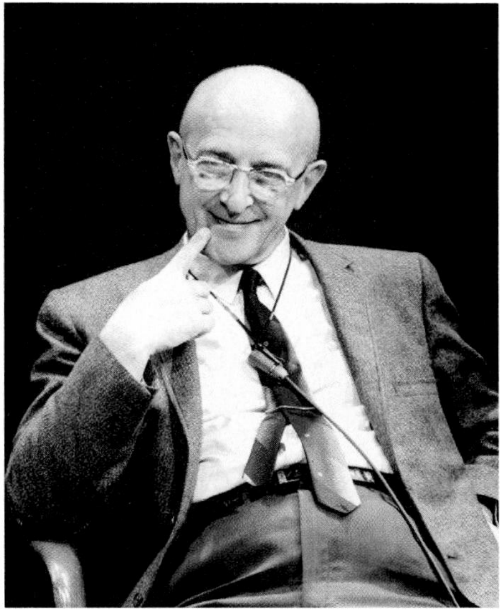

I Believe in You
Carl Rogers leads a group therapy session in 1966. One of the founders of humanism, Rogers firmly believed that all people are fundamentally good and capable of self-actualization, or becoming all that they can be. Michael Rougier/The LIFE Picture Collection/Getty Images.

abuse and neglect, and so just beyond their crimes, they have had circumstances and interactions with people that are negative at best." Some inmates have never experienced unconditional positive regard, she notes, but this approach makes them feel more comfortable, enables them to talk openly, and ultimately helps them develop more self-awareness.

TAKING STOCK: AN APPRAISAL OF INSIGHT THERAPY The insight therapies we have explored—psychoanalysis, psychodynamic therapy, and humanistic therapy—have had a profound impact on the field. Freudian theories help therapists understand how past experiences and conflicts influence behavior; psychodynamic therapy may be effective for treating a variety of disorders; humanistic therapy is useful for people dealing with complex and diverse problems, and in many cases its success rivals that of other methods (Angus, Watson, Elliott, Schneider, & Timulak, 2015; Corey, 2017). Humanist techniques, in particular, have helped therapists of all persuasions build stronger relationships with clients and create positive therapeutic environments.

As with all approaches, the insight therapies have their limitations. Freud's theories, in particular, have come under sharp criticism because they lack scientific support. Neither therapists nor patients know if they are tapping into the patients' unconscious because it is made up of thoughts, memories, and desires that are often beyond awareness and hard to operationalize (Parth & Loeffler-Stastka, 2015). Humanistic therapy is difficult to study for similar reasons: The methodology has not been operationalized, and its use varies from one therapist to the next. Finally, insight therapies demand high levels of verbal expression and awareness of self and environment. Symptoms like hallucinations or delusions might interfere with these requirements.

show what you know

1. ______________ therapy focuses on the positive nature of human beings and on the here and now.
   a. Humanistic
   b. Psychoanalytic
   c. Psychodynamic
   d. Free association

2. How do psychoanalytic and psychodynamic therapies differ?

3. Seeing the world through a client's eyes and understanding how it feels to be that person is referred to as:
   a. interpretation.
   b. genuineness.
   c. empathy.
   d. self-actualization.

✓CHECK YOUR ANSWERS IN APPENDIX C.

Behavior and Cognitive Therapies

Insight therapies help clients develop a deeper understanding of self, which often leads to positive changes in behavior and mental processes. But is it possible to alter those variables directly? This is the goal of behavior and cognitive therapies.

Get to Work! Behavior Therapy

LO 6 Outline the principles and characteristics of behavior therapy.

Using the principles of classical conditioning, operant conditioning, and observational learning (Chapter 5), behavior therapy aims to replace maladaptive behaviors with those that are adaptive. If behaviors are learned, who says they can't be changed through the same mechanisms?

EXPOSURE AND RESPONSE PREVENTION To help a person overcome a fear or phobia, a behavior therapist might use **exposure,** a technique of placing clients in the situations they fear—without any physical risks involved. Take, for example, a client struggling with a rat phobia. Rats cause this person extreme anxiety; the mere thought of seeing one scamper beneath a dumpster causes considerable distress. The client usually goes to great lengths to avoid the rodents, and this makes his anxiety drop. The reduced anxiety **negatively reinforces** his avoidance behavior. With exposure therapy, the therapist might arrange for the client to be in a room with a very friendly pet rat. After a positive experience with the animal, the client's anxiety diminishes (along with his efforts to avoid it), and he learns that the situation needn't be anxiety-provoking. Ideally, both the anxiety and the avoidance behavior are extinguished. This process of stamping out learned associations is called *extinction.* The theory behind this *response prevention* technique is that if you encourage someone to confront a feared object or situation, and prevent him from responding the way he normally does, the fear response eventually diminishes or disappears.

CONNECTIONS In **Chapter 5,** we learned about negative reinforcement; behaviors followed by a reduction in something unpleasant are likely to recur. If avoiding a feared object leads to a decrease in anxiety, the avoidance will likely be repeated.

A particularly intense form of exposure is to *flood* the client with an anxiety-provoking stimulus that cannot be escaped, causing a high degree of arousal. In one study, for example, women with snake phobias sat very close to a garter snake in a glass aquarium for 30 minutes without a break (Girodo & Henry, 1976). Flooding is potentially stressful for some therapists, which may be one reason this technique is not commonly used (Schumacher et al., 2015). Just imagine being a therapist and watching your client become extremely anxious or frightened during a flooding session you orchestrated.

For some clients, it's better to approach a feared scenario with "baby steps," upping the exposure with each movement forward (Prochaska & Norcross, 2014). This can be accomplished with an *anxiety hierarchy,* which is essentially a list of experiences ordered from least to most anxiety-provoking (**INFOGRAPHIC 14.2**). If the feared object is rats, the process might go something like this. Step 1: Think about a caged rat. Step 2: Look at a caged rat from afar. Step 3: Walk toward the cage, and so on.

But take note: Working up the anxiety hierarchy needn't involve actual rodents. With technologies available today, you could put on some fancy goggles and travel into a virtual "rat world," where it is possible to reach out and "touch" that creepy crawly animal with the simple click of a mouse. Virtual reality exposure therapy has become a popular way of reducing anxiety associated with various disorders, including specific phobias. Let's see how it works.

exposure A therapeutic technique that brings a person into contact with a feared object or situation while in a safe environment, with the goal of extinguishing or eliminating the fear response.

Classical Conditioning in Behavior Therapy

Behavior therapists believe that most behaviors—either desirable or undesirable—are learned. When a behavior is maladaptive, a new, more adaptive behavior can be learned to replace it. Behavior therapists use learning principles to help clients eliminate unwanted behaviors. The two behavior therapies highlighted here rely upon classical conditioning techniques. In exposure therapy, a therapist might use an approach known as *systematic desensitization* to reduce an unwanted response, such as a fear of needles, by pairing it with relaxation. In *aversion therapy,* an unwanted behavior such as excessive drinking is paired with unpleasant reactions, creating an association that prompts avoidance of that behavior.

SYSTEMATIC DESENSITIZATION

A client practices relaxation techniques while engaging in situations listed on her anxiety hierarchy, beginning with the least anxiety-provoking situation. After repeated pairings, the client learns to associate the anxiety-provoking situation with the desirable, conditioned response (calm), which is incompatible with fear or anxiety. The process is repeated for every step on the hierarchy.

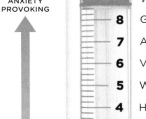

Anxiety Hierarchy for Fear of Needles

MOST ANXIETY PROVOKING

8 Getting a flu shot.
7 Allowing someone to prep your arm for a shot.
6 Visiting a health clinic to discuss getting a shot.
5 Watching someone get a shot.
4 Holding a hypodermic needle.
3 Touching a hypodermic needle in its packaging.
2 Looking at an actual hypodermic needle.
1 Looking at a photo of a hypodermic needle.

LEAST ANXIETY PROVOKING

During conditioning, two stimuli that produce incompatible responses are repeatedly paired.

+ relaxation

ANXIETY calm

Because the responses are incompatible, one response will eventually be extinguished. Starting at the bottom of the hierarchy with the least anxiety-provoking situation enables the desired response (calm) to prevail.

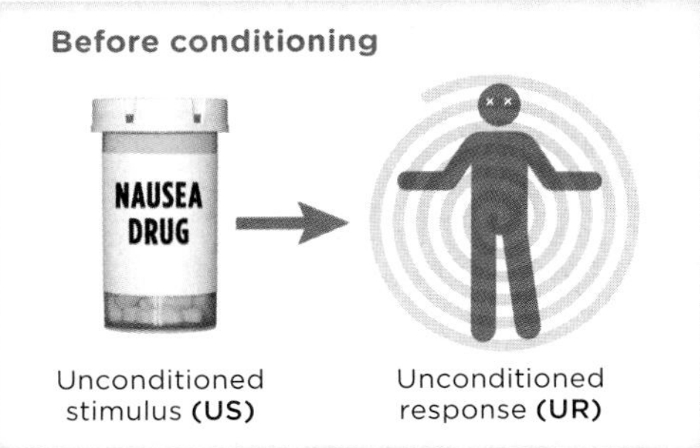

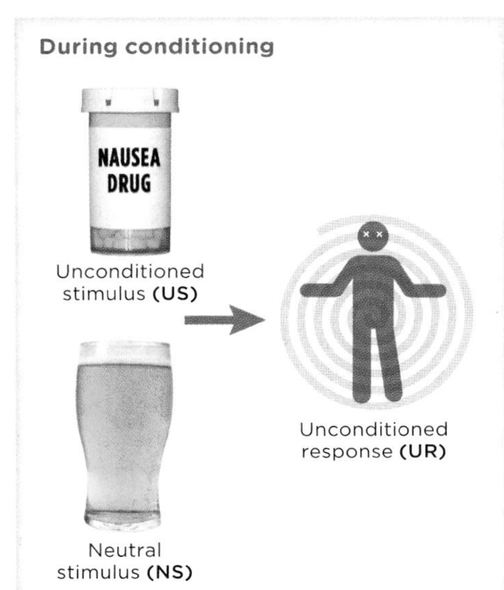

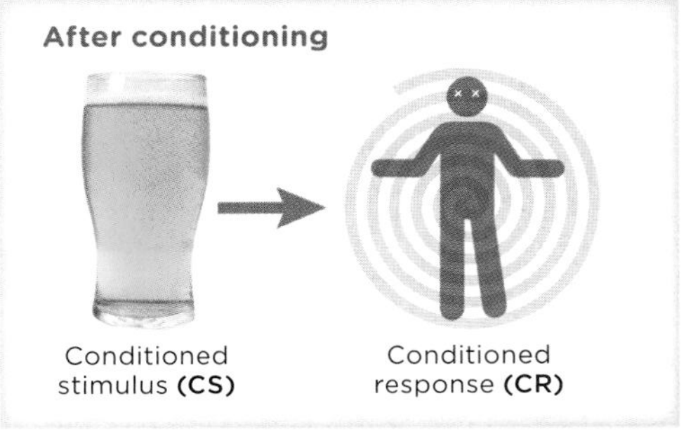

AVERSION THERAPY

Aversion therapy seeks to diminish a behavior by linking it with an unpleasant reaction. To reduce alcohol consumption, alcohol is consumed with a drug that causes feelings of nausea. Eventually, alcohol becomes a conditioned stimulus, prompting the unpleasant physical reaction all on its own.

It's a Long Way Down—But Not Really Wearing a headset like the one shown above, a client can enter a virtual reality and face feared objects or situations—in this case, driving over a bridge. The goal of exposure therapy (virtual or otherwise) is to reduce the fear response by exposing clients to situations they fear. When nothing bad happens, their anxiety diminishes and they are less likely to avoid the feared situations in the future. Top: Courtesy Limbix. Bottom: Limbix.

DIDN'T SEE THAT COMING

VIRTUAL REALITY EXPOSURE THERAPY Imagine you suffer from an intense and irrational fear of airplane travel (aviaphobia), and your therapist develops a treatment plan that includes virtual reality exposure therapy. Wearing a head-mounted display (HMD) or a headset like Google Cardboard, you are suddenly transported into the virtual interior of a jumbo jet (Powers & Carlbring, 2016; Rothbaum, Hodges, Smith, Lee, & Price, 2000). The rows of blue seats, the luggage compartments overhead, everything seems so real. So, too, do the movements of the plane, thanks to the hydraulic chair supporting you. Turn your head to the side or look toward the ceiling, and the computer creating this experience automatically adjusts to show you the part of the "plane" you are viewing (Shiban et al., 2016).

SOUNDS LIKE A GREAT IDEA, BUT DOES IT WORK?

A few feet away, your therapist sits at her desk clicking away at a keyboard or swiping and typing on a screen; she is moving you through the virtual airplane and monitoring your reports of anxiety every step of the way (Krijn, Emmelkamp, Olafsson, & Biemond, 2004). It's time to take your seat. Next, prepare for takeoff. If you're really feeling comfortable, your therapist might simulate some turbulence or a bumpy landing.

Studies suggest that virtual reality exposure therapy is effective for treating posttraumatic stress disorder (PTSD; Norrholm et al., 2016; Rothbaum et al., 2014) and various phobias, including fear of airplane travel, spiders, and heights (Krijn et al., 2004; Seinfeld et al., 2016; Shiban, Schelhorn, Pauli, & Mühlberger, 2015). More randomized controlled trials are needed to determine how it compares to other treatments (McCann et al., 2014), but researchers seem optimistic: "[Virtual reality exposure therapy] can produce significant behavior change in real-life situations," and it may be as effective as real-world exposure therapy (Morina, Ijntema, Meyerbröker, & Emmelkamp, 2015, p. 18).

Now that we have a general understanding of exposure therapy—and how it can be delivered through virtual worlds—let's explore an emerging area of research on this topic.

FOR ARACHNOPHOBIA, A NEW TWIST ON EXPOSURE THERAPY

Seeing photos of these eight-legged nasties soon after being reminded of your phobia could destabilize fear memories.

The sight of a spider casts dread into some people's hearts. This fear, known as arachnophobia, is perturbing, irrational and debilitating. But at its essence, fear is rooted in memory, and memory is plastic.

For years the mainstay treatment for phobias has been exposure therapy—gradually familiarizing a patient with the source of his or her fear by repeatedly presenting it in a safe environment. A related approach aims to disrupt the fear memory itself. In a study published in . . . *Current Biology*, a team of researchers in Sweden successfully did just that with chronic arachnophobia sufferers.

The researchers showed 45 arachnophobes photographs of spiders for several seconds to trigger their fear. Half the participants were shown images of these arthropods again 10 minutes later; the other half saw them again after six hours. Functional MRI revealed increased activity in the basolateral amygdala—a brain region that responds to scary stimuli—when subjects in both groups were looking at the creepy crawlers. On seeing the pictures again, however, the 10-minute-interval group had lower amygdala activity than the six-hour group and avoided spider images less in behavioral tests days later.

The key to this difference may lie in how memory works. When subjects first see the photos and are reminded of their fear, the memory "destabilizes, and it has to be resaved," says Johannes Björkstrand, a psychologist at Uppsala University who led the study. Subjects in the 10-minute-interval group did not have enough time to resave their fear memory, he says, before being shown more spider pictures, whereas the other subjects had plenty of time and retained their original fear.

Memory-disruption therapy might one day be used in the clinic. For example, patients would be reminded of their fear for one minute and, 10 minutes later, would receive three hours of exposure. This could be repeated over several sessions, as with traditional exposure therapy. Larger, longer-term trials are needed to determine if the method works better than standard exposure therapy. If successful, the researchers say the treatment could be investigated for other phobias, as well as post-traumatic stress disorder and related anxiety disorders. **Abdul-Kareem Ahmed. Reproduced with permission. Copyright © 2017 Scientific American, a division of Nature America, Inc. All rights reserved.**

SYSTEMATIC DESENSITIZATION One technique commonly used in behavior therapy is **systematic desensitization,** which takes advantage of the fact that we can't be relaxed and anxious at the same time. The therapist begins by teaching clients how to relax their muscles. This can be accomplished through **progressive muscle relaxation,** the process of tensing and then relaxing muscle groups, starting at the head and ending at the toes. Using this method, clients can learn to release all the tension in their body. It's very simple—want to try it?

CONNECTIONS

In **Chapter 12,** we described progressive muscle relaxation for relieving stress and reducing anxiety. Here, we see it can also be used in the treatment of anxiety.

try this Sit in a comfortable chair in a quiet room. Start by tensing the muscles controlling your scalp: After 10 seconds, relax the muscles and focus on the tension dissipating. Next follow the same procedure for the muscles in your face. Continue tensing and releasing muscles all the way down to your toes and see what happens.

Once a client has learned how to relax, it's time to face an anxiety hierarchy (either in the real world or via imagination) while trying to maintain a sense of calm. Imagine a client who fears flying, moving through an anxiety hierarchy with her therapist. Starting with the least-feared scenario at the bottom of her hierarchy, she imagines purchasing a ticket online. If she can stay relaxed through the first step, then she moves to the second item in the hierarchy, thinking about boarding a plane. At some point in the process, she might start to feel jittery or unable to take the next step. If this happens, the therapist guides her back a step or two in the hierarchy, or as many steps as she needs to feel calm again, using the relaxation technique described above. Then it's back up the hierarchy she goes. This process does not happen in one session, but over the course of many.

CONNECTIONS

In **Chapter 5,** we described classical conditioning. Here, we see how this type of learning could lead to decreases in alcohol use. The neutral stimulus is drinking alcohol; the unconditioned stimulus is the nausea-inducing drug; and the unconditioned response is nausea. After repeated pairings with the drug, alcohol becomes the conditioned stimulus, and nausea the conditioned response.

AVERSION THERAPY Exposure therapy focuses on *extinguishing* or eliminating associations, but there is another behavior therapy aimed at producing them. It's called **aversion therapy.** Seizing on the power of classical conditioning, aversion therapy seeks to link problematic behaviors, such as drug use, to unpleasant physical reactions like sickness and pain (Infographic 14.2). One type of aversion therapy uses the drug Antabuse, which has helped some people with alcoholism stop drinking, at least temporarily (Cannon, Baker, Gino, & Nathan, 1986; Gaval-Cruz & Weinshenker, 2009). Antabuse interferes with the body's ability to break down alcohol, so combining this drug with even a small amount of alcohol brings on an immediate unpleasant reaction (vomiting, throbbing headache, and so on). With **repeated pairings** of alcohol consumption and physical misery, one is less inclined to drink in the future. But aversion therapies like this are only effective if the client is motivated to change and comply with treatment (Newton-Howes, Levack, McBride, Gilmor, & Tester, 2016).

systematic desensitization A treatment that combines anxiety hierarchies with relaxation techniques.

aversion therapy Therapeutic approach that uses the principles of classical conditioning to link problematic behaviors to unpleasant physical reactions.

IT'S ABOUT CHANGING BEHAVIOR Another form of behavior therapy is **behavior modification**, which draws on the principles of operant conditioning. Therapists practicing behavior modification use **positive and negative reinforcement**, as well as punishment, to help clients increase adaptive behaviors and reduce maladaptive ones. In difficult cases, therapists might use successive approximations, that is, reinforce incremental changes toward the desired behaviors. Some will incorporate observational learning (that is, learning by watching and imitating others) to help clients change their behaviors.

CONNECTIONS

In **Chapter 5,** we described how positive reinforcement (a desirable consequence) increases the likelihood of a behavior being repeated. With behavior modification, therapists use reinforcers to replace maladaptive behaviors with adaptive ones.

In a **token economy,** people are given tokens as positive reinforcement for desired behaviors. **Tokens** can be exchanged for candy, outings, privileges, and other perks. They can also be taken away as a punishment to reduce undesirable behaviors. This behavior modification approach has proven successful for a variety of populations, including psychiatric patients in residential treatment facilities and hospitals, children in classrooms, and prison inmates (Dickerson, Tenhula, & Green-Paden, 2005; Kazdin, 1982; Walker, Pann, Shapiro, & Van Hasselt, 2016). In a residential treatment facility, for example, patients with schizophrenia may earn tokens for socializing with each other or cleaning up after themselves. Critics contend that token economies manipulate the people they intend to help. (You might agree that giving adults play money for good behavior is degrading.) We also have to consider what happens to those residents who move on to less structured settings—do the changes in their behavior persist? From a practical standpoint, however, these systems can help people adopt healthier behaviors.

CONNECTIONS

Tokens are an excellent example of secondary reinforcers. In **Chapter 5,** we reported that secondary reinforcers derive their power from their connection with primary reinforcers, which satisfy biological needs.

synonyms

behavior modification applied behavior analysis

Jon Schulte/Getty Images.

You Are What You Think: Cognitive Therapies

FOLLOW-UP Earlier in the chapter, we described Dr. Foster's initial encounter with Chepa, a young woman facing schizophrenia. After being discharged from the psychiatric hospital, Chepa returns to the reservation, where Dr. Foster and his colleagues from Indian Health Service follow her progress. Every month, she goes to the medical clinic for an injection to quell her psychosis. This is also when she is most likely to have a therapy session with Dr. Foster. One of his main goals is to turn Chepa's negative thought patterns into healthier ones. To help clients recognize the maladaptive nature of their thoughts, Dr. Foster might provide an analogy as he does here:

Dr. Foster: If we had a blizzard in February and it's 20 degrees below for 4 days in a row, would you consider that a strange winter?

Chepa: No.

Dr. Foster: If we had a day that's 105 degrees in August, would you consider that an odd summer?

Chepa: Well, no.

Dr. Foster: Yet you're talking about a difference of 125 degrees, and we're in the same place and we're saying this is normal weather. . . . We're part of nature. You and I are part of this natural world, and so you might have a day today where you're very distressed, very upset, and a week from now where you're very calm and very at peace, and both of those are normal. Both of those are appropriate.

Dr. Foster might also remind Chepa that her symptoms result from her psychological condition. "Your response is a normal response [for] a human being with this [psychological disorder]," he says, "and so of course you're scared, of course you're upset."

behavior modification Therapeutic approach in which behaviors are shaped through reinforcement and punishment.

token economy A type of behavior modification that uses tokens to reinforce desired behaviors.

LO 7 Outline the principles and characteristics of cognitive therapy.

Dr. Foster has identified his client's maladaptive thoughts and is beginning to help her change the way she views her world and her relationships. This is the basic goal of **cognitive therapy,** an approach advanced by psychiatrist Aaron Beck.

Beck's Cognitive Approach The father of cognitive therapy, Aaron Beck, believes that distorted thought processes lie at the heart of psychological problems. Macmillan Learning.

BECK'S COGNITIVE THERAPY Beck was trained in psychoanalysis, but he opted to develop his own approach after trying (without luck) to produce scientific evidence showing that Freud's methods worked (Beck & Weishaar, 2014). Beck believes that patterns of *automatic thoughts* lie at the root of psychological disturbances. These *cognitive distortions,* or errors, cause individuals to misinterpret events in their lives and are associated with psychological problems like depression (Beck, Rush, Shaw, & Emory, 1979; **Table 14.3**). One such distortion is **overgeneralization,** or thinking that self-contained events will have major repercussions in life (Prochaska & Norcross, 2014). For example, a person assumes that something is always true just because it happens to be true under one set of circumstances. (*I have had difficulty working for a male boss, so I will never be able to work effectively under a male supervisor.*) Beck suggests that **cognitive schemas** underlie such patterns of automatic thoughts, directing the way we interpret events. His cognitive therapy aims to dismantle, or take apart, the schemas harboring these errors and replace them with beliefs that nurture more positive, realistic thoughts.

CONNECTIONS

In **Chapter 8,** we presented Piaget's concept of the schema, a collection of ideas or notions representing a basic unit of understanding. Young children form schemas based on functional relationships they observe in the environment. Beck suggests that schemas can also direct the way we interpret events, not always in a realistic or rational manner.

The restructuring of schemas can be facilitated by client homework. For example, the therapist may challenge clients to test "hypotheses" related to their dysfunctional thinking. ("If it's true you don't work effectively under male bosses, then why did your previous boss give you a promotion?") Client homework is an important component

TABLE 14.3 COGNITIVE DISTORTIONS

Cognitive Distortion	Explanation	Example
Arbitrary inference	Coming to a conclusion even when there is no evidence to support it	*I am a horrible student.*
Selective abstraction	Ignoring information and assuming something has happened based on details taken out of context	*I know he is cheating because he is e-mailing a woman at work.*
Overgeneralizing	Belief that something may always occur because it has occurred before	*My boss doesn't like me; I will never be liked.*
Magnification/ minimization	Belief that something is more or less critical than it really is	*If I don't pass this first quiz, I will fail the course.*
Dichotomous thinking	Viewing experiences in extremes	*I can either be at the top of my class, or I can get married and have a family.*
Personalizing	Taking other people's behaviors too personally	*I waved at her, but she didn't even acknowledge me. I must have upset her.*

Aaron Beck contends that psychological problems stem from distorted patterns of thought. Cognitive therapy aims to replace these cognitive distortions with more realistic and constructive ways of thinking. Information from Beck & Weishaar (2014).

cognitive therapy A type of therapy aimed at addressing the maladaptive thinking that leads to maladaptive behaviors and feelings.

overgeneralization A cognitive distortion that assumes self-contained events will have major repercussions.

of cognitive therapy. So, too, is psychoeducation, which might include sharing websites and reading materials that help clients understand their disorders and thus adopt more realistic attitudes and expectations.

ELLIS' RATIONAL EMOTIVE BEHAVIOR THERAPY The other major figure in cognitive therapy is psychologist Albert Ellis (1913–2007). Like Beck, Ellis was trained in psychoanalysis but was disappointed by its results, so he created his own treatment approach: **rational emotive behavior therapy (REBT).** The goal of REBT is to help people identify their irrational or illogical thoughts and convert them into rational ones. An REBT therapist uses the ABC model to understand a client's problems. Point A represents an *Activating event* in the client's life: "My boss fired me." Point B stands for the *irrational Beliefs* that follow: "I will never be able to hold a steady job." And point C represents the *emotional Consequences*: "I feel hopeless and depressed." Therapy focuses on addressing point B, the irrational beliefs causing distress. If all goes well, the client successfully reaches point D, *Disputing flawed beliefs:* "Losing one job does not spell the end of my career." That leads to point E, an *Effective new philosophy*: "I am capable of being successful in another job" (Ellis & Dryden, 1997; **Figure 14.2**).

According to Ellis, people tend to have unrealistic beliefs, often perfectionist in nature, about how they and others should think and act. This inevitably leads to disappointment, as no one is perfect. The ultimate goal of REBT is to arrive at self-acceptance, that is, to change these irrational thoughts to realistic ones. This often involves letting go of the "I shoulds" and "I musts," what Ellis called "musturbatory thinking" (Prochaska & Norcross, 2014, p. 266). Through REBT, one develops a rational way of thinking that helps reduce suffering and amplify enjoyment: "The purpose of life," as Ellis was known to say, "is to have a $&%#@ good time" (p. 263). Ellis took a hard line with clients, forcefully challenging them to provide evidence for their irrational ideas and often shocking people with his direct manner (Kaufman, 2007, July 25; Prochaska & Norcross, 2014).

As Ellis developed his therapy throughout the years, he realized it was important to focus on cognitive processing as well as behavior. Thus, REBT therapists focus on changing both cognitions and behaviors, assigning homework to implement the insights clients gain during therapy. Because Ellis and Beck incorporated both cognitive and behavior therapy methods, their approaches are commonly referred to as **cognitive behavioral therapy (CBT).** Both are action-oriented, as they require clients to confront and resist their illogical thinking.

TAKING STOCK: AN APPRAISAL OF BEHAVIOR AND COGNITIVE THERAPIES

Behavior and cognitive therapies offer a few key advantages over insight therapies. Behavior therapy tends to work fast, producing quick resolutions to stressful situations, sometimes in a single session (Oar, Farrell, & Ollendick, 2015; Öst, 1989). And reduced time in therapy typically translates to a lower cost. What's more, the procedures used in behavior therapy are often easy to operationalize (remember, the focus is on modifying observable behavior), so evaluating the outcome is more straightforward. There are some drawbacks to behavior therapy, however. The goal is to change learned behaviors, but not all behaviors and symptoms are learned. (For example, you can't "learn" to have hallucinations.) And because the reinforcement comes from an external source, newly learned behaviors may disappear when reinforcement stops. Finally, the emphasis on observable behavior may downplay the social, biological, and cognitive roots of psychological disorders. This narrow approach works well for treating phobias and other behavior problems, but not as well for addressing far-reaching, complex issues arising from disorders such as schizophrenia.

The cognitive approaches of Beck and Ellis have the advantage of being short-term (usually no more than about 20 one-hour sessions). For clients with obsessive-compulsive disorder (OCD), major depressive disorder, and posttraumatic stress

rational emotive behavior therapy (REBT) A type of cognitive therapy, developed by Ellis, that identifies illogical thoughts and attempts to convert them into rational ones.

cognitive behavioral therapy (CBT) An action-oriented type of therapy that requires clients to confront and resist their illogical thinking.

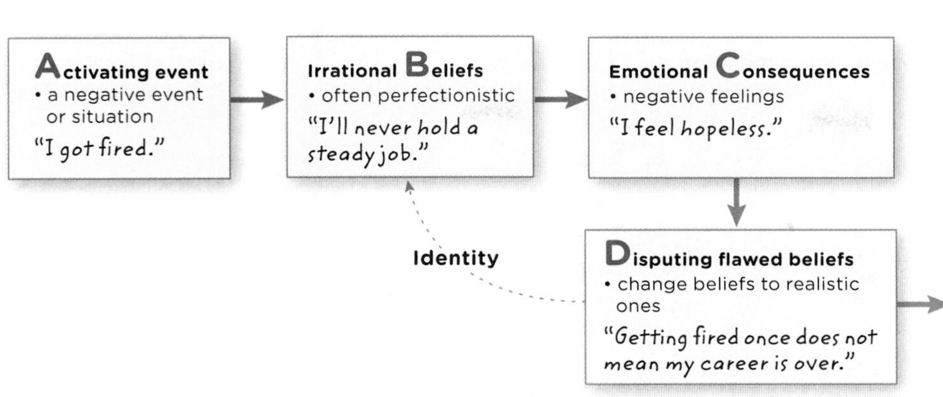

FIGURE 14.2
The ABCs of REBT
A rational emotive behavior therapist uses the ABC model (depicted in blue) to understand a client's problems. Therapy, shown in green, helps a client identify and address irrational beliefs—and ultimately develop a mature and realistic perspective.

disorder (PTSD), cognitive behavioral therapy (CBT) is not only effective; it produces measurable changes in the brain (Moody et al., 2017; Shou et al., 2017). Even when administered online, CBT may benefit clients with a variety of psychological problems (Carlbring, Andersson, Cuijpers, Riper, & Hedman-Lagerlöf, 2018). Still, every approach has its limitations. Cognitive models that focus on flawed assumptions and attitudes may present a chicken-and-egg problem. People experiencing depression often have distorted beliefs, but are distorted beliefs causing their depression or is depression causing their distorted beliefs? Perhaps it is a combination of both.

All the therapies we have discussed thus far involve interactions among therapists and clients. But in many cases, psychotherapy is not enough; a biological approach is also needed.

show what you know

1. The goal of ________ therapy is to replace maladaptive behaviors with more adaptive ones.
   a. behavior
   b. exposure
   c. humanistic
   d. psychodynamic
2. Describe the similarities and differences between cognitive and behavior therapy.
3. The basic goal of ________ is to help clients identify maladaptive thoughts and change the way they view the world and their relationships.

✓ CHECK YOUR ANSWERS IN APPENDIX C.

Biomedical Therapies

LO 8 Summarize the biomedical interventions and identify their common goal.

People with severe disorders like depression, schizophrenia, and bipolar disorder can benefit from talk therapy, but this may not be enough. Their symptoms are driven by biological processes that can be directly targeted with biomedical therapies. These therapies take three basic forms: (1) drugs, or *psychotropic* medications; (2) electroconvulsive therapy; and (3) surgery.

Psychologists Who Prescribe
Psychotropic medications are typically prescribed by psychiatrists, but a small number of psychologists have prescription privileges as well. New Mexico, Louisiana, Iowa, Illinois, and Idaho have passed laws giving psychologists the green light to prescribe, provided they have "advanced specialized training," including a postdoctoral master's degree in clinical psychopharmacology (APA, 2017b, para. 1). The same is true for psychologists working in federal agencies, such as the Defense Department or Indian Health Service (DeAngelis, 2017, November 9).
Wavebreakmedia Ltd/Getty Images.

Medicines That Help

Psychotropic medications are used to treat psychological disorders and their symptoms. Prescribing these drugs is generally the domain of *psychiatrists,*

TABLE 14.4 MEDICATIONS FOR PSYCHOLOGICAL DISORDERS

Category	Commonly Used Medication		Target of Treatment
Antidepressant	Fluoxetine (Prozac) Citalopram (Celexa) Sertraline (Zoloft) Paroxetine (Paxil)	Escitalopram (Lexapro) Venlafaxine (Effexor) Duloxetine (Cymbalta) Bupropion (Wellbutrin)	Depression
Mood-stabilizing	Lithium Valproic acid (Valproic)	Carbamazepine (Tegretol) Lamotrignine (Lamictal) Oxcarbazepine (Trileptal)	Mania and depression
Traditional antipsychotics	Chlorpromazine (Thorazine, Largactil) Haloperidol (Haldol)	Perphenazine (Trilafon) Fluphenazine (Prolixin)	Psychosis
Atypical antipsychotics	Risperidone (Risperdal) Olanzapine (Zyprexa) Quetiapine (Seroquel) Ziprasidon (Geodon)	Aripiprazole (Abilify) Paliperidone (Invega) Lurasidone (Latuda)	Psychosis
Anti-anxiety	Clonazepam (Klonopin) Alprazolam (Xanax) Lorazapam (Ativan)	Diazepam (Valium) Buspirone (Buspar)	Anxiety

Listed here are some of the medications commonly used for treating psychological disorders. In many cases, psychotropic drugs are most effective when used alongside psychotherapy. Information from Cuijpers, De Wit, Weitz, Andersson, & Huibers (2015); Manber et al. (2008).

physicians who specialize in treating people with disorders. (Psychiatrists are medical doctors, whereas clinical psychologists have PhDs or PsyDs and generally cannot prescribe medication.) *Psychopharmacology* is the scientific study of how psychotropic medications alter perceptions, moods, behaviors, and other aspects of psychological functioning. These drugs can be divided into four types: *antidepressant, mood-stabilizing, antipsychotic,* and *anti-anxiety* (**Table 14.4**).

ANTIDEPRESSANT DRUGS Major depressive disorder is commonly treated with **antidepressant drugs,** medication used to improve mood (and to treat anxiety and eating disorders in certain individuals). Essentially, there are three classes of antidepressant drugs: monoamine oxidase inhibitors (MAOIs), such as Nardil (phenelzine); tricyclic antidepressants, such as Elavil (amitriptyline); and selective serotonin reuptake inhibitors (SSRIs), such as Prozac (fluoxetine). All these antidepressants are thought to work by influencing the activity of **neurotransmitters** hypothesized to be involved in depression and other disorders (**INFOGRAPHIC 14.3**). (Keep in mind, no one has pinpointed the exact neurological mechanisms underlying depression.)

CONNECTIONS

In **Chapter 2,** we described how sending neurons release neurotransmitters into the synapse, where they bind to receptors on the receiving neuron. Neurotransmitters that do not immediately attach are reabsorbed by the sending neuron (reuptake) or broken down in the synapse. Here, we see how medications can influence this process.

The monoamine oxidase inhibitors (MAOIs) help people with major depressive disorder by slowing the breakdown of certain neurotransmitters known as monoamines: norepinephrine, serotonin, and dopamine. MAOIs extend the amount of time these neurotransmitters remain in the synapse by hindering the normal activity of monoamine oxidase, whose natural role is to break them down. By making these neurotransmitters more available (that is, allowing them more time in the synapse), MAOIs might lessen symptoms of depression. These drugs have fallen out of use due to safety concerns and side effects, as they require great attention to diet. MAOIs can trigger a life-threatening jump in blood pressure when ingested alongside tyramine, a substance found in many everyday foods, including cheddar cheese, salami, and wine (Anastasio et al., 2010; Horwitz, Lovenberg, Engelman, & Sjoerdsma, 1964; Larsen, Krogh-Nielsen, & Brøsen, 2016).

antidepressant drugs Psychotropic medications used for the treatment of depression.

Biomedical Therapies

Biomedical therapies use physical interventions to treat psychological disorders. These therapies can be categorized according to the method by which they influence the brain's functioning: chemical, electrical, or structural.

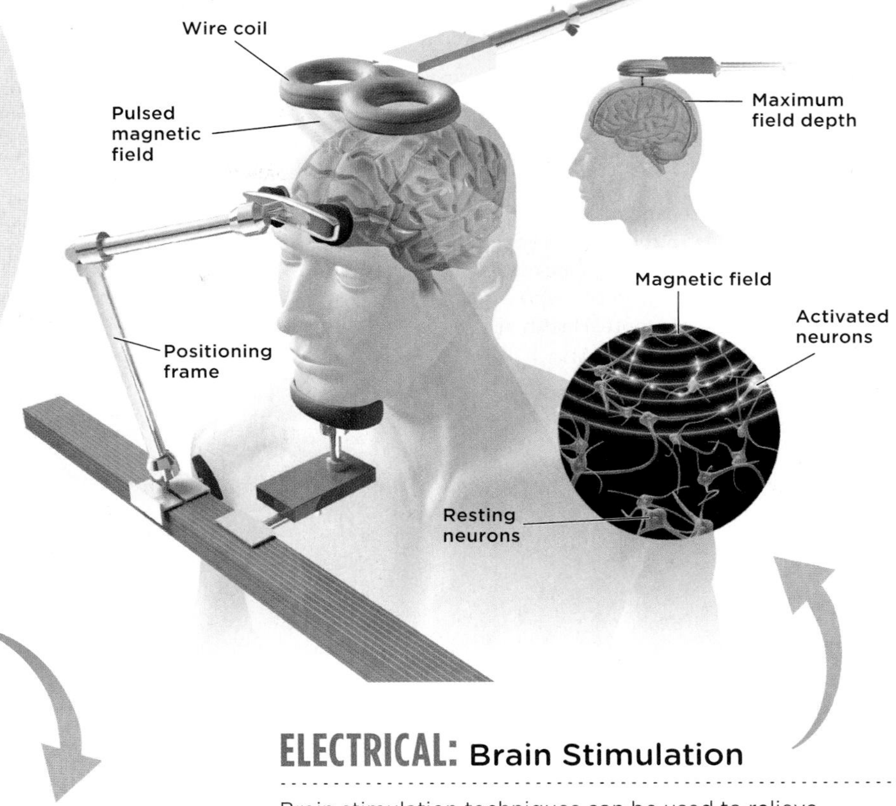

STRUCTURAL: Neurosurgery

Modern surgical techniques are able to target a very precise area of the brain known to be directly involved in the condition being treated. For example, the black circles on these scans mark areas typically targeted for a form of surgery known as anterior cingulotomy, which has been shown to reduce symptoms in patients suffering severe cases of major depression (Steele, Christmas, Elijamel, & Matthews, 2008). Using radio frequencies emitted from a 6-millimeter probe, the surgeon destroys part of the anterior cingulate cortex, an area known to be associated with emotions (Faria, 2013).

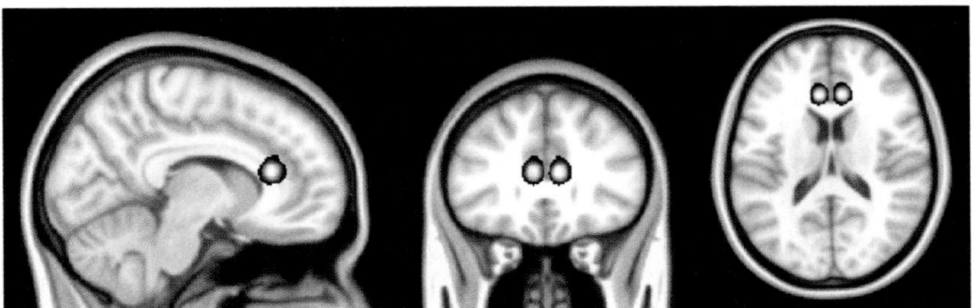

ELECTRICAL: Brain Stimulation

Brain stimulation techniques can be used to relieve symptoms by affecting the electrical activity of the brain. Research on electroconvulsive therapy found a greater than 80% remission rate for those with severe major depression (Fink, 2014). Repetitive transcranial magnetic stimulation (rTMS), shown here, is a noninvasive procedure. A coil pulses a magnetic field that passes painlessly through scalp and bone, penetrating just to the outer cortex. The field induces electric current in nearby neurons, activating targeted regions in the brain (National Institute of Mental Health, 2016).

CHEMICAL: Psychotropic Medications

Drug therapies, which alter the brain's chemistry, are the most commonly prescribed biomedical treatment. Each works to influence neurotransmitters thought to be associated with certain disorders. This illustration shows the action of a class of antidepressants known as selective serotonin reuptake inhibitors (SSRIs).

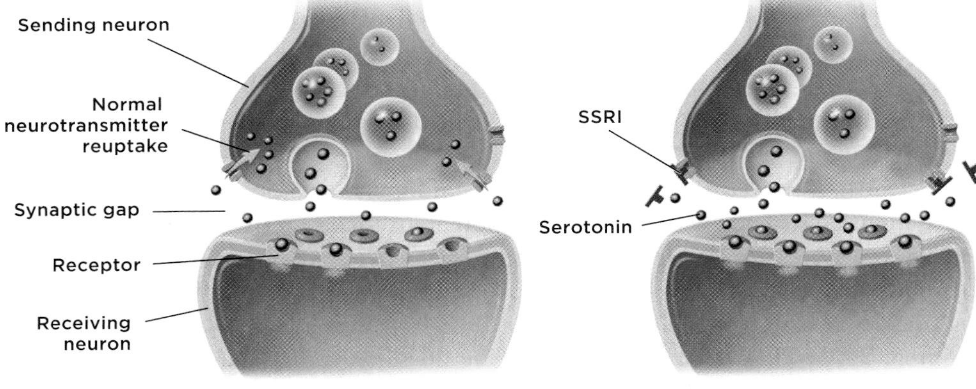

In normal communication between neurons, neurotransmitters released into the synaptic gap bind to the receiving neuron, sending a message. Excess neurotransmitters are reabsorbed into the sending neurons through the process of reuptake.

As indicated by their name, SSRIs inhibit the reuptake of the neurotransmitter serotonin. Allowed to remain longer in the synapse, serotonin can achieve a greater effect.

Credits: (Illustration) Graphic by Bryan Christie Design. Stimulating the Brain by Mark S. George. *Scientific American*, September 2003, page 69; (Brain photo) Reprinted by permission from Macmillan Publishers Ltd: Tractographic analysis of historical lesion surgery for depression. Schoene-Bake JC, Parpaley Y, Weber B, Panksepp J, Hurwitz TA, Coenen VA. *Neuropsychopharmacology.* 2010 December; 35(13): 2553–2563.

Black Box
A growing number of children and teenagers are taking SSRIs to combat depression, but these medications may increase the risk of suicidal behaviors and thoughts for a small percentage of youth. For this reason, the U.S. Food and Drug Administration (FDA) requires manufacturers to include a "black box" warning on the packaging of these drugs (National Institute of Mental Health, n.d.-a). Todor Tsvetkov/Getty Images.

The tricyclic antidepressants, named for their three-ringed molecular structure, inhibit the reuptake of serotonin and norepinephrine in the synaptic gap. This allows these neurotransmitters more time to be active, which appears to reduce symptoms. The tricyclic drugs are not always well tolerated by patients and can cause a host of side effects, including sexual dysfunction, confusion, and increased risk of heart attack (Cohen, Gibson, & Alderman, 2000; Coupland et al., 2016; Higgins, Nash, & Lynch, 2010). Overdoses can be fatal.

Newer, more popular pharmaceutical interventions include selective serotonin reuptake inhibitors (SSRIs)—brands such as Prozac, Paxil (paroxetine), and Zoloft (sertraline)—that inhibit the reuptake of serotonin specifically. SSRIs may reduce the potentially devastating symptoms of depression, and are generally safer and have fewer negative effects than the older generation of antidepressants, but they are far from perfect. Weight gain, fatigue, hot flashes, chills, insomnia, nausea, and sexual dysfunction are all possible side effects. Some research suggests that SSRIs are not better than a **placebo** when it comes to treating mild to moderate depression (Fournier et al., 2010; Khan & Brown, 2015). A recent analysis of studies concluded that antidepressants of various types (not just SSRIs) "were more efficacious than placebo in adults with major depressive disorder," although these effects were "mostly modest" (Cipriani et al., 2018, p. 1362).

synonyms
mood-stabilizing drugs anti-manic drugs

CONNECTIONS
In **Chapter 1,** we stated that a placebo is a fake treatment used to explore the effectiveness of an actual treatment. The placebo effect is the tendency to feel better if we believe we are being treated with a real medication. Expectations about getting better can change treatment outcomes.

MOOD-STABILIZING DRUGS People with bipolar disorder may find some degree of symptom relief in **mood-stabilizing drugs**. Lithium, for instance, helps smooth the mood swings of people with bipolar disorder, leveling out the dramatic peaks (mania) and valleys (depression) (Song et al., 2016). For this reason, it is sometimes called a "mood normalizer" (Bech, 2006), and it has been widely used to treat bipolar disorder for decades. Unlike many standard drugs that chemists cobble together in laboratories, lithium is a naturally occurring mineral salt. Doctors must be very careful when prescribing lithium, monitoring the blood levels of their patients. Too small a dose will fall short of controlling bipolar symptoms, while too large a dose can be lethal.

Scientists have yet to determine the cause of bipolar disorder and how its symptoms might be lessened with lithium. But numerous theories exist, some pointing to imbalances in neurotransmitters such as glutamate and serotonin (Cho et al., 2005; Dixon & Hokin, 1998; Song et al., 2015). Lithium also seems to be effective in lowering suicide risk among people with bipolar disorder (Angst, Angst, Gerber-Werder, & Gamma, 2005; Hayes et al., 2016), who are 20 times more likely than people in the general population to die by suicide (Inder et al., 2016; Tondo, Isacsson, & Baldessarini, 2003).

You Asked, Dr. Foster Answers

http://qrs.ly/m65a5fy

How might medication impact the effectiveness of psychotherapy?

mood-stabilizing drugs Psychotropic medications that minimize the lows of depression and the highs of mania.

Anticonvulsant medications are also used to treat bipolar disorder. These drugs were originally created to alleviate symptoms of seizure disorders, but scientists discovered they might also function as mood stabilizers, and some research suggests that they can reduce the symptoms of mania (Bowden et al., 2000). Unfortunately, certain anticonvulsants may increase the risk of suicide or of possible suicide masked as violent death through injury or accident (Muller et al., 2015; Patorno et al., 2010). For this reason, the U.S. Food and Drug Administration (FDA, 2008) requires drug companies to place warnings on their labels.

ANTIPSYCHOTIC DRUGS The hallucinations and delusions of people with disorders like schizophrenia can be subdued with **antipsychotic drugs.** Both ***traditional antipsychotics*** and ***atypical antipsychotics*** seek to reduce dopamine activity in certain areas of the brain, as abnormal activity of this neurotransmitter is believed to contribute to the psychotic symptoms of schizophrenia and other disorders (Blasi et al., 2015; Schnider, Guggisberg, Nahum, Gabriel, & Morand, 2010). Antipsychotics accomplish this by acting as dopamine **antagonists**, meaning they "pose" as dopamine, binding to receptors normally reserved for dopamine (sort of like stealing someone's parking space). By blocking dopamine's receptors, antipsychotic drugs reduce dopamine's excitatory effect on neurons. The main difference between atypical antipsychotics and the traditional variety is that the atypical antipsychotics *also* interfere with neural pathways involving other neurotransmitters, such as serotonin (also associated with psychotic symptoms).

synonyms

traditional antipsychotics first-generation antipsychotic medications, typical antipsychotic medications

atypical antipsychotics second-generation antipsychotic medications

CONNECTIONS

In **Chapter 2,** we described how drugs influence behavior by changing what is happening in the synapse. Agonists increase the normal activity of a neurotransmitter, and antagonists block normal neurotransmitter activity. Here, we see how antipsychotics can act as antagonists.

Antipsychotics have helped many people achieve higher levels of functioning, but these drugs have unwanted side effects. After about a year of taking traditional antipsychotics, some patients have developed a neurological condition called *tardive dyskinesia,* whose symptoms include shaking, restlessness, and bizarre facial grimaces. Atypical antipsychotics like Risperdal (risperidone) usually do not cause tardive dyskinesia (Correll, Leucht, & Kane, 2004; Jacobsen, 2015), but they have other potential side effects, such as weight gain, increased risk for Type 2 diabetes, sexual dysfunction, and heart disease (Ücok & Gaebel, 2008). And although these drugs reduce symptoms in 60–85% of patients, they do not provide a cure.

Community in Pain
A young man stands among the graves of relatives on the Pine Ridge Indian Reservation in South Dakota. In the United States, the suicide rate among American Indian and Alaska Native youth (ages 10 to 24) exceeds that of all other racial groups. Both youth and adult suicides have increased substantially over the last two decades (Leavitt et al., 2018; Willis, DeLeon, Haldane, & Heldring, 2014). Traumatic incidents like suicides inevitably have witnesses, and those witnesses suffer from what they see and hear. Their pain often manifests itself in the form of anxiety. Matthew Ryan Williams/Redux.

ANTI-ANXIETY DRUGS Most of today's **anti-anxiety drugs** are *benzodiazepines* such as Xanax (alprazolam) and Ativan (lorazepam). Also called "minor tranquilizers," these anti-anxiety drugs are used for a continuum of anxiety, from fear of flying to extreme panic attacks. In high doses, benzodiazepines promote sleep, so they can also be used to treat insomnia.

Benzodiazepines ease anxiety by enhancing the effect of GABA, an inhibitory neurotransmitter that decreases or stops some types of neural activity. By giving GABA a boost, these drugs inhibit the firing of neurons that normally induce anxiety reactions. Fast-acting and dangerously addictive, benzodiazepines are potentially lethal when mixed with alcohol. Between 1996 and 2013, there was a 67% increase in the number of people filling prescriptions for benzodiazepines, and the rate of deaths from overdosing on these drugs nearly quadrupled (Bachhuber, Hennessy, Cunningham, & Starrels, 2016). Valium and Xanax are the most commonly abused anti-anxiety drugs (Phillips, 2013).

MEDICATION PLUS PSYCHOTHERAPY Psychotropic medications have helped countless people get back on their feet and enjoy life, but drugs alone don't produce the best long-term outcomes. Studies suggest that psychotropic drugs are most effective when used alongside talk therapy. For example, combining medication with an integrative approach to psychotherapy, including cognitive, behavioral, and psychodynamic

antipsychotic drugs Psychotropic medication used in the treatment of psychotic symptoms, such as hallucinations and delusions.

anti-anxiety drugs Psychotropic medications used for treating the symptoms of anxiety.

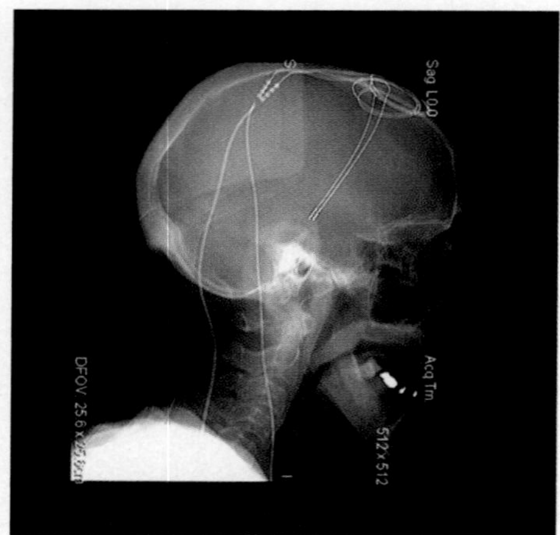

Stimulate the Brain
An X-ray image of a person undergoing deep brain stimulation reveals two electrodes—one implanted in each hemisphere. These electrodes send electrical impulses through certain neural networks, inducing changes that may lead to reduced symptoms. This treatment has produced promising results in patients with depression, but further research is needed to identify its long-term effects (Bergfeld et al., 2016; Schlaepfer et al., 2013). Medical Body Scans/Science Source.

perspectives, may reduce major depressive symptoms faster than either approach alone (Cuijpers, De Wit, Weitz, Andersson, & Huibers, 2015; Manber et al., 2008). With therapy, Dr. Foster says, "The person feels greater self-efficacy. They're not relying on a pill to manage depression."

Another key point to remember: Medications affect people in different ways. A drug that works for one person may have no effect on another, and could produce distinct side effects. We metabolize (break down) drugs at different rates, which means dosages must be assessed on a case-by-case basis. To complicate matters further, many people take multiple medications at once, and some drugs interact in harmful ways.

Other Biomedical Therapies

Sometimes, the symptoms of psychological disorders do not improve with medication. In these extreme cases, there are other biomedical options. For example, repetitive transcranial magnetic stimulation (rTMS) appears to be effective in treating symptoms of depression and some types of hallucinations (Sommer & Neggers, 2014). With rTMS, electromagnetic coils are put on (or above) a person's head, directing brief electrical current into a particular area of the brain (Slotema, Blom, Hoek, & Sommer, 2010). Another technique under investigation is deep brain stimulation, which involves implanting a device that supplies weak electrical stimulation to specific areas of the brain thought to be linked to depression (Bergfeld et al., 2016; Schlaepfer, Bewernick, Kayser, Mädler, & Coenen, 2013). These technologies show great promise, but more research is required to determine their long-term impact.

ELECTROCONVULSIVE THERAPY Severely depressed people who have not responded to psychotropic medications or psychotherapy may benefit from **electroconvulsive therapy (ECT),** a biomedical approach that essentially causes seizures in the brain. If you've ever seen ECT, or "shock therapy," portrayed in movies, you might think it's a barbaric form of abuse. Truth be told, ECT was a brutal and overly used treatment in the mid-20th century (Glass, 2001; Smith, 2001). Doctors jolted patients (in some cases, a dozen times a day) with powerful electric currents, creating seizures violent enough to break bones and erase weeks or months of memories (Smith, 2001). Today, ECT is much more humane, administered according to guidelines developed by the American Psychiatric Association (2001). Patients take painkillers and muscle relaxants before the treatment, and general anesthesia can be used during the procedure. The electrical currents are weaker, inducing seizures only in the brain. In the United States, patients typically undergo three treatments per week for up to a month (Glass, 2001; National Institute of Mental Health, 2016).

Scientists don't know exactly how ECT reduces the symptoms of depression, although a variety of theories have been proposed (Cyrzyk, 2013; Pirnia et al., 2016). And despite its enduring "bad rap," ECT can be an effective treatment for depression, bipolar disorder, and schizophrenia in people who haven't responded well to psychotherapy or drugs (Glass, 2001; Oremus et al., 2015). The major downside of ECT is its tendency to induce confusion and memory loss, including **anterograde and retrograde amnesia** (American Psychiatric Association, 2001; Moirand et al., 2018; Read & Bentall, 2010).

CONNECTIONS
In **Chapter 6,** we discussed amnesia, which is memory loss due to physical or psychological conditions. Retrograde amnesia is the inability to access old memories; anterograde amnesia is the inability to make new memories. ECT can cause these types of amnesia, which is one reason the American Psychiatric Association developed guidelines for its use.

NEUROSURGERY Another extreme option for patients who don't show substantial improvement with psychotherapy or psychotropic drugs is **neurosurgery,** which destroys some portion of the brain or severs connections between different areas of the brain. Like ECT, neurosurgery is tarnished by an unethical past. During the

synonyms
neurosurgery psychosurgery, brain surgery

1930s, 40s, and 50s, doctors performed *prefrontal lobotomies,* destroying part of the frontal lobes or disconnecting them from lower areas of the brain (Kucharski, 1984; Wickens, 2015). But lobotomies may have severe side effects, including permanent impairments to everyday functioning. In the past, this procedure lacked precision, frequently resulting in personality changes and diminished function. The consequences of lobotomy were often worse than the disorders they aimed to fix. The popularity of this surgery plummeted in the 1950s when the first-generation antipsychotics were introduced, offering a safer alternative to surgery (Caruso & Sheehan, 2017; Schlich, 2015, May).

Today, brain surgeries are a last-resort treatment for psychological disorders, and they are far more precise than the archaic lobotomy. Surgeons focus on a small target, destroying only tiny tracts of tissue. One of these surgeries has been a lifesaver for a select few suffering from a severe, drug-resistant form of obsessive-compulsive disorder (OCD), but the precise effects have yet to be determined (Castle, Bosanac, & Rossell, 2015; Mashour et al., 2005). People struggling with severe seizure disorders (as opposed to psychological disorders) sometimes undergo **split-brain operations**—the surgical separation of the right and left hemispheres. With the corpus callosum severed, the two hemispheres are disconnected, preventing the spread of electrical storms responsible for seizures. These more invasive biomedical therapies are seldom used, but they can make a difference in the quality of life for some individuals.

CONNECTIONS

Chapter 2 describes the split-brain operation, a treatment for drug-resistant seizures. When the hemispheres are disconnected, researchers can study them separately to explore their unique capabilities. People who undergo this operation have fewer seizures, and can have normal cognitive abilities and no obvious changes in temperament or personality.

Put Your Heads Together

In your group, **A)** identify the pros and cons of using psychotropic medications, **B)** discuss why people in the United States are so quick to use drugs as the first line of treatment for psychological disorders, and **C)** consider how this approach to treating psychological disorders differs across cultures.

show what you know

1. A young man is taking psychotropic medications for major depression, but the drugs do not seem to be alleviating his symptoms. Which of the following biomedical approaches might his psychiatrist try next?
   a. split-brain operation
   b. tardive dyskinesia
   c. prefrontal lobotomy
   d. electroconvulsive therapy
2. Psychotropic drugs can be divided into four categories, including mood-stabilizing, antipsychotic, anti-anxiety, and:
   a. mood normalizer.
   b. antidepressant.
   c. antagonist.
   d. atypical antipsychotic.
3. Patients with serious disorders who don't show substantial improvement with psychotherapy or psychotropic drugs may benefit from ______________, which involves destroying some portion of the brain or severing connections between different areas of the brain.
4. How do biomedical interventions differ from psychotherapy? Compare their goals.

✓CHECK YOUR ANSWERS IN APPENDIX C.

Psychotherapy: Who's in the Mix?

LO 9 Describe how culture interacts with the therapy process.

WHEN TO LISTEN, WHEN TO TALK One of the challenges of providing therapy in a country like the United States, where ethnic minorities comprise over a third of the population (SAMHSA, 2018), is meeting the needs of clients from vastly different cultures. For Dr. Foster, this part of the job is relatively straightforward. All his clients are Northern Plains Indians, which means they follow similar social rules. And because Dr. Foster belongs to this culture, its norms are

electroconvulsive therapy (ECT) A biomedical treatment for severe disorders that induces seizures in the brain through electrical currents.

neurosurgery A biomedical therapy that involves the destruction of some portion of the brain or connections between different areas of the brain.

The Power of Culture
Residents of the Rosebud Reservation gather for a cultural event. Dr. Foster believes and hopes that Indian language, spiritual ceremony, and culture can act somewhat like a shield, protecting people from psychological problems. But centuries of assaults by Western society have eroded American Indian cultures. Robert VAN DER HILST/Gamma-Rapho via Getty Images.

second nature to him. He has come to expect, for example, that a young Lakota client will not begin talking until he, the therapist, has spoken first. Dr. Foster is an elder, and elders are shown respect. Thus, he might begin a session by talking for 3 or 4 minutes. Once the client does open up, he limits his verbal and nonverbal feedback, sitting quietly and avoiding eye contact. In mainstream American culture, people continuously respond to each other with facial animation and filler words like "wow" and "uh-huh," but the Lakota find this ongoing feedback intrusive.

Another facet of Lakota communication—one that often eludes therapists from outside the culture—is the tendency to pause for long periods in the middle of a conversation. If Dr. Foster poses the question "How are you doing?" a client might take 20 to 30 seconds to respond. These long pauses make some non-Indians very uncomfortable, according to Dr. Foster. "I've found that an outside provider will feel awkward, will start talking within 3 to 5 seconds," he adds. "The client will feel that they never have a chance to speak, and they'll leave frustrated because the person wouldn't be quiet [and] listen."

ACROSS THE WORLD

KNOW THY CLIENT Clearly, it is important for therapists to understand the cultural context in which they work. But does that mean therapists and clients should be matched according to ethnicity? Some clients prefer to discuss private thoughts and feelings with a therapist who shares their experience—someone who knows firsthand how it feels to be, say, African American or Hispanic (Cabral & Smith, 2011). For clients with certain disorders (severe PTSD), treatment outcomes may be better when the therapist and client belong to the same ethnicity. However, it's important to remember that a common ethnic background does not always translate to shared experiences and perspectives. People of the same ethnicity may belong to different religions and socioeconomic groups, and their views on psychotherapy may conflict (Ruglass et al., 2014). Working with a therapist of the same background may be helpful in some instances, but it is not essential.

SHOULD THERAPISTS AND CLIENTS BE MATCHED ACCORDING TO ETHNICITY?

When the therapist and client do come from different worlds, it is the therapist's job to get in touch with the client's unique perspective. That includes being respectful of cultural norms. Western therapists working in Sri Lanka, for example, should be aware that mental illness is highly stigmatized in this cultural setting, and that intense emotional displays (crying in group therapy, for example) are taboo (Christopher, Wendt, Marecek, & Goodman, 2014). Therapists must also be cognizant of their own cultural biases and sensitive to the many forms of prejudice and discrimination people experience.

Within any group, there is vast variation from one individual to the next, but cultural themes do emerge. The Sioux and Blackfeet Indians, for example, are very relationship-oriented. "What kind of car you drive or how nice your home is, and so forth, is not even important," Dr. Foster says. "Relationships matter." Some therapists working with American Indian groups report that entire families may show up at sessions to express support for the client (Prochaska & Norcross, 2014). Similarly, Latino and Polynesian cultures place a high value on family, often prioritizing relationships with relatives over individual needs (Allen & Smith, 2015; Greenfield & Quiroz, 2013). These groups are generally more collectivist, or community-minded, whereas European American cultures tend to be more individualistic (Greenfield & Quiroz, 2013).

Therapists should also be mindful of the challenges facing immigrant populations. Men often have a difficult time adjusting to the declining social status and

You Asked, Dr. Foster Answers

http://qrs.ly/m65a5fy

What are the risks if a psychologist fails to pay appropriate attention to both therapy methods and cultural tradition?

income that comes with moving to a new country. Women tend to fare better, adapting to the new culture and finding jobs more quickly, which can lead to tension between spouses (Prochaska & Norcross, 2014). Keep in mind that these are only general trends; assuming they apply to an entire population promotes stereotyping.

When it comes to psychological treatment, there is no "one-size-fits-all." Every client has a unique story and a singular set of psychological needs. Responding to the needs of the person—her culture, religious beliefs, and unique personal qualities—is essential for successful therapy (Lakes, Lopez, & Garro, 2006; Norcross & Wampold, 2011).

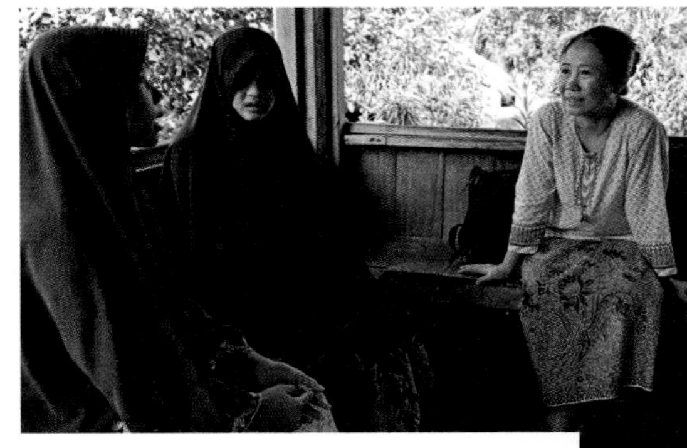

Culture-Conscious
A psychologist meets with two young Muslim women at the Centre for Needy Orphans and Poor Children in Thailand. Psychologists must always be mindful of cultural factors that may come into play during therapy. Thierry Falise/LightRocket via Getty Images.

Let's Get Through This Together

For some people, group therapy is a better fit than individual therapy. First developed in the 1940s, group therapy has adapted to the ever-changing demands of clinical work (Yalom & Leszcz, 2005). Usually, group therapy is led by one or two therapists trained in any of the various approaches (for example, psychoanalytic or cognitive). Sessions can include as few as 3 clients, or upwards of 10, and members share their problems as openly as possible. There are groups to help people cope with shyness, panic disorder, compulsive gambling, grief, and sexual identity issues, just to name a few. Working in a group, clients often realize that they are not alone in their struggles to improve. It is not always a psychological disorder that brings people to group therapy, but instead a desire to work on a specific issue.

LO 10 Identify the benefits and challenges of group therapy.

GROUP THERAPY Research shows that group therapy is as effective as individual therapy for addressing many problems. In fact, it is the preferred approach for interpersonal issues, because it allows therapists to observe clients interacting with others. The therapist's skills play an important role in the success of group sessions, and the dynamics between clients and therapists may be similar to those that arise in individual therapy. (Clients may demonstrate resistance or transference, for example.)

SELF-HELP GROUPS* Another type of group that offers opportunities for personal growth is the ***self-help group***. Alcoholics Anonymous (AA), Al-Anon, Parents without Partners, and Weight Watchers are commonly known examples, but self-help groups provide support for people facing a host of issues, including bereavement, divorce, infertility, HIV/AIDS, and cancer. Some evidence suggests that self-help groups can even benefit people who struggle with psychosis (Scott, Webb, & Rowse, 2015).

synonyms
self-help groups mutual help groups, support groups

With over 2 million active members, AA is the most widely used self-help group in the world (Alcoholics Anonymous, 2016a). Group meetings are open to anyone who wants help overcoming an alcohol problem. AA does not provide counseling, but one-on-one support called "sponsorship" (Alcoholics Anonymous, 2016b). Known as a "twelve-step program," AA bases its model on 12 steps that members must follow in order to take control of their drinking problem. Groups like Al-Anon and Alateen are based on the 12 steps of AA, but provide support for friends and family of people with alcohol problems. Other 12-step programs include Debtors Anonymous, Narcotics Anonymous, Overeaters Anonymous, and Sex Addicts Anonymous. These groups strive to ensure a high level of confidentiality for all participants.

*You can learn more about self-help groups in your area from the National Mental Health Consumers' Self-Help Clearinghouse, at www.mhselfhelp.org.

Self-help groups are *not* typically run by a psychiatrist, licensed psychologist, or other mental health professional, but by a mental health advisor or *paraprofessional* trained to run the groups. The typical AA leader, for example, is a "recovering alcoholic" who grasps the complexities of alcoholism and recovery, but is not necessarily a mental health professional. How effective are 12-step programs like AA? The answer to that question is still under investigation (Glaser, 2015, April). One large review concluded that "no experimental studies unequivocally demonstrated the effectiveness of AA or [12-step] approaches for reducing alcohol dependence or problems" (Ferri, Amato, & Davoli, 2006, p. 2). Even so, many people claim that AA has helped them turn their life around (Alcoholics Anonymous Australia, 2016; Alcoholics Anonymous Great Britain, 2016; David, 2015, August 13).

synonyms

family therapy family counseling

FAMILY THERAPY Introduced in North America in the 1940s, **family therapy** focuses on the family as an integrated system, recognizing how the interactions within it can create instability or lead to collapse of the entire unit (Corey, 2017). Family therapy explores relationship problems rather than the symptoms of particular disorders, teaching communication skills in the process. The family is viewed as a dynamic, holistic entity, and the goal is to understand each person's role in the system, not to root out troublemakers, assign blame, or identify one member who must be "fixed." Because families typically seek the resolution of a specific problem, the course of therapy tends to be brief (Corey, 2017). Suppose a teenage girl has become withdrawn at home and is acting out in school, and the whole family decides to participate in therapy. The therapist begins by helping the parents identify ways they encourage her behaviors (not following through with consequences, for example), and may examine how their marital dynamics affect their children.

TAKING STOCK: AN APPRAISAL OF GROUP AND FAMILY THERAPY Like any treatment, group therapy has its strengths and limitations (**Table 14.5**). Group members may not get along, or they may feel uncomfortable discussing sensitive issues. But conflict and discomfort are not necessarily bad when it comes to therapy (group or otherwise), because such feelings often motivate people to reevaluate how they interact with others, and perhaps try new approaches.

TABLE 14.5 BENEFITS AND DRAWBACKS OF GROUP THERAPY

Strengths	Weaknesses
Sessions generally cost about half as much as individual therapy (Helliker, 2009, March 24).	Not everyone feels at ease discussing personal troubles in a room full of people.
People find relief and comfort knowing that others face similar struggles.	Group members may not always get along. This friction can inhibit the therapeutic process.
Group members offer support and encouragement. They also challenge one another to think and behave in new ways.	Groups may include members who show resistance to group therapy, resulting in poor attendance, tardiness, or dropouts (Yalom & Leszcz, 2005).
Seeing others improve offers hope and inspiration.	Some group therapy participants have had negative family experiences, and thus maintain negative expectations of the group setting (Yalom & Leszcz, 2005).

Listed above are some of the pros and cons of group therapy.

family therapy A type of therapy that focuses on the family as an integrated system, recognizing that the interactions within it can create instability or lead to the breakdown of the family unit.

Evaluating group therapies can be difficult because there is so much variation in approach (psychodynamic, cognitive behavioral, and so on). For many types of clients and problems, the outcomes of group therapy rival those of individual therapy (Barrera, Mott, Hofstein, & Teng, 2013; Burlingame & Baldwin, 2011; Yalom & Leszcz, 2005). As with individual therapies, the role of the therapist is of critical importance: Empathy, good facilitation skills, listening, and careful observation are important predictors of successful outcomes. So, too, are the preparation of the group members, the therapist's verbal style, and the "climate" and cohesion of the group (Burlingame & Baldwin, 2011).

Finding Strength in Others
Cook County inmates participate in a session at the jail's Mental Health Transition Center. There are over a dozen mental health professionals working at the jail, and they often provide therapy in group settings. "We have such a large number of people that receive mental health treatment services here . . . while they may have individualized treatment plans, it's very difficult to individualize the actual care that they receive," Dr. Jones Tapia explains. "So you have to do more group work and rely on group activities to really get the person to the level of stability that they should be at." Joshua Lott/The New York Times/Redux.

Put Your Heads Together

Team up and **A**) discuss the advantages and disadvantages of group therapy. **B**) Looking back at Chapter 13, identify which psychological disorders would be best addressed through group therapy, and explain your reasoning. **C**) Identify disorders that would be best addressed in private sessions, again explaining your reasoning.

Does Psychotherapy Work?

LO 11 Evaluate the effectiveness of psychotherapy.

So far, we have familiarized ourselves with the strengths and weaknesses of various therapeutic approaches, but now let's direct our attention to overall outcomes. How effective is psychotherapy in general? This question is not easily answered, partly because therapeutic "success" is so difficult to quantify. What constitutes success in one context may not be the same in another. And for therapists trying to measure the efficacy of their own methods, eliminating bias can be very challenging.

That being said, decades of research have established that psychotherapy is effective (Campbell, Norcross, Vasquez, & Kaslow, 2013). For many disorders, the benefits derived from psychotherapy may actually surpass those provided by medication (Decker, 2016a). In one large study investigating the effects of psychotherapy, all therapeutic approaches performed equally well across all disorders. But there is one caveat: Individuals who were limited by their insurance companies in terms of therapist choice and treatment duration did not see the same improvement as those who were less restricted by insurance (Seligman, 1995). Perhaps this is not surprising, since people who start therapy but then quit prematurely tend to experience less successful outcomes (Swift & Greenberg, 2012). Given the many therapeutic approaches, the unique qualities of each client, and the variety of therapists, identifying the best type of therapy can be challenging (Pope & Wedding, 2014). But it is relatively safe to say that psychotherapy is "cost-effective, reduces disability, morbidity, and mortality, improves work functioning, decreases uses of psychiatric hospitalization, and . . . leads to reduction in unnecessary use of medical and surgical services" (American Psychological Association [APA], 2012b, para. 19).

How much therapy is enough? The answer to this question depends on the specific needs of the client and the ability of the therapist to help reduce symptoms and improve functioning (Owen, Adelson, Budge, Kopta, & Reese, 2016). Around 50% of clients show "clinically significant improvement" after 21 psychotherapy sessions, whereas some 75% show the same degree of improvement after twice as many sessions (Lambert, Hansen, & Finch, 2001).

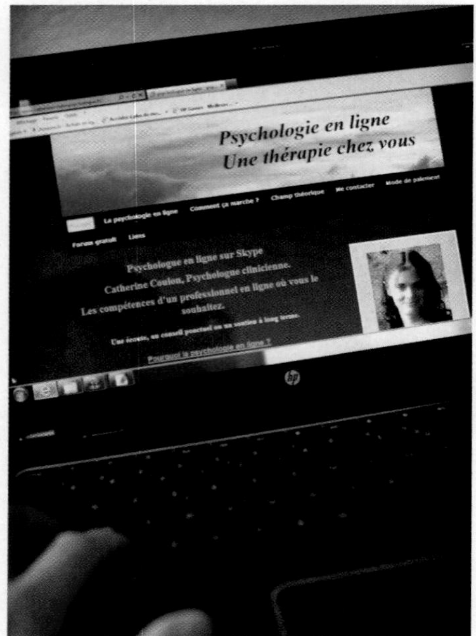

Online Therapy
A clinical psychologist conducts an online consultation with a client. With digital communication technologies such as Skype and Google Hangouts, therapists can conduct sessions with clients on the opposite side of the globe. But problems may arise when therapy occurs online; for example, certain types of "non-verbal communication" may be difficult to detect (de Bitencourt Machado et al., 2016). HAMILTON/REA/Redux.

Help When You Need It

If you suspect you or someone you care about is suffering from a psychological disorder or needs support coping with a divorce, death, or major life change, do not hesitate to seek professional help. The first step is figuring out what kind of therapy best fits the person and the situation (individual, family, group, and so on). Then there is the issue of cost: Therapy can be expensive. These days, one 60-minute therapy session can cost anywhere from $80 to $250 (or more). If you attend a college or university, however, your student fees may cover services at a student counseling center.

Many people have health insurance that helps pay for medication and psychotherapy. In 2010 the Mental Health Parity and Addiction Equity Act (MHPAEA) took effect, requiring all group health insurance plans (with 50 employees or more) to provide mental health treatment benefits equal to those provided for medical treatment. Essentially, this means that mental health problems merit the same attention and resources as physical health problems. Co-payments must be the same, limits on treatment must be the same, and so on. If your insurance plan does not restrict the number of times you can see your family physician, it also cannot limit the number of visits you have with a psychologist (American Psychological Association, 2014, May). For those without insurance, community-based mental health centers provide quality care to all in need, often with a sliding scale for fees.

The next step is finding the right therapist, that is, the right qualified therapist. Helping others manage their mental health issues is a tremendous responsibility that only licensed professionals should take on. Licensing requirements differ from state to state, so we encourage you to verify the standing of a therapist's license with your state's Department of Regulatory Agencies. The pool of potential therapists might include clinical psychologists with PhDs or PsyDs, counseling psychologists, psychiatrists, psychiatric nurses, social workers, marriage and family therapists, pastoral counselors, people with EdDs (doctorates in education), and more. (See Appendix B for additional information about education and careers in psychology.) If you decide to seek professional help online, you should be very cautious.

From Self-Help to Smartphones

Type "psychology" or "self-help" into Google, and you will find thousands of books, articles, and YouTube channels designed to help eliminate stress, boost self-esteem, and beat depression. Some self-help resources contain valuable information, but others make claims that lack scientific support or propagate myths (Kayes & Bailey, 2018, February 2). Keep an open mind, but proceed with skepticism, especially when it comes to the research cited by self-help purveyors. As you have learned, determining the efficacy of therapy is a difficult business, even when studies are impeccably designed. Consumer beware.

LO 12 Summarize the strengths and weaknesses of online psychotherapy.

With 89% of U.S. adults using the Internet and 77% owning smartphones (Pew Research Center, 2018, January 31a & b), online therapies are multiplying like never before. Online therapy, or **e-therapy,** can mean anything from e-mail communication between client and therapist to real-time sessions via webcam. Digital tools are valuable for serving rural areas and providing services to those who would otherwise have no access. But online psychotherapy and telehealth raise concerns about licensing and privacy, and difficulties may arise with "nonverbal communication" and the development of therapeutic relationships (Barak, Hen, Boniel-Nissim, & Shapira, 2008; de Bitencourt Machado et al., 2016; Maheu, Pulier, McMenamin, & Posen, 2012; Sucala et al., 2012).

e-therapy A category of treatment that utilizes the Internet to provide support and therapy.

Can Instagram Help Diagnose Depression?
Which photo is more likely to be posted by a person suffering from depression? One group of researchers used "machine learning tools" to identify signs of depression in Instagram posts. They found that "photos posted by depressed individuals tended to be bluer, darker, and grayer" than those posted by non-depressed people (Reece & Danforth, 2017, p. 7). Republished with permission of Reece and Danforth, from EPJ Data Science (2017) 6:15 DOI 10.1140/epjds/s13688-017-0110-z, permission conveyed through Copyright Clearance Center, Inc.

Some mental health experts believe that smartphones can help identify mental health issues and facilitate the treatment of psychological disorders. Unlike therapists, who only see their clients once or twice a week, smartphones stay with their owners almost all hours of the day. These devices also have built-in technologies like GPS that could be used to monitor behaviors associated with mental health, such as sleep patterns, physical activity, and social interactions. For example, a person who is becoming depressed may be less likely to leave home, respond to phone calls, and be active on social media—all activities that could be recorded by a smartphone. What's more, that same smartphone could be used to connect people to peer support networks and therapists (Dobbs, 2017, July/August). Some research suggests these apps can be effective, especially when used in combination with talk therapy. However, most commercially available options "do not have demonstrated efficacy or adhere to evidence-based practice" (Firth et al., 2017). The bottom line: Mental health apps hold promise, but more research is needed.

While we are on the topic of digital technologies, we cannot resist a tie-in to social media. What role do Facebook, LinkedIn, and other forms of social media play in the lives of therapists and clients?

SOCIAL MEDIA AND PSYCHOLOGY

THERAPIST OR FRIEND? Imagine that you are the psychotherapist serving a small community college. You talk to students about their deepest fears and conflicts. They tell you about their mothers, fathers, lovers, and enemies. In some respects, you know these students better than their closest friends do. But your clients are not your buddies. So what do you say when a client asks you to become a friend on Facebook, a contact on LinkedIn, or a follower on Instagram?

DOES FACEBOOK HAVE A PLACE IN THERAPY?

Our answer to that question is a definitive no. Psychotherapy is a private affair, social media is very public, and "when psychologists interact in both spheres, they do risk violating clients' confidentiality or crossing boundaries" (Lannin & Scott, 2014, February, p. 56). However, that does not mean social media has no place in the mental health field. Like other health professionals, psychologists use social media to connect with colleagues, distribute credible information, and market their services (Gagnon & Sabus, 2015; Moorhead et al., 2013). These platforms may even come in handy during therapy; imagine a client with public speaking anxiety who shows his therapist a video of himself giving a speech (Kolmes, 2012).

The emergence of social media presents new opportunities and risks for mental health professionals. Therapists who use social media would be wise to create two separate profiles (one personal, and the other professional) and to establish a formal policy outlining the parameters of their social media use (Lannin & Scott, 2014).

Put Your Heads Together

Team up and decide which of the theoretical approaches presented in this chapter would be most compatible with online therapy. Which should never be used online? Explain your reasoning.

PASSIONATE PROVIDERS Before wrapping up, we thought you might like to know what Dr. Dan Foster and Dr. Nneka Jones Tapia are doing these days. Dr. Foster is now working as a full-time consultant in Montana. He and his wife Becky (also a doctorate level psychologist) work with the Rosebud Sioux Tribe Methamphetamine Program, and Dr. Foster sees clients once a week at Montana State Hospital in Warm Springs. One of their daughters, also a clinical psychologist, provides telemedicine services to the Blackfeet Tribal Clinic.

Dr. Dan Foster with his wife, Dr. Becky Foster. Macmillan Learning.

Dr. Nneka Jones Tapia. Courtesy Dr. Nneka Jones Tapia.

After many years of service at Cook County Jail, Dr. Jones Tapia has decided to take her career in a new direction. Looking back on her days at the jail, Dr. Jones Tapia thinks about the remarkable change she witnessed in some inmates. She remembers how they appeared in their mugshots when they first came into custody. "I can't even describe it. It's almost like they look humiliated; they look angry; it's every negative emotion you can think of," she says. Helping these men and women change their outlook and move in a more positive direction, and seeing that transformation in their faces is "an intrinsic reward that is like none other," Dr. Jones Tapia says. "I try to encourage as many clinical professionals as I can to go into working in jails and prisons. . . . To me, there is true value in really helping a human being at their worst, to see life in a different way."

show what you know

1. Under what conditions might group therapy fail or be inappropriate?
2. What are some concerns regarding online psychotherapy?
3. If you were trying to convince a friend that psychological treatment works for many people, what evidence would you provide? What would you say about the role of culture in its outcome?
4. Studies indicate that psychotherapy is generally effective, but which of the following factors has been linked to less successful outcomes?
   a. type of therapeutic approach
   b. client's disorder
   c. limits imposed by an insurance company
   d. Mental Health Parity and Addiction Equity Act

✓ CHECK YOUR ANSWERS IN APPENDIX C.

YOUR SCIENTIFIC WORLD is a new application-based feature appearing in every chapter. In these online activities, you will take on role-playing scenarios that encourage you to think critically and apply your knowledge of psychological science to solve a real-world problem. For example: Have you ever had a panic attack? In this activity, you explore the different types of therapy that can help someone who suffers from an overwhelming fear of public speaking. You can access Your Scientific World activities in LaunchPad. Have fun!

SUMMARY OF CONCEPTS

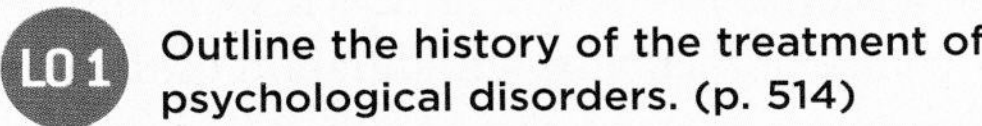

LO 1 Outline the history of the treatment of psychological disorders. (p. 514)

Early "treatments" for psychological disorders were often inhumane. According to one theory, Stone Age people may have used trephination (drilling holes through the skull) to let demons escape. In the late 1700s, Philippe Pinel advanced the idea of "moral treatment," which eventually spread throughout Europe and America. In the mid- to late 1800s, Dorothea Dix supported the "mental hygiene movement," a campaign to reform asylums in America. The mid-1900s witnessed deinstitutionalization, a mass movement of people with psychological disorders out of America's mental institutions and into the community.

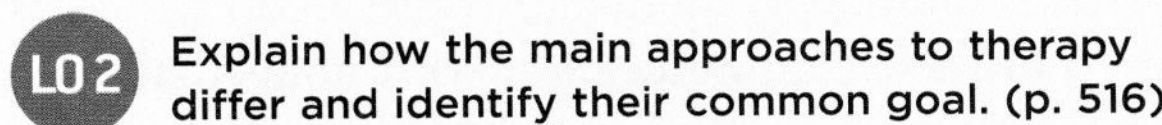

LO 2 Explain how the main approaches to therapy differ and identify their common goal. (p. 516)

The insight therapies—psychoanalysis, psychodynamic therapy, and humanistic therapy—aim to increase awareness of self and environment. Behavior therapy focuses on behavioral change. Cognitive therapy seeks to change maladaptive thoughts. Biomedical therapy targets the biological basis of disorders, often with the use of medication. All these approaches share a common goal: to reduce symptoms and increase quality of life, whether the person suffers from a debilitating psychological disorder or simply wants to lead a happier existence.

LO 3 Describe how psychoanalysis differs from psychodynamic therapy. (p. 519)

Psychoanalysis, the first formal system of psychotherapy, attempts to uncover unconscious conflicts, making it possible to address and work through them. Psychodynamic therapy is an updated form of psychoanalysis that incorporates many of Freud's core themes, including the notion that personality characteristics and behavior problems often can be traced to unconscious conflicts. With psychodynamic therapy, therapists see clients once a week for several months rather than many times a week for years. And instead of sitting quietly off to the side, therapists sit facing clients and engage in dialogue.

LO 4 Outline the principles and characteristics of humanistic therapy. (p. 521)

Humanistic therapy concentrates on the positive aspects of human nature: our powerful desires to form close relationships, treat others with warmth and empathy, and grow as individuals. Instead of digging up unconscious thoughts and feelings, humanistic therapy emphasizes conscious experience and problems in the present.

LO 5 Describe person-centered therapy. (p. 522)

Person-centered therapy aims to help clients reach their full potential. Sitting face-to-face with the client, the therapist's main job is to "be there" for the client through empathy, unconditional positive regard, genuineness, and active listening, all important components of building a therapeutic alliance. The goals of treatments are to reduce incongruence between the ideal and real self, to create a warm and accepting relationship between therapist and client, and to help clients see they have the power to make changes in their lives and follow a path of positive growth.

LO 6 Outline the principles and characteristics of behavior therapy. (p. 524)

Using the principles of classical conditioning, operant conditioning, and observational learning, behavior therapy aims to replace maladaptive behaviors with more adaptive behaviors. It incorporates a variety of techniques, including exposure therapy, aversion therapy, systematic desensitization, and behavior modification. Behavior therapy focuses on observable behaviors in the present.

LO 7 Outline the principles and characteristics of cognitive therapy. (p. 529)

The goal of cognitive therapy is to identify maladaptive thinking and help clients change the way they view the world and relationships. Aaron Beck believed patterns of automatic thoughts, or cognitive distortions, lie at the root of psychological disturbances. The aim of cognitive therapy is to help clients recognize and challenge cognitive distortions. Sessions are short-term, action-oriented, and homework-intensive. Albert Ellis created rational emotive behavior therapy (REBT), another form of cognitive therapy, to help people identify and correct irrational and illogical ways of thinking.

LO 8 Summarize the biomedical interventions and identify their common goal. (p. 531)

Psychopharmacology is the scientific study of how psychotropic medications alter perception, mood, behavior, and other aspects of psychological functioning. Psychotropic drugs include antidepressant, mood-stabilizing, antipsychotic, and anti-anxiety medications. When severe symptoms do not improve with medication and psychotherapy, other biomedical options are available: electroconvulsive therapy (ECT), which causes seizures in the brain; and neurosurgery, which destroys some portion of the brain or severs connections between different brain areas. Biomedical interventions target the biological roots of psychological disorders.

Describe how culture interacts with the therapy process. (p. 537)

Therapists work with clients from a vast array of cultures. Every client has a unique story and a singular set of psychological needs, but therapists should know the cultural context in which they work. This includes being respectful of cultural norms and sensitive to the many forms of prejudice and discrimination that people can experience.

LO 10 Identify the benefits and challenges of group therapy. (p. 539)

The benefits of group therapy include cost-effectiveness, identification with others, accountability, support, encouragement, and a sense of hope. Challenges include potential conflict among group members and discomfort expressing feelings in the presence of others.

Evaluate the effectiveness of psychotherapy. (p. 541)

Psychotherapy generally "works," with different approaches achieving comparable success across disorders. Clients with insurance plans that limit choice of therapists and duration of therapy do not see the same improvement as those with less restrictive insurance. In addition, people who start therapy but then quit prematurely experience less successful outcomes.

LO 12 Summarize the strengths and weaknesses of online psychotherapy. (p. 542)

As more people have gained access to the Internet, online therapies have multiplied. E-therapy can mean anything from an e-mail communication between client and therapist to real-time sessions via webcam. Digital tools are valuable for serving rural areas and providing services to those who would otherwise have no access. However, online psychotherapy raises many concerns about licensing, privacy, communication with nonverbal cues, and the development of therapeutic relationships.

KEY TERMS

active listening, p. 522
anti-anxiety drugs, p. 535
antidepressant drugs, p. 532
antipsychotic drugs, p. 535
aversion therapy, p. 527
behavior modification, p. 528
behavior therapy, p. 516
biomedical therapy, p. 516
cognitive behavioral therapy (CBT), p. 530
cognitive therapy, p. 529
deinstitutionalization, p. 514
eclectic approach to therapy, p. 518
electroconvulsive therapy (ECT), p. 536
empathy, p. 522
e-therapy, p. 542
evidence-based practice, p. 518
exposure, p. 524
family therapy, p. 540
free association, p. 519
genuineness, p. 522
humanistic therapy, p. 522
insight therapies, p. 516
interpretation, p. 520
mood-stabilizing drugs, p. 534
neurosurgery, p. 536
nondirective, p. 522
overgeneralization, p. 529
person-centered therapy, p. 522
psychodynamic therapy, p. 520
psychotherapy, p. 516
rational emotive behavior therapy (REBT), p. 530
resistance, p. 520
systematic desensitization, p. 527
therapeutic alliance, p. 522
token economy, p. 528
transference, p. 520

TEST PREP ARE YOU READY?

1. Philippe Pinel worked to improve the living conditions of people in mental institutions, removing their chains and showing them respect and care. This ____________ eventually spread throughout Europe and America.
   a. trephination
   b. moral treatment
   c. psychoanalysis
   d. deinstitutionalization
2. Which of the following goals are shared by the main approaches to therapy?
   a. increase awareness of self and environment
   b. use medications to target biological basis of disorder
   c. focus on behavioral change
   d. reduce symptoms and increase quality of life
3. Lorena has three weekly sessions with her therapist. She generally lies on a couch while her therapist sits off to the side, out of Lorena's sight. The goal of her therapy is to uncover unconscious conflicts influencing her behavior. Which type of therapy is Lorena receiving?
   a. psychodynamic
   b. psychoanalysis
   c. behavioral
   d. humanistic
4. A friend tells you about his therapist, who is nondirective, uses active listening, and shows empathy and unconditional positive regard. This therapist is most likely conducting:
   a. cognitive therapy.
   b. behavior therapy.
   c. psychoanalysis.
   d. person-centered therapy.
5. Systematic desensitization uses ____________ that represent gradual increases in clients' anxiety.
   a. hierarchies
   b. token economies
   c. behavior modification
   d. free association
6. Which of the following statements would not qualify as one of Beck's cognitive errors?
   a. My friend stole from me; therefore, everyone will steal from me.
   b. Getting fired once does not mean my career is over.
   c. I forgot to vote; that's why the president lost.
   d. My hairdresser added $20 to my Visa charge. You can't trust salons.
7. Which of the following claims about group therapy is true?
   a. It generally costs twice as much as one-on-one therapy.
   b. Everyone feels comfortable sharing their troubles with a group.
   c. Group members avoid pushing others to own up to their mistakes.
   d. Seeing others improve offers hope and inspiration.
8. Humanistic therapy emphasizes the positive nature of humans, with a focus on:
   a. the unconscious.
   b. rational emotive behavior.
   c. past problems.
   d. the present.
9. ____________ is the scientific study of how medication alters perceptions, moods, behaviors, and other aspects of psychological functioning.
   a. Biomedical therapy
   b. Psychoeducation
   c. Therapeutic alliance
   d. Psychopharmacology
10. Overall, psychotherapy is cost-effective and helps to decrease disability, hospitalization, and problems at work. Which of the following factors may reduce its effectiveness?
    a. unlimited number of sessions
    b. insurance-mandated limitations on choice of therapist
    c. number of people in a therapy session
    d. gender of therapist
11. Compare and contrast cognitive behavioral therapy and insight therapies.
12. Beck identified a collection of common cognitive distortions. Describe two of these distortions and give examples of each.
13. How might a behavior therapist help someone overcome a fear of spiders?
14. How does culture influence the therapeutic process?
15. Describe the strengths and weaknesses of online psychotherapy.

✓ CHECK YOUR ANSWERS IN APPENDIX C.

Go to **LaunchPad** or **Achieve: Read & Practice** to test your understanding with **LearningCurve**.

APPENDIX

A

Introduction to Statistics

The vast knowledge base that defines the field of psychology is the result of rigorous and meticulous scientific research, most of which entails careful collection of data. In Chapter 1, we presented various methods used to gather this data, but we only touched upon statistical approaches for analyzing it. Here, we will discover how we can use data meaningfully: Welcome to **statistics,** the science of collecting, organizing, analyzing, displaying, and interpreting data.

Data are everywhere—not just in the academic materials published by psychologists. Newspapers, websites, and television shows report on statistical findings every day, though they sometimes make mistakes, exaggerate, or leave out important information. You can detect these types of errors if you understand statistics. It is important for everyone (not just psychology students) to think critically about how data are presented.

Descriptive and Inferential Statistics

There are two basic types of statistics: descriptive and inferential. With *descriptive statistics,* researchers summarize information they have gleaned from their studies. The raw data can be organized and presented through tables, graphs, and charts, examples of which we provide in this appendix. We can also use descriptive statistics to represent the average and the spread of the data (how dispersed the values are), a topic we will explore later. The goal of descriptive statistics is to describe data, or provide a snapshot of what is observed in a study. **Inferential statistics**, on the other hand, go beyond simple data presentation. With inferential statistics, for example, we can determine the probability of events and make predictions about general trends. The goals are to generalize findings from studies, make predictions based on relationships among variables, and test hypotheses. Inferential statistics also can be used to make statements about how confident we are in our findings based on the data collected.

In Chapter 1, we defined a *hypothesis* as a statement used to test a prediction. Once a researcher develops a hypothesis, she gathers data and uses statistics to test it. **Hypothesis testing** involves mathematical procedures to determine whether data support a hypothesis or simply result from chance. Let's look at an example to see how this works. (And you might find it useful to review Chapter 1 if your knowledge of research methods is a little rusty.)

Suppose a researcher wants to determine whether taking vitamin D supplements can boost cognitive function. The researcher designs an experiment to test if giving participants vitamin D pills (the independent variable) leads to better performance on some sort of cognitive task, such as a memory test (the test score being the dependent variable). Participants in the experimental group receive doses of vitamin D and participants in the control group receive a placebo. Neither the participants nor the researchers working directly with those participants know who is getting the vitamin D

CONNECTIONS

In **Chapter 1,** we presented a study examining the impact of fast-paced cartoons on executive functioning. The researchers tested the following hypothesis: Children who watch 9 minutes of *SpongeBob SquarePants* will be more likely to show a decrease in cognitive function than children who watch an educational program or simply draw. The researchers used inferential statistics to determine that the children in the *SpongeBob* group did show a lapse in cognitive functioning in comparison to the other two groups in the study.

statistics A science that focuses on how to collect, organize, analyze, display, and interpret data; numbers that describe characteristics of a sample.

hypothesis testing Mathematical procedures used to determine the likelihood that a researcher's predictions are supported by the data collected.

and who is getting the placebo, so we call it a **double-blind procedure**. After the data have been collected, the researcher needs to compare the memory scores for the two groups to see if the treatment worked. In all likelihood, the average test scores of the two groups will differ simply because they include two different groups of people. So how does the researcher know whether the difference is sufficient to conclude that vitamin D had an effect? Using statistical procedures, the researcher can state with a chosen level of certainty (for example, with 95% confidence) that the disparity in average scores resulted from the vitamin D treatment. In other words, there is a slight possibility (in this case, 5%) that the difference was merely due to chance.

Using statistical methods, researchers can establish **statistical significance,** indicating that **differences between groups** in a study (for example, the average scores for experimental and control groups) are so great that they are likely due to the researchers' manipulations. In other words, the mathematical analyses suggest a minimal probability that the findings were due to chance. When we use the experimental method (that is, randomly assign individuals, manipulate an independent variable, and control extraneous variables) and find *statistically* significant differences between our experimental and control groups, we can be assured that these differences are very likely due to how we treated the participants (for example, administering vitamin D treatment versus a placebo).

In addition to determining statistical significance, we also have to consider the *practical importance* of findings, meaning the degree to which the results of a study can be used in a meaningful way. In other words, do the findings have any relevance to real life? If the vitamin D regimen produces statistically significant results (with a performance gap between the experimental and control groups most likely not due to chance), the researcher still must determine its practical importance. Suppose the two groups differ by only a few points on the cognitive test; then the question is whether vitamin D supplementation is really worth the trouble. We should note that big samples are more likely to result in *statistically* significant results (small differences between groups can be amplified by a large sample) even though the results might not provide much practical information.

CONNECTIONS

In **Chapter 14,** we presented the biomedical approach to treating psychological disorders. Many researchers use a double-blind procedure to determine whether psychotropic drugs reduce the symptoms of psychological disorders. For example, Palgi and colleagues (2017) used a randomized double-blind procedure to determine the impact of oxytocin and a placebo on participants' "empathic abilities" (p. 70). The researchers used a double-blind procedure to ensure that neither the participants' nor the researchers' expectations unduly influenced the results.

CONNECTIONS

In **Chapter 5,** we presented Bandura's work on observational learning and aggressive models. Bandura and colleagues (1961) divided participants into experimental and control groups and found that the average "expression of aggression" for children who viewed aggressive models was statistically significantly greater than for the control group children who did not observe an aggressive model. The difference in the amount of expressed aggression for the two groups was large enough to be attributed to the experimenters' manipulation as opposed to chance (for example, simply based on the children who were assigned randomly to each group).

Sampling Techniques

Long before data are collected and analyzed, researchers must select people to participate in their studies. Depending on what a psychologist is interested in studying, the probability of being able to include all members of a *population* is not likely, so generally a *sample,* or subset of the population, is chosen. The characteristics of the sample members must closely reflect those of the population of interest so that the researcher can generalize, or apply, her findings to the population at large.

In an effort to ensure that the sample accurately reflects the larger population, a researcher may use *random sampling,* which means that all members of the population have an equal chance of being invited to participate in the study. If the researcher has a numbered list of the population members, she could generate random numbers on a computer and then contact the individuals with those numbers. Because the numbers are randomly picked, everyone on the list has an equal chance of being selected. Another approach is *stratified sampling.* A researcher chooses this method if she wants a certain variable to be well represented—car ownership in urban areas, for example. She divides the population into four groups or *strata* (no car, one car, two cars, more than two cars), and then picks randomly from within each group or *stratum,* ensuring that all the different types of car ownership are included in the sample. Researchers use strata such as ethnicity, gender, and age group to ensure a sample has appropriate representation of these important factors.

Some researchers use a method called *convenience sampling,* which involves choosing a sample from a group that is readily available or convenient. If a student researcher is interested in collecting data on coffee-drinking behavior from people

statistical significance The probability that the findings of a study were due to chance.

who frequent coffee shops, he might be tempted to go to the Starbucks and Peet's Coffee shops in his neighborhood. But this approach does not use random sampling (just think of all the Dunkin' Donuts and Caribou Coffee drinkers who would be excluded), so the likelihood that it results in a *representative sample* is very slim. In other words, a randomly picked sample is more likely than a convenience sample to include members with characteristics similar to the population. Only if a sample is representative can a researcher use his findings to make accurate *inferences* or valid generalizations about the characteristics of the population. But it's important to note that even a randomly selected sample is not foolproof. There is always the possibility that the chosen participants have characteristics that are not typical for the population. The smaller the sample, the less likely it will be representative and the less reliable the results. Larger samples tend to provide more accurate reflections of the population being studied.

The ultimate goal of most studies is to provide results that can be used to make inferences about a population. We can describe a population using various **parameters,** or numbers that delineate its characteristics—for example, the average number of cars owned by *all* households in urban areas in the United States. When the same characteristics are determined for a sample, they are referred to as *statistics*—in this case, the average number of cars owned by households in the sample. (Recall that the word "statistics" can also refer to the scientific discipline of collecting, organizing, analyzing, displaying, and interpreting data.) We will introduce you to some of these numerical characteristics later when we discuss *measures of central tendency* and *measures of variation.*

Understanding sampling techniques can help you become a more critical consumer of scientific information. When reading or watching media reports on scientific studies, ask yourself whether the samples are truly representative. If not, the use of statistics to make inferences about parameters is suspect; the findings might only be true for the sample, not the population.

Variables

Once a sample is selected, researchers can begin studying and manipulating the variables of interest. Variables are measurable characteristics that vary over time or across people, situations, or objects. In psychology, variables may include cognitive abilities, social behaviors, or even the font size in books. Statisticians often refer to two types of variables. *Quantitative variables* are numerical, meaning they have values that can be represented by numbered units or ranks. Midterm exam scores, age at graduation, and number of students in a class are all quantitative variables. ***Qualitative variables*** are characteristics that enable us to place participants in categories, but they cannot be assigned numbered units or ranks. An example might be college major; you can ask all the students in the library to line up under signs for psychology, biology, chemistry, undeclared, and so on, and thereby categorize them by their majors. We can rank how much we like the majors based on the courses associated with them, but the majors cannot be ordered or ranked in and of themselves. We can alphabetize them, but that is a ranking based on their labels. We can even order the majors in terms of how many students are pursuing them, but that is a different variable (number of students). Other examples of qualitative variables include eye color, ethnicity, and religious faith.

synonyms
qualitative variables categorical variables

Throughout this textbook, we have identified multiple characteristics and traits that can be used as variables in studies. Pick two chapters and see if you can identify five variables that are quantitative and five that are qualitative.

✓ CHECK YOUR ANSWERS IN APPENDIX C.

parameters Numbers that describe characteristics of a population.

Variables are the focal point of experiments in psychology. Typically, the goal is to determine how one variable (the dependent variable) is affected by changes in another (the independent variable). Many studies focus on similar topics, so you might imagine it's easy to compare their results. But this is not necessarily the case. Sometimes psychologists define variables in different ways, or study the same variables with vastly different samples, methods of measurement, and experimental designs. How do we reconcile all their findings? We rely on a **meta-analysis,** a statistical approach that allows researchers to combine the findings of different studies and draw general conclusions. A meta-analysis is an objective, quantitative (measurable) mechanism for gathering and analyzing findings from a set of studies on the same topic (Conroy & Hagger, 2018; Montoya, Kershaw, & Prosser, 2018).

The Presentation of Data

Conducting an experiment is a major accomplishment, but it has little impact if researchers cannot devise an effective way to present their data. If they share only raw data that has not been organized in any way, others will find it difficult to draw valuable conclusions. Imagine you have collected the data presented in **Table A.1,** which represents the number of minutes of REM sleep (the dependent variable) each of your 44 participants ($n = 44$; n is the symbol for sample size) had during one night spent in your sleep lab. Looking at this table, you can barely tell what variable is being studied.

TABLE A.1 RAW DATA FROM REM SLEEP STUDY

77	114	40	18	68	96	81	142	62	80	117
81	98	76	22	71	35	85	49	105	99	49
20	70	35	83	150	57	112	131	104	121	47
31	47	39	92	73	122	68	58	100	52	101

Quantitative Data Displays

A common and simple way to display data is to use a **frequency distribution,** which shows how often the various values in a data set are present. In **Table A.2,** we have

TABLE A.2 FREQUENCY DISTRIBUTION FOR REM SLEEP STUDY

Minutes of REM (Class Limits)	Raw Frequency	Relative Frequency
4 to 24	3	.068
25 to 45	5	.114
46 to 66	8	.182
67 to 87	12	.273
88 to 108	8	.182
109 to 129	5	.114
130 to 150	3	.068

meta-analysis A type of statistical analysis that combines findings from many studies on a single topic; statistics used to merge the outcomes of many studies.

frequency distribution A simple way to portray data that displays how often various values in a data set are present.

displayed the data in seven *classes,* or groups, of equal width. The frequency for each class is tallied up and appears in the middle column. The first class goes from 4 to 24 minutes, and in our sample of 44 participants, only 3 had a total amount of REM in this class (18, 20, 22 minutes). The greatest number of participants experienced between 67 and 87 minutes of REM sleep. By looking at the frequency for each class, you begin to see patterns. In this case, the greatest number of participants had REM sleep within the middle of the distribution, and fewer appear on the ends. We will come back to this pattern shortly.

Frequency distributions can also be presented with a **histogram,** which displays the classes of a variable on the *x-axis* and the frequency of the data on the *y-axis* (portrayed by the height of the vertical bars). The values on the *y*-axis can be either the raw frequency (actual number) or the relative frequency (proportion of the whole set; see Table A.2, right column). The example portrayed in **Figure A.1** is a histogram of the minutes of REM sleep, with the classes representing the number of minutes in REM on the *x*-axis and the raw frequency on the *y*-axis. Looking at a histogram makes it easier to see how the data are distributed across classes. In this case, you can see that the most frequent duration of REM is in the middle of the distribution (the 67- to 87-minute class), and that the frequency tapers off toward both ends. Histograms are often used to display quantitative variables that have a wide range of values that would be difficult to interpret if they weren't grouped in classes.

Similar to a histogram is a **frequency polygon,** which uses lines instead of bars to represent the frequency of the data values, and shows midpoints of the classes (rather than class boundaries) along the *x*-axis. The same data displayed in the histogram (Figure A.1) appear in the frequency polygon in **Figure A.2** We see the same general shape in the frequency polygon, but instead of raw frequency, we have used the relative frequency to represent the proportion of participants in each of the classes (Table A.2, right column). Thus, rather than saying 12 participants had 67 to 87 minutes of REM sleep, we can state that the proportion of participants in this class was approximately .27, or 27%. Relative frequencies are especially useful when comparing data sets with different sample sizes. Imagine we wanted to compare two different studies examining REM sleep: one with a sample size of 500, and the other with a sample size of 44. The larger sample might have a greater number of

FIGURE A.1
Histogram of REM sleep study

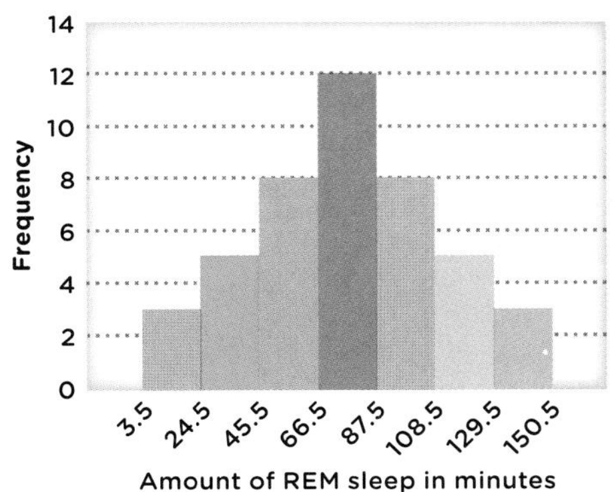

FIGURE A.2
Frequency polygon of REM sleep study

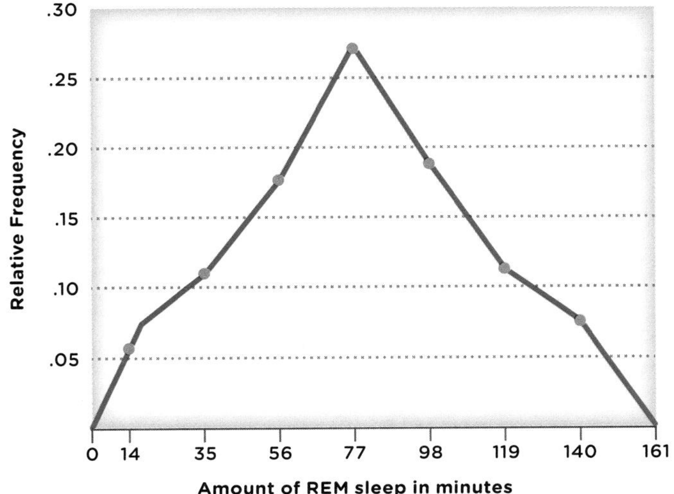

histogram Displays the classes of a variable on the *x*-axis and the frequency of the data on the *y*-axis; frequency is indicated by the height of the vertical bars.

frequency polygon A type of graphic display that uses lines to represent the frequency of data values.

Stem	Leaf
1	8
2	0 2
3	1 5 5 9
4	0 7 7 9 9
5	2 7 8
6	2 8 8
7	0 1 3 6 7
8	0 1 1 3 5
9	2 6 8 9
10	0 1 4 5
11	2 4 7
12	1 2
13	1
14	2
15	0

FIGURE A.3
Stem-and-leaf plot for REM sleep study

participants in the 67- to 87-minute class (let's say 50 participants out of 500 [.10] versus 12 out of 44 participants [.27] in the smaller sample), making the raw frequency of this class (50) in the larger sample greater than the raw frequency of this class (12) in the smaller sample. But the proportion for the smaller sample would still be greater (smaller sample = .27 versus larger sample = .10). The relative frequency makes it easier to detect these differences in proportion.

Another common way to display quantitative data is through a **stem-and-leaf plot,** which uses the actual data values in its display. The *stem* is made up of the first digits in a number, and the *leaf* is made up of the last digit in each number. This allows us to group numbers by 10s, 20s, 30s, and so on. In **Figure A.3,** we display the REM sleep data in a stem-and-leaf plot using the first part of the number (either the 10s and/or the 100s) as the stem, and the ones column as the leaf. In the top row, for example, 8 is from the ones column of the smallest number in the data set, 18; 0 and 2 in the second row represent the ones column from the numbers 20 and 22; the 0 in the bottom row comes from 150.

Distribution Shapes

Once the data have been displayed on a graph, researchers look very closely at the **distribution shape,** which is just what it sounds like—how the data are spread along the *x*-axis. (That is, the shape is based on the variable represented along the *x*-axis and the frequency of its values portrayed on the *y*-axis.) A symmetric shape is apparent in the histogram in **Figure A.4a,** which shows a distribution for a sample that is high in the middle, but tapers off at the same rate on each end. The bell-shaped or normal curve on the right (b) also has a symmetric shape, and this type of curve is fairly typical in psychology. (Curves generally represent the distribution of the entire population.) Many human characteristics have this type of distribution, including cognitive abilities, personality characteristics, and a variety of physical characteristics such as height and weight. Through many years of study, we have found that measurements for the great majority of people fall in the middle of the distribution, and a smaller proportion have characteristics represented on the ends (tails) of the distribution. For example, if you look at the IQ scores displayed in **Figure A.4b,** you can see that 68% of people have scores between 85 and 115, about 95% have scores between 70 and 130, around 99.7% fall between 55 and 145, and only a tiny percentage (.3%) are below 55 or above 145. These percentages are true for many other characteristics.

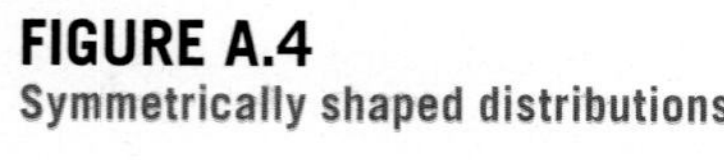

FIGURE A.4
Symmetrically shaped distributions

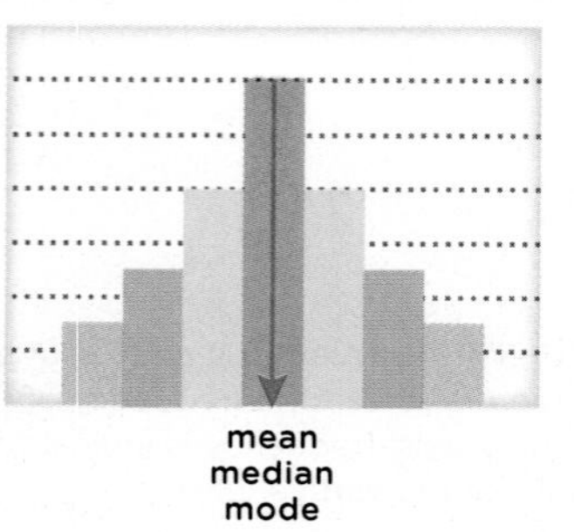

(a)

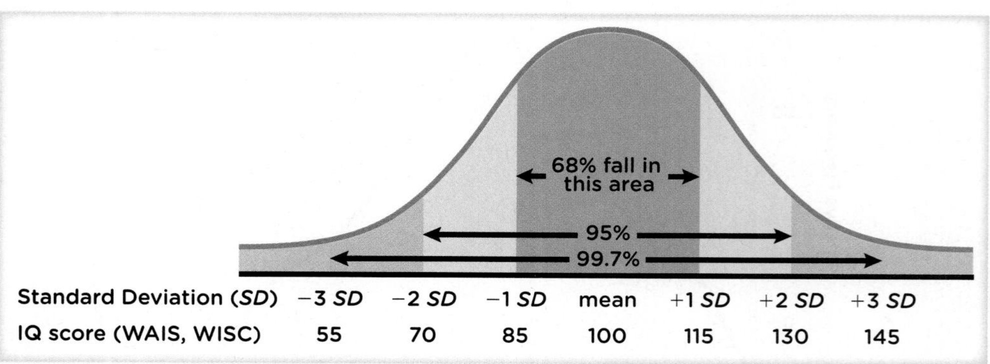

(b)

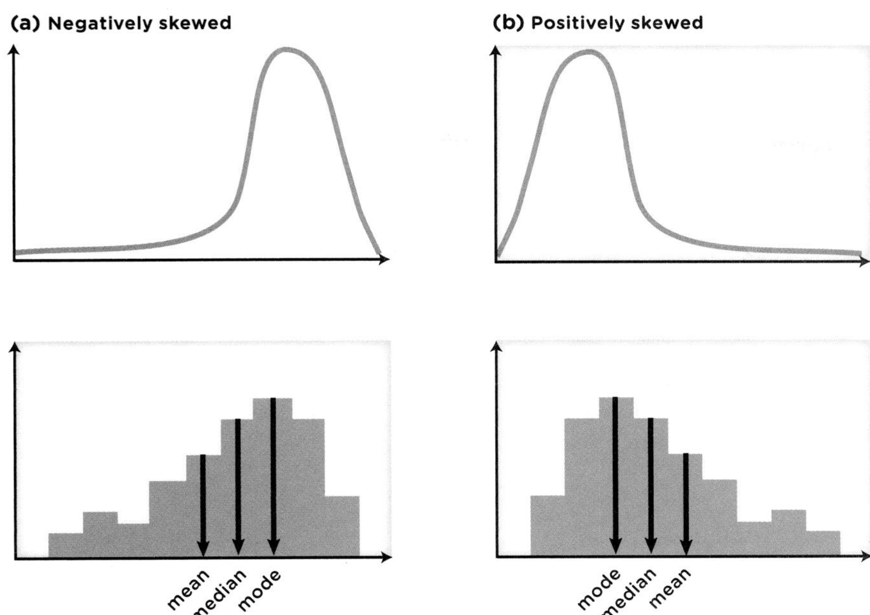

FIGURE A.5
Skewed distributions

Some data have a **skewed distribution,** which is not symmetrical. As you can see in **Figure A.5a,** a **negatively skewed** or *left-skewed* distribution has a longer tail to the left side of the distribution. A **positively skewed** or *right-skewed* distribution (**Figure A.5b**) has a longer tail to the right side of the distribution. Determining whether a distribution is skewed is particularly important because it informs our decision about what type of statistical analysis to conduct. Later, we will see how certain types of data values can play a role in *skewing* a distribution.

Qualitative Data Displays

Thus far, we have discussed several ways to represent quantitative data. With qualitative data, a frequency distribution lists the various categories and the number of members in each. For example, if we wanted to display the college major data on the 44 students interviewed at the library, we could use a frequency distribution (**Table A.3**).

TABLE A.3 FREQUENCY DISTRIBUTION OF COLLEGE MAJORS

College Major	Raw Frequency	Percent
Biology	3	7
Chemistry	5	11.5
Culinary Arts	8	18
English	5	11.5
Nursing	12	27
Psychology	3	7
Undecided	8	18

stem-and-leaf plot A type of graphical display that uses the actual data values in the form of leading digits and trailing digits.

distribution shape How the frequencies of the values are shaped along the *x*-axis.

skewed distribution Nonsymmetrical frequency distribution.

negatively skewed A nonsymmetric distribution with a longer tail to the left side of the distribution; left-skewed distribution.

positively skewed A nonsymmetric distribution with a longer tail to the right side of the distribution; right-skewed distribution.

FIGURE A.6
Bar graph for college majors

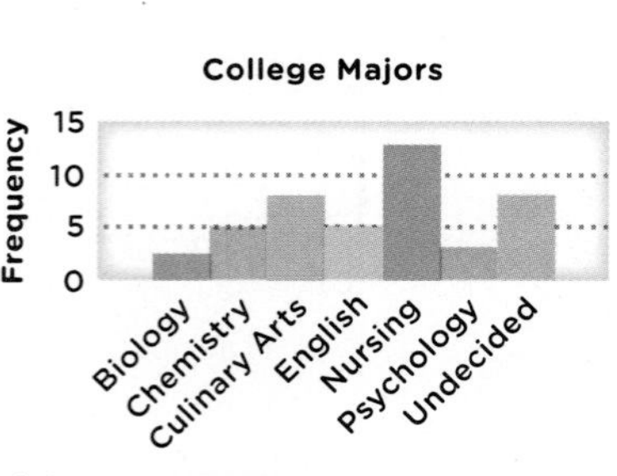

(a) Data on majors collected from library interviews

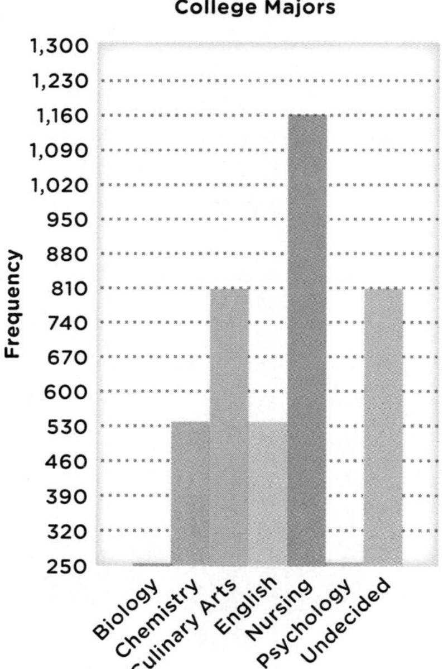

(b) Data on majors collected campus-wide

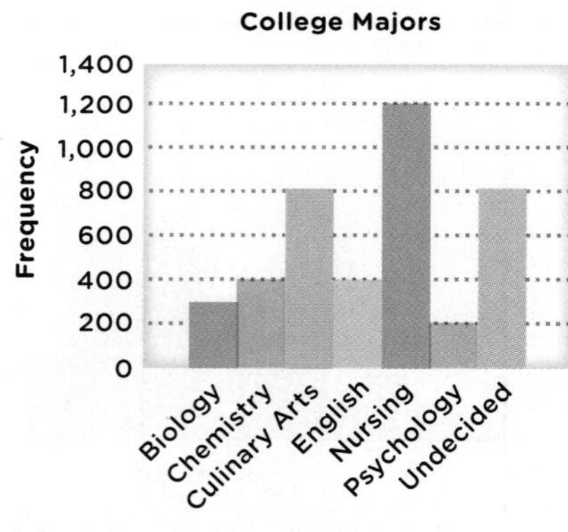

(c) Data on majors collected campus-wide

Another common way to present qualitative data is through a **bar graph,** which displays the categories of interest on the *x*-axis and their frequencies on the *y*-axis. **Figure A.6** shows how the data collected in the library can be presented in a bar graph. Bar graphs are useful for comparing several different populations on the same variable (for example, comparing college majors by gender or ethnicity).

FIGURE A.7
Pie chart for college majors

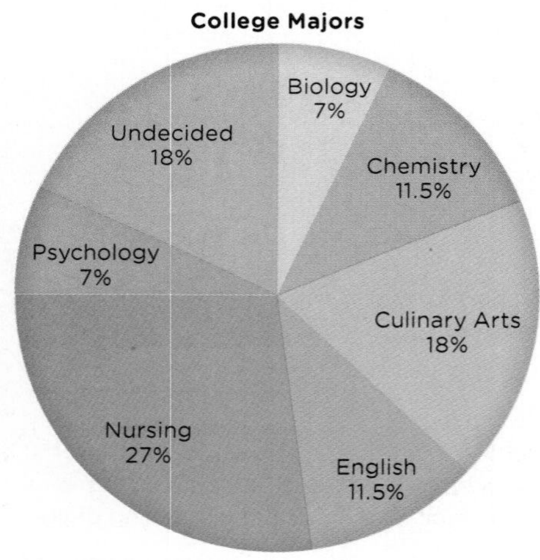

Pie charts can also be used to display qualitative data, with pie slices representing the proportion of the data set belonging to each category (**Figure A.7**). As you can see, the biggest percentage is nursing (27%), followed by culinary arts (18%) and undecided (18%). The smallest percentage is shared by biology and psychology (both 7%). Often researchers use pie charts to display data when it is important to know the relative proportion of each category (for example, a psychology department trying to gain support for funding its courses might want to display the relative number of psychologists in particular subfields; see Figure 0.2 on page 0-2).

With any type of data display, one must be on the lookout for misleading portrayals. In Figure A.6a, we display data for the 44 students interviewed in the library. Notice that, while Figures A.6b and A.6c look different, they display the same data for the same campus of 4,400 students. Look at parts (b) and (c) of the figure and decide, if you were head of the psychology department, which bar chart you would use to demonstrate the popularity of the psychology major. In (b), the size of the department (as measured by number of students) looks fairly small compared to that of other departments, particularly the nursing program. But notice that the scale on the *y*-axis starts at 250 in (b), whereas it begins at 0 in (c). In this third bar chart, it appears that the student count for the psychology program is not far behind that for other programs like chemistry and English. An important aspect of *critical thinking* is being able to evaluate the source of evidence, something one must consider when reading graphs and charts. (For example, does the author of the bar chart in Figure A.6b have a particular agenda to reduce funding for the psychology and biology departments?) It is important to recognize that manipulating the presentation of data can lead to faulty interpretations. (The data on the 4,400 students are valid, but the way they are presented in A.6b is not.)

bar graph Displays qualitative data with categories of interest on the *x*-axis and frequency on the *y*-axis.

pie chart Displays qualitative data with categories of interest represented by slices of the pie.

The Description of Data

In addition to using graphs and charts, psychologists can describe their data sets using numbers that express important characteristics: measures of central tendency, measures of variation, and measures of position. These numbers are an important component of descriptive statistics, as they provide a current snapshot of a data set.

Measures of Central Tendency

If you want to understand human behaviors and mental processes, it helps to know what is typical, or standard, for the population. What is the average level of intelligence? At what age do most people experience first love? To answer these types of questions, psychologists can describe their data sets by calculating **measures of central tendency,** which are numbers representing the "middle" of data sets. There are several ways of doing this. The **mean** is the arithmetic average of a data set. Most students learn how to calculate a mean, or "average," early in their schooling, using the following formula:

$\overline{X} = \frac{\Sigma X}{n}$ where $\overline{X}$ is the sample mean; X is a value in the data set; Σ, or sigma, tells us to take the sum of the values; and n represents the sample size

or

$$\text{Sample mean} = \frac{\text{Sum of all of the values in the data set}}{\text{Number of values}}$$

To calculate the sample mean ($\overline{X}$) for minutes of REM sleep, you would plug the numbers into the formula

$$\begin{aligned}\overline{X} &= (18 + 20 + 22 + 31 + 35 + 35 + 39 + \cdots + 131 + 142 + 150) \div 44 \\ &= 76.8 \text{ minutes}\end{aligned}$$

Another measure of central tendency is the **median**—the number representing the position in the middle of a data set. In other words, 50% of the data values are greater than the median, and 50% are smaller. To find the median for a small set of numbers, start by ordering the values, and then determine which number lies exactly in the center. This is relatively simple when the data set is odd-numbered; all you have to do is find the value that has the same number of values above and below it. For a data set that has an even number of values, however, there is one additional step. You must take the average of the two middle numbers: Add them together and divide by 2. With an odd number of values in a data set, the median will always be a member of the set. With an even number of values, the median may or may not be a member of the data set.

Here is how you would determine the median (*Mdn*) for the minutes of REM sleep:

1. Order the numbers in the data set from smallest to largest. We can use the stem-and-leaf plot for this purpose (Figure A.3 on page A-6).
2. Find the value in the data set that has 50% of the other values below it and 50% above it. Because we have an even number for our sample size ($n = 44$), we will have to find the middle two data values and calculate their average. We divide our sample size of 44 by 2, which is 22, indicating that the median is midway between the 22nd and 23rd values in our set. We count (starting at 18 in the stem-and-leaf plot) to the 22nd and 23rd numbers in our ordered list (76 and 77; there are 21 values below 76 and 21 values above 77):
3. $Mdn = \frac{76 + 77}{2} = 76.5$ minutes

measures of central tendency Numbers that represent the middle of a data set.

mean The arithmetic average of a data set; a measure of central tendency.

median A number that represents the position in the data set for which 50% of the values are above it, and 50% are below it; a measure of central tendency.

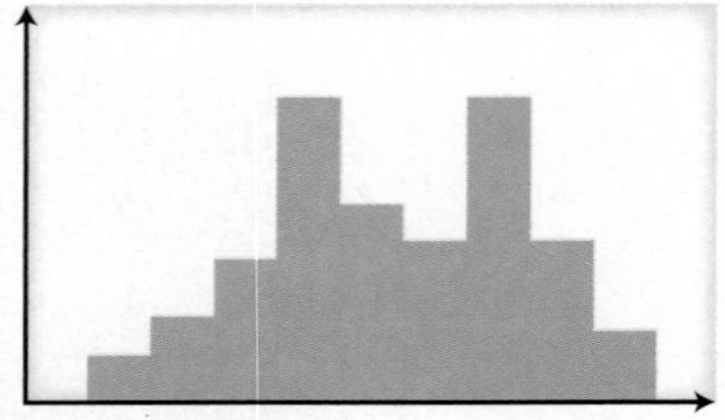

FIGURE A.8
Bimodal distribution

A third measure of central tendency is the **mode,** which is the most frequently occurring value in a data set. If there is only one such value, we call it a *unimodal* distribution. With a symmetric distribution, the mean, median, and mode are the same (Figure A.4a on page A-6). Sometimes there are two modes evident in a histogram, indicating a **bimodal distribution,** and the shape of the distribution exhibits two vertical bars of equal height (**Figure A.8**). In our example of REM sleep data, we cannot see a clear mode, as there are several values that occur twice (35, 47, 49, 68, and 81 minutes). In bimodal distributions, the mode is often a better representation of the central tendency, because neither the mean nor median will indicate that there are, in essence, two "centers" for the data set.

Under other circumstances, the median is better than the mean for representing the middle of the data set. This is especially true when the data set includes one or more *outliers,* or values that are very different from the rest of the set. We can see why this is true by replacing just one value in our data set on REM sleep. See what happens to the mean and median when you swap 150 for 400. First calculate the mean:

1. $\overline{X} = (18 + 20 + 22 + 31 + 35 + 35 + 39 + \cdots + 131 + 142 + 400) \div 44$
   $= 82.5$ minutes (greater than the original mean of 76.8)
2. And now calculate the median. The numbers in the data set are ordered from smallest to largest. The middle two values have not changed (76 and 77).

   Mdn = 76.5 minutes (identical to the original median of 76.5)

No matter how large (or small) a single value is, it does not change the median, but it can have a great influence on the mean. When this occurs, psychologists often present both of these statistics, and discuss the possibility that an outlier is pulling the mean toward it. Look again at the skewed distributions in Figure A.5 on page A-7 and see how the mean is "pulled" toward the side of the distribution that has a possible outlier in its tail. When data are skewed, it is often a good idea to use the median as a measure of central tendency, particularly if a problem exists with outliers.

Measures of Variation

In addition to information on the central tendency, psychologists are interested in **measures of variation,** which describe how much variation or dispersion there is in a data set. If you look at the two data sets in **Figure A.9** (number of miles commuting to school), you can see that they have the same central tendency: The mean commute for both samples is 30 miles ($\overline{X}$ is 30.0). Yet, their dispersion is very different. One data set looks spread out (Sample A), and the other closely packed (Sample B).

There are several measures we can use to characterize the *variability,* or variation, of a data set. The **range** represents the length of a data set and is calculated by taking

Data Values from Sample A

Stem	Leaves
0	9
1	0 5
2	3 5
3	2 5
4	5 8
5	8

$\overline{X}$ = 30.0 miles, *Mdn* = 28.5 miles

Data Values from Sample B

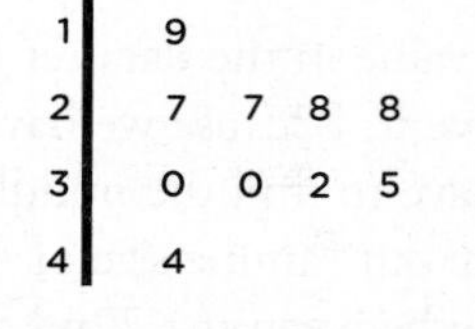

$\overline{X}$ = 30.0 miles, *Mdn* = 29.0 miles

FIGURE A.9
Same mean, different variability for Sample A and Sample B
Data Values from Sample A (daily commute to school in miles): 9, 10, 15, 23, 25, 32, 35, 45, 48, 58.
Data Values from Sample B (daily commute to school): 19, 27, 27, 28, 28, 30, 30, 32, 35, 44.

mode The value of the data set that is most frequent; a measure of central tendency.

bimodal distribution A distribution with two modes, which are the two most frequently occurring values.

measures of variation Numbers that describe the variation or dispersion in a data set.

range A number that represents the length of the data set and is a rough depiction of dispersion; a measure of variation.

the highest value minus the lowest value. The range is a rough depiction of variability, but it's useful for comparing data on the same variable measured in two samples. For the data sets presented in Figure A.9, we can compare the ranges of the two samples and see that Sample A has a range of 49 miles and Sample B has a smaller range of 25 miles:

Sample A	**Sample B**
Range = 58 − 9	Range = 44 − 19
Range = 49 miles	Range = 25 miles

Another measure of variation is the **standard deviation** (referred to by the symbol s when describing samples), which essentially represents the average distance the data points are from their mean. Think about it like this: If the values in a data set are very close to each other, they will also be very close to their mean, and the dispersion will be small. Their average distance from the mean is small. If the values are widely spread, they will not all be clustered around the mean, and their dispersion will be great. Their average distance from the mean is large. One way we can calculate the standard deviation of a sample is by using the following formula:

$$s = \sqrt{\frac{\Sigma(X - \overline{X})^2}{n - 1}}$$

This formula does the following: (1) Subtract the mean from a value in the data set, then square the result. Do this for every value in the set and calculate the sum of the results. (2) Divide this sum by the sample size minus 1. (3) Take the square root of the result. In **Table A.4,** we have gone through each of these steps for Sample A.

The standard deviation for Sample A is 16.7 miles and the standard deviation for Sample B is 6.4 miles. (The calculation is not shown here.) These standard deviations are consistent with what we expect from looking at the stem-and-leaf plots in Figure A.9. Sample A is more variable, or spread out, than Sample B.

TABLE A.4 STANDARD DEVIATION FOR SAMPLE A

X	$X - \overline{X}$	$(X - \overline{X})^2$
9	9 − 30 = −21	$-21^2 = 441$
10	10 − 30 = −20	$220^2 = 400$
15	15 − 30 = 215	$215^2 = 225$
23	23 − 30 = −7	$27^2 = 49$
25	25 − 30 = −5	$25^2 = 25$
32	32 − 30 = 2	$2^2 = 4$
35	35 − 30 = 5	$5^2 = 25$
45	45 − 30 = 15	$15^2 = 225$
48	48 − 30 = 18	$18^2 = 324$
58	58 − 30 = 28	$28^2 = 784$

$\Sigma(X - \overline{X})^2 = 441 + 400 + 225 + 49 + 25 + 4 + 25 + 225 + 324 + 784$

$= 2{,}502$

$n - 1 = (10 - 1) = 9$

$s = \sqrt{\frac{2{,}502}{9}}$

$s = 16.7$

standard deviation A number that represents the average distance the values in a data set are from their mean; a measure of variation.

TABLE A.5 SYMBOLS COMMONLY USED IN STATISTICS

Concept	Symbol	Description
Sample correlation coefficient	r	Represents the strength and direction of the relationship between two variables
F-test value	F	Used to measure the statistical significance of the differences among 3 or more means
t-test value	t	Used to measure the statistical significance of the difference between 2 means
p-value	p	An indication of the probability of getting a test statistic of a certain size by chance
Population mean	μ	The mean of a population (pronounced "mew")
Sample mean	M (or $\overline{X}$)	The mean of a sample (pronounced "X-bar")
Population standard deviation	σ	The standard deviation of the population (pronounced "sigma")
Sample standard deviation	s	The standard deviation of a sample
Population size	N	Indicates the size of a population
Sample size	n	Indicates the size of a sample
z-score	z	Indicates a standard score; number of standard deviations from the mean

The standard deviation is useful for making predictions about the probability of a particular value occurring (Figure A.4b on page A-6). The *empirical rule* tells us that we can expect approximately 68% of all values to fall within 1 standard deviation below or above their mean on a normal curve. We can expect approximately 95% of all values to fall within 2 standard deviations below or above their mean. And we can expect approximately 99.7% of all values to fall within 3 standard deviations below or above their mean. Only .3% of the values will fall above or below 3 standard deviations—these values are extremely rare, as you can see in Figure A.4b.

Measures of Position

Another way to describe data is by looking at **measures of position,** which represent where particular data values fall in relation to other values in a set. You have probably heard of *percentiles,* which indicate the percentage of values occurring above and below a certain point in a data set. A value at the 50th percentile is at the median, which indicates that 50% of the values fall above it, and 50% fall below it. A value at the 10th percentile indicates that 90% fall above it, and 10% fall below it. Often you will see percentiles in reports from standardized tests, weight charts, height charts, and so on.

Statistics Is a Language

This introduction to statistics was created to provide you with an overview of the "language" of statistics that psychologists use to collect, organize, analyze, display, and interpret data. Like any foreign language, statistics is not something you master by reading a brief overview. To become proficient in statistical methods, you must study and practice them. And the best way to become fluent in this language is to immerse yourself in it. For starters, we recommend taking a course in elementary statistics and reading articles published in psychology journals. (See **Table A.5** for some commonly

measures of position Numbers that represent where particular data values fall in relation to other values in the data set.

used symbols.) If you find statistics is your forte, keep taking classes, and consider the possibility of becoming a researcher. Perhaps your work will be published in a scientific journal one day—and cited in an introductory psychology textbook!

Using the data below, calculate the mean, median, range, and standard deviation. Also create a stem-and-leaf plot to display the data and then describe the shape of the distribution.

10 10 11 16 18 18 20 20 24 24 25 25 26 29 29 39 40 41 41 42 43 46 48 49 50 50 51 52 53 56 36 37 38 66 71 75 31 34 34 35 57 59 61 61 38

✓ CHECK YOUR ANSWERS IN APPENDIX C.

KEY TERMS

bar graph, p. A-8
bimodal distribution, p. A-10
distribution shape, p. A-6
frequency distribution, p. A-4
frequency polygon, p. A-5
histogram, p. A-5
hypothesis testing, p. A-1
mean, p. A-9
measures of central tendency, p. A-9
measures of position, p. A-12
measures of variation, p. A-10
median, p. A-9
meta-analysis, p. A-4
mode, p. A-10
negatively skewed, p. A-7
parameters, p. A-3
pie chart, p. A-8
positively skewed, p. A-7
range, p. A-10
skewed distribution, p. A-7
standard deviation, p. A-11
statistical significance, p. A-2
statistics, p. A-1
stem-and-leaf plot, p. A-6

TEST PREP ARE YOU READY?

1. ________ is the science of collecting, organizing, analyzing, displaying, and interpreting data.

2. With descriptive statistics, researchers use tables, graphs, and charts to:
   a. summarize data.
   b. make inferences about data.
   c. make predictions.
   d. test hypotheses.

3. A classmate is collecting data for a research project incorporating an experimental group and a control group. When the data collection is complete, she will check for ____________ to see if the differences between the two groups are due to the researcher's manipulations.
   a. random sampling
   b. descriptive statistics
   c. standard deviations
   d. statistical significance

4. In each item below, identify the variable as quantitative (1) or qualitative (2):
   a. political affiliation
   b. hair color
   c. yearly income
   d. weight in pounds

5. One common way to present data is to use a ____________, which displays how often various values in a data set are present.
   a. qualitative variable
   b. meta-analysis
   c. frequency distribution
   d. measure of variation

6. A researcher is looking to measure cognitive ability in a large representative sample. She can expect that the distribution will be symmetric and have a bell shape. This type of distribution is also known as a:
   a. normal curve.
   b. stem-and-leaf plot.
   c. qualitative variable.
   d. parameter.

7. Some data will have a skewed distribution, which is not symmetrical. A ____________ distribution has a longer tail to the left side, and a ____________ distribution has a longer tail to the right side.

8. Numbers that represent the "middle" of data sets are known as:
   a. standard deviations.
   b. measures of central tendency.
   c. measures of variability.
   d. misleading.

9. What is the mean for a sample that includes the following values: 4, 4, 6, 3, 8?
   a. 4
   b. 5
   c. 6
   d. 7

10. What is the median for a sample that includes the following values: 4, 4, 6, 3, 8?
   a. 4
   b. 5
   c. 6
   d. 7

11. What is the mode for a sample that includes the following values: 4, 4, 6, 3, 8?
   a. 4
   b. 5
   c. 6
   d. 7

12. A value that is very different from the rest of the data set is called a(n) ____________, and it can have a great influence on the ____________.
   a. mode; median
   b. variable; mode
   c. outlier; mean
   d. outlier; median

13. A classmate is trying to calculate a measure of variability. He takes the highest value in the data set and subtracts the lowest value from it. This is considered the _____________ of the data set.

a. range
b. central tendency
c. median
d. standard deviation

14. What is the standard deviation for a sample that includes the following values: 4, 4, 6, 3, 8?

a. 2
b. 3
c. 4
d. 5

15. When you look at a graph in a newspaper, online, or elsewhere, you need to determine if it is a valid representation of the data being described. Graphic representations can be misleading; it depends on the values chosen for the *y*-axis. Find two examples of graphs in the media and examine their *y*-axes to see how the units are portrayed.

✔ CHECK YOUR ANSWERS IN APPENDIX C.

APPENDIX B

Careers in Psychology

Most people hear the word "psychologist" and automatically think of therapy, counseling, and Freud, but as we noted in Chapter 0, psychologists perform a variety of roles in society. Psychology is a vast field, and there is no shortage of career paths. If you are considering psychology, or even if you have already chosen psychology as your major, it is important to determine if this is the right career choice for you and to figure out which subfield matches your interests, skills, and abilities. Then there is the issue of money. Will the career you choose allow you to reach your financial goals? Psychologists' salaries are highly variable and depend on many factors, including education level, specialty, and type of employer.

Any career in psychology will require some degree of specialized education. The question is, how much are you willing and able to attain? For many students, the answer depends on age, family responsibilities, financial concerns, and life experiences. In psychology, there are three types of degrees you can consider at the undergraduate and graduate level: bachelor's, master's, and doctoral.

What Can I Do with a Bachelor's Degree in Psychology?

Many students begin their journey by obtaining a 2-year associate's degree and then go on to earn a bachelor's degree from a 4-year institution. A bachelor's degree in psychology is a great step toward understanding the scientific study of behavior and mental processes. It can prepare you to enter a graduate program, or it may serve as the foundation for your career. The psychology bachelor's degree is exceptionally popular, with 118,000 awarded in 2015–2016 (Snyder, de Bray, & Dillow, 2018), which could mean substantial competition in the job market. This is where the decision between entering the workforce or attending graduate school becomes important. **Table B.1** on the next page gives you a sense of which jobs you can obtain with a bachelor's degree in psychology.

According to the Bureau of Labor Statistics (2017–2018), the median salary for psychologists in 2017 was $77,030, but that figure can be misleading because there is a huge range in earning potential. When it comes to making money, educational attainment matters. People with a bachelor's degree in psychology can expect to earn an annual starting salary of $30,000–$35,000. Those with a master's degree typically start at $40,000, while doctorate-level professionals generally begin around $70,000 (Morgan & Korschgen, 2014). Another factor that makes a difference is psychological subfield. Median salaries at the doctoral level range from $125,000 for psychologists trained in industrial/organizational psychology to $75,000 for those trained in educational psychology (American Psychological Association [APA], 2017c).

TABLE B.1 BACHELOR'S DEGREES AND CAREERS IN PSYCHOLOGY

Psychology Focus	Median Annual Salary	Business Focus	Median Annual Salary	Other Focus	Median Annual Salary
Correctional treatment specialist	$51,140	Administrative assistant	$37,870	Child-care employee	$22,290
Probation officer	$51,140	Customer relations	$32,890	Health services manager	$98,350
Social services assistant	$33,120	Insurance agent	$49,710	High school teacher	$59,170
Social and community service manager	$63,500	Human resource specialist	$60,350	Law enforcement	$62,960
Substance abuse counselor	$43,300	Public relations	$59,300	Recreation	$24,540

A bachelor's degree in psychology prepares you for many types of employment opportunities. Here, we see how this type of degree is not limited to the field of psychology. Information from Landrum (2001, 2018 January) and Lloyd (1997, July 16). Salary information from Bureau of Labor Statistics (2017–2018).

What Can I Do with a Master's Degree in Psychology?

Choosing to pursue a graduate degree in psychology requires a great deal of research. There are many types of degrees and a multitude of colleges and universities that offer them. The American Psychological Association (APA) publishes a valuable resource for students thinking about this next step. This guide, *Graduate Study in Psychology* (2018), is routinely updated and includes information on approximately 600 psychology graduate programs offered in the United States and Canada. In it you can find application deadlines, tuition costs, graduate employment data, and other useful information.

A master's degree in psychology is flexible and can prepare you to work in areas outside the field of psychology, including government, health care, business, marketing, and education. Many master's-level psychologists devote their careers to research, working under PhD-level researchers at universities and other institutions. Others become therapists. Typically, this means earning a master's degree, with an emphasis on counseling, and securing a state license to practice.

Table B.2 provides some general information about the types of degrees and training required of various mental health professions. In most states, master's-level clinicians must obtain a license to practice and share details about their education, training, and licensing status with their clients. One can also earn a master's degree in nonclinical specialties such as industrial/organizational psychology, engineering psychology, and leadership psychology. Some of these applied fields offer lucrative careers in business and industry. Finally, many students earning a master's degree in psychology go on to complete their doctorate degrees.

Doctorate Degrees: PhD and PsyD

Whether you need a degree at the doctoral level really depends on your interests. A PhD (doctor of philosophy) psychologist typically focuses on research, though

TABLE B.2 MENTAL HEALTH PROFESSIONALS

Degree	Occupation	Training	Focus	Approximate Years of Post-Bachelor's Degree
Medical doctor, MD	Psychiatrist	Medical school and residency training in mental health	Treatment of psychiatric disorders; may include research focus	8 years total (including residency)
Doctor of philosophy, PhD	Clinical or counseling psychologist	Graduate school; includes dissertation and internship	Research-oriented and clinical practice	3 to 6 years
Doctor of psychology, PsyD	Clinical or counseling psychologist	Graduate school; includes internship; may include dissertation	Focus on professional practice	3 to 5 years
Master's degree, MA or MS	Mental health counselor	Graduate school; includes internship	Focus on professional practice	2 years

Mental health professionals have a variety of backgrounds. Here, we present a handful of these career choices, including general information on training, focus, and the length of education.

some may provide therapy (APA, n.d.-i; Norcross & Sayette, 2016). Earning a PhD requires graduate-level course work: 3 to 6 years of advanced college courses and training in addition to a bachelor's degree. PhD coursework and research culminate in a dissertation, which you might think of as a huge research paper in your field of study. PhD programs are highly competitive; it is not unusual for an applicant to apply to multiple schools, but only gain acceptance to one or two. The good news is that programs typically provide 70–100% of students with tuition assistance (Norcross & Sayette, 2016). For some helpful tips on applying to PhD programs, you can visit the APA website at www.apa.org/education/grad/applying.aspx.

If your interest is more clinically focused, then you may consider the other doctoral-level degree in psychology, a PsyD (doctor of psychology). This degree emphasizes clinical practice rather than research, and typically requires 1 to 1.5 fewer years than a PhD program. This is not to say that PsyD programs do not require course work in statistics and research methods; it is just not the primary focus. PsyD programs traditionally emphasize clinical study, practice, and experience (Norcross & Sayette, 2016). Because most PsyD degrees are offered by professional schools of psychology or private colleges and universities, students in these programs graduate with an average debt of $173,000 (Doran, Kraha, Marks, Ameen, & El-Ghoroury, 2016). There also tends to be less financial aid available for PsyD students. After graduating, PhD psychologists tend to earn more money than PsyDs, their median salaries being $85,000 and $75,000, respectively (APA, 2017c).

Doctor of Psychology
David Brantley III celebrates with his daughter after receiving a doctor of psychology degree (PsyD) from Rutgers Graduate School of Applied and Professional Psychology. Unlike PhD programs, which are highly research focused, PsyD programs emphasize the clinical side of things—that is, the diagnosis and treatment of psychological disorders. MIKE DERER/AP Images.

Subfields of Psychology

Psychologists provide treatment for people with mental disorders, examine cognitive processes, study changes across the life span, work with children in schools, help corporations develop

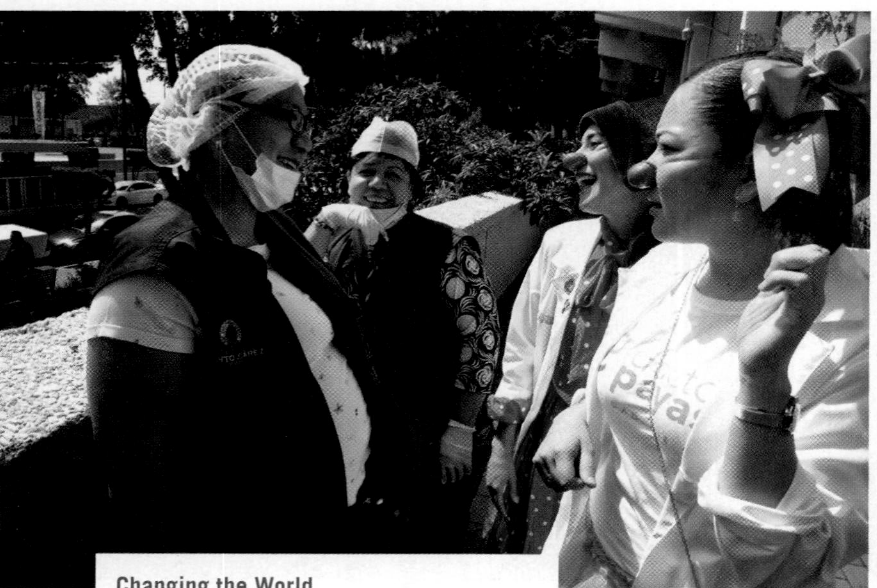

Changing the World
Therapists wearing clown outfits provide support for victims of a 7.1-magnitude earthquake that hit Mexico City and its surrounding areas on September 19, 2017. The quake claimed over 200 lives, damaged many buildings, and left almost 5 million people without power (Chavez, Almasy, Sanchez, & Simon, 2017, September 20). During times like these, many people benefit from the support of psychological professionals. ALFREDO ESTRELLA/Getty Images.

marketing strategies, and much more. Let's explore careers in some of the subfields of psychology.

CLIMATE AND ENVIRONMENTAL PSYCHOLOGY Environmental psychologists study the connection between behavior and the world around us. "The world around us" can refer to any place humans spend time, be it at home, in a college dorm, or on a city block. Climate and environmental psychologists explore ways to encourage environmentally friendly behaviors. They also try to understand why some people engage in behaviors that are not sustainable (APA, n.d.-f).

CLINICAL PSYCHOLOGY Clinical psychologists focus on the diagnosis and treatment of people with psychological disorders. In addition to providing therapy, many of these professionals also conduct research. They may, for example, use brain-scanning technologies to better understand the causes of depression, or design studies to compare the effects of different treatments. Some work as professors in colleges or universities, others as clinicians in medical facilities, schools, counseling centers, or private practice. Still others work in industries that focus on health care, program development, and public policy (APA, n.d.-b, 2011, 2014b).

COGNITIVE PSYCHOLOGY Cognitive psychologists, also known as brain scientists, examine thinking, memory, language, attention, and problem solving. Using the scientific method, these psychologists study how people make decisions and interpret events, explore the relationship between cognition and emotion, and investigate treatments for diseases that impact memory, speech, and perception (APA, n.d.-c, 2011, 2014b). Cognitive psychologists work in college and university settings, but many are employed as consultants in curriculum design, public health, safety, architecture, graphic design, and other fields.

COUNSELING PSYCHOLOGY Like clinical psychologists, counseling psychologists provide treatment for people with psychological disorders. They also work with individuals across the life span needing support with day-to-day problems; this may include helping clients identify their strengths and take advantage of useful resources (APA, n.d.-a). These psychologists tend to focus on relationship issues, career exploration, and stress management. They can be found in academic settings, clinical practice, and hospitals (APA, 2011). The work of clinical and counseling psychologists overlaps to some degree. In some cases, counseling programs are located in a psychology department, which is also the case for most clinical programs. However, some counseling psychology programs are affiliated with education departments, which might conduct different types of research and training than psychology departments (APA, n.d.-a). Counseling psychologists may work in community mental health centers, medical facilities, VA hospitals, rehabilitation facilities, and business sectors (APA, n.d.-n, 2014c).

DEVELOPMENTAL PSYCHOLOGY Developmental psychologists are primarily concerned with growth, development, and change over the life span (APA, n.d.-d). Research in this field provides information about people from conception to death, influencing decisions about how children are treated in day-care settings, how students are educated in classrooms, and how elderly people are advised to manage their health, among other things. In the past, this field focused primarily on children from birth to adolescence, but developmental psychologists have become increasingly aware of the need to study adults as they age. They are especially concerned with helping people remain independent throughout life (APA, 2011, 2014d).

EDUCATIONAL AND SCHOOL PSYCHOLOGY Educational psychologists examine methods of learning and how memory relates to learning. These specialists play a key role in developing teaching strategies and curricula. School psychologists working in the classroom often apply lessons gleaned by educational psychologists. Research findings may inform decisions about how to classify students academically, for example. Educational and school psychologists work at colleges and universities, and in school districts, government, and the private sector (APA, 2014j). Psychologists specializing in teaching and learning may collaborate with school administrators, teachers, and parents to provide an effective and safe learning environment. They may assist students who are having learning difficulties, students identified as gifted, or teachers dealing with classroom management and student behavior problems (APA, 2014j).

EXPERIMENTAL PSYCHOLOGY Experimental psychologists are science enthusiasts. They spend their days conducting basic and applied research on people, animals, and data. These researchers typically focus on a particular area of study, such as cognitive psychology, neuroscience, or animal behavior. Experimental psychologists may teach at colleges and universities, or conduct research for government and industry (APA, n.d.-h; 2014e).

FORENSIC PSYCHOLOGY Forensic psychologists apply the principles of psychology to the legal system, working in diverse environments including criminal, family, and civil courts. These experts often are called upon in legal cases involving decisions about child custody, or situations in which a person's "mental competence to stand trial" is in question (APA, 2011, p. 2). Some forensic psychologists are trained in law as well as in psychology, and they may conduct research on topics such as jury behavior or eyewitness testimony. Forensic psychologists may be employed in prisons, police departments, law offices, and government agencies (APA, 2014f).

HEALTH PSYCHOLOGY Health psychologists focus their efforts on promoting positive health behaviors and preventing illness. They explore questions such as *Why do people smoke?* and *What drives people to overeat?* and their findings are used to promote good health practices. Health psychologists examine how individuals deal with sickness, pain, and medical treatment. They look at the interaction of biological, psychological, and social factors in relation to health and well-being. Health psychologists may be employed by hospitals, clinics, and rehabilitation centers, or they might work in private practice (APA, n.d.-j, 2011, 2014g).

HUMAN FACTORS AND ENGINEERING PSYCHOLOGY Human factors and engineering psychologists use research to improve work environments by optimizing processes, systems, and equipment. These specialists observe on-the-job activities, conduct surveys, and recommend changes to facilitate optimal work environments with high productivity and safety. They may recommend changes in equipment, workload, personnel, or training (APA, n.d.-k, 2011, 2014h).

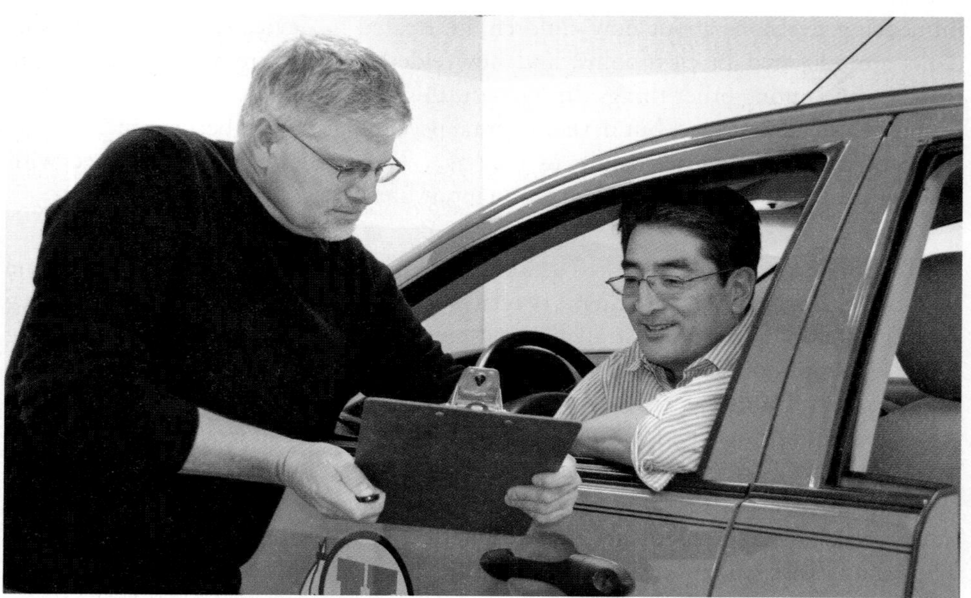

Lifesaving Human Factors Research? Cognitive neuroscientist David Strayer (left) studies the brains of distracted drivers using technologies such as electroencephalography (EEG). His research underscores the dangers of talking on the phone, texting, and performing other digital tasks, even with the use of voice-activated technologies (AAA, 2015, October 22). Newer cars have more buttons, touch screens, and other attention-demanding features, and these technologies do not appear to be making us any safer. As Strayer observes, "It's adding more and more layers of complexity and information at drivers' fingertips without often considering whether it's a good idea to put it at their fingertips" (Lowy, 2017, October 5, para. 4). Dr. David Strayer.

INDUSTRIAL AND ORGANIZATIONAL (I/O) PSYCHOLOGY Industrial and organizational psychologists examine the relationships of people working in organizations. They are particularly interested in employee job satisfaction, productivity, organizational structure and change, and the interface between humans and machines. In addition, I/O psychologists work with administrators to assist in hiring, training, and educating employees. These specialists are often employed in industry, government, business, and academic settings (APA, n.d.-l, 2011, 2014i).

MEDIA PSYCHOLOGY Media psychologists examine human responses to the interactions among graphics, images, and sound. They study how psychology relates to the development, production, and use of technology. Media psychologists investigate all forms of media (print, radio, television, social media) and different formats (mobile, interactive, virtual; APA, n.d.-r). They are particularly interested in how social media,

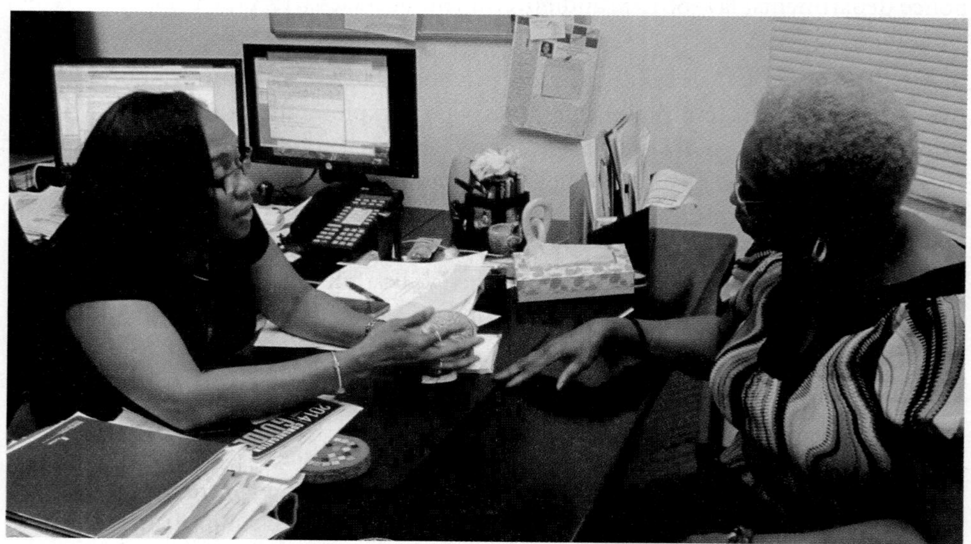

Neuropsychologist at Work Cognitive neuropsychologist Dr. Lisa Barnes (left) studies the social factors involved in age-related cognitive decline in minority populations. A professor at Rush University Medical Center in Chicago, Dr. Barnes aims to understand why African Americans are disproportionately affected by Alzheimer's disease. Dr. Lisa L Barnes.

text messaging, and other digital technologies shape the way we spend our time and relate to one another. Media psychologists might also examine the way reality TV shows can elevate ordinary people to celebrity status.

NEUROPSYCHOLOGY Neuropsychologists are interested in the link between human behavior and the body (neural activity, hormonal changes, and so on; 2011). These psychologists work with people recovering from strokes and brain traumas or struggling with learning disabilities and developmental delays. They investigate how the structure and function of the brain relate to behavior, cognition, and emotion. Neuropsychologists often conduct research at colleges or universities, but they may also be employed by hospitals or other medical facilities (APA, 2011).

REHABILITATION PSYCHOLOGY Rehabilitation psychologists either study or work with patients who have lost functioning as a result of stroke, epilepsy, autism, depression, chronic pain, or accidents, for example. These psychologists are particularly concerned with helping people adjust to work, relationships, and day-to-day living. Their workplaces include hospitals, physical rehabilitation facilities, assisted living centers, and community organizations, and their research may impact the development of public programs (APA, n.d.-p, 2011, 2014k).

SOCIAL PSYCHOLOGY Social psychologists examine the behaviors, thoughts, and emotions of people in groups. They may study attitudes, bullying, persuasion, discrimination, conformity, or group behavior. Social psychologists are interested in the many factors that influence interpersonal relationships, including those associated with attraction and love. While often employed by colleges and universities, these psychologists may also work in government, nonprofit organizations, hospitals, and corporations (APA, n.d.-q, 2011, 2014l).

SPORT PSYCHOLOGY Sport psychologists help athletes and their coaches set constructive goals, increase motivation, facilitate communication and conflict resolution (among teammates or with leadership), as well as cope with anxiety related to athletic performance (APA, 2011, 2014m). As any sport psychologist can testify, being physically fit is not the only requirement for athletic excellence; mental fitness is also critical. Sport psychologists also work in many corporations, helping to build their "teams" and supporting efforts to manage stress, build confidence, and improve job performance (APA, 2015a).

Psychological Fitness
BMX rider Brooke Crain (left) meets with sport psychologist Jason Richardson (middle) and coach Tony Hoffman a couple weeks before the 2016 Olympics in Rio. Sport psychologists help athletes and coaches contend with the psychological challenges of their sport. Kris Arciaga/ KPBS Public Broadcasting.

The science of psychology is relatively young compared to other sciences, and it is growing and changing with the advancement of technology and interdisciplinary research. If you are considering a career in psychology, keep up with the exciting developments in the field. A good way to stay abreast is by visiting the websites of the field's professional organizations: the Association for Psychological Science and the American Psychological Association.

Check Your Answers

1 Introduction to the Science of Psychology

show what you know

What Is Psychology and How Did It Begin?

1. basic research; applied research
2. d. change
3. b. functionalism.
4. Answers will vary. *Sociocultural* and *biopsychosocial* perspectives are similar in that both examine how interactions with other people influence behaviors and mental processes. *Cognitive* and *biological* perspectives differ in that the cognitive perspective focuses on the thought processes underlying behavior, while the biological perspective emphasizes physiological processes.

How Do Psychologists Do Research?

1. c. representative sample
2. operational definitions
3. Answers will vary. If the population is large, the researcher will need to select a sample. A random sample is a subset of the population chosen through a procedure that ensures all members have an equal chance of being selected. Random sampling increases the likelihood of achieving a representative sample, or subgroup, whose characteristics are similar to the population of interest. If the sample is small relative to the population size, we must be careful about drawing inferences from sample to population. Representative samples help ensure that our inferences are meaningful in these cases.

Descriptive and Correlational Methods

1. c. new or unexplored topics.
2. The correlational method is useful for illuminating links between variables, and it helps researchers make predictions, but it cannot determine cause and effect. Even if variables *X* and *Y* are strongly correlated, we cannot assume that changes in *X* are driving changes in *Y* (or vice versa); there may be some third variable influencing both *X* and *Y*. Some possible third variables that may be involved in the correlation between smartphone use and absenteeism might include: boredom on the job, an ill family member, apathy about work.
3. naturalistic observation

The Experimental Method

1. b. debriefing.
2. In a *double-blind study*, neither the participants nor the researchers working directly with those participants know who is getting the treatment and who is getting the placebo. This type of study is designed to reduce expectations and biases that can arise when either participants or experimenters know what they've received or distributed. This use of deception is necessary so that neither experimenter nor participant consciously or unconsciously alters his or her behaviors, that is, unknowingly changes the outcome of the experiment.

TEST PREP ARE YOU READY?

1. b. applied research.
2. b. critical thinking.
3. c. the nature side of the nature–nurture issue.
4. d. Humanistic psychology
5. c. the scientific method
6. c. variables.
7. d. an equal chance of being picked to participate.
8. b. case study
9. a. double-blind
10. d. random sample
11. Answers will vary. The goals of psychology are to describe, explain, predict, and change behavior. These goals lay the foundation for the scientific approach and the research designs used to carry out experiments in psychology. A researcher might conduct a study to describe differences in children's food preferences.

If the researcher saw a pattern of food preferences among children within families, she might explain it by considering the children's home environment. She might conduct a study that predicted children's food preferences based on other close family members. The researcher might apply the findings to help experts create a campaign for healthy eating.

12. Answers will vary. Read through other studies on aggression and exposure to media violence to see how they ensured ethical treatment. She will also need to study the ethical guidelines of the professional organizations and submit her proposal to the Institutional Review Board.
13. Answers will vary. See Table 1.1.
14. Answers will vary. Look for studies on topics that would be very hard for researchers to manipulate in an ethical manner (for example, breast feeding, amount of television watched, attitudes).
15. Answers will vary. The researchers used the experimental method to establish a cause-and-effect relationship between watching the cartoons and changes in cognitive function. The children were randomly assigned to the groups, and the researchers manipulated the activities they were involved in. Other variables were held constant. One way to change the study is to use a different age group.

2 Biology and Behavior

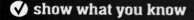

 show what you know 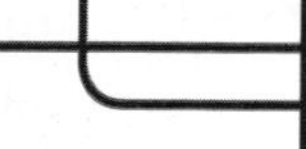

Introducing the Brain

1. c. tracks changes of radioactive substances; uses X-rays to create cross-sectional images
2. neuroscience

Neurons and Neural Communication

1. myelin sheath
2. b. Neurotransmitters; synapse
3. Answers will vary. See Table 2.1 for examples.

The Brain Can't Do It Alone

1. c. autonomic nervous system
2. pituitary
3. Brandon would display a reflex. Remember that the knee jerk is an involuntary reaction carried out by neurons outside of the brain.

The Amazing Brain

1. d. lateralization.
2. b. Broca's area.
3. The *corpus callosum* is a bundle of nerve fibers that allows the two halves of the brain to communicate and work together to process information. For example, with visual information each eye receives visual sensations, but that information is sent to the opposite hemisphere, and shared between the hemispheres via the corpus callosum. Specifically, information presented in the right visual field is processed in the left hemisphere, and information presented in the left visual field is processed in the right hemisphere. Because the hemispheres are disconnected through the surgery, researchers can study each hemisphere separately to explore its own unique capabilities (or specializations). In a split-brain individual, communication between the hemispheres is limited.
4. a. neuroplasticity.
5. b. frontal lobes
6. The frontal lobes organize information among the other lobes of the brain. They are responsible for higher-level cognitive functions, such as thinking, perception, and impulse control. The occipital lobes process visual information, and help us see. The parietal lobes receive and process sensory information, and orient the body in space. The temporal lobes are instrumental in the comprehension of hearing and language. They process auditory stimuli, recognize visual objects, and play a key role in language comprehension and memory.

Let's Dig a Little Deeper

1. amygdala
2. a. relay sensory information.
3. cerebellum

TEST PREP ARE YOU READY?

1. a. cell body; dendrites; axon terminals
2. 1. acetylcholine: c. movement; 2. glutamate: b. learning, memory; 3. endorphins: a. reduction of pain; 4. serotonin: d. mood, aggression, appetite
3. a. central nervous system.
4. b. spinal cord
5. d. parasympathetic nervous system
6. b. endocrine system; glands
7. b. The right hemisphere is more competent handling visual tasks.
8. b. limbic system
9. 1. association areas: b. integration of information from all over brain; 2. temporal lobes: c. hearing and language comprehension; 3. meninges: a. three thin membranes protect brain; 4. occipital lobes: e. process visual information; 5. parietal lobes: d. receive sensory information, such as touch
10. d. reticular formation
11. Neuroplasticity is the brain's ability to heal, grow new connections, and reorganize in order to adapt to the environment. Examples of neuroplasticity will vary, but Brandon Burns and Christina Santhouse provide compelling examples.
12. Diagrams will vary; see Figure 2.2. A *reflex* is an involuntary reaction that often protects us from bodily harm. For example, we automatically pull away when we touch a hot surface.

Sensory neurons are activated and carry information from the environment to interneurons in the spinal cord, which activates motor neurons. The motor neurons excite the muscle and initiate the motion of pulling away.

13. *Neurotransmitters* are chemical messengers produced by neurons, which enable those neurons to communicate with each other. *Hormones* are chemical messengers produced by the endocrine system and released into the bloodstream. The effects of neurotransmitters are almost instantaneous, whereas those of hormones are usually delayed and longer lasting. Both influence thoughts, emotions, and behaviors. Neurotransmitters and hormones can work together, for example, directing the fight-or-flight response to stress.
14. Sperry and Gazzaniga's research demonstrated that the hemispheres of the human brain, while strikingly similar in appearance, specialize in different functions. The left hemisphere excels in language processing, and the right hemisphere excels at visuospatial tasks. The corpus callosum normally allows the two hemispheres to share and integrate information.
15. The *EEG* detects electrical impulses in the brain. The *CAT* uses X-rays to create many cross-sectional images of the brain. The *MRI* uses powerful magnets to produce more detailed cross-sectional images than those of a CAT scan, but both MRI and CAT are used to study the structure of the brain. The *PET* uses radioactivity to track glucose consumption and construct a map of brain activity. The *fMRI* also captures changes in brain activity, but instead of tracking glucose consumption, it reveals patterns of blood flow in the brain, which is a good indicator of how much oxygen is being used. All these tools have strengths and limitations (see Infographic 2.1).

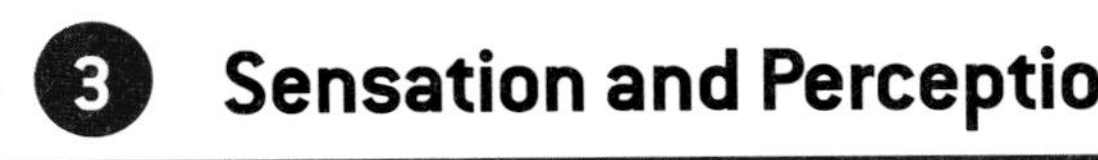

3 Sensation and Perception

show what you know

An Introduction to Sensation and Perception

1. a. perception
2. Answers will vary, but can include examples such as hearing the honking of a car outside, or smelling food cooking in the kitchen, or a lamp illuminating your book, which enables you to see the words on the page.
3. d. sensory adaptation.

Vision

1. wavelength
2. The *trichromatic theory of color vision* suggests there are three types of cones, each sensitive to particular wavelengths in the red, green, and blue spectrums. The brain identifies a precise hue by calculating patterns of excitement among the three types of cones, that is, the relative activity of the three types.

   The opponent-process theory of color vision suggests that in addition to the color-sensitive cones, we also have neurons that respond to opponent colors (for example, red–green, blue–yellow). One neuron in an opponent pair fires in response to red but not green, for example. Both the trichromatic and opponent-process theories clarify different aspects of color vision, as color perception occurs in the light-sensing cones in the retina and in the opponent cells serving the brain.
3. d. rods.

Hearing

1. a. pitch
2. b. transduction.
3. The place theory of pitch perception suggests that it is the location of neural activity along the cochlea that allows us to sense the different pitches of high-frequency sounds. Hair cells toward the oval-window end of the basilar membrane vibrate more when exposed to higher-frequency sounds, and this is what the researcher found.

Smell, Taste, Touch

1. b. transduction.
2. Answers will vary, but may include examples such as typing on my keyboard, holding my head upright, moving my head to look outside, sitting upright in my chair, moving my hand to scratch my head.
3. c. the gate-control theory

Perception: Is It All in Your Head?

1. Gestalt
2. a. convergence
3. *ESP* is the purported ability to obtain information about the world in the absence of sensory stimuli. There is a lack of scientific evidence to support the existence of ESP, and most so-called evidence comes in the form of personal anecdotes. Subjective information can be biased. Using critical thinking, we must determine the credibility of the source and validity of the evidence. Despite ESP's lack of scientific credibility, many people still believe in its existence in part because of illusory correlations, which appear to be links between variables that are not closely related at all.

TEST PREP ARE YOU READY?

1. c. sensation.
2. a. transduction.
3. d. cornea
4. a. afterimage effect; trichromatic
5. c. neural impulses firing
6. a. thalamus
7. a. proprioceptors
8. d. cones
9. d. proximity.

10. c. relative size.

11. Answers will vary. Tastes push us toward foods we need and away from those that could harm us. We gravitate toward sweet, calorie-rich foods for their life-sustaining energy. We are also drawn to salty foods, which tend to contain valuable minerals, and to umami, which signals the presence of proteins essential for cellular health and growth. Bitter and sour tastes we tend to avoid. This also gives us an evolutionary edge because poisonous plants or rancid foods are often bitter or sour.

12. Answers will vary. Subliminal stimuli are well beneath our absolute thresholds (such as light too dim to see and sounds too faint to hear). Extrasensory perception (ESP) is the purported ability to obtain information about the world without any sensory stimuli (absolutely no measurable sensory data).

13. Diagrams will vary; see Infographic 3.2. The pinna funnels sound waves into the auditory canal, focusing them toward the eardrum. Vibrations in the eardrum cause the malleus to push the incus, which moves the stapes, which presses on the oval window, amplifying waves. Pressure on the oval window causes fluid in the cochlea to vibrate and bend the hair cells on the basilar membrane. If the vibration is sufficiently strong, the hair cells bend enough to initiate the firing of nearby nerve cells. The auditory nerve carries signals to the auditory cortex in the brain, where sounds are given meaning.

14. The *gate-control theory of pain* suggests that the perception of pain can either increase or decrease through the interaction of biopsychosocial factors. Signals are sent to open or close the "gates" that control the neurological pathways for pain. When large myelinated fibers are active, the gates are more likely to close, which then inhibits pain messages from being sent. With a sore shoulder, applying ice to the injured area can stimulate the temperature and pressure receptors of the large fibers. This activity closes the gates, temporarily interfering with the pain message that would have been sent to the brain.

15. An absolute threshold is the weakest stimuli that can be detected 50% of the time. Difference thresholds indicate the minimum difference between two stimuli noticed 50% of the time. Weber's law states the ratios that determine these difference thresholds. The ability to detect weak signals in the environment is based on many factors.

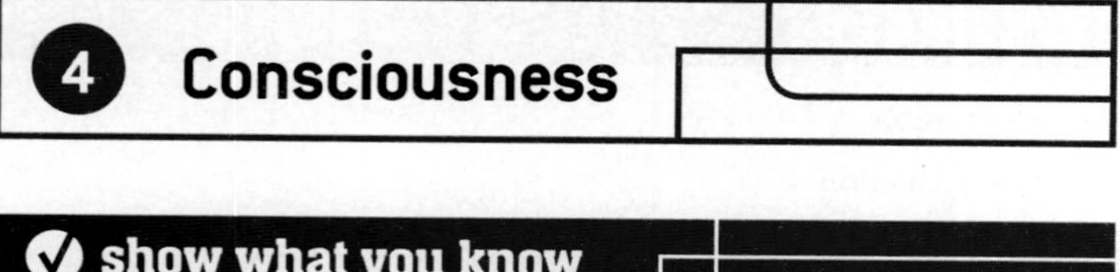

show what you know

An Introduction to Consciousness

1. b. automatic processing

2. Answers will vary. The ability to focus awareness on a small segment of information that is available through our sensory systems is called selective attention. Although we are exposed to many different stimuli at once, we tend to pay particular attention to abrupt or unexpected changes in the environment. Such events may pose a danger and we need to be aware of them. However, selective attention can cause us to be blind to objects directly in our line of vision. This "looking without seeing" can have serious consequences, as we fail to see important occurrences in our surroundings. Our advice would be to try to remain aware of the possibility of inattentional blindness, in particular when you are in situations that could involve serious injury.

3. Consciousness

Sleep

1. circadian rhythm
2. b. Stage N2
3. cataplexy

Dreams

1. c. activation–synthesis model

2. Electroencephalogram (EEG) and positron emission tomography (PET) can demonstrate neural activity of the sleeping brain. During REM sleep, the motor areas of the brain are inhibited, but a great deal of neural activity is occurring in the sensory areas of the brain. The activation–synthesis model suggests dreams result when the brain responds to this random neural activity as if it has meaning. The creative human mind makes up stories to match the neural activity. The vestibular system is also active during REM sleep, resulting in sensations of floating or flying. The neurocognitive theory of dreams proposes that a network of neurons in the brain (including some areas in the limbic system and forebrain) is necessary for dreaming to occur.

3. manifest content; latent content

What Are Altered States?

1. 1. depressant: b. slows down activity in the CNS; 2. opioid: a. blocks pain; 3. alcohol: d. cirrhosis of the liver; 4. cocaine: c. increases activity in the CNS

2. c. LSD

3. psychoactive drugs

4. Answers will vary. One could evaluate the presence of tolerance or withdrawal, both signs of physiological dependence. With tolerance, one's system adapts to a drug over time and therefore needs more and more of the substance to re-create the original effect. Withdrawal can occur with constant use of some psychoactive drugs, when the body has become dependent and then reacts when the drug is withheld. Psychological dependence is indicated by a host of problematic symptoms distinct from tolerance and withdrawal. It is a strong urge or craving, not a physical need to continue using the substance. People with psychological dependence believe, for example, they need the drug because it increases their emotional or mental well-being. In some cases, with psychological dependence, behaviors may be problematic when there is a strong desire or need to continue the behavior. Physiological dependence is physical and has serious health consequences.

TEST PREP ARE YOU READY?

1. b. selective attention.
2. d. circadian rhythm.
3. a. insomnia
4. b. hallucinogen
5. d. REM sleep
6. b. wish fulfillment.
7. c. Psychoactive drugs
8. a. dopamine
9. c. Short-term amnesia can occur if the hypnotist suggests something will be forgotten.
10. c. Physiological; withdrawal
11. Answers will vary. If someone walks into your room while you are asleep, you wake up immediately if there is a noise. You hear a text message come in during the night and immediately wake up to answer the message.
12. Without one's awareness, the brain determines what is important, what requires immediate attention, and what can be processed and stored for later use if necessary. This automatic processing happens involuntarily, with little or no conscious effort, and is important because our sensory systems absorb large amounts of information that need to be processed. Automatic processing also enables sensory adaption, which is the tendency to become less sensitive to and less aware of constant stimuli after a period of time.
13. We might not want a doctor with such a schedule to care for us because staying up for 48 hours can result in problems with memory, attention, reaction time, and decision making, all important processes that doctors use in caring for patients. Sleep deprivation impairs the ability to focus attention on a single activity, such as delivering medical care.
14. Answers will vary. See Table 4.2 for information on sleep disturbances and their defining characteristics.
15. Answers will vary. There are many different drugs that people use legally on an everyday basis. Caffeine is a psychoactive drug found in coffee, soda, tea, and some medicines. Over-the-counter painkillers are legal drugs used to treat a range of aches and pains. Nicotine is a highly addictive drug found in cigarettes or cigars. Alcohol is a legal psychoactive drug used daily by many people, as they drink a glass of wine or beer with an evening meal.

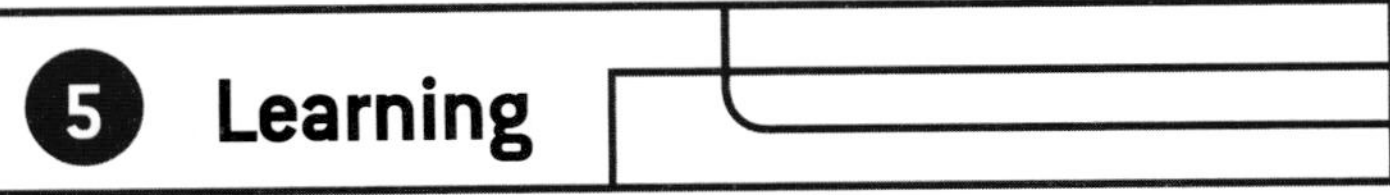

5 Learning

show what you know

An Introduction to Learning

1. Learning
2. Answers will vary. Learning that your tongue will get burned if you put your coffee in the microwave for too long; studying hard for a test after getting a good score on the last test you studied for.

Classical Conditioning

1. conditioned
2. a. salmonella
3. When Little Albert heard the loud bang, it was an unconditioned stimulus (US) that elicited fear, the unconditioned response (UR). Through conditioning, the sight of the rat became paired with the loud noise, and thus the rat went from being a *neutral stimulus* to a conditioned stimulus (CS). Little Albert's fear of the rat became a conditioned response (CR). Little Albert showed stimulus generalization, as he not only began to fear rats, but he generalized this fear to other furry objects, including a sealskin coat and a rabbit.
4. biological preparedness

Operant Conditioning

1. law of effect
2. d. stimulus generalization.
3. a. positive punishment
4. Answers will vary, but can be based on the following definitions. *Reinforcers* are events, stimuli, and other consequences that increase the likelihood of a behavior reoccurring. *Positive reinforcement* is the process by which reinforcers are presented following a target behavior. *Negative reinforcement* occurs with the removal of an unpleasant stimulus following a target behavior. *Successive approximation* is a method that uses reinforcers to condition a series of small steps that gradually approach the target behavior. We could consider using food as a primary reinforcer (meeting a biological need). Good grades, or money, are examples of secondary reinforcers.
5. *Continuous reinforcement* is a schedule of reinforcement in which every target behavior is reinforced. *Partial reinforcement* is a schedule of reinforcement in which target behaviors are reinforced intermittently, not continuously. Continuous reinforcement is generally more effective for establishing a behavior, whereas learning through partial reinforcement is more resistant to extinction and useful for maintaining behavior.

Observational Learning and Cognition

1. a. observational learning.
2. Answers will vary, but can be based on the following definitions. A *model* is an individual or character whose behavior is being imitated. *Observational learning* occurs as a result of watching the behavior of others.
3. c. latent learning.

TEST PREP ARE YOU READY?

1. b. habituation
2. c. responses to positive reinforcement.
3. a. involuntary; voluntary
4. b. conditioned response.
5. c. conditioned emotional response.

6. d. The law of effect
7. c. a dog whining in the morning, leading an owner to wake up and take it outside
8. b. positive reinforcement.
9. a. were more likely to display aggressive behavior.
10. a. latent learning.
11. With stimulus generalization, once an association is forged between a conditioned stimulus and a conditioned response, the learner often responds to similar stimuli as if they were the conditioned stimulus. Stimulus discrimination is the ability to differentiate between the conditioned stimulus and other sufficiently different stimuli.
12. Answers will vary. See Infographics 5.2 through 5.4, and Table 5.3.
13. Answers will vary, but can be based on the following definitions. *Primary reinforcers* are reinforcers that satisfy biological needs. Food, water, and physical contact are considered primary reinforcers. *Secondary reinforcers* do not satisfy biological needs, but often gain their power through their association with primary reinforcers. A primary reinforcer used to change behavior might be food. A college tries to increase student participation by providing food at important school functions. Money can be used as a secondary reinforcer. Employees are paid money, which increases attendance at work.
14. Answers will vary, but can be based on the following. *Punishment decreases* the likelihood of a behavior recurring. On the other hand, *negative reinforcement increases* the likelihood of a behavior recurring. See Table 5.3 for examples.
15. Answers can vary. A conditioned taste aversion is a form of classical conditioning that occurs when an organism learns to associate the taste of a particular food or drink with illness. Avoiding foods that induce sickness increases the odds the organism will survive and reproduce, passing its genes along to the next generation. Imagine a grizzly bear that avoids poisonous berries after vomiting from eating them. In this case, the unconditioned stimulus (US) is the poison in the berries; the unconditioned response (UR) is the vomiting. After acquisition, the conditioned stimulus (CS) would be the sight of the berries, and the conditioned response (CR) would be a nauseous feeling.

try this **page 171**

ANSWER: The neutral stimulus (NS) is the sight of a hot dog, the unconditioned stimulus (US) is the virus, the unconditioned response (UR) is the upset stomach, the conditioned stimulus (CS) is the sight or thought of a hot dog, and the conditioned response (CR) is the sick feeling you get even after you have recovered.

try this **page 192**

ANSWER: Independent variable: exposure to an adult displaying aggressive or nonaggressive behavior. Dependent variable: child's level of aggression. Ideas for altering the study: Conducting the same study with older or younger children; exposing the children to other children (as opposed to adults) behaving aggressively; pairing children with adults of the same and different ethnicities to determine the impact of ethnic background.

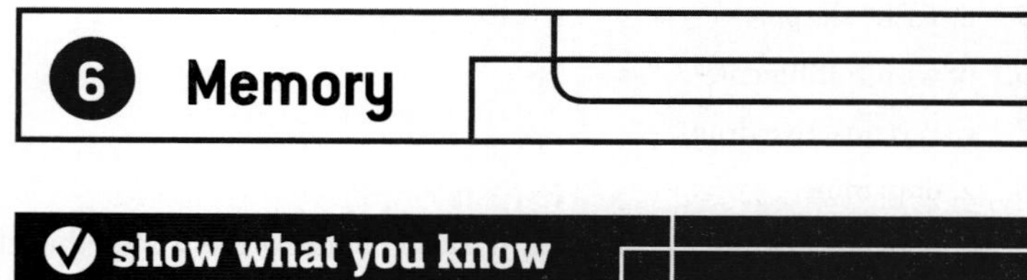

6 Memory

show what you know

What Is Memory?

1. b. Encoding
2. Paying little attention to data entering our sensory system results in *shallow processing*. For example, you remember seeing a word that has been boldfaced in the text while studying. You might even be able to recall the page that it appears on, and where on the page it is located. *Deeper-level processing* relies on characteristics related to patterns and meaning, and generally results in longer-lasting and easier to retrieve memories. As we study, if we contemplate incoming information and relate it to memories we already have, deeper processing occurs and the new memories are more likely to persist.
3. Memory

Stages of Memory

1. b. 30 seconds
2. b. working memory.
3. chunking
4. Answers will vary. **Ex**quisitely **Se**rious **Ep**isodes **Fl**ashed **Im**possible **P**roteins **L**ightning **S**tyle

   Explicit memory, **Se**mantic memory, **Ep**isodic memory, **Fl**ash-bulb memory, **Im**plicit memory, **Pr**ocedural memory, **L**ong-term memory, **S**ensory memory.

Retrieval and Forgetting

1. d. rich false memory.
2. misinformation effect
3. A *reconstructionist model* of memory suggests that memories are a combination of "fact and fiction." Over time, memories can fade, and because they are permeable, they become more vulnerable to the invasion of new information. In other words, memory of an event might include revisions to what really happened, based on knowledge, opinions, and information you have gained since the event occurred. The Loftus and Palmer experiment indicates that the wording of questions can significantly influence recall, demonstrating that memories can change in response to new information (that is, they are malleable).

The Biology of Memory

1. a. Anterograde amnesia
2. c. hippocampus
3. Alzheimer's disease
4. Answers will vary, but can be based on the following information. *Infantile amnesia* is the inability to remember events from one's earliest years. Most adults cannot remember events before the age of 3.

TEST PREP ARE YOU READY?

1. d. retrieval
2. a. neurofibrillary tangles
3. d. chunking
4. b. working memory
5. a. the encoding specificity principle.
6. c. Proactive interference; retroactive interference
7. d. a reconstructionist model of memory
8. b. rich false memory
9. b. access memories of events created before the damage.
10. d. hippocampus
11. Information enters sensory memory, which includes an overwhelming array of sensory stimuli. If it is not lost in sensory memory, it enters the short-term memory stage. The amount of time information is maintained and processed in short-term memory can be about 30 seconds. And short-term memory has a limited capacity. Because short-term memories cannot last for a couple of hours, it is more likely your friend's grandmother is having difficulty encoding, storing, and/or recalling information that should be held in long-term memory.
12. *Iconic memories* are visual impressions that are photograph-like in their accuracy but dissolve in less than a second. *Echoic memories* are exact copies of the sounds we hear, lasting about 1–10 seconds. Iconic memory uses our visual system, whereas echoic memory uses our auditory system.
13. *Short-term memory* is a stage of memory that temporarily maintains and processes a limited amount of information. *Working memory* is the active processing of information in short-term memory. Working memory refers to what is going on in short-term memory.
14. Answers will vary. **E**very **S**tudent **R**emembers.
15. The teacher should list the most important rules first and last in the list. The *serial position effect* suggests items at the beginning and at the end of a list are more likely to be recalled. The *primacy effect* suggests we are more likely to remember items at the beginning of a list, because they have a better chance of moving into long-term memory. The *recency effect* suggests we are more likely to remember items at the end of a list because they linger in short-term memory.

7 Cognition, Language, and Intelligence

show what you know

What Is Cognition?

1. Cognition
2. b. concept
3. c. formal concept
4. Answers will vary. Structures in the brain are associated with cognition. For example, the association areas integrate information from all over the brain. Broca's and Wernicke's areas work with other parts of the brain to generate and understand language.

   The biology of cognition can be found at the neural level as well. For example, changes at the level of neurons make it possible to store and retrieve information. It is also at the neuronal level where we see the plasticity of the brain at work.

Problem Solving and Decision Making

1. c. trial and error.
2. heuristic
3. d. availability heuristic.
4. Answers will vary. A *heuristic* uses a "rule of thumb" or a broad application of a strategy to solve a problem, but it can also be used to help predict the probability of an event occurring. However, heuristics can lead us astray in our assessment of situations or predictions of outcomes. In the current example, you can present information to your friend that indicates flying is the safest form of travel. But you can also describe how the *availability heuristic* might lead him to believe that air travel is not safe. The vividness of airplane crashes can influence his recall; even though they are rare events, he is likely to overestimate the probability of them happening again due to the ease with which he recalls similar events. Highly detailed media reports of an airplane crash are likely to linger in his memory.

The Power of Language

1. Phonemes
2. b. thinking and perception.
3. Answers will vary. Bilingualism is associated with enhanced creativity, abstract thought, and working memory. And knowing more than one language has been found to be associated with more efficient executive functioning, including abilities related to planning ahead and solving problems. Thus, bilingualism may actually improve performance on cognitive tasks, such as deciphering unknown and untranslatable words.

Intelligence

1. c. analytic, creative, practical.
2. aptitude; achievement
3. The *intelligence quotient* (*IQ*) is a score from an intelligence assessment; it provides a way to compare levels of intelligence across ages. Originally, an IQ score was derived by dividing mental age by chronological age and multiplying that number by 100. Modern intelligence tests still assign a numerical score, although they no longer use the actual quotient score.
4. divergent thinking

TEST PREP ARE YOU READY?

1. d. Cognition; thinking
2. a. Concepts
3. c. natural concepts
4. b. the plasticity
5. d. an algorithm
6. d. linguistic relativity hypothesis
7. b. availability heuristic
8. b. phonemes
9. d. Intelligence
10. c. genetic hypothesis
11. *Formal concepts* are created through rigid and logical rules, or features of a concept. *Natural concepts* are acquired through everyday experience, and they do not have the same types of rigid rules for identification that formal concepts have.

    Examples will vary. An example of a formal concept is the pitch of a sound, which is defined by the frequency of the sound wave. The concept of family is an example of a natural concept. Is a family a group of people who just live together, or do they have to be related genetically? Family is a natural concept that can change based on individual experiences.
12. See Table 7.2. Charles Spearman speculated that intelligence consists of a *general intelligence* (or *g*-factor), which refers to a singular underlying aptitude or intellectual ability. Howard Gardner suggested we have *multiple intelligences,* proposing nine different types of intelligences or "frames of mind": linguistic (verbal), logical-mathematical, spatial, bodily-kinesthetic, musical, intrapersonal, interpersonal, naturalist, and existential. Robert Sternberg proposed three kinds of intelligences. His *triarchic theory of intelligence* suggests that humans have varying degrees of analytical, creative, and practical abilities.
13. Using the *availability heuristic,* we predict the probability of something happening in the future based on how easily we can recall a similar type of event from the past. The availability heuristic is essentially a decision-making strategy that relies on memory. The Jersey Shore residents remembered a recent storm in which they did not have to leave their homes, so they decided it was safe to stay.
14. *Reliability* is the ability of an assessment to provide consistent, reproducible results. *Validity* is the degree to which an assessment measures what it intends to measure. An unreliable IQ test might result in getting different scores for the IQ test taken now and again in a few months; it would not be consistent across time, which is counter to what you would expect (we expect level of intelligence to remain fairly stable over time). An IQ test that is not valid would not be able to predict future performance on tasks related to intellectual ability.
15. Answers will vary. *Divergent thinking* is the ability to devise many solutions to a problem.

    Possible solutions: As a doorstop, icebreaker, paperweight, shovel, or axe; for putting out cigarettes; for breaking glass; for crushing ingredients for a recipe; for putting out a candle; and so on.

8 Human Development

show what you know

Why Study Human Development?

1. maturation
2. Developmental psychologists' longstanding discussions have centered on three major themes: stages and continuity; nature and nurture; and stability and change. Each of these themes relates to a basic question: (1) Does development occur in separate or discrete stages, or is it a steady, continuous process? (2) What are the relative roles of heredity and environment in human development? (3) How stable is one's personality over a lifetime and across situations?
3. c. cross-sectional

Inside the Womb

1. d. Chromosomes
2. Genotype; phenotype
3. a. embryonic period

Infants and Children

1. rooting; sucking
2. d. assimilation.
3. scaffolding
4. c. developmental tasks or emotional crises.
5. There is a universal sequence of language development. At around 2–3 months, infants typically start to produce vowel-like sounds known as *cooing.* At 4–6 months, in the *babbling stage,* infants combine consonants with vowels. This progresses to the *one-word stage* around 12 months, followed by *two-word telegraphic speech* at approximately 18 months. As children mature, they start to use

more complete sentences. Infants pay more attention to adults who use infant-directed speech and are more likely to provide them with chances to learn and interact, thus allowing more exposure to language. Parents and caregivers should talk with their infants and children as much as possible, as babies benefit from a lot of chatter.

The Teenage Years

1. b. secondary sex characteristics.
2. Answers will vary. During the stage of *ego identity versus role confusion,* an adolescent seeks to define himself through his values, beliefs, and goals. If a helicopter parent has been troubleshooting all of her child's problems, the child has never had to learn to take care of things for himself. Thus, he may feel helpless and unsure of how to handle a problem that arises. The parent might also have ensured the child was successful in every endeavor, but this, too, could cause the child to be unable to identify his true strengths, again interfering with the creation of an adult identity.
3. Preconventional
4. a. formal operational stage.
5. c. gender role

Adulthood

1. a. physical exercise
2. fluid; crystallized
3. d. acceptance
4. integrity; despair

TEST PREP ARE YOU READY?

1. b. longitudinal research.
2. d. nature and nurture
3. d. genes
4. a. epigenetics.
5. c. synaptic pruning
6. b. scaffolding
7. d. Teratogens
8. c. Primary sex characteristics
9. a. formal operational stage.
10. c. coo; babble; first words
11. Answers will vary, but can be based on the following. Gender refers to the categories or dimensions of masculinity and femininity based on social, cultural, and psychological characteristics. Men are expected to be masculine, while women are expected to be more feminine. We learn how to behave in gender-conforming ways through the gender roles designated by our cultures, and from observations of people around us, particularly those of the same gender. One component of identity is gender identity, which is the feeling or sense of being either male or female, and compatibility, contentment, and conformity with one's gender. Adolescents explore who they are by trying out different ideas in a variety of categories, including politics and religion. Then they begin to commit to a particular set of beliefs and attitudes, making decisions to engage in activities related to their evolving identity. Concepts of masculine and feminine vary according to culture, social context, and the individual.
12. The adult body experiences many changes as we age. During early adulthood, hearing declines and there is a reduction in fertility. Middle adulthood brings about skin wrinkles and skin spots, graying or loss of hair, weakened bones, and decline in eyesight. For women, middle adulthood brings about a decrease in estrogen and the transition toward menopause. Men experience a reduction in testosterone production. Late adulthood can result in cataracts and impaired night vision, increased reaction time, and deterioration of memory.
13. Answers will vary. See Infographics 8.3 and 8.4, and Table 8.3.
14. Answers will vary, but can be based on the following definitions. *Crystallized intelligence* refers to the knowledge we gain through experience, and *fluid intelligence* refers to the ability to think in the abstract and create associations among concepts. As we age, the speed with which we learn new material and create associations decreases, but crystallized intelligence increases.
15. Answers will vary. See Infographic 8.4.

9 Motivation and Emotion

show what you know

Motivation

1. Motivation
2. b. intrinsic motivation
3. hierarchy of needs
4. The *drive-reduction theory* of motivation suggests that human behaviors are driven by the need to maintain homeostasis—that is, to fulfill basic biological needs. If a need is not fulfilled, this creates a drive, or state of tension, that pushes us or motivates behaviors to meet the need. Once a need is met, the drive is reduced, at least temporarily, because this is an ongoing process, as the need inevitably returns. *Arousal theory* suggests that humans seek an optimal level of arousal, and what is optimal is based on individual differences. Behaviors can arise out of the simple desire for stimulation, or arousal, which is a level of alertness and engagement in the world, and people are motivated to seek out activities that fulfill this need. Drive-reduction theory suggests that the motivation is to reduce tension, but arousal theory suggests that in some cases the motivation is to increase tension.

Sexuality

1. a. excitement, plateau, orgasm, and resolution.
2. fraternal birth order effect

Hunger

1. a. stomach was contracting.
2. When glucose levels dip, the stomach and liver send signals to the brain that something must be done about this reduced energy source. The brain, in turn, initiates a sense of hunger. When the lateral hypothalamus is activated, appetite increases. On the other hand, if the ventromedial hypothalamus becomes activated, appetite declines, causing an animal to stop eating.

Emotion

1. Answers will vary, but can be based on the following definitions. *Emotion* is a psychological state that includes a subjective or inner experience. It also has a physiological component and entails a behavioral expression. Emotions are quite strong, but they don't generally last as long as moods. In addition, emotions are more likely to have an identifiable cause (that is, a reaction to a stimulus that provoked it), which has a greater probability of motivating a person to take some sort of action. *Moods* are longer-term emotional states that are less intense than emotions and do not appear to have distinct beginnings or ends. It is very likely that on your way to a wedding you are in a happy mood, and you have been that way for quite a while. If you were to get mud on your clothing, it is likely that you would experience an emotion such as anger, which might have been triggered by someone jumping in a large mud puddle and splashing you. Your anger would have a subjective experience (your feeling of anger), a physiological component (you felt your face flush with heat), and a behavioral expression (you glared angrily at the person who splashed you).
2. b. Display rules
3. Answers may vary. See Infographic 9.2. The *Cannon–Bard* theory of emotion suggests that environmental stimuli are the starting point for emotions, and that body changes and emotions happen together. The *Schachter–Singer* theory of emotion suggests there is a general pattern of physiological arousal caused by the sympathetic nervous system, and this pattern is common to a variety of emotions. Unlike the Cannon–Bard theory, the Schachter–Singer theory suggests our thoughts about our body changes can lead to emotions. The experience of emotion is the result of two factors: physiological arousal and a cognitive label for this physiological state (the arousal). Cannon–Bard did not suggest that a cognitive label is necessary for emotions to be experienced.
4. Darwin suggested that interpreting facial expressions is not something we learn but rather is an innate ability that evolved because it promotes survival. Sharing the same facial expressions allows for communication. Research on an isolated group of indigenous peoples in New Guinea suggests that the same facial expressions represent the same basic emotions across cultures. In addition, the fact that children born deaf and blind have the same types of emotional expressions as children with normal sensory abilities indicates that these displays, and the emotions behind them, may be universal.
5. amygdala
6. *Heritability* is the degree to which heredity is responsible for a particular characteristic in a population. In this case, the heritability for happiness is as high as 80%, indicating that around 80% of the population-wide variation in happiness can be attributed to genes, and 20% to environmental influences. In other words, we can explain a high proportion of the variation in happiness, life satisfaction, and well-being by considering genetic make-up, as opposed to environmental factors.

TEST PREP ARE YOU READY?

1. d. an incentive
2. a. extrinsic motivation
3. b. drive-reduction
4. a. sensation seekers
5. a. excitement
6. c. behavioral expression.
7. b. could identify the facial expressions common across the world.
8. c. physiological arousal and cognitive labeling.
9. b. cognitive-appraisal approach
10. b. heritability estimates
11. Because monozygotic twins share nearly 100% of their genetic make-up, we expect them to share more genetically influenced characteristics than dizygotic twins, who only share about 50% of their genes. Using twins, researchers explored the impact of genes and environment on same-sex sexual behavior. Monozygotic twins were moderately more likely than dizygotic twins to have the same sexual orientation. They found men and women differ in terms of the heritability of same-sex sexual behavior. These studies highlight that the influence of the environment is substantial with regard to same-sex sexual behavior.
12. Answers will vary, but can be based on the following. Maslow's hierarchy of needs is considered universal. Needs are ordered according to the strength of their associated drives, with more critical needs at the base of the hierarchy and nonessential, higher-level needs at the top: physiological needs; safety needs; love and belongingness needs; esteem needs; self-actualization; self-transcendence. Maslow suggested that one's most basic needs must be met before higher-level needs motivate behavior. An example of someone not following the prescribed order of needs might be a martyr who is motivated by self-transcendence needs, ignoring safety needs altogether.
13. Answers will vary. Stomach contractions accompany feelings of hunger, and the stomach (and liver) send signals to the brain when glucose levels in the blood decrease. The brain, in turn, initiates a sense of hunger. When the lateral hypothalamus is activated, appetite increases. If the ventromedial hypothalamus becomes activated, appetite declines, causing an animal to stop eating. A variety of social and cultural factors, including exposure to large portion sizes and the presence of eating companions, may impact eating behaviors.
14. The amygdala is found in the limbic system and appears to be central to our experience of fear. When people view threatening images, or even look at an image of a frightened face, the amygdala is activated. When confronted with a fear-provoking situation, the amygdala enables an ultrafast and unconscious response.

The direct route (thalamus to amygdala, causing an emotional reaction) enables us to react quickly to threats for which we are biologically prepared (snakes, spiders, aggressive faces). The other pathway allows us to evaluate more complex threats (such as nuclear weapons, job layoffs) with our cortex, overriding the fast-response pathway when necessary.

15. Answers will vary but may be based on the following. There is relatively little fluctuation in adult weight over time. The communication between the brain and the appetite hormones helps regulate the body's set point, or stable weight that we tend to maintain despite variability in day-to-day exercise and intake of food. The set point helps to maintain a consistent weight in part through changes in metabolism. Research suggests that the biological basis of happiness may include a "set point," similar to the set point for body weight. Happiness tends to fluctuate around a fixed level, which is influenced by genes and related to temperament. We may experience periodic ups and downs, but ultimately we move back toward that fixed level of happiness. However, the set points for body weight and happiness may not be as powerful as researchers once suspected. To some degree, they depend on our conscious choices and behaviors.

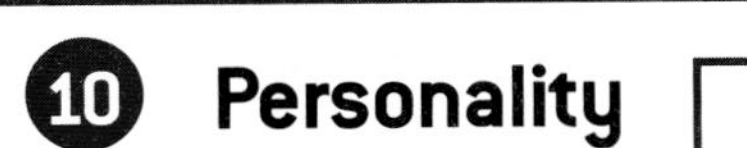

10 Personality

show what you know

An Introduction to Personality

1. Personality
2. Answers will vary (see Table 10.1).

Psychoanalytic Theories

1. psychosexual; fixation
2. Answers will vary, but could include the following. Some of *Freud's followers* branched out on their own due to disagreements about certain issues, such as his focus on the instincts of sex and aggression, his idea that personality is determined by the end of childhood, and his somewhat negative view of human nature. *Adler* proposed that humans are conscious and intentional in their behaviors. *Jung* suggested that we are driven by a psychological energy (as opposed to sexual energy), which encourages positive growth, self-understanding, and balance. *Horney* emphasized the role of relationships between children and their caregivers, not erogenous zones and psychosexual stages.
3. d. topographical model of the mind

Humanistic, Learning, and Trait Theories

1. d. unconditional positive regard.
2. Answers will vary (also see Table 10.4). The *Big Five* traits include openness, conscientiousness, extraversion, agreeableness, and neuroticism. Three decades of research suggest the five factors are influenced by genes, brain structures, and other biological factors. The proportion of population-wide variation in the Big Five traits attributed to genetic make-up is substantial (ranging from .41 to .61), suggesting that the remainder can be attributed to environmental influences.
3. b. locus of control
4. Answers will vary, but can be based on the following definition (also see Infographic 10.2). *Reciprocal determinism* refers to the multidirectional interactions among cognition, behaviors, and the environment guiding our behavior patterns and personality.
5. a. traits.
6. learning theory

Personality Testing

1. b. Projective
2. Answers will vary, but can be based on the following definitions. A *valid measure* is one that can be shown to measure what it intends to measure. If a measure is not valid, a client might be given information that is not meaningful because the findings have not been shown to measure their intended topic. A *reliable measure* provides consistent results across time as well as across raters or people scoring the measure. If findings from a personality test are not reliable, a client may be given information that will not reflect a consistent pattern, or may be questionable due to problems with scoring.
3. a. standardization

TEST PREP ARE YOU READY?

1. d. behavioral
2. d. mental processes that occur at three levels of consciousness.
3. a. psychosexual stages; fixation
4. a. incongruent
5. c. self-efficacy
6. a. Personality
7. a. source traits
8. b. the stability of personality characteristics over time.
9. c. Reliability
10. c. his intense emphasis on sex and aggression
11. Answers will vary, but can be based on the following information. According to behaviorists and learning theory, the *environment* shapes personality through *operant* conditioning. *Observation* and *modeling* also play a role in personality development.
12. Answers will vary. The *humanistic perspective* suggests that we are innately good and that we have capabilities we can and should take advantage of as we strive for personal growth. The choices we make in life influence our personalities. The *social-cognitive perspective* focuses on relationships, environmental influences, cognitive activity, and individual behavior as they come together to form personality. The humanistic perspective views personality as what we are able to do, whereas the social-cognitive perspective views personality, in part, as how we react to the environment.
13. Both the Oedipus (for boys) and Electra (for girls) complex represent an important conflict that occurs during the phallic stage.

For both boys and girls, the conflict can be resolved through the process of identification. Although basic urges and developmental processes underlie both of these complexes, there are several important differences. The *Oedipus complex* is the attraction a boy feels toward his mother, along with resentment or envy directed toward his father. When a little boy becomes aware of his attraction to his mother, he realizes his father is a formidable rival and experiences jealousy and anger toward him. With the *Electra complex,* a little girl feels an attraction to her father and becomes jealous and angry toward her mother. Realizing she doesn't have a penis, she may respond with anger, blaming her mother for her missing penis.

14. Answers will vary, but can be based on the following definitions. An *internal locus of control* suggests that the causes of life events reside within an individual, and that one has some control over them. An *external locus of control* suggests that causes for outcomes reside outside of an individual, and that one has little control over them.
15. *Objective assessments* of personality are based on a standardized procedure in which the scoring is free of opinions, beliefs, expectations, and values. Critics of objective assessments contend they do not allow flexibility or fully appreciate individual differences in experiences. Findings from *subjective assessments* of personality are based, in part, on personal intuition, opinions, and interpretations. Critics of the subjective assessments suggest there is not enough consistency across findings because of nonstandard scoring procedures.

11 Social Psychology

show what you know

An Introduction to Social Psychology

1. b. Social psychology; sociology
2. a. Attributions
3. d. disposition of the person.
4. Social psychology studies often involve confederates, who are working for the researchers. Playing the role of participants, confederates say what the researchers tell them to say and do what the researchers tell them to do. They are, unknown to the other participants, just part of the researchers' experimental manipulation. In a double-blind study, neither participants nor researchers administering a treatment know who is getting the real treatment. Participants are told ahead of time that they might receive a placebo, but do not necessarily know about confederates until after the study is complete.

Social Influence

1. a. social influence; b. persuasion; c. compliance; d. foot-in-the-door technique; e. conformity
2. d. Obedience
3. Answers will vary. Examples may include resisting the urge to eat dessert when others at the table are doing so, saying no to a cigarette when others offer one, and so forth.

Groups and Aggression

1. c. The bystander effect
2. Males tend to show more direct aggression (physical displays of aggression), whereas females are more likely to engage in relational aggression (gossip, exclusion, ignoring), perhaps because females have a higher risk for physical or bodily harm than males do.
3. Answers will vary, but may be based on the following information. *Discrimination* is showing favoritism or hostility to others because of their affiliation with a group. *Prejudice* is holding hostile or negative attitudes toward an individual or group. *Stereotypes* are conclusions or inferences we make about people who are different from us based on their group membership, such as their race, religion, age, or gender. Discrimination, prejudice, and stereotypes involve making assumptions about others we may not know. They often lead to unfair treatment of others.

Prosocial Behavior, Attraction, and Love

1. d. prosocial behavior.
2. b. proximity; similarity; physical attractiveness
3. According to this model, decisions to stay together or part ways are based on how happy people are in their relationship, their notion of what life would be like without it, and their investment in the relationship. People may stay in unsatisfying or unhealthy relationships if they feel there are no better alternatives or believe they have too much to lose. This model helps us understand why people remain in destructive relationships. These principles may also apply to friendships, positions at work, or loyalty to institutions. We tend to stay in jobs and friendships that may not be in our best interest because we are invested and feel there are no better alternatives.

TEST PREP ARE YOU READY?

1. d. school board policies regarding support for children with disabilities
2. b. Social cognition
3. d. the fundamental attribution error.
4. c. altruism.
5. a. conformity.
6. c. compliance.
7. d. stereotypes
8. c. aggression
9. b. expectations
10. d. passion, intimacy, and commitment.
11. Answers will vary, but may be based on the following information. *Social psychology* is the study of human cognition, emotion, and

behavior in relation to others. It focuses on studying individuals in relation to others and groups, whereas *sociology* studies the groups themselves—their cultures, societies, and subcultures.

12. Answers will vary. *Obedience* occurs when we change our behavior, or act in a way that we might not normally act, because we have been ordered to do so by an authority figure. An imbalance of power exists, and the person with more power generally has an advantage over a person with less power. It is important for us to pay attention to how we react when under the influence of an authority figure as we could inflict harm on others. One person can make a difference when he or she stands up for what is right.
13. Answers will vary. When a person is in trouble, bystanders have the tendency to assume that someone else will help—and therefore they stand by and do nothing, a phenomenon that is partly due to the diffusion of responsibility. This *bystander effect* is particularly common when there are many other people present. Individuals are more likely to aid a person in distress if no one else is present.
14. Answers will vary, but can be based on the following. *Stereotypes* are the conclusions or inferences we make about people who are different from us, based on their group membership (such as race, religion, age, or gender). We tend to see the world in terms of *in-groups* (the group to which we belong) and *out-groups* (people who are outside the group to which we belong), which can impact the stereotypes we hold.
15. Answers will vary, but can be based on the following. *Proximity* means nearness, which may play an important role in the formation of relationships. *Similarity* has to do with how much you have in common with someone else. We tend to prefer those who share our interests, viewpoints, ethnicity, values, and other characteristics. *Physical attractiveness* can be an important part of interpersonal attraction, with facial symmetry and signs of fertility generally considered desirable.

12 Stress and Health

show what you know

What Is Stress?

1. Stress
2. d. illness.
3. b. Acculturative stress
4. Answers will vary, but can be based on the following definitions. *Daily hassles* are the minor problems or irritants we deal with on a regular basis (for example, heavy traffic, financial worries, messy roommates). *Uplifts* are positive experiences that have the potential to make us happy (for example, a humorous text message, small gift).

Stress and Your Health

1. a. alarm stage
2. c. The hypothalamic–pituitary–adrenal system
3. general adaptation syndrome (GAS)
4. c. cortisol.
5. When the body is expending its resources to deal with an ongoing stressor, the immune system is less powerful, and the work of the lymphocytes becomes compromised. During times of stress, people tend to sleep poorly, eat erratically, and may increase their drug and alcohol use, along with other poor behavioral choices. These tendencies can lead to health problems.

Can You Deal?

1. d. Problem-focused coping
2. Answers may vary. *Stress management* incorporates tools to lower the impact of possible stressors. Exercise, meditation, progressive muscle relaxation, biofeedback, and social support all have positive physical and psychological effects on the response to stressors. In addition, looking out for the well-being of others by caring and giving of yourself is an effective way to reduce the impact of stress.
3. b. Type B personality.

TEST PREP ARE YOU READY?

1. d. stressors.
2. b. cortisol; the immune system
3. d. life-changing events
4. c. exhaustion stage
5. d. sympathetic nervous system
6. a. immune system
7. b. Coping
8. d. progressive muscle relaxation
9. a. Type A personality
10. b. hardiness.
11. Answers will vary, but can be based on the following explanation. There are various ways people respond to acculturative stress. Some try to assimilate into the culture, letting go of old ways and adopting those of the new culture. Another approach is to cling to one's roots and remain separated from the new culture. Such an approach can be very problematic if the new culture does not support this type of separation and requires assimilation. A combination of these two approaches is integration, or holding onto some elements of the old culture, but also adopting aspects of the new one.
12. Answers will vary, but can be based on the following definitions. *Daily hassles* are the minor problems or irritants we deal with on a regular basis. *Life-changing events* are occurrences that require a life adjustment (for example, marriage, change in school status). During times of stress, people tend to sleep poorly, eat erratically, and may increase their drug and alcohol use, along with other poor behavioral choices. These tendencies can lead to health problems. Exercise, mindfulness meditation, progressive muscle relaxation, biofeedback, and social support all have positive physical and psychological effects on the response to stressors.

13. Answers will vary, but can be based on the following information. Reactions associated with the fight-or-flight response include increased pulse, breathing rate, and mental alertness. A coordinated effort of the sympathetic nervous system and the endocrine system, the fight-or-flight reaction primes the body to respond to danger, either by escaping or confronting the threat head-on.
14. Answers will vary, but can be based on the following definitions. One major source of stress is conflict, which can be defined as the discomfort felt when making tough choices. Often two choices presented are both attractive to you (*approach–approach conflict*); at times a choice or situation has favorable and unfavorable characteristics (*approach–avoidance conflict*); and at other times the two alternatives are both unattractive (*avoidance–avoidance conflict*).
15. Answers will vary, but can be based on the following definitions. Someone with an *internal locus of control* generally feels as if she is in control of life and its circumstances; she probably believes it is important to take charge and make changes when problems occur. A person with an *external locus of control* generally feels as if chance, luck, or fate is responsible for her circumstances; there is no need to try to change things or make them better. Any decisions related to healthy choices can be influenced by locus of control.

13 Psychological Disorders

show what you know

An Introduction to Psychological Disorders

1. a. dysfunction
2. psychological disorder
3. Answers will vary (see Figure 13.1). The *biopsychosocial perspective* suggests that psychological disorders result from a complex interaction of factors: *biological* (for example, genes, neurotransmitter and hormone activity, structures in the brain), *psychological* (for example, learned associations, thinking patterns, personality traits), and *sociocultural* (for example, media, cultural beliefs).

When Anxiety Is Extreme

1. c. panic attacks.
2. d. compulsions.
3. Repeatedly locking the car temporarily reduced Melissa's anxiety, making her more likely to perform this behavior in the future; thus, negative reinforcement promoted this maladaptive behavior. The therapist probably expected that if Melissa was not able to repeatedly check the locks and nothing bad happened, eventually Melissa would not need to continue locking her car repeatedly.

From Depression to Mania

1. b. major depressive disorder
2. Answers will vary, but can be based on the following information. The symptoms of major depressive disorder can include feelings of sadness or hopelessness, reduced pleasure, sleeping excessively or not at all, loss of energy, feelings of worthlessness, or difficulties thinking or concentrating. The hallmarks of major depressive disorder are the "substantial" severity of symptoms and impairment in the ability to perform expected roles. *Biological theories* suggest the disorder results from a genetic predisposition, neurotransmitters, and hormones. *Psychological theories* suggest that feelings of learned helplessness and negative thinking may play a role. Not just one factor is involved in major depressive disorder, but rather the interplay of several.
3. b. manic episodes.
4. A diagnosis of *bipolar I disorder* requires that a person experience at least one manic episode, substantial distress, and great impairment. *Bipolar II disorder* requires at least one major depressive episode as well as a hypomanic episode, which is associated with some of the same symptoms as a manic episode, but is not as severe and does not impair one's ability to function. People with bipolar disorder cycle between extreme highs and lows of emotion and energy that last for days, weeks, or even months. Individuals with *major depressive disorder,* on the other hand, tend to experience a persistent low mood, loss of energy, and feelings of worthlessness.

Schizophrenia and Autism

1. psychosis
2. a. hallucination.
3. Answers will vary, but can be based on the following information. Schizophrenia is a complex psychological disorder that results from a combination of biological, psychological, and social factors. This disorder springs from a complex interaction of genes and environment. The diathesis–stress model takes these factors into account, with *diathesis* referring to an inherited disposition (for example, to schizophrenia) and *stress* referring to the stressors in the environment (internal and external). Genes, neurotransmitters, differences in the brain, and exposure to a virus in utero are all possible influences in the development of schizophrenia. There are some sociocultural and environmental factors that may play a minor role in one's risk for developing the disorder, as well as the severity of symptoms. Evidence exists, for instance, that complications at birth, social stress, and cannabis abuse are related to a slightly increased risk of schizophrenia onset.

Personality, Dissociative, and Eating Disorders

1. borderline personality disorder
2. Answers will vary, but can be based on the following information (see Table 13.1). *Distress* is the degree to which behavior or emotions cause an individual to feel upset or uncomfortable. *Impairment* or *dysfunction* is the degree to which behavior interferes with daily life and relationships. *Deviance* means violating the norms, or rules, of society. Personality disorders are a group of psychological disorders that can include impairments in cognition, emotional responses, interpersonal functioning, and impulse control. Thus, they involve issues that meet three of the criteria of abnormal behavior: dysfunction (they interfere with daily life and relationships), distress (from problems in interpersonal relationships, anxiety), and deviance (behaviors often considered outside the standards of society).
3. Dissociative identity disorder
4. d. extreme overeating followed by purging.

TEST PREP ARE YOU READY?

1. b. the medical model.
2. a. obsessions; compulsions
3. b. biopsychosocial
4. b. agoraphobia
5. b. antisocial personality disorder.
6. d. binge-eating disorder.
7. c. problems associated with sleep.
8. b. psychosis.
9. a. borderline personality disorder
10. b. personalities
11. Answers will vary, but can be based on the following information. *Dysfunction* is the degree to which a behavior interferes with one's life or ability to function (for example, washing one's hands to the point of making them raw). *Distress* is feeling regularly upset or uncomfortable because of unwanted behaviors or emotions (for example, continually feeling sad and hopeless). *Deviance* is the degree to which a behavior is considered to be outside of the standards or rules of a society (for example, removing one's clothes in inappropriate settings).
12. Answers will vary. This statement does not follow the suggestion of using "people-first language." Instead, it defines an individual by the disorder. People are much more than their diagnoses. The diagnosis does not describe who your friend is, but only what is causing the distress or discomfort.
13. Classical conditioning can play a role in the development of a panic disorder by pairing an initially neutral stimulus (for example, a mall) with an unexpected panic attack (the unconditioned stimulus). The panic attack location then becomes a conditioned stimulus. When the location is visited or even considered, a panic attack can ensue (now the conditioned response).
14. Cognitive therapist Aaron Beck suggested that depression is a product of a cognitive triad, which includes a negative view of experiences, self, and the future. Negative thinking may lead to self-defeating behaviors, which, in turn, reinforce the beliefs.
15. Answers will vary, but can be based on the following information. Schizophrenia is a complex psychological disorder that results from biological, psychological, and social factors. Because this disorder springs from a complex interaction of genes and environment, researchers have a hard time predicting who will be affected. The diathesis–stress model takes these factors into account, with *diathesis* referring to an inherited disposition (for example, to schizophrenia) and *stress* referring to the stressors in the environment (internal and external). Genes, neurotransmitters, differences in the brain, and exposure to a virus in utero are all possible biological factors. Neurotransmitters are also thought to play a role in schizophrenia. The *dopamine hypothesis,* for example, suggests that the synthesis, release, and concentrations of dopamine are all elevated in people who have been diagnosed with schizophrenia and are suffering from psychosis. There are several environmental triggers thought to be involved in one's risk for developing the disorder as well as the severity of symptoms (for example, complications at birth, social stress, and cannabis abuse are related to a slightly increased risk of schizophrenia onset).

14 Treatment of Psychological Disorders

show what you know

An Introduction to Treatment

1. a. symptoms
2. mental hygiene movement
3. *Deinstitutionalization* was the mass movement of patients with psychological disorders out of mental institutions, in an attempt to reintegrate them into the community. Deinstitutionalization was partially the result of a movement to reduce the social isolation of people with psychological disorders. This movement marked the beginning of new treatment modalities that allowed individuals to better care for themselves and function in society. However, many former patients ended up living on the streets or behind bars. Many people locked up in American jails and prisons are suffering from mental health problems.

Insight Therapies

1. a. Humanistic
2. *Psychoanalysis,* the first formal system of psychotherapy, attempts to increase awareness of unconscious conflicts, making it possible to address and work through them. The therapist's goal is to uncover these unconscious conflicts. *Psychodynamic therapy* is an updated form of psychoanalysis; it incorporates many of Freud's core themes, including the notion that personality characteristics and behavior problems often can be traced to unconscious conflicts. In psychodynamic therapy, therapists see clients once a week for several months rather than many times a week for years. And instead of sitting quietly off to the side, therapists and clients sit face-to-face and engage in a two-way dialogue.
3. c. empathy.

Behavior and Cognitive Therapies

1. a. behavior
2. Answers will vary, but may be based on the following information. *Behavior therapy* focuses on behavioral change, with the belief that the key to resolving problems is not understanding their origins. Using the learning principles of classical conditioning, operant conditioning, and observational learning, behavior therapy aims to replace maladaptive behaviors with more adaptive behaviors. It incorporates a variety of techniques, including exposure therapy, aversion therapy, systematic desensitization, and behavior modification. Behavior therapy covers a broad range of treatment approaches, and focuses on observable behaviors in the present. *Cognitive therapy* is a type of therapy aimed at addressing the maladaptive thinking that leads to negative behaviors and feelings. The aim of cognitive therapy is to help clients recognize and resist their own cognitive distortions and illogical thoughts in short-term, action-oriented, and homework-intensive therapy sessions. The goal of both approaches is to change the way an individual works or functions in the world. One major difference is that behavioral

therapy focuses on behaviors, whereas cognitive therapy focuses on thinking—the way an individual views the world, and views himself/herself in the world.

3. cognitive therapy

Biomedical Therapies

1. d. electroconvulsive therapy
2. b. antidepressant.
3. neurosurgery
4. Answers will vary. *Biomedical therapies* use physical interventions to treat psychological disorders. These therapies can be categorized according to the method by which they influence the brain's functioning: chemical, electrical, or structural. *Psychotherapy* is a treatment approach in which a client works with a mental health professional to reduce psychological symptoms and increase his or her quality of life. These approaches share common features: The relationship between the client and the treatment provider is of utmost importance, as is a sense of hope that things will get better. And these approaches generally seek to reduce symptoms and increase the quality of life, whether a person is struggling with a psychological disorder or simply wants to be more fulfilled.

Psychotherapy: Who's in the Mix?

1. Answers will vary (see Table 14.5). Group therapy would be inappropriate for an individual who is not comfortable talking or interacting with others and is unwilling to share his or her own thoughts, feelings, or problems. A group may fail if group members do not get along, are continually late for meetings, or drop out. The skills of the group therapist also play a role in the success of treatment (for example, empathy, facilitation skills, observation skills).
2. Answers will vary, but may include: licensing and privacy issues; difficulties with nonverbal communication; difficulties with the development of therapeutic relationships.
3. Answers will vary, but may be based on the following information. In general, therapy "works," especially if it is long-term. All approaches to psychotherapy perform equally well across all disorders. But individuals whose insurance companies limit their choice of therapists and how long they can receive treatment do not experience the same improvement as those who are less restricted. In addition, people who start therapy but then decide to stop it experience less successful outcomes. The client's cultural experience is important to keep in mind. Within any group, there is vast variation from one individual to the next, but it is still necessary for therapists to understand the cultural context in which they work. This includes being respectful of cultural norms and sensitive to the many forms of prejudice and discrimination that people can experience.
4. c. limits placed by an insurance company

TEST PREP ARE YOU READY?

1. b. moral treatment
2. d. reduce symptoms and increase quality of life
3. b. psychoanalysis
4. d. person-centered therapy.
5. a. hierarchies
6. b. Getting fired once does not mean my career is over.
7. d. Seeing others improve offers hope and inspiration.
8. d. the present.
9. d. Psychopharmacology
10. b. insurance-mandated limitations on choice of therapist
11. Answers will vary, but may be based on the following information. *Cognitive behavioral therapy* is an action-oriented type of therapy that requires clients to confront and resist their illogical thinking. *Insight therapies* aim to increase awareness of self and the environment. These approaches share common features: The relationship between the client and the treatment provider is of utmost importance, as is a sense of hope that things will get better. And these approaches generally seek to reduce symptoms and increase the quality of life, whether a person is struggling with a psychological disorder or simply wants to be more fulfilled.
12. Answers will vary (see Table 14.3).
13. Answers will vary, but may be based on the following information. *Exposure* is a therapeutic technique that brings a person into contact with a feared object or situation while in a safe environment, with the goal of extinguishing or eliminating the fear response. An anxiety hierarchy (a list of activities ordered from least to most anxiety-provoking) can be used to help with exposure. *Aversion therapy* is an approach that uses principles of classical conditioning to link problematic behaviors to unpleasant physical reactions.
14. Answers will vary, but may be based on the following information. One challenge of providing therapy is to meet the needs of clients from vastly different cultures. Within any group, there is great variation from one individual to the next, but it is still necessary for the therapist to keep in mind the client's cultural experience. This includes being respectful of cultural norms and sensitive to the many forms of prejudice and discrimination that people can experience. Every client has a unique story and a singular set of psychological needs. Responding to those needs and determining which approach will be most effective are key to successful therapy.
15. Answers will vary, but may be based on the following information. As more people gain access to the Internet and own smartphones, online therapies are multiplying. Online therapy can mean anything from e-mail communications between client and therapist to real-time sessions via a webcam. These digital tools are valuable for serving rural areas and providing treatment to those who would otherwise have no access. Videoconferencing is also useful for consultation and supervision. But online psychotherapy raises many concerns, including licensing and privacy issues, lack of nonverbal cues, and potential problems with developing therapeutic relationships.

Appendix A

Introduction to Statistics

TEST PREP ARE YOU READY?

1. Statistics
2. a. summarize data.
3. d. statistical significance
4. a. 2; b. 2; c. 1; d. 1
5. c. frequency distribution
6. a. normal curve.
7. negatively skewed; positively skewed
8. b. measures of central tendency.
9. b. 5
10. a. 4
11. a. 4
12. c. outlier; mean
13. a. range
14. a. 2
15. Answers will vary, but it is important to consider what is being measured, how that measurement is actually being depicted, where the data come from, and the purpose of gathering the data.

try this **p. A-3**

Answers will vary, but here are examples from Chapter 3:

quantitative variables: frequency of sound waves, pitch of sound, number of hair cells, color wavelength, sound intensity

qualitative variables: gender, religious affiliation, supertaster status, carpentered worlds versus traditional settings

try this **p. A-13**

The mean for the sample is 38.6, the median is 38, the range is 65, and the standard deviation is 16.5. A stem-and-leaf plot would look like the following, and it appears the sample data might be positively skewed:

1	001688
2	004455699
3	144567889
4	01123689
5	00123679
6	116
7	15

Glossary

abnormal behavior Behavior that is atypical, dysfunctional, distressful, and/or deviant. (p. 473)

absolute thresholds The weakest stimuli that can be detected 50% of the time. (p. 83)

accommodation The process by which the lens changes shape in order to focus on objects near and far. (p. 88)

accommodation A restructuring of old ideas to make a place for new information. (p. 296)

acculturation The process of cultural adjustment and adaptation, including changes to one's language, values, cultural behaviors, and sometimes national identity. (p. 447)

acculturative stress Stress that occurs when people move to new countries or cultures and must adjust to a new way of life. (p. 447)

achievement Acquired knowledge, or what has been learned. (p. 266)

acquired immunodeficiency syndrome (AIDS) This condition, caused by HIV, generally results in a severely compromised immune system, which makes the body vulnerable to other infections. (p. 445)

acquisition The initial learning phase in both classical and operant conditioning. (p. 166)

action potential The spike in voltage that passes through the axon of a neuron, the purpose of which is to convey information. (p. 47)

activation–synthesis model The theory proposing that humans respond to random neural activity while in REM sleep as if it has meaning. (p. 141)

active listening The ability to pick up on the content and emotions behind words in order to understand a client's perspective, often by echoing the main point of what the client says. (p. 522)

adaptive value The degree to which a trait or behavior helps an organism survive. (p. 171)

adolescence The transition period between late childhood and early adulthood. (p. 305)

adrenal glands Endocrine glands involved in responses to stress as well as the regulation of salt balance. (p. 57)

afterimage An image that appears to linger in the visual field after its stimulus, or source, is removed. (p. 92)

aggression Intimidating or threatening behavior or attitudes intended to hurt someone. (p. 427)

agoraphobia Extreme fear of situations involving public transportation, open spaces, or other public settings. (p. 485)

algorithm An approach to problem solving using a formula or set of rules that, if followed, ensures a solution. (p. 249)

all-or-none A neuron either fires or does not fire; action potentials are always the same strength. (p. 47)

alpha waves Brain waves that indicate a relaxed, drowsy state. (p. 130)

altruism A desire or motivation to help others with no expectation of anything in return. (p. 432)

amphetamines Stimulant drugs; methamphetamine is an example of a drug in this class. (p. 149)

amplitude The height of a wave; distance from midpoint to peak, or from midpoint to trough. (p. 87)

amygdala A pair of almond-shaped structures in the limbic system that processes aggression and basic emotions such as fear, as well as associated memories. (p. 71)

androgens The male hormones secreted by the testes in males and by the adrenal glands in both males and females. (p. 285)

androgyny The tendency to cross gender-role boundaries, exhibiting behaviors associated with both genders. (p. 312)

anorexia nervosa An eating disorder identified by significant weight loss, an intense fear of being overweight, a false sense of body image, and a refusal to eat the proper amount of calories to achieve a healthy weight. (p. 505)

anterograde amnesia A type of memory loss; an inability to create new memories following damage to the brain. (p. 229)

anti-anxiety drugs Psychotropic medications used for treating the symptoms of anxiety. (p. 535)

antidepressant drugs Psychotropic medications used for the treatment of depression. (p. 532)

antipsychotic drugs Psychotropic medication used in the treatment of psychotic symptoms, such as hallucinations and delusions. (p. 535)

antisocial personality disorder A psychological disorder distinguished by unethical behavior, deceitfulness, impulsivity, irritability, aggressiveness, disregard for others, and lack of remorse. (p. 501)

anxiety disorders A group of psychological disorders associated with extreme anxiety and/or debilitating, irrational fears. (p. 483)

approach–approach conflict A type of conflict in which one must choose between two or more options that are attractive. (p. 449)

approach–avoidance conflict A type of conflict that occurs when one faces a choice or situation that has favorable and unfavorable characteristics. (p. 449)

aptitude An individual's potential for learning. (p. 266)

archetypes Primal images, patterns of thoughts, and storylines stored in the collective unconscious, with themes that may be found in art, literature, music, dreams, and religions. (p. 379)

arousal theory Suggests that humans are motivated to seek an optimal level of arousal, or alertness and engagement in the world. (p. 330)

assimilation Using existing knowledge and ideas to understand new information and experiences. (p. 296)

association areas Regions of the cortex that integrate information from all over the brain, allowing us to learn, think in abstract terms, and carry out other intellectual tasks. (p. 69)

attachment The degree to which an infant feels an emotional connection with primary caregivers. (p. 301)

attitudes The relatively stable thoughts, feelings, and responses one has toward people, situations, ideas, and things. (p. 409)

attributions Beliefs one develops to explain human behaviors and characteristics, as well as situations. (p. 405)

audition The sense of hearing. (p. 94)

authoritarian parenting A rigid parenting style characterized by strict rules and poor communication skills. (p. 319)

authoritative parenting A parenting style characterized by high expectations, strong support, and respect for children. (p. 319)

automatic processing Collection and sometimes storage of information without conscious effort or awareness. (p. 124)

autonomic nervous system The branch of the peripheral nervous system that controls involuntary processes within the body, such as contractions in the digestive tract and activity of glands. (p. 55)

availability heuristic A decision-making strategy that predicts the likelihood of something happening based on how easily a similar type of event from the past can be recalled. (p. 253)

aversion therapy Therapeutic approach that uses the principles of classical conditioning to link problematic behaviors to unpleasant physical reactions. (p. 527)

avoidance–avoidance conflict A type of conflict in which one must choose between two or more options that are unattractive. (p. 449)

axon Skinny tube-like structure of a neuron that extends from the cell body, and that sends messages to other neurons through its axon terminals. (p. 45)

bar graph Displays qualitative data with categories of interest on the *x*-axis and frequency on the *y*-axis. (p. A-8)

barbiturate Depressant drug that decreases neural activity and reduces anxiety; a type of sedative. (p. 144)

behavior modification Therapeutic approach in which behaviors are shaped through reinforcement and punishment. (p. 528)

behavior therapy A type of therapy that focuses on behavioral change. (p. 516)

behavioral perspective An approach suggesting that behavior is primarily learned through associations, reinforcers, and observation. (p. 8)

behaviorism The scientific study of observable behavior. (p. 8)

beta waves Brain waves that indicate an alert, awake state. (p. 130)

bimodal distribution A distribution with two modes, which are the two most frequently occurring values. (p. A-10)

binge-eating disorder An eating disorder characterized by episodes of extreme overeating, during which a larger amount of food is consumed than most people would eat in a similar amount of time under similar circumstances. (p. 506)

binocular cues Information gathered from both eyes to help judge depth and distance. (p. 112)

biofeedback A technique that involves providing visual or auditory information about biological processes, allowing a person to control physiological activity (for example, heart rate, blood pressure, and skin temperature). (p. 467)

biological perspective An approach that uses knowledge about underlying physiology to explain behavior and mental processes. (p. 9)

biological preparedness The tendency for animals to be predisposed or inclined to form certain kinds of associations through classical conditioning. (p. 172)

biological psychology The branch of psychology that focuses on how the brain and other biological systems influence human behavior. (p. 42)

biomedical therapy Drugs and other physical interventions that target the biological processes underlying psychological disorders; primary goal is to reduce symptoms. (p. 516)

biopsychosocial perspective Explains behavior through the interaction of biological, psychological, and sociocultural factors. (p. 10)

bipolar disorder A psychological disorder marked by dramatic swings in mood, ranging from manic episodes to depressive episodes. (p. 473)

bisexual Attraction to members of both the same and opposite sex. (p. 337)

blind spot A hole in the visual field caused by the optic disc (the location where the optic nerve exits the retina). (p. 90)

borderline personality disorder A psychological disorder distinguished by an incomplete sense of self, extreme self-criticism, unstable emotions, and feelings of emptiness. (p. 502)

bottom-up processing Taking basic information about incoming sensory stimuli and processing it for further interpretation. (p. 81)

Broca's area A region of the cortex that is critical for speech production. (p. 61)

bulimia nervosa An eating disorder characterized by extreme overeating followed by purging, with serious health risks. (p. 505)

burnout Emotional, mental, and physical fatigue that results in reduced motivation, enthusiasm, and performance. (p. 460)

bystander effect The tendency for people to avoid getting involved in an emergency they witness because they assume someone else will help. (p. 426)

Cannon–Bard theory of emotion Suggests that environmental stimuli are the starting point for emotions, and physiological or behavioral responses occur at the same time emotions are felt. (p. 350)

case study A type of descriptive research that closely examines an individual or small group. (p. 20)

cell body The region of the neuron that includes structures that nourish the cell, and a nucleus containing DNA. (p. 45)

central nervous system (CNS) A major component of the human nervous system that includes the brain and spinal cord. (p. 52)

cerebellum A structure located behind the brainstem that is responsible for muscle coordination and balance; Latin for "little brain." (p. 73)

cerebral cortex The wrinkled outermost layer of the cerebrum, responsible for higher mental functions, such as decision making, language, and processing visual information. (p. 64)

cerebrum The largest part of the brain, includes virtually all parts of the brain except brainstem structures; has two distinct hemispheres. (p. 58)

chromosomes Inherited threadlike structures composed of deoxyribonucleic acid (DNA). (p. 284)

chronic traumatic encephalopathy (CTE) A neurodegenerative disease that leads to atypical deposits of tau protein throughout various regions in the brain as a result of repeated mild traumatic brain injury. (p. 234)

chunking Grouping numbers, letters, or other items into recognizable subsets as a strategy for increasing the quantity of information that can be maintained in short-term memory. (p. 208)

circadian rhythm The daily patterns roughly following the 24-hour cycle of daylight and darkness; a 24-hour cycle of physiological and behavioral functioning. (p. 127)

classical conditioning Learning process in which two stimuli become associated with each other; when an originally neutral stimulus is conditioned to elicit an involuntary response. (p. 166)

cochlea Fluid-filled, snail-shaped organ of the inner ear lined with the basilar membrane. (p. 97)

cognition The mental activity associated with obtaining, converting, and using knowledge. (p. 242)

cognitive appraisal approach Suggests that the appraisal or interpretation of interactions with surroundings causes an emotional reaction. (p. 352)

cognitive behavioral therapy (CBT) An action-oriented type of therapy that requires clients to confront and resist their illogical thinking. (p. 530)

cognitive dissonance A state of tension that results when behaviors are inconsistent with attitudes. (p. 410)

cognitive map A mental representation of physical space. (p. 194)

cognitive perspective An approach examining the mental processes that direct behavior. (p. 9)

cognitive psychology The scientific study of mental processes such as thinking, problem solving, and language. (p. 122)

cognitive therapy A type of therapy aimed at addressing the maladaptive thinking that leads to maladaptive behaviors and feelings. (p. 529)

cohort effect The differences across groups that result from common experiences within the groups. (p. 281)

collective unconscious According to Jung, the universal experiences of humankind passed from generation to generation, including memories. (p. 379)

color constancy Objects are perceived as maintaining their color, even with changing sensory data. (p. 115)

comorbidity The occurrence of two or more disorders at the same time. (p. 480)

companionate love Love that consists of profound fondness, camaraderie, understanding, and emotional closeness. (p. 436)

compliance Changes in behavior at the request or direction of another person or group, who in general does not have any true authority. (p. 415)

compulsion A behavior or "mental act" that a person repeats over and over in an effort to reduce anxiety. (p. 486)

concepts Mental representations of categories of objects, situations, and ideas that belong together based on their central features or characteristics. (p. 242)

concrete operational stage Piaget's stage of cognitive development during which children begin to think more logically, but mainly in reference to concrete objects and circumstances. (p. 298)

conditioned emotional response An emotional reaction acquired through classical conditioning; process by which an emotional reaction becomes associated with a previously neutral stimulus. (p. 173)

conditioned response (CR) A learned response to a conditioned stimulus. (p. 166)

conditioned stimulus (CS) A previously neutral stimulus that an organism learns to associate with an unconditioned stimulus. (p. 166)

conditioned taste aversion A form of classical conditioning that occurs when an organism learns to associate the taste of a particular food or drink with illness. (p. 171)

cones Photoreceptors that enable us to sense color and minute details. (p. 88)

confirmation bias The tendency to look for evidence that upholds our beliefs and to overlook evidence that runs counter to them. (p. 254)

conformity The tendency to modify behaviors, attitudes, beliefs, and opinions to match those of others. (p. 416)

confounding variable A type of extraneous variable that changes in sync with the independent variable, making it difficult to discern which one is causing changes in the dependent variable. (p. 29)

consciousness The state of being aware of oneself, one's thoughts, and/or the environment; includes various levels of conscious awareness. (p. 121)

conservation Refers to the unchanging properties of volume, mass, or amount in relation to appearance. (p. 298)

consummate love Love that combines intimacy, commitment, and passion. (p. 436)

continuous reinforcement A schedule of reinforcement in which every target behavior is reinforced. (p. 181)

control group The participants in an experiment who are not exposed to the treatment variable; this is the comparison group. (p. 28)

convergence A binocular cue used to judge distance and depth based on the tension of the muscles that direct where the eyes are focusing. (p. 112)

convergent thinking A conventional approach to problem solving that focuses on finding a single best solution to a problem by using previous experience and knowledge. (p. 274)

coping The cognitive, behavioral, and emotional abilities used to manage something that is perceived as difficult or challenging. (p. 461)

cornea The clear, outer layer of the eye that shields it from damage and focuses incoming light waves. (p. 87)

corpus callosum The thick band of nerve fibers connecting the right and left cerebral hemispheres; principal structure for information shared between the two hemispheres. (p. 58)

correlation An association or relationship between two (or more) variables. (p. 23)

correlation coefficient The statistical measure (symbolized as r) that indicates the strength and direction of the relationship between two variables. (p. 23)

correlational method A type of descriptive research examining the relationships among variables. (p. 23)

creativity In problem solving, the ability to construct valuable results in innovative ways; the ability to generate original ideas. (p. 273)

critical period Specific time frame in which an organism is sensitive to environmental factors, and certain behaviors and abilities are readily shaped or altered by events or experiences. (p. 280)

critical thinking The process of weighing various pieces of evidence, synthesizing them, and evaluating and determining the contributions of each; disciplined thinking that is clear, rational, open-minded, and informed by evidence. (p. 15)

cross-sectional method A research design that examines people of different ages at a single point in time. (p. 281)

cross-sequential method A research design that examines groups of people of different ages, following them across time. (p. 283)

crystallized intelligence Knowledge gained through learning and experience. (p. 317)

culture-fair intelligence tests Assessments designed to minimize cultural bias. (p. 270)

daily hassles Minor and regularly occurring problems that can act as stressors. (p. 448)

dark adaptation Ability of the eyes to adjust to dark after exposure to bright light. (p. 90)

debriefing Sharing information with participants after their involvement in a study has ended, including the purpose of the research and any deception used. (p. 34)

decision making The cognitive process of choosing from alternatives that might be used to reach a goal. (p. 253)

deindividuation The diminished sense of personal responsibility, inhibition, or adherence to social norms that occurs when group members are not treated as individuals. (p. 424)

deinstitutionalization The mass movement of patients with psychological disorders out of institutions, and the attempt to reintegrate them into the community. (p. 514)

delirium tremens (DTs) Withdrawal symptoms that can occur when a person who is physiologically dependent on alcohol suddenly stops drinking; can include sweating, restlessness, hallucinations, severe tremors, and seizures. (p. 156)

delta waves Brain waves that indicate a deep sleep. (p. 131)

delusions Strange or false beliefs that a person firmly maintains even when presented with evidence to the contrary. (p. 496)

dendrites Tiny, branchlike fibers extending from the cell body that receive messages from other neurons and send information in the direction of the cell body. (p. 45)

deoxyribonucleic acid (DNA) A molecule that provides instructions for the development of an organism. (p. 284)

dependent variable (DV) In the experimental method, the characteristic or response that is measured to determine the effect of the researcher's manipulation. (p. 29)

depressants A class of psychoactive drugs that *depress* or slow down activity in the central nervous system. (p. 144)

depth perception The ability to perceive three-dimensional objects and judge distances. (p. 112)

descriptive research Research methods that describe and explore behaviors, but with findings that cannot definitively state cause-and-effect relationships. (p. 19)

developmental psychology A field of psychology that examines age-related physical, cognitive, and socioemotional changes across the life span. (p. 279)

difference thresholds The minimum differences between two stimuli that can be noticed 50% of the time. (p. 84)

diffusion of responsibility The sharing of duties and responsibilities among all group members that can lead to feelings of decreased accountability and motivation. (p. 423)

discrimination Showing favoritism or hostility to others because of their affiliation with a group. (p. 428)

display rules Framework or guidelines for when, how, and where an emotion is expressed. (p. 355)

dispositional attribution A belief that some characteristic of an individual is involved in the cause of an event or activity. (p. 406)

dissociation A disturbance in the normally integrated experience of psychological functions involved in memory, consciousness, perception, or identity. (p. 503)

dissociative amnesia A psychological disorder marked by difficulty remembering important personal information and life events. (p. 503)

dissociative disorders Psychological disorders distinguished by disturbances in normal psychological functioning; may include problems with memory, identity, consciousness, perception, and motor control. (p. 503)

dissociative fugue A condition in which a person with dissociative amnesia or dissociative identity disorder wanders about in a confused and unexpected manner. (p. 503)

dissociative identity disorder A psychological disorder that involves the occurrence of two or more distinct personalities within an individual. (p. 504)

distress The stress response to unpleasant and undesirable stressors. (p. 444)

distributed practice Spreading out study sessions over time with breaks in between. (p. 213)

distribution shape How the frequencies of the values are shaped along the *x*-axis. (p. A-6)

divergent thinking The ability to devise many solutions to a problem; a component of creativity. (p. 274)

dizygotic twins Fraternal twins who develop from two eggs inseminated by two sperm, and are as genetically similar as any sibling pair. (p. 284)

dominant gene One of a pair of genes that has power over the expression of an inherited characteristic. (p. 286)

door-in-the-face technique A compliance technique that involves making a large request first, followed by a smaller request. (p. 415)

dopamine hypothesis A theory suggesting that the synthesis, release, and concentrations of the neurotransmitter dopamine play a role in schizophrenia. (p. 499)

double-blind study Type of study in which neither the researchers who are administering the independent variable nor the participants know what type of treatment is being given. (p. 29)

drive A state of tension that pushes us or motivates behaviors to meet a need. (p. 330)

drive-reduction theory Suggests that homeostasis motivates us to meet biological needs. (p. 330)

echoic memory Exact copies of the sounds we hear; a form of sensory memory. (p. 207)

eclectic approach to therapy Drawing on multiple theories and approaches to tailor treatment for a client. (p. 518)

effortful processing The encoding and storage of information with conscious effort or awareness. (p. 213)

ego According to Freud, the structure of the mind that uses the reality principle to manipulate situations, plan for the future, solve problems, and make decisions. (p. 372)

ego defense mechanisms Unconscious processes the ego uses to distort perceptions and memories and thereby reduce anxiety created by the id-superego conflict. (p. 373)

egocentrism When a person is only able to imagine the world from his or her own perspective. (p. 296)

elaborative rehearsal The method of connecting incoming information to knowledge in long-term memory; a deep level of encoding. (p. 213)

electroconvulsive therapy (ECT) A biomedical treatment for severe disorders that induces seizures in the brain through electrical currents. (p. 536)

embryo The unborn human from the beginning of the 3rd week of pregnancy, lasting through the 8th week of prenatal development. (p. 286)

emerging adulthood A phase of life between 18 and 25 years that includes exploration and opportunity. (p. 313)

emotion A psychological state that includes a subjective or inner experience, physiological component, and behavioral expression. (p. 347)

emotional intelligence The capacity to perceive, understand, regulate, and use emotions to adapt to social situations. (p. 271)

emotion-focused coping A coping strategy in which a person addresses the emotions that surround a problem, as opposed to trying to solve it. (p. 461)

empathy The ability to feel what a person is experiencing by attempting to observe the world through his or her eyes. (p. 522)

encoding The process through which information enters our memory system. (p. 203)

encoding specificity principle Memories are more easily recalled when the context and cues at the time of encoding are similar to those at the time of retrieval. (p. 219)

endocrine system The communication system that uses glands to convey messages by releasing hormones into the bloodstream. (p. 56)

epigenetics A field of study that examines the processes involved in the development of phenotypes. (p. 286)

episodic memory The record of memorable experiences or "episodes," including when and where an experience occurred; a type of explicit memory. (p. 211)

estrogens The female hormones secreted primarily by the ovaries and by the adrenal glands in both males and females. (p. 285)

e-therapy A category of treatment that utilizes the Internet to provide support and therapy. (p. 542)

ethnocentrism Seeing the world only from the perspective of one's own group. (p. 428)

eustress The stress response to agreeable or positive stressors. (p. 444)

evidence-based practice Making decisions about treatment that integrate valuable research findings, clinical expertise, and knowledge of a patient's culture, values, and preferences. (p. 518)

evolutionary perspective An approach that uses knowledge about evolutionary forces, such as natural selection, to understand behavior. (p. 9)

expectancy A person's predictions about the consequences or outcomes of behavior. (p. 384)

experiment A controlled procedure that involves careful examination through the use of scientific observation and/or manipulation of variables (measurable characteristics). (p. 11)

experimental group The members of an experiment who are exposed to the treatment variable or manipulation by the researcher; represents the treatment group. (p. 28)

experimental method A type of research that manipulates a variable of interest (independent variable) to uncover cause-and-effect relationships. (p. 27)

experimenter bias Researchers' expectations that influence the outcome of a study. (p. 31)

explicit memory A type of memory you are aware of having and can consciously express in words or declare, including memories of facts and experiences. (p. 211)

exposure A therapeutic technique that brings a person into contact with a feared object or situation while in a safe environment, with the goal of extinguishing or eliminating the fear response. (p. 524)

extinction In classical conditioning, the process by which the conditioned response decreases after repeated exposure to the conditioned stimulus in the absence of the unconditioned stimulus; in operant conditioning, the disappearance of a learned behavior through the removal of its reinforcer. (p. 169)

extraneous variable A characteristic of participants or the environment that could unexpectedly influence the outcome of a study. (p. 29)

extrasensory perception (ESP) The purported ability to obtain information about the world without any sensory stimuli. (p. 116)

extrinsic motivation The drive or urge to continue a behavior because of external reinforcers. (p. 328)

facial feedback hypothesis The facial expression of an emotion can affect the experience of that emotion. (p. 356)

false consensus effect The tendency to overestimate the degree to which others think or act like we do. (p. 407)

family therapy A type of therapy that focuses on the family as an integrated system, recognizing that the interactions within it can create instability or lead to the breakdown of the family unit. (p. 540)

feature detectors Neurons in the visual cortex specialized in detecting specific features of the visual experience, such as angles, lines, and movements. (p. 91)

fetal alcohol syndrome (FAS) Delays in development that result from moderate to heavy alcohol use during pregnancy. (p. 287)

fetus The unborn human from 2 months following conception to birth. (p. 288)

figure-ground A central principle of Gestalt psychology, involving the shifting of focus; as attention is focused on one object, all other features drop or recede into the background. (p. 112)

five-factor model of personality A trait approach to explaining personality, including dimensions of openness to experience, conscientiousness, extraversion, agreeableness, and neuroticism; also known as "the Big Five." (p. 388)

fixation Being stuck in a particular psychosexual stage of development as a result of unsuccessfully dealing with the conflict characteristic of that stage. (p. 375)

fixed-interval schedule A schedule in which the reinforcer comes after a preestablished interval of time; the behavior is only reinforced after the given interval is over. (p. 183)

fixed-ratio schedule A schedule in which the subject must exhibit a predetermined number of desired behaviors before a reinforcer is given. (p. 182)

flashbulb memory A detailed account of circumstances surrounding an emotionally significant or shocking, sometimes historic, event. (p. 211)

fluid intelligence The ability to think in the abstract and create associations among concepts. (p. 317)

foot-in-the-door technique A compliance technique that involves making a small request first, followed by a larger request. (p. 415)

formal concepts The mental representations of categories that are created through rigid and logical rules or features. (p. 244)

formal operational stage Piaget's stage of cognitive development during which children begin to think more logically and systematically. (p. 298)

framing effect Occurs when the wording of questions or the context of a problem influences the outcome of a decision. (p. 255)

free association A psychoanalytic technique in which a patient says anything that comes to mind. (p. 519)

frequency The number of sound waves passing a given point per unit of time; higher frequency is perceived as higher pitch, and lower frequency is perceived as lower pitch. (p. 95)

frequency distribution A simple way to portray data that displays how often various values in a data set are present. (p. A-4)

frequency polygon A type of graphic display that uses lines to represent the frequency of data values. (p. A-5)

frequency theory States that pitch is determined by the vibrating frequency of the sound wave, basilar membrane, and associated neural impulses. (p. 98)

frontal lobes The area of the cortex that organizes information among the other lobes of the brain and is responsible for cognitive functions, such as thinking, perception, and impulse control. (p. 64)

frustration–aggression hypothesis Suggests that aggression may occur in response to frustration. (p. 427)

functional fixedness A barrier to problem solving that occurs when familiar objects can only be imagined to function in their normal or usual way. (p. 250)

functionalism An early school of psychology that focused on the function of thought processes, feelings, and behaviors and how they help us adapt to the environment. (p. 7)

fundamental attribution error The tendency to overestimate the degree to which the characteristics of an individual are the cause of an event, and to underestimate the involvement of situational factors. (p. 406)

gate-control theory Suggests that the perception of pain will either increase or decrease through the interaction of biopsychosocial factors; signals are sent to open or close "gates" that control the neurological pathways for pain. (p. 106)

gender The dimension of masculinity and femininity based on social, cultural, and psychological characteristics. (p. 310)

gender identity The feeling or sense of being either male or female, and compatibility, contentment, and conformity with one's gender. (p. 310)

gender roles The collection of actions, beliefs, and characteristics that a culture associates with masculinity and femininity. (p. 310)

gender schemas The psychological or mental guidelines that dictate how to be masculine and feminine. (p. 311)

gene Specified segment of a DNA molecule. (p. 284)

general adaptation syndrome (GAS) A specific pattern of physiological reactions to stressors that includes the alarm stage, resistance stage, and exhaustion stage. (p. 451)

general intelligence (*g*-factor) A singular underlying aptitude or intellectual ability that drives capabilities in many areas, including verbal, spatial, and reasoning competencies. (p. 264)

generalized anxiety disorder A psychological disorder characterized by an excessive amount of worry and anxiety about activities relating to family, health, school, and other aspects of daily life. (p. 485)

genotype An individual's complete collection of genes. (p. 285)

genuineness The ability to respond to a client in an authentic way rather than hiding behind a polite or professional mask. (p. 522)

gestalt The natural tendency for the brain to organize stimuli into a whole, rather than perceiving the parts and pieces. (p. 112)

gifted Highly intelligent; defined as having an IQ score of 130 or above. (p. 270)

glial cells Cells that support, nourish, and protect neurons; some produce myelin that covers axons. (p. 45)

grammar The rules associated with word and sentence structure. (p. 259)

group polarization The tendency for a group to take a more extreme stance than originally held after deliberations and discussion. (p. 425)

groupthink The tendency for group members to maintain cohesiveness and agreement in their decision making, failing to consider possible alternatives and related viewpoints. (p. 425)

gustation The sense of taste. (p. 102)

habituation A basic form of learning evident when an organism does not respond as strongly or as often to an event following multiple exposures to it. (p. 164)

hallucinations Perception-like experiences that an individual believes are real, but that are not evident to others. (p. 497)

hallucinogens A group of psychoactive drugs that can produce hallucinations, distorted sensory experiences, alterations of mood, and distorted thinking. (p. 151)

hardiness A personality characteristic indicating an ability to remain resilient and optimistic despite intensely stressful situations. (p. 463)

health psychology The study of the biological, psychological, and social factors that contribute to health and illness. (p. 451)

heritability The degree to which hereditary factors (genes) are responsible for a particular characteristic observed within a population; the proportion of variation in a characteristic attributed to genetic factors. (p. 272)

heterosexual Attraction to members of the opposite sex. (p. 337)

heuristics Problem-solving approaches that incorporate a rule of thumb or broad application of a strategy. (p. 249)

hierarchy of needs A continuum of needs that are universal and ordered in terms of the strength of their associated drives. (p. 332)

higher order conditioning With repeated pairings of a conditioned stimulus and a second neutral stimulus, that second neutral stimulus becomes a conditioned stimulus as well. (p. 169)

hindbrain Includes areas of the brain responsible for fundamental life-sustaining processes. (p. 73)

hindsight bias The mistaken belief that an outcome could have been predicted easily; the "I knew it all along" feeling. (p. 255)

hippocampus A pair of structures located in the limbic system; primarily responsible for creating new memories. (p. 71)

histogram Displays the classes of a variable on the *x*-axis and the frequency of the data on the *y*-axis; frequency is indicated by the height of the vertical bars. (p. A-5)

homeostasis The tendency for bodies to maintain constant states through internal controls. (p. 329)

homosexual Attraction to members of the same sex. (p. 337)

hormones Chemical messengers released into the bloodstream that influence mood, cognition, appetite, and many other processes and behaviors. (p. 56)

hue The color of an object, determined by the wavelength of light it reflects. (p. 86)

human immunodeficiency virus (HIV) A virus transferred via bodily fluids (blood, semen, vaginal fluid, or breast milk) that causes the breakdown of the immune system, eventually resulting in AIDS. (p. 445)

humanistic psychology An approach suggesting that human nature is by and large positive, and the human direction is toward growth. (p. 9)

humanistic therapy A type of insight therapy that emphasizes the positive nature of humankind. (p. 522)

hypnosis An altered state of consciousness allowing for changes in perceptions and behaviors, which result from suggestions made by a hypnotist. (p. 157)

hypothalamus A small structure located below the thalamus that maintains a constant internal environment within a healthy range; helps regulate sleep–wake cycles, sexual behavior, and appetite. (p. 72)

hypothesis A statement that can be used to test a prediction. (p. 11)

hypothesis testing Mathematical procedures used to determine the likelihood that a researcher's predictions are supported by the data collected. (p. A-1)

iconic memory Visual impressions that are photograph-like in their accuracy but dissolve in less than a second; a form of sensory memory. (p. 206)

id According to Freud, the most primitive structure of the mind, the activities of which occur at the unconscious level and are guided by the pleasure principle. (p. 371)

ideal self The self-concept a person strives for and fervently wishes to achieve. (p. 382)

identity A sense of self based on values, beliefs, and goals. (p. 307)

illusion A perception that is inconsistent with sensory data. (p. 110)

implicit memory A memory of something you know or know how to do, which may be automatic, unconscious, and difficult to bring to awareness and express. (p. 211)

incentive An association established between a behavior and its consequences, which then motivates that behavior. (p. 327)

independent variable (IV) In the experimental method, the variable manipulated by the researcher to determine its effect on the dependent variable. (p. 28)

informed consent Acknowledgment from study participants that they understand what their participation will entail. (p. 34)

in-group The group to which we belong. (p. 428)

insanity A legal determination of the degree to which a person is responsible for criminal behaviors. (p. 476)

insight An understanding or solution that occurs in a sudden stroke of clarity (the feeling of "aha!"). (p. 250)

insight therapies Psychotherapies aimed at increasing awareness of self and environment. (p. 516)

insomnia Sleep disturbance characterized by an inability to fall asleep or stay asleep, impacting both the quality and quantity of sleep. (p. 136)

instinctive drift The tendency for animals to revert to instinctual behaviors after a behavior pattern has been learned. (p. 181)

instincts Complex behaviors that are fixed, unlearned, and consistent within a species. (p. 329)

Institutional Review Board (IRB) A committee that reviews research proposals to protect the rights and welfare of all participants. (p. 34)

intelligence Innate ability to solve problems, adapt to the environment, and learn from experiences. (p. 263)

intelligence quotient (IQ) A score from an intelligence assessment; originally based on mental age divided by chronological age, multiplied by 100. (p. 266)

interneurons Neurons that reside exclusively in the brain and spinal cord; act as a bridge connecting sensory and motor neurons. (p. 53)

interpersonal attraction The factors that lead us to form friendships or romantic relationships with others. (p. 433)

interpretation A psychoanalytic technique used to explore unconscious conflicts driving behavior. (p. 520)

intersexual Having ambiguous or inconsistent biological indicators of male or female in the sexual structures and organs. (p. 285)

intrinsic motivation The drive or urge to continue a behavior because of internal reinforcers. (p. 328)

introspection The examination of one's own conscious activities. (p. 6)

iris The muscle responsible for changing the size of the pupil. (p. 88)

James–Lange theory of emotion Suggests that a stimulus initiates the experience of a physiological and/or behavioral reaction, and this reaction leads to the feeling of an emotion. (p. 350)

just-world hypothesis The tendency to believe the world is a fair place and individuals generally get what they deserve. (p. 407)

kinesthesia Sensory system that conveys information about body position and movement. (p. 107)

language A system for using symbols to think and communicate. (p. 258)

latent content The hidden meaning of a dream, often concealed by the manifest content of the dream. (p. 141)

latent learning Learning that occurs without awareness and regardless of reinforcement, and is not evident until needed. (p. 194)

lateralization The idea that each cerebral hemisphere processes certain types of information and excels in certain activities. (p. 60)

law of effect Thorndike's principle stating that behaviors are more likely to be repeated when followed by pleasurable outcomes, and less likely to be repeated when followed by unpleasant outcomes. (p. 176)

learned helplessness A tendency for people to believe they have no control over the consequences of their behaviors, resulting in passive behavior. (p. 493)

learning A relatively enduring change in behavior or thinking that results from experiences. (p. 163)

light adaptation Ability of the eyes to adjust to light after being in the dark. (p. 90)

limbic system A collection of structures that regulates emotions and basic drives like hunger, and aids in the creation of memories. (p. 71)

longitudinal method A research design that examines one sample of people over a period of time to determine age-related changes. (p. 281)

long-term memory A stage of memory with essentially unlimited capacity and the ability to store information indefinitely. (p. 205)

long-term potentiation The increased efficiency of neural communication over time, resulting in learning and the formation of memories. (p. 233)

lymphocyte Type of white blood cell produced in the bone marrow whose job is to battle enemies such as viruses and bacteria. (p. 454)

lysergic acid diethylamide (LSD) A synthetically produced, odorless, tasteless, and colorless hallucinogen that is very potent; produces extreme changes in sensations and perceptions. (p. 152)

maintenance rehearsal Technique of repeating information to be remembered, increasing the length of time it can be held in short-term memory. (p. 207)

major depressive disorder A psychological disorder that includes at least one major depressive episode, with symptoms such as depressed mood, problems with sleep, and loss of energy. (p. 489)

manic episodes States of continuous elation that are out of proportion to the setting, and can include irritability, very high and sustained levels of energy, and an "expansive" mood. (p. 494)

manifest content The apparent meaning of a dream; the remembered story line of a dream. (p. 141)

massed practice Studying for long periods of time without breaks. (p. 213)

maturation Physical growth beginning with conception and ending when the body stops growing. (p. 279)

mean The arithmetic average of a data set; a measure of central tendency. (p. A-9)

means–ends analysis Heuristic used to determine how to decrease the distance between a goal and the current status (the means), leading to the solution of a problem (the end). (p. 249)

measures of central tendency Numbers that represent the middle of a data set. (p. A-9)

measures of position Numbers that represent where particular data values fall in relation to other values in the data set. (p. A-12)

measures of variation Numbers that describe the variation or dispersion in a data set. (p. A-10)

median A number that represents the position in the data set for which 50% of the values are above it, and 50% are below it; a measure of central tendency. (p. A-9)

medical model An approach suggesting that psychological disorders are illnesses that have underlying biological causes. (p. 481)

medulla A structure that oversees vital functions, including breathing, digestion, and heart rate. (p. 73)

memory Brain processes involved in the encoding, storage, and retrieval of information. (p. 202)

memory trace The location where memories are etched in the brain via physiological changes. (p. 230)

menarche The point at which menstruation begins. (p. 305)

menopause The time when a woman no longer ovulates, her menstrual cycle stops, and she is no longer capable of reproduction. (p. 316)

mental age (MA) A score representing the mental abilities of an individual in relation to others of a similar chronological age. (p. 266)

mere-exposure effect The more we are exposed to someone or something, the more positive our reaction to it becomes. (p. 434)

meta-analysis A type of statistical analysis that combines findings from many studies on a single topic; statistics used to merge the outcomes of many studies. (p. A-4)

methylenedioxymethamphetamine (MDMA) A synthetic drug that produces a combination of stimulant and hallucinogenic effects. (p. 152)

midbrain The part of the brainstem involved in levels of arousal; responsible for generating movement patterns in response to sensory input. (p. 73)

mindfulness meditation Being fully present in the moment; focusing attention on the here and now without passing judgment. (p. 468)

misinformation effect The tendency for new and misleading information obtained after an incident to distort one's memory of it. (p. 225)

mnemonic Technique to improve memory. (p. 213)

mode The value of the data set that is most frequent; a measure of central tendency. (p. A-10)

model The individual or character whose behavior is being imitated. (p. 191)

monocular cues Depth and distance cues that require the use of only one eye. (p. 114)

monozygotic twins Identical twins who develop from one egg inseminated at conception, which then splits into two separate cells. (p. 284)

mood-stabilizing drugs Psychotropic medications that minimize the lows of depression and the highs of mania. (p. 534)

morphemes The fundamental units that bring meaning to language. (p. 259)

motivation A stimulus that can direct behavior, thinking, and feeling. (p. 327)

motor cortex A band of tissue toward the rear of the frontal lobes that works with other brain regions to plan and execute voluntary movements. (p. 66)

motor neurons Neurons that transmit information from the central nervous system to the muscles and glands. (p. 53)

myelin sheath Fatty substance that insulates the axon and speeds the transmission of neural messages. (p. 45)

narcolepsy A neurological disorder characterized by excessive daytime sleepiness, which includes lapses into sleep and napping. (p. 134)

natural concepts The mental representations of categories resulting from experiences in daily life. (p. 244)

natural selection The process through which inherited traits in a given population either increase in frequency because they are adaptive or decrease in frequency because they are maladaptive. (p. 9)

naturalistic observation A type of descriptive research that studies participants in their natural environment through systematic observation. (p. 19)

nature The inherited biological factors that shape behaviors, personality, and other characteristics. (p. 5)

need for achievement (n-Ach) A drive to reach attainable and challenging goals, especially in the face of competition. (p. 334)

need for power (n-Pow) A drive to control and influence others. (p. 334)

needs Physiological or psychological requirements that must be maintained at some baseline or constant state. (p. 330)

negative punishment The removal of something desirable following an unwanted behavior, with the intention of decreasing that behavior. (p. 185)

negative reinforcement The removal of an unpleasant stimulus following a target behavior, which increases the likelihood of it occurring again. (p. 178)

negative symptoms Behaviors or characteristics that are limited or absent; examples are social withdrawal, diminished speech, limited or no emotions, and loss of energy and follow-up. (p. 497)

negatively skewed A nonsymmetric distribution with a longer tail to the left side of the distribution; left-skewed distribution. (p. A-7)

nerves Bundles of neurons that carry information to and from the central nervous system; provide communication between the central nervous system and the muscles, glands, and sensory receptors. (p. 54)

neurogenesis The generation of new neurons in the brain. (p. 63)

neurons Specialized cells of the nervous system that transmit electrical and chemical signals in the body; nerve cells. (p. 45)

neuroplasticity The brain's ability to heal, grow new connections, and reorganize in order to adapt to the environment. (p. 63)

neuroscience The study of the brain and nervous system. (p. 42)

neurosurgery A biomedical therapy that involves the destruction of some portion of the brain or connections between different areas of the brain. (p. 536)

neurotransmitters Chemical messengers that neurons use to communicate at the synapse. (p. 48)

neutral stimulus (NS) A stimulus that does not cause a relevant automatic or reflexive response. (p. 166)

nightmares Frightening dreams that occur during REM sleep. (p. 136)

nondirective A technique used in person-centered therapy whereby the therapist follows the lead of the client during treatment sessions. (p. 522)

non-rapid eye movement (non-REM) The nondreaming sleep that occurs during sleep Stages N1 to N3. (p. 130)

normal curve Depicts the frequency of values of a variable along a continuum; bell-shaped symmetrical distribution, with the highest point reflecting the average score. (p. 269)

norms Standards of the social environment. (p. 416)

nurture The environmental factors that shape behaviors, personality, and other characteristics. (p. 5)

obedience Changing behavior because we have been ordered to do so by an authority figure. (p. 419)

object permanence A milestone of the sensorimotor stage of cognitive development; an infant's realization that objects and people still exist even when out of sight or touch. (p. 296)

observational learning Learning that occurs as a result of watching the behavior of others. (p. 191)

observer bias Errors in the recording of observations, the result of a researcher's value system, expectations, or attitudes. (p. 20)

obsession A thought, an urge, or an image that happens repeatedly, is intrusive and unwelcome, and often causes anxiety and distress. (p. 486)

obsessive-compulsive disorder (OCD) A psychological disorder characterized by obsessions and/or compulsions that are time-consuming and cause a great deal of distress. (p. 486)

obstructive sleep apnea hypopnea A serious disturbance of non-REM sleep characterized by complete absence of air flow (apnea) or reduced air flow (hypopnea). (p. 135)

occipital lobes The area of the cortex in the back of the head that processes visual information. (p. 64)

Oedipus complex According to Freud, the attraction a boy feels toward his mother, along with the resentment or envy directed toward his father. (p. 376)

olfaction The sense of smell. (p. 100)

operant conditioning Learning that occurs when voluntary actions become associated with their consequences. (p. 176)

operational definition The precise manner in which a variable of interest is defined and measured. (p. 13)

opiates A class of psychoactive drugs that cause a sense of euphoria; drugs that imitate the endorphins naturally produced in the brain. (p. 146)

opponent-process theory Perception of color derives from a special group of neurons that respond to opponent colors (red–green, blue–yellow). (p. 93)

optic nerve The bundle of axons from ganglion cells leading to the visual cortex. (p. 88)

orgasm A powerful combination of extremely gratifying sensations and a series of rhythmic muscular contractions. (p. 336)

out-group People outside the group to which we belong. (p. 428)

overgeneralization A cognitive distortion that assumes self-contained events will have major repercussions. (p. 529)

panic attack Sudden, extreme fear or discomfort that escalates quickly, often with no obvious trigger, and includes symptoms such as increased heart rate, sweating, shortness of breath, chest pain, nausea, lightheadedness, and fear of dying. (p. 483)

panic disorder A psychological disorder that includes recurrent, unexpected panic attacks and fear that can cause significant changes in behavior. (p. 483)

parameters Numbers that describe characteristics of a population. (p. A-3)

parapsychology The study of extrasensory perception. (p. 116)

parasympathetic nervous system The division of the autonomic nervous system that orchestrates the "rest-and-digest" response to bring the body back to a noncrisis mode. (p. 56)

parietal lobes The area of the cortex that receives and processes sensory information such as touch, pressure, temperature, and spatial orientation. (p. 64)

partial reinforcement A schedule of reinforcement in which target behaviors are reinforced intermittently, not continuously. (p. 182)

partial reinforcement effect The tendency for behaviors acquired through intermittent reinforcement to be more resistant to extinction than those acquired through continuous reinforcement. (p. 182)

passionate love Love that is based on zealous emotion, leading to intense longing and sexual attraction. (p. 436)

perception The organization and interpretation of sensory stimuli by the brain. (p. 81)

perceptual constancy The tendency to perceive objects in our environment as stable in terms of shape, size, and color, regardless of changes in the sensory data received. (p. 115)

perceptual set The tendency to perceive stimuli in a specific manner based on past experiences and expectations. (p. 115)

peripheral nervous system (PNS) The part of the nervous system that connects the central nervous system to the rest of the body. (p. 52)

permissive parenting A parenting style characterized by low demands of children and few limitations. (p. 319)

personality The unique, core set of characteristics that influence the way one thinks, acts, and feels, and that are relatively consistent and enduring throughout the life span. (p. 367)

personality disorders A group of psychological disorders that can include impairments in cognition, emotional responses, interpersonal functioning, and impulse control. (p. 501)

person-centered therapy A form of humanistic therapy developed by Rogers; aimed at helping clients achieve their full potential. (p. 522)

persuasion Intentionally trying to make people change their attitudes and beliefs, which may lead to changes in their behaviors. (p. 413)

phenotype The observable expression or characteristics of one's genetic inheritance. (p. 285)

phonemes The basic building blocks of spoken language. (p. 258)

photoreceptors Specialized cells in the retina that absorb light energy and turn it into electrical and chemical signals for the brain to process. (p. 88)

phrenology An early approach to explaining the functions of the brain by trying to link the physical structure of the skull with a variety of characteristics. (p. 42)

physiological dependence With constant use of some psychoactive drugs, the body no longer functions normally without the drug. (p. 155)

pie chart Displays qualitative data with categories of interest represented by slices of the pie. (p. A-8)

pitch The degree to which a sound is high or low, determined by the frequency of its sound wave. (p. 95)

pituitary gland The small endocrine gland located in the center of the brain just under the hypothalamus; known as the master gland. (p. 57)

place theory States that pitch corresponds to the location of the vibrating hair cells along the cochlea. (p. 98)

placebo An inert substance given to members of the control group; the fake treatment has no benefit, but is administered as if it did. (p. 31)

pleasure principle A principle that guides the id, directing behavior toward instant gratification and away from contemplating consequences. (p. 372)

pons A hindbrain structure that helps regulate sleep–wake cycles and coordinate movement between the right and left sides of the body. (p. 73)

population All members of an identified group about which a researcher is interested. (p. 18)

positive psychology An approach that focuses on the positive aspects of human beings, seeking to understand their strengths and uncover the roots of happiness, creativity, humor, and so on. (p. 37)

positive punishment The addition of something unpleasant following an unwanted behavior, with the intention of decreasing that behavior. (p. 185)

positive reinforcement The process by which reinforcers are added or presented following a target behavior, increasing the likelihood of it occurring again. (p. 177)

positive symptoms Excesses or distortions of normal behavior; examples are delusions, hallucinations, and disorganized speech. (p. 497)

positively skewed A nonsymmetric distribution with a longer tail to the right side of the distribution; right-skewed distribution. (p. A-7)

posttraumatic stress disorder (PTSD) A psychological disorder characterized by exposure to or being threatened by an event involving death, serious injury, or violence; can include disturbing memories, nightmares, flashbacks, and other distressing symptoms. (p. 487)

pragmatics The social rules that help to organize language. (p. 260)

prejudice Holding hostile or negative attitudes toward an individual or group. (p. 428)

preoperational stage Piaget's stage of cognitive development during which children can start to use language to explore and understand their worlds. (p. 296)

primacy effect The tendency to remember items at the beginning of a list. (p. 217)

primary appraisal One's initial assessment of a situation to determine its personal impact and whether it is irrelevant, positive, challenging, or harmful. (p. 461)

primary reinforcer A reinforcer that satisfies a biological need; innate reinforcer. (p. 179)

primary sex characteristics Organs associated with reproduction, including the ovaries, uterus, vagina, penis, scrotum, and testes. (p. 305)

priming The stimulation of memories as a result of retrieval cues in the environment. (p. 216)

proactive interference The tendency for information learned in the past to interfere with the retrieval of new material. (p. 221)

problem solving The variety of approaches that can be used to achieve a goal. (p. 248)

problem-focused coping A coping strategy in which a person deals directly with a problem by attempting to solve and address it head-on. (p. 461)

procedural memory The unconscious memory of how to carry out a variety of skills and activities; a type of implicit memory. (p. 212)

projective personality tests Assessments used to explore characteristics that might not be accessible through interview or observation; the test taker is presented with ambiguous stimuli and then projects meaning onto them. (p. 394)

proprioceptors Specialized nerve endings primarily located in the muscles and joints that provide information about body location and orientation. (p. 107)

prosocial behaviors Actions that are kind, generous, and beneficial to others. (p. 193)

prototype The ideal or most representative example of a natural concept; helps us categorize or identify specific members of a concept. (p. 244)

proximity Nearness; plays an important role in the formation of relationships. (p. 433)

psychoactive drugs Substances that can cause changes in psychological activities such as sensation, perception, attention, judgment, memory, self-control, emotion, thinking, and behavior; substances that cause changes in conscious experiences. (p. 143)

psychoanalysis Freud's views regarding personality as well as his system of psychotherapy and tools for the exploration of the unconscious. (p. 370)

psychoanalytic perspective An approach developed by Freud suggesting that behavior and personality are shaped by unconscious conflicts. (p. 8)

psychodynamic therapy A type of insight therapy that incorporates core psychoanalytic themes, including the importance of unconscious conflicts and experiences from the past. (p. 520)

psychological dependence With constant use of some psychoactive drugs, a strong desire or need to continue using the substance occurs without the evidence of tolerance or withdrawal symptoms. (p. 156)

psychological disorder A set of behavioral, emotional, and cognitive symptoms that are significantly distressing or disabling in terms of social functioning, work endeavors, and other aspects of life. (p. 473)

psychologists Scientists who study behavior and mental processes. (p. 2)

psychology The scientific study of behavior and mental processes. (p. 2)

psychoneuroimmunology The field that studies the relationships among psychological factors, the nervous system, and immune system functioning. (p. 456)

psychosexual stages According to Freud, the stages of development of sexuality and personality, from birth to adulthood, each of which has an erogenous zone as well as a conflict that must be dealt with. (p. 375)

psychosis Loss of contact with reality that is severe and chronic. (p. 496)

psychotherapy "Talk therapy"; a treatment approach in which a client works with a mental health professional to reduce psychological symptoms and improve his or her quality of life. (p. 516)

puberty The period of development during which the body changes and becomes sexually mature and capable of reproduction. (p. 305)

punishment The application of a consequence that decreases the likelihood of a behavior recurring. (p. 183)

random assignment The process of appointing study participants to the experimental or control groups, ensuring that every person has an equal chance of being assigned to either. (p. 28)

random sample A subset of the population chosen through a procedure that ensures all members of the population have an equal chance of being selected to participate in the study. (p. 18)

range A number that represents the length of the data set and is a rough depiction of dispersion; a measure of variation. (p. A-10)

rapid eye movement (REM) The stage of sleep associated with dreaming; sleep characterized by bursts of eye movements, with brain activity similar to that of a waking state, but with a lack of muscle tone. (p. 131)

rational emotive behavior therapy (REBT) A type of cognitive therapy, developed by Ellis, that identifies illogical thoughts and attempts to convert them into rational ones. (p. 530)

reality principle A principle that guides the ego as it negotiates between the id and the environment, directing behavior to follow society's rules. (p. 372)

recall The process of retrieving information held in long-term memory without the help of explicit retrieval cues. (p. 217)

recency effect The tendency to remember items at the end of a list. (p. 217)

receptor sites Locations on the receiving neuron's dendrites where neurotransmitters attach. (p. 48)

recessive gene One of a pair of genes that is overpowered by a dominant gene. (p. 286)

reciprocal determinism According to Bandura, multidirectional interactions among cognition, behaviors, and the environment. (p. 386)

recognition The process of matching incoming data to information stored in long-term memory. (p. 217)

reflex arc An automatic response to a sensory stimulus, such as the "knee-jerk" reaction; a simple pathway of communication from sensory neurons through interneurons in the spinal cord back out through motor neurons. (p. 54)

refractory period An interval of time during which a man cannot attain another orgasm. (p. 336)

reinforcement Process of increasing the frequency of behaviors with consequences. (p. 176)

reinforcers Events, stimuli, and other consequences that increase the likelihood of a behavior reoccurring. (p. 176)

relearning Material learned previously is acquired more quickly in subsequent exposures. (p. 219)

reliability The ability of an assessment to provide consistent, reproducible results. (p. 267)

REM rebound An increased amount of time spent in REM after sleep deprivation. (p. 138)

REM sleep behavior disorder A sleep disturbance in which the mechanism responsible for paralyzing the body during REM sleep does not function, resulting in the acting out of dreams. (p. 135)

replicate To repeat an experiment, generally with a new sample and/or other changes to the procedures, the goal of which is to provide further support for the findings of the first study. (p. 15)

representative sample A subgroup of a population selected so that its members have characteristics similar to those of the population of interest. (p. 18)

representativeness heuristic A decision-making strategy that evaluates the degree to which the primary characteristics of a person or situation are similar to our prototype of that type of person or situation. (p. 254)

resistance A patient's unwillingness to cooperate in therapy; a sign of unconscious conflict. (p. 520)

resting potential The electrical potential of a cell "at rest"; the state of a cell when it is not activated. (p. 47)

reticular formation A network of neurons running through the midbrain that controls levels of arousal and quickly analyzes sensory information on its way to the cortex. (p. 73)

retina The layer of the eye containing photoreceptor cells, which transduce light energy into neural activity. (p. 88)

retinal disparity A binocular cue that uses the difference between the images the two eyes see to determine the distance of objects. (p. 114)

retrieval The process of accessing information encoded and stored in memory. (p. 203)

retrieval cues Stimuli that help in the retrieval of stored information that is difficult to access. (p. 216)

retroactive interference The tendency for recently learned information to interfere with the retrieval of things learned in the past. (p. 222)

retrograde amnesia A type of memory loss; an inability to access memories formed prior to damage to the brain. (p. 229)

reuptake Process by which neurotransmitters are reabsorbed by the sending axon terminal. (p. 48)

rich false memories Recollections of events that never occurred, which are expressed with emotions and confidence and include details. (p. 225)

risky shift The tendency for groups to recommend uncertain and risky options. (p. 425)

rods Photoreceptors that enable us to see in dim lighting; not sensitive to color, but useful for night vision. (p. 88)

romantic love Love that is a combination of connection, concern, care, and intimacy. (p. 436)

sample A subset of a population chosen for inclusion in an experiment. (p. 18)

saturation Color purity. (p. 87)

scaffolding Pushing children to go just beyond what they are competent and comfortable doing, while providing help in a decreasing manner. (p. 299)

scapegoat A target of negative emotions, beliefs, and behaviors; typically, a member of the out-group who receives blame for an upsetting social situation. (p. 428)

Schachter–Singer theory of emotion Suggests that the experience of emotion is the result of physiological arousal and a cognitive label for this physiological state. (p. 351)

schema A collection of ideas that represents a basic unit of understanding. (p. 295)

schizophrenia A disabling psychological disorder that can include delusions, hallucinations, disorganized speech, and abnormal motor behavior. (p. 496)

scientific method The process scientists use to conduct research, which includes a continuing cycle of exploration, critical thinking, and systematic observation. (p. 11)

secondary appraisal An assessment to determine how to respond to a challenging or threatening situation. (p. 461)

secondary reinforcer Reinforcers that do not satisfy biological needs but often gain power through their association with primary reinforcers. (p. 179)

secondary sex characteristics Body characteristics, such as pubic hair, underarm hair, and enlarged breasts, that develop in puberty but are not associated with reproduction. (p. 305)

selective attention The ability to focus awareness on a small segment of information that is available through our sensory systems. (p. 125)

self-actualization The need to be one's best and strive for one's fullest potential. (p. 333)

self-concept The knowledge an individual has about his strengths, abilities, behavior patterns, and temperament. (p. 382)

self-determination theory (SDT) Suggests that humans are born with the needs for competence, relatedness, and autonomy, which are always driving us in the direction of growth and optimal functioning. (p. 334)

self-efficacy Beliefs one has regarding how effective he or she will be in reaching a goal. (p. 386)

self-serving bias The tendency to attribute our successes to personal characteristics and our failures to environmental factors. (p. 407)

semantic memory The memory of information theoretically available to anyone, which pertains to general facts about the world; a type of explicit memory. (p. 211)

semantics The rules used to bring meaning to words and sentences. (p. 259)

sensation The process by which sensory organs in the eyes, ears, nose, mouth, skin, and other tissues receive and detect stimuli. (p. 81)

sensorimotor stage Piaget's stage of cognitive development during which infants use their sensory capabilities and motor skills to learn about the surrounding world. (p. 296)

sensory adaptation The process through which sensory receptors become less sensitive to constant stimuli. (p. 83)

sensory memory A stage of memory that captures near-exact copies of vast amounts of sensory stimuli for a very brief period of time. (p. 205)

sensory neurons Neurons that receive information from the sensory systems and convey it to the brain for further processing. (p. 53)

serial position effect The ability to recall items in a list depends on where they are in the series. (p. 217)

set point The stable weight that is maintained despite variability in exercise and food intake. (p. 345)

sexual dysfunction A significant disturbance in the ability to respond sexually or to gain pleasure from sex. (p. 341)

sexual orientation A person's enduring sexual attraction to individuals of the same sex, opposite sex, or both sexes; a continuum that includes dimensions of sexuality, attraction, desire, and emotions. (p. 337)

sexuality A dimension of human nature encompassing everything that makes us sexual beings: sexual activities, attitudes, and behaviors. (p. 335)

sexually transmitted infections (STIs) Diseases or illnesses transmitted through sexual activity. (p. 341)

shape constancy An object is perceived as maintaining its shape, regardless of the image projected on the retina. (p. 115)

shaping Process by which a person observes the behaviors of another organism, providing reinforcers if the organism performs at a required level. (p. 179)

short-term memory A stage of memory that temporarily maintains and processes a limited amount of information. (p. 205)

signal detection theory Explains how internal and external factors influence our ability to detect weak signals in the environment. (p. 85)

situational attribution A belief that some environmental factor is involved in the cause of an event or activity. (p. 406)

size constancy An object is perceived as maintaining its size, regardless of the image projected on the retina. (p. 115)

skewed distribution Nonsymmetrical frequency distribution. (p. A-7)

sleep terrors A disturbance of non-REM sleep, generally occurring in children; characterized by screaming, staring fearfully, and usually no memory of the episode the following morning. (p. 136)

social cognition The way people think about others, attend to social information, and use this information in their lives, both consciously and unconsciously. (p. 405)

social facilitation The tendency for the presence of others to improve personal performance when the task or event is fairly uncomplicated and a person is adequately prepared. (p. 423)

social identity How we view ourselves within our social group. (p. 428)

social influence How a person is affected by others as evidenced in behaviors, emotions, and cognition. (p. 412)

social loafing The tendency for group members to put forth less than their best effort when individual contributions are too complicated to measure. (p. 423)

social psychology The study of human cognition, emotion, and behavior in relation to others. (p. 403)

social roles The positions we hold in social groups, and the responsibilities and expectations associated with those roles. (p. 431)

social support The assistance we acquire from others. (p. 448)

social-cognitive perspective Suggests that personality results from relationships and other environmental factors (social) and patterns of thinking (cognitive). (p. 384)

sociocultural perspective An approach examining how social interactions and culture influence behavior and mental processes. (p. 9)

somatic nervous system The branch of the peripheral nervous system that includes sensory nerves and motor nerves; gathers information from sensory receptors and controls the skeletal muscles responsible for voluntary movement. (p. 54)

somatosensory cortex A band of tissue running parallel to the motor cortex that receives and integrates sensory information from all over the body. (p. 67)

source traits Basic underlying or foundational characteristics of personality. (p. 387)

specific phobia A psychological disorder that includes a distinct fear or anxiety in relation to an object or situation. (p. 484)

spermarche A boy's first ejaculation. (p. 305)

spinal cord The bundle of neurons that allows communication between the brain and peripheral nervous system. (p. 53)

split-brain operation A rare procedure used to disconnect the right and left hemispheres by cutting the corpus callosum. (p. 59)

spontaneous recovery The reappearance of a conditioned response following its extinction. (p. 169)

standard deviation A number that represents the average distance the values in a data set are from their mean; a measure of variation. (p. A-11)

standardization Occurs when test developers administer a test to a large sample and then publish the average scores for specified groups. (p. 269)

statistical significance The probability that the findings of a study were due to chance. (p. A-2)

statistics A science that focuses on how to collect, organize, analyze, display, and interpret data; numbers that describe characteristics of a sample. (p. A-1)

stem cells Cells responsible for producing new neurons. (p. 63)

stem-and-leaf plot A type of graphical display that uses the actual data values in the form of leading digits and trailing digits. (p. A-6)

stereotype threat A "situational threat" in which individuals are aware of others' negative expectations, which leads to a fear of being judged or treated as inferior. (p. 430)

stereotypes Conclusions or inferences we make about people who are different from us based on their group membership, such as race, religion, age, or gender. (p. 428)

stigma A negative attitude or opinion about a group of people based on certain traits or characteristics. (p. 476)

stimulants A class of drugs that increase neural activity in the central nervous system. (p. 149)

stimulus An event or object that generally leads to a response. (p. 164)

stimulus discrimination The ability to differentiate between a conditioned stimulus and other stimuli sufficiently different from it. (p. 167)

stimulus generalization The tendency for stimuli similar to the conditioned stimulus to elicit the conditioned response. (p. 167)

storage The process of preserving information for possible recollection in the future. (p. 203)

stress The response to perceived threats or challenges resulting from stimuli or events that cause strain. (p. 443)

stressors Stimuli that cause both psychological and physiological reactions. (p. 443)

structuralism An early school of psychology that used introspection to determine the structure and most basic elements of the mind. (p. 6)

successive approximations A method that uses reinforcers to condition a series of small steps that gradually approach the target behavior. (p. 179)

superego According to Freud, the structure of the mind that guides behavior to follow the rules of society, parents, or other authority figures. (p. 372)

surface traits Easily observable characteristics that derive from source traits. (p. 387)

survey method A type of descriptive research that uses questionnaires or interviews to gather data. (p. 21)

sympathetic nervous system The division of the autonomic nervous system that mobilizes the "fight-or-flight" response to stressful or crisis situations. (p. 55)

synapse The tiny gap between the axon terminal of one axon and a dendrite of a neighboring neuron; junction between neurons where communication occurs. (p. 45)

syntax The collection of rules concerning where to place words or phrases. (p. 259)

systematic desensitization A treatment that combines anxiety hierarchies with relaxation techniques. (p. 527)

telegraphic speech Two-word phrases typically used by infants around the age of 18 months. (p. 294)

temperament Characteristic differences in behavioral patterns and emotional reactions that are evident from birth. (p. 300)

temporal lobes The area of the cortex that processes auditory stimuli and language. (p. 64)

teratogens Environmental agents that can damage the growing zygote, embryo, or fetus. (p. 287)

testosterone An androgen produced by the testes. (p. 285)

tetrahydrocannabinol (THC) The active ingredient of marijuana. (p. 153)

thalamus A structure in the limbic system that processes and relays sensory information to the appropriate areas of the cortex. (p. 71)

theory Synthesizes observations in order to explain phenomena and guide predictions to be tested through research. (p. 13)

therapeutic alliance A warm and accepting client–therapist relationship that serves as a safe place for self-exploration. (p. 522)

theta waves Brain waves that indicate light sleep. (p. 130)

thinking Mental activity associated with coming to a decision, reaching a solution, or forming a belief. (p. 242)

third variable An unaccounted for characteristic of participants or the environment that explains changes in the variables of interest. (p. 25)

thyroid gland Endocrine gland that regulates the rate of metabolism by secreting thyroxin. (p. 57)

token economy A type of behavior modification that uses tokens to reinforce desired behaviors. (p. 528)

tolerance With constant use of some psychoactive drugs, the body requires more and more of the drug to create the original effect; a sign of physiological dependence. (p. 156)

top-down processing Drawing on past experiences and knowledge to understand and interpret sensory information. (p. 81)

trait theories Theories that focus on personality dimensions and their influence on behavior; can be used to predict behaviors. (p. 386)

traits The relatively stable properties that describe elements of personality. (p. 386)

transduction The process of transforming stimuli into neural signals. (p. 82)

transference A type of resistance that occurs when a patient reacts to a therapist as if dealing with parents or other caregivers from childhood. (p. 520)

transgender Refers to people whose gender identity and expression do not match the gender assigned to them at birth. (p. 313)

transsexual An individual who seeks or undergoes a social transition to the other gender, and who may make changes to his or her body through surgery and medical treatment. (p. 313)

trial and error An approach to problem solving that involves finding a solution through a series of attempts and eliminating those that do not work. (p. 249)

triarchic theory of intelligence Sternberg's theory suggesting that humans have varying degrees of analytical, creative, and practical abilities. (p. 265)

trichromatic theory The perception of color is the result of three types of cones, each sensitive to wavelengths in the red, green, or blue spectrums. (p. 91)

Type A personality A person who exhibits a competitive, aggressive, impatient, and often hostile pattern of behaviors. (p. 461)

Type B personality A person who exhibits a relaxed, patient, and nonaggressive pattern of behaviors. (p. 463)

unconditional positive regard According to Rogers, the total acceptance or valuing of a person, regardless of behavior. (p. 382)

unconditioned response (UR) A reflexive, involuntary response to an unconditioned stimulus. (p. 166)

unconditioned stimulus (US) A stimulus that automatically triggers an involuntary response without any learning needed. (p. 166)

unconscious According to Freud, the level of consciousness outside of awareness, which is difficult to access without effort or therapy. (p. 371)

uninvolved parenting A parenting style characterized by a parent's indifference to a child, including a lack of emotional involvement. (p. 319)

uplifts Experiences that are positive and have the potential to make one happy. (p. 449)

validity The degree to which an assessment measures what it intends to measure. (p. 267)

variable-interval schedule A schedule in which a behavior is reinforced after an interval of time, but the length of the interval changes from trial to trial. (p. 183)

variable-ratio schedule A schedule in which the number of desired behaviors that must occur before a reinforcer is given changes across trials and is based on an average number of behaviors to be reinforced. (p. 183)

variables Measurable characteristics that can vary over time or across people. (p. 17)

vestibular sense The sense of balance and equilibrium. (p. 107)

volley principle States that the perception of pitches between 400 Hz and 4,000 Hz is made possible by neurons working together to fire in volleys. (p. 99)

wavelength The distance between wave peaks (or troughs). (p. 86)

weber's law States that each of the senses has its own constant ratio determining difference thresholds. (p. 84)

Wernicke's area A region of the cortex that plays a pivotal role in language comprehension. (p. 62)

withdrawal With constant use of some psychoactive drugs, the body becomes dependent and then reacts when the drug is withheld; a sign of physiological dependence. (p. 156)

working memory The active processing of information in short-term memory; the maintenance and manipulation of information in the memory system. (p. 208)

zone of proximal development The range of cognitive tasks that can be accomplished alone and those that require the guidance and help of others. (p. 299)

zygote A single cell formed by the union of a sperm and egg. (p. 284)

References

AAA. (2015, October 22). *New hands-free technologies pose hidden dangers for drivers.* Retrieved from https://newsroom.aaa.com/2015/10/new-hands-free-technologies-pose-hidden-dangers-for-drivers/

Abdellaoui, A., Ehli, E. A., Hottenga, J. J., Weber, Z., Mbarek, H., Willemsen, G., . . . De Geus, E. J. (2015). CNV concordance in 1,097 MZ twin pairs. *Twin Research and Human Genetics, 18,* 1–12.

Abel, A., Hayes, A. M., Henley, W., & Kuyken, W. (2016). Sudden gains in cognitive-behavior therapy for treatment-resistant depression: Processes of change. *Journal of Consulting and Clinical Psychology, 84,* 726–737.

Abel, K. M., Drake, R., & Goldstein, J. M. (2010). Sex differences in schizophrenia. *International Review of Psychiatry, 22,* 417–428.

Abou-Khalil, B. W. (2010). When should corpus callosotomy be offered as palliative therapy? *Epilepsy Currents, 10,* 9–10.

Abramovitch, A., & McKay, D. (2016). Behavioral impulsivity in obsessive-compulsive disorder. *Journal of Behavioral Addictions, 5,* 1–3.

Adams, T. D., Davidson, L. E., Litwin, S. E., Kolotkin, R. L., LaMonte, M. J., Pendleton, R. C., . . . Hunt, S. C. (2012). Health benefits of gastric bypass surgery after 6 years. *Journal of the American Medical Association, 308,* 1122–1131.

Adinolfi, B., & Gava, N. (2013). Controlled outcome studies of child clinical hypnosis. *Acta Bio Medica Atenei Parmensis, 84,* 94–97.

Adler, A. (1994). *Understanding human nature.* Oxford, UK: Oneworld. (Original work published 1927).

Adolphs, R. (2008). Fear, faces, and the human amygdala. *Current Opinion in Neurobiology, 18,* 166–172.

Adolphs, R. (2013). The biology of fear. *Current Biology, 23,* R79–R93.

Afshin, A., Forouzanfar, M. H., Reitsma, M. B., Sur, P., Estep, K., Lee, A., . . . Salama, J. S. (2017). Health effects of overweight and obesity in 195 countries over 25 years. *New England Journal of Medicine, 377,* 13–27.

Agence France Presse. (2010, October 14). In Chile mine rescue 33 is lucky number. *The Sydney Morning Herald.* Retrieved from http://www.smh.com.au/world/in-chile-mine-rescue-33-is-lucky-number-20101014-16kxg.html

Agüera, Z., Brewin, N., Chen, J., Granero, R., Kang, Q., Fernandez-Aranda, F., & Arcelus, J. (2017). Eating symptomatology and general psychopathology in patients with anorexia nervosa from China, UK and Spain: A cross-cultural study examining the role of social attitudes. *PloS One, 12,* e0173781. doi:10.1371/journal.pone.0173781

Ahmed, A.-K. (2016, December). For arachnophobia, a new twist on exposure therapy. *Scientific American Mind, 28,* 17.

Aiello, J. R., & Douthitt, E. A. (2001). Social facilitation from Triplett to electronic performance monitoring. *Group Dynamics: Theory, Research, and Practice, 5,* 163–180.

Ailshire, J. A., & Clarke, P. (2014). Fine particulate matter air pollution and cognitive function among U.S. older adults. *Journals of Gerontology, Series B: Psychological Sciences and Social Sciences, 70,* 322–328.

Ainsworth, M. D. S. (1979). Infant–mother attachment. *American Psychologist, 34,* 932–937.

Ainsworth, M. D. (1985). Patterns of attachment. *Clinical Psychologist, 38,* 27–29.

Ainsworth, M. D. S., & Bell, S. M. (1970). Attachment, exploration, and separation: Illustrated by the behavior of one-year-olds in a strange situation. *Child Development, 41,* 49–67.

Ainsworth, M. D. S., Blehar, M. C., Waters, E., & Wall, S. (1978). *Patterns of attachment: A psychological study of the strange situation.* Hillsdale, NJ: Lawrence Erlbaum Associates.

Ainsworth, S. E., & Maner, J. K. (2012). Sex begets violence: Mating motives, social dominance, and physical aggression in men. *Journal of Personality and Social Psychology, 103,* 819–829. doi:10.1037/a0029428

Ajzen, I. (2001). Nature and operation of attitudes. *Annual Review of Psychology, 52,* 27–58.

Akinola, M., & Mendes, W. B. (2012). Stress-induced cortisol facilitates threat-related decision making among police officers. *Behavioral Neuroscience, 126,* 167–174.

Al Firdaus, M. M. (2012). SQ3R strategy for increasing students' retention of reading and written information. *Majalah Ilmiah Dinamika, 31,* 49–63.

Albert, D., Chein, J., & Steinberg, L. (2013). The teenage brain: Peer influences on adolescent decision making. *Current Directions in Psychological Science, 22,* 114–120.

Albuquerque, D., Stice, E., Rodríguez-López, R., Manco, L., & Nóbrega, C. (2015). Current review of genetics of human obesity: From molecular mechanisms to an evolutionary perspective. *Molecular Genetics and Genomics, 290,* 1191–1221.

Alcoholics Anonymous. (2016a). *Estimated worldwide A.A. individual and group membership* [Service Material]. General Service Office. Retrieved from http://www.aa.org/assets/en_US/smf-132_en.pdf

Alcoholics Anonymous. (2016b). *Information on Alcoholics Anonymous.* Retrieved from http://www.aa.org/assets/en_US/f-2_InfoonAA.pdf

Alcoholics Anonymous Australia. (2016). *Members' stories.* Retrieved from http://www.aa.org.au/new-to-aa/personal-stories.php

Alcoholics Anonymous Great Britain. (2016). *Personal stories.* Retrieved from http://www.alcoholics-anonymous.org.uk/About-AA/Newcomers/Members'-Stories

Alexander, B. (2017, July 20). "Dunkirk": How historically accurate is Christopher Nolan's WWII battle film? *USA Today.* Retrieved from https://www.usatoday.com/story/life/movies/2017/07/20/dunkirk-how-historically-accurate-christopher-nolans-wwii-film/493068001/

Alexander, D. A., & Klein, S. (2001). Ambulance personnel and critical incidents: Impact of accident and emergency work on mental health and emotional well-being. *British Journal of Psychiatry, 178,* 76–81.

Alexander, G. M., & Hines, M. (2002). Sex differences in response to children's toys in nonhuman primates (*Cercopithecus aethiops sabaeus*). *Evolution and Human Behavior, 23,* 467–479.

Alexander, G. M., Wilcox, T., & Woods, R. (2009). Sex differences in infants' visual interest in toys. *Archives of Sexual Behavior, 38,* 427–433.

Alexander, S. A., Frohlich, K. L., & Fusco, C. (2014). Playing for health? Revisiting health promotion to examine the emerging public health position on children's play. *Health Promotion International, 29,* 155–164.

Alfano, A. (2015, June 1). Too much praise promotes narcissism. *Scientific American.* Retrieved from https://www.scientificamerican.com/article/too-much-praise-promotes-narcissism/

Allemand, M., Steiger, A. E., & Hill, P. L. (2013). Stability of personality traits in adulthood: Mechanisms and implications. *GeroPsych: The Journal of Gerontopsychology and Geriatric Psychiatry, 26*(1), 5–13.

Allen, G. E., & Smith, T. B. (2015). Collectivistic coping strategies for distress among Polynesian Americans. *Psychological Services, 12,* 322–329.

Allen, K. (2003). Are pets a healthy pleasure? The influence of pets on blood pressure. *Current Directions in Psychological Science, 12,* 236–239.

Allen, M. S., & McCarthy, P. J. (2016). Be happy in your work: The role of positive psychology in working with change and performance. *Journal of Change Management, 16,* 55–74.

Allen, S. (2009, October 30). 11 famous people who overcame dyslexia. *CNN.* Retrieved from http://www.cnn.com/2009/LIVING/10/30/mf.dyslexia.famous.celebrities/

Allik, J., & McCrae, R. R. (2004). Toward a geography of personality traits patterns of profiles across 36 cultures. *Journal of Cross-Cultural Psychology, 35,* 13–28.

Allik, J., Church, A. T., Ortiz, F. A., Rossier, J., Hřebíčková, M., de Fruyt, F., . . . McCrae, R. R. (2017). Mean profiles of the NEO Personality Inventory. *Journal of Cross-Cultural Psychology, 48,* 402–420.

Allport, G. W., & Odbert, H. S. (1936). Trait-names: A psycho-lexical study. *Psychological Monographs, 47*(211), i–171.

Alosco, M. L., Kasimis, A. B., Stamm, J. M., Chua, A. S., Baugh, C. M., Daneshvar, D. H., . . . Au, R. (2017). Age of first exposure to American football and long-term neuropsychiatric and cognitive outcomes. *Translational Psychiatry, 7*(9), e1236.

Al-Rousan, T., Rubenstein, L., Sieleni, B., Deol, H., & Wallace, R. B. (2017). Inside the nation's largest mental health institution: A prevalence study in a state prison system. *BMC Public Health, 17*(1), 342.

Altschul, I., Lee, S. J., & Gershoff, E. T. (2016). Hugs, not hits: Warmth and spanking as predictors of child social competence. *Journal of Marriage and Family, 78*(13), 695–714.

Altshuler, L. L., Kuaka, R. W., Hellemann, G., Frye, M. A., Sugar, C. A., McElroy, S. L., . . . Suppes, T. (2010). Bipolar disorder evaluated prospectively in the Stanley Foundation Bipolar Treatment Outcome Network. *American Journal of Psychiatry, 167,* 708–715.

Alzheimer's Association. (2013a). *Alzheimer's and dementia testing for earlier diagnosis.* Retrieved from http://www.alz.org/research/science/earlier_alzheimers_diagnosis.asp#Brain

Alzheimer's Association. (2013b). Alzheimer's disease facts and figures. *Alzheimer's & Dementia, 9,* 208–245.

America's Got Talent. (2017, June 6). Mandy Harvey: Deaf singer earns Simon's golden buzzer with original song. *America's Got Talent 2017* [Video file]. Retrieved from https://www.youtube.com/watch?v=ZKSWXzAnVe0

American Academy of Ophthalmology. (2014a). *EyeSmart: Preventing eye injuries.* Retrieved from http://www.geteyesmart.org/eyesmart/living/eye-injuries/preventing.cfm

American Academy of Ophthalmology. (2014b). *EyeSmart: Smoking and eye health.* Retrieved from http://www.geteyesmart.org/eyesmart/living/smokers.cfm

American Academy of Ophthalmology. (2014c). *EyeSmart: The sun, UV radiation and your eyes.* Retrieved from http://www.geteyesmart.org/eyesmart/living/sun.cfm

American Academy of Pediatrics (AAP). (2009). Policy statement: Media violence. *Pediatrics, 124,* 1495–1503.

American Academy of Pediatrics (AAP). (2015). *Newborn eyesight.* Retrieved from https://www.healthychildren.org/English/ages-stages/baby/Pages/Your-Baby's-Vision-1-Month.aspx

American Academy of Pediatrics (AAP). (2016a). Media and young minds. *Pediatrics, 138,* e20162399. doi:10.1542/peds.2016–2591

American Academy of Pediatrics (AAP). (2016b). Media use in school-aged children and adolescents. *Pediatrics, 138,* e20162592. doi:10.1542/peds.2016–2592

American Academy of Pediatrics (AAP). (n.d.). *Media and children.* Retrieved from https: //www.aap.org/en-us/advocacy-and-policy/aap-health-initiatives/pages/media-and- children.aspx

American Foundation for Suicide Prevention. (n.d.). *Suicide: Facts and figures.* Retrieved from https://afsp.org/wp-content/uploads/2017/06/US_FactsFigures_Flyer.pdf

American Heart Association. (2014). *Overweight in children.* Retrieved from http://www.heart.org/HEARTORG/GettingHealthy/Overweight-in-Children_UCM_304054_Article.jsp

American Heart Association. (2015). *Alcohol and heart health.* Retrieved from http://www.heart.org/HEARTORG/HealthyLiving/HealthyEating/Nutrition/Alcohol-and-Heart-Health_UCM_305173_Article.jsp#.V1mI7mQrI34

American Heart Association. (2017). *Atherosclerosis.* Retrieved from http://www.heart.org/HEARTORG/Conditions/Cholesterol/AboutCholesterol/Atherosclerosis_UCM_305564_Article.jsp#.WiV6_raZOks

American Psychiatric Association. (1952). *Diagnostic and statistical manual of mental disorders.* Arlington, VA: Author.

American Psychiatric Association. (2001). *The practice of ECT: A task force report* (2nd ed.). Washington, DC: Author.

American Psychiatric Association. (2013). *Diagnostic and statistical manual of mental disorders* (5th ed., *DSM-5*). Arlington, VA: Author.

American Psychological Association (APA). (1998). Final conclusions of the American Psychological Association's working group on investigation of memories of childhood abuse. *Psychology, Public Policy, and Law, 4,* 933–940.

American Psychological Association (APA). (2006). *Answers to your questions about individuals with intersex conditions.* Retrieved from http://www.apa.org/topics/lgbt/intersex.aspx

American Psychological Association (APA). (2008). *Answers to your questions: For a better understanding of sexual orientation and homosexuality.* Retrieved from http://www.apa.org/topics/sorientation.pdf

American Psychological Association (APA). (2010). *Publication manual of the American Psychological Association* (6th ed.). Washington, DC: Author.

American Psychological Association (APA). (2011). *Careers in psychology: Some of the subfields in psychology.* Retrieved from http://www.apa.org/careers/resources/guides/careers.aspx?item=3#

American Psychological Association (APA). (2012, March). *Understanding alcohol use disorders and their treatment.* Retrieved February 20, 2013, from http://www.apa.org/helpcenter/alcohol-disorders.aspx

American Psychological Association (APA). (2012a). Guidelines for psychological practice with lesbian, gay, and bisexual clients. *American Psychologist, 67,* 10–42.

American Psychological Association (APA). (2012b). *Resolution on the recognition of psychotherapy effectiveness.* Retrieved June 23, 2015 from http://www.apa.org/about/policy/resolution-psychotherapy.aspx

American Psychological Association (APA). (2013a). *Graduate study in psychology, 2014 edition.* Washington, DC: Author.

American Psychological Association (APA). (2013b). *Roper v. Simmons.* Retrieved from http://www.apa.org/about/offices/ogc/amicus/roper.aspx

American Psychological Association (APA). (2013c). *Stress in America: Missing the health care connection.* Retrieved from http://www.apa.org/news/press/releases/stress/2012/full-report.pdf

American Psychological Association (APA). (2014, May). *Resources on mental health parity law.* Retrieved from http://www.apa.org/helpcenter/parity-lawresources.aspx

American Psychological Association (APA). (2014a). *Answers to your questions about transgender people, gender identity, and gender expression.* Retrieved from http://www.apa.org/topics/sexuality/transgender.pdf

American Psychological Association (APA). (2014b). *Psychology: Science in action. Pursuing a career in clinical or counseling psychology.* Retrieved from http://www.apa.org/action/science/clinical/education-training.pdf

American Psychological Association (APA). (2014c). *Psychology: Science in action. Pursuing a career in counseling psychology.* Retrieved from http://www.apa.org/action/science/counseling/education-training.pdf

American Psychological Association (APA). (2014d). *Psychology: Science in action. Pursuing a career in developmental psychology.* Retrieved from http://www.apa.org/action/science/developmental/education-training.pdf

American Psychological Association (APA). (2014e). *Psychology: Science in action. Pursuing a career in experimental psychology.* Retrieved from http://www.apa.org/action/science/experimental/education-training.pdf

American Psychological Association (APA). (2014f). *Psychology: Science in action. Pursuing a career in forensic and public service psychology.* Retrieved from http://www.apa.org/action/science/forensic/education-training.pdf

American Psychological Association (APA). (2014g). *Psychology: Science in action. Pursuing a career in health psychology.* Retrieved from http://www.apa.org/action/science/health/education-training.pdf

American Psychological Association (APA). (2014h). *Psychology: Science in action. Pursuing a career in human factors and engineering psychology.* Retrieved from http://www.apa.org/action/science/human-factors/education-training.pdf

American Psychological Association (APA). (2014i). *Psychology: Science in action. Pursuing a career in industrial and organizational psychology.* Retrieved from http://www.apa.org/action/science/organizational/education-training.pdf

American Psychological Association (APA). (2014j). *Psychology: Science in action. Pursuing a career in the psychology of teaching and learning.* Retrieved from http://www.apa.org/action/science/teaching-learning/education-training.pdf

American Psychological Association (APA). (2014k). *Psychology: Science in action. Pursuing a career in rehabilitation psychology.* Retrieved from http://www.apa.org/action/science/rehabilitation/education-training.pdf

American Psychological Association (APA). (2014l). *Psychology: Science in action. Pursuing a career in social psychology.* Retrieved from http://www.apa.org/action/science/social/education-training.pdf

American Psychological Association (APA). (2014m). *Psychology: Science in action. Pursuing a career in sport and performance psychology.* Retrieved from http://www.apa.org/action/science/performance/education-training.pdf

American Psychological Association (APA). (2015a). *Demographics of the U.S. psychology workforce: Findings from the American Community Survey.* Washington, DC: Author.

American Psychological Association (APA). (2015b). *Key terms and concepts in understanding gender diversity and sexual orientation among students.* Retrieved from http://dx.doi.org/10.1037/e527502015-001

American Psychological Association (APA). (2015c). Psychology & global climate change: Addressing a multifaceted phenomenon and set of challenges. *Task Force on the Interface Between Psychology and Global Climate Change.* Retrieved from http://www.apa.org/science/about/publications/climate-change.aspx

American Psychological Association (APA). (2017a). *Ethical principles of psychologists and code of conduct.* Retrieved from http://www.apa.org/ethics/code/?item=6#210

American Psychological Association (APA). (2017b). Idaho becomes fifth state to allow psychologists to prescribe medications [Press release]. Retrieved from http://www.apa.org/news/press/releases/2017/04/idaho-psychologists-medications.aspx

American Psychological Association (APA). (2017c). *Salaries in psychology: Findings from the National Science Foundation's 2015 National Survey of College Graduates.* Washington, DC: Author.

American Psychological Association (APA). (2018). *Graduate study in psychology, 2019 edition.* Washington, DC: Author.

American Psychological Association (APA). (n.d.-a). *A career in counseling psychology.* Retrieved from http://www.apa.org/action/science/counseling/index.aspx

American Psychological Association (APA). (n.d.-b). *Clinical psychology solves complex human problems.* Retrieved from http://www.apa.org/action/science/clinical/index.aspx

American Psychological Association (APA). (n.d.-c). *Cognitive psychology explores our mental processes.* Retrieved from http://www.apa.org/action/science/brain-science/index.aspx

American Psychological Association (APA). (n.d.-d). *Developmental psychology studies humans across the lifespan.* Retrieved from http://www.apa.org/action/science/developmental/index.aspx

American Psychological Association (APA). (n.d.-e). *Divisions of the APA.* Retrieved from http://www.apa.org/about/division/index.aspx

American Psychological Association (APA). (n.d.-f). *Environmental psychology makes a better world.* Retrieved from http://www.apa.org/action/science/environment/index.aspx

American Psychological Association (APA). (n.d.-g). *Even a bit of lead is bad for kids' development.* Retrieved from http://www.apa.org/action/resources/research-in-action/lead.aspx.

American Psychological Association (APA). (n.d.-h). *Experimental psychology studies humans and animals.* Retrieved from http://www.apa.org/action/science/experimental/index.aspx

American Psychological Association (APA). (n.d.-i). *Frequently asked questions about graduate school.* Retrieved from http://www.apa.org/education/grad/faqs.aspx

American Psychological Association (APA). (n.d.-j). *Health psychology promotes wellness.* Retrieved from http://www.apa.org/action/science/health/index.aspx

American Psychological Association (APA). (n.d.-k). *Human factors psychology studies humans and machines.* Retrieved from http://www.apa.org/action/science/human-factors/index.aspx

American Psychological Association (APA). (n.d.-l). *I/O psychology provides workplace solutions.* Retrieved from http://www.apa.org/action/science/organizational/index.aspx

American Psychological Association (APA). (n.d.-m). *Protecting your privacy: Understanding confidentiality.* Retrieved from www.apa.org/helpcenter/confidentiality.aspx

American Psychological Association (APA). (n.d.-n). *Pursuing a career in counseling psychology.* Retrieved from http://www.apa.org/action/science/counseling/education-training.aspx

American Psychological Association (APA). (n.d.-o). *Questions and answers about memories of childhood abuse.* Retrieved from http://apa.org/topics/trauma/memories.aspx

American Psychological Association (APA). (n.d.-p). *Rehabilitation psychology tackles challenges.* Retrieved from http://www.apa.org/action/science/rehabilitation/index.aspx

American Psychological Association (APA). (n.d.-q). *Social psychology studies human interactions.* Retrieved from http://www.apa.org/action/science/social/index.aspx

American Psychological Association (APA). (n.d.-r). *What is media psychology?* Retrieved from http://www.apadivisions.org/division-46/about/what-is.aspx

American Speech-Language-Hearing Association. (n.d.). *Who should be screened for hearing loss?* Retrieved from http://www.asha.org/public/hearing/Who-Should-be-Screened/

Ames, M. E., Leadbeater, B. J., & MacDonald, S. W. S. (2018). Health behavior changes in adolescence and young adulthood: Implications for cardiometabolic risk. *Health Psychology, 37,* 103–113.

Amesbury, E. C., & Schallhorn, S. C. (2003). Contrast sensitivity and limits of vision. *International Ophthalmology Clinics, 43,* 31–42.

Amso, D. (2017, January/February). Ask the brains: When do children start making long-term memories? *Scientific American Mind, 28,* 72–73.

Anastasi, A., & Urbina, S. (1997). *Psychological testing* (7th ed.). Upper Saddle River, NJ: Prentice Hall.

Anastasio, A., Draisci, R., Pepe, T., Mercogliano, R., Quadri, F. D., Luppi, G., & Cortesi, M. L. (2010). Development of biogenic amines during the ripening of Italian dry sausages. *Journal of Food Protection, 73,* 114–118.

Anderson, R. C. (1971). Encoding processes in the storage and retrieval of sentences. *Journal of Experimental Psychology, 91,* 338–340.

Anderson, S. R. (2017). The place of human language in the animal world. In J. Blochowiak, C. Grisot, S. Durriemann-Tame, & C. Laenzlinger (Eds.), *Formal models in the study of language* (pp. 339–351). New York, NY: Springer.

Anderson, W. E. (2016, June 15). Herpes simplex encephalitis. Medscape. Retrieved from http://emedicine.medscape.com/article/1165183-overview#a6

Anderson, W. E. (2017, August 23). Herpes simplex encephalitis. Medscape. Retrieved from https://emedicine.medscape.com/article/1165183-overview#a5

André, M. A. E., Güntürkün, O., & Manahan-Vaughan, D. (2015). The metabotropic glutamate receptor, mGlu5, is required for extinction learning that occurs in the absence of a context change. *Hippocampus, 25,* 149–158.

Andreotti, C., Root, J. C., Ahles, T. A., McEwen, B. S., & Compas, B. E. (2015). Cancer, coping, and cognition: A model for the role of stress reactivity in cancer-related cognitive decline. *Psycho-Oncology, 24,* 617–623.

Andrus, B. M., Blizinsky, K., Vedell, P. T., Dennis, K., Shukla, P. K., Schaffer, D. J., . . . Redei, E. E. (2012). Gene expression patterns in the hippocampus and amygdala of endogenous depression and chronic stress models. *Molecular Psychiatry, 17,* 49–61.

Angst, J., Angst, F., Gerber-Werder, R., & Gamma, A. (2005). Suicide in 406 mood-disorder patients with and without long-term medication: A 40 to 44 years' follow-up. *Archives of Suicide Research, 9,* 279–300.

Angst, J., Paksarian, D., Cui, L., Merikangas, K. R., Hengartner, M. P., Ajdacic-Gross, V., & Rössler, W. (2016). The epidemiology of common mental disorders from age 20 to 50: results from the prospective Zurich cohort Study. *Epidemiology and Psychiatric Sciences, 25,* 24–32.

Angus, L., Watson, J. C., Elliott, R., Schneider, K., & Timulak, L. (2015). Humanistic psychotherapy research 1990–2015: From methodological innovation to evidence-supported treatment outcomes and beyond. *Psychotherapy Research, 25,* 330–347.

Annan, J., Blattman, C., & Horton, R. (2006). *The state of youth and youth protection in northern Uganda: Findings from the Survey for War Affected Youth* [Report for UNICEF Uganda, pp. ii–89]. Retrieved from http://chrisblattman.com/documents/policy/sway/SWAY.Phase1.FinalReport.pdf

Annese, J., Schenker-Ahmed, N. M., Bartsch, H., Maechler, P., Sheh, C., Thomas, N., . . . Corkin, S. (2014). Postmortem examination of patient H.M.'s brain based on histological sectioning and digital 3D reconstruction. *Nature Communications, 5,* 3122. doi:10.1038/ncomms4122

Anokhin, A. P., Grant, J. D., Mulligan, R. C., & Heath, A. C. (2015). The genetics of impulsivity: Evidence for the heritability of delay discounting. *Biological Psychiatry, 77*(10), 887–894.

Ansbacher, H. L., & Ansbacher, R. R. (Eds.). (1956). *The individual psychology of Alfred Adler.* New York, NY: Harper & Row.

Anton, M. T., Jones, D. J., & Youngstrom, E. A. (2015). Socioeconomic status, parenting, and externalizing problems in African American single-mother homes: A person-oriented approach. *Journal of Family Psychology, 29,* 405–415.

Anusic, I., Yap, S. C., & Lucas, R. E. (2014). Testing set-point theory in a Swiss national sample: Reaction and adaptation to major life events. *Social Indicators Research, 119,* 1265–1288.

APA Center for Workforce Studies. (2015). Table 3: Current major field of APA members by membership status. *APA Directory.* Retrieved from http://www.apa.org/workforce/publications/15-member/table-3.pdf

APA Presidential Task Force on Evidence-Based Practice. (2006). Evidence-based practice in psychology. *American Psychologist, 61,* 271–285.

Aranake, A., Mashour, G. A., & Avidan, M. S. (2013). Minimum alveolar concentration: Ongoing relevance and clinical utility. *Anaesthesia, 68,* 512–522.

Araque, A., & Navarrete, M. (2010). Glial cells in neuronal network function. *Philosophical Transactions of the Royal Society of Biological Sciences, 365,* 2375–2381.

Archer, J., & Coyne, S. M. (2005). An integrated review of indirect, relational, and social aggression. *Personality and Social Psychology Review, 9,* 212–230.

Arganini, C., & Sinesio, F. (2015). Chemosensory impairment does not diminish eating pleasure and appetite in independently living older adults. *Maturitas, 82,* 241–244.

Arkes, H. R. (2013). The consequences of the hindsight bias in medical decision making. *Current Directions in Psychological Science, 22,* 356–360.

Arkowitz, H., & Lilienfeld, S. O. (2011, July/August). Deranged and dangerous? *Scientific American Mind, 22,* 64–65.

Arlin, P. K. (1975). Cognitive development in adulthood: A fifth stage? *Developmental Psychology, 11,* 602–606.

Armitage, C. J., & Christian, J. (2003). From attitudes to behaviour: Basic and applied research on the theory of planned behaviour. *Current Psychology: Developmental, Learning, Personality, Social, 22,* 187–195.

Armstrong, T. (2015). The myth of the normal brain: Embracing neurodiversity. *AMA Journal of Ethics, 17,* 348–352.

Arnett, J. J. (2000). Emerging adulthood: A theory of development from the late teens through the twenties. *American Psychologist, 55,* 469–480.

Aronson, E. (2015). *Jigsaw classroom.* Retrieved from http://www.jigsaw.org

Aronson, E. (2018). *The social animal* (12th ed.). New York, NY: Worth.

Aronson, E., & Festinger, L. (1958). *Some attempts to measure tolerance for dissonance* (WADC.TR-58.492ASTIA Document No. AD 207 337). San Antonio, TX: Lackland Air Force Base.

Arora, M., Reichenberg, A., Willfors, C., Austin, C., Gennings, C., Berggren, S., . . . Bölte, S. (2017). Fetal and postnatal metal dysregulation in autism. *Nature Communications, 8.* doi:10.1038/ncomms15493

Asch, S. E. (1955). Opinions and social pressure. *Scientific American, 193,* 31–35.

Asch, S. E. (1956). Studies of independence and conformity: I. A minority of one against a unanimous majority. *Psychological Monographs: General and Applied, 70,* 1–70.

Assefa, S. Z., Diaz-Abad, M., Wickwire, E. M., & Scharf, S. M. (2015). The functions of sleep. *AIMS Neuroscience, 2*(3), 155–171.

Assistant Secretary for Public Affairs (ASPA), U.S. Department of Health and Human Services. (2017). *The opioid epidemic in the U.S.* Retrieved from https://www.hhs.gov/opioids/about-the-epidemic/index.html

Associated Press. (2010, August 25). Geology of Chilean gold and copper mine helped miners survive with air, water and warmth. *Fox News.* Retrieved from http://www.foxnews.com/world/2010/08/25/geology-chilean-gold-copper-helped-miners-survive-air-water-warmth/

Associated Press. (2014, May 8). Therapy dogs help troops deal with postwar stress. *CBS News.* Retrieved from http://www.cbsnews.com/news/therapy-dog-help-stroops-deal-with-postwar-stress/

Associated Press. (2015, August 26). James Holmes trial: Judge formally sentences Aurora gunman to life in prison. *NBC News.* Retrieved from http://www.nbcnews.com/news/us-news/james-holmes-trial-judge-formally-sentences-aurora-gunmanlife-prison-n416396

Association for Psychological Science (APS). (n.d.). *Psychology links.* Retrieved from http://www.psychologicalscience.org/index.php/about/psychology-links

Atance, C. M., & Caza, J. S. (2018). "Will I know more in the future than I know now?" Preschoolers' judgments about changes in general knowledge. *Developmental Psychology, 54,* 857–865.

Athanasopoulos, P., Bylund, E., Montero-Melis, G., Damjanovic, L., Schartner, A., Kibbe, A., . . . Thierry, G. (2015). Two languages, two minds: Flexible cognitive processing driven by language of operation. *Psychological Science, 26,* 518–526.

Atkinson, R. C., & Shiffrin, R. M. (1968, January 31–February 2). Some speculations on storage and retrieval processes in long-term memory (Technical Report No. 127). Paper presented at Conference on Research on Human Decision Making sponsored by NASA-Ames Research Center, Moffett Field, CA.

Attarian, H. P., Schenck, C. H., & Mahowald, M. W. (2000). Presumed REM sleep behavior disorder arising from cataplexy and wakeful dreaming. *Sleep Medicine, 1,* 131–133.

Aurora, R. N., Zak, R. S., Maganti, R. K., Auerbach, S. H., Casey, K. R., Chowdhuri, S., . . . American Academy of Sleep Medicine. (2010). Best practice guide for the treatment of REM sleep behavior disorder (RED). *Journal of Clinical Sleep Medicine, 15,* 85–95.

Auster, C. J., & Mansbach, C. S. (2012). The gender marketing of toys: An analysis of color and type of toy on the Disney store website. *Sex Roles, 67,* 375–388.

Australian Department of Health. (2016, May 27). *Tobacco control key facts and figures.* Retrieved from http://www.health.gov.au/internet/main/publishing.nsf/Content/tobacco-kff

Axelrod, V., Bar, M., Rees, G., & Yovel, G. (2014). Neural correlates of subliminal language processing. *Cerebral Cortex.* doi:10.1093/cercor/bhu022

Axson, S. (2017, August 8). "Concussion" doctor: Letting kids play football is "definition of child abuse." *Sports Illustrated.* Retrieved from https://www.si.com/nfl/2017/08/08/bennet-omalu-cte-football

Aydin, N., Agthe, M., Pfundmair, M., Frey, D., & DeWall, N. (2017). Safety in beauty: Social exclusion, antisocial responses, and the desire to reconnect. *Social Psychology, 48,* 208–225.

Bachhuber, M. A., Hennessy, S., Cunningham, C. O., & Starrels, J. L. (2016). Increasing benzodiazepine prescriptions and overdose mortality in the United States, 1996–2013. *American Journal of Public Health, 106,* 686–688.

Back, M. D., Schmukle, S. C., & Egloff, B. (2008). Becoming friends by chance. *Psychological Science, 19,* 439–440.

Back, M. D., Stopfer, J. M., Vazire, S., Gaddis, S., Schmukle, S. C., Egloff, B., & Gosling, S. D. (2010). Facebook profiles reflect actual personality, not self-idealization. *Psychological Science, 21,* 372–374.

Backeljauw, P., & Hwa, V. (2016). Growth hormone physiology. In L. E. Cohen (Ed.), *Growth hormone deficiency: Physiology and clinical management.* Cham, Switzerland: Springer International.

Baddeley, A. (1995). Working memory. In M. S. Gazzaniga (Ed.), *The cognitive neurosciences* (pp. 755–764). Cambridge, MA: MIT Press.

Baddeley, A. (1999). *Essentials of human memory.* East Sussex, UK: Psychology Press.

Baddeley, A. (2000). The episodic buffer: A new component of working memory? *Trends in Cognitive Sciences, 4,* 417–423.

Baddeley, A. (2002). Is working memory still working? *European Psychologist, 7,* 85–97.

Baddeley, A. (2006). Working memory: An overview. In S. J. Pickering (Ed.), *Working memory in education* (pp. 3–31). Burlington, MA: Elsevier.

Baddeley, A. (2012). Working memory: Theories, models, and controversies. *Annual Review of Psychology, 63,* 1–29.

Baddeley, A. D., & Hitch, G. J. (1974). Working memory. In G. Bower (Ed.), *Recent advances in learning and memory* (Vol. 8, pp. 47–90). New York, NY: Academic Press.

Badie, D. (2010). Groupthink, Iraq, and the war on terror: Explaining US policy shift toward Iraq. *Foreign Policy Analysis, 6,* 277–296.

Baer, J. M. (1993). *Creativity and divergent thinking.* Hillsdale, NJ: Erlbaum.

Baggetto, M. (2010). Meet the women of the administration: Claudia Gordon [Web log post]. Retrieved from https://www.whitehouse.gov/blog/2010/08/30/meet-women-administration-claudia-gordon

Bahrick, H. P., Hall, L. K., & Da Costa, L. A. (2008). Fifty years of memory of college grades: Accuracy and distortions. *Emotion, 8,* 13–22.

Bahrick, L. E., Gogate, L. J., & Ruiz, I. (2002). Attention and memory for faces and actions in infancy: The salience of actions over faces in dynamic events. *Child Development, 73,* 1629–1643.

Bahrick, L. E., & Newell, L. C. (2008). Infant discrimination of faces in naturalistic events: Actions are more salient than faces. *Developmental Psychology, 44,* 983–996.

Baibazarova, E., van de Beek, C., Cohen-Kettenis, P. T., Buitelaar, J., Shelton, K. H., & van Goozen, S. H. M. (2013). Influence of prenatal maternal stress, maternal plasma cortisol and cortisol in the amniotic fluid on birth outcomes and child temperament at 3 months. *Psychoneuroendocrinology, 38,* 907–915.

Bailey, C. (2017, October 4). More Americans killed by guns since 1968 than in all U.S. wars—combined. *NBC News.* Retrieved from https://www.nbcnews.com/storyline/las-vegas-shooting/more-americans-killed-guns-1968-all-u-s-wars-combined-n807156

Bailey, S. J., & Covell, K. (2011). Pathways among abuse, daily hassles, depression and substance use in adolescents. *The New School Psychology Bulletin, 8,* 4–14.

Baillargeon, R., Spelke, E. S., & Wasserman, S. (1985). Object permanence in five-month-old infants. *Cognition, 20,* 191–208.

Bakalar, N. (2015, October 28). Don't blame it on birth order [Web log post]. Retrieved from http://well.blogs.nytimes.com/2015/10/28/dont-blame-it-on-birth-order/?_r=0

Balliet, D., & Ferris, D. L. (2013). Ostracism and prosocial behavior: A social dilemma perspective. *Organizational Behavior and Human Decision Processes, 120,* 298–308.

Balter, M. (2017, July/August). Schizophrenia's unyielding mysteries. *Scientific American Mind, 28,* 50–60.

Banaji, M. R., & Greenwald, A. G. (2013). *Blindspot: Hidden biases of good people.* New York, NY: Delacorte Press.

Bandell, M., Macpherson, L. J., & Patapoutian, A. (2007). From chills to chilis: Mechanisms for thermosensation and chemesthesis via thermoTRPs. *Current Opinion in Neurobiology, 17,* 490–497.

Bandura, A. (1977a). Self-efficacy: Toward a unifying theory of behavioral change. *Psychological Review, 84,* 191–215.

Bandura, A. (1977b). *Social learning theory.* Englewood Cliffs, NJ: Prentice Hall.

Bandura, A. (1978). The self system in reciprocal determinism. *American Psychologist, 33,* 344–358.

Bandura, A. (1986). *Social foundations of thought and action: A social cognitive theory.* Englewood Cliffs, NJ: Prentice Hall.

Bandura, A. (2001). Social cognitive theory: An agentic perspective. *Annual Review of Psychology, 52,* 1–26.

Bandura, A. (2006). Toward a psychology of human agency. *Perspectives on Psychological Science, 1,* 164–180.

Bandura, A., Ross, D., & Ross, S. A. (1961). Transmission of aggression through imitation of aggressive models. *Journal of Abnormal and Social Psychology, 63,* 575–582.

Banissy, M. J., Jonas, C., & Kadosh, R. C. (2014). Synesthesia: An introduction. *Frontiers in Psychology, 5,* 1414. doi:10.3389/fpsyg.2014.01414

Banks, M. S., & Salapatek, P. (1978). Acuity and contrast sensitivity in 1-, 2-, and 3-month-old human infants. *Investigative Ophthalmology & Visual Science, 17,* 361–365.

Banuazizi, A., & Movahedi, S. (1975). Interpersonal dynamics in a simulated prison: A methodological analysis. *American Psychologist, 30,* 152–160.

Banyard, V. L., & Moynihan, M. M. (2011). Variation in bystander behavior related to sexual and intimate partner violence prevention: Correlates in a sample of college students. *Psychology of Violence, 1,* 287–301.

Barak, A., Hen, L., Boniel-Nissim, M., & Shapira, N. A. (2008). A comprehensive review and a meta-analysis of the effectiveness of Internet-based psychotherapeutic interventions. *Journal of Technology in Human Services, 26,* 109–160.

Baraona, E., Abittan, C. S., Dohmen, K., Moretti, M., Pozzato, G., Chayes, Z. W., . . . Lieber, C. S. (2001). Gender differences in pharmacokinetics of alcohol. *Alcoholism: Clinical and Experimental Research, 25,* 502–507.

Barash, P. G., Cullen, B. F., Stoelting, R. K., & Cahalan, M. (2009). *Clinical anesthesia* (6th ed.). Philadelphia: Lippincott Williams & Wilkins.

Barber, R. (2012, October 27). Yes, I give dogs electric shocks and use spike chokers . . . but I'm NOT cruel, says Hollywood's favourite pet guru. *Daily Mail.* Retrieved from http://www.dailymail.co.uk/news/article-2224252/Yes-I-dogs-electric-shocks-use-spike-chokers--Im-NOT-cruel-says-Hollywoods-favourite-pet-guru-Cesar-Millan.html

Bard, P. (1934). Emotion I: The neuro-humoral basis of emotional reactions. In C. Murchison (Ed.), *Handbook of general experimental psychology* (pp. 264–311) (International University Series in Psychology). Worcester, MA: Clark University Press.

Bargh, J. A., & McKenna, K. Y. A. (2004). The Internet and social life. *Annual Review of Psychology, 55,* 573–590.

Bar-Hillel, M. (2015). Position effects in choice from simultaneous displays: A conundrum solved. *Perspectives on Psychological Science, 10,* 419–433.

Barlé, N., Wortman, C. B., & Latack, J. A. (2016). Traumatic bereavement: Basic research and clinical implications. *Journal of Psychotherapy Integration.* Retrieved from http://dx.doi. org/10.1037/int0000013

Barnes, S. K. (2010). Sign language with babies: What difference does it make? *Dimensions of Early Childhood, 38,* 21–30.

Barnett, M. L., Olenski, A. R., & Jena, A. B. (2017). Opioid-prescribing patterns of emergency physicians and risk of long-term use. *New England Journal of Medicine, 376,* 663–673.

Baron, K. G., & Reid, K. J. (2014). Circadian misalignment and health. *International Review of Psychiatry, 26,* 139–154.

Barr, T. F., Dixon, A. L., & Gassenheimer, J. B. (2005). Exploring the "lone wolf" phenomenon in student teams. *Journal of Marketing Education, 27,* 81–90.

Barredo, J. L., & Deeg, K. E. (2009, February 24). Could living in a mentally enriching environment change your genes? *Scientific American.* Retrieved from http://www.scientificamerican.com/article.cfm?id=enriched-environments-memory

Barrera, T. L., Mott, J. M., Hofstein, R. F., & Teng, E. J. (2013). A meta-analytic review of exposure in group cognitive behavioral therapy for posttraumatic stress disorder. *Clinical Psychology Review, 33,* 24–32.

Barrett, L. F. (2017, June 4). Poverty on the brain [Web log post]. Retrieved from https://lisafeldmanbarrett.com/2017/06/04/poverty-on-the-brain/

Barss, T. S., Pearcey, G. E., & Zehr, E. P. (2016). Cross-education of strength and skill: An old idea with applications in the aging nervous system. *The Yale Journal of Biology and Medicine, 89,* 81–86.

Bartels, M. (2015). Genetics of wellbeing and its components satisfaction with life, happiness, and quality of life: A review and meta-analysis of heritability studies. *Behavior Genetics, 45,* 137–156.

Bartels, M., Saviouk, V., De Moor, M. H. M., Willemsen, G., van Beijsterveldt, T. C. E. M., Hottenga, J.-J., . . . Boomsma, D. I. (2010). Heritability and genome-wide linkage scan of subjective happiness. *Twin Research and Human Genetics, 13,* 135–142.

Bartlett, T. (2014). The search for psychology's lost boy. *Chronicle of Higher Education, 60* (38). Retrieved from http://chronicle.com/interactives/littlealbert

Barton, R. A., & Capellini, I. (2016). Sleep, evolution and brains. *Brain, Behavior and Evolution, 87,* 65–68. doi:10.1159/000443716

Bates, M. (2012, September 18). Super powers for the blind and deaf. *Scientific American.* Retrieved from https://www.scientificamerican.com/article/superpowers-for-the-blind-and-deaf/

Batsell, W. R., Jr., Perry, J. L., Hanley, E., & Hostetter, A. B. (2017). Ecological validity of the testing effect: The use of daily quizzes in introductory psychology. *Teaching of Psychology, 44,* 18–23.

Batson, C. D., & Powell, A. A. (2003). Altruism and prosocial behavior. In I. B. Weiner, T. Millon, & M. J. Lerner (Eds.), *Handbook of psychology: Vol. 5. Personality and social psychology* (pp. 463–484). Hoboken, NJ: John Wiley & Sons.

Bauchner, H., Rivara, F. P., Bonow, R. O., Bressler, N. M., Disis, M. L. N., Heckers, S., . . . Rhee, J. S. (2017). Death by gun violence—a public health crisis. *JAMA Psychiatry, 318,* 1763–1764.

Bauer, P. J. (2006). Constructing a past in infancy: A neuro-developmental account. *Trends in Cognitive Sciences, 10,* 175–181.

Bauer, P. J. (2015). A complementary processes account of the development of childhood amnesia and a personal past. *Psychological Review, 122,* 204–231.

Bauer, P. J., & Larkina, M. (2014). The onset of childhood amnesia in childhood: A prospective investigation of the course and determinants of forgetting of early-life events. *Memory, 22,* 907–924.

Baughman, H. M., Giammarco, E. A., Veselka, L., Schermer, J. A., Martin, N. G., Lynskey, M., & Vernon, P. A. (2012). A behavioral genetic study of humor styles in an Australian sample. *Twin Research and Human Genetics, 15,* 663–667.

Baumeister, R. F., Maranges, H. M., & Vohs, K. D. (2018). Human self as information agent: Functioning in a social environment based on shared meanings. *Review of General Psychology, 22,* 36–47.

Baumrind, D. (1966). Effects of authoritative parental control on child behavior. *Child Development, 37,* 887–907.

Baumrind, D. (1971). Current patterns of parental authority. *Developmental Psychology Monograph, 4,* 1–103.

Baumrind, D. (1991). The influence of parenting style on adolescent competence and substance use. *Journal of Early Adolescence, 11,* 56–95.

Baumrind, D. (2013). Is a pejorative view of power assertion in the socialization process justified? *Review of General Psychology, 17,* 420–427.

Bayley, N. (1993). *The Bayley Scales of Infant Development* (2nd ed.). San Antonio, TX: Psychological Test Corporation.

BBC. (2014, September 17). *Dr. Money and the boy with no penis—programme transcript.* Retrieved from http://www.bbc.co.uk/sn/tvradio/programmes/horizon/dr_money_trans.shtml

BBC News. (2017, July 13). Brazil corruption scandals: All you need to know. Retrieved from http://www.bbc.com/news/world-latin-america-35810578

BBC News. (2017, May 12). Singer finds her sound after going deaf [Video file]. Retrieved from http://www.bbc.com/news/av/world-us-canada-39901298/mandy-harvey-singer-finds-her-sound-after-going-deaf

Beauchamp, M. H., & Anderson, V. (2010). Social: An integrative framework for the development of social skills. *Psychological Bulletin, 136,* 39–64.

Bech, P. (2006). The full story of lithium. *Psychotherapy and Psychosomatics, 75,* 265–269.

Beck, A. T. (1976). *Cognitive therapy and the emotional disorders.* New York, NY: International Universities Press.

Beck, A. T., Rush, A. J., Shaw, B. F., & Emory, G. (1979). *Cognitive therapy of depression.* New York, NY: Guilford Press.

Beck, A. T., & Weishaar, M. E. (2014). Cognitive therapy. In R. J. Corsini & D. Wedding (Eds.), *Current psychotherapies* (10th ed., pp. 231–264). Belmont, CA: Brooks/Cole, Cengage Learning.

Beck, H. P., & Irons, G. (2011). Finding Little Albert: A seven-year search for psychology's lost boy. *The Psychologist, 24,* 392–395.

Beck, H. P., Levinson, S., & Irons, G. (2009). Finding Little Albert: A journey to John B. Watson's infant laboratory. *American Psychologist, 64,* 605–614.

Becker, K. A. (2003). History of the Stanford-Binet intelligence scales: Content and psychometrics. In *Stanford-Binet intelligence scales, Fifth Edition Assessment Service Bulletin* (No. 1). Itasca, IL: Riverside.

Bedrosian, T. A., Fonken, L. K., & Nelson, R. J. (2016). Endocrine effects of circadian disruption. *Annual Review of Physiology, 78,* 1.1–1.23.

Beebe-Center, J. G. (1951). Feeling and emotion. In H. Helson (Ed.), *Theoretical foundations of psychology* (pp. 254–317). Princeton, NJ: Van Nostrand.

Bekk, M., & Spörrle, M. (2010). The influence of perceived personality characteristics on positive attitude towards and suitability of a celebrity as a marketing campaign endorser. *Open Psychology Journal, 3,* 54–66.

Belizaire, L. S., & Fuertes, J. N. (2011). Attachment, coping, acculturative stress, and quality of life among Haitian immigrants. *Journal of Counseling & Development, 89,* 89–97.

Bellieni, C. V., Alagna, M. G., & Buonocore, G. (2013). Analgesia for infants' circumcision. *Italian Journal of Pediatrics, 39*(38). doi:10.1186/1824-7288-39-38

Belmaker, R. H. (2004). Bipolar disorder. *New England Journal of Medicine, 351,* 476–486.

Belmaker, R. H., & Agam, G. (2008). Major depressive disorder. *New England Journal of Medicine, 358,* 55–68.

Bem, D. J. (2011). Feeling the future: Experimental evidence for anomalous retroactive influences on cognition and affect. *Journal of Personality and Social Psychology, 100,* 407–425.

Bem, D. J., Utts, J., & Johnson, W. O. (2011). Must psychologists change the way they analyze their data? *Journal of Personality and Social Psychology, 101,* 716–719.

Bem, S. L. (1981). Gender schema theory: A cognitive account of sex typing. *Psychological Review, 88,* 354–364.

Benedek, M., Franz, F., Heene, M., & Neubauer, A. C. (2012). Differential effects of cognitive inhibition and intelligence on creativity. *Personality and Individual Differences, 53,* 480–485.

Benestad, R. E., Nuccitelli, D., Lewandowsky, S., Hayhoe, K., Hygen, H. O., van Dorland, R., & Cook, J. (2016). Learning from mistakes in climate research. *Theoretical and Applied Climatology, 126,* 699–703.

Benham, G. (2010). Sleep: An important factor in stress-health models. *Stress and Health, 26,* 201–214.

Benjamin, L. T. (2007). *A brief history of modern psychology.* Malden, MA: Blackwell.

Bennett, A. T. D., Cuthill, I. C., Partridge, J. C., & Maier, E. J. (1996). Ultraviolet vision and mate choice in zebra finches. *Nature, 380,* 433–435.

Ben-Porath, Y. S. (2012). *Interpreting the MMPI 2 RF.* Minneapolis, MN: University of Minnesota Press.

Bensky, M. K., Gosling, S. D., & Sinn, D. L. (2013). The world from a dog's point of view: A review and synthesis of dog cognition research. *Advances in the Study of Behavior, 45,* 209–406.

Benson, H. (2000). *The relaxation response.* New York, NY: Avon Books.

Ben-Zvi, A., Vernon, S. D., & Broderick, G. (2009). Model-based therapeutic correction of hypothalamic-pituitary-adrenal axis dysfunction. *PLoS Computational Biology, 5,* e1000273. doi:10.1371/journal.pcbi.1000273

Berdan, B. (2016, October 6). Participation trophies send a dangerous message. *The New York Times.* Retrieved from https://www.nytimes.com/roomfordebate/2016/10/06/should-every-young-athlete-get-a-trophy/participation-trophies-send-a-dangerous-message

Berenbaum, S. A., Blakemore, J. E. O., & Beltz, A. M. (2011). A role for biology in gender-related behavior. *Sex Roles, 64,* 804–825.

Beresin, E. V. (2015). The impact of media violence on children and adolescents: Opportunities for clinical interventions. *American Academy of Child and Adolescent Psychiatry.* Retrieved from https://www.aacap.org/aacap/Medical_Students_and_Residents/Mentorship_Matters/DevelopMentor/The_Impact_of_Media_Violence_on_Children_and_Adolescents_Opportunities_for_Clinical_Interventions.aspx

Berger, W., Coutinho, E. S. F., Figueira, I., Marques-Portella, C., Luz, M. P., Neylan, T. C., . . . Mendlowicz, M. V. (2011). Rescuers at risk: A systematic review and meta-regression analysis of the worldwide current prevalence and correlates of PTSD in rescue workers. *Social Psychiatry and Psychiatric Epidemiology, 47,* 1001–1011.

Bergfeld, I. O., Mantione, M., Hoogendoorn, M. L., Ruhé, H. G., Notten, P., van Laarhoven, J., . . . Schene, A. H. (2016). Deep brain stimulation of the ventral anterior limb of the internal capsule for treatment-resistant depression: A randomized clinical trial. *JAMA Psychiatry, 73,* 456–464.

Bergh, C., Sjöstedt, S., Hellers, G., Zandian, M., & Södersten, P. (2003). Meal size, satiety and cholecystokinin in gastrectomized humans. *Physiology & Behavior, 78,* 143–147.

Bernard, L. L. (1926). *An introduction to social psychology.* New York, NY: Henry Holt.

Bernier, A., Carlson, S. M., & Whipple, N. (2010). From external regulation to self-regulation: Early parenting precursors of young children's executive functioning. *Child Development, 81,* 326–229.

Berry, J. W. (1997). Immigration, acculturation, and adaptation. *Applied Psychology: An International Review, 46,* 5–68.

Berry, R. B., Brooks, R., Gamald, C. E., Harding, S. M., Lloyd, R. M., Marcus, C. L., & Vaughn, B. V., for the American Academy of Sleep Medicine. (2016). *The AASM manual for the scoring of sleep and associated events: Rules, terminology, and technical specifications* (Version 2.3). Darien, IL: American Academy of Sleep Medicine.

Berry, T. D., Mitteer, D. R., & Fournier, A. K. (2015). Examining hand-washing rates and durations in public restrooms: A study of gender differences via personal, environmental, and behavioral determinants. *Environment and Behavior, 47,* 923–944.

Berscheid, E. (2010). Love in the fourth dimension. *Annual Review of Psychology, 61,* 1–25.

Berthoz, S., Blair, R. J. R., Le Clec'h, G., & Martinot, J.-L. (2002). Emotions: From neuropsychology to functional imaging. *International Journal of Psychology, 37,* 193–203.

Berwick, R. C., Friederici, A. D., Chomsky, N., & Bolhuis, J. J. (2013). Evolution, brain, and the nature of language. *Trends in Cognitive Sciences, 17,* 89–98.

Besedovsky, L., Lange, T., & Born, J. (2012). Sleep and immune function. *Pflügers Archiv—European Journal of Physiology, 463,* 1–17.

Bezdjian, S., Baker, L. A., & Tuvblad, C. (2011). Genetic and environmental influences on impulsivity: A meta-analysis of twin, family and adoption studies. *Clinical Psychology Review, 31,* 1209–1223.

Bezdjian, S., Tuvblad, C., Raine, A., & Baker, L. A. (2011). The genetic and environmental covariation among psychopathic personality traits, and reactive and proactive aggression in childhood. *Child Development, 82,* 1267–1281.

Bialystok, E. (2011). Reshaping the mind: The benefits of bilingualism. *Canadian Journal of Experimental Psychology, 65,* 229–235.

Bialystok, E., Poarch, G., Luo, L., & Craik, F. I. (2014). Effects of bilingualism and aging on executive function and working memory. *Psychology and Aging, 29,* 696–705.

Bieniek, K. F., Ross, O. A., Cormier, K. A., Walton, R. L., Soto-Ortolaza, A., Johnston, A. E., . . . Rademakers, R. (2015). Chronic traumatic encephalopathy pathology in a neurodegenerative disorders brain bank. *Acta Neuropathologica, 130,* 877–889.

Bignall, W. J. R., Jacquez, F., & Vaughn, L. M. (2015). Attributions of mental illness: An ethnically diverse community perspective. *Community Mental Health Journal, 51,* 540–545.

Bihm, E. M., Gillaspy, J. A., Lammers, W. J., & Huffman, S. P. (2010). IQ zoo and teaching operant concepts. *Psychological Record, 60,* 523–526.

Binda, P., Pereverzeva, M., & Murray, S. O. (2013). Pupil constrictions to photographs of the sun. *Journal of Vision, 13*(6), 8, 1–9.

Birch, J. (2012). Worldwide prevalence of red-green color deficiency. *Journal of the Optical Society of America A, 29,* 313–320.

Bishara, D., Sauer, J., & Taylor, D. (2015). The pharmacological management of Alzheimer's disease. *Progress in Neurology and Psychiatry, 19,* 9–16.

Blackmore, S. J. (2005). *Consciousness: A very short introduction.* New York, NY: Oxford University Press.

Blair, C., & Raver, C. C. (2012). Child development in the context of adversity: Experiential canalization of brain and behavior. *American Psychologist, 67,* 309–318. doi:10.1037/a0027493

Blair, C., & Raver, C. C. (2015). School readiness and self-regulation: A developmental psychobiological approach. *Annual Review of Psychology, 66,* 711–731.

Blake, A. B., Nazarian, M., & Castel, A. D. (2015). The Apple of the mind's eye: Everyday attention, metamemory, and reconstructive memory for the Apple logo. *Quarterly Journal of Experimental Psychology, 68,* 858–865.

Blakemore, E. (2016, June 9). The world's "ugliest" color could help people quit smoking. *Smithsonian.com.* Retrieved from http://www.smithsonianmag.com/smartnews/worlds-ugliest-color-could-help-people-quit-smoking-180959364/?no-ist

Blanchard, R. (2008). Review and theory of handedness, birth order, and homosexuality in men. *Laterality, 13,* 51–70.

Blanchard, R. (2014). Detecting and correcting for family size differences in the study of sexual orientation and fraternal birth order. *Archives of Sexual Behavior, 43*(5), 845–852.

Blanchard, S., & Muller, C. (2015). Gatekeepers of the American dream: How teachers' perceptions shape the academic outcomes of immigrant and language minority students. *Social Science Research, 51,* 262–275.

Blasi, A. (1980). Bridging moral cognition and moral action: A critical review of the literature. *Psychological Bulletin, 88,* 1–45.

Blasi, G., Selvaggi, P., Fazio, L., Antonucci, L. A., Taurisano, P., Maşellis, R., . . . Popolizio, T. (2015). Variation in dopamine D2 and serotonin 5-HT2A receptor genes is associated with working memory processing and response to treatment with antipsychotics. *Neuropsychopharmacology, 40,* 1600–1608.

Blass, T. (1991). Understanding behavior in the Milgram obedience experiment: The role of personality, situations, and their interactions. *Journal of Personality and Social Psychology, 60,* 398–413.

Blass, T. (1999). The Milgram paradigm after 35 years: Some things we now know about obedience to authority. *Journal of Applied Social Psychology, 25,* 955–978.

Blass, T. (2004). *The man who shocked the world: The life and legacy of Stanley Milgram.* New York, NY: Basic Books.

Blaszczak-Boxe, A. (2017, February/March). The dark side of emotional intelligence. *Scientific American Mind, 28,* 9.

Blatchley, B., & O'Brien, K. R. (2007). Deceiving the participant: Are we creating the reputational spillover effect? *North American Journal of Psychology, 9,* 519–534.

Bliese, P. D., Edwards, J. R., & Sonnentag, S. (2017). Stress and well-being at work: A century of empirical trends reflecting theoretical and societal influences. *Journal of Applied Psychology, 102,* 389–402.

BlinkNow. (n.d.). *Women's Center.* Retrieved from http://www.blinknow.org/pages/womens-center

Bliss-Moreau, E., Bauman, M. D., & Amaral, D. G. (2011). Neonatal amygdala lesions result in globally blunted affect in adult rhesus macaques. *Behavioral Neuroscience, 125,* 848–858.

Bloch, M. H., McGuire, J., Landeros-Weisenberger, A., Leckman, J. F., & Pittenger, C. (2010). Meta-analysis of the dose-reponse relationship of SSRI in obsessive-compulsive disorder. *Molecular Psychiatry, 15,* 850–855.

Block, C. J., Koch, S. M., Liberman, B. E., Merriweather, T. J., & Roberson, L. (2011). Contending with stereotype threat at work: A model of long-term responses. *Counseling Psychologist, 39,* 570–600.

Blom E., Boerma T., Bosma E., Cornips, L., & Everaert, E. (2017). Cognitive advantages of bilingual children in different sociolinguistic contexts. *Frontiers in Psychology, 8.* doi:10.3389/fpsyg.2017.00552

Bloom, D. (2016, November 8). Instead of detention, these students get meditation. *CNN.* Retrieved from http://www.cnn.com/2016/11/04/health/meditation-in-schools-baltimore/

Blumenthal, H., Leen-Feldner, E. W., Babson, K. A., Gahr, J. L., Trainor, C. D., & Frala, J. L. (2011). Elevated social anxiety among early maturing girls. *Developmental Psychology, 47,* 1133–1140.

Boardman, M. (2015, April 3). Kendrick Lamar opens up about depression, suicidal thoughts: Watch. *US Weekly.* Retrieved from http://www.usmagazine.com/celebrity-news/news/kendrick-lamar-opens-up-about-depression-suicidal-thoughtswatch-201534

Boccella, K. (2012, May 6). Blindness is no barrier for Center City triathlete. *The Philadelphia Inquirer.* Retrieved from http://articles.philly.com/2012-05-06/news/31587179_1_husband-retinal-cancer-guide/3

Boehnke, K. F., Litinas, E., & Clauw, D. J. (2016). Medical cannabis use is associated with decreased opiate medication use in a retrospective cross-sectional survey of patients with chronic pain. *The Journal of Pain, 17,* 739–744.

Boeve, B. F., Silber, M. H., Saper, C. B., Ferman, T. J., Dickson, D. W., Parisi, J. E., . . . Braak, H. (2007). Pathophysiology of REM sleep behaviour disorder and relevance to neurodegenerative disease. *Brain, 130,* 2770–2788.

Bold, K. W., Kong, G., Camenga, D. R., Simon, P., Cavallo, D. A., Morean, M. E., & Krishnan-Sarin, S. (2017). Trajectories of e-cigarette and conventional cigarette use among youth. *Pediatrics, 141*(1). doi:10.1542/peds.2017-1832

Bold, K. W., Yoon, H., Chapman, G. B., & McCarthy, D. E. (2013). Factors predicting smoking in a laboratory-based smoking-choice task. *Experimental and Clinical Psychopharmacology, 21,* 133–143. doi:10.1037/a0031559

Bonanno, G. A., Westphal, M., & Mancini, A. D. (2011). Resilience to loss and potential trauma. *Annual Review of Clinical Psychology, 7,* 1.1–1.25.

Bond, R., & Smith, P. B. (1996). Culture and conformity: A meta-analysis of studies using Asch's (1952b, 1956) line judgment task. *Psychological Bulletin, 119,* 111–137.

Bongers, P., van den Akker, K., Havermans, R., & Jansen, A. (2015). Emotional eating and Pavlovian learning: Does negative mood facilitate appetitive conditioning? *Appetite, 89,* 226–236.

Bonnet, L., Comte, A., Tatu, L., Millot, J. L., Moulin, T., & de Bustos, E. M. (2015). The role of the amygdala in the perception of positive emotions: An "intensity detector." *Frontiers in Behavioral Neuroscience, 9.* doi:10.3389/fnbeh.2015.00178

Bonnie, R. J., & Scott, E. S. (2013). The teenage brain: Adolescent brain research and the law. *Current Directions in Psychological Science, 22,* 158–161.

Boomsma, D. I., Helmer, Q., Nieuwboer, H. A., Hottenga, J. J., de Moor, M. H., van den Berg, S. M., . . . de Geus, E. J. (2018). An extended twin-pedigree study of neuroticism in the Netherlands Twin Register. *Behavior Genetics, 48,* 1–11.

Boothroyd, L. G., Meins, E., Vukovic, J., & Burt, D. M. (2014). Developmental changes in children's facial preferences. *Evolution and Human Behavior, 35,* 376–383.

Borbély, A. A., Daan, S., Wirz-Justice, A., & Deboer, T. (2016). The two-process model of sleep regulation: A reappraisal. *Journal of Sleep Research, 25,* 131–143.

Bordier, A., Futerman, S., & Pulitzer, L. (2014). *Separated @ birth: A true love story of twin sisters reunited.* New York, NY: G.P. Putnam's Sons.

Borges, G., Nock, M. K., Abad, J. M. H., Hwang, I., Sampson, N. A., Alonso, J., . . . Kessler, R. C. (2010). Twelve month prevalence of and risk factors for suicide attempts in the WHO world mental health surveys. *Journal of Clinical Psychiatry, 71,* 1617–1628.

Boring, E. G. (1953). A history of introspection. *Psychological Bulletin, 50,* 169–189.

Borota, D., Murray, E., Keceli, G., Chang, A., Watabe, J. M., Ly, M., Toscano, J. P., & Yassa, M. A. (2014). Post-study caffeine administration enhances memory consolidation in humans. *Nature Neuroscience, 17,* 201–203.

Borra, J. E. (2005). *Roper v. Simmons. Journal of Gender, Social Policy, & the Law, 13,* 707–715.

Bos, H., van Gelderen, L., & Gartrell, N. (2015). Lesbian and heterosexual two-parent families: Adolescent–parent relationship quality and adolescent well-being. *Journal of Child and Family Studies, 24,* 1031–1046.

Boscamp, E. (2013, July 11). Dining etiquette from around the world. *Huffington Post.* Retrieved from http://www.huffingtonpost.com/2013/07/11/dining-etiquette-around-the-world_n_3567015.html

Botta, P., Demmou, L., Kasugai, Y., Markovic, M., Xu, C., Fadok, J. P., . . . Lüthi, A. (2015). Regulating anxiety with extrasynaptic inhibition. *Nature Neuroscience, 18,* 1493–1500.

Bouchard, T. J., Jr., Lykken, D. T., McGue, M., Segal, N. L., & Tellegen, A. (1990). Sources of human psychological differences: The Minnesota Study of Twins Reared Apart. *Science, 250,* 223–228.

Boureau, Y. L., Sokol-Hessner, P., & Daw, N. D. (2015). Deciding how to decide: Self-control and meta-decision making. *Trends in Cognitive Sciences, 19,* 700–710.

Bourgeois, A., Neveu, R., & Vuilleumier, P. (2016). How does awareness modulate goal-directed and stimulus-driven shifts of attention triggered by value learning? *PLoS One, 11*(8), e0160469.

Bouton, C. E., Shaikhouni, A., Annetta, N. V., Bockbrader, M. A., Friedenberg, D. A., Nielson, D. M., . . . Rezai, A. R. (2016). Restoring cortical control of functional movement in a human with quadriplegia. *Nature, 533,* 247–250.

Bouton, M. E., Mineka, S., & Barlow, D. H. (2001). A modern learning theory perspective on the etiology of panic disorder. *Psychological Review, 108,* 4–32.

Bowden, C. L., Calabrese, J. R., McElroy, S. L., Gyulai, L., Wassef, A., Petty, F., . . . Wozniak, P. J. (2000). A randomized, placebo-controlled 12-month trial of divalproex and lithium in treatment of outpatients with bipolar I disorder. *Archives of General Psychiatry, 57,* 481–489.

Bower, B. (2013, May 21). Dog sniffs out grammar. *ScienceNews.* Retrieved from https://www.sciencenews.org/article/dog-sniffs-out-grammar

Bower, G. H., Clark, M. C., Lesgold, A. M., & Winzenz, D. (1969). Hierarchical retrieval schemes and recall of categorized word lists. *Journal of Verbal Learning and Verbal Behavior, 8,* 323–343.

Bower, G. H., Gilligan, S. G., & Menteiro, K. P. (1981). Selectivity of learning caused by affective states. *Journal of Experimental Psychology: General, 110,* 451–473.

Bowers, J. S., Mattys, S. L., & Gage, S. H. (2009). Preserved implicit knowledge of a forgotten childhood language. *Psychological Science, 20,* 1064–1069.

Bradley, L. A. (2011). Culture, gender and clothing. *Paideusis-Journal for Interdisciplinary and Cross-Cultural Studies, 5,* A1–A6.

Brady, S. T., Reeves, S. L., Garcia, J., Purdie-Vaughns, V., Cook, J. E., Taborsky-Barba, S., . . . Cohen, G. L. (2016). The psychology of the affirmed learner: Spontaneous self-affirmation in the face of stress. *Journal of Educational Psychology, 108,* 353–373.

Bragard, I., Dupuis, G., & Fleet, R. (2015). Quality of work life, burnout, and stress in emergency department physicians: A qualitative review. *European Journal of Emergency Medicine, 22,* 227–234.

Branch, J. (2016, March 3). Brandi Chastain to donate her brain for C.T.E. research. *The New York Times.* Retrieved from http://www.nytimes.com/2016/03/04/sports/soccer/brandi-chastain-to-donate-her-brain-for-cte-research.html?_r=0

Brandone, A. C., Salkind, S. J., Golinkoff, R. M., & Hirsh-Pasek, K. (2006). Language development. In G. G. Bear & K. M. Minke (Eds.), *Children's needs III: Development, prevention, and intervention* (pp. 499–514). Washington, DC: National Association of School Psychologists.

Brandt, J., & Benedict, R. H. B. (1993). Assessment of retrograde amnesia: Findings with a new public events procedure. *Neuropsychology, 7,* 217–227.

Branje, S. (2018). Development of parent–adolescent relationships: Conflict interactions as a mechanism of change. *Child Development Perspectives. 12*(3), 171–176.

Brann, J. H., & Firestein, S. J. (2014). A lifetime of neurogenesis in the olfactory system. *Frontiers in Neuroscience, 8.* Retrieved from http://dx.doi.org/10.3389/fnins.2014.00182

Brascamp, J. W., Blake, R., & Kristjánsson, A. (2011). Deciding where to attend: Priming of pop-out drives target selection. *Journal of Experimental Psychology: Human Perception and Performance, 37,* 1700–1707.

Brase, G. L. (2017). Emotional reactions to conditional rules of reciprocal altruism. *Evolutionary Behavioral Sciences, 11,* 294–308.

Breastcancer.org. (2017, March 10). *U.S. breast cancer statistics.* Retrieved from http://www.breastcancer.org/symptoms/understand_bc/statistics

Breeden, P. (n.d.). Dog whispering in the 20th century [Web log post]. Retrieved from https://biologyofbehavior.wordpress.com/dog-whispering-in-the-21st-century/

Breedlove, S. M. (2017). Prenatal influences on human sexual orientation: Expectations versus data. *Archives of Sexual Behavior, 46,* 1583–1592.

Breland, K., & Breland, M. (1951). A field of applied animal psychology. *American Psychologist, 6,* 202–204.

Breland, K., & Breland, M. (1961). The misbehavior of organisms. *American Psychologist, 16,* 681–684.

Bremner, J. G., Slater, A., & Johnson, S. (2015). Perception of object persistence: The origins of object permanence in infancy. *Child Development Perspectives, 9,* 7–13.

Brendgen, M., Dionne, G., Girard, A., Boivin, M., Vitaro, F., & Pérusse, D. (2005). Examining genetic and environmental effects on social aggression: A study of 6-year-old twins. *Child Development, 76,* 930–946.

Brent, R. L. (2004). Environmental causes of human congenital malformations: The pediatrician's role in dealing with these complex clinical problems caused by a multiplicity of environmental and genetic factors. *Pediatrics, 113,* 957–968.

Breslau, J., Cefalu, M., Wong, E. C., Burnam, M. A., Hunter, G. P., & Collins, R. L. (2017). Racial/ethnic differences in perception of need for mental health treatment in a US national sample. *Social Psychiatry and Psychiatric Epidemiology, 52,* 929–937.

Breus, M. J. (2009, May 6). Are you fooling yourself? [Huffpost Healthy Living]. *Huffington Post.* Retrieved from http://www.huffingtonpost.com/dr-michael-jbreus/are-you-fooling-yourself_b_198525.html

Brewin, C. R., & Andrews, B. (2014). Why it is scientifically respectable to believe in repression: A response to Patihis, Ho, Tingen, Lilienfeld, and Loftus (2014). *Psychological Science, 25,* 1964–1966.

Bridge, H., Harrold, S., Holmes, E. A., Stokes, M., & Kennard, C. (2012). Vivid visual mental imagery in the absence of the primary visual cortex. *Journal of Neurology, 259,* 1062–1070.

Briere, J., Agee, E., & Dietrich, A. (2016). Cumulative trauma and current posttraumatic stress disorder status in general population and inmate samples. *Psychological Trauma: Theory, Research, Practice, and Policy, 8,* 439–446.

Briggs, K. C., & Myers, I. B. (1998). *Myers–Briggs type indicator.* Palo Alto, CA: Consulting Psychologists Press.

Briley, D. A., & Tucker-Drob, E. M. (2014). Genetic and environmental continuity in personality development: A meta-analysis. *Psychological Bulletin, 140,* 1303–1331.

Britton, W. B., Lepp, N. E., Niles, H. F., Rocha, T., Fisher, N., & Gold, J. (2014). A randomized controlled pilot trial of classroom-based mindfulness meditation compared to an active control condition in 6th grade children. *Journal of School Psychology, 52,* 263–278.

Broadbelt, K. G., Paterson, D. S., Rivera, K. D., Trachtenberg, F. L., & Kinney, H. C. (2010). Neuroanatomic relationships between the GABAergic and serotonergic systems in the developing human medulla. *Autonomic Neuroscience: Basic & Clinical, 154,* 30–41.

Brody, S. (2010). The relative health benefits of different sexual activities. *Journal of Sexual Medicine, 7,* 1336–1361.

Brody, S., & Costa, R. M. (2009). Satisfaction (sexual, life, relationship, and mental health) is associated directly with penile-vaginal intercourse, but inversely with other sexual behavior frequencies. *The Journal of Sexual Medicine, 6,* 1947–1954.

Brogaard, P., & Marlow, K. (2012, December 11). Kim Peek, the real rain man [Web log post]. Retrieved from http://www.psychologytoday.com/blog/the-superhuman-mind/201212/kim-peek-the-real-rain-man

Brooks, A. C. (2018, January 21). Empathize with your political foe. *The New York Times.* Retrieved from https://www.nytimes.com/2018/01/21/opinion/empathize-with-your-political-foe.html

Brooks, J. E., & Neville, H. A. (2016). Interracial attraction among college men: The influence of ideologies, familiarity, and similarity. *Journal of Social and Personal Relationships.* doi:10.1177/0265407515627508

Brothers, J. R., & Lohmann, K. J. (2015). Evidence for geomagnetic imprinting and magnetic navigation in the natal homing of sea turtles. *Current Biology, 25,* 392–396.

Brotto, L. A. (2010). The DSM diagnostic criteria for hypoactive sexual desire disorder in men. *Journal of Sex Medicine, 7,* 2015–2030.

Brouwer, R. M., Koenis, M. M. G., Schnack, H. G., van Baal, G. C., van Soelen, I. L., Boomsma, D. I., & Pol, H. E. H. (2015). Longitudinal development of hormone levels and grey matter density in 9- and 12-year-old twins. *Behavior Genetics, 45,* 313–323.

Brown, A. S., & Nix, L. A. (1996). Age-related changes in the tip-of-the-tongue experience. *American Journal of Psychology, 109,* 79–91.

Brown, A. S., & Patterson, P. H. (2011). Maternal infection and schizophrenia: Implications for prevention. *Schizophrenia Bulletin, 37,* 284–290.

Brown, C. C., Raio, C. M., & Neta, M. (2017). Cortisol responses enhance negative valence perception for ambiguous facial expressions. *Scientific Reports, 7,* 15107. doi:http://10.1038/s41598-017-14846-3

Brown, P. K., & Wald, G. (1964). Visual pigments in single rods and cones of the human retina. *Science, 144,* 45.

Brown, R. (2017, May 4). Your iPhone could really mess up your baby. *New York Post.* Retrieved from http://nypost.com/2017/05/04/your-iphone-could-really-mess-up-your-baby/

Brown, R., & Kulik, J. (1977). Flashbulb memories. *Cognition, 5,* 73–99.

Brown, S. L., Nesse, R. M., Vinokur, A. D., & Smith, D. M. (2003). Providing social support may be more beneficial than receiving it: Results from a prospective study of mortality. *Psychological Science, 14,* 320–327.

Brown, T. T., & Dobs, A. S. (2002). Endocrine effects of marijuana. *Journal of Clinical Pharmacology, 42,* 90S–96S.

Brownell, P. (2010). *Gestalt therapy: A guide to contemporary practice.* New York, NY: Springer.

Brownlee, W. J., Hardy, T. A., Fazekas, F., & Miller, D. H. (2017). Diagnosis of multiple sclerosis: Progress and challenges. *The Lancet, 389,* 1336–1346.

Brummelman, E., Thomaes, S., Nelemans, S. A., Orobio de Castro, B., Overbeek, G., & Bushmane, B. J. (2015). Origins of narcissism in children. *Proceedings of the National Academy of Sciences, 112,* 3659–3662.

Brusewitz, G., Cherkas, L., Harris, J., & Parker, A. (2013). Exceptional experiences amongst twins. *Journal of the Society for Psychical Research, 77,* 220–235.

Buchanan, L. R., Rooks-Peck, C. R., Finnie, R. K., Wethington, H. R., Jacob, V., Fulton, J. E., . . . Glanz, K. (2016). Reducing recreational sedentary screen time: A community guide systematic review. *American Journal of Preventive Medicine, 50,* 402–415.

Buchanan, T. W., Tranel, D., & Adolphs, R. (2004). Anteromedial temporal lobe damage blocks startle modulation by fear and disgust. *Behavioral Neuroscience, 188,* 429–437.

Buck, R. (1980). Nonverbal behavior and the theory of emotion: The facial feedback hypothesis. *Journal of Personality and Social Psychology, 38,* 811–824.

Buckle, C. E., Udawatta, V., & Straus, C. M. (2013). Now you see it, now you don't: Visual illusions in radiology. *Radiographics, 33,* 2087–2102.

Buettner, D. (2015). *The Blue Zones solution.* Washington, DC: National Geographic.

Buffardi, L. E., & Campbell, W. K. (2008). Narcissism and social networking web sites. *Personality and Social Psychology Bulletin, 34,* 1303–1314.

Bufka, L. F., & Halfond, R. (2016). Professional standards and guidelines. In J. C. Norcross, G. R. VandenBos, D. K. Freedheim, & L. E. Campbell (Eds.), *APA handbook of clinical psychology: Education and profession* (Vol. 5, pp. 355–373). Washington, DC: American Psychological Association.

Bui, N. H. (2012). False consensus in attitudes toward celebrities. *Psychology of Popular Media Culture, 1,* 236–243. doi:10.1037/a0028569

Bulik, C. M., Kleiman, S. C., & Yilmaz, Z. (2016). Genetic epidemiology of eating disorders. *Current Opinion in Psychiatry, 29,* 383.

Bulpitt, C. J., Markowe, H. L. J., & Shipley, M. J. (2001). Why do some people look older than they should? *Postgraduate Medical Journal, 77,* 578–581.

Burda, J. E., Bernstein, A. M., & Sofroniew, M. V. (2016). Astrocyte roles in traumatic brain injury. *Experimental Neurology, 275,* 305–315.

Bureau of Labor Statistics, U.S. Department of Labor. (2014). *Employment Projections Program. Employment by industry, occupation, and percent distribution, 2014 and projected 2024: 19-3030 Psychologists.* Retrieved from http://www.bls.gov/emp/ind-occ-matrix/occ_xlsx/occ_19-3030.xlsx

Bureau of Labor Statistics, U.S. Department of Labor. (2017–2018). *Occupational outlook handbook.* Retrieved from http://www.bls.gov/ooh

Burger, J. M. (2009). Replicating Milgram: Would people still obey today? *American Psychologist, 64,* 1–11.

Burger, J. M. (2015). *Personality* (9th ed.). Belmont, CA: Wadsworth, Cengage Learning.

Burlingame, G. M., & Baldwin, S. (2011). Group therapy. In J. C. Norcross, G. R. VandenBos, & D. K. Freedheim (Eds.), *History of psychotherapy: Continuity and change* (2nd ed., pp. 505–515). Washington, DC: American Psychological Association.

Burnette, J. L., Pollack, J. M., & Forsyth, D. R. (2011). Leadership in extreme contexts: A groupthink analysis of the May 1996 Mount Everest disaster. *Journal of Leadership Studies, 4,* 29–40.

Burstein, A. G., & Loucks, S. (1989). *Rorschach's test: Scoring and interpretation.* New York, NY: Hemisphere.

Burton, H. (2003). Visual cortex activity in early and late blind people. *Journal of Neuroscience, 23,* 4005–4011.

Burzynska, A. Z., Jiao, Y., Knecht, A. M., Fanning, J., Awick, E. A., Chen, T., . . . Kramer, A.F. (2017). White matter integrity declined over 6-months, but dance intervention improved integrity of the fornix of older adults. *Frontiers in Aging Neuroscience, 9*(59). doi:10.3389/fnagi.2017.00059

Bushdid, C., Magnasco, M. O., Vosshall, L. B., & Keller, A. (2014). Humans can discriminate more than 1 trillion olfactory stimuli. *Science, 343,* 1370–1372.

Bushman, B. J., Newman, K., Calvert, S. L., Downey, G., Dredze, M., Gottfredson, M., . . . Romer, D. (2016). Youth violence: What we know and what we need to know. *American Psychologist, 71,* 17–39.

Buss, D. M., & Penke, L. (2015). Evolutionary personality psychology. In M. Mikulincer, P. R. Shaver, M. L. Cooper, & R. J. Larsen (Eds.), *APA handbook of personality and social psychology* (Vol. 4, pp. 3–29). Washington, DC: American Psychological Association.

Buss, L., Tolstrup, J., Munk, C., Bergholt, T., Ottensen, B., Grønbæk, M., & Kjaer, S. K. (2006). Spontaneous abortion: A prospective cohort study of younger women from the general population in Denmark. Validation, occurrence and risk determinants. *Acta Obstetricia et Gynecologic, 85,* 467–475.

Bussey, K., & Bandura, A. (1999). Social cognitive theory of gender development and differentiation. *Psychological Review, 106,* 676–713.

Butcher, J. N., & Rouse, S. V. (1996). Personality: Individual differences and clinical assessment. *Annual Review of Psychology, 47,* 87–111.

Butler, A. C., Zaromb, F. M., Lyle, K. B., & Roediger, H. L. (2009). Using popular films to enhance classroom learning. *Psychological Science, 20*(9), 1161–1168.

Butler, J. (2015). Hypnosis for dental professionals. *BDJ Team, 1.* doi:10.1038/bdjteam.2015.28

Butler, R. A. (1960). Acquired drives and the curiosity-investigative motives. In R. H. Waters, D. A. Rethlingshafer, & W. E. Caldwell (Eds.), *Principles of comparative psychology* (pp. 144–176) (McGraw-Hill Series in Psychology). New York, NY: McGraw-Hill.

Cabral, R. R., & Smith, T. B. (2011). Racial/ethnic matching of clients and therapists in mental health services: A meta-analytic review of preferences, perceptions, and outcomes. *Journal of Counseling Psychology, 58,* 537–554.

Cain, M. S., Leonard, J. A., Gabrieli, J. D., & Finn, A. S. (2016). Media multitasking in adolescence. *Psychonomic Bulletin & Review,* 1–10. doi:10.3758/s13423-016- 1036-3

Calabrese, M., Magliozzi, R., Ciccarelli, O., Geurts, J. J., Reynolds, R., & Martin, R. (2015). Exploring the origins of grey matter damage in multiple sclerosis. *Nature Reviews Neuroscience, 16,* 147–158.

Calfas, J. (2017, May 11). Do fidget spinners really help with ADHD? Nope, experts say. *Money.* Retrieved from http://time.com/money/4774133/fidget-spinners-adhd-anxiety-stress/

Callan, M. J., Ferguson, H. J., & Bindemann, M. (2013). Eye movements to audiovisual scenes reveal expectations of a just world. *Journal of Experimental Psychology: General, 142,* 34–40. doi:10.1037/a0028261

Camarota, S. A., & Zeigler, K. (2016, October). Immigrants in the United States: A profile of the foreign-born using 2014 and 2015 Census Bureau data. Center for Immigration Studies. Retrieved from https://cis.org/sites/cis.org/files/immigrant-profile_0.pdf

Campbell, A. (1999). Staying alive: Evolution, culture, and women's intrasexual aggression. *Behavioral and Brain Sciences, 22,* 203–252.

Campbell, G. A., & Rosner, M. H. (2008). The agony of ecstasy: MDMA (3,4-Methylenedioxymethamphetamine) and the kidney. *Clinical Journal of the American Society of Nephrology, 3,* 1852–1860.

Campbell, L. F., Norcross, J. C., Vasquez, M. J. T., & Kaslow, N. J. (2013). Recognition of psychotherapy effectiveness: The APA resolution. *Psychotherapy, 50,* 98–101.

Campos, F., Sobrino, T., Ramos-Cabrer, P., Argibay, B., Agulla, J., Pérez-Mato, M., . . . Castillo, J. (2011). Neuroprotection by glutamate oxaloacetate transaminase in ischemic stroke: An experimental study. *Journal of Cerebral Blood Flow & Metabolism, 31,* 1378–1386.

Cannon, D. S., Baker, T. B., Gino, A., & Nathan, P. E. (1986). Alcohol-aversion therapy: Relation between strength of aversion and abstinence. *Journal of Consulting and Clinical Psychology, 54,* 825–830.

Cannon, W. B. (1927). The James-Lange theory of emotions: A critical examination and an alternative theory. *American Journal of Psychology, 39,* 106–124.

Cannon, W. B., & Washburn, A. L. (1912). An explanation of hunger. *American Journal of Physiology, 29,* 441–454.

Cantero, J. L., Atienza, M., Salas, R. M., & Gómez, C. M. (1999). Alpha EEG coherence in different brain states: An electrophysiological index of the arousal level in human subjects. *Neuroscience Letters, 271,* 167–170.

Caporro, M., Haneef, Z., Yeh, H. J., Lenartowicz, A., Buttinelli, C., Parvizi, J., & Stern, J. M. (2012). Functional MRI of sleep spindles and K-complexes. *Clinical Neurophysiology, 123*(2), 303–309.

Carbon, C. C. (2014). Understanding human perception by human-made illusions. *Frontiers in Human Neuroscience, 8.* Retrieved from http://dx.doi.org/10.3389/fnhum.2014.00566

Cardno, A. G., & Owen, M. J. (2014). Genetic relationships between schizophrenia, bipolar disorder, and schizoaffective disorder. *Schizophrenia Bulletin, 40,* 504–515.

Carey, B. (2008, December 4). H.M., an unforgettable amnesiac, dies at 82. *The New York Times.* Retrieved from http://www.nytimes.com/2008/12/05/us/05hm.html?pagewanted=all&_r=0

Carlbring, P., Andersson, G., Cuijpers, P., Riper, H., & Hedman-Lagerlöf, E. (2018). Internet-based vs. face-to-face cognitive behavior therapy for psychiatric and somatic disorders: An updated systematic review and meta-analysis. *Cognitive Behaviour Therapy, 47,* 1–18. doi:10.1080/16506073.2017.1401115

Carr, K., Kendal, R. L., & Flynn, E. G. (2015). Imitate or innovate? Children's innovation is influenced by the efficacy of observed behaviour. *Cognition, 142,* 322–332.

Carr, P. B., Dweck, C. S., & Pauker, K. (2012). "Prejudiced" behavior without prejudice? Beliefs about the malleability of prejudice affect interracial interactions. *Journal of Personality and Social Psychology, 103,* 452–471.

Carrier, L. M., Rosen, L. D., Cheever, N. A., & Lim, A. F. (2015). Causes, effects, and practicalities of everyday multitasking. *Developmental Review, 35,* 64–78.

Carroll, R. (2016, July 14). Starved, tortured, forgotten: Genie, the feral child who left a mark on researchers. *The Guardian.* Retrieved from https://www.theguardian.com/society/2016/jul/14/genie-feral-child-los-angeles-researchers

Carson, H. (2011). *Captain for life: My story as a Hall of Fame linebacker.* New York, NY: St. Martin's Press.

Carstensen, L. L., Turan, B., Scheibe, S., Ram, N., Ersner-Hershfield, H., Samanez-Larkin, G. R., . . . Nesselroade, J. R. (2011). Emotional experience improves with age: Evidence based on over 10 years of experience sampling. *Psychology and Aging, 26,* 21–33.

Carter, B. D., Abnet, C. C., Feskanich, D., Freedman, N. D., Hartge, P., Lewis, C. D., . . . Jacobs, E. J. (2015). Smoking and mortality—beyond established causes. *New England Journal of Medicine, 372,* 631–640.

Carter, C. J. (2007). eIF2B and oligodendrocyte survival: Where nature and nurture meet in bipolar disorder and schizophrenia? *Schizophrenia Bulletin, 33,* 1343–1353.

Caruso, C. (2017, February/March). Slo-mo made him do it. *Scientific American Mind, 28,* 13.

Caruso, E. M., Burns, Z. C., & Converse, B. A. (2016). Slow motion increases perceived intent. *Proceedings of the National Academy of Sciences USA, 113*(33), 9250–9255.

Caruso, J. P., & Sheehan, J. P. (2017). Psychosurgery, ethics, and media: A history of Walter Freeman and the lobotomy. *Neurosurgical Focus, 43.* doi:10.3171/2017.6.FOCUS17257

Caruso, R. (2007, August 13). Why does it take so long for our vision to adjust to a darkened theater after we come in from bright sunlight? *Scientific American Online.* Retrieved from http://www.scientificamerican.com/article.cfm?id=experts-eyes-adjust-to-darkness

Case, B. G., Bertollo, D. N., Laska, E. M., Price, L. H., Siegel, C. E., Olfson, M., & Marcus, S. C. (2013). Declining use of electroconvulsive therapy in United States general hospitals. *Biological Psychiatry, 73,* 119–126.

Caspi, A., Roberts, B. W., & Shiner, R. L. (2005). Personality development: Stability and change. *Annual Review of Psychology, 56,* 453–484.

Cassidy, J. (2001). Truth, lies, and intimacy: An attachment perspective. *Attachment & Human Development, 3,* 121–155.

Castle, D. J., Bosanac, P., & Rossell, S. (2015). Treating OCD: What to do when first-line therapies fail. *Australasian Psychiatry, 23,* 350–353.

Catalino, L. I., & Fredrickson, B. L. (2011). A Tuesday in the life of a flourisher: The role of positive emotional reactivity in optimal mental health. *Emotion, 11,* 938–950.

Catanzaro, D., Chesbro, E. C., & Velkey, A. J. (2013). Relationship between food preferences and PROP taster status of college students. *Appetite, 68,* 124–131.

Cattell, R. B. (1950). *Personality: A systematic theoretical and factual study.* New York, NY: McGraw-Hill.

Cattell, R. B. (1973a). *Personality and mood by questionnaire.* San Francisco, CA: Jossey-Bass.

Cattell, R. B. (1973b). Personality pinned down. *Psychology Today, 7,* 40–46.

Cattell, R. B., Eber, H. W., & Tatsuoka, M. M. (1970). *Handbook for the sixteen personality factor questionnaire (16PF).* Champaign, IL: Institute for Personality and Ability Testing.

Catts, V. S., Lai, Y. L., Weickert, C. S., Weickert, T. W., & Catts, S. V. (2016). A quantitative review of the postmortem evidence for decreased cortical N-methyl-daspartate receptor expression levels in schizophrenia: How can we link molecular abnormalities to mismatch negativity deficits? *Biological Psychology, 116,* 57–67.

Cavadel, E. W., & Frye, D. A. (2017). Not just numeracy and literacy: Theory of mind development and school readiness among low-income children. *Developmental Psychology, 53,* 2290–2303.

Cavallini, A., Fazzi, E., Viviani, V., Astori, M. G., Zaverio, S., Bianchi, P. E., & Lanzi, G. (2002). Visual acuity in the first two years of life in healthy term newborns: An experience with the teller acuity cards. *Functional Neurology, 17,* 87–92.

Ceci, S., & Williams, W. M. (2009). Yes: The scientific truth must be pursued. *Nature, 457,* 788–789.

Celizic, M. (2010, June 7). Al's fit club: Roker on 115-pound loss. *Today Health.* Retrieved from http://www.today.com/id/37550535/ns/today-today_health/t/als-fit-club-roker-115-pound-loss/#.V7XCDpMrKkt

Center for Behavioral Health Statistics and Quality. (2015). *Behavioral health trends in the United States: Results from the 2014 National Survey on Drug Use and Health* (HHS Publication No. SMA 15-4927, NSDUH Series H-50). Retrieved from http://www.samhsa.gov/data/

Center for Behavioral Health Statistics and Quality. (2017). *2016 National Survey on Drug Use and Health: Detailed tables.* Rockville, MD: Substance Abuse and Mental Health Services Administration.

Centers for Disease Control and Prevention (CDC). (2013a). *Incidence, prevalence, and cost of sexually transmitted infections in the United States.* Retrieved from http://www.cdc.gov/std/stats/STI-Estimates-Fact-Sheet-Feb-2013.pdf

Centers for Disease Control and Prevention (CDC). (2013b). *Suicide myths.* Retrieved from https://www.cdc.gov/violenceprevention/suicide/holiday.html

Centers for Disease Control and Prevention (CDC). (2014). *Nursing home care.* Retrieved from http://www.cdc.gov/nchs/fastats/nursing-home-care.htm

Centers for Disease Control and Prevention (CDC). (2015a). *Genital herpes.* Retrieved from http://www.cdc.gov/std/Herpes/STDFact-Herpes.htm

Centers for Disease Control and Prevention (CDC). (2015b). *Gonorrhea.* Retrieved from http://www.cdc.gov/std/gonorrhea/STDFact-gonorrhea.htm

Centers for Disease Control and Prevention (CDC). (2015c). *Tobacco-related mortality* [Fact sheet]. Retrieved from http://www.cdc.gov/tobacco/data_statistics/fact_sheets/health_effects/tobacco_related_mortality/index.htm

Centers for Disease Control and Prevention (CDC). (2016a). *About teen pregnancy.* Retrieved from http://www.cdc.gov/teenpregnancy/about/index.htm

Centers for Disease Control and Prevention (CDC). (2016b). *Autism spectrum disorder: Data and statistics.* Retrieved from http://www.cdc.gov/ncbddd/autism/data.html

Centers for Disease Control and Prevention (CDC). (2016c). *Chlamydia.* Retrieved from http://www.cdc.gov/std/chlamydia/STDFact-chlamydia-detailed.htm

Centers for Disease Control and Prevention (CDC). (2016d). *Genital HPV infection.* Retrieved from http://www.cdc.gov/std/HPV/STDFact-HPV.htm

Centers for Disease Control and Prevention (CDC). (2016e). *Important milestones: Your baby at six months.* Retrieved from http://www.cdc.gov/ncbddd/actearly/milestones/milestones-6mo.html

Centers for Disease Control and Prevention (CDC). (2016f). *Syphilis.* Retrieved from http://www.cdc.gov/std/syphilis/STDFact-Syphilis.htm

Centers for Disease Control and Prevention (CDC). (2017). *Sexually transmitted diseases: Adolescents and young adults.* Retrieved from https://www.cdc.gov/std/life-stages-populations/adolescents-youngadults.htm

Centers for Disease Control and Prevention (CDC). (2017, January). *Health effects of secondhand smoke.* Retrieved from https://www.cdc.gov/tobacco/data_statistics/fact_sheets/secondhand_smoke/health_effects/index.htm

Centers for Disease Control and Prevention (CDC). (2017, June 16). *Impaired driving: Get the facts.* Retrieved from https://www.cdc.gov/motorvehiclesafety/impaired_driving/impaired-drv_factsheet.html

Centers for Disease Control and Prevention (CDC). (2017, March 17). *Leading causes of death.* Retrieved from https://www.cdc.gov/nchs/fastats/leading-causes-of-death.htm

Centers for Disease Control and Prevention (CDC). (2017, May 15). *Health effects of cigarette smoking.* Retrieved from https://www.cdc.gov/tobacco/data_statistics/fact_sheets/health_effects/effects_cig_smoking/index.htm

Centers for Disease Control and Prevention (CDC). (2017, October 3). *Suicide: Risk and protective factors.* Retrieved from https://www.cdc.gov/violenceprevention/suicide/riskprotectivefactors.html

Centers for Disease Control and Prevention (CDC). (2017, October 6). *Infant immunizations FAQs.* Retrieved from https://www.cdc.gov/vaccines/parents/parent-questions.html

Centers for Disease Control and Prevention (CDC). (2017, October 11). *HIV in the United States: At a glance.* Retrieved from https://www.cdc.gov/hiv/statistics/overview/ataglance.html

Centers for Disease Control and Prevention (CDC). (2018, June 7). Suicide rising across the US. *CDC Vitalsigns.* Retrieved from https://www.cdc.gov/vitalsigns/pdf/vs-0618-suicide-H.pdf

Centers for Disease Control and Prevention (CDC). (n.d.). *Current cigarette smoking among adults in the United States.* Retrieved from https://www.cdc.gov/tobacco/data_statistics/fact_sheets/adult_data/cig_smoking/index.htm

Centers for Disease Control and Prevention and National Center for Health Statistics (CDC/NCHS), National Vital Statistics System, Mortality. (2016). Overdose deaths involving opioids, United States, 2000–2015. *CDC WONDER.* Atlanta, GA: US Department of Health and Human Services, CDC. Retrieved from https://www.cdc.gov/drugoverdose/data/index.html

Centers for Disease Control and Prevention (CDC), National Center for Injury Prevention and Control. (2018, April 18). *WISQARS fatal injury and nonfatal injury: 10 leading causes of injury deaths by age group highlighting unintentional injury deaths, United States—2016.* Retrieved from https://www.cdc.gov/injury/wisqars/leadingcauses.html

Centola, D. (2010). The spread of behavior in an online social network experiment. *Science, 329,* 1194–1197.

Centre for Addiction and Mental Health. (2010). *LSD.* Retrieved from https://www.camh.ca/en/health-info/mental-illness-and-addiction-index/lsd

Cerasoli, C. P., Nicklin, J. M., & Ford, M. T. (2014). Intrinsic motivation and extrinsic incentives jointly predict performance: A 40-year meta-analysis. *Psychological Bulletin, 140,* 980–1008. Retrieved from http://dx.doi.org/10.1037/a0035661

Cerda-Molina, A. L., Hernández-López, L., de la O, C. E., Chavira-Ramírez, R., & Mondragón-Ceballos, R. (2013). Changes in men's salivary testosterone and cortisol levels, and in sexual desire after smelling female axillary and vulvar scents. *Frontiers in Endocrinology, 28,* Article 159. doi:10.3389/fendo.2013.00159

Cevallos, D. (2015, July 17). Don't rely on insanity defense. *CNN.* Retrieved from http://www.cnn.com/2015/02/11/opinion/cevallos-insanity-defense/

Chae, Y., Goodman, M., Goodman, G. S., Troxel, N., McWilliams, K., Thompson, R. A., . . . Widaman, K. F. (2018). How children remember the Strange Situation: The role of attachment. *Journal of Experimental Child Psychology, 166,* 360–379.

Chaiken, S., & Eagly, A. H. (1976). Communication modality as a determinant of message persuasiveness and message comprehensibility. *Journal of Personality and Social Psychology, 34,* 605–614.

Chaimay, B. (2011). Influence of breastfeeding practices on children's cognitive development—systematic review. *Asia Journal of Public Health, 2,* 40–44.

Chamberlain, R., Drake, J. E., Kozbelt, A., Hickman, R., Siev, J., & Wagemans, J. (2018). Artists as experts in visual cognition: An update. *Psychology of Aesthetics, Creativity, and the Arts.* Advance online publication. Retrieved from http://dx.doi.org/10.1037/aca0000156

Chambers, J. (2015, October 13). Chile miners reflect on changed lives five years on. *BBC News.* Retrieved from http://www.bbc.com/news/world-latin-america-34463547

Chan, D. K., Zhang, X., Fung, H. H., & Hagger, M. S. (2015). Does emotion and its daily fluctuation correlate with depression? A cross-cultural analysis among six developing countries. *Journal of Epidemiology and Global Health, 5,* 65–74.

Chander, D., Garcia, P. S., MacColl, J. N., Illing, S., & Sleigh, J. W. (2014). Electroencephalographic variation during end maintenance and emergence from surgical anesthesia. *PLoS ONE, 9*(9), e106291. doi:10.1371/journal.pone.0106291

Chandrashekar, J., Hoon, M. A., Ryba, N. J., & Zuker, C. S. (2006). The receptors and cells for mammalian taste. *Nature, 444,* 288–294.

Charlton, B., & Verghese, A. (2010). Caring for Ivan Ilyich. *Journal of General Internal Medicine, 25,* 93–95.

Chatterjee, R. (2015). Out of the darkness. *Science, 350*(6259), 372–375.

Chavez, N., Almasy, S., Sanchez, R., & Simon, D. (2017, September 20). Central Mexico earthquake kills more than 200, topples buildings. *CNN.* Retrieved from https://www.cnn.com/2017/09/19/americas/mexico-earthquake/index.html

Chawla, J. (2017, April 12). Neurologic effects of caffeine. *Medscape.* Retrieved from http://emedicine.medscape.com/article/1182710-overview

Chechik, G., Meilijson, I., & Ruppin, E. (1998). Synaptic pruning in development: A computational account. *Neural Computation, 10,* 1759–1777.

Chen, A. C. H., Chang, R. Y. H., Besherat, A., & Baack, D. W. (2013). Who benefits from multiple brand celebrity endorsements? An experimental investigation. *Psychology & Marketing, 30,* 850–860.

Chen, C.-Y., Lin, Y.-H., & Hsaio, C.-L. (2012). Celebrity endorsement for sporting events using classical conditioning. *International Journal of Sports Marketing and Sponsorship, 13,* 209–219.

Chen, H., Chen, S., Zeng, L., Zhou, L., & Hou, S. (2014). Revisiting Einstein's brain in Brain Awareness Week. *Bioscience Trends, 8*(5), 286–289.

Chen, P., Chavez, O., Ong, D. C., & Gunderson, B. (2017). Strategic resource use for learning: A self-administered intervention that guides self-reflection on effective resource use enhances academic performance. *Psychological Science, 28,* 774–485.

Chen, P. W. (2014, June 26). Putting us all at risk for measles [Web log post]. Retrieved from http://well.blogs.nytimes.com/2014/06/26/putting-us-all-at-riskfor-measles/?_r=0

Cheng, C., Cheung, S.-F., Chio, J. H.-M., & Chan, M.-P. S. (2013). Cultural meaning of perceived control: A meta-analysis of locus of control and psychological symptoms across 18 cultural regions. *Psychological Bulletin 139,* 152–188. doi:10.1037/a0028596

Cheng, D. T., Knight, D. C., Smith, C. N., & Helmstetter, F. J. (2006). Human amygdala activity during the expression of fear responses. *Behavioral Neuroscience, 120,* 1187–1195.

Cheng, S. Y., Suh, S. Y., Morita, T., Oyama, Y., Chiu, T. Y., Koh, S. J., . . . Tsuneto, S. (2015). A cross-cultural study on behaviors when death is approaching in East Asian countries: What are the physician-perceived common beliefs and practices? *Medicine, 94,* e1573.

Cheng, T. L., Johnson, S. B., & Goodman, E. (2016). Breaking the intergenerational cycle of disadvantage: The three generation approach. *Pediatrics,* e20152467.

Cheyne, J. A. (2002). Situational factors affecting sleep paralysis and associated hallucinations: Position and timing effects. *Journal of Sleep Research, 11,* 169–177.

Chiandetti, C., & Turatto, M. (2017). Context-specific habituation of the freezing response in newborn chicks. *Behavioral Neuroscience, 131,* 437–446.

Chiao, J. Y., Iidka, T., Gordon, H. L., Nogawa, J., Bar, M., Aminoff, E., . . . Ambady, N. (2008). Cultural specificity in amygdala response to fear faces. *Journal of Cognitive Neuroscience, 20,* 2167–2174.

Chiras, D. D. (2015). *Human biology* (8th ed.). Burlington, MA: Jones & Bartlett Learning.

Chirawatkul, S., Prakhaw, P., & Chomnirat, W. (2011). Perceptions of depression among people of Khon Kaen City: A gender perspective. *Journal of Nursing Science & Health, 34,* 66–75.

Cho, H. J., Meira-Lima, I., Cordeiro, Q., Michelon, L., Sham, P., Vallada, H., & Collie, D. A. (2005). Population-based and family-based studies on the serotonin transporter gene polymorphisms and bipolar disorder: A systematic review and meta-analysis. *Molecular Psychiatry, 10,* 771–781.

Chodosh, S. (2017, January/February). Stop sending yourself reminder e-mails. *Scientific American Mind, 28,* 12.

Choi, C. Q. (2008, March). Do you need only half your brain? *Scientific American, 298,* 104.

Chomsky, N. (1959). Verbal behavior. *Language, 35,* 26–58.

Chomsky, N. (2000). *New horizons in the study of language and mind.* Cambridge, UK: Cambridge University Press.

Chouchou, F., Khoury, S., Chauny, J. M., Denis, R., & Lavigne, G. J. (2014). Postoperative sleep disruptions: A potential catalyst of acute pain? *Sleep Medicine Reviews, 18,* 273–282.

Christakis, D. A., Garrison, M. M., Herrenkohl, T., Haggerty, K., Rivara, F. P., Zhou, C., & Liekweg, K. (2013). Modifying media content for preschool children: A randomized controlled trial. *Pediatrics, 131,* 431–438.

Christopher, J. C., Wendt, D. C., Marecek, J., & Goodman, D. M. (2014). Critical cultural awareness: Contributions to a globalizing psychology. *American Psychologist, 69,* 645–655.

Chung, F., & Elsaid, H. (2009). Screening for obstructive sleep apnea before surgery: Why is it important? *Current Opinion in Anesthesiology, 22,* 405–411.

Cialdini, R. B., & Goldstein, N. J. (2004). Social influence: Compliance and conformity. *Annual Review of Psychology, 55,* 591–621.

Cipriani, A., Furukawa, T. A., Salanti, G., Chaimani, A., Atkinson, L. Z., Ogawa, Y., . . . Egger, M. (2018). Comparative efficacy and acceptability of 21 antidepressant drugs for the acute treatment of adults with major depressive disorder: A systematic review and network meta-analysis. *The Lancet, 391,* 1357–1366.

Cirelli, C. (2012). Brain plasticity, sleep and aging. *Gerontology, 58*(5), 441–445.

Cisler, J. M., Brady, R. E., Olatunji, B. O., & Lohr, J. M. (2010). Disgust and obsessive beliefs in contamination-related OCD. *Cognitive Therapy Research, 34,* 439–448.

Clark, A. M., DesMeules, M., Luo, W., Duncan, A. S., & Wielgosz, A. (2009). Socioeconomic status and cardiovascular disease: Risk and implications for care. *Nature Reviews Cardiology, 6,* 712–722.

Clark, I., & Landolt, H. P. (2017). Coffee, caffeine, and sleep: A systematic review of epidemiological studies and randomized controlled trials. *Sleep Medicine Reviews, 31,* 70–78.

Clarkin, J. F., Meehan, K. B., & Lenzenweger, M. F. (2015). Emerging approaches to the conceptualization and treatment of personality disorder. *Canadian Psychology/Psychologie Canadienne, 56,* 155–167.

Coan, J. A. (2010). Emergent ghosts of the emotion machine. *Emotion Review, 2,* 274–285.

Cochrane, R. E., Tett, R. P., & Vandecreek, L. (2003). Psychological testing and the selection of police officers: A national survey. In C. R. Bartol & A. M. Bartol (Eds.), *Current perspectives in forensic psychology and criminal justice* (pp. 25–34). Thousand Oaks, CA: SAGE.

Coffey, H. (2017, June 19). Is London safe to visit? Statistics and official advice for travelers. *The Independent.* Retrieved from http://www.independent.co.uk/travel/news-and-advice/is-london-safe-terror-attacks-finsbury-park-westminster-visit-travel-tourist-advice-stats-a7796946.html

Cohen, D. (2011). Applied knowledge: NASA aids the Chilean rescue effort. *ASK Magazine, 41,* 5–9.

Cohen, D. A., Wang, W., Wyatt, J. K., Kronauer, R. E., Dijk, D. J., Czeisler, C. A., & Klerman, E. B. (2010). Uncovering residual effects of chronic sleep loss on human performance. *Science Translational Medicine, 13,* 14ra3.

Cohen, H. W., Gibson, G., & Alderman, M. H. (2000). Excess risk of myocardial infarction in patients treated with antidepressant medications: Association with use of tricyclic agents. *American Journal of Medicine, 108,* 2–8.

Cohen, S., Doyle, W., Frank, E., Gwaltney, J. M., Jr., Rabin, B. S., & Skoner, D. P. (1998). Types of stressors that increase susceptibility to the common cold in healthy adults. *Health Psychology, 17,* 214–223.

Cohen, S., Janicki-Deverts, D., Doyle, W. J., Miller, G. E., Frank, E., Rabin, B. S, & Turner, R. B. (2012). Chronic stress, glucocorticoid receptor resistance in inflammation and disease risk. *PNAS Proceedings of the National Academy of Sciences of the United States of America, 109,* 5995–5999.

Cohen, S., Janicki-Deverts, D., Turner, R. B., & Doyle, W. J. (2015). Does hugging provide stress-buffering social support? A study of susceptibility to upper respiratory infection and illness. *Psychological Science, 26,* 135–147.

Cohen, S., Miller, G. E., & Rabin, B. S. (2001). Psychological stress and antibody response to immunization: A critical review of the human literature. *Psychosomatic Medicine, 63,* 7–18.

Coker, T. R., Elliott, M. N., Schwebel, D. C., Windle, M., Toomey, S. L., Tortolero, S. R., . . . Schuster, M. A. (2015, January/February). Media violence exposure and physical aggression in fifth-grade children. *Academic Pediatrics, 15*(1), 82–88.

Colapinto, J. (2000). *As nature made him: The boy who was raised as a girl.* New York, NY: HarperCollins.

Cole, C. F., Labin, D. B., & del Rocio Galarza, M. (2008). Begin with the children: What research on *Sesame Street*'s international coproductions reveals about using media to promote a new more peaceful world. *International Journal of Behavioral Development, 32*(4), 359–365.

Coleman-Jensen, A., Rabbitt, M., Gregory, C., & Singh, A. (2017). *Household food security in the United States in 2016* (ERR-237). Washington, DC: United States Department of Agriculture. Retrieved from https://www.ers.usda.gov/webdocs/publications/84973/err237_summary.pdf?v=42979

Colloca, L. (2017). Nocebo effects can make you feel pain. *Science, 358,* 44.

Colrain, I. M. (2005). The K-complex: A 7-decade history. *SLEEP, 28,* 255–273.

Common Sense Media. (2015). *The Common Sense census: Media use by tweens and teens.* Retrieved from https://www.commonsensemedia.org/sites/default/files/uploads/research/census_researchreport.pdf

Common Sense Media. (2016). *Executive summary, May 2016—Technology addiction: Concern, controversy, and finding balance.* Retrieved from https://www.commonsensemedia.org/sites/default/files/uploads/research/2016_csm_technology_addiction_executive_summary.pdf

Compton, W. M. (2017, June 30). *Research on the use and misuse of fentanyl and other synthetic opioids.* Retrieved from https://www.drugabuse.gov/about-nida/legislative-activities/testimony-to-congress/2017/research-use-misuse-fentanyl-other-synthetic-opioids

Congdon, E., Service, S., Wessman, J., Seppänen, J. K., Schönauer, S., Miettunen, J., . . . Nelson B. (2012). Early environment and neurobehavioral development predict adult temperament clusters. *PLoS ONE, 7,* e38065. doi:10.1371/journal.pone.0038065

Conroy, D., & Hagger, M. S. (2018). Imagery interventions in health behavior: A meta-analysis. *Health Psychology, 37,* 668–679.

Consortium, I. S. (2009). Common polygenic variation contributes to risk of schizophrenia that overlaps with bipolar disorder. *Nature, 460,* 748.

Contie, V., Defibaugh, A., Steinberg, D., & Wein, H. (2013, April). Sleep on it. How snoozing strengthens memories. *NIH News in Health.* Retrieved from https://newsinhealth.nih.gov/issue/apr2013/feature2

Contrera, J. (2017, September 4). "These are all fake news," said the honor student. He was wrong. *The Washington Post.* Retrieved from https://www.washingtonpost.com/lifestyle/style/these-are-all-fake-news-said-the-honor-student-he-was-wrong/2017/09/01/e2db60be-890a-11e7-961d-2f373b3977ee_story.html?utm_term=.486f3c192659

Convento, S., Russo, C., Zigiotto, L., & Bolognini, N. (2016). Transcranial electrical stimulation in post-stroke cognitive rehabilitation. *European Psychologist, 21,* 55–64.

Conway, M. A., Cohen, G., & Stanhope, N. (1991). On the very long-term retention of knowledge acquired through formal education: Twelve years of cognitive psychology. *Journal of Experimental Psychology: General, 120,* 395–409.

Cook County Sheriff's Office. (n.d.). *Corrections.* Retrieved from https://www.cookcountysheriff.org/cook-county-department-of-corrections/

Cook, P. F., Prichard, A., Spivak, M., & Berns, G. S. (2016). Awake canine fMRI predicts dogs' preference for praise vs food. *Social Cognitive and Affective Neuroscience, 11,* 1853–1862.

Cook, T. M., Andrade, J., Bogod, D. G., Hitchman, J. M., Jonker, W. R., Lucas, N., . . . Pandit, J. J. (2014). The 5th National Audit Project (NAP5) on accidental awareness during general anaesthesia: Patient experiences, human factors, sedation, consent and medicolegal issues. *Anaesthesia, 69,* 1102–1116.

Corballis, M. C. (2014). Left brain, right brain: Facts and fantasies. *PLoS Biology, 12,* e1001767. doi:10.1371/journal.pbio.1001767

Corey, G. (2017). *Theory and practice of counseling and psychotherapy* (10th ed.). Belmont, CA: Brooks/Cole, Cengage Learning.

Corkin, S. (2002). What's new with the amnesic patient H.M.? *Nature Reviews Neuroscience, 3,* 153–160.

Cornelius, S. W., & Caspi, A. (1987). Everyday problem solving in adulthood and old age. *Psychology and Aging, 2,* 144–153.

Correia, I., Alves, H., Morais, R., & Ramos, M. (2015). The legitimation of wife abuse among women: The impact of belief in a just world and gender identification. *Personality and Individual Differences, 76,* 7–12.

Correll, C. U., Leucht, S., & Kane, J. M. (2004). Lower risk for tardive dyskinesia associated with second-generation antipsychotics: A systematic review of 1-year studies. *American Journal of Psychiatry, 161,* 414–425.

Corrigan, P. W., & Al-Khouja, M. A. (2018). Three agendas for changing the public stigma of mental illness. *Psychiatric Rehabilitation Journal, 41,* 1–7.

Corrigan, P. W., & Penn, D. L. (2015). Lessons from social psychology on discrediting psychiatric stigma. *Stigma and Health, 1*(S), 2–15.

Costa, P. T., Jr., Terracciano, A., & McCrae, R. R. (2001). Gender differences in personality traits across cultures: Robust and surprising findings. *Journal of Personality and Social Psychology, 81,* 322–331.

Costandi, M. (2009, February 10). Where are old memories stored in the brain? *Scientific American Online.* Retrieved from http://www.scientificamerican.com/article/the-memory-trace/

Costandi, M. (2017, May 4). Is the baby in pain? Brain scans can tell. *Scientific American.* Retrieved from https://www.scientificamerican.com/article/is-the-baby-in-pain-brain-scans-can-tell/

Costandi, M. (2017, November/December). Striking evidence linking football to brain disease sparks calls for more research. *Scientific American Mind, 28,* 9–11.

Costanzo, E. S., Lutgendorf, S. K., & Roeder, S. L. (2011). Common-sense beliefs about cancer and health practices among women completing treatment for breast cancer. *Psychooncology, 20,* 53–61.

Cotman, C. W., & Berchtold, N. C. (2002). Exercise: A behavioral intervention to enhance brain health and plasticity. *Trends in Neurosciences, 25,* 295–301.

Cottrell, J. M., Newman, D. A., & Roisman, G. I. (2015). Explaining the Black–White gap in cognitive test scores: Toward a theory of adverse impact. *Journal of Applied Psychology, 100,* 1713–1736.

Coulson, J. (2016, October 20). The negative effects of time-out on children [Web log post]. Retrieved from https://ifstudies.org/blog/the-negative-effects-of-time-out-on-children

Coulson, S., & Van Petten, C. (2007). A special role for the right hemisphere in metaphor comprehension? ERP evidence from hemifield presentation. *Brain Research, 1146,* 128–145.

County of Los Angeles, Department of Medical Examiner-Coroner. (2017, May 15). *Autopsy report* [Case no. 09419]. Los Angeles, CA: Author. Retrieved from http://documents.latimes.com/read-carrie-fishers-autopsy/

Couperus, J. W. (2011). Perceptual load influences selective attention across development. *Developmental Psychology, 47,* 1431–1439.

Coupland, C., Hill, T., Morriss, R., Moore, M., Arthur, A., & Hippisley-Cox, J. (2016). Antidepressant use and risk of cardiovascular outcomes in people aged 20 to 64: Cohort study using primary care database. *BMJ Open, 352,* i1350.

Cowan, N. (1988). Evolving conceptions of memory storage, selective attention, and their mutual constraints within the human information-processing system. *Psychological Bulletin, 104,* 163–191.

Cowan, N. (2015). George Miller's magical number of immediate memory in retrospect: Observations on the faltering progression of science. *Psychological Review, 122,* 536–541.

Cowan, N., Chen, Z., & Rouder, J. N. R. (2004). Constant capacity in an immediate serial-recall task: A logical sequel to Miller (1956). *Psychological Science, 15,* 634–640.

Cowan, N., Nugent, L. D., & Elliott, E. M. (2000). Memory-search and rehearsal processes and the word length effect in immediate recall: A synthesis in reply to service. *Quarterly Journal of Experimental Psychology, 53,* 666–670.

Coyne, S. M. (2016). Effects of viewing relational aggression on television on aggressive behavior in adolescents: A three-year longitudinal study. *Developmental Psychology, 52,* 284–295.

Craddock, N., O'Donovan, M. C., & Owen, M. J. (2005). The genetics of schizophrenia and bipolar disorder: Dissecting psychosis. *Journal of Medical Genetics, 42,* 193–204.

Craik, F. I. M., & Lockhart, R. S. (1972). Levels of processing: A framework for memory research. *Journal of Verbal Learning and Verbal Behavior, 11,* 671–684.

Craik, F. I. M., & Tulving, E. (1975). Depth of processing and the retention of words in episodic memory. *Journal of Experimental Psychology, 104,* 268–294.

Craker, N., & March, E. (2016). The dark side of Facebook®: The Dark Tetrad, negative social potency, and trolling behaviours. *Personality and Individual Differences, 102,* 79–84.

Cramer, P. (2000). Defense mechanisms in psychology today: Further processes for adaptation. *American Psychologist, 55,* 637–646.

Cramer, P. (2008). Identification and the development of competence: A 44-year longitudinal study from late adolescence to late middle age. *Psychology and Aging, 23,* 410–421.

Cramer, P. (2015). Defense mechanisms: 40 years of empirical research. *Journal of Personality Assessment, 97,* 114–122.

Craske, M. G., Kircanski, K., Epstein, A., Wittchen, H.-U., Pine, D. S., Lewis-Fernández, R., . . . DSM-V Anxiety, OC Spectrum, Posttraumatic and Dissociative Disorder Work Group. (2010). Panic disorder: A review of DSM-IV panic disorder and proposals for DSM-V. *Depression and Anxiety, 27,* 93–112.

Craze, M., & Crooks, N. (2010, October 13). Chile frees 12 of 33 miners in underground rescue. *Bloomberg.com.* Retrieved from http://www.bloomberg.com/news/2010-10-13/chile-frees-first-of-33-miners-in-world-s-longest-underground-mine-rescue.html

Crisco, J. J., Fiore, R., Beckwith, J. G., Chu, J. J., Brolinson, P. G., Duma, S., . . . Greenwald, R. M. (2010). Frequency and location of head impact exposures in individual collegiate football players. *Journal of Athletic Training, 45,* 549–559.

Crivello, C., Kuzyk, O., Rodrigues, M., Friend, M., Zesiger, P., & Poulin-Dobois, D. (2016). The effects of bilingual growth on toddlers' executive function. *Journal of Experimental Child Psychology, 141,* 121–132.

Croce, P. J. (2010). Reaching beyond Uncle William: A century of William James in theory and in life. *History of Psychology, 13,* 351–377.

Crooks, R., & Baur, K. (2017). *Our sexuality* (13th ed.). Boston, MA: Cengage Learning.

Cropanzano, R., Anthony, E. L., Daniels, S. R., & Hall, A. V. (2017). Social exchange theory: A critical review with theoretical remedies. *The Academy of Management Annals, 11,* 479–516.

Crosby, L. E., Quinn, C. T., & Kalinyak, K. A. (2015). A biopsychosocial model for the management of patients with sickle-cell disease transitioning to adult medical care. *Advances in Therapy, 32,* 293–305.

Crowell, S. E., Beauchaine, T. P., & Linehan, M. M. (2009). A biosocial developmental model of borderline personality: Elaborating and extending Linehan's theory. *Psychological Bulletin, 135,* 495–510.

Crowley, R., Kirschner, N., Dunn, A. S., & Bornstein, S. S. (2017). Health and public policy to facilitate effective prevention and treatment of substance use disorders involving illicit and prescription drugs: An American College of Physicians position paper. *Annals of Internal Medicine, 166,* 733–736.

Csikszentmihalyi, M. (1975). Play and intrinsic rewards. *Journal of Humanistic Psychology, 15,* 41–63.

Csikszentmihalyi, M. (1990). *Flow: The psychology of optimal experience.* New York, NY: Harper Perennial.

Csikszentmihalyi, M. (1999). If we are so rich, why aren't we happy? *American Psychologist, 54,* 821–827.

Cuijpers, P., De Wit, L., Weitz, E., Andersson, G., & Huibers, M. J. H. (2015). The combination of psychotherapy and pharmacotherapy in the treatment of adult depression: A comprehensive meta-analysis. *Journal of Evidence-Based Psychotherapies, 15,* 147–168.

Culbertson, S. S., Fullagar, C. J., Simmons, M. J., & Zhu, M. (2015). Contagious flow antecedents and consequences of optimal experience in the classroom. *Journal of Management Education, 39,* 319–349.

Cummins, R. A., Li, N., Wooden, M., & Stokes, M. (2014). A demonstration of set-points for subjective wellbeing. *Journal of Happiness Studies, 15,* 183–206.

Cunha, J. P., & Stöppler, M. C. (Eds.). (2016, June 6). Jetlag. *Medicine.net.com.* Retrieved from http://www.medicinenet.com/jet_lag/article.htm

Cunningham, J. H., & Edelman, A. (2012, December 17). Comfort dogs help ease the pain of mourning Newtown community. *New York Daily News.* Retrieved from http://www.nydailynews.com/news/national/comfort-dogs-helping-ease-pain-sandy-hook-tragedy-article-1.1222295

Cunningham, M. R., Shamblen, S. R., Barbee, A. P., & Ault, L. K. (2005). Social allergies in romantic relationships: Behavioral repetition, emotional sensitization, and dissatisfaction in dating couples. *Personal Relationships, 12,* 273–295.

Currin, J. M., Gibson, L., & Hubach, R. D. (2015). Multidimensional assessment of sexual orientation and the fraternal birth order effect. *Psychology of Sexual Orientation and Gender Diversity, 2,* 113–122.

Curtiss, S., Fromkin, V., Krashen, S., Rigler, D., & Rigler, M. (1974). The linguistic development of Genie. *Language, 50,* 528–554.

Cuttler, C., & Ryckman, M. (2018). Don't call me delusional: Stigmatizing effects of noun labels on people with mental disorders. *Stigma and Health.* Advance online publication. Retrieved from http://dx.doi.org/10.1037/sah0000132

Cyna, A., Crowther, C., Robinson, J., Andrew, M., Antoniou, G., & Baghurst, P. (2013). Hypnosis antenatal training for childbirth: A randomized controlled trial. *BJOG: An International Journal of Obstetrics & Gynaecology, 120,* 1248–1259.

Cyna, A. M., McAuliffe, G. L., & Andrew, M. I. (2004). Hypnosis for pain relief in labour and childbirth: A systematic review. *British Journal of Anesthesia, 93,* 505–511.

Cyrzyk, T. (2013). Electroconvulsive therapy: Why it is still controversial. *Mental Health Practice, 16,* 22–27.

Czarnowski, C., Bailey, J., & Bal, S. (2007). Curare and a Canadian connection. *Canadian Family Physician, 53,* 1531–1532.

D'Souza, J., & Gurin, M. (2016). The universal significance of Maslow's concept of self-actualization. *The Humanistic Psychologist, 44,* 210–214.

Daenen, L., Varkey, E., Kellmann, M., & Nijs, J. (2015). Exercise, not to exercise, or how to exercise in patients with chronic pain? Applying science to practice. *The Clinical Journal of Pain, 31,* 108–114.

Daffner, K. R., Chong, H., Riis, J., Rentz, D. M., Wolk, D. A., Budson, A. E., & Holcomb, P. J. (2007). Cognitive status impacts age-related changes in attention to novel and target events. *Neuropsychology, 21,* 291–300.

Dalenberg, C. J., Brand, B. L., Loewenstein, R. J., Gleaves, D. H., Dorahy, M. J., Cardeña, E., . . . Spiegel, D. (2014). Reality versus fantasy: Reply to Lynn et al. (2014). *Psychological Bulletin, 140,* 911–920.

Damasio, A. R., Grabowski, T. J., Bechara, A., Damasio, H., Ponto, L. L. B., Parvizi, J., & Hichwa, R. D. (2000). Subcortical and cortical brain activity during the feeling of self-generated emotions. *Nature Neuroscience, 3,* 1049–1056.

Damian, R. I., & Roberts, B. W. (2015). Settling the debate on birth order and personality. *Proceedings of the National Academy of Sciences, 112,* 14119–14120.

Damour, L. (2017, September 21). How technology changes teen romance. *The New York Times.* Retrieved from https://www.nytimes.com/2017/09/21/well/family/the-love-lives-of-digital-natives.html?mcubz=1&_r=0

Dan, A., Mondal, T., Chakraborty, K., Chaudhuri, A., & Biswas, A. (2017). Clinical course and treatment outcome of Koro: A follow-up study from a Koro epidemic reported from West Bengal, India. *Asian Journal of Psychiatry, 26,* 14–20.

Danker, J. F., & Anderson, J. R. (2010). The ghosts of brain states past: Remembering reactivates the brain regions engaged during encoding. *Psychological Bulletin, 136,* 87–102.

Dapretto, M., Lee, S. S., & Caplan, R. (2005). A functional magnetic resonance imaging study of discourse coherence in typically developing children. *NeuroReport, 16,* 1661–1665.

Darcy, A. M., Doyle, A. C., Lock, J., Peebles, R., Doyle, P., & Le Grange, D. (2012). The eating disorders examination in adolescent males with anorexia nervosa: How does it compare to adolescent females? *International Journal of Eating Disorders, 45,* 110–114.

Darley, J. M., & Latané, B. (1968). Bystander intervention in emergencies: Diffusion of responsibility. *Journal of Personality and Social Psychology, 8,* 377–383.

Dar-Nimrod, I., & Heine, S. J. (2011). Genetic essentialism: On the deceptive determinism of DNA. *Psychological Bulletin, 137,* 800–818.

Darwin, C. (2002). *The expression of the emotions in man and animals.* New York, NY: Oxford University Press. (Original work published 1872)

Daskalopoulou, C., Stubbs, B., Kralj, C., Koukounari, A., Prince, M., & Prina, A. M. (2017). Physical activity and healthy ageing: A systematic review and meta-analysis of longitudinal cohort studies. *Ageing Research Reviews, 38,* 6–17.

David, A. (2015, August 13). AA saved my life (and I get why you hate it). *Huffington Post.* Retrieved from http://www.huffingtonpost.com/anna-david/aa-saved- my-life-and-i-get-why-you-hate-it_b_7978690.html

Davidson, R. J., Scherer, K. R., & Goldsmith, H. H. (Eds.). (2002). *Handbook of affective sciences.* New York, NY: Oxford University Press.

Davies, G., Tenesa, A., Payton, A., Yang, J., Harris, S. E., Liewald, D., . . . McGhee, K. (2011). Genome-wide association studies establish that human intelligence is highly heritable and polygenic. *Molecular Psychiatry, 16,* 996–1005.

Davies, M. (2015). A model of critical thinking in higher education. In M. B. Paulsen (Ed.), *Higher education: Handbook of theory and research* (Vol. 30, pp. 41–92). Cham, Switzerland: Springer International.

Davis, E. P., & Sandman, C. A. (2010). The timing of prenatal exposure to maternal cortisol and psychosocial stress is associated with human infant cognitive development. *Child Development, 81,* 131–148.

Davis, K. (2015, October 20). Federal judge says neuroscience is not ready for the courtroom—yet. *ABA Journal.* Retrieved from http://www.abajournal.com/news/artcle/federal_judge_says_neuroscience_is_not_ready_for_the_courtroom_yet

Davis, M., & Whalen, P. J. (2001). The amygdala: Vigilance and emotion. *Molecular Psychiatry, 6,* 13–34.

de Bitencourt Machado, D., Braga Laskoski, P., Trelles Severo, C., Margareth Bassols, A., Sfoggia, A., & Kowacs, C. (2016). A psychodynamic perspective on a systematic review of online psychotherapy for adults. *British Journal of Psychotherapy, 32,* 79–108.

De Boeck, P., & Jeon, M. (2018). Perceived crisis and reforms: Issues, explanations, and remedies. *Psychological Bulletin, 144,* 757–777.

de Boysson-Bardies, B., Halle, P., Sagart, L., & Durand, C. (1989). A cross-linguistic investigation of vowel formats in babbling. *Journal of Child Language, 16,* 1–17.

de Gelder, D. B., Hortensius, R., & Tamietto, M. (2012). Attention and awareness each influence amygdala activity for dynamic bodily expressions—a short review. *Frontiers in Integrative Neuroscience, 6.* doi:10.3389fnint.2012.00054

de Lauzon-Guillain, B., Wijndaele, K., Clark, M., Acerini, C. L., Hughes, I. A., Dunger, D. B., . . . Ong, K. K. (2012). Breastfeeding and infant temperament at age three months. *PLoS ONE, 7*(1), e29326. doi:10.1371/journal.pone.0029326

de Raad, B., & Mlačić, B. (2017). The lexical foundation of the Big Five Factor Model. In T. A. Widiger (Ed.), *Oxford library of psychology. The Oxford handbook of the Five Factor Model* (pp. 191–216). New York, NY: Oxford University Press.

De Winter, F. L., Zhu, Q., Van den Stock, J., Nelissen, K., Peeters, R., de Gelder, B., . . . Vandenbulcke, M. (2015). Lateralization for dynamic facial expressions in human superior temporal sulcus. *NeuroImage, 106,* 340–352.

de Wit, H., Gorka, S. M., & Phan, K. L. (2015). The ups and downs of 3,4-methylenedioxymethamphetamine: Linking subjective effects to spontaneous brain function. *Biological Psychiatry, 78,* 519–521.

de Zambotti, M., Willoughby, A. R., Franzen, P. L., Clark, D. B., Baker, F. C., & Colrain, I. M. (2016). K-Complexes: Interaction between the central and autonomic nervous systems during sleep. *Sleep, 39,* 1129–1137.

DeAngelis, T. (2017, November 9). Prescribing psychologists working in the federal system. *PracticeUpdate.* Retrieved from http://www.apapracticecentral.org/update/2017/11-09/psychologists-federal-system.aspx

DeAngelis, T. (2018, January). Practice makes perfect: Strategies that hone practitioners' skills. *Monitor on Psychology, 29*(1). Retrieved from http://www.apa.org/monitor/2018/01/ce-corner.aspx

DeCaro, M. S., Van Stockum, C. A., Jr., & Wieth, M. B. (2016). When higher working memory capacity hinders insight. *Journal of Experimental Psychology: Learning, Memory, and Cognition, 42,* 39–49.

DeCasper, A. J., & Fifer, W. P. (1980). Of human bonding: Newborns prefer their mothers' voices. *Science, 208,* 1174–1176.

Deci, E. L., Koestner, R., & Ryan, R. M. (1999). A meta-analytic review of experiments examining the effects of extrinsic rewards on intrinsic motivation. *Psychological Bulletin, 125,* 627–668.

Deci, E. L., Koestner, R., & Ryan, R. M. (2001). Extrinsic rewards and intrinsic motivation in education: Reconsidered once again. *Review of Educational Research, 71,* 1–27.

Deci, E. L., Olafsen, A. H., & Ryan, R. M. (2017). Self-determination theory in work organizations: The state of a science. *Annual Review of Organizational Psychology and Organizational Behavior, 4,* 19–43.

Deci, E. L., & Ryan, R. M. (2008). Self-determination theory: A macrotheory of human motivation, development, and health. *Canadian Psychology, 49,* 182–185.

Decker, H. S. (2016a). Cyclical swings: The bête noire of psychiatry. *History of Psychology, 19,* 52–56.

Decker, H. S. (2016b). Professor Decker replies. *History of Psychology, 19,* 66–67.

Deer, B. (2011). How the case against the MMR vaccine was fixed. *British Medical Journal, 342,* 77–82.

Deese, J., & Kaufman, R. A. (1957). Serial effects in recall of unorganized and sequentially organized verbal material. *Journal of Experimental Psychology, 54,* 180–187.

Degnan, K. A., Hane, A. A., Henderson, H. A., Moas, O. L., Reeb-Sutherland, B. C., & Fox, N. A. (2011). Longitudinal stability of temperamental exuberance and social-emotional outcomes in early childhood. *Developmental Psychology, 47,* 765–780.

DeGregory, L. (2008, July 31). The girl in the window. *Tampa Bay Times.* Retrieved from http://www.tampabay.com/specials/2008/reports/danielle/

Deisseroth, K. (2015). Optogenetics: 10 years of microbial opsins in neuroscience. *Nature Neuroscience, 18*(9), 1213–1225.

Del Giudice, M., Booth, T., & Irwing, P. (2012). The distance between Mars and Venus: Measuring global sex differences in personality. *PLoS ONE, 7*(1), e29265. doi:10.1371/journal.pone.0029265

Delmonte, R., Lucchetti, G., Moreira-Almeida, A., & Farias, M. (2016). Can the DSM-5 differentiate between nonpathological possession and dissociative identity disorder? A case study from an Afro-Brazilian religion. *Journal of Trauma & Dissociation, 17,* 322–337.

DeLongis, A., Coyne, J. C., Dakof, G., Folkman, S., & Lazarus, R. S. (1982). Relationship of daily hassles, uplifts, and major life events to health status. *Health Psychology, 1,* 119–136.

DeLongis, A., Folkman, S., & Lazarus, R. S. (1988). The impact of daily stress on health and mood: Psychological and social resources as mediators. *Journal of Personality and Social Psychology, 54,* 486–495.

DelPriore, D. J., Bradshaw, H. K., & Hill, S. E. (2018). Appearance enhancement produces a strategic beautification penalty among women. *Evolutionary Behavioral Sciences, 12,* 348–366.

Dement, W., & Kleitman, N. (1957). The relation of eye movements during sleep to dream activity: An objective method for the study of dreaming. *Journal of Experimental Psychology, 53,* 339–346.

Dement, W. C., & Vaughan, C. (1999). *The promise of sleep.* New York, NY: Delacorte Press.

Denollet, J., & Conraads, V. M. (2011). Type D personality and vulnerability to adverse outcomes in heart disease. *Cleveland Clinic Journal of Medicine, 78,* S13–S19.

Denson, T. F., O'Dean, S. M., Blake, K. R., & Beames, J. R. (2018). Aggression in women: Behavior, brain and hormones. *Frontiers in Behavioral Neuroscience, 12,* Article ID 81. Retrieved from http://dx.doi.org/10.3389/fnbeh.2018.00081

Denworth, L. (2014, April 25). Science gave my son the gift of sound. *Time.* Retrieved from http://time.com/76154/deaf-culture-cochlear-implants/

Department of Justice. (2006). *Use of polygraph examinations in the Department of Justice* (I-2006-008). Washington, DC: Office of the Inspector General, Evaluation and Inspections Division.

DeRobertis, E. M. (2016). On framing the future of humanistic psychology. *The Humanistic Psychologist, 44,* 18–41.

Derr, M. (2016, March 9). Cesar Millan crosses the line again. *Psychology Today.* Retrieved from https://www.psychologytoday.com/blog/dogs-best-friend/201603/cesar-millan-crosses-the-line-again

Desco, M., Navas-Sanchez, F. J., Sanchez-González, J., Reig, S., Robles, O., Franco, C., . . . Arango, C. (2011). Mathematically gifted adolescents use more extensive and more bilateral areas of the fronto-parietal network than controls during executive functioning and fluid reasoning tasks. *NeuroImage, 57,* 281–292.

deShazo, R. D., Hall, J. E., & Skipworth, L. B. (2015). Obesity bias, medical technology, and the hormonal hypothesis: Should we stop demonizing fat people? *American Journal of Medicine, 128,* 456–460.

Deslandes, A., Moraes, H., Ferreira, C., Veiga, H., Silverira, H., Mouta, R., . . . Laks, J. (2009). Exercise and mental health: Many reasons to move. *Neuropsychobiology, 59,* 191–198.

Desmarais, S. L., Van Dom, R. A., Johnson, K. L., Grimm, K. J., Douglas, K. S., & Swartz, M. S. (2014). Community violence perpetration and victimization among adults with mental illness. *American Journal of Public Health, 104,* 2342–2349.

Despins, L. A., Scott-Cawiezell, J., & Rouder, J. N. (2010). Detection of patient risk by nurses: A theoretical framework. *Journal of Advanced Nursing, 66,* 465–474.

Detrick, P., & Chibnall, J. T. (2014). Underreporting on the MMPI-2-RF in a high-demand police officer selection context: An illustration. *Psychological Assessment, 26,* 1044–1049.

DeValois, R. L., & DeValois, K. K. (1975). Neural coding of color. *Handbook of Perception, 5,* 117–166.

Devaney, S. A., Palomaki, G. E., Scott, J. A., & Bianchi, D. W. (2011). Noninvasive fetal sex determination using cell-free fetal DNA. *Journal of American Medical Association, 306,* 627–636.

Devinsky, O., Cross, J. H., Laux, L., Marsh, E., Miller, I., Nabbout, R., . . . Wright, S. (2017). Trial of cannabidiol for drug-resistant seizures in the Dravet syndrome. *New England Journal of Medicine, 376,* 2011–2020.

DeWall, C. N., Baumeister, R. F., & Vohs, K. D. (2008). Satiated with belongingness? Effects of acceptance, rejection, and task framing on self-regulatory performance. *Journal of Personality Social Psychology, 95,* 1367–1382.

Dewar, M., Alber, J., Butler, C., Cowan, N., & Della Sala, S. (2012). Brief wakeful resting boosts new memories over the long term. *Psychological Science, 23,* 955–960.

DeYoung, C. G., Carey, B. E., Krueger, R. F., & Ross, S. R. (2016). Ten aspects of the Big Five in the Personality Inventory for DSM–5. *Personality Disorders: Theory, Research, and Treatment, 7,* 113–123.

Dhabhar, F. S. (2014). Effects of stress on immune function: The good, the bad, and the beautiful. *Immunologic Research, 58,* 193–210.

Dhindsa, R. S., & Goldstein, D. B. (2016). Schizophrenia: From genetics to physiology at last. *Nature, 530,* 162–163.

Di Lorenzo, L., De Pergola, G., Zocchetti, C., L'Abbate, N., Basso, A., Pannacciulli, N., . . . Soleo, L. (2003). Effect of shift work on body mass index: Results of a study performed in 319 glucose-tolerant men working in a Southern Italian industry. *International Journal of Obesity, 21,* 1353–1358.

Diamond, E. L. (1982). The role of anger and hostility in essential hypertension and coronary heart disease. *Psychological Bulletin, 92,* 410–433.

Diamond, M. (2004). Sex, gender, and identity over the years: A changing perspective. *Child and Adolescent Psychiatric Clinics of North America, 13,* 591–607.

Diamond, M., & Sigmundson, H. K. (1997). Sex reassignment at birth: Long-term review and clinical implications. *Archives of Pediatric & Adolescent Medicine, 151,* 298–304.

Dickens, W. T., & Flynn, J. R. (2001). Heritability estimates vs. large environmental effects: The IQ paradox resolved. *Psychological Review, 108,* 346–369.

Dickens, W. T., & Flynn, J. R. (2006). Black Americans reduce the racial IQ gap: Evidence from standardization samples. *Psychological Science, 17,* 913–920.

Dickerson, F. B., Tenhula, W. N., & Green-Paden, L. D. (2005). The token economy for schizophrenia: Review of the literature and recommendations for future research. *Schizophrenia Research, 75,* 405–416.

Diekelmann, S., & Born, J. (2010). The memory function of sleep. *Nature Reviews Neuroscience, 11,* 114–126.

Diener, E. (1979). Deindividuation, self-awareness, and disinhibition. *Journal of Personality and Social Psychology, 3,* 1160–1171.

Diener, E., Fraser, S. C., Beaman, A. L., & Kelem, R. T. (1976). Effects of deindividuation variables on stealing among Halloween trick-or-treaters. *Journal of Personality and Social Psychology, 33,* 178–183.

Diener, E., Lucas, R. E., & Scollon, C. N. (2006). Beyond the hedonic treadmill. *American Psychologist, 6,* 305–314.

Digdon, N., Powell R. A., & Harris, B. (2014). Little Albert's alleged neurological impairment: Watson, Rayner, and historical revision. *History of Psychology, 17*(4), 312–324.

DiLalla, L. F. (2002). Behavior genetics of aggression in children: Review and future directions. *Developmental Review, 22,* 593–622.

Dimberg, U., Thunberg, M., & Elmehed, K. (2000). Unconscious facial reactions to emotional facial expressions. *Psychological Science, 11,* 86–89.

Dimidjian, S., Goodman, S. H., Felder, J. N., Gallop, R., Brown, A. P., & Beck, A. (2016). Staying well during pregnancy and the postpartum: A pilot randomized trial of mindfulness-based cognitive therapy for the prevention of depressive relapse/recurrence. *Journal of Consulting and Clinical Psychology, 84,* 134–145.

Dimsdale, J. E. (2008). Psychological stress and cardiovascular disease. *Journal of the American College of Cardiology, 51,* 1237–1247.

Ding, M., Bhupathiraju, S. N., Chen, M., van Dam, R. M., & Hu, F. B. (2014). Caffeinated and decaffeinated coffee consumption and risk of type 2 diabetes: A systematic review and a dose-response meta-analysis. *Diabetes Care, 37,* 569–586.

Dingfelder, S. F. (2011, February). Reflecting on narcissism. *Monitor on Psychology.* Retrieved from http://www.apa.org/monitor/2011/02/narcissism.aspx

DiorVargas.com. (n.d.). *People of color & mental illness photo project.* Retrieved from http://diorvargas.com/poc-mental-illness/

Dissel, S., Melnattur, K., & Shaw, P. J. (2015). Sleep, performance, and memory in flies. *Current Sleep Medicine Reports, 1*(1), 47–54.

Dixon, J. F., & Hokin, L. E. (1998). Lithium acutely inhibits and chronically up-regulates and stabilizes glutamate uptake by presynaptic nerve endings in mouse cerebral cortex. *Proceedings of the National Academy of Sciences, 95,* 8363–8368.

Dixson, B. J., & Brooks, R. C. (2013). The role of facial hair in women's perceptions of men's attractiveness, health, masculinity and parenting abilities. *Evolution and Human Behavior, 34,* 236–241.

Dobbs, D. (2017, July/August). The smartphone psychiatrist. *The Atlantic.* Retrieved from https://www.theatlantic.com/magazine/archive/2017/07/the-smartphone-psychiatrist/528726/

Dobkin, B. H. (2005). Rehabilitation after stroke. *New England Journal of Medicine, 352,* 1677–1684.

Doherty-Sneddon, G. (2008). The great baby signing debate. *Psychologist, 21,* 300–303. doi:10.1371/journal.pone.0029265

Dolbier, C. L., & Rush, T. E. (2012). Efficacy of abbreviated progressive muscle relaxation in a high-stress college sample. *International Journal of Stress Management, 19,* 48–68.

Dolgin, E. (2017, November 22). The most popular genes in the human genome. *Nature News.* Retrieved from https://www.nature.com/articles/d41586-017-07291-9

Doliński, D., Grzyb, T., Folwarczny, M., Grzybała, P., Krzyszycha, K., Martynowska, K., & Trojanowski, J. (2017). Would you deliver an electric shock in 2015? Obedience in the experimental paradigm developed by Stanley Milgram in the 50 years following the original studies. *Social Psychological and Personality Science, 8,* 927–933.

Dollard, J., Miller, N. E., Doob, L. W., Mowrer, O. H., & Sears, R. R. (1939). *Frustration and aggression.* New Haven, CT: Yale University Press.

Domenici, E. (2017). Schizophrenia genetics comes to translation. *NPJ Schizophrenia, 3.* doi:10.1038/s41537-017-0011-y

Domhoff, G. W. (2001). A new neurocognitive theory of dreams. *Dreaming, 11,* 13–33.

Domhoff, G. W. (2017a). Now an invasion by a Freudian concept-snatcher: Reply to Erdelyi. *Dreaming, 27,* 345–350.

Domhoff, G. W. (2017b). The invasion of the concept snatchers: The origins, distortions, and future of the continuity hypothesis. *Dreaming, 27,* 14–39.

Domhoff, G. W., & Fox, K. C. (2015). Dreaming and the default network: A review, synthesis, and counterintuitive research proposal. *Consciousness and Cognition, 33,* 342–353.

Donaldson, S. I., Dollwet, M., & Rao, M. A. (2015). Happiness, excellence, and optimal human functioning revisited: Examining the peer-reviewed literature linked to positive psychology. *The Journal of Positive Psychology, 10,* 185–195.

Donnelly, G. E., Ksendzova, M., Howell, R. T., Vohs, K. D., & Baumeister, R. F. (2016). Buying to blunt negative feelings: Materialistic escape from the self. *Review of General Psychology, 3,* 272–316.

Donovan, N. J., Amariglio, R. E., Zoller, A. S., Rudel, R. K., Gomez-Isla, T., Blacker, D., . . . Rentz, D. M. (2014). Subjective cognitive concerns and neuropsychiatric predictors of progression to the early clinical stages of Alzheimer's disease. *The American Journal of Geriatric Psychiatry, 22,* 1642–1651.

Doom, J. R., Cook, S. H., Sturza, J., Kaciroti, N., Gearhardt, A. N., Vazquez, D. M., . . . Miller, A. L. (2018). Family conflict, chaos, and negative life events predict cortisol activity in low-income children. *Developmental Psychobiology, 60,* 364–379.

Dorahy, M. J., Brand, B. L., Şar, V., Krüger, C., Stavropoulos, P., Martínez-Taboas, A., . . . Middleton, W. (2014). Dissociative identity disorder: An empirical overview. *Australian & New Zealand Journal of Psychiatry, 48,* 402–417.

Doran, J. M., Kraha, A., Marks, L. R., Ameen, E. J., & El-Ghoroury, N. H. (2016). Graduate debt in psychology: A quantitative analysis. *Training and Education in Professional Psychology, 10,* 3–13.

Doucleff, M. (2014, October 23). What's my risk of catching ebola? *NPR.* Retrieved from http://www.npr.org/sections/goatsandsoda/2014/10/23/358349882/an-answer-for-americans-who-ask-whats-my-risk-of-catching-ebola

Dougherty, L. R., Klein, D. N., Olino, T. M., Dyson, M., & Rose, S. (2009). Increased waking salivary cortisol and depression risk in preschoolers: The role of maternal history of melancholic depression and early child temperament. *Journal of Child Psychology and Psychiatry, 50,* 1495–1503.

Dovidio, J. F., Kawakami, K., & Gaertner, S. L. (2002). Implicit and explicit prejudice and interracial interaction. *Journal of Personality and Social Psychology, 82,* 62–68.

Drace, S., Ric, F., & Desrichard, O. (2010). Affective biases in likelihood perception: A possible role of experimental demand in mood-congruence effects. *International Review of Social Psychology, 23*(1), 93–109.

Drake, C., Roehrs T., Shambroom, J., & Roth, T. (2013). Caffeine effects on sleep taken 0, 3, or 6 hours before going to bed. *Journal of Clinical Sleep Medicine, 9,* 1195–1200.

Drew, T., Vo, M. L. H., & Wolfe, J. M. (2013). The invisible gorilla strikes again: Sustained inattentional blindness in expert observers. *Psychological Science, 24,* 1848–1853.

Drexler, B., Zinser, S., Huang, S., Poe, M. M., Rudolph, U., Cook, J. M., & Antkowiak, B. (2013). Enhancing the function of alpha5-subunit-containing GABAA receptors promotes action potential firing of neocortical neurons during up-states. *European Journal of Pharmacology, 702,* 18–24.

Driessen, E., Van, H. L., Peen, J., Don, F. J., Kool, S., Westra, D., . . . Dekker, J. J. (2015). Therapist-rated outcomes in a randomized clinical trial comparing cognitive behavioral therapy and psychodynamic therapy for major depression. *Journal of Affective Disorders, 170,* 112–118.

Driver, H. S., & Taylor, S. R. (2000). Exercise and sleep. *Sleep Medicine Reviews, 4,* 387–402.

drjilltaylor.com. (n.d.). *Dr. Jill Bolte Taylor.* Retrieved from http://drjilltaylor.com/about.html

Drougard, A., Fournel, A., Valet, P., & Knauf, C. (2015). Impact of hypothalamic reactive oxygen species in the regulation of energy metabolism and food intake. *Frontiers in Neuroscience, 9,* 1–12. doi:10.3389/fnins.2015.00056

Druckman, D., & Bjork, R. A. (Eds.). (1994). *Learning, remembering, believing: Enhancing human performance* [Study conducted by the National Research Council]. Washington, DC: National Academy Press.

Drug Abuse Warning Network. (2011). *Drug Abuse Warning Network, 2011: National estimates of drug-related emergency department visits.* Retrieved from http://www.samhsa.gov/data/2k13/DAWN2k11ED/DAWN2k11ED.htm#high

Drug Enforcement Administration. (n.d.). *Drug schedules.* Retrieved from https://www.dea.gov/druginfo/ds.shtml

Druss, B. G., Hwang, I., Petukhova, M., Sampson, N. A., Wang, P. S., & Keller, R. C. (2009). Impairment in role functioning in mental and chronic medical disorders in the United States: Results from the National Comorbidity Survey Replication. *Molecular Psychiatry, 14,* 728–737.

Duckworth, A. L., Gendler, T. S., & Gross, J. J. (2016). Situational strategies for self-control. *Perspectives on Psychological Science, 11,* 35–55.

Duckworth, A. L., & Seligman, M. E. P. (2005). Self-discipline outdoes IQ in predicting academic performance of adolescents. *Psychological Science, 16,* 939–944.

Duckworth, A. L., Weir, D., Tsukayama, E., & Kwok, D. (2012). Who does well in life? Conscientious adults excel in both objective and subjective success. *Frontiers in Psychology, 3*(356). doi:10.3389/fpsyg.2012.00356

Duggan, K. A., McDevitt, E. A., Whitehurst, L. N., & Mednick, S. C. (2016). To nap, perchance to DREAM: A factor analysis of college students' self-reported reasons for napping. *Behavioral Sleep Medicine,* 1–19. doi:10.1080/15402002.2016.1178115

Duits, P., Cath, D. C., Lissek, S., Hox, J. J., Hamm, A. O., Engelhard, I. M., . . . Baas, J. M. (2015). Updated meta-analysis of classical fear conditioning in the anxiety disorders. *Depression and Anxiety, 32,* 239–253.

Dunlop, G. (2017, January 19). Saroo Brierley: The real-life search behind the film Lion. *BBC News.* Retrieved http://www.bbc.com/news/world-australia-38645840

Dunlosky, J., Rawson, K. A., Marsh, E. J., Nathan, M. J., & Willingham, D. T. (2013). Improving students' learning with effective learning techniques promising directions from cognitive and educational psychology. *Psychological Science in the Public Interest, 14,* 4–58.

Dunn, E. W., Aknin, L. B., & Norton, M. I. (2014). Prosocial spending and happiness: Using money to benefit others pays off. *Current Directions in Psychological Science, 23,* 41–47.

Duregotti, E., Zanetti, G., Scorzeto, M., Megighian, A., Montecucco, C., Pirazzini, M., & Rigoni, M. (2015). Snake and spider toxins induce a rapid recovery of function of botulinum neurotoxin paralysed neuromuscular junction. *Toxins, 7,* 5322–5336.

Dusek, J. A., Out, H. H., Wohlhueter, A. L., Bhasin, M., Zerbini, L. F., Joseph, M. G., . . . Libermann, T. A. (2008). Genomic counter-stress changes induced by the relaxation response. *PLoS ONE, 3,* e2576. doi:10.1371/journal.pone.0002576

Duzel, E., van Praag, H., & Sendtner, M. (2016). Can physical exercise in old age improve memory and hippocampal function? *Brain, 139,* 662–673.

Dwyer, C., Sowerby, L., & Rotenberg, B. W. (2016). Is cocaine a safe topical agent for use during endoscopic sinus surgery? *Laryngoscope, 126,* 1721–1723.

Eagly, A. H., & Crowley, M. (1986). Gender and helping behavior: A meta-analytic review of the social psychological literature. *Psychological Bulletin, 100,* 283–308.

Eastside College Preparatory School. (n.d.). *History.* Retrieved from http://www.eastside.org/_about/history.html

Eastwick, P. W., Eagly, A. H., Finkel, E. J., & Johnson, S. E. (2011). Implicit and explicit preferences for physical attractiveness in a romantic partner: A double dissociation in predictive validity. *Journal of Personality and Social Psychology, 101,* 993–1011.

Eastwick, P. W., Luchies, L. B., Finkel, E. J., & Hunt, L. L. (2014). The predictive validity of ideal partner preferences: A review and meta-analysis. *Psychological Bulletin, 140,* 623–665.

Eaton, N. R., Keyes, K. M., Krueger, R. F., Balsis, S., Skodol, A. E., Markon, K. E., . . . Hasin, D. S. (2012). An invariant dimensional liability model of gender differences in mental disorder prevalence: Evidence from a national sample. *Journal of Abnormal Psychology, 121,* 282–288.

Ebbinghaus, H. (1913). *Memory: A contribution to experimental psychology* (H. A. Ruger & C. E. Bussenius, Trans.). New York, NY: Teachers College, Columbia University. (Original work published 1885)

Ebrahim, I. O., Shapiro, C. M., Williams, A. J., & Fenwick, P. B. (2013). Alcohol and sleep I: Effects on normal sleep. *Alcoholism: Clinical and Experimental Research, 37,* 539–549.

Eckert, M. A., Keren, N. I., Roberts, D. R., Calhoun, V. D., & Harris, K. C. (2010). Age-related changes in processing speed: Unique contributions of cerebellar and prefrontal cortex. *Frontiers in Human Neuroscience, 4,* 1–14.

Eckstein, D., Aycock, K. J., Sperber, M. A., McDonald, J., Van Wiesner, V., III, Watts, R. E., & Ginsburg, P. (2010). A review of 200 birth-order studies: Lifestyle characteristics. *Journal of Individual Psychology, 6,* 408–434.

Edens, J. F., Kelley, S. E., Lilienfeld, S. O., Skeem, J. L., & Douglas, K. S. (2015). DSM-5 antisocial personality disorder: Predictive validity in a prison sample. *Law and Human Behavior, 39,* 123–129.

Editors of *The Lancet.* (2010). Retraction—Ileal-lymphoid-nodular hyperplasia, non-specific colitis, and pervasive developmental disorder in children. *The Lancet, 375,* 445.

Edsall, T. B. (2018, April 12). Trump wants America to revert to the Queens of his childhood. *The New York Times.* Retrieved from https://www.nytimes.com/2018/04/12/opinion/trump-queens-childhood-america.html

Edwards, A. C., Bigdeli, T. B., Docherty, A. R., Bacanu, S., Lee, D., De Candia, T. R., . . . Walsh, D. (2016). Meta-analysis of positive and negative symptoms reveals schizophrenia modifier genes. *Schizophrenia Bulletin, 42,* 279–287.

Egan, S. K., & Perry, D. G. (2001). Gender identity: A multidimensional analysis with implications for psychosocial adjustment. *Developmental Psychology, 37,* 451–463.

Eichenbaum, H. (2004). Hippocampus: Cognitive processes and neural representations that underlie declarative memory. *Neuron, 44,* 109–120.

Ekman, P. (1992). Are there basic emotions? *Psychological Review, 99,* 550–553.

Ekman, P. (2003). *Emotions revealed.* New York, NY: Times Books.

Ekman, P. (2016). What scientists who study emotion agree about. *Perspectives on Psychological Science, 11,* 31–34.

Ekman, P., & Friesen, W. V. (1971). Constants across cultures in the face and emotion. *Journal of Personality and Social Psychology, 17,* 124–129.

Ekman, P., & Keltner, D. (2014, April 10). Darwin's claim of universals in facial expressions not challenged. *Huffington Post.* Retrieved from http://www.huffingtonpost.com/paul-ekman/darwins-claim-of-universals-in-facial-expression-not-challenged_b_5121383.html

Ekman, P., Levenson, R. W., & Friesen, W. V. (1983). Autonomic nervous system activity distinguishes among emotions. *Science, 221,* 1208–1210.

El Mansari, M., Guiard, B. P., Chernoloz, O., Ghanbari, R., Katz, N., & Blier, P. (2010). Relevance of norepinephrine-dopamine interactions in the treatment of major depressive disorder. *CNS Neuroscience & Therapeutics, 16,* e1–e17. doi:10.1111/j.1755-5949.2010.00146.x

Elder, B. L., Ammar, E. M., & Pile, D. (2015). Sleep duration, activity levels, and measures of obesity in adults. *Public Health Nursing, 33,* 200–205.

Elder, C. R., Gullion, C. M., Funk, K. L., DeBar, L. L., Lindberg, N. M., & Stevens, V. J. (2012). Impact of sleep, screen time, depression and stress on weight change in the intensive weight loss phase of the LIFE study. *International Journal of Obesity, 36,* 86–92.

Elkind, D. (1967). Egocentrism in adolescence. *Child Development, 38,* 1025–1034.

Elliott, D. B., Krivickas, K., Brault, M. W., & Kreider, R. M. (2012, May 3–5). Historical marriage trends from 1890–2010: A focus on race differences. Paper presented at the annual meeting of the Population Association of America, San Francisco, CA.

Ellis, A., & Dryden, W. (1997). *The practice of rational emotive behavior therapy* (2nd ed.). New York, NY: Springer.

Else-Quest, N. M., Higgins, A., Allison, C., & Morton, L. C. (2012). Gender differences in self-conscious emotional experience: A meta-analysis. *Psychological Bulletin, 138,* 947–981.

Emmons, R. A., & McCullough, M. E. (2003). Counting blessings versus burdens: An experimental investigation of gratitude and subjective well-being in daily life. *Journal of Personality and Social Psychology, 84,* 377–389. doi:10.1037/0022-3514.84.2.377

Emmorey, K. (2015). The neurobiology of sign language. *Brain Mapping: An Encyclopedic Reference, 3,* 475–479.

Emotion. (n.d.). In *Online etymology dictionary.* Retrieved from http://www.etymonline.com/index.php?term=emotion

Endicott, L., Bock, T., & Narvaez, D. (2003). Moral reasoning, intercultural development, and multicultural experiences: Relations and cognitive underpinnings. *International Journal of Intercultural Relations, 27,* 403–419.

Englander, E., & McCoy, M. (2018). Sexting: Prevalence, age, sex, and outcomes. *JAMA Pediatrics, 172,* 317–318. doi:10.1001/jamapediatrics.2017.5682

Epstein, L., & Mardon, S. (2007). *The Harvard Medical School guide to a good night's sleep.* New York, NY: McGraw-Hill.

Epstein, R. (2016). Do gays have a choice? *Scientific American, 25,* 56–63.

Erdberg, P. (1990). Rorschach assessment. In G. Goldstein & M. Hersen (Eds.), *Handbook of psychological assessment* (2nd ed.). New York, NY: Pergamon.

Erickson, K. I., Voss, M. W., Prakash, R. S., Basak, C., Szabo, A., Chaddock, L., . . . Kramer, A. F. (2011). Exercise training increases size of hippocampus and improves memory. *Proceedings of the National Academy of Sciences, 108*(7), 3017–3022.

Ericsson, K. A. (2003). The acquisition of expert performance as problem solving. In J. E. Davidson & R. J. Sternberg (Eds.), *The psychology of problem solving* (pp. 31–83). Cambridge, UK: Cambridge University Press.

Erikson, E. H. (1993). *Childhood and society.* New York, NY: W. W. Norton.

Erikson, E. H., & Erikson, J. M. (1997). *The life cycle completed.* New York, NY: W. W. Norton.

Eriksson, P. S., Perfilieva, E., Bjork-Eriksson, T., Alborn, A. M., Nordborg, C., Peterson, D. A., & Gage, F. H. (1998). Neurogenesis in the adult human hippocampus. *Nature Medicine, 4,* 1313–1317.

Erland, L. A., & Saxena, P. K. (2017). Melatonin natural health products and supplements: Presence of serotonin and significant variability of melatonin content. *Journal of Clinical Sleep Medicine, 13,* 275–281.

Erol, A., & Karpyak, V. M. (2015). Sex and gender-related differences in alcohol use and its consequences: Contemporary knowledge and future research considerations. *Drug and Alcohol Dependence, 156,* 1–13.

Eskreis-Winkler, L., Shulman, E. P., Young, V., Tsukayama, E., Brunwasser, S. M., & Duckworth, A. L. (2016). Using wise interventions to motivate deliberate practice. *Journal of Personality and Social Psychology, 111,* 728–744.

Etaugh, C. (2008). Women in the middle and later years. In F. L. Denmark & M. Paludi (Eds.), *Psychology of women: Handbook of issues and theories* (2nd ed., pp. 271–302). Westport, CT: Praeger.

Evans, J. S. B., & Stanovich, K. E. (2013). Dual-process theories of higher cognition: Advancing the debate. *Perspectives on Psychological Science, 8,* 223–241.

Evans, V., & Green, M. (2006). *Cognitive linguistics: An introduction.* Mahwah, NJ: Erlbaum.

Evensen, S., Wisløff, T., Lystad, J. U., Bull, H., Ueland, T., & Falkum, E. (2016). Prevalence, employment rate, and cost of schizophrenia in a high-income welfare society: A population-based study using comprehensive health and welfare registers. *Schizophrenia Bulletin, 42,* 476–483.

Exner, J. E. (1980). But it's only an inkblot. *Journal of Personality Assessment, 44,* 562–577.

Exner, J. E. (1986). *The Rorschach: A comprehensive system* (Vol. 1, 2nd ed.). New York, NY: John Wiley & Sons.

Eysenck, H. J. (1967). *The biological basis of personality.* Springfield, IL: C. C. Thomas.

Eysenck, H. J. (1990). Biological dimensions of personality. In L. A. Pervin (Ed.), *Handbook of personality: Theory of research* (pp. 244–276). New York, NY: Guilford Press.

Eysenck, H. J., & Eysenck, B. G. (1968). *Manual for the Eysenck Personality Inventory.* San Diego, CA: Educational Industrial Testing Service.

Fabian, J. (2015, June 19). Obama goofs in speech at Tyler Perry's house. *The Hill.* Retrieved from http://thehill.com/homenews/administration/245512-obama-goofs-in-speech-at-tyler-perrys-house

Facebook Help Center. (2015). *What is the maximum number of friends that we can add on Facebook?* Retrieved from https://www.facebook.com/help/community/question/?id=567604083305019

Facer-Childs, E., & Brandstaetter, R. (2015). The impact of circadian phenotype and time since awakening on diurnal performance in athletes. *Current Biology, 25*(4), 518–522.

Fainaru, S. (2016, March 15). NFL acknowledges, for first time, link between football, brain disease. *ESPN.* Retrieved from http://espn.go.com/espn/otl/story/_/id/14972296/top-nfl-official-acknowledges-link-football-related-head-trauma-cte-first

Fainaru-Wada, M. (2013, February 15). League of denial: The NFL's concussion crisis. In M. Kirk (Producer & Director), J. Gilmore (Producer), & M. Wiser (Producer), *The Frontline interviews.* Boston, MA: PBS. Available from http://www.pbs.org/wgbh/pages/frontline/sports/league-of-denial/the-frontline-interview-sydney-seau-2/

Falk, D., Lepore, F. E., & Noe, A. (2013). The cerebral cortex of Albert Einstein: A description and preliminary analysis of unpublished photographs. *Brain, 136,* 1304–1327.

Fan, S. P., Liberman, Z., Keysar, B., & Kinzler, K. D. (2015). The exposure advantage: Early exposure to a multilingual environment promotes effective communication. *Psychological Science, 26,* 1090–1097.

Fancher, R. E., & Rutherford, A. (2012). *Pioneers of psychology: A history* (4th ed.). New York, NY: W. W. Norton.

Fantini, M. L., Corona, A., Clerici, S., & Ferini-Strambi, L. (2005). Aggressive dream content without daytime aggressiveness in REM sleep behavior disorder. *Neurology, 65,* 1010–1015.

Farah, M. J., Hutchinson, J., Phelps, E. A., & Wagner, A. D. (2014). Functional MRI-based lie detection: Scientific and societal challenges. *Nature Reviews Neuroscience, 15,* 123–131.

Farb, N. A., Chapman, H. A., & Anderson, A. K. (2013). Emotions: Form follows function. *Current Opinion in Neurobiology, 23,* 393–398.

Farha, B. (2007). *Paranormal claims: A critical analysis.* Lanham, MD: University Press of America.

Faria, M. A. (2013). Violence, mental illness, and the brain. A brief history of psychosurgery: Part 2–From the limbic system and cingulotomy to deep brain stimulation. *Surgical Neurology International, 4.* http://doi.org/10.4103/2152-7806.112825

Farthing, G. W. (1992). *The psychology of consciousness.* Upper Saddle River, NJ: Prentice Hall.

Fawal, J. (2015, November 23). After an 11-mile journey, a lost dog finds his way back to his foster mom. *Woman's Day.* Retrieved from http://www.womansday.com/life/pet-care/a52822/dog-walks-11-miles-back-to-foster-mom/

Faymonville, M. E., Laureys, S., Degueldre, C., DelFiore, G., Luxen, A., Franck, G., . . . Maquet, P. (2000). Neural mechanisms of antinociceptive effects of hypnosis. *Anesthesiology, 2,* 1257–1267.

Fazel, S., Gulati, G., Linsell, L., Geddes, J. R., & Grann, M. (2009). Schizophrenia and violence: Systematic review and meta-analysis. *PLOS Medicine, 6,* e1000120. doi:10.1371/journal.pmed.1000120

FBI Uniform Crime Reports. (n.d.). *Crime in the United States 2001, Section II—Crime index offenses reported.* Retrieved from https://ucr.fbi.gov/crime-in-the-u.s/2001/01sec2.pdf

Federal Bureau of Investigation. (n.d.). *Special agent selection process candidate information packet.* Retrieved from https://www.fbijobs.gov/sites/default/les/Special_Agent_Candidate_Information_Packet.pdf

Feigelman, S. (2011). The first year. In R. M. Kliegman, R. E. Behrman, H. B. Jenson, & B. F. Stanton (Eds.), *Nelson textbook of pediatrics* (19th ed., pp. 26–30). Philadelphia, PA: Saunders Elsevier.

Feinstein, A., Freeman, J., & Lo, A. C. (2015). Treatment of progressive multiple sclerosis: What works, what does not, and what is needed. *The Lancet Neurology, 14,* 194–207.

Feinstein, J. S., Adolphs, R., Damasio, A., & Tranel, D. (2011). The human amygdala and the induction and experience of fear. *Current Biology, 21,* 34–38.

Feinstein, R., Heiman, N., & Yager, J. (2015). Common factors affecting psychotherapy outcomes: Some implications for teaching psychotherapy. *Journal of Psychiatric Practice, 21,* 180–189.

Feist, G. J. (2004). Creativity and the frontal lobes. *Bulletin of Psychology and the Arts, 5,* 21–28.

Feldman, G., Lian, H., Kosinski, M., & Stillwell, D. (2017). Frankly, we do give a damn: The relationship between profanity and honesty. *Social Psychological and Personality Science, 8,* 816–826.

Feng, P., Huang, L., & Wang, H. (2013). Taste bud homeostasis in health, disease, and aging. *Chemical Senses, 39,* 3–16.

Ferguson, C. J. (2010). Genetic contributions to antisocial personality and behavior: A meta-analytic review from an evolutionary perspective. *Journal of Social Psychology, 150,* 160–180.

Ferguson, C. J. (2015). "Everybody knows psychology is not a real science": Public perceptions of psychology and how we can improve our relationship with policymakers, the scientific community, and the general public. *American Psychologist, 70,* 527–542.

Fernald, A., Marchman, V. A., & Weisleder, A. (2014). SES differences in language processing skill and vocabulary are evident at 18 months. *Developmental Science, 16,* 234–248.

Ferrante, A., Gellerman, D., Ay, A., Woods, K. P., Filipowica, A. M., Jain, K., . . . Ingram, K. K. (2015). Diurnal preference predicts phase differences in expression of human peripheral circadian clock genes. *Journal of Circadian Rhythms, 13,* 1–7.

Ferri, M., Amato, L., & Davoli, M. (2006). Alcoholics Anonymous and other 12-step programmes for alcohol dependence. *Cochrane Database of Systematic Reviews.* doi:10.1002/14651858.CD005032.pub2

Ferris, P. A., Kline, T. J. B., & Bourdage, J. S. (2012). He said, she said: Work, biopsychosocial, and lifestyle contributions to coronary heart disease risk. *Health Psychology, 31,* 503–511.

Fessler, L. (2017, June 22). Good managers give constructive criticism—but truly masterful leaders offer constructive praise. *Quartz.* Retrieved from https://qz.com/1010784/good-managers-give-constructive-criticism-but-truly-masterful-leaders-give-constructive-praise/

Festinger, L. (1957). *A theory of cognitive dissonance.* New York, NY: Harper & Row.

Festinger, L., & Carlsmith, J. M. (1959). Cognitive consequences of forced compliance. *Journal of Abnormal and Social Psychology, 58,* 203–210.

Festinger, L., Schachter, S., & Back, K. (1950). *Social pressures in informal groups: A study of human factors in housing.* Stanford, CA: Stanford University Press.

Fiegl, A. (2012, December 12). The healing power of dogs. *National Geographic News.* Retrieved from http://news.nationalgeographic.com/news/2012/12/121221-comfort-dogs-newtown-tragedy-animal-therapy/

Field, T. (1996). Attachment and separation in young children. *Annual Review of Psychology, 47,* 541–561.

Filkins, D. (2004, November 21). In Falluja, young Marines saw the savagery of an urban war. *The New York Times.* Retrieved from http://www.nytimes.com/2004/11/21/international/middleeast/21battle.html?_r=0

Fincham, F. D., & May, R. W. (2017). Infidelity in romantic relationships. *Current Opinion in Psychology, 13,* 70–74.

Fine, E. J., Ionita, C. C., & Lohr, L. (2002). The history of the development of the cerebellar examination. *Seminars in Neurology, 22,* 375–384.

Fine, J. (2013, February 7). Rescuing Cesar Millan. *Men's Journal.* Retrieved from http://www.mensjournal.com/magazine/rescuing-dog-whisperer-cesar-millan-20130207

Fink, G. (2011). Stress controversies: Post-traumatic stress disorder, hippocampal volume, gastroduodenal ulceration. *Journal of Neuroendocrinology, 23,* 107–117.

Fink, G. (2017). Selye's general adaptation syndrome: Stress-induced gastroduodenal ulceration and inflammatory bowel disease. *Journal of Endocrinology, 232,* F1–F5.

Fink, M. (2014). What was learned: Studies by the consortium for research in ECT (CORE) 1997–2011. *Acta Psychiatrica Scandinavica, 129,* 417–4226.

Finucane, A. M. (2011). The effect of fear and anger on selective attention. *Emotion, 11,* 970–974.

Firestein, S. (2001). How the olfactory system makes sense of scents. *Nature, 413,* 211–218.

Firth, J., Torous, J., Nicholas, J., Carney, R., Rosenbaum, S., & Sarris, J. (2017). Can smartphone mental health interventions reduce symptoms of anxiety? A meta-analysis of randomized controlled trials. *Journal of Affective Disorders, 218,* 15–22.

Firth, S. (2005). End-of-life: A Hindu view. *The Lancet, 366,* 682–686.

Fischer, B., & Rehm, J. (2007). Illicit opioid use in the 21st century: Witnessing a paradigm shift? *Addiction, 102,* 499–501.

Fischer, P., Krueger, J. I., Greitemeyer, T., Vogrincic, C., Kastenmüller, A., Frey, D., . . . Kainbacher, M. (2011). The bystander-effect: A meta-analytic review on bystander intervention in dangerous and non-dangerous emergencies. *Psychological Bulletin, 137,* 517–537.

Fisher, L. B., Overholser, J. C., Ridley, J., Braden, A., & Rosoff, C. (2015). From the outside looking in: Sense of belonging, depression, and suicide risk. *Psychiatry, 78,* 29–41.

Fisher, T. D., & Brunell, A. B. (2014). A bogus pipeline approach to studying gender differences in cheating behavior. *Personality and Individual Differences, 61,* 91–96.

Fitzpatrick, M. J., & McPherson, B. J. (2010). Coloring within the lines: Gender stereotypes in contemporary coloring books. *Sex Roles, 62,* 127–137.

Flaherty, B. (2017, May 27). Bryce Harper to young players: "No participation trophies, okay. First place only." *The Washington Post.* Retrieved from https://www.washingtonpost.com/news/dc-sports-bog/wp/2017/05/27/bryce-harper-to-young-players-no-participation-trophies-okay-first-place-only/?utm_term=.ddc08fc3c2e5

Flor, H., & Birbaumer, N. (1993). Comparison of the efficacy of electromyographic biofeedback, cognitive-behavioral therapy, and conservative medical interventions in the treatment of chronic musculoskeletal pain. *Journal of Consulting and Clinical Psychology, 61,* 653–658.

Flor, H., Nikolajsen, L., & Jensen, T. S. (2006). Phantom limb pain: A case of maladaptive CNS plasticity? *Nature Reviews Neuroscience, 7,* 873–881.

Flora, C. (2018). Are smartphones really destroying the adolescent brain? *Scientific American, 318,* 30–37.

Flueck, J. L., Schaufelberger, F., Lienert, M., Schäfer Olstad, D., Wilhelm, M., & Perret, C. (2016). Acute effects of caffeine on heart rate variability, blood pressure and tidal volume in paraplegic and tetraplegic compared to able-bodied individuals: A randomized, blinded trial. *PLoS One, 11,* e0165034.

Flynn, J. R. (2009). *What is intelligence? Beyond the Flynn effect.* Cambridge, UK: Cambridge University Press.

Flynn, J. R. (2012). *Are we getting smarter? Rising IQ in the twenty-first century.* Cambridge, UK: Cambridge University Press.

Fogel, S. M., & Smith, C. T. (2011). The function of the sleep spindle: A psychological index of intelligence and a mechanism for sleep-dependent memory consolidation. *Neuroscience & Biobehavioral Reviews, 35,* 1154–1165.

Folkman, S., & Lazarus, R. S. (1985). If it changes it must be a process: Study of emotion and coping during three stages of a college examination. *Journal of Personality and Social Psychology, 48,* 150–170.

Foos, P. W., & Goolkasian, P. (2008). Presentation format effects in a levels-of-processing task. *Experimental Psychology, 55,* 215–227.

Forbes, C. E., Poore, J. C., Krueger, F., Barbey, A. K., Solomon, J., & Grafman, J. (2014). The role of executive function and the dorsolateral prefrontal cortex in the expression of neuroticism and conscientiousness. *Social Neuroscience, 9,* 139–151.

Ford, M., Acosta, A., & Sutcliffe, T. J. (2013). Beyond terminology: The policy impact of a grassroots movement. *Intellectual and Developmental Disabilities, 51,* 108–112.

Forgas, J. P. (2008). Affect and cognition. *Perspectives on Psychological Science, 3,* 94–101.

Forger, D. B., & Peskin, C. S. (2003). A detailed predictive model of the mammalian circadian clock. *Proceedings of the National Academy of Sciences, 100,* 14806–14811.

Foroughi, C. K, Werner, N. E., Barragán, D., & Boehm-Davis, D. A. (2015). Interruptions disrupt reading comprehension. *Journal of Experimental Psychology: General, 144,* 704–709.

Foss, D. J., & Pirozzolo, J. W. (2017). Four semesters investigating frequency of testing, the testing effect, and transfer of training. *Journal of Educational Psychology, 109*(8), 1067–1083.

Fournier, J. C., DeRubeis, R. J., Hollon, S. D., Dimidjian, S., Amsterdam, J. D., Shelton, R. C., & Fawcett, J. (2010). Antidepressant drug effects and depression severity. *Journal of the American Medical Association, 303,* 47–53.

Fowlkes, C. C., Martin, D. R., & Malik, J. (2007). Local figure–ground cues are valid for natural images. *Journal of Vision, 7,* 1–9.

Fox, M. (2013, July 25). Virginia Johnson, Masters' collaborator in sex research, dies at 88. The New York Times. Retrieved from http://www.nytimes.com/2013/07/26/us/virginia-johnson-masterss-collaborator-in-sex-research-diesat-88.html–pagewanted=all&_r=0

Fox, N. A., Snidman, N., Haas, S. A., Degnan, K. A., & Kagan, J. (2015). The relations between reactivity at 4 months and behavioral inhibition in the second year: Replication across three independent samples. *Infancy, 20,* 98-114.

Fozard, J. L. (1990). Vision and hearing in aging. *Handbook of the Psychology of Aging, 3,* 143–156.

Frances, A. (2016). Entrenched reductionisms: The bete noire of psychiatry. *History of Psychology, 19,* 57–59.

Francis, W. S., & Gutiérrez, M. (2012). Bilingual recognition memory: Stronger performance but weaker levels-of-processing effects in the less fluent language. *Memory Cognition, 40,* 496–503.

Frankenburg, W. K., Dodds, J., Archer, P., Shapiro, H., & Bresnick, B. (1992). The Denver II: A major revision and restandardization of the Denver Developmental Screening Test. *Pediatrics, 89,* 91–97.

Franklin, J. (2011). *33 Men: Inside the miraculous survival and dramatic rescue of the Chilean miners.* New York, NY: G.P. Putnam's Sons.

Franklin, K. A., & Lindberg, E. (2015). Obstructive sleep apnea is a common disorder in the population—a review on the epidemiology of sleep apnea. *Journal of Thoracic Disease, 7,* 1311–1322.

Fratiglioni, L., Paillard-Borg, S., & Winblad, B. (2004). An active and socially integrated lifestyle in late life might protect against dementia. *The Lancet Neurology, 3,* 343–353.

Freedman, J. L., & Fraser, S. C. (1966). Compliance without pressures: The foot-in-the-door technique. *Journal of Personality and Social Psychology, 4,* 195–202.

Frequently asked questions about chronic traumatic encephalopathy. (n.d.). Retrieved from http://www.bu.edu/cte/about/what-is-cte/

Freud Museum. (n.d.). About the museum. Retrieved from http://www.freud.org.uk/about/

Freud, S. (1949). *An outline of psychoanalysis* (James Strachey, Trans.). New York, NY: W. W. Norton. (Original work published 1940)

Freud, S. (1953). The interpretation of dreams. In J. Strachey (Ed. and Trans.), *The standard edition of the complete psychological works of Sigmund Freud* (Vol. 4, pp. 1–338; Vol. 5, pp. 339–621). London, UK: Hogarth Press. (Original work published 1900)

Freud, S. (1953). Three essays on the theory of sexuality. In J. Strachey (Ed. and Trans.), *The standard edition of the complete psychological works of Sigmund Freud* (Vol. 7, pp. 123–245). London, UK: Hogarth Press. (Original work published 1905)

Freud, S. (1960). *The ego and the id.* (Joan Riviere, Trans., & James Strachey, Ed.). New York, NY: W. W. Norton. (Original work published 1923)

Freud, S. (1961). The ego and the id. In J. Strachey (Ed. and Trans.), *The standard edition of the complete psychological works of Sigmund Freud* (Vol. 19, pp. 1–66). London, UK: Hogarth Press. (Original work published 1923)

Freud, S. (1964). New introductory lectures on psycho-analysis. In J. Strachey (Ed. and Trans.), *The standard edition of the complete psychological works of Sigmund Freud* (Vol. 22, pp. 1–182). London, UK: Hogarth Press. (Original work published 1933)

Freud, S. (1966). *Introductory lectures on psycho-analysis: The standard edition.* New York, NY: W. W. Norton. (Original work published 1917)

Fridlund, A. J., Beck, H. P., Goldie, W. D., & Irons, G. (2012). Little Albert: A neurologically impaired child. *History of Psychology, 15*(4), 302–327.

Friedman, B. H., Stephens, C. L., & Thayer, J. F. (2014). Redundancy analysis of autonomic and self-reported, responses to induced emotions. *Biological Psychology, 98,* 19–28.

Friedman, H. (2014). Are humanistic and positive psychology really incommensurate? *American Psychologist, 69,* 89–90. Retrieved from http://dx.doi.org/10.1037/a0034865

Friedman, M., & Rosenman, R. H. (1974). *Type A behavior and your heart.* New York, NY: Knopf.

Friedman, R. A. (2017, February 13). LSD to cure depression? Not so fast. *The New York Times.* Retrieved from https://www.nytimes.com/2017/02/13/opinion/lsd-to-cure-depression-not-so-fast.html?_r=0

Friedmann, N., & Rusou, D. (2015). Critical period for first language: The crucial role of language input during the first year of life. *Current Opinion in Neurobiology, 35,* 27–34.

Fry, R. (2015, November 11). Record share of young women are living with their parents, relatives. *Pew Research Center.* Retrieved from http://www.pewresearch.org/fact-tank/2015/11/11/record-share-of-young-women-are-living-with-their-parents-relatives/

Fukada, M., Kano, E., Miyoshi, M., Komaki, R., & Watanabe, T. (2012). Effect of "rose essential oil" inhalation on stress-induced skin-barrier disruption in rats and humans. *Chemical Senses, 37,* 347–356.

Fuller, D. A., Sinclair, E., Geller, J., Quanbeck, C., & Snook, J. (2016). *Going, going, gone: Trends and consequences of eliminating state psychiatric beds, 2016.* Arlington, VA: Treatment Advocacy Center.

Fully present: The book. (2010, August 3). Fully present: The book-meditation [Video file]. Retrieved from https://www.youtube.com/watch?v=k8ARntepT6g

Furnham, A., & Hughes, D. J. (2014). Myths and misconceptions in popular psychology: Comparing psychology students and the general public. *Teaching of Psychology, 4,* 256–261.

Furtado, A. (Writer). (2014). Boss with a bark [Television series episode]. In D. Leepson & C. Millan (Producers), *Cesar 911.* Washington, DC: Nat Geo Wild.

Fusar-Poli, P., Papanastasiou, E., Stahl, D., Rocchetti, M., Carpenter, W., Shergill, S., & McGuire, P. (2015). Treatments of negative symptoms in schizophrenia: Meta-analysis of 168 randomized placebo-controlled trials. *Schizophrenia Bulletin, 41,* 892–899.

Fusar-Poli, P., Smieskova, R., Kempton, M. J., Ho, B. C., Andreasen, N. C., & Borgwardt, S. (2013). Progressive brain changes in schizophrenia related to antipsychotic treatment? A meta-analysis of longitudinal MRI studies. *Neuroscience & Biobehavioral Reviews, 37,* 1680–1691.

Füzesi, T., & Bains, J. S. (2015). A tonic for anxiety. *Nature Neuroscience, 18,* 1434–1435.

Gabrieli, J. D. E., Corkin, S., Mickel, S. F., & Growdon, J. H. (1993). Intact acquisition and long-term retention of mirror-tracing skill in Alzheimer's disease and in global amnesia. *Behavioral Neuroscience, 107,* 899–910.

Gackenbach, J., & LaBerge, S. (Eds.). (1988). *Conscious mind, sleeping brain: Perspectives on lucid dreaming.* New York, NY: Plenum Press.

Gagnon, K., & Sabus, C. (2015). Professionalism in a digital age: Opportunities and considerations for using social media in health care. *Physical Therapy, 95,* 406–414.

Galanter, E. (1962). Contemporary psychophysics. In R. Brown, E. Galanter, E. H. Hess, & G. Mandler (Eds.), *New directions in psychology* (pp. 87–156). New York, NY: Holt, Rinehart & Winston.

Galati, D., Scherer, K. R., & Ricci-Bitti, P. E. (1997). Voluntary facial expression of emotion: Comparing congenitally blind with normally sighted encoders. *Journal of Personality and Social Psychology, 73,* 1363–1379.

Galbraith, K. (2015, April 7). Can orange glasses help you sleep better? [Web log post]. Retrieved from http://well.blogs.nytimes.com/2015/04/07/can-orange- glasses-help-you-sleep-better/?_r=1

Gale, C. R., Batty, G. D., & Deary, I. J. (2008). Locus of control at age 10 years and health outcomes and behaviors at age 30 years: The 1970 British Cohort Study. *Psychosomatic Medicine, 70,* 397–403.

Gamer, M. (2009). Portrait of a lie. *Scientific American Mind, 20,* 50–55.

Gandhi, T., Kalia, A., Ganesh, S., & Sinha, P. (2015). Immediate susceptibility to visual illusions after sight onset. *Current Biology, 25*(9), R358–R359.

Gandolphe, M. C., & El Haj, M. (2017). Flashbulb memories of the Paris attacks. *Scandinavian Journal of Psychology, 58,* 199–204.

Gangestad, S. W., & Haselton, M. G. (2015). Human estrus: Implications for relationship science. *Current Opinion in Psychology, 1,* 45–51.

Gangestad, S. W., & Scheyd, G. J. (2005). The evolution of human physical attractiveness. *Annual Review of Anthropology, 34,* 523–548.

Ganim, S., Grinberg, E., & Welch, C. (2017, June 13). In video of Penn State hazing death, victim looked "like a corpse." *CNN.* Retrieved from http://www.cnn.com/2017/06/12/us/penn-state-hearing-video-timothy-piazza/index.html

Ganis, G., Thompson, W. L., & Kosslyn, S. M. (2004). Brain areas underlying visual mental imagery and visual perception: An fMRI study. *Cognitive Brain Research, 20,* 226–241.

Gannon, M. (2016, February 5). Race is a social construct, scientists argue. *Scientific American.* Retrieved from https://www.scientificamerican.com/article/race-is-a-social-construct-scientists-argue/

Ganzel, B. L., Morris, P. A., & Wethington, E. (2010). Allostasis and the human brain: Integrating models of stress from the social and life sciences. *Psychological Review, 117,* 134–174.

Garcia, J., Ervin, F. R., & Koelling, R. A. (1966). Learning with prolonged delay of reinforcement. *Psychonomic Science, 5,* 121–122.

Garcia, J. R., Reiber, C., Massey, S. G., & Merriwether, A. M. (2012). Sexual hookup culture: A review. *Review of General Psychology, 16,* 161–176.

García-Lázaro, H., Ramirez-Carmona, R., Lara-Romero, R., & Roldan-Valadez, E. (2012). Neuroanatomy of episodic and semantic memory in humans: A brief review of neuroimaging studies. *Neurology India, 60,* 613–617.

Gardner, H. (1999). *Intelligence reframed: Multiple intelligences for the 21st century.* New York, NY: Basic Books.

Gardner, H. (2003, April). Multiple intelligences after twenty years. Paper presented at the annual meeting of the American Educational Research Association, Chicago, IL.

Gardner, H. (2011). *Frames of mind: The theory of multiple intelligences.* New York, NY: Basic Books.

Gardner, H., & Hatch, T. (1989). Educational implications of the theory of multiple intelligences. *Educational Researcher, 18,* 4–10.

Garry, M., & Gerrie, M. P. (2005). When photographs create false memories. *Current Directions in Psychological Science, 14,* 321–325.

Gary, J., & Rubin, N.S. (2014, December). A first person account of the refugee experience: Identifying psychosocial stressors and formulating psychological responses. *Psychology International.* Retrieved from http://www.apa.org/international/pi/2014/12/global-violence.aspx

Gastil, J. (1990). Generic pronouns and sexist language: The oxymoronic character of masculine generics. *Sex Roles, 23,* 629–643.

Gatchel, R. J., Haggard, R., Thomas, C., & Howard, K. J. (2013). Biopsychosocial approaches to understanding chronic pain and disability. In R. J. Moore (Ed.), *Handbook of pain and palliative care* (pp. 1–16). New York, NY: Springer.

Gatchel, R. J., & Maddrey, A. M. (2004). The biopsychosocial perspective of pain. In J. M. Raczynski & L. C. Leviton (Eds.), *Handbook of clinical health psychology: Vol 2. Disorders of behavior and health* (pp. 357–378). Washington, DC: American Psychological Association.

Gatchel, R. J., Peng, Y. B., Peters, M. L., Fuchs, P. N., & Turk, D. C. (2007). The biopsychosocial approach to chronic pain: Scientific advances and future directions. *Psychological Bulletin, 133,* 581–624.

Gates, G. J. (2011). *How many people are lesbian, gay, bisexual, and transgendered?* Los Angeles, CA: Williams Institute, UCLA School of Law. Retrieved from http://williamsinstitute.law.ucla.edu/research/census-lgbt-demographics-studies/how-many-people-are-lesbian-gay-bisexual-and-transgender/

Gatto, N. M., Henderson, V. W., Hodis, H. N., St John, J., Lurmann, F., Chen, J. C., & Mack, W. J. (2014). Components of air pollution and cognitive function in middle-aged and older adults in Los Angeles. *Neurotoxicology, 40,* 1–7.

Gaval-Cruz, M., & Weinshenker, D. (2009). Mechanisms of disulfiram-induced cocaine abstinence: Antabuse and cocaine relapse. *Molecular Interventions, 9,* 175–187.

Gavie, J., & Revonsuo, A. (2010). The future of lucid dreaming treatment [Commentary on "The neurobiology of consciousness: Lucid dreaming wakes up" by J. Allan Hobson]. *International Journal of Dream Research, 3,* 13–15.

Gay, P. (1988). *Freud: A life for our time.* New York, NY: W. W. Norton.

Gayton, S. D., & Lovell, G. P. (2012). Resilience in ambulance service paramedics and its relationships with well-being and general health. *Traumatology, 18,* 58–64. doi:10.1177/1534765610396727

Gazzaniga, M. S. (1967). The split brain in man. *Scientific American, 217,* 24–29.

Gazzaniga, M. S. (1998). The split brain revisited. *Scientific American, 279,* 50–55.

Gazzaniga, M. S. (2005). Forty-five years of split-brain research and still going strong. *Nature Reviews Neuroscience, 6,* 653–659.

Gazzaniga, M. S., Bogen, J. E., & Sperry, R. W. (1965). Observations on visual perception after disconnection of the cerebral hemispheres in man. *Brain, 88,* 221–236.

Genetics Home Reference. (2017, July 13). *Congenital insensitivity to pain with anhidrosis.* Retrieved from https://ghr.nlm.nih.gov/condition/congenital-insensitivity-to-pain-with-anhidrosis

Genetics Home Reference. (2017, July 5). *Narcolepsy.* Retrieved from https://ghr.nlm.nih.gov/condition/narcolepsy

Gentile, D. A., Reimer, R. A., Nathanson, A. I., Walsh, D. A., & Eisenmann, J. C. (2014). Protective the effects of parental monitoring of children's media use: A prospective study. *JAMA Pediatrics, 168*(5), 479–484.

Genzel, L., Rossato, J. I., Jacobse, J., Grieves, R. M., Spooner, P. A., Battaglia, F. P., . . . Morris, R. G. (2017). The yin and yang of memory consolidation: Hippocampal and neocortical. *PLoS Biology, 15*(1), e2000531. doi:10.1371/journal.pbio.2000531

George, M. J., Russell, M. A., Piontak, J. R., & Odgers, C. L. (2018). Concurrent and subsequent associations between daily digital technology use and high risk adolescents' mental health symptoms. *Child Development, 89,* 78-88.

George, M. S. (2003, September). Stimulating the brain. *Scientific American,* 69.

Georgiadis, J. R., Reinders, A. A. T., Paans, A. M., Renken, R., & Kortekaas, R. (2009). Men versus women on sexual brain function: Prominent differences during tactile genital stimulation, but not during orgasm. *Human Brain Mapping, 30,* 3089–3101.

Gerbasi, M. E., Richards, L. K., Thomas, J. J., Agnew-Blais, J. C., Thompson-Brenner, H., Gilman, S. E., & Becker, A. E. (2014). Globalization and eating disorder risk: Peer influence, perceived social norms, and adolescent disordered eating in Fiji. *International Journal of Eating Disorders, 47, 727–737.*

Gerhart, B., & Fang, M. (2015). Pay, intrinsic motivation, extrinsic motivation, performance, and creativity in the workplace: Revisiting long-held beliefs. *Annual Reviews of Organizational Psychology and Organizational Behavior, 2,* 489–521.

German, T. P., & Defeyter, M. A. (2000). Immunity to functional fixedness in young children. *Psychonomic Bulletin & Review, 7,* 707–712.

Gershoff, E. T. (2016). Should parents' physical punishment of children be considered a source of toxic stress that affects brain development? *Family Relations, 65,* 151–162.

Gershoff, E. T., & Grogan-Kaylor, A. (2016). Spanking and child outcomes: Old controversies and new meta-analyses. *Journal of Family Psychology, 30,* 453–469.

Gerstein, J. (2017, July 27). Justice Department says no LGBT protection in federal sex-discrimination law. *Politico.* Retrieved from https://www.politico.com/story/2017/07/27/lgbt-protection-sex-discrimination-law-241039

Gerstorf, D., Ram, N., Hoppmann, C., Willis, S. L., & Schaie, K. W. (2011). Cohort differences in cognitive aging and terminal decline in the Seattle Longitudinal Study. *Developmental Psychology, 47,* 1026–1041.

Ghose, T. (2014, August 18). Botox: Uses and side effects. *LiveScience.* Retrieved from http://www.livescience.com/44222-botox-uses-side-effects.html

Gibson, E. J., & Walk, R. D. (1960). The "visual cliff." *Scientific American, 202,* 80–92.

Giedd, J. N., Lalonde, F. M., Celano, M. J., White, S. L., Wallace, G. L., Lee, N. R., & Lenroot, R. K. (2009). Anatomical brain magnetic resonance imaging of typically developing children and adolescents. *Journal of the American Academy of Child and Adolescent Psychiatry, 48,* 465–475.

Gifford, K. (2013, March 22). Meditation saved my job and changed my life. *Huffington Post.* Retrieved from http://www.huffingtonpost.com/karen-gifford/meditation-saved-my-job_b_2932819.html

Gilger, J. W., Allen, K., & Castillo, A. (2016). Reading disability and enhanced dynamic spatial reasoning: A review of the literature. *Brain and Cognition, 105,* 55–65.

Gillan, C. M., & Robbins, T. W. (2014). Goal-directed learning and obsessive-compulsive disorder. *Philosophical Transactions of the Royal Society B, 369,* 1–11.

Gilligan, C. (1982). *In a different voice: Psychological theory and women's development.* Cambridge, MA: Harvard University Press.

Gillin, J. C. (2002, March 25). How long can humans stay awake? *Scientific American.* Retrieved from http://www.scientificamerican.com/article.cfm?id=how-long-can-humans-stay

Gilman, S. E., & Becker, A. E. (2014). Globalization and eating disorder risk: Peer influence, perceived social norms, and adolescent disordered eating in Fiji. *International Journal of Eating Disorders, 47,* 727–737.

Gilovich, T., & Kumar, A. (2015). We'll always have Paris: The hedonic payoff from experiential and material investments. *Advances in Experimental Social Psychology, 51,* 147–187.

Girodo, M., & Henry, D. R. (1976). Cognitive, physiological and behavioural components of anxiety in flooding. *Canadian Journal of Behavioural Science, 8,* 224–231.

Glahn, D. C., Laird, A. R., Ellison-Wright, I., Thelen, S. M., Robinson, J. L., Lancaster, J. L., . . . Fox, P. (2008). Meta-analysis of gray matter anomalies in schizophrenia: Application of anatomic likelihood estimation and network analysis. *Biological Psychiatry, 64,* 774–781.

Glaser, G. (2015, April). The irrationality of alcoholics anonymous. *The Atlantic.* Retrieved from http://www.theatlantic.com/magazine/archive/2015/04/the-irrationality-of-alcoholics-anonymous/386255/

Glaser, R., & Kiecolt-Glaser, J. K. (2005). Stress-induced immune dysfunction: Implications for health. *Nature Reviews Immunology, 5,* 243–251.

Glass, R. M. (2001). Electroconvulsive therapy: Time to bring it out of the shadows. *Journal of the American Medical Association, 285,* 1346–1348.

Glass, S. T., Lingg, E., & Heuberger, E. (2015). Do ambient urban odors evoke basic emotions? *Frontiers in Psychology, 5.* doi:10.3389/fpsyg.2014.00340

Glenn, A. L., Raine, A., Schug, R. A., Gao, Y., & Granger, D. A. (2011). Increased testosterone-to-cortisol ration in psychopathy. *Journal of Abnormal Psychology, 120,* 389–399.

Glikson, E., Cheshin, A., & van Kleef, G. A. (2017). The dark side of a smiley: Effects of smiling emoticons on virtual first impressions. *Social Psychological and Personality Science.* doi:10.1177/1948550617720269

Global Initiative to End All Corporal Punishment of Children. (n.d.). Retrieved from http://www.endcorporalpunishment.org

Go, A. S., Mozaffarian, D., Roger, V. L., Benjamin, E. J., Berry, J. D., Borden, W. B., . . . Turner, M. B. (2013). Heart disease and stroke statistics—2013 update: A report from the American Heart Association. *Circulation, 127,* e6–e245.

Godden, D. R., & Baddeley, A. D. (1975). Context-dependent memory in two natural environments: On land and underwater. *British Journal of Psychology, 66,* 325–331.

Godlee, F., Smith, J., & Marcovitch, H. (2011). Wakefield's article linking MMR vaccine and autism was fraudulent. *British Medical Journal, 342,* c7452.

Goel, N., Rao, H., Durmer, J. S., & Dinges, D. F. (2009, September). Neurocognitive consequences of sleep deprivation. *Seminars in Neurology, 29,* 320–339.

Goes, F. S., Pirooznia, M., Parla, J. S., Kramer, M., Ghiban, E., Mavruk, S., . . . Potash, J. B. (2016). Exome sequencing of familial bipolar disorder. *JAMA Psychiatry, 73,* 590–597.

Goforth, A. N., Oka, E. R., Leong, F. T. L., & Denis, D. J. (2014). Acculturation, acculturative stress, religiosity and psychological adjustment among Muslim Arab American adolescents. *Journal of Muslim Mental Health, 8,* 3–19.

Gogtay, N., Vyas, N. S., Testa, R., Wood, S. J., & Pantelis, C. (2011). Age of onset of schizophrenia: Perspectives from neural structural neuroimaging studies. *Schizophrenia Bulletin, 37,* 504–513.

Goksan, S., Hartley, C., Emery, F., Cockrill, N., Poorun, R., Moultrie, F., . . . Slater, R. (2015). fMRI reveals neural activity overlap between adult and infant pain. *eLife, 4,* e06356. doi:10.7554/eLife.06356

Gold, R. B. (2005). The implications of defining when a woman is pregnant. *Guttmacher Report on Public Policy, 8*(2), 7–10.

Goldin, P. R., Morrison, A., Jazaieri, H., Brozovich, F., Heimberg, R., & Gross, J. J. (2016). Group CBT versus MBSR for social anxiety disorder: A randomized controlled trial. *Journal of Consulting and Clinical Psychology, 84,* 427–437.

Goldin-Meadow, S. (1978). Review: A study in human capacities. *Science, 200,* 649–651.

Goldman, B. (2017, Spring). Two minds. Stanford Medicine. Retrieved from https://stanmed.stanford.edu/2017spring/how-mens-and-womens-brains-are-different.html

Goldman, J. G. (2012, December 13). What is operant conditioning? (And how does it explain driving dogs?) [Web log post]. Retrieved from http://blogs.scientificamerican.com/thoughtful-animal/what-is-operant-conditioning-and-how-does-it-explain-driving-dogs/

Goldsmith, H. H., Buss, A. H., Plomin, R., Rothbart, M. K., Chess, S., Hinde, R. A., & McCall, R. B. (1987). What is temperament? Four approaches. *Child Development, 58,* 505–529.

Goldstein, E. B. (2011). *Cognitive psychology: Connecting mind, research, and everyday experience* (3rd ed.). Belmont, CA: Wadsworth, Cengage Learning.

Goleman, D. (1995). *Emotional intelligence.* New York, NY: Bantam.

Golinkoff, R. M., Can, D. D., Soderstrom, M., & Hirsh-Pasek, K. (2015). (Baby) Talk to me: The social context of infant-directed speech and its effects on early language acquisition. *Current Directions in Psychological Science, 24,* 339–344.

Gollwitzer, A., & Bargh, J. A. (2018). Social psychological skill and its correlates. *Social Psychology, 49,* 88–102.

Golumbic, E. M. Z., Ding, N., Bickel, S., Lakatos, P., Schevon, C. A., McKhann, G. M., . . . Poeppel, D. (2013). Mechanisms underlying selective neuronal tracking of attended speech at a "cocktail party." *Neuron, 77*(5), 980–991.

Gonzales, R., & Raphelson, S. (2018, March 23). Trump memo disqualifies certain transgender people from military service. NPR. Retrieved from https://www.npr.org/sections/thetwo-way/2018/03/23/596594346/trump-memo-disqualifies-certain-transgender-people-from-military-service

Gonzalez, A. M., Steele, J. R., & Baron, A. S. (2017). Reducing children's implicit racial bias through exposure to positive out-group exemplars. *Child Development, 88,* 123–130.

Goodnough, A. (2017, July 6). Opioid prescriptions fall after 2010 peak, C.D.C. report finds. *The New York Times.* Retrieved from https://www.nytimes.com/2017/07/06/health/opioid-painkillers-prescriptions-united-states.html

Gooriah, R., & Ahmed, F. (2015). Therapeutic uses of botulinum toxin. *Journal of Clinical Toxicology, 5.* doi:10.4172/2161-0495.1000225

Gordon, B. (2013, January 1). Does photographic memory exist? *Scientific American Mind, 23.* Retrieved from http://www.scientificamerican.com/article/i-developed-what-appears-to-be-a-ph/

Gordon, B. (2013, January/February). I developed what appears to be a photographic memory when I was 16 years old. Does this kind of memory truly exist, and, if so, how did I develop it? *Scientific American Mind, 23,* 70.

Gordon, S. M. (2001, July 5). What are the effects of the drug ecstasy? *Scientific American Online.* Retrieved from http://www.scientificamerican.com/article/what-are-the-effects-of-t/

Gordon-Messer, D., Bauermeister, J. A., Grodzinski, A., & Zimmerman, M. A. (2013). Sexting among young adults. *Journal of Adolescent Health, 52,* 301–306. doi:10.1016/j.jadohealth.2012.05.013

Gottesman, I. I. (2001). Psychopathology through a life span–genetic prism. *American Psychologist, 56,* 867–878.

Gottesman, I. I., Laursen, T. M., Bertelsen, A., & Mortensen, P. B. (2010). Severe mental disorders in offspring with 2 psychiatrically ill parents. *Archives of General Psychiatry, 67,* 252–257.

Gottfried, J. A., Smith, A. P. R., Rugg, M. D., & Dolan, R. J. (2004). Remembrance of odors past: Human olfactory cortex in cross-modal recognition memory. *Neuron, 42,* 687–895.

Gottschalk, M. G., & Domschke, K. (2017). Genetics of generalized anxiety disorder and related traits. *Dialogues in Clinical Neuroscience, 19*(2), 159–168.

Gould, E., Beylin, A., Tanapat, P., Reeves, A., & Shors, T. J. (1999). Learning enhances adult neurogenesis in the hippocampal formation. *Nature Neuroscience, 2,* 260–265.

Govindaraju, D., Atzmon, G., & Barzilai, N. (2015). Genetics, lifestyle and longevity: Lessons from centenarians. *Applied & Translational Genomics, 4,* 23–32.

Goyal, M., Singh, S., Sibinga, E. M. S., Gould, N. F., Rowland-Seymour, A., Sharma, R., . . . Haythornthwaite, J. A. (2014). Meditation programs for psychological stress and well-being. *JAMA Internal Medicine, 174,* 357–368.

Grabner, R. H., Ansari, D., Reishofer, G., Stern, E., Ebner, F., & Neuper, C. (2007). Individual differences in mathematical competence predict parietal brain activation during mental calculation. *NeuroImage, 38,* 346–356.

Grace, A. (2016). Dysregulation of the dopamine system in the pathophysiology of schizophrenia and depression. *Nature Reviews: Neuroscience, 17,* 524–532.

Gracheva, E. O., Ingolia, N. T., Kelly, Y. M., Cordero-Morales, J. F., Hollopeter, G., Chesler, A. T., . . . Julius, D. (2010). Molecular basis of infrared detection by snakes. *Nature, 464,* 1006–1011.

Gradin, M., & Eriksson, M. (2011). Neonatal pain assessment in Sweden—a fifteen-year follow up. *Acta Pædiatrica, 100,* 204–208.

Graham, L. C., Harder, J. M., Soto, I., de Vries, W. N., John, S. W., & Howell, G. R. (2016). Chronic consumption of a western diet induces robust glial activation in aging mice and in a mouse model of Alzheimer's disease. *Scientific Reports, 6,* 1–13.

Grammer, K., & Thornhill, R. (1994). Human (*Homo sapiens*) facial attractiveness and sexual selection: The role of symmetry and averageness. *Journal of Comparative Psychology, 108,* 233–242.

Granello, D. H., & Gibbs, T. A. (2016). The power of language and labels: "The mentally ill" versus "people with mental illnesses." *Journal of Counseling & Development, 94,* 31–40.

Granrud, C. E. (2009). Development of size constancy in children: A test of the metacognitive theory. *Perception & Psychophysics, 71,* 644–654.

Grant, B. F., Stinson, F. S., Dawson, D. A., Chou, S. P., Dufour, M. C., Compton, W., . . . Kaplan, K. (2004). Prevalence and co-occurrence of substance use disorders and independent mood and anxiety disorders: Results from the National Epidemiologic Survey on Alcohol and Related Conditions. *Archives of General Psychiatry, 61,* 807–816.

Grant, P. R. (1991). Natural selection and Darwin's finches. *Scientific American, 265,* 82–87.

Gray, P. B., & Brogdon, E. (2017). Do step- and biological grandparents show differences in investment and emotional closeness with their grandchildren? *Evolutionary Psychology, 15,* Article ID 1474704917694367.

Green, J. P. (1999). Hypnosis and the treatment of smoking cessation and weight loss. In I. Kirsch, A. Capafons, E. Cardeña-Buelna, & S. Amigó (Eds.), *Clinical hypnosis and self-regulation: Cognitive-behavioral perspectives* (pp. 249–276; Dissociation, Trauma, Memory, and Hypnosis Book Series). Washington, DC: American Psychological Association.

Green, M., & Elliott, M. (2010). Religion, health, and psychological well-being. *Journal of Religious Health, 49,* 149–163.

Greenberg, P. E., Fournier, A. A., Sisitsky, T., Pike, C. T., & Kessler, R. C. (2015). The economic burden of adults with major depressive disorder in the United States (2005 and 2010). *Journal of Clinical Psychiatry, 76,* 155–162.

Greenblatt, S. H., Dagi, T. F., & Epstein, M. H. (1997). *A history of neurosurgery.* Park Ridge, IL: American Association of Neurological Surgeons.

Greenfield, P. M., & Quiroz, B. (2013). Context and culture in the socialization and development of personal achievement values: Comparing Latino immigrant families, European American families, and elementary schoolteachers. *Journal of Applied Developmental Psychology, 34,* 108–118.

Greenstein, L. (2017, October 11). 9 Ways to fight mental health stigma [Web log post]. Retrieved from https://www.nami.org/blogs/nami-blog/october-2017/9-ways-to-fight-mental-health-stigma

Greenwood, V. (2016, January 26). Why some cultures love the tastes you hate. *BBC Future.* Retrieved from http://www.bbc.com/future/story/20160125-why-some-cultures-love-the-tastes-you-hate

Greitemeyer, T., & Mügge, D. O. (2015). When bystanders increase rather than decrease intentions to help. *Social Psychology, 46,* 116–119. https://doi.org/10.1027/1864-9335/a000215

Griebe, M., Nees, F., Gerber, B., Ebert, A., Flor, H., Wolf, O. T., . . . Szabo, K. (2015). Stronger pharmacological cortisol suppression and anticipatory cortisol stress response in transient global amnesia. *Frontiers in Behavioral Neuroscience, 9.* doi:10.3389/fnbeh.2015.00063

Grigg-Damberger, M. M., & Ianakieva, D. (2017). Poor quality control of over-the-counter melatonin: What they say is often not what you get. *Journal of Clinical Sleep Medicine, 13,* 163–165.

Griggs, R. A. (2014a). The continuing saga of Little Albert in introductory psychology textbooks. *Teaching of Psychology, 41,* 309–317.

Griggs, R. A. (2014b). Coverage of the Stanford Prison experiment in introductory psychology textbooks. *Teaching of Psychology, 41,* 195–203.

Griggs, R. A. (2015a). Coverage of the Phineas Gage story in introductory psychology textbooks: Was Gage no longer Gage? *Teaching of Psychology, 42,* 195–202.

Griggs, R. A. (2015b). The disappearance of independence in textbook coverage of Asch's social pressure experiments. *Teaching of Psychology, 42,* 137–142.

Griggs, R. A. (2015c). The Kitty Genovese story in introductory psychology textbooks fifty years later. *Teaching of Psychology, 42,* 149–152.

Griggs, R. A. (2015d). Psychology's lost boy. Will the real Little Albert please stand up? *Teaching of Psychology, 42,* 14–18.

Griggs, R. A., & Christopher, A. N. (2016). Who's who in introductory psychology textbooks: A citation analysis redux. *Teaching of Psychology, 43,* 108–119.

Griggs, R. A., & Whitehead, G. I., III. (2014). Coverage of the Stanford Prison experiment in introductory social psychology textbooks. *Teaching of Psychology, 41,* 318–324.

Griggs, R. A., & Whitehead, G. I., III. (2015). Coverage of Milgram's obedience experiments in social psychology textbooks: Where have all the criticisms gone? *Teaching of Psychology, 42,* 315–322.

Griskevicius, V., Haselton, M. G., & Ackerman, J. M. (2015). Evolution and close relationships. In M. Mikulincer, P. R. Shaver, J. A. Simpson, & J. F. Dovidio (Eds.), *APA handbook of personality and social psychology: Vol. 3. Interpersonal relation* (pp. 3–32). Washington, DC: American Psychological Association.

Griswold, A. (2013, December 27). 20 low-paying jobs that workers love. *Business Insider.* Retrieved from http://www.businessinsider.com/happy-low-paying-jobs-2013-12

Groopman, J. (2008). *How doctors think.* Boston, MA: Houghton Mifflin.

Grossman, A. J. (2012, June 9). The science of Cesar Millan's dog training: Good timing and hard kicks in the stomach. *Huffington Post.* Retrieved from http://www.huffingtonpost.com/anna-jane-grossman/the-dog-whisperer-technique_b_1406337. html

Grossman, R. P., & Till, B. D. (1998). The persistence of classically conditioned brand attitudes. *Journal of Advertising, 21,* 23–31.

Grotenhermen, F., & Müller-Vahl, K. (2012). The therapeutic potential of cannabis and cannabinoids. *Deutsches Ärzteblatt International, 109,* 495–501.

Gruber, D. F. (2009). Three's company. *Nature Medicine, 15,* 232–235.

Gruber, S. A., Dahlgren, M. K., Sagar, K. A., Gönenç A., & Lukas, S. E. (2014). Worth the wait: Effects of age of onset of marijuana use on white matter and impulsivity. *Psychopharmacology, 231,* 1455–1465.

Grusec, J. E., & Goodnow, J. J. (1994). Impact of parental discipline methods on the child's internalization of values: A reconceptualization of current points of view. *Developmental Psychology, 30,* 4–19.

Grusec, J. E., Goodnow, J. J., & Kuczynski, L. (2000). New directions in analyses of parenting contributions to children's acquisition of values. *Child Development, 71,* 205–211.

Guilford, J. P. (1967). *The nature of human intelligence.* New York, NY: McGraw-Hill.

Guilford, J. P., Christensen, P. R., Merrifield, P. R., & Wilson, R. C. (1960). *Alternate uses.* Beverly Hills, CA: Sheridan Psychological Services.

Guillot, C. (2007). Is recreational ecstasy (MDMA) use associated with higher levels of depressive symptoms? *Journal of Psychoactive Drugs, 39,* 31–39.

Guiney, H., & Machado, L. (2013). Benefits of regular aerobic exercise for executive functioning in healthy populations. *Psychonomic Bulletin & Review, 20,* 73–86.

Gulevich, G., Dement, W., & Johnson, L. (1966). Psychiatric and EEG observations on a case of prolonged (264 hours) wakefulness. *Archives of General Psychiatry, 15,* 29–35.

Gunderson, E. A., Hamdan, N., Sorhagen, N. S., & D'Esterre, A. P. (2017). Who needs innate ability to succeed in math and literacy? Academic-domain-specific theories of intelligence about peers versus adults. *Developmental Psychology, 53,* 1188-1205.

Gunderson, E. A., Ramirez, G., Levine, S. C., & Beilock, S. L. (2012). The role of parents and teachers in the development of gender-related math attitudes. *Sex Roles, 66,* 153–166.

Gundlach, H. (2018). William James and the Heidelberg fiasco. *History of Psychology, 21,* 47–72.

Gurven, M., von Rueden, C., Massenkoff, M., Kaplan, H., & Lero Vie, M. (2013). How universal is the Big Five? Testing the five-factor model of personality variation among forager-farmers in the Bolivian Amazon. *Journal of Personality and Social Psychology, 104,* 354–370.

Gushanas, T. (2015, April 14). Twins study—about. NASA. Retrieved from https://www.nasa.gov/twins-study/about

Haedt-Matt, A. A., & Keel, P. K. (2011). Revisiting the affect regulation model of binge eating: A meta-analysis of studies using ecological momentary assessment. *Psychological Bulletin, 137,* 660–681.

Hagan, L. K. (2016). History of child development. In W. D. Woody, R. L. Miller, & W. J. Wozniak (Eds.), *Psychological specialties in historical context: Enriching the classroom experience for teachers and students.* Retrieved from the Society for the Teaching of Psychology web site: http://teachpsych.org/ebooks/

Haijma, S. V., Van Haren, N., Cahn, W., Koolschijn, P. C. M., Pol, H. E. H., & Kahn, R. S. (2013). Brain volumes in schizophrenia: A meta-analysis in over 18,000 subjects. *Schizophrenia Bulletin, 39,* 1129–1138.

Hall, D., & Buzwell, S. (2012). The problem of free-riding in group projects: Looking beyond social loafing as reason for non-contribution. *Active Learning in Higher Education, 14,* 37–49.

Hall, J. A., & Matsumoto, D. (2004). Gender differences in judgments of multiple emotions from facial expressions. *Emotion, 4,* 201–206.

Hall, J. K., Hutton, S. B., & Morgan, M. J. (2010). Sex differences in scanning faces: Does attention to the eyes explain female superiority in facial expression recognition? *Cognition and Emotion, 24,* 629–637.

Hall, J. W., Smith, S. D., & Popelka, G. R. (2004). Newborn hearing screening with combined otoacoustic emissions and auditory brainstem responses. *Journal of the American Academy of Audiology, 15,* 414–425.

Hallfors, D. D., Iritani, B. J., Zhang, L., Hartman, S., Lueseno, W. K., Mpofu, E., & Rusakaniko, S. (2016). "I thought if I marry the prophet I would not die": The significance of religious affiliation on marriage, HIV testing, and reproductive health practices among young married women in Zimbabwe. *Journal of Social Aspects of HIV/AIDS, 13,* 178–189.

Hameed, M. A., & Lewis, A. J. (2016). Offspring of parents with schizophrenia: A systematic review of developmental features across childhood. *Harvard Review of Psychiatry, 24*(2), 104–117.

Hamilton, W. D. (1964). The genetical evolution of social behavior. *Journal of Theoretical Biology, 12,* 12–45.

Hammond, S. I., Müller, U., Carpendale, J. I. M., Bibok, M. B., & Liebermann-Finestone, D. P. (2012). The effects of parental scaffolding on preschoolers' executive function. *Developmental Psychology, 48,* 271–281.

Hampton, J. A. (1998). Similarity-based categorization and fuzziness of natural categories. *Cognition, 65,* 137–165.

Hamzelou, J. (2015, January 26). Is MSG a silent killer or useful flavour booster? *NewScientist.* Retrieved from https://www.newscientist.com/article/dn26854-ismsg-a-silent-killer-or-useful-flavour-booster/

Haney, C., Banks, C., & Zimbardo, P. (1973). Interpersonal dynamics in a simulated prison. *International Journal of Criminology and Penology, 1,* 69–97.

Haney, C., & Zimbardo, P. (1998). The past and future of U.S. prison policy: Twenty-five years after the Stanford prison experiment. *American Psychologist, 53,* 709–727.

Hanford, L. C., Nazarov, A., Hall, G. B., & Sassi, R. B. (2016). Cortical thickness in bipolar disorder: A systematic review. *Bipolar Disorders, 18,* 4–18.

Hanish, L. D., Sallquist, J., DiDonato, M., Fabes, R. A., & Martin, C. L. (2012, September). Aggression by whom–aggression toward whom: Behavioral predictors of same- and other-gender aggression in early childhood. *Developmental Psychology, 48,* 1450–1462. doi:10.1037/a0027510

Hanley, A. W., Warner, A. R., Dehili, V. M., Canto, A. I., & Garland, E. L. (2015). Washing dishes to wash the dishes: Brief instruction in an informal mindfulness practice. *Mindfulness, 6,* 1095–1103.

Hanley, J. R., & Chapman, E. (2008). Partial knowledge in a tip-of-the-tongue state about two- and three-word proper names. *Psychonomic Bulletin & Review, 15,* 156–160.

Hanna, C. (2012, October 27). Dog whisperer Cesar Millan accused of punching dogs and using shock collars. *Examiner.com.* Retrieved from https://web.archive.org/web/20160422035235/http://www.examiner.com/article/dog-whisperer-cesar-milan-accused-of-punching-dogs-and-using-shock-collars

Hanna-Pladdy, B., & MacKay, A. (2011). The relation between instrumental musical activity and cognitive aging. *Neuropsychology, 25,* 378–386.

Hanscombe, K. B., Trzaskowski, M., Haworth, C. M. A., Davis, O. S. P., Dale, P. S., & Plomin, R. (2012). Socioeconomic status (SES) and children's intelligence (IQ): In a UK-representative sample SES moderates the environmental, not genetic, effect on IQ. *PLoS ONE, 7,* e30320. doi:10.1371/journal.pone.0030320

Hansen, C. J., Stevens, L. C., & Coast, J. R. (2001). Exercise duration and mood state: How much is enough to feel better? *Health Psychology, 20,* 267–275.

Hanson, H. (2017, July 1). The scary reason animal shelters get so busy on the Fourth of July. *Huffington Post.* Retrieved from http://www.huffingtonpost.com/entry/fourth-of-july-animal-shelters-busy-pet-safety_us_5956a9d6e4b0da2c732379a6

Happiness Research Institute. (2015). *The Facebook experiment.* Retrieved from http://www.happinessresearchinstitute.com/publications/4579836749

Hareli, S., Kafetsios, K., & Hess, U. (2015). A cross-cultural study on emotion expression and the learning of social norms. *Frontiers in Psychology, 6.* doi:10.3389/fpsyg.2015.01501

Hariri, A. R., Tessitore, A., Mattay, V. S., Fera, F., & Weinberger, D. R. (2002). The amygdala response to emotional stimuli: A comparison of faces and scenes. *NeuroImage, 17,* 317–323.

Harlow, H. F. (1958). The nature of love. *American Psychologist, 13,* 673–685.

Harlow, H. F., Harlow, M. K., & Meyer, D. R. (1950). Learning motivated by a manipulation drive. *Journal of Experimental Psychology, 40,* 228–234.

Harlow, H. F., Harlow, M. K., & Suomi, S. J. (1971). From thought to therapy: Lessons from a primate laboratory. *American Scientist, 59,* 538–549.

Harlow, H. F., & Zimmerman, R. R. (1959). Affectional responses in the infant monkey. *Science, 130,* 421–432.

Harmon, K. G., Drezner, J., Gammons, M., Guskiewicz, K., Halstead, M., Herring, S., . . . Roberts, W. (2013). American Medical Society for Sports Medicine position statement: Concussion in sport. *Clinical Journal of Sports Medicine, 23,* 1–18.

HarnEnz, Z. (2016, November 14). *Fighting stigma: How to respond to inappropriate and insensitive comments.* Retrieved from https://www.psychiatry.org/news-room/apa-blogs/apa-blog/2016/11/fighting-stigma-how-to-respond-to-inappropriate-and-insensitive-comments-about-mental-health

Harper, R. S. (1950). The first psychological laboratory. *Isis, 41,* 158–161.

Harrington, A. (2012). The fall of the schizophrenogenic mother. *The Lancet, 379,* 1292–1293.

Harrington, A., & Dunne, J. D. (2015). When mindfulness is therapy: Ethical qualms, historical perspectives. *American Psychologist, 70,* 621–631.

Harrington, R. (2013). *Stress, health & well-being: Thriving in the 21st century.* Belmont, CA: Wadsworth, Cengage Learning.

Harris, B. (1979). Whatever happened to Little Albert? *American Psychologist, 34,* 151–160.

Hart, B., & Risley, T. R. (1995). *Meaningful differences in the everyday experience of young American children.* Baltimore, MD: Paul H. Brookes.

Harter, J., & Adkinds, A. (2015, April 8). Employees want a lot more from their managers. Gallup. Retrieved from http://www.gallup.com/businessjournal/182321/employees-lot-managers.aspx

Harvard Medical School. (2007). *Healthy sleep: Jet lag and shift work.* Retrieved from http://healthysleep.med.harvard.edu/healthy/science/variations/jet-lag-and-shift-work

Harvey, M. A., Sellman, J. D., Porter, R. J., & Frampton, C. M. (2007). The relationship between non-acute adolescent cannabis use and cognition. *Drug and Alcohol Review, 26,* 309–319.

Haslam, S. A., & Reicher, S. D. (2012). When prisoners take over the prison: A social psychology of resistance. *Personality and Social Psychology Review, 16,* 154–179.

Hassett, J. M., Siebert, E. R., & Wallen, K. (2008). Sex differences in rhesus monkey toy preferences parallel those of children. *Hormones and Behavior, 54,* 359–364.

Hasson, U., Andric, M., Atilgan, H., & Collignon, O. (2016). Congenital blindness is associated with large-scale reorganization of anatomical networks. *NeuroImage, 128,* 362–372.

Hatch, S. L., & Dohrenwend, B. P. (2007). Distribution of traumatic and other stressful life events by race/ethnicity, gender, SES and age: A review of the research. *American Journal of Community Psychology, 40,* 313–332.

Hatemi, P. K., McDermott, R., & Eaves, L. (2015). Genetic and environmental contributions to relationships and divorce attitudes. *Personality and Individual Differences, 72,* 135–140.

Hatemi, P. K., Medland, S. E., Klemmensen, R., Oskarsson, S., Littvay, L., Dawes, C. T., . . . Martin, N. G. (2014). Genetic influences on political ideologies: Twin analyses of 19 measures of political ideologies from five democracies and genome-wide findings from three populations. *Behavior Genetics, 44,* 282–294.

Hatfield, E., Bensman, L., & Rapson, R. L. (2012). A brief history of social scientists' attempts to measure passionate love. *Journal of Social and Personal Relationships, 29,* 143–164.

Hauck, C., Wei, A., Schulte, E. M., Meule, A., & Ellrott, T. (2017). Prevalence of "food addiction" as measured with the Yale Food Addiction Scale 2.0 in a representative German sample and its association with sex, age and weight categories. *Obesity Facts, 10,* 12–24.

Häuser, W., Hagl, M., Schmierer, A., & Hansen, E. (2016). The efficacy, safety and applications of medical hypnosis: A systematic review of meta-analyses. *Deutsches Ärzteblatt International, 113,* 289.

Havelka, M., Lučanin, J. D., & Lučanin, D. (2009). Biopsychosocial model-the integrated approach to health and disease. *Collegium Antropologicum, 33,* 303–310.

Hawi, N. S., & Samaha, M. (2016). To excel or not to excel: Strong evidence on the adverse effect of smartphone addiction on academic performance. *Computers & Education, 98,* 81–89.

Hay, D. F. (2017). The early development of human aggression. *Child Development Perspectives, 11,* 102–106.

Hay, J., Johnson, V. E., Smith, D. H., & Stewart, W. (2016). Chronic traumatic encephalopathy: The neuropathological legacy of traumatic brain injury. *Annual Review of Pathology: Mechanisms of Disease, 11,* 21–45.

Hayes, J. E., & Keast, R. E. (2011). Two decades of supertasting: Where do we stand? *Physiology & Behavior, 104,* 1072–1074.

Hayes, J. F., Pitman, A., Marston, L., Walters, K., Geddes, J. R., King, M., & Osborn, D. P. (2016). Self-harm, unintentional injury, and suicide in bipolar disorder during maintenance mood stabilizer treatment: A UK population-based electronic health records study. *JAMA Psychiatry, 73,* 630–637.

He's one smart puppy. (2004, June 20). *Newsweek.* Retrieved from http://www.newsweek.com/hes-one-smart-puppy-128631

Healy, J. (2010, August 23). Chileans will work to sustain miners. *The New York Times.* Retrieved from http://www.nytimes.com/2010/08/24/world/americas/24chile.html?_r=0

Hecht, S., & Mandelbaum, J. (1938). Rod-cone dark adaptation and vitamin A. *Science, 88,* 219–221.

Hegarty, P., & Buechel, C. (2006). Androcentric reporting of gender differences in APA journals: 1965–2004. *Review of General Psychology, 10,* 377–389.

Heijnen, S., Hommel, B., Kibele, A., & Colzato, L. S. (2015). Neuromodulation of aerobic exercise—a review. *Frontiers in Psychology, 6.* Retrieved from http://doi.org/10.3389/fpsyg.2015.01890

Heil, M., Krüger, M., Krist, H., Johnson, S. P., & Moore, D. S. (2018). Adults' sex difference in a dynamic Mental Rotation Task: Validating infant results. *Journal of Individual Differences, 39,* 48–52. Retrieved from http://dx.doi.org/10.1027/1614-0001/a000248

Heiman, J. R. (2002). Sexual dysfunction: Overview of prevalence, etiological factors, and treatments. *Journal of Sex Research, 39,* 73–78.

Heiser, C. (2015, May 28). Demi Lovato speaks up about living with bipolar disorder. *Women's Health.* Retrieved from http://www.womenshealthmag.com/health/demi-lovato-be-vocal-campaign

Helliker, K. (2009, March 24). No joke: Group therapy offers savings in numbers. *Wall Street Journal.* Retrieved from http://www.wsj.com/articles/SB123785686766020551

Helliwell, J. F., Layard, R., & Sachs, J. (Eds.). (2015). *World happiness report 2015.* New York, NY: Sustainable Development Solutions Network.

Helliwell, J. F., Layard, R., & Sachs, J. (Eds.). (2017). *World happiness report 2017.* New York, NY: Sustainable Development Solutions Network.

Helliwell, J. F., Layard, R., & Sachs, J. (Eds.). (2018). *World happiness report 2018.* New York, NY: Sustainable Development Solutions Network.

Henderson, S. N., Van Hasselt, V. B., LeDuc, T. J., & Couwels, J. (2016). Firefighter suicide: Understanding cultural challenges for mental health professionals. *Professional Psychology: Research and Practice, 47,* 224–230.

Henneman, W. J., Sluimer, J. D., Barnes, J., van der Flier, W. M., Sluimer, I. C., Fox, N. C., . . . Barkhof, F. (2009). Hippocampal atrophy rates in Alzheimer disease: Added value over whole brain volume measures. *Neurology, 72,* 999–1007.

Hensch, T. K. (2004). Critical period regulation. *Annual Review of Neuroscience, 27,* 549–579.

Herbenick, D., Reece, M., Schick, V., Sanders, S. A., Dodge, B., & Fortenberry, J. D. (2010). Sexual behavior in the United States: Results from a national probability sample of men and women ages 14–94. *Journal of Sexual Medicine, 7*(Suppl. 5), 255–265.

Herculano-Houzel, S. (2012). The remarkable, yet not extraordinary, human brain as a scaled-up primate brain and its associated cost. *Proceedings of the National Academy of Sciences, 109*(Suppl. 1), 10661–10668.

Herculano-Houzel, S. (2014). The glia/neuron ratio: How it varies uniformly across brain structures and species and what that means for brain physiology and evolution. *Glia, 62,* 1377–1391.

Herman, C. P., Roth, D. A., & Polivy, J. (2003). Effects of the presence of others on food intake: A normative interpretation. *Psychological Bulletin, 129,* 873–886.

Hersh, S. M. (2004, May 10). Torture at Abu Ghraib. *The New Yorker.* Retrieved from http://www.newyorker.com/archive/2004/05/10/040510fa_fact?printable=true¤tPage=all

Hertenstein, M. J., & McCullough, M. A. (2005). Separation anxiety. In N. J. Salkind (Ed.), *Encyclopedia of human development* (Vol. 3, pp. 1146–1147). Thousand Oaks, CA: Sage.

Hertzog, C., Kramer, A. F., Wilson, R. S., & Lindenberger, U. (2009, July/August). Fit body, fit mind? *Scientific American Mind, 20,* 24–31.

Herz, R. (2007). *The scent of desire: Discovering our enigmatic sense of smell.* New York, NY: William Morrow/HarperCollins.

Herzog, T. K., Hill-Chapman, C., Hardy, T. K., Wrighten, S. A., & El-Khabbaz, R. (2015). Trait emotion, emotional regulation, and parenting styles. *Journal of Educational and Developmental Psychology, 5,* 119–135.

Hettema, J. M., Kettenmann, B., Ahluwalia, V., McCarthy, C., Kates, W. R., Schmitt, J. E., . . . Fatouros, P. (2012). Pilot multimodal twin imaging study of generalized anxiety disorder. *Depression and Anxiety, 29,* 202–209.

Hey, J. (2009). Why should we care about species? *Nature Education, 2,* 2.

Hickok, G., & Poeppel, D. (2000). Towards a functional neuroanatomy of speech perception. *Trends in Cognitive Sciences, 4,* 131–138.

Higgins, A., Nash, M., & Lynch, A. M. (2010, September 8). Antidepressant-associated sexual dysfunction: Impact, effects, and treatment. *Drug, Healthcare and Patient Safety, 2,* 141–150.

Hilgard, E. R. (1987). *Psychology in America: A historical survey.* Orlando, FL: Harcourt Brace Jovanovich.

Hilgard, E. R., Morgan, A. H., & Macdonald, H. (1975). Pain and dissociation in the cold pressor test: A study of hypnotic analgesia with "hidden reports" through automatic key pressing and automatic talking. *Journal of Abnormal Psychology, 84,* 280–289.

Hines, M. (2011a). Gender development and the human brain. *Annual Review of Neuroscience, 34,* 69–88.

Hines, M. (2011b). Prenatal endocrine influences on sexual orientation and on sexually differentiated childhood behavior. *Frontiers in Neuroendocrinology, 32,* 170–182.

Hines, R. (2015, May 27). Howie Mandel says "AGT" hypnotism didn't cure him, it sent him to therapy. *Today.* Retrieved from http://www.today.com/popculture/howie-mandel-says-agt-hypnotism-act-didnt-cure-him-t23106

Hingson, R. W., Zha, W., & White, A. M. (2017). Drinking beyond the binge threshold: Predictors, consequences, and changes in the U.S. *American Journal of Preventive Medicine, 52,* 717–727.

Hinton, C., Fischer, K. W., & Glennon, C. (2012). Mind, brain, and education: The students at the center series. In *Students at the center: Teaching and learning in the era of the Common Core* (pp. 1–27). Retrieved from http://www.howyouthlearn.org/pdf/Mind%20Brain%20Education.pdf

Hirshkowitz, M., Whiton, K., Albert, S. M., Alessi, C., Bruni, O., DonCarols, L., . . .Ware, J. C. (2015). National Sleep Foundation's updated sleep duration recommendations: Final report. *Sleep Health, 1,* 233–243.

Hirsh-Pasek, K., Adamson, L. B., Bakeman, R., Owen, M. T., Golinko , R. M., Pace, A., . . . Suma, K. (2015). The contribution of early communication quality to low-income children's language success. *Psychological Science, 26,* 1071–1083.

Hirsh-Pasek, K., Golinkoff, R. M., & Eyer, D. (2003). *Einstein never used flash cards.* Emmaus, PA: Rodale.

Hirst, W., & Phelps, E. A. (2016). Flashbulb memories. *Current Directions in Psychological Science, 25,* 36–41.

Hirst, W., Phelps, E. A., Meksin, R., Vaidya, C. J., Johnson, M. K., Mitchell, K. J., . . . Mather, M. (2015). A ten-year follow-up of a study of memory for the attack of September 11, 2001: Flashbulb memories and memories for flashbulb events. *Journal of Experimental Psychology: General, 144,* 604–623.

Hobson, J. A. (1989). *Sleep.* New York, NY: Scientific American Library.

Hobson, J. A. (2006, April/May). Freud returns? Like a bad dream. *Scientific American Mind, 17,* 35.

Hobson, J. A., & McCarley, R. W. (1977). The brain as a dream state generator: An activation–synthesis hypothesis of the dream process. *American Journal of Psychiatry, 134,* 1335–1348.

Hobson, J. A., & Pace-Schott, E. F. (2002). The cognitive neuroscience of sleep: Neuronal systems, consciousness and learning. *Nature Reviews Neuroscience, 3,* 679–693.

Hochard, K. D., Heym, N., & Townsend, E. (2016). The behavioral effects of frequent nightmares on objective stress tolerance. *Dreaming, 26,* 42–49.

Hock, R. R. (2016). *Human sexuality* (4th ed.). Upper Saddle River, NJ: Pearson Education.

Hodgson, A. B., Randell, R. K., & Jeukendrup, A. E. (2013). The metabolic and performance effects of caffeine compared to coffee during endurance exercise. *PLoS ONE, 8,* e59561. doi:10.1371/journal.pone.0059561

Hoeft, F., Gabrieli, J. D., Whitfield-Gabrieli, S., Haas, B. W., Bammer, R., Menon, V., & Spiegel, D. (2012). Functional brain basis of hypnotizability. *Archives of General Psychiatry, 69,* 1064–1072.

Høeg, B. L., Johansen, C., Christensen, J., Frederiksen, K., Dalton, S. O., Dyregrov, A., . . . Bidstrup, P. E. (2018). Early parental loss and intimate relationships in adulthood: A nationwide study. *Developmental Psychology, 54,* 963–974.

Hoff, E. (2003). The specificity of environmental influence: Socioeconomic status affects early vocabulary development via maternal speech. *Child Development, 74,* 1368–1378.

Hoff, E. H., & Core, C. C. (2015). What clinicians need to know about bilingual development. *Seminars in Speech and Language, 36,* 89–99.

Hoffman, I. Z. (2009). Therapeutic passion in the countertransference. *Psychoanalytic Dialogues, 19,* 617–636.

Hoffman, S. J., & Tan, C. (2013). Following celebrities' medical advice: Metanarrative analysis. *BMJ, 347,* f7151.

Hofmann, L., & Palczewski, K. (2015). Advances in understanding the molecular basis of the first steps in color vision. *Progress in Retinal and Eye Research, 49,* 46–66.

Hofmann, S. G., & Hinton, D. E. (2014). Cross-cultural aspects of anxiety disorders. *Current Psychiatry Reports, 16,* 1–5. doi:10.1007/s11920014-0450-3

Hofmann, W., Vohs, K. D., & Baumeister, R. F. (2012). What people desire, feel conflicted about, and try to resist in everyday life. *Psychological Science, 23,* 582–588.

Hogan, C. L., Mata, J., & Carstensen, L. L. (2013). Exercise holds immediate benefits for affect and cognition in younger and older adults. *Psychology and Aging, 28,* 587–594. doi:10.1037/a0032634

Hoge, C. W., & Warner, C. H. (2014). Estimating PTSD prevalence in US veterans: Considering combat exposure, PTSD checklist cutpoints, and DSM-5. *Journal of Clinical Psychiatry, 75,* 1439–1441.

Holahan, C. K., & Sears, R. R. (1995). *The gifted group in later maturity.* Stanford, CA: Stanford University Press.

Holliday, E., & Gould, T. J. (2016). Nicotine, adolescence, and stress: A review of how stress can modulate the negative consequences of adolescent nicotine abuse. *Neuroscience & Biobehavioral Reviews, 65,* 173–184.

Holmes, T. H., & Rahe, R. H. (1967). The Social Readjustment Rating Scale. *Journal of Psychosomatic Research, 11,* 213–318.

Holowka, S., & Petitto, L. A. (2002). Left hemisphere cerebral specialization for babies while babbling. *Science, 297,* 1515.

Holsen, L. M., Spaeth, S. B., Lee, J.-H., Ogden, L. A., Klibanski, A., Whitfield-Gabrieli, S., & Goldstein, J. M. (2011). Stress response circuitry hypoactivation related to hormonal dysfunction in women with major depression. *Journal of Affective Disorders, 131,* 379–387.

Holtgraves, T. (2015). I think I am doing great but I feel pretty bad about it: Affective versus cognitive verbs and self-reports. *Personality & Social Psychology Bulletin, 41,* 677–686.

Homa, D. M., Neff, L. J., King, B. A., Caraballo, R. S., Bunnell, R. E., Babb, S. D., Garrett, B. E., Sosnoff, C. S., & Want, L. (2015, February 6). Vital signs: Disparities in nonsomokers' exposure to secondhand smoke—United States, 1999–2012. *MMWR Morbidity and Mortality Weekly Report, 64,* 103–108.

Honda, H., Shimizu, Y., & Rutter, M. (2005). No effect of MMR withdrawal on the incidence of autism: A total population study. *Journal of Child Psychology and Psychiatry, 46,* 572–579.

Hong, Y.-Y., Wyer, R. S., Jr., & Fong, C. P. S. (2008). Chinese working in groups: Effort dispensability versus normative influence. *Asian Journal of Social Psychology, 11,* 187–195.

Hoogland, T. M., & Parpura, V. (2015). Editorial: The role of glia in plasticity and behavior. *Frontiers in Cellular Neuroscience, 9.* doi:10.3389/fncel.2015.00356

Hooper, J., Sharpe, D., & Roberts, S. G. B. (2016). Are men funnier than women, or do we just think they are? *Translational Issues in Psychological Science, 2,* 54–62.

Horgan, J. (2017, March 10). Why Freud still isn't dead [Web log post]. Retrieved from https://blogs.scientificamerican.com/cross-check/why-freud-still-isnt-dead/

Horikawa, T., Tamaki, M., Miyawaki, Y., & Kamitani, Y. (2013). Neural decoding of visual imagery during sleep. *Science, 340,* 639–642.

Horne, J. (2006). *Sleepfaring.* Oxford, UK: Oxford University Press.

Horney, K. (1945). *Our inner conflicts: A constructive theory of neurosis.* New York, NY: W. W. Norton.

Horney, K. (1967). The flight from womanhood: The masculinity-complex in women as viewed by men and by women. In H. Kelmam (Ed.), *Feminine psychology* (pp. 54–70). New York, NY: W. W. Norton. (Original work published 1926)

Horoscope.com. (2017). *Monthly horoscope: Taurus.* Retrieved from https://www.horoscope.com/us/horoscopes/general/horoscope-general-monthly.aspx?sign=2

Horwitz, B., Amunts, K., Bhattacharyya R., Patkin, D., Jeffries, K., Zilles, K., & Braun, A. R. (2003). Activation of Broca's area during the production of spoken and signed language: A combined cytoarchitectonic mapping and PET analysis. *Neuropsychologia, 41,* 1868–1876.

Horwitz, D., Lovenberg, W., Engelman, K., & Sjoerdsma, A. (1964). Monoamine oxidase inhibitors, tyramine, and cheese. *Journal of the American Medical Association, 188,* 1108–1110.

Horwood, L. J., & Fergusson, D. M. (1998). Breastfeeding and later cognitive and academic outcomes. *Pediatrics, 101,* 1–7.

Hothersall, D. (2004). *History of psychology* (4th ed.). New York, NY: McGraw-Hill.

House, J. S., Landis, K. R., & Umberson, D. (1988). Social relationships and health. *Science, 241,* 540–545.

Hovland, C. I., Janis, I. L., & Kelley, H. H. (1953). *Communication and persuasion: Psychological studies of opinion change.* New Haven, CT: Yale University Press.

Hovland, C. I., & Weiss, W. (1951). The influence of source credibility on communication effectiveness. *Public Opinion Quarterly, 15,* 635–650.

Howe, L. C., Goyer, J. P., & Crum, A. J. (2017). Harnessing the placebo effect: Exploring the influence of physician characteristics on placebo response. *Health Psychology.* http://dx.doi.org/10.1037/hea0000499

Howes, O. D., & Kapur, S. (2009). The dopamine hypothesis of schizophrenia: Version III—the final common pathway. *Schizophrenia Bulletin, 35,* 549–562.

Howland, J., Rohsenow, D. J., Greece, J. A., Littefield, C. A., Almeida, A., Heeren, T., . . . Hermos, J. (2010). The effects of binge drinking on college students' next-day academic test-taking performance and mood state. *Addiction, 105,* 655–665.

Hsu, C.-T., Jacobs, A. M., Altmann, U., & Conrad, M. (2015). The magical activation of left amygdala when reading Harry Potter: An fMRI study on how descriptions of supra-natural events entertain and enchant. *PLoS ONE, 10,* e0118179. doi:10.1371/journal.pone.0118179

Hsu, P. J., Shoud, H., Benzinger, T., Marcus, D., Durbin, T., Morris, J. C., & Sheline, Y. I. (2015). Amyloid burden in cognitively normal elderly is associated with preferential hippocampal subfield volume loss. *Journal of Alzheimer's Diseases, 45,* 27–33.

Huang, Z. J., & Luo, L. (2015). It takes the world to understand the brain. *Science, 350*(6256), 42–44.

Hubbard, T. L. (2010). Auditory imagery: Empirical findings. *Psychological Bulletin, 136,* 302–329.

Hubel, D. H., & Wiesel, T. N. (1979, September). Brain mechanisms of vision. *Scientific American, 241,* 150–162.

Huesmann, L. R., Moise-Titus, J., Podolski, C., & Eron, L. D. (2003). Longitudinal relations between children's exposure to TV violence and their aggressive and violent behavior in young adulthood: 1977–1992. *Developmental Psychology, 33,* 201–221.

Huffman, J. C., Beale, E. E., Celano, C. M., Beach, S. R., Belcher, A. M., Moore, S. V., . . . Januzzi, J. L. (2016). Effects of optimism and gratitude on physical activity, biomarkers, and readmissions after an acute coronary syndrome: the gratitude research in acute coronary events study. *Circulation: Cardiovascular Quality and Outcomes, 9,* 55–63.

Hughes, S., Lyddy, F., & Lambe, S. (2013). Misconceptions about psychological science: A review. *Psychology Learning and Teaching, 12,* 20–31.

Huguelet, P., & Perroud, N. (2005). Wolfgang Amadeus Mozart's psychopathology in light of the current conceptualization of psychiatric disorders. *Psychiatry, 68,* 130–139.

Huizink, A. C. (2014). Prenatal cannabis exposure and infant outcomes: Overview of studies. *Progress in Neuro-Psychopharmacology and Biological Psychiatry, 52,* 45–52.

Hull, C. L. (1952). *A behavior system: An introduction to behavior theory concerning the individual organism.* New Haven, CT: Yale University Press.

Hulsegge, G., Looman, M., Smit, H. A., Daviglus, M. L., van der Schouw, Y. T., & Verschuren, W. M. (2016). Lifestyle changes in young adulthood and middle age and risk of cardiovascular disease and all-cause mortality: The Doetinchem Cohort Study. *Journal of the American Heart Association, 5.* Retrieved from http://dx.doi.org/10.1161/JAHA.115.002432

Humphreys, H., Fitzpatick, F., & Harvey, B. J. (2015). Gender differences in rates of carriage and bloodstream infection caused by methicillin-resistant *Staphylococcus aureus*: Are they real, do they matter and why? *Clinical Infectious Diseases, 61,* 1708–1714.

Humphries, T., Kushalnagar, P., Mathur, G., Napoli, D. J., Padden, C., Rathmann, C., & Smith, S. R. (2012). Language acquisition for deaf children: Reducing the harms of zero tolerance to the use of alternative approaches. *Harm Reduction Journal, 3,* 1–9.

Hunsley, J., Lee, C. M., & Wood, J. M. (2003). Controversial and questionable assessment techniques. In S. O. Lilienfeld, J. M. Lohr, & S. J. Lynn (Eds.), *Science and pseudoscience in clinical psychology* (pp. 39–76). New York, NY: Guilford Press.

Hunt, W. A. (1939). A critical review of current approaches to affectivity. *Psychological Bulletin, 36,* 807–828.

Hunter, S. C., Fox, C. L., & Jones, S. E. (2016). Humor style similarity and difference in friendship dyads. *Journal of Adolescence, 46,* 30–37.

Huppertz, C., Bartels, M., Jansen, I. E., Boomsma, D. I., Willemsen, G., de Moor, M. H. M., & de Geus, E. J. C. (2014). A twin-sibling study on the relationship between exercise attitudes and exercise behavior. *Behavior Genetics, 44,* 45–55.

Hurley, S. W., & Johnson, A. K. (2014). The role of the lateral hypothalamus and orexin in ingestive behavior: A model for the translation of past experience and sensed deficits into motivated behaviors. *Frontiers in Systems Neuroscience, 8.* http://dx.doi.org/10.3389/fnsys.2014.00216

Hutson, M. (2016, November/December). The more rituals the merrier. *Scientific American Mind, 27,* 8.

Hyde, J. S. (2016). Sex and cognition: Gender and cognitive functions. *Current Opinion in Neurobiology, 38,* 53–56.

Hyde, J. S., & Linn, M. C. (1988). Gender differences in verbal ability: A meta-analysis. *Psychological Bulletin, 104,* 53–69.

Hyman, I. E., Jr. (2016). Unaware observers: The impact of inattentional blindness on walkers, drivers, and eyewitnesses. *Journal of Applied Research in Memory and Cognition, 5,* 264–269.

Hyman, I. E., Jr., Husband, T. H., & Billings, F. J. (1995). False memories of childhood experiences. *Applied Cognitive Psychology, 3,* 181–197.

Ilias, I., Tayeh, L. S., & Pachoundakis, I. (2016). Diversity in endocrinology practice: The case of Ramadan. *Hormones, 15,* 147–148.

IMDB. (n.d.). *Biography for Gloria Delgado-Pritchett (character).* Retrieved from http://www.imdb.com/character/ch0170388/bio

iminmotion.net. (n.d.). *Ivonne Marcela Mosquera-Schmidt.* Retrieved from http://www.iminmotion.net

Impey, C., Buxner, S., & Antonellis, J. (2012). Non-scientific beliefs among undergraduate students. *Astronomy Education Review, 11.* doi:10.3847/AER2012016

Inder, M. L., Crowe, M. T., Luty, S. E., Carter, J. D., Moor, S., Frampton, C. M., & Joyce, P. R. (2016). Prospective rates of suicide attempts and nonsuicidal self-injury by young people with bipolar disorder participating in a psychotherapy study. *Australian and New Zealand Journal of Psychiatry, 50,* 167–173.

Indicrat. (2017, September 21). Trump supporters allow freedom of speech for #BlackLivesMatter on stage at MOAR rally [Video file]. Retrieved from https://www.youtube.com/watch?time_continue=44&v=3tWPMbQ_PCA

Ingold, J. (2013, September 30). Sides debate lengthy witness lists for James Holmes trial. *The Denver Post.* Retrieved from http://www.denverpost.com/breakingnews/ci_24205468/psychiatric-exam-up-debate-new-aurora-theater-shooting#

Isbister, K. (2017, May 18). Fidget toys aren't just hype. *Scientific American.* Retrieved from https://www.scientificamerican.com/article/fidget-toys-arent-just-hype/

Isen, A. (2008). Some ways in which positive affect influences decision making and problem solving. In M. Lewis, J. M. Haviland-Jones, & L. F. Barrett (Eds.), *Handbook of emotions* (3rd ed., pp. 548–573). New York, NY: Guilford Press.

Ismail, Z., Smith, E. E., Geda, Y., Sultzer, D., Brodaty, H., Smith, G., . . . Lyketsos, C. G. (2016). Neuropsychiatric symptoms as early manifestations of emergent dementia: Provisional diagnostic criteria for mild behavioral impairment. *Alzheimer's & Dementia, 12,* 195–202.

Ito, T. A., Friedman, N. P., Bartholow, B. D., Correll, J., Loersch, C., Altamirano, L. J., & Miyake, A. (2015). Toward a comprehensive understanding of executive cognitive function in implicit racial bias. *Journal of Personality and Social Psychology, 108,* 187–218.

Iurato, S., Carrillo-Roa, T., Arloth, J., Czamara, D., Diener-Hölzl, L., Lange, J., . . . Erhardt, A. (2017). DNA Methylation signatures in panic disorder. *Translational Psychiatry, 7.* doi:10.1038/s41398-017-0026-1

Iversen, L. (2003). Cannabis and the brain. *Brain, 126,* 1252–1270.

Ivey-Stephenson, A. Z., Crosby, A. E., Jack, S. P., Haileyesus, T., & Kresnow-Sedacca, M. J. (2017). Suicide trends among and within urbanization levels by sex, race/ethnicity, age group, and mechanism of death—United States, 2001–2015. *MMWR Surveillance Summaries, 66*(18), 1–9.

Izadi, E. (2017, July 27). Justin Bieber 'Purpose' timeline: Pinkeye, punching dudes and posing with controversial tigers. *The Washington Post.* Retrieved from https://www.washingtonpost.com/news/arts-and-entertainment/wp/2017/07/26/justin-bieber-purpose-timeline-pink-eye-punching-dudes-and-posing-with-controversial-tigers/?utm_term=.433868b68a3a

Izard, C. E. (1992). Basic emotions, relations among emotions, and emotion-cognition relations. *Psychological Review, 99,* 561–565.

Izard, C. E. (2007). Basic emotions, natural kinds, emotion schemas, and a new paradigm. *Perspectives on Psychological Science, 2,* 260–280.

Jaaro-Peled, H., Ayhan, Y., Pletnikov, M. V., & Sawa, A. (2010). Review of pathological hallmarks of schizophrenia: Comparison of genetic models with patients and nongenetic models. *Schizophrenia Bulletin, 36,* 301–313.

Jaarsveld, S., Fink, A., Rinner, M., Schwab, D., Benedek, M., & Lachmann, T. (2015). Intelligence in creative processes: An EEG study. *Intelligence, 49,* 171–178.

Jabr, F. (2017, May 12). Can prairie dogs talk? *The New York Times.* Retrieved from https://www.nytimes.com/2017/05/12/magazine/can-prairie-dogs-talk.html?_r=0

Jack, R. E., Sun, W., Delis, I., Garrod, O. G., & Schyns, P. G. (2016). Four not six: Revealing culturally common facial expressions of emotion. *Journal of Experimental Psychology, 145,* 708–730.

Jacobs, H. (2012). Don't ask, don't tell, don't publish. *EMBO Reports, 13*(5), 393.

Jacobsen, F. M. (2015). Second-generation antipsychotics and tardive syndromes in affective illness: A public health problem with neuropsychiatric consequences. *American Journal of Public Health, 105,* e10–e16.

Jacobson, E. (1938). *Progressive relaxation.* Chicago, IL: University of Chicago Press.

Jain, A., Marshall, J., Buikema, A., Bancroft, T., Kelly J. P., & Newschaffer, C. J. (2015). Autism occurrence by MMR vaccine status among US children with older siblings with and without autism. *Journal of the American Medical Association, 313,* 1534–1540.

Jäkel, S., & Dimou, L. (2017). Glial cells and their function in the adult brain: A journey through the history of their ablation. *Frontiers in Cellular Neuroscience, 11.* doi:10.3389/fncel.2017.00024

Jamal, A., King, B. A., Neff, L. J., Whitmill, J., Babb, S. D., & Graffunder, C. M. (2016). Current cigarette smoking among adults—United States, 2005–2015. *Morbidity and Mortality Weekly Report, 65,* 1205–1211.

James, L. E., & Burke, D. M. (2000). Phonological priming effects on word retrieval and tip-of-the-tongue experiences in young and older adults. *Journal of Experimental Psychology: Learning, Memory, and Cognition, 26,* 1378–1391.

James, W. J. (1983). *The principles of psychology.* Cambridge, MA: Harvard University Press. (Original work published 1890)

Jameson, D., & Hurvich, L. M. (1989). Essay concerning color constancy. *Annual Review of Psychology, 40,* 1–24.

Jamkhande, P. G., Chintawar, K. D., & Chandak, P. G. (2014). Teratogenicity: A mechanism based short review on common teratogenic agents. *Asian Pacific Journal of Tropical Disease, 4,* 421–432.

Janak, P. H., & Tye, K. M. (2015). From circuits to behaviour in the amygdala. *Nature, 517,* 284–292.

Janata, P., & Paroo, K. (2006). Acuity of auditory images in pitch and time. *Perception & Psychophysics, 68,* 829–844.

Jang, K. L., Livesley, W. J., & Vernon, P. A. (1996). Heritability of the Big Five personality dimensions and their facets: A twin study. *Journal of Personality, 64,* 577–592.

Janis, I. L. (1972). *Victims of groupthink: A psychological study of foreign-policy decisions and fiascoes.* Oxford, UK: Houghton Mifflin.

Janis, I. L., & Feshbach, S. (1953). Effects of fear-arousing communications. *Journal of Abnormal and Social Psychology, 48,* 78–92.

Janis, I. L., Kaye, D., & Kirschner, P. (1965). Facilitating effects of "eating-while-reading" on responsiveness to persuasive communication. *Journal of Personality and Social Psychology, 1,* 181–186.

Jankovic, N., Geelen, A., Streppel, M. T., de Groot, L. C., Orfanos, P., van den Hooven, E. H., . . . Feskens, E. J. (2014). Adherence to a healthy diet according to the World Health Organization guidelines and all-cause mortality in elderly adults from Europe and the United States. *American Journal of Epidemology, 180,* 978–988.

Javanbakht, A., King, A. P., Evans, G. W., Swain, J. E., Angstadt, M., Phan, K. L., & Liberzon, I. (2015). Childhood poverty predicts adult amygdala and frontal activity and connectivity in response to emotional faces. *Frontiers in Behavioral Neuroscience, 9,* 1–8.

Javitt, D. C., & Sweet, R. A. (2015). Auditory dysfunction in schizophrenia: Integrating clinical and basic features. *Nature Reviews Neuroscience, 16,* 535–550.

Jensen, E. (2016, April 11). Nyle DiMarco on his "DWTS" Disney Night performance, #RedefiningDance. *USA Today.* Retrieved from https://www.usatoday.com/story/life/entertainthis/2016/04/11/nyle-dimarco-his-dwts-disney-night-performance-redefiningdance/82878866/

Jensen, M. P., Adachi, T., Tomé-Pires, C., Lee, J., Osman, Z. J., & Miró, J. (2015). Mechanisms of hypnosis: Toward the development of a biopsychosocial model. *International Journal of Clinical and Experimental Hypnosis, 63*(1), 34–75.

Jerald, C. D. (2009). Defining a 21st century education. Center for Public Education. Retrieved from http://www. centerforpubliceducation.org/LearnAbout/21st-Century/Defining-a-21st-CenturyEducation-Full-Report-PDF.pdf

Jessberger, S., & Gage, F. H. (2014). Adult neurogenesis: Bridging the gap between mice and humans. *Trends in Cell Biology, 24*(10), 558–563.

Jeste, D. V., Savla, G. N., Thompson, W. K., Vahia, I. V., Glorioso, D. K., Palmer, B. W., . . . Depp, C. A. (2013). Association between older age and more successful aging: Critical role of resilience and depression. *American Journal of Psychiatry, 170,* 188–196. doi:10.1176/appi.ajp.2012.12030386

Jia, F., Gottardo, A., Chen, X., Koh, P., & Pasquarella, A. (2016). English proficiency and acculturation among Chinese immigrant youth in Canada: A reciprocal relationship. *Journal of Multilingual and Multicultural Development, 37,* 774–782.

Jiang, W., Liu, H., Zeng, L., Liao, J., Shen, H., Luo, A., . . . Wang, W. (2015). Decoding the processing of lying using functional connectivity MRI. *Behavioral and Brain Functions,* 11. doi:10.1186/s12993-014-0046-4

Jiang, Y., Chew, S. H., & Ebstein, R. P. (2013). The role of D4 receptor gene exon lll polymorphisms in shaping human altruism and prosocial behavior. *Frontiers in Human Neuroscience, 7,* 1–7.

Johannsson, M., Snaedal, J., Johannesson, G. H., Gudmundsson, T. E., & Johnsen, K. (2015). The acetylcholine index: An electroencephalographic marker of cholinergic activity in the living human brain applied to Alzheimer's disease and other dementias. *Dementia and Geriatric Cognitive Disorders, 39,* 132–142.

John-Henderson, N. A., Stellar, J. E., Mendoza-Denton, R., & Francis, D. D. (2015). Socioeconomic status and social support: Social support reduces inflammatory reactivity for individuals whose early-life socioeconomic status was low. *Psychological Science, 26,* 1620–1629.

Johnson, D. M. (2005). *Introduction to and review of simulator sickness research* (Research Report 1832, Army Project No. 2O262785A790). Arlington, VA: U.S. Army Research Institute for the Behavioral and Social Sciences. Retrieved from http://www.dtic.mil/cgi-bin/GetTRDoc?AD=ADA434495

Johnson, H. D., McNair, R., Vojick, A., Congdon, D., Monacelli, J., & Lamont, J. (2006). Categorical and continuous measurement of sex-role orientation: Differences in associations with young adults' reports of well-being. *Social Behavior and Personality, 34,* 59–76.

Johnson, K. (2017, May 28). Dyeing your armpits bright colors is still a thing. Popsugar. Retrieved from https://www.popsugar.com/beauty/Dyeing-Your-Armpit-Hair-Colors-36178686

Johnson, L. R., LeDoux, J. E., & Doyère, V. (2009). Hebbian reverberations in emotional memory micro circuits. *Frontiers in Neuroscience, 3,* 198–205.

Johnson, P. L., Truitt, W., Fitz, S. D., Minick, P. E., Dietrich, A., Sanghani, S., . . . Shekhar, A. (2010). A key role for orexin in panic anxiety. *Nature Medicine, 16,* 111–115.

Johnson, R. D. (1987). Making judgments when information is missing: Inferences, biases, and framing effects. *Acta Psychologica, 66,* 69–72.

Johnson, S. B., Riis, J. L., & Noble, K. G. (2016). State of the art review: Poverty and the developing brain. *Pediatrics, 137.* doi:10.1542/peds.2015-3075

Johnson, W., & Bouchard, T. J. (2011). The MISTR A data: Forty-two mental ability tests in three batteries. *Intelligence, 39,* 82–88.

Johnston, L. D., O'Malley, P. M., Bachman, J. G., & Schulenberg, J. E. (2012). *Monitoring the future national results on adolescent drug use: Overview of key findings, 2011.* Ann Arbor, MI: Institute for Social Research, University of Michigan.

Johnston, M. V. (2009). Plasticity in the developing brain: Implications for rehabilitation. *Developmental Disabilities Research Reviews, 15,* 94–101.

Jones, K. (2013). Discouraging social loafing during team-based assessments. *Teaching Innovation Projects, 3,* Art. 13.

Jones, S., Boisvert, A., Naghi, A., Hullin-Matsuda, F., Greimel, P., Kobayashi, T., . . . Culty, M. (2016). Stimulatory effects of combined endocrine disruptors on MA-10 Leydig cell steroid production and lipid homeostasis. *Toxicology, 355,* 21–30.

Jordan, J. (2009, May 13). Wanda Sykes becomes mom of twins! *People.* Retrieved from http://www.people.com/people/article/0,,20278746,00.html

Jordan-Young, R. M. (2012). Hormones, context, and "brain gender": A review of evidence from congenital adrenal hyperplasia. *Social Science & Medicine, 74,* 1738–1744.

Joseph, D. L., Jin, J., Newman, D. A., & O'Boyle, E. H. (2015). Why does self-reported emotional intelligence predict job performance? A meta-analytic investigation of mixed EI. *Journal of Applied Psychology, 100,* 298–342.

Joseph, N. T., Matthews, K. A., & Myers, H. F. (2014). Conceptualizing health consequences of Hurricane Katrina from the perspective of socioeconomic status decline. *Health Psychology, 33,* 139–146.

Joy, E., Kussman, A., & Nattiv, A. (2016). 2016 Update on eating disorders in athletes: A comprehensive narrative review with a focus on clinical assessment and management. *British Journal of Sports Medicine, 50,* 154–162.

Juberg, D. R., Alfano, K., Coughlin, R. J., & Thompson, K. M. (2001). An observational study of object mouthing behavior by young children. *Pediatrics, 107,* 135–142.

Judge, T. A., Piccolo, R. F., Podsakoff, N. P., Shaw, J. C., & Rich, B. L. (2010). The relationship between pay and job satisfaction: A meta-analysis of the literature. *Journal of Vocational Behavior, 77,* 157–167.

Julien, R. M., Advokat, C. D., & Comaty, J. E. (2014). *A primer of drug action* (13th ed.). New York, NY: Worth.

Junco, R. (2015). Student class standing, Facebook use, and academic performance. *Journal of Applied Developmental Psychology, 36,* 18–29.

Junco, R., & Cotten, S. R. (2012). No A 4 U: The relationship between multitasking and academic performance. *Computers and Education, 59,* 505–514.

Jung, A. (n.d.). The scary reason you need to limit your child's screen time ASAP. *Reader's Digest.* Retrieved from http://www.rd.com/advice/parenting/toddler-screen-use-and-speech-delays/

Jung, C. G. (1969). *Collected works: Vol. 8. The structure and dynamics of the psyche* (2nd ed., Ed. R. F. C. Hull). Princeton, NJ: Princeton University Press.

Jussim, L., & Harber, K. D. (2005). Teacher expectations and self-fulfilling prophecies: Knowns and unknowns, resolved and unresolved controversies. *Personality and Social Psychology Review, 9,* 131–155.

Kaczmarek, M. (2015). On the doorstep to senility: Physical changes, health status and well-being in midlife. *Anthropological Review, 78,* 269–287.

Kadohisa, M. (2013). Effects of odor on emotion, with implications. *Frontiers in Systems Neuroscience, 7.* doi:10.3389/fnsys.2013.00066

Kaduvettoor-Davidson, A., & Inman, A. G. (2013). South Asian Americans: Perceived discrimination, stress, and well-being. *Asian American Journal of Psychology, 4,* 155–165. doi:10.1037/a0030634

Kagan, J. (1985). The human infant. In A. M. Rogers & C. J. Scheirer (Eds.), *The G. Stanley Hall lecture series* (Vol. 5, pp. 55–86). Washington, DC: American Psychological Association.

Kagan, J. (2003). Biology, context, and developmental inquiry. *Annual Review of Psychology, 54,* 1–23.

Kagan, J. (2016). An overly permissive extension. *Perspectives on Psychological Science, 11,* 442–450.

Kagan, J., & Snidman, N. (1991). Temperamental factors in human development. *American Psychologist, 46,* 856–862.

Kahlenberg, S. G., & Hein, M. M. (2010). Progression on Nickelodeon? Gender-role stereotypes in toy commercials. *Sex Roles, 62,* 830–847.

Kahn, J. (2012, January). Born to run back. *Runner's World.* Retrieved from http://rw.runnersworld.com/selects/born-to-run-back.html

Kahneman, D., & Tversky, A. (1973). On the psychology of prediction. *Psychological Review, 80,* 238–251.

Kahneman, D., & Tversky, A. (1984). Choices, values, and frames. *American Psychologist, 39,* 341–350.

Kahneman, D., & Tversky, A. (1996). On the reality of cognitive illusions. *Psychological Review, 103,* 582–591.

Kajonius, P. J., & Johnson, J. (2018). Sex differences in 30 facets of the five factor model of personality in the large public (N = 320,128). *Personality and Individual Differences, 129,* 126–130.

Kalant, H. (2015). Cannabis in the treatment of rheumatic diseases: Suggestions for a reasoned approach. *Journal of Rheumatology, 42,* 146–148.

Kambeitz, J. P., & Howes, O. D. (2015). The serotonin transporter in depression: Meta-analysis of in vivo and post mortem findings and implications for understanding and treating depression. *Journal of Affective Disorders, 186,* 358–366.

Kamilar-Britt, P., & Bedi, G. (2015). The prosocial effects of 3, 4-methylenedioxymethamphetamine (MDMA): Controlled studies in humans and laboratory animals. *Neuroscience & Biobehavioral Reviews, 57,* 433–446.

Kamimori, G. H., McLellan, T. M., Tate, C. M., Voss, D. M., Niro, P., & Lieberman, H. R. (2015). Caffeine improves reaction time, vigilance and logical reasoning during extended periods with restricted opportunities for sleep. *Psychopharmacology, 232,* 2031–2042.

Kaminski, J., Call, J., & Fischer, J. (2004). Word learning in a domestic dog: Evidence for "fast mapping." *Science, 304,* 1682–1683.

Kanai, R., Bahrami, B., Roylance, R., & Rees, G. (2012). Online social network size is reflected in human brain structure. *Proceedings of the Royal Society B, 279,* 1327–1334.

Kandel, E. R. (2009). The biology of memory: A forty-year perspective. *Journal of Neuroscience, 29,* 12748–12756.

Kandel, E. R., & Pittenger, C. (1999). The past, the future and the biology of memory storage. *Philosophical Transactions: Biological Sciences, 354,* 2027–2052.

Kandler, C., Bleidorn, W., & Riemann, R. (2012). Left or right? Sources of political orientation: The roles of genetic factors, cultural transmission, assortative mating, and personality. *Journal of Personality and Social Psychology, 102,* 633–645.

Kandler, C., Bleidorn, W., Riemann, R., Spinath, F. M., Thiel, W., & Angleitner, A. (2010). Sources of cumulative continuity in personality: A longitudinal multiple-rater twin study. *Journal of Personality and Social Psychology, 98,* 995–1008.

Kandler, C., Kornadt, A. E., Hagemeyer, B., & Neyer, F. J. (2015). Patterns and sources of personality development in old age. *Journal of Personality and Social Psychology, 109,* 175–191.

Kaneda, H., Maeshima, K., Goto, N., Kobayakawa, T., Ayabe-Kanamura, S., & Saito, S. (2000). Decline in taste and odor discrimination abilities with age, and relationship between gustation and olfaction. *Chemical Senses, 25,* 331–337.

Kantor, J. (2014, October 10). Malala Yousafzai, youngest Nobel Peace Prize winner, adds to her achievements and expectations. *The New York Times.* Retrieved from http://www.nytimes.com/2014/10/11/world/asia/malala-yousafzai-youngest-nobel-peace-prize-winner-adds-to-her-achievements-and-expectations.html

Kanwisher, N., McDermott, J., & Chun, M. M. (1997). The fusiform face area: A module in human extrastriate cortex specialized for face perception. *Journal of Neuroscience, 17,* 4302–4311.

Kapler, I. V., Weston, T., & Wiseheart, M. (2015). Spacing in a simulated undergraduate classroom: Long-term benefits for factual and higher-level learning. *Learning and Instruction, 36,* 38–45.

Kaptchuk, T. J., & Miller, F. G. (2015). Placebo effects in medicine. *New England Journal of Medicine, 373,* 8–9.

Karanicolas, P. J., Graham, D., Gönen, M., Strong, V. E., Brennan, M. F., & Coit, D. G. (2013). Quality of life after gastrectomy for adenocarcinoma: A prospective cohort study. *Annals of Surgery, 257,* 1039–1046.

Karlen, S. J., Kahn, D. M., & Krubitzer, L. (2006). Early blindness results in abnormal cortico-cortical and thalamocortical connections. *Neuroscience, 142,* 843–858.

Karau, S. J., & Williams, K. D. (1993). Social loafing: A meta-analytic review and theoretical integration. *Journal of Personality and Social Psychology, 65,* 681.

Karpinski, A. C., Kirschner, P. A., Ozer, I., Mellott, J. A., & Ochwo, P. (2013). An exploration of social networking site use, multitasking, and academic performance among United States and European university students. *Computers in Human Behavior, 29,* 1182–1192.

Karremans, J. C., Stroebe, W., & Claus, J. (2006). Beyond Vicary's fantasies: The impact of subliminal priming and brand choice. *Journal of Experimental Social Psychology, 42,* 792–798.

Karwowski, M., & Lebuda, I. (2016). The Big Five, the Huge Two, and creative self-beliefs: A meta-analysis. *Psychology of Aesthetics, Creativity, and the Arts, 10,* 214–232.

Kassin, S., Fein, S., & Markus, H. R. (2011). *Social psychology* (8th ed.). Belmont, CA: Wadsworth, Cengage Learning.

Kassin, S. M. (2017). The killing of Kitty Genovese: What else does this case tell us? *Perspectives on Psychological Science, 12*(3), 374–381.

Kastenbaum, R., & Costa, P. T., Jr. (1977). Psychological perspectives on death. *Annual Review of Psychology, 28,* 225–249.

Katotomichelakis, M., Balatsouras, D., Tripsianis, G., Davris, S., Maroudias, N., Danielides, V., & Simopoulos, C. (2007). The effect of smoking on the olfactory function. *Rhinology, 45,* 273–280.

Katz, J. (2017, April 14). You draw it: Just how bad is the drug overdose epidemic? *The New York Times.* Retrieved from https://www.nytimes.com/interactive/2017/04/14/upshot/drug-overdose-epidemic-you-draw-it.html

Katz, J. (2017, June 5). Drug deaths in America are rising faster than ever. *The New York Times.* Retrieved from https://www.nytimes.com/interactive/2017/06/05/upshot/opioid-epidemic-drug-overdose-deaths-are-rising-faster-than-ever.html

Kaufman, M. T. (2007, July 25). Albert Ellis, 93, influential psychotherapist, dies. *The New York Times.* Retrieved from http://www.nytimes.com/2007/07/25/nyregion/25ellis.html?pagewanted=all&_r=0

Kaul, G. (2017, July 17). How Minnesota determines who's fit—and unfit—to be a police officer. *MinnPost.* Retrieved from https://www.minnpost.com/politics-policy/2017/07/how-minnesota-determines-who-s-fit-and-unfit-be-police-officer

Kauten, R. L., Lui, J. H., Stary, A. K., & Barry, C. T. (2015). "Purging my friends list. Good luck making the cut": Perceptions of narcissism on Facebook. *Computers in Human Behavior, 51,* 244–254.

Kavšek, M., & Granrud, C. E. (2012). Children's and adults' size estimates at near and far distances: A test of the perceptual learning theory of size constancy development. *i-Perception, 3*(7), 459–466.

Kawa, S., & Giordano, J. (2012). A brief historicity of the Diagnostic and Statistical Manual of Mental Disorders: Issues and implications for the future of psychiatric canon and practice. *Philosophy, Ethics, and Humanities in Medicine, 7.* doi: 10.1186/1747-5341-7-2

Kay, L. M., & Sherman, S. M. (2007). An argument for an olfactory thalamus. *Trends in Neurosciences, 30,* 47–53.

Kay, M. B., Proudfoot, D., & Larrick, R. P. (2018). There's no team in I: How observers perceive individual creativity in a team setting. *Journal of Applied Psychology, 103,* 432–442.

Kayes, D. C., & Bailey, J. R. (2018, February 2). 4 Self-improvement myths that may be holding you back. *Harvard Business Review.* Retrieved from https://hbr.org/2018/02/4-self-improvement-myths-that-may-be-holding-you-back

Kaysen, R. (2017, February 10). Light bulbs that help you sleep. *The New York Times.* Retrieved from https://www.nytimes.com/2017/02/10/realestate/light-bulbs-that-help-you-sleep.html

Kazdin, A. E. (1982). The token economy: A decade later. *Journal of Applied Behavior Analysis, 15,* 431–445.

Keel, P. K., & Klump, K. L. (2003). Are eating disorders culture-bound syndromes? Implications for conceptualizing their etiology. *Psychological Bulletin, 129,* 747–769.

Keesey, R. E., & Hirvonen, M. D. (1997). Body weight set-points: Determination and adjustment. *Journal of Nutrition, 127,* 1875S–1883S.

Kegel, M. (2017, April). First dose group in Parkinson's stem cell trial successfully transplanted. *Parkinson's News Today.* Retrieved from https://parkinsonsnewstoday.com/2017/04/26/first-dose-group-parkinsons-stem-cell-trial-successfully-transplanted/

Keirstead, H. S., Nistor, G., Bernal, G., Totoiu, M., Cloutier, F., Sharp, K., & Oswald, S. (2005). Human embryonic stem cell-derived oligodendrocyte progenitor cell transplants remyelinate and restore locomotion after spinal cord injury. *Journal of Neuroscience, 25,* 4694–4705.

Keith, S. E., Michaud, D. S., & Chiu, V. (2008). Evaluating the maximum playback sound levels from portable digital audio players. *Journal of the Acoustical Society of America, 123,* 4227–4237.

Keller, A., & Malaspina, D. (2013). Hidden consequences of olfactory dysfunction: A patient report series. *BMC Ear, Nose and Throat Disorders, 13*(8). doi:10.1186/1472-6815-13-8

Kelley, M. R., Neath, I., & Surprenant, A. M. (2015). Serial position functions in general knowledge. *Journal of Experimental Psychology: Learning, Memory, and Cognition, 41,* 1715–1727.

Kelly, M. L., Peters, R. A., Tisdale, R. K., & Lesku, J. A. (2015). Unihemispheric sleep in crocodilians? *Journal of Experimental Biology, 218,* 3175–3178.

Kember, D., Ho, A., & Hong, C. (2008). The importance of establishing relevance in motivating student learning. *Active Learning in Higher Education, 9,* 249–263.

Kemeny, M. E., & Shestyuk, A. (2008). Emotions, the neuroendocrine and immune systems, and health. In M. Lewis, J. M. Haviland-Jones, & L. F. Barrett (Eds.), *Handbook of emotions* (3rd ed., pp. 661–675). New York, NY: Guilford Press.

Kendall, A. E. (2012, June). *U.S. response to the global threat of HIV/AIDS: Basic facts.* Washington, DC: Congressional Research Service.

Kennedy, M., Kreppner, J., Knights, N., Kumsta, R., Maughan, B., Golm, D., . . . Sonuga-Barke, E. J. (2016). Early severe institutional deprivation is associated with a persistent variant of adult attention-deficit/hyperactivity disorder: Clinical presentation, developmental continuities and life circumstances in the English and Romanian adoptees study. *Journal of Child Psychology and Psychiatry, 57,* 1113–1125.

Kennedy, N., Boydell, J., Kalidindi, S., Fearon, P., Jones, P. B., van Os, J., & Murray, R. M. (2005). Gender differences in incidence and age at onset of mania and bipolar disorder over a 35-year period in Camberwell, England. *American Journal of Psychiatry, 162,* 257–262.

Kennedy, P. (2017, April 7). To be a genius, think like a 94-year-old. *The New York Times.* Retrieved from https://www.nytimes.com/2017/04/07/opinion/sunday/to-be-a-genius-think-like-a-94-year-old.html?mcubz=0

Kerr, N. L., & Tindale, R. S. (2004). Group performance and decision making. *Annual Review of Psychology, 55,* 623–655.

Kershaw, K. N., Robinson, W. R., Gordon-Larsen, P., Hicken, M. T., Goff, D. C., Carnethon, M. R., . . . Roux, A. V. D. (2017). Association of changes in neighborhood-level racial residential segregation with changes in blood pressure among black adults: The CARDIA study. *JAMA Internal Medicine, 177,* 996–1002.

Kersten, A. W., Meissner, C. A., Lechuga, J., Schwartz, B. L., Albrechtsen, J. S., & Iglesias, A. (2010). English speakers attend more strongly than Spanish speakers to manner of motion when classifying novel objects and events. *Journal of Experimental Psychology: General, 139,* 638–653.

Kessler, R. C. (2010). The prevalence of mental illness. In T. L. Scheid & T. N. Brown (Eds.), *A handbook for the study of mental health: Social contexts, theories, and systems* (2nd ed., pp. 46–63). Cambridge, UK: Cambridge University Press.

Kessler, R. C., Berglund, P. A., Coulouvrat, C., Fitzgerald, T., Hajak, G., Roth, T., . . . Walsh, J. K. (2012). Insomnia, comorbidity, and risk of injury among insured Americans: Results from the America Insomnia Survey. *SLEEP, 35,* 825–834.

Kessler, R. C., Berglund, P., Demler, O., Jin, R., Merikangas, K. R., & Walters, E. E. (2005). Lifetime prevalence and age-of-onset distributions of DSM-IV disorders in the National Comorbidity Survey Replication. *Archives of General Psychiatry, 62,* 593–602.

Kessler, R. C., Berglund, P., Demler, O., Jin, R., Koretz, D., Merikangas, K. R., . . . Wang, P. S. (2003). The epidemiology of major depressive disorder: Results from the National Comorbidity Survey Replication (NCS-R). *Journal of the American Medical Association, 289,* 3095–3105.

Kessler, R. C., Chiu, W. T., Demler, O., & Walters, E. E. (2005). Prevalence, severity, and comorbidity of 12-month DSM-IV disorders in the National Comorbidity Survey Replication. *Archives of General Psychiatry, 62,* 617–627.

Kessler, S. (2016, January 8). What I learned in 12 weeks of therapy for social media addiction. *Fast Company.* Retrieved from https://www.fastcompany.com/3055149/what-i-learned-in-12-weeks-of-therapy-for-social-media-addiction

Kessler, R. C., & Wang, P. S. (2008). The descriptive epidemiology of commonly occurring mental disorders in the United States. *Annual Review of Public Health, 29,* 115–129.

Key, M. S., Edlund, J. E., Sagarin, B. J., & Bizer, G. Y. (2009). Individual differences in susceptibility to mindlessness. *Personality and Individual Differences, 46,* 261–264.

Keys, T. E. (1945). *The history of surgical anesthesia.* New York, NY: Schuman's.

Khan, A., & Brown, W. A. (2015). Antidepressants versus placebo in major depression: An overview. *World Psychiatry, 14,* 294–300.

Khan, N. A., & Hillman, C. H. (2014). The relation of childhood physical activity and aerobic fitness to brain function and cognition: A review. *Pediatric Exercise Science, 26,* 138–146.

Khan, R. F., & Sutcliffe, A. (2014). Attractive agents are more persuasive. *International Journal of Human-Computer Interaction, 30,* 142–150.

Kidd, S. A., Eskenazi, B., & Wyrobek, A. J. (2001). Effects of male age on semen quality and fertility: A review of the literature. *Fertility and Sterility, 75,* 237–248.

Kihlstrom, J. F. (1985). Hypnosis. *Annual Review of Psychology, 36,* 385–418.

Kilmartin, C. T., & Dervin, D. (1997). Inaccurate representation of the Electra complex in psychology textbooks. *Teaching of Psychology, 24,* 269–270.

Kim, J., & Anagondahalli, D. (2017). The effects of temporal perspective on college students' energy drink consumption. *Health Psychology, 36,* 898.

Kim, J. S., Jin, M. J., Jung, W., Hahn, S. W., & Lee, S. H. (2017). Rumination as a mediator between childhood trauma and adulthood depression/anxiety in non-clinical participants. *Frontiers in Psychology, 8.* doi:10.3389/fpsyg.2017.01597

Kim, P., Strathearn, L., & Swain, J. E. (2016). The maternal brain and its plasticity in humans. *Hormones and Behavior, 77,* 113–123.

Kindred. (n.d.). *Mission.* Retrieved from http://www.kindredadoption.org

King, B. M. (2006). The rise, fall, and resurrection of the ventromedial hypothalamus in the regulation of feeding behavior and body weight [Invited review]. *Physiology & Behavior, 87,* 221–244.

King, C., & Laurent, O. (2016, February 6). Meet the photographer who found how to balance a life of love and war. *Time.* Retrieved from http://time.com/3699030/lynsey-addario-war-photographer/

Kingsbury, M. K., & Coplan, R. J. (2012). Mothers' gender-role attitudes and their responses to young children's hypothetical display of shy and aggressive behaviors. *Sex Roles, 66,* 506.

Kinsella, E. L., Ritchie, T. D., & Igou, E. R. (2015). Zeroing in on heroes: A prototype analysis of hero features. *Journal of Personality and Social Psychology, 108,* 114–127.

Kinsey, A. C., Pomeroy, W. B., & Martin, C. E. (1948). *Sexual behavior in the human male.* Philadelphia, PA: W. B. Saunders.

Kinsey, A. C., Pomeroy, W. B., Martin, C. E., & Gebhard, P. H. (1953). *Sexual behavior in the human female.* Philadelphia, PA: W. B. Saunders.

Kircher, M. (2017, February 28). This baffling picture of strawberries actually doesn't contain any red pixels. *Select All.* Retrieved from http://nymag.com/selectall/2017/02/strawberries-look-red-without-red-pixels-color-constancy.html

Kirk, M. (Interviewer), & Carson, H. (Interviewee). (2013, September 4). Harry Carson [Interview transcript]. *Frontline.* PBS. Retrieved from http://www.pbs.org/wgbh/pages/frontline/sports/league-of-denial/the-frontline-interview-harry-carson/#seg10

Kirk, M. (Producer & Director), Gilmore, J. (Producer), & Wiser, M. (Producer). (2013). *League of denial: The NFL's concussion crisis* [Documentary movie]. Boston, MA: WGBH. Retrieved from http://www.pbs.org/wgbh/frontline/lm/league-of-denial/

Kirschner, M., Aleman, A., & Kaiser, S. (2016). Secondary negative symptoms: A review of mechanisms, assessment and treatment. *Schizophrenia Research.* doi:http://dx.doi.org/10.1016/j.schres.2016.05.003

Kishida, M., & Rahman, Q. (2015). Fraternal birth order and extreme right-handedness as predictors of sexual orientation and gender nonconformity in men. *Archives of Sexual Behavior, 44,* 1493–1501.

Kisilevsky, B. S., Hains, S. M. J., Lee, K., Xie, X., Huang, H., Ye, H. H., . . . Wang, Z. (2003). Effects of experience on fetal voice recognition. *Psychological Science, 14,* 220–224.

Kitamura, T., Ogawa, S. K., Roy, D. S., Okuyama, T., Morrissey, M. D., Smith, L. M., Redondo, R. L., & Tonegawa, S. (2017). Engrams and circuits crucial for systems consolidation of a memory. *Science, 356,* 73–78.

Klass, P. (2011, October 10). Hearing bilingual: How babies sort out language. *The New York Times.* Retrieved from http://www.nytimes.com/2011/10/11/health/views/11klass.html?_r=1

Klaver, C. C., Wolfs, R. C., Vingerling, J. R., Hoffman, A., & de Jong, P. T. (1998). Age-specific prevalence and causes of blindness and visual impairment in an older population: The Rotterdam Study. *Archives of Opthamology, 116,* 653–658.

Kleber, H. D., & DuPont, R. (2012). Physicians and medical marijuana. *American Journal of Psychiatry, 169,* 564–568.

Klein, J. D. (2018). E-cigarettes: A 1-way street to traditional smoking and nicotine addiction for youth. *Pediatrics, 141*(1). doi:10.1542/peds.2017-2850

Kleinman, A. (2004). Culture and depression. *New England Journal of Medicine, 351,* 951–953.

Klettke, B., Hallford, D., & Mellor, D. J. (2014). Sexting prevalence and correlates: A systematic literature review. *Clinical Psychology Review, 34,* 44–53.

Klimstra, T. A., Luyckx, K., Hale, W. W., III, Frijns, T., van Lier, P. A. C., & Meeus, W. H. J. (2010). Short-term fluctuations in identity: Introducing a micro-level approach to identity formation. *Journal of Personality and Social Psychology, 99,* 191–202.

Kluen, L. M., Agorastos, A., Wiedemann, K., & Schwabe, L. (2017). Cortisol boosts risky decision-making behavior in men but not in women. *Psychoneuroendocrinology, 84,* 181–189.

Klugman, A., & Gruzelier, J. (2003). Chronic cognitive impairment in users of "ecstasy" and cannabis. *World Psychiatry, 2,* 184–190.

Kluver, H., & Bucy, P. (1939). Preliminary analysis of function of the temporal lobe in monkeys. *Archives of Neurology, 42,* 979–1000.

Knafo, A., & Israel, S. (2010). Genetic and environmental influences on prosocial behavior. In M. Mikulincer & P. R. Shaver (Eds.), *Prosocial motives, emotions, and behavior: The better angels of our nature* (pp. 149–167). Washington, DC: American Psychological Association.

Knapp, S., & VandeCreek, L. (2000). Recovered memories of childhood abuse: Is there an underlying professional consensus? *Professional Psychology: Research and Practice, 31,* 365–371.

Knapton, S. (2017, May 4). Tablets and smartphones damage toddlers' speech development. *The Telegraph.* Retrieved from http://www.telegraph.co.uk/science/2017/05/04/tablets-smartphones-damage-toddlers-speech-development/

Knettel, B. A. (2016). Exploring diverse mental illness attributions in a multinational sample: A mixed-methods survey of scholars in international psychology. *International Perspectives in Psychology: Research, Practice, Consultation, 5,* 128–140.

Knorr, A. C., Tull, M. T., Anestis, M. D., Dixon-Gordon, K. L., Bennett, M. F., & Gratz, K. L. (2016). The interactive effect of major depression and nonsuicidal self-injury on current suicide risk and lifetime suicide attempts. *Archives of Suicide Research, 20,* 539–552.

Knudsen, E. I. (2004). Sensitive periods in the development of the brain and behavior. *Journal of Cognitive Neuroscience, 16,* 1412–1425.

Knvul, S. (2017). Digital hypocrisy. *Scientific American Mind, 28,* 10–11.

Ko, K. H. (2015). Brain reorganization allowed for the development of human language: Lunate sulcus. *International Journal of Biology, 7,* 59–65.

Kobasa, S. C. (1979). Stressful life events, personality, and health: An inquiry into hardiness. *Journal of Personality and Social Psychology, 37,* 1–11.

Koch, I., Lawo, V., Fels, J., & Vorländer, M. (2011). Switching in the cocktail party: Exploring intentional control of auditory selective attention. *Journal of Experimental Psychology: Human Perception and Performance, 37,* 1140–1147.

Kochanek, K. D., Murphy, S. L, Xu, J., & Tejada-Vera, B. (2017, April 3). Deaths: Final data for 2014. *National Vital Statistics Reports, 65,* 1–122.

Kochanek, K. D., Xu, J., Murphy, S. L., Miniño, A. M., & Kung, H.-C. (2011). *Deaths: Final data for 2009* (National Vital Statistics Reports, Vol. 60, No. 3). Hyattsville, MD: National Center for Health Statistics. Retrieved from http://www.cdc.gov/nchs/data/nvsr/nvsr59/nvsr59_04.pdf

Kochanska, G., Kim, S., & Boldt, L. J. (2015). (Positive) power to the child: The role of children's willing stance toward parents in developmental cascades from toddler age to early preadolescence. *Development and Psychopathology, 27,* 987–1005.

Koenig, B. A., & Gates-Williams, J. (1995). Understanding cultural difference in caring for dying patients. *Western Journal of Medicine, 163,* 244–249.

Kogan, S. M., Cho, J., Simons, L. G., Allen, K. A., Beach, S. R., Simons, R. L., & Gibbons, F. X. (2015). Pubertal timing and sexual risk behaviors among rural African American male youth: Testing a model based on life history theory. *Archives of Sexual Behavior, 44,* 609–618.

Kohl, S., Jägle, H., & Wissinger, B. (2013). Achromatopsia. In R. A. Pagon, M. P. Adam, H. H. Ardinger, T. D. Bird, C. R. Dolan, C. T. Fong, . . . B. Wissinger (Eds.), *GeneReviews* [Internet]. Seattle, WA: University of Washington. Retrieved from https://www.ncbi.nlm.nih.gov/books/NBK1418/

Kohlberg, L. (1981). *The philosophy of moral development: Vol. 1. Essays on moral development.* San Francisco, CA: Harper & Row.

Kohlberg, L., & Hersh, R. H. (1977). Moral development: A review of the theory. *Theory into Practice, 16,* 53–59.

Köhler, W. (1925). *The mentality of apes.* New York, NY: Harcourt Brace Jovanovich.

Kolar, D. R., Rodriguez, D. L. M., Chams, M. M., & Hoek, H. W. (2016). Epidemiology of eating disorders in Latin America: A systematic review and meta-analysis. *Current Opinion in Psychiatry, 29,* 363–371.

Kolb, B., & Gibb, R. (2011). Brain plasticity and behaviour in the developing brain. *Journal of the Canadian Academy of Child and Adolescent Psychiatry, 20,* 265–276.

Kolb, B., & Gibb, R. (2015). Childhood poverty and brain development. *Human Development, 58,* 215–217.

Kolb, B., & Whishaw, I. Q. (1998). Brain plasticity and behavior. *Annual Review of Psychology, 49,* 43–64.

Kolb, B., & Whishaw, I. Q. (2015). *Fundamentals of human neuropsychology* (7th ed.). New York, NY: Worth.

Kolb, B., Whishaw, I. Q., & Teskey, G. C. (2016). *An introduction to brain and behavior* (5th ed.). New York, NY: Worth.

Kolmes, K. (2012). Social media in the future of professional psychology. *Professional Psychology: Research and Practice, 43,* 606–612.

Koopman, P., Sinclair, A., & Lovell-Badge, R. (2016). Of sex and determination: Marking 25 years of Randy, the sex-reversed mouse. *Development, 143,* 1633–1637.

Koopmann-Holm, B., & Matsumoto, D. (2011). Values and display rules for specific emotions. *Journal of Cross-Cultural Psychology, 42,* 355–371.

Koopmann-Holm, B., & Tsai, J. L. (2014). Focusing on the negative: Cultural differences in expressions of sympathy. *Journal of Personality and Social Psychology, 107,* 1092–1115.

Kornheiser, A. S. (1976). Adaptation to laterally displaced vision: A review. *Psychological Bulletin, 5,* 783–816.

Kosslyn, S. M., Ball, T. M., & Reiser, B. J. (1978). Visual images preserve metric spatial information: Evidence from studies of image scanning. *Journal of Experimental Psychology: Human Perception and Performance, 4,* 47–60.

Kosslyn, S. M., Thompson, W. L., Costantini-Ferrando, M. F., Alpert, N. M., & Spiegel, D. (2000). Hypnotic visual illusion alters color processing in the brain. *American Journal of Psychiatry, 157,* 1279–1284.

Kossoff, E. H., Vining, E. P. G., Pillas, D. J., Pyzik, P. L., Avellino, A. M., Carson, B. S., & Freeman, J. M. (2003). Hemispherectomy for intractable unihemispheric epilepsy: Epilepsy vs. outcome. *Neurology, 61,* 887–890.

Kostora, N. (2012, May 16). 25 Craziest football terms and where they come from. *Bleacher Report.* Retrieved from http://bleacherreport.com/articles/1184750-25-craziest-football-terms-and-where-they-come-from

Kothadia, J. P., Chhabra, S., Marcus, A., May, M., Saraiya, B., & Jabbour, S. K. (2012). Anterior mediastinal mass in a young marijuana smoker: A rare case of small-cell lung cancer. *Case Reports in Medicine,* Article 754231, 1–4.

Kouider, S., & Dehaene, S. (2007). Levels of processing during non-conscious perception: A critical review of visual masking. *Philosophical Transactions of the Royal Society B: Biological Sciences, 362,* 857–875.

Kounios, J., & Beeman, M. (2009). The *Aha!* moment: The cognitive neuroscience of insight. *Current Directions in Psychological Science, 18,* 210–216.

Kovács, A. M., & Mehler, J. (2009). Cognitive gains in 7-month-old bilingual infants. *Proceedings of the National Academy of Sciences, 106,* 6556–6560.

Kozusznik, M. W., Rodríguez, I., & Peiró, J. M. (2015). Eustress and distress climates in teams: Patterns and outcomes. *International Journal of Stress Management, 22,* 1–23.

Kraft, D. (2012). Successful treatment of heavy smoker in one hour using split screen imagery, aversion, and suggestions to eliminate cravings. *Contemporary Hypnosis and Integrative Therapy, 29,* 175–188.

Kramer, A. F., Erickson, K. I., & Colcombe, S. J. (2006). Exercise, cognition, and the aging brain. *Journal of Applied Physiology, 101,* 1237–1242.

Krämer, N. C., Feurstein, M., Kluck, J. P., Meier, Y., Rother, M., & Winter, S. (2017). Beware of selfies: The impact of photo type on impression formation based on social networking profiles. *Frontiers in Psychology, 8.* doi:10.3389/fpsyg.2017.00188

Krapohl, E., Rimfeld, K., Shakeshaft, N. G., Trzaskowski, M., McMillan, A., Pingault, J. B., . . . Plomin, R. (2014). The high heritability of educational achievement reflects many genetically influenced traits, not just intelligence. *Proceedings of the National Academy of Sciences, 111,* 15273–15278.

Krebs, D. L., & Denton, K. (2005). Toward a more pragmatic approach to morality: A critical evaluation of Kohlberg's model. *Psychological Review, 112,* 629–649.

Kreiman, G., Koch, C., & Fried, I. (2000). Imagery neurons in the human brain. *Nature, 408,* 357–361.

Krejtz, I., Nezlek, J. B., Michnicka, A., Holas, P., & Rusanowska, M. (2016). Counting one's blessings can reduce the impact of daily stress. *Journal of Happiness Studies, 17*(1), 25–39.

Kremen, W. S., Panizzon, M. S., & Cannon, T. D. (2016). Genetics and neuropsychology: A merger whose time has come. *Neuropsychology, 30*(1), 1–5.

Krijn, M., Emmelkamp, P. M. G., Olafsson, R. P., & Biemond, R. (2004). Virtual reality exposure therapy of anxiety disorders: A review. *Clinical Psychology Review, 24,* 259–281.

Kripke, D. F. (2015). Mortality risk of hypnotics: Strengths and limits of evidence. *Drug Safety, 39,* 93–107.

Kripke, D. F., Langer, R. D., & Kline, L. E. (2012). Hypnotics' association with mortality or cancer: A matched cohort study. *BMJ Open, 2,* e000850.

Krizan, Z., & Windschitl, P. D. (2007). The influence of outcome desirability on optimism. *Psychological Bulletin, 133,* 95–121.

Krosnick, J. A., Betz, A. L., Jussim, L. J., & Lynn, A. R. (1992). Subliminal conditioning of attitudes. *Personality and Social Psychology Bulletin, 18,* 152–162.

Krueger, E. T., & Reckless, W. C. (1931). The theory of human motivation. In *Longmans' Social Science Series: Social psychology* (pp. 142–170). New York, NY: Longmans, Green and Co.

Kruger, J., Blanck, H. M., & Gillespie, C. (2006). Dietary and physical activity behaviors among adults successful at weight loss maintenance. *International Journal of Behavioral Nutrition and Physical Activity, 3,* 17–27.

Kübler-Ross, E. (2009). *On death and dying: What the dying have to teach doctors, nurses, clergy, and their own families* (40th anniversary ed.). London, UK: Routledge.

Kucharski, A. (1984). History of frontal lobotomy in the United States, 1935–1955. *Neurosurgery, 14,* 765–772.

Kuhl, P. K. (2015). Baby talk. *Scientific American, 313,* 64–69.

Kuhl, P. K., Conboy, B. T., Padden, D., Nelson, T., & Pruitt, J. (2005). Early speech perception and later language development: Implications for the "Critical Period." *Language Learning and Development, 1,* 237–264.

Kujawa, S. G., & Liberman, M. C. (2006). Acceleration of age-related hearing loss by early noise exposure: evidence of a misspent youth. *Journal of Neuroscience, 26,* 2115–2123.

Kumsta, R., Marzi, S. J., Viana, J., Dempster, E. L., Crawford, B., Rutter, M., . . . Sonuga-Barke, E. J. S. (2016). Severe psychosocial deprivation in early childhood is associated with increased DNA methylation across a region spanning the transcription start site of CYP2E1. *Translational Psychiatry, 6,* e830. doi:10.1038/tp.2016.95

Kuo, B. C. (2014). Coping, acculturation, and psychological adaptation among migrants: A theoretical and empirical review and synthesis of the literature. *Health Psychology and Behavioral Medicine: An Open Access Journal, 2,* 16–33.

Kuo, Z. Y. (1921). Giving up instincts in psychology. *Journal of Philosophy, 18,* 654–664.

Kwon, D. (2016, July 1). Financial stress hurts, literally. *Scientific American Mind.* Retrieved from https://www.scientificamerican.com/article/financial-stress-hurts-literally/

LaBerge, S. (2014). Lucid dreaming: Paradoxes of dreaming consciousness. In C. Etzel, S. J. Lynn, & S. Krippner (Eds.), *Dissociation, Trauma, Memory, and Hypnosis Series: Varieties of anomalous experience: Examining the scientific evidence* (2nd ed., pp. 145–173). Washington, DC: American Psychological Association.

Lackner, J. R. (2014). Motion sickness: More than nausea and vomiting. *Experimental Brain Research, 232,* 2493–2510.

Ladouceur, C. D. (2012). Neural systems supporting cognitive-affective interactions in adolescence: The role of puberty and implications for affective disorders. *Frontiers in Integrative Neuroscience, 6,* 1–11.

Laeng, B., & Falkenberg, L. (2007). Women's pupillary responses to sexually significant others during the hormonal cycle. *Hormones and Behavior, 52,* 520–530.

Laeng, B., Profeti, I., Sæther, L., Adolfsdottir, S., Lundervold, A. J., Vangberg, T., . . . Waterloo, K. (2010). Invisible expressions evoke core impressions. *Emotion, 10,* 573–386.

Laird, J. D., & Lacasse, K. (2014). Bodily influences on emotional feelings: Accumulating evidence and extensions of William James's theory of emotion. *Emotion Review, 6,* 27–34.

Lakes, K., Lopez, S. R., & Garro, L. C. (2006). Cultural competence and psychotherapy: Applying anthropologically informed conceptions of culture. *Psychotherapy: Theory, Research, Practice, Training, 43,* 380–396.

Lambert, M. J., Hansen, N. B., & Finch, A. E. (2001). Patient-focused research: Using patient outcome data to enhance treatment effects. *Journal of Consulting and Clinical Psychology, 69,* 159–172.

Lamia, M. C. (2016, June 25). Why time-outs need a time out [Web log post]. Retrieved from https://www.psychologytoday.com/blog/intense-emotions-and-strong-feelings/201606/why-time-outs-need-time-out

Lanagan-Leitzel, L. K. (2012). Identification of critical events by lifeguards, instructors, and non-lifeguards. *International Journal of Aquatic Research and Education, 6,* 203–214.

Lanagan-Leitzel, L. K., Skow, E., & Moore, C. M. (2015). Great expectations: Perceptual challenges of visual surveillance in lifeguarding. *Applied Cognitive Psychology, 29,* 425–435.

Landgren, M. (2017). How much is too much? The implication of recognizing alcohol as a teratogen. *Acta Paediatrica, 106,* 353–355.

Lando, H. A. (1976). On being sane in insane places: A supplemental report. *Professional Psychology, 7,* 47–52.

Landrum, R. E. (2001). I'm getting my bachelor's degree in psychology—what can I do with it? *Eye on Psi Chi, 6,* 22–24.

Landrum, R. E. (2016). The history of the teaching of psychology: Or, what was old is new again. In W. D. Woody, R. L. Miller, & W. J. Wozniak (Eds.), *Psychological specialties in historical context: Enriching the classroom experience for teachers and students.* Society for the Teaching of Psychology. Retrieved from http://teachpsych.org/ebooks/

Landrum, R. E. (2018, January). *What can you do with a bachelor's degree in psychology? Like this title, the actual answer is complicated.* Retrieved from http://www.apa.org/ed/precollege/psn/2018/01/bachelors-degree.aspx

Landrum, R. E., & Gurung, R. A. (2013). The memorability of introductory psychology revisited. *Teaching of Psychology, 40,* 222–227.

Lange, C. G., & James, W. (1922). The emotions. In K. Dunlap (Ed.), *Psychology classics: A series of reprints and translations.* Baltimore, MD: Williams & Wilkins.

Langer, E., Blank, A., & Chanowitz, B. (1978). The mindlessness of ostensibly thoughtful action: The role of "placebic" information in interpersonal interaction. *Journal of Personality and Social Psychology, 36,* 635–642.

Langer, E. J., & Rodin, J. (1976). The effects of choice and enhanced personal responsibility for the aged: A field experiment in an institutional setting. *Journal of Personality and Social Psychology, 34,* 191–198.

Langeslag, S. J. E., & van Strien, J. W. (2018). Early visual processing of snakes and angry faces: An ERP study. *Brain Research, 1678,* 297–303.

Langley, T. (2016, February 10). Star Wars psychology: The problems with diagnosing Kylo Ren [Web log post]. *Psychology Today.* Retrieved from https://www.psychologytoday.com/blog/beyond-heroes-and-villains/201602/star-wars-psychology-the-problems-diagnosing-kylo-ren

Langlois, J. H., Kalakanis, L., Rubenstein, A. J., Larson, A., Hallam, M., & Smoot, M. (2000). Maxims or myths of beauty? A meta-analytic and theoretical review. *Psychological Bulletin, 126,* 390–423.

Långström, N., Rahman, Q., Carlström, E., & Lichtenstein, P. (2010). Genetic and environmental effects on same-sex sexual behavior: A population study of twins in Sweden. *Archives of Sexual Behavior, 39,* 75–80.

Lannin, D. G., Ludwikowski, W. M. A., Vogel, D. L., Seidman, A. J., & Anello, K. (2018). Reducing psychological barriers to therapy via contemplation and self-affirmation. *Stigma and Health.* Advance online publication. http://dx.doi.org/10.1037/sah0000139

Lannin, D. G., & Scott, N. A. (2014, February). Best practices for an online world. *Monitor on Psychology, 45,* 56–61.

Lanza, A., Roysircar, G., & Rodgers, S. (2018). First responder mental healthcare: Evidence-based prevention, postvention, and treatment. *Professional Psychology: Research and Practice, 49*(3), 193–204.

Lara, D. R. (2010). Caffeine, mental health, and psychiatric disorders. *Journal of Alzheimer's Disease, 20,* S239–S248.

Larsen, J. K., Krogh-Nielsen, L., & Brøsen, K. (2016). The monoamine oxidase inhibitor isocarboxazid is a relevant treatment option in treatment-resistant depression-experience-based strategies in Danish psychiatry. *Health Care: Current Reviews, 4.* doi:10.4172/2375-4273.1000168

Larsen, L., Hartmann, P., & Nyborg, H. (2008). The stability of general intelligence from early adulthood to middle-age. *Intelligence, 36,* 29–34.

Larsson, M., & Willander, J. (2009). Autobiographical odor memory. *Annals of the New York Academy of Sciences, 1170,* 318–323.

Larzelere, R. E. (2016, October 31). Positive parenting is ideal, but many children need time-outs, too [Web log post]. Retrieved from https://ifstudies.org/blog/positive-parenting-is-ideal-but-many-children-need-time-outs-too

LaSalle, J. M. (2013). Epigenomic strategies at the interface of genetic and environmental risk factors for autism. *Journal of Human Genetics, 58,* 396–401.

Lashley, K. S. (1950). In search of the engram. *Symposia of the Society for Experimental Biology, 4,* 454–482.

Lashley, K. S., & Wiley, L. E. (1933). Studies of cerebral function in learning IX. Mass action in relation to the number of elements in the problem to be learned. *The Journal of Comparative Neurology, 57,* 3–55.

Latané, B., Williams, K., & Harkins, S. (1979). Many hands make light the work: The causes and consequences of social loafing. *Journal of Personality and Social Psychology, 37,* 822–832.

Lathia, N., Sandstrom, G. M., Mascolo, C., & Rentfrow, P. J. (2017). Happier people live more active lives: Using smartphones to link happiness and physical activity. *PLoS One, 12*(1), e0160589. doi:10.1371/journal.pone.0160589

Laumann, E. O., Gagnon, J. H., Michael, R. T., & Michaels, S. (1994). *The social organization of sexuality: Sexual practices in the United States.* Chicago, IL: University of Chicago Press.

Laumann, E. O., Paik, A., & Rosen, R. C. (1999). Sexual dysfunction in the United States: Prevalence and predictors. *Journal of the American Medical Association, 281,* 537–544.

Lauriola, M., Panno, A., Levin, I. P., & Lejuez, C. W. (2014). Individual differences in risky decision making: A meta-analysis of sensation seeking and impulsivity with the Balloon Analogue Risk Task. *Journal of Behavioral Decision Making, 27,* 20–26.

Laventure, S., Fogel, S., Lungu, O., Albouy, G., Sévigny-Dupont, P., Vien, C., . . . Doyon, J. (2016). NREM2 and sleep spindles are instrumental to the consolidation of motor sequence memories. *PLoS Biology, 14.* Retrieved from http://dx.doi.org/10.1371/journal.pbio.1002429

Lawler-Row, K. A., & Elliott, J. (2009). The role of religious activity and spirituality in the health and well-being of older adults. *Journal of Health Psychology, 14,* 43–52.

Lazarus, R. S. (1984). On the primacy of cognition. *American Psychologist, 39,* 124–129.

Lazarus, R. S. (1991a). Cognition and motivation in emotion. *American Psychologist, 46,* 352–367.

Lazarus, R. S. (1991b). Progress on a cognitive-motivational-relational theory of emotion. *American Psychologist, 46,* 819–834.

Lazarus, R. S. (1993). From psychological stress to the emotions: A history of changing outlooks. *Annual Review of Psychology, 44,* 1–21.

Lazarus, R. S., & Folkman, S. (1984). *Stress, appraisal, and coping.* New York, NY: Springer.

Lazzouni, L., & Lepore, F. (2014). Compensatory plasticity: Time matters. *Frontiers in Human Neuroscience, 8.* http://dx.doi.org/10.3389/fnhum.2014.00340

Leavitt, R. A., Ertl, A., Sheats, K., Petrosky, E., Ivey-Stephenson, A., & Fowler, K. A. (2018). Suicides among American Indian/Alaska Natives—National Violent Death Reporting System, 18 states, 2003–2014. *Morbidity and Mortality Weekly Report, 67,* 237–242.

LeBeau, R. T., Glenn, D., Liao, B., Wittchen, H.-U., Beesdo-Baum, K., Ollendick,T., & Craske, M. G. (2010). Specific phobia: A review of DSM-IV specific phobia and preliminary recommendations for DSM-V. *Depression and Anxiety, 27,* 148–167.

Lecendreux, M., Churlaud, G., Pitoiset, F., Regnault, A., Tran, T. A., Liblau, R., . . . Rosenzwajg, M. (2017). Narcolepsy type 1 is associated with a systemic increase and activation of regulatory T cells and with a systemic activation of global T cells. *PLoS ONE, 12,* e0169836.

LeDoux, J. (2012). Rethinking the emotional brain. *Neuron, 73,* 653–676.

LeDoux, J. E. (1996). *The emotional brain: The mysterious underpinnings of emotional life.* New York, NY: Simon & Schuster.

LeDoux, J. E. (2000). Emotion circuits in the brain. *Annual Review of Neuroscience, 23,* 155–184.

Lee, B. K., Magnusson, C., Gardner, R. M., Blomström, Å., Newschaffer, C. J., Burstyn I., . . . Dalman, C. (2015). Maternal hospitalization with infection during pregnancy and risk of autism spectrum disorders. *Brain, Behavior, and Immunity, 44,* 100–105.

Lee, J. H., Chang, Y. S., Yoo, H. S., Ahn, S. Y., Seo, H. J., Choi, S. H., . . . Park, W. S. (2011). Swallowing dysfunction in very low birth weight infants with oral feeding desaturation. *World Journal of Pediatrics, 7,* 337–343.

Lee, K. M., Lindquist, K. A., & Payne, B. K. (2018). Constructing bias: Conceptualization breaks the link between implicit bias and fear of Black Americans. *Emotion, 18,* 855–871.

Lee, P. A., Houk, C. P., Ahmed, S. F., & Hughes, I. A. (2006). Consensus statement on management of intersex disorders. *Pediatrics, 118,* e488–e500.

Lee, S. W. S., & Schwarz, N. (2014). Framing love: When it hurts to think we were made for each other. *Journal of Experimental Social Psychology, 54,* 61–67.

Lee, V. E., & Burkan, D. T. (2002). *Inequality at the starting gate.* Washington, DC: Economic Policy Institute.

Legome, E. L. (2016, September 12). Postconcussive syndrome in the ED. Medscape. Retrieved from http://emedicine.medscape.com/article/828904-overview

Leichsenring, F., Abbass, A., Gottdiener, W., Hilsenroth, M., Keefe, J. R., Luyten, P., . . . Steinert, C. (2016). Psychodynamic therapy: A well-defined concept with increasing evidence. *Evidence Based Mental Health, 19.* doi:10.1136/eb-2016-102372

Leichsenring, F., Luyten, P., Hilsenroth, M. J., Abbass, A., Barber, J. P., Keefe, J. R., . . . Steinert, C. (2015). Psychodynamic therapy meets evidence-based medicine: A systematic review using updated criteria. *The Lancet Psychiatry, 2,* 648–660.

Leichsenring, F., & Rabung, S. (2008). Effectiveness of long-term psychodynamic psychotherapy. *Journal of the American Medical Association, 300,* 1551–1565.

Leighty, K. A., Grand, A. P., Pittman Courte, V. L., Maloney, M. A., & Bettinger, T. L. (2013). Relational responding by eastern box turtles (*Terrapene carolina*) in a series of color discrimination tasks. *Journal of Comparative Psychology, 127,* 256–264. doi:10.1037/a0030942

Leinninger, G. (2011). Lateral thinking about leptin: A review of leptin action via the lateral hypothalamus. *Physiology & Behavior, 104,* 572–581.

Leiserowitz, A., Feinberg, G., Rosenthal, S., Smith, N., Anderson A., Roser-Renouf, C., & Maibach, E. (2014). *What's in a name? Global warming vs. climate change.* Yale University and George Mason University. New Haven, CT: Yale Project on Climate Change Communication.

Lembke, A., Papac, J., & Humphreys, K. (2018). Our other prescription drug problem. *New England Journal of Medicine, 378,* 693–695.

Lenzenweger, M. F., Lane, M. C., Loranger, A. W., & Kessler, R. C. (2007). DSM-IV personality disorders in the national comorbidity survey replication. *Biological Psychiatry, 62,* 553–564.

Leo, J. (1987, January 12). Behavior: Exploring the traits of twins. *Time.* Retrieved from http://content.time.com/time/magazine/article/0,9171,963211,00.html

Leontovich, O. (2016). Garlic and love: Gastronomic communication in an intercultural family. *Procedia—Social and Behavioral Sciences, 236,* 89–94.

LePort, A. K., Mattfeld, A. T., Dickinson-Anson, H., Fallon, J. H., Stark, C. E., Kruggel, F., . . . McGaugh, J. L. (2012). Behavioral and neuroanatomical investigation of highly superior autobiographical memory (HSAM). *Neurobiology of Learning and Memory, 98,* 78–92.

Lerman, C., & Audrain-McGovern, J. (2010). Reinforcing effects of smoking: More than a feeling. *Biological Psychiatry, 67,* 699–701.

Lerner, D., Lyson, M., Sandberg, E., & Rogers, W. H. (n.d.). The high cost of mental disorders: Facts for employers. One Mind Initiative. Retrieved from https://onemindinitiative.org/wp-content/uploads/2018/02/OMI-White-Paper-R18.pdf

Lerner, J. S., Li, Y., Valdesolo, P., & Kassam, K. S. (2015). Emotion and decision making: Online supplement. *Annual Review of Psychology, 66,* 799–823.

Lerner, L. (2016, March 16). Adventures of the first neuroscientist at Argonne. Argonne National Laboratory. Retrieved from https://www.anl.gov/articles/adventures-first-neuroscientist-argonne

Leshner, A. I., & Dzau, V. J. (2018). Good gun policy needs research. *Science, 359*(6381), 1195.

Levendosky, A. A., Bogat, G. A., Lonstein, J. S., Martinez-Torteya, C., Muzik, M., Granger, D. A., & Von Eye, A. (2016). Infant adrenocortical reactivity and behavioral functioning: Relation to early exposure to maternal intimate partner violence. *Stress, 19,* 37–44.

Levett-Jones, T., Sundin, D., Bagnall, M., Hague, K., Schuman, W., Taylor, C., & Wink, J. (2010). Learning to think like a nurse. *HNE Handover: For Nurses and Midwives, 3,* 15–20.

Levine, B. (2002, September 25). Redeeming Rover. *Los Angeles Times.* Retrieved from http://articles.latimes.com/2002/sep/25/news/lv-dogtherapy25

Levine, H., Jørgensen, N., Martino-Andrade, A., Mendiola, J., Weksler-Derri, D., Mindlis, I., . . . Swan, S. H. (2017). Temporal trends in sperm count: A systematic review and meta-regression analysis. *Human Reproduction Update.* doi:10.1093/humupd/dmx022

Levinson, D. F. (2006). The genetics of depression: A review. *Biological Psychiatry, 60,* 84–92.

Levy, B. R., & Bavishi, A. (2016). Survival advantage mechanism: Inflammation as a mediator of positive self-perceptions of aging on longevity. *Journals of Gerontology Series B: Psychological Sciences and Social Sciences,* gbw035. doi:http://10.1093/geronb/gbw035

Levy, B. R., Pilver, C., Chung, P. H., & Slade, M. D. (2014). Subliminal strengthening: Improving older individuals' physical function over time with an implicit-age-stereotype intervention. *Psychological Science, 25,* 2127–2135.

Levy, F., & Rodkin, J. (2015). The Bloomberg recruiter report: Job skills companies want but can't get. *Bloomberg.* Retrieved from http://www.bloomberg.com/graphics/2015-job-skills-report/

Levy, R. A., & Ablon, S. J. (2010, February 23). Talk therapy: Off the couch and into the lab. *Scientific American.* Retrieved from http://www.scientificamerican.com/article/talk-therapy-off-couch-into-lab/

Levy, S. R., Hilsenroth, M. J., & Owen, J. J. (2015). Relationship between interpretation, alliance, and outcome in psychodynamic psychotherapy: Control of therapist effects and assessment of moderator variable impact. *The Journal of Nervous and Mental Disease, 203,* 418–424.

Lew, S. M. (2014). Hemispherectomy in the treatment of seizures: A review. *Translational Pediatrics, 3,* 208–217.

Lewis, D. J., & Duncan, C. P. (1956). Effect of different percentages of money reward on extinction of a lever-pulling response. *Journal of Experimental Psychology, 52,* 23–27.

Lewis, T. (2017, May/June). The "Goldilocks" level of teen screen use. *Scientific American Mind, 28,* 16.

Ley, J., Bennett, P., & Coleman, G. (2008). Personality dimensions that emerge in companion canines. *Applied Animal Behaviour Science, 110,* 305–317.

Li, J. (2005). Mind or virtue: Western and Chinese beliefs about learning. *Current Directions in Psychological Science, 14,* 190–194.

Li, J. (J.), Chen, X.-P., Kotha, S., & Fisher, G. (2017). Catching fire and spreading it: A glimpse into displayed entrepreneurial passion in crowdfunding campaigns. *Journal of Applied Psychology, 102,* 1075–1090.

Li, W., Ma, L., Yang, G., & Gan, W. B. (2017). REM sleep selectively prunes and maintains new synapses in development and learning. *Nature Neuroscience, 20*(3), 427–437.

Liberles, S. B. (2015). Mammalian pheromones. *Annual Review of Physiology, 76,* 151–175.

Liberman, M. C. (2015). Hidden hearing loss. *Scientific American, 313,* 48–53.

Libourel, P. A., & Herrel, A. (2016). Sleep in amphibians and reptiles: A review and a preliminary analysis of evolutionary patterns. *Biological Reviews, 91,* 833–866.

Lichtwarck-Aschoff, A., Kunnen, S. E., & van Geert, P. L. C. (2009). Here we go again: A dynamic systems perspective on emotional rigidity across parent-adolescent conflicts. *Developmental Psychology, 45,* 1364–1375.

Licis, A. K., Desruisseau, D. M., Yamada, K. A., Duntley, S. P., & Gurnett, C. A. (2011). Novel findings in an extended family pedigree with sleepwalking. *Neurology, 76,* 49–52.

Liddle, J. R., Shackelford, T. K., & Weekes-Shackelford, V. A. (2012). Why can't we all just get along? Evolutionary perspectives on violence, homicide, and war. *Review of General Psychology, 16,* 24–36.

Lieberson, A. D. (2004, November 8). How long can a person survive without food? *Scientific American.* Retrieved from http://www.scientificamerican.com/article.cfm?id=how-long-can-a-person-sur

Likhtik, E., Stujenske, J. M., Topiwala, M. A., Harris, A. Z., & Gordon, J. A. (2014). Prefrontal entrainment of amygdala activity signals safety in learned fear and innate anxiety. *Nature Neuroscience, 17,* 106–113.

Lilienfeld, S. O. (2012). Public skepticism of psychology: Why many people perceive the study of human behavior as unscientific. *American Psychologist, 67,* 111–129.

Lilienfeld, S. O., & Arkowitz, H. (2012, September 1). Are all psychotherapies created equal? *Scientific American.* Retrieved from http://www.scientificamerican.com/article/are-all-psychotherapies-created-equal/

Lilienfeld, S. O., Lynn, S. J., Ruscio, J., & Beyerstein, B. L. (2010). Busting big myths in popular psychology. *Scientific American Mind, 21,* 42–49.

Lilienfeld, S. O., Wood, J. M., & Garb, H. N. (2005). What's wrong with this picture? *Scientific American Mind, 16,* 50–57.

Lillard, A. S., Drell, M. B., Richey, E. M., Boguszewski, K., & Smith, E. D. (2015). Further examination of the immediate impact of television on children's executive function. *Developmental Psychology, 51,* 792–805. doi:10.1037/a0039097

Lillard, A. S., & Peterson, J. (2011). The immediate impact of different types of television on young children's executive function. *Pediatrics, 128,* 644–649.

Lim, J., & Dinges, D. F. (2010). A meta-analysis of the impact of short-term sleep deprivation on cognitive variables. *Psychological Bulletin, 136,* 375–389.

Lin, P. (2016). Risky behaviors: Integrating adolescent egocentrism with the theory of planned behavior. *Review of General Psychology, 20,* 392–398.

Lina, J., Epel, E., & Blackburn, E. (2012). Telomeres and lifestyle factors: Roles in cellular aging. *Mutation Research, 730,* 85–89.

Lind, O., & Delhey, K. (2015). Visual modelling suggests a weak relationship between the evolution of ultraviolet vision and plumage coloration in birds. *Journal of Evolutionary Biology, 28,* 715–722.

Lindau, S. T., Schumm, L. P., Laumann, E. O., Levinson, W., O'Muircheartaigh, C. A., & Waite, L. J. (2007). A study of sexuality and health among older adults in the United States. *New England Journal of Medicine, 357,* 762–774.

Lindquist, K. A., Satpute, A. B., & Gendron, M. (2015). Does language do more than communicate emotion? *Current Directions in Psychological Science, 24,* 99–108.

Lineberry, T. W., & Bostwick, J. M. (2006). Methamphetamine abuse: A perfect storm of complications. *Mayo Clinic Proceedings, 81,* 77–84.

Linhares, J. M., Pinto, P. D., & Nascimento, S. M. (2008). The number of discernible colors in natural scenes. *Journal of the Optical Society of America, 25,* 2918–2924.

Linnerooth, P. J., Mrdjenovich, A. J., & Moore, B. A. (2011). Professional burnout in clinical military psychologists: Recommendations before, during, and after deployment. *Professional Psychology: Research and Practice, 42,* 87–93.

Linthicum, K. (2017, June 25). Mexican soccer fans are reluctant to give up a favorite chant—an anti-gay slur. *Los Angeles Times.* Retrieved from http://www.latimes.com/world/mexico-americas/la-fg-mexico-soccer-slur-20170623-story.html

Lisman, J. (2015). The challenge of understanding the brain: Where we stand in 2015. *Neuron, 86,* 864–882.

Liu, C. C., Kanekiyo, T., Xu, H., & Bu, G. (2013). Apolipoprotein E and Alzheimer disease: Risk, mechanisms and therapy. *Nature Reviews Neurology, 9,* 106–118.

Liu, K., Daviglus, M. L., Loria, C. M., Colangelo, L. A., Spring, B., Moller, A. C., & Lloyd-Jones, D. M. (2012). Healthy lifestyle through young adulthood and the presence of low cardiovascular disease risk profile in middle age: The coronary artery risk development in (young) adults (cardia) study. *Circulation, 125,* 996–1004.

Liu, L., Preotiuc-Pietro, D., Samani, Z. R., Moghaddam, M. E., & Ungar, L. H. (2016). Analyzing personality through social media profile picture choice. In *Proceedings of the Tenth International AAAI Conference on Web and Social Media* (pp. 211–220). Cologne, Germany: Association for the Advancement of Artificial Intelligence.

Liu, R. T., Kleiman, E. M., Nestor, B. A., & Cheek, S. M. (2015). The hopelessness theory of depression: A quarter-century in review. *Clinical Psychology: Science and Practice, 22,* 345–365.

Liu, Y., Wheaton, A. G., Chapman, D. P., Cunningham, T. J., Lu, H., & Croft, J. B. (2016). Prevalence of healthy sleep duration among adults—United States, 2014. *Morbidity and Mortality Weekly Report (MMWR), 65,* 137–141.

Liu, Y., Yu, C., Liang, M., Li, J., Tian, L., Zhou, Y., . . . Jiang, T. (2007). Whole brain functional connectivity in the early blind. *Brain, 130,* 2085–2096.

Livingston, I., Doyle, J., & Mangan, D. (2010, April 25). Stabbed hero dies as more than 20 people stroll past him. *New York Post.* Retrieved from http://www.nypost.com/p/news/local/queens/passers_by_let_good_sam_die_5SGkf5XDP5ooudVuEd8fbI

Lloyd, M. A. (1997, July 16). Entry level positions obtained by psychology majors. Psych Web. Retrieved from http://www.psywww.com/careers/entry.htm

Loftus, E. F. (1994). The repressed memory controversy. *American Psychologist, 49,* 443–445.

Loftus, E. F. (1997). Creating false memories. *Scientific American, 277,* 70–75.

Loftus, E. F. (2005). Planting misinformation in the human mind: A 30-year investigation of the malleability of memory. *Learning and Memory, 12,* 361–366.

Loftus, E. F., & Bernstein, D. M. (2005). Rich false memories. In A. F. Healy (Ed.), *Experimental cognitive psychology and its applications* (pp. 101–113). Washington, DC: American Psychological Association Press.

Loftus, E. F., Miller, D. G., & Burns, H. J. (1978). Semantic integration of verbal information into a visual memory. *Journal of Experimental Psychology: Human Learning and Memory, 4,* 19–31.

Loftus, E. F., & Palmer, J. C. (1974). Reconstruction of automobile destruction. *Journal of Verbal Learning and Verbal Behavior, 13,* 585–589.

Loftus, E. F., & Pickrell, J. E. (1995). The formation of false memories. *Psychiatric Annals, 25,* 720–725.

Loftus, E., & Ketcham, K. (1994). *The myth of repressed memory.* New York, NY: St. Martin's Griffin.

Lohr, J. (2015, September/October). Does napping really help cognitive function? *Scientific American Mind, 26,* 70.

Lois, C., & Kelsch, W. (2014). Adult neurogenesis and its promise as a hope for brain repair. *Frontiers in Neuroscience, 8.* Retrieved from http://dx.doi.org/10.3389/fnins.2014.00165

Lopez, F. G., Ramos, K., & Kim, M. (2018). Development and initial validation of a measure of attachment security in late adulthood. *Psychological Assessment, 30,* 1214–1225.

Lopez, R. (2012, March 18). "Dog Whisperer" Cesar Millan grooms his canine-training empire. *Los Angeles Times.* Retrieved from http://articles.latimes.com/2012/mar/18/business/la-fi-himi-millan-20120318

Lorang, M. R., McNiel, D. E., & Binder, R. L. (2016). Minors and sexting: Legal implications. *Journal of the American Academy of Psychiatry and the Law Online, 44,* 73–81.

Lorenz, K. Z. (1937). The companion in the bird's world. *The Auk, 54,* 245–273.

Lott, A. J., & Lott, B. E. (1965). Group cohesiveness as interpersonal attraction: A review of relationships with antecedent and consequent variables. *Psychological Bulletin, 64,* 259–309.

Lou, S., & Zhang, G. (2009). What leads to romantic attractions: Similarity, reciprocity, security, or beauty? Evidence from a speed-dating study. *Journal of Personality, 77,* 933–964.

Loughrey, D. G., Kelly, M. E., Kelley, G. A., Brennan, S., & Lawlor, B. A. (2018). Association of age-related hearing loss with cognitive function, cognitive impairment, and dementia: A systematic review and meta-analysis. *JAMA Otolaryngology–Head & Neck Surgery, 144*(2), 115–126.

Louie, J. Y., Oh, B. J., & Lau, A. S. (2013). Cultural differences in the links between parental control and children's emotional expressivity. *Cultural Diversity and Ethnic Minority Psychology, 19,* 424–434.

Lowenstein, J. A., Blank, H., & Sauer, J. D. (2010). Uniforms affect the accuracy of children's eyewitness identification and decisions. *Journal of Investigative Psychology and Offender Profiling, 7,* 59–73.

Lowy, J. (2017, October 5). Technology crammed into cars worsens driver distraction. Associated Press. Retrieved from https://apnews.com/23e2fbcf837348b69e5b5a8d1e3f2963

Lu, Z.-L., Williamson, S. J., & Kaufman, L. (1992). Behavioral lifetime of human auditory sensory memory predicted by physiological measures. *Science, 258,* 1668–1670.

Lubke, G. H., McArtor, D. B., Boomsma, D. I., & Bartels, M. (2018). Genetic and environmental contributions to the development of childhood aggression. *Developmental Psychology, 54,* 39–50.

Lucasfilm (Producer), & Marquand, R. (Director). (1983). *Star wars: Episode VI—return of the Jedi* [Motion picture]. United States: Twentieth Century Fox Film Corporation.

Ludel, J. (1978). *Introduction to sensory processes.* San Francisco, CA: W. H. Freeman.

Luers, J. C., & Hüttenbrink, K.-B. (2016). Surgical anatomy and pathology of the middle ear. *Journal of Anatomy, 228,* 338–353.

Luk, J. W., Patock-Peckham, J. A., Medina, M., Terrell, N., Belton, D., & King, K. M. (2016). Bullying perpetration and victimization as externalizing and internalizing pathways: A retrospective study linking parenting styles and self-esteem to depression, alcohol use, and alcohol-related problems. *Substance Use & Misuse, 51,* 113–125.

Lund, C., De Silva, M., Plagerson, S., Cooper, S., Chisholm, D., Das, J., . . . Patel, V. (2011). Poverty and mental disorders: Breaking the cycle in low-income and middle-income countries. *The Lancet, 78,* 1502–1514.

Lundin, R. W. (1963). Personality theory in behavioristic psychology. In J. M. Wepman & R. W. Heine (Eds.), *Concepts of personality* (pp. 257–290). Hawthorne, NY: Aldine.

Luo, Y. H.-L., & da Cruz, L. (2014). A review and update on the current status of retinal prostheses (bionic eye). *British Medical Bulletin, 109,* 31–44.

Lussier, K. (2018). Temperamental workers: Psychology, business, and the Humm-Wadsworth Temperament Scale in interwar America. *History of Psychology, 21,* 79–99.

Luttrell, A., Petty, R. E., & Briñol, P. (2016). Ambivalence and certainty can interact to predict attitude stability over time. *Journal of Experimental Social Psychology, 63,* 56–68.

Luyster, F. S., Strollo, P. J., Jr., Zee, P. C., & Walsh, J. K. (2012). Sleep: A health imperative. *SLEEP, 35,* 727–734.

Lyall, S. (2007, November 4). In Stetson or wig, he's hard to pin down. *The New York Times.* Retrieved from http://www.nytimes.com/2007/11/04/movies/moviesspecial/04lyal.html

Lyckholm, L. J. (2004). Thirty years later: An oncologist reflects on Kübler-Ross's work. *American Journal of Bioethics, 4,* 29–31.

Lynch, G. (2002). Memory enhancement: The search for mechanism-based drugs. *Nature Neuroscience, 5*(Suppl.), 1035–1038.

Lynch, K. (1960). *The image of the city.* Cambridge, MA: MIT Press.

Lynn, S. J., Lilienfeld, S. O., Merckelbach, H., Giesbrecht, T., & van der Kloet, D. (2012). Dissociation and dissociative disorders: Challenging conventional wisdom. *Current Directions in Psychological Science, 21,* 48–53.

Lyoo, I. K., Yoon, S., Kim, T. S., Lim, S. M., Choi, Y., Kim, J. E., . . . Rnshaw, P. F. (2015). Predisposition to and effects of methamphetamine use on the adolescent brain. *Molecular Psychiatry, 20,* 1516–1524.

Lyubomirsky, S., Dickerhoof, R., Boehm, J. K., & Sheldon, K. M. (2011). Becoming happier takes both a will and a proper way: An experimental longitudinal intervention to boost well-being. *Emotion, 11,* 391–402.

Lyubomirsky, S., & Layous, K. (2013). How do simple positive activities increase well-being? *Current Directions in Psychological Science, 22,* 57–62.

Lyubomirsky, S., Sheldon, S. M., & Schkade, D. (2005). Pursuing happiness: The architecture of sustainable change. *Review of General Psychology, 9,* 111–131.

Ma, J., van den Heuvel, M., Maguire, J., Parkin, P., & Birken, C. (2017). Is handheld screen time use associated with language delay in infants? Poster session presented at the Pediatric Academic Societies meeting, San Francisco, CA.

Maass, A., Düzel, S., Brigadski, T., Goerke, M., Becke, A., Sobieray, U., . . . Düzel, E. (2016). Relationships of peripheral IGF-1, VEGF and BDNF levels to exercise-related changes in memory, hippocampal perfusion and volumes in older adults. *NeuroImage, 131,* 142–154.

MacCann, C., Fogarty, G. J., Zeidner, M., & Roberts, R. D. (2011). Coping mediates the relationship between emotional intelligence (EI) and academic achievement. *Contemporary Educational Psychology, 36,* 60–70.

Maccoby, E. E., & Martin, J. A. (1983). Socialization in the context of the family: Parent-child interaction. In P. Mussen & E. M. Hetherington (Eds.), *Handbook of child psychology: Vol. IV. Socialization, personality and social development* (pp. 1–101). New York, NY: John Wiley & Sons.

Mack, A. (2003). Inattentional blindness: Looking without seeing. *Current Directions in Psychological Science, 12,* 180–184.

MacLean, E. L., & Hare, B. (2015). Dogs hijack the human bonding pathway. *Science, 348*(6232), 280–281.

MacLeod, C. M., Jonker, T. R., & James, G. (2013). Individual differences in remembering. In T. J. Perfect & D. S. Lindsay (Eds.), *The SAGE handbook of applied memory* (pp. 385–403). Thousand Oaks, CA: Sage.

Macmillan, M. (2000). Restoring Phineas Gage: A 150th retrospective. *Journal of the History of the Neurosciences, 9,* 46–66.

Madsen, K. M., Hviid, A., Vestergaard, M., Schendel, D., Wohlfahrt, J., Thorsen, P., . . . Melbye, M. (2002). A population-based study of measles, mumps, and rubella vaccination and autism. *New England Journal of Medicine, 347,* 1477–1482.

Maguire, E. A., Valentine, E.R., Wilding, J. M., & Kapur, N. (2003). Routes to remembering: The brains behind superior memory. *Nature Neuroscience, 6,* 90–95.

Maguire, E. A., Woollett, K., & Spiers, H. J. (2006). London taxi drivers and bus drivers: A structural MRI and neuropsychological analysis. *Hippocampus, 16,* 1091–1101.

Mah, K., & Binik, Y. M. (2001). Do all orgasms feel alike? Evaluating a two-dimensional model of orgasm experience across gender and sexual context. *Journal of Sex Research, 39,* 104–113.

Maher, C. A., Lewis, L. K., Ferrar, K., Marshall, S., De Bourdeaudhuij, I., & Vandelanotte, C. (2014). Are health behavior change interventions that use online social networks effective? A systematic review. *Journal of Medical Internet Research, 16,* e40. doi:10.2196/jmir.2952

Maher, W. B., & Maher, B. A. (2003). Abnormal psychology. In D. K. Freedheim (Ed.), *Handbook of psychology: History of psychology* (Vol. 1, pp. 303–336). New York, NY: John Wiley & Sons.

Maheu, M. M., Pulier, M. L., McMenamin, J. P., & Posen, L. (2012). Future of telepsychology, telehealth, and various technologies in psychological research and practice. *Professional Psychology: Research and Practice, 43,* 613–621.

Mahmood, N. (2010, March 31). Here's how easily a hacker can crack your weak passwords. *Tech Journal.* Retrieved from http://thetechjournal.com/electronics/computer/security-computer-electronics/heres-how-easily-a-hacker-can-crack-your-weak-passwords.xhtml#ixzz1F7chbAEr

Mahoney, J. (2010). Strategic communication and anti-smoking campaigns. *Public Communication Review, 1,* 33–48.

Mai, E., & Buysse, D. J. (2008). Insomnia: Prevalence, impact, pathogenesis, differential diagnosis, and evaluation. *Sleep Medicine Clinics, 3,* 167–174.

Maiden, B., & Perry, B. (2011). Dealing with free-riders in assessed group work: Results from a study at a UK university. *Assessment & Evaluation in Higher Education, 36,* 451–464.

Majid, A. (2012). Current emotion research in the language sciences. *Emotion Review, 4,* 432–443.

Ma-Kellams, C., & Blascovich, J. (2012). Enjoying life in the face of death: East-West differences in responses to mortality salience. *Journal of Personality and Social Psychology, 103,* 773–386.

Makin, J. W., & Porter, R. H. (1989). Attractiveness of lactating females' breast odors to neonates. *Child Development, 60,* 803–810.

Makin, T. R., Scholz, J., Slater, D. H., Johansen-Berg, H., & Tracey, I. (2015). Reassessing cortical reorganization in the primary sensorimotor cortex following arm amputation. *Brain, 138,* 2140–2146.

Malani, P., Clark, S., Solway, E., Singer, D., & Kirch, M. (2018, May). Let's talk about sex. National Poll on Healthy Aging, University of Michigan. Retrieved from https://www.healthyagingpoll.org/sites/default/files/2018-05/NPHA-Sexual-Health-Report_050118_final2.pdf

Malekmohammadi, M., Elias, W. J., & Pouratian, N. (2015). Human thalamus regulates cortical activity via spatially specific and structurally constrained phase-amplitude coupling. *Cerebral Cortex, 25,* 1618–1628.

Malenka, R. C., & Nicoll, R. A. (1999). Long-term potentiation: A decade of progress? *Science, 285,* 1870–1874.

Malik, Z. (2016, October 31). Zayn Malik: Why I went public with my anxiety issues. *Time.* Retrieved from http://time.com/4551320/zayn-malik-anxiety/

Malinowski, J., & Horton, C. L. (2014). Evidence for the preferential incorporation of emotional waking-life experiences into dreams. *Dreaming, 24,* 18–31.

Malkemus, S. A. (2015). Reclaiming instinct: Exploring the phylogenetic unfolding of animate being. *Journal of Humanistic Psychology, 55,* 3–29.

Malkoff-Schwartz, S., Frank, E., Anderson, B, Sherrill, J. T., Siegel, L., Patterson, D., & Kupfer, D. J. (1998). Stressful life events and social rhythm disruption in the onset of manic and depressive bipolar episodes. *Archives of General Psychiatry, 55,* 702–707.

Manber, R., Kraemer, H. C., Arnow, B. A., Trivedi, M. H., Rush, A. J., Thase, M. E., . . . Keller, M. E. (2008). Faster remission of chronic depression with combined psychotherapy and medication than with each therapy alone. *Journal of Consulting and Clinical Psychology, 76,* 459–467.

Mancini, A. D., Bonanno, G. A., & Clark, A. E. (2011). Stepping off the hedonic treadmill: Individual differences in response to major life events. *Journal of Individual Differences, 32,* 144–152.

Mandler, J. M. (2008). On the birth and growth of concepts. *Philosophical Psychology, 21,* 207–230.

Manninen, B. A. (2011). Parental, medical, and sociological responsibilities: "Octomom" as a case study in the ethics of fertility treatments. *Journal of Clinical Research & Bioethics, S1,* 1–11.

Manning, R., Levine, M., & Collins, A. (2007). The Kitty Genovese murder and the social psychology of helping: The parable of the 38 witnesses. *American Psychologist, 62,* 555–562.

Manns, J. R., Hopkins, R. O., & Squire, L. R. (2003). Semantic memory and the human hippocampus. *Neuron, 38,* 127–133.

Maquet, P. (2000). Functional neuroimaging of normal human sleep by positron emission tomography. *Journal of Sleep Research, 3,* 208–231.

Marceau, K., Ram, N., Houts, R. M., Grimm, K. J., & Susman, E. J. (2011). Individual differences in boys' and girls' timing and tempo of puberty: Modeling development with nonlinear growth models. *Developmental Psychology, 47,* 1389–1409.

Marcus, A., & Oransky, I. (2015, May 22). What's behind big science frauds? *The New York Times.* Retrieved from http://www.nytimes.com/2015/05/23/opinion/whats-behind-big-science-frauds.html?_r=0

Marcus, J., & Le, H. (2013). Interactive effects of levels of individualism–collectivism on cooperation: A meta-analysis. *Journal of Organizational Behavior, 34,* 813–834.

Marczinski, C. A., Fillmore, M. T., Maloney, S. F., & Stamates, A. L. (2017). Faster self-paced rate of drinking for alcohol mixed with energy drinks versus alcohol alone. *Psychology of Addictive Behaviors, 31,* 154–161.

Marczinski, C. A., Stamates, A. L., & Maloney, S. F. (2018, January 15). Differential development of acute tolerance may explain heightened rates of impaired driving after consumption of alcohol mixed with energy drinks versus alcohol alone. *Experimental and Clinical Psychopharmacology, 26,* 147–155.

Mariën, P., Ackermann, H., Adamaszek, M., Barwood, C. H., Beaton, A., Desmond, J., . . . Ziegler, W. (2014). Consensus paper: Language and the cerebellum: An ongoing enigma. *The Cerebellum, 13,* 386–410.

Marin, M. M., Rapisardi, G., & Tani, F. (2015). Two-day-old newborn infants recognise their mother by her axillary odour. *Acta Paediatrica, 104,* 237–240.

Marinsek, N., Turner, B. O., Gazzaniga, M., & Miller, M. B. (2014). Divergent hemispheric reasoning strategies: Reducing uncertainty versus resolving inconsistency. *Frontiers in Human Neuroscience, 8.* Retrieved from http://dx.doi.org10.3389/fnhum.2014.00839

Markovitch, N., Luyckx, K., Klimstra, T., Abramson, L., & Knafo-Noam, A. (2017). Identity exploration and commitment in early adolescence: Genetic and environmental contributions. *Developmental Psychology, 53,* 2092–2102.

Maron, E., Hettema, J. M., & Shlik, J. (2010). Advances in molecular genetics of panic disorder. *Molecular Psychiatry, 15,* 681–701.

Maroon, J. C., Winkelman, R., Bost, J., Amos, A., Mathyssek, C., & Miele, V. (2015). Chronic traumatic encephalopathy in contact sports: A systematic review of all reported pathological cases. *PLoS ONE, 10,* e0117338.

Marsh, H. W., Nagengast, B., & Morin, A. J. (2013). Measurement invariance of Big-Five factors over the life span: ESEM tests of gender, age, plasticity, maturity, and La Dolce Vita effects. *Developmental Psychology, 49,* 1194–1218.

Marshall, L., & Born, L. (2007). The contribution of sleep to hippocampus-dependent memory consolidation. *Trends in Cognitive Sciences, 10,* 442–450.

Martin, C. (2013). Memorable outliers. *Current Biology, 23*(17), R731–R733.

Martin, C. L., & Cook, R. E. (2018). Cognitive perspectives on children's toy choices. In E. S. Weisgram & L. M. Dinella (Eds.), *Gender typing of children's toys: How early play experiences impact development* (pp. 141–164). Washington, DC, US: American Psychological Association.

Martin, C. L., & Ruble, D. N. (2010). Patterns of gender development. *Annual Review of Psychology, 61,* 353–381.

Martin, J. (2016). Ernest Becker and Stanley Milgram: Twentieth-century students of evil. *History of Psychology, 19,* 3–21.

Martin, L. A., Doster, J. A., Critelli, J. W., Purdum, M., Powers, C., Lambert, P. L., & Miranda, V. (2011). The "Distressed" personality, coping and cardiovascular risk. *Stress and Health, 27,* 64–72.

Martin, R. A., Puhlik-Doris, P., Larsen, G., Gray, J., & Weir, K. (2003). Individual differences in uses of humor and their relation to psychological well-being: Development of the Humor Styles Questionnaire. *Journal of Research in Personality, 37,* 48–75.

Martin, R., & Kuiper, N. A. (2016). Three decades investigating humor and laughter: An interview with professor Rod Martin. *Europe's Journal of Psychology, 12,* 498–512.

Martins, S. S., Sarvet, A., Santaella-Tenorio, J., Saha, T., Grant, B. F., & Hasin, D. S. (2017). Changes in US lifetime heroin use and heroin use disorder: Prevalence from the 2001–2002 to 2012–2013 National Epidemiologic Survey on Alcohol and Related Conditions. *JAMA Psychiatry, 74,* 445–455.

Marx, V., & Nagy, E. (2015). Fetal behavioural responses to maternal voice and touch. *PLoS ONE, 10,* e0129118.

Masaoka, K., Berns, R. S., Fairchild, M. D., & Moghareh Abed, F. (2013). Number of discernible object colors is a conundrum. *Journal of the Optical Society of America A, 30,* 264–277.

Mashour, G. A., & Avidan, M. S. (2015). Intraoperative awareness: Controversies and non-controversies. *British Journal of Anesthesia, 115*(Suppl.), i20–i26.

Mashour, G. A., Walker, E. E., & Martuza, R. L. (2005). Psychosurgery: Past, present, and future. *Brain Research Reviews, 48,* 409–419.

Maslow, A. H. (1943). A theory of human motivation. *Psychological Review, 50,* 370–396.

Massen, J. J., Dusch, K., Eldakar, O. T., & Gallup, A. C. (2014). A thermal window for yawning in humans: Yawning as a brain cooling mechanism. *Physiology & Behavior, 130,* 145–148.

Masters, W., & Johnson, V. (1966). *Human sexual response.* Boston, MA: Little, Brown.

Mather, V. (2016, May 24). The BMX rider Dave Mirra, who died in a suicide, had C.T.E. *The New York Times.* Retrieved from http://www.nytimes.com/2016/05/25/sports/dave-mirra-cte-bmx.html?_r=0

Mathes, J., Schredl, M., & Göritz, A. S. (2014). Frequency of typical dream themes in most recent dreams: An online study. *Dreaming, 24,* 57–66.

Matheson, S. L., Shepherd, A. M., & Carr, V. J. (2014). How much do we know about schizophrenia and how well do we know it? Evidence from the schizophrenia library. *Psychological Medicine, 44,* 3387–3405.

Matlin, M. W., & Farmer, T. A. (2016). *Cognition* (9th ed.). Hoboken, NJ: John Wiley & Sons.

Matloubian, M., Lo, C. G., Cinamon, G., Lesneski, M. J., Xu, Y., Brinkmann, V., . . . Cyster, J. G. (2004). Lymphocyte egress from thymus and peripheral lymphoid organs is dependent on S1P receptor 1. *Nature, 427,* 355–360.

Matsumoto, D., & Willingham, B. (2009). Spontaneous facial expressions of emotion of congenitally and noncongenitally blind individuals. *Journal of Personality and Social Psychology, 96,* 1–10.

Matsumura, S., Bito, S., Liu, H., Kahn, K., Fukuhara, S., Kagawa-Singer, M., & Wenger, N. (2002). Acculturation of attitudes toward end-of-life care: A cross-cultural survey of Japanese Americans and Japanese. *Journal of General Internal Medicine, 17,* 531–539.

Max-Planck-Gesellschaft. (2015). *Optogenetics.* Retrieved from https://www.mpg.de/18011/Optogenetics.

Mayo Clinic. (2014, July 18). *Transient global amnesia.* Retrieved from http://www.mayoclinic.org/diseases-conditions/transient-global-amnesia/basics/definition/con-20032746

Mayo Clinic. (2014, June 2). *Fetal alcohol syndrome: Symptoms.* Retrieved from http://www.mayoclinic.com/health/fetal-alcohol-syndrome/DS00184/DSECTION=symptoms

Mayo Clinic. (2014, October 17). *Presbyopia.* Retrieved from http://www.mayoclinic.org/diseases-conditions/presbyopia/basics/definition/con-20032261

Mayo Clinic. (2015, September 3). *Hearing loss.* Retrieved from http://www.mayoclinic.org/diseases-conditions/hearing-loss/basics/definition/con-20027684

Mayo Clinic. (2018, January 31). *Suicide: What to do when someone is suicidal.* Retrieved from https://www.mayoclinic.org/diseases-conditions/suicide/in-depth/suicide/art-20044707

McAdams, D. P., & Olson, B. D. (2010). Personality development: Continuity and change over the life course. *Annual Review of Psychology, 61,* 5.1–5.26.

McAra, L., & McVie, S. (2016). Understanding youth violence: The mediating effects of gender, poverty and vulnerability. *Journal of Criminal Justice, 45,* 71–77.

McCaffrey, J., & Machery, E. (2012). Philosophical issues about concepts. *Wiley Interdisciplinary Reviews: Cognitive Science, 3,* 265–279.

McCann, R. A., Armstrong, C. M., Skopp, N. A., Edwards-Stewart, A., Smolenski, D. J., June, J. D., . . . Reger, G. M. (2014). Virtual reality exposure therapy for the treatment of anxiety disorders: An evaluation of research quality. *Journal of Anxiety Disorders, 28,* 625–631.

McCarthy, C. (2013). Pediatricians and television: It's time to rethink our messaging and our efforts. *Pediatrics, 131,* 589–590.

McCarthy, J. (2017, May 15). U.S. support for gay marriage edges to new high. *Gallup News.* Retrieved from http://news.gallup.com/poll/210566/support-gay-marriage-edges-new-high.aspx

McCarthy, J. R., & Skowronski, J. J. (2011). The interplay of controlled and automatic processing in the expression of spontaneously inferred traits: A PDP analysis. *Journal of Personality and Social Psychology, 100,* 229–240.

McClain, S., & Cokley, K. (2017). Academic disidentification in Black college students: The role of teacher trust and gender. *Cultural Diversity and Ethnic Minority Psychology, 23,* 125–133.

McClelland, D. C., Atkinson, J. W., Clark, R. W., & Lowell, E. L. (1976). *The achievement motive.* New York, NY: Irvington.

McClintock, M. K. (1971). Menstrual synchrony and suppression. *Nature, 229,* 244–245.

McCosker, B., & Moran, C. C. (2012). Differential effects of self-esteem and interpersonal competence on humor styles. *Psychology Research and Behavior Management, 5,* 143–150.

McCrae, R. R. (2011). Personality theories for the 21st century. *Teaching of Psychology, 38,* 209–214.

McCrae, R. R., Chan, W., Jussim, L., De Fruyt, F., Löckenhoff, C. E., De Bolle, M., . . . Allik, J. (2013). The inaccuracy of national character stereotypes. *Journal of Research in Personality, 47,* 831–842.

McCrae, R. R., & Costa, P. T., Jr. (1987). Validation of the five-factor model of personality across instruments and observers. *Journal of Personality and Social Psychology, 49,* 81–90.

McCrae, R. R., & Costa, P. T., Jr. (1990). *Personality in adulthood.* New York, NY: Guilford Press.

McCrae, R. R., Costa, P. T., Jr., Ostendorf, F., Angleitner, A., Hřebíčková, M., Avia, M. D., . . . Smith, P. B. (2000). Nature over nurture: Temperament, personality, and life span development. *Journal of Personality and Social Psychology, 78,* 173–186.

McCrae, R. R., Scally, M., Terracciano, A., Abecasis, G. R., & Costa, P. T., Jr. (2010). An alternative to the search for single polymorphisms: Toward molecular personality scales for the five-factor model. *Journal of Personality and Social Psychology, 99,* 1014–1024.

McCrae, R. R., Terracciano, A., & 78 Members of the Personality Profiles of Cultures Project. (2005). Universal features of personality traits from the observer's perspective: Data from 50 cultures. *Journal of Personality and Social Psychology, 88,* 547–561.

McDermott, R. C., Schwartz, J. P., & Rislin, J. L. (2016). Men's mental health: A biopsychosocial critique. In Y. J. Wong & S. R. Wester (Eds.), *APA Handbooks in Psychology Series: APA handbook of men and masculinities* (pp. 731–751). Washington, DC: American Psychological Association.

McDougall, W. (1912). *An introduction to social psychology* (Rev. 4th ed.). Boston, MA: John W. Luce.

McEwen, B. S. (2000). The neurobiology of stress: From serendipity to clinical relevance. *Brain Research, 886,* 172–189.

McFadden, P., Mallett, J., & Leiter, M. (2018). Extending the two-process model of burnout in child protection workers: The role of resilience in mediating burnout via organizational factors of control, values, fairness, reward, workload, and community relationships. *Stress and Health, 34,* 72–83.

McFadden, R. D. (2016, April 4). Winston Moseley, who killed Kitty Genovese, dies in prison at 81. *The New York Times.* Retrieved from http://www.nytimes.com/2016/04/05/nyregion/winston-moseley-81-killer-of-kitty-genovese-dies-inprison.html?_r=0

McGaugh, J. L., & LePort, A. (2014). Remembrance of all things past. *Scientific American, 310,* 40–45.

McGue, M., Bouchard, T. J., Jr., Iacono, W. G., & Lykken, D. T. (1993). Behavioral genetics of cognitive ability: A life-span perspective. In R. Plomin & G. E. McClearn (Eds.), *Nature, nurture & psychology* (pp. 59–76). Washington, DC: American Psychological Association.

McKee, A. C., Cairns, N. J., Dickson, D. W., Folkerth, R. D., Keene, C. D., Litvan, I., . . . Tripodis, Y. (2016). The first NINDS/NIBIB consensus meeting to define neuropathological criteria for the diagnosis of chronic traumatic encephalopathy. *Acta Neuropathologica, 131,* 75–86.

McKee, A. C., Cantu, R. C., Nowinski, C. J., Hedley-Whyte, E. T., Gavett, B. E., Budson, A. E., . . . Stern, R. A. (2009). Chronic traumatic encephalopathy in athletes: Progressive tauopathy after repetitive head injury. *Journal of Neuropathology & Experimental Neurology, 68*(7), 709–735.

McKee, A. C., Stein, T. D., Nowinski, C. J., Stern, R. A., Daneshvar, D. H., Alvarez, V. E., . . . Riley, D. O. (2013). The spectrum of disease in chronic traumatic encephalopathy. *Brain, 136,* 43–64.

McKinney, A., & Coyle, K. (2006). Alcohol hangover effects on measures of affect the morning after a normal night's drinking. *Alcohol & Alcoholism, 41,* 54–60.

McLean, W. J., Yin, X., Lu, L., Lenz, D. R., McLean, D., Langer, R. D., . . . Edge, A. S. (2017). Clonal expansion of Lgr5-positive cells from mammalian cochlea and high-purity generation of sensory hair cells. *Cell Reports, 18,* 1917–1929.

McLellan, T. M., Caldwell, J. A., & Lieberman, H. R. (2016). A review of caffeine's effects on cognitive, physical and occupational performance. *Neuroscience & Biobehavioral Reviews, 71,* 294–312.

McMurray, B. (2007). Defusing the childhood vocabulary explosion. *Science, 317,* 631.

McMurtrie, B. (2017, November 27). Should laptops be banned in class? An op-ed fires up the debate. *The Chronicle of Higher Education.* Retrieved from https://www.chronicle.com/article/Should-Laptops-Be-Banned-in/241878

McNally, R. J., & Clancy, S. A. (2005). Sleep paralysis, sexual abuse, and space alien abduction. *Transcultural Psychiatry, 42,* 113–122.

McPherson, M., Smith-Lovin, L., & Cook, J. M. (2001). Birds of a feather: Homophily in social networks. *Annual Review of Sociology, 27,* 415–444.

McRae, A. F., Visscher, P. M., Montgomery, G. W., & Martin, N. G. (2015). Large autosomal copy-number differences within unselected monozygotic twin pairs are rare. *Twin Research and Human Genetics, 18,* 13–18.

McRobbie, L. R. (2017, February 8). Total recall: The people who never forget. *The Guardian.* Retrieved from https://www.theguardian.com/science/2017/feb/08/total-recall-the-people-who-never-forget

Meczkowski, E. J., Dillard, J. P., & Shen, L. (2016). Threat appeals and persuasion: Seeking and finding the elusive curvilinear effect. *Communication Monographs, 83,* 373–395.

Medeiros-Ward, N., Watson, J. M., & Strayer, D. L. (2015). On supertaskers and the neural basis of efficient multitasking. *Psychonomic Bulletin & Review, 22,* 876–883.

Medline Plus. (2015, April 25). *Caffeine in the diet.* Retrieved from https://www.nlm.nih.gov/medlineplus/ency/article/002445.htm

Medline Plus. (2015, March 31). *Gastric bypass surgery.* Retrieved from https://medlineplus.gov/ency/article/007199.htm

Meerwijk, E. L., & Sevelius, J. M. (2017). Transgender population size in the United States: A meta-regression of population-based probability samples. *American Journal of Public Health, 107,* e1–e8.

Mehler, P. S., & Brown, C. (2015). Anorexia nervosa—medical complications. *Journal of Eating Disorders, 3.* doi:10.1186/s40337-015-0040-8

Mekawi, Y., & Bresin, K. (2015). Is the evidence from racial bias shooting task studies a smoking gun? Results from a meta-analysis. *Journal of Experimental Social Psychology, 61,* 120–130.

Melchert, T. P. (2015). Physical health. In T. P. Melchert, *Biopsychosocial practice: A science-based framework for behavioral health care* (pp. 123–132). Washington, DC: APA Books.

Mele, C. (2017, May 5). Minnesota sees largest outbreak of measles in almost 30 years. *The New York Times.* Retrieved from https://www.nytimes.com/2017/05/05/us/measles-minnesota-vaccines.html?_r=0

Melin, A. D., Hiramatsu, C., Parr, N. A., Matsushita, Y., Kawamura, S., & Fedigan, L. M. (2014). The behavioral ecology of color vision: Considering fruit conspicuity, detection distance and dietary importance. *International Journal of Primatology, 35,* 258–287.

Melnikova, N., Welles, W. L., Wilburn, R. E., Rice, N., Wu, J., & Stanbury, M. (2011). Hazards of illicit methamphetamine production and efforts at reduction: Data from the hazardous substances emergency events surveillance system. *Public Health Reports, 126,* 116–123.

Melzack, R. (1993). Pain: Past, present and future. *Canadian Journal of Experimental Psychology, 47,* 615–629.

Melzack, R. (2008). The future of pain. *Nature Reviews, 7,* 629.

Melzack, R., & Wall, P. D. (1965). Pain mechanisms: A new theory. *Science, 150,* 971–979.

Méndez-Bértolo, C., Moratti, S., Toledano, R., Lopez-Sosa, F., Martínez-Alvarez, R., Mah, Y. H., . . . Strange, B. A. (2016). A fast pathway for fear in human amygdala. *Nature Neuroscience, 19,* 1041–1049.

Mendle, J., & Ferrero, J. (2012). Detrimental psychological outcomes associated with pubertal timing in adolescent boys. *Developmental Review, 32,* 49–66.

Mendle, J., Harden, K. P., Brooks-Gunn, J., & Graber, J. A. (2010). Development's tortoise and hare: Pubertal timing, pubertal tempo, and depressive symptoms in boys and girls. *Developmental Psychology, 46,* 1341–1353.

Mendrek, A., & Mancini-Marïe, A. (2016). Sex/gender differences in the brain and cognition in schizophrenia. *Neuroscience & Biobehavioral Reviews, 67,* 57–78.

Menken, J., Trussell, J., & Larsen, U. (1986). Age and infertility. *Science, 233,* 1389–1394.

Mennella, J. A., Coren, P., Jagnow, M. S., & Beauchamp, G. K. (2001). Prenatal and postnatal flavor learning by human infants. *Pediatrics, 107,* e88.

Menolascino, N., & Jenkins, L. N. (2018). Predicting bystander intervention among middle school students. *School Psychology Quarterly, 33,* 305–313.

Merikangas, K. R., Akiskal, H. S., Angst, J., Greenberg, P. E., Hirschfeld, R. M., Petukhova, M., & Kessler, R. C. (2007). Lifetime and 12-month prevalence of bipolar spectrum disorder in the national comorbidity survey replication. *Archives of General Psychiatry, 64,* 543–552.

Mervis, C. B., & Rosch, E. (1981). Categorization of natural objects. *Annual Review of Psychology, 32,* 89–115.

Meshi, D., Tamir, D. I., & Heekeren, H. R. (2015). The emerging neuroscience of social media. *Trends in Cognitive Sciences, 19,* 771–782.

Mez, J., Daneshvar, D. H., Kiernan, P. T., Abdolmohammadi, B., Alvarez, V. E., Huber, B. R., . . . McKee, A. C. (2017). Clinicopathological evaluation of chronic traumatic encephalopathy in players of American football. *JAMA, 318,* 360–370.

Michael, R. T., Laumann, E. O., Kolata, G. B., & Gagnon, J. H. (1994). *Sex in America: A definitive survey.* Boston, MA: Little, Brown.

Michals, D. (2015). *Harriet Tubman.* Retrieved from https://www.nwhm.org/education-resources/biography/biographies/harriet-tubman/

Michikyan, M., Subrahmanyam, K., & Dennis, J. (2015). Facebook use and academic performance among college students: A mixed-methods study with a multiethnic sample. *Computers in Human Behavior, 45,* 265–272.

Milani, R. V., & Lavie, C. J. (2009). Reducing psychosocial stress: A novel mechanism of improving survival from exercise training. *The American Journal of Medicine, 122,* 931–938. doi:10.1016/j.amjmed.2009.03.028

Milar, K. S. (2016). Unknown, untold, unsung: Women in the history of psychology. In W. D. Woody, R. L. Miller, & W. J. Wozniak (Eds.), *Psychological specialties in historical context: Enriching the classroom experience for teachers and students.* Society for the Teaching of Psychology. Retrieved from http://teachpsych.org/ebooks/

Milgram, S. (1963). Behavioral study of obedience. *Journal of Abnormal and Social Psychology, 67,* 371–378.

Milgram, S. (1964). Issues in the study of obedience: A reply to Baumrind. *American Psychologist, 19,* 848–852.

Milgram, S. (1965). Some conditions of obedience and disobedience to authority. *Human Relations, 18*(1), 57–76.

Milgram, S. (1974). *Obedience to authority: An experimental view.* New York, NY: Harper & Row.

Millan, C. (2013). *Cesar Millan's short guide to a happy dog.* Washington, DC: National Geographic Society.

Millan, C. (2013, March 26). It isn't always about the dog. *Huffington Post.* Retrieved from http://www.huffingtonpost.com/cesar-millan/it-isnt-always-about-the-_b_2541801.html

Millan, C. (n.d.). The Dog Psychology Center: Evolution of a dream. [Web log comment]. Retrieved from https://www.cesarsway.com/cesar-millan/cesars-blog/dog-psychology-center-evolution-of-a-dream

Millan, C., & Peltier, M. J. (2006). *Cesar's way: The natural, everyday guide to understanding & correcting common dog problems.* New York, NY: Random House.

Millan, C., & Peltier, M. J. (2010). *Cesar's rules: Your way to train a well-behaved dog.* New York, NY: Three Rivers Press.

Miller, D. I., & Halpern, D. F. (2014). The new science of cognitive sex differences. *Trends in Cognitive Sciences, 18,* 37–45.

Miller, G. (1956). The magical number seven, plus or minus two: Some limits on our capacity for processing information. *Psychological Review, 63,* 81–97.

Miller, H. (2016, April 5). Investigating the potential for miscommunication using emoji [Web log post]. Retrieved from https://grouplens.org/blog/investigating-the-potential-for-miscommunication-using-emoji/

Miller, H., Thebault-Spieker, J., Chang, S., Johnson, I., Terveen, L., & Hecht, B. (2016). "Blissfully happy" or "ready to fight": Varying interpretations in emoji. In *Proceedings of the Tenth International AAAI Conference on Web and Social Media (ICWSM 2016),* pp. 259–268.

Miller, S. L., & Maner, J. K. (2010). Scent of a woman: Men's testosterone responses to olfactory ovulation cues. *Psychological Science, 21,* 276–283.

Mills, C. (2015). The psychiatrization of poverty: Rethinking the mental health-poverty nexus. *Social and Personality Psychology Compass, 9,* 213–222.

Milrod, B., Leon, A. C., Busch, F., Rudden, M., Schwalberg, M., Clarkin, J., . . . Shear, M. K. (2007). A randomized control trial of psychoanalytic psychotherapy for panic disorder. *American Journal of Psychiatry, 164,* 265–272.

Mirsky, A. F., Bieliauskas, L. A., French, L. M., Van Kammen, D. P., Jönsson, E., & Sedvall, G. A. (2000). A 39-year followup of the Genain quadruplets. *Schizophrenia Bulletin, 26,* 699–708.

Mirsky, A. F., Bieliauskas, L. A., Duncan, C. C., & French, L. M. (2013). Letter to the editor. *Schizophrenia Research, 148,* 186–187.

Mirsky, A. F., & Quinn, O. W. (1988). The Genain triplets. *Schizophrenia Bulletin, 14,* 595–612.

Mischel, W., & Shoda, Y. (1995). A cognitive-affective system theory of personality: Reconceptualizing the invariances in personality and the role of situations. *Psychological Review, 102,* 229–258.

Mischkowski, D., Crocker, J., & Way, B. M. (2016). From painkiller to empathy killer: Acetaminophen (paracetamol) reduces empathy for pain. *Social Cognitive and Affective Neuroscience, 11*(9), 1345–1353.

Mistry, R. S., & Wadsworth, M. E. (2011). Family functioning and child development in the context of poverty. *Prevention Researcher, 18,* 11–15.

Mitchell, A. S., Sherman, S. M., Sommer, M. A., Mair, R. G., Vertes, R. P., & Chudasama, Y. (2014b). Advances in understanding mechanisms of thalamic relays in cognition and behavior. *The Journal of Neuroscience, 34,* 15340–15346.

Mitchell, D. C., Knight, C. A., Hockenberry, J., Teplansky, R., & Hartman, T. J. (2014a). Beverage caffeine intakes in the U.S. *Food and Chemical Toxicology, 63,* 136–142.

Mitchell, H. A., & Weinshenker, D. (2010). Good night and good luck: Norepinephrine in sleep pharmacology. *Biochemical Pharmacology, 79,* 801–809.

Mitchell, J. (2018, January 29). With 175 Americans dying a day, what are the solutions to the opioid epidemic? *The Clarion-Ledger.* Retrieved from https://www.usatoday.com/story/news/nation-now/2018/01/29/175-americans-dying-day-what-solutions-opioid-epidemic/1074336001/

Mitler, M. M., & Miller, J. C. (1996). Methods of testing for sleeplessness. *Behavioral Medicine, 21,* 171–183.

Mizuno, K. (2014). Human circadian rhythms and exercise: Significance and application in real-life situations. *The Journal of Physical Fitness and Sports Medicine, 3,* 307–315.

Moed, A., Gershoff, E. T., Eisenberg, N., Hofer, C., Losoya, S., Spinrad, T. L., & Liew, J. (2015). Parent–adolescent conflict as sequences of reciprocal negative emotion: Links with conflict resolution and adolescents' behavior problems. *Journal of Youth and Adolescence, 44,* 1607–1622.

Mogilner, C., & Norton, M. I. (2016). Time, money, and happiness. *Current Opinion in Psychology, 10,* 12–16.

Moinuddin, K. A., Bruck, D., & Shi, L. (2017). An experimental study on timely activation of smoke alarms and their effective notification in typical residential buildings. *Fire Safety Journal, 93,* 1–11.

Moirand, R., Galvao, F., Lecompte, M., Poulet, E., Haesebaert, F., & Brunelin, J. (2018). Usefulness of the Montreal Cognitive Assessment (MoCA) to monitor cognitive impairments in depressed patients receiving electroconvulsive therapy. *Psychiatry Research, 259,* 476–481.

Mollon, J. D. (1982). Color vision. *Annual Review of Psychology, 33,* 41–85.

Molloy, L. E., Gest, S. D., Feinberg, M. E., & Osgood, D. W. (2014). Emergence of mixed-sex friendship groups during adolescence: Developmental associations with substance use and delinquency. *Developmental Psychology, 50,* 2449–2461.

Monk, T. H., & Buysse, D. J. (2013). Exposure to shift work as a risk factor for diabetes. *Journal of Biological Rhythms, 28,* 356–359.

Monroe, S. M., & Harkness, K. L. (2011). Recurrence in major depression: A conceptual analysis. *Psychological Review, 118,* 655–674.

Monteleone, G. T., Phan, L., Nusbaum, H. C., Gitzgerald, D., Irick, J.-S., Fienberg, S. E., & Cacioppo, J. T. (2009). Detection of deception using fMRI: Better than chance, but well below perfection. *Social Neuroscience, 4,* 528–538.

Montemayor, R. (1983). Parents and adolescents in conflict: All families some of the time and some families most of the time. *Journal of Early Adolescence, 3,* 83–103.

Montoya, E. R., Terburg, D., Bos, P. A., & van Honk, J. (2012). Testosterone, cortisol, and serotonin as key regulators of social aggression: A review and theoretical perspective. *Motivation and Emotion, 36,* 65–73.

Montoya, R. M., Horton, R. S., Vevea, J. L., Citkowicz, M., & Lauber, E. A. (2017). A re-examination of the mere exposure effect: The influence of repeated exposure on recognition, familiarity, and liking. *Psychological Bulletin, 143,* 459–498.

Montoya, R. M., Kershaw, C., & Prosser, J. L. (2018). A meta-analytic investigation of the relation between interpersonal attraction and enacted behavior. *Psychological Bulletin, 144,* 673–709.

Moody, T. D., Morfini, F., Cheng, G., Sheen, C., Tadayonnejad, R., Reggente, N., . . . Feusner, J. D. (2017). Mechanisms of cognitive-behavioral therapy for obsessive-compulsive disorder involve robust and extensive increases in brain network connectivity. *Translational Psychiatry, 7,* e1230. doi:10.1038/tp.2017.192

Moon, C., Lagercrantz, H., & Kuhl, P. K. (2013). Language experienced in utero affects vowel perception after birth: A two-country study. *Acta Paediatrica, 102*(2), 156–160.

Moon, C., Zernzach, R. C., & Kuhl, P. K. (2015). Mothers say "baby" and their newborns do not choose to listen: A behavioral preference study to compare with ERP results. *Frontiers in Human Neuroscience, 9.* Retrieved from http://journal.frontiersin.org/article/10.3389/fnhum.2015.00153/full

Moore, D. S. (2013). Current thinking about nature and nurture. In K. Kampourakis (Ed.), *The philosophy of biology: A companion for educators* (pp. 629–652). Dordrecht, the Netherlands: Springer Science.

Moore, D. S., & Johnson, S. P. (2008). Mental rotation in human infants: A sex difference. *Psychological Science, 19,* 1063–1066.

Moore, S. R., & Depue, R. A. (2016). Neurobehavioral foundation of environmental reactivity. *Psychological Bulletin, 142,* 107–164.

Moorhead, S. A., Hazlett, D. E., Harrison, L., Carroll, J. K., Irwin, A., & Hoving, C. (2013). A new dimension of health care: Systematic review of the uses, benefits, and limitations of social media for health communication. *Journal of Medical Internet Research, 15.* doi:10.2196/jmir.1933

Moosa, A. N., Jehi, L., Marashly, A., Cosmo, G., Lachhwani, D., Wyllie, E., . . . Gupta, A. (2013). Long-term functional outcomes and their predictors after hemispherectomy in 115 children. *Epilepsia, 54,* 1771–1779.

Morales, A., Heaton, J. P. W., & Carson, C. C., III. (2000). Andropause: A misnomer for a true clinical entity. *Journal of Urology, 163,* 705–712.

Morales Ayma, E. (2009, March 13). Let me chew my coca leaves. *The New York Times.* Retrieved from http://www.nytimes.com/2009/03/14/opinion/14morales.html

Moran, B. (2015, February 23). Untangling the connectome. *Research.* Retrieved from http://www.bu.edu/research/articles/untangling-the-connectome/

Mora-Rodriguez, R., & Pallarés, J. G. (2014). Performance outcomes and unwanted side effects associated with energy drinks. *Nutrition Reviews, 72*(Suppl. 1), 108–120.

Moreira-Almeida, A., Neto, F. L., & Cardeña, E. (2008). Comparison of Brazilian spiritist mediumship and dissociative identity disorder. *Journal of Nervous and Mental Disease, 196,* 420–424.

Moreland, R. L., & Zajonc, R. B. (1982). Exposure effects in person perception: Familiarity, similarity, and attraction. *Journal of Experimental Social Psychology, 18,* 395–415.

Morewedge, C. K., Yoon, H., Scopelliti, I., Symborski, C. W., Korris, J. H., & Kassam, K. S. (2015). Debiasing decisions improved decision making with a single training intervention. *Policy Insights from the Behavioral and Brain Sciences, 2,* 129–140.

Morgan, B. L., & Korschgen, A. J. (2014). *Majoring in psych? Career options for psychology undergraduates* (5th ed.). Boston, MA: Pearson.

Morina, N., Ijntema, H., Meyerbröker, K., & Emmelkamp, P. M. (2015). Can virtual reality exposure therapy gains be generalized to real-life? A meta-analysis of studies applying behavioral assessments. *Behaviour Research and Therapy, 74,* 18–24.

Morita, T., Oyama, Y., Cheng, S. Y., Suh, S. Y., Koh, S. J., Kim, H. S., . . . Tsuneto, S. (2015). Palliative care physicians' attitudes toward patient autonomy and a good death in East Asian countries. *Journal of Pain and Symptom Management, 50,* 190–199.

Morone, N. E., & Greco, C. M. (2007). Mind–body interventions for chronic pain in older adults: A structured review. *Pain Medicine, 8,* 359–375.

Morry, M. M., Kito, M., & Ortiz, L. (2011). The attraction-similarity model and dating couples: Projection, perceived similarity, and psychological benefits. *Personal Relationships, 18,* 125–143.

Moshagen, M., Hilbig, B. E., Erdfelder, E., & Moritz, A. (2014). An experimental validation method for questioning techniques that assess sensitive issues. *Experimental Psychology, 61,* 48–54.

Mosher, W. D., Chandra, A., & Jones, J. (2005, September 15). Sexual behavior and selected health measures: Men and women 15–44 years of age, United States, 2002. In *Advance data from vital and health statistics* (No. 362). Washington, DC: Centers for Disease Control and Prevention, National Center for Health Statistics. Retrieved from http://www.cdc.gov/nchs/data/ad/ad362.pdf

Moss, D. (2015). The roots and genealogy of humanistic psychology. In K. J. Schneider, J. F. Pierson, & J. F. T. Bugental (Eds.), *The handbook of humanistic psychology: Theory, research, and practice* (2nd ed., pp. 5–20). Thousand Oaks, CA: Sage.

Most, S. B., Simons, D. J., Scholl, B. J., Jimenez, R., Clifford, E., & Chabris, C. F. (2001). How not to be seen: The contribution of similarity and selective ignoring to sustained inattentional blindness. *Psychological Science, 12,* 9–17.

Motive. (n.d.). In *Online etymology dictionary.* Retrieved from https://www.etymonline.com/word/motive

Moyer, M. W. (2016, September 1). What science says—and doesn't—about spanking. *Scientific American.* Retrieved from https://www.scientificamerican.com/article/what-science-says-and-doesn-t-about-spanking/

Moyer, M. W. (2017, May/June). Once dependable, always dependable? *Scientific American Mind, 28,* 10.

Mueller, P. A., & Oppenheimer, D. M. (2014). The pen is mightier than the keyboard: Advantages of longhand over laptop note taking. *Psychological Science, 25,* 1159–1168.

Mukherjee, S., & Manahan-Vaughan, D. (2013). Role of metabotropic glutamate receptors in persistent forms of hippocampal plasticity and learning. *Neuropharmacology, 66,* 65–81.

Müller, K. W., Dreier, M., Beutel, M. E., Duven, E., Giralt, S., & Wölfling, K. (2016). A hidden type of internet addiction? Intense and addictive use of social networking sites in adolescents. *Computers in Human Behavior, 55,* 172–177.

Muller, P. Y., Dambach, D., Gemzik, B., Hartmann, A., Ratcliffe, S., Trendelenburg, C., & Urban, L. (2015). Integrated risk assessment of suicidal ideation and behavior in drug development. *Drug Discovery Today, 20,* 1135–1142.

Müllerová, J., Hansen, M., Contractor, A. A., Elhai, J. D., & Armour, C. (2016). Dissociative features in posttraumatic stress disorder: A latent profile analysis. *Psychological Trauma: Theory, Research, Practice, and Policy, 8*(5), 601–608.

Mulvey, S. (2006, May 15). Cakes and jokes at Cafe d'Europe. *BBC News.* Retrieved from http://news.bbc.co.uk/2/hi/europe/4755659.stm

Murdoch, D. D. (2016). Psychological literacy: Proceed with caution, construction ahead. *Psychology Research and Behavior Management, 9,* 189–199.

Murdock, B. (1962). The serial position effect of free recall. *Journal of Experimental Psychology, 64,* 482–488.

Murkar, A., Smith, C., Dale, A., & Miller, N. (2014). A neuro-cognitive model of sleep mentation and memory consolidation. *International Journal of Dream Research, 7,* 85–89.

Murphy, D., & Joseph, S. (2016). Person-centered therapy: Past, present, and future orientations. In D. J. Cain, K. Keenan, & S. Rubin (Eds.), *Humanistic psychotherapies: Handbook of research and practice* (2nd ed., pp. 185–218). Washington, DC: American Psychological Association.

Murray, R. M., Morrison, P. D., Henquet, C., & Di Forti, M. (2007). Cannabis, the mind and society: The hash realities. *Nature Reviews Neuroscience, 8,* 885–895.

Murray, S. B., Nagata, J. M., Griffiths, S., Calzo, J. P., Brown, T. A., Mitchison, D., . . . Mond, J. M. (2017). The enigma of male eating disorders: A critical review and synthesis. *Clinical Psychology Review, 57,* 1–11.

Murre, J. M., & Dros, J. (2015). Replication and analysis of Ebbinghaus' forgetting curve. *PLoS ONE, 10,* e0120644. doi:10.1371/journal.pone.0120644

Murthy, V. H. (2016). Ending the opioid epidemic—a call to action. *New England Journal of Medicine, 375,* 2413–2415.

Musaiger, A. O., Al-Mannai, M., Tayyem, R., Al-Lalla, O., Ali, E. Y., Kalam, F., . . . Chirane, M. (2013). Risk of disordered eating attitudes among adolescents in seven Arab countries by gender and obesity: A cross cultural study. *Appetite, 60,* 162–167.

Musto, D. F. (1991). Opium, cocaine and marijuana in American history. *Scientific American, 265,* 41–47.

Myers, B. J. (2014). Mother–infant boding as a critical period. In M. H. Bornstein (Ed.), *Sensitive periods in development: Interdisciplinary perspectives* (pp. 223–245). New York, NY: Psychology Press. (Original work published 1987)

Myers, D. G., & Lamm, H. (1976). The group polarization phenomenon. *Psychological Bulletin, 83,* 602–627.

Mysterud, I. (2003). Long live nature via nurture! *Evolutionary Psychology, 1,* 188–191.

Nadorff, M. R., Nadorff, D. K., & Germain, A. (2015). Nightmares: Under-reported, undetected, and therefore untreated. *Journal of Clinical Sleep Medicine, 11*(7), 747–750.

Nagasawa, M., Mitsui, S., En, S., Ohtani, N., Ohta, M., Sakuma, Y., . . . Kikusui, T. (2015). Oxytocin-gaze positive loop and the coevolution of human–dog bonds. *Science, 348*(6232), 333–336.

Nagel, I. E., Chicherio, C., Li, S., von Oertzen, T., Sander, T., Villringer, A., . . . Lindenberger, U. (2008). Human aging magnifies genetic effects on executive functioning and working memory. *Frontiers in Human Neuroscience, 2,* 1–8.

Nahemow, L., & Lawton, M. P. (1975). Similarity and propinquity in friendship formation. *Journal of Personality and Social Psychology, 32,* 205–213.

Nash, M. R. (2001). The truth and the hype of hypnosis. *Scientific American, 285,* 44–55.

National Academies of Sciences, Engineering, and Medicine. (2016). *Ending discrimination against people with mental and substance use disorders: The evidence for stigma change.* Washington, DC: National Academies Press. doi:10.17226/23442

National Academies of Sciences, Engineering, and Medicine. (2017, January). *The health effects of cannabis and cannabinoids: Committee's conclusions.* Retrieved from http://nationalacademies.org/hmd/~/media/Files/Report%20Files/2017/Cannabis-Health-Effects/cannabis-conclusions.pdf?_ga=2.247507972.2083320254.1499706356-1581552225.1499706356

National Alliance on Mental Illness (NAMI). (n.d.). *Frankie & Alice: Inspired by an amazing true story* [NAMI Film Discussion Guide]. Retrieved from https://www.nami.org/getattachment/Get-Involved/What-Can-I-Do/Movies-to-Watch/frankie-alice-viewingguide.pdf

National Conference of State Legislatures. (2017, June 5). *Drug overdose immunity and Good Samaritan laws.* Retrieved from http://www.ncsl.org/research/civil-and-criminal-justice/drug-overdose-immunity-good-samaritan-laws.aspx

National Eye Institute. (n.d.). *Facts about the cornea and corneal disease.* Retrieved from https://nei.nih.gov/health/cornealdisease

National Geographic. (2015). *Dia de los Muertos.* Retrieved from http://education.nationalgeographic.com/education/media/dia-de-los-muertos/?ar_a=1

National Highway Traffic Safety Administration. (2017, March). *Distracted driving 2015.* Retrieved from https://www.nhtsa.gov/risky-driving/distracted-driving

National Institute of Mental Health. (2016). *Brain stimulation therapies.* Retrieved from https://www.nimh.nih.gov/health/topics/brain-stimulation-therapies/brain-stimulation-therapies.shtml

National Institute of Mental Health. (2018, May). *Suicide.* Retrieved from https://www.nimh.nih.gov/health/statistics/suicide.shtml#part_154969

National Institute of Mental Health. (n.d.-a). *Antidepressant medications for children and adolescents: Information for parents and caregivers.* Retrieved from http://www.nimh.nih.gov/health/topics/child-and-adolescent-mental-health/antidepressant-medications-for-children-and-adolescents-information-for-parents-and-caregivers.shtml

National Institute of Mental Health. (n.d.-b). *Eating disorders.* http://www.nimh.nih.gov/health/topics/eating-disorders/index.shtml

National Institute of Neurological Disorders and Stroke (2013, January 10). *NIH statement.* Retrieved from http://espn.go.com/pdf/2013/0110/espn_otl_NIH_Statement.pdf

National Institute of Neurological Disorders and Stroke. (2013, September). *Narcolepsy* [Fact sheet]. Retrieved from http://www.ninds.nih.gov/disorders/narcolepsy/detail_narcolepsy.htm

National Institute of Neurological Disorders and Stroke. (2017). *Arteriovenous malformations and other vascular lesions of the central nervous system fact sheet.* Retrieved from https://www.ninds.nih.gov/Disorders/Patient-Caregiver-Education/Fact-Sheets/Arteriovenous-Malformation-Fact-Sheet#3052_1

National Institute of Neurological Disorders and Stroke. (2017, May 9). *Narcolepsy fact sheet.* Retrieved from https://www.ninds.nih.gov/Disorders/Patient-Caregiver-Education/Fact-Sheets/Narcolepsy-Fact-Sheet

National Institute of Neurological Disorders and Stroke. (n.d.). *Arteriovenous malformations and other vascular lesions of the central nervous system* [Fact sheet]. Retrieved from http://www.ninds.nih.gov/disorders/avms/detail_avms.htm

National Institute on Aging. (n.d.). *About Alzheimer's disease: Alzheimer's basics.* Retrieved from http://www.nia.nih.gov/alzheimers/topics/alzheimers-basics

National Institute on Alcohol Abuse and Alcoholism. (n.d.). *Alcohol facts and statistics.* Retrieved from https://www.niaaa.nih.gov/alcohol-health/overview-alcohol-consumption/alcohol-facts-and-statistics

National Institute on Deafness and Other Communication Disorders. (2017, March 6). *Cochlear implants.* Retrieved from https://www.nidcd.nih.gov/health/cochlear-implants

National Institute on Drug Abuse (NIDA). (2016, June). *What is cocaine?* Retrieved from https://www.drugabuse.gov/publications/drugfacts/cocaine

National Institute on Drug Abuse (NIDA). (2016, October). *Most commonly used addictive drugs.* Retrieved from https://www.drugabuse.gov/publications/media-guide/most-commonly-used-addictive-drugs

National Institute on Drug Abuse (NIDA). (2017, February). *What is methamphetamine?* Retrieved from https://www.drugabuse.gov/publications/drugfacts/methamphetamine

National Institute on Drug Abuse (NIDA). (2018, February). *Synthetic cannabinoids.* Retrieved from https://www.drugabuse.gov/publications/drugfacts/synthetic-cannabinoids-k2spice

National Institutes of Health (NIH). (2012). Tips for getting a good night's sleep. *Medline Plus, 7,* 20.

National Institutes of Health (NIH). (2017, May 17). Study finds tens of millions of Americans drink alcohol at dangerously high levels [Press release]. Retrieved from https://www.nih.gov/news-events/news-releases/study-finds-tens-millions-americans-drink-alcohol-dangerously-high-levels

National Institutes of Health, National Institute on Alcohol Abuse and Alcoholism. (2013). *Alcohol use disorder.* Retrieved from http://www.niaaa.nih.gov/alcohol-health/overview-alcohol-consumption/alcohol-use-disorders

National Library of Medicine (NLM). (2016, February 22). *Natal teeth.* Retrieved from https://www.nlm.nih.gov/medlineplus/ency/article/003268.htm

National Safety Council. (2015). *Annual estimate of cell phone crashes 2013.* Retrieved from http://www.nsc.org/DistractedDrivingDocuments/Attributable-Risk-Estimate.pdf

National Safety Council. (2016). *Injury facts 2016 edition.* Itasca, IL: Author.

National Safety Council. (n.d.). *Hands-free is not risk-free.* Retrieved from http://www.nsc.org/learn/NSC-Initiatives/Pages/distracted-driving-hands-free-is-not-risk-free-infographic.aspx

National Sleep Foundation. (2016). *See: A great night's sleep can depend on the visual conditions in your bedroom environment.* Retrieved from https://sleepfoundation.org/bedroom/see.php

National Sleep Foundation. (n.d.). *Excessive sleepiness: How much sleep do babies and kids need?* Retrieved from https://sleepfoundation.org/excessivesleepiness/content/how-much-sleep-do-babies-and-kids-need

National Science Foundation, National Center for Science and Engineering Statistics. (2018). Doctorate recipients from U.S. universities: 2016. In *Special Report NSF 18-304.* Arlington, VA: Author. Available at https://www.nsf.gov/statistics/2018/nsf18304/data.cfm

Nazir, A., Smalbrugge, M., Moser, A., Karuza, J., Crecelius, C., Hertogh, C., . . . Katz, P. R. (2018). The prevalence of burnout among nursing home physicians: An international perspective. *Journal of the American Medical Directors Association, 19,* 86–88.

Needleman, H. L., Gunnoe, C., Leviton, A., Reed, R., Peresie, H., Maher, C., & Barrett, P. (1979). Deficits in psychologic and classroom performance of children with elevated dentine lead levels. *New England Journal of Medicine, 300,* 689–695.

Neisser, U. (1979). The control of information pickup in selective looking. In A. D. Pick (Ed.), *Perception and its development: A tribute to Eleanor J. Gibson* (pp. 201–219). Hillsdale, NJ: Erlbaum.

Neisser, U. (1991). A place of misplaced nostalgia. *American Psychologist, 46,* 34–36.

Neisser, U., & Becklen, R. (1975). Selective looking: Attending to visually specified events. *Cognitive Psychology, 7,* 480–494.

Neligan, A. (2014). Temporal trends in epilepsy surgery. *European Journal of Neurology, 21,* 814–815.

Nelson, L. D., Simmons, J., & Simonsohn, U. (2018). Psychology's renaissance. *Annual Review of Psychology, 69,* 511–534.

Nelson, R. (2014). Scientific basis for polygraph testing. *Polygraph, 44,* 28–61.

Nelson, R., & Handler, M. (2013). A brief history of scientific reviews of polygraph accuracy research. *APA Magazine, 46,* 22–28.

Nelson, S. K., Layous, K., Cole, S. W., & Lyubomirsky, S. (2016). Do unto others or treat yourself? The effects of prosocial and self-focused behavior on psychological flourishing. *Emotion, 16*(6), 850–861. doi:10.1037/emo0000178

Nelson, S. M., Telfer, E. E., & Anderson, R. A. (2013). The ageing ovary and uterus: New biological insights. *Human Reproduction Update, 19,* 67–83.

Nes, R. B., Czajkowski, N., & Tambs, K. (2010). Family matters: Happiness in nuclear families and twins. *Behavioral Genetics, 40,* 577–590.

Nesi, J., & Prinstein, M. J. (2015). Using social media for social comparison and feedback-seeking: Gender and popularity moderate associations with depressive symptoms. *Journal of Abnormal Child Psychology, 43,* 1427–1438.

Nevison, C. D. (2014). A comparison of temporal trends in United States autism prevalence to trends in suspected environmental factors. *Environmental Health, 13,* 73. doi:10.1186/1476-069X-13-73

Newell, A., Shaw, J. C., & Simon, H. A. (1958). Elements of a theory of human problem solving. *Psychological Review, 65,* 151–166.

Newell, B. R., & Andrews, S. (2004). Levels of processing effects on implicit and explicit memory tasks: Using question position to investigate the lexical-processing hypothesis. *Experimental Psychology, 51,* 132–144.

Newton, K. M., Reed, S. D., LaCroix, A. Z., Grothaus, L. C., Ehrlich, K., & Guiltinan, J. (2006). Treatment of vasomotor symptoms of menopause with black cohosh, multibotanicals, soy, hormone therapy, or placebo. *Annals of Internal Medicine, 145,* 869–879.

Newton-Howes, G., Levack, W. M., McBride, S., Gilmor, M., & Tester, R. (2016). Non-physiological mechanisms influencing disulfiram treatment of alcohol use disorder: A grounded theory study. *Drug and Alcohol Dependence, 165,* 126–131.

Neylan, T. C. (1999). Frontal lobe function: Mr. Phineas Gage's famous injury. *Journal of Neuropsychiatry and Clinical Neurosciences, 11,* 280–281.

Ng, C. (2016, August 18). Andre De Grasse, Usain Bolt set to clash in 200 nal. *CBC News.* Retrieved from http://feed.cbc.ca/sports/olympics/rio2016/track-eld/de-grasse-bolt-semis-1.3725866

Ng, D. M., & Jeffery, R. W. (2003). Relationships between perceived stress and health behaviors in a sample of working adults. *Health Psychology, 22,* 638–642.

Ngun, T. C., Ghahramani, N., Sánchez, F. J., Bocklandt, S., & Vilain, E. (2011). The genetics of sex differences in brain and behavior. *Frontiers in Neuroendocrinology, 32,* 227–248.

Nichols, A. L., & Edlund, J. E. (2015). Practicing what we preach (and sometimes study): Methodological issues in experimental laboratory research. *Review of General Psychology, 19,* 191–202. Retrieved from http://dx.doi.org/10.1037/gpr0000027

NIDA Blog Team. (2015, March 16). What are date rape drugs and how do you avoid them? [Web log post]. Retrieved from https://teens.drugabuse.gov/blog/post/what-are-date-rape-drugs-and-how-do-you-avoid-them

Nielsen, J. A., Zielinski, B. A., Ferguson, M. A., Lainhart, J. E., & Anderson, J. S. (2013). An evaluation of the left-brain vs. right-brain hypothesis with resting state functional connectivity magnetic resonance imaging. *PLoS One, 8,* e71275.

Nir, S. M. (2016, February 23). Woman exonerated after serving 10 years for manslaughter conviction. *The New York Times.* Retrieved from http://www.nytimes.com/2016/02/24/nyregion/womans-manslaughter-conviction-in-1991-death-to-be-vacated.html?_r=0

Nisbett, R. E., Aronson, J., Blair, C., Dickens, W., Flynn, J., Halpern, D. F., & Turkehimer, E. (2012). Intelligence: New findings and theoretical developments. *American Psychologist, 67,* 130–159.

Nishitani, S., Miyamura, T., Tagawa, M., Sumi, M., Takase, R., Doi, H., . . . Shinohara, K. (2009). The calming effect of a maternal breast milk odor on the human newborn infant. *Neuroscience Research, 63,* 66–71.

Niskar, A. S., Kieszak, S. M., Holmes, A. E., Esteban, E., Rubin, C., & Brody, D. J. (2001). Estimated prevalence of noise-induced hearing threshold shifts among children 6 to 19 years of age: The Third National Health and Nutrition Examination Survey, 1988–1994, United States. *Pediatrics, 108,* 40–43.

Niven, K. (2015). Can music with prosocial lyrics heal the working world? A field intervention in a call center. *Journal of Applied Social Psychology, 45*(3), 132–138.

No Barriers (No Barriers USA). (2015, July 29). No Barriers Summit 2015—Mandy Harvey singing "Try" [Video file]. Retrieved from https://www.youtube.com/watch?v=z-DRYk0OxCo

NobelPrize.org. (2009, October 9). *Facts on the Nobel Prize in Literature.* Retrieved from https://www.nobelprize.org/nobel_prizes/facts/literature/

NobelPrize.org. (2014). *Malala Yousafzai—biographical.* Retrieved from https://www.nobelprize.org/nobel_prizes/peace/laureates/2014/yousafzai-bio.html

Nolen-Hoeksema, S. (1991). Responses to depression and their effects on the duration of depressive episodes. *Journal of Abnormal Psychology, 100,* 569–582.

Noller, G. (2009). *Literature review and assessment report on MDMA/ecstasy.* Wellington, New Zealand: Ministry of Health. Retrieved from http://www.moh.govt.nz/notebook/nbbooks.nsf/0/EE5BDDAA39721D6ACC257B8000708A11/$file/July2010Literature-Review-Assessment-Report-MDMA-Ecstasy.pdf

Nonnemaker, J., Hersey, J., Homsi, G., Busey, A., Hyland, A., Juster, H., & Farrelly, M. (2011). Self-reported exposure to policy and environmental influences on smoking cessation and relapse: A 2-year longitudinal population-based study. *International Journal of Environmental Research and Public Health, 8,* 3591–3608.

Norcross, J. C., & Beutler, L. E. (2014). Integrative psychotherapies. In R. J. Corsini & D. Wedding (Eds.), *Current psychotherapies* (10th ed., pp. 499–532). Belmont, CA: Brooks/Cole, Cengage Learning.

Norcross, J. C., & Sayette, M. A. (2016). *Insider's guide to graduate programs in clinical and counseling psychology 2016–2017 edition.* New York, NY: Guilford Press.

Norcross, J. C., & Wampold, B. E. (2011). What works for whom: Tailoring psychotherapy to the person. *Journal of Clinical Psychology, 67,* 127–132.

Norrholm, S. D., Jovanovic, T., Gerardi, M., Breazeale, K. G., Price, M., Davis, M., . . . Tuerk, P. W. (2016). Baseline psychophysiological and cortisol reactivity as a predictor of PTSD treatment outcome in virtual reality exposure therapy. *Behaviour Research and Therapy, 82,* 28–37.

North, A. (2014, August 1). Here's the thing that "lasting love" is really about [Web log post]. Retrieved from http://op-talk.blogs.nytimes.com/2014/08/01/heresthe-thing-that-lasting-love-is-really-about/?_r=0

Northoff, G., Schneider, F., Rotte, M., Matthiae, C., Tempelmann, C., Wiebking, C., . . . Panksepp, J. (2009). Differential parametric modulation of self-relatedness and emotions in different brain regions. *Human Brain Mapping, 30,* 369–382.

Nour, N. M. (2009). Child marriage: A silent health and human rights issue. *Reviews in Obstetrics & Gynecology, 2,* 51–56.

NPR Staff. (2011, August 8). A year later, Chilean miners sift through trauma. *NPR Books.* Retrieved from http://www.npr.org/2011/08/08/139003770/a-year-later-chilean-miners-sift-through-trauma

NPR Staff. (2014, June 22). With memories and online maps, a man finds his "way home." NPR. Retrieved from http://www.npr.org/2014/06/22/323355643/with-memories-and-online-maps-a-man-finds-his-way-home

NPR. (2013, December 31). *Pharrell Williams on juxtaposition and seeing sounds.* Retrieved from http://www.npr.org/sections/therecord/2013/12/31/258406317/pharrell-williams-on-juxtaposition-and-seeing-sounds

NPR. (2014, March 30). *Cesar Millan's long walk to becoming the "Dog Whisperer."* Retrieved from http://www.npr.org/2014/03/30/295796786/cesar-millans-long-walk-to-becoming-the-dog-whisperer

NPR. (2016, June 13). *How YouTube videos help people cope with mental illness.* Retrieved from https://www.npr.org/sections/health-shots/2016/06/13/481547500/how-seeing-youtube-videos-helped-me-understand-my-schizophrenia

Nusbaum, E. C., & Silvia, P. J. (2011). Are intelligence and creativity really so different? Fluid intelligence, executive processes, and strategy use in divergent thinking. *Intelligence, 39,* 36–45.

Nutt, D. J., Lingford-Hughes, A., Erritzoe, D., & Stokes, P. R. A. (2015). The dopamine theory of addiction: 40 years of highs and lows. *Nature Reviews Neuroscience, 16,* 305–312.

O'Brien, D. (2013). *How to develop a brilliant memory week by week: 50 Proven ways to enhance your memory skills.* London, UK: Watkins Publishing.

O'Brien, P. (2007). Is it all right for women to drink small amounts of alcohol in pregnancy? Yes. *British Journal of Medicine, 335,* 857.

O'Keefe, D. J. (2008). Elaboration likelihood model. In W. Donsbach (Ed.), *International encyclopedia of communication* (Vol. IV, pp. 1475–1480). Malden, MA: Blackwell.

Oakley, S. (2012, May 30). Mayo Clinic medical edge: Cochlear implants a good next step when hearing aids are no longer effective. *The Chicago Tribune.* Retrieved from http://articles.chicagotribune.com/2012-05-30/lifestyle/sns-201205291800-tms-premhnstr-k-b20120530-20120530_1_cochlear-auditory-nerve-implant-device

Oar, E. L., Farrell, L. J., & Ollendick, T. H. (2015). One session treatment for specific phobias: An adaptation for paediatric blood-injection-injury phobia in youth. *Clinical Child and Family Psychology Review, 18,* 370–394.

Oatley, K., Keltner, D., & Jenkins, J. (2006). *Understanding emotions.* Malden, MA: Blackwell.

Öberg, M., Jaakkola, M. S., Woodward, A., Peruga, A., & Prüss-Ustün, A. (2011). Worldwide burden of disease from exposure to second-hand smoke: A retrospective analysis of data from 192 countries. *The Lancet, 311,* 139–146.

Occupational Safety & Health Administration. (n.d.). *Occupational noise exposure.* Retrieved from https://www.osha.gov/SLTC/noisehearingconservation/

Oda, R., Matsumoto-Oda, A., & Kurashima, O. (2005). Effects of belief in genetic relatedness on resemblance judgments by Japanese raters. *Evolution of Human Behavior, 26,* 441–450.

Oerlemans, W. G. M., Bakker, A. B., & Veenhoven, R. (2011). Finding the key to happy aging: A day reconstruction study of happiness. *Journal of Gerontology: Psychological Sciences, 6*(6), 665–674. doi:10.1093/geronb/gbr040

Oexman, R. (2013, May 5). Better sleep month: Top 10 sleep myths debunked. *Huffington Post Healthy Living.* Retrieved from http://www.huffingtonpost.com/dr-robert- oexman/sleep-myths_b_3177375.html

Oh, D. L., Jerman, P., Marques, S. S., Koita, K., Boparai, S. K. P., Harris, N. B., & Bucci, M. (2018). Systematic review of pediatric health outcomes associated with childhood adversity. *BMC Pediatrics, 18*(1). doi:10.1186/s12887-018-1037-7

Ohayon, M. (2011). Epidemiological overview of sleep disorders in the general population. *Sleep Medicine Reviews, 2,* 1–9.

Ohayon, M., Carskadon, M. A., Guilleminault, C., & Vitiello, M. V. (2004). Meta-analysis of quantitative sleep parameters from childhood to old age in healthy individuals: Developing normative sleep values across the human lifespan. *Sleep, 21,* 1255–1273.

Oishi, S., Talhelm, T., & Lee, M. (2015). Personality and geography: Introverts prefer mountains. *Journal of Research in Personality, 58,* 55–68.

Olatunde, O., & Balogun, F. (2017). Sexting: Prevalence, predictors, and associated sexual risk behaviors among postsecondary school young people in Ibadan, Nigeria. *Frontiers in Public Health, 5*(96). doi:10.3389/fpubh.2017.00096

Olenik-Shemesh, D., Heiman, T., & Eden, S. (2015). Bystanders' behavior in cyberbullying episodes: Active and passive patterns in the context of personal–socio-emotional factors. *Journal of Interpersonal Violence.* doi:10.1177/0886260515585531

Olivo, A. (2018, January 10). Danica Roem sworn into office as Virginia's first openly transgender lawmaker. *The Washington Post.* Retrieved from https://www.washingtonpost.com/local/virginia-politics/her-rainbow-scarf-wasnt-visible-but-she-had-it-with-her/2018/01/10/2684c4a6-f4ac-11e7-beb6-c8d48830c54d_story.html?utm_term=.1eecc5484636

Olson, J. M., Vernon, P. A., Harris, J. A., & Jang, K. L. (2001). The heritability of attitudes: A study of twins. *Journal of Personality and Social Psychology, 80,* 845–860.

Omalu, B. I., DeKosky, S. T., Minster, R. L., Kamboh, M. I., Hamilton, R. L., & Wecht, C. H. (2005). Chronic traumatic encephalopathy in a National Football League player. *Neurosurgery, 57,* 128–134.

Oppedal, B., & Idsoe, T. (2015). The role of social support in the acculturation and mental health of unaccompanied minor asylum seekers. *Scandinavian Journal of Psychology, 56,* 203–211.

Oremus, C., Oremus, M., McNeely, H., Losier, B., Parlar, M., King, M., . . . Hanford, L. (2015). Effects of electroconvulsive therapy on cognitive functioning in patients with depression: Protocol for a systematic review and meta-analysis. *BMJ Open, 5,* e006966.

Ornish, D., Lin, J., Chan, J. M., Epel, E., Kemp, C., Weidner, G., . . . Estay, I. (2013). Effect of comprehensive lifestyle changes on telomerase activity and telomere length in men with biopsy-proven low-risk prostate cancer: 5-year follow-up of a descriptive pilot study. *The Lancet Oncology, 14,* 1112–1120.

Oskin, B. (2013, May 17). Fighting to save an endangered bird—with vomit. *LiveScience.* Retrieved from http://www.livescience.com/32092-saving-marbled-murrelet-with-vomit-eggs.html

Öst, L. G. (1989). One-session treatment for specific phobias. *Behaviour Research and Therapy, 27,* 1–7.

Overmier, J. B., & Seligman, M. E. P. (1967). Effects of inescapable shock upon subsequent escape and avoidance responding. *Journal of Comparative and Physiological Psychology, 63,* 28–33.

Owen, E. (2016, June 22). Girl endures childhood neglect, makes amazing progress with adoptive family. *The San Francisco Globe.* Retrieved from http://sfglobe.com/2015/09/20/girl-endures-childhood-neglect-makes-amazing-progress-with-adoptive-family/

Owen, J. J., Adelson, J., Budge, S., Kopta, S. M., & Reese, R. J. (2016). Good-enough level and dose-effect models: Variation among outcomes and therapists. *Psychotherapy Research, 26,* 22–30.

Owen, P. R., & Padron, M. (2016). The language of toys: Gendered language in toy advertisements. *Journal of Research on Women and Gender, 6,* 67–80.

Oxford Royale Academy. (2014, October 15). *11 Great jokes to help you remember English grammar rules.* Retrieved from https://www.oxford-royale.co.uk/articles/11-great-jokes-remember-english-grammar-rules.html

Özkan, M., Yıldırım, N., Dişçi, R., İlgün, A. S., Sarsenov, D., Alço, G., . . . Özmen, V. (2017). Roles of biopsychosocial factors in the development of breast cancer. *European Journal of Breast Health, 13*(4), 206–212. http://doi.org/10.5152/ejbh.2017.3519

Pace, A., Luo, R., Hirsh-Pasek, K., & Golinkoff, R. M. (2017). Identifying pathways between socioeconomic status and language development. *Annual Review of Linguistics, 3,* 285–308.

Pachana, N. A., Brilleman, S. L., & Dobson, A. J. (2011). Reporting of life events over time: Methodological issues in a longitudinal sample of women. *Psychological Assessment, 23,* 277–281.

Padden, C., & Humphries, T. (1988). *Deaf in America: Voices from a culture.* Cambridge, MA: Harvard University Press.

Pagnini, F., Bercovitz, K., & Langer, E. (2016). Perceived control and mindfulness: Implications for clinical practice. *Journal of Psychotherapy Integration, 26,* 91–102.

Paikoff, R. L., & Brooks-Gunn, J. (1991). Do parent-child relationships change during puberty? *Psychological Bulletin, 110,* 47–66.

Palermo, T. M., Eccleston, C., Lewandowski, A. S., Williams, A. C. D. C., & Morley, S. (2010). Randomized controlled trials of psychological therapies for management of chronic pain in children and adolescents: An updated meta-analytic review. *Pain, 148,* 387–397.

Palgi, S., Klein, E., & Shamay-Tsoory, S. (2017). The role of oxytocin in empathy in PTSD. *Psychological Trauma: Theory, Research, Practice, and Policy, 9,* 70–75.

Palmatier, J. J., & Rovner, L. (2015). Credibility assessment: Preliminary process theory, the polygraph process, and construct validity. *International Journal of Psychophysiology, 95,* 3–13.

Palmer, K. M. (2015, January 26). Why did vaccinated people get measles at Disneyland? Blame the unvaccinated. *Wired.* Retrieved from http://www.wired.com/2015/01/vaccinated-people-get-measles-disneyland-blame-unvaccinated/

Pan, J.-Y., & Wong, D. F. K. (2011). Acculturative stressors and acculturative strategies as predictors of negative affect among Chinese international students in Australia and Hong Kong: A cross-cultural comparative study. *Academic Psychiatry, 35,* 376–381.

Panza, G. A., Taylor, B. A., Thompson, P. D., White, C. M., & Pescatello, L. S. (2017). Physical activity intensity and subjective well-being in healthy adults. *Journal of Health Psychology.* doi:10.1177/1359105317691589.

Pape, H.-C., & Pare, D. (2010). Plastic synaptic networks of the amygdala for the acquisition, expression, and extinction of conditioned fear. *Physiological Review, 90,* 419–463.

Paris, J. (2014). Modernity and narcissistic personality disorder. *Personality Disorders: Theory, Research, and Treatment, 5,* 220–226.

Paris, J. (2015). Antisocial personality disorder. In J. Paris, *A concise guide to personality disorders* (pp. 65–71). Washington, DC: American Psychological Association.

Park, S., Guo, Y., Jia, X., Choe, H. K., Grena, B., Kang, J., . . . Yim, Y. S. (2017). One-step optogenetics with multifunctional flexible polymer fibers. *Nature Neuroscience, 20,* 612–619.

Parmentier, F. B. R., & Andrés, P. (2010). The involuntary capture of attention by sound: Novelty and postnovelty distraction in young and older adults. *Experimental Psychology, 57,* 68–76.

Parrott, A. C. (2004). MDMA (3,4-Methylenedioxymethamphetamine) or ecstasy: The neuropsychobiological implications of taking it at dances and raves. *Neuropsychobiology, 50,* 329–335.

Parrott, A. C. (2015). Why all stimulant drugs are damaging to recreational users: An empirical overview and psychobiological explanation. *Human Psychopharmacology: Clinical and Experimental, 30*(4), 213–224.

Parry, M. S. (2006). Dorothea Dix (1802–1887). *American Journal of Public Health, 96,* 624–625.

Parsaik, A. K., Mascarenhas, S. S., Khosh-Chashm, D., Hashmi, A., John, V., Okusaga, O., & Singh, B. (2016). Mortality associated with anxiolytic and hypnotic drug: A systematic review and meta-analysis. *Australian & New Zealand Journal of Psychiatry, 50,* 520–533.

Partanen, E., Kujala, T., Näätänen, R., Liitola, A., Sambeth, A., & Huotilainen, M. (2013). Learning-induced neural plasticity of speech processing before birth. *Proceedings of the National Academy of Sciences, 110*(37), 15145–15150.

Parth, K., & Loeffler-Stastka, H. (2015). Psychoanalytic core competence. *Frontiers in Psychology, 6.* doi:10.3389/fpsyg.2015.00356

Partisan Pictures. (Producer). (2012). *Cesar Millan: The real story* [DVD]. Available from https://www.amazon.com/Cesar-Millan-Real-Story-Milan/dp/B00A4Y61SC

Pasanen, T. P., Tyrväinen, L., & Korpela, K. M. (2014). The relationship between perceived health and physical activity indoors, outdoors in built environments, and outdoors in nature. *Applied Psychology: Health and Well-Being, 6,* 324–346.

Pashler, H., Rohrer, D., Cepeda, N. J., & Carpenter, S. K. (2007). Enhancing learning and retarding forgetting: Choices and consequences. *Psychonomic Bulletin & Review, 14,* 187–193.

Passel, J. S., & Cohen, D. (2017, February 9). 20 metro areas are home to six-in-ten unauthorized immigrants in U.S. *Pew Research Center.* Retrieved from http://www.pewresearch.org/fact-tank/2017/02/09/us-metro-areas-unauthorized-immigrants/

Patihis, L. (2016). Individual differences and correlates of highly superior autobiographical memory. *Memory, 24,* 961–978.

Patihis, L., Frenda, S. J., LePort, A. K., Petersen, N., Nichols, R. M., Stark, C. E., . . . Loftus, E. F. (2013). False memories in highly superior autobiographical memory individuals. *Proceedings of the National Academy of Sciences, 110,* 20947–20952.

Patihis, L., Ho, L. Y., Lilienfeld, S. O., & Loftus, E. F. (2014). Unconscious repressed memory is scientifically questionable. *Psychological Science, 25,* 1967–1968.

Patihis, L., Ho, L. Y., Tingen, I. W., Lilienfeld, S. O., & Loftus, E. F. (2014). Are the "Memory Wars" over? A scientist-practitioner gap in beliefs about repressed memory. *Psychological Science, 25,* 519–530.

Patil, K., Pressnitzer, D., Shamma, S., & Elhilali, M. (2012). Music in our ears: The biological bases of musical timbre perception. *PLoS Computational Biology, 8,* e1002759. doi:10.1371/journal.pcbi.1002759

Patorno, E., Bohn, R. L., Wahl, P. M., Avorn, J., Patrick, A. R., Liu, J., & Schneeweiss, S. (2010). Anticonvulsant medications and the risk of suicide, attempted suicide, or violent death. *Journal of the American Medical Association, 303,* 1401–1409.

Patrick, M. E., & Schulenberg, J. E. (2014). Prevalence and predictors of adolescent alcohol use and binge drinking in the United States. *Alcohol Research: Current Reviews, 35,* 193–200.

Patterson, M. C. (2017). A naturalistic investigation of media multitasking while studying and the effects on exam performance. *Teaching of Psychology, 44,* 51–57.

Pauls, D. L., Abramovitch, A., Rauch, S. L., & Geller, D. A. (2014). Obsessive compulsive disorder: An integrative genetic and neurobiological perspective. *Nature Reviews Neuroscience, 15,* 410–424.

Pavlos, P., Vasilios, N., Antonia, A., Dimitrios, K., Georgios, K., & Georgios, A. (2009). Evaluation of young smokers and non-smokers with electrogustometry and contact endoscopy. *BMC Ear, Nose and Throat Disorders, 9*(9). doi:10.1186/1472-6815-9-9

Pavlov, I. (1906). The scientific investigation of the psychical faculties or processes in the higher animals. *Science, 24,* 613–619.

Pavlov, I. (1960). *Conditioned reflexes.* New York, NY: Dover. (Original work published 1927)

Pavlovich-Danis, S. J., & Patterson, K. (2006, January 9). For a good night's sleep. *Nurseweek News.*

Payne, E., Ford, D., & Morris, J. (2015, February 25). Jury finds Eddie Ray Routh guilty in "American Sniper" case. *CNN.* Retrieved from http://www.cnn.com/2015/02/24/us/american-sniper-chris-kyle-trial/

Pazzaglia, M. (2015). Body and odors not just molecules, after all. *Current Directions in Psychological Science, 24,* 329–333.

PBS. (1997, March 4). Secret of the wild child. *NOVA: Transcripts.* Retrieved from http://www.pbs.org/wgbh/nova/transcripts/2112gchild.html

PBS. (2005, January 27). Kinsey. *American Experience.* Retrieved from http://www.pbs.org/wgbh/amex/kinsey/peopleevents/p_kinsey.html

PBS. (2014). Other notorious insanity cases. *Frontline.* Retrieved from http://www.pbs.org/wgbh/pages/frontline/shows/crime/trial/other.html

Peever, J., Luppi, P. H., & Montplaisir, J. (2014). Breakdown in REM sleep circuitry underlies REM sleep behavior disorder. *Trends in Neuroscience, 7,* 279–288.

Penfield, W., & Boldrey, E. (1937). Somatic motor and sensory representation in the cerebral cortex of man as studied by electrical stimulation. *Brain, 60,* 389–443.

Pennisi, E. (2012, September 5). Human genome is much more than just genes. *Science NOW.* Retrieved from http://news.sciencemag.org/sciencenow/2012/09/human-genome-is-much-more-than-j.html

Peplau, L. A. (2003). Human sexuality: How do men and women differ? *Current Directions in Psychological Science, 12,* 37–40.

Peretto, P., & Bonfanti, L. (2015). Adult neurogenesis 20 years later: Physiological function vs. brain repair. *Frontiers in Neuroscience, 9.*

Perkins, K. A., Karelitz, J. L., Conklin, C. A., Sayette, M. A., & Giedgowd, G. E. (2010). Acute negative affect relief from smoking depends on the affect measure and situation, but not on nicotine. *Biological Psychiatry, 67,* 707–714.

Perlman, L. M., & Segal, N. L. (2005). Memories of the Child Development Center study of adopted monozygotic twins reared apart: An unfulfilled promise. *Twin Research and Human Genetics, 8,* 271–381.

Perrin, A. J., Cohen, P. N., & Caren, N. (2013). Are children of parents who had same-sex relationships disadvantaged? A scientific evaluation of the no-differences hypothesis. *Journal of Gay & Lesbian Mental Health, 17,* 327–336.

Peschel, S. K., Feeling, N. R., Vögele, C., Kaess, M., Thayer, J. F., & Koenig, J. (2016). A systematic review on heart rate variability in bulimia nervosa. *Neuroscience & Biobehavioral Reviews, 63,* 78–97.

Peters, W. (1971). *A class divided: Then and now.* New Haven, CT: Yale University Press.

Peterson, G. B. (2000). The discovery of shaping: B. F. Skinner's big surprise. *The Clicker Journal: The Magazine for Animal Trainers, 43,* 6–13.

Peterson, G. B. (2004). A day of great illumination: B. F. Skinner's discovery of shaping. *Journal of the Experimental Analysis of Behavior, 82,* 317–328.

Peterson, J. K., Skeem, J., Kennealy, P., Bray, B., & Zvonkovic, A. (2014). How often and how consistently do symptoms directly precede criminal behavior among offenders with mental illness? *Law and Human Behavior, 38,* 439–449.

Peterson, L. R., & Peterson, M. J. (1959). Short-term retention of individual verbal items. *Journal of Experimental Psychology, 58,* 193–198.

Peterson, M. J., Meagher, R. B., Jr., & Ellsbury, S. W. (1970). Repetition effects in sensory memory. *Journal of Experimental Psychology, 84,* 15–23.

Petit, D., Pennestri, M. H., Paquet, J., Desautels, A., Zadra, A., Vitaro, F., . . . Montplaisir, J. (2015). Childhood sleepwalking and sleep terrors: A longitudinal study of prevalence and familial aggregation. *JAMA Pediatrics, 169,* 653–658.

Petitto, L. A. (1994). Are signed languages "real" languages? *International Quarterly of the Sign Linguistics Association, 7,* 1–10.

Petitto, L. A., & Marentette, P. F. (1991). Babbling in the manual mode: Evidence for the ontogeny of language. *Science, 251,* 1493–1496.

Petronis, A. (2004). The origin of schizophrenia: Genetic thesis, epigenetic antithesis, and resolving synthesis. *Biological Psychiatry, 55,* 965–970.

Petty, R. E., & Cacioppo, J. T. (1986). The elaboration likelihood model of persuasion. *Advances in Experimental Social Psychology, 19,* 123–205.

Pew Research Center. (2014, February 3). *6 New facts about Facebook.* Retrieved from http://www.pewresearch.org/fact-tank/2014/02/03/6-new-facts-about-facebook/

Pew Research Center. (2015, September 28). *Modern immigration wave brings 59 million to U.S., driving population growth and change through 2065: Views of immigration's impact on U.S. society mixed.* Retrieved from http://www.pewhispanic.org/2015/09/28/chapter-5-u-s-foreign-born-population-trends/

Pew Research Center. (2017, January 12). *Social media fact sheet.* Retrieved from http://www.pewinternet.org/fact-sheet/social-media/

Pew Research Center. (2018, January 31a). *Internet/broadband fact sheet.* Retrieved from http://www.pewinternet.org/fact-sheet/internet-broadband/

Pew Research Center. (2018, January 31b). *Mobile fact sheet.* Retrieved from http://www.pewinternet.org/fact-sheet/mobile/

Pfeifer, C. (2012). Physical attractiveness, employment and earnings. *Applied Economics Letters, 19,* 505–510.

Pfungst, O. (1911). *Clever Hans (the horse of Mr. Von Osten): A contribution to experimental, animal, and human psychology* (C. L. Rahn, Trans.). New York, NY: Holt.

Phillips, J. (2013). Prescription drug abuse: Problem, policies, and implications. *Nursing Outlook, 61,* 78–84.

Phillips, R. G., & LeDoux, J. E. (1992). Differential contribution of amygdala and hippocampus to cued and contextual fear conditioning. *Behavioral Neuroscience, 106,* 274–285.

Piaget, J. (1952). *The origins of intelligence in children.* New York, NY: Norton. (Original work published 1936)

Pich, E. M., Pagliusi, S. R., Tessari, M., Talabot-Ayer, D., Van Huijsduijnen, R. H., & Chiamulera, C. (1997). Common neural substrates for the addictive properties of nicotine and cocaine. *Science, 275,* 83–86.

Pickren, W. E., & Burchett, C. (2014). Making psychology inclusive: A history of education and training for diversity in American psychology. In W. E. Pickren, C. Burchett, F. T. L. Leong, L. Comas-Díaz, G. C. Nagayama Hall, C. Gordon, . . . J. E. Trimble (Eds.), *APA handbook of multicultural psychology: Vol. 2. Applications and training. APA handbooks in psychology* (pp. 3–18). Washington, DC, US: American Psychological Association.

Pierre, J. M. (2012). Mental illness and mental health: Is the glass half empty or half full? *Canadian Journal of Psychiatry, 57,* 651–658.

Pietromonaco, P. R., & Collins, N. L. (2017). Interpersonal mechanisms linking close relationships to health. *American Psychologist, 72*(6), 531–542.

Pike, K. M., & Dunne, P. E. (2015). The rise of eating disorders in Asia: A review. *Journal of Eating Disorders, 3,* 33. doi:10.1186/s40337-015-0070-2

Pilley, J. W., & Reid, A. K. (2011). Border collie comprehends object names as verbal referents. *Behavioural Processes, 86,* 184–195.

Pine Ridge Indian Reservation. (2016). Retrieved from http://www.re-member.org/pine-ridge-reservation.aspx

Pines, A. (2011). Male menopause: Is it a real clinical syndrome? *Climacteric, 14,* 15–17.

Pinker, S. (1994). *The language instinct.* New York, NY: Harper Perennial.

Pinker, S. (2003). Language as an adaptation to the cognitive niche. In M. H. Christiansen & S. Kirby (Eds.), *Language evolution: The states of the art* (pp. 16–37). New York, NY: Oxford University Press.

Pinto, Y., Neville, D. A., Otten, M., Corballis, P. M., Lamme, V. A., de Haan, E. H., . . . Fabri, M. (2017). Split brain: Divided perception but undivided consciousness. *Brain, 140,* 1231–1237.

Piper, A., Lillevik, L., & Kritzer, R. (2008). What's wrong with believing in repression? A review for legal professionals. *Psychology, Public Policy, and Law, 14,* 223–242.

Piper Jaffray. (2017, Spring). *Taking stock with teens: A collaborative consumer insights project.* Retrieved from http://www.piperjaffray.com/3col.aspx?id=4359

Pirnia, T., Joshi, S. H., Leaver, A. M., Vasavada, M., Njau, S., Woods, R. P., . . . Narr, K. L. (2016). Electroconvulsive therapy and structural neuroplasticity in neocortical, limbic and paralimbic cortex. *Translational Psychiatry, 6,* e832. doi:10.1038/tp.2016.102

Pison, G., Monden, C., & Smits, J. (2015). Twinning rates in developed countries: Trends and explanations. *Population and Development Review, 41*(4), 629–649.

Pittenger, C. (2010). Meta-analysis of the dose-response relationship of SSRI in obsessive-compulsive disorder. *Molecular Psychiatry, 15,* 850–855.

Pittenger, C., Adams, T. G., Gallezot, J. D., Crowley, M. J., Nabulsi, N., Ropchan, J., . . . Hannestad, J. (2016). OCD is associated with an altered association between sensorimotor gating and cortical and subcortical 5-HT1b receptor binding. *Journal of Affective Disorders, 196,* 87–96.

Pittenger, D. J. (1993, November). Measuring the MBTI and coming up short. *Journal of Career Planning & Placement, 54*(1), 48–52.

Pittenger, D. J. (2005). Cautionary comments regarding the Myers-Briggs Type Indicator. *Consulting Psychology Journal: Practice and Research, 57,* 210–221.

Pittman, M., & Reich, B. (2016). Social media and loneliness: Why an Instagram picture may be worth more than a thousand Twitter words. *Computers in Human Behavior, 62,* 155–167.

Plante, C., & Anderson, C. A. (2017, February). Global warming and violent behavior. *Observer, 30*(2). Retrieved from https://www.psychologicalscience.org/observer/global-warming-and-violent-behavior

Plata, M. (2017, December 19). 3 narcissistic traits in Kylo Ren [Web log post]. *Psychology Today.* Retrieved from https://www.psychologytoday.com/blog/the-gen-y-psy/201712/3-narcissistic-traits-in-kylo-ren

Platt, J. R. (2011, December 27). Lions vs. cattle: Taste aversion could solve African predator problem [Web log post]. Retrieved from http://blogs.scientificamerican.com/extinction-countdown/lions-vs-cattle-taste-aversion/

Platt, J. R. (2015, June 24). African lion populations drop 42 percent in past 21 years [Web log post]. Retrieved from http://blogs.scientificamerican.com/extinction-countdown/african-lion-populations-drop-42-percent-in-past-21-years/

Pletcher, M. J., Vittinghoff, E., Kalhan, R., Richman, J., Safford, M., Sidney, S., . . . Kertesz, S. (2012). Association between marijuana exposure and pulmonary function over 20 years. *Journal of the American Medical Association, 307,* 173–181.

Plomin, R., & DeFries, J. C. (1998). Genetics of cognitive abilities and disabilities. *Scientific American, 218*(5), 62–69.

Plomin, R., DeFries, J. C., Knopik, V. S., & Neiderhiser, J. M. (2013). *Behavioral genetics* (6th ed.). New York, NY: Worth.

Plomin, R., DeFries, J. C., Knopik, V. S., & Neiderhiser, J. M. (2016). Top 10 replicated endings from behavioral genetics. *Perspectives on Psychological Science, 11,* 3–23.

Polat, B. (2017). Before attachment theory: Separation research at the Tavistock Clinic, 1948–1956. *Journal of the History of the Behavioral Sciences, 53,* 48–70.

Polderman, T. J., Benyamin, B., de Leeuw, C. A., Sullivan, P. F., van Bochoven, A., Visscher, P. M., & Posthuma, D. (2015). Meta-analysis of the heritability of human traits based on fifty years of twin studies. *Nature Genetics, 47*(7), 702–709.

Polidori, M. C., Nelles, G., & Pientka, L. (2010). Prevention of dementia: Focus on lifestyle. *International Journal of Alzheimer's Disease, 2010,* 1–9. doi:10.406112010/393579

Pongrácz, P., Ujvári, V., Faragó, T., Miklósi, Á., & Péter, A. (2017). Do you see what I see? The difference between dog and human visual perception may affect the outcome of experiments. *Behavioural Processes, 140,* 53–60.

Poole, S. (2016, April 20). 20 Things you probably didn't know about Harriet Tubman. *The Atlanta Journal-Constitution.* Retrieved from http://www.ajc.com/news/lifestyles/think-you-know-everything-about-harriet-tubman-thi/nq8Xd/

Pope, K. S., & Wedding, D. (2014). Contemporary challenges and controversies. In R. J. Corsini & D. Wedding (Eds.), *Current psychotherapies* (10th ed., pp. 569–604). Belmont, CA: Brooks/Cole, Cengage Learning.

Popova, S., Lange, S., Probst, C., Gmel, G., & Rehm, J. (2017). Estimation of national, regional, and global prevalence of alcohol use during pregnancy and fetal alcohol syndrome: A systematic review and meta-analysis. *The Lancet Global Health, 5,* 290–299.

Porsch, R. M., Middeldorp, C. M., Cherny, S. S., Krapohl, E., Van Beijsterveldt, C. E., Loukola, A., . . . Kaprio, J. (2016). Longitudinal heritability of childhood aggression. *American Journal of Medical Genetics Part B: Neuropsychiatric Genetics, 171B,* 697–707.

Porter, J. S., Stern, M., & Zak-Piace, J. (2009). Prematurity, stereotyping, and perceived vulnerability at 5 months: Relations with mothers and their premature and full-term infants at 9 months. *Journal of Reproductive and Infant Psychology, 27,* 168–181.

Porter, R. H., & Winberg, J. (1999). Unique salience of maternal breast odors for newborn infants. *Neuroscience & Biobehavioral Reviews, 23,* 439–449.

Porter, S. B., & Baker, A. T. (2015). CSI (Crime Scene Induction): Creating false memories of committing crime. *Trends in Cognitive Sciences, 19,* 716–718.

Portnuff, C. D. F. (2016). Reducing the risk of music-induced hearing loss from overuse of portable listening devices: understanding the problems and establishing strategies for improving awareness in adolescents. *Adolescent Health, Medicine and Therapeutics, 7,* 27–35.

Postuma, R. B., Gagnon, J. F., Vendette, M., Fantini, M. L., Massicotte-Marquez, J., & Montplaisir, J. (2009). Quantifying the risk of neurodegenerative disease in idiopathic REM sleep behavior disorder. *Neurology, 72,* 1296–1300.

Potter, R. H. (2006). "As firecrackers to atom bombs": Kinsey, science, and authority. *Sexuality & Culture, 10,* 29–38.

Poulain, M., Herm, A., & Pes, G. (2013). The Blue Zones: Areas of exceptional longevity around the world. *Vienna Yearbook of Population Research, 11,* 87–108.

Poulton, E. C. (1967). Population norms of top sensory magnitudes and SS Stevens' exponents. *Perception & Psychophysics, 2,* 312–316.

Powell, R. A. (2010). Little Albert still missing. *American Psychologist, 65,* 299–300.

Powell, R. A., Digdon, N., Harris, B., & Smithson, C. (2014). Correcting the record on Watson, Rayner and Little Albert: Albert Barger as "Psychology's Lost Boy." *American Psychologist, 69,* 600–611.

Powers, A., Cross, D., Fani, N., & Bradley, B. (2015). PTSD, emotion dysregulation, and dissociative symptoms in a highly traumatized sample. *Journal of Psychiatric Research, 61,* 174–179.

Powers, J. (2015, August 28). Science says participation trophies are a big win for the little ones [Web log post]. Retrieved from http://www.huffingtonpost.com/jason-powers/science-says-participatio_b_8054046.html

Powers, M. B., & Carlbring, P. (2016). Technology: Bridging the gap from research to practice. *Cognitive Behaviour Therapy, 45,* 1–4.

Prather, A. A., Janicki-Deverts, D., Hall, M. H., & Cohen, S. (2015). Behaviorally assessed sleep and susceptibility to the common cold. *Sleep, 38,* 1353–1359.

Premack, A. J., & Premack, D. (1972). Teaching language to an ape. *Scientific American, 227,* 92–99.

Price, M. (2016, October 17). Facial expressions—including fear—may not be as universal as we thought. *Brain & Behavior.* doi:10.1126/science/aal0271

Pro Football Hall of Fame. (n.d.). *Harry Carson enshrinement speech.* Retrieved from http://www.profootballhof.com/players/harry-carson/enshrinement/

Prochaska, J. J., Velicer, W. F., Prochaska, J. O., Delucchi, K., & Hall, S. M. (2006). Comparing intervention outcomes in smokers treated for single versus multiple behavioral risks. *Health Psychology, 25,* 380–388.

Prochaska, J. O., & Norcross, J. C. (2014). *Systems of psychotherapy* (8th ed.). Pacific Grove, CA: Brooks/Cole, Cengage Learning.

Przybylski, A. K., & Weinstein, N. (2012). Can you connect with me now? How the presence of mobile communication technology influences face-to-face conversation quality. *Journal of Social and Personal Relationships, 30,* 237–246.

PubMed Health. (2016, August 17). *How does our sense of taste work?* Retrieved from https://www.ncbi.nlm.nih.gov/pubmedhealth/PMH0072592/

PubMed Health. (2016, July 28). *How does skin work?* Retrieved from https://www.ncbi.nlm.nih.gov/pubmedhealth/PMH0072439/?report=printable

Puce, A., & Carey, L. (2010). Somatosensory function. In I. B. Weiner & W. E. Craighead (Eds.), *The Corsini encyclopedia of psychology* (4th ed., Vol. 4, pp. 1678–1680). Hoboken, NJ: John Wiley & Sons.

Pugh, J., Kahane, G., Maslen, H., & Savulescu, J. (2016). Lay attitudes toward deception in medicine: Theoretical considerations and empirical evidence. *AJOB Empirical Bioethics, 7,* 31–38.

Puig, J., Englund, M. M., Simpson, J. A., & Collins, W. A. (2013). Predicting adult physical illness from infant attachment: A prospective longitudinal study. *Health Psychology, 32,* 409–417.

Pullum, G. K. (1991). *The great Eskimo vocabulary hoax and other irreverent essays on the study of language.* Chicago, IL: University of Chicago Press.

Qin, S., Ge, S., Yin, H., Xia, J., & Heynderickx, I. (2010). Just noticeable difference in black level, white level and chroma for natural images measured in two different countries. *Displays, 31,* 25–34.

Quinn, O. W. (1963). The public image of the family. In D. Rosenthal (Ed.), *The Genain quadruplets: A case study and theoretical analysis of heredity and environment in schizophrenia* (pp. 355–372). New York, NY: Basic Books.

Rabinowitz, M., Latella, L., Stern, C., & Jost, J. T. (2016). Beliefs about childhood vaccination in the United States: Political ideology, false consensus, and the illusion of uniqueness. *PLoS ONE, 11,* e0158382.

Rabkin, J. G., & Struening, E. L. (1976). Life events, stress, and illness. *Science, 194,* 1013–1020.

RACHELSTARLIVE. (2018, January 11). I feel nothing—anhedonia [Video file]. Retrieved from https://www.youtube.com/watch?v=5oD7gKfCL6w

Radak, Z., Hart, N., Sarga, L., Koltai, E., Atalay, M., Ohno, H., & Boldough, I. (2010). Exercise plays a preventive role against Alzheimer's disease. *Journal of Alzheimer's Disease, 20,* 777–783.

Radua, J., & Mataix-Cols, D. (2009). Voxel-wise meta-analysis of grey matter changes in obsessive-compulsive disorder. *British Journal of Psychiatry, 195,* 393–402.

Raevuori, A., Keski-Rahkonen, A., & Hoek, H. W. (2014). A review of eating disorders in males. *Current Opinion in Psychiatry, 27,* 426–430.

Raichle, K. A., Hanley, M., Jensen, M. P., & Cardenas, D. D. (2007). Cognitions, coping, and social environment predict adjustment to pain in spinal cord injury. *Journal of Pain, 8,* 718–729.

Raichlen, D. A., & Alexander, G. E. (2017). Adaptive capacity: An evolutionary neuroscience model linking exercise, cognition, and brain health. *Trends in Neurosciences, 40,* 408–421.

Raine, A., Lencz, T., Bihrle, S., LaCasse, L., & Colletti, P. (2000). Reduced prefrontal gray matter volume and reduced autonomic activity in antisocial personality disorder. *Archives of General Psychiatry, 57,* 119–127.

Rainville, P., Duncan, G. H., Price, D. D., Carrier, B., & Bushnell, M. C. (1997, August 15). Pain affect encoded in human anterior cingulate but not somatosensory cortex. *Science, 277*(5328), 968–971.

Ramachandran, V. S., & Brang, D. (2009). Sensations evoked in patients with amputation from watching an individual whose corresponding intact limb is being touched. *Archives of Neurology, 66,* 1281–1284.

Ramachandran, V. S., & Rogers-Ramachandran, D. (2008). Right side up. *Scientific American, 18,* 22–25.

Ramachandran, V. S., & Rogers-Ramachandran, D. (2009). I see, but I don't know. Patients with unusual visual deficits provide insights into how we normally see. *Scientific American Mind, 19,* 20–22.

Ramchandran, K., & Hauser, J. (2010). Phantom limb pain #212. *Journal of Palliative Medicine, 13,* 1285–1287.

Randall, D. K. (2012, September 22). Rethinking sleep. *The New York Times.* Retrieved from http://www.nytimes.com/2012/09/23/opinion/sunday/rethinking-sleep.html

Raphelson, S. (2017, November 30). How the loss of U.S. psychiatric hospitals led to a mental health crisis. NPR. Retrieved from https://www.npr.org/2017/11/30/567477160/how-the-loss-of-u-s-psychiatric-hospitals-led-to-a-mental-health-crisis

Rasch, B., & Born, J. (2013). About sleep's role in memory. *Physiological Reviews, 93,* 681–766.

Ratiu, P., Talos, I. F., Haker, S., Lieberman, D., & Everett, P. (2004). The tale of Phineas Gage, digitally remastered. *Journal of Neurotrauma, 21,* 637–643.

Ratnesar, R. (2011, July/August). The menace within. *Stanford Magazine.* Retrieved from http://alumni.stanford.edu/get/page/magazine/article/?article_id=40741

Rauh, V. A. (2018). Polluting developing brains—EPA failure on chlorpyrifos. *New England Journal of Medicine, 378,* 1171–1174.

Rawson, R. (1979, May 7). Two Ohio strangers find they're twins at 39—and a dream to psychologists. *People.* Retrieved from http://www.people.com/people/archive/article/0,,20073583,00.html

Re, D. E., Wang, S. A., He, J. C., & Rule, N. O. (2016). Selfie indulgence: Self-favoring biases in perceptions of selfies. *Social Psychological and Personality Science, 7,* 588–596.

Read, J., & Bentall, R. (2010). The effectiveness of electroconvulsive therapy: A literature review. *Epidemiologia e Psichiatria Sociale, 19,* 333–347.

Reber, P. (2010, May/June). Ask the brains: What is the memory capacity of the human brain? Is there a physical limit to the amount of information it can store? *Scientific American Mind, 21,* 70.

Reber, S., Allen, R., & Reber, E. S. (2009). Appendix A: Simple phobias. In S. Reber, R. Allen, & E. S. Reber (Eds.), *The Penguin dictionary of psychology* (4th ed.). London, UK: Penguin.

Reby, D., Levréro, F., Gustafsson, E., & Mathevon, N. (2016). Sex stereotypes influence adults' perception of babies' cries. *BioMed Central Psychology, 4*(19). doi:10.1186/s40359-016-0123-6

Rechtschaffen, A., & Bergmann, B. M. (1995). Sleep deprivation in the rat by the disk-over-water method. *Behavioural Brain Research, 69,* 55–63.

Reece, A. G., & Danforth, C. M. (2017). Instagram photos reveal predictive markers of depression. *EPJ Data Science, 6,* 15.

Reece, A. S. (2009). Chronic toxicology of cannabis. *Clinical Toxicology, 47,* 517–524.

Rees, J. L. (2003). Genetics of hair and skin color. *Annual Review of Genetics, 37,* 67–90.

Reese, H. W. (2010). Regarding Little Albert. *American Psychologist, 65,* 300–301.

Regnerus, M., & Gordon, D. (2013). *Social, emotional, and relational distinctions in patterns of recent masturbation among young adults.* Austin, TX: Austin Institute for the Study of Family and Culture. Retrieved from http://www.austin-institute.org/wp-content/uploads/2014/02/M-word-manuscript-for-website-working-paper-v2.pdf

Rehm, J., Shield, K. D., Roerecke, M., & Gmel, G. (2016). Modelling the impact of alcohol consumption on cardiovascular disease mortality for comparative risk assessments: An overview. *BMC Public Health, 16,* 363–372. doi:10.1186/s12889-016-3026-9

Reiche, E. M. V., Nunes, S. O. V., & Morimoto, H. K. (2004). Stress, depression, the immune system, and cancer. *The Lancet Oncology, 5,* 617–625.

Reichert, C., Fendrich, R., Bernarding, J., Tempelmann, C., Hinrichs, H., & Rieger, J. W. (2014). Online tracking of the contents of conscious perception using real-time fMRI. *Probing Auditory Scene Analysis, 69.* Retrieved from http://dx.doi.org/10.3389/fnins.2014.00116

Reichert, J. L., & Schöpf, V. (2017). Olfactory loss and regain: Lessons for neuroplasticity. *The Neuroscientist.* doi:10.1177/1073858417703910

Reifsteck, E. J., Gill, D. L., & Labban, J. D. (2016). "Athletes" and "exercisers": Understanding identity, motivation, and physical activity participation in former college athletes. *Sport, Exercise, and Performance Psychology, 5,* 25–38.

Reisenzein, R. (1983). The Schachter theory of emotion: Two decades later. *Psychological Bulletin, 94,* 239–264.

Ren, J., Wu, Y. D., Chan, J. S., & Yan, J. H. (2013). Cognitive aging affects motor performance and learning. *Geriatrics & Gerontology International, 13,* 19–27. doi:10.1111/j.1447-0594.2012.00914.x

Reneman, L., Booij, J., de Bruin, K., Reitsma, J. B., de Wolff, F. A., Gunning, W. B., . . . van den Brink, W. (2001). Effects of dose, sex, and long-term abstention from use on toxic effects of MDMA (ecstasy) on brain serotonin neurons. *The Lancet, 358,* 1864–1869.

Renner, M. J., & Mackin, R. S. (1998). A life stress instrument for classroom use. *Teaching of Psychology, 25,* 46–48.

Renner, W., Laireiter, A.-R., & Maier, M. (2012). Social support as a moderator of acculturative stress among refugees and asylum seekers. *Social Behavior and Personality, 40,* 129–146.

Rentzeperis, I., Nikolaev, A. R., Kiper, D. C., & van Leeuwen, C. (2014). Distributed processing of color and form in the visual cortex. *Frontiers in Psychology, 5.* doi:10.3389/fpsyg.2014.00932

Reuter-Lorenz, P. A. (2013). Aging and cognitive neuroimaging: A fertile union. *Perspectives on Psychological Science, 8,* 68–71.

Reynard, J., Brewster, S., & Biers, S. (2013). *Oxford handbook of urology* (3rd ed.). Oxford, UK: Oxford University Press.

Reynolds, B. A., & Weiss, S. (1992). Generation of neurons and astrocytes from isolated cells of the adult mammalian central nervous system. *Science, 255,* 1707–1710.

Reynolds, G., Field, A. P., & Askew, C. (2015). Learning to fear a second-order stimulus following vicarious learning. *Cognition and Emotion.* doi:1080/02699931.2015.1116978

Riccelli, R., Toschi, N., Nigro, S., Terracciano, A., & Passamonti, L. (2017). Surface-based morphometry reveals the neuroanatomical basis of the five-factor model of personality. *Social Cognitive and Affective Neuroscience, 12,* 671–684.

Rice, E., Rhoades, H., Winetrobe, H., Sanchez, M., Montoya, J., Plant, A., & Kordic, T. (2012). Sexually explicit cell phone messaging associated with sexual risk among adolescents. *Pediatrics, 130,* 667–673.

Richardson, E. G., & Hemenway, D. (2011). Homicide, suicide, and unintentional firearm fatality: Comparing the United States with other high-income countries, 2003. *Journal of Trauma, 70,* 238–243.

Richtel, M. (2016, April 27). Texting and driving? Watch out for the textalyzer. *The New York Times.* Retrieved from http://www.nytimes.com/2016/04/28/science/driving-texting-safety-textalyzer.html

Richtel, M. (2017, March 13). Are teenagers replacing drugs with smartphones? *The New York Times.* Retrieved from https://www.nytimes.com/2017/03/13/health/teenagers-drugs-smartphones.html?mcubz=0&_r=0

Ridout, K. K., Carpenter, L. L., & Tyrka, A. R. (2016). The cellular sequelae of early stress: Focus on aging and mitochondria. *Neuropsychopharmacology, 41,* 388–389.

Rieger, G., Cash, B. M., Merrill, S. M., Jones-Rounds, J., Dharmavaram, S. M., & Savin-Williams, R. C. (2015). Sexual arousal: The correspondence of eyes and genitals. *Biological Psychology, 104,* 56–64.

Rieke, F., & Baylor, D. A. (1998). Single-photon detection by rod cells of the retina. *Reviews of Modern Physics, 70,* 1027–1036.

Riggio, H. R., & Garcia, A. L. (2009). The power of situations: Jonestown and the fundamental attribution error. *Teaching of Psychology, 36,* 108–112.

Ringo, A. (2013, August 9). Understanding deafness: Not everyone wants to be "fixed." *The Atlantic.* Retrieved from http://www.theatlantic.com/health/archive/2013/08/understanding-deafness-not-everyone-wants-to-be-fixed/278527

Ripke, S., Neale, B. M., Corvin, A., Walters, J. T., Farh, K. H., Holmans, P. A., . . . Pers, T. H. (2014). Biological insights from 108 schizophrenia-associated genetic loci. *Nature, 511,* 421–427.

Ritchie, J. (2009, January 12). Fact or fiction: Elephants never forget. *Scientific American Online.* Retrieved from http://www.scientificamerican.com/article.cfm?id=elephants-never-forget

Ritchie, S. J., Wiseman, R., & French, C. C. (2012). Replication, replication, replication. *Psychologist, 25*(5), 346–348.

Robbins, B. D. (2008). What is the good life? Positive psychology and the renaissance of humanistic psychology. *The Humanistic Psychologist, 36,* 96–112.

Robbins, R. N., & Bryan, A. (2004). Relationships between future orientation, impulsive sensation seeking, and risk behavior among adjudicated adolescents. *Journal of Adolescent Research, 19,* 428–445.

Roberson, R. (2013, September). Helping students find relevance. *Psychology Teacher Network, 23,* 18–20. Retrieved from http://apa.org/ed/precollege/ptn/2013/09/students-relevance.aspx

Roberti, J. W. (2004). A review of behavioral and biological correlates of sensation seeking. *Journal of Research in Personality, 38,* 256–279.

Roberts, B. W., & DelVecchio, W. F. (2000). The rank-order consistency of personality traits from childhood to old age: A quantitative review of longitudinal studies. *Psychological Bulletin, 126,* 3–25.

Roberts, C. A., Jones, A., & Montgomery, C. (2016). Meta-analysis of molecular imaging of serotonin transporters in ecstasy/polydrug users. *Neuroscience & Biobehavioral Reviews, 63,* 158–167.

Roberts, J. A., & David, M. E. (2017). Put down your phone and listen to me: How boss phubbing undermines the psychological conditions necessary for employee engagement. *Computers in Human Behavior, 75,* 206-217.

Robertson, L. A., McAnally, H. M., & Hancox, R. J. (2013). Childhood and adolescent television viewing and antisocial behavior in early adulthood. *Pediatrics, 131,* 439–446.

Robinson, D. K. (2010). Gustav Fechner: 150 years of Elemente der Psychophysik. *History of Psychology, 13,* 409–410.

Robinson, E., Oldham, M., Cuckson, I., Brunstrom, J. M., Rogers, P. J., & Hardman, C. A. (2016). Visual exposure to large and small portion sizes and perceptions of portion size normality: Three experimental studies. *Appetite, 98,* 28–34.

Rodin, J. (1986). Aging and health: Effects of the sense of control. *Science, 233,* 1271–1276. doi:10.1126/science.3749877

Rodin, J., & Langer, E. J. (1977). Long-term effects of a control-relevant intervention with the institutionalized aged. *Journal of Personality and Social Psychology, 12,* 897–902.

Rodkey, E. N. (2015). The visual cliff's forgotten menagerie: Rats, goats, babies, and myth-making in the history of psychology. *Journal of the History of the Behavioral Sciences, 51,* 113–140.

Rodriguez, T. (2012). Open mind, longer life. *Scientific American Mind, 23,* 18.

Rodriguez, T. (2016, September 1). Harsh parents raise bullies—so do permissive ones. *Scientific American.* Retrieved from https://www.scientificamerican.com/article/harsh-parents-raise-bullies-so-do-permissive-ones/

Roediger, H. L., & Bergman, E. T. (1998). The controversy over recovered memories. *Psychology, Public Policy, and Law, 4,* 1091–1109.

Roediger, H. L., III, Putnam, A. L., & Smith, M. A. (2011). Ten benefits of testing and their applications to educational practice. *Psychology of Learning and Motivation: Advances in Research and Theory, 55,* 1–36.

Roenigk, A. (2016, May 24). Doctors say late BMX legend Dave Mirra had CTE. ESPN. Retrieved from http://espn.go.com/action/story/_/id/15614274/bmx-legend-dave-mirra-diagnosed-cte

Rofé, Y., & Rofé, Y. (2015). Fear and phobia: A critical review and the rational choice theory of neurosis. *International Journal of Psychological Studies, 7,* 37–73.

Rogers, C. R. (1951). *Client-centered therapy: Its current practice, implications, and theory.* Boston, MA: Houghton Mifflin.

Rogers, C. R. (1959). A theory of therapy, personality, and interpersonal relationships as developed in the client-centered framework. In S. Koch (Ed.), *Psychology: A study of a science: Vol. 3. Formulations of the person and the social context* (pp. 184–256). New York, NY: McGraw-Hill.

Rogers, C. R. (1961). *On becoming a person.* New York, NY: Houghton Mifflin.

Rogers, C. R. (1979). The foundations of the person-centered approach. *Education, 100,* 98–107.

Roghanizad, M. M., & Bohns, V. K. (2017). Ask in person: You're less persuasive than you think over email. *Journal of Experimental Social Psychology, 69,* 223–226.

Rohr, M. K., Wieck, C., & Kunzmann, U. (2017). Age differences in positive feelings and their expression. *Psychology and Aging, 32,* 608–620.

Rohrer, D., & Taylor, K. (2006). The effects of overlearning and distributed practice on the retention of mathematics knowledge. *Applied Cognitive Psychology, 20,* 1209–1224.

Rohrer, J. M., Egloff, B., & Schmukle, S. C. (2015). Examining the effects of birth order on personality. *Proceedings of the National Academy of Sciences, 112,* 14224–14229.

Rohwedder, S., & Willis, R. J. (2010). Mental retirement. *Journal of Economic Perspective, 24,* 119–138.

Roid, G. H. (2003). *Stanford-Binet Intelligence Scales* (5th ed.). Itasca, IL: Riverside.

Romero, J. R., Mercado, M., Beiser, A. S., Pikula, A., Seshadri, S., Kelly-Hayes, M., . . . Kase, C. S. (2013). Transient global amnesia and neurological events: The Framingham Heart Study. *Frontiers in Neurology, 4,* 1–2.

Rosales-Lagarde, A., Armony, J. L., del Rio-Portilla, Y., Trejo-Mardnez, D., Conde, R., & Corsi-Cabrera, M. (2012). Enhanced emotional reactivity after selective REM sleep deprivation in humans: An fMRI study. *Frontiers in Behavioral Neuroscience, 6,* 1–13.

Rosch, E. (1973). Natural categories. *Cognitive Psychology, 4,* 328–350.

Rosch, E., & Mervis, C. B. (1975). Family resemblances: Studies in the internal structure of categories. *Cognitive Psychology, 7,* 573–605.

Rosch, E., Mervis, C. B., Gray, W. D., Johnson, D. M., & Boyes-Braem, P. (1976). Basic objects in natural categories. *Cognitive Psychology, 8,* 382–439.

Rose, J. D. (2011). Diverse perspectives on the groupthink theory: A literary review. *Emerging Leadership Journeys, 4,* 37–57.

Rosen, J. (2014, November 10). The knowledge, London's legendary taxi-driver test, puts up a fight in the age of GPS. *The New York Times.* Retrieved from http://www.nytimes.com/2014/11/10/t-magazine/london-taxi-test-knowledge.html

Rosenblum, L. D. (2010). *See what I'm saying: The extraordinary powers of our five senses.* New York, NY: W. W. Norton.

Rosenhan, D. L. (1973). On being sane in insane places. *Science, 179,* 250–258.

Rosenkranz, M. A. (2007). Substance P at the nexus of mind and body in chronic inflammation and affective disorders. *Psychological Bulletin, 133,* 1007–1037.

Rosenman, R. H., Brand, R. J., Jenkins, D., Friedman, M., Straus, R., & Wurm, M. (1975). Coronary heart disease in the Western Collaborative Group Study: Final follow-up experience of 8½ years. *Journal of the American Medical Association, 233,* 872–877.

Rosenthal, R. (1965). *Clever Hans: A case study of scientific method, introduction to Clever Hans.* New York, NY: Holt, Rinehart & Winston.

Rosenthal, R. (2002a). Covert communication in classrooms, clinics, courtrooms, and cubicles. *American Psychologist, 57,* 839–849.

Rosenthal, R. (2002b). Experimenter and clinician effects in scientific inquiry and clinical practice. *Prevention & Treatment, 5,* 1–12.

Rosenthal, R. (2003). Covert communication in laboratories, classrooms, and the truly real world. *Current Directions in Psychological Science, 12,* 151–154.

Rosenthal, R., & Jacobson, L. (1966). Teachers' expectancies: Determinants of pupils' IQ gains. *Psychological Reports, 19,* 115–118.

Rosenthal, R., & Jacobson, L. (1968). *Pygmalion in the classroom: Teacher expectation and pupils' intellectual development.* New York, NY: Holt, Rinehart & Winston.

Rosenzweig, M. R. (1984). Experience, memory, and the brain. *American Psychologist, 39,* 365–376.

Roseth, C. J., Johnson, D. W., & Johnson, R. T. (2008). Promoting early adolescents' achievement and peer relationships: The effects of cooperative, competitive, and individualistic goal structures. *Psychological Bulletin, 134,* 223–246.

Rosky, J. W. (2013). The (f)utility of post-conviction polygraph testing. *Sexual Abuse, 25,* 259–281.

Ross, L. (1977). The intuitive psychologist and his shortcomings: Distortions in the attribution process. In L. Berkowitz (Ed.), *Advances in experimental social psychology* (Vol. 10, pp. 173–220). New York, NY: Academic Press.

Ross, L., Greene, D., & House, P. (1977). The "false consensus effect": An egocentric bias in social perception and attribution processes. *Journal of Experimental Social Psychology, 13,* 279–301.

Ross, L. D., Amabile, T. M., & Steinmetz, J. L. (1977). Social roles, social control, and biases in social-perception processes. *Journal of Personality and Social Psychology, 33,* 485–494.

Rossen, L. M., Ahrens, K. A., & Branum, A. M. (2017). Trends in risk of pregnancy loss among US women, 1990–2011 [Abstract]. *Paediatric and Perinatal Epidemiology, 32,* 19–29.

Rossion, B. (2014). Understanding face perception by means of prosopagnosia and neuroimaging. *Frontiers in Bioscience (Elite edition), 6,* 258–307.

Rosso, A., Mossey, J., & Lippa, C. F. (2008). Review: Caffeine: Neuroprotective functions in cognition and Alzheimer's disease. *American Journal of Alzheimer's Disease and Other Dementias, 23,* 417–422.

Rotge, J.-Y., Guehl, D., Dilharreguy, B., Tignol, J., Bioulac, B., Allard, M., . . . Aouizerate, B. (2009). Meta-analysis of brain volume changes in obsessive-compulsive disorder. *Biological Psychiatry, 65,* 75–83.

Roth, T. (2007). Insomnia: Definition, prevalence, etiology, and consequences. *Journal of Clinical Sleep Medicine, 3,* 7–10.

Rothbaum, B. O., Hodges, L., Smith, S., Lee, J. H., & Price, L. (2000). A controlled study of virtual reality exposure therapy for the fear of flying. *Journal of Consulting and Clinical Psychology, 68,* 1020–1026.

Rothbaum, B. O., Price, M., Jovanovic, T., Norrholm, S. D., Gerardi, M., Dunlop, B., . . . Ressler, K. J. (2014). A randomized, double-blind evaluation of D-cycloserine or alprazolam combined with virtual reality exposure therapy for posttraumatic stress disorder in Iraq and Afghanistan War veterans. *American Journal of Psychiatry, 171,* 640–648.

Rothbaum, F., Weisz, J., Pott, M., Miyake, K., & Morelli, G. (2000). Attachment and culture: Security in the United States and Japan. *American Psychologist, 55,* 1093–1104.

Rotter, J. B. (1966). Generalized expectancies for internal versus external control of reinforcement. *Psychological Monographs: General and Applied, 80,* 1–28.

Rotter, J. B. (1990). Internal versus external control of reinforcement: A case history of a variable. *American Psychologist, 45,* 489–493.

Rouder, J. N., & Morey, R. D. (2011). A Bayes factor meta-analysis of Bem's ESP claim. *Psychonomic Bulletin and Review, 18,* 682–689.

Routh, D. K., & Reisman, J. M. (2003). Clinical psychology. In D. K. Freedheim (Ed.), *Handbook of psychology: Vol. 1. History of psychology* (pp. 337–355). Hoboken, NJ: John Wiley & Sons.

Rowe, M. H. (2002). Trichromatic color vision in primates. *News in Physiological Sciences, 17,* 93–98.

Rowe, M. L. (2012). A longitudinal investigation of the role of quantity and quality of child-directed speech in vocabulary development. *Child Development, 83,* 1762–1774.

Rubin, Z., & Peplau, L. A. (1975). Who believes in a just world? *Journal of Social Issues, 31,* 65–89.

Ruglass, L. M., Hien, D. A., Hu, M. C., Campbell, A. N., Caldeira, N. A., Miele, G. M., & Chang, D. F. (2014). Racial/ethnic match and treatment outcomes for women with PTSD and substance use disorders receiving community-based treatment. *Community Mental Health Journal, 50,* 811–822.

Running, C. A., Craig, B. A., & Mattes, R. D. (2015). Oleogustus: The unique taste of fat. *Chemical Senses, 40,* 507–516. doi:10.1093/chemse/bjv036

Rupp, R. (2014, September 30). Are you a supertaster? *National Geographic.* Retrieved from http://theplate.nationalgeographic.com/2014/09/30/are-you-a-supertaster/

Rusbult, C. E. (1983). A longitudinal test of the investment model: The development (and deterioration) of satisfaction and commitment in heterosexual involvements. *Journal of Personality and Social Psychology, 45,* 101–117.

Rusbult, C. E., & Martz, J. M. (1995). Remaining in an abusive relationship: An investment model analysis of nonvoluntary dependence. *Personality and Social Psychology Bulletin, 21,* 558–571.

Ruscio, A. M., Stein, D. J., Chiu, W. T., & Kessler, R. C. (2010). The epidemiology of obsessive-compulsive disorder in the National Comorbidity Survey Replication. *Molecular Psychiatry, 15,* 53–63.

Rushton, J. P., & Jensen, A. R. (2010). Race and IQ: A theory-based review of the research in Richard Nisbett's *Intelligence and How to Get It. Open Psychology Journal, 3,* 9–35.

Ruxton, C. H. S. (2008). The impact of caffeine on mood, cognitive function, performance and hydration: A review of benefits and risks. *Nutrition Bulletin, 33,* 15–25.

Ryan, R. M., & Deci, E. L. (2017). *Self-determination theory: Basic psychological needs in motivation, development, and wellness.* New York, NY: Guilford.

Sabah, M., Mulcahy, J., & Zeman, A. (2012). Herpes simplex encephalitis. *British Medical Journal, 344,* e3166. doi:10.1136/bmj.e3166

Sabia, S., Dugravot, A., Dartigues, J.-F., Abell, J., Elbaz, A., Kivimäki, M., & Singh-Manoux, A. (2017). Physical activity, cognitive decline, and risk of dementia: 28 year follow-up of Whitehall II cohort study. *British Medical Journal, 357,* Article ID j2709.

Sachdeva, A., Choudhary, M., & Chandra, M. (2015). Alcohol withdrawal syndrome: Benzodiazepines and beyond. *Journal of Clinical and Diagnostic Research, 9,* VE01–VE07.

Sacks, O. (2007, September 24). The abyss. *The New Yorker.* Retrieved from http://www.newyorker.com/reporting/2007/09/24/070924fa_fact_sacks

Sagiv, M., Vogelaere, P. P., Soudry, M., & Ehrsam, R. (2000). Role of physical activity training in attenuation of height loss through aging. *Gerontology, 46,* 266–270.

Saha, S., Chant, D., Welham, J., & McGrath, J. (2005). A systematic review of the prevalence of schizophrenia. *PLoS Medicine, 2,* e141.

Saikia, G. (2017, April 19). Addiction to internet and social media on the rise. NewsBytes. Retrieved from https://www.newsbytesapp.com/timeline/Science/6273/37962/the-dark-world-of-internet-addiction

Sailor, K. A., Schinder, A. F., & Lledo, P. M. (2017). Adult neurogenesis beyond the niche: Its potential for driving brain plasticity. *Current Opinion in Neurobiology, 42,* 111–117.

Salam, M. (2017, August 16). Sperm count in Western men has dropped over 50 percent since 1973, paper finds. *The New York Times.* Retrieved from https://www.nytimes.com/2017/08/16/health/male-sperm-count-problem.html?mcubz=0&_r=0

Salk, R. H., Hyde, J. S., & Abramson, L. Y. (2017). Gender differences in depression in representative national samples: Meta-analyses of diagnoses and symptoms. *Psychological Bulletin, 143,* 783–822.

Salmon, C., Cuthbertson, A. M., & Figueredo, A. J. (2016). The relationship between birth order and prosociality: An evolutionary perspective. *Personality and Individual Differences, 96,* 18–22.

Salmon, P. (2001). Effects of physical exercise on anxiety, depression, and sensitivity to stress: A unifying theory. *Clinical Psychology Review, 21,* 33–61.

Salovey, P., Mayer, J. D., & Caruso, D. (2002). The positive psychology of emotional intelligence. In C. R. Snyder & S. J. Lopez (Eds.), *Handbook of positive psychology* (pp. 159–171). New York, NY: Oxford University Press.

Salthouse, T. A. (2006). Mental exercise and mental aging: Evaluating the validity of the "use it or lose it" hypothesis. *Perspectives on Psychological Science, 1,* 68–87.

Salva, O. R., Farroni, T., Regolin, L., Vallortigara, G., & Johnson, M. H. (2011). The evolution of social orienting: Evidence from chicks (*Gallus gallus*) and human newborns. *PLoS ONE, 6,* e18802. doi:10.1371/journal.pone.0018802

Samaha, A. (2014, August 7). The rise and fall of crime in New York City: A timeline. *The Village Voice.* Retrieved from https://www.villagevoice.com/2014/08/07/the-rise-and-fall-of-crime-in-new-york-city-a-timeline/

Samaha, M., & Hawi, N. S. (2016). Relationships among smartphone addiction, stress, academic performance, and satisfaction with life. *Computers in Human Behavior, 57,* 321–325.

Samhita, L., & Gross, H. J. (2013). The "Clever Hans phenomenon" revisited. *Communicative & Integrative Biology, 6,* e27122.

Sampasa-Kanyinga, H., & Lewis, R. F. (2015). Frequent use of social networking sites is associated with poor psychological functioning among children and adolescents. *Cyberpsychology, Behavior, and Social Networking, 18,* 380–385.

Sandin, S., Lichtenstein, P., Kuja-Halkola, R., Larsson, H., Hultman, C. M., & Reichenberg, A. (2014). The familial risk of autism. *Journal of the American Medical Association, 311,* 1770–1777.

Sansom-Daly, U. M., Peate, M., Wakefield, C. E., Bryant, R. A., & Cohn, R. (2012). A systematic review of psychological interventions for adolescents and young adults living with chronic illness. *Health Psychology, 31,* 380–393.

Saper, C. B., Scammell, T. E., & Lu, J. (2005). Hypothalamic regulation of sleep and circadian rhythms. *Nature, 437,* 1257–1263.

Sar, V. (2011). Epidemiology of dissociative disorders: An overview. *Epidemiology Research International, 2011.* http://dx.doi.org/10.1155/2011/404538

Sattler, J. M. (1990). *Assessment of children* (3rd ed.). San Diego, CA: Author.

Saunders, B., de Oliveira, L. F., da Silva, R. P., de Salles Painelli, V., Gonçalves, L. S., Yamaguchi, G., . . . Gualano, B. (2016). Placebo in sports nutrition: A proof-of-principle study involving caffeine supplementation. *Scandinavian Journal of Medicine & Science in Sports, 27,* 1240–1247.

Saunders, D. T., Roe, C. A., Smith, G., & Clegg, H. (2016). Lucid dreaming incidence: A quality effects meta-analysis of 50 years of research. *Consciousness and Cognition, 43,* 197–215.

Saxbe, D. E. (2017). Birth of a new perspective? A call for biopsychosocial research on childbirth. *Current Directions in Psychological Science, 26,* 81–86.

Scarr, S., & McCartney, K. (1983). How people make their own environments: A theory of genotype–environment effects. *Child Development, 54,* 424–435.

Schachner, A., & Hannon, E. E. (2011). Infant-directed speech drives social preferences in 5-month-old infants. *Developmental Psychology, 47,* 19–25.

Schachter, S., & Singer, J. E. (1962). Cognitive, social, and physiological determinants of emotional state. *Psychological Review, 69,* 379–399.

Schaefer, J. D., Caspi, A., Belsky, D. W., Harrington, H., Houts, R., Horwood, L. J., . . . Moffitt, T. E. (2017). Enduring mental health: Prevalence and prediction. *Journal of Abnormal Psychology, 126,* 212–224.

Schaie, K. W. (1993). The Seattle longitudinal studies of adult intelligence. *Current Directions in Psychological Science, 2,* 171–175.

Schaie, K. W. (2008). Historical processes and patterns of cognitive aging. In S. M. Hofer & D. F. Alwin (Eds.), *Handbook of cognitive aging: Interdisciplinary perspectives.* Thousand Oaks, CA: Sage.

Schalock, R. L., Borthwick-Duffy, S., Bradley, V. J., Bunting, W. H. E., Coulter, D. L., & Craig, E. M. (2010). *Intellectual disability: Definition classification, and systems of supports* (11th ed.). Washington, DC: American Association on Intellectual and Developmental Disabilities.

Scheffer, P. G., van der Schoot, C. E., Page-Christiaens, G. C., Bossers, B., van Erp, F., & de Haas, M. (2010). Reliability of fetal sex determination using maternal plasma. *Obstetrics & Gynecology, 115,* 117–126.

Scherer, A. M., Windschitl, P. D., O'Rourke, J., & Smith, A. R. (2012). Hoping for more: The influence of outcome desirability on information seeking and predictions about relative quantities. *Cognition, 125,* 113–117.

Schermer, J. A., Martin, R. A., Vernon, P. A., Martin, N. G., Conde, L. C., Statham, D., & Lynskeye, M. T. (2017). Lonely people tend to make fun of themselves: A behavior genetic analysis of humor styles and loneliness. *Personality and Individual Differences, 117,* 71–73.

Schickedanz, A., Dreyer, B. P., & Halfon, N. (2015). Childhood poverty: Understanding and preventing the adverse impacts of a most-prevalent risk to pediatric health and well-being. *Pediatric Clinics of North America, 62,* 1111–1135.

Schiffman, S. S. (1997). Taste and smell losses in normal aging and disease. *Journal of American Medical Association, 278,* 1357–1362.

Schiller, C. E., Meltzer-Brody, S., & Rubinow, D. R. (2015). The role of reproductive hormones in postpartum depression. *CNS Spectrums, 20,* 48–59.

Schilling, O. K., Wahl, H. W., Boerner, K., Horowitz, A., Reinhardt, J. P., Cimarolli, V. R., . . . Heckhausen, J. (2016). Developmental regulation with progressive vision loss: Use of control strategies and affective well-being. *Developmental Psychology, 52,* 679–694.

Schizophrenia Working Group of the Psychiatric Genomics Consortium. (2014). Biological insights from 108 schizophrenia-associated genetic loci. *Nature, 511,* 421–427.

Schlaepfer, T. E., Bewernick, B. H., Kayser, S., Mädler, B., & Coenen, V. A. (2013). Rapid effects of deep brain stimulation for treatment-resistant major depression. *Biological Psychiatry, 73,* 1204–1212.

Schlaug, G. (2015). Musicians and music making as a model for the study of brain plasticity. *Progress in Brain Research, 217,* 37–55.

Schleppenbach, M., Flevares, L. M., Sims, L. M., & Perry, M. (2007). Teachers' responses to student mistakes in Chinese and U.S. mathematics classrooms. *The Elementary School Journal, 108,* 131–147.

Schlich, T. (2015, May). Cutting the body to cure the mind. *The Lancet, 2,* 390–392.

Schlichting, A., & Bäuml, K. H. T. (2017). Brief wakeful resting can eliminate directed forgetting. *Memory, 25,* 254–260.

Schmaal, L., Hibar, D. P., Sämann, P. G., Hall, G. B., Baune, B. T., Jahanshad, N., . . . Vernooij, M. W. (2017). Cortical abnormalities in adults and adolescents with major depression based on brain scans from 20 cohorts worldwide in the ENIGMA Major Depressive Disorder Working Group. *Molecular Psychiatry, 22,* 900–909.

Schmaal, L., Veltman, D. J., van Erp, T. G., Sämann, P. G., Frodl, T., Jahanshad, N., . . . Vernooij, M. W. (2016). Subcortical brain alterations in major depressive disorder: Findings from the ENIGMA Major Depressive Disorder working group. *Molecular Psychiatry, 21,* 806–812.

Schmaltz, R., & Lilienfeld, S. O. (2014). Hauntings, homeopathy, and the Hopkinsville Goblins: Using pseudoscience to teach scientific thinking. *Frontiers in Psychology, 5,* 1–5.

Schmerling, R. H. (2017, August). Right brain/left brain, right? https://www.health.harvard.edu/blog/right-brainleft-brain-right-2017082512222

Schmidt, H. G., Peeck, V. H., Paas, F., & van Breukelen, G. J. P. (2000). Remembering the street names of one's childhood neighbourhood: A study of very long-term retention. *Memory, 8,* 37–49.

Schmidt-Daffy, M. (2011). Modeling automatic threat detection: Development of a face-in-the-crowd task. *Emotion, 11,* 153–168.

Schmitt, D. P., Realo, A., Voracek, M., & Allik, J. (2008). Why can't a man be more like a woman? Sex differences in Big Five personality traits across 55 cultures. *Journal of Personality and Social Psychology, 94,* 168–182.

Schnall, S., Roper, J., & Fessler, D. M. (2010). Elevation leads to altruistic behavior. *Psychological Science, 21,* 315–320.

Schneidman, E. S. (1973). *Deaths of man.* New York, NY: Quadrangle/The New York Times Book Co.

Schneps, M. H., Brockmole, J. R., Sonnert, G., & Pomplun, M. (2012). History of reading struggles linked to enhanced learning in low spatial frequency scenes. *PLoS One, 7*(4), e35724.

Schnider, A., Guggisberg, A., Nahum, L., Gabriel, D., & Morand, S. (2010). Dopaminergic modulation of rapid reality adaptation in thinking. *Neuroscience, 167,* 583–587.

Schoemaker, M. J., Jones, M. E., Wright, L. B., Griffin, J., McFadden, E., Ashworth, A., & Swerdlow, A. J. (2016). Psychological stress, adverse life events and breast cancer incidence: A cohort investigation in 106,000 women in the United Kingdom. *Breast Cancer Research, 18,* 72. doi:10.1186/s13058-016-0733-1

Schoenborn, C. A., Adams, P. F., & Peregoy, J. A. (2013). Health behaviors of adults: United States, 2008–2010. *Vital Health Stat, 10*(257), 1–184.

Schoene-Bake, J. C., Parpaley, Y., Weber, B., Panksepp, J., Hurwitz, T. A., & Coenen, V. A. (2010, December). Tractographic analysis of historical lesion surgery for depression. *Neuropsychopharmacology, 35*(13), 2553–2563.

Schreiner, A. M., & Dunn, M. E. (2012). Residual effects of cannabis use on neurocognitive performance after prolonged abstinence: A meta-analysis. *Experimental and Clinical Psychopharmacology, 20,* 420–429.

Schroeder, G. D., Kepler, C. K., & Vaccaro, A. R. (2016). The use of cell transplantation in spinal cord injuries. *Journal of the American Academy of Orthopaedic Surgeons, 24,* 266–275.

Schulenberg, J. E., Johnston, L. D., O'Malley, P. M., Bachman, J. G., Miech, R. A., & Patrick, M. E. (2017). *Monitoring the Future national survey results on drug use, 1975–2016: Vol. 2. College students and adults ages 19–55.* Ann Arbor, MI: Institute for Social Research, The University of Michigan. Available at http://monitoringthefuture.org/pubs.html#monographs

Schultheiss, O. C., & Schiepe-Tiska, A. (2013). The role of the dorsoanterior striatum in implicit motivation: The case of the need for power. *Frontiers in Human Neuroscience, 7,* 141.

Schultz, D. P., & Schultz, S. E. (2013). *Theories of personality* (10th ed.). Belmont, CA: Wadsworth, Cengage Learning.

Schultz, D. P., & Schultz, S. E. (2016). *A history of modern psychology* (11th ed.). Belmont, CA: Wadsworth, Cengage Learning.

Schultz, D. P., & Schultz, S. E. (2017). *Theories of personality* (11th ed.). Boston, MA: Cengage Learning.

Schumacher, S., Miller, R., Fehm, L., Kirschbaum, C., Fydrich, T., & Ströhle, A. (2015). Therapists' and patients' stress responses during graduated versus flooding in vivo exposure in the treatment of specific phobia: A preliminary observational study. *Psychiatry Research, 230,* 668–675.

Schutte, N. M., Nederend, I., Hudziak, J. J., de Geus, E. J., & Bartels, M. (2016). Differences in adolescent physical fitness: A multivariate approach and meta-analysis. *Behavior Genetics, 46,* 217–227.

Schwartz, B. L. (2012). *Tip-of-the-tongue states: Phenomenology, mechanism, and lexical retrieval.* Mahwah, NJ: Psychology Press.

Schwartz, C., Meisenhelder, J. B., Yunsheng, M., & Reed, G. (2003). Altruistic social interest behaviors are associated with better mental health. *Psychosomatic Medicine, 65,* 778–785.

Schwartz, C. E., Keyl, P. M., Marcum, J. P., & Bode, R. (2009). Helping others shows differential benefits on health and well-being for male and female teens. *Journal of Happiness Studies, 10,* 431–448.

Schwartz, S. J. (2001). The evolution of Eriksonian and Neo-Eriksonian identity theory and research: A review and integration. *Identity: An International Journal of Theory and Research, 1,* 7–58.

Schwartz, S. J., Benet-Martínez, V., Knight, G. P., Unger, J. B., Zamboanga, B. L., Des Rosiers, S. E., . . . Szapocznik, J. (2014). Effects of language of assessment on the measurement of acculturation: Measurement equivalence and cultural frame switching. *Psychological Assessment, 26,* 100–114.

Schweinsburg, A. D., Brown, S. A., & Tapert, S. F. (2008). The influence of marijuana use on neurocognitive functioning in adolescents. *Current Drug Abuse Reviews, 1,* 99–111.

Schweizer, A., Brunner, F., Handford, C., & Richter-Appelt, H. (2014). Gender experience and satisfaction with gender allocation in adults with diverse intersex conditions (divergences of sex development, DSD). *Psychology & Sexuality, 5,* 56–82.

Scoboria, A., Wade, K. A., Lindsay, D. S., Azad, T., Strange, D., Ost, J., & Hyman, I. E. (2017). A mega-analysis of memory reports from eight peer-reviewed false memory implantation studies. *Memory, 25,* 146–163.

Scott, A. J., Webb, T. L., & Rowse, G. (2015). Self-help interventions for psychosis: A meta-analysis. *Clinical Psychology Review, 39,* 96–112.

Scott, S. B., Rhoades, G. K., Stanley, S. M., Allen, E. S., & Markman, H. J. (2013). Reasons for divorce and recollections of premarital intervention: Implications for improving relationship education. *Couple and Family Psychology: Research and Practice, 2,* 131–145.

Scott, S. K., Blank, C. C., Rosen, S., & Wise, R. J. S. (2000). Identification of a pathway for intelligible speech in the left temporal lobe. *Brain, 123,* 2400–2406.

Scoville, W. B., & Milner, B. (1957). Loss of recent memory after bilateral hippocampal lesions. *Journal of Neurology, Neurosurgery, & Psychiatry, 20,* 11–21.

Scullin, M. K., & Bliwise, D. L. (2015). Sleep, cognition, and normal aging integrating a half century of multidisciplinary research. *Perspectives on Psychological Science, 10,* 97–137.

Scully, J. A., Tosi, H., & Banning, K. (2000). Life event checklists: Revisiting the Social Readjustment Rating Scale after 30 years. *Educational and Psychological Measurement, 60,* 864–876.

Searight, H. R., & Gafford, J. (2005). Cultural diversity at the end of life: Issues and guidelines for family physicians. *American Family Physician, 71,* 515–522.

Searleman, A. (2007, March 12). Is there such a thing as a photographic memory? And if so, can it be learned? *Scientific American Online.* Retrieved from http://www.scientificamerican.com/article/is-there-such-a-thing-as/

Sedgewick, J. R., Flath, M. E., & Elias, L. J. (2017). Presenting your best self(ie): The Influence of gender on vertical orientation of selfies on Tinder. *Frontiers in Psychology, 8.* doi:10.3389/fpsyg.2017.00604

Seery, M. D. (2011). Resilience: A silver lining to experiencing adverse life events? *Current Directions in Psychological Science, 20,* 390–394.

Segal, D. L., Coolidge, F. L., & Mizuno, H. (2007). Defense mechanism differences between younger and older adults: A cross-sectional investigation. *Aging and Mental Health, 11,* 415–422.

Segal, N. (1984). Cooperation, competition, and altruism within twin sets: A reappraisal. *Ethology and Sociobiology, 5,* 163–177.

Segal, N. L. (1999). *Entwined lives: Twins and what they tell us about human behavior.* New York, NY: Dutton/Penguin Books.

Segal, N. L. (2012). *Born together—reared apart: The landmark Minnesota Twin Study.* Cambridge, MA: Harvard University Press.

Segal, N. L., & Cortez, F. A. (2014). Born in Korea—adopted apart: Behavioral development of monozygotic twins raised in the United States and France. *Personality and Individual Differences, 70,* 97–104.

Segall, M. H., Campbell, D. T., & Herskovits, M. J. (1968). The influence of culture on visual perception. In H. Toch & C. Smith (Eds.), *Social perception* (pp. 1–5). Oxford, UK: Bobbs-Merrill.

Segerstrom, S. C., & Miller, G. E. (2004). Psychological stress and the human immune system: A meta-analytic study of 30 years of inquiry. *Psychological Bulletin, 130,* 601–630.

Segraves, R. T. (2010). Considerations for a better definition of male orgasmic disorder in *DSM V. Journal of Sexual Medicine, 7,* 690–699.

Seidel, J. (2018). Convergence of placenta biology and genetic risk for schizophrenia. *Nature Medicine, 24*(6), 792–801.

Seinfeld, S., Bergstrom, I., Pomes, A., Arroyo-Palacios, J., Vico, F., Slater, M., & Sanchez-Vives, M. V. (2016). Influence of music on anxiety induced by fear of heights in virtual reality. *Frontiers in Psychology, 6.* doi:10.3389/fpsyg.2015.01969

Seligman, M. E. P. (1975). *Helplessness: On depression, development, and death.* San Francisco, CA: W. H. Freeman.

Seligman, M. E. P. (1995). The effectiveness of psychotherapy: The *Consumer Reports* study. *American Psychologist, 50,* 965–974.

Seligman, M. E. P., & Csikszentmihalyi, M. (2000). Positive psychology: An introduction. *American Psychologist, 55,* 5–14.

Seligman, M. E. P., & Maier, S. F. (1967). Failure to escape traumatic shock. *Journal of Experimental Psychology, 74,* 1–9.

Seligman, M. E. P., & Steen, T. A. (2005). Positive psychology progress. *American Psychologist, 60,* 410–421.

Seltenrich, N. (2015, October). POPs and pubertal timing: Evidence of delayed development. *Environmental Health Perspectives, 123,* A266.

Selye, H. (1936). A syndrome produced by diverse nocuous agents. *Nature, 138,* 32.

Selye, H. (1953). The General-Adaptation-Syndrome in its relationships to neurology, psychology, and psychopathology. In A. Weider (Ed.), *Contributions toward medical psychology: Vol. 1. Theory and psychodiagnostic methods* (pp. 234–274). New York, NY: Ronald Press.

Selye, H. (1956). *The stress of life.* New York, NY: McGraw-Hill.

Selye, H. (1976). Forty years of stress research: Principal remaining problems and misconceptions. *Canadian Medical Association Journal, 115,* 53–56.

Selye, H., & Fortier, C. (1950). Adaptive reaction to stress. *Psychosomatic Medicine, 12,* 149–157.

Semega, J. L., Fontenot, K. R., & Kollar, M. A. (2017, September). Income and poverty in the United States: 2016. United States Census Bureau. Retrieved from https://www.census.gov/content/dam/Census/library/publications/2017/demo/P60-259.pdf

Seri, I., & Evans, J. (2008). Limits of viability: Definition of the gray zone. *Journal of Perinatology, 28,* S4–S8.

Serrano, R. A. (2002, November 26). Hate crimes against Muslims soar, report says. *Los Angeles Times.* Retrieved from http://articles.latimes.com/2002/nov/26/nation/na-hate26

Seubert, J., Freiherr, J., Djordjevic, J., & Lundström, J. N. (2013). Statistical-localization of human olfactory cortex. *Neuroimage, 66,* 333–342.

Shackelford, T. K., & Liddle, J. R. (2014). Understanding the mind from an evolutionary perspective: An overview of evolutionary psychology. *Wiley Interdisciplinary Reviews: Cognitive Science, 5,* 247–260.

Shah, A. K., & Oppenheimer, D. M. (2008). Heuristics made easy: An effort-reduction framework. *Psychological Bulletin, 134,* 207–222.

Shahani, A. (2017, June 9). Changing pay rates keep Uber drivers on the road longer. NPR. Retrieved from http://www.npr.org/2017/06/09/532196932/changing-pay-rates-keep-uber-drivers-on-the-road-longer

Shahkhase, M. S., Gharaei, A., Fathi, M., Yaghoobi, H., & Bayazi, M. H. (2014). The study of hypnosis effectiveness in the treatment of headaches. *Reef Resources Assessment and Management Technical Paper, 40,* 426–432.

Shakeshaft, N. G., Trzaskowski, M., McMillan, A., Krapohl, E., Simpson, M. A., Reichenberg, A., . . . Plomin, R. (2015). Thinking positively: The genetics of high intelligence. *Intelligence, 48,* 123–132.

Shams, M. (Mansoor Shams). (2016, December 2). Stories of Muslims in US Armed Forces (Ibrahim Hashi) [Video file]. Retrieved from https://www.youtube.com/watch?v=EV38RkjljhA

Shapiro, D. H., Jr., Schwartz, C. E., & Astin, J. A. (1996). Controlling ourselves, controlling our world: Psychology's role in understanding positive and negative consequences of seeking and gaining control. *American Psychologist, 51,* 1213–1230.

Shapiro, L. A. S., & Margolin, G. (2014). Growing up wired: Social networking sites and adolescent psychosocial development. *Clinical Child and Family Psychology Review 17*(1), 1–18. doi:10.1007/s10567-013-0135-1

Shargorodsky, J., Curhan, S. G., Curhan, G. C., & Eavey, R. (2010). Change in prevalence of hearing loss in US adolescents. *Journal of the American Medical Association, 304,* 772–778.

Sharp, C., & Kim, S. (2015). Recent advances in the developmental aspects of borderline personality disorder. *Current Psychiatry Reports, 17.* doi:10.1007/s11920-015-0556-2

Shaw, J. (2016, January 8). 9 things you probably didn't know about Sigmund Freud [Web log post]. Retrieved from https://blogs.scientificamerican.com/mind-guest-blog/9-things-you-probably-didn-t-know-about-sigmund-freud/

Shaw, J., & Porter, S. (2015). Constructing rich false memories of committing crime. *Psychological Science, 26,* 291–301.

Shaywitz, S. E. (1996). Dyslexia. *Scientific American, 275,* 98–104.

Shaywitz, S. E. (2003). *Overcoming dyslexia: A new and complete science-based program for reading problems at any level.* New York, NY: Vintage Books.

Shaywitz, S. E., & Shaywitz, B. A. (2005). Dyslexia (specific reading disability). *Biological Psychiatry, 57,* 1301–1309.

Shea, B. (n.d.). Karl Popper: Philosophy of science. In *Internet encyclopedia of philosophy.* Retrieved from http://www.iep.utm.edu/pop-sci/

Shearer, A., Hunt, M., Chowdhury, M., & Nicol, L. (2016). Effects of a brief mindfulness meditation intervention on student stress and heart rate variability. *International Journal of Stress Management, 23,* 232–254.

Shedler, J. (2010). The efficacy of psychodynamic psychotherapy. *American Psychologist, 63,* 98–109.

Sheikh, K. (2017, February/March). Digital hypocrisy. *Scientific American Mind, 28,* 10–11.

Sheikh, K. (2017, February/March). "Super agers" have brains that look young. *Scientific American Mind, 28,* 13.

Sheldon, P., & Bryant, K. (2016). Instagram: Motives for its use and relationship to narcissism and contextual age. *Computers in Human Behavior, 58,* 89–97.

Shelton, J. F., Geraghty, E. M., Tancredi, D. J., Delwiche, L. D., Schmidt, R. J., Ritz, B., . . . Hertz-Picciotto, I. (2014). Neurodevelopmental disorders and prenatal residential proximity to agricultural pesticides: The CHARGE study. *Environmental Health Perspectives, 122,* 1103–1109.

Shelton, K. H., & van den Bree, M. B. M. (2010). The moderating effects of pubertal timing on the longitudinal associations between parent-child relationships' quality and adolescent substance use. *Journal of Research on Adolescence, 20,* 1044–1064.

Shepard, R. N., & Metzler, J. (1971). Mental rotation of three-dimensional objects. *Science, 171,* 701–703.

Sherman, S. M., Buckley, T. P., Baena, E., & Ryan, L. (2016). Caffeine enhances memory performance in young adults during their non-optimal time of day. *Frontiers in Psychology, 7.* doi:10.3389/fpsyg.2016.01764

Shernoff, D. J., Csikszentmihalyi, M., Shneider, B., & Shernoff, E. S. (2003). Student engagement in high school classrooms from the perspective of flow theory. *School Psychology Quarterly, 18,* 158–176.

Sherwood, L. (2016). *Human physiology: From cells to systems* (9th ed.). Boston, MA: Cengage Learning.

Shi, F., Yap, P. T., Wu, G., Jia, H., Gilmore, J. H., Lin, W., & Shen, D. (2011). Infant brain atlases from neonates to 1- and 2-year-olds. *PLoS One, 6.* doi:10.1371/journal.pone.0018746

Shiban, Y., Diemer, J., Müller, J., Brütting-Schick, J., Pauli, P., & Mühlberger, A. (2017). Diaphragmatic breathing during virtual reality exposure therapy for aviophobia: Functional coping strategy or avoidance behavior? A pilot study. *BMC Psychiatry, 17(1),* 29. doi:10.1186/s12888-016-1181-2

Shiban, Y., Schelhorn, I., Pauli, P., & Mühlberger, A. (2015). Effect of combined multiple contexts and multiple stimuli exposure in spider phobia: A randomized clinical trial in virtual reality. *Behaviour Research and Therapy, 71,* 45–53.

Shorter, E. (2015). The history of nosology and the rise of the *Diagnostic and Statistical Manual of Mental Disorders. Dialogues in Clinical Neuroscience, 17,* 59–67.

Shou, H., Yang, Z., Satterthwaite, T. D., Cook, P. A., Bruce, S. E., Shinohara, R. T., . . . Sheline, Y. I. (2017). Cognitive behavioral therapy increases amygdala connectivity with the cognitive control network in both MDD and PTSD. *NeuroImage: Clinical, 14,* 464–470.

Shultz, J. M., Thoresen, S., & Galea, S. (2017). The Las Vegas shootings—underscoring key features of the firearm epidemic. *JAMA, 318,* 1753–1754.

Siclari, F., Baird, B., Perogamvros, L., Bernardi, G., LaRocque, J. J., Riedner, B., . . . Tononi, G. (2017). The neural correlates of dreaming. *Nature Neuroscience, 20,* 872–878.

Siegel, J. M. (2005). Clues to the functions of mammalian sleep. *Nature, 437,* 1264–1271.

Siegel, J. M. (2008). Do all animals sleep? *Trends in Neurosciences, 31,* 208–213.

Sierp, A., & Karner, C. (2017). National stereotypes in the context of the European crisis. *National Identities, 19.* Retrieved from http://dx.doi.org/10.1080/14608944.2016.1209646

Silber, M. H., Ancoli-Israel, S., Bonnet, M. H., Chokroverty, S., Grigg-Damberger, M. M., Hirshkowitz, M., . . . Pressman, M. R. (2007). The visual scoring of sleep in adults. *Journal of Clinical Sleep Medicine, 3*(2), 121–131.

Sili, U., Kaya, A., Mert, A., & HSV Encephalitis Study Group. (2014). Herpes simplex virus encephalitis: Clinical manifestations, diagnosis and outcome in 106 adult patients. *Journal of Clinical Virology, 60,* 112–118.

Silva, C. E., & Kirsch, I. (1992). Interpretive sets, expectancy, fantasy proneness, and dissociation predictors of hypnotic response. *Journal of Personality and Social Psychology, 63,* 847–856.

Simion, F., & Di Giorgio, E. (2015). Face perception and processing in early infancy: Inborn predispositions and developmental changes. *Frontiers in Psychology, 6.* doi:10.3389/fpsyg.2015.00969

Simms, A., & Nichols, T. (2014). Social loafing: A review of the literature. *Journal of Management Policy and Practice, 15,* 58–67.

Simon, S. (2015, January 16). 6 Steps to help lower your cancer risk. American Cancer Society. Retrieved from http://www.cancer.org/cancer/news/features/6-steps-to-help-lower-your-cancer-risk

Simons, D. J. (2010). Monkeying around with the gorillas in our midst: Familiarity with an inattentional-blindness task does not improve the detection of unexpected events. *i-Perception, 1,* 3–6.

Simonton, D. K. (2000). Creativity: Cognitive, personal, developmental, and social aspects. *American Psychologist, 55,* 151–158.

Simonton, D. K. (2012, November/December). The science of genius. *Scientific American Mind, 23,* 35–41.

Simpson, J. A., & Rholes, W. S. (2010). Attachment and relationships: Milestones and future directions. *Journal of Social and Personal Relationships, 27,* 173–180.

Singh, L., Nestor, S., Parikh, C., & Yull, A. (2009). Influences of infant-directed speech on early word recognition. *Infancy, 14,* 654–666.

Singh, P. B., Hummel, T., Gerber, J. C., Landis, B. N., & Iannilli, E. (2015). Cerebral processing of umami: A pilot study on the effects of familiarity. *Brain Research, 1614,* 67–74.

Singh-Manoux, A., Kivimaki, M., Glymour, M. M., Elbaz, A., Berr, C., Ebmeier, K. P., . . . Dugravot, A. (2012). Timing of onset of cognitive decline: Results from Whitehall II prospective cohort study. *British Medical Journal, 334,* 1–8.

Sinha, A., Hurakadli, M., & Yadav, P. (2015). Botox and derma fillers: The twin face of cosmetic dentistry. *International Journal of Contemporary Dental and Medical Reviews, 2015.* doi:10.15713/ins.ijcdmr.27

Sinn, D. L., & Moltschaniwskyj, N. A. (2005). Personality traits in dumpling squid (*Euprymna Tasmania*): Context-specific traits and their correlation with biological characteristics. *Journal of Comparative Psychology, 119,* 99–110.

Sio, U. N., & Ormerod, T. C. (2009). Does incubation enhance problem solving? A meta-analytic review. *Psychological Bulletin, 135,* 94–120.

Sisti, D. A., Segal, A. G., & Emanuel, E. J. (2015). Improving long-term psychiatric care: Bring back the asylum. *Journal of the American Medical Association, 313,* 243–244.

Sivacek, J., & Crano, W. D. (1982). Vested interest as a moderator of attitude-behavior consistency. *Journal of Personality and Social Psychology, 43,* 210–221.

Skeem, J., Kennealy, P., Monahan, J., Peterson J., & Appelbaum, P. (2016). Psychosis uncommonly and inconsistently precedes violence among high-risk individuals. *Clinical Psychological Science, 4,* 40–49.

Skeldon, A. C., Derks, G., & Dijk, D. J. (2016). Modelling changes in sleep timing and duration across the lifespan: Changes in circadian rhythmicity or sleep homeostasis? *Sleep Medicine Reviews, 28,* 92–103.

Skinner, B. F. (1953). *Science and human behavior.* New York, NY: Macmillan.

Skinner, B. F. (1956). A case history in scientific method. *American Psychologist, 11,* 221–233.

Skinner, B. F. (1957). *Verbal behavior.* New York, NY: Macmillan.

Skinner, B. F. (1976). *Particulars of my life.* New York, NY: Knopf.

Skinner, N. F. (2009). Academic folk wisdom: Fact, fiction and falderal. *Psychology Learning and Teaching, 8,* 46–50.

Skoog, G., & Skoog, I. (1999). A 20-year follow-up of patients with obsessive compulsive disorder. *Archives of General Psychiatry, 56,* 121–127.

Slaney, K. L., & Racine, T. P. (2011). On the ambiguity of concept use in psychology: Is the concept "concept" a useful concept? *Journal of Theoretical and Philosophical Psychology, 31,* 73–89.

Slatcher, R. B., & Robles, T. F. (2012). Preschoolers' everyday conflict at home and diurnal cortisol patterns. *Health Psychology, 31,* 834–838. doi:10.1037/a0026774

Slavich, G. M. (2016). Life stress and health: A review of conceptual issues and recent findings. *Teaching of Psychology, 43,* 346–355.

Slepecky, M., Kotianova, A., Prasko, J., Majercak, I., Gyorgyova, E., Kotian, M., . . . Tonhajzerova, I. (2017). Which psychological, psychophysiological, and anthropometric factors are connected with life events, depression, and quality of life in patients with cardiovascular disease. *Neuropsychiatric Disease and Treatment, 13,* 2093–2104.

Slife, B. D. (1990). Introduction and overview of the special issue on Aristotle. *Theoretical & Philosophical Psychology, 10,* 3–6.

Slobodchikoff, C. N., Paseka, A., & Verdolin, J. L. (2008). Prairie dog alarm calls encode labels about predator colors. *Animal Cognition, 12,* 435–443.

Slotema, C. W., Blom, J. D., Hoek, H. W., & Sommer, I. E. C. (2010). Should we expand the toolbox of psychiatric treatment methods to include Repetitive Transcranial Magnetic Stimulation (rTMS)? A meta-analysis of the efficacy of rTMS in psychiatric disorders. *Journal of Clinical Psychiatry, 71,* 873–884.

Sloter, E., Schmid, T. E., Marchetti, F., Eskenazi, B., Nath, J., & Wyrobek, A. J. (2006). Quantitative effects of male age on sperm motion. *Human Reproduction, 21,* 2868–2875.

Slovic, P., & Weber, E. U. (2002, April). Perception of risk posed by extreme events. Paper presented at Conference on Risk Management Strategies in an Uncertain World, Palisades, NY.

Small, B. J., Dixon, R. A., McArdle, J. J., & Grimm, K. J. (2012). Do changes in lifestyle engagement moderate cognitive decline in normal aging? Evidence from the Victoria Longitudinal Study. *Neuropsychology, 26,* 144–155. doi:10.1037/a0026579

Smink, F. R., van Hoeken, D., & Hoek, H. W. (2012). Epidemiology of eating disorders: Incidence, prevalence and mortality rates. *Current Psychiatry Reports, 14,* 406–414.

Smith, C. N., & Squire, L. R. (2009). Medial temporal lobe activity during retrieval of semantic memory is related to the age of the memory. *Journal of Neuroscience, 29,* 930–938.

Smith, D. (2001). Shock and disbelief. *Atlantic Monthly, 287,* 79–90.

Smith, M. (2016, July 13). Can social media help prevent opioid abuse? *Science.* Retrieved from http://www.sciencemag.org/news/2016/07/can-social-media-help-prevent-opioid-abuse

Smith, S. M., Glenberg, A. M., & Bjork, R. A. (1978). Environmental context and human memory. *Memory and Cognition, 6,* 342–353.

Smith, T. W., Birmingham, W., & Uchino, B. N. (2012). Evaluative threat and ambulatory blood pressure: Cardiovascular effects of social stress in daily experience. *Health Psychology, 31,* 763–766.

Smith, T. W., & MacKenzie, J. (2006). Personality and risk of physical illness. *Annual Review of Clinical Psychology, 2,* 435–467.

Smith, T. W., & Ruiz, J. M. (2002). Psychosocial influences on the development and course of coronary heart disease: Current status and implications for research and practice. *Journal of Consulting and Clinical Psychology, 70,* 548–568.

Smrt, D. L., & Karau, S. J. (2011). Protestant work ethic moderates social loafing. *Group Dynamics: Theory, Research, and Practice, 15,* 267–274.

Sniekers, S., Stringer, S., Watanabe, K., Jansen, P. R., Coleman, J. R., Krapohl, E., . . . Amin, N. (2017). Genome-wide association meta-analysis of 78,308 individuals identifies new loci and genes influencing human intelligence. *Nature Genetics, 49,* 1107–1112.

Snyder, C. R., Ilardi, S. S., Cheavens, J., Michael, S. T., Yamhure, L., & Sympson, S. (2000). The role of hope in cognitive-behavior therapies. *Cognitive Therapy and Research, 24,* 747–762.

Snyder, T. D., de Brey, C., and Dillow, S. A. (2018). *Digest of education statistics 2016* (NCES 2017-094). Washington, DC: National Center for Education Statistics, Institute of Education Sciences, U.S. Department of Education. Retrieved from https://nces.ed.gov/pubs2017/2017094.pdf

Solivan, A. E., Wallace, M. E., Kaplan, K. C., & Harville, E. W. (2015). Use of a resiliency framework to examine pregnancy and birth outcomes among adolescents: A qualitative study. *Families, Systems, & Health, 33,* 349–355.

Solms, M. (2006, April/May). Freud returns. *Scientific American,* 82–88.

Solomon, B. C., & Jackson, J. J. (2014). The long reach of one's spouse: Spouses' personality influences occupational success. *Psychological Science, 25,* 2189–2198.

Solomon, S. G., & Lennie, P. (2007). The machinery of color vision. *Nature Reviews Neuroscience, 8,* 276–286.

Sommer, I. E., & Neggers, S. F. W. (2014). Repetitive transcranial magnetic stimulation as a treatment for auditory hallucinations. *Neuropsychopharmacology Reviews, 39,* 239–240.

Song, C., & Knöpfel, T. (2016). Optogenetics enlightens neuroscience drug discovery. *Nature Reviews Drug Discovery, 15,* 97–109.

Song, J., Bergen, S. E., Di Florio, A., Karlsson, R., Charney, A., Ruderfer, D. M., . . . Forty, L. (2016). Genome-wide association study identifies SESTD1 as a novel risk gene for lithium-responsive bipolar disorder. *Molecular Psychiatry, 21,* 1290–1297.

Sørensen, K., Aksglaede, L., Petersen, J. H., & Juul, A. (2010). Recent changes in pubertal timing in healthy Danish boys: Associations with Body Mass Index. *Journal of Clinical Endocrinology & Metabolism, 95,* 263–270.

Sorhagen, N. S. (2013). Early teacher expectations disproportionately affect poor children's high school performance. *Journal of Educational Psychology, 105,* 465–477.

Sorkin, N., Rosenblatt, A., Cohen, E., Ohana, O., Stolovitch, C., & Dotan, G. (2016). Comparison of Ishihara booklet with color vision smartphone applications. *Optometry and Vision Science, 93,* 667–672.

Sorrells, S. F., Paredes, M. F., Cebrian-Silla, A., Sandoval, K., Qi, D., Kelley, K. W., . . . Chang, E. F. (2018). Human hippocampal neurogenesis drops sharply in children to undetectable levels in adults. *Nature, 555,* 377–381.

Soto, C. J. (2016). The Little Six personality dimensions from early childhood to early adulthood: Mean-level age and gender differences in parents' reports. *Journal of Personality, 84,* 409–422.

Soto, C. J., & John, O. P. (2017). The next Big Five Inventory (BFI-2): Developing and assessing a hierarchical model with 15 facets to enhance bandwidth, fidelity, and predictive power. *Journal of Personality and Social Psychology, 113,* 117–143.

Soto, C. J., & Tackett, J. L. (2015). Personality traits in childhood and adolescence structure, development, and outcomes. *Current Directions in Psychological Science, 24,* 358–362.

Sparling, J., Wilder, D. A., Kondash, J., Boyle, M., & Compton, M. (2011). Effects of interviewer behavior on accuracy of children's responses. *Journal of Applied Behavior Analysis, 44,* 587–592.

Speakman, J. R., Levitsky, D. A., Allison, D. B., Bray, M. S., de Castro, J. M., Clegg, D. J., . . . Westerterp-Plantenga, M. S. (2011). Set points, settling points and some alternative models: Theoretical options to understand how genes and environments combine to regulate body adiposity. *Disease Models & Mechanisms, 4,* 733–745.

Spear, L. P. (2013). Adolescent neurodevelopment. *Journal of Adolescent Health, 52,* S7–S13.

Specht, J., Egloff, B., & Schmukle, S. C. (2011). Stability and change of personality across the life course: The impact of age and major life events on mean-level and rank-order stability of the Big Five. *Journal of Personality and Social Psychology, 101,* 862–882.

Spencer, S. J., Emmerzaal, T. L., Kozicz, T., & Andrews, Z. B. (2015). Ghrelin's role in the hypothalamic-pituitary-adrenal axis stress response: Implications for mood disorders. *Biological Psychiatry, 78,* 19–27.

Sperling, G. (1960). The information available in brief visual presentations. *Psychological Monographs: General and Applied, 74,* 1–29.

Spiegel, D., Loewenstein, R. J., Lewis-Fernández, R., Sar, V., Simeon, D., Vermetten, E., . . . Dell, P. F. (2011). Dissociative disorders in *DSM-5. Depression and Anxiety, 28,* 824–852.

Spiegel, D. R., Smith, J., Wade, R. R., Cherukuru, N., Ursani, A., Dobruskina, Y., . . . Dreyer, N. (2017). Transient global amnesia: Current perspectives. *Neuropsychiatric Disease and Treatment, 13,* 2691–2703. http://dx.doi.org/10.2147/NDT.S130710

Spinelli, M., Fasolo, M., & Mesman, J. (2017). Does prosody make the difference? A meta-analysis on relations between prosodic aspects of infant-directed speech and infant outcomes. *Developmental Review, 44,* 1–18.

Spitzer, R. L. (1975). On pseudoscience in science, logic in remission, and psychiatric diagnosis: A critique of Rosenhan's "On Being Sane in Insane Places." *Journal of Abnormal Psychology, 84,* 442–451.

Spong, C. Y. (2013). Defining "term" pregnancy: Recommendations from the Defining "Term" Pregnancy Workgroup. *Journal of the American Medical Association, 309*(23), 2445–2446.

Squire, L. R., & Bayley, P. J. (2007). The neuroscience of remote memory. *Current Opinion in Neurobiology, 17,* 185–196.

Squire, L. R., Stark, C. E. L., & Clark, R. E. (2004). The medial temporal lobe. *Annual Review of Neuroscience, 27,* 279–306.

Squire, L. R., & Wixted, J. T. (2011). The cognitive neuroscience of human memory since HM. *Annual Review of Neuroscience, 34,* 259–288.

Staff, R. T., Murray, A. D., Ahearn, T. S., Mustafa, N., Fox, H. C., & Whalley, L. J. (2012). Childhood socioeconomic status and adult brain size: Childhood socioeconomic status influences adult hippocampal size. *Annals of Neurology, 71,* 653–660.

Stahre, M., Roeber, J., Kanny, D., Brewer, R. D., & Zhang, X. (2014). Contribution of excessive alcohol consumption to deaths and years of potential life lost in the United States. *Preventing Chronic Disease, 11.* Retrieved from http://dx.doi.org/10.5888/pcd11.130293

Stamatakis, A. M., Van Swieten, M., Basiri, M. L., Blair, G. A., Kantak, P., & Stuber, G. D. (2016). Lateral hypothalamic area glutamatergic neurons and their projections to the lateral habenula regulate feeding and reward. *The Journal of Neuroscience, 36,* 302–311.

Stanford School of Medicine. (n.d.). About narcolepsy. Center for Narcolepsy. Retrieved from http://med.stanford.edu/narcolepsy/symptoms.html

Stanger, S., Abaied, J., & Wagner, C. (2016). Predicting heavy alcohol use in college students: Interactions among socialization of coping, alcohol use onset, and physiological reactivity. *Journal of Studies on Alcohol and Drugs, 77,* 483–494.

Staniloiu, A., & Markowitsch, H. J. (2012). The remains of the day in dissociative amnesia. *Brain Sciences, 2,* 101–129.

Stanovich, K. E. (2013). *How to think straight about psychology* (10th ed.). Upper Saddle River, NJ: Pearson.

Staub, M. E. (2016). The other side of the brain: The politics of split-brain research in the 1970s–1980s. *History of Psychology, 19,* 259–273.

Steel, Z., Marnane, C., Iranpour, C., Chey, T., Jackson, J. W., Patel, V., & Silove, D. (2014). The global prevalence of common mental disorders: A systematic review and meta-analysis 1980–2013. *International Journal of Epidemiology, 43,* 476–493.

Steele, C. M. (1997). A threat in the air: How stereotypes shape intellectual identity and performance. *American Psychologist, 52,* 613–629.

Steele, C. M. (2010). *Whistling Vivaldi: How stereotypes affect us and what we can do.* New York, NY: W. W. Norton.

Steele, H., Bate, J., Steele, M., Dube, S. R., Danskin, K., Knafo, H., . . . Murphy, A. (2016). Adverse childhood experiences, poverty, and parenting stress. *Canadian Journal of Behavioural Science/Revue Canadienne des Sciences du Comportement, 48,* 32–38.

Steele, J. D., Christmas, D., Elijamel, M. S., & Matthews, K. (2008). Anterior cingulotomy for major depression: Clinical outcome and relationship to lesion characteristics. *Biological Psychology, 63,* 670–677.

Stein, B. E., Stanford, T. R., & Rowland, B. A. (2009). The neural basis of multisensory integration in the midbrain: Its organization and maturation. *Hearing Research, 258,* 4–15.

Steinberg, L. (2010). Commentary: A behavioral scientist looks at the science of adolescent brain development. *Brain and Cognition, 72,* 160–164.

Steinberg, L. (2012). Should the science of adolescent brain development inform public policy? *Issues in Science & Technology, 28,* 76–78.

Steindl, C., & Jonas, E. (2015). The dynamic reactance interaction: How vested interests affect people's experience, behavior, and cognition in social interactions. *Frontiers in Psychology, 6.* doi:10.3389/fpsyg.2015.01752

Steiner, M. (2012, September 4). The importance of pragmatic communication. *Monocracy Neurodevelopmental Center.* Retrieved from http://monocacycenter.com/the-importance-of-pragmatic-communication/

Steiner-Adair, C. (2013). *The big disconnect.* New York, NY: HarperCollins.

Steinmetz, J., Xu, Q., Fishbach, A., & Zhang, Y. (2016). Being observed magnifies action. *Journal of Personality and Social Psychology, 111,* 852–865.

Stenseng, F., Belsky, J., Skalicka, V., & Wichstrøm, L. (2014). Preschool social exclusion, aggression, and cooperation: A longitudinal evaluation of the need-to-belong and the social-reconnection hypotheses. *Personality and Social Psychology Bulletin, 40,* 1637–1647.

Stern, E. M. (2016). Foreword to the second edition. In K. J. Schneider, J. F. Pierson, & J. F. T. Bugental (Eds.), *The handbook of humanistic psychology: Theory, research, and practice* (2nd ed., p. xi). Thousand Oaks, CA: Sage.

Stern, K., & McClintock, M. K. (1998). Regulation of ovulation by human pheromones. *Nature, 392,* 177–179.

Sternberg, R. J. (1986). A triangular theory of love. *Psychological Review, 93,* 119–135.

Sternberg, R. J. (1988). *The triarchic mind: A new theory of human intelligence.* New York, NY: Viking.

Sternberg, R. J. (2004). Culture and intelligence. *American Psychologist, 59,* 325–338.

Sternberg, R. J. (2006a). Creating a vision of creativity: The first 25 years. *Psychology of Aesthetics, Creativity, and the Arts, S*(1), 2–12.

Sternberg, R. J. (2006b). The nature of creativity. *Creativity Research Journal, 18,* 87–98.

Sternberg, R. J., & Grigorenko, E. L. (2005). Intelligence and wisdom. In M. L. Johnson (Ed.), *The Cambridge handbook of age and ageing* (pp. 209–213). Cambridge, UK: Cambridge University Press.

Stetka, B. (2017, October 11). Where's the proof that mindfulness meditation works? *Scientific American.* Retrieved from https://www.scientificamerican.com/article/wheres-the-proof-that-mindfulness-meditation-works1/

Stieff, M., Origenes, A., DeSutter, D., Lira, M., Banevicius, L., Tabang, D., & Cabel, G. (2018). Operational constraints on the mental rotation of STEM representations. *Journal of Educational Psychology.* Advance online publication. Retrieved from http://dx.doi.org/10.1037/edu0000258

Stix, G. (2014, May/June). My brain made me pull the trigger. *Scientific American Mind, 25,* 14.

Stoet, G., & Geary, D. C. (2013). Sex differences in mathematics and reading achievement are inversely related: Within- and across-nation assessment of 10 years of PISA data. *PLoS One, 8,* e57988. doi:10.1371/journal.pone.0057988

Stoltenborgh, M., Bakermans-Kranenburg, M. J., Alink, L. R. A., & van IJzendoorn, M. H. (2015). The prevalence of child maltreatment across the globe: Review of a series of meta-analyses. *Child Abuse Review, 24,* 37–50.

Stone, A. A., Schwartz, J. E., Broderick, J. E., & Deaton, A. (2010). A snapshot of the age distribution of psychological well-being in the United States. *Proceedings of the National Academy of Sciences, 107,* 9985–9990.

Stone, D. (2009). Brainy Bonnie. *Smithsonian Zoogoer.* Retrieved from http://nationalzoo.si.edu/Publications/ZooGoer/2009/1/BrainyBonnie.cfm

Stone, D. N., Deci, E. L., & Ryan, R. M. (2009). Beyond talk: Creating autonomous motivation through self-determination theory. *Journal of General Management, 34,* 75–102.

Stoner, J. A. F. (1961). *A comparison of individual and group decisions involving risk* (Unpublished master's thesis, Alfred P. Sloan School of Management, Massachusetts Institute of Technology). Retrieved from http://dspace.mit.edu/bitstream/handle/1721.1/11330/33120544-MIT.pdf?sequence=2

Stoner, J. A. F. (1968). Risky and cautious shifts in group decisions: The influence of widely held values. *Journal of Experimental Psychology, 4,* 442–459.

Storm, B. C., Bjork, E. L., & Bjork, R. A. (2008). Accelerated relearning after retrieval-induced forgetting: The benefit of being forgotten. *Journal of Experimental Psychology: Learning, Memory, and Cognition, 34,* 230–236.

Storrs, C. (2017, July 13). How poverty affects the brain. *Nature News, 547,* 150–152.

Strack, F., Martin, L. L., & Stepper, S. (1988). Inhibiting and facilitating conditions of the human smile: A nonobtrusive test of the facial feedback hypothesis. *Journal of Personality and Social Psychology, 54,* 768–777.

Strain, G. M. (2003). *How well do dogs and other animals hear?* Department of Comparative Biomedical Sciences, School of Veterinary Medicine, Louisiana State University. Retrieved from http://www.lsu.edu/deafness/HearingRange.html

Strassberg, D. S., McKinnon, R. K., Sustaíta, M. A., & Rullo, J. (2013). Sexting by high school students: An exploratory and descriptive study. *Archives of Sexual Behavior, 42,* 15–21.

Stratton, G. (1896, August). Some preliminary experiments on vision without inversion of the retinal image. Paper presented at the Third International Congress for Psychology, Munich.

Straub, R. O. (2017). *Health psychology: A biopsychosocial approach* (5th ed.). New York, NY: Worth.

Strawser, M. G., & McCormick, J. K. (2017). Adapting the basic communication course for a globally and technologically mediated 21st century context. *Basic Communication Course Annual, 29,* 83–89.

Strayer, D. L., & Watson, J. M. (2012, March). Top multitaskers help explain how brain juggles thoughts. *Scientific American Mind, 23,* 22–29.

Streit, W. J. (2000). Microglial response to brain injury: A brief synopsis. *Toxicologic Pathology, 28,* 28–30.

Strelan, P. (2018). Justice and forgiveness in interpersonal relationships. *Current Directions in Psychological Science, 27,* 20–24.

Strenger, C. (2015). Can psychoanalysis reclaim the public sphere? *Psychoanalytic Psychology, 32,* 293–306.

Strickland, B. R. (2014). Julian B. Rotter (1916–2014). *American Psychologist, 69,* 545–546.

Stroebe, W., van Koningsbruggen, G. M., Papies, E. K., & Aarts, H. (2013). Why most dieters fail but some succeed: A goal conflict model of eating behavior. *Psychological Review, 120,* 110–138.

Stroud, M. (2015, February 2). Will lie detectors ever get their day in court again? *Bloomberg.* Retrieved from http://www.bloomberg.com/news/articles/2015-02-02/will-lie-detectors-ever-get-their-day-in-court-again-

Stuart, H. (2003). Violence and mental illness: An overview. *World Psychiatry, 2,* 121–124.

Stull, A. T., & Hegarty, M. (2016). Model manipulation and learning: Fostering representational competence with virtual and concrete models. *Journal of Educational Psychology, 108,* 509–527.

Stuss, D. T., & Alexander, M. P. (2000). Executive functions and the frontal lobes: A conceptual view. *Psychological Research, 63,* 289–298.

Su, Y. S., Veeravagu, A., & Grant, G. (2016). Neuroplasticity after traumatic brain injury. In D. Laskowitz & G. Grant (Eds.), Translational research in traumatic brain injury (Chap. 8). Boca Raton, FL: CRC Press/Taylor and Francis. Available from https://www.ncbi.nlm.nih.gov/books/NBK326735/

Suardi, A., Sotgiu, I., Costa, T., Cauda, F., & Rusconi, M. (2016). The neural correlates of happiness: A review of PET and fMRI studies using autobiographical recall methods. *Cognitive, Affective, & Behavioral Neuroscience, 16,* 383–392.

Substance Abuse and Mental Health Services Administration (SAMHSA). (2010). *The DAWN report: Trends in emergency department visits involving nonmedical use of narcotic pain relievers.* Retrieved from http://oas.samhsa.gov/2k10/DAWN016/OpioidED.htm

Substance Abuse and Mental Health Services Administration (SAMHSA). (2012). *Results from the 2011 National Survey on Drug Use and Health: Summary of national findings* (NSDUH Series H-44, HHS Publication No. SMA 12-4713). Retrieved from http://www.samhsa.gov/data/nsduh/2k11results/nsduhresults2011.htm

Substance Abuse and Mental Health Services Administration (SAMHSA). (2017). *Key substance use and mental health indicators in the United States: Results from the 2016 National Survey on Drug Use and Health* (HHS Publication No. SMA 17-5044, NSDUH Series H-52). Rockville, MD: Office of Applied Studies.

Substance Abuse and Mental Health Services Administration (SAMHSA). (2018). *Racial and ethnic minority populations.* Retrieved from https://www.samhsa.gov/specific-populations/racial-ethnic-minority

Sucala, M., Schnur, J. B., Constantino, M. J., Miller, S. J., Brackman, E. H., & Montgomery, G. H. (2012). The therapeutic relationship in e-therapy for mental health: A systematic review. *Journal of Medical Internet Research, 14,* e110. doi:10.2196/jmir.2084

Summa, K. C., & Turek, F. W. (2015, February). The clocks within us. *Scientific American, 312,* 50–55.

Sumner, R. C., & Gallagher, S. (2017). Unemployment as a chronic stressor: A systematic review of cortisol studies. *Psychology & Health, 32,* 289–311.

Sun-Edelstein, C., & Mauskop, A. (2011). Alternative headache treatments: Nutraceuticals, behavioral, and physical treatments. *Headache, 25,* 469–483.

Susuki, K. (2010). Myelin: A specialized membrane for cell communication. *Nature Education, 3,* 59–63.

Sutherland, C. A., Liu, X., Zhang, L., Chu, Y., Oldmeadow, J. A., & Young, A. W. (2018). Facial first impressions across culture: Data-driven modeling of Chinese and British perceivers' unconstrained facial impressions. *Personality and Social Psychology Bulletin, 44,* 521–537.

Sutherland, S. (2017, May/June). Rethinking relief. *Scientific American Mind, 28,* 28–35.

Suwanrath, C., & Suntharasaj, T. (2010). Sleep-wake cycles in normal fetuses. *Archives of Gynecology and Obstetrics, 281,* 449–454.

Svrakic, D. M., Zorumski, C. F., Svrakic, N. M., Zwir, I., & Cloninger, C. R. (2013). Risk architecture of schizophrenia: The role of epigenetics. *Current Opinion in Psychiatry, 26,* 188–195.

Swan, S. H., Liu, F., Hines, M., Kruse, R. L., Wang, C., Redmon, J. B., . . . Weiss, B. (2010). Prenatal phthalate exposure and reduced masculine play in boys. *International Journal of Andrology, 3,* 259–269.

Swanson, L. (1997). Cochlear implants: The head-on collision between medical technology and the right to be deaf. *Canadian Medical Association Journal, 157,* 929–932.

Swendsen, J. D., Tennen, H., Carney, M. A., Affleck, G., Willard, A., & Hromi, A. (2000). Mood and alcohol consumption: An experience sampling test of the self-medication hypothesis. *Journal of Abnormal Psychology, 109,* 198–204.

Swift, J. K., & Greenberg, R. P. (2012). Premature discontinuation in adult psychotherapy: A meta-analysis. *Journal of Consulting and Clinical Psychology, 80,* 547–559.

Syracuse University. (n.d.). *InclusiveU.* Retrieved from http://taishoffcenter.syr.edu/inclusiveu/

Szabo, R., & Hall, M. (2007). *Behind happy faces.* Los Angeles, CA: Volt Press.

Szasz, T. (2011). The myth of mental illness: 50 years later. *Psychiatrist Online, 35,* 179–182.

Tackett, J. L., Waldman, I. D., & Lahey, B. B. (2009). Etiology and measurement of relational aggression: A multi-informant behavior genetic investigation. *Journal of Abnormal Psychology, 118,* 722–733.

Talbert, J. J. (2014). Club drugs: Coming to a patient near you. *The Nurse Practitioner, 39,* 20–25.

Talbot, M. (2018, March 12). The gun-control debate after Parkland. *The New Yorker.* Retrieved from https://www.newyorker.com/magazine/2018/03/12/the-gun-control-debate-after-parkland

Tallandini, M. A., & Caudek, C. (2010). Defense mechanisms development in typical children. *Psychotherapy Research, 20,* 535–545.

Tan, R., & Goldman, M. S. (2015). Exposure to female fertility pheromones influences men's drinking. *Experimental and Clinical Psychopharmacology, 23,* 139–146.

Tandon, R., Keshavan, M. S., & Nasrallah, H. A. (2008a). Schizophrenia, "just the facts": What we know in 2008. Part 1: Overview. *Schizophrenia Research, 100,* 4–19.

Tandon, R., Keshavan, M. S., & Nasrallah, H. A. (2008b). Schizophrenia, "just the facts": What we know in 2008. 2. Epidemiology and etiology. *Schizophrenia Research, 102,* 1–18.

Tandon, R., Nasrallah, H. A., & Keshavan, M. S. (2009). Schizophrenia, "just the facts." 4. Clinical features and conceptualization. *Schizophrenia Research, 110,* 1–23.

Tang, Y. Y., Hölzel, B. K., & Posner, M. I. (2015). The neuroscience of mindfulness meditation. *Nature Reviews Neuroscience, 16,* 213–225.

Tanis, M., Beukeboom, C. J., Hartmann, T., & Vermeulen, I. E. (2015). Phantom phone signals: An investigation into the prevalence and predictors of imagined cell phone signals. *Computers in Human Behavior, 51,* 356–362.

Tate, M. C., Herbet, G., Moritz-Gasser, S., Tate, J. E., & Duffau, H. (2014). Probabilistic map of critical functional regions of the human cerebral cortex: Broca's area revisited. *Brain, 137,* 2773–2782.

Tauer, J. (2009). *Monday morning quarterbacking: The case of the hindsight bias.* Retrieved from https://www.psychologytoday.com/blog/goal-posts/200911/monday-morning-quarterbacking-the-case-the-hindsight-bias

Taverniers, J., Smeets, T., Van Ruysseveldt, J., Syroit, J., & von Grumbkow, J. (2011). The risk of being shot at: Stress, cortisol secretion, and their impact memory and perceived learning during reality-based practice for armed officers. *International Journal of Stress Management, 18,* 113–132.

Taylor, J. B. (2006). *My stroke of insight.* New York, NY: Plume.

Taylor, J. B. (2008, February). Jill Bolte Taylor: My stroke of insight [Video file]. Retrieved from http://www.ted.com/talks/jill_bolte_taylor_s_powerful_stroke_of_insight

TEDxDirigo. (2015, December 8). Salim Salim: Taking risks is risky [Video file]. Retrieved from https://www.youtube.com/watch?v=FyL9OkVgZA4

Teghtsoonian, R. (1971). On the exponents in Stevens' law and the constant in Ekman's law. *Psychological Review, 78,* 71–80.

Teigen, C. (2017, March 6). Chrissy Teigen opens up for the first time about her postpartum depression. *Glamour.* Retrieved from https://www.glamour.com/story/chrissy-teigen-postpartum-depression

Teigen, K. H. (1994). Yerkes-Dodson: A law for all seasons. *Theory & Psychology, 4,* 525–547.

Temmel, A. F., Quint, C., Schickinger-Fischer, B., Klimek, L., Stoller, E., & Hummel, T. (2002). Characteristics of olfactory disorders in relation to major causes of olfactory loss. *Archives of Otolaryngology—Head & Neck Surgery, 128,* 635–641.

Tenenbaum, H. R., & Leaper, C. (2002). Are parents' gender schemas related to their children's gender-related cognitions? A meta-analysis. *Developmental Psychology, 38,* 615–630.

Teodorescu, M., Barnet, J. H., Hagen, E. W., Palta, M., Young, T. B., & Peppard, P. E. (2015). Association between asthma and risk of developing obstructive sleep apnea. *Journal of the American Medical Association, 313,* 156–164.

Terman, L. M. (1916). *The measurement of intelligence.* Boston, MA: Houghton Mifflin.

Terman, L. M. (1925). *Genetic studies of genius. Mental and physical traits of a thousand gifted children.* Palo Alto, CA: Stanford University Press.

Terman, L. M., & Oden, M. H. (1947). *The gifted child grows up: Twenty-five years' follow-up of a superior group.* Palo Alto, CA: Stanford University Press.

Terracciano, A., Abdel-Khalek, A. M., Ádám, N., Adamovová, L., Ahn, C. K., Ahn, H. N., . . . McCrae, R. R. (2005). National character does not reflect mean personality trait levels in 49 cultures. *Science, 310,* 96–100.

Terracciano, A., Costa, P. T., & McCrae, R. R. (2006). Personality plasticity after age 30. *Personality and Social Psychology Bulletin, 32,* 999–1009.

Tesla. (n.d.). *Solar roof.* Retrieved from https://www.tesla.com/solarroof

The insanity defense among the states. (n.d.). Retrieved from https://criminal.findlaw.com/criminal-procedure/the-insanity-defense-among-the-states.html

Thelen, E., & Fisher, D. M. (1982). Newborn stepping: An explanation for a "disappearing" reflex. *Developmental Psychology, 18,* 760–775.

Thibaut, J., & Kelly, H. (1959). *The social psychology of groups.* New York, NY: John Wiley & Sons.

Thomas, A., & Chess, S. (1986). The New York Longitudinal Study: From infancy to early adult life. In R. Plomin & J. Dunn (Eds.), *The study of temperament: Changes, continuities, and challenges* (pp. 39–52). Hillsdale, NJ: Lawrence Erlbaum Associates.

Thomas, I., & Bruck, D. (2010). Awakening of sleeping people: A decade of research. *Fire Technology, 46,* 743–761.

Thomas, K. A., De Freitas, J., De Scioli, P., & Pinker, S. (2016). Recursive mentalizing and common knowledge in the bystander effect. *Journal of Experimental Psychology: General, 145,* 621–629.

Thompson, P. M., Giedd, J. N., Woods, R. P., MacDonald, D., Evans, A. C., & Toga, A. W. (2000). Growth patterns in the developing brain detected by using continuum mechanical tensor maps. *Nature, 404,* 190–193.

Thompson, R. F., & Kim, J. J. (1996). Memory systems in the brain and localization of a memory. *Proceedings of the National Academy of Sciences, USA, 93,* 13438–13444.

Thompson, R. F., & Steinmetz, J. E. (2009). The role of the cerebellum in classical conditioning of discrete behavioral responses. *Neuroscience, 162,* 732–755.

Thorndike, E. L. (1898). Animal intelligence: An experimental study of the associative process in animals. *Psychological Review Monograph Supplement, 2*(8).

Thorne, M., & Henley, T. B. (2005). *Connections in the history and systems of psychology* (3rd ed.). Boston, MA: Houghton Mifflin.

Thurfjell, H., Ciuti, S., & Boyce, M. S. (2017). Learning from the mistakes of others: How female elk (*Cervus elaphus*) adjust behaviour with age to avoid hunters. *PLoS One, 12,* e0178082. doi:10.1371/journal.pone.0178082

Time Magazine Staff. (2016, November 17). The 25 best inventions of 2016. *Time.* Retrieved from http://time.com/4572079/best-inventions-2016/

Times Staff Writer. (2014, June 18). Now 15, the "Girl in the Window" is featured on Oprah show (w/video). *Tampa Bay Times.* Retrieved from http://www.tampabay.com/features/humaninterest/now-15-the-girl-in-the-window-is-featured-on-oprah-show/2184949

Tirindelli, R., Dibattista, M., Pifferi, S., & Menini, A. (2009). From pheromones to behavior. *Physiological Reviews, 89,* 921–956.

Tobaldini, E., Costantino, G., Solbiati, M., Cogliati, C., Kara T., Nobili, L., & Montano, N. (2016). Sleep, sleep deprivation, autonomic nervous system and cardiovascular diseases. *Neuroscience and Biobehavioral Reviews, 74*(Pt. B), 321–329.

Tobar, H. (2014). *Deep down dark: The untold stories of 33 men buried in a Chilean mine, and the miracle that set them free.* New York, NY: Farrar, Straus and Giroux.

Tobar, H. (2014, July 7). Sixty-nine days. *The New Yorker.* Retrieved from http://www.newyorker.com/magazine/2014/07/07/sixty-nine-days

Tobin, D. D., Menon, M., Menon, M., Spatta, B. C., Hodges, E. V. E., & Perry, D. G. (2010). The intrapsychics of gender: A model of self-socialization. *Psychological Review, 117,* 601–622.

Todes, D. P. (2014). *Ivan Pavlov: A Russian life in science.* New York, NY: Oxford University Press.

Toga, A. W., Thompson, P. M., & Sowell, E. R. (2006). Mapping brain maturation. *Trends in Neuroscience, 29,* 148–159.

Tollenaar, M. S., Beijers, R., Jansen, J., Riksen-Walraven, J. M. A., & De Weerth, C. (2011). Maternal prenatal stress and cortisol reactivity to stressors in human infants. *Stress, 14,* 53–65.

Tolman, E. C. (1948). Cognitive maps in rats and men. *Psychological Review, 55*(4), 189–208.

Tolman, E. C., & Honzik, C. H. (1930). Introduction and removal of reward, and maze performance in rats. *University of California Publications in Psychology, 4,* 257–275.

Tondo, L., Isacsson, G., & Baldessarini, R. J. (2003). Suicidal behaviour in bipolar disorder: Risk and prevention. *CNS Drugs, 17,* 491–511.

Tononi, G., & Cirelli, C. (2014). Sleep and the price of plasticity: From synaptic and cellular homeostasis to memory consolidation and integration. *Neuron, 81,* 12–34.

Topp, S. S. (2013). Against the quiet revolution: The rhetorical construction of intersex individuals as disordered. *Sexualities, 16,* 180–194.

Torrente, M. P., Gelenberg, A. J., & Vrana, K. E. (2012). Boosting serotonin in the brain: Is it time to revamp the treatment of depression? *Journal of Psychopharmacology, 26,* 629–635.

Torrey, E. F., Fuller, D. A., Geller, J., Jacobs, C., & Rogasta, K. (2012). *No room at the inn: Trends and consequences of closing public psychiatric hospitals.* Arlington, VA: Treatment Advocacy Center.

Torrey, E. F., Kennard, A. D., Eslinger, D., Lamb, R., & Pavle, J. (2010). *More mentally ill persons are in jails and prisons than hospitals: A survey of the states.* Arlington, VA: Treatment Advocacy Center.

Torry, Z. D., & Billick, S. B. (2010). Overlapping universe: Understanding legal insanity and psychosis. *Psychiatric Quarterly, 81,* 253–262.

Tourangeau, R., & Yan, T. (2007). Sensitive questions in surveys. *Psychological Bulletin, 133,* 859–883.

Tränkner, D., Jägle, H., Kohl, S., Apfelstedt-Sylla, E., Sharpe, L. T., Kaupp, U. B., . . . Wissinger, B. (2004). Molecular basis of an inherited form of incomplete achromatopsia. *Journal of Neuroscience, 24,* 138–147.

Treffers-Daller, J., & Milton, J. (2013). Vocabulary size revisited: The link between vocabulary size and academic achievement. *Applied Linguistics Review, 4,* 151–172.

Treffert, D. A. (2015). Accidental genius. *Scientific American, 23,* 54–59.

Tremayne, P., & Norton, W. (2017). Sexuality and the older woman. *British Journal of Nursing, 26,* 819–824.

Trivers, R. L. (1971). The evolution of reciprocal altruism. *Quarterly Review of Biology, 46,* 35–57.

Trostel, P. (2015, October 14). *It's not just the money: The benefits of college education to individuals and to society.* Retrieved from https://www.luminafoundation.org/resources/its-not-just-the-money

True lies. (2004, April 15). *Nature.* Retrieved from http://www.nature.com/nature/journal/v428/n6984/full/428679a.html

Tsaw, D., Murphy, S., & Detgen, J. (2011). Social loafing and culture: Does gender matter? *International Review of Business Research, 7,* 1–8.

Tsuang, M. T., Stone, W. S., & Faraone, S. V. (2001). Genes, environment and schizophrenia. *British Journal of Psychiatry, 178,* s18–s24.

Tullis, J. G., & Benjamin, A. S. (2015). Cue generation: How learners exibly support future retrieval. *Memory & Cognition, 43,* 922–938.

Tulving, E. (1972). Episodic and semantic memory. In E. Tulving & W. Donaldson (Eds.), *Organization of memory* (pp. 381–403). New York, NY: Academic Press.

Tulving, E. (1985). Memory and consciousness. *Canadian Psychology/Psychologice Canadienne, 26,* 1–11.

Tulving, E., & Osler, S. (1968). Effectiveness of retrieval cues in memory forwords. *Journal of Experimental Psychology, 77,* 593–601.

Tulving, E., & Thomson, D. M. (1973). Encoding specificity and retrieval processes in episodic memory. *Psychological Review, 80,* 352–373.

Tummala-Narra, P. (2016). A historical overview and critique of the psychoanalytic approach to culture and context. In P. Tummala-Narra, *Psychoanalytic theory and cultural competence in psychotherapy* (pp. 7–29). Washington, DC: American Psychological Association. Retrieved from http://dx.doi.org/10.1037/14800-002

Tummala-Narra, P., Alegria, M., & Chen, C.-N. (2012). Perceived discrimination, acculturative stress, and depression among South Asians: Mixed findings. *Asian American Journal of Psychology, 3,* 3–16.

Turiano, N. A., Spiro, A., III, & Mroczek, D. K. (2012). Openness to experience and mortality in men: Analysis of trait and facets. *Journal of Aging and Health, 24,* 654–672.

Turner, R. C., Lucke-Wold, B. P., Robson, M. J., Omalu, B. I., Petraglia, A. L., & Bailes, J. E. (2013). Repetitive traumatic brain injury and development of chronic traumatic encephalopathy: A potential role for biomarkers in diagnosis, prognosis, and treatment? *Frontiers in Neurology, 3*(186). doi:10.3389/fneur.2012.00186

Turpin, C. (2017, June 14). Penn State fraternity hazing death hearing continues in July. *NJ.com.* Retrieved from http://www.nj.com/hunterdon/index.ssf/2017/06/penn_state_fraternity_hazing_death_hearing_continu.html

Turrini, G., Purgato, M., Ballette, F., Nosè, M., Ostuzzi, G., & Barbui, C. (2017). Common mental disorders in asylum seekers and refugees: Umbrella review of prevalence and intervention studies. *International Journal of Mental Health Systems, 11,* 51.

Tversky, A., & Kahneman, D. (1981). The framing of decisions and the psychology of choice. *Science, 211,* 453–458.

Tversky, A., & Kahneman, D. (1982). Judgment under uncertainty: Heuristics and biases. In D. Kahneman, P. Slovic, & A. Tversky (Eds.), *Judgment under uncertainty: Heuristics and biases* (pp. 3–20). New York, NY: Cambridge University Press.

Twenge, J. M. (2014). *Generation me—revised and updated: Why today's young Americans are more confident, assertive, entitled—and more miserable than ever before.* New York, NY: Simon & Schuster

Twenge, J. M. (2017, September). Have smartphones destroyed a generation? *The Atlantic.* Retrieved from https://www.theatlantic.com/magazine/archive/2017/09/has-the-smartphone-destroyed-a-generation/534198/

Twenge, J. M., Baumeister, R. F., DeWall, C. N., Ciarocco, N. J., & Bartels, J. M. (2007). Social exclusion decreases prosocial behavior. *Journal of Personality and Social Psychology, 92,* 56–66.

Twenge, J. M., & Park, H. (2017). The decline in adult activities among US adolescents, 1976–2016. *Child development.* Advance online publication. doi:10.1111/cdev.12930

Twenge, J. M., Sherman, R. A., & Wells, B. E. (2017). Declines in sexual frequency among American adults, 1989–2014. *Archives of Sexual Behavior, 46,* 2389–2401.

U.S. Census Bureau. (2015). *Figure MS-2. Median age at first marriage: 1890 to present.* Retrieved from https://www.census.gov/hhes/families/les/graphics/MS-2.pdf

U.S. Census Bureau. (2017). *Facts for features: American Indian and Alaska Native Heritage Month: November 2017.* Retrieved from https://www.census.gov/newsroom/facts-for-features/2017/aian-month.html

U.S. Department of Defense. (2015, July 23). *National security implications of climate-related risks and a changing climate* (Report No. 8-6475571). Retrieved from http://archive.defense.gov/pubs/150724-congressional-report-on-national-implications-of-climate-change.pdf?source=govdelivery

U.S. Department of Health and Human Services. (2016). *E-cigarette use among youth and young adults. A report of the Surgeon General.* Atlanta, GA: U.S. Department of Health and Human Services, Centers for Disease Control and Prevention, National Center for Chronic Disease Prevention and Health Promotion, Office on Smoking and Health.

U.S. Department of Housing and Urban Development. (2017). *HUD 2017 continuum of care homeless assistance programs homeless populations and subpopulations.* Retrieved from https://www.hudexchange.info/resource/reportmanagement/published/CoC_PopSub_NatlTerrDC_2017.pdf

U.S. Fish & Wildlife Service. (2006). *Laysan Albatross* Phoebastria immutabilis *conservation status* (Alaska Seabird Information Series, 3–4). Retrieved from http://www.fws.gov/alaska/mbsp/mbm/seabirds/pdf/laal.pdf

U.S. Food and Drug Administration. (2008). *Drugs: Information for healthcare professionals: Suicidal behavior and ideation and antiepileptic drugs.* Retrieved from http://www.fda.gov/Drugs/DrugSafety/PostmarketDrugSafetyInformationforPatientsandProviders/ucm100192.htm

U.S. Food and Drug Administration. (n.d.). *For consumers: Side effects of sleep drugs.* Retrieved from http://www.fda.gov/forconsumers/consumerupdates/ucm107757.htm

U.S. Olympic Committee. (n.d.). Psychology. Retrieved from http://www.teamusa.org/About-the-USOC/Athlete-Development/Sport-Performance/Psychology

Uchida, S., Shioda, K., Morita, Y., Kubota, C., Ganeko, M., & Takeda, N. (2012). Exercise effects on sleep physiology. *Frontiers in Neurology, 3.* Retrieved from http://dx.doi.org/10.3389/fneur.2012.00048

Ücok, A., & Gaebel, W. (2008). Side effects of atypical antipsychotics: A brief overview. *World Psychiatry, 7,* 58–62.

Uhls, Y. T., Ellison, N. B., & Subrahmanyam, K. (2017). Benefits and costs of social media in adolescence. *Pediatrics, 140,* S67–S70. doi:10.1542/peds.2016-1758E

Ujvari, B., & Madsen, T. (2009). Increased mortality of naive varanid lizards after the invasion of non-native cane toads (*Bufo marinus*). *Herpetological Conservation and Biology, 4,* 248–251.

UNAIDS. (2017, July). *Global HIV statistics.* Retrieved from http://www.unaids.org/sites/default/files/media_asset/UNAIDS_FactSheet_en.pdf

Underwood, E. (2014). The taste of things to come. *Science, 345*(6198), 750–751.

Underwood, E. (2016). How the body learns to hurt. *Science, 354,* 694.

United Nations Office on Drugs and Crime. (2017). *World drug report 2017.* Retrieved from https://www.unodc.org/wdr2017/field/Booklet_2_HEALTH.pdf

United Nations, Department of Economic and Social Affairs, Population Division. (2017). *International migration report 2017: Highlights* (ST/ESA/SER.A/404).

United Nations, General Assembly. (1987, August 4). *Report of the World Commission on Environment and Development: Our common future* (A/42/427). Retrieved from http://www.un-documents.net/our-common-future.pdf

University of Notre Dame. (n.d.). *Blood alcohol concentration.* Retrieved from https://mcwell.nd.edu/your-well-being/physical-well-being/alcohol/blood-alcohol-concentration/

Ursini, G., Punzi, G., Chen, Q., Marenco, S., Robinson, J. F., Porcelli, A., . . . Seidel, J. (2018). Convergence of placenta biology and genetic risk for schizophrenia. *Nature Medicine, 24*(6), 792–801.

Vadeboncoeur, C., Townsend, N., & Foster, C. (2015). A meta-analysis of weight gain in first year university students: Is freshman 15 a myth? *BMC Obesity, 2.* doi:10.1186/s40608-015-0051-7

Vaillant, G. E. (1992). *Ego mechanisms of defense: A guide for clinicians and researchers.* Arlington, VA: American Psychiatric Association.

Vaillant, G. E. (2000). Adaptive mental mechanisms: Their role in a positive psychology. *American Psychologist, 55,* 89–98.

Vainchtein, I. D., Chin, G., Cho, F. S., Kelley, K. W., Miller, J. G., Chien, E. C., . . . Akil, O. (2018). Astrocyte-derived interleukin-33 promotes microglial synapse engulfment and neural circuit development. *Science, 359*(6381), 1269–1273.

Valenza, E., Leo, I., Gava, L., & Simion, F. (2006). Perceptual completion in newborn human infants. *Child Development, 77,* 1810–1821.

Vall, O., Salat-Batlle, J., & Garcia-Algar, O. (2015). Alcohol consumption during pregnancy and adverse neurodevelopmental outcomes. *Journal of Epidemiology and Community Health, 69*(10), 927–929.

Van den Akker, A. L., Deković, M., Asscher, J., & Prinzie, P. (2014). Mean-level personality development across childhood and adolescence: A temporary defiance of the maturity principle and bidirectional associations with parenting. *Journal of Personality and Social Psychology, 107,* 736–750.

van den Eijnden, R. J. J. M., Lemmens, J. S., & Valkenburg, P. M. (2016). The social media disorder scale. *Computers in Human Behavior, 61,* 478–487.

Van Doorn, M. D., Branje, S. J. T., & Meeus, W. H. (2011). Developmental changes in conflict resolution styles in parent-adolescent relationships: A four-wave longitudinal study. *Journal of Youth and Adolescence, 40,* 97–107.

van Erp, T. G. M., Hibar, D. P., Rasmussen, J. M., Glahn, D. C., Pearlson, G. D., Andreassen, O. A., . . . Melle, I. (2016). Subcortical brain volume abnormalities in 2028 individuals with schizophrenia and 2540 healthy controls via the ENIGMA consortium. *Molecular Psychiatry, 21,* 547–553.

Van Horn, J. D., Irimia, A., Torgerson, C. M., Chambers, M. C., Kikinis, R., & Toga, A. W. (2012). Mapping connectivity damage in the case of Phineas Gage. *PLoS ONE, 7*(5), e37454.

van Os, J., & Kapur, S. (2009). Schizophrenia. *The Lancet, 374,* 635–645.

Van Petegem, S., Soenens, B., Vansteenkiste, M., & Beyers, W. (2015). Rebels with a cause? Adolescent defiance from the perspective of reactance theory and self-determination theory. *Child Development, 86,* 903–918.

van Praag, H., Kempermann, G., & Gage, F. H. (2000). Neural consequences of environmental enrichment. *Nature Reviews Neuroscience, 1,* 191–198.

van Rooij, A. J., Ferguson, C. J., van de Mheen, D., & Schoenmakers, T. M. (2017). Time to abandon Internet addiction? Predicting problematic Internet, game, and social media use from psychosocial well-being and application use. *Clinical Neuropsychiatry, 14,* 113–121.

Van Rosmalen, L., van der Horst, F. C., & Van der Veer, R. (2016). From secure dependency to attachment: Mary Ainsworth's integration of Blatz's security theory into Bowlby's attachment theory. *History of Psychology, 19,* 22–39.

Van Someren, E. J. W., Cirelli, C., Dijk, D. J., Van Cauter, E., Schwartz, S., & Chee, M. W. (2015). Disrupted sleep: From molecules to cognition. *The Journal of Neuroscience, 35,* 13889–13895.

Van Strien, J. W., Franken, I. H., & Huijding, J. (2014). Testing the snake-detection hypothesis: Larger early posterior negativity in humans to pictures of snakes than to pictures of other reptiles, spiders and slugs. *Frontiers in Human Neuroscience, 8.* doi:10.3389/fnhum.2014.00691

Vanhoenacker, M. (2016, May 31). Become a pilot. *Slate.* Retrieved from http://www.slate.com/articles/technology/technology/2016/05/become_a_pilot_seriously_it_s_a_great_job.html

Vanini, G., Lydic, R., & Baghdoyan, H. A. (2012). GABA-to-ACh ratio in basal forebrain and cerebral cortex varies significantly during sleep. *SLEEP, 35,* 1325–1334.

Vaquero, L., Hartmann, K., Ripollés, P., Rojo, N., Sierpowska, J., François, C., . . . Münte, T. F. (2016). Structural neuroplasticity in expert pianists depends on the age of musical training onset. *NeuroImage, 126,* 106–119.

Varadkar, S., Bien, C. G., Kruse, C. A., Jensen, F. E., Bauer, J., Pardo, C. A., . . . Cross, J. H. (2014). Rasmussen's encephalitis: Clinical features, pathobiology, and treatment advances. *The Lancet Neurology, 13,* 195–205.

Vartanian, L. R. (2015). Impression management and food intake. Current directions in research. *Appetite, 86,* 74–80.

Vartanian, L. R., Herman, C. P., & Polivy, J. (2016). What does it mean to eat an appropriate amount of food? *Eating Behaviors, 23,* 24–27.

Vartanian, L. R., Spanos, S., Herman, C. P., & Polivy, J. (2015). Modeling of food intake: A meta-analytic review. *Social Influence, 10,* 119–136.

Vas, A. K., Chapman, S. B., & Cook, L. G. (2015). Language impairments in traumatic brain injury: A window into complex cognitive performance. In J. Grafman & A. M. Salazar (Eds.), *Handbook of clinical neurology: Traumatic brain injury, part II* (pp. 497–510). Amsterdam: Elsevier.

Vasalou, A., Joinson, A. N., & Courvoisier, D. (2010). Cultural differences, experience with social networks and the nature of "true commitment" in Facebook. *International Journal of Human Computer Studies, 68,* 719–728.

Velagaleti, G. V. N., & Moore, C. M. (2011). Role of array comparative genomic hybridization of cytogenetic causes of pregnancy loss. *Pathology Case Reviews, 16,* 214–221.

Vennard, M. (2011, November 21). How can musicians keep playing despite amnesia? *BBC World Service.* Retrieved from http://www.bbc.co.uk/news/magazine-15791973

Verduyn, P., Lee, D. S., Park, J., Shablack, H., Orvell, A., Bayer, J., . . . Kross, E. (2015). Passive Facebook usage undermines affective well-being: Experimental and longitudinal evidence. *Journal of Experimental Psychology: General, 144,* 480–488.

Vernon, P. A., Martin, R. A., Schermer, J. A., Cherkas, L. F., & Spector, T. D. (2008). Genetic and environmental contributions to humor styles: A replication study. *Twin Research and Human Genetics, 11,* 44–47.

Vervecken, D., & Hannover, B. (2015). Effects of gender fair job descriptions on children's perceptions of job status, job difficulty, and vocational self-efficacy. *Social Psychology, 46*(2), 76–92.

Vicedo, M. (2017). Putting attachment in its place: Disciplinary and cultural contexts. *European Journal of Developmental Psychology, 14,* 684–699.

Victora, C. G., Bahl, R., Barros, A. J., França, G. V., Horton, S., Krasevec, J., . . . Rollins, N. C. (2016). Breastfeeding in the 21st century: Epidemiology, mechanisms, and lifelong effect. *The Lancet, 387*(10017), 475–490.

Vigilant Citizen. (2010, October 14). *The odd masonic imagery of the 33 Chilean miners' rescue.* Retrieved from http://vigilantcitizen.com/latestnews/the-odd-masonic-imagery-surrounding-the-33-chilean-miners-rescue/

Vilain, E. J. N. (2008). Genetics of sexual development and differentiation. In D. L. Rowland & L. Incrocci (Eds.), *Handbook of sexual and gender identity disorders* (pp. 329–353). Hoboken, NJ: John Wiley & Sons.

Vingtdeux, V., Davies, P., Dickson, D. W., & Marambaud, P. (2011). AMPK is abnormally activated in tangle- and pre-tangle-bearing neurons in Alzheimer's disease and other tauopathies. *Acta Neuropathologica, 121,* 337–349.

Visser, B. A., Ashton, M. C., & Vernon, P. A. (2006). Beyond *g:* Putting multiple intelligences theory to the test. *Intelligence, 34,* 487–502.

Visser, P. L., & Hirsch, J. K. (2014). Health behaviors among college students: The influence of future time perspective and basic psychological need satisfaction. *Health Psychology and Behavioral Medicine, 2,* 88–99.

Vogel, G. (2014, October 6). Updated: Brain's GPS earns three neuroscientists a Nobel Prize. *Science.* Retrieved from http://www.sciencemag.org/news/2014/10/updated-brains-gps-earns-three-neuroscientists-nobel-prize

von Stumm, S., & Deary, I. J. (2012). Typical intellectual engagement and cognition in the ninth decade of life: The Lothian Birth Cohort 1921. *Psychology and Aging, 27,* 761–767.

von Stumm, S., & Plomin, R. (2015). Socioeconomic status and the growth of intelligence from infancy through adolescence. *Intelligence, 48,* 30–36.

Voyles, E. C., Bailey, S. F., & Durik, A. M. (2015). New pieces of the jigsaw classroom: Increasing accountability to reduce social loafing in student group projects. *The New School Psychology Bulletin, 13,* 11–20.

Vredeveldt, A., Baddeley, A. D., & Hitch, G. J. (2014). The effectiveness of eye-closure in repeated interviews. *Legal and Criminological Psychology, 19,* 282–295.

Vygotsky, L. S. (1962). *Thought and language* (E. Hanfmann & G. Vakar, Eds. & Trans.). Cambridge, MA: Massachusetts Institute of Technology. (Original work published 1934)

Wagenmakers, E. J., Wetzels, R., Borsboom, D., & van der Maas, H. L. (2011). Why psychologists must change the way they analyze their data: The case of psi [Peer commentary on the paper "Feeling the future: Experimental evidence for anomalous retroactive influences on cognition and affect" by D. J. Bem]. *Journal of Personality and Social Psychology, 100,* 426–432.

Wagner, H. S., Ahlstrom, B., Redden, J. P., Vickers, Z., & Mann, T. (2014). The myth of comfort food. *Health Psychology, 33,* 1552–1557.

Wagner, S. L., Cepeda, I., Krieger, D., Maggi, S., D'Angiulli, A., Weinberg, J., & Grunau, R. E. (2016). Higher cortisol is associated with poorer executive functioning in preschool children: The role of parenting stress, parent coping and quality of daycare. *Child Neuropsychology, 22,* 853–869.

Wahlstrom, K., Dretzke, B., Gordon, M., Peterson, K., Edwards, K., & Gdula, J. (2014). *Examining the impact of later high school start times on the health and academic performance of high school students: A multi-site study.* Retrieved from http://hdl.handle.net/11299/162769

Wakefield, A. J., Murch, S. H., Anthony, A., Linnell, J., Casson, D. M., Malik, M., . . . Walker-Smith, J. A. (1998). Ileal-lymphoid-nodular hyperplasia, non-specific colitis, and pervasive developmental disorder in children. *The Lancet, 28,* 637–641.

Wakefield, J. C. (1992). The concept of mental disorder: On the boundary between biological facts and social values. *American Psychologist, 47,* 373–388.

Wakeman, J. (2018, January 15). Your favorite selfie filter could be contributing to a mental health crisis. *NBC News: Think.* Retrieved from https://www.nbcnews.com/think/opinion/your-favorite-selfie-filter-could-be-contributing-mental-health-crisis-ncna837376

Walker, L. E., Pann, J. M., Shapiro, D. L., & Van Hasselt, V. B. (2016). A review of best practices for the treatment of persons with mental illness in jail. In *Best practices for the mentally ill in the criminal justice system* (pp. 57–69). Cham, Switzerland: Springer International.

Wall, S. S. (2015). Standing at the intersections: Navigating life as a black intersex man. *Narrative Inquiry in Bioethics, 5,* 117–119.

Wallin, P. (1949). An appraisal of some methodological aspects of the Kinsey report. *American Sociological Review, 14,* 197–210.

Walsh, R. (2011). Lifestyle and mental health. *American Psychologist, 66,* 579–592.

Walton, R. G., & Monte, W. C. (2015). Dietary methanol and autism. *Medical Hypotheses, 85,* 441–446.

Wang, H.-X., Karp, A., Winblad, B., & Fratiglioni, L. (2002). Late-life engagement in social and leisure activities is associated with a decreased risk of dementia: A longitudinal study from the Kungsholmen Project. *American Journal of Epidemiology, 155,* 1081–1087.

Wang, Q. (2016). Remebering the self in cultural contexts: A cultural dynamic theory of autobiographical memory. *Memory Studies, 9,* 295–304.

Wang, Q., & Conway, M. A. (2004). The stories we keep: Autobiographical memory in American and Chinese middle-aged adults. *Journal of Personality, 72,* 911–938.

Wang, S. W., & Repetti, R. L. (2016). Who gives to whom? Testing the support gap hypothesis with naturalistic observations of couple interactions. *Journal of Family Psychology, 30,* 492–504.

Wansink, B., Cao, Y., Saini, P., Shimizu, M., & Just, D. R. (2013). College cafeteria snack food purchases become less healthy with each passing week of the semester. *Public Health Nutrition, 16,* 1291–1295.

Wansink, B., & Kim, J. (2005). Bad popcorn in big buckets: Portion size can influence intake as much as taste. *Journal of Nutrition Education and Behavior, 37,* 242–245.

Warburton, D. E. R., Charlesworth, S., Ivey, A., Nettlefold, L., & Bredin, S. S. D. (2010). A systematic review of the evidence for Canada's physical activity guidelines for adults. *International Journal of Behavioral Nutrition and Physical Activity, 7,* 1–220.

Ward, E., Wiltshire, J. C., Detry, M. A., & Brown, R. L. (2013). African American men and women's attitude toward mental illness, perceptions of stigma, and preferred coping behaviors. *Nursing Research, 62,* 185–194.

Ward-Fear, G., Pearson, D. J., Brown, G. P., Rangers, B., & Shine, R. (2016). Ecological immunization: in situ training of free-ranging predatory lizards reduces their vulnerability to invasive toxic prey. *Biology Letters, 12,* 20150863.

Warneken, F., & Tomasello, M. (2006). Altruistic helping in human infants and young chimpanzees. *Science, 311,* 1301–1303.

Washburn, D. A. (2010). Book reviews: The animal mind at 100. *Psychological Record, 60,* 369–376.

Washburn, M. F. (1908). *The animal mind: A textbook of comparative psychology.* New York, NY: Macmillan.

Watson, J. B., & Rayner, R. (1920). Conditioned emotional reactions. *Journal of Experimental Psychology, 3,* 1–14. (Reprinted in *American Psychologist, 55,* 313–317)

Watson, J. M., & Strayer, D. L. (2010). Supertaskers: Profiles in extraordinary multi-tasking ability. *Psychonomic Bulletin and Review, 17,* 479–485.

Watson, N. F., Morgenthaler, T., Chervin, R., Carden, K., Kirsch, D., Kristo, D., . . . Weaver, T. (2015). Confronting drowsy driving: The American Academy of Sleep Medicine perspective. *Journal of Clinical Sleep Medicine, 11*(11), 1335–1336.

Watson, R. I. (1968). *The great psychologists* (2nd ed.). Philadelphia, PA: J. B. Lippincott.

Waugh, N. C., & Norman, D. A. (1965). Primary memory. *Psychological Review, 72,* 89–104.

Wearing, D. (2005). *Forever today: A memoir of love and amnesia.* London, UK: Corgi Books.

Webb, S. J., Monk, C. S., & Nelson, C. A. (2001). Mechanisms of postnatal neurobiological development: Implications for human development. *Developmental Neuropsychology, 19,* 147–171.

Weber, H., Scholz, C. J., Domschke, K., Baumann, C., Klauke, B., Jacob, C. P., . . . Reif, A. (2012). Gender differences in associations of glutamate decarboxylase 1 gene (GAD1) variants with panic disorder. *PLoS ONE, 7,* e37651.

Webster's New International Dictionary of the English Language. (1925). W. T. Harris & F. Sturges Allen (Eds.). Springfield, MA: G. & C. Merriam.

Weidner, R., Plewan, T., Chen, Q., Buchner, A., Weiss, P. H., & Fink, G. R. (2014). The moon illusion and size–distance scaling—evidence for shared neural patterns. *Journal of Cognitive Neuroscience, 26,* 1871–1882.

Weingarten, J. A., & Collop, N. A. (2013). Air travel: Effects of sleep deprivation and jet lag. *Chest, 144,* 1394–1401.

Weintraub, K. (2017, January 4). How to control aging. *Scientific American.* Retrieved from https://www.scientificamerican.com/article/how-to-control-aging/

Weir, F. W., Hatch, J. L., Muus, J. S., Wallace, S., & Meyer, T. A. (2016). Audiologic outcomes in Ehlers-Danlos Syndrome. *Otology & Neurotology, 37,* 748–752.

Weir, K. (2015, November). Marijuana and the developing brain. *Monitor on Psychology, 46,* 48.

Weisberg, S. M., & Newcombe, N. S. (2016). How do (some) people make a cognitive map? Routes, places, and working memory. *Journal of Experimental Psychology: Learning, Memory, and Cognition, 42*(5), 768–785.

Weisel, O., & Shalvi, S. (2015). The collaborative roots of corruption. *Proceedings of the National Academy of Sciences, 112,* 10651–10656.

Weisgram, E. S., Fulcher, M., & Dinella, L. M. (2014). Pink gives girls permission: Exploring the roles of explicit gender labels and gender-typed colors on preschool children's toy preferences. *Journal of Applied Developmental Psychology, 35*(5), 401–409.

Weiss, A., Wilson, M. L., Collins, D. A., Mjungu, D., Kamenya, S., Foerster, S., & Pusey, A. E. (2017). Personality in the chimpanzees of Gombe National Park. *Scientific Data, 4.* doi:10.1038/sdata.2017.146

Weiss, R. B., Stange, J. P., Boland, E. M., Black, S. K., LaBelle, D. R., Abramson, L. Y., & Alloy, L. B. (2015). Kindling of life stress in bipolar disorder: Comparison of sensitization and autonomy models. *Journal of Abnormal Psychology, 124,* 4–16.

Weisskirch, R. S., & Delevi, R. (2011). "Sexting" and adult romantic attachment. *Computers in Human Behavior, 27,* 1697–1701.

Wemer, A., Uldbjerg, N., Zachariae, R., Rosen, G., & Nohr, E. (2013). Self-hypnosis for coping with labour pain: A randomised controlled trial. *BJOG, 120,* 346–353.

Wen, C. P., Wai, J. P., Tsai, M. K., Yang, Y. C., Cheng, T. Y., Lee, M. C., . . . Wu, X. (2011). Minimum amount of physical activity for reduced mortality and extended life expectancy: A prospective cohort study. *The Lancet, 378,* 1244–1253.

Wentzel, K. R., McNamara Barry, C., & Caldwell, K. A. (2004). Friendships in middle school: Influences on motivation and school adjustment. *Journal of Educational Psychology, 96,* 195–203.

Werker, J. F., & Hensch, T. K. (2015). Critical periods in speech perception: New directions. *Annual Review of Psychology, 66,* 173–196.

Werker, J. F., & Tees, R. C. (1984). Cross-language speech perception: Evidence for perceptual reorganization during the first year of life. *Infant Behavior and Development, 7,* 49–63.

Werner, K. B., Few, L. R., & Bucholz, K. K. (2015). Epidemiology, comorbidity, and behavioral genetics of antisocial personality disorder and psychopathy. *Psychiatric Annals, 45,* 195–199.

Wernig, M., Zhao, J. P., Pruszak, J., Hedlund, E., Fu, D., Soldner, F., . . . Jaenisch, R. (2008). Neurons derived from reprogrammed fibroblasts functionally integrate into the fetal brain and improve symptoms of rats with Parkinson's disease. *Proceedings of the National Academy of Sciences, 105,* 5856–5861.

Wertheimer, M. (2012). *A brief history of psychology* (5th ed.). New York, NY: Taylor & Francis.

Wertheimer, M. (2014). Music, thinking, perceived motion: The emergence of Gestalt theory. *History of Psychology, 17,* 131–133.

Westbrook, A., & Braver, T. S. (2015). Cognitive effort: A neuroeconomic approach. *Cognitive, Affective, & Behavioral Neuroscience, 15,* 395–415.

Westen, D. (1990). Psychoanalytic approaches to personality. In L. A. Pervin (Ed.), *Handbook of personality* (pp. 21–65). New York, NY: Guilford Press.

Westen, D., Gabbard, G. O., & Ortigo, K. M. (2008). Psychoanalytic approaches to personality. In O. P. John, R. W. Robins, & L. A. Pervin (Eds.), *Handbook of personality: Theory of research* (pp. 61–113). New York, NY: Guilford Press.

Westly, E. (2011, July/August). The bilingual advantage. *Scientific American Mind.*

Weuve, J., Puett, R. C., Schwartz, J., Yanosky, J. D., Laden, F., & Grodstein, F. (2012). Exposure to particulate air pollution and cognitive decline in older women. *Archives of Internal Medicine, 172,* 219–227.

Whillans, A. V., Dunn, E. W., Smeets, P., Bekkers, R., & Norton, M. I. (2017). Buying time promotes happiness. *Proceedings of the National Academy of Sciences,* 201706541. doi:10.1073/pnas.1706541114

Whisman, M. A., & Synder, D. K. (2007). Sexual infidelity in a national survey of American women: Differences in prevalence and correlates as a function of method of assessment. *Journal of Family Psychology, 21,* 147–154.

Whitaker, R. (2015). The triumph of American psychiatry: How it created the modern therapeutic state. *European Journal of Psychotherapy & Counselling, 17,* 326–341.

White, A. M., Slater, M. E., Ng, G., Hingson, R., & Breslow, R. (2018). Trends in alcohol-related emergency department visits in the United States: Results from the Nationwide Emergency Department Sample, 2006 to 2014. *Alcoholism: Clinical and Experimental Research, 42,* 352–359.

Whitlock, J. R., Heynen, A. J., Shuler, M. G., & Bear, M. F. (2006). Learning induces long-term potentiation in the hippocampus. *Science, 313,* 1093–1097.

Who gets the most sleep? (2016, September/October). *Scientific American Mind, 27,* 9.

Whorf, B. L. (1956). *Language, thought, and reality.* Cambridge, MA: MIT Press.

Wich, S. A., Swartz, K. B., Hardus, M. E., Lameira, A. R., Stromberg, E., & Shumaker, R. W. (2009). Case of spontaneous acquisition of a human sound by an orangutan. *Primates, 50,* 56–64.

Wickens, A. P. (2015). *A history of the brain: From stone age surgery to modern neuroscience.* New York, NY: Psychology Press.

Wicker, A. W. (1969). Attitudes versus actions: The relationship of verbal and overt behavioral responses to attitude objects. *Journal of Social Issues, 24,* 41–78.

Wilhelmus, M. M., Hay, J. L., Zuiker, R. G., Okkerse, P., Perdrieu, C., Sauser, J., . . . Silber, B. Y. (2017). Effects of a single, oral 60 mg caffeine dose on attention in healthy adult subjects. *Journal of Psychopharmacology, 31,* 222–232. doi:0269881116668593

Williams, C. (Writer), & Whittingham, K. (Director). (2007, February 8). Phyllis' wedding (G. Daniels, Producer). In *The Office* [television series]. Los Angeles, CA: NBC.

Williams, D. R., & Mohammed, S. A. (2009). Discrimination and racial disparities in health: Evidence and needed research. *Journal of Behavioral Medicine, 32,* 20–47. doi:10.1007/s10865-008-9185-0

Williams, M., Hong, S. W., Kang, M.-S., Carlisle, N. B., & Woodman, G. F. (2013). The benefit of forgetting. *Psychonomic Bulletin & Review, 20,* 348–355.

Williams, P. G., Suchy, Y., & Kraybill, M. L. (2010). Five-factor model personality traits and executive functioning among older adults. *Journal of Research in Personality, 44,* 485–491.

Williamson, A. M., & Feyer, A. M. (2000). Moderate sleep deprivation produces impairments in cognitive and motor performance equivalent to legally prescribed levels of alcohol intoxication. *Occupational and Environmental Medicine, 57,* 649–655.

Willis, D. J., DeLeon, P. H., Haldane, S., & Heldring, M. B. (2014). A policy article—personal perspectives on the public policy process: Making a difference. *Professional Psychology: Research and Practice, 45,* 143–151.

Willoughby, K. A., Desrocher, M., Levine, B., & Rovet, J. F. (2012). Episodic and semantic autobiographical memory and everyday memory during late childhood and early adolescence. *Frontiers in Psychology, 3,* 1–15.

Willyard, C. (2008). Hungry for sleep. *Nature Medicine, 14,* 477–480.

Wilson, B. A., Baddeley, A. D., & Kapur, N. (1995). Dense amnesia in a professional musician following herpes simplex virus encephalitis. *Journal of Clinical and Experimental Neuropsychology, 17,* 668–681.

Wilson, B. A., Kopelman, M., & Kapur, N. (2008). Prominent and persistent loss of past awareness in amnesia: Delusion, impaired consciousness or coping strategy. *Neuropsychological Rehabilitation, 18,* 527–540.

Wilson, B. A., & Wearing, D. (1995). Prisoner of consciousness: A state of just awakening following herpes simplex encephalitis. In R. Campbell & M. Conway (Eds.), *Broken memories: Case studies in memory impairment* (pp. 14–30). Oxford, UK: Blackwell.

Wilson, R. (2018, February 24). Gun debate shows signs of change in Florida. *The Hill.* Retrieved from http://thehill.com/homenews/state-watch/375361-gun-debate-shows-signs-of-change-in-florida

Wilson, R. S., & Bennett, D. A. (2003). Cognitive activity and risk of Alzheimer's disease. *Current Directions in Psychological Science, 12,* 87–91.

Wimber, M., Alink, A., Charest, I., Kriegeskorte, N., & Anderson, M. C. (2015). Retrieval induces adaptive forgetting of competing memories via cortical pattern suppression. *Nature Neuroscience, 18,* 582–589.

Windham, G. C., Pinney, S. M., Voss, R. W., Sjödin, A., Biro, F. M., Greenspan, L. C., . . . Kushi, L. H. (2015). Brominated flame retardants and other persistent organohalogenated compounds in relation to timing of puberty in a longitudinal study of girls. *Environmental Health Perspectives, 123,* 1046–1052.

Winerman, L. (2015). A double life. *Monitor on Psychology, 46,* 30.

Wintermann, G.-B., Kirschbaum, C., & Petrowski, K. (2016). Predisposition or side effect of the duration: The reactivity of the HPA-axis under psychosocial stress in panic disorder. *International Journal of Psychophysiology, 107,* 9–15.

Winton, W. M. (1987). Do introductory textbooks present the Yerkes-Dodson Law correctly? *American Psychologist, 42,* 202–203.

Wipfli, B., Landers, D., Nagoshi, C., & Ringenbach, S. (2011). An examination of serotonin and psychological variables in the relationship between exercise and mental health. *Scandinavian Journal of Medicine and Science in Sports, 21,* 474–481.

Wirth, M. M. (2015). Hormones, stress, and cognition: The effects of glucocorticoids and oxytocin on memory. *Adaptive Human Behavior and Physiology, 1,* 177–201.

Wise, N. J., Frangos, E., & Komisaruk, B. R. (2017). Brain activity unique to orgasm in women: An fMRI analysis. *The Journal of Sexual Medicine, 14,* 1380–1391.

Wiseman, R., & Watt, C. (2006). Belief in psychic ability and the misattribution hypothesis: A qualitative review. *British Journal of Psychology, 91,* 323–338.

Witelson S., Kigar, D., & Harvey, T. (1999). The exceptional brain of Albert Einstein. *The Lancet, 353,* 2149–2153.

Withers, R. S., & Barnes, Z. (2015, September 11). What it's really like to live with schizophrenia. *Women's Health.* Retrieved from https://www.womenshealthmag.com/health/living-with-schizophrenia

Witherspoon, D. J., Wooding, S., Rogers, A. R., Marchani, E. E., Watkins, W. S., Batzer, M. A., & Jorde, L. B. (2007). Genetic similarities within and between human populations. *Genetics, 176,* 351–359.

Wixted, J., & Mickes, L. (2017, November/December). Eyewitness memory is a lot more reliable than you think. *Scientific American Mind, 28,* 35–38.

Wixted, J. T., Mickes, L., Clark, S. E., Gronlund, S. D., & Roediger, H. L., III. (2015). Initial eyewitness confidence reliably predicts eyewitness identification accuracy. *American Psychologist, 70,* 515–526.

Wobst, A. H. K. (2007). Hypnosis and surgery: Past, present, and future. *Anesthesia & Analgesia, 104,* 1199–1208.

Wohlfahrt-Veje, C., Korsholm Mouritsen, A., Hagen, C. P., Tinggaard, J., Grunnet Mieritz, M., Boas, M., . . . Main, K. M. (2016). Pubertal onset in boys and girls is influenced by pubertal timing of both parents. *The Journal of Clinical Endocrinology & Metabolism.* Retrieved from http://dx.doi.org/10.1210/jc.2016-1073#sthash.6PNVCAkZ.dpuf

Wojcicki, J. M., van der Straten, A., & Padian, N. (2010). Bridewealth and sexual and reproductive practices among women in Harare, Zimbabwe. *AIDS Care, 22,* 705–710.

Wolfe, U., & Ali, N. (2015). Dark adaptation and Purkinje shift: A laboratory exercise in perceptual neuroscience. *The Journal of Undergraduate Neuroscience Education, 13,* A59–A63.

Wolfson, G. (2017, May 30). Dr. Ben Carson: Poverty is "a state of mind." SiriusXM. Retrieved from http://blog.siriusxm.com/dr-ben-carson-poverty-is-a-state-of-mind/

Wolman, D. (2012, March 15). The split brain: A tale of two halves. *Nature, 483,* 260–263.

Wolpert, D. M., Goodbody, S. J., & Husain, M. (1998). Maintaining internal representations: The role of the human superior parietal lobe. *Nature Neuroscience, 1,* 529–533.

Wong, B. (2011). Point of view: Color blindness. *Nature Methods, 8,* 441.

Wood, B., Rea, M. S., Plitnick, B., & Figueiro, M. G. (2013). Light level and duration of exposure determine the impact of self-luminous tablets on melatonin suppression. *Applied Ergonomics, 44,* 237–240.

Wood, E., Zivcakova, L., Gentile, P., Archer, K., De Pasquale, D., & Nosko, A. (2011). Examining the impact of off-task multi-tasking with technology on real-time classroom learning. *Computers & Education, 58,* 365–374.

Wood, G., & Pennington, J. (1973). Encoding and retrieval from long-term storage. *Journal of Experimental Psychology, 99,* 243–254.

Wood, W., & Eagly, A. H. (2015). Two traditions of research on gender identity. *Sex Roles, 73,* 461–473.

Woolley, K., & Fishbach, A. (2018). It's about time: Earlier rewards increase intrinsic motivation. *Journal of Personality and Social Psychology, 114,* 877–890.

Workowski, K. A., & Bolan, G. A. (2015). Sexually transmitted diseases treatment guidelines, 2015. Centers for Disease Control and Prevention. *MMWR Recommendations and Reports, 64,* 1–138.

World Health Organization (WHO). (2014, November). *Information sheet on opioid overdose.* Retrieved from http://www.who.int/substance_abuse/information-sheet/en/

World Health Organization (WHO). (2015). *Hearing loss due to recreational exposure to loud sounds: A review.* Retrieved from http://apps.who.int/iris/bitstream/10665/154589/1/9789241508513_eng.pdf

Worringham, C. J., & Messick, D. M. (1983). Social facilitation of running: An unobtrusive study. *Journal of Social Psychology, 121,* 23–29.

Wray, N. R., Pergadia, M. L., Blackwood, D. H. R., Penninx, B. W. J. H., Gordon, S. D., Nyholt, D. R., . . . Smit, J. H. (2012). Genome-wide association study of major depressive disorder: New results, meta-analysis, and lessons learned. *Molecular Psychiatry, 17,* 36–48.

Wright, K. (2002). The times of our lives. *Scientific American, 287,* 59–65.

Wright, K. P., Bogan, R. K., & Wyatt, J. K. (2013). Shift work and the assessment and management of shift work disorder (SWD). *Sleep Medicine Reviews, 17,* 41–54.

Wu, C., Odden, M. C., Fisher, G. G., & Stawski, R. S. (2016). Association of retirement age with mortality: A population-based longitudinal study among older adults in the USA. *Journal of Epidemiology and Community Health, 70,* 917–923.

Wyatt, T. D. (2015). The search for human pheromones: The lost decades and the necessity of returning to first principles. *Proceedings of the Royal Society B, 282,* 20142994. doi:10.1098/rspb.2014.2994

Wynn, K., Bloom, P., Jordan, A., Marshall, J., & Sheskin, M. (2018). Not noble savages after all: Limits to early altruism. *Current Directions in Psychological Science, 27,* 3–8.

Xu, H., Wen, L. M., Hardy, L. L., & Rissel, C. (2016). Associations of outdoor play and screen time with nocturnal sleep duration and pattern among young children. *Acta Paediatrica, 105,* 297–303.

Xu, J., Gannon, P. J., Emmorey, K., Smith, J. F., & Braun, A. R. (2009). Symbolic gestures and spoken language are processed by a common neural system. *Proceedings of the National Academy of Sciences, USA, 106,* 20664–20669.

Xu, M., Chung, S., Zhang, S., Zhong, P., Ma, C., Chang, W.-C., . . . Dan, Y. (2015). Basal forebrain circuit for sleep–wake control. *Nature Neuroscience, 18,* 1641–1647.

Xu, Y., & Zheng, Y. (2017). Fraternal birth order, handedness, and sexual orientation in a Chinese population. *The Journal of Sex Research, 54,* 10–18.

Yagil, D. (2015). Display rules for kindness: Outcomes of suppressing benevolent emotions. *Motivation and Emotion, 39,* 156–166.

Yalom, I. D., & Leszcz, M. (2005). *The theory and practice of group psychotherapy* (5th ed.). New York, NY: Basic Books.

Yam, K. C., Fehr, R., & Barnes, C. M. (2014). Morning employees are perceived as better employees: Employees' start times influence supervisor performance ratings. *Journal of Applied Psychology, 99,* 1288–1299.

Yamagata, S., Suzuki, A., Ando, J., Ono, Y., Kijima, N., Yoshimura, K., . . . Jang, K. (2006). Is the genetic structure of human personality universal? A cross-cultural twin study from North America, Europe, and Asia. *Journal of Personality and Social Psychology, 90,* 987–998.

Yanchar, S. C., Slife, B. D., & Warne, R. (2008). Critical thinking as disciplinary practice. *Review of General Psychology, 12,* 265–281.

Yee, E., & Thompson-Schill, S. L. (2016). Putting concepts into context. *Psychonomic Bulletin & Review, 23,* 1015–1027.

Yee, M., & Brown, R. (1994). The development of gender differentiation in young children. *British Journal of Social Psychology, 33,* 183–196.

Yerkes, R. M., & Dodson, J. D. (1908). The relation of strength of stimulus to rapidity of habit-formation. *Journal of Comparative Neurology, 18,* 459–482.

Yetish, G., Kaplan, H., Gurven, M., Wood, B., Pontzer, H., Manger, P. R., . . . Siegel, J. M. (2015). Natural sleep and its seasonal variations in three pre-industrial societies. *Current Biology, 25*(21), 2862–2868.

Yolken, R. H., & Torrey, E. F. (1995). Viruses, schizophrenia, and bipolar disorder. *Clinical Microbiology Reviews, 8,* 131–145.

Yoon, S., Kim, J. E., Kim, G. H., Kang, H. J., Kim, B. R., Jeon, S., . . . Lyoo, I. K. (2016). Subregional shape alterations in the amygdala in patients with panic disorder. *PLoS One, 11,* e0157856.

Young, M. E., Mizzau, M., Mai, N. T., Sirisegaram, A., & Wilson, M. (2009). Food for thought: What you eat depends on your sex and eating companions. *Appetite, 53,* 268–271.

Youngstedt, S. D., & Kline, C. E. (2006). Epidemiology of exercise and sleep. *Sleep and Biological Rhythms, 4,* 215–221.

Youyou, W., Stillwell, D., Schwartz, H. A., & Kosinski, M. (2017). Birds of a feather do flock together: Behavior-based personality assessment method reveals personality similarity among couples and friends. *Psychological Science, 28,* 276–284.

Yu, C. K. C. (2014). Toward 100% dream retrieval by rapid-eye-movement sleep awakening: A high-density electroencephalographic study. *Dreaming, 24,* 1–17.

Yu, C. K. C. (2015). One hundred typical themes in most recent dreams, diary dreams, and dreams spontaneously recollected from last night. *Dreaming, 25,* 206–219.

Yudell, M., Roberts, D., DeSalle, R., & Tishkoff, S. (2016). Taking race out of human genetics. *Science, 351,* 564–565.

Yuhas, D., & Jabr, F. (2012). *Know your neurons: What is the ratio of glia to neurons in the brain?* Retrieved from http://blogs.scientificamerican.com/brainwaves/2012/06/13/know-your-neurons-what-is-the-ratio-of-glia-to-neurons-in-the-brain/

Yule, G. (1996). *Pragmatics.* Oxford, UK: Oxford University Press.

Zacks, J. M. (2015, February 13). Why movie "facts" prevail. *The New York Times.* Retrieved from http://www.nytimes.com/2015/02/15/opinion/sunday/why-movie-facts-prevail.html?_r=0

Zafeiriou, D. I. (2004). Primitive reflexes and postural reactions in the neurodevelopmental examination. *Pediatric Neurology, 31,* 1–8.

Zajonc, R. B. (1980). Feeling and thinking: Preferences need no inferences. *American Psychologist, 35,* 151–175.

Zajonc, R. B. (1984). On the primacy of affect. *American Psychologist, 39,* 117–123.

Zaraska, M. (2017, January/February). In human attraction, you are what you eat. *Scientific American Mind, 28,* 15.

Zaretskii, V. K. (2009). The zone of proximal development: What Vygotsky did not have time to write. *Journal of Russian and East European Psychology, 47,* 70–93.

Zenger, J., & Folkman, J. (2017, May 2). Why do so many managers avoid giving praise? *Harvard Business Review.* Retrieved from https://hbr.org/2017/05/why-do-so-many-managers-avoid-giving-praise

Zhang, L., Dong, Y., Doyon, W. M., & Dani, J. A. (2012). Withdrawal from chronic nicotine exposure alters dopamine signaling dynamics in the nucleus accumbens. *Biological Psychiatry, 71,* 184–191.

Zhang, T.-Y., & Meaney, M. J. (2010). Epigenetics and the environmental regulation of the genome and its function. *Annual Review of Psychology, 61,* 439–466.

Zhao, H. (2017). Recent progress of development of optogenetic implantable neural probes. *International Journal of Molecular Sciences, 18,* 1751.

Zimbardo, P. (2007). *The Lucifer effect: Understanding how good people turn evil.* New York, NY: Random House.

Zimmerman, A., Bai, L., & Ginty, D. D. (2014). The gentle touch receptors of mammalian skin. *Science, 346,* 950–954.

Zingoni, A., Fionda, C., Borrelli, C., Cippitelli, M., Santoni, A., & Soriani, A. (2017). Natural killer cell response to chemotherapy-stressed cancer cells: Role in tumor immunosurveillance. *Frontiers in Immunology, 8.* doi:10.3389/fimmu.2017.01194

Zosuls, K. M., Miller, C. F., Ruble, D. N., Martin, C. L., & Fabes, R. A. (2011). Gender development research in sex roles: Historical trends and future directions. *Sex Roles, 64,* 826–842.

Zuckerman, M. (1979). *Sensation seeking: Beyond the optimal level of arousal.* Hillsdale, NJ: Lawrence Erlbaum Associates.

Zuckerman, M. (1994). *Behavioral expressions and biosocial bases of sensation seeking.* Cambridge, UK: Cambridge University Press.

Zuckerman, M. (2015). Behavior and biology: Research on sensation seeking and reactions to the media. In L. Donohew, H. Sypher, & E. T. Higgins (Eds.), *Communication, social cognition and affect* (pp. 173–194). Hillsdale, NJ: Psychology Press.

Zvolensky, M. J., Rosenfield, D., Garey, L., Kauffman, B. Y., Langdon, K. J., Powers, M. B., . . . Smits, J. A. J. (2018). Does exercise aid smoking cessation through reductions in anxiety sensitivity and dysphoria? *Health Psychology, 37*(7), 647–657. http://dx.doi.org/10.1037/hea0000588

Name Index

Note: Page numbers followed by f indicate figures; t indicates tables; i indicates Infographics; c indicates Connections.

Subject Index

Note: Boldface indicates key terms; *italics* indicate features; f indicates figures; t indicates tables; i indicates Infographics; c indicates Connections.

INTRODUCING THE INFOGRAPHICS: Full-page visual presentations of each chapter's most challenging concepts.